Handbook of Depression
Treatment, Assessment, and Research

Handbook of Depression
Treatment, Assessment, and Research

Edited by
Ernest Edward Beckham
and
William R. Leber

 DORSEY PROFESSIONAL BOOKS 1985

THE DORSEY PRESS
HOMEWOOD, ILLINOIS 60430

ISBN 0-256-03490-7

Library of Congress Catalog Card No. 85–70980

Printed in the United States of America

1 2 3 4 5 6 7 8 9 0 K 2 1 0 9 8 7 6 5

Preface

The field of depression and affective disorders has become so large that no one person can keep abreast of all of the literature that is being published. In just the last 35 years there has been tremendous progress in diagnosing and treating depression, with exciting advances in both the psychological and biological realms. This book has followed traditional conceptual boundaries in specifying chapter topics—some focusing mainly on psychological aspects of depression and others focusing primarily on biological aspects. However, the philosophy behind this book is that psychology and biology interact in a very complex fashion in depression and that a body/mind dualism is not, in the final analysis, the most valuable heuristic for understanding depression.

We believe that clinicians and researchers have much to gain from working closely together. In our original letters to authors we requested that they write in a way that would not only address the areas of research and practice individually but would also attempt to bridge the gap between them. We hope that this book has accomplished that goal and that it will be a useful tool for those who research and treat depression.

There are many people who have assisted us in one way or another with this undertaking. Most of all we would like to thank our authors, who have provided such high-quality contributions. Second, we would like to thank our colleagues in the Treatment of Depression Collaborative Research Program, who have encouraged us in this project. John Watkins and Irene Elkin were supportive of the project from the very beginning. We are also indebted to Gene Walker for his initial encouragement to undertake this task and for his invaluable assistance throughout. Finally, we are very appreciative of our secretary for this project, Judy Short, for her efficient handling of the voluminous correspondence that has been involved.

Ernest Edward Beckham

William R. Leber

Russell L. Adams, Ph.D.
Professor and Director, Psychological Assessment Laboratory
Department of Psychiatry and Behavioral Sciences
University of Oklahoma Health Sciences Center
Oklahoma City, Oklahoma

Arthur Anastopoulos, Ph.D.
Pediatric Psychologist
University of Iowa College of Medicine
Iowa City, Iowa

Hagop S. Akiskal, M.D.
Professor and Director of Affective Disorders Program
Department of Psychiatry
University of Tennessee College of Medicine
Memphis, Tennessee

Paul Bebbington, M.A., M.Phil., M.R.C.P., M.R.C.Psych.
Senior Lecturer
Institute of Psychiatry
London, England

Aaron T. Beck, M.D.
Professor, Department of Psychiatry
University of Pennsylvania
Philadelphia, Pennsylvania

Ernest Edward Beckham, Ph.D.
Assistant Professor
Department of Psychiatry and Behavioral Sciences
University of Oklahoma Health Sciences Center
Oklahoma City, Oklahoma

Alan S. Bellack, Ph.D.
Professor, The Medical College of Pennsylvania at Eastern State Psychiatric Institute
Department of Psychiatry
Philadelphia, Pennsylvania

Jules R. Bemporad, M.D.
Director of Training and Education
Massachusetts Mental Health Center
Boston, Massachusetts

Andrew G. Billings, Ph.D.
Research Psychologist
Social Ecology Laboratory, Department of Psychiatry and Behavioral Sciences
Stanford University School of Medicine
Stanford, California

Dan G. Blazer, M.D., Ph.D.
Associate Professor of Psychiatry and Head, Division of Social and
*   Community Psychiatry*
Duke University Medical Center
Durham, North Carolina

Jenny L. Boyer, Ph.D., J.D.
Assistant Professor
Department of Psychiatry and Behavioral Sciences
University of Oklahoma Health Sciences Center
Oklahoma City, Oklahoma

David D. Burns, M.D.
Clinical Assistant Professor of Psychiatry
University of Pennsylvania School of Medicine
Philadelphia, Pennsylvania

Eve S. Chevron, M.S.
Clinical Psychologist, Department of Psychiatry
Yale University School of Medicine
New Haven, Connecticut

John F. Clarkin, Ph.D.
Department of Psychiatry
Cornell University
New York, New York

Pamela Danker-Brown, Ph.D.
North Care Center
Department of Psychiatry
University of Oklahoma Health Sciences Center
Oklahoma City, Oklahoma

John M. Davis, M.D.
Director, Research Department
Illinois State Psychiatric Institute
Chicago, Illinois

Frank DeLeon-Jones, M.D.
Associate Chief of Staff, Department of Research and Development
West Side Veterans Administration Medical Center
Chicago, Illinois

Jan Fawcett, M.D.
Professor and Chairman, Department of Psychiatry
Rush-Presbyterian-St. Luke's Medical Center
Chicago, Illinois

Ellen Frank, Ph.D.
Associate Professor of Psychiatry and Psychology
Western Psychiatric Institute and Clinic
University of Pittsburg School of Medicine
Pittsburgh, Pennsylvania

Ira D. Glick, Ph.D.
Department of Psychiatry
Cornell University Medical College
New York, New York

Lesley Guthrie, Ph.D.
Red Rock Comprehensive Mental Health Center
Oklahoma City, Oklahoma

Gretchen L. Haas, Ph.D.
Department of Psychiatry
Cornell University Medical College
New York, New York

Constance Hammen, Ph.D.
Department of Psychology
University of California at Los Angeles
Los Angeles, California

Harry M. Hoberman, Ph.D.
Psychologist/Clinical Researcher
Division of Child and Adolescent Psychiatry
University of Minnesota Medical School
Minneapolis, Minnesota

Kay Kline Hodges, Ph.D.
Associate Professor, Department of Psychiatry
University of Missouri School of Medicine—Columbia
Columbia, Missouri

Roger G. Kathol, M.D.
Assistant Professor of Psychiatry and Internal Medicine
College of Medicine, The University of Iowa
Iowa City, Iowa

Gerald L. Klerman, M.D.
George Harrington Professor of Psychiatry
Department of Psychiatry
Harvard Medical School
Boston, Massachusetts

Doreen Kotik, Ph.D.
Department of Neurology
Baylor College of Medicine
Houston, Texas

Susan E. Krantz, Ph.D.
VA Medical Center
Palo Alto, California

Howard M. Kravitz, D.O.
Assistant Professor, Department of Psychiatry
Medical Director, Sleep Disorder Service and Research Center
Rush-Presbyterian-St. Luke's Medical Center
Chicago, Illinois

David J. Kupfer, M.D.
Professor and Chairman, Department of Psychiatry
Western Psychiatric Institute and Clinic
University of Pittsburgh School of Medicine
Pittsburgh, Pennsylvania

William R. Leber, Ph.D.
Assistant Professor
Department of Psychiatry and Behavioral Sciences
University of Oklahoma Health Sciences Center
Oklahoma City, Oklahoma

Laurent Lehmann, M.D.
Chief, Mental Health Services
Oklahoma City VA Medical Center
Oklahoma City, Oklahoma

Gregory W. Lester, Ph.D.
Psychologist in Private Practice
Houston, Texas

Peter M. Lewinsohn, Ph.D.
Department of Psychology
University of Oregon
Eugene, Oregon

Scott B. McCabe, B.A.
Clarke Institute of Psychiatry
Toronto, Ontario

J. Mendlewicz, M.D., Ph.D.
Chef de service
Hopital Erasme
Bruxelles, Belgique

Theodore Millon, Ph.D.
Professor and Director of Clinical Training
Department of Psychology
University of Miami
Coral Gables, Florida

Rudolf H. Moos, Ph.D.
Research Career Scientist and Professor
Veterans Administration and Stanford University Medical Centers
Palo Alto, California

Katherine M. Noll, Ph.D.
Assistant Professor of Psychology
Elmhurst College
Elmhurst, Illinois

Christopher Peterson, Ph.D.
Associate Professor
Department of Psychology
Virginia Polytechnic Institute and State University
Blacksburg, Virginia

Saul E. Rosenberg, Ph.D.
Assistant Clinical Professor, Medical Psychology
University of California at San Francisco
San Francisco, California

Bruce J. Rounsaville, M.D.
Associate Professor, Department of Psychiatry
Yale University School of Medicine
New Haven, Connecticut

William P. Sacco, Ph.D.
Associate Professor
University of South Florida
Tampa, Florida

Martin E. P. Seligman, Ph.D.
Professor, Department of Psychology
University of Pennsylvania
Philadelphia, Pennsylvania

Brian F. Shaw, Ph.D.
Associate Professor, Department of Psychiatry
University of Toronto
Director, Cognitive and Behaviour Therapies Section
Clarke Institute of Psychiatry
Toronto, Ontario

Lawrence J. Siegel, Ph.D.
Associate Professor, Department of Pediatrics
University of Texas Medical Branch
Galveston, Texas

Rebecca C. Simmons, M.D.
Department of Psychiatry
University of Tennessee
Memphis, Tennessee

Alan Stoudemire, M.D.
Assistant Professor of Psychiatry
Emory University School of Medicine
Atlanta, Georgia

Michael E. Thase, M.D.
Assistant Professor of Psychiatry
Western Psychiatric Institute and Clinic
University of Pittsburgh School of Medicine
Pittsburgh, Pennsylvania

T. Michael Vallis, Ph.D.
Lecturer, Department of Psychiatry
University of Toronto
Toronto, Ontario

Myrna M. Weissman, Ph.D.
Professor, Departments of Psychiatry and Epidemiology
Yale University School of Medicine
New Haven, Connecticut

John K. Wing, M.D., Ph.D.
Director, Medical Research Council
Social Psychiatry Unit
Professor of Social Psychiatry
University of London
London, England

Contents

Part 1
Treatment

1. *Cognitive Therapy of Depression*   William P. Sacco and
   Aaron T. Beck   **3**

   The Cognitive Theory of Depression. Cognitive Therapy of Depression:
   Basic Treatment Strategies: *Step 1—Identify and Monitor Dysfunc-*
   tional Automatic Thoughts. Step 2—Recognize the Connection between
   Thoughts, Emotion, and Behavior. Step 3—Evaluate the Reasonable-
   ness of the Automatic Thoughts. Step 4—Substitute More Reasonable
   Thoughts for the Dysfunctional Automatic Thoughts. Step 5—Identify
   and Alter Dysfunctional Silent Assumptions. Behavioral Techniques.
   Research Bearing on the Validity of the Cognitive Theory of Depression
   and the Efficacy of Cognitive Therapy: *Correlational Studies.* Causal
   Evidence. Efficacy of Cognitive Therapy for Depression. Conclusion.

2. *The Behavioral Treatment of Depression*
   Harry M. Hoberman and Peter M. Lewinsohn   **39**

   Conceptual and Historical Perspectives: *Conceptual Foundations of Be-*
   havior Therapy. History of Behavioral Approaches to Depression. Behavioral Theories of Depression. Behavioral Strategies for Treating Depression: *Diagnostic and Functional Assessment.* Conceptualization of
   Presenting Problems: *Monitoring of Mood and Activities.* Progressive
   Goal Attainment and Behavioral Productivity. Contracting and Self-Reinforcement. Specific Skills—Remediation and Therapeutic Decision
   Making. Structural Parameters of Therapy. Outcome Evaluation. Practical Concerns in Implementing Behavioral Treatments. Behavioral Tactics for Treating Depression: *Decreasing Unpleasant Events and In-*
   creasing Pleasant Events: An Individualized Approach to Depression.
   The Coping with Depression Course. Social Interaction Therapy. Self-
   Control Therapy. Social Skills Training for Depression. An Operant

Reinforcement Approach. Final Comments on Behavioral Treatment Programs. Current and Future Directions in Behavioral Treatments for Depression.

3. *Long-Term Analytic Treatment of Depression*
    Jules R. Bemporad   82

Historical Review. The Depressive Personality. Psychoanalytic Psychotherapy. Effectiveness of Long-Term Analytic Treatment.

4. *Brief Dynamic Psychotherapy for Depression*
    Saul E. Rosenberg   100

Principles of Selection: *Diagnostic Contraindications for Brief Dynamic Psychotherapy. An Appropriate Focus for Short-Term Dynamic Psychotherapy. The Patient's Psychological Resources.* Principles of Brief Dynamic Psychotherapy for Depression: *Establishing a Time Limit. Maintaining and Elaborating a Focus. The Therapist Adopts an Active Role. Analysis of Transference. Analysis of Defense and Resistance. Working through Feelings about Termination. Working with Themes of Loss and Grief. Working with Oedipal Themes in Depressed Patients. Adjusting Technique to Suit the Personality Style of the Depressed Patient. Themes of Guilt. The Use of Adjunctive Antidepressant Medication.* Research: *Methodological Problems. Studies of the Efficacy of Brief Dynamic Therapy for Depression. Recommendations for Future Research.* Summary.

5. *Short-Term Interpersonal Psychotherapy (IPT) for Depression*
    Bruce J. Rounsaville, Gerald L. Klerman, Myrna M. Weissman,
    and Eve S. Chevron   124

Introduction. Elements of IPT: *A Medical Model of Depression. Social Influences on Depression/Social Interventions to Bring about Improvement. Need for an Effective Short-Term Treatment. The IPT Therapist's Use of an Exploratory Stance.* A Description of IPT Strategies: *Managing the Depression. Intervening in the Patient's Current Interpersonal Functioning.* Efficacy Data on IPT: *IPT as Maintenance Treatment. IPT as Acute Treatment. IPT with Methadone Maintained Opiate Addicts.* Conclusion.

6. *Marital and Family Treatment of Depression*
    Gretchen L. Haas, John F. Clarkin, and Ira D. Glick   151

Introduction. The Psychosocial Context of Depression: *The Interpersonal Element in Contemporary Models of Depression. Psychosocial Dysfunction in a Clinically Depressed Population. The Functional Relationship between Marital/Family Stress and Depression. Patterns of Psychosocial Dysfunction: Exogenous versus Endogenous Depression. Patterns of Psychosocial Dysfunction: Patient/Spouse Communication.*

Outcome Studies of Family/Marital Therapy for Depression. Theoretical and Practical Considerations in Family/Marital Treatment with Depressed Patients. A General Approach to the Family/Marital Treatment of Affective Disorders. Assessment Strategies. Treatment Goals and Strategies. Typical Issues in Family/Marital Treatment of Depressive Disorders. Case Illustrations. Family/Marital Treatment in the Prevention of Family Psychiatric Disorder.

7. *Alternate Psychotherapies for Depression: Transactional Analysis, Gestalt Therapy, and Reality Therapy* Gregory W. Lester **184**

Transactional Analysis: *Background. TA Personality Theory. The Role of Parent Ego-State Injunctions in Depression. The Role of Child Ego-State Decisions in Depression. Life Positions and Depression. Stroking Patterns and Depression. Psychological Games and Depression. Racket Feelings and Depression. The Adult Ego-State and Depression. Depressive Life Scripts. TA Treatment of Depression. Increasing Adult Awareness. Changing the "Don't Exist" Injunction. Changing the Early Depressive Decision. The Role of Strokes in Treating Depression.* Gestalt Therapy: *Background. The Cycle of Needs. Awareness and the Need/Satisfaction Cycle. Mechanisms which Interfere with Gestalt Formation. Unfinished Business. Gestalt Treatment of Depression.* Reality Therapy: *Background. Human Needs and Responsible Behavior. Reality Therapy and the Treatment of Depression.* Discussion

8. *Psychotherapy Research in Depression: An Overview* **Alan S. Bellack** **204**

Specific Issues with General Relevance: *Interpersonal Psychotherapy. Cognitive Therapy. Behavior Therapy. Other Psychotherapies.* General Issues: *Diagnosis. Assessment of Outcome. Do Current Treatments Really Differ?*

9. *Medication and Somatic Therapies in the Treatment of Depression* Katherine M. Noll, John M. Davis, and **Frank DeLeon-Jones** **220**

Introduction. History. Differential Diagnosis and the Issue of "Depressive Equivalents" or "Masked Depression." Medication in the Treatment of Depression. Tricyclic Antidepressants: *Effectiveness. Mode of Use. Proposed Mechanisms of Action. Side Effects and Adverse Effects of TCA Treatment.* "Second-Generation" Antidepressants: *Effectiveness. Dosage. Special Issues in the Use of New Antidepressants. Proposed Mechanisms of Action of New Antidepressants.* Monoamine Oxidase Inhibitors: *Effectiveness. Mode of Use. Special Issues in the Use of MAO Inhibitors. Mechanisms of the MAOI Antidepressant Action.* Lithium: *Effectiveness. Mode of Use. Special Issues in the Use of Lithium. Proposed Mechanism of Lithium Action.* Other Medications: *Stimulants. Endocrine Treat-*

ments. Anticonvulsants. Transmitter Precursors. Methylation. Other Drug Treatments with Reported Antidepressant Effects. Somatic Therapies for Depression: *Electroconvulsive Therapy. Effectiveness. Mode of Use. Special Issues in the Use of ECT. Proposed Mechanisms of Action of ECT.* Sleep, Light and Circadian Rhythm Manipulations.

10. *The Comparative Efficacy of Psychotherapy and Pharmacotherapy for Depression* **Ernest Edward Beckham and William R. Leber 316**

Summary of Studies Comparing Medication and Psychotherapy: *Early Studies. Treatment of Acute Depression with Interpersonal Therapy. Comparisons of Cognitive Therapy with Pharmacotherapy. Studies Comparing Behavior Therapy and Pharmacotherapy. Comparisons of Short-Term Analytic Therapy with Medication. Meta-Analysis of Comparative Efficacy. The NIMH Treatment of Depression Collaborative Research Program. Summary of Outcome Studies.* Limitations on the Generalizability of Research Findings. Issues in Research. Future Research Directions. Clinical Implications. Conclusion.

Part 2
Assessment

11. *Diagnostic Criteria for Depression* **William R. Leber, Ernest Edward Beckham, and Pamela Danker-Brown 343**

Introduction. Issues in the Classification of Depression and Other Mental Disorders. Definitions and Assumptions. The Purpose of Diagnosis. Classifications of Depression: *The Neurotic-Psychotic Distinction. The Reactive-Endogenous Distinction. The Primary-Secondary Distinction. The Unipolar-Bipolar Distinction. The Winokur-Iowa Classification System. The Akiskal Classification of Dysthymia. Endogenomorphic Depression and Hysteroid Dysphoria. Current-American Classifications of Depression—RDC and DSM-III. Current Issues with DSM-III.* Future Directions: *A Biological Classification of Depression? Classification Based on Psychosocial Processes.* Criteria for Evaluating Classification Systems. Conclusion. Appendix: Practical Diagnostic Interviewing.

12. *The Assessment of the Severity and Symptom Patterns in Depression* **Brian F. Shaw, T. Michael Vallis, and Scott B. McCabe 372**

Introduction. Interviewing the Depressed Patient. Interview Methods of Assessing Depression: *Schedule for Affective Disorders and Schizophrenia. The Hamilton Rating Scale for Depression. The Present State Examination.* Self-Report Methods of Assessment: *Beck Depression Inventory.*

Minnesota Multiphasic Personality Inventory. The Carroll Rating Scale for Depression. Zung Self-Rating Depression Scale (SDS). Center for Epidemiologic Studies Depression Scale. Depression Adjective Checklist. Visual Analogue Scale (VAS). Comparative Value of Self-Report and Interview Measures. Special Considerations. Conclusion. Summary. Appendix: Brief Review of Selected Mania Measures.

13. *Measures of Psychological Processes in Depression*
    Constance Hammen and Susan E. Krantz   **408**

Cognitive Approaches to Depression: *Cognitive Distortion Model of Depression. Attributional Model of Depression. Self-Control Model of Depression.* Behavioral Approaches to Depression: *Level of Reinforcement. Social Skill Assessment. Coping and Depression.* Issues in the Assessment of Cognitions. Implications for Appropriate Research and Clinical Use of Measures.

14. *New Medical Diagnostic Procedures for Depression*
    Jan Fawcett and Howard M. Kravitz   **445**

Introduction. In the Beginning: Biogenic Amines—Past, Present, and (?) Future: *Monoamine Hypotheses. Catecholamine Measures. Indoleamine Measures. PEA Measures, Central Cholinergic Factors. Conclusions. Summary.* Psychoneuroendocrine Studies of Depressive Disorders: *Introduction. Cortisol and the Dexamethasone Suppression Test (DST).* Other Tests of Limbic System-Hypothalamic-Pituitary Function: *Thyroid-Releasing Hormone (TRH) Stimulation Test. Growth Hormone. Prolactin. Gonadotropins. Summary and Conclusions.* The Stimulant Challenge Test and Depression: *Summary and Conclusions.* Lithium Transport. Neurophysiological Studies: *Sleep Markers in Depression.* Other Electrophysiological and Neuroradiologic Studies: *Brain Imaging: A Glimpse at Things to Come.* Conclusions.

Part 3
Special Topics

15. *Depression in Children and Adolescents*
    Kay Kline Hodges and Lawrence J. Siegel   **517**

Issues of Diagnosis/Classification. Prevalence and Epidemiology. Developmental Issues. Assessment: *Self-Rating Scales. Clinician-Rated Scales. Diagnostic Interviews. Peer Inventories. Parent Scales. Future Research Needs.* Cognitive Features of Childhood Depression. Suicidal Behavior and Depression: *Suicides. Suicide Attempts. Suicide Ideation and Threats.* Treatment of Childhood Depression.

16. *Depession in the Elderly*   Alan Stoudemire and Dan G. Blazer   **556**

Introduction. The Epidemiology of Late Life Depression. Biological Aspects of Aging in the Elderly. Psychological Aspects of Aging and Depression: *Sociological Aspects of Aging.* Diagnosis of Depression in the Elderly. Differential Diagnosis: *The Aprosodias: A Possible Complication in the Evaluation of Brain Damaged Depressed Patients.* Normal and Pathological Grief. Treatment of Depression: *Evaluation. Psychopharmacologic Considerations. MAO Inhibitors. Lithium Carbonate. The Use of Electrotherapy in the Elderly.* Psychotherapy: *Psychotherapy Outcome Research with the Depressed Elderly.* Conclusion: Psychotherapy with the Elderly.

17. *Chronic and Refractory Depressions: Evaluation and Management*   Hagop S. Akiskal and Rebecca C. Simmons   **587**

Introduction. Definitional Issues. Classification. Treatment Implications of Proposed Chronic Depressive Subtypes: *Chronic Residual Phase of Unipolar Depression. Chronic Secondary Dysphorias. Characterologic Depressions.* The Question of Intractable Depressions: *Terminologic Aspects. Recommendations in the Literature. The University of Tennessee Approach.* Summary.

18. *Assessment and Treatment of the Suicidal Patient*   Jenny L. Boyer and Lesley Guthrie   **606**

Introduction. Assessment of Suicidal Risk: *Risk Factors. Environmental Stressors. Medical History. Psychiatric History. Diagnosis. Personality Factors.* Psychological Assessment Instruments. Biochemical Assessment. Treatment of Suicide: *Outcome Studies.* Treatment Approaches: *Support Strategies. Control Strategies. Therapist Reactions. Medication. Conclusion.* Suicide in Children and Adolescents. Legal Issues: *Involuntary Commitment. Malpractice. Confidentiality.* Ethics. Appendix: The Clinical Checklist of Suicidality.

19. *The Role of Self-Help Assignments in the Treatment of Depression*   David D. Burns, Russell L. Adams, and Arthur D. Anastopoulos   **634**

Historical Overview. Prevalence. Rationale. Empirical Support. How to Introduce the Concept of Self-Help to the Patient. Self-Help Methods. Signs of Therapeutic Resistance. Ways of Motivating Resistant Patients. Appendix: The Concept of Self-Help.

20. *The Relationship of Depression to Other DSM-III Axis I Disorders*   Laurent Lehmann   **669**

Introduction: The Nature of Depression. Depression and Anxiety Disorders. Depression and Schizophrenia. Depression and Schizoaffective Disorder. Depression and Paranoid Disorders. Depression and Substance Use Disorders. Depression and Eating Disorders. Depression and Organic Mental Disorders. Depression and Somatoform Disorders. Depression and Dissociative Disorders. Depression and Psychosexual Disorders. Depression and Impulse Control Disorders. Conclusion.

21. *The Relationship of Depression to Disorders of Personality* **Theodore Millon and Doreen Kotik** **700**

The Dependent Personality. The Histrionic Personality. The Schizoid Personality. The Avoidant Personality. The Schizotypal Personality. The Antisocial Personality. The Narcissistic Personality. The Paranoid Personality. The Passive-Aggressive Personality. The Borderline Personality. The Compulsive Personality. Conclusions.

22. *Depression Associated with Physical Disease* **Roger G. Kathol 745**

Introduction. Defining Depression in the Medically Ill: *Common Symptoms. The Question of Obscure Affective Illness.* Medical Illness in Depressed Patients. Depression in the Medically Ill. Psychological Reaction to Physical Illness. Treatment. Summary.

Part 4
Basic Research

23. *Epidemiology of Depression* **John K. Wing and Paul Bebbington** **765**

The Epidemiological Approach. The Concept of Disease. Clinical Syndromes of Depression. Methods of Case Finding in Epidemiological Surveys. The Frequency of Depressive Disorders. Macrosocial Factors—Sex, Marital Status, Family Responsibility, Employment. Precipitation and Vulnerability: *Measurement of Life Events and Chronic Problems. Does Adversity Precipitate Depression? Vulnerability to Stress. Psychosocial Support.* Cross-Cultural Studies. Summary and Conclusions.

24. *Genetic Research in Depressive Disorders* **J. Mendlewicz** **795**

Depressive Disorders: Epidemiology and Heredity: *Prevalence. Twin Studies. Linkage Studies. Adoption Studies. Mode of Inheritance. Affective Disorders, Schizophrenia and Schizoaffective Illness: Genetic Considerations.* Practical Applications of Genetic Research in Depression: *Genetic Criteria of Lithium Response. Genetic Counseling.*

25. *Biological Processes in Major Depression* **Michael E. Thase, Ellen Frank, and David J. Kupfer** **816**

Historical Perspectives. Conceptual Issues. Methodologic Issues. Neurochemical Abnormalities: *Monoamines (MA). Summary. Acetylcholine. Summary. Other Neurochemical Studies.* Neurophysiological Abnormalities: *Electroencephalographic Sleep Studies. Other Electroencephalographic Studies. Abnormalities of Smooth Pursuit Eye Movements. Neuroradiological Abnormalities. Measurement of Psychomotor Disturbances. Electrodermal Activity Recording. Colonic Motility Studies. Summary.* Neuroendocrine Abnormalities: *HYPAC Axis Abnormalities. Thyroid Axis Disturbances. Insulin Tolerance Test Findings. Growth Hormone Regulation. Prolactin Secretion. Sex Differences in Depression. Summary.* Chronobiology and Depression. Summary of Research on the Biology of Major Depression.

26. The Learned Helplessness Model of Depression: Current Status of Theory and Research   Christopher Peterson and Martin E. P. Seligman   914

Basic Issues and Questions for a Theory of Depression. The Original Helplessness Model: *Original Helplessness Theory and the 13 Issues.* The Attributional Reformulation: *The Reformulation and the 13 Issues.* Future Directions.

27. *Psychosocial Stressors, Coping, and Depression*
Andrew G. Billings and Rudolf H. Moos   940

Introduction. An Integrative Framework: *Framework Boundaries.* Stressful Life Circumstances: *Stressful Events. Life Strains. Microstressors.* Personal Resources: *Sense of Environmental Mastery. Attributional Styles. Interpersonal Skills and Orientation. Personal Resources: Directions for Research.* Environmental Resources: *Family Support. Work Support. Indirect and Reciprocal Effects.* Appraisal and Coping Responses: *Appraisal of Stressors. Stressor-Appraisal Specificity. Coping Responses. Help-Seeking.* Social Background Factors: *Social Status. Gender Differences.* Clinical and Research Applications: *Assessment of the Domains in the Framework. Developing and Evaluating Psychosocial Treatments. Exploring the Determinants of Posttreatment Functioning. Developing Prevention Programs.* Summary.

Part 5
Appendixes

Appendix 1   DSM-III Criteria for Major Depressive Episode and Dysthymic Disorder   977

Appendix 2   Interview Questions for Symptoms of Major Depression and Endogenous Subtype from the Schedule for Affective Disorders and Schizophrenia   980

Appendix 3   Beck Depression Inventory   984

Appendix 4 Hamilton Rating Scale for Depression **987**

Appendix 5 Carroll Rating Scale for Depression **996**

Appendix 6 Rosenbaum Self-Control Schedule **998**

Appendix 7 Dysfunctional Attitude Scale (Form A) **1000**

Appendix 8 Pleasant Events Schedule Form III-S **1005**

Appendix 9 A Selected Listing of Other Depression Inventories and
Depression-Related Instruments for Adults **1012**

Appendix 10 A Selected Listing of Measures of Depression for
Children **1018**

Name Index **1027**

Subject Index **1065**

PART 1

Treatment

Chapter 1

Cognitive Therapy of Depression

William P. Sacco
Aaron T. Beck

The cognitive theory of depression (Beck, 1967, 1976) and the psychotherapeutic strategies that have grown from the theory (Beck, Rush, Shaw, & Emery, 1979) represent the product of over 20 years of theory and research. In a very early study, Beck (1961) first reported on the dream content of depressed patients. The purpose of the study was to evaluate the psychoanalytic view that depression was the result of inverted hostility. Following from the psychoanalytic position, it was hypothesized that depressed patients would show more hostility in their dreams than nondepressed patients. Surprisingly, the psychoanalytic hypothesis was not supported. Rather, it was observed that depressed patients had a greater than normal incidence of dreams with content that centered around being deprived, thwarted, depreciated, excluded, or punished in some way. This serendipitous finding has been replicated on several occasions (e.g., Beck & Ward, 1961; Hauri, 1976). Extending these observations, Beck (1963) began to analyze the free associations and verbal reports of depressed patients. The idiosyncratic cognitive content and cognitive distortions he observed (Beck, 1963) led to a clinically based theory that depressed persons view the self, the world, and the future negatively and that a theme of loss permeates their cognitive distortions. Further, it was theorized that these cognitive propensities play a central role in the development and maintenance of depression.

Since then, a tremendous amount of energy and enthusiasm has been directed toward empirical examination of the cognitive theory, development of a cognitive-based treatment program for depressed patients (Beck et al., 1979), and empirical examination of the efficacy of the cognitive therapy of depression (e.g., Rush, Beck, Kovacs, & Hollon, 1977). Today, the cognitive theory remains one of the most widely supported theories of depression. Outcome studies have provided strong evidence of the effects of cognitive therapy relative to other psychosocial therapies, and early studies have shown cognitive therapy to be more effective than pharmacological treatment (e.g., Rush et al., 1977).

In this chapter we first describe the cognitive theory of depression. Next, we outline the stages of cognitive therapy of depression. In our description of the therapy we attempt to communicate the underlying structure which

3

guides the cognitive therapist. As will be seen, cognitive therapy of depression is designed to be "transportable." That is, a treatment manual has been designed so that with adequate training and supervision, cognitive therapy, and its apparent effectiveness, can be replicated by therapists at large. Finally, we provide a summary of the large body of empirical evidence bearing on the validity of the cognitive theory and the efficacy of cognitive therapy for depression.

THE COGNITIVE THEORY OF DEPRESSION

Simply stated, the cognitive theory of depression proposes that depression is primarily a result of the tendency to view the self, the future, and the world in an unrealistically negative manner. This distorted, negative view of self, future, and world is termed the *negative triad* (Beck, 1967). Depressed persons regard themselves as unworthy, incapable, and undesirable. They expect failure, rejection, and dissatisfaction and perceive most experiences as confirming these negative expectations. The major symptoms of a depressive disorder (affective, behavioral, somatic, and motivational) are viewed as a direct consequence of this negative cognitive set.

A central feature of this theory is that the depressed individual's negative view is usually a distortion of reality. Idiosyncratic cognitive schemas are proposed as hypothetical structures serving to maintain the depressogenic cognitive triad despite contradictory evidence. Schemas are viewed as stable cognitive patterns through which events are processed. Functioning like a template, schemas actively screen, code, categorize, and evaluate stimuli. In depression these schemas or response categories, especially those related to the self-concept and personal expectations, tend to be global, rigid, and negatively toned (Hollon & Beck, 1979). Once activated, these depressive schemas influence how external stimuli are interpreted, resulting in the cognitive distortions commonly found in depressed persons.

Beck (1967) has described several common systematic errors in the way depressed individuals process information (cognitive distortions), which reflect the activity of depressogenic cognitive schemas. The systematic errors in logic are listed below:

1. Arbitrary inference (a response set)—drawing a conclusion in the absence of evidence or when the evidence is contrary to the conclusion.
2. Selective abstraction (a stimulus set)—the tendency to focus on a negative detail in a situation and to conceptualize the entire experience on the basis of this negative fragment.
3. Overgeneralization (a response set)—the tendency to draw a general rule or conclusion on the basis of one isolated incident and to apply the concept indiscriminately to both related and unrelated situations.

4. Magnification and minimization (a response set)—the tendency to overestimate the significance or magnitude of undesirable events and underestimate the significance or magnitude of desirable events.
5. Personalization (a response set)—the tendency to relate external events to oneself without evidence.
6. All-or-none thinking (a response set)—the tendency to think in absolute black or white, all-or-none terms.

These errors in logic are considered causally related to the depression-prone individual's tendency to interpret events in extreme, negative, categorical, absolute, and judgmental ways and reflect more primitive, immature levels of cognitive processing (Beck et al., 1979).

It is important to point out that the cognitive theory of depression represents a diathesis-stress model of psychopathology although many writers and researchers fail to acknowledge this important feature. It proposes that individuals who are prone to depression have acquired a psychological predisposition toward depression through early experiences that shape the development of cognitive schemas in a negative, self-referential manner. The depressogenic cognitive schemas will remain latent until activated by stressors (precipitating factors) to which the individual is sensitized. For example, due to the loss of a parent in childhood, some individuals may be predisposed to develop a depressive disorder upon the termination of a love relationship in adult life. These same individuals may not develop a depressive disorder in response to loss of employment, a stressor which might precipitate a depression in an individual who has been sensitized to failing to live up to excessively high standards imposed by parents in early childhood. This concept of specific vulnerability may help explain why the relationship between life stressors and depression is not as strong as many have expected (e.g., Paykel, 1979). Moreover, this view also suggests that individuals who are predisposed to depressive disorders will tend to avoid depression if experiences to which they are sensitized are absent from their environment. In such cases the negative cognitive schemas remain latent and inactive. Consequently, fewer negative thoughts will occur (see Eaves & Rush, 1984).

Although the cognitive theory of depression focuses on an intrapsychic mechanism to describe the development and maintenance of depression, the role of interpersonal factors in the development of depressive disorders is acknowledged (Beck et al., 1979). Recent evidence points to the fact that depressed individuals create a powerful impact on their social environment (e.g., Coyne, 1976; Lewinsohn, 1974; Sacco, Milana, & Dunn, in press). However, the specific role played by interpersonal factors must be examined for each individual case. Data suggests that in some situations, the depressed individual's social behavior may elicit rejection by others, serving to exacerbate the depression (Coyne, 1976). Alternatively, in some situations depressed persons elicit increased social support which may help to alleviate the severity of their depression (e.g., Hokanson, Sacco, Blumberg, & Landrum, 1980). Cognitive therapists are encouraged to assess the potential benefits to be gained from involving significant others in the therapy process (Beck et al., 1979; Bedrosian, 1981). Significant others are often useful for helping depressed patients test the validity of their thinking (Rush, Shaw, & Khatami, 1980). However, if the depressed patient's significant interpersonal relationships appear dysfunctional and are acting to maintain or exacerbate the depression, it may be necessary to initiate some form of interpersonal therapy (e.g., couples or family therapy). Still, in many cases cognitive therapy appears to provide additional benefits even after interpersonal difficulties have been resolved.

COGNITIVE THERAPY OF DEPRESSION: BASIC TREATMENT STRATEGIES

Cognitive therapy for depression is an active, directive, structured, psychoeducational approach based upon Beck's cognitive theory of depression (Beck et al., 1979). Three theoretical assumptions underlie cognitive therapy interventions. The principal underlying assumption is that an individual's affect and behavior are largely determined by the way in which he/she views the world. A second assumption is that cognitions (thoughts, beliefs, fantasies, images, and so on) can be self-monitored by the patient and communicated. Identification and self-monitoring of cognitions may require training, but these cognitions are not unconscious, and the concept of unconscious processes is largely irrelevant to cognitive therapy. Finally, it is assumed that the modification of cognitions will lead to changes in affect and behavior. Research bearing on the validity of these assumptions will be reviewed in a later section.

The cognitive therapist employs a variety of cognitive and behavioral techniques to alter the depressed patient's depressogenic style of thought. To accomplish this goal, a series of highly specific learning experiences are incorporated into treatment. The steps are outlined below. However, before describing the basic treatment approach, a few points of clarification are necessary.

Prior to beginning treatment, it is recommended that all patients receive a thorough diagnostic evaluation. Insuring that the patient is suitable for cognitive treatment is of utmost importance (Beck, et al., 1979). Generally speaking, nonbipolar, nonpsychotic depressed patients are well suited for cognitive therapy (see outcome study results in a later section of this chapter). Suicidal patients and severely depressed patients, however, may require hospitalization and/or "somatic" therapy, though these approaches may be used in conjunction with cognitive therapy.

Cognitive therapy is designed to be a time-limited, short-term treatment. General guidelines suggest 15 to 25 (50-minute) sessions at weekly intervals, with more seriously depressed patients usually requiring twice weekly meetings for the initial four to five weeks. To avoid an abrupt termination, a "tapering off" process is recommended, with the last few sessions occurring once every two weeks. After termination, some patients may also need a few (four or five is common) "booster sessions."

It is recommended that the patient's level of depression be assessed throughout treatment. The Beck Depression Inventory ([BDI]; Beck, 1967; see Appendix 3 at end of book) is useful for this purpose, as it has demonstrated reliability and validity and can be completed by patients prior to each session in approximately 10 minutes. The BDI thus provides a useful method for monitoring patients' progress. It also includes items relevant to assessing suicidal ideation and intent. Obviously, substantial increases or decreases in depression level provide important information and suggest that the therapist and patient try to determine possible causes for the changes.

Before every session, the patient and therapist should establish an agenda of prioritized issues that each would like to deal with during the session. It is the therapist's responsibility to control the therapy session so that, to the extent it is possible, the high-priority agenda items are covered. Those items not discussed should be brought up in the following session. The agenda achieves a variety of goals, including enhancing the efficiency of each session, providing a structure for the sessions which seems in itself to be therapeutic for depressed patients, and actively involving the patient in the direction of each session.

Although cognitive therapy adopts a psychoeducational approach, utilizing structure and a variety of techniques designed to modify cognitive-behavioral habits, the therapeutic process itself is also considered important. Effective cognitive therapy requires, first of all, the development of a strong therapeutic relationship; for example, development of trust, genuine concern for and acceptance of the patient, and accurate empathy. Thus, the cognitive therapist must possess the basic characteristics of an effective psychotherapist. Moreover, although cognitive therapy is described below as a very structured therapy, when properly conducted the implicit structure of cognitive therapy is melded into the therapy process such that the goals of each session are accomplished within a therapeutic context that involves a natural and effective flow of communication between the therapist and patient. Similarly, although it is accurate to infer that therapy proceeds in stepwise progression, the boundaries between the steps described below typically are blurred during the actual therapeutic process.

The pace at which the therapist and patient proceed through the steps of cognitive therapy is likely to vary, primarily due to patient characteristics such as the severity of depression, motivation, and suitability for cognitively oriented interventions. However, guidelines can be extrapolated from the research protocol for outcome studies conducted at the Center for Cognitive Therapy (see Beck et al., 1979). These guidelines are presented here simply to provide the reader with an approximate time frame for the steps outlined below. Note that these guidelines were developed for an outcome study that limited treatment to a maximum of 20 sessions. Thus in nonresearch settings, the pace and duration of treatment is likely to vary to a much greater extent.

With these caveats in mind, the research protocol suggests that steps 1 and 2 should occur during sessions 1–4; steps 3 and 4 should occur during sessions 6–8; and step 5 should occur during sessions 8–12. The remaining sessions (up to 20 for the outcome study) are designed to prepare the patient for termination. During these sessions the principles and strategies learned previously are practiced, with the patient taking on a greater responsibility for enacting self-help strategies so that he/she is prepared for termination of treatment.

Step 1—Identify and Monitor Dysfunctional Automatic Thoughts

One of the first goals of cognitive therapy is to teach the patient to identify and monitor automatic dysfunctional thoughts. Automatic thoughts are specific subvocalizations or self-statements which occur automatically and without conscious effort. Patients are often unaware of having these thoughts unless taught to recognize them. When brought to their attention, depressed persons usually see their automatic thoughts as accurate representations of reality even though they are often unreasonably negative. Clinical experience and recent data also indicate that the degree to which an individual believes his/her negative dysfunctional ideation is related to the strength of his/her negative emotional response (Rogers & Craighead, 1977).

A variety of interventions are made in an effort to teach patients to identify and monitor dysfunctional ideation. First, patients are taught the basic concepts of cognitive theory and cognitive therapy. Automatic thoughts are described to patients in a didactic manner, and patients are provided relevant reading material to increase their intellectual understanding of cognitive therapy; for example a booklet titled "Coping with Depression," (Beck & Greenberg, 1974). The therapist then attempts to engage the patient as a collaborator, or fellow scientist, to work together to discover if the patient does indeed tend to experience a great number of these negative thoughts. Beck et al. (1979) consider the enactment of collaborative empiricism to be essential for effective cognitive therapy with depressed individuals. By joining in the collaborative-empirical venture, patients learn under nonthreatening conditions to evaluate their thinking more objectively. Thus, the idea that the patient may be thinking in an unrealistically negative manner should be raised as a tentative hypothesis to be decided by various data-gathering techniques. No attempt is made to argue the veracity or reasonableness of the patient's thoughts in these initial sessions. The therapist simply reinforces the patient for identifying and monitoring his/her negative automatic thoughts.

Several techniques are useful in helping the therapist and patient identify dysfunctional thoughts. The therapist may make direct inquiries about cognitive reactions to events leading to strong emotional responses. For example, during the first session, patients may be asked about thoughts they had prior to meeting the therapist. This questioning often elicits a variety of automatic thoughts about expectations of therapy outcome, the therapist's characteristics, how the therapist will view the patient and so on. Past events associated with negative mood can also be examined by asking patients to imagine the chain of events occurring just prior to a particular negative reaction and then focusing on the patient's specific thoughts during that time. Role-playing may be utilized to facilitate accurate recall of past events and associated cognitions. Mood shifts during the session (e.g., tearful eyes) are also very effective cues for the therapist to inquire about the patient's thoughts.

A variety of homework assignments are used to promote recognition of automatic thoughts between sessions. For instance, the Dysfunctional Thoughts Record (see Tables 1–3) is especially helpful in teaching patients to dissect emotion-producing situations into three components—the objective situation, the emotion, and the automatic thoughts that lead to the emotion. Another homework assignment, "thought counting," is designed to help patients monitor the frequency of certain automatic thoughts. Patients may use either a wrist counter or an index card to simply count thoughts of a specific theme (e.g., guilt-inducing thoughts).

Weekly homework is an integral feature of cognitive therapy. Cognitive therapy is designed to be a short-term treatment and work done by the patient between therapy sessions serves to facilitate progress. The idea of weekly homework is presented to the patient at the beginning of treatment. Most patients are quite receptive to the idea of working outside of the therapy session, and some experience increased optimism simply because they themselves can do something that may alleviate their depressed condition. Only in the very early sessions does the therapist take responsibility for suggesting a homework assignment. In keeping with the spirit of "collaborative empiricism," the therapist should soon begin to involve the patient more and more in planning the weekly homework until finally the patient is taking a major role in determining what work will be done between therapy sessions.

Step 2—Recognize the Connection between Thoughts, Emotion, and Behavior

The next step of cognitive therapy involves teaching patients to recognize the connection between thoughts, emotion, and behavior. Frequently the patient will discover this connection while learning to identify automatic thoughts. It is again important to point out that a hypothesis testing attitude is recommended when trying to establish this connection. Thus the therapist should ask "How did you feel (or what did you do) when you had those thoughts?" In almost all cases, patients easily see the connection between their thoughts, emotions, and behaviors. Patients may also be told at this point that most people experiencing the same thoughts as the patient would probably have similar behavioral and emotional reactions. Thus, the connection between thoughts, emotion, and behavior is presented as a general principle, applicable to all people and situations.

TABLE 1
Daily record of dysfunctional thoughts

Date	Situation	Emotion(s)	Automatic thought(s)	Rational response	Outcome
	Describe: 1. Actual event leading to un-pleasant emotion, or 2. Stream of thoughts, daydream, or recollection, leading to unpleasant emotion.	1. Specify sad/anxious/angry, etc. 2. Rate degree of emotion, 1–100.	1. Write automatic thought(s) that preceded emotion(s). 2. Rate belief in automatic thought(s), 0–100 percent.	1. Write rational response to automatic thought(s). 2. Rate belief in rational response, 0–100 percent.	1. Re-rate belief in automatic thought(s), 0–100 percent. 2. Specify and rate subsequent emotions, 0–100.

Explanation: When you experience an unpleasant emotion, note the situation that seemed to stimulate the emotion. (If the emotion occurred while you were thinking, daydreaming, etc., please note this.) Then note the automatic thought associated with the emotion. Record the degree to which you believe this thought: 0 percent = not at all; 100 percent = completely. In rating degree of emotion: 1 = a trace; 100 = the most intense possible.

TABLE 2
Instructions for completing the daily record of dysfunctional thoughts

The Daily Record of Dysfunctional Thoughts is designed to help you analyze and resolve situations that cause you to feel or act in a way that is not in your best interest.

Column 1: Situation.   In this column you describe the actual events that led to the unpleasant emotion. In filling out this column you must be objective. That is, briefly describe what happened as a videotape would have recorded it. Sometimes there is no specific event that led to the unpleasant emotion. Rather, unpleasant emotions often result from just daydreaming about something. In that case, briefly describe the daydream or stream of thought leading to the unpleasant emotion.

Column 2: Emotion(s).   Indicate how you felt (feel) at the time. Emotions are feelings such as sad, angry, depressed, lonely, afraid, and anxious. These are your emotions, *not your thoughts.* Remember that thoughts are really words, phrases, or sentences that we say to ourselves. It may take some practice to be able to distinguish between thoughts and emotions, but you will be able to do so. Also, indicate the degree that you felt these emotions using the 0–100 scale described on the bottom of the form.

Column 3: Automatic Thought(s).   Most people assume that it is the situation that causes the feeling. In actuality, it is our thoughts about the situation that lead to our feelings. For this column you are to write down the automatic thoughts that preceded the emotion.

Sometimes it is easy for you to identify your automatic thoughts. Sometimes, they are harder to identify because they are so automatic. For these cases, you have to concentrate on what happened and your reaction to the event. Then, write down all your thoughts, exactly as they came to you, verbatim. Then, rate how strongly you believe the automatic thoughts to be true using the 0–100 scale described on the bottom of the form.

Column 4: Rational Response.   After you have written down your automatic thoughts, you need to examine the reasonableness of each thought. Is the thought accurate? What is the evidence to support it? Is there another less depression-producing interpretation of the event? Is there another way of looking at the situation that would not make you feel so bad? Work hard at these rational responses. It may help to ask someone who may be more objective and rational about an event that you feel emotionally upset over. Also, rate the degree to which you believe the rational response to be true using the 0–100 scale described on the bottom of the form.

Column 5: Outcome.   After you have completed columns 1–4, re-rate how strongly you believe the automatic thoughts to be true and how you now feel.

Practice this technique often.

TABLE 3
Daily record of negative automatic thoughts

Date	Situation	Emotion(s)	Automatic Thought(s)	Questioning the evidence	REASONABLE/ADAPTIVE RESPONSE(S)		
					Alternative therapy	Re-attribution	De-catastrophizing
5/23	At home, reading—waiting for Bob to call—it's now 10 P.M.—he hasn't called.	Sad Miserable Abandoned Lonely	Why didn't he call? Why is he rejecting me? I feel so miserable, I don't know what to do—why can't I hold on to a guy? Why does this always happen to me—I just *can't* go on like this—what did I do wrong?	Just because he didn't call doesn't mean he is rejecting me—I have no *real* proof of that—I already saw him twice this week—if he didn't like me he would not have spent that much time with me—I *shouldn't* jump to crazy conclusions like	There could be many reasons why he didn't call—besides rejection? He could be tied up with his clients, he could be trying to set bail for someone—it may have skipped his mind—he may not be feeling well—he could be with friends—he may have had something to do! But even if he *is*	Why should I assume that his not calling has to do with *me*? He may have a lot of reasons for doing what he does—things that have nothing to do with me. It doesn't make sense to think that everything happens be-cause of *me*—that I did	Here I go *again*! thinking that I am rejected! —but even if I am (which I don't know for sure)—even if he doesn't want to see me it's *not true* that I can't go on! It's just a feeling that I have—I have survived before even if this doesn't work—the worst that can happen is that I'll be sad,

unhappy but it's not the end of the world—there are other men out there, and I have my friends, my job—I *can* go on.

something wrong! He must have his *own* feelings, ideas and fears—just like I. If things don't work out the way I'd like them, it could be because of his *own* things—it doesn't make sense to believe that I am *solely* responsible for what happens between the TWO OF US!

having second thoughts about me—we could talk about it—it doesn't automatically mean that I can't hold on to him.

that—and it's *not* true that "this" *always* happens to me. With John, *I* was the one who didn't want to keep up the relationship!

Source Adapted from Kovacs (1977).

Step 3—Evaluate the Reasonableness of the Automatic Thoughts

After the therapist and patient have demonstrated the patient's tendency to experience negative automatic thoughts (negative view of self, world, future) and that these thoughts appear causally related to negative affect and dysfunctional behavior, the empirical approach is extended to examining the reasonableness of the patient's thoughts. In essence, therapist and patient test the hypothesis that the automatic thoughts are either illogical, inconsistent with the facts of the situation, or are self-defeating because there is little or no advantage to thinking them. The goal of this step is to teach the patient to think as a scientist; that is, to view thoughts and conclusions more tentatively as hypotheses that should be examined in light of the available evidence. This goal is to be contrasted with directly attacking the irrationality of the patient's thoughts.

This third stage represents the quintessential element of Beck's cognitive therapy. Hence, the majority of therapist-patient interactions center around achieving this psychoeducational goal. Depression-inducing situations and concomitant automatic thoughts are examined closely to evaluate their accuracy and logic. A variety of cognitive cues are taught to facilitate the search for possible cognitive distortions and erroneous conclusions. For example, it is helpful to teach patients to ask themselves four questions regarding their automatic thoughts:

First, patients should be taught to ask themselves "What is the evidence to support this thought?" The therapist may use Socratic questioning to examine the logic or the premises upon which conclusions are based. This type of questioning helps clarify the patient's thinking in response to the particular situation. In addition, perhaps a greater value comes from the therapist modeling rational thinking processes. Another very effective mechanism to help the patient critically examine the evidence regarding a thought is to conduct "mini-experiments" designed to gather data bearing on the validity of the patient's thoughts. For example, a new grandmother reported feeling very depressed after being irritated with her new grandchild. Examining her automatic thoughts revealed the thought that "other grandmothers never have negative reactions to their grandchildren; therefore, because I felt irritation with my grandchild, I am a bad grandmother." Rather than trying to verbally attack the logic or reasonableness of these thoughts, the therapist asked the patient how she could test her thought and basic premise. Together they devised a plan to ask several grandmothers if they ever felt annoyed or irritated with their grandchildren. By doing so, the patient discovered that her peers frequently had similar feelings and at times felt relief when their grandchildren left at the end of a visit.

A second important question for patients to learn to ask themselves is "Are there any alternative interpretations of this event?" Depressed patients are notorious for reaching singular and negative interpretations of ambiguous situations when in actuality a host of alternative less depression-inducing views are quite possible and often accurate. The therapist encourages the patient to "brainstorm" about other interpretations in hopes of teaching the patient to maintain an open mind until more data is obtained.

A third question is designed to help the depressed patients recognize their tendency to erroneously attribute the cause of negative events entirely to internal factors rather than to factors in the environment or in other people. Patients are taught to ask "Am I totally to blame for this negative event?" This tendency in depressives resembles the central thesis of the reformulated learned helplessness model (Abramson, Seligman, & Teasdale, 1978), which posits that depression results from the tendency to attribute negative events to internal, stable, global causes. In cognitive therapy it has been noted that depressed persons often make such attributions (Beck, 1976). For example, depressed persons often attribute any response even remotely resembling a symptom of depression to a stable defect within them. This tendency was exemplified by a patient who felt depressed for several days because she had decided against attending a social gathering with her teammates following a tennis match. Rather than attributing her decision to the fact that she was hot, sweaty, and wanted to go home to relax and cool down, she perceived it as evidence of her hopelessly depressed condition. This tendency to make depression-inducing attributions can often be demonstrated to patients by having them make attributions for hypothetical others in the same situation. Depressed individuals often have a "double standard," making more tolerant attributions for others.

Finally, patients are taught to ask themselves a fourth question—"So what if my negative interpretation of reality is true, why is that so terrible?" This strategy is designed to help patients realize that they can cope with the negative events that sometimes occur to all people. For example, "even if it is true that your boyfriend is going to leave you, why is that so terrible?" By confronting the worst possibility, patients often gain a more realistic perspective. The therapist and patient acknowledge that losing a boyfriend is a negative event which is likely to be disruptive and lead to unpleasant emotions; however, it is also something that people live through.

Step 4—Substitute More Reasonable Thoughts for the Dysfunctional Automatic Thoughts

Learning to substitute more reasonable thoughts for dysfunctional automatic thoughts typically occurs as a direct result of step 3. Patients are taught to change their self-statements to be more in accord with available evidence and logic. The Dysfunctional Thoughts Record is frequently used to attain this goal. Tables 1–3 display the Dysfunctional Thoughts Record, instructions for completion, and a sample demonstrating its use. Initially, patients are strongly encouraged to write down their dysfunctional thoughts and rational counter-responses rather than simply answering them in their heads. Indeed, written dissection of emotion-producing situations seems essential in the beginning stages of this learning process. Later, patients can learn to answer their dysfunctional automatic thoughts without writing them down. It is important that the patient truly believe the rational counterresponse. Simple parroting of rational responses provided by the therapist is usually ineffective; and thus, the therapist must involve the patient in the process of developing rational responses. The therapist should be sensitive to unstated reservations about the accuracy of the rational response. These reservations often take the form of additional negative automatic thoughts in reaction to proposed rational responses. These automatic thoughts must also be examined until the patient believes in the rational responses. Table 3 provides a sample of rational responses that might result from evaluating automatic thoughts in light of the four questions discussed in step 3 (derived from Kovacs, 1977).

Step 5—Identify and Alter Dysfunctional Silent Assumptions

Toward the latter part of treatment, when symptoms have lessened, the therapist should begin to focus on identifying and modifying the basic underlying beliefs that predispose the person toward depressogenic thinking. Depressed individuals often harbor dysfunctional premises or silent assumptions which predispose them to distort and negatively evaluate life events. These assumptions are "silent" in that the individual is typically unaware of their existence and of their impact on the way he/she views the world. Although each individual's silent assumptions or rules are idiosyncratic, common themes are found in the belief system of depressed patients, which tend to be rigid and excessive. For example, a common belief is that one must be loved or life is meaningless. Such a belief is likely to result in hyperdependency, hypervigilence and anxiety regarding possible rejection by loved ones. If an important relationship ends, depression is likely to ensue. Other dysfunctional assumptions which predispose individuals to excessive depression or sadness have been described by Beck (1976). Examples are:

1. In order to be happy, I have to be successful in whatever I undertake.
2. To be happy, I must be accepted by all people at all times.
3. If I make a mistake, it means that I am inept.
4. I can't live without you.
5. If somebody disagrees with me, it means that person doesn't like me.
6. My value as a person depends on what others think of me.

The final step of cognitive therapy involves the identification and modification of these "silent assumptions." Identification of these underlying beliefs usually occurs as a product of the examination of automatic thoughts. An individual's automatic thoughts typically center around one or two themes which reflect dysfunctional premises. For example, a patient who believes it is necessary to be approved of by all people will usually have dysfunctional automatic thoughts in response to social interactions which the patient has perceived as evidence of rejection or disapproval. The Dysfunctional Attitude Scale (Weissman & Beck, 1978; see Appendix 7 at end of book), which has been developed to identify an individual's silent assumptions, is useful in helping the therapist and patient conceptualize these assumptions.

Modification of silent assumptions involves basically the same process as modification of automatic dysfunctional thoughts, and a variety of strategies are described by Beck et al. (1979) and Burns (1981). For example, patients may be asked to list the advantages and disadvantages of holding the beliefs. Or, "response prevention" may be effectively used. This technique involves having patients perform an experiment in which they behave opposite to the way their dysfunctional silent assumption would dictate. For example, patients driven by perfectionistic tendencies would be urged to perform tasks in an "only satisfactory" manner to learn that excessively high standards are not necessary to be happy and may often interfere with performance and satisfaction.

BEHAVIORAL TECHNIQUES

A variety of behavioral techniques are employed in cognitive therapy (Beck et al., 1979). Behavioral techniques are used primarily in the early stages of treatment and are particularly helpful with more severely depressed patients who are less able to view their thoughts objectively. Although one immediate purpose of the behavioral techniques is to alter various behavioral symptoms (e.g., avoidance, reduced activity levels), the ultimate goal is cognitive change. That is, the cognitive therapist uses behavioral change primarily as a method to identify and alter dysfunctional cognitions. For example, "pleasure prediction experiments" (Burns, 1981) are designed to identify and modify the tendency of depressed persons to expect relatively little satisfaction from potentially pleasant events (Sacco, 1985). The patient and therapist plan activities for the patient to engage in during the week. The activity scheduling is presented in part as a data-gathering exercise to see if the patient's expectations about the activities are accurate. Thus, prior to scheduling an activity the patient is asked to make a prediction about how much satisfaction he/she expects from engaging in the event. After completing the event, the patient records the amount of satisfaction actually obtained. Because depressed patients often underestimate the actual satisfaction obtained from the experience, this "mini-experiment" helps to demonstrate and alter the tendency to make unrealistically negative expectations about future events. In addition, patients begin to see the role that negative expectations play in affecting their motivation.

Sometimes, however, the depressed person's negative expectation will be accurate. That is, activities will result in no change in mood or, in some cases, more negative mood. In this case it is necessary for the therapist to help the patient identify the various dysfunctional cognitions that are associated with the activity and which are responsible for induction of the negative moods.

Other behavioral techniques utilized in cognitive therapy are listed below:

1. *Weekly Activity Schedule.* This technique involves having patients monitor their daily activities on an hour-by-hour basis. Such monitoring helps depressed patients test their beliefs that they "never accomplish anything." Ratings of mastery and pleasure are used in conjunction with the activity schedule. These ratings force the patient to attend to any degree of reward experienced. If it is found that the depressed individual does indeed remain inactive throughout the week, the therapist and patient collaboratively schedule activities on an hour-by-hour basis for each day of the week. This technique is especially useful for suicidal patients and serves to counter a loss of motivation, inactivity, and rumination or worrying. Engaging in activities is often therapeutic simply because it distracts the depressed person from de-pressogenic thinking (Teasdale & Rezin, 1978).

2. *Graded Task Assignments.* This behavioral technique involves three steps. First, the patient and therapist identify a goal that the patient wishes to attain but believes to be impossible. Second, the goal is broken down into simple component tasks. Third, the patient is assigned a simple task that is highly likely to provide immediate and unambiguous success feedback. This technique is designed to counter negative expectations and to alter the way in which the patient conceptualizes future tasks so that they no longer seem insurmountable.

RESEARCH BEARING ON THE VALIDITY OF THE COGNITIVE THEORY OF DEPRESSION AND THE EFFICACY OF COGNITIVE THERAPY

The cognitive theory of depression and the treatment developed from the theory have received considerable attention from researchers. In 1979, Beck et al. noted that recent reviews (Beck & Rush, 1978; Hollon & Beck, 1979) had cited over 35 correlational and experimental studies supporting hypotheses derived from the cognitive theory. Since those earlier reviews, at least that many additional supporting studies have been published. This large body of data can be conveniently broken down into three general areas—studies correlating depression level with relevant cognitive variables; studies utilizing designs which provide evidence that the symptoms of depression occur primarily as a consequence of a negative cognitive set; and finally, studies reporting on the efficacy of cognitive therapy interventions. The present review is not intended to be an entirely comprehensive or critical review of these studies. Rather the purpose here is to provide to the reader an overview of the empirical literature related to cognitive theory and therapy of depression.

Correlational Studies

Correlational studies are clearly the most prolific of those published in support of the cognitive model. Numerous studies have reported significant covariation between level of depression and a variety of response categories reflective of the cognitive processes described by the cognitive theory. For convenience of presentation, the correlational research will be categorized according to the particular aspects of the cognitive theory upon which they reflect—the negative view of the self; the negative view of the future; the negative view of the world/experience; and general cognitive processes and content. It is important to note, however, that often the focus of a particular study or a particular measure does not clearly fit into one of the categories used here. Thus at times the categorization of a study was somewhat arbitrarily determined.

Negative View of the Self. Numerous studies provide evidence that depressed persons view themselves more negatively than do nondepressed persons. Measurement of self-esteem provides a direct assessment of this aspect of the cognitive triad. As predicted, depressed persons score significantly lower than nondepressed individuals on a variety of measures of self-esteem (e.g., Altman & Wittenborn, 1980; Beck, 1974; Feather & Barber, 1983; Karoly & Ruehlman, 1983; Lewinsohn, Larson, & Muñoz, 1982; Sacco & Hokanson, 1978). Kazdin, French, Unis, Esveldt-Dawson, and Sherick (1983) found a similar relationship between self-esteem and childhood depression. Other studies have found that depression level is significantly related to feelings of guilt, helplessness, and lower confidence (Cofer & Wittenborn, 1980; Peterson, 1979); less perceived ability to deal with sources of stress (Hammen & DeMayo, 1982); less perceived control and accomplishments (Warren & McEachren, 1983); more negative and less positive self-verbalizations (Missel & Sommer, 1983); judgments of being less self-efficacious in interpersonal functioning (Kanfer & Zeiss, 1983); and the tendency to generalize a single failure to a more generally negative view of other aspects of the self (Carver & Ganellen, 1983). This latter finding also provides direct support for Beck's (1976) assertion that depressives are prone to commit the cognitive distortion of overgeneralization. Finally, recent studies by Davis and Unruh (1981), and Derry and Kuiper (1981), provide evidence of an organized negative self-schema in long-term depressed patients.

Negative View of the Future. According to the cognitive model, the depressed person expects failure, dissatisfaction, and indefinite continuation of current difficulties. A number of studies have provided evidence that negative expectations are related to depression level. Several studies have found depression scores to be significantly related to self-report measures of hopelessness (Beck, 1974; Beck, Kovacs, & Weissman, 1975; Fibel and Hale, 1978; Karoly & Ruehlman, 1983; Layne, Lefton, Walters, & Merry, 1983). A later study (Kazdin et al., 1983) has also found depression in children to be related to scores on a modification of the adult hopelessness scale (Beck, Weissman, Lester, & Trexler, 1974). Lewinsohn et al. (1982) found that depressives have more negative expectancies for future events pertaining to self but not to the world. Depression level has also been related to lower expectancies for achievement and affection (Gurtman, 1981); lower expectations of satisfaction from planned pleasant activities (Sacco, 1985); and lower expectations for success on a skill task (Lobitz & Post, 1979).

Negative View of the World/Experience.   The third component of the negative cognitive triad postulated by Beck (1974) is that depressed individuals are prone to view their experiences in the world negatively. A variety of measures of cognitions about experience have indeed found depression level to be significantly correlated with more negative perceptions. Depressed persons view significant others in a more negative manner than do nondepressed persons. Specifically, more negative ratings of parents (Blatt, Wein, Chevron, & Quinlan, 1979) and of friends and family (Karoly & Ruehlman, 1983) have been related to depression level. Rogers and Forehand (1983) found that depression level of mothers of clinic-referred children was related to perceptions of greater child maladjustment despite the fact that objective raters were unable to distinguish the children of depressed mothers from those of nondepressed mothers on levels of compliance and deviant behavior.

Depressed individuals cognitively process their task performance in a more negative manner. Studies of depressed persons indicate that they reward themselves less and punish themselves more for their skill-task performance (e.g., Gotlib, 1981; Lobitz & Post, 1979; Rozensky, Rehm, Pry, & Roth, 1977); underestimate the amount of reinforcement they have received (De-Monbreun & Craighead, 1977; Dobson & Shaw, 1981; Nelson & Craighead, 1977; Wener & Rehm, 1975); recall fewer self-rewards and more self-punishments than is objectively the case (Gotlib, 1981); recall more uncompleted tasks than completed tasks (Johnson, Petzel, Hartney, & Morgan, 1983); recall material of a negatively toned content more easily and readily than material of a more positive nature (Lishman, 1972; Lloyd & Lishman, 1975); and prefer to attend to negative feedback rather than positive feedback about themselves (Roth & Rehm, 1980). Finally, Sacco and Graves (1984) have found that depression level in children is related to lower self-ratings of interpersonal problem-solving performance. Taken together these studies provide strong evidence that depression is related to more negative perceptions of experiences in the world.

General Cognitive Processes and Content.   Several studies have utilized more general measures of cognitive processes and content that encompass several aspects of the negative cognitive set. Cognitive distortions are considered a central mechanism explaining the development and maintenance of negative cognitions despite contradictory evidence. Several studies utilizing different measures of cognitive distortions find that depressed persons exhibit a variety of the cognitive distortions or biases predicted by the cognitive theory (Blaney, Behar, & Head, 1980; Krantz & Hammen, 1979; Lefebvre, 1981; Norman, Miller, & Klee, 1983). Another group of studies has examined the way that depressed individuals make attributions about the causes of unpleasant events. It has been theorized that depressed persons exhibit a depressive attributional style, the tendency to attribute unpleasant events to internal, stable, and global causes (Abramson et al., 1978). This style of information processing is quite consistent with that expected by the cognitive theory. A large number of studies have provided evidence or partial evidence that such an attributional style appears more often in depressed persons than in nondepressed persons (e.g., Blaney et al., 1980; Golin, Sweeney, & Shaeffer, 1981; Hamilton & Abramson, 1983; Miller, Klee, & Norman, 1982; Raps, Peterson, Reinhard, Abramson, & Seligman, 1982).

The Automatic Thoughts Questionnaire was designed to measure the extent to which people experience negative cognitions (Hollon & Kendall, 1980). Cross-validation studies show that depressed persons report experiencing more negative cognitions than nondepressed persons (Dobson & Breiter, 1983; Hollon & Kendall, 1980).

Several studies have demonstrated that depressed persons ascribe to more dysfunctional attitudes, which directly correspond to what the cognitive model terms *silent assumptions* (Hamilton & Abramson, 1983; Lapointe & Crandell, 1980; Nelson, 1977; O'Hara, Rehm, & Campbell, 1982; Weissman & Beck, 1978). Finally, a more direct measure of cognitive processes was utilized in several early studies (Beck & Hurvich, 1959; Beck & Ward, 1961; Hauri, 1976) which found that relative to nondepressed subjects, the reported manifest dream content of depressed subjects more often contained themes of personal loss and failure.

CAUSAL EVIDENCE

The large number of studies reported above provide convincing evidence that depressed persons perceive their self, their world, and their future more negatively than do nondepressed persons. According to the cognitive theory, these perceptions result in the development and maintenance of the affective, motivational, somatic, and behavioral symptoms associated with depression. However, correlational evidence fails to provide evidence of causality; it is equally plausible to argue that negative cognitions occur as a result of the other symptoms of depression. For example, negative affect or reduced behaviors may be responsible for the negative perceptions found in depressed persons (Bower, 1981; Lewinsohn, 1974; Teasdale, 1983).

The following section describes studies which provide support for the notion that negative perceptions are causally related to the other symptoms of depression. This research typically utilizes experimental designs in which some independent variable presumed to alter cognitive content or processes is experimentally manipulated to see if changes in cognitions do indeed alter affective, physiological, and behavioral responses. Another group of studies employs methodologies that utilize correlational data to provide support for the notion that cognitive variables precede or predict later manifestations of depression.[1]

The use of experimental designs in which subjects are induced to alter cognitive content is a common methodology employed to test the role of cognition as a causal agent in the development and maintenance of depressive symptoms. By far, the Velten-Mood Induction Procedure ([VMIP]; Velten, 1968) is the most popular procedure in this area. Velten (1968) reported that when subjects were asked to read and "try to feel the mood suggested by" statements with depressed, elated, or neutral content, mood-relevant responses were altered in the expected directions. Since then, the effect of this experimental manipulation has been replicated and extended. Studies utilizing the VMIP, or variations thereof, have related the experimental induction of negative versus positive thought content to a variety of dependent variables relevant to depression including changes in mood, physiology, and behavior.

Over 15 studies have demonstrated that self-reported dysphoric mood can be induced by manipulations designed to increase the negative content of subjects' thoughts (e.g., Natale, 1977a, 1977b; Riskind, Rholes, & Eggers, 1982; Sherwood, Schroeder, Abrami, & Alden, 1981; Teasdale & Bancroft, 1977). Likewise, many of these studies have simultaneously demonstrated that inducing subjects to think positive, or "elated," thoughts results in self-reports of decreased negative mood states.

Another group of studies has assessed the effect of such manipulations of thought content on physiological responding. Changes in a variety of physiological responses (e.g., heart rate, galvanic skin response) have been experimentally induced by instructions to alter cognitive content (May & Johnson, 1973; Rimm & Litvak, 1969; Rogers & Craighead, 1977; Russell & Brandsma, 1974; Schuele & Wiesenfeld, 1983; Teasdale & Bancroft, 1977). These studies lend credence to the cognitive theory's assertion that negative cognitive content could be responsible for the physiological and somatic changes associated with depression. In addition, these studies provide important evidence in support of the validity of other VMIP studies that have only measured self-reported moods. Whereas changes in self-reported moods could be attributed to the demand characteristics of the procedure, physiological responses are less likely to be due to subjects' desire to conform to the experimental

---

[1] It is important to point out that the cognitive theory acknowledges that behavior, affect, or physiological responses may also influence cognition in a reciprocal manner. For example, the cognitive model recognizes that an individual who experiences a large number of failures is likely to experience negative self-referential cognitions, and that negative affect may increase the probability of negative thoughts. The cognitive model simply asserts that the cognitive habits of the depressive are prepotent factors in the development and maintenance of the depressed state. It follows from this proposition that treatment of depression would be most effective if attempts were made to directly modify these cognitive habits.

hypothesis (Orton, Beiman, Lapointe, & Lankford, 1983). It is also noteworthy that both Velten (1968) and Coleman (1975) have provided additional evidence that demand characteristics are not responsible for the changes in mood found in studies of this nature.

Changes in behavioral responses have also been demonstrated to occur as a result of experimental alterations of cognitive content. Inductions of depressed cognitive content have been related to retarded speech rate (Natale, 1977a; Teasdale & Fogerty, 1979); reduced gaze behavior (Natale, 1977b); and altered writing speed (Alloy & Abramson, 1981). In contrast, Raps, Reinhard, and Seligman (1980) found that administering the elation portion of the VMIP to depressed patients significantly improved anagram performance. Miller and Norman (1981) found that inducing depressed patients to make internal attributions for success on a task that was said to be indicative of general intellectual ability resulted in significantly better subsequent anagram performance.

Finally, inductions of negative thought content have been related to a variety of other dependent variables related to depressive responding, including more rapid retrieval of unpleasant memories relative to pleasant memories (Teasdale & Fogerty, 1979), decreased ratings of the enjoyability of pleasant events (Carson & Adams, 1980), self-reports of increased desire for social withdrawal (Wilson & Krane, 1980), decreased perceptions of control (Alloy & Abramson, 1981), and lower expectancies for success (Miller & Norman, 1981).

Recent studies have suggested some clarification of the way in which manipulations of thought content work. Rogers and Craighead (1977) found that changes in physiological and affective responses were associated with the degree to which subjects believe in the content of the self-statement. As Hollon and Beck (1979) point out, these data suggest that simply repeating positive covert self-statements will have little or no effect if the self-statements are viewed as inaccurate. Sherwood et al. (1981) verified that self-referential positive and negative thoughts induced appropriate changes in mood level, while positive and negative nonself-referent statements did not significantly alter mood. Finally, a recent study by Frost, Graff, and Becker (1979) provided evidence that the somatic items of the VMIP (e.g., "I feel tired") had a much greater impact on mood than did the self-devaluation items. These data suggest that, in contrast to the prediction of the cognitive theory of depression, negative self-referential items of the VMIP may not be responsible for the changes in mood, behavior, and physiology reported in earlier studies. However, a recent study by Riskind et al. (1982) did not replicate the Frost et al. (1979) findings. Riskind et al. (1982) found that both the self-devaluation and the somatic items induced depressed mood relative to the elation condition. This pattern of results confirms the support for the cognitive theory provided by earlier studies using the VMIP.

The role of cognitions as causally related to mood was examined in two novel studies employing interactions between therapist and patient. In a case report of a single subject, Peterson, Luborsky, and Seligman (1983) found that attributions in therapy sessions predicted mood swings as measured by the symptom-context method. Teasdale and Fennell (1982) used a within-subjects design and systematically varied whether the therapist attempted to change depressive thought or simply explored the depressive thought of chronically depressed patients. Consistent with cognitive theory, modification of depressive thinking was consistently accompanied by reductions in self-reported depressed mood while thought exploration produced minimal reduction. These data are consistent with earlier studies by Teasdale and his colleagues which have shown that the mood of depressed patients deteriorates when instructed to think thoughts with a negative content (Teasdale & Bancroft, 1977) and improves when they are sufficiently distracted to reduce the frequency of their negative thought (Teasdale & Rezin, 1978).

A second group of studies attempting to evaluate the causal relationship between cognitive content and depression have utilized designs in which cognitive content at one point in time is correlated with depression levels at some later time. These studies still utilize correlational data and therefore are weaker relative to those utilizing experimental manipulations. However, they do provide further evidence bearing on the validity of the cognitive theory of depression. Hammen, Krantz, and Cochran (1981), found support for the notion that cognitive appraisals of stressful events mediate the development of depression. Perceptions of low controllability and globality (the belief that the event would affect other areas of a person's life) were predictive of later depression. Similarly, Golin et al. (1981) used a cross-lagged panel correlational analysis to assess the possible causal role of attributional style in depression. Their results indicated that global and stable attributions for failure were causally related to subsequent depression level.

Two studies have related cognitive variables to later postpartum depression. O'Hara et al. (1982) found that scores obtained during the second trimester of pregnancy on scales designed to assess depressive attributional style and dysfunctional attitude were significantly related to depression level approximately four months postpartum. Cutrona (1983) found that depressive attributional style in the third trimester was significantly related to depression level two months postpartum.

EFFICACY OF COGNITIVE THERAPY FOR DEPRESSION

In the last decade, there has been a steady increase in the number of experiments conducted to evaluate the efficacy of psychotherapeutic interventions for depression. Included are a relatively large number of experiments evaluating the effectiveness of what may be termed *cognitive* interventions. Most, if not all, of these cognitive interventions were developed on the basis of Beck's (1967, 1976) cognitive theory of depression. However, the actual cognitive therapeutic strategies employed in *cognitive* treatments often differ in many ways from each other and from that explicitly prescribed by Beck et al. (1979) in their manual for cognitive therapy of depression. This variation among cognitive treatments and deviations from the Beck et al. (1979) prescription are understandable given that many evaluation studies were conducted prior to the complete development and availability of the cognitive therapy manual. Thus, the reader should be aware that the common use of the term *cognitive therapy* does not necessarily imply uniformity in procedures.

These outcome studies also vary in terms of whether subjects were exposed to cognitive techniques alone or a combination of cognitive and behavioral techniques. As noted earlier, the cognitive therapy recommended by Beck et al. (1979) does employ techniques which are intended to directly modify behavior (e.g., activity scheduling), though the primary purpose of these behavioral strategies is identification and modification of dysfunctional cognitive responses said to mediate the behavioral disturbances of depression. In contrast, therapies of depression based on a behavioral theory (e.g., Lewinsohn, 1974) usually employ some of the same behavioral techniques (e.g., activity scheduling) but without direct attempts to modify cognitions. As a result of this overlap in techniques, many studies have attempted to compare the relative efficacy of cognitive versus behavioral treatments by utilizing only cognitive techniques in the cognitive modality and only behavioral techniques in the behavioral modality. While this procedure is necessary to examine the relative efficacy of a purely cognitive versus a purely behavioral therapy, such a procedure does not properly evaluate the entire treatment package recommended by Beck et al. (1979).

It is also necessary to clarify the use of the terms *cognitive* and *cognitive-behavioral therapy* in the present review. To avoid confusion, the term *cognitive therapy* will refer to therapeutic strategies that solely utilize techniques designed to alter cognitive habits without employing behavioral techniques. *Cognitive-behavioral therapy* will refer to the use of both cognitive and behavioral techniques, which is recommended by Beck et al. (1979).

The present review does not include all possible outcome studies. Inclusion or exclusion of studies was based on several criteria.[2] Only controlled outcome studies are presented. Studies employing treatments of extremely low magnitude and intensity were excluded (e.g., if not more than three sessions or more than three hours of therapist-patient contact; see Yeaton & Sechrest, 1981). Studies of cognitive treatment bearing little resemblance to that which would have evolved from Beck's cognitive theory were also omitted (e.g., Zeiss, Lewinsohn, & Muñoz, 1979). Also excluded were studies examining the effectiveness of self-control therapy (e.g., Fuchs & Rehm, 1977). Although self-control therapy does utilize cognitive techniques that are consistent with Beck's cognitive theory (e.g., encouraging depressed patients to attend to positive events and evaluate oneself appropriately), it seems that sufficient theoretical and procedural differences remain to justify distinguishing between these two forms of therapy for depression.

---

[2] For additional reviews, see Blaney (1981) and Hollon & Beck (1979). Hollon (1981) provides an excellent discussion of methodological issues relevant to outcome research on depression.

The evaluation studies included in the present review are listed in Table 4 in chronological order. Inspection of these studies reveals, first, that all cognitive and cognitive-behavioral treatments led to reduced depression levels relative to pretest and, when included, relative to no-treatment control groups. This finding is true for studies that used either group or individual administrations of therapy, and generalizes to a variety of patient samples; for example, college students, outpatients, and general practice patients. Thus, there is overwhelming evidence that cognitive and cognitive-behavioral therapy inverventions are effective relative to no treatment.

Several other patterns of results characterize the studies in Table 4. Cognitive and cognitive-behavior therapy have been compared with behavioral, interpersonal, insight/relational, and pharmacological therapy. In studies comparing a strictly cognitive approach (not cognitive-behavioral) with behavioral therapy, cognitive and behavioral therapies appear equivalent in effectiveness (e.g., Gallagher & Thompson, 1982; Taylor & Marshall, 1977; Wilson, Goldin, & Charbonneau-Powis, 1983) In studies that have compared cognitive-behavioral therapy with behavioral therapy alone, cognitive-behavioral therapy was more effective (Shaw, 1977a; Taylor & Marshall, 1977). Cognitive therapy was more effective than insight or relational/insight in two studies (Gallagher & Thompson, 1982; Morris, 1975) and as effective in one study (Lapointe, 1977). Cognitive-behavioral therapy was more effective than nondirective therapy (Shaw, 1977a). Compared with therapy focusing on interpersonal factors, cognitive therapy was equivalent in one study (Lapointe, 1977) and less effective at posttest but equivalent at follow-up in another (Hodgson, 1981).[3]

Evidence of the comparability of group and individual administrations is limited. A study by Rush & Watkins (1981) compared group versus individual administration of cognitive-behavior therapy and found that individual therapy was more effective than group administration. This study is not listed in Table 4 because subjects were not assigned on a strictly random basis. However, assignment of subjects was determined prior to and independent of the evaluation of specific subjects. Shaw & Hollon (1978) conducted a similar study and also found that group therapy was less effective than individual although, again, subjects were not randomly assigned from the same research pool. Thus, while these two studies suggest that individual administration of cognitive-behavior therapy is superior to group administration, a study in which subjects are randomly assigned to treatment is necessary before such a conclusion may be reached with confidence. Nevertheless, both group and individual cognitive-behavior therapy appear more effective than no treatment.

Because pharmacological therapy is so easily administered and relatively inexpensive, it has stood as the standard by which to compare psychological

---

[3] In Hodgson (1981) the cognitive therapy group focused exclusively on subjects' perceptions of interpersonal interactions and thus had a very limited focus relative to the more typical administration of cognitive therapy.

TABLE 4
Outcome studies of cognitive therapy

Author(s)	Sample	Intervention	Outcome
Morris (1975)	Female, clinic patients, n = 51, Group n's 12-17	Group treatment: 1. Cognitively oriented 2. Insight 3. Waiting list Six, 90-minute sessions over three weeks	Cognitive treatment was more effective than insight and waiting list at posttreatment and six-week follow-up.
Lapointe (1977)	Female, community volunteers, n = 33, Group n's 5-6	Group treatment: 1. Cognitive 2. Assertion 3. Insight Six, two-hour sessions for six weeks	Improvement in all groups at posttreatment and two-month follow-up.
Taylor & Marshall (1977)	College student volunteers, n = 45	Individual treatment: 1. Cognitive 2. Behavioral 3. Cognitive-behavioral 4. Waiting list Six, 40-minute sessions for six weeks	Cognitive-behavioral combination was more effective than other treatments; cognitive and behavioral treatments alone were more effective than waiting list.
Shaw (1977a)	Student health patients, n = 32	Group treatment: 1. Cognitive-behavioral 2. Behavioral 3. Nondirective 4. Waiting List Four, two-hour sessions over four weeks	Cognitive-behavioral was more effective than others; behavioral and nondirective were more effective than the waiting list.
Rush, Beck, Kovacs, & Hollon (1977) and Kovacs, Rush, Beck, & Hollon (1981)	Adult outpatients, n = 44	Individual treatment: 1. Cognitive-behavioral 2. Pharmacotherapy (imipramine) 20 sessions of cognitive-behavioral therapy over a 12-week period; 20-	Cognitive-behavioral was more effective than pharmacotherapy; cognitive-behavioral had lower dropout rate; cognitive-behavioral maintained greater effectiveness at 12-month follow-up.

TABLE 4 (concluded)

Author(s)	Sample	Intervention	Outcome
Hollon, Bedrosian, & Beck (1979)	Adult outpatients, $n = 26$	minute weekly pharmacotherapy sessions for 12 weeks Individual treatment: 1. Cognitive-behavioral 2. Cognitive-behavioral and pharma-cotherapy (amitriptyline, up to 300mg/day) 20 sessions over 12 weeks	Both treatments were effective relative to pretest; no differences between treatments.
Blackburn, Bishop, Glen, Whalley, & Christie (1981)	Hospital outpatients and general practice patients, $n = 64$	Individual treatment: 1. Cognitive-behavioral 2. Pharmacotherapy ("usually ami-triptyline or chlomipramine" variable dose) 3. Combination of cognitive-behav-ioral and pharmacotherapy 16–17 sessions over 12–15 weeks	For hospital patients, combination was more effective than cognitive-behavioral or pharmacotherapy alone; cognitive-behav-ioral alone and pharmacotherapy alone were equivalent; no difference in dropout rates. For general practice patients, cogni-tive-behavioral and combination treatment was more effective than pharmacotherapy alone.
Hodgson (1981)	Volunteer college students, $n = 38$	Group treatment: 1. Interpersonal skills 2. Cognitive (focus was on percep-tions of interpersonal interactions) Seven, two-hour sessions	Both treatments were effective relative to pretest; interpersonal was more effective than cognitive at posttest; no differences between interpersonal and cognitive at follow-up.
Gallagher & Thompson (1982)	Elderly outpatients, $n = 30$	Individual treatment: 1. Cognitive 2. Behavioral 3. Relational/insight Sixteen, 90-minute sessions over 12 weeks	All treatments led to reduced depression at posttest; at one-year follow-up, cognitive and behavioral groups showed greater maintenance of gain than Relational/in-sight.

Study	Sample	Treatment	Results
Wilson, Goldin, & Charbonneau-Powis (1983)	Adult outpatient, $n = 25$	Individual treatment: 1. Behavioral 2. Cognitive 3. Waiting list Over eight-week period	Cognitive and behavioral more effective than waiting list at posttest; treatment effects maintained at five-month follow-up.
Teasdale, Fennell, Hibbert, & Amies (1983)	Adult general practice, $n = 34$	Individual treatment: 1. "Treatment as usual" by general practitioner (usually antidepressant medication) 2. Cognitive-behavioral therapy in addition to "Treatment as usual" Average of 15.2 one-hour cognitive-behavioral sessions during main treatment phase; one additional "booster" session at six weeks and three months after treatment	Cognitive-behavioral was more effective in reducing depression than general practitioner treatment alone at posttest. At three-month follow-up, there were no differences between treatments.
Murphy, Simons, Wetzel, & Lustman (1984)	Adult outpatients, $n = 87$	1. Cognitive-behavioral 2. Pharmacotherapy (nortriptyline) 3. Cognitive-behavioral and pharmacotherapy 4. Cognitive-behavioral and placebo Average of 17.1, 50-minute cognitive-behavioral sessions, over 11.2 weeks. Pharmacotherapy-alone treatment administered for 12 weeks, with 20-minute weekly medication sessions.	All treatments effective in reducing depression at posttreatment and one-month follow-up. All treatment conditions were equally effective.

interventions. Indeed, it can be said that the most controversial issue surrounding the treatment of depression today is the comparative efficacy of pharmacological and psychosocial interventions. Studies evaluating the efficacy of pharmacological therapy for depression generally find that 60–65 percent show definite improvement. However, a number of problems occur with sole use of pharmacological treatment modalities. First of all, 35–40 percent of the patients do not show clear improvement, and recent reviews have raised questions about the absolute magnitude of the improvement of those who do respond to medication (e.g., Hollon, 1981; Hollon & Beck, 1979). Moreover, many depressed individuals refuse medical treatment because of adverse side effects and personal objections. A review of controlled drug studies indicates that an average of 30 percent of the subjects drop out (Shaw, 1977b; cited by Hollon & Beck, 1979). Also troublesome is the very real possibility that the patient may attribute changes in depressive symptoms to an external agent (Shapiro & Morris, 1978), which may reduce the person's tendency to develop or utilize psychological coping strategies. Furthermore, most pharmacological therapies are lethal in large doses, necessitating extreme caution with potentially suicidal individuals (Hollon & Beck, 1979). Finally, depression tends to be a cyclical disorder. Spontaneous recovery is common; however, approximately 50 percent of those whose depression has remitted will again suffer from the disorder (American Psychiatric Association, 1980). It is not surprising, therefore, that when drug therapy is terminated there is a high-relapse rate (often as high as 50 percent in the year following termination). The high-relapse rate of depression requires that all treatments be evaluated in terms of both speed of recovery and the degree to which recurrence of depression occurs.

In recent years a number of controlled outcome studies have compared the relative efficacy of psychosocial interventions for depression with that of pharmacological therapies (see Kovacs, 1983, and Chapter 10 by Beckham and Leber in this book for a review). Table 4 presents the results of four studies which have compared cognitive-behavior therapy with the effects of a pharmacological therapy for depression. The first study of this nature was conducted by Rush et al. (1977), and Kovacs et al. (1981) provide additional follow-up data. In the Rush et al. (1977) study, moderately to severely depressed outpatients were randomly assigned to receive either 20 sessions of individual cognitive-behavior therapy over a 12-week period, or pharmacotherapy (imipramine up to 250 mg/day). The drug treatment group had weekly 20-minute pharmacotherapy sessions over the same 12-week period. Both treatments resulted in significant improvement in depressive symptoms over the 12-week treatment period; however cognitive-behavior therapy was more effective than imipramine on several measures of depressive symptomology and in treatment completion rate. Follow-up assessments at three months, six months, and one year indicated continued differences between the groups. In addition, pharmacotherapy subjects relapsed approximately 2.1 times more than cognitive-behavior therapy subjects.

Blackburn et al. (1981) compared the effectiveness of cognitive-behavior therapy, pharmacotherapy ("usually amitriptyline or clomipramine, in variable dose"), and a combination of the pharmacotherapy and cognitive-behavior therapy. Two patient samples were tested—hospital outpatients and general practice patients. Results differed according to the sample studied. For hospital outpatients, the combination of drug therapy and cognitive-behavior therapy was more effective than either of the treatments alone. Cognitive-behavior therapy and drug therapy were equivalent in effectiveness. No differences in dropout rates were found. In contrast, for general practice patients cognitive-behavior therapy and the combination of cognitive-behavior and pharmacotherapy were equivalent in effectiveness and both of those groups were more effective than the drug-alone group. Again, no differences in dropout rates were found.

Hollon et al. (1979) compared the effectiveness of cognitive-behavior therapy and a combination of cognitive-behavior therapy and pharmacotherapy (amitriptyline, up to 300mg/day). They found both treatments equally effective at reducing depression levels. It is noteworthy, however, that both treatments showed greater absolute change in measures of depressive symptomology than the group-administered pharmacotherapy-alone treatment in the Rush et al. (1977) study. This finding, along with the results from Blackburn et al. (1981), suggests that the addition of drug therapy to cognitive-behavior therapy provides no additional improvements in symptoms.

Teasdale et al. (1983) compared treatment "as usual" by general practice physicians (usually antidepressant medication) to the effects of adding cognitive-behavior therapy to the treatment "as usual." At posttest cognitive-behavior therapy was more effective in reducing depression than treatment by the general practitioner only. At the three-month follow-up, the differences between the groups disappeared due to continuing improvement in the general practitioner-only treatment group.

Finally, Murphy et al. (1984) also report a controlled outcome study comparing cognitive-behavior therapy, pharmacotherapy (nortriptyline), and cognitive-behavior therapy with a placebo drug. Subjects were outpatients. All treatment conditions produced significant reductions on measures of depression at posttreatment and one-month follow-up. All treatments were equally effective, suggesting that combining drug and cognitive-behavioral therapy produces no additional therapeutic effect and no negative interactions.

CONCLUSION

In the last 20 years, the cognitive therapy of depression and the treatment package that has been derived from the theory have passed numerous criteria by which any scientific theory should be evaluated. The theory explains in a parsimonious manner the development and maintenance of depression, which is a significant and pervasive problem faced by mental health professionals. The theory has heuristic value and is testable, as is evidenced by the very large number of studies conducted to test hypotheses derived from the cognitive theory. Moreover, the cognitive theory has an excellent batting average with respect to the number of studies providing evidence consistent with its postulates, thus providing support for the empirical validity of the theory. Finally, the cognitive theory has utility. Based upon this theory a clearly articulated set of operations has evolved which, judging from the results of initial outcome studies, appears to be a very promising treatment for depression.

References

Abramson, L. Y., Seligman, M. E. P., & Teasdale J. D. (1978). Learned helplessness in humans: Critique and reformulation. *Journal of Abnormal Psychology, 87,* 102–109.

Alloy, L. B., & Abramson, L. Y. (1981). Induced mood and the illusion of control. *Journal of Personality and Social Psychology, 41,* 1129–1140.

Altman, J. H., & Wittenborn, J. R. (1980). Depression-prone personality in women. *Journal of Abnormal Psychology, 89,* 303–329.

American Psychiatric Association. (1980). *Diagnostic and statistical manual of mental disorders* (3rd. ed.) Washington, D.C.: Author.

Beck, A. T. (1961). A systematic investigation of depression. *Comprehensive Psychiatry, 2,* 163–170.

Beck, A. T. (1963). Thinking and depression: 1. Idiosyncratic content and cognitive distortions. *Archives of General Psychiatry, 9,* 324–333.

Beck, A. T. (1967). *Depression: Clinical, experimental, and theoretical aspects.* New York: Harper & Row.

Beck, A. T. (1974). The development of depression: A cognitive model. In R. Friedman & M. Katz (Eds.), *Psychology of depression: Contemporary theory and research* (pp. 3–28). Washington, DC: Winston-Wiley.

Beck, A. T. (1976). *Cognitive theory and the emotional disorders.* New York: International Universities Press.

Beck, A. T., & Greenberg, R. L. (1974). *Coping with depression.* New York: Institute for Rational Living.

Beck, A. T., & Hurvich, M. S. (1959). Psychological correlates of depression. 1. Frequency of "masochistic" dream content in a private practice sample. *Psychosomatic Medicine, 21,* 50–55.

Beck, A. T., Kovacs, M., & Weissman, A. (1975). Hopelessness and suicidal behavior: An overview. *Journal of the American Medical Association, 234,* 1146–1149.

Beck, A. T., & Rush, A. J. (1978). Cognitive approaches to depression and suicide. In G. Serban (Ed.), *Cognitive defects in the development of mental illness* (pp. 235–257). New York: Brunner/Mazel.

Beck, A. T., Rush, A. J., Shaw, B. F., & Emery, G. (1979). *Cognitive therapy of depression: A treatment manual.* New York: Guilford Press.

Beck, A. T., & Ward, C. H. (1961). Dreams of depressed patients: Characteristic themes in manifest content. *Archives of General Psychiatry, 5,* 462–571.

Beck, A. T., Weissman, A., Lester, D., & Trexler, L. (1974). The measurement of pessimism: The Hopelessness Scale. *Journal of Consulting and Clinical Psychology, 42,* 861–865.

Bedrosian, R. C. (1981). The application of cognitive therapy techniques with adolescents. In G. Emery, S. D. Hollon, & R. C. Bedrosian (Eds.), *New directions in cognitive therapy* (pp. 63–83). New York: Guilford Press.

Blackburn, I. M., Bishop, S., Glen, A. I. M., Whalley, L. J., & Christie, J. E. (1981). The efficacy of cognitive therapy in depression: A treatment trial using cognitive therapy and pharmacotherapy, each alone and in combination. *British Journal of Psychiatry, 139,* 181–189.

Blaney, P. H. The effectiveness of cognitive and behavioral therapies. In L. P. Rehm (Ed.), *Behavior Therapy for depression* (pp. 1–32). New York: Academic Press.

Blaney, P. H., Behar, V., & Head, R. (1980). Two measures of depressive cognitions: Their association with depression and with each other. *Journal of Abnormal Psychology, 89,* 678–682.

Blatt, S. J., Wein, S. J., Chevron, E., & Quinlan, D. M. (1979). Parental representations and depression in normal young adults. *Journal of Abnormal Psychology, 88,* 388–397.

Bower, G. H. (1981). Mood and memory. *American Psychologist, 36,* 129–148.

Burns, D. (1981). *Feeling good: The new mood therapy.* New York: Signet.

Carson, T. P., & Adams, H. E. (1980). Activity valence as a function of mood change. *Journal of Abnormal Psychology, 89,* 368–377.

Carver, C. S., & Ganellen, R. J. (1983). Depression and components of self-punitiveness: High standards, self-criticism, and overgeneralization. *Journal of Consulting and Clinical Psychology, 92,* 330–337.

Cofer, D. H., & Wittenborn, J. R. (1980). Personality characteristics of formerly depressed women. *Journal of Abnormal Psychology, 89,* 309–314.

Coleman, R. E. (1975). Manipulation of self-esteem as a determinant of mood of elated and depressed women. *Journal of Abnormal Psychology, 84,* 693–700.

Coyne, J. C. (1976). Depression and the response of others. *Journal of Abnormal Psychology, 85,* 186–193.

Cutrona, C. E. (1983). Causal attributions and perinatal depression. *Journal of Abnormal Psychology, 92,* 161–172.

Davis, H., & Unruh, W. R. (1981). The development of the self-schema in adult depression. *Journal of Abnormal Psychology, 90,* 125–133.

DeMonbreun, B. G., & Craighead, W. E. (1977). Distortion of perception and recall of positive and neutral feedback in depression. *Cognitive Therapy and Research, 1,* 311–330.

Derry, P. A., & Kuiper, N. A. (1981). Schematic processing and self-reference in clinical depression. *Journal of Abnormal Psychology, 90,* 286–297.

Dobson, K. S., & Breiter, H. J. (1983). Cognitive assessment of depression: Reliability and validity of three measures. *Journal of Abnormal Psychology, 92,* 107–109.

Dobson, K. S., & Shaw, B. F. (1981). The effects of self-correction on cognitive distortions in depression. *Cognitive Therapy and Research, 5,* 391–404.

Eaves, G., & Rush, A. J. (1984). Cognitive patterns in symptomatic and remitted unipolar major depression. *Journal of Abnormal Psychology, 93,* 31–40.

Feather, N. T., & Barber, J. G. (1983). Depressive reactions and unemployment. *Journal of Abnormal Psychology, 92,* 185–195.

Fibel, B., & Hale, W. D. (1978). The generalized expectancy for success scale: A new measure. *Journal of Consulting and Clinical Psychology, 46,* 924–931.

Frost, R. O., Graff, M., & Becker, J. (1979). Self-evaluation and depressed moods. *Journal of Consulting and Clinical Psychology, 47,* 958–962.

Fuchs, C. Z., & Rehm, L. P. (1977). A self-control behavior therapy program for depression. *Journal of Consulting and Clinical Psychology, 45,* 206–215.

Gallagher, D. E., & Thompson, L. W. (1982). Treatment of major depressive disorder in older adult outpatients with brief psychotherapies. *Psychotherapy: Theory, Research and Practice, 19,* 482–490.

Golin, S., Sweeney, P. D., & Shaeffer, D. E. (1981). The causality of causal attributions in depression: A cross-lagged panel correlational analysis. *Journal of Abnormal Psychology, 90,* 14–22.

Gotlib, I. H. (1981). Self-reinforcement and recall: Differential deficits in depressed and nondepressed psychiatric inpatients. *Journal of Abnormal Psychology, 90,* 521–530.

Gurtman, M. B. (1981). The relationship of expectancies for need attainment to depression and hopelessness in college students. *Cognitive Therapy and Research, 5,* 313–316.

Hamilton, E. W., & Abramson, L. Y. (1983). Cognitive patterns and major depressive disorder: A longitudinal study in a hospital setting. *Journal of Abnormal Psychology, 92,* 173–184.

Hammen, C., & DeMayo, R. (1982). Cognitive correlates of teacher stress and depressive symptoms: Implications for attributional models of depression. *Journal of Abnormal Psychology, 91,* 96–101.

Hammen, C., Krantz, S. E., & Cochran, S. D. (1981). Relationships between depression and causal attributions about stressful life events. *Cognitive Therapy and Research, 5,* 351–358.

Hauri, P. (1976). Dreams in patients remitted from reactive depression. *Journal of Abnormal Psychology, 85,* 1–10.

Hodgson, J. W. (1981). Cognitive versus behavioral-interpersonal approaches to the group treatment of depressed college students. *Journal of Counseling Psychology, 28,* 243–249.

Hokanson, J. E., Sacco, W. P., Blumberg, S., & Landrum, G. (1980). Interpersonal behavior of depressive individuals in a mix-motive game. *Journal of Abnormal Psychology, 89,* 320–332.

Hollon, S. D. (1981). Comparisons and combinations with alternative approaches. In L. P. Rehm (Ed.), *Behavior therapy for depression* (pp. 33–72). New York: Academic Press.

Hollon, S. D., & Beck, A. T. (1979). Cognitive therapy of depression. In P. C. Kendall & S. D. Hollon (Eds.), *Cognitive-behavioral interventions: Theory, research, and procedures* (pp. 153–204). New York: Academic Press.

Hollon, S. D., Bedrosian, R. C., & Beck, A. T. (1979, July). *Combined cognitive-pharmacotherapy vs. cognitive therapy in the treatment of depression.* Paper presented at the Annual Meeting of the Society of Psychotherapy Research, Oxford, Eng.

Hollon, S. D., & Kendall, P. C. (1980). Cognitive self-statements in depression: Development of an automatic thoughts questionnaire. *Cognitive Therapy and Research, 3,* 383–396.

Johnson, J. E., Petzel, T. P., Hartney, L. M., & Morgan, R. A. (1983). Recall of importance ratings of completed and uncompleted tasks as a function of depression. *Cognitive Therapy and Research, 7,* 51–56.

Kanfer, R., & Zeiss, A. M. (1983). Depression, interpersonal standard setting, and judgments of self-efficacy. *Journal of Abnormal Psychology, 92,* 319–329.

Karoly, P., & Ruehlman, L. (1983). Affective meaning and depression: A semantic differential analysis. *Cognitive Therapy and Research, 7,* 41–50.

Kazdin, A. E., French, N. H., Unis, A. S., Esveldt-Dawson, K., & Sherick, R. B. (1983). Hopelessness, depression, and suicidal intent among psychiatrically disturbed inpatient children. *Journal of Consulting and Clinical Psychology, 51,* 504–510.

Kovacs, M. (1977, August). *Cognitive therapy of depression: Rationale and basic strategies.* Paper presented at the annual meeting of the American Psychological Association, San Francisco, CA.

Kovacs, M. (1983). Psychotherapy versus drug therapy of depression. In J. Korf & L. Pepplinkhuizen (Eds.), *Depression: Molecular and psychologically-based therapies.* Drachten, Neth.: TGO Foundation.

Kovacs, M., Rush, A. J., Beck, A. T., & Hollon, S. D. (1981). Depressed outpatients treated with cognitive therapy or pharmacotherapy: A one-year follow-up. *Archives of General Psychiatry, 38,* 33–39.

Krantz, S., & Hammen, C. (1979). Assessment of cognitive bias in depression. *Journal of Abnormal Psychology, 88,* 611–619.

Lapointe, K. A. (1977). Cognitive therapy versus assertive training in the treatment of depression. (Doctoral dissertation, Southern Illinois University, Carbondale, IL 1976). *Dissertation Abstracts International, 37,* 4689B. (University Microfilms No. 77-6232).

Lapointe, K. A., & Crandell, C. J. (1980). Relationship of irrational beliefs to self-reported depression. *Cognitive Therapy and Research, 4,* 247–250.

Layne, C., Lefton, W., Walters, D., & Merry, J. (1983). Depression: motivational deficits versus social manipulation. *Cognitive Therapy and Research, 7,* 125–132.

Lefebvre, M. F. (1981). Cognitive distortion and cognitive errors in depressed psychiatric and low back pain patients. *Journal of Consulting and Clinical Psychology, 49,* 517–525.

Lewinsohn, P. M. (1974). A behavioral approach to depression. In R. M. Friedman & M. M. Katz (Eds.), *The psychology of depression: Contemporary theory and research* (pp. 157–186). Washington, DC: Winston-Wiley.

Lewinsohn, P. M., Larson, D. W., & Muñoz, R. F. (1982). The measurement of expectancies and other cognitions in depressed individuals. *Cognitive Therapy and Research, 6,* 437–446.

Lishman, W. A. (1972). Selective factors in memory: II. Affective disorders. *Psychological Medicine, 2,* 248–253.

Lloyd, G. G., & Lishman, W. A. (1975). Effect of depression on the speed of recall of pleasant and unpleasant experiences. *Psychological Medicine, 5,* 173–180.

Lobitz, C., & Post, D. (1979). Parameters of self-reinforcement and depression. *Journal of Abnormal Psychology, 88,* 33–41.

May, J. R., & Johnson, J. J. (1973). Physiological activity to internally elicited arousal and inhibitory thoughts. *Journal of Abnormal Psychology, 82,* 239–245.

Miller, I. W., Klee, S. H., & Norman, W. H. (1982). Depressed and nondepressed inpatients' cognitions of hypothetical events, experimental tasks, and stressful life events. *Journal of Abnormal Psychology, 91,* 78–81.

Miller, I. W., & Norman, W. H. (1981). Affects of attributions of success of alleviation of learned helplessness and depression. *Journal of Abnormal Psychology, 90,* 113–124.

Missel, T., & Sommer, D. (1983). Depression and self-verbalization. *Cognitive Therapy and Research, 7,* 141–148.

Morris, N. E. (1975). *A group of self-instruction methods for the treatment of depressed outpatients.* Unpublished doctoral dissertation, University of Toronto.

Murphy, G. E., Simons, A. D., Wetzel, R. D., & Lustman, P. J. (1984). Cognitive therapy and pharmacotherapy. *Archives of General Psychiatry, 41,* 33–41.

Natale, M. (1977a). Effects of induced elation-depression on speech in the initial interview. *Journal of Consulting and Clinical Psychology, 45,* 45–52.

Natale, M. (1977b). Induction of mood states and their effect on gaze behavior. *Journal of Consulting and Clinical Psychology, 45,* 717–723.

Nelson, R. E. (1977). Irrational beliefs in depression. *Journal of Consulting and Clinical Psychology, 45,* 1190–1191.

Nelson, R. E., & Craighead, W. E. (1977). Selective recall of positive and negative feedback, self-control behaviors, and depression. *Journal of Abnormal Psychology, 86,* 379–388.

Norman, W. H., Miller, I. W., & Klee, S. H. (1983). Assessment of cognitive distortion in a clinically depressed population. *Cognitive Therapy and Research, 7,* 133–140.

O'Hara, M. W., Rehm, L. P., & Campbell, S. B. (1982). Predicting depressive symptomotology: Cognitive-behavioral models and postpartum depression. *Journal of Abnormal Psychology, 91,* 457–461.

Orton, I. K., Beiman, I., Lapointe, K., & Lankford, A. (1983). Induced states of anxiety and depression: Effects on self-reported affect and tonic psychophysiological response. *Cognitive Therapy and Research, 7,* 233–244.

Paykel, E. S. (1979). Recent life events in the development of depressive disorders. In R. A. Depue (Ed.), *The psychobiology of the depressive disorders* (pp. 245–262). New York: Academic Press.

Peterson, C. (1979). Uncontrollability and self-blame in depression: Investigation of the paradox in a college population. *Journal of Abnormal Psychology, 88,* 620–624.

Peterson, C., Luborsky, L., & Seligman, M. E. P. (1983). Attributions and depressive mood shifts: Case study using the symptom-context method. *Journal of Abnormal Psychology, 92,* 96–103.

Raps, C. S., Peterson, C., Reinhard, K. E., Abramson, L. Y., & Seligman, M. E. P. (1982). Attributional style among depressed patients. *Journal of Abnormal Psychology, 91,* 102–108.

Raps, C. S., Reinhard, K. E., & Seligman, M. E. P. (1980). Reversal of cognitive and affective deficits associated with depression and learned helplessness by mood elevation in patients. *Journal of Abnormal Psychology, 89,* 342–349.

Rimm, D. C., & Litvak, S. B. (1969). Self-verbalization and emotional arousal. *Journal of Abnormal Psychology, 74,* 181–187.

Riskind, J. H., Rholes, W. S., & Eggers, J. (1982). The Velten Mood Induction Procedure: Effects on mood and memory. *Journal of Consulting and Clinical Psychology, 50,* 3–13.

Rogers, T., & Craighead, W. E. (1977). Physiological responses to self-statements: The effects of statement valence and discrepancy. *Cognitive Therapy and Research, 1,* 99–120.

Rogers, T. R., & Forehand, R. (1983). The role of parent depression in interactions between mothers and their clinic-referred children. *Cognitive Therapy and Research, 7,* 315–324.

Roth, D., & Rehm, L. P. (1980). Relationships among self-monitoring processes, memory, and depression. *Cognitive Therapy and Research, 4,* 149–158.

Rozensky, R. H., Rehm, L., Pry, G., & Roth, D. (1977). Depression and self-depression and self-reinforcement behavior in hospitalized patients. *Journal of Behavior Therapy and Experimental Psychiatry, 8,* 31–34.

Rush, A. J., Beck, A. T., Kovacs, M., & Hollon, S. D. (1977). Comparative efficacy of cognitive therapy versus pharmacotherapy in outpatient depressives. *Cognitive Therapy and Research, 1,* 17–37.

Rush, A. J., Shaw, B., & Khatami, M. (1980). Cognitive therapy of depression: Utilizing the couples' system. *Cognitive Therapy and Research, 4,* 103–114.

Rush, A. J. & Watkins, J. T. (1981). Group versus individual cognitive therapy: A pilot study. *Cognitive Therapy and Research, 5,* 95–104.

Russell, P. L., & Brandsma, J. M. (1974). A theoretical and empirical investigation of the rational-emotive and classical conditioning theories. *Journal of Consulting and Clinical Psychology, 42,* 389–397.

Sacco, W. P. (1985). *Depression and expectations of satisfaction.* Manuscript submitted for publication.

Sacco, W. P., & Graves, D. J. (1984). Childhood depression, interpersonal problem-solving, and self-ratings of performance. *Journal of Clinical Child Psychology, 13,* 10–15.

Sacco, W. P., & Hokanson, J. E. (1978). Expectations of success and anagram performance of depressives in a public and private setting. *Journal of Abnormal Psychology, 87,* 122–130.

Sacco, W. P., Milana, S. A., & Dunn, V. (in press). Effect of depression level and length of acquaintance on reactions of others to a request for help. *Journal of Personality and Social Psychology.*

Schuele, J. G., & Wiesenfeld, A. R. (1983). Automatic response to self-critical thoughts. *Cognitive Therapy and Research, 7,* 189–194.

Shapiro, A. K., & Morris, L. A. (1978). Placebo effects in medical and psychological therapies. In S. L. Garfield & A. E. Bergin (Eds.), *Handbook of psychotherapy and behavior change: An empirical analysis* (2nd ed.) (pp. 369–410). New York: John Wiley & Sons.

Shaw, B. F. (1977a). Comparison of cognitive therapy and behavior therapy in the treatment of depression. *Journal of Consulting and Clinical Psychology, 45,* 543–551.

Shaw, B. F. (1977b). *Drug trials in depression: An analysis of premature termination rates.* Unpublished manuscript, University of Pennsylvania, Philadelphia.

Shaw, B. F., & Hollon, S. D., (1978). *Cognitive therapy in a group format with depressed outpatients.* Unpublished manuscript, University of Western Ontario, London.

Sherwood, G. G., Schroeder, K. G., Abrami, D. L., & Alden, L. E. (1981). Self-referent versus nonself-referent statements in the induction of mood states. *Cognitive Therapy and Research, 5,* 105–108.

Taylor, F. G., & Marshall, W. L. (1977). Experimental analysis of a cognitive-behavioral therapy for depression. *Cognitive Therapy and Research, 1,* 59–72.

Teasdale, J. D. (1983, February 7). *Changing cognition during depression: Psychopathological implications.* Paper presented to the section of Psychiatry of Royal Society of Medicine.

Teasdale, J. D., & Bancroft, J. (1977). Manipulation of thought content as a determinant of mood and corrugator electromyographic activity in depressed patients. *Journal of Abnormal Psychology, 86,* 235–241.

Teasdale, J. D., & Fennell, M. J. V. (1982). Immediate effects on depression of cognitive therapy interventions. *Cognitive Therapy and Research, 6,* 343–352.

Teasdale, J. D., Fennell, M. J. V., Hibbert, G. A., & Amies, P. L. (1983). *Cognitive therapy for major depressive disorder and primary care.* Unpublished manuscript, University of Oxford, Oxford, England.

Teasdale, J. D., & Fogerty, S. J. (1979). Differential effects of induced mood on retrieval of pleasant and unpleasant events from episodic memory. *Journal of Abnormal Psychology, 88,* 248–257.

Teasdale, J. D., & Rezin, V. (1978). The effects of reducing frequency of negative thoughts on the mood of depressed patients—Tests of a cognitive model of depression. *British Journal of Social and Clinical Psychology, 17,* 65–74.

Velten, E. (1968). A laboratory task for induction of mood states. *Behavior Research and Therapy. 6,* 473–482.

Warren, L. W., & McEachren, L. (1983). Psychosocial correlates of depressive symptomatology in adult women. *Journal of Abnormal Psychology, 92,* 151–160.

Weissman, A., & Beck, A. T. (1978, November). *Development and validation of the dysfunctional attitude scale.* Paper presented at the meeting of the Association for Advancement of Behavior Therapy, Chicago.

Wener, A. E., & Rehm, L. P. (1975). Depressive affect: A test of behavioral hypotheses. *Journal of Abnormal Psychology, 84,* 221–227.

Wilson, P. H., Goldin, J. C., & Charbonneau-Powis, M. (1983). Comparative efficacy of behavioral and cognitive treatments of depression. *Cognitive Therapy and Research, 7,* 111–124.

Wilson, A. R., & Krane, R. V. (1980). Change in self-esteem and its effects on symptoms of depression. *Cognitive Therapy and Research, 4,* 419–422.

Yeaton, W. H., & Sechrest, L. (1981). Critical dimensions in the choice and maintenance of successful treatments: Strength, integrity, and effectiveness. *Journal of Consulting and Clinical Psychology, 49,* 156–157.

Zeiss, A. M., Lewinsohn, P. M., & Muñoz, R. F. (1979). Nonspecific improvement effects in depression using interpersonal skills training, pleasant activity schedules, or cognitive training. *Journal of Consulting and Clinical Psychology, 47,* 427–439.

Chapter 2

The Behavioral Treatment of Depression

Harry M. Hoberman
University of Minnesota Medical School

Peter M. Lewinsohn
University of Oregon

The past 10 years have witnessed a veritable explosion in the development and study of behavioral treatments for unipolar depression. As recently as 1975, Lieberman concluded that there was little scientific evidence to the efficacy of verbal psychotherapy in treating depressive disorders, including behavioral interventions. Similarly, Becker (1974) observed that behavioral theorists had relatively little to say about depression. As we have noted elsewhere (Lewinsohn & Hoberman, 1982a), behavior researchers were particularly late in attempting to study and treat depression, relative to other psychiatric disorders. Consequently, it is especially striking that, at present, there are a variety of behaviorally oriented treatment packages for depressive disorders and well over 50 outcome studies of behavioral approaches for ameliorating depression. In a short time, both the quantity and the sophistication of behavioral treatments for depression have increased dramatically. Additionally, a number of thoughtful and comprehensive reviews of this literature have appeared (e.g., Blaney, 1981; Craighead, 1981; DeRubeis & Hollon, 1981; Hersen & Bellack, 1982; Lewinsohn & Hoberman, 1982b; Rehm & Kornblith, 1979; Rush & Beck, 1978). Stimulated by the increasing evidence that a variety of structured behavioral therapies are effective in treating depression, this prolific activity has resulted in an increased acceptance of such approaches among clinicians. Indeed, the problem facing the practitioner in this area is one of sifting and choosing from a range of promising therapeutic formulations and approaches.

Beyond the cumulative support for their efficacy, behavioral approaches are worth considering for several more specific reasons (Rush & Beck, 1978). First, such therapies offer the patient new behavior skills and/or new ways of thinking about him or herself. Additionally, behavioral methods may significantly decrease the dropout rate for outpatient treatment. Relatedly, in conjunction with chemotherapy specific behavior techniques may be utilized to increase compliance with medical prescriptions and to decrease premature termination from biological treatments. Still another advantage of behavioral therapies, when applied in a patient's social system, is that they may modify predisposing or etiologically critical interactions by restructuring the content of these problematic interactions. Finally, depressed persons who either refuse or cannot take antidepressant medication, or who do not respond to adequate trials of chemotherapy, may respond to behavior therapies.

The purposes of this chapter are twofold. First, we aim to provide the reader with an understanding of the foundations and practices of behavioral approaches to the treatment of unipolar depression. The second goal is to review the research literature available both as to the efficacy and clinical parameters of these interventions. To these ends, we begin with a brief discussion of the conceptual foundations of behavior therapy in general and then of early behavioral attempts to explain and treat depression. Following this, we systematically explicate current behavioral theories, strategies, and tactics for the treatment of depressive disorders. In particular, we shall focus on two treatment packages for unipolar depression developed at the Depression Research Unit of the University of Oregon; the first of these therapy programs is an individual approach, while the other is a psychoeducational group intervention. Other behavioral treatment approaches will then be described for contrast. Last, a brief review of current research programs investigating aspects of behavioral treatments for depression will be presented.

CONCEPTUAL AND HISTORICAL PERSPECTIVES

Current behavioral approaches to the treatment of depression can best be understood and appreciated against the background of the conceptual foundations of behavior therapy in general, as well as early attempts by behaviorists to generate and test theory-based treatments for depression. Contemporary behavioral approaches for depression follow fairly directly both from the generic behavioral perspective and initial endeavors both to understand and modify depression within a behavioral framework.

Conceptual Foundations of Behavior Therapy

The development of behavioral approaches to the treatment of psychological disorders had its basis in two initially distinct but sequential movements within psychology. First, beginning in the early part of this century, investigators increasingly attempted to explain human behavior on the basis of experimental studies of learning. Thus, psychologists such as Thorndike (1931) and Skinner (1953) argued for the importance of the "law of effect" and the role of behavioral consequences in learning, with Skinner also emphasizing the role of the environment rather than undocumented mental entities in determining behavior. A second and somewhat later force in the genesis of behavior therapy was rooted in an increasing dissatisfaction with the predominant intrapsychic conceptions of abnormal behavior (e.g., a disease model) and related treatment approaches. More particularly certain theorists and practitioners were motivated to explore alternative models of treatment primarily because of three reasons: (1) there was difficulty in testing critical assumptions of psychodynamic approaches and a lack of empirical support when those assumptions could be tested; (2) the current diagnostic schemes had few implications for understanding the etiology, prognosis, or treatment of the disorders they defined; and (3) there was a general belief that, as Eysenck's (1952) study had suggested, the efficacy of traditional psychotherapy had yet to be established. As a result of the dissatisfaction with available psychotherapeutic orientations, a variety of theorists and therapists endeavored to develop therapeutic approaches based on the clinical utility of learning concepts. These initial theories and practices based on experimental studies of behavior constituted the basis for the field of behavior therapy.

Currently, behavior therapy can best be understood more as a scientific approach to the understanding of behavior and its treatment, rather than having a specific theoretical basis or consisting of a specific set of techniques. Kazdin (1982) has suggested that behavior therapy can best be characterized by a number of assumptions:

1. A reliance on findings or techniques derived from general psychology, especially the psychology of learning.
2. A view of the continuity of normal and abnormal behavior.
3. A direct focus on the maladaptive behavior for which an individual seeks treatment.
4. An emphasis on the assessment of behavior across response modalities for delineation of an individual's behavior and of the influences which may contribute to or be used to modify that behavior.
5. A belief that the process of treatment should be closely tied to the continual assessment of problematic target behaviors so that the outcome of therapy can be measured by monitoring changes in target behaviors.

Additionally, behavior therapy is marked by its focus on current rather than historical determinants of behavior and the specification of treatment in objective and operational terms so that procedures can be replicated.

History of Behavioral Approaches to Depression

The first attempt at a behavioral analysis of depression is contained in Skinner's *Science and Human Behavior* (1953), in which depression is described as a weakening of behavior due to the interruption of established sequences of behavior that have been positively reinforced by the social environment. This conceptualization of depression as an extinction phenomenon and as reduced frequency of emission of positively reinforced behavior has been central to all behavioral positions. Ferster (1966) provided more detail by suggesting that such diverse factors as sudden environmental changes, punishment, and aversive control, and shifts in reinforcement contingencies can give rise to depression (e.g., to a reduced rate of behavior). Costello (1972) argued that depression results not from the loss of reinforcers per se but instead from the loss of reinforcer effectiveness. Lewinsohn (e.g., Lewinsohn & Shaw, 1969) also maintained that a low rate of response-contingent positive reinforcement constituted a sufficient explanation for parts of the depressive syndrome, such as the low rate of behavior. Lewinsohn and his colleagues amplified the behavioral position through several additional hypotheses:

1. A causal relationship between the low rate of response-contingent positive reinforcement and the feeling of dysphoria.
2. An emphasis on the maintenance of depressive behaviors by the social environment through the provision of contingencies in the form of sympathy, interest, and concern.
3. An emphasis on deficiencies in social skill as an important antecedent to the low rate of positive reinforcement.

Early attempts to treat depression from a behavioral perspective typically involved small numbers of individuals and employed a single or limited number of therapeutic interventions. These simple treatments were focused on one of four aspects of behavior: (*a*) the individual's affective experience; (*b*) the individual's activity level; (*c*) the individual's social skills or interpersonal style; and (*d*) obsessive negative thoughts. Lazarus (1968) reported on the use of two techniques to induce affect incompatible with dysphoria: affective expression, where attempts were made to stimulate feelings of amusement, affection, and sexual excitement in the depressed individual; and time projection, where the individual was asked to imagine her/himself engaging in rewarding activities six months in the future. Seitz (1971) described the use of relaxation training to induce nondysphoric affect. With regard to the individual's activity level, the practice of reinforcing simple, graduated tasks in depressives was first described by Burgess (1969). Lewinsohn, Weinstein, and Shaw (1969) had patients keep a daily record of their behavior, while Lewinsohn (1975a) reported on the success of having patients increase their rate of activities. A number of early studies of depressed individuals targeted social behavior as the focus of intervention. Wolpe and Lazarus (1966) described the use of assertiveness training to reduce depression, while Lewinsohn, Weinstein, and Alper (1970) employed a group treatment paradigm to provide information to depressed individuals about their behavior and its interpersonal consequences upon them. The group was also used to assist the depressed patients in defining new interpersonal behavior goals and to reinforce behavior changes. In addition, Robinson and Lewinsohn (1973) utilized contingent reinforcement to increase the speaking rate and quality of a severely depressed individual. In a series of case studies, Lewinsohn and his colleagues (e.g., Lewinsohn & Atwood, 1969; Lewinsohn & Shaw, 1969) utilized home observations to provide interactional feedback to depressed individuals; this feedback then served as the basis for individual and conjoint therapy sessions aimed at improving marital communication and depression. Finally, Lazarus (1968) and Wanderer (1972) described the use of thought stopping techniques to reduce the rate of a depressed individual's negative obsessive thoughts. Thus, early behavioral approaches to treating depression employed a variety of interventions in treating several aspects of the depressed individual's behavior. As will be seen later in this chapter, the variety of interventions utilized by behavior therapists in their initial attempts to treat depression would come to serve as the basis for treatment packages developed and studied in later years.

BEHAVIORAL THEORIES OF DEPRESSION

Perhaps the most important role that a theory of depression plays, at least from a clinical perspective, is to provide a useful guide for treatment efforts. In general terms, a theory specifies functional relationships between certain antecedent events and the occurrence of depression. These events presumably account for, or "explain" depression. For a given patient, a theory represents a statement about the likely reasons for the patient's depression. Consequently, a theory dictates the intermediate goals for therapy. To the extent that the theory is valid, accomplishing the goals should lead to a change in the level of depression. The predominant behavioral theories of depression fall in the domain of what is known as social learning theory. First introduced by Rotter (1954), it has more recently been extended by Bandura (1977). Social learning theory assumes that psychological functioning can best be understood in terms of continuous reciprocal interactions among personal factors (e.g., cognitive processes, expectancies), behavioral factors, and environmental factors, all operating as interdependant determinants of one another. From the perspective of social learning theory, people are seen as capable of exercising considerable control over their own behavior, not just as reactors to external influences; rather they are viewed as selecting, organizing, and transforming the stimuli that impinge upon them. People and their environments are seen as reciprocal determinants of one another.

Over the years, Lewinsohn and his colleagues (e.g., Lewinsohn et al., 1969; Lewinsohn, Youngren, & Grosscup, 1979) have argued that depression and reinforcement are related phenomena. Depressed behavior and affect is seen as a function of the reduction in the rate of response-contingent positive reinforcement, where reinforcement is defined in terms of the quality of one's interactions with one's environment. The critical assumption of behavioral theories of depression is that the low rate of behavioral output and the associated dysphoric feelings are elicited by a low rate of positive reinforcement and/or a high rate of aversive experience; that is, it is assumed that the behavior of depressed persons does not lead to positive reinforcement to a degree sufficient to maintain their behavior. A low rate of positive reinforcement, by virtue of providing little or no rewarding interactions with the environment, is assumed to cause the dysphoric feelings that are so central to the phenomenology of depression. Thus, the key notion of behavioral theories of depression is that being depressed is a consequence of some combination of a decrease in person-environment interactions with positive outcomes for a person and/or an increase in the rate of punishing experiences.

According to Lewinsohn's initial theory of depression (Lewinsohn, Biglan, & Zeiss, 1976), low rates of positive reinforcement and/or high rates of aversive experience in the person-environment interaction were postulated as occuring for several reasons: (1) The person's immediate environment may have few available positive reinforcers or may have many punishing aspects (availability); (2) the person may lack the skills to obtain available positive reinforcers and/or cope effectively with aversive events (skill deficits); (3) the positive reinforcement potency of events may be reduced and/or the negative impact of punishing events may be heightened. These notions, and research results consistent with them, have been discussed elsewhere in more detail (Grosscup & Lewinsohn, 1980; Lewinsohn & Amenson, 1978; Lewinsohn et al., 1976; Lewinsohn & Talkington, 1979; Lewinsohn et al., 1979; MacPhillamy & Lewinsohn, 1974).

Recently, Lewinsohn, Hoberman, Teri, and Hautzinger (1985) have proposed a new theoretical model of the etiology and maintenance of depression. This model is presented schematically in Figure 1. This integrative model of depression represents an attempt to intergrate the findings of our epidemiological (e.g., Lewinsohn & Hoberman, 1982c) and treatment outcome studies (e.g., Zeiss, Lewinsohn, & Muñoz, 1979) with an increasing body of work in social psychology on the phenomenon of self-awareness (e.g., Carver & Scheier, 1982, Duval & Wicklund, 1973). The proposed etiological model, while tentative, represents the phenomena and conditions which we believe are most often involved in the development and maintenance of

FIGURE 1
Schematic representation of variables involved in the occurrence of unipolar depression

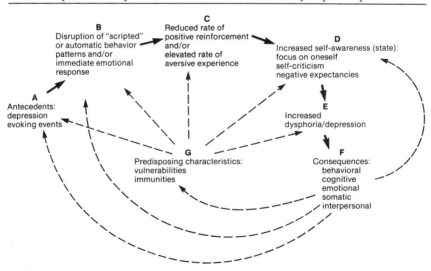

depression. One of the strengths of this model is its incorporation of a number of different characteristics and processes which can influence the occurrence of depression. In so doing, we believe that we are able to account for the great heterogeneity that characterizes both depression and depressives.

As we see it, the depressogenic process consists of the following components:

1. Antecedents are empirically defined as all events which increase the probability for the future occurrence of depression. In the literature to date, all of these "evoking events" fall under the general rubric of stressors, including life events, microstressors, and chronic difficulties. In particular, stressors related to marital distress, social exits, and work problems exhibit an especially strong relationship to the later development of depression.

2. The occurrence of *antecedents* is assumed to initiate the depressogenic process to the extent that they disrupt substantial, important, and relatively automatic behavior patterns of individuals. Langer (1978) has suggested that much of everyday behavior is "scripted" (e.g., Schank & Abelson, 1975), and consequently automatic requiring very little mental effort. Yet these "scripted" patterns constitute aspects of an individual's behavior repertoire which are typical and crucial to a person's everyday interactions with the environment. Consequently, if antecedent or depression-evoking events do disrupt expected, automatic patterns of behavior, they are likely to elicit an immediate negative emotional response (e.g., dysphoria).

3. Such disruptions and emotional upset are assumed to be related to depression to the extent that they lead to a reduction of positive reinforcement and/or to an elevated rate of aversive experience; that is, they shift the balance of the quality of a person's interactions with the environment in a negative direction (e.g., Lewinsohn et al., 1979).

4. A continued inability to reverse the depressogenic process to this point (e.g., through decreasing negative reinforcement or increasing positive reinforcement and consequently, producing a resumption of scripted behavior and/or neutral or positive affect) is hypothesized to lead to a heightened state of self-awareness. Such a state of self-awareness has been shown to have a number of relevant ramifications to depressive onset. First, given a situation which involves a behavioral standard (e.g., coping with evoking events and their subsequent emotional and behavioral disruption), self-awareness has been shown to increase self-evaluation and self-criticism when such a standard is not matched (e.g., Ickes, Wicklund, & Ferris, 1973). Second, when an individual is made self-aware on the basis of negative outcome expectancies (e.g., about future efforts to reverse the depressive cycle) his/her response is likely to be one of behavioral withdrawal (Carver, Blaney, & Scheier, 1979a, 1979b) and further self-criticism. In addition, heightened self-awareness has been shown to result in greater acceptance of responsibility for outcomes (e.g., self-attribution) (Buss & Scheier, 1976, Duval & Wicklund, 1973). In short, the elicitation of a state of self-awareness breaks through an individual's self-protective, self-enhancing cognitive schema (e.g., Alloy & Abramson, 1979; Lewinsohn, Mischel, Chaplin, & Barton, 1980) and increases an individual's awareness of his or her failure to live up to his/her expected standards of coping, and consequently engenders a state of self-denigration and behavioral withdrawal.

5. Another important consequence of a heightened state of self-awareness is an intensification or magnification of affective reactions (Scheier & Carver, 1977). As we have noted, antecedents typically evoke some negative affect (e.g., sadness). Given a situation where an individual feels responsible for the occurrence of a stressor and/or attributes his/her inability to reverse the depressive cycle to him/herself, dysphoria is likely to be the predominant emotional response. Thus, self-awareness will serve to magnify the initial and continuing dysphoria.

6. Feeling increasingly dysphoric, in turn, is assumed to lead to many of the behavioral, cognitive, emotional, and interpersonal changes that have previously been shown to be correlated with depression (e.g., appetite loss, slowed behavior, social withdrawal). These changes are presumed to "lock" the heightened state of self-awareness and heightened dysphoria into a "vicious cycle" which serves to maintain the depressive state.

7. The proposed model also allows for a great variety of individual and environmental differences to both increase and decrease the risk of a depressive episode at a number of points during the depressogenic process. We assume that there are both predisposing vulnerabilities (e.g., being female, ages 20–40, previous history of depression, and so on) and protective immunities (e.g., high self-perceived social competence, competence in social interaction, generalized coping skills, high frequency of pleasant events, and so on).

We believe that this model, in addition to taking into account much of what is empirically known about depression, provides potential explanations for a number of important aspects of depression. The explanatory value of this integrative theory of depression, a more detailed description of the model, and a more elaborated empirical documentation of the processes implicated in the model is presented in Lewinsohn et al. (1985). The utility of the integrative model of depression for the clinician is twofold: First, it takes into account much of what has been learned through treatment outcome studies of depression, and second it provides direction to the practitioner for the development and application of efficacious treatment programs.

BEHAVIORAL STRATEGIES FOR TREATING DEPRESSION

A theory, however, is only a set of abstract statements suggesting general treatment goals for depressed persons (or at least certain kinds of depressives). A comprehensive treatment approach must also have a strategy. A treatment strategy translates the theory into a set of specific operations and procedures which can be used to formulate treatment goals for the depressed person and to direct the parameters of the treatment process. Research studies to investigate the behavioral theory of depression as well as clinical experience in applying the theory during treatment have generated a set of procedures useful for work with depressed patients. The guiding assumption in the treatment of depressed patients is that the restoration of an adequate schedule of positive reinforcement is essential to the reduction of dysphoria, and thus depression. Alterations in the frequency, quality, and range of the patient's activities and social interactions are the most common foci for achieving such a change in a schedule of reinforcement. What follows is a description of a number of assessment and treatment strategies which in the experience of behavior therapists have proven useful in ameliorating depression.

Diagnostic and Functional Assessment

When an individual presents him or herself to a clinic with apparent symptoms of depression, there are two important assessment goals which must be met: differential diagnosis and a functional analysis of depressive behavior. First, an assessment for differential diagnosis must occur to determine whether or not depression is *the,* or at least *a,* problem for the individual. Individuals who are experiencing an episode of depression may manifest a heterogeneity of symptoms; additionally, symptoms of depression, and depression itself, occurs in a large number of patients suffering from medical and other psychiatric disorders. Consequently, if depression is a presenting problem, an adequate medical and psychiatric history must be obtained to determine whether the depression is secondary to physical illness or a medical regime, or subsequent to a manic or hypomanic episode. In all these cases, it would be important to recommend an individual for specific additional assessment and treatment for the primary condition (e.g., lithium for a bipolar patient) before proceeding with behavioral treatment for the depression. Existing assessment instruments allow a clinician to describe a patient in regard to depression severity, to delineate the specific constellation of symptoms shown by that patient, and to evaluate the absence or presence of other psychiatric symptoms and conditions. In this regard, we have utilized the Schedule for Affective Disorders and Schizophrenia ([SADS]; Endicott & Spitzer, 1978) and the Research Diagnostic Criteria ([RDC]; Spitzer, Endicott, & Robins, 1978), by means of which it is possible to assign patients to diagnostic categories with considerable reliability. In addition, we recommend the use of one of the many convenient short, and easy to use, self-report measures of depression level such as the Beck Depression Inventory ([BDI]; Beck, Ward, Mendelson, Mock, & Erbaugh, 1961), the Zung Self-Rating Depression Scale ([SDS]; Zung, 1965), and the Center for Epidemiologic Studies-Depression

Scale ([CES-D]; Radloff, 1977). These instruments are particularly useful for measuring both the severity of depression and for assessing the outcome of treatment.

While differential diagnosis may be common to behavioral as well as other treatment approaches, the second stage of assessment is relatively specific to behavioral interventions. A functional diagnosis or analysis of depressive behavior involves pinpointing specific person-environment interactions and events related to a particular patient's depression. This part of the diagnostic process is needed to guide the formulation of a treatment plan designed to change the events contributing to the patient's depression. Behavior patterns may be postulated as being functionally related to depression on the basis of three criteria: (1) if the pattern occurs with increased, or decreased frequency in depressed vis-à-vis appropriate control groups; (2) if the behavior-environment interaction is present when the person is depressed but is absent or attenuated when the person is not depressed; and (3) if the occurrence of the person-environment interaction covaries with fluctuations in daily mood. The prototypical means of identifying behavioral events and activities functionally related to depression involves the use of the Pleasant Events Schedule ([PES]; MacPhillamy & Lewinsohn, 1971) and the Unpleasant Events Schedule ([UES]; Lewinsohn, 1975c). Both of these tests have been described in greater detail elsewhere and test manuals providing normative data are available (Lewinsohn, 1975b,c; MacPhillamy & Lewinsohn, 1982). Briefly, each schedule consists of 320 items assumed to represent an exhaustive sample of interactions with the environment which many people find pleasant or unpleasant. The client first rates the frequency of each event's occurrence during the past month, and then rates the subjective impact of the events. The frequency ratings are assumed to reflect the rate of occurrence of the events during the past month. The subjective impact ratings are assumed to indicate the individual's potential for positive reinforcement and for punishment. Cross product scores of the frequency and impact ratings are assumed to reflect the total amount of positive reinforcement and of aversiveness experienced during the past month.

Normative data on both schedules allow evaluation of the client's scores relative to others of the same sex and age. PES scores below norms and UES scores above the norms on various subscales suggest the kinds of reinforcing and punishing events potentially related to the client's depression. Patterns among scores are often important. For example, a client may have a low score for pleasant sexual events but a high score for marital distress events. This immediately suggests potential reasons for this client's depression and even some potential treatment tactics. In addition, the analysis of PES and UES scores also provides individualized lists of specific events which are potentially pleasant or unpleasant for a patient. We share these working hypotheses with the patient and use them to formulate some intermediate treatment goals.

An additional means of delineating behavioral and environmental targets for intervention is through the use of home observations. Home visits, lasting about an hour, should be scheduled around mealtimes, when all members of the family are present. Detailed case descriptions illustrating the use of the home visit as part of the initial assessment are available elsewhere (Lewinsohn & Shaffer, 1971). Although costly in terms of the therapist's time, home observations can be very valuable in identifying interpersonal behavior patterns in the family that the therapist may hypothesize to be causally related to the depression. If for practical reasons, the therapist is unable to conduct home observations, it might be advisable to schedule an interview with the spouse.

CONCEPTUALIZATION OF PRESENTING PROBLEMS

Another important strategy essential to behavior therapy for depression involves the development of a shared conceptualization of a patient's presenting problems between the therapist and the patient. Patients usually enter therapy with conceptualizations or definitions of their problems. As McLean (1981) has written, depressed patients often see themselves as victims of their moods or of environmental forces. Rarely do patients see their behaviors and/ or their interpretations of their behaviors and/or the behaviors of others as causes for the depression. To complicate things further, fairly substantial numbers of the professional community are convinced that there is a biogenic cause of unipolar depression. This is often meant to imply the insignificance of psychological and environmental variables as causal factors. Thus, depressed patients often initially assume a passive stance; that is, they believe that something analogous to a physical disease has happened to them. Although they may emphasize specific behavioral problems (e.g., sleeplessness, lack of social involvement, obsessive thoughts), typically the focus is on "depression." Thus, it usually takes a considerable amount of work to move patients from a construct usage of the term *depression* to a recognition of the importance of specific problematic behavioral events that may be related to their dysphoria.

One goal of the initial phase of treatment is for therapist and patient to redefine the patient's problems in terms that will give the patient a sense of control and a feeling of hope, especially in terms that will lead to specific behavioral interventions. Thus the therapist tries to understand the patient's description and definition of the problem, but the therapist does not uncritically accept the patient's view of the problem. Instead, therapist and patient attempt to redefine the problem in terms that are acceptable to both of them. Information obtained through the functional assessment of depressive behavior may be especially useful in developing a shared understanding of the genesis and maintenance of patient's depression. It is the reformulation or conceptualization phase then that sets the stage for behavioral change. We see it as essential for successful treatment that the patient and the therapist evolve a common conceptualization with common expectations. This conceptualization should be such as to lead naturally to specific behavioral changes that will benefit the patient in real-life situations.

There are numerous ways in which the patient and therapist can evolve a common conceptualization. Some therapists are very directive, forcing on the patient a particular conceptualization by the power of personality, jargon, or position. In some cases, such a hard-sell approach may prove successful. A preferred way to proceed is to have the patient and the therapist evolve a common conceptualization that will increase the patient's feeling of being an active participant in making a contribution to the therapy process. The manner in which the therapist discusses the presenting problem, the kinds of questions asked, the type of assessment procedure employed, the content of the therapy rationale, and the kinds of initial homework assignments given are all used to evolve a common patient-therapist conceptualization. It is important to do a great deal of "structuring" in the initial phase of treatment of depressed patients so that there will be a clear and mutual understanding of expectations, goals, time commitments, and other conditions.

Monitoring of Mood and Activities

As noted earlier in this chapter, an essential element of behavior therapy in general is the continual feedback between ongoing assessment and treatment interventions. This characteristic is especially true of behavioral treatments for depression. From the first day of therapy, the depressed patient is typically asked to monitor and rate his/her mood on a daily basis for the duration of treatment. These ratings can be made on a simple nine-point visual analog scale (where one indicates very happy and nine indicates very depressed) or on the Depressive Adjective Checklist ([DACL]; Lubin, 1965). In rating their moods on a daily basis, depressed individuals are provided the opportunity to note variations in their mood. Daily mood ratings also permit the therapist to note particular days when a patient is more or less depressed and to explore the specific circumstances and/or repeated patterns influencing fluctuations in an individual's mood.

Similarly, patients are asked to monitor the occurrences of pleasant and aversive events on a daily basis. Generic activity schedules can be used for this purpose, although behavior therapists typically prefer to generate an individualized list of events and activities for the individual to keep track of. The main purpose of daily monitoring of activities and mood is to enable the patient and the therapist to become aware of the covariance that typically exists between mood and the rates of occurrences of pleasant and unpleasant activities. This covariance permits the evaluation of the functional diagnosis and further specification of the person-environment interactions influencing the patient's mood. Inspection of a graph of the daily mood and event scores provides an easy means of estimating concommitant changes in the levels of these variables.

Lewinsohn and his associates (Lewinsohn, 1976; Lewinsohn et al., 1976; Lewinsohn, Sullivan, & Grosscup, 1980) have pioneered the use of computerized analysis of PES and UES ratings to provide the basis for constructing a personalized activity schedule. Each patient's activity schedule consists of the 80 items the patient rated as most pleasant on the PES and the 80 items the patient rated as most unpleasant and most frequent on the UES. This computer analysis provides the means of pinpointing precisely the specific events most highly correlated with mood fluctuations. The therapist and patient can then use this information to fine-tune the diagnosis and the associated therapy goals.

PROGRESSIVE GOAL ATTAINMENT AND BEHAVIORAL PRODUCTIVITY

An increase in goal-defined behavior is essential to all behavioral treatments for depression. McLean (1981) has described a number of issues concerning goals common to depressed patients. He notes that many depressives are often problem or crisis focused and are unable to identify goals they wish to pursue. Typically, when depressed persons are able to formulate personal goals, their goals are often unrealistic and their criteria for achievement are expressed in an "all-or-none" manner. Depressed individuals, thus, are frequently characterized by frustration in attempting goals which have a low probability of attainment or, in those cases where goals are absent or undefined, by an aimless reactivity to the environment. In both cases, the general result of these deficiencies in goal setting is likely to be a decrease in purposeful behavior, particularly behavior which might have antidepressive consequences.

Given these deficits in goal setting and goal-related behavior, a major behavioral treatment strategy involves educating depressed individuals with regard to goals and goal-directed behavior. Depressives are taught to routinely set, plan, and review their goals. Each goal that is defined must be clearly relevant to the patient's needs. As Biglan and Dow (1981) note, patients are encouraged to decide on their own priorities among goals since this is likely to enhance their involvement in therapy. Additionally, patients are encouraged to take global goals (e.g., happiness, success) and break them down into smaller and more attainable goals. After defining realistic objectives (e.g., aspects of the person or environment that can be changed), performance tasks are graduated "into as small untis as are necessary in order to reduce the task demands to the point that successful performance is relatively guaranteed" (McLean, 1976, p. 80). Throughout treatment, an ongoing effort is made to keep intermediate treatment goals mutually meaningful and specific.

Although the reciprocal interaction between thoughts, feelings, and behavior is acknowledged, the emphasis in behavior therapy for depression is that thoughts and feelings can be most effectively influenced by behavior change. Consequently, a graduated goal-oriented behavioral focus is established early in treatment and the utility of this position is identified throughout the course of therapy. The focus on behavioral productivity is accomplished through the employment of regular homework assignments which emphasize gradual behavior change designed to ensure a high probability of successful performance on the part of the depressive.

CONTRACTING AND SELF-REINFORCEMENT

Another central element of behavioral treatments for depression involves the "activation" of the depressed/individual's motivation via an increase in their behavioral output. Both the assessment and the treatment of a depressed patient require effort on the patient's part. For example, the patient may be asked to fill out the PES, to keep track of mood variations, to monitor activities on a daily basis, and so on throughout the course of treatment. Moreover, the patient may be asked to take steps that involve substantial changes in daily activities. A variety of response-induction procedures can be used to mobilize initial behavior, which can then be shaped into distinct performance steps. It has been found useful to take advantage of various contingencies that may motivate the patient to engage in treatment-relevant activities. We advise patients to make specific agreements with themselves to give themselves rewards, but only if they perform the specifics of the agreements. The purpose of the contract is to arrange in advance the specific positive consequence (reinforcement) to follow the achievement of a goal. For example, a contract might state that the patient will have dinner at a favorite restaurant if and only if baseline observations are faithfully carried out for one week. We recommend the inclusion of contracting because it has been our experience that it makes the accomplishment of goals easier for many patients.

Reinforcers may take many forms: (1) material rewards that are available in the patient's environment (e.g., favorite meals, magazines, books, clothes, records, and other objects requiring money), and (2) time (e.g., earning time to do things the patient likes to do but rarely has time for, such as taking a relaxing bath, sleeping late, sunbathing, talking on the phone, or just "wasting time"). A patient's responses on the PES also suggest appropriate reinforcers.

Another important means of cultivating motivation in depressed patients involves developing their ability and inclination to self-reinforce. The relative importance of a performance task and the criteria for acknowledging its achievement are determined at the time of goal setting. If and when the goal is accomplished, the behavior therapist provides appropriate social reinforcement for this success. More importantly, the patient is encouraged (and reinforced) for employing any of a number of self-reinforcing practices (e.g., self-praise for a completed task, a pat on the back, thinking about one's own good points and accomplishments, good relationships with others) or mental "treats" (e.g., daydreaming about pleasurable things, meditating, listening to music).

Other motivational tactics we have used include making the next appointment contingent on the completion of certain tasks and reducing patient fees for keeping appointments and for completing assignments. Frequently, at the beginning of treatment, a depressed patient is asked to generate a "reward menu" consisting of 5 or 10 potentially pleasurable rewards. The reward menu consists of events the patient would like to do and is capable of doing. The patient then specifies the degree of goal satisfaction needed to earn each reward and then self-rewards him/herself for engaging in and completing treatment-relevant activities.

In summary, we use contingency contracts and self-reinforcement schedules in ways that are consistent with the overall goal of treatment, which is to increase the amount of response-contingent reinforcement. Contingency contracts can also serve to clarify progress toward the accomplishment of goals.

SPECIFIC SKILLS—REMEDIATION AND THERAPEUTIC DECISION MAKING

Behavioral theories of depression place considerable weight, etiologically speaking, on a decrease in response-contingent pleasurable activities, particularly as a result of specific performance and skill deficits. As a review of the empirical literature on depression has demonstrated, depressed individuals as a group show marked deficiencies in the areas of social skills, coping with stressors, and cognitive self-regulation, among other areas (Lewinsohn & Hoberman, 1982a). Hence, a significant aspect of all behavioral treatment programs for depression involve the systematic remediation of the performance and skill deficits presented by depressed patients. Treatment approaches thus focus on teaching depressed patients skills they can use to change detrimental patterns of interaction with their environment, as well as the skills needed to maintain these changes after the termination of therapy. Specific skills training interventions will vary from case to case, ranging from highly structured standardized programs to individually designed ad hoc procedures. Training typically involves the following processes: didactic introduction to the skills involved; modeling and coaching by the therapist; role-playing and rehearsal; practice by the patient during and after treatment sessions; and, application of the skills in the real world. A wide variety of specific skills are available to a therapist to employ in treating depressed individuals. Among the variety of specific skills which may be included in behavioral treatment programs for depression are: self-change skills; contingency management skills; social skills, such as assertiveness and communication skills; relaxation and stress management skills; identifying and increasing rewarding activities; and a number of cognitive and self-control skills. Consequently, this is the aspect of therapy on which behavioral treatment programs differ the most from each other in that different programs (and different therapists) often emphasize the application of different skills to reach similar strategic goals.

While depressives as a group show a number of performance and skill deficits, it must be remembered that as individuals depressed persons are remarkably heterogeneous with regard to symptoms, presenting problems, and functional difficulties. This fact points to the importance of therapeutic decision making in the behavior therapy of depressed individuals. Treatment decision making must necessarily be a dynamic process involving the nature of a patient's performance deficits, the nature of a patient's personal and social environmental resources, and ongoing treatment response (McLean, 1976).

STRUCTURAL PARAMETERS OF THERAPY

Behavioral treatment approaches are typically designed to be applied within a prespecified number of moderately well-structured sessions. A time limit for treatment is always part of the initial contract. Time limits have ranged from four weeks to three months, typically involving 12 treatment sessions. The time limit should be determined for each patient on the basis of the period of time that likely will be required to achieve the treatment goals. The existence of a time limit makes it essential for both the therapist and the patient to define and accept treatment goals they can reasonably expect to be accomplished during the allotted time. Of course, when deemed necessary by the patient or the therapist, treatment goals and time limits can be and are renegotiated.

OUTCOME EVALUATION

A paramount concern of behavior therapy is the accountability of the therapist to the patient. While this is true on a general level of treatment, so that the therapist employs procedures which have been previously demonstrated to be efficacious, it is also true on the level of individual patient needs. This means that the selection and continuation of specific treatment techniques must be justified on the basis of the ongoing evaluation of the patient's progress. Evaluation involves periodic assessment not only of changes in depression level but also the concommitant changes in the events presumed to be related to the patient's depression. This two-pronged approach to assessment allows the therapist to evaluate the effectiveness of treatment and to change the targeted behavior patterns and then to determine whether these are accompanied by changes in depression level. Typically, at the end of therapy and at some point after the end of treatment (e.g., one month later), patients are asked to repeat the various intake questionnaires, for example the Pleasant Events and Unpleasant Events Schedules, as well as some measure of depression level (e.g., the Beck Depression Inventory). Comparison of the pre- and postscores of the patient allows assessment of the direction and amount of change in person-environment interactions and depression level.

PRACTICAL CONCERNS IN IMPLEMENTING BEHAVIORAL TREATMENTS

Patient compliance with the procedures suggested by behavioral strategies for treating depression is the critical element in the actualization of behavior change. The behavioral approach requires considerable effort on the part of the patient and is dependent on the patient's keeping accurate records, being willing to learn how to chart the daily monitoring data, and agreeing to carry out other assignments from time to time. While reservations regarding the ability of depressed individuals to carry out such assignments are frequently expressed, this is generally found not to be a problem. Patients typically are quite cooperative, as long as they are convinced that the procedures suggested are an integral part of a treatment program designed to benefit them. Thus the crucial factor in eliciting a patient's cooperation is the therapist's ability to present a convincing rationale for the procedures. The therapist must be able to convince the patient that the self-monitoring and other assignments are an integral part of treatment that will help him or her pinpoint specific goals, learn self-management of depression techniques, and evaluate progress.

McLean (1981) has pointed to a number of high-frequency "complications" which interfere with rationale acceptance and compliance on the part of patients in behavioral treatment programs. He notes that depressives are prone to become preoccupied in attempts to understand the causes of their depression. In particular, critical analysis of one's life history (as well as any number of other hypotheses regarding depression onset offered in the popular media) may exacerbate existing self-preoccupation and self-devaluation. Further, depressed patients, like many people, generally do not understand the relationships between personal behavior and social interaction, thought content, and mood. Consequently, as we discussed earlier, it is essential in the beginning of treatment for the therapist to thoroughly discuss and illustrate the elements of the behavioral rationale for the onset, maintenance, and improvement in depressed mood.

BEHAVIORAL TACTICS FOR TREATING DEPRESSION

The final major component of a comprehensive approach to the treatment of depression is a set of tactics with which to accomplish the goals that have been pinpointed during the diagnostic process. Tactics are the specific interventions used to accomplish the strategic goals of therapy. Useful tactics are those that dependably produce clinically desired changes in the events related to the depression. In general terms, behavioral treatment tactics are aimed at increasing the person's pleasant interactions with the environment and decreasing unpleasant ones. Tactics thus fall into three general categories: (1) those that focus on implementing changes in the actual environment of a patient (e.g., having someone move from an isolated home into a more populated area); (2) those that focus on teaching depressed individuals skills that they can use to change problematic patterns of interaction with the environment (e.g., assertiveness training); and (3) those that focus on enhancing the pleasantness and decreasing the aversiveness of person-environment interactions (e.g., relaxation training). Some combination of these types of tactics constitutes the different behavioral treatment programs for depression.

To best illustrate how behavioral theories of depression and strategies for treating the disorder inform the actual choice of tactics, a description of two behavioral treatments for unipolar depression developed at the Depression Research Unit at the University of Oregon will be presented. The first treatment approach is one geared for the individual therapy of the depressed person, while the second treatment makes use of similar, albeit more formalized, techniques for the group treatment of depressed individuals. Following this, other behavioral treatment programs for depression will be reviewed. For each therapy program discussed, outcome literature will be described as well in order to document the efficacy of these approaches.

Decreasing Unpleasant Events and Increasing Pleasant Events: An Individualized Approach to Depression

Lewinsohn et al., (1980, 1982) have described a behavioral program which aims to change the quality and the quantity of the depressed patient's interactions with the environment in the direction of increasing positive and decreasing negative ones. This program has been utilized with the range of types and severity of depressive disorders. The treatment is time limited (12 sessions), highly structured, and a therapist manual is available to assist in the implementation of specific tactics. While the therapist manual is relatively specific in suggesting what should be done in each therapy session, it is meant to serve as a flexible guide and not as a rigid schedule.

During the diagnostic phase, which precedes treatment, extensive use is made of the Pleasant Events Schedule (MacPhillamy & Lewinsohn, 1971) and of the Unpleasant Events Schedule (Lewinsohn, 1975c) to begin to pinpoint specific person-environment interactions related to the patient's depression. An activity schedule (Lewinsohn, 1976), consisting of 80 items rated by the patient as most pleasant and frequent and 80 items rated by the patient as most unpleasant and frequent, is constructed and patients begin daily monitoring of the occurrence of pleasant and unpleasant activities and their mood. They continue this daily monitoring for the duration of treatment. The covariation of certain pleasant and unpleasant events with changes in mood is used to pinpoint specific person-environment interactions influencing the person's dysphoria. Subsequently, the treatment proceeds in two phases: in the first phase, treatment provides assistance to the patient in decreasing the frequency and subjective aversiveness of unpleasant events in his or her life, and then in the second phase, concentrates on increasing pleasant ones. The typical order of treatment tactics is described below.

Daily Monitoring.   Patients are first taught to graph and to interpret their daily monitoring data. They seem to understand intuitively the relationship between unpleasant events and mood. However the covariation between pleasant events and mood is typically a revelation to patients. *Seeing* these relationships on a day-to-day basis impresses on patients in a powerful way how the quantity and the quality of their daily interactions have an important impact on their depression. Now, the depression is no longer a mysterious force, but a reasonable experience. The graphing and interpretation provides patients with a framework for understanding their depression and suggests ways of dealing with it. Monitoring specific events helps a patient focus on coping with particular unpleasant aspects of their daily lives and, of equal importance, makes them aware of the range of pleasant experiences potentially accessible to them. Patients, in a very real sense, learn to diagnose their own depression.

Relaxation Training.   Relaxation training is provided because feelings of anxiety and tension tend to make unpleasant events more aversive and to reduce patients' enjoyment of pleasant activities. Anxiety and tension also tend to impair the clear thinking required for making decisions, planning, and learning new skills.

In our experience in the treatment of depressed patients, relaxation training has become a multipurpose tactic. It is a procedure that is easy to master, and patients tend to become particularly involved with it. Without exception, our patients have reported benefiting from the skill of being able to relax themselves, and they realize the long-term value of this skill. Relaxation training (in particular the practice sessions with the therapist) also seems to enhance certain nonspecific but positive components in the therapeutic process (e.g., feelings of liking, respect, and trust toward the therapist) and thus increases, mutual communication and openness between the therapist and patient, and makes the patient more open to persuasion. This in turn often produces a more significant change in the patient's outlook. The relaxation methods we use in our clinic represent a modified version of the technique developed by Jacobson (1929) for inducing deep muscular relaxation. Following the traditional method in progressive relaxation training, the patient learns to identify the feeling of muscular relaxation by alternately tensing and relaxing different muscle groups. We also give the patient the assignment of reading a book (e.g., Benson, 1975; Rosen, 1977) that presents all the rules one needs to know and follow in practicing progressive muscular relaxation. The procedures are relatively easy to learn and are readily adaptable to a self-administered program.

During the first relaxation training session it may be helpful for the therapist to practice the relaxation procedure with the patient so that the patient can see how to perform particular steps. It is important that the therapist pace the presentation to the patient's facility in performing the steps. It is also important to stress that progressive relaxation is a skill, and like any other skill it can be learned only through practice. The patient is asked to schedule practice sessions once or twice each day at a regular time and place, in addition to the therapist-assisted relaxation training. We recommend that patients collect baseline data on how tense thay are each day and how frequently they experience tension-related symptoms. By keeping records each day for one week, patients are able to accomplish two important preliminary steps: (1) they will have baselines against which to compare progress as they learn to relax more effectively, and (2) they can identify particular situations that make them more tense and particular times of the day when they are more tense.

Managing Aversive Events.   The therapy next moves to teaching patients to manage aversive events. Patients often overreact to unpleasant events and allow themselves to interfere with their engagement in and enjoyment of pleasant activities. Relaxation training is, therefore, introduced early in treatment with the goal of teaching patients to be more relaxed generally but especially in specific situations in which they feel tense.

The "decreasing unpleasant events" aspect of therapy then proceeds with pinpointing a small number of negative interactions or situations that trigger the patient's dysphoria. In order to reduce the aversiveness of these situations, the therapist has available a wide range of tactics which typically fall into three categories: stress management skills; reducing aversive social interactions; and reducing aversive thoughts.

Stress management skills are based on techniques and procedures described by Meichenbaum and Turk (1976) and by Novaco (1975). Stress management training also involves teaching patients to recognize objective signs of dysphoria early in the provocative sequence. After the patients become aware of pending aversive situations and the effect that they are having on them, they may begin to pinpoint specific irrational beliefs, automatic thoughts, expectancies, and negative self-statements and self-appraisals. Other components of "cognitive preparation" involve teaching patients specific skills needed for dealing with aversive situations and preparing for aversive encounters: self-instruction; in vivo relaxation; problem-solving skills; and other task-oriented skills.

Tactics aimed at allowing the patient to change the quantity and the quality of his or her interpersonal relationships typically cover two aspects of interpersonal behavior: assertion, and interpersonal style of expessive behavior. For assertion, a covert modeling procedure based on Kazdin's works (1974, 1976) has been utilized in a sequence involving instruction, modeling, rehearsal, and feedback. After the concept of assertion is presented, patients read *Your Perfect Right* (Alberti & Emmons, 1974) and a personalized list of problematic situations is developed by the patient and the therapist. The therapist may model some assertive possibilities for the patient; after that, the patient is encouraged to take over and to rehearse assertiveness using the covert modeling procedure. Transfer to in vivo practices is planned and monitored during later sessions.

Work on the interpersonal style of the patient involves the same format of instruction, modeling, rehearsal, and feedback. Patients and therapists together set goals, usually small and easily attained ones, based on preassessment problems and patient's preferences. Typical goals may include responding with more positive interest to others, reducing complaints or "whining," increasing activity level and discussion, or changing other verbal aspects of behavior.

Cognitive skills are intended to facilitate changes in the way patients think about reality. The locus of control over thoughts can clearly be identified as being in the patient, since only the patient can observe his or her thoughts. Patients may monitor their thoughts every day. They are taught to discriminate between positive and negative thoughts, necessary and unnecessary thoughts, and constructive and destructive thoughts.

A number of cognitive self-management techniques have been utilized including thought stopping and "premacking" positive thoughts (described in Mahoney & Thoresen, 1974) and Meichenbaum's "self-talk" procedure (1977). Patients may be asked to schedule a "worrying time" or to engage in a "blowup" technique, whereby potentially negative consequences are progressively exaggerated. Rational-emotive concepts may be covered, and a procedure for disputing irrational thoughts may be presented (Ellis & Harper, 1961; Kranzler, 1974). All techniques are presented as skills to be learned and practiced to become maximally useful.

Time Management.   Daily planning and time management training is another general tactic included in the program. At this stage, patients read and make considerable use of selected chapters from Lakein's *How to Get Control of Your Time and Your Life* (1974). Depressed individuals typically make poor use of their time, do not plan ahead, and therefore have not made the preparations (e.g., getting a baby-sitter) needed in order to take advantage of opportunities for pleasant events. The training aims also to assist patients to achieve a better balance between activities they want to do and activities they feel they have to do. Using a daily time schedule, patients are asked to preplan each day and each week. Initially this planning is done in the sessions with the therapist's assistance; gradually patients are expected to do the planning at home.

Increasing Pleasant Activities.   The weekly and daily planning also lays the groundwork for patients to schedule specific pleasant events which become the focus of the second phase of treatment. In helping patients to increase their rate of engagement in pleasant activities, the emphasis is on setting concrete goals for this increase and on developing specific plans for things patients will do. Patients make use of their activity schedule to identify events which they enjoy and specific goals for increasing the actual amount of enjoyment are established and monitored. Patients are taught to distinguish events, behaviors, and feelings which interfere with the enjoyment of activities and to use relaxation, cognitive techniques, social skills and so on to increase their enjoyment of these activities. Small but systematic increases in the number of pleasant activities are implemented by each patient over a period of several weeks and the effects on their mood are self-monitored.

Beyond increasing simply the number of pleasant events, patients are assisted in distinguishing and enacting pleasant events which have a particularly strong relationship to a more positive mood. Patients are especially encouraged to increase their pleasant social activities. Patients and therapists set goals for such increases based on the patient's current frequency of social activity. Goals are gradually increased over several sessions. In this phase of treatment, a manual prepared by Gambrill and Richey (1976) is useful for specific help in areas such as initiating conversations or finding out about activities available in the local community.

Some writers have questioned the causal relationship between mood and positive reinforcement or engagement in pleasant activities. Hammen and Glass (1975) reported a study using 40 college students who, on the basis of self-report questionnaires, were described as mildly to moderately depressed. These subjects were instructed to increase their participation in events they had rated as pleasurable or were assigned to one of several control groups. Hammen and Glass found that increasing participation in pleasant activities did not have an effect on dysphoria. Lewinsohn (1975a) presented a methodological critique of the Hammen and Glass study based upon how events are scored as pleasant, classification of subjects as depressed, and the types of instruments employed to assess mood. Early studies by Lewinsohn and his colleagues (Lewinsohn & Graf, 1973; MacPhillamy & Lewinsohn, 1974) clearly demonstrated that a consistent relationship between mood and the rate of engagement in pleasant activities and that clinically depressed individuals engage in a relatively smaller number of such activities. More recently, Rehm (1978) also found a significant association between the number of pleasant events which a person engaged in and their mood. Harmon, Nelson, and Hayes (1980) showed that simply self-monitoring activity produced an increase in self-reported pleasant activities and a decrease in depressed mood.

For those interested, a more detailed description of this individualized treatment procedure and case illustrations are presented in papers by Lewinsohn et al. (1980).

With regard to the efficacy of "Decreasing Unpleasant Events and Increasing Pleasant Events" treatment approach, Lewinsohn et al. (1979) examined the relationship between reinforcement and depression across four samples of depressives. Over the course of treatment, they found that the rate of positive reinforcement increased as a function of improvement in clinical depression level. Similarly, the rate of experienced aversiveness, or the reaction to unpleasant events, diminished as clinical depression decreased. Further, the increase in the rate of response-contingent positive reinforcement was greater for patients who improved more than for those who improved less; that is, those persons who showed the most improvement were the individuals who increased pleasant events the most.

The outcome of two different treatment modules for depression was reported in Lewinsohn et al., (1980). A program of increasing pleasant events was tested across two samples of depressed individuals, while another sample of patients received therapy emphasizing both decreasing unpleasant events and increasing pleasant events. All three samples demonstrated significant amounts of clinical improvement, but no program was significantly more effective than the other.

THE COPING WITH DEPRESSION COURSE

The Coping with Depression (CWD) course is a multimodal, psychoeducational group treatment for unipolar depression. The major vehicle for treatment is an explicit educational experience designed to teach people techniques and strategies for coping with the problems that are assumed to be related to their depression. Thus the course emphasizes the attainment of knowledge and skills over an intensive relationship with a therapist. The CWD course consists of 12 two-hour sessions conducted over eight weeks. Sessions are held twice a week during the first four weeks of treatment, and once a week for the final four weeks. One-month and six-month follow-up sessions, called "class reunions," are held to encourage maintenance of treatment gains.

The first two sessions of the CWD course are devoted to the definition of course ground rules, the presentation of the social learning view of depression, and instruction in basic self-help skills. The next eight sessions are devoted to the acquisition of skills in four specific areas: (1) learning how to relax; (2) increasing pleasant activities; (3) changing aspects of one's thinking; (4) and improving both the quality and quantity of one's social interactions. Each of the sessions in these four specific areas makes use of similar skills and techniques described earlier as part of the individualized treatment program for depression. Two sessions are devoted to each skill. The final two sessions focus on maintenance and prevention issues.

The course is a highly structured, time-limited, skill-training program that makes use of a text, *Control Your Depression* (Lewinsohn, Mūnoz, Youngren, & Zeiss, 1978) from which reading assignments are made; a participant workbook (Brown & Lewinsohn, 1979) which was developed to supplement the text; and an Instructor's Manual (Steinmetz, Antonuccio, Bond, McKay, Brown, & Lewinsohn, 1979) to ensure comparability of treatment across instructors. A more detailed description of the course is provided in Lewinsohn, Antonuccio, Steinmetz, and Teri (1984).

The Participant Workbook contains goal statements, assignments for each session, and monitoring forms for recording specific behaviors, thoughts, and feelings relevant to the class assignments. Group time is divided between lecture, review of the assignments, discussion, role-play, and structured exercises. The instructor's main goals are to deliver the course information accurately, to promote the effective application of the information, to help participants solve problems related to the material, and to facilitate a supportive group interaction.

An important feature of the CWD course is that participants are able to meet effectively in groups to assist each other in overcoming their depression. With relatively few exceptions (Barrera, 1979; Fuchs & Rehm, 1977; Lewinsohn et al., 1970), previous cognitive behavioral treatments have been offered exclusively in an individual therapy mode. This is not surprising since most authorities in the area of group therapy (e.g., Yalom, 1975) advise against homogeneous groups of depressed patients. Our results indicate that within the structure presented by the course depressives work together very effectively. Another feature of the course is that it presents a cost-effective, community-oriented outreach approach to impact on the great majority of depressives who never avail themselves of the services of clinics and mental health professionals. The educational focus reduces the stigma involved in seeking "psychiatric" or "psychological" treatment, which is especially important to the elderly depressed.

Three treatment outcome studies on the CWD course have been completed (Brown & Lewinsohn, 1979; Steinmetz, Lewinsohn, & Antonuccio, 1983; Teri & Lewinsohn, 1981), and two are currently in progress (Saenz, Lewinsohn, & Hoberman, 1985; Hoberman, Lewinsohn, & Tilson, 1985). In each of these studies course participants were carefully assessed on a wide range of variables at four points in time: pretreatment, posttreatment, one month, and six months following treatment. Each of these studies assessed somewhat different variables depending on the specific hypotheses under investigation; however, a core assessment battery was constant across studies.

The CWD course was compared to individual tutoring based on the CWD manual, a minimal phone contact procedure (Brown & Lewinsohn, 1979), and individual behavior therapy (Teri & Lewinsohn, 1981). The results indicated that the differences between all the active treatment conditions were small. In each study, depressed individuals participating in the CWD course showed substantial improvement at posttreatment and maintained improvement at both one-month and six-month follow-ups. This was true on both self-report and clinical diagnoses. Improvement from the CWD course has been comparable in magnitude to that shown by subjects in individual therapy in our own (e.g., Lewinsohn et al., 1980) as well as in other studies of cognitive-behavioral therapy for depression. Additionally, the CWD course is considerably more cost effective than individual (one-to-one) treatment.

In addition, studies have been conducted to examine whether individual participant characteristics or group leader characteristics were predictive of outcome in the CWD course. Antonuccio, Lewinsohn, and Steinmetz (1982) evaluated group leaders on a large number of variables which were hypothesized to be related to outcome. The major finding was that even though the leaders differed significantly on many of the therapist variables (e.g., therapist warmth, therapist enthusiasm, and so on) there was no significant main effect for instructor differences. That is, the instructors did not differ in how much improvement their respective students showed at the end of the course. Similarly, Steinmetz et al., (1983) attempted to examine participant variables related to successful treatment outcome. As one might expect the single strongest predictor of postcourse depression level (as measured by the Beck

Depression Inventory [BDI]) is pretreatment depression level. Those who are most depressed at the beginning are still, relatively, the most depressed at the end of treatment. After correcting for initial severity of depression, a number of other variables were also shown to be consistently related to treatment outcome: (1) expected improvement: participants who expect to be the most symptom free at the end of treatment were the most improved; (2) satisfaction with major life roles: participants who expressed more satisfaction in regard to 18 life areas deemed to be generally important were also most improved; (3) lack of concurrent treatment: participants who were not currently receiving additional psychotherapy and/or antidepressive medicines for depression were more improved; (4) perceived social support from family members: better treatment outcome resulted for those with more perceived social support; and (5) age: younger participants were more likely to improve. Each of these five characteristics associated with successful treatment outcome were also found to predict treatment responses in studies by Brown and Lewinsohn (1979) and Teri and Lewinsohn (1981).

Variables that consistently did not predict treatment outcome after correcting for pretreatment depression level were: (1) symptoms: endogeneity, number of previous episodes, previous alcohol, or drug abuse; (2) demographics: sex, income, occupational level, number of children, or marital status; (3) cognitions: locus of control or irrational beliefs, or acceptance of course rationale; (4) stressful life events as measured by the Holmes and Rahe (1967) scale; (5) other participant characteristics: manageability, treatability, likeability, motivation, social skill, or emotional reliance on others.

In our studies the predictor variables accounted for a little more than half the variance in posttreatment BDI scores. Studies are currently under way (Hoberman et al., 1985; Saenz et al., 1985) to evaluate the contribution of other variables predicting improvement as well as to cross validate the findings obtained thus far.

SOCIAL INTERACTION THERAPY

The social interaction theory of depression postulated by McLean (1976, 1981) considers the depressed person's interaction with his or her social environment to be crucial for the development and for the reversal of depression. As McLean views it, depression results when individuals lose the ability to control their interpersonal environment. When ineffective coping techniques are utilized to remedy situational life problems, the consequence may be a decrease in positive events and thus depression. Social interaction therapy aims to maximize the patient's competence in specific coping skills.

Social interaction therapy incorporates behavioral and cognitive techniques. Consequently, social interaction therapy places a marked emphasis on therapeutic decision making regarding appropriate intervention components. It is also distinguished by its incorporation of procedures for including relevant social network members (e.g., spouse) as integral components of

treatment. The therapist's evaluation includes the patient's living arrangements, marital status and satisfaction, and employment status and satisfaction.
McLean stresses the importance of obtaining the patient's own criteria
for improvement, and treatment maintains a focus on data management;
explicit performance criteria are monitored by the patient throughout
therapy.

Six specific therapeutic components are suggested by McLean: communication training, behavioral productivity, social interaction training, assertiveness training, decision-making and problem-solving training, and cognitive
self-control. While the first three components are utilized in the treatment of
all depressed patients, the latter three are optional, depending upon assessment of a patient's particular deficiencies in the problem areas. Perhaps the
most distinctive component of social interaction therapy involves communication training between the patient and his/her spouse, or significant other.
Therapy includes a structured form of communication training to counteract
aversive marital interactions and a constricted quantity in range of interactions. Communication exercises aim to provide opportunities for positive
feedback, to enhance self-esteem, and to facilitate other forms of social interaction. Additionally, the inclusion of a relevant social network member
is important in the promotion of social interaction and in maintaining treatment effects. At the end of treatment, patients are assisted to prepare for
future episodes of depression and contingency plans are established and
rehearsed.

McLean, Ogston, and Grauer (1973) developed a therapeutic program
based on the aforementioned components and found it to produce significant
changes in problematic behaviors and in verbal communication styles. More
recently, McLean and Hakstian (1979) conducted a large-scale treatment outcome study. One hundred seventy-eight moderately clinically depressed patients were selected by interview screening and psychometric criteria. Subjects were randomly assigned to one of four treatment conditions: behavior
therapy as described by McLean (1976), short-term traditional psychotherapy,
relaxation training, and medication (amitriptyline). Therapists were selected
on the basis of their preferred treatment modality. Patients encouraged their
spouses or significant others to participate in treatment sessions; treatment
took place over 10 weeks of weekly sessions. The results obtained demonstrated the unequivocal superiority of the behavioral intervention. Behavior
therapy was best on 9 out of 10 outcome measures immediately after treatment, and marginally superior at a three-month follow-up (best on 7 of 10
outcome measures). Additionally, behavior therapy conditions showed a significantly lower attrition rate (5 percent) than the other conditions which had
dropout rates of 26 to 36 percent. In particular, the medication condition was
found to have the highest attrition rate. The traditional psychotherapy treatment proved to be the least effective at both the posttreatment and follow-up
evaluation periods; generally, it faired worse than a control condition (relaxation training).

SELF-CONTROL THERAPY

Rehm's (1977) self-control theory of depression emphasizes the importance of self-administered reinforcement and punishment. According to this formulation, depressed individuals selectively attend to negative aspects in their experience, set very high perfectionistic standards for themselves, and consequently self-reinforce at a very low rate and self-punish at a very high rate.

A treatment based on a self-control theory has been described by Fuchs and Rehm (1977). The treatment consists of six sessions with two sessions devoted to each of three self-control processes (self-monitoring, self-evaluation, and self-reinforcement). The original treatment package was administered over a six-week period. Rehm and Kornblith (1978) presented a revised self-control therapy protocol which expanded treatment from 6 to 12 sessions. The revised program reflects an increased emphasis on self-monitoring. The first session of each phase of treatment involves a didactic presentation and discussion of self-control principles relevant to the assumed deficits of depressives plus a behavioral homework assignment. In the second session, patients review the preceding week's assignment. The principles of self-control are reiterated by the therapist and appropriate use of these concepts by patients is reinforced. For example, the homework given to patients at the end of the first session typically involves a log form on which to monitor each day's positive activities. Patients are asked to turn in a list of 20 potentially positive activities. In addition, patients are asked to write one-line descriptions of each of their day's positive activities as well as to rate their mood after each event. Patients are also asked to graph their daily average mood and total number of positive activities. As part of the revised self-control therapy program, depressed patients are also assigned exercises examining the immediate and delayed effects of activities, increasing activities associated with improved mood, and modifying self-attribution for successes and failures. Self-monitoring activities are continued throughout the rest of therapy.

During the self-evaluation phase of treatment patients are directed to develop realistic criteria for specific goals in regard to increasing their positive activities. Such goals are developed to be discrete, attainable, overt, and discernible in terms of the patient's own behavior. A point system is introduced for self-evaluation. Patients are asked to assign a weight to each subgoal they have set. As homework, patients are instructed to record the point values of accomplished behaviors in a column on their logs.

During the self-reinforcement phase, patients develop individual "reward menus" stressing immediate and available rewards; on the basis of their self-monitoring and self-evaluation, patients are instructed to self-administer rewards as points are earned with the completion of specific goal-related positive activities. At the end of treatment patients are encouraged to continue using explicit self-control procedures after termination and are given extra copies of log sheets and graphs. Several studies have been conducted to assess the efficacy of self-control therapy programs. Comparing a group version of a self-control therapy program to a nonspecific group therapy condition and waiting list control group, Fuchs and Rehm (1977) found that a self-control group showed significantly more improvement than the other conditions at termination and at the six-month follow-up. Rehm, Fuchs, Roth, Kornblith, and Romano (1979) compared two treatment conditions: self-control therapy, and a social skills treatment (essentially assertion training). Results indicated that social skill subjects improved more in social skills, while self-control subjects improve more on self-control dependent measures. At six-week follow-up, treatment effects were maintained. More recently, Roth, Bielski, Jones, Parker, and Osborne (1982) compared self-control therapy program alone to self-control therapy plus antidepressant medication. Both treatment conditions produced marked decreases in depression symptomatology. No significant benefit was obtained with the addition of medication except that the combined therapy group did evidence a more rapid improvement in depressive symptoms.

SOCIAL SKILLS TRAINING FOR DEPRESSION

Based on Lewinsohn's (1975b) writing on depression, a behavioral program for treating depression was developed by combining social skill techniques utilized in Lewinsohn's (1975b) early research with social skill procedures developed in other treatment situations (e.g., other types of psychiatric patients) (Hersen, Bellack, & Himmelhoch, 1982). This approach (Bellack, Hersen, & Himmelhoch, 1981a) assumes that the depressed patient has either lost socially skillful responses as the result of anxiety, the course of psychiatric illness, or hospitalization, or that the patient never possessed social skills in his/her behavioral repertoire. Consequently, treatment is conceived of as a reeducation or education for depressed patients and employs instruction, feedback, social reinforcement, modeling, coaching, behavioral rehearsal, and graded homework assignments. The actual implementation of therapeutic interventions is based on a careful behavioral analysis of social skill deficits. Typically, treatment takes place over 12 weekly therapy sessions, followed by 6–8 booster sessions spread over a six-month period. Social skill training can best be understood as focusing on a matrix of types of social situations by types of social skills. Since social skills tend to be situation specific, training is provided in each of four social contexts: (1) with strangers; (2) with friends; (3) with family members or in heterosocial interactions; (4) at work or school. The importance of each of these four contexts is prioritized by each individual. Within each area, specific social problems are delineated and dealt with hierarchically in order of increasing difficulty. Treatment across the different social contexts is seen as ensuring generalization of social skills across a variety of situations. Three types of social skills, which are viewed as being especially relevant to depression, are the primary focus of social skills training. Positive assertion refers to the expression of positive feelings toward others. Instruction in positive assertion concentrates on giving compliments, expression of affection, offering approval and praise, and making apologies; particular emphasis is placed on responding at appropriate times with the appropriate nonverbal components. Negative assertion refers to the expression of displeasure and standing up for one's own rights. Training in this skill concerns the refusal of unrealistic requests, requesting new behavior from others, compromise and negotiation, and the expression of disapproval and annoyance. Here treatment aims to demonstrate that the reactions of others will be less negative than expected and less painful than continuing passivity and submissiveness. Finally, the third target skill of this treatment is conversational skills, including the ability to initiate, maintain, and end conversations. Patients are coached to avoid "sick talk" and to be more positively reinforcing to others.

For each social context by social skill deficit, the training program emphasizes four individual components. The skills training component involves training in specific response skills. Assessment is conducted through a role-play task. Intervention targets are identified and the patient is provided with a rationale for his/her responding. Specific succinct instructions are provided for what the patient should do in a given situation. Following this, a number of serial trials occur in which the patient observes the therapist model a response and then the patient performs the response him/herself. Discrete response behaviors are taught singly and sequentially, with regular feedback and positive reinforcement. Since behaviors which are not overlearned have been shown to drop out in stressful situations, the second component of social skills training involves practice both within therapy sessions and outside therapy. Appropriate homework assignments designed to lead to reinforcement are made and monitored by the patient and therapist. Social perception training is an additional treatment component and includes instruction in the social meaning of various response cues and familiarity with social mores, attention to the relevant aspects of interaction context, and ability to accurately predict interpersonal consequences. Finally, in the self-evaluation and reinforcement component depressives are trained to evaluate their responding more objectively and to employ self-reinforcements; here the therapist provides objective and appropriate criteria for judgment if the patient is too negative in self-evaluation.

Two pilot studies of social skills training (Hersen, Bellack, & Himmelhoch, 1980; Wells, Hersen, Bellack, & Himmelhoch, 1979) demonstrated that this intervention resulted in improvement in both specific social skills as well as on self-report and psychiatric rating scales. A larger study of social skills training was reported by Bellack et al. (1981b). Four different treatments (amitriptyline, social skills training plus amitriptyline, social skills training plus placebo, and psychotherapy plus placebo) were employed across 72 female outpatients. All treatments produced statistically significant and clinically meaningful changes in symptoms and social functioning. Thus, social skills training and placebo was as effective as amitriptyline alone or psychotherapy plus placebo. However, a greater proportion of patients were significantly improved in the social skills training plus placebo condition.

Further, there was a significant difference in dropout rate across the treatment conditions from a low of 15 percent in the social skills training and placebo to as high as 56 percent in the amytriptyline alone condition.

AN OPERANT REINFORCEMENT APPROACH

An operant reinforcement method of treating depression was described by Azrin and Besalel (1981). Like other behavioral programs, this one stresses an increase of reinforcement and it tends to directly modify verbal behavior associated with depression. However, Azrin and Besalel also report on a number of distinctive tactics designed to facilitate the amelioration of depression.

To begin with, depressed individuals are asked to identify at least four changes they desire, with the objective to be stated in behavioral terms if possible, and in terms of specific frequency or duration. Patients are asked to rate their degree of happiness in each of eight areas: household responsibilities, sex, communication, social activities, finances, care of children, independence, and personal habits. On the basis of these assessment procedures, a variety of treatment tactics are discussed with the patient and role-played and a behavioral contract is signed by both the therapist and patient, outlining their responsibilities to one another.

More specifically, a number of instruments are presented to the patient which emphasize positive reinforcements rather than problematic aspects of his/her life; these forms serve as the basis for the management of positive reinforcements during the course of treatment. Patients indicate which of 15 attitudinal statements, reflecting quasi-universal positive attributes, apply to them. On the basis of this desirable attitude list, patients write down as many "nice qualities about themselves" as they can think of. Next, a "happiness-reminder" list of 18 items, reflecting generally positive types of events or situations, is utilized as a basis for generating a personalized list of activities and events that have been pleasant, meaningful, or previously interesting to the patient. Additionally, patients are asked to indicate which events on a possible pleasant activities list of 50 recreational activities apply to them. A list of 43 probably pleasant activities is constructed for each patient and each item is rated on a 1–4 scale as to degree of enjoyment obtained for each activity. Another list, this one of all persons liked by the patient, is also constructed. Employing these various lists of potentially reinforcing events, activities, and persons, the therapist helps the patient to arrange a daily and weekly schedule for engagement in reinforcing activities.

Azrin and Besalel (1981) also reported on the results of techniques to directly combat the negative mood of depression. Employing an overcorrection rationale, the therapist teaches the depressed individual to engage in compensatory, positive statements whenever a depressive state or response occurs. Each positive statement is derived from the "nice qualities" list described earlier and serve the purpose of self-praise. Patients are also asked to review a list of 42 severe traumatic events (e.g., "My house burned down"), few if any of which apply to a given person; this tactic is designed to induce behavioral contrasts with the patient's own life situation. Similarly, the depressed person is asked to respond to a form emphasizing positive aspects of stress-related severe depression, including possibly negative aspects of their life situation if the problem had not occurred and any benefits that occurred because of this problem. Each of these procedures is intended to refocus the patient's affective experience.

Reinforcer-facilitating social skills are taught to depressed persons whose depression is influenced by unsatisfactory social relationships. Individuals are taught to give compliments and show appreciation, to request reinforcers (e.g., compliments or appreciation) from others, to react to annoyance caused by others, to make agreements with others, and to identify probable reinforcers of friends. In addition, patients are encouraged to engage in "happy talk" with friends, focusing on pleasant topics of mutual interest and not problem solving.

Finally, common sources of depression were addressed directly through skill remediation. Individuals with marital, vocational, employment, and other specific problems were assisted in translating amorphous complaints into specific behavioral objectives. Patients were then helped to implement those objectives through condensed interventions for marital, vocational, employment, and academic concerns.

Treatment utilizing these tactics takes place over 4–10 sessions. Particular procedures are discussed and practiced throughout treatment as necessary. Patients utilize self-reminder forms on which to record activities assigned to be carried out for each day between treatment sessions. These activities include each of the individualized goals, the activities scheduled by the therapist, and various positive interactional activities relevant to the specific individual. During treatment meetings this form serves as the starting point of discussion and emphasizes what the depressed individual had done to help him/herself. The therapist reviews the forms and accomplishments of the previous week, and then assigns and helps the patient to practice further intervention tactics. In contrast to other behavioral interventions, there is no attempt to have the patient master one procedure before proceeding to the next one. Rather, as noted earlier, all potentially relevant techniques are introduced initially and then applied as appropriate.

Azrin and Besalel (1981) also reported on the results of an outcome study of their operant reinforcement approach to treating depression. The study employed a waiting list, within-subjects design, in which a two-week waiting period was scheduled after an intake session. A total of 29 subjects were treated. While little or no change occurred after the waiting period, significant and substantial changes from pre- to posttreatment were demonstrated on traditional depression measures. Additionally, patients indicated a decrease in the percentage of time spent feeling unhappy and reported that they attained, on an average, 75 percent of their specified individual treatment goals. In absolute sense, 62 percent of the subjects had very favorable outcome measures on all assessment measures. Treatment gains were shown to persist at a seven-week follow-up and there was no significant difference in improvement for persons with more or less severe depression. The average number of sessions was seven and the reduction in depression was most pronounced after the second session of treatment.

FINAL COMMENTS ON BEHAVIORAL TREATMENT PROGRAMS

As we noted at the beginning of this chapter, a number of well-defined behavioral treatment programs for unipolar depression presently exist. All of these treatment programs share a conceptualization of the etiology of depression which emphasizes changes in the quality of an individual's interactions with the environment. Behavioral theories assume that the depressed patient has acquired maladaptive reaction patterns which can be unlearned. Symptoms are seen as important in their own right, rather than as manifestations of underlying conflicts, and treatments are aimed at the modification of relatively specific behaviors and cognitions rather than a general reorganization of the patient's personality. All behavioral treatments are structured and time limited. For each specific behavioral treatment program, empirical support for its therapeutic efficacy has been demonstrated. Each program appears to produce significant decreases in depression level and depressive symptomatology, although relatively little difference in outcome measures has been observed between treatment programs. It seems clear that at least certain behavioral treatment programs ameliorate depression in the same degree or better than antidepressive medications and that a significantly lower number of patients drop out of behavioral treatments.

In fact, a recent study by Steinbrueck, Maxwell, and Howard (1983) presented a meta-analysis of 56 outcome studies of drug therapy and psychotherapy (most of which were cognitive and/or behavioral in nature) in the treatment of unipolar depression in adults. Their results suggest that psychotherapy had an average effectiveness almost twice that of chemotherapy. The question can be raised as to how all the different behavioral treatment programs can be similarly effective. Several possibilities might account for these findings. Clearly, there is great commonality across the behavioral approaches with regard to specific tactics employed to reduce depression level. However, even when specific behavioral techniques are employed and assessed, there appears to be no selective impact on target behaviors. Zeiss et al. (1979) compared brief behavioral interventions based on increasing pleasant activities, improving social skills, or reducing negative cognitions, and found that participants receiving different treatments all improved equally in their activity, social skills, and cognitions. Similar results were reported by Rehm, Rabin, Kaslow, and Willard (1982). Given these results, it may be argued that behavioral treatment packages as currently implemented may include some common "core" of strategies or tactics. For example, Rosenbaum and Merbaum (1984) have suggested that self-control procedures may account for the therapeutic success of behavioral treatments of depression and anxiety. Similarly, in a study attempting to disassemble a behavioral treatment program, Rehm, Kornblith, O'Hara, Lamparski, Romano, and Volkin (1981) found that self-monitoring procedures alone produced a treatment effect similar to the complete self-control treatment package. Thus there seems to be some empirical support for the importance of self-monitoring as a critical element in behavioral treatment programs.

The authors of two treatment outcome studies for behavioral treatments of depression have offered their hypotheses as to the critical components for successful short-term behavioral treatments for depression. Zeiss et al. (1979) concluded that efficacious behavioral treatments should include the following characteristics:

1. Therapy should begin with an elaborated, well-planned rationale.
2. Therapy should provide training in skills that the patient can utilize to feel more effective in handling his/her daily life.
3. Therapy should emphasize independent use of these skills by the patient outside of the therapy context, and thus provide enough structure so that the attainment of independent skills is possible for the patient.
4. Therapy should encourage the patient's attribution that improvement in mood is caused by the patient's increased skillfulness, and not by the therapist's skillfulness.

Similarly, McLean and Hakstian (1979) noted that high structure, a social learning rationale, goal attainment focus, and increasing social interaction were significant elements in the behavioral treatment of depression.

CURRENT AND FUTURE DIRECTIONS IN BEHAVIORAL TREATMENTS FOR DEPRESSION

Buoyed by initial progress in developing a variety of behavior therapy programs for treating depression and in demonstrating their efficacy, researchers are continuing to systematically expand their studies of therapy for depressed individuals. Presently efforts are being made in a number of different directions including: refining the strategies and tactics of behavioral treatments; identifying those depressives most and least likely to benefit from behavioral treatments; and modifying existing treatment programs to ameliorate depression in groups other than the typical middle-aged depressive.

Several studies have attempted to identify and evaluate the contribution of individual components of behavioral treatment programs. Rehm et al. (1981) conducted a study of "disassembled" elements of the self-control treatment package. They compared five treatment conditions: self-monitoring alone; self-monitoring and self-evaluation together; self-monitoring and self-reinforcement together; the full self-control treatment package; and a waiting list control condition. Results indicated that all treatment conditions produced significant change relative to the control condition. A slightly different component study was conducted by Turner, Ward, and Turner (1979). They compared an increased activities condition and a self-monitoring condition to both an expectancy- and an attention-control group. Their findings showed that the "increasing activities" condition produced significantly greater improvement. Taken together, these studies suggest that critical components of behavioral treatment programs include both self-monitoring relationship between mood and activities and increasing activity level.

A number of writers have discussed the potential value of matching treatment components to patient characteristics to provide a problem-specific approach to treating depression (Biglan & Dow, 1981; McLean, 1981). A recent study by McKnight, Nelson, Hayes, and Jarrett (1983) compared the relative efficacy of treatments which were directly related or unrelated to initial target problem areas. Depressed patients with social skills difficulties or irrational cognitions improved more after receiving specific interventions for those deficits than interventions not related to their presenting problem areas. Unfortunately, this study utilized only a small number of subjects, and it remains for later studies to replicate and extend this finding. However, the study does suggest that it may be clinically efficacious to match particular treatment components to the types of target problem areas the patients do present.

Other studies have examined the amount of therapist contact needed to produce clinical improvement. Brown and Lewinsohn (1979) showed that a minimal phone contact produced an equivalent amount of improvement, relative to individual tutoring based on the Coping with Depression course and the course itself. Similarly, Schmidt and Miller (1983) demonstrated that a bibliotherapy condition (e.g., where patients receive only self-help treatment manuals) produced similar levels of improvement compared to individual and group treatment; patients in this study were severely depressed, with mean BDI scores of 24.6. These studies indicate that valid clinical improvement in depression can be accomplished with behavioral procedures that use relatively little client/clinician contact. Along these same lines, Selmi, Klein, Greist, Johnson, and Harris (1982) have reported on their endeavors to develop a computer-assisted, cognitive-behavior therapy program for treating depression, although no outcome results are presently available.

Predictors of treatment response, nonresponse, and recurrence have also been the focus of studies. As noted earlier, five variables have consistently emerged as predictors of improvement for depressives participating in the Coping with Depression course (Brown & Lewinsohn, 1979; Steinmetz et al., 1983; Teri & Lewinsohn, 1981): expected improvement; greater life satisfaction; lack of concurrent psychotherapy of antidepressive medication; high levels of perceived family social support; and younger age. Steinmetz, Breckenridge, Thompson, and Gallagher (1982) found that depressed individuals with greater perceived control of their symptoms *and* expected improvement were most improved at the end of treatment. Zeiss and Jones (1982) reanalyzed data collected as part of a study by Zeiss et al. (1979) with regard to treatment failures from behavioral treatments of depression. Their results show that treatment dropouts were more likely to be single, younger, and male, while treatment failures were more likely to be married and older. Both dropouts and failures tended to report a predominance of depression with relatively little anxiety, as measured by the Minnesota Multiphasic Personality Inventory (MMPI). Overall, Zeiss and Jones concluded that the more extreme the deficits and maladaptive behavior patterns exhibited by the depressed patient, the greater the chance of treatment failure. In a study of life events and symptom course for depressed women who participated in a behavioral treatment program, Monroe, Bellack, Hersen, and Himmelhoch (1983) showed that an increase in entrances into the individual social field (e.g., making new friends) in the prior year were consistently predictive of fewer symptoms at follow-up. Finally, in a long-term follow-up study of participants in the Coping with Depression course, Gonzales, Lewinsohn, and Clarke (in press) have attempted to identify distinguishing characteristics of persons who do or do not experience recurrent episodes of depression after treatment.

Several investigators have in recent years attempted to examine the efficacy of behavioral treatments with a number of special groups. Thompson, Gallagher, Nies, and Epstein (1983) modified the CWD course to make it better suited for elderly adults. This intervention, also described by Steinmetz, Zeiss, and Thompson, 1984) was shown to be efficacious with clinically depressed elderly by Hedlund and Thompson (1980). Similarly, Antonuccio, Akins, Chatham, Monagan, and Zeigler (1983) conducted a pilot study which indicated that inpatients with "drug refractory" depression responded favorably to a modified version of the CWD program. Turner, Wehl, Cannon, and Craig (1980) have shown that a behavior therapy program was successful in treating depressed inpatient alcoholics. Finally, Clarke and Lewinsohn (1985) are presently conducting an outcome study for depressed adolescents based on the CWD program. In short, behavioral treatments for depression are increasingly being demonstrated as having efficacy with a variety of depressed persons, suggesting a widespread applicability of behavior therapy approaches for treating depression.

In conclusion, the last 10 years have been a period of exciting progress in the development and study of behavioral treatments for unipolar depression. Treatment strategies and tactics have been hypothesized and tested, with a now considerable number of studies demonstrating the efficacy of behavioral programs for ameliorating depression. Presently, these approaches are being refined, outcome studies are endeavoring to become more precise in identifying those most likely to improve from behavioral treatments, and behavioral programs are being generalized across special populations of depressives. Given the rapid strides made to date, the field of behavior therapy for depression can likely look forward to increasing advances in the future.

References

Alberti, R. E., & Emmons, M. L. (1974). *Your perfect right.* San Luis Obispo, CA: Impact Pubs.

Alloy, L. B., & Abramson, L. Y. (1979). Judgment of contingency in depressed and nondepressed students: Sadder but wiser? *Journal of Experimental Psychology: General, 108,* 441–485.

Antonuccio, D. O., Akins, W. T., Chatham, T., Monagan, B., & Ziegler, B. (1983). *An exploratory study: The psychoeducational group treatment of chronically depressed veterans.* Reno, NV: VA Medical Center.

Antonuccio, D. O., Lewinsohn, P. M., & Steinmetz, J. L. (1982). Identification of therapist differences in a group treatment for depression. *Journal of Consulting and Clinical Psychology, 50,* 433–435.

Azrin, N. H., & Besalel, V. A. (1981). An operant reinforcement method of treating depression. *Journal of Behavior Therapy and Experimental Psychiatry, 12,* 145–151.

Bandura, A. (1977). *Social learning theory.* Englewood Cliffs, NJ: Prentice–Hall.

Barerra, M. (1979). An evaluation of a brief group therapy for depression. *Journal of Consulting and Clinical Psychology, 47,* 413–415.

Beck, A. T., Ward, G. H., Mendelson, M., Mock, J., & Erbaugh, J. (1961). An inventory for measuring depression. *Archives of General Psychiatry, 4,* 561–571.

Becker, J. (1974). *Depression: Theory and research.* New York: Holt, Rinehart & Winston.

Bellack, A. S., Hersen, M., & Himmelhoch, J. (1981a). Social skills training for depression: A treatment manual. *Journal Supplement Abstract Service Catalog of Selected Documents, 11,* 36.

Bellack, A. S., Hersen, M., & Himmelhoch, J. (1981b). Social skills training, pharmacotherapy, and psychotherapy for unipolar depression. *American Journal of Psychiatry, 138,* 1562–1567.

Benson, H. (1975) *The relaxation response.* New York: William Morrow.

Biglan, A., & Dow, M. G. (1981). Toward a "second generation" model of depression treatment: A problem specific approach. In L. P. Rehm (Ed.), *Behavior therapy for depression: Present status and future directions.* New York: Academic Press.

Blaney, P. H. (1981). The effectiveness of cognitive and behavior therapies. In L. P. Rehm (Ed.), *Behavior therapy for depression: Present status and future directions.* New York: Academic Press.

Brown, R., & Lewinsohn, P. M. (1979). *A psychoeducational approach to the treatment of depression: Comparison of group, individual, and minimal contact procedures.* Unpublished mimeo, University of Oregon, Eugene.

Burgess, E. (1969). The modification of depressive behaviors. In R. Rubin & C. Franks (Eds.), *Advances in behavior therapy, 1968.* New York: Academic Press.

Buss, D. M., & Scheier, M. (1976). Self-consciousness, self-awareness, and self-attribution. *Journal of Research in Personality, 10,* 463–468.

Carver, C. S. (1979). A cybernetic model of self-attention processes. *Journal of Personality and Social Psychology, 37,* 1251–1281.

Carver, C. S., Blaney, P. H., & Scheier, M. F. (1979a). Focus of attention, chronic expectancy, and responses to a feared stimulus. *Journal of Personality and Social Psychology, 37,* 1186–1195.

Carver, C. S., Blaney, P. H., & Scheier, M. F. (1979b). Reassertion and giving up: The interactive role of self-directed attention and outcome expectancy. *Journal of Personality and Social Psychology, 37,* 1859–1870.

Carver, C. S., & Scheier, M. F. (1982). Control theory: A useful conceptual framework for personality, social, clinical, and health psychology. *Psychological Bulletin, 92,* 111–135.

Clarke, G., & Lewinsohn, P. M. (1985). *A psychoeducational approach to treating depression in high school adolescents.* Manuscript in preparation, University of Oregon, Eugene.

Costello, C. G. (1972). Depression: Loss of reinforcers or loss of reinforcer effectiveness? *Behavior Therapy, 3,* 240–247.

Craighead, W. E. (1981). Behavior therapy for depression: Issues resulting from treatment studies. In L. P. Rehm (Ed.), *Behavior therapy for depression: Present status and future directions.* New York: Academic Press.

DeRubeis, R. J., & Hollon, S. D. (1981). Behavioral treatment of affective disorders. In L. Michelson, M. Hersen, & S. Turner (Eds.), *Future perspectives in behavior therapy* (pp. 103–129). New York: Plenum, Publishing.

Duval, S., & Wicklund, R. (1973). Effects of objective self-awareness on attribution of causality. *Journal of Experimental Social Psychology, 9,* 17–31.

Ellis, A., & Harper, R. A. (1961). *A guide to rational living.* Hollywood, CA: Wilshire Book.

Endicott, J., & Spitzer, R. L. (1978). A diagnostic interview: The Schedule for Affective Disorders and Schizophrenia. *Archives of General Psychiatry, 35,* 837–844.

Eysenck, H. J. (1952). The effects of psychotherapy: An evaluation. *Journal of Consulting Psychology, 16,* 319–324.

Ferster, C. B. (1966). Animal behavior and mental illness. *Psychological Record, 16,* 345–356.

Fuchs, C. Z., & Rehm, O. P. (1977). A self-control behavior therapy program for depression. *Journal of Consulting and Clinical Psychology, 45,* 206–215.

Gambrill, E., & Richey, C. A. (1976). *It's up to you. The development of assertive social skills.* Millbrae, CA: Les Femmes Publishing.

Gonzales, L., Lewinsohn, P. M., & Clarke, G. (in press). Long-term effectiveness of the Coping with Depression course. *Journal of Consulting and Clinical Psychology.*

Grosscup, S. J., & Lewinsohn, P. M. (1980). Unpleasant and pleasant events and mood. *Journal of Clinical Psychology, 36,* 252–259.

Hammen, C. L., & Glass, D. R. (1975). Depression, activity, and evaluation of reinforcement. *Journal of Abnormal Psychology, 84,* 718–721.

Harmon, T. M., Nelson, R. O., & Hayes, S. C. (1980). Self-monitoring of mood versus activity by depressed clients. *Journal of Consulting and Clinical Psychology, 48,* 30–38.

Hedlund, B., & Thompson, L. W. (1980). *Teaching the elderly to control depression using an educational format.* Paper presented at the meeting of the American Psychological Association, Montreal, Can.

Hersen, M., & Bellack, A. S. (1982). Perspectives in the behavioral treatment of depression. *Behavior Modification, 6,* 95–106.

Hersen, M., Bellack, A. S., & Himmelhoch, J. M. (1980). Treatment of unipolar depression with social skills training. *Behavior Modification, 4,* 547–556.

Hersen, M., Bellack, A. S., & Himmelhoch, J. M. (1982). Skills training with unipolar depressed women. In J. P. Curran & P. M. Monti (Eds.), *Social competence and psychiatric disorders: Theory and practice.* New York: Guilford Press.

Hoberman, H., Lewinsohn, P. M., & Tilson, M. (1985). *Predictors of treatment response in the Coping with Depression course.* Manuscript in preparation, University of Oregon, Eugene.

Holmes, T. H., & Rahe, R. H. (1967). The Social Readjustment Rating Scale. *Psychosomatic Medicine, 11,* 213–218.

Ickes, J., Wicklund, A., & Ferris, C. (1973). Objective self-awareness and self-esteem. *Journal of Experimental Social Psychology, 9,* 202–219.

Jacobson, E. (1929). *Progressive relaxation.* Chicago: University of Chicago Press.

Kazdin, A. E. (1974). Effects of covert modeling and model reinforcement on assertive behavior. *Journal of Abnormal Psychology, 83,* 240–252.

Kazdin, A. E. (1976). Effects of covert modeling, multiple models, and model reinforcement on assertive behavior. *Behavior Therapy, 7,* 211–222.

Kranzler, G. (1974). *You can change how you feel.* Eugene, OR: Author.

Lakein, A. (1974). *How to get control of your time and your life.* New York: New American Library.

Langer, E. (1978). Rethinking the role of thought in social interaction. In J. H. Harvey, W. J. Ickes, & R. Kidd (Eds.), *New directions in attribution research* (vol. 2). Hillsdale, NJ: Erlbaum.

Lazarus, A. A. (1968). Learning theory and the treatment of depression. *Behavior Research and Therapy, 6,* 83–89.

Lewinsohn, P. M. (1975a). Engagement in pleasant activites and depression level. *Journal of Abnormal Psychology, 84,* 729–731.

Lewinsohn, P. M. (1975b). The behavioral study and treatment of depression. In M. Hersen, R. M. Eisler, & P. M. Miller (Eds.), *Progress in behavior modification (Vol. 1).* New York: Academic Press.

Lewinsohn, P. M. (1975c). *The Unpleasant Events Schedule.* Unpublished manuscript, University of Oregon.

Lewinsohn, P. M. (1976). Activity schedules in the treatment of depression. In C. E. Thoreson & J. D. Kromholtz (Eds.), *Counseling methods.* New York: Holt, Rinehart, & Winston.

Lewinsohn, P. M., & Amenson, C. S. (1978). Some relations between pleasant and unpleasant mood-related events and depression. *Journal of Abnormal Psychology, 87,* 655–664.

Lewinsohn, P. M., Antonuccio, D. O., Steinmetz, J. L., & Teri, L. (1984). *The Coping with Depression course: A psychoeducational intervention for unipolar depression.* Eugene, OR: Castalia Publishing.

Lewinsohn, P. M., & Atwood, G. (1969). Depression: A clinical-research approach. The case of Mrs. G. *Psychotherapy: Theory, Research and Practice, 6,* 166–171.

Lewinsohn, P. M., Biglan, T., & Zeiss, A. (1976). Behavioral treatment of depression. In P. Davidson (Ed.), *Behavioral management of anxiety, depression, and pain* (pp. 91–146). New York: Brunner/Mazel.

Lewinsohn, P. M., & Graf, M. (1973). Pleasant activities and depression. *Journal of Consulting and Clinical Psychology, 41,* 261–268.

Lewinsohn, P. M., & Hoberman, H. M. (1982a). Depression. In A. S. Bellack, M. Hersen, & A. E. Kazdin (Eds.), *International handbook of behavior modification and therapy* (pp. 397–429). New York: Plenum.

Lewinsohn, P. M., & Hoberman, H. M. (1982b). Behavioral and cognitive approaches to treatment. In E. S. Paykel (Ed.), *Handbook of affective disorders*. Edinburgh, Churchill-Livingston.

Lewinsohn, P. M., & Hoberman, H. M. (1982c). *Stress, moderator variables and depression: A prospective perspective.* Paper presented at Western Psychological Association, Sacramento, CA.

Lewinsohn, P. M., Hoberman, H. M., Teri, L., & Hautzinger, M. (1985). An integrative theory of depression. In S. Reiss & R. Bootzin (Eds.), *Theoretical issues in behavior therapy*. New York: Academic Press.

Lewinsohn, P. M., Mermelstein, R. M., Alexander, C., & MacPhillamy, D. J. (1983). *The unpleasant events schedule: A scale for the measurement of aversive events.* Unpublished mimeo, University of Oregon, Eugene.

Lewinsohn, P. M., Mischel, W., Chaplin, W., & Barton, R. (1980). Social competence, and depression: The role of illusory self-perceptions. *Journal of Abnormal Psychology, 89,* 203–212.

Lewinsohn, P. M., Muñoz, R. F., Youngren, M. A., & Zeiss, A. M. (1978). *Control Your Depression.* Englewood Cliffs, NJ: Prentice-Hall.

Lewinsohn, P. M., & Shaffer, M. (1971). Use of home observations as an integral part of the treatment of depression: Preliminary report and case studies. *Journal of Consulting and Clinical Psychology, 37,* 87–94.

Lewinsohn, P. M., & Shaw, D. A. (1969). Feedback about interpersonal behavior as an agent of behavior change: A case study in the treatment of depression. *Psychotherapy and Psychosomatics, 17,* 82–88.

Lewinsohn, P. M., Sullivan, J. M., & Grosscup, S. J. (1980). Changing reinforcing events: An approach to the treatment of depression. *Psychotherapy: Theory, Research, and Practice, 47,* 322–334.

Lewinsohn, P. M., Sullivan, J. M., & Grosscup, S. J. (1982). Behavioral therapy: Clinical applications. In A. J. Rush (Ed.), *Short-term psychotherapies for the depressed patient.* New York: Guilford Press.

Lewinsohn, P. M., & Talkington, J. (1979). Studies on the measurement of unpleasant events and relations with depression. *Applied Psychological Measurement, 3,* 83–101.

Lewinsohn, P. M., Weinstein, M., & Alper, T. (1970). A behavioral approach to the group treatment of depressed persons: A methodological contribution. *Journal of Clinical Psychology, 26,* 525–532.

Lewinsohn, P. M., Weinstein, M., & Shaw, D. (1969). Depression: A clinical-research approach. In R. D. Rubin & C. M. Frank (Eds.), *Advances in behavior therapy, 1968.* New York: Academic Press.

Lewinsohn, P. M., Youngren, M. A., & Grosscup, S. J. (1979). Reinforcement and depression. In R. A. Dupue (Ed.), *The psychobiology of depressive disorders: Implications for the effects of stress.* New York: Academic Press.

Lieberman, M. A. (1975). *Survey and evaluation of the literature in verbal psychotherapy of depressive disorders.* Clinical Research Branch, NIMH.

Lubin, B. (1965). Adjective check lists for the measurement of depression. *Archives of General Psychiatry, 12,* 57–62.

MacPhillamy, D. J., & Lewinsohn, P. M. (1971). *The Pleasant Events Schedule.* Unpublished technical paper, University of Oregon, Eugene.

MacPhillamy, D. J., & Lewinsohn, P. M. (1974). Depression as a function of levels of desired and obtained pleasure. *Journal of Abnormal Psychology, 83,* 651–657.

MacPhillamy, D. J., & Lewinsohn, P. M. (1982). The Pleasant Events Schedule: Studies on reliability, validity, and scale intercorrelations. *Journal of Consulting and Clinical Psychology, 50,* 363–380.

Mahoney, M. J., & Thoresen, C. E. (1974). *Self-control: Power to the person.* Monterey, CA: Brooks/Cole Publishing.

McKnight, D. L., Nelson, R. O., Hayes, S. C., & Jarrett, R. B. (1983). *Importance of treating individually assessed response classes in the amelioration of depression.* Unpublished mimeo, University of North Carolina, Greensboro.

McLean, P. (1976). Therapeutic decision-making in the behavioral treatment of depression. In P. Davidson (Ed.), *Behavioral management of anxiety, depression, and pain* (pp. 54–89). New York, Brunner/Mazel.

McLean, P. (1981). Remediation of skills and performance deficits in depression: Clinical steps and research findings. In J. Clarkin & H. Glazer (Eds.), *Behavioral and directive strategies* (pp. 172–204). New York: Garland Publishing.

McLean, P. (1982). Behavioral therapy: Theory and research. In A. J. Rush (Ed.), *Short-term psychotherapies for the depressed patient* (pp. 19–49). New York: Guilford Press.

McLean, P. D., & Hakstian, A. R. (1979). Clinical depression: Comparative efficacy of outpatient treatments. *Journal of Clinical and Consulting Psychology, 47,* 818–836.

McLean, P. D., Ogston, K., & Grauer, L. (1973). A behavioral approach to the treatment of depression. *Journal of Behavior Therapy and Experimental Psychiatry, 4,* 323–330.

Meichenbaum, D. (1977). *Cognitive behavior modification.* New York: Plenum Publishing.

Meichenbaum, D., & Turk, D. (1976). *The cognitive-behavioral management of anxiety, depression and pain.* New York: Brunner/Mazel.

Monroe, S. M., Bellack, A. S., Hersen, M., & Himmelhoch, J. M. (1983). Life events, symptom course, and treatment outcome in depressed women. *Journal of Consulting and Clinical Psychology, 51,* 604–615.

Novaco, R. W. (1975). *Anger control.* Lexington, MA: D. C. Heath.

Radloff, L. S. (1977). The CES-D scale: A self-report depression scale for research in the general population. *Applied Psychological Measurement, 1,* 358–401.

Rehm, L. P. (1977). A self-control model of depression. *Behavior Therapy, 8,* 787–804.

Rehm, L. P. (1978). Mood, pleasant events, and unpleasant events: Two pilot studies. *Journal of Consulting and Clinical Psychology, 46,* 854–859.

Rehm, L. P., Fuchs, C. Z., Roth, D. M., Kornblith, S. J., & Romano, J. M. (1979). A comparison of self-control and social skills treatments of depression. *Behavior Therapy, 10,* 429–442.

Rehm, L. P., & Kornblith, S. J. (1978). *Self-control therapy manual, V-2 session manual.* Unpublished mimeo, University of Pittsburgh.

Rehm, L. P., & Kornblith, S. J. (1979). Behavior therapy for depression: A review of recent developments. In M. Hersen, R. M. Eisler, & P. M. Miller (Eds.), *Progress in behavior modification.* New York: Academic Press.

Rehm, L. P., Kornblith, S. J., O'Hara, M. W., Lamparski, D. M., Romano, J. M., & Volkin, J. I. (1981). An evaluation of major components in a self-control therapy program for depression. *Behavior Modification, 5,* 459–490.

Rehm, L. P., Rabin, A. S., Kaslow, N. J., & Willard, R. (1982). *Cognitive and behavioral targets in a self-control therapy program for depression.* Paper presented at the Annual Meeting of the Association for the Advancement of Behavior Therapy, Los Angeles.

Robinson, J. C., & Lewinsohn, P. M. (1973). Behavior modification of speech characteristics in a chronically depressed man. *Behavior Therapy, 4,* 291–295.

Rosen, G. M. (1971). *The relaxation response.* Englewood Cliffs, NJ: Prentice-Hall.

Rosen, G. M. (1977). *The relaxation book.* Englewood-Cliffs, NJ: Prentice-Hall.

Rosenbaum, M., & Merbaum, M. (1984). Self-control of anxiety and depression: An evaluative review of treatments. In Cyril M. Franks (Ed.), *New developments in behavior therapy: From research to clinical application* (pp. 105–155). New York: Haworth.

Roth, D., Bielski, R., Jones, M., Parker, W., & Osborne, G. (1982). A comparison of self-control therapy and combined self-control therapy and antidepressant medication in the treatment of depression. *Behavior Therapy, 13,* 133–144.

Rotter, J. B. (1954). *Social learning and clinical psychology.* Englewood Cliffs, NJ: Prentice-Hall.

Rush, A. J., & Beck, A. T. (1978). Behavior therapy in adults with affective disorders. In M. Hersen & A. S. Bellack (Eds.), *Behavior therapy in the psychiatric setting.* Baltimore: Williams & Wilkins.

Saenz, M., Lewinsohn, P. M., & Hoberman, H. M. (1985). *Prediction of outcome in the Coping with Depression course.* In preparation, University of Oregon, Eugene.

Schank, R., & Ableson, R. P. (1975). *Scripts, plans and knowledge.* Prepared to present at the 4th International Conference on artificial intelligence. Tbilisi, USSR.

Scheier, M. F., & Carver, C. S. (1977). Self-focused attention and the experience of emotion: Attraction, repulsion, elation, and depression. *Journal of Personality and Social Psychology, 35,* 624–636.

Schmidt, M., & Miller, W. R. (1983). Amount of therapist contact and outcome in a multidimensional depression treatment program. *Acta Psychiatrica Scandinavica, 67,* 319–332.

Seitz, F. C. (1971). Behavior modification techniques for treating depression. *Psychotherapy: Theory, Research and Practice, 8,* 181–184.

Selmi, P. M., Klein, M. H., Greist, J. H., Johnson, J. H., & Harris, W. G. (1982). An investigation of computer-assisted cognitive-behavior therapy in the treatment of depression. *Behavior Research Methods and Instrumentation, 14,* 181–185.

Skinner, B. F. (1953). *Science and human behavior.* New York: Free Press.

Spitzer, R. L., Endicott, J., & Robins, E. (1978). Research diagnostic criteria: Rationale and reliability. *Archives of General Psychiatry, 35,* 773–782.

Steinbrueck, S. M., Maxwell, S. E., & Howard, G. S. (1983). A meta-analysis of psychotherapy and drug therapy in the treatment of unipolar depression with adults. *Journal of Consulting and Clinical Psychology, 51,* 856–863.

Steinmetz, J. L., Antonuccio, D. O., Bond, M., McKay, G., Brown, R., & Lewinsohn, P. M. (1979). *Instructor's manual for Coping with Depression course.* Unpublished mimeo, University of Oregon, Eugene.

Steinmetz, J. L., Breckenridge, J. N., Thompson, L. W., & Gallagher, D. (1982). *The role of client expectations in predicting treatment outcome for elderly depressives.* Paper presented at the Annual Meeting of the Gerontological Society of America, Boston.

Steinmetz, J. L., Lewinsohn, P. M., & Antonuccio, D. O. (1983). Prediction of individual outcome in a group intervention for depression. *Journal of Consulting and Clinical Psychology, 51,* 331–337.

Steinmetz, J. L., Zeiss, A. N., & Thompson, L. W. (1984). The life satisfaction course: An intervention for the elderly. In D. Upper & S. M. Ross (Eds.), *Handbook of behavioral group therapy.* New York: Plenum Publishing.

Teri, L., & Lewinsohn, P. M. (1981). *Comparative efficacy of group vs. individual treatment of unipolar depression.* Paper presented at meeting of the Association for the Advancement of Behavior Therapy, San Francisco, CA.

Teri, L., & Lewinsohn, P. M. (1982). Modification of the pleasant and unpleasant events schedules for use with the elderly. *Journal of Consulting and Clinical Psychology, 50,* 444–445.

Thompson, L. W., Gallagher, D., Nies, G., & Epstein, D. (1983). Evaluation of the effectiveness of professionals and nonprofessionals as instructors of Coping with Depression classes for elders. *Gerontologist, 23,* 390–396.

Thorndike, E. L. (1931). *Human learning.* New York: Appleton, Century, Crofts.

Turner, R. W., & Wehl, C. W. (1983). *Cognitive-behavioral vs. other treatments of depressed alcoholics and inpatients.* Paper presented at 17th Annual Convention of the Association for the Advancement of Behavior Therapy, Washington, DC.

Turner, R. W., Ward, M. F., & Turner, D. J. (1979). Behavioral treatment for depression: An evaluation of therapeutic components. *Journal of Clinical Psychology, 35,* 166–175.

Turner, R. W., Wehl, C. K., Cannon, D. S., & Craig, K. A. (1980). *Individual treatment for depression in alcoholics: A comparison of behavioral, cognitive, and nonspecific therapy.* Unpublished mimeo, VA Medical Center, Salt Lake City, UT.

Wanderer, Z. W. (1972). Existential depression treated by desensitization of phobias: Strategy and transcript. *Journal of Behavior Therapy and Experimental Psychiatry, 3,* 111–116.

Wells, K. C., Hersen, M., Bellack, A. S., & Himmelhoch, J. (1979). *Social skills training for unipolar depressive females.* Paper presented at the meetings of the Association for the Advancement of Behavior Therapy, Atlanta, GA.

Wolpe, J., & Lazarus, A. A. (1966). *Behavior therapy techniques.* New York: Pergamon Press.

Yalom, I. D. (1975). *The theory and practice of group psychotherapy.* New York: Basic Books.

Zeiss, A. M., & Jones, S. L. (1982). Behavioral treatment of depression: Examining treatment failures. In E. B. Foa & M. G. Emmelkamp (Eds.), *Failures in behavior therapy.* New York: Wiley.

Zeiss, A. M., Lewinsohn, P. M., & Muñoz, R. F. (1979). Nonspecific improvement effects in depression using interpersonal, cognitive, and pleasant events focused treatments. *Journal of Consulting and Clinical Psychology, 47,* 427–439.

Zung, W. W. K. (1965). A Self-Rating Depression Scale. *Archives of General Psychiatry, 123,* 62–70.

Chapter 3

Long-Term Analytic Treatment of Depression

Jules R. Bemporad

The analytic treatment of depression is based on the belief that this clinical disorder is the result of a particular personality structure and so embedded in the everyday functioning of the individual that less radical forms of therapy would be ineffective. While the clinical manifestations of a single episode might be alleviated with other forms of treatment, the individual would remain vulnerable to future recurrences. Therefore, analytic treatment aims at preventing future depressions and not simply treating the presenting episode. At the same time, not all depressions warrant extensive treatment (as will be discussed below), and analytic therapy is usually restricted to those depressions which are termed *characterological*, meaning that this form of pathological response to frustration or loss is extreme, repetitive and results from the atavistic retention to childhood modes of estimating one's self and significant others. Such individuals are believed to be predisposed to recurrent depressions as a result of specific childhood experiences which so shape the individual that he cannot withstand the everyday vicissitudes of adult life. Throughout the history of psychoanalytic theory, this predisposition to depression has been described in various ways, reflecting the more fundamental evolution of a general theory of psychopathology.

During the early years of the psychoanalytic movement, Freud's prime intent was to prove the existence of the unconscious by demonstrating its effect on conscious thought and manifest behavior. Therefore, disorders such as hysteria and obsessive compulsive neurosis, which were believed to reveal blatantly the power of unconscious forces, were initially investigated. Depressive states, which lacked the dramatic presentations of other disorders, came late to the attention of psychoanalysts.

HISTORICAL REVIEW

The first truly psychoanalytic interpretation of depression was published by Abraham in 1911 (1960a). In this pioneer paper, Abraham interpreted depressive symptoms as resulting from repression of libidinal drives, in a manner similar to the mechanisms underlying anxiety. However, in the latter, gratification was thought to be still possible while in melancholia any hope of gratification had been abandoned. Abraham was impressed by the similarity between obsessional and depressed individuals. In both, he preceived a profound ambivalence toward others with positive and negative feelings alternating and blocking the expression of each other. In his later works Abraham explained the occurrence of this ambivalent form of relating as due to a regression to a fixated mode of object-relationships in childhood. The depressive is quick to feel hatred toward others over slights and frustration. This propensity for hatred blocks the individual's capacity to love or to express his libidinal urges. Abraham believed that the depressive could not accept his hatred of others and projected this hatred onto others so that "I hate them" became "They hate me." The depressive then invents some imagined fault or defect which justifies others hating him. Simultaneously, the depressive feels himself alone and alienated from others since he has, in effect severed both libidinal and aggressive ties with them.

Aside from its theoretical exposition, this early contribution contains a wealth of astute clinical observations. Abraham mentions the ambivalence, the inability to love genuinely, the manipulative use of guilt, and the underlying hostility of the depressive. He also includes valuable suggestions on treatment. There is no mention in this early work, however, of the role of object loss or orality, which where later to play a significant role in psychodynamic theories of depression. Finally, Abraham concludes that depression is ultimately caused by the individual's inability to fulfill the demands of adult life, ironically a formulation that was later adopted by the culturalists who had rejected much of Freudian psychoanalysis.

Abraham's later contributions on depression (1916/1960b, 1924/1960c) also reflect the current developments in psychoanalytic theory of the time. In these works, Abraham focuses on aspects of depression which would indicate a regression to the oral psychosexual stage and attempts to interpret depressive symptoms as expressions of oral and anal drives. In his last work on this subject, Abraham also centered on the role of childhood object loss, echoing Freud's more recent contributions on depression.

In a summary statement given in this same monograph (1924/1960c), Abraham lists the multiple variables that predispose to depression. These are: (1) a constitutional factor that results in an increased amount of oral eroticism; (2) a libidinal fixation at the oral stage, leading to not only "oral" symptoms but an unconscious predilection to incorporate objects; (3) a disappointment in love before the Oedipal complex; (4) the occurrence of a childhood form of depression called "primal parathymia"; and (5) the recurrence of this childhood experience following disappointments in later life.

Abraham's contributions to the application of psychoanalytic theory to depression may be summarized as: (1) pointing out the role of ambivalence; (2) indicating the importance of significant others in the predisposition to depression; and (3) viewing the clinical episode as a recurrence of a childhood experience which is inappropriate to adult behavior; and (4) elaborating the role of early love relations in later psychopathology.

While Abraham's contributions are regarded as the pioneer works in depression, the most influential psychoanalytic work on this disorder is Freud's "Mourning and Melancholia." Although written in 1915, World War I delayed publication until 1917 (1961a). This short paper is unique in many ways: it is the first psychoanalytic contribution that does not mention inhibition of erotic drives as a causative factor for illness and may be seen as the harbinger of Freud's so-called mature works. This paper also presages the entire object relations school by enlarging the contents of the unconscious to include introjected objects as well as drives. In it may also be found the conceptual forerunner of what later became the superego.

The paper begins with an investigation of the clinical differences between grief and depression. Freud notes that in grief the person's loss is clearly external and there is no effect on his self-esteem, while in the latter there is often difficulty in determining what has been lost and that there appears to have been an internal impoverishment whatever the environmental deprivation. In addition, in melancholia, in contrast to mourning, the individual is full of self-recriminations which are loudly proclaimed without shame and do not seem to apply to oneself. Rather, these recriminations seem to better describe the object whose loss precipitated the depressive episode.

On the basis of these astute observations, Freud formulated a view of depression that was to influence psychiatry for half a century. He postulated that the self-recriminations are actually directed at an introject of the lost object which has become part of the melancholic's own ego. This introjection of the object would also account for the internal sense of loss and inner emptiness of the melancholic since, when he has lost the external object, he has also, in essence, lost a part of himself.

The predisposition to this reaction to object loss was said to derive from a particular childhood experience which Freud described as the young child suffering a loss of the mother or loss of love from the mother and not being able to find an appropriate substitute. In order to rectify this major loss, the child does not find a new love object but creates within himself or herself an effigy of the forsaken object, predisposing for future depressive episodes following significant losses. From this time forward, the individual will tend to react to losses of love objects with a reactivation of the anger which accompanied the original loss. However, since the object has become part of the ego, the anger is directed inward toward the introjected object rather than outward toward the real object. This retroflected anger results in the depressive manifestation of self-debasements and recriminations which are really aimed at the internalized object.

This ingenious theory explained depression as a misdirection of anger and influenced therapists to get their patients to redirect the anger outward. It also created a logical relationship between early object loss and depression even though Freud stressed that the mother need not be absent and that a loss of her love was sufficient to create the pathological incorporation. Finally, the predisposition to depression was seen as the tendency to introject the love object rather than the cathexis of a new object.

This formulation exerted an enormous effect on the interpretation and treatment of depression for many years although Freud cautioned that it applied only to a small segment of all melancholics and, of greater importance, later rejected his own theory. In subsequent works (1923/1961b, 1933/1961c), Freud stated that the tendency to internalize lost objects was a normal, ubiquitous way by which the child deals with losses and, therefore, cannot be specific to future depressives. The punishing agency was also seen as no longer limited to melancholics but became the familiar superego of Freud's later writings. In his "New Introductory Lectures on Psychoanalysis" (1933/1961c), written almost two decades after "Mourning and Melancholia," Freud suggests that depression is simply due to an excessive severity of the superego, possibly resulting from constitutional excess of death instinct.

Despite these later alterations in theory, a good many psychoanalysts continued to utilize the original retroflected anger formulation in their understanding of depression. One of the authors who attempted to integrate the changes brought about by the structural theory with its familiar division of the psyche into id, ego, and superego, was Sandor Rado (1956), who published a revised theory of depression in 1928. In this paper, Rado also depicted the abnormal relationship of the depressive to his adult love objects. He speculated that prior to the onset of depression, the individual will punish the love object and push this significant other to the limits of patience. When the other is driven away by his hostile behavior, the depressive will attempt to regain the object by suffering, self-negation, and all of the symptoms that define the early stages of a depressive episode. Rado mentions that the depressive is like a love addict who cannot do without the object, although once he/she has the love of the object he/she will test the other continuously. This behavior is a recapitulation in adult life of a childhood pattern of relating to the mother typified by an anger-guilt-atonement sequence in which the object is utilized to absorb the rage of the depressive as well as being necessary for an adequate sense of self-esteem.

If the depressive is able to regain the love object via contrition, then his depression subsides and the episode clears. However, if the object cannot be regained, then the depressive regresses to a psychotic position and gives up the world of real objects, attempting to gain love from the internalized childhood object which has become part of the superego. Eventually, when the individual has suffered sufficiently, he gains the forgiveness of the superego and recovers from his melancholia.

The significant aspects of Rado's theory are that it describes depression as a process of repair that allows the individual to either win back a lost object or gain forgiveness from within the self. It also describes the depressive's own participation in his illness, relates the clinical episode to the everyday mode of life of the depressive and attempts to describe the transition from neurotic to psychotic depression. Finally, in keeping with the structural theory, Rado emphasizes the role of the superego in severe melancholia.

These papers describe the classical literature on depression, written at a time when psychoanalysis was still evolving its basic concepts. Later works no longer present new postulates of psychoanalysis but rather reflect refinements in theory using the fundamental structures and concepts which had become universally accepted. These newer works on depression reveal the increasing importance given to the ego in psychic functioning as well as a return to fomulations which, while less imaginative, seem closer to manifest clinical data.

Fenichel summarized this ego-oriented view of depression in his encyclopedic text on psychoanalysis which was published in 1945. In the section on melancholia, Fenichel focuses on a fall in self-esteem secondary to frustration of narcissistic needs as a cardinal feature of depression. The depressive-prone individual was described as living in constant need of external narcissistic supplies in order to maintain a satisfactory sense of self. The significant role of the ego can be appreciated when it is understood that it is this psychic structure that is responsible for self-esteem by indicating the degree of disparity between an ego ideal and the actual state of self. Therefore, when the individual fails significantly to achieve an ego ideal or suffers an experience that shatters the belief that he has fulfilled his ego ideal and has to confront an unsatisfying state of self, a failure in self-esteem, and clinical depression, ensue.

Bibring (1953) elaborated this position in his own innovative formulations of depression. Bibring argued that depression may result from a variety of life's circumstances which share one basic common pattern: a breakdown of the mechanisms which establish self-esteem. Different individuals may be susceptible to different negative life events depending on the particular sources of esteem. For Bibring, the conscious experience of depression is representative of the ego's helplessness and powerlessness to fulfill urgent narcissistic needs. Therefore, Bibring does not view depression as a result of a complex intersystemic conflict between psychic agencies but as being the direct emotional correlate of a basis state of the ego when faced with a specific situation of deprivation.

Although Bibring's position may appear as a commonsense observation, it has far-reaching ramifications. By viewing depression as a primary ego state, Bibring shifts the emphasis in the understanding of depression from its alleged intrapsychic mechanisms to external precipitants and antecedent personality characteristics. The experience of depression is taken as a fundamental given, which arises whenever the ego finds itself helpless to satisfy narcissistic needs in the maintenance of self-esteem. Some individuals may be more prone to depressive episodes because they harbor unrealistic ambitions which can never be met or because they have learned to capitulate in the face of adversity and too readily lapse into hopelessness and helplessness. Finally, if depression is seen as a basic ego state, it is possible to create defenses against this painful experience, or that in milder forms depression may serve some sort of alerting function which could mobilize the individual to alter patterns of functioning. On the other hand, Bibring's view is that the symptoms of clinical depression are not reparative and do not have special symbolic meanings as described in the classical literature.

Sandler and Joffee (1965) have furthered the view of depression as an experiential state by proposing that depression be conceptualized as a fundamental affect, much like anxiety. While acknowledging their debt to Bibring, Sandler and Joffee consider "loss of self-esteem" as too elaborate or intellectual a concept to indicate the primal nature of the depressive experience. Rather, they propose that depression results whenever the individual has lost a former state of well-being. When depression occurs following the loss of a love object, they postulate that what is lost is the sense of well-being that the object supplied rather than the loss of the object in itself.

Sandler and Joffee also differentiate between the initial dysphoric reaction which immediately follows upon the loss of a state of well-being and clinical depression. The former is seen as a "psychobiological" reaction that occurs in everyone, while the latter represents an individual's failure to work through the loss. The initial reaction is somewhat analogous to signal anxiety in alerting the individual to somehow compensate for his loss. If he cannot do this, for internal or environmental reasons, the depression escalates to clinical proportions and no longer serves any homeostatic purpose.

Arieti (1978) also conceived of depression as a basic affect that was a psychological equivalent to physical pain and proposed that its evolutionary purpose was to alarm the individual to alter his psychological self, much as pain forces the individual to alter his behavior. Arieti believed that the individual overcomes depression by going through "sorrow work," during which he realigns his expectation, views of himself and of others, and modes of obtaining meaning to conform to a new environmental situation. If the individual cannot go through this process adequately, his depression remains, intensifies and loses its original purpose by overwhelming the individual and preventing any fruitful action.

The foregoing review of theory reveals a lessening of interest in the possible meaning of depressive symptoms themselves, and an increasing appreciation of the character structure that underlies the clinical manifestations. Recent theorists direct their enquiry to those factors which predispose to frequent or severe bouts of depression in terms of the individual's inability to reconstitute satisfactory sources of meaning, gratification and self-esteem following a narcissistic blow.[1] Espisodes of depression are seen as a commonplace and often appropriate reaction to life's vicissitudes. Most individuals can, in time, recover from these painful experiences by themselves and go on to live relatively satisfying lives. Others, however, appear vulnerable to repeated and/or chronic states of melancholia which are so integrated into their everyday functioning that their very personality structure predisposes to re-

---

[1] Not all currently practicing psychoanalysts would agree with this simplified view. Jacobson (1971) has evolved a theory of depression as the aggressive cathexis of the self-representation, together with a libidinal cathexis of the object representation and a personification of the superego. Similarly, Kleinian psychoanalysts also propose a more intricate formulation, having to do with excessive guilt experienced over the destruction of good inner objects by one's hostile fantasies. See Bemporad (1978) for a more extensive exposition of these views.

current psychopathology. It is for these individuals that analytic treatment, which aims at modifying the underlying personality, is the treatment of choice.

THE DEPRESSIVE PERSONALITY

The two attributes that are cited repeatedly in the psychodynamic literature on depression are pathological dependency and self-inhibition. These qualities describe the character of the chronic depressive and are not limited to the clinical episode. The discovery of these underlying personality configurations may be in surprising contrast to the notable achievements and superficial maturity manifested by many depressives. In fact, objectively one could have considered those who succumb to depression as paragons of psychological health. The depressive is often stable, reliable, and hard working. He or she is the one who gets the job done and does not shirk from onerous or unglamorous tasks. Yet the depressive appears to derive little direct pleasure from such accomplishments or his/her exemplary moral standards. Rather, the depressive's arduous efforts were aimed at wrenching praise from idealized others, and his/her exemplary behavior is not based on altruism or high ethical principles, but on the fear of guilt or abandonment.

Over 20 years ago, Arieti (1962) noted the tendency of some depressives to idealize and to need a particular individual in order to function without sever dysphoria. He wrote that while schizophrenic decompensation appeared to involve a detachment from a negation of the whole interpersonal world, depressives became markedly symptomatic following the failure of just one highly prized relationship. This led him to propose the term *dominant other* to describe the highly influential other who holds such sway over the mental health of the depressive. This pathological relationship is utilized by the depressive to derive a sense of worth but is not so overwhelmingly narcissistic as to supply a sense of identity or reality as in borderline or psychotic conditions. Rather, the dominant other is the resurrection of the moral parent who rewards industry and self-sacrifice and can punish laziness or frivolity. The depressive reinstates this child-parent relationship with others in adult life and then strives to become special in their eyes by hard work and self-denial. When the relationship is threatened, the depressive may work all the harder in an effort to win back the needed praise and nurturance from the dominant other. If these efforts fail, then a clinical episode may ensue. Some depressives need a flesh and blood dominant other to allow them to feel worthy and free from guilt and anxiety. For some, however, the dominant other is not a person but an organization such as the army, church, or corporation which is personified and provides structure, rewards, and meaning in life.

Another variant of this basic form of depressive personality is that which Arieti and Bemporad (1980) called the "dominant goal" type. In this case, the individual is obsessed with the pursuit of some fantastic achievement, deriving almost all his/her gratification from this quest and shunning other avenues of pleasure or meaning because they would detract from the possibility of realizing his/her dream. The person so dangerously limits other means of obtaining worth or meaning that he or she is left painfully vulnerable to depression if or when he or she realizes that the magical goal is not attainable. The individual then senses him/herself an abysmal failure and succumbs to a clinical depressive episode. The underlying similarity to the dominant other type of depressive is manifested in the inhibition over pleasurable activity but more so in the meaning that the goal has for the individual. The pursuit of his/her fantasied objectives brings the person no pleasure. The meaning of the goal resides in the changes that are believed to take place after it is attained: the individual believes that he/she will now be loved and will be a worthy individual. This lack of enjoyment in one's activities per se may lead to depression even when one achieves the all-important goal and finds he is not given the nurturance and approval he feels he deserves and needs. He may then feel that no matter what he does, he can never obtain the love he desires.

These aspects of the depressive personality also demonstrate the massive inhibitions that he or she imposes on him or herself and the fear inherent in obtaining gratification directly from activity. The depressive looks for justification for any indulgence and experiences anxiety when faced with the prospect of pure enjoyment for its own sake. One depressed woman, for example, could only bring herself to spend money on attractive clothes if she could convince herself that she needed them for work. Another woman who traveled frequently on business became overwhelmed with morbid fears of her parents dying or her apartment being vandalized when she was rewarded for her excellent work performance with a company-paid vacation.

This obsessive anxiety over pleasure also pervades those depressive individuals who do not demonstrate a predominant pattern of striving toward a dominant other or dominant goal. These depressives overvalue the opinions of others and also strive toward objectives that are not inherently meaningful; but they are not able to defend against depressive episodes by even these pathological processes. Their sense of worth derives from fending off a dreaded sense of self by constantly attempting to reassure themselves that they measure up to some lofty moral ideal. Leff, Roatch, and Bunney (1970) give a penetrating description of such an individual in their study of precipitants in depression. After being hospitalized following a serious suicide attempt, their patient exhibited a severe depression with vegetative signs. A reconstruction of her history revealed the following significant factors. She was the product of an illegitimate pregnancy by a sexually promiscuous mother. The patient vowed to be a "pure person" and never to allow herself to follow in her mother's footsteps. She was intensely ashamed of her mother's way of life and derived a sense of worth from her higher standards of virtue. Nevertheless, she consented to premarital intercourse with her future husband. When their first child was born prematurely and died, she believed she had caused the death of the child. At this time, she developed clinical symptoms of anxiety and phobias as her concept of self was challenged. There followed a period of further stresses in her relationship with relatives, her mother, and her husband, but her final collapse came when her husband slapped her during an argument and said, "You're a whore, just like your mother." This accusation crystallized her greatest fear and her greatest shame. After hearing these words spoken by her husband, she took a massive overdose of drugs which caused her to remain in a coma for three days and from which she barely survived.

This case illustrates the depressive's labile sense of self and his/her need to ward off feelings of shame, unworthiness, and guilt. Some depressives accomplish this by exemplary behavior, others by pursuit of some magical goal and yet others by a relationship with a transferentially overidealized other. For all, however, there is an excessive dependence on others for one's view of one's worth and an extreme inhibition in terms of self-gratification. If one loses and external source of esteem and, because of one's limited alternatives, cannot find new avenues of meaning, then the affect of depression automatically arises and in time escalates to clinical proportions. Ernest Becker (1964) has poetically and accurately described the plight of the depressive as being "left in the hopeless despair of the actor who knows only one set of lines, and loses the one audience who wants to hear it" (p. 127).

Alice Miller (1979) has recently presented her own formulation of depression which is not greatly dissimilar from that presented above. Miller postulates that the future depressive is forced to create an overblown false self in order to please and obtain love from a narcissistic mother. This false self often works well in everyday society in bringing the individual the public success demanded by the mother. However, a large portion of the basic personality, which Miller calls the real self, is suppressed and split off. Therefore, the individual does not have access to his true desires and views the real self with dread and disdain. At the same time, the success of the false self gives the depressive a sense of grandiosity and well-being. However, this false self must be reaffirmed constantly and when the individual encounters obstacles that prevent its efficient functioning, the real self reasserts itself into consciousness, causing a radical restructuring of the personality and causing the symptoms of depression.

Therefore, Miller also stresses the distorted evaluations of the self and others, the overreliance on external supplies for narcissistic equilibrium and the massive inhibition over experiences of gratification and meaning.

PSYCHOANALYTIC PSYCHOTHERAPY

The task of psychoanalytic psychotherapy is to alter these patterns of personality structure so as to prevent future recurrences of clinical depression as well as to improve the everyday functioning and feeling of the individual. While this form of therapy attempts to go beyond the immediate clinical manifestations to underlying maladaptive patterns of self-estimation, the symptoms of the illness cannot be ignored. In mild forms of depression, the painful dysphoria may be used to motivate the patient to persevere at times, in the unpleasant process of change. In severe depression, however, the symptoms may so overwhelm the individual that they prevent productive analytic work. Therefore, symptom relief by any useful means is the first task of therapy with severely depressed individuals. Pharmacological treatments are certainly indicated to ease the burden of melancholia and to allow the depressive a respite from torment, Experienced analysts, such as Arieti (1977) and Jacobson (1975), who spent decades treating severely depressed patients, recommend the usage of medication to allay those symptoms which block the engagement of the individual in psychoanalysis. A number of research studies indicate that drugs and psychotherapy affect different aspects of the depressive syndrome (APA Commission on Psychotherapy, 1982). Medication ameliorates the more biologically based symptoms such as early morning insomnia, anorexia or anergia, while psychotherapy exerts an effect on the individual's more psychological functions, improving social withdrawal, suicidality, or low self-esteem. The use of medication in depressions which include vegetative symptoms, and most severe depressions do, is recommended. These very symptoms may become the focus of the patient's concerns and justifiably cause him or her to resist engaging in a mutual search, with the analyst, for the causes of his/her unhappiness.

Whatever the severity of the depression, one of the major tasks of the initial sessions is to interrupt the depressive's litany of complaints and protestations. Spiegel (1965) has described how the depressive's monotonous repetition of his or her preoccupations frustrate the therapist and may lead to a negative countertransference. Levine (1965) has labeled the depressive's continuous reporting of misery as the "broken record response" which must be interrupted if therapy is ever to be initiated. The usual silent or detached analytic stance or the use of the couch are to be avoided since, if left to his/her own devices, the patient will fill the entire session with repetitious complaints.

A middle-aged businessman (whose treatment will be referred to as an illustration of long-term analytic therapy) presented with a moderately severe depressive episode when his firm started doing badly. This man continuously dwelled on his physical symptoms or his fear of losing all of his money and of ending up in the poor house. While his concerns over a financial loss were somewhat justified, he greatly exaggerated the magnitude of its possible consequences in terms of how his life would be affected. He was so obsessed and overwhelmed by the prospect of a financial failure that he had to be encouraged to talk about his wife, children, friends, or anything other than his symptoms or his worries. If left on his own, he would have filled each session with his grim foreboding of utter poverty and an endless repetition of his various complaints. It was explained to him that the therapist was cognizant of his worries and suffering but that dwelling on these matters would lead nowhere and that if therapy were to proceed other aspects of his life had to be considered.

The other pitfall in adopting too analytic a posture is that this stance may lead to an eventually countertherapeutic idealization of the therapist. A depressive will seek out treatment when in the throws of a painful clinical episode and, whatever he or she may verbalize, there is always a wish for magical surcease from his/her torment. This relief often takes the form of depending on a strong parentified figure who will take care of the depressive and nurture him or her in time of need. The patient may say that the therapist is the only one who can help or that the sessions make him or her feel so much better. The therapist must be wary of these narcissistically gratifying remarks and realize that he or she is being set up as a new dominant other who will have to shoulder the burden of the patient's problems and eventually will have to disappoint the patient's unrealistic expectations.

In the treatment of the businessman described above, it became apparent that his recent business venture which was in danger of failing represented the first time that he had worked alone; in the past he had always worked with a partner or with his father. During this stressful time, he wished to again have a partner who, like his prior associates, would buoy up his spirits, reassure him that things would turn out well and eventually salvage the situation. Without consciously being aware of it, he wanted the therapist to become his missed senior partner and he tried to obtain reassurances that his business would do well, that he would feel better, and that he would be taken care of, by praising his therapy and the alleged benefit he had already received from it. His unrealistic expectations were interpreted as well as his idealization of the analytic situation. At the same time, the realistic beneficial aspects of therapy such as the opportunity to be completely honest, to look at the reasons for one's difficulties and, through understanding, to alter aspects of the personality that created difficulties or blocked a full expression of oneself, were repeatedly indicated to him.

The initial sessions are crucial, for they set the course for the rest of the therapy. The therapist has to tread a difficult path between a reflective analytic posture and his or her innate wish to reassure and help a fellow human being in distress. The therapist should be warm and encouraging but consistently make clear that the burden of therapy and cure is the patient's responsibility. New topics can be introduced to break the repetitive cycle of complaints and misery. Idealization should be detected early and transference distortions corrected as these arise. The therapist must be honest about his/her own shortcomings and the limitations of analysis to produce miraculous or rapid cures. This openness, which has been recommended by Kolb (1956), is very important since the depressive has all too often been raised in an atmosphere of deceit, manipulation, and secret obligations and he or she must be shown that it is possible to be honest and forthright without being criticized or abandoned.

Once analysis has begun on the proper course, the patient should be encouraged to look inward toward the causes of the dysphoria. This search involves the patient relating the precipitating factor of the clinical episode to his/her particular personality organization. The environmental loss, frustration, or rejection that provokes a severe depression has a deeper meaning for the individual which threatens his/her needed sense of self and his or hers sources of narcissism. Therefore, what appears to the casual observer as a trivial event may reverberate with a deep-seated fear and shame in the vulnerable individual. The precipitating event sets off a chain reaction which alters the psychic equilibrium of the individual and reevokes childhood modes of self-evaluation and adaptation.

The patient described above began to relate his current fears of financial failure to older feelings of being inadequate and worthless when, as a child, he had been unable to please his parents, and particularly his father. He remembered that he had created a facade of compliance and diligence to ward off criticism and in order to obtain the approval which he so deeply desired. His manner of gaining praise from his father, and later of feeling good about himself, was to achieve financial success. To actually suffer a monetary loss meant the realization of a sense of self that he despised and of which he was intensely ashamed. He also remembered that he has suffered from mild depressive episodes for years although he had managed to suppress this painful feeling by bolstering a specious sense of self through manipulating others to laud his ability in business or to declare their love for him. Whenever this facade of competence and attractiveness was challenged, he began to feel dysphoric. He then required specific others—his partners, his wife and, particularly, his father, to dispel his sense of sadness by telling him he was capable, worthwhile, and lovable.

The realistic possibility of a financial setback threatened this needed sense of self and caused him to see himself in an acutely painful manner. This man gradually was able to relate the current precipitant to his particular personality structure in terms of how the threat of financial loss meant a possible shattering of his way of obtaining self-esteem. The failure of his financial venture represented the failure of himself as a worthy person.

During this time, the sessions were directed toward uncovering why this particular threat so jeopardized his usual sense of self as a responsible and capable adult. Dreams, memories, and possible transferential reactions were utilized to further the mutual understanding of the shaky sources of his self-esteem and his needing a facade to hide painful older feelings which the depression had laid bare.

He remembered that as a child he always wished for his father's approval and would defend the father in arguments with his sister, who took their mother's side. The father was remembered as a despotic parent who ruled the house through criticizing and shaming. He remembered his mother as a sweet but weak person who was no match for the father and who was repeatedly hospitalized for numerous illnesses, including depression, until her death when the patient was in his 20s. The father praised the values of the marketplace where the sentimental or feeling person could not survive and only the strong and domineering prevailed. He consciously tried to be what the father wanted since this allowed him a favored place in the household. Later, when he went to work for his father, he felt he could not please him, eventually became angry and resentful at his lack of recognition and left to start businesses on his own with various partners. At the same time, he adopted many of his father's tyrannical qualities toward his own wife and children.

In this reconstruction of his life, the patient reviewed his past in terms of appreciating those forces which led him to adopt certain defenses in order to maintain esteem at the cost of suppressing and repressing valuable and gratifying aspects of his personality. This public self had to be reaffirmed by the praise of his partners, the obedience of his immediate family, and the continued success of his financial ventures.

The setting of the proper course of therapy in terms of dependency and transference, the relating of the clinical episode to a particular premorbid personality organization, and the connecting of the precipitating events with particular maladaptive modes of gaining and maintaining a sense of worth, comprise the major objectives of the first stage of therapy.

The next stage involves the process of relinquishing these ingrained modes of behavior, which, while pathological, offer the patient a sense of security, gratification, and predictability. This is the time of "working through," which is the real battleground of therapy with frequent advances, regressions, and stalemates. The fundamental struggle involves the depressive giving up his excessive reliance on external props for self-esteem and his risking to venture into new modes of deriving pleasure and meaning. The patient has often evolved a facade which may succeed in obtaining social rewards, just as it succeeded in obtaining parental praise, but restricts his life excessively and excludes experiencing the full range of his potential. The resistances that are usually encountered are a fear that one's life will be totally empty without the familiar, if stifling, structure that the former beliefs and adaptations had provided and a crippling anxiety that one will be abandoned or ridiculed if one dares to break the childhood taboos.

During this stage of therapy, the patient remembered that he had once greatly enjoyed playing the piano but gave it up as a frivolous waste of time. He also recalled feeling painfully alone as a child and secretly bringing home stray animals for comfort and company.

The majority of his associations and recollections, however, centered on his relationship with his parents. He remembered an aching sense of abandonment with each of his mother's illnesses and hospitalizations. Eventually, he shifted his affections toward his father, who was perceived as more powerful and consistently available. However, the father demanded exemplary behavior in return for attention so that the patient had to be constantly on guard lest he provoke a shattering rebuke for being too soft or weak. The father gradually became his barometer of self-worth and his waking efforts were directed toward wresting a rare word of acknowledgement from him. Later, the patient required continuous reaffirmation of his worth from other esteemed environmental figures, such as teachers or senior colleagues who transferentially replaced the father. He demonstrated this distortion in therapy as he unrealistically idealized the analyst and attempted to manipulate him to gain reassurance and support. These projections and defensive maneuvers were pointed out as they occurred and interpreted as his need to have an external figure who was irrationally endowed with great power approve of him in order for him to feel whole and meaningful. This sense of fulfillment, however, was labeled as basically maladaptive since (1) it served to repress further unacknowledged parts of the self which were basically healthy, (2) it continued a shaky and unrealistic manner of obtaining self-esteem, (3) it often caused other symptoms such as massive anxiety when he believed he had displeased the powerful others (these symptoms had, in fact, caused him to drop out of college), and (4) predisposed him to further depressive episodes. The most radical flaw in this manner of functioning was that he constantly needed inordinate reinforcement to prop up a fraudulent facade which had become harder and harder to maintain and which prevented enjoyment of many aspects of existence. The patient would remain unable to really enjoy his family or his lost aesthetic interests. He would never feel sufficiently free to be spontaneous or creative or to be confident to venture through life without a parent-surrogate in the guise of a partner. Finally, he would not be able to appreciate others in their own right, aside from their ability to support or threaten his facade.

As therapy progressed, this man protested that he was not improving any longer and, indeed, was losing the initial gains he had achieved in therapy. He complained of feeling more depressed, empty, and confused, and questioned the advisability of further treatment. At the same time, he was less driven by the need to succeed at all costs; he treated his wife in a more egalitarian manner; and he started spending time on pursuits that were simply enjoyable and not solely practical or self-aggrandizing.

His protestations of increased discomfort were acknowledged and related to his giving up old ways of obtaining esteem and of structuring his life, so that he would be expected to feel himself somewhat lost and unhappy. The older transactions, beliefs, and evaluations were stifling and ultimately unproductive but did offer transient gratifications and a sense of order. As such, the relinquishing of defenses is always accompanied by a sense of loss and sadness. However, the formerly disallowed aspects of the self were permitted to emerge and give new forms of satisfaction and meaning. These qualities which had been for so long hidden away in order to please and placate the original dominant other and his later substitutes were now beginning to be seen as valid and valuable. Therefore, as the old "shoulds" are challenged and the usual manipulative ways of obtaining affirmation are discarded, more appropriate sources of worth and pleasure arise spontaneously. As these new ventures solidify, they form the nucleus for a new system of estimating the self and others that will protect the individual from future episodes of illness.

During the process of accepting repressed aspects of the self and in relinquishing an unworkable facade, the patient began to dream of his mother and to recall his longing for her as well as his constant fears of being abandoned by her. She was first hospitalized when he was eight and had suffered prolonged bouts of physical and psychological illness before then.

He realized that his tyrannical hold on his wife served to reassure him that she would not abandon him as had his mother. He came to see his ambition, arrogance, and manipulations as supporting defenses, hiding fears, and resisting a valid apprehension of himself and others. His various distortions supported a specious grandiosity but also deprived him of true satisfaction and meaning. He was able to separate his financial difficulties from his sense of worth and eventually to feel confident about his business abilities without the necessity of a senior partner to supply a false sense of security. He also began to enjoy the process of his endeavors rather than only the result which had been intended to impress others or to defend against feelings of inferiority.

Each individual presents personally idiosyncratic distortions, fears, and resistances that relate to the different past histories that he has experienced. However, the basic theme is that of real assertion and gratification versus inhibition and guilt or fear. A dream of a depressed middle-aged woman accurately illustrates this core conflict. She dreamt of two women in a beautiful room. One woman was thin, sad, and unattractive, while the other was voluptuous and beautiful, with intricate tatoos all over her body. The voluptuous woman said, "Use my body and I'm happy," and went into a luxurious bathroom, exuding a great sexual aura. This woman then did something "disgusting," which could not be specified by the patient. Suddenly, the scene changed to a hospital room where the patient learns from a boy who had pursued her during her adolescence that her father is dying. The patient feels terribly guilty when the father dies in the dream. The boyfriend consoles her and says, "I've always loved you." Whereupon she woke up.

This dream expresses the conflict between the pleasure-seeking, sensuous "bad" self and the ascetic, self-depriving "good" self. Daring to become the gratified self results in abandonment and death of needed authority figures. It might be mentioned here that this woman's father had been dead for many years but his dictates lived on. The dream also indicates that she was beginning to realize that it is possible to find love outside the family orbit. This reference to adolescent suitors or to adolescent aspirations is not uncommon in depressives as they are well along the process of change. It would seem that the normal pressure for independence and individuation at adolescence had stirred up a desire to break out of the familial bonds but that this aspiration was routinely squelched by intimidation or guilt. These adolescent dreams for freedom often are revived years later as the patient reexperiences a new desire for personal liberation from internalized shoulds.

The obstacles to healthy change are not all internal, but often derive from others who have become comfortable with the depressive's prior mode of living. Significant others will react negatively to the new and, for them, alarming or irritating sense of self that emerges in the therapeutic process. This resistance to change may be found in parents, colleagues, or employers of depressives but is most strongly manifested in the spouses of older patients. These marital partners truly want the patient to be cured and certainly do not wish him to suffer the terrible episodes of clinical depression. At the same time, they do not want to give up the type of relationship which fostered recurrent episodes of melancholia. This interlocking reinforcement of depression between marital partners is seen so frequently that Forrest (1967) recommends starting marital couples therapy in addition to individual psychotherapy with married depressives at the time of initial referral for optimal results.

If therapy has proceeded well to this point, the depressive will exhibit a new integrity in his relationships and will show his feelings of anger as well as spontaneous enjoyment openly and no longer resort to devious manipulations that typified so many of his previous interpersonal transactions. Other characteristics that are indicative of more profound change include a sense of spontaneity and humor in behavior as well as a more philosophic attitude toward the failures and rejections that are inevitable in everyday life. Another positive sign is the relinquishing of a hypermoral view of all events so that everything that occurs has to be someone's fault. Most significant is the evolving ability to achieve genuine empathy with others and to cease viewing other people transferentially as bestowers of praise or rewards or dispensers of temptation and evil.

Finally, there should be a coming to terms with the ghosts of the past. Just as the patient begins to perceive others in his/her current life as necessarily imperfect beings who are struggling against their own difficulties to find a satisfactory mode of life, he or she should also understand that the significant others in his/her past had to deal with their own problems and shortcomings. Too often there is a rapid reversal from idealization of parents or teachers to bitter recriminations and unproductive anger. The psychological significance of the past is for one to understand those events and forces that helped shape the personality and not to serve as ammunition to cast at the important personages of childhood. Hopefully, this understanding will correct past distortions and help the individual from having to repeat errors in living that ultimately result in clinically significant illness.

EFFECTIVENESS OF LONG-TERM ANALYTIC TREATMENT

There are no large follow-up studies of depressed patients who received long-term analytic treatment reported in the literature nor are there controlled studies comparing this form of therapy against other types of treatment. Most psychoanalytic therapists, by the very nature of the intensity of their work, can see only a few patients at one time and so do not compile a sizable treatment sample. Also, these clinicians usually are not inclined to perform research studies. Finally, some believe that each patient engaged in analysis is unique with his or her own particular constellation of defenses, memories, fantasies, and life situation, so that any comparison between individuals would not be valid. Others may doubt that the true efficacy of therapy resulting in a different appreciation of one's inner self or the freeing of neurotic inhibitions could be measured accurately.

Nevertheless, two senior psychoanalysts with decades of experience in the therapy of severe depressives have reported their results, albeit not in a research design format. Jacobson (1971) reported follow-up status of severely depressed patients in an anecdotal manner without giving the size or selection of her sample. She found that severely depressed patients often did well for 20 or more years after analysis. They continued to experience episodes of dysphoria secondary to life stresses but these instances were much milder than those before treatment. She remarks that almost all showed marked improvement in their social functioning and were able to initiate satisfying relationships, raise families, and perform rewarding and productive work. Some returned for more treatment after a major change in their lives which she described as beneficial. The two types of depressives who did not do well at follow-up were those with chronic rather than episodic severe depression and those who experienced depression with suicidal ideation in childhood.

Arieti (1977) presented a more systematic report of a three- (or more) year follow-up of his psychoanalytic therapy of 12 severely depressed patients, all of whom were treated on an ambulatory basis. Of the 12 patients, 9 were female and 3 male; 10 had suicidal ideation. Arieti found that seven showed full recovery with no relapses, four showed marked improvement and one was classified as a treatment failure.

While these two reports are neither sufficiently large nor scientific, they do suggest that long-term analytic therapy can be a most effective treatment modality in both the amelioration of the acute episode, the attenuation of future episodes, and in improving social functioning. Obviously, one must carefully select appropriate patients for this type of treatment. Although the cost of analysis may seem unconscionable when there are quicker, cheaper ways to reduce symptoms, this form of treatment may well be more cost effective for certain patients in preventing a lifetime of repeated short-term treatments, loss of income due to illness, and extensive personal suffering.

References

Abraham, K. (1960a). Notes on the psychoanalytic treatment of manic depressive insanity and allied conditions. In *Selected papers on psychoanalysis*. New York: Basic Books. (Original work published 1911)

Abraham, K. (1969b). The first pregenital stage of libido. In *Selected papers on psychoanalysis*. New York: Basic Books. (Original work published 1916)

Abraham, K. (1960c). A short study of the development of libido. In *Selected papers on psychoanalysis*. New York: Basic Books. (Original work published 1924)

APA Commission on Psychotherapies (1982). *Psychotherapy research: Methodological and efficacy issues*. Washington, DC: American Psychiatric Association.

Arieti, S. (1962). The psychotherapeutic approach to depression. *American Journal of Psychiatry, 16,* 397–406.

Arieti, S. (1977). Psychotherapy of severe depression. *American Journal of Psychiatry, 134,* 864–868.

Arieti, S. (1978). Psychobiology of sadness. In S. Arieti and J. R. Bemporad (Eds.), *Severe and mild depression.* New York: Basic Books.

Arieti, S., & Bemporad, J. R. (1980). Psychological organization of depression. *American Journal of Psychiatry, 137,* 1360–1365.

Becker, E. (1964). *The revolution in psychiatry.* New York: Free Press.

Bemporad, J. R. (1971). New views on the psychodynamics of the depressive character. In S. Arieti (Ed.), *World biennial of psychiatry and psychotherapy* (Vol. 1), New York: Basic Books.

Bemporad, J. R. (1978). Critical review of major concepts of depression. In S. Arieti and J. R. Bemporad (Eds.), *Severe and mild depression.* New York: Basic Books.

Bibring, E. (1953). The mechanism of depression. In P. Greenacre (Ed.), *Affective disorders.* New York: International Universities Press.

Fenichel, O. (1945). *The psychoanalytic theory of neurosis.* New York: W. W. Norton.

Forrest, T. (1967). The combined use of marital and individual therapy in depression. *Contemporary Psychoanalysis, 6,* 76–83.

Freud, S. (1961a). Mourning and melancholia. In J. Strachey (Ed. and Trans.), *The standard edition of the complete psychological works of Sigmund Freud* (Vol. 14). London: Hogarth Press. (Original work published 1917)

Freud, S. (1961b). The ego and the id. In J. Strachey (Ed. and Trans.), *The standard edition of the complete psychological works of Sigmund Freud* (Vol. 19). London: Hogarth Press. (Original work published 1923)

Freud, S. (1961c). New introductory lectures on psychoanalysis. In J. Strachey (Ed. and Trans.), *The standard edition of the complete psychological works of Sigmund Freud,* (Vol. 22). London: Hogarth Press. (Original work published 1933)

Jacobon, E. (1971). *Depression.* New York: International Universities Press.

Jacobson, E. (1975). The psychoanalytic treatment of depressed patients. In E. J. Anthony & T. Benedek (Eds.), *Depression and human existence.* Boston: Little, Brown.

Kolb, L. C. (1956). Psychotherapeutic evolution and its implications. *Psychiatric Quarterly, 30,* 1–19.

Leff, M. L., Roatch, J. F., & Bunney, W. E. (1970). Environmental factors preceding the onset of severe depression. *Psychiatry, 33,* 293–311.

Levine, S. (1965). Some suggestions for treating the depressed patient. *Psychoanalytic Quarterly, 34,* 37–65.

Miller, A. (1979). Depression and grandiosity as related forms of narcissistic disturbances. *International Review of Psychoanalysis, 6,* 61–76.

Rado, S. (1956). The problem of melancholia. In *Collected papers* (Vol. 1). New York: Grune & Stratton. (Original work published 1927)

Sandler, J., & Joffee, W. G. (1965). Notes on childhood depression. *International Journal of Psychoanalysis, 46,* 80–96.

Spiegel, R. (1965). Communications with depressed patients. *Contemporary Psychoanalysis, 2,* 30–35.

Chapter 4

Brief Dynamic Psychotherapy for Depression

Saul E. Rosenberg

Kaiser Permanente Medical Center, South San Francisco; Langley Porter
Psychiatric Institute, University of California, San Francisco

All treatments for depression share the goal of alleviating depressive symptoms. In addition to providing symptom relief, the short-term dynamic therapist attempts to alter, as much as possible within a limited time, the patient's underlying neurotic conflicts, characterological defenses, maladaptive relationship patterns, and unconscious irrational ideas. The methods employed to achieve these ambitious aims include careful selection of patients, setting a time limit, and employing an active focused technique. The rapid pace and intensity of short-term dynamic therapy place special demands on both the patient and the therapist. The patient must have sufficient psychological resources and motivation to become quickly involved in the therapeutic process. The therapist must explore the patient's avoided and conflicted feelings in relation to a selected focus while maintaining the therapeutic alliance.

This chapter will review the principles of short-term dynamic therapy that are relevant to the treatment of unipolar, nonpsychotic depression. These principles are extrapolated from descriptions of case studies of depression and discussions about technique from the literature on the short-term psychotherapy of neurotic and personality disorders. There is little systematic discussion of the treatment of depression in the brief therapy literature since that literature emphasizes methods for understanding and interpreting the patient's underlying psychodynamic conflicts which are presumed to be the cause of depressive symptoms. This chapter will discuss those principles that are widely applied by many brief dynamic therapists as well as reviewing some of the distinctive elements in the treatment approaches of Malan (1976, 1979); Sifneos (1972, 1978); Davanloo (1978, 1980); Mann (1973) and Mann

Preparation of this manuscript was supported in part by a grant, MH34052, from the National Institute of Mental Health for a study conducted at Mount Zion Hospital and Medical Center, San Francisco.

I would like to thank Michael Hoyt, David Glotzer, Terese Schulman, and Bruce Johnston for their valuable suggestions and editorial assistance.

and Goldman (1982); Strupp and Binder (1984); and M. Horowitz, Marmar, Krupnick, Wilner, Kaltreider, and Wallerstein (1984). In addition, pertinent research and methodological issues will be covered. General historical reviews of the history of short-term dynamic therapy are beyond the scope of this chapter and can be found in Marmor (1979); M. Horowitz et al. (1984); Bauer and Kobos (1984); and Strupp and Binder (1984).

PRINCIPLES OF SELECTION

A diagnosis of depressive disorder does not offer sufficient information to determine whether a particular patient is suitable for brief dynamic therapy. The patient should meet the following three conditions to be considered an appropriate candidate for brief therapy: (1) there are no diagnostic contraindications; (2) there is an appropriate focus for short-term work; and (3) the patient has the required psychological resources.

Diagnostic Contraindications for Brief Dynamic Psychotherapy

Most brief dynamic therapists exclude depressed patients who are severely disturbed, for example, psychotic, manic-depressive, borderline, narcissistic, or impulsive. Patients are also excluded who are suicidal, alcoholic, or chronically depressed.

The Suicidal Patient. Suicidal ideation is not a contraindication for brief dynamic therapy. However, a patient who is acutely suicidal, agitated, has made suicidal plans, or has impaired reality testing is not a candidate for brief dynamic therapy. These patients may require crisis intervention, hospitalization, or supportive therapy rather than a psychodynamic approach (further discussion of the evaluation of suicide risk can be found in Chapter 18).

Alcohol and Drug Abuse Problems. For the majority of patients suffering from chronic alcoholism or substance abuse, specialized treatment programs are more appropriate than brief dynamic psychotherapy. These patients are often unable to deal with the anxiety-arousing aspects of an insight-oriented psychotherapy without resorting to substance abuse. However, if the patient is abusing alcohol or drugs as a response to a recent crisis and is able to stop the substance abuse at the beginning of treatment and meets the selection criteria, brief dynamic therapy may be appropriate. A trial therapy model can be used in which interpretive work can be initiated to determine if the patient has the requisite ego strength to make use of insight-oriented techniques. If the patient responds well to interpretive work without becoming intolerably anxious or depressed and without resuming alcohol or drug use, a full course of short-term dynamic psychotherapy can be considered. This kind of treatment is best conducted by therapists who have specialized knowledge and familiarity with the psychodynamics of drug abuse and the techniques of short-term dynamic psychotherapy (Skuja, 1982).

Chronic Depression.   When a patient has a history of chronic depression, brief therapy is usually inappropriate. Patients whose chronic depression is associated with severe and repeated trauma, deprivation, or abuse which have left the patient with a chronic feeling of emptiness and a constant need for emotional supplies from others presents a major obstacle to a brief therapy approach. Patients who have felt chronically deprived may have difficulty forming a rapid therapeutic alliance and resist termination.

Exclusion Criteria Employed by Different Approaches to Brief Therapy.   Each school of brief dynamic therapy emphasizes particular aspects of psychopathology which suggest a patient may be inappropriate for their type of treatment. Malan (1976) based his exclusion criteria on whether the patient's diagnosis or personality characteristics were likely to impede treatment, such as difficulty in motivating the patient, prolonged work to penetrate rigid defenses, getting stuck in deep-seated psychopathology, severe dependency, or intensification of psychotic or depressive disturbance. For patients with these characteristics, an inability to begin work quickly and difficulty in terminating would be likely complications. Malan (1979) quoted in Gustafson (1984), expressed one of his most important principles about patient selection as follows: "We should expect to revisit the worst states the patient has known in intensive psychotherapy. If these worst states of mind brought about dangerous actions by the patient in the past or if they required more support than the patient's present environment can provide, then their reactivation is too much of a risk and the patient cannot be offered brief therapy" (p. 941). Davanloo (personal communication, 1984) has emphasized that the depressed patient has to have the available energy to interact with the therapist; that is, if he or she cannot mobilize sufficient energy to get involved, he/she is more appropriate for another treatment. Sifneos (1978) distinguishes between those patients who have Oedipal problems in which predominantly positive feelings for both parents exist with conflicts about choosing between them (good prognosis) versus patients whose negative feelings predominate (poorer prognosis for Sifneos's short-term anxiety-provoking psychotherapy). Mann (1973) excludes patients who have vegetative signs of depression and no central issue or anxiety. (The potential for experiencing anxiety implies concern about a possible future, according to Mann, and thus is a better sign than no manifest anxiety). Mann also suggests that patients with a diagnosis of depressive character may pose considerable difficulties for time-limited psychotherapy. Strupp and Binder (1984) rule out the traditionally excluded patients with more severe psychopathology (e.g., the suicidal or psychotic patient), while treating patients with personality disorders who have depressive symptoms. Similarly, M. Horowitz et al. (1984) also rule out the more disturbed patients while treating depressed patients following major stressful life events who also may have underlying personality disorders.

An Appropriate Focus for Short-Term Dynamic Psychotherapy

Themes of unresolved grief, reactions to loss and disappointment, poor self-esteem, guilt, and problems with aggression are prominent issues for many depressed patients. In contrast to long-term psychodynamic therapy where many of these themes might be explored, in brief therapy one or two themes are selected and investigated in regard to significant past and current relationships and the relationship with the therapist.

Each of the major contributors to the brief dynamic therapy literature has a unique approach for selecting a focus. To illustrate the particular approaches of the various writers, examples of focal themes from the work of Mann, Strupp and Binder, and Malan will be described below.

According to Mann (1973), a central issue should be framed that captures the patient's "chronically endured pain." In presenting the central issue to the patient, the therapist, in Mann's approach, conveys a recognition of the patient's active coping maneuvers toward gaining satisfaction, describes the patient's feeling of failure and victimization and relates the patient's experiences to his or her lack of self-esteem. An example of a central issue from Mann and Goldman (1982) is the following: "You have always given of yourself to so many others, and yet you always feel that you are both undeserving and unrewarded" (p. 33).

Strupp and Binder (1984) provide the following example of a dynamic focus with a depressed patient that illustrates their approach to the focus in regard to the patient's maladaptive relationship pattern which gets evoked in the therapeutic relationship, particularly the patient's negative expectations about her "fate" in relationships:

> A married woman in her middle 30s sought psychotherapy to cope with periodic depressive episodes which she feared would become as incapacitating as those that had been endured by her father in his later years. Rather than make the depression per se the focus of the treatment, the therapist attempted to understand the interpersonal context within which it occurred. During the course of the initial interview the therapist learned that as a child the patient, the middle of three sisters, felt that her parents paid more attention to her sisters than to her. Finally, as he explored the patient's expectations of therapy and her immediate experience in the therapeutic relationship, the therapist helped her acknowledge that she could not imagine that anything she said could be of interest to the therapist. Her defense of "steeling" herself against feeling hurt consisted of an aloof and curt manner, which evoked an urge in the therapist to pursue "facts" instead of attending to the patient's emotional experience. Although the therapist might have formulated a dynamic hypothesis that this woman's passive resignation was a reaction-formation against aggressive competitive feelings, the initial therapeutic focus consisted of exploring the expectation that her feelings and needs were of no interest to anyone.[1]

---

[1] Quotation from pre-publication manuscript deleted from published book.

In Malan's approach, the focus provides the patient with a connection between a current conflict and one in childhood. A case description from Malan (1976) called "the Almoner" (someone who dispenses alms) illustrates this point. The patient was a 22-year-old single girl who complained of mild depressive symptoms including early morning awakening, poor self-esteem, social inhibition, and difficulties over aggression. Her entrance into therapy was precipitated by an incident at work where a man of whom she was fond threw something at her. It was noted that her interactional style was to maintain a smiling and proper attitude and to be "nice" as a defense against aggressive feelings. Her history revealed that she admired her father but felt he was distant and was closer to her mother whom she idealized. Among the themes revealed by projective psychological testing were her wish to have a man but her fear that a woman would be jealous, and anger toward a father figure for not devoting himself exclusively to her. The therapist's focus was on her feeling of anger at her parents when they were close and she felt excluded and feared that her mother would be angry if she had her own man. An additional formulation was that she felt guilty about her angry feelings toward both parents and defended against her aggressive feelings by idealization of them.

These examples of focal themes from Strupp and Binder (1984) and Malan (1976) illustrate how dynamic therapists investigate depressive symptoms within the context of recurrent maladaptive interpersonal patterns. To develop an understanding of this context the evaluator assesses the patient's presenting problem, history, and interactional style in the evaluation interview which will be discussed below.

The Selection Interview.   To determine if there is a focus for brief dynamic psychotherapy, brief dynamic therapists gather information from the patient in four areas: (*a*) the presenting complaint, (*b*) the precipitants of the depressive episode, (*c*) the history, and (*d*) reaction to trial interpretations or trial therapy.

Clarifying the Presenting Complaint.   A patient's statement about feeling "depressed" or "guilty" is too vague and incomplete for dynamic therapy. Further questioning is carried out to understand how, when, and with whom a patient experiences feelings of depression or guilt. In addition to clarifying the major presenting problem, the dynamic therapist elicits all of the patient's other problems and disturbances. After the presenting problem is clarified, the interviewer gathers further evidence from the precipitating stress and the history to construct a psychodynamic formulation to account for a patient's symptoms and complaints.

Investigating the Precipitating Stress.   A clear precipitating stress is often a good prognostic sign for brief therapy, particularly if the patient's previous adjustment was good. A patient in acute distress or crisis may be highly motivated to make a change in his or her life. The anxiety or depression associated with a crisis (provided it is not too severe) can be a powerful motivator for the often difficult work of self-scrutiny. However, while a clear precipitant is often a good prognostic sign for brief therapy, patients without a clear precipitant may also be good candidates. For some patients the stimulus for depression is not a clear external event but an internal, emotional connection between some current event and one from the past—a connection that becomes clearer in the process of assessment for dynamic therapy.

The precipitants for the most recent depressive episode provide information about the patient's areas of psychological vulnerability. The most frequent precipitants for depression are serious life events such as a loss (M. Horowitz et al., 1984), or any change or disappointment that affects the patient's self-esteem.

The dynamic therapist is also interested in any recent life changes including events that would be conventionally viewed as positive, such as a job promotion or the advent of a new relationship. For many depressed patients, successes can have a paradoxical effect—the patient feels guilty and undeserving rather than proud of an accomplishment.

History of Depression and Childhood Memories. Inquiring about childhood family relationships, traumas, and losses provides crucial information for developing a dynamic focus. Since the focus is based on recurrent problems or patterns, identifying the roots of a current problem in the past offers valuable information. It is useful to inquire about a history of depression in family members. From a psychodynamic persepective, the patient may be identifying unconsciously with depressed parents. Of course, depression in family members may suggest biological factors in addition to psychological ones (see Chapter 25).

Trial Interpretation and Trial Therapy. One of the hallmarks of brief dynamic therapy is the rapid uncovering of painful and conflicted feelings. Since the awareness of painful ideas and feelings is often strenuously defended against, the brief dynamic therapist must determine if the patient can tolerate relinquishing certain defenses without developing intolerable anxiety or decompensating. In addition, the brief therapist must determine if the patient can benefit from an insight-oriented approach. For many patients, determining suitability from the history is difficult and the best method is to offer a trial interpretation around the focal theme and observe the patient's response. Malan advocates making trial interpretations to test how psychologically-minded the patient is. Two studies of dynamic therapy have suggested that motivation and psychological mindedness may increase as a result of successful early interventions (Malan, 1976, Kernberg et al., 1972). The patient's response to trial interpretations is a valuable prognostic sign; if the rapport is deepened, defensiveness reduced, and new material obtained, the prognosis for a favorable response to brief therapy is enhanced. On the other hand, if the patient becomes more anxious, constricted, and withdrawn the prognosis for brief therapy is poorer.

The brief therapist is also alert to the fact that the patient's response to a single interpretation, particularly one formed with little information about the patient, is often inadequate. In those cases, a period of trial therapy is appropriate. Davanloo (1980) has advocated a trial therapy approach to the initial interview which is generally conducted in one or two hours but may last up to three to four hours with highly resistant patients. Gustafson (1984) has also advocated a trial therapy as one of the best indicators of the patient's suitability for brief dynamic therapy.

The Patient's Psychological Resources

Estimating the patient's motivation and interpersonal capacity while he or she is deeply depressed is a difficult undertaking. It may not be possible to forecast accurately how a patient with little energy for interpersonal relationships would be able to relate if more energy were available. The interviewer must forecast whether the patient has the *potential* to develop a therapeutic alliance. This prediction is difficult since in part it depends on the patient's character and in part depends upon how the qualities and interventions of the particular therapist match the personality style of the patient (Strupp, 1980a).

Sifneos conducts a systematic evaluation in which patients must fulfill a number of criteria to be considered suitable candidates. The patient must have a circumscribed problem (and be able to set one as a priority), a history of a good relationship in early life (i.e., reciprocating and nonexploitive), a good capacity to express feelings in the interview, and adequate motivation for change. The patient's motivation for change is scrutinized particularly closely. Motivation includes psychological-mindedness, honesty, introspectiveness, willingness to explore oneself, realistic expectations of therapy, and willingness to make some sacrifice in the therapy arrangements.

The more the patient has shown evidence of reciprocal relationships, the give-and-take quality emphasized by Sifneos, the better. In addition to Sifneos's criteria, the more a patient shows a capacity for intimacy, trust, and involvement with others, the more favorable the prognosis; the more distant and exploitive of others, the worse the prognosis for brief therapy. This criteria should not be taken to imply that the patient has to have exemplary interpersonal skills as a requirement for entering brief therapy. Rather, the key issue is whether the patient's interpersonal capacities are sufficient to allow him/her to form a relationship with the therapist that facilitates change.

PRINCIPLES OF BRIEF DYNAMIC PSYCHOTHERAPY FOR DEPRESSION

This section will provide an overview of the therapeutic strategies and issues that are most pertinent to the treatment of depression. The emphasis placed on the following techniques and themes varies according to the schools of brief dynamic therapy: (1) establishing a time limit; (2) the focus; (3) therapist activity; (4) transference; (5) defense and resistance; (6) termination; (7) themes of loss and grief; (8) working with Oedipal themes; (9) adjusting technique to fit the personality style of the patient; (10) guilt; (11) adjunctive antidepressant medication.

Establishing a Time Limit

Brief therapy begins with the idea that there is a limited period of time in which to accomplish the therapeutic work. It is this awareness of a deadline—even more than the number of sessions—that provides the structure for brief treatment. The number of sessions, usually varying from 12–25 and up to 40, is somewhat arbitrary. There is no consensus about how a time limit is set or even if an exact number of sessions is specified (Budman & Gurman, 1983). The critical distinction is between the time-limited arrangement of brief therapy compared with the open-ended sense of "timelessness" in psychoanalytic psychotherapy. When there is a deadline, both patient and therapist have a powerful motivation to complete the work in the allotted time (Appelbaum, 1975).

Maintaining and Elaborating a Focus

During the evaluation, or trial therapy, the therapist establishes a therapeutic focus based on his initial understanding of the patient's current disturbance and how it is related to earlier conflicts. The focus is not based on symptoms but on the underlying conflicts, characteristic ways the patient avoids facing painful feelings and the particular relationship patterns that are reenacted. At the end of the evaluation phase the therapist conveys all or part of the focus to the patient. The focus is conveyed in a manner which helps the patient feel that his or her conflictual position is understandable given a particular background or history. It is valuable to get across to the depressed patient that he or she is not to blame for the problem and that the task of the therapy is to understand how the patient is predisposed to act automatically or unconsciously in self-defeating ways.

After the evaluation period the therapist elaborates on this focus while not allowing the exploration to become too diffuse. The therapist responds in Malan's phrase with "selective attention" and "selective neglect." Areas not related to the focus are avoided. For example, if the focus is based on conflicts over competitiveness in a triangular situation, then issues around dependency in dyadic relationships are ignored.

In determining a focus, it is important to note that it is a construction by the clinician to give meaning to the patient's problem in terms of the therapist's theory and technique. There is more than one way to render the patterns of a patient's life meaningful, and interpretive styles differ from one brief therapist to another. The therapist's task is to establish a focus that the therapist and patient can work on productively. Brief therapists vary with regard to how much they value providing the patient with a cognitive explanation. However, the focus must be more than an intellectual conception; the patient should be able to resonate emotionally with the theme.

Ordinarily, a formulation based on inferences about unconscious processes would not be offered until sufficient evidence had been gathered from the patient. Through preparatory work on the patient's resistances and defenses, the way is prepared for deep interpretive work. The therapist's initial inferences about wishes that are warded off and strongly defended against are not presented directly to the patient (although a derivative form might be suitable) until sufficient preliminary work has been done. Interpretations about deep conflicts are offered tentatively, since premature interpretations can strengthen the patient's defensiveness and render subsequent interpretative work more difficult. The brief therapists differ with regard to their emphasis on the patient's avoidance of primitive aggressive and sexual impulses. Mann, Strupp, and Horowitz place less emphasis on the patient's impulses than Sifneos, Davanloo, and Malan.

For example, a patient who was depressed following the death of a loved one felt guilty that he had not done enough for that person while he was alive. This therapeutic issue might be handled differently depending on whether or not a confrontational approach was adopted. The less confrontational approaches might interpret mixed feelings of love and hate toward the deceased. In the less confrontational approach, first the therapeutic alliance has to be established, then evidence is gathered, and the patient's ability to tolerate painful insights tested. In the first interview the patient might be told that the focus of the therapy will be to explore the meanings of the loss of the loved one and his guilty (and by implication excessive) feelings of responsibility for the person's death. In such an interpretation, the therapist would be alleviating the patient's tendency toward harsh self-criticism while avoiding direct interpretation of hostile impulses until work on defenses against aggression was done. As the therapy unfolds the therapist might work more on the patient's defensive style of avoiding the fearful consequences of expressing anger by exploring such instances in the patient's current life, his past, and in the transference prior to making any interpretations about murderous impulses. Therapists who emphasize the understanding of maladaptive interpersonal patterns (cf., Strupp & Binder, 1984) would not emphasize interpretations of conflictual impulses but focus on the manifestation of the patient's problems in the therapeutic relationship. On the other hand, therapists who use a more confrontational approach, such as Davanloo, might interpret defenses against the awareness of feelings of murderous rage.

Sometimes the therapist's understanding of the patient's problem changes radically after treatment has begun. It is sobering to note that even the most exhaustive diagnostic evaluations conducted in the Menninger Psychotherapy Research Project (Wallerstein, in press) failed to discover major areas of patient's psychopathology which only came to light after psychotherapy was long under way. While the original focus is not casually dismissed, the difficulties of psychodynamic diagnosis require some flexibility on the part of the therapist. Sometimes the focus is modified and the plan for and duration of therapy altered if the original focus proves incorrect or unworkable.

The Therapist Adopts an Active Role

Brief dynamic therapists are active from early sessions in guiding the treatment, and interpreting defenses, resistance, and transference. This stance is in contrast to traditional psychoanalytic therapy in which the psychoanalyst does not want to interfere with the patient's free associations by being too active. Too much activity might interfere with the development of a transference neurosis which is considered the best vehicle for understanding the patient's infantile neurosis. In contrast, the brief dynamic therapist limits free association, actively guides the patient and wants to avoid the development of a regressive transference neurosis.

Analysis of Transference

The early and repeated interpretation of manifestations of the patient's problem in the therapeutic relationship is frequently used in brief dynamic therapy. Brief dynamic therapists address negative feelings evoked in the transference directly rather than ignore or reflect them onto another current figure in the patient's life. Tranference interpretations provide an opportunity for the patient to realize how he or she brings maladaptive interpersonal predispositions into relationships including that with the therapist. Old patterns, when evoked and analyzed in the immediate therapeutic relationship, can provide a powerful affective learning experience. Malan (1976) has advocated linking conflictual feelings toward the patient's parents with those felt toward the therapist as a particularly powerful intervention.

Analysis of Defense and Resistance

Most brief therapists adhere to the psychoanalytic concept of interpreting defenses prior to identifying the ideas that the patient is avoiding. This principle is relevant for working with many depressed patients who avoid aggressive feelings. A patient's characterological defenses, for example, passive compliance, excessive politeness, or obsessional rumination, may pose a barrier to the direct experience of feelings.

Davanloo has developed a confrontational technique for dealing with the patient's defenses and resistance. The first step is clarifying the patient's feelings. At the beginning of therapy, the patient is often vague, equivocal, and noncommittal in his/her language. Intellectual descriptions of feelings and problems are common. Davanloo does not accept vague or intellectualized answers to his questions about how the patient feels. If the patient replies he/she feels "angry" or "guilty," Davanloo questions the patient about how the patient *experiences* that feeling. Abstract descriptions are not accepted; rather Davanloo is attempting to get the patient to use more concrete, visceral language. Many times Davanloo will get the patient to recreate a scene by evoking visual images and descriptions. During this period, the patient may be confused about what the therapist wants. The patient may try to comply with what is perceived as the therapist's demand only to find that the therapist does not want compliance and submission; rather the therapist wants the patient to become aware of how distant he or she is from true feelings and what the cost has been. Davanloo may also point out that if the patient persists in being so vague he or she will not discover anything about themselves and the therapy will be useless. During the initial phase in such a treatment, Davanloo may seem contentious and the therapeutic climate often appears tense or strained leading to a perception by some observers that Davanloo is badgering the patient. However, Davanloo conducts his interviews in a way that conveys to the patient that he is opposing their defenses—not them. According to Davanloo, the patients, although they may get angry, actually feel relieved that the therapist is trying to break through the wall that they erect to keep themselves distant from their feelings and other people.

Although Davanloo's technique is often viewed as synonomous with his noted ability to break down defensive barriers to relatedness, that is only one part of this technique. Moreover, it is not always the central therapeutic strategy; for patients who are highly motivated and not highly defensive, Davanloo does not relentlessly pursue their resistances. With the more highly motivated patients, he gets directly to the therapeutic work of reconstruction of the patient's feelings in relation to significant childhood figures.

Case Example of Davanloo's Technique.   The following vignette illustrates Davanloo's (1980) technique with a 29-year-old female teacher who presented with problems of depression, anxiety, job difficulties and interpersonal relationship difficulties with men. In this sample of an early session, the therapist focuses on the patient's passivity outside and within the therapeutic relationship:

> **Patient:** Uh. In terms of the relationship. But she (mother) is passive, and she is not. There were situations where she knew what she wanted and wasn't passive.
>
> **Therapist:** Going back to yourself, do you see yourself as a passive person?
>
> **Patient:** Yeah.
>
> **Therapist:** You do . . .
>
> **Patient:** In certain situations where I don't feel . . . when I get involved with a man . . . I find I tend to take a passive role, and I don't like that.
>
> **Therapist:** What specifically do you mean by not liking it?
>
> **Patient:** I feel upset inside.
>
> **Therapist:** What is that you experience when you say "upset?"
>
> **Patient:** Perhaps irritated . . . something like that . . .
>
> **Therapist:** But you say "perhaps" . . . Is it that you experience irritation and anger, or isn't it?
>
> **Patient:** Ummm. Yeah. Yeah . . . . I do.
>
> **Therapist:** You say you take a passive role in relationship to men. Are you doing that here with me?
>
> **Patient:** I would say so.

Therapist: You "would" say so, but still you are not committing yourself.

Patient: [*Long, awkward pause*]: Well . . . I don't . . . you see, I don't know how to . . . uh . . . I don't know about the situation . . . you know . . . I am here, and I am a passive recipient or a passive participant. I am not passive, really. I am active; I am participating, but I am . . .

Therapist: Are you participating?

Patient: Well, sure.

Therapist: Um-hmm. To what extent?

Patient: [*pause*]: I am answering your questions.

Therapist: What comes to my mind is, if I don't question you, what do you think would happen here?

Patient: Well . . . I might . . . I might start to tell . . . I might start something which would indicate . . . would tell you where I am going. It might be very intellectual, though, because I don't really know . . . I don't really understand the source of my depression.

Therapist: Uh-hum. In relationship with me then you are passive; and it is the same with all men. [*Patient is silent, pause*].

Therapist: How do you feel when I indicate to you that you are passive?

Patient: I don't like it [*The patient is laughing, but it is quite evident that she is irritated.*]

Therapist: But you are smiling.

Patient: I know. Well . . . maybe that is my way of expressing my irritation.

Therapist: Then you are irritated?

Patient: A little bit . . . yeah . . .

Therapist: A little bit?

Patient: Actually, quite a bit.

Therapist: Let's look at what happened here. I brought to your attention your passivity, your noninvolvement. You got irritated and angry with me, and the way you dealt with your irritation was by smiling (p. 48).[2]

The therapist then goes on to explore, after the patient's angry feelings toward him have been clarified, whether their relationship reminds her of any other situations or relationships. This sample of Davanloo's approach illustrates how he confronts a passive patient with her vague and noncommital use of language. The vignette also illustrates that the therapist is not a neutral object for the patient to project her fantasies onto. Rather the therapist is a highly active participant confronting the patient at all points.

Working through Feelings about Termination

Since a time limit has been specified in advance, termination is always an issue. How much of an issue depends upon the patient's psychodynamics and the particular school of treatment. Some exponents of brief therapy (Mann,

---

[2] Reprinted by permission of the publisher from SHORT-TERM DYNAMIC PSYCHOTHER-APY by Habib Davanloo (ed.) Copyright 1980, Jason Aronson, New York.

1973; Mann & Goldman, 1982) make dealing with termination a major theme for the whole therapy. For those depressed patients who have suffered multiple losses or who have a posttraumatic stress disorder, the loss of the therapist may be another major disappointment which should be worked through well in advance (M. Horowitz, 1976; Hoyt, 1979).

For Mann (1973) the termination phase is distinguished by the patient's unconscious attempt to separate without facing the true ambivalence that existed in past separations or currently with the therapist. At the end of therapy, Mann will firmly insist that the time is up and if necessary he will reassure the patient that he believes the patient can manage without the therapist.

Working with Themes of Loss and Grief

Frequent themes in working with depressed patients are their reactions to loss and grief. Malan (1979), in describing technical issues of working with a patient who has suffered a loss, points out the importance of helping the patient to face the grief directly. For patients whose loss has occurred long before treatment, the therapist must determine if the patient has sufficient motivation and ego strength to face the painful feelings. Malan suggests that grief often goes unexpressed because the patient feels angry and resentful toward the lost person around whom feelings of guilt arise. According to Malan, these ambivalent feelings about a lost person are a very common dynamic in depression.

Example of Malan's Technique.   This example of Malan's (1978) treatment of a young depressed woman illustrates his technique of interpreting the patient's resistance to facing her grief, including how she uses the transference as a resistance.

Patient: I feel better than I did on Friday.

Therapist: I imagined you might, but it was an important session on Friday. It seemed to indicate that you'd been hiding from yourself—no, to put it another way, that you had been making out to yourself that you were much better than you were.

Patient: I felt much better, and I thought, now I'll start getting better and better. It's the whole business of thinking that it's just time. I seemed to be meeting more people in the last six weeks, but it seems to be so unsatisfying—that's what I felt. And this isn't right. I'm sort of feeling that with people I thought were beyond superficial, it's not very satisfying with them either. I guess I was struck when you said you thought I hadn't really realized or been sad about leaving America, and I thought about that quite a bit, and I think there's a lot there, but somehow I seem to feel, although I used to get depressed and have bad times—but I didn't think it was like this; this bad.

Therapist: Before you left America?

Patient: Yes, when I was there. It's hard to say because I was changing all the time. But I couldn't understand it last week when I felt so bad, just as much as, as I've said, after Simon, and after W———, which were hard times, and you know, I hadn't lost anyone then, last week, so I didn't understand why I felt so bad. I just felt like I'd lost everything. I just didn't care much. I felt bad for the next day or two, and then J_____ called me, and I wasn't tearful any more after that, and I haven't been since. I saw him, and it went well.

Therapist: It sounded to me, thinking about it afterward, as if you might be using each new relationship, including the one with J_____ and with me, and in the sense of putting so much hope in them, you forgot about the past sadness, you see, as if you're using the new relationships as a defense against facing the sadnesses which hadn't yet been dealt with.

Patient: Yes, that's what you said, and I thought a lot about that. I think that might be right (p. 455).[3]

Themes of loss and grief have traditionally been a major topic for brief dynamic psychotherapy. M. Horowitz et al. (1984) have stressed the importance of assisting the bereaved patient to affectively reexperience the loss and to complete the grief process by dealing with the meanings of the loss in terms of the patient's self and other object representations.

Working with Oedipal Themes in Depressed Patients

Sifneos selects patients who have unresolved conflicts originating in Oedipal or triangular situations. The core of the Oedipal conflict is the competitive struggle with a parent of the same sex for the love and affection of the opposite sex parent. By selecting appropriate patients for his technique Sifneos is able to interpret this Oedipal struggle directly without much prior defense analysis. He avoids pre-Oedipal issues, for example, unresolved dependency issues arising from the early mother-infant dyad, and interprets the patient's conflicts and feelings of loss in terms of the Oedipal situation.

Example of Sifneos's Technique. The patient described in the vignette below is a young female student who complained of depression and difficulties in her relationships. The following is an excerpt from an evaluation interview (Sifneos, 1978).

Patient: [describing first relationship at 17]: We dated for a few years. I . . . I just decided that I was too close, I guess. I didn't want to go out with anybody. I felt I was too young to be involved with one person, which really wasn't that good for him. But that tends to be my pattern. I do that with everybody I go out with. I make sure I get to the point where I know they really love me and then I just don't want them any more, which is really negative because I probably hurt a lot of people by doing that.

Therapist: Which is a little bit like it was with your father, isn't it?

Patient: Yeah, I guess so.

---

[3] Reprinted by permission of the publisher from BASIC PRINCIPLES AND TECHNIQUES IN SHORT-TERM DYNAMIC PSYCHOTHERAPY by Habib Davanloo (ed.) Copyright 1978, Spectrum Publications, Inc., Jamaica, New York.

Therapist: Is that really the prototype? And then there is the pattern that repeats itself. Have you thought of it that way?

Patient: No, I've never thought of it in terms of my father, but I've thought of it in terms of my boyfriends.

Therapist: You see, when you said that you know that your father loved you and he wants to express himself physically but that there is something that you find repugnant and you withdraw then and you are caught in this situation, I have a little bit of feeling that the same thing happens with that boy, that you know he loves you and you are very close to him, but somehow it is you who wants to put a distance between you (p. 155).[4]

The above vignette illustrates the use of an Oedipal focus in understanding a patient's presenting problem of difficulties in current relationships. Sifneos draws a parallel between her anxious withdrawal from her father's physical affection and her withdrawal from boys she dates.

Adjusting Technique to Suit the Personality Style of the Depressed Patient

In therapies of short duration the patient's personality style must be effectively countered with the appropriate interpretive and empathic stance. M. Horowitz et al. (1984) have provided specific guidelines for treating patients with different personality styles. For example, patients with an hysterical personality style may have magical expectations of having all past injustices and hurts remedied by the therapist. The therapist, while responding empathically, has to give no indication that gratification of all needs is to be forthcoming.

The compulsive patient may be helped by the therapist's consistent focus on affectively laden ideas rather than on intellectualized discussions which do not allow the patient to complete the mourning process. The therapist helps the patient to avoid shifting from an idea to avoid pain and to stay with an idea long enough to master the problem.

Patients with a narcissistic style may vacillate between expecting to be admired and expecting to be criticized and made to feel ashamed. These patients require extreme tact so as to not injure further their precarious self-esteem while maintaining a realistic sense of themselves and the therapist.

Themes of Guilt

Many psychoanalytic writers have stressed the role of guilt in depressive disorders (Mendelson, 1974). Recently, Weiss and Sampson (1984) have discussed how feelings of guilt impede patients from pursuing their goals. Guilt can take many different forms: guilt about being independent and separate from a parent, guilt about success, guilt about surpassing a parent or

---

[4] Reprinted by permission of the publisher from BASIC PRINCIPLES AND TECHNIQUES IN SHORT-TERM DYNAMIC PSYCHOTHERAPY by Habib Davanloo (ed.) Copyright 1978, Spectrum Publications, Inc., Jamaica, New York.

sibling, to name just a few. Weiss and Sampson (1984) have emphasized the role of unconscious irrational ideas of guilt which arise in early childhood interactions with parents. For example, the patient may believe that if he or she acts too independent the parent will feel not needed and be terribly hurt. According to their theory, the patient will "test" these beliefs in his or her relationship with the therapist to see if the beliefs will be disconfirmed. For example, the patient might behave in an independent manner to see if the therapist, like the patient's parent, acts hurt. If the therapist does not act threatened by the patient's independence, the therapist "passes the test" and the patient's irrational belief that others will be hurt by his/her independence will be disconfirmed and the patient will feel emboldened to pursue his/her goals. In contrast, if the therapist "fails the test" and acts hurt by the patient's independence the patient's pathogenic belief will be confirmed and the patient is likely to become more anxious and constricted.

The Use of Adjunctive Antidepressant Medication

From the paucity of references to antidepressant medication in the writings of the brief dynamic therapists, it can be inferred that medication has played a relatively minor role. Most brief dynamic therapists prefer to treat the patients most suitable for brief therapy (that is, patients with reactive depression or with neurotic depression [DSM-III Dysthymic Disorder]) without medication. Lowry (1980) has provided a clinical classification in which he recommends medication for bipolar affective disorder and unipolar depressive disorders. Lowry recommends brief psychotherapy for neurotic and reactive depression, and long-term treatment for chronic, intermittent depressions with personality disorders. Weissman (1979) suggests from research evidence that pharmacotherapy is most effective on sleep disturbance and appetite loss and psychotherapy is most effective for treating suicidal feelings, guilt, loss, and social and interpersonal problems. A comparative efficacy study of the type done on interpersonal therapy with and without medication (Weissman, Klerman, Prusoff, Sholomskas, & Padian, 1981) which would yield more definitive guidelines but has not yet been conducted for dynamic psychotherapy (see Chapters 5, 9, and 10).

RESEARCH

Research in brief dynamic psychotherapy for depression has been hindered by the same problems of lack of specificity of patient, therapist, and interactional variables that affects much of the research on psychodynamic therapy. In addition, researchers have generally not addressed the issue of the effectiveness of brief dynamic therapy for homogeneous groups of patients, including depressed patients, for two reasons: (1) depression is treated as a symptom of an underlying disorder; and (2) patients are selected according to criteria for brief dynamic psychotherapy rather than on diagnostic grounds. In this section, I will address three major methodological problems and review empirical research on brief dynamic treatment of depression. For broader reviews of research on brief therapy, see Butcher and Koss (1978).

Methodological Problems

I will focus on three major methodological problems: (1) the therapeutic techniques psychodynamic psychotherapists employ have not been clearly specified; (2) descriptive diagnostic systems such as *DSM-III* are limited as tools for categorizing patients for dynamic therapy; (3) the diagnostic concepts of greatest use to dynamic clinicians have been difficult to operationalize.

The Therapeutic Techniques Psychodynamic Psychotherapists Employ Have Not Been Clearly Specified.   As Orlinsky and Howard (1978) have pointed out, therapists' in-session behavior does not always reflect their professed orientation. Descriptions of therapist technique have been so global and vague that the relationship between therapist interventions and the mechanisms of therapeutic change is obscure (Parloff, Waskow, & Wolfe, 1978).

It has proved difficult to specify whether a therapist is practicing a particular technique and how skillfully it is performed. Previous studies have not often distinguished between the therapist's adherence to a technique on the one hand and its effect on the patient on the other (Schaffer, 1983). One solution to the problem of lack of specificity in describing therapist technique is a treatment manual such as Strupp and Binder (1984) have developed. By defining guidelines for practice, and using rating scales to measure adherence to those guidelines, researchers have a powerful methodology for describing whether a particular technique is being practiced. In addition to treatment manuals, which are intended to cover a heterogeneous group of patients, addendums or new manuals may need to be written to cover a specific diagnostic group such as depression.

Descriptive Diagnostic Systems Such as DSM-III Are Limited as Tools for Categorizing Patients for Dynamic Therapy.   Patients with the same *DSM-III* diagnosis are often dissimilar in ways that are crucial for planning dynamic psychotherapy. For example, Karasu and Skodol (1980) described three patients with the same *DSM-III* diagnosis who differ in their original and present conflicts, life histories, relations with others, defenses and coping styles, needs, weaknesses, and assets. They suggest that psychodynamic criteria should be made clearer, more precise, and reliable to serve as an additional axis for *DSM-III* diagnoses. L. Horowitz, Weckler, and Doren (1983) have described two patients who were equally depressed but who had very different interpersonal problems and underlying psychopathology which necessitated very different kinds of treatment. Descriptive criteria should be supplemented by measures of dynamic conflicts, personality, and interpersonal functioning which are relevant to treatment planning.

There is a growing consensus that the patient's personality style (which is only partially captured by *DSM-III* Axis 2 personality disorders) is a crucial determinant of treatment response. Strupp (1980a, 1980b) has clearly illustrated this point in two papers that describe a brief treatment technique applied by the same therapist to two patients who were both anxious, depressed, and socially withdrawn but whose personalities differed. One patient was highly negativistic, hostile, and resistant; it was difficult to achieve a therapeutic alliance and the outcome was poor. The other patient enjoyed the work of self-scrutiny and felt positive about the therapy process; a smooth working relationship ensued and the outcome was excellent. If the results from these two patients were averaged in a group statistical design, it might appear that the technique had no effect when, in fact, the technique had important differential effects that depended, apparently, upon the personality structure of the particular client.

The Diagnostic Concepts of Greatest Use to Dynamic Clinicians Have Been Difficult to Operationalize. The measurement of patients' underlying conflicts, defensive styles, maladaptive relationship patterns, and transference potentials are a top priority for future research. Since these concepts have not been readily operationalizable, previous comparative studies have contrasted dynamic with other therapies on primarily symptomatic or global measures leading to the conclusion that the results on symptom criteria were the same (cf., Luborsky, Singer, & Luborsky, 1975; Smith, Glass, & Miller, 1980). However, as Parloff (1984) points out, it is premature to view all therapies as producing similar results when most comparative studies have not included measures that would be sensitive to psychodynamic or characterological change.

Studies of the Efficacy of Brief Dynamic Therapy for Depression

In a previous review, Strupp, Sandell, Waterhouse, O'Malley, and Anderson (1982) found very little research specifically on the brief dynamic therapy of depression. Strupp et al. (1982) pointed out an additional problem—that although the therapists were experienced in psychoanalytic psychotherapy they were not generally expert in short-term dynamic techniques.

Two comparative studies have been conducted comparing brief psychotherapy to other modalities for depressed patients. McLean and Hakstian (1979) compared short-term therapy based on the work of Marmor (1973, 1975) and Wolberg (1967) to behavior therapy, drug therapy, and relaxation therapy. In the dynamic therapy, the goals were amelioration of presenting symptomatic complaints and returning the patient to his/her previous equilibrium. The techniques were catharsis, insight, reality testing, support, advice, and conjoint marital therapy for more than a third of the cases. The therapists were experienced and working with a treatment they preferred. Surprisingly, the brief therapy was the least effective of all the treatments at termination and follow-up evaluation periods. The brief treatment generally did even worse than a muscle relaxation treatment. How can this poor showing for brief therapy be accounted for? There are several reasons for caution in interpreting the results of this study: (1) no specific selection criteria for brief dynamic therapy were employed; (2) in the brief psychotherapy, a wide variety of techniques both dynamic and nondynamic were employed (suggestion and advice, conjoint marital interviews); and (3) the training of the therapists in specialized techniques of brief therapy was not reported.

A study by Bellack, Hersen, and Himmelhoch (1981) compared four treatments including brief dynamic psychotherapy for unipolar (nonpsychotic) depression. The brief dynamic psychotherapy was described as 12 sessions of individual psychotherapy with a pill placebo. Therapists had at least five years of experience and were committed to the treatment they employed. Therapists practiced their usual techniques with no constraints. The approach was described as time-limited dynamic therapy focused primarily on the patient's current concerns rather than an investigation of deep-seated conflicts.

All of the four treatments, including dynamic psychotherapy, were effective in producing significant change in distress, symptoms, and social functioning. The psychotherapy and social skills training were as effective as antidepressant medication (amitriptyline) in producing improvement on symptoms. In conclusion: (1) the brief dynamic therapy treatment appeared to be effective; (2) since the study was conducted before treatment manuals for brief therapy were available it is not known what the specific treatment interventions were; (3) the description of the therapy as focused on current problems rather than in-depth psychodynamic exploration means that the technique was fundamentally different than that advocated by all of the brief dynamic therapists surveyed in this chapter; and (4) it is not known whether the therapists had specialized training in brief treatment techniques.

A recent process-outcome study (M. Horowitz, Marmar, Weiss, DeWitt, & Rosenbaum, 1984) conducted on a sample of bereaved patients overcomes some of the methodological problems that have limited previous studies. Most of the patients studied had elevated scores on the depression subscale of the Symptom Checklist 90 (SCL90-R). The majority of the diagnoses were adjustment disorder, posttraumatic stress disorder and major depressive episode. The results, therefore, cannot be understood as a basis for generalizing about depressed patients as a group; however, they provide the best available evidence about the relationship between patient dispositional variables, therapist technique, and outcome.

The treatment in the M. Horowitz et al. (1984) study was a time-limited, 12-session psychotherapy employing techniques advocated by Mann for dealing with separation and loss themes, principles of dynamic brief therapy enunciated by Malan and Sifneos, and specialized techniques for working through the meaning of the loss in terms of the patient's self-concept and internalized models of role relationships. M. Horowitz et al. (1984) found that patients who were rated higher on developmental level of the self-concept at the pretherapy evaluation had a more favorable outcome in work and interpersonal functioning at outcome.

Correlational tests of a variety of therapist actions with outcome were overwhelmingly nonsignificant. This finding is similar to Piper's results (1984) which showed nonsignificant linear relationships between therapist transference interpretations and outcome. Both of these studies as well as clinical knowledge supports the idea that the effect of a therapist intervention probably depends on characteristics of the patient and the interactional context. For example, in the Horowitz et al. study patients with high motivation benefited more from interpretive work than patients with low motivation.

M. Horowitz et al. (1984) used a hierarchical regression model to examine the interaction of patient dispositional variables, process variables, and outcome. They found that for patients with low motivation, greater therapist emphasis on establishing a positive attitude toward the therapeutic alliance is associated with better outcomes; whereas for patients with initial high motivation whose therapists placed greater emphasis on establishing a positive alliance, the outcome was relatively poorer.

The clinical implications drawn by the authors are as follows: for patients with high motivation the discussion of negative reactions to the therapist may be highly productive. However, for patients with lower levels of motivation negative reactions toward the therapist may not be easily worked on because the patient may be too threatened or disappointed to want to engage in a difficult and uncomfortable process.

The therapist action of differentiating fantasized from realistic meaning of the stress event—an essentially psychodynamic uncovering technique—was strongly related to outcome for patients with high motivation and a stable self-concept; conversely, such therapist techniques may have been detrimental for more vulnerable patients. For the therapist action of encouraging change in self-image—an essentially supportive technique—patients who were typically considered poorer candidates did better with these techniques. However, these supportive techniques may slow progress in highly motivated patients. For patients low in initial motivation, therapist interpretations dealing with termination were positively related to good outcome; for patients with higher initial motivation, focusing on termination was counterproductive, consistent with the approach of Sifneos and Davanloo.

This study offers two methodological advances that remedy many of the problems in the previous literature. First, it examines outcome as a product of interaction between therapist technique and patient dispositional variables; for example, level of motivation and developmental level of the self-concept. Such a strategy is crucial for moving research design beyond simple linear models to account for outcome based on either patient or therapist characteristics taken in isolation. While it is clinically obvious that the same technique cannot be used with all patients, research efforts have not reflected this clinical reality. Second, the study measured change beyond symptoms, for example, intimacy in relationships, as measured by the Patterns of Individual Change Scores (Kaltreider, DeWitt, Weiss, & Horowitz, 1981) which provides ratings that are relevant to the goals of affecting changes in dynamic therapy.

Recommendations for Future Research

Research efforts on the brief dynamic therapy of depression could be improved with greater specification of the interaction between patient disorders, dispositional characteristics, and therapist techniques. The following recommendations would improve future research efforts:

1. The use of treatment manuals that define therapist technique with rating scales to measure adherence to the techniques. Specific guidelines for applying general principles in a manual to the treatment of depression would add greater precision.
2. Developing operationalized measures for psychodynamic therapy that reflect psychodynamic concepts such as dynamic focus, transference, defenses, and characterological change.
3. Employing interactional models in which patient dispositional factors and personality styles are codeterminants with therapist technique in producing outcome.
4. Employing contrast group designs to test hypotheses, for example, brief compared to long-term dynamic therapy for depression; dynamic therapy with and without antidepressant medication; dynamic compared to nondynamic psychotherapy.

SUMMARY

The clinical and research literature on the brief dynamic therapy of depression supports the following conclusions:

1. Brief dynamic therapy is distinct from other treatments for depression in its goals (alteration of underlying psychopathology as well as symptoms) and strategies (interpretation and confrontation of defenses, transference, and underlying conflict).
2. There is not a clear clinical consensus about which depressed patients are most appropriate for brief dynamic therapy and there is virtually no research evidence to guide the clinician. At this point it appears brief dynamic therapy is most appropriate for neurotic and reactive depression (dysthymic disorders) and some unipolar, nonpsychotic disorders and inappropriate for bipolar and psychotic disorders. The treatment of patients who have coexisting personality disorders is still an open question.
3. A diagnosis of depressive disorder is not sufficient for selecting a patient for brief dynamic psychotherapy. Other conditions, namely,

the absence of diagnostic contraindications, the presence of a focus, and adequate psychological resources are necessary.

4. There are some similarities among the brief therapists; namely, selecting appropriate patients, setting a time limit, and an active technical approach. However, there are also numerous differences with regard to the amount of confrontation of defenses, the emphasis on transference, and the range of characterological pathology that is treated.

5. There is a trend toward developing manuals and greater specification of therapist technique.

6. More complex models of the patient-therapist dyadic interaction are being proposed to explain outcome.

References

American Psychiatric Association. (1980). *Diagnostic and statistical manual of mental disorders* (3rd ed.). Washington, DC: American Psychiatric Association.

Appelbaum, S. A. (1975). "Parkinson's Law" in psychotherapy. *International Journal of Psychoanalytic Psychotherapy, 4,* 426–436.

Bauer, G. P., & Kobos, J. C. (1984). Short-term psychodynamic psychotherapy: Reflections on the past and current practice. *Psychotherapy, 21*(2), 153–170.

Bellack, A. S., Hersen, M., & Himmelhoch, J. (1981). Social skills training compared with pharmacotherapy and psychotherapy in the treatment of unipolar depression. *American Journal of Psychiatry, 138*(12), 1562–1567.

Budman, S. (Ed.). (1981). *Forms of brief therapy.* New York: Guilford Press.

Budman, S., & Gurman, A. (1983). The practice of brief therapy. *Professional Psychology: Research and Practice, 14*(3), 277–292.

Butcher, J. N., & Koss, M. P. (1978). Research on brief and crisis-oriented therapies. In S. L. Garfield & A. E. Bergin (Eds.), *Handbook of psychotherapy and behavior change* (2nd ed). New York: John Wiley & Sons.

Davanloo, H. (Ed.). (1978). *Basic principles and techniques in short-term dynamic psychotherapy.* Jamaica, NY: Spectrum Publications.

Davanloo, H. (Ed.). (1980). *Short-term dynamic psychotherapy.* New York: Jason Aronson.

Gustafson, J. P. (1984). An integration of brief dynamic psychotherapy. *American Journal of Psychiatry, 141*(8), 935–944.

Horowitz, L. M., Weckler, D. A., & Doren, R. (1983). Interpersonal problems and symptoms: A cognitive approach. In P. C. Kendall (Ed.), *Advances in cognitive-behavioral research and therapy, 2,* 81–125.

Horowitz, M. J. (1976). *Stress response syndromes.* New York: Jason Aronson.

Horowitz, M. J., Marmar, C., Krupnick, J., Wilner, N., Kaltreider, N., & Wallerstein, R. (1984). *Personality styles and brief psychotherapy.* New York: Basic Books.

Horowitz, M. J., Marmar, C., Weiss, D. S., DeWitt, K., & Rosenbaum, R. (1984). Brief psychotherapy of bereavement reactions. *Archives of General Psychiatry, 41,* 438–448.

Hoyt, M. F. (1979). Aspects of termination in a time-limited brief psychotherapy. *Psychiatry, 42,* 208–219.

Kaltreider, N., DeWitt, K., Weiss, D. S., & Horowitz, M. J. (1981). Patterns of Individual Change Scales. *Archives of General Psychiatry, 38,* 1263–69.

Karasu, T. B., & Skodol, A. E. (1980). VIth axis for *DSM-III:* Psychodynamic evaluation. *American Journal of Psychiatry, 137,* 607–610.

Kernberg, O., Burstein, E. D., Coyne, L., Applebaum, A., Horwitz, L., & Voth, H. (1972). Psychotherapy and psychoanalysis: Final report of the Menninger Foundation's psychotherapy research project. *Bulletin Menninger Clinic, 36,* 1–278.

Lowry, F. (1980). The use of drugs and other treatments in depression. In F. J. Ayd, Jr. (Ed.), *Clinical depression: Diagnostic and therapeutic challenges.* Baltimore: Ayd Medical Communications.

Luborsky, L., Singer, B., & Luborsky, L. (1975). Comparative studies of psychotherapies. *Archives of General Psychiatry, 32,* 995–1008.

Malan, D. (1976). *The frontier of brief psychotherapy.* New York: Plenum Publishing.

Malan, D. (1978). The case of the woman in mourning. In H. Davanloo (Ed.), *Basic principles and techniques in short-term dynamic psychotherapy.* Jamaica, NY: Spectrum Publications.

Malan, D. (1979). *Individual psychotherapy and the science of psychodynamics.* London: Butterworths.

Mann, J. (1973). *Time-limited psychotherapy.* Cambridge, MA: Harvard University Press.

Mann, J., & Goldman, R. (1982). *A casebook in time-limited psychotherapy.* New York: McGraw-Hill.

Marmor, J. (1973). *Psychiatry in transition.* New York: Brunner/Mazel.

Marmor, J. (1975). Academic lecture: The nature of the psychotherapeutic process revisited. *Canadian Psychiatric Association Journal, 20,* 557–565.

Marmor, J. (1979). Historical aspects of short-term dynamic psychotherapy. *Psychiatric Clinics of North America, 2,* 3–9.

McLean, P. D., & Hakstian, A. R. (1979). Clinical depression: Comparative efficacy of outpatient treatments. *Journal of Consulting and Clinical Psychology, 47*(5), 818–836.

Mendelson, M. (1974). *Psychoanlaytic concepts of depression* (2nd ed.). Jamaica, NY: Spectrum Publications.

Orlinsky, D. E., & Howard, K. I. (1978). The relation of process to outcome. In S. L. Garfield & A. E. Bergin (Eds.), *Handbook of psychotherapy and behavior change* (2nd ed). New York: John Wiley & Sons.

Parloff, M. B. (1984). Psychotherapy research and its incredible credibility crisis. *Clinical Psychology Review, 4*(1), 95–109.

Parloff, M. B., Waskow, I., & Wolfe, B. E. (1978). Research on therapist variables in relationship to process and outcome. In S. L. Garfield & A. E. Bergin (Eds.), *Handbook of psychotherapy and behavior change* (2nd ed). New York: John Wiley & Sons.

Piper, W. E. (1984, June). *Relationships between the focus of therapist interpretations and outcome in short-term individual psychotherapy.* Paper delivered at the annual meeting of the Society for Psychotherapy Research, Lake Louise, Alberta, Canada.

Schaffer, N. (1983). The utility of measuring the skillfulness of therapeutic techniques. *Psychotherapy: Theory, Research and Practice, 20,* 330–339.

Sifneos, P. (1972). Short-term psychotherapy and emotional crisis. Cambridge, MA: Harvard University Press.

Sifneos, P. (1978). Short-term anxiety provoking psychotherapy. In H. Davanloo (Ed.), *Basic principles and techniques in short-term dynamic psychotherapy.* Jamaica, NY: Spectrum Publications.

Skuja, A. (1982, April). *Short-term dynamic psychotherapy with alcohol patients: An overview of theoretical and practical issues.* Presented at Western Psychological Association, Sacramento, CA.

Smith, M. L., Glass, G. V., & Miller, T. I. (1980). *The benefits of psychotherapy.* Baltimore: The Johns Hopkins Press.

Strupp, H. H. (1980a). Success and failure in time-limited psychotherapy: A systematic comparison of two cases (Comparison 1). *Archives of General Psychiatry, 37,* 595–603.

Strupp, H. H. (1980b). Success and failure in time-limited psychotherapy: A systematic comparison of two cases (Comparison 2). *Archives of General Psychiatry, 37,* 708–716.

Strupp, H. H., & Binder, J. (1984). *Psychotherapy in a new key: Time-limited dynamic psychotherapy.* New York: Basic Books.

Strupp, H. H., Sandell, J. A., Watherhouse, G. J., O'Malley, S. S., & Anderson, J. L. (1982). Short-term dynamic psychotherapies for the depressed patient. In A. J. Rush (Ed.). *Short-term psychotherapies for depression.* New York: Guilford Press.

Wallerstein, R. S. (in press). *42 Lives in treatment: A study of psychoanalysis and psychotherapy.* New York: Guilford Press.

Weiss, J., & Sampson, H. (1984). Testing alternative psychoanalytic explanations of the therapeutic process. In J. M. Masling (Ed.), *Empirical studies of psychoanalytical theories* (Vol 2). Hillsdale, NJ: Analytic Press.

Weissman, M. M. (1979). Psychological treatment of depression: Evidence for the efficacy of psychotherapy alone, in comparison with and in combination with pharmacotherapy. *Archives of General Psychiatry, 36,* 1262–1269.

Weissman, M. M., Klerman, G. L., Prusoff, B. A., Sholomskas D., & Padian N. (1981). Depressed outpatients. Results one year after treatment with drugs and/or interpersonal psychotherapy. *Archives of General Psychiatry. 38*(1), 51–55.

Wolberg, L. R. (1967) *Short-term psychotherapy.* New York: Grune & Stratton.

Chapter 5

Short-Term Interpersonal Psychotherapy (IPT) for Depression

Bruce J. Rounsaville
Gerald L. Klerman
Myrna M. Weissman
Eve S. Chevron

INTRODUCTION

Short-term interpersonal psychotherapy (IPT) is a brief psychological treatment aimed at reducing symptoms and improving social functioning in ambulatory patients with a diagnoses of major depression, according to either Research Diagnostic Criteria (Spitzer, Endicott, & Robins, 1978) or the American Psychiatric Association's *DSM-III* Criteria (1980). IPT was developed over a course of 12 years for use in the Boston-New Haven Collaborative Depression Project (DiMascio, Weissman, Prusoff, Neu, Zwilling, & Klerman, 1979; Klerman, DiMascio, Weissman, Prusoff, & Paykel, 1974; Weissman, Klerman, Paykel, Prusoff, & Hanson, 1974; Weissman, Prusoff, DiMascio, Neu, Goklaney, & Klerman, 1979). The central focus of IPT is on current interpersonal functioning. This is based on the concept that depression is associated with impaired social relationships which either precipitate or perpetuate the disorder. As described below the specific techniques and strategies of IPT are explicitly eclectic and contain four major elements:

1. Adherence to a medical model of depression.
2. Emphasis on the importance of interpersonal functioning to psychotherapy.
3. The attempt to provide effective treatment in a short term.
4. Use of an exploratory stance by the psychotherapist which is similar to that used with experiential and insight-oriented psychotherapies.

IPT is suitable for use, following a period of training, by experienced psychiatrists, psychologists, or social workers. It is designed to be used alone or in conjunction with pharmacologic agents. Variants of IPT have been tested in two clinical trials of depressed patients—one of maintenance treatment (Klerman et al., 1974; Weissman et al., 1974) and one of acute treatment (DiMascio et al., 1979b; Weissman et al., 1979). A third study testing IPT in a sample of Methadone-maintained patients, has also been completed (Rounsaville, Glazer, Wilber, Weissman, & Kleber, 1983). IPT has been tested with and without the addition of a tricyclic antidepressant. A further testing of IPT against cognitive therapy and a tricyclic antidepressant is currently under way in a collaborative clinical trial sponsored by the National Institute of Mental Health (Elkin, Hadley, Parloff, & Autry, 1985).

An important aspect of IPT is that it was developed to be used in a research context. We believe that psychotherapists can be maximally effective only when they know that the techniques that they are using are likely to be useful for the particular type of patients that they are attempting to treat. In order to evaluate the efficacy of a given psychotherapy, controlled clinical trials are needed. In order to evaluate a form of psychotherapy in a clinical trial, its strategies and techniques must be sufficiently specified so that it can be practiced uniformly by different psychotherapists and with different patients. At the time IPT was developed, few therapies for depression were sufficiently specified in procedural manuals to enable serious replication trials to be conducted. These were based on more highly structured cognitive (e.g., Beck, Rush, Shaw, & Emery, 1979) or behavioral (e.g., Lewinsohn, Biglan, and Zeiss, 1976) approaches. In that many practitioners in the field base their therapeutic methods on exploratory and interpersonal approaches, IPT was designed to allow a representative type of psychotherapy to be empirically evaluated.

To enable a rigorous testing of IPT, its procedures and methods have been specified in a procedural manual (Klerman, Weissman, Rounsaville, & Chevron, 1984). In addition a program has been developed to train experienced psychotherapists to perform IPT in clinical trials (Rounsaville, Chevron, & Weissman, 1983). Rating procedures have also been developed to determine that trainees are performing IPT in a manner consistent with the training manual and to monitor therapist performance over the course of a research project to prevent therapist drift (Chevron & Rounsaville, 1983; Rounsaville et al., 1983b).

It is our belief that a variety of treatments may be suitable for depression. The depressed patient's interests are best served by the availability and scientific testing of different psychological as well as pharmacologic treatments that can be used alone or in combination. The ultimate aim of these studies is to determine which are the best treatments for particular subgroups of depressed patients.

In this chapter we will describe the defining characteristics of IPT, outline the clinical strategies used, and summarize the efficacy data available at this time.

ELEMENTS OF IPT

A Medical Model of Depression

For the IPT practitioner depression is seen as a psychiatric disorder and shares characteristics with other mental disorders as described in the American Psychiatric Associations' *Diagnostic and Statistical Manual of Mental Disorders,* ([*DSM-III*]; 1980), as follows:

> Each of the mental disorders is conceptualized as a clinically significant behavior or psychological syndrome or pattern that occurs in an individual and that is typically associated with either a painful symptom (distress) or impairment in one or more important areas of functioning (disability). In addition, there is an inference that there is a behavioral, psychological, or biological dysfunction, and that the disturbance is not only in the relationship between the individual and society.

One important corollary to the syndrome approach in IPT is that the depression is not a part of normal functioning but represents significantly *abnormal behavior or function. Depression* as a term is often used to cover a broad spectrum of moods and behaviors that range from the disappointment and sadness of normal life to bizarre suicidal acts of severe melancholia. There are at least three meanings to the term: a mood, a symptom, and a syndrome. Depression as a normal mood is a universal and transient phenomenon from which no one escapes. As a symptom or abnormal mood, depression is also common, and the differentiation between the normal and pathological can be indistinct. Depression of mood that is unduly persistent and pervasive is generally considered pathological. Depressive symptoms are common. They occur in many persons who do not have psychiatric disorders, as well as in those with other medical psychiatric disorders. IPT has been designed for patients who meet the criteria of depression as a clinical syndrome, not just a mood or symptom. A clinical syndrome includes a number of specific symptoms of certain severity and persistence which produce impairment and/or disability, and occur in the absence of other symptoms or disorders which may better explain the condition.

A second important corollary to the medical model concept is that the use of the syndrome is *part of the treatment itself.* This involves educating the patient about characteristics that are known about the depressive syndrome such as its prognosis, prevalance, course, symptom constellation, and effects on interpersonal functioning. It also involves refraining from forcefully proposing an elaborated theory about the origins of depression. Like all psychiatric disorders, the precise etiologies of depression are not known although theories are abundant and often contradictory. Focusing on the syndrome as an entity in and of itself, allows the patient to realize that he may have limited control over changing the symptoms. Whatever the psychological, social, and biochemical influences on the development of any given patient's depression, the syndrome probably results as an end product of a final common pathway and has characteristics which are not necessarily related to the features which caused it (e.g., an oak tree cannot be described as essentially "acornish"). Moreover, the improvement of depression may involve steps which do not simply retrace and reverse those which led to the depression in the first place. Rather the depression has a "life of its own" with a characteristic course and symptom constellation. Because of the common characteristics to most depressions, the patient is in need of professional help and is entitled to the "sick role," which involves being temporarily relieved of some social obligations and the need to make allowances for impairment in day-to-day living.

Social Influences on Depression/Social Interventions to Bring about Improvement

A second major feature of interpersonal psychotherapy is an emphasis on the relationship between depression and impaired interpersonal functioning. Based on the theoretical and empirical work described below, problems in interpersonal relationships are seen as a contributant to the cause or perpetuation of the patient's depression disorder and many of the interventions of interpersonal psychotherapy are aimed at detecting and resolving these problems.

Theoretical Framework.   IPT is derived from a number of theoretical sources. The earliest source is Adolph Meyer whose psychobiological approach to understanding psychiatric disorders placed great emphasis on the patient's current psychosocial and interpersonal experiences (Meyer, 1957). In contrast to Kraeplin and the biomedical model of illness, derived from Continental European psychiatry, Meyer saw psychiatric disorders as part of the patient's attempt to adapt to the environment, usually the psychosocial environment. He viewed the patient's response to environmental change and stress as determined by early developmental experiences in the family and by the patient's membership in various social groups. Meyer attempted to apply the concepts of role adaptation to understanding psychiatric illness.

Among Meyer's associates, Harry Stack Sullivan stands out for his theory on interpersonal relations (Sullivan, 1953a, 1953b). He asserted that psychiatry was the scientific study of people and the processes that involve or go on between people, in contrast to the study of only the mind, society, the brain, or the glands. Hence the unit of study is the interpersonal situation at any one time.

The interpersonal conceptualization was applied to therapeutic strategies in the writings of J. Frank (1973) who stressed mastery of current interpersonal situations as an important social psychological component in psychotherapy. Among others, Becker (1974) and Chodoff (1970) have also emphasized the social roots of depression and the need to attend to the interpersonal aspects of the disorder.

Empirical Basis for Understanding Depression in an Interpersonal Context. The empirical basis for understanding and treating depression in an interpersonal context derives from several divergent sources.

First, there is the research on the relationship of disruption of attachment bonds to depression. The seminal work of Bowlby has demonstrated the importance of attachment and social bonds to human functioning, the vulnerability of individuals to impaired interpersonal relations if strong attachment bonds do not develop early, and the vulnerability to depression or despair during disruption of attachment bonds (Bowlby, 1969). Along these lines, the work of Henderson et al. (1978a, 1978b, 1978c) has found that deficiencies in social bonds in the current environment is associated with neurosis.

Second, another source is the sophisticated empirical work by Brown, Harris, & Copeland (1977) aimed at defining an aspect of attachment bonding (intimacy—a confiding relationship) and defining its relationship to the development of depression. In a community survey of women living in the Camberwell section of London, this group found that women who reported having an intimate, confiding relationship with a man had less depression in the face of life stress than did women who did not have a close relationship.

A third source links recent social stress to the onset of depression. Based on the work of Holmes, Goodell, and Woolf (1950) demonstrating the impact of recent life events on illness, several investigators have gone on to show a link between stressful life events in the interpersonal sphere and depressive symptoms (Ilfeld, 1977; Paykel et al., 1969; Pearlin & Lieberman, 1977).

A fourth source is the body of work which has attempted to evaluate the social functioning of patients with depressive illness. Such individuals have been shown to have impaired intimate relationships (Briscoe & Smith, 1973; Weissman & Paykel, 1974) and even to elicit characteristic, unhelpful responses from others (Coyne, 1976).

Need for an Effective Short-Term Treatment

A third major factor influencing the nature of IPT is its attempt to bring about change in a short-term treatment. Short-term treatments for depression are needed because many patients do not need a longer term treatment or cannot use, afford, or accept it. Moreover, depression is a condition which frequently remits without treatment in a relatively brief time period and it may be counterproductive to offer a treatment which lasts longer than the disorder which it is intended to relieve.

Many of the characteristics of IPT are determined by its short-term nature. In this respect, it is similar to other forms of brief treatment. These include the following:

1. Setting limited goals.   In this regard, the depression is viewed as having three interrelated components.
   a. Symptom formation, which involves the development of depressive affect and the negative signs and symptoms, and may derive from psychobiological and/or psychodynamic mechanisms.

 b. Social and interpersonal relations, which involve interactions in social roles with other persons and derives from learning based on childhood experiences, concurrent social reinforcement, and/or personal mastery and competence.

 c. Personality, which involves the enduring traits such as severe dependency tendencies to interact with others in a passive aggressive style, or a tendency to invariably allow oneself to be exploited in relationships. These traits determine the person's unique reactions to interpersonal experience. Personality patterns may provide part of the person's predisposition to manifest symptom episodes.

  IPT attempts to intervene in the first two processes—symptom formation and social and interpersonal relations. Although personality functioning is assessed in IPT, this treatment does not attempt to change enduring aspects of personality structure because of the relatively short duration of treatment.

2. Developing a structured and comparatively concrete treatment plan. In IPT, goals are made relatively explicit and are not left unformulated.

3. Attempting a prompt reestablishment of equilibrium. Initial focus of treatment on management of depressive symptoms is an attempt to reduce the impact of the depression quickly.

4. Not seeking a full understanding of determinants. Because the emphasis of a short-term treatment is on change, there is less ambition that all important antecedents to a patient's depression will be identified and dealt with.

5. Intervening promptly. The therapist in IPT is always keeping in mind the focus and goals of treatment and takes actions at the earliest opportunity to help the patient reach them.

6. Having the therapist take an active and directive stance. Going along with the prompt intervention the therapist does not simply wait for the patient to bring in issues related to treatment goals at the patient's own pace but attempts to redirect the focus of the treatment periodically when sessions seem to be offtrack.

7. Undertaking an early and rapid assessment of the general problem. As part of the formulating goals, the therapist engages in relatively active, thorough, and structured interventions in early sessions.

8. Fostering an early positive relationship. The IPT therapist attempts to offer him/herself as a helpful ally, and not make analysis of the patient/therapist relationship the key focus of the treatment unless major resistances arise which make this focus necessary.

9. Focusing on the here and now. Although there is a recognition that patients have often learned dysfunctional ways of handling and thinking about interpersonal relationships in childhood or in the past, the major focus of IPT is on the interpersonal problems associated with the current episode of depression

10. Encouraging behavioral practice. The IPT therapist uses some directive techniques such as decision analysis and direct advice in order to provide a direct link between the activities that are taking place in treatment sessions and the patient's initiating changes in interpersonal relationships outside of the session.

The IPT Therapist's Use of an Exploratory Stance

The fourth major influence on IPT is the fact that all of its practitioners have had prior training and experience in an insight-oriented, exploratory approach to psychotherapy. Those trained in more structured, behavioral treatments are less likely to be appropriate candidates for this type of psychotherapy. The most important way that this has influenced IPT is through the use of techniques and a therapeutic stance that are common to many types of exploratory therapies. For example, although the therapist is comparatively active, he/she takes the patient's lead in choosing the topics in any given hour. The therapist adopts a comparatively neutral role and attempts to encourage the patient to talk freely and in an exploratory manner about a given interpersonal topic in order to discover unexpected thoughts or affects that are associated with it. Although advice may be offered this is sparing and homework is not assigned. To distinguish IPT from brief insight-oriented psychotherapies (e.g., Davenloo, 1982; Malan, 1963; Sifneos, 1979) it includes more active, practical interventions and is less ambitious in the nature of change sought. The IPT therapist does not attempt to bring about major personality change through the achievement of insight into underlying conflicts. Rather, change is sought through education, combating demoralization, social manipulation or problem solving, and the IPT therapist addresses underlying psychological conflict only if work at these levels is stalled or if the patient is showing strong resistance to the treatment which must be managed.

A DESCRIPTION OF IPT STRATEGIES

Interpersonal psychotherapy has two goals: (*a*) alleviation of depressive symptoms; and (*b*) improvement of interpersonal functioning. Although these goals may be interdependent, specific techniques and strategies are used to reach each goal. Change in IPT is seen as taking place as a result of increased understanding of one's problems and learning of new ways to approach them.

Managing the Depression

The key to understanding the IPT strategy for managing depression is to see it as an attempt to combat demoralization. Typically, the depressed patient has three types of problems: (*a*) interpersonal problems associated with the depression; (*b*) depressive symptoms; and (*c*) demoralization that takes place in reaction to (*a*) and (*b*).

The combat demoralization and to help the patient manage the depression the IPT therapist does the following:

1. Reviewing symptoms.
2. Giving the symptoms a name.
3. Explaining that depression has a positive prognosis.
4. Evaluating the need for medication.
5. Giving the patient the "sick role."
6. Helping the patient manage his/her day and tasks around the constraints placed on him/her by depressive symptoms.
7. Helping the patient recognize and avoid depressing situations in the short term.
8. Helping the patient recognize and seek out situations in which depressive symptoms are mitigated.

Reviewing Symptoms.   In the initial session the IPT therapist systematically reviews the full range of depressive symptoms, possibly with the structured guidance of systematic depression scales, such as the Hamilton Depression Scale (Hamilton, 1960) or the Schedule for Affective Disorders and Schizophrenia (Endicott & Spitzer, 1978). As the symptoms are reviewed, the therapist is careful to note the context in which the symptoms arise, the immediate precipitants, and the interpersonal impact of the symptoms, including the reactions of others to them. The symptom review then provides the basis around which all other strategies for immediate management of depression are derived.

Giving the Symptoms a Name.   Education of the patient regarding depression as a psychiatric disorder can often be highly reassuring. The patient frequently finds the depression baffling and frightening and has a tendency to exaggerate its negative prognostic implications or to minimize its importance. There may also be a tendency to place excessive blame on him/herself. Educating the patient about depression is aimed at combating demoralization through correcting dysfunctional misapprehensions about depression.

An important step is giving the syndrome a name and explaining the constellation of disparate symptoms as being related to the depressive episode. In listing the patient's depressive symptoms, it is important for the therapist to emphasize those which have interpersonal import such as lack of energy, irritability, inability to experience interest or pleasure in usual activities or sex, the tendency to evaluate oneself and the future negatively, and loss of ability to concentrate and remember. Although those features of depression are frequently recognized by the patient, they are often not evaluated as being part of the depression.

Explaining That Depression Has a Positive Prognosis.   To instill hope, the patient should be informed of the relatively good prognosis of depression. This may be done by informing the patient that: (*a*) depression is very common with around 4 percent being depressed at any given time and around 15–20 percent having a significant depression in their lifetime; and (*b*) that depression usually has a good prognosis. It is very useful to emphasize that pessimism is part of the depressive syndrome and that such pessimism frequently takes the form of feeling that one will never recover. Moreover, despite the suffering that the patient is experiencing now, that is not indicative of a serious organic illness or a sign that the patient is going to go out of his/her mind. Regarding treatment, it can be emphasized that a number of different types of treatment are effective and the patients should not feel hopeless if the first approach is ineffective. Psychotherapy is one of the standard treatments for depression which has been shown to be effective in a number of research trials.

Evaluating the Need for Medication.   The need for pharmacologic treatment, usually a tricyclic antidepressant, will depend on the severity of symptoms, the patient's preference, medical contraindications, and previous response. It is beyond the scope of this chapter to provide details regarding the decision of who should receive antidepressant pharmacotherapy and which agents to use. In general, patients with severe sleep and appetite disturbance, or agitation and lack of reactivity are good candidates for antidepressants in addition to psychotherapy. Patients with these endogenous features to their depression, in fact, may not respond as rapidly to psychotherapy if psychotherapy is the sole treatment modality. These patients typically do best when treated with combined psychotherapy and tricyclic antidepressants (Prusoff, Weissman, Klerman, & Rounsaville, 1980).

The presence of life stress does not preclude the use of medication in addition to psychotherapy. In fact, the majority of patients, even those with endogenous features of melancholia, will identify a stress associated with the onset of depression. Nor does an acute depression superimposed on chronic depression or depressive personality preclude the use of tricyclic antidepressants in addition to psychotherapy (Rounsaville, Sholomskas, & Prusoff, 1980).

In order to prevent interference between the psychotherapy and the pharmacotherapy, it is important for the psychotherapist to explain the rationale for the use of the two types of treatment in somewhat the following fashion:

> We see the depressive syndrome which you have as having two main interrelated parts: (1) the depressed mood accompanied by physical types of symptoms such as low energy, loss of appetite, and poor sleep, and (2) problems in ways of interacting with others and thinking about yourself. Treatment with medications has been shown to be most effective in treating the depressed mood and symptoms of sleep and appetite disturbance, while psychotherapy is intended to help you to develop improved ways of dealing with others and solving problems so that you can prevent future depressions. If you feel better and have more energy, you are more likely to be able to settle your problems with _____ (important individual in patient's life). On the other hand, if, in psychotherapy you are better able to deal with _____, then you may find yourself with less to be upset about.

Giving the Identified Patient the "Sick Role." While depressed, the patient is entitled to the sick role. The idea of the "sick role" was first presented by Talcott Parsons (1951), who noted that "illness is not merely a condition but also a social role."

Parsons described four features of the "sick role":

1. To exempt the sick person from certain normal social obligations. This function must be socially defined and validated.
2. To exempt the patient from certain types of responsibility.
3. To be considered in a state which is socially defined as undesirable, to be gotten out of as expeditiously as possible.
4. To be defined as "in need of help" and assuming the role of patient who carries certain obligations. These include cooperating with the helper in the process of getting well and affirming that he/she is ill.

A key element of the sick role which becomes the focus of treatment is assisting the patient to relinquish the sick role and recover. If the review of symptoms is understood within the context of the sick role concept, the therapist can then demonstrate that the patient is entitled to the sick role, at least initially.

In order to give the identified patient the sick role within the context of IPT, the therapist asserts that the patient has only a limited amount of control over his/her depressive symptoms. The patient does not wish to be sick, but has developed a disorder because of circumstances, stresses, feelings, and/or biochemical imbalances that are not in his/her control. Although the patient must play an important role in getting him/herself out of the depression, the depression renders him/her at least partially disabled on a temporary basis and allowances need to be made for the patient's decreased capabilities. The patient and those around him or her must have decreased expectations of the patient's functioning and both make allowances for failure to perform ordinary roles and to lighten the load on the patient by taking on some of his or her functions while the depression persists. A useful metaphor is to describe the depressed patient as someone who is caught in quicksand. If he/she makes quick, impulsive, energetic, and desperate efforts to free himself he will get further entrapped. However, if slow but deliberate efforts to free oneself are made it can be successful. It is important to note to the patient that the sick role is a temporarily, undesirable one and that cooperating with the treatment means efforts to gradually give it up. Some patients may be tempted to remain in this role indefinitely and this tendency is to be prevented through the short-term nature of the treatment.

Planning Activities around the Constraints of Depression. As a follow-through of giving the patient the sick role, it is useful for the therapist to review the patient's day-to-day functioning with him in order to help him manage his daily activities taking depressive symptoms into consideration. Many depressed patients expect that they will be able to perform their normal routine even though they have decreased energy, reduced motivation, and so on. With such patients it is important to identify priorities for daily tasks and to eliminate those with low priority. In addition it is useful to determine on which parts of the day the patient is most symptomatic and to help the patient plan activities around times when symptoms are less pressing.

Sensitive clinical judgment is needed to determine the degree to which the patient is impaired by depressive symptoms. Encouraging the patient to excuse him/herself from too many activities or social obligations, can exacerbate symptoms by increasing guilt and by providing the patient with blocks of unfilled time which may be spent ruminating about his or her dysphoric state. A particular example where the patient should not be encouraged to relax is in the case of early morning awakening. Patients with this symptom frequently describe an agitated feeling of increased energy accompanying the early awakening and they may make futile efforts to get back to sleep. In this case the patient should be encouraged to get up and occupy him/herself with whatever activities are possible at that time. Another potential exception to excusing patients from expectations of themselves relates to activities which involve getting together with others such as parties and dates. Patients who are mild/moderately depressed and those whose level of depression is beginning to lift frequently continue to avoid social contacts. This avoidance has a phobic quality to it and it frequently greatly exaggerates the actual difficulty involved in participating in the activity. In fact, many depressives are surprised that they can actually enjoy an activity that they had fearful anticipations about.

Helping the Patient Recognize and Avoid Dysphoric Situations.   In the initial, short-term management of depressive symptoms, it is frequently useful to simply advise the patient to avoid situations which are upsetting. If, for example, the patient experiences increased depressive symptoms while alone or in the company of particular friends or relative, the patient may be asked to explore ways of avoiding these situations, at least until depressive symptoms have been alleviated to a degree that would allow them to be managed more successfully. This intervention may be seen by the patient as advice to "run away from my problems," especially when depression is exacerbated in the context of relating to those with whom the patient has a disturbed relationship. The therapist can counter this objection by explaining that, in the patient's current, debilitated condition, his energy must be focused on getting better and there will be time for handling this problem when he feels stronger.

Helping the Patient Recognize and Seek out Situations in Which Depressive Symptoms Are Relieved.   Depressed patients characteristically take poor care of themselves and it is important for the therapist to help the patient combat this tendency. In reviewing the patient's day-to-day activities, it is important for the therapist to be alert to those situations which are associated with symptom relief and to help the patient to seek them out frequently. This approach may meet with resistance from depressed patients who feel guilty and unworthy as they describe such an approach as "selfish."

The therapist can counter this by emphasizing the need to be temporarily selfish in order to restore a level of functioning which will enable the patient to help others more effectively.

Intervening in the Patient's Current Interpersonal Functioning

Because IPT is short term, it is usually concentrated on one or two current interpersonal problems. A definition of problem areas is needed as a first step in formulating a treatment strategy with the patient. In this section, we describe four major interpersonal problem areas commonly presented by depressed patients. Each problem area will be defined and related to the therapeutic goals and treatment strategies of IPT. The problem areas are: (1) grief; (2) interpersonal role disputes; (3) role transitions; and (4) interpersonal deficits.

These problem areas are not necessarily mutually exclusive. Patients may present with a combination of problems in several areas, or there may be no clear-cut significant difficulty in any one area. For a patient with wide-ranging problems, the therapist may be guided in the choice of focus by the precipitating events of the current depressive episode and by the identification of areas in which change can most readily take place.

The area of focus may change as therapy progresses. Occasionally, the patient and the therapist will not agree about the most appropriate focus. Patients are often unwilling or unable to recognize the degree to which a particular problem is bothering them. For instance, patients with marital role disputes may be reluctant to complain of problems, because they feel threatened by the possibility of endangering the marital relationship. Patients with pathological grief reactions may be totally unaware of the source of their annual episodes of depression. In cases in which the therapist and the patient do not agree about the preferred focus of treatment, the therapist can take one of three choices: (1) delay setting treatment goals until the patient realizes the importance of the issue; (2) set very general goals in the hope of being able to focus the treatment more specifically as therapy progresses; or (3) accept the patient's priorities in the hope that, after these issues are looked into, the focus can shift to more central issues. For example, F.A., a middle-aged woman, came in with a complaint that "My children are driving me crazy." Several sessions later, she brought up her more pressing distress over her husband's extramarital affairs.

Grief

Definition and Description. Grief in association with the death of a loved one can be either normal or abnormal. IPT deals with the depression associated with abnormal grief reactions, which result from the failure to go through normal mourning following the death of a person important to the patient.

Normal Grief.   The experience of normal grief following the death of a loved one has much in common with depression, but these conditions are not equivalent, and IPT is not used to treat normal grief reactions. Grieving normally occurs when a person sustains an important loss of a significant other and, during the bereavement period, experiences symptoms such as sadness, disturbed sleep, agitation, and decreased ability to carry out day-to-day tasks. These symptoms are considered normal and tend to resolve themselves without treatment in two to four months. In normal grief, the bereaved characteristically goes through a process of gradual weaning from remembered experiences with the loved one. A detailed account of the normal grieving process has been provided elsewhere (Lindemann, 1944; Siggins, 1966).

Abnormal Grief.   The principal assumption behind the therapeutic strategy described in this section is that inadequate normal grieving can lead to depression, either immediately after the loss or at some delayed time when the patient is somehow reminded of the loss. Abnormal grief processes of two general kinds are commonly noted in depressed persons: delayed grief and distorted grief.

Grief can be postponed and experienced long after the loss. When grieving is delayed, it may not be recognized as a reaction to the original loss. However, the symptoms are those of normal grieving. A delayed or unresolved grief reaction may be precipitated by a more recent, less important loss. In some cases, delayed reactions are precipitated when the patient achieves the age at which the unmourned loved on died. Questioning the grieving person about earlier losses may reveal these dynamics.

Distorted grief reactions do not resemble normal grieving and may occur immediately following the loss or years afterward. There may be no sadness or dysphoric mood. Instead, nonaffective symptoms may be present. These manifestations may involve different medical specialists before a psychiatrist is called to the task of deciphering the nature of such reactions.

Diagnosing Abnormal Grief.   Frequently, it is clear that the patient's depression began with a significant loss, but in other cases there may be only an indirect relationship between the current depression and a previous loss. In reviewing the patient's interpersonal relationships, it is essential to obtain a history of significant relationships with those who are now dead or otherwise absent. This should include the circumstances of the death and the patient's behavioral and emotional reaction to the death in each case.

Goals and Strategies of Treatment.   The two general goals of the treatment of depression that centers around grief are: (1) to facilitate the mourning process, and (2) to help patients to reestablish interests and relationships that can substitute for the ones they have lost. The therapist's major task is to help the bereaved patient to assess the significance of the loss realistically and to emancipate himself or herself from a crippling attachment to the dead person, thus facilitating the cultivation of new interests and the formation of satisfying new relationships. The therapist adopts and utilizes strategies and techniques that help the patient bring into focus memories and emotions related to the patient's experiences with the lost person.

Nonjudgmental Exploration and Elicitation of Feelings. Abnormal grief reactions are often associated with the lack of a supportive social network that, when present, tends to help the bereaved with the normal process of mourning. Consequently, the major psychotherapeutic strategy is to encourage the patient: (1) to think about the loss; (2) to present the sequence and consequence of events prior, during, and after the death; and (3) to explore associated feelings, with the psychotherapist substituting for the missing social network.

Reassurance. Often the patient expresses the fear of bringing up that which "has been buried." The patient may express fears of "cracking up," of not being able to stop crying, or of otherwise losing control. In such instances, the psychotherapist may let the patient know that these fears are not uncommon and that mourning in psychotherapy rarely leads to decompensation.

Horowitz (1976) has identified some common themes that are typical of the dysphoric thoughts of those who have experienced stressful events such as a painful loss:

—Fear of repetition of the event even in thought.
—Shame over helplessness at being unable to prevent or stop the event.
—Rage at the person who is the source of the event (in this case, the deceased).
—Guilt or shame over aggressive impulses such as destructive fantasies.
—Survivor guilt (i.e., guilt that the loved one has died and that the survivor is relieved to remain alive).
—Fear of identification or merging with the victim.
—Sadness in relationship to the loss.

Reconstruction of the Patient's Relationship with the Deceased. Patients with abnormal grief reactions are frequently fixated on the death itself, thus avoiding the complexities of their relationship with the deceased. The therapist should lead a thorough, exhaustive, factual, and affective exploration of the patient's relationship to the deceased, both during the period when the deceased was alive and in the present context. The patient may not wish to acknowledge angry or hostile feelings toward the deceased. When the mourning process is blocked by strongly negative feelings toward the deceased, the psychotherapist should encourage the patient to express these feelings. The feelings should not be encouraged to emerge in confrontation because this may provoke a shift in the hostility from the deceased to the psychotherapist. If negative feelings emerge too rapidly, the patient may not return to psychotherapy because of the guilt that will have developed. However, if the psychotherapist reassures the patient that these negative feelings will be followed by positive and comforting feelings, as well as by a positive attitude toward the deceased, the patient will be much better prepared to acknowledge mixed feelings.

Development of Awareness.   Following the above steps, the patient may formulate a new and healthier way of understanding memories of the deceased. For instance, a particular patient may no longer regard his father as a villain but instead may come to realize that he was a sick person; the patient may thus be able to accept the father's behavior and his own reaction to it. To help patients achieve a new understanding the psychotherapist may attempt to elicit both affective and factual responses that lead the patient to a better understanding of the elements contributing to difficulties in mourning the loved one. The therapist may need to confront patients in regard to their felt need to maintain a pathologically strong bond to the deceased.

Behavioral Change.   As the patient becomes less invested in maintaining continued abnormal grieving, they may be more open to developing new relationships to "fill the empty space" left by lost loved ones. At this point, the therapist may be very active in leading the patient to consider various alternative ways (e.g., dating, church, organizations, work) to become more involved with others again.

Interpersonal Role Disputes

Definition and Description.   An "interpersonal role dispute" refers to a situation in which the patient and at least one significant other have nonreciprocal expectations about their relationship. This definition would probably pertain to every relationship at least part of the time, because role disputes are an inevitable part of life. However, IPT therapists choose to focus on role disputes only if, in their judgment, these are important in the genesis and perpetuation of a depression. Typically, these sorts of disputes are stalled or repetitious, with little perceived hope for improvement. In such circumstances, patients lose self-esteem because they feel that they can no longer control the disputes. There is a threatened loss of what others provide for them, or of their feeling of competence in managing their lives. Typical features that perpetuate role disputes are patients' demoralized sense that nothing can be done, poor habits of communication, and/or truly irreconcilable differences.

Diagnosis of Interpersonal Role Disputes.   In order for a therapist to choose role disputes as the focus of IPT, a patient must give strong evidence that he or she is currently having overt or covert conflicts with a rather significant person. Role disputes are usually revealed in the patient's initial complaints. In previous trials of IPT, role disputes with the spouse were the most frequent problem area presented (Rounsaville, Weissman, Prusoff, & Herceg-Baron, 1979). In practice, however, recognition of important interpersonal disputes in the lives of depressed patients may be difficult. Typically, patients when depressed are preoccupied with their hopeless feelings and feel that they alone are responsible for their condition. When there is no clear precipitant for a depressive episode, and when the patient does not identify problems in current interpersonal relationships, it is important for the therapist performing an assessment of past and present relationships to listen as much for what is omitted as for what is said. Failure to elaborate on a current or recent relationship that seems to be important, or the presentation of a relationship in overly idealized terms, may be clues to difficulties that the patient is unwilling to recognize and/or explore in treatment. To understand the interpersonal impact of the patient's depression, it is important to question the patient carefully about ways in which relationships may have changed prior to the onset of depressive symptoms. An understanding of ways in which interpersonal problems may have precipitated the depression, or of ways in which they are involved in preventing recovery, may suggest a strategy for therapy.

Goals and Strategies of Treatment. The general goals for treatment of an interpersonal role dispute are: (1) to help the patient identify the dispute; (2) to guide him or her in making choices about a plan of action; and (3) to encourage the patient to modify maladaptive communication patterns (if present), or to reassess expectations in order to bring about a satisfactory resolution of the dispute. Improvements in role disputes may result from behavioral changes by the patient and/or the significant other, from attitude changes by the patient (with or without attempts to satisfy needs outside the relationship), or from a satisfactory dissolution of the relationship. IPT therapists have no particular commitment to guiding patients to any particular resolution of difficulties, and they make no attempt to preserve unworkable relationships.

In developing a treatment plan, the therapist first determines the stage of the role dispute. *Renegotiation* implies that the patient and the significant other are openly aware of difficulties and are actively attempting, even if unsuccessfully, to bring about changes. *Impasse* implies that discussion between the patient and the significant other has stopped and that the smoldering, low-level resentment typical of "cold marriages" exists. *Dissolution* implies that the relationship is irretrievably disrupted. The therapist's tasks and expectations at these three stages differ. For example, intervening in an impasse situation may involve increasing apparent disharmony in order to reopen negotiations, while the task of treating a dispute at the stage of unsatisfactory negotiations may be to calm down the participants in order to facilitate conflict resolution. As with treatment of grief described above, the therapist attempts to help the patient to put the relationship in perspective, and even to become free to form new attachments if the role dispute is at the stage of dissolution.

The IPT therapist's general treatment strategy with interpersonal disputes is to help patients understand how nonreciprocal role expectation relate to the disputes and to help them to begin steps that will bring about resolution of disputes and constructive role negotiations. This movement from exploration to action may take place over the entire course of therapy, with early sessions devoted to exploration and communication analysis, and later sessions to systematic review of options for change. In dealing with particular, circumscribed problems, however, the movement from exploration to decision making may take place in a single session.

In exploring a role dispute, the therapist seeks information on different levels. At a practical level, the following questions should be answered: What are the ostensible issues in the dispute? What are the differences in expectations and values between the patient and the significant other? What are the patient's wishes in the relationship? What are the patient's options? What is the likelihood of alternatives coming about? What resources does the patient have at his or her command to bring about change in the relationship?

In understanding the emotional importance of the particular dispute, the therapist attempts to discover parallels in previous relationships. The parallels may be obvious (as in a female patient who repeatedly becomes involved with alcoholic men), or subtle (as in a man who, with apparently disparate individuals and relationships, manipulates others to reject him). When parallels are discovered, the key questions to explore are these: What does the patient gain by this behavior? What are the central unspoken assumptions that lie behind the patient's behavior?

In understanding how disputes are perpetuated, special attention to the interpersonal strategies of the disputants frequently reveals problems in communication patterns. For instance, repetitious, painful disputes are frequently perpetuated when participants are overly afraid of confrontation and expression of negative feelings. They may prefer to ignore solvable problems by simply waiting for things to "blow over."

Finally, helping the patient become aware of his or her personality style (as well as of the style of the significant other) may result in greater acceptance of conflicts, even if disputes recur in truncated form. In brief therapy, a patient may not discover and resolve unconscious conflicts underlying a tendency toward a pathological personality trait or pattern, such as pathological jealousy of a spouse. However, short of this, the treatment can be helpful if, for example, the patient can come to recognize the irrational nature of these suspicions and to devise strategies for managing these feelings, such as avoiding situations in which they arise or reducing impulsive behavior based on irrational suspicions.

When the patient has developed a sufficiently clear understanding of role disputes, including the part he or she plays in them, the process of decision analysis can be fruitfully taken up. In this process, the therapist's role is not to suggest any particular plan of action, but to assist the patient in considering the consequences of a number of alternatives thoroughly before proceeding.

Role Transitions

Definition and Description. Depressions associated with role transitions occur when patients experience great difficulty in trying to cope with life changes. Role-transition problems are most commonly associated with changes that are perceived by the patient as losses. The transition may be immediately apparent, as in the case of divorce, or it may be more symbolic, as with the sense of loss of freedom following the birth of a child or a change in social or professional status. In either, case, patients feel unable to cope with these role changes, possibly because the situations are experienced as threatening to their self-esteem and senses of identity. In general, patients' difficulties in coping with role transitions are associated with the following issues: (1) loss of familiar social supports; (2) management of accompanying affect (e.g., anger or fear); (3) demands for a new repertoire of social skills; and (4) cognitive factors (e.g., diminished self-esteem or a sense of anomie).

Individuals have multiple roles in the social system, and these roles become indelibly interwoven with the sense of self. The roles held by individuals, as well as the status attached to these roles, have an important influence on the individual's social behavior and patterns of interpersonal relationships. Impairment in social functioning frequently occurs in response to demands on the individual for rapid adaptation to new and initially strange roles, especially to roles that are perceived by the individual as representing diminished status.

Individuals undoubtedly differ in their overall vulnerability to the stress associated with role transitions. In addition, individuals differ in regard to the particular kinds of changes that are likely to produce stress, depending on the meaning of the event to the individual's self-esteem. For example, a lawyer whose sense of fulfillment and self-esteem is derived largely from his professional affiliations may not be as likely to be affected by a divorce as his wife may be, particularly if her status in the community and sense of identity are derived in large part from being "Attorney _____'s wife." In general, women tend to be more vulnerable to role transitions involving separations. Because of the way in which women are socialized, their sense of identity is more frequently derived from their connections to other people (e.g., as wife, mother). By the same token, role changes resulting from retirement are likely to place greater stresses on men than on women, since the socialization of men in our society places great emphasis on achievement and instrumentality.

Diagnosis of Role-Transition Problems.   In order for the therapist to choose role-transition problems as the focus of treatment, there must be evidence that recent events in the life of the patient has produced major changes in the patient's constellation of roles, or alternatively, the patient has become stuck and unable to negotiate expected, normative transitions (e.g., separation from parents in early adulthood). Evidence of change per se is not necessarily predictive of problems in the area of role transition. It is the significance of the change to the individual, as reflected in impaired interpersonal relationships and reduced self-esteem, that is associated with depression. It is essential, therefore, that the therapist carefully investigate both the factual nature of the changes in the patient's lifestyle and, even more importantly, the impact these changes have had on the patient in terms of social supports, role definitions, and the affects associated with the transition.

For IPT, two components of role-transition problems are distinguished: (1) the patient's feelings about the actual person or thing that has been lost (e.g., spouse, job), and (2) the patient's reaction to the concomitant role changes occasioned by the loss. The former is similar to a grief reaction in that the patient is unable to deal with the loss as such and tends to remain fixated around the lost *object*. It is the second component of the role-transition problem, involving the inability to cope with the *change* itself, that distinguishes this problem from a traditional grief reaction. For example, a patient presenting for treatment following the dissolution of her marriage may report that her marriage was intolerable for many years, and that is was she who initiated the divorce proceedings, with the expectation that her life would markedly improve if only she could extricate herself from an essentially "impossible relationship." Following the divorce, however, she may find that her married female friends, who have hitherto been an important source of support, begin to withdraw from her because they perceive her as a threat to their own marriages. In addition, the patient may experience feelings of inadequacy as a mother because her children seem to blame her for "sending Daddy away." She begins to feel increasingly unable to discipline her teenage children now that her husband is no longer providing "backup." Feeling lonely, abandoned, inadequate, and deprived of her usual social supports, she seeks treatment. What distinguishes this patient's problem from a grief reaction is that she is not mourning her husband so much as her former *role* of "married woman"; her depression is not related to the separation from her husband as such, but to her difficulty in coping with the transition from the role of wife and mother to the role of single parent.

Ordinarily, patients with role-transition problems will spontaneously relate their depression to the recent change in their life situation. However, they may not be aware of the connection between the psychological significance of the change and their diminished self-esteem. As the therapist explores such a patient's perception of the old and new role requirements and the feelings associated with each, he or she will be better able to formulate a realistic treatment plan.

Goals and Strategies of Treatment.   The two general goals in the treatment of depression associated with role transitions are: (1) to enable the patient to regard the new role in a more positive, less restrictive manner, perhaps as an opportunity for growth; and (2) to restore self-esteem by developing in the patient a sense of mastery vis-à-vis the demands of the new role-related attitudes and behaviors.

Abnormal grief and role-transition problems have much in common, in that both involve a reaction to a life change, frequently associated with a loss of some kind. Thus, the IPT strategies and techniques for dealing with problems associated with giving up old roles are similar to those recommended for grief. The therapeutic tasks are to facilitate the patient's realistic evaluation of what has been lost; to encourage the appropriate expression of affect; and, to help the patient develop a social support system and the repertoire of social skills that are called for in the new role.

The therapist will help the patient in a systematic review of the positive and negative aspects of both the old role and possible new roles. Patients will frequently feel frightened by the change itself, and, as a result, will tend to romanticize the positive aspects of what has been lost. For this reason, they need to be encouraged to explore the opportunities offered in the new role. As a rule, patients' resistances to change make it difficult for them to imagine themselves functioning efficiently in different ways. The therapist must actively support these patients as they gradually disengage themselves from the familiar old roles and begin to venture out into new, and as yet unexplored, ways of feeling and behaving.

Interpersonal Deficits

Definition and Description.   Interpersonal deficits are chosen as the focus of treatment when a patient presents with a history of social impoverishment involving inadequate or unsustaining interpersonal relationships. These patients may never have established lasting or intimate relationships as adults and have frequently experienced severe disruptions of important relationships as children. In general, patients who present with a history of severe social isolation tend to be more severely disturbed than do those with other presenting problems and may meet diagnostic criteria for personality disorders such as schizotypal, schizoid, or borderline personality.

Diagnosis of Interpersonal Deficits.   Optimal social functioning would include close relationships with intimates or family members, less intense but satisfying relationships with friends and acquaintances, and adequate performance and relationships in some sort of work role. It may be useful to distinguish three types of patients with interpersonal deficits:

1. Those who are *socially isolated* and lack relationships with either intimates, friends, or in a work role. These patients may have longstanding or temporary deficiencies in social skills.
2. Those who have an adequate number and range of relationships but who are *socially unfulfilled.* Such individuals may have chronic low self-esteem, despite apparent interpersonal or occupational success.
3. Those who are *chronically depressed* from a lingering depressive episode that was untreated or inadequately treated in the past. Although some of such patients' acute symptoms may have resolved, persistent multiple symptoms of low intensity continue to cause distress. For these patients, interpersonal functioning may have become impaired only after the onset of an apparently unprecipitated depressive episode. In such individuals, role impairment may take place in one or a number of roles, but this difficulty has not led to disputes with the significant other.

Persons with interpersonal deficits may become depressed during periods of change or transition, when the absence of satisfying social relations becomes more critical.

Goals and Strategies of Treatment.   The goal of treatment of interpersonal deficits is to reduce the patients' social isolation. Because many of these patients have no current meaningful relationships, the focus of treatment is on past relationships, the relationship with the therapist, and the tentative formation of new relationships.

Review of past significant relationships, particularly childhood relationships with family members, assumes a greater importance with these patients. As each relationship is reviewed, it is important to determine about each both the best and the worst part of the relationship discussed. Discussion of past relationships at their best may provide a model for helping the patient to develop satisfying new relationships.

Detailed evaluation of failed relationships or of past interpersonal difficulties may alert the therapist to predictable problem areas that may arise in new relationships. The therapist should look for regularities in the kinds of situations that led to difficulty for the patient and should help the patient identify these situations, with the hope either of avoiding them in the future or of working on gradual resolution of these difficulties.

For socially isolated patients, the attention paid to the patient-therapist relationship is more important than for patients with other types of problems. This relationship provides the therapist with the most direct data about such a patient's style of relating to others. In addition, solving problems that arise in the patient-therapist relationship may provide a model for the patient to follow in developing intimacy in other relationships. Of particular importance is the open discussion of the patient's distorted or unrealistic negative feelings about the therapist or the therapy. Typically, such patients prefer severing relationships to openly confronting other persons and resolving issues.

For a patient with interpersonal impoverishment, dealing with negative feelings toward the therapist not only provides a model of interpersonal learning, but also acts as a safety valve to prevent the patient from terminating therapy prematurely because of some imagined slight.

In helping these patients apply the learning taking place in treatment to outside situations, therapists may make extensive use of *communication analysis* and *role-playing*. When patients have attempted, successfully or unsuccessfully, to increase their interactions with others, a detailed review of these attempts may reveal easily correctable deficits in the patients' communication skills. In helping the patients overcome their hesitations in approaching others, therapists may invite the patients to role-play difficult situations with them.

In conclusion, it should be emphasized that the brief treatment of interpersonal deficits is a most difficult task, and, therefore, goal setting should be limited to starting to work on these issues, not necessarily solving them.

EFFICACY DATA ON IPT

Two trials of IPT with depressed patients and one with methadone-maintained opiate addicts have been completed by the New Haven-Boston Collaborative Depression Project.

IPT as Maintenance Treatment

Description of Study. The first study began in 1967 and was an eight-month maintenance trial of 150 women who were recovering from an acute depressive episode treated for six to eight weeks with a tricyclic antidepressant (amitriptyline). Criteria for entrance into the study of acute treatment was definite depression of at least two weeks' duration and of sufficient intensity to reach a total score of 7 or more on the Raskin Depression Scale (range 3–15; see Raskin, Schulterbrandt, Reatig et al., 1970). The majority of patients (88 percent) were diagnosed as having a neurotic depression according to *DSM-II*, (American Psychiatric Association, 1968).

This study tested the efficacy of IPT (administered weekly by experienced psychiatric social workers), as compared with low contact (brief monthly visits for assessments [the control for IPT]), with either amitriptyline, placebo, or no pill using random assignment in a 2 × 3 factorial design. The full design, methodology, and results have been reported elsewhere (Klerman et al., 1974; Weissman et al., 1974). For this discussion we will focus on the results of IPT as compared to low contact.

Results. The findings showed that maintenance IPT as compared with low contact had no significant differential impact on prevention of relapse or symptom return, but enhanced social and interpersonal functioning for patients who did not relapse. IPT's effects on social functioning, assessed by the Social Adjustment Scale (Weissman & Paykel, 1974), took six to eight months to become statistically apparent, possibly indicating the need for a longer time period to bring about changes in complex social relationships. Patients receiving IPT as compared to low contact were significantly less impaired in work performance, in the extended family, and in marriage. The percent store of improvement in social adjustment was substantially greater in IPT (44 percent) as contrasted with 28 percent in low contact.

There were several problems in this maintenance study. First, the sample of depressed patients, while all women, was not diagnostically homogeneous. In 1967 the new research diagnostic approaches which included operationalized diagnostic criteria and systematic methods for collecting information on signs and symptoms to make these diagnoses, were not available. The main diagnostic criteria used for depression was the *DSM-II,* accompanied by a symptoms severity measure. Second, although the psychotherapy was as described, in terms of conceptual framework, goals, frequency of contact, and criteria for therapist's suitability, the techniques and strategies had not yet been operationalized in a procedural manual. Finally, the maintenance study was not the best design for testing out the efficacy of a psychological treatment. Patients who entered into maintenance treatment were all drug responders. The IPT did not begin until the patient had had at least four weeks of drug treatment. Thus, the patient had already established a therapeutic relationship with the psychiatrist who was not administering IPT and the patient was not acutely depressed at the point of randomization to the social worker for IPT.

IPT as Acute Treatment

Description of Study. In 1973 we initiated a study of the acute treatment of ambulatory depressed men and women, using IPT, Amitriptyline, each alone and in combination against a nonscheduled treatment group for 16 weeks. IPT was administered weekly by experienced psychiatrists. Eighty-one patients entered the study and accepted the randomized treatment assignment.

Based on the experience in the maintenance study, changes were incorporated into this acute treatment study which resulted in a better design for a clinical trial, testing out psychotherapy. By 1973 the Schedule for Affective Disorders and Shizophrenia (SADS) and Research Diagnostic Criteria (RDC) (Endicott & Spitzer, 1978; Spitzer, Endicott, & Robins, 1978) were available for making more precise diagnostic judgments, therefore allowing the inclusion of a more homogenous sample of depressed patients. Based on the SADS-RDC approach, the inclusion criteria were nonbipolar, nonpsychotic, ambulatory patients who were experiencing an acute primary, major depression of sufficient intensity to reach a score of at least 7 on the Raskin Depression Scale.

A procedural manual for IPT was developed. Patients were randomized into IPT at the beginning of treatment. The treatment was limited to 16 weeks since this was an acute and not a maintenance treatment trial. There was a follow-up one year after treatment had ended to determine any long-term effects of treatment. The assessment of outcome was made by a clinical evaluator who was independent of and blind to the treatment the patient had received. The full details of this study have been described elsewhere (DiMascio et al., 1979b; Weissman et al., 1979). The control for IPT was nonscheduled treatment.

For this discussion, we will focus on IPT as compared to nonscheduled treatment. In nonscheduled treatment, patients were assigned a psychiatrist whom they were told to contact whenever they felt a need for treatment. No active treatment was scheduled but the patient could telephone if his/her needs were of sufficient intensity, and a 50-minute session (maximum of one a month) was scheduled. Patients requiring further treatment, who were still symptomatic after eight weeks, or whose clinical condition worsened sufficiently to require other treatment were considered failures of this treatment and were withdrawn from the study. This procedure served as an ethically feasible control for psychotherapy in that it allowed a patient to receive periodic supportive help "on demand" (DiMascio et al., 1979a).

Results. The probability of symptomatic failure over 16 weeks, as assessed by the Hamilton Scale (Hamilton, 1960), was significantly lower in IPT as compared to nonscheduled treatment. These results were upheld using other symptom outcome measures, both self-report and clinical ratings. As noted earlier, there were no differential effects of IPT on the patient's social functioning at the end of four months of maintenance treatment; they took six to eight months to develop. Similarly, in the acute treatment study, which ended at four months, no differential effects of IPT on social functioning were found. However, at one-year follow-up, patients who received IPT as compared to those who had not, were functioning at a less impaired level in social activities, as parents, and in the family unit; this difference was reflected in the rater's global assessment.

IPT with Methadone Maintained Opiate Addicts

The purpose of this study was to evaluate short-term interpersonal psychotherapy (IPT) as treatment for psychiatric disorders in opiate addicts who were also participating in a full service methadone-maintained program (Rounsaville et al., 1983a).

Seventy-two opiate addicts were randomly assigned to one of two treatment conditions for six months: (1) IPT, consisting of weekly individual psychotherapy, and (2) low contact, consisting of one brief meeting per month.

Recruitment was a problem as only 5 percent of eligible clients agreed to participate and only about half of the subjects completed study treatment. The major finding was the similarity of outcome in addicts receiving the two study treatments. However, in many of the outcome areas, subjects in both treatment conditions attained significant clinical improvement. Several factors may limit the generalizability of findings and may have biased against showing the psychotherapy effect. First, subjects in the control condition were receiving relatively intensive treatment in that the New Haven Methadone Clinic requires that all clients attend at least one 90-minute group psychotherapy session per week in addition to daily contact with the Methadone Clinic monitoring of urine specimens, and meetings with the program counselor on an as-needed basis. Second, the timing of recruitment into the study was such that clients may have resolved acute symptoms before getting engaged in the psychotherapy and this may have reduced motivation. Third, there was not a close administrative link between the clinic program and the psychotherapy, thereby undercutting the client's perception of the psychotherapy as an integral part of his/her treatment. Fourth, the recruitment rate into the psychotherapy study was low resulting in a small number of clients participating who seemed to represent those who were refractory to ordinary treatment methods.

Despite the limitations of the study, there was little in the findings to suggest that individual weekly short-term interpersonal psychotherapy provided additional benefit when added to a methadone program which already provided weekly group psychotherapy.

CONCLUSION

The field of psychotherapy outcome research is rapidly developing. In addition to the use of randomized treatment assignment and independent and blind clinical assessment of outcome, the work presented here has attempted to incorporate two important methodologic advances for psychotherapy clinical trials. There are operationalized defined diagnostic criteria to allow for relatively homogenous patient groups and operationalized and defined psychotherapeutic procedures to facilitate comparability of goals and focus between therapies and to allow for replication. This work has been evolving as we gain experience and new methodology becomes available. IPT has been refined further since the studies were completed and is being used in replication studies outside of the New Haven-Boston centers (Elkin et al., 1985).

Substantively, we have demonstrated the efficacy of: (1) maintenance IPT as compared to low contact in recovering depressives in enhancing social functioning; and (2) IPT as compared to nonscheduled treatment in acute depressives on symptom reduction and later on social functioning. The effects on social functioning take at least six to eight months to become apparent. It is not known at present which subtypes of depression (e.g., chronic, acute) are most likely to benefit from this treatment.

References

American Psychiatric Association (1968). *DSM-II: Diagnostic and statistical manual of mental disorders* (2nd ed.) Washington, DC: Author.

American Psychiatric Association. (1980). *DSM-III: Diagnostic and statistical manual of mental disorders* (3rd ed.) Washington, DC: Author.

Beck, A. T., Rush, A. J., Shaw, B. F., & Emery, G. (1979). *Cognitive therapy of depression.* New York: Guilford Press.

Becker, J. (1974). *Depression: Theory and research.* New York: Wiley.

Bloom, B. L., Asher, S. J., & White, S. W. (1978). Marital disruption as a stressor: A review and analysis. *Psychological Bulletin, 85,* 867–894.

Bowlby, J. (1969). *Attachment and loss.* London: Hogarth.

Briscoe, C. W., & Smith, J. B. (1973). Depression and marital turmoil. *Archives of General Psychiatry, 28,* 811–817.

Brown, G. W., Harris, T., & Copeland, J. R. (1977). Depression and loss. *British Journal of Psychiatry, 130,* 1–18.

Chevron, E. S., & Rounsaville, B. J. (1983). Evaluating the clinical skills of psychotherapists: A comparison of techniques. *Archives of General Psychiatry, 40,* 1129–1132.

Chodoff, P. (1970). The core problem in depression. In J. Masserman (Ed.), *Science and psychoanalysis* (Vol. 17). New York: Grune & Stratton.

Coyne, J. C. (1976). Depression and the response of others. *Journal of Abnormal Psychology, 85,* 186–193.

Davenloo, H. (1982). *Short-term dynamic psychotherapy.* New York: Jason Aronson.

DiMascio, A., Klerman, G. L., Weissman, M. M., Prusoff, B. A., Neu, C., & Moore, P. (1979a). A control group for psychotherapy research in acute depression: One solution to ethical and methodologic issues. *Journal of Psychiatric Research, 15,* 189–197.

DiMascio, A., Weissman, M. M., Prusoff, A. B., Neu, C., Zwilling, M., & Klerman, G. L. (1979b). Differential symptom reduction by drugs and psychotherapy in acute depression. *Archives of General Psychiatry, 36,* 1450–1456.

Elkin, I. E., Parloff, M. B., Hadley, S. W., & Autry, A. H. (1985). N.I.M.H. Treatment of depression collaborative research program: Background and research plan. *Archives of General Psychiatry, 42,* 305–316.

Endicott, J., & Spitzer, R. L. (1978). A diagnostic interview—The schedule for affective disorders and schizophrenia. *Archives of General Psychiatry, 37,* 837–844.

Frank, J. D. (1973). *Persuasion and healing: A comparative study of psychotherapy.* Baltimore: Johns Hopkins University Press.

Hamilton, M. (1960). A rating scale for depression. *Journal of Neurology, Neurosurgery, and Psychiatry, 23,* 56–62.

Henderson, S., Byrne, D. G., Duncan-Jones, P., Adcock, S., Scott, R., & Steele, G. P. (1978a). Special bonds in the epidemiology of neurosis. *British Journal of Psychiatry, 132,* 463–466.

Henderson, S., Duncan-Jones, P., Byrne, D. G., Scott, R., & Adcock, S. (1978b, October). *Social bonds, adversity, and neurosis.* Paper presented at W.P.A. Section on Epidemiology and Community Psychiatry, St. Louis.

Henderson, S., Duncan-Jones, P., McAuley, H., & Richie, K. (1978c). The patient's primary group. *British Journal of Psychiatry, 132,* 74–86.

Holmes, T. H., Goodell, H., & Woolf, S. (1950). *The nose: An experimental study of reactions within the nose of human subjects during varying life experience.* Springfield, IL: Charles C Thomas.

Horowitz, M. J. (1976). *Stress response syndrome.* New York: Jason Aronson.

Ilfeld, F. W. (1977). Current social stressors and symptoms of depression. *American Journal of Psychiatry, 134,* 161–166.

Klerman, G. L., DiMascio, A., Weissman, M. M., Prusoff, B. A., & Paykel, E. S. (1974). Treatment of depression by drugs and psychotherapy. *American Journal of Psychiatry, 131,* 186–191.

Klerman, G. L., Weissman, M. M., Rounsaville, B. J., & Chevron, E. (1984). *Interpersonal psychotherapy of depression.* New York: Basic Books.

Lewinsohn, P. M., Biglan, T., & Zeiss, A. (1976). Behavioral treatment of depression. In P. Davidson (Ed.), *Behavioral management of anxiety, depression, and pain.* New York: Brunner/Mazel.

Lindemann, E. (1944). Symptomatology and management of acute grief. *American Journal of Psychiatry, 101,* 141–148.

Malan, D. H. (1963). *A study of brief psychotherapy.* London: Tavistock Publications.

Meyer, A. (1957). *Psychobiology: A science of man.* Springfield, IL: Charles C Thomas.

Parsons, T. (1951). Illness and the role of the physician: A sociological perspective. *American Journal of Orthopsychiatry, 21,* 452–460.

Paykel, E. S., Myers, J. K., Dienelt, M. N., Klerman, G. L., Lindenthal, J. J., & Pepper, M. P. (1969). Life events and depression: A controlled study. *Archives of General Psychiatry, 21,* 753–760.

Prusoff, B. A., Weissman, M. M., Klerman, G. L., & Rounsaville, B. J. (1980). Research diagnostic criteria and differential response to psychotherapy and drug treatment. *Archives of General Psychiatry, 37,* 796–803.

Raskin, A., Schulterbrandt, J. G., Reatig, N., & McKeon, J. J. (1970). Differential response of hospitalized depressed patients. *Archives of General Psychiatry, 23,* 164–173.

Rounsaville, B. J., Weissman, M. M., Prusoff, B. A., & Herceg-Baron, R. (1979). Marital disputes and treatment outcome in depressed women. *Comprehensive Psychiatry, 20,* 473–490.

Rounsaville, B. J., Sholomskas, D., & Prusoff, B. A. (1980). Chronic minor mood disorders in depressed outpatients: Diagnosis and response to pharmacotherapy. *Journal of Affective Disorders, 2,* 73–88.

Rounsaville, B. J., Glazer, W., Wilber, C. H., Weissman, M. M., & Kleber, H. D. (1983). Short-term interpersonal psychotherapy in methadone-maintained opiate addicts. *Archives of General Psychiatry, 40,* 629–636.

Rounsaville, B. J., Chevron, E., & Weissman, M. M. (1983). Specification of techniques in interpersonal psychotherapy. In R. L. Spitzer & J. R. W. Williams (Eds.), *Psychotherapy research: Where are we and where should we go?* (pp. 160–172). New York: Guilford Press.

Sifneos, P. E. (1979). *Short-term dynamic psychotherapy evaluation and technique.* New York: Plenum Publications.

Siggins, L. (1966). Mourning: A critical survery of the literature. *International Journal of Psychoanalysis, 47,* 14–25.

Spitzer, R. L., Endicott, J., & Robins, E. (1978). Research Diagnostic Criteria: Rational and reliability. *Archives of General Psychiatry, 35,* 773–782.

Sullivan, H. S. (1953a). *Conceptions of modern psychiatry.* New York: Norton.

Sullivan, H. S. (1953b). *The interpersonal theory of psychiatry.* New York: Norton.

Weissman, M. M., Klerman, G. L., Paykel, E. S., Prusoff, B. A., & Hauson, B. (1974). Treatment effects on the social adjustment of depressed patients. *Archives of General Psychiatry, 30,* 771–778.

Weissman, M. M., & Paykel, E. S. (1974). *The depressed woman: A study of social relationships.* Chicago: University of Chicago Press.

Weissman, M. M., Prusoff, B. A., DiMascio, A., Neu, C., Goklaney, M., & Klerman, G. L. (1979). The efficacy of drugs and psychotherapy in the treatment of acute depressive episodes. *American Journal of Psychiatry, 136,* 555–558.

Chapter 6

Marital and Family Treatment of Depression

Gretchen L. Haas

Assistant Professor of Psychology in Psychiatry, Department of Psychiatry, Cornell University Medical College and Payne Whitney Clinic, The New York Hospital

John F. Clarkin

Associate Professor of Clinical Psychology in Psychiatry, Department of Psychiatry, Cornell University Medical College and Westchester Division, The New York Hospital

Ira D. Glick

Professor of Psychiatry, Department of Psychiatry, Cornell University Medical College and Payne Whitney Clinic, The New York Hospital

INTRODUCTION

Historical trends in the psychiatric treatment of depression reflect concomitant shifts in perspective regarding the nature and origins of depressive disorders. With the advent of effective psychopharmacological treatments for affective disorders, there has been a shift from more psychogenic models of depression to interactional models describing the joint contributions of psychosocial and biological determinants.

Current clinical wisdom holds that the treatment of choice for endogenous depression involves the combination of psychopharmacological and psychosocial treatments (Klerman, DiMascio, Weissman, Prusoff, & Paykel, 1974). The rationale for this is based, in part, on the finding that interpersonal problems are associated with depressive symptomatology and/or character structure (Akiskal, 1983; Akiskal, Hirschfeld, & Yerevanian, 1983; Briscoe & Smith, 1969; Brown, Harris, & Copeland, 1977; Coleman & Miller, 1975; Paykel, Myers, Dienelt, Klerman, Lindethal, & Pepper, 1969). Hence, individual treatment which focuses on the marital and/or family problems (Rounsaville, Weissman, Prusoff, & Herceg-Baron, 1979) or alternately, marital/family treatment is indicated to be of greatest potential benefit to depressed patients.

This review will focus on current theory and practice of marital/family therapy for the broad spectrum of depressive disorders. The theoretical rationale for applications of marital/family therapy will be presented followed by findings from several lines of empirical investigation bearing on the relationship between social functioning and depressive disorders. Three major areas of investigation will be discussed: (*a*) the association between marital dysfunction and depressive symptoms in a clinically depressed population; (*b*) clinical observations of specific life history patterns of psychosocial dysfunction associated with the various subtypes of depression; and (*c*) communication patterns of the depressed patient and spouse. Next, empirical findings on the use of family/marital therapy for treatment of depressive disorders will be reviewed. Finally, implications for the application of family/ marital interventions with depressives will be discussed, including (*a*) the description of the goals, strategies, and techniques of family/marital therapy with depressives; and (*b*) the use of family/marital therapies for prevention of psychiatric disorders.

THE PSYCHOSOCIAL CONTEXT OF DEPRESSION

The Interpersonal Element in Contemporary Models of Depression

Recent developments in social psychiatry have stimulated interest in the relationship of mental illness to certain parameters of the social environment and units of social organization, including, in particular, the family (Kreitman, 1964). In contrast to traditional intrapsychic models of depression, the interpersonal models, evolving from general systems theory and communication theory perspectives, place a growing emphasis on the social origins and complex interpersonal processes associated with depressive symptomatology. Several authors in the field of psychiatry have presented interpersonal models of depression (Coyne, 1976), many of which focus specifically on family and marital interaction as an essential aspect of the depressive process (Feldman, 1976; Haley, 1963; Hogan & Hogan, 1975; Rubenstein & Timmens, 1978; Watzlawick & Coyne, 1980). Hence, the communication theorists (Bateson, 1972; Lidz, Cornelison, & Terry, 1960; Watzlawick, Jackson, & Beavin, 1967), the systems theory therapists (Bowen, 1966; Haley, 1963; Wynne, 1961), the strategic therapists (Bateson, 1972; Erickson cited in Haley, 1963; Watzlawick, Weakland, & Fisch, 1974), and the structural family therapists (Minuchin, 1974) derive from the same evolutionary cybernetic model (Hoffman, 1981) a focus on the interpersonal components of the depressive symptomatology; the depressive symptoms are viewed as functional links in an interpersonal interactive process; diagnosis and intervention are defined in terms of the larger structures and dynamics of the family/marital systems. It is on the basis of this theoretical perspective that family/marital therapies have been selected as the *preferred* mode of intervention.

Reinforcement Theories. Behavioral and social learning theory perspectives have provided a framework for cognitive-behavioral models of depression. Among these, reinforcement theories specifically attribute depression to inadequate rates of positive reinforcement, secondary to a low frequency of social activity (Youngren & Lewinsohn, 1980), poor social skills (Lewinsohn, Weinstein, & Alper, 1970; Lewinsohn & Shaffer, 1971; Libet & Lewinsohn, 1973); and the tendency to elicit negative affect and rejecting behavior from others (Coyne, 1976).

Cognitive Theories. Cognitive theories of depression (Beck, 1967; Ellis & Harper, 1961; Rehm, 1977; Seligman, 1974) cite evidence of disorders of thinking and perception (Beck, Rush, Shaw, & Emery, 1978) as the primary components of a constellation of depressive symptoms, including depressive mood, lowered self-esteem (Filippo & Lewinsohn, 1971) and lowered expectations for success (Weintraub, Segal, & Beck, 1974). Cognitive approaches to marital/family therapy for depression (Russell, Russell, & Waring, 1980; Waring & Russell, 1982) promote cognitive self-disclosure among family members; the aim is to increase intimacy via enhanced knowledge and understanding of the ideas, attitudes, and beliefs of the marital partner and/or other family members. Personal theories of family members regarding the nature of marital/family maladjustment are actively explored. Horowitz, Weckler, and Doren (1983) advocate a bifocal approach to the treatment of depression, one which focuses on modification of cognitions *or* resolution of interpersonal conflicts/discord or a combination of the two. Thus, for the depressed patient who manifests distortions in his perceptions of self, other, and future events (Beck, 1967; Ellis & Harper, 1961; Rehm, 1977; Seligman, 1974), the active exploration of his/her perceptions of self and other in the context of a social group (such as the family or marital unit), offers the possibility of correcting misperceptions, faulty logic, and unrealistic expectations that tend to inhibit constructive and gratifying social activity. Here the family/marital partners provide feedback and a context for observing and testing the realistic/unrealistic nature of the depressed family members' perception and thinking.

Cognitive-Behavioral Theories. Seligman's (1974) model of depression is based on an experimental paradigm of "learned helplessness"; according to his theory, the depressive syndrome originates under environmental conditions which generate an expectation that responding is independent of reinforcement. Hence, the term *learned helplessness* refers to the development of a cognitive set in which reinforcements are viewed as response-independent; that is, independent of the respondent's behavior. Viewed from within a social or interpersonal context, this phenomenon is manifested as the belief that one's actions have little or no significant effect upon the people and events in one's surrounding social environment and day-to-day living. Such attributions appear to generate a sense of personal helplessness, and this attitude may generalize to future events (Abramson,

Seligman, & Teasdale, 1978). Family/marital therapy based on Seligman's model of learned helplessness would be directed toward modifying the depressed person's feelings of personal ineffectuality (and the motivational deficits which accompany such feelings). Hence, training in the use of effective social skills is viewed as prerequisite to enhancing one's ability to generate response-contingent social reinforcements. Thus, from this perspective, the objective of marital/family interventions is to induce more frequent and pleasurable (i.e., reinforcement-generating) relations between the depressed patient and members of his/her family and to enhance his patient's sense of control over the occurrence of pleasurable events. Similarly, the use of operant learning principles (Stuart, 1969), experiential techniques (Satir, 1967), and the specific application of cognitive-behavioral principles, as in marital contracting strategies (Sager, 1976), is directed toward enhancement of the depressed patient's capacity for pleasure.

Lewinsohn and his group (Lewinsohn & Hoberman, 1982) emphasize the training in, and acquisition of, effective social skills to enable the depressive patient to: (1) enter the domain of social interaction, and (2) function effectively; that is, in a manner which enables the patient to generate necessary social reinforcements.

Other social learning theories suggest that the quality of marital/family relations is determined by the ratio of positive to negative exchanges (Jacobson & Moore, 1981; Stuart, 1969; Weiss, Hops, & Patterson, 1973). The depressive's tendency to be aversive to others in social situations (Coyne, 1976) is associated with his/her tendency to receive aversive responses from others (Jacobson & Moore, 1981); the depressed individual tends to give and receive aversive stimulation at higher rates than evidenced by other members of the family (Reid, 1967, cited in Lewinsohn & Hoberman, 1982); similarly, there is some evidence that a depressed partner and his mate tend to engage in negative (aversive) exchanges more frequently than do nondistressed, "normal" couples (Birchler & Webb, 1975; Birchler et al., 1972; Weiss et al., 1973; Wills, Weiss, & Patterson, 1974). Furthermore, "distressed" couples are more reactive to recent events, positive or negative, than are their nondistressed counterpart (Jacobson, Follette, & McDonald, 1982).

Based on these findings, marital therapy for the depressed patient and mate would be directed to: (1) reducing the frequency of aversive communications between partners, and (2) inducing more frequent mutual reinforcement (Stuart, 1969), as well as modification of distorted cognitive and perceptual responses to the behavior of the partner (Jacobson et al., 1982). Viewed from a broader perspective, the *general goals* of behavioral approaches to marital/family therapy are to: (1) increase the rate of rewarding interactions; (2) decrease the rate of aversive interactions; and (3) enhance the active conflict-resolution and problem-solving strategies and skills (Gurman & Kniskern, 1978).

In summary, the influence of broad-based paradigm shifts in the conception of depressive processes (as represented by systems theories and behavioral/social learning theories), there has been an upsurge of interest in identifying and utilizing social and interpersonal forces in the treatment of depressive disorders. Hence, a technology of interpersonal therapies has emerged, as represented by such generic treatment modalities as group, family and marital therapies which work, in large part, to alter the interpersonal components of the depressive disorder. The specific utility of marital and family therapy approaches to the treatment of depression can be evaluated in terms of their relevance to the specific psychosocial deficits associated with depressive disorders. The following discussion deals with the empirical evidence of psychosocial dysfunction among samples of clinically depressed patients. Such data is presented in order to substantiate the *need* for and *validity* of psychosocial/interpersonal treatments of depression.

Psychosocial Dysfunction in a Clinically Depressed Population

A substantial body of evidence is accumulating which indicates that patients with depressive disorders experience impairment of psychosocial functioning at various stages of the life history (Brown, Bhrolchain, & Harris, 1975; Paykel & Weissman, 1973; Rutter & Quinton, 1977; Weissman, Klerman, & Paykel, 1974). For example, Paykel et al. (1969) observed that marital friction was the most common event reported to occur during the six months prior to the onset of depressive symptoms. Moreover, stress in marital and parental role-functioning has been identified as a principle correlate of depressive symptoms (Ilfeld, 1977).

Birtchnell & Kennard (1983a, 1983b) present evidence that, among a series of depressed psychiatric patients in the United Kingdom, marital maladjustment occurred more frequently among the *neurotic* depressed than among the *endogenous* depressed; in a majority of these cases, marital maladjustment antedates the onset of depressive symptoms. Furthermore, evidence of a temporal association between premorbid marital adjustment and the age of onset of depressive symptoms has been cited (Paykel & Weissman, 1973).

Several lines of investigation further substantiate the association between depression and social adjustment. These include studies which reveal: (*a*) evidence of social dysfunction *during the acute phase* of the depressive disorder (Weissman & Paykel, 1974); (*b*) the temporal association of recent life events and, in particular, marital stress, with the *onset* of depression (Ilfeld, 1977; Paykel et al., 1969; Paykel et al., 1973; Pearlin & Lieberman, 1977; Weissman & Paykel, 1974); (*c*) lower levels of social and marital role-functioning among depressives as compared with normals (Birtchnell & Kennard, 1983b); (*d*) differential levels of depressive symptoms for individuals with "good" versus "poor" marital adjustment (Birtchnell & Kennard, 1983a); (*e*) an association between neurotic depression, age, and length of marriage (Baldwin, 1971; Birtchnell & Kennard, 1983a); and (*f*) an apparent prophylactic influence of a close, intimate relationship on potential depressive symptoms (Brown et al., 1975; Brown & Harris, 1978b).

The Functional Relationship between Marital/Family Stress and Depression

The work of Vaughn and Leff (1976) on the "expressed emotion" of family members of psychiatric patients is relevant to a discussion of the psychosocial functioning of depressed patients. In a study of family relations of 32 hospitalized primary depressed patients, these investigators found that the frequency of critical remarks made by key relatives in reference to the depressed patient, was related to the rate of patient relapse. Results indicated that the depressed patients were more sensitive to criticism from relatives than were schizophrenic patients for whom criticism and emotional overreactivity of relatives are highly correlated with rates of relapse and hospital readmission (Brown, Birley, & Wing, 1972).

Evidence of an association between marital/family conflict and depression prompts one to question the specific nature and direction of any causal connections underlying this association. Several alternative types of causal relationships are suggested by the available data: (1) consistent with a diathesis-stress model of psychopathology, marital/family stressors may *elicit* or *precipitate* the onset of depressive symptoms in a biologically, predisposed individual; (2) alternately, marital/family stress, or the lack of a sufficiently supportive, intimate relationship, may *potentiate* the effects of other environmental stressors, as suggested by the results of Vaughn and Leff (1976) and the Brown and Harris (1978a) longitudinal study; (3) depressive symptoms may trigger maladaptive behavior and negative responses from family members (Paykel & Weissman, 1973), thus acting to elicit marital/family conflict (Bullock, Siegel, Weissman, & Paykel, 1972; Cammer, 1971; Henderson, Byrne, & Duncan-Jones, 1981; Ineichen, 1976); and (4) subclinical depressive or characterological traits, behavior patterns, etc., may potentiate marital/family discord which, in turn, tends to trigger the onset of a depressive episode (Akiskal, Bitar, Puzantian, Rosenthal, & Walker, 1978; Akiskal et al., 1983).

The various "linkages" of depression and psychosocial dysfunction can be viewed as consonant with the major subtypes of depressive disorder: primary (endogenous) forms (both unipolar and bipolar) represented by the diathesis-stress model or model which combines *both* the diathesis-stress and characterological-predisposition models (Akiskal et al., 1983), secondary (nonendogenous) forms represented by the precursor-potentiator model (e.g., Brown & Harris, 1978b), and characterological forms represented by the personality trait characterological-predisposition models of depression.

Among some endogenous depressives social dysfunction appears *not* to antedate onset of depressive symptoms. Certain chronic forms of personality change and social maladjustment appear to develop over the course of repeated depressive episodes (Akiskal et al., 1978; Cassano, Maggini & Akiskal, 1983; Klein, 1974). However, the more traditional view of primary affective disorder as presented by Kraepelin (1921) describes the disorder in terms of an underlying personality structure which predisposes these individuals to affective episodes. By way of illustration of this latter perspective, we consider the following line of investigation. Evidence of a pattern of chronic social dysfunction among a subset of depressed (primary affective disorder) patients suggests that, for this group, the chronic baseline impairment of social functioning is antecedent to, or coextensive with, the expression of the depressive symptoms. Weissman and Paykel (1974), in their longitudinal study of depressed women, note that clinically recovered depressives continued to experience problems functioning in their parental and spousal roles several months after recovery from the depressive symptoms. Moreover, the differential benefits of an interpersonally oriented psychotherapy over drugs alone in a sample of depressed women were shown to be specifically in the area of social functioning, manifest only in *long-term* outcome at six- and eight-month follow-up, and only several months after patients experienced relief from the depressive symptoms (DiMascio, Weissman, Prusoff, Neu, Swilling, & Klerman, 1979; Klerman et al., 1974; Weissman & Paykel, 1974; Weissman, Prusoff, DiMascio, Neu, & Klerman, 1979). Hence, the presence of depressive symptoms is *not* a necessary precondition to marital/familial distress in these patients. Instead, interpersonal dysfunction is viewed as one of several *components* of a depressive personality disorder and a relatively constant "background" to the affective episodes.

The linkage of characterological traits with depressive symptoms is richly described in several clinical reports of the marital relationships of primary affective disorder patients. For example, a characteristic lack of autonomy and a tendency to "cling" to relationship partners has been noted among endogenous depressives (Akiskal et al., 1978), as has a characteristic wish for the partner to be strong (Wadeson & Fitzgerald, 1971) and to control or set limits for the depressed spouse (Greene, Lustig, & Lee, 1976; Mayo, 1979). Moreover, there is evidence that the depressive episodes of the unipolar endogenous depressive patient tend to occur *during* a relationship rather then *after separation* or breakup of partners, the latter occurring more frequently among the nonendogenous depressives (Akiskal et al., 1983). The temporal contiguity of unipolar depressive episodes with involvement in what may be malignant patterns of marital interaction, suggests that, for this group of patients, marital/family relations constitute an important component of what could be viewed as a biosocial disorder; that is, one in which interpersonal relations are intimately linked to the clinical manifestations of the depression.

The research findings on assortative mating among endogenous depressive patients would further support this model of a transactional relationship between biological and psychosocial determinants of depression. The well-documented tendency for affective disorder patients to select similarly disposed individuals as mates (Baron, Mendlewicz, Gruen, Asnis, & Fieve, 1981; Crow, 1968; Merikangas, Bromet, & Spiker, 1983; Merikangas & Spiker, 1982; Negri, Melica, Zuliani, Gasperini, Macciardi, & Smeraldi, 1981) would suggest that the social maladjustment of the endogenous depressed patient predisposes such patients to maladaptive selection of a marital partner and marital maladjustment (Merikangas et al., 1983). Conversely, the apparent "protective" functions of an intimate relationship with a "normal" partner, as described by Brown and Harris (1978b), are manifest among those endogenous depressed patients who marry a psychiatrically "well" partner and experience subsequent remission or reduction of their depressive symptoms (Merikangas et al., 1983).

Patterns of Psychosocial Dysfunction: Exogenous versus Endogenous Depression

The constellation of psychosocial problems manifest in exogenous precipitated forms of depression contrasts with those of the endogenous depressive disorders. For example, episodes of neurotic depression are frequently preceded by separation, or breakup, of a conjugal relationship; this is less frequently found among cases of endogenous depression, which tend to occur within the context of an intact relationship (Matussek & Feil, 1983). The character of psychosocial deficits differs for the two groups; Matussek and Feil (1983) suggest that among nonendogenous depressives, dysfunctional interpersonal coping tends to take the form of a mistrust and pseudo-independence or pseudo-autonomy as protection against potential frustration or disappointment in their interpersonal relations. The negative reactions of the neurotic depressive's mate may, in turn, reinforce the guilt feelings or fear characteristic of these patients.

In contrast, the constellation of marital/family problems experienced by the endogenous unipolar depressives appears to be associated with a characterological form of over accommodation, submissiveness, and lack of self-assertiveness associated with feelings of neediness and dependency. Due to passivity and fear of abandonment, these patients are likely to be ineffective in coping with interpersonal conflicts, tending to avoid overt expressions of anger and lacking the capacity to engage in active approaches to interpersonal problem solving (Matussek & Feil, 1983). Psychological stress of interpersonal intimacy may, for these patients, explain the tendency for depressive episodes to occur within the context of a conjugal relationship. Matussek and Feil (1983) speculate that loss or permanent separation from a mate is unlikely to trigger a depressive episode among endogenous depressive patients; these patients are, these authors suggest, more likely to seek out new partners relatively soon after a breakup, thus reestablishing the socioemotional situation which appears to give rise to their depressive state.

Based on clinical observations, these findings, as reported by Matussek and Feil (1983), are speculative. Nonetheless, the formulations presented by these investigators lend integrative power to the organization and interpretation of a broad spectrum of psychosocial phenomena associated with depressive disorders. As such, they are provocative and appear to be worthy of empirical investigation.

Patterns of Psychosocial Dysfunction: Patient/Spouse Communication

One line of investigation has focused on the specific patterns of communication of depressed patients and their spouses. Experimental paradigms have been designed to test the hypothesis that the communicative interactions between the depressed patient and the spouse contribute to, and sustain, depressive symptomatology. Hinchcliffe, Hooper, Roberts, and Vaughan (1975) compared a sample of depressed psychiatric inpatients and spouses with a control sample of surgical inpatients and spouses on several dimensions of interpersonal communication: expressiveness, responsiveness, personal control, and tension, as well as certain dimensions of nonverbal communication. These patients and their spouses were studied in an experimental situation in which discussion was generated and recorded during an acute episode of depression, and at posttreatment follow-up. Recordings of the dialogues within the control group of surgical patients and spouses were also made. These investigators observed that depressed couples verbalized their personal (subjective) experiences more frequently than did control couples who tended to be more task oriented in their discussions (Hooper, Roberts, Hinchcliffe, & Vaughan, 1977). In addition, the depressed patient couples expressed more negative affect in their verbal communications than did the control couples. Finally, indirect indexes of tension between speakers suggested that during discussion the depressed couples experienced significantly more negative tension than did the control couples (Hinchcliffe et al., 1975).

Contrary to theoretical assumptions regarding the passivity and dependency of the depressed spouse, Hooper, Roberts, Hinchcliffe, and Vaughan (1977) reported that the depressed patients in their sample produced more control-oriented communications with the spouse during the acute depressive episode as compared with the posttreatment follow-up period. Likewise, the investigators observed that during the acute phase of depression patients demonstrated a slightly higher rate of speech and a greater use of eye gaze than during the recovery phase. These findings prompted the investigators to suggest that the concept of the "powerless" and "subordinate" depressed spouse needs revision.

Paykel and Weissman (1973) followed 40 depressed women and controls over an eight-month period. Whereas work performance and clinical symptoms showed the most rapid recovery, several aspects of the women's interpersonal relations improved less rapidly or showed little change over the eight-month period. Interpersonal friction, inhibited communication, and the expression of hostility endured over the course of the eight months, despite symptom improvement. Consistent with these findings are the findings of Hooper et al. (1977) who observed that high levels of tension and negative comments persist unchanged over time in the conversations of female depressed patients and their husbands. Male patients were found to have difficulty confronting their wives; frustration and aggression were communicated by tone of voice; male patients also attempted to camouflage negative affects by using words with a more positive or euphemistic connotation. Hinchcliffe et al. (1977) noted that these behavior patterns tended to persist unchanged, suggesting that they are more enduring characteristics of personality and social functioning rather than consequences of the depressive episode.

In summary, the specific "linkages" of psychosocial problems with the depressive symptoms will tend to dictate the nature and timing of any psycho-social intervention in the treatment of depressed patients. While we have talked about the intricacies of combined psychopharmalogical and psychoso-cial treatments elsewhere (Glick & Clarkin, 1981) treatment of endogenous depression would be directed to: (1) reducing symptoms with psychophar-macological agents; and (2) using marital family therapies to treat the psycho-social component of the disorder. The focus of marital/family treatment would be: (*a*) reducing marital/family stressors that tend to elicit the onset of a depressive episode; (*b*) enlisting the support of family members to assure patient compliance with any prescribed medication regimen; and (*c*) promot-ing understanding of the nature of the illness and the development of the "support" functions (a la Brown & Harris, 1978b) of the family/marital rela-tionship. For (nonendogenous) depressions, marital/family therapies would aim to: (*a*) enhance intrafamilial communication and problem-solving func-tions, in general; and (*b*) more specifically, reduce misperceptions, faulty communications, and ineffective problem-solving strategies which appear to support or exacerbate the depressive symptoms. Finally, in cases of character-ological depressive conditions, therapy would be directed toward altering the structural aspects of the marital/family relationship that support and maintain the depressive symptoms.

Outcome Studies of Family/Marital Therapy for Depression

Despite the fact that there have been many studies of the efficacy of marital and family therapies (Gurman & Kniskern, 1978), there are only two con-trolled studies in which the identified patient suffers from affective disorder. The best designed study is by Friedman (1975). This was a random-assign-ment, placebo-controlled, 12-week clinical trial designed to assess the relative effectiveness of amitriptyline and marital therapy, administered separately and in combination. Subjects were 196 patients with a primary diagnosis of "depression" (including 172 "neurotic or reactive depression" types, 15 with "psychotic depressions," and 9 with either manic-depressive psychosis or involutional psychotic reactions). Outcome was assessed in the following areas: symptom severity, global improvement, family and marital relations, and attitudes toward medication. Results indicated that both drug and marital therapies had beneficial effects compared to their respective control treat-ments (placebo drug and minimal contact, individual therapy). Of particular interest, however, was evidence of some differential effects of these two major modes of treatment; whereas drug therapy was associated with signifi-cant early improvement in clinical symptoms, marital therapy was associated with significant long-term positive changes in patient self-report measures of family role-functioning and marital relations.

McLean, Ogston, and Grauer (1973) used behavioral techniques to re-cord and intervene in verbal interactions between couples, one member of which was clinically depressed. With a total number of 20 couples, half of the couples were given feedback boxes designed to signal positive and negative feedback during ongoing conversation. Not only did the feedback procedure significantly reduce remarks considered negative, but couples in this intervention group showed significantly reduced negative interchanges, while comparison group couples did not. The total behavioral treatment package, including the feedback procedure, training in the use of behavioral contracting and social learning principles, produced significantly more improvement on target complaints for the experimental treatment group as compared to the nontreatment comparison group.

There are several controlled studies of marital and family therapies for treatment of depression in progress. Weissman, Rounsaville, Prusoff, and Chevron (1983, personal communication) are in the process of assessing the relative efficacy of individual marital therapy as compared to conjoint marital therapy for women (outpatients) who present with depression and marital disputes.

Glick and colleagues in New York City (Glick, Haas, Spencer, Clarkin, Lewis, Newman, DeMane, Good-Ellis, & Harris, 1983) are in the process of assessing the relative efficacy of including inpatient family intervention (IFI) with hospitalization versus hospitalization alone for patients diagnosed as having either major affective disorder or schizophrenic disorder. Inpatient family intervention, of at least six-session duration, is designed to: (*a*) modify maladaptive family patterns associated with the problems of the identified patient, (*b*) facilitate family communication, and (*c*) promote more adaptive family role-functioning and attitudes toward the identified patient.

Preliminary results with the first half of the sample (Glick et al., 1983) suggest that at six-month follow-up, there is an overall significant treatment effect favoring family intervention for all patients combined, and a significantly better outcome for the good prehospital functioning schizophrenics treated with family intervention than for those treated with the comparison hospital treatment without family intervention.

Theoretical and Practical Considerations in Family/Marital Treatment with Depressed Patients

The temporal and functional relationship between depression and aspects of marital/family interaction has important implications for the design and implementation of marital/family treatment of depressive disorders. As noted earlier, in cases of neurotic depression, marital/family conflict is often reported as the primary precipitant in episodes of clinical depression. In such cases, marital or family therapy would be indicated for treatment of the interpersonal problems; antidepressant medication can be combined with these therapies for symptom relief without risk of compromising their effectiveness (Rounsaville, Klerman, & Weissman, 1981).

In cases where marital or family conflict appears not to be a contributing factor in the depressive episode, the identified patient should be treated with appropriate medication and then reevaluated for psychotherapy. The addition of short-term supportive marital and/or family therapies may be useful in helping to engage the patient in the recommended medication regimen and in establishing a social support system which provides the increased positive reinforcement and/or insulation from excessive stressors.

With cases of endogenous depression, the stress of intimate relations and the negative impact of the patient's symptoms on other members of the family (Targum, Dibble, Davenport, & Gershon, 1981) suggest the need for a biphasic program of marital or family intervention. During the initial phase, psychopharmacological treatments are begun and short-term supportive marital or family therapy is introduced to ameliorate the family's negative reactions to the symptoms (thus reducing secondary stress reactions) and to educate the patient and family as to the nature of the disorder, the recommended treatment, and strategies for coping with residual symptoms and possible relapse. It is only after the florid symptoms have "cleared" and the patient and family have reached a "plateau" or relatively stable stage of adjustment that a second phase of therapy can be initiated with the family. Efforts to modify maladaptive communication patterns and problem-solving strategies, deal with resistances and effect structural changes are best reserved for this second phase of intervention with the family.

A General Approach to the Family/Marital Treatment of Affective Disorders

In this section, we will briefly describe some of the general principles of treatment for families or marital couples in which one or more members presents with depression. These principles, while applicable to the treatment of certain other conditions, have been adapted for treatment of depressive symptomatology and the related psychosocial dysfunctions in the patient's marital and family relations.

Assessment Strategies

Given that depression accompanies a broad spectrum of disorders, with diverse etiologies, phenotypic symptom constellations and developmental courses, the role of assessment in the planning and implementation of a coordinated treatment program is crucial. The multifaceted nature of the depressive disorders, characterized as they are by a complex of biological, psychosocial, and intrapsychic components, call for a multifocal approach to assessment and treatment. (See Table 1.)

Assessment procedures are implemented during *all* phases of treatment for the primary purposes of: (1) understanding the specific nature of the disorder; (2) designing and modifying treatment strategies; and (3) systematically assessing patient/family responses to specific treatment interventions. The selection of appropriate assessment procedures is guided in general principle by the need to evaluate the depressed patient and his/her family

TABLE 1
Differential treatment planning for depression

Family context	Type of depression		
	Endogenous	*Nonendogenous*	*Nonendogenous with life stress*
Chronic, hostile, intrusive interactions	Pharmacotherapy followed by family intervention Attention to children at risk	Family intervention Consider pharmacotherapy	Family intervention Consider pharmacotherapy
Negative reaction to current depressive episode	Pharmacotherapy Brief family therapy and psychoeducation	Brief family therapy and psychoeducation Consider pharmacotherapy	Brief family therapy Consider pharmacotherapy
Cooperative, nondisturbed, family interaction	Pharmacotherapy Brief family psychoeducation	Individual therapy Consider pharmacotherapy	Individual or family therapy depending on nature of stresses Consider pharmacotherapy

along each of three principle axes: (1) the *biological* axis including assessment of current medical status, patient and family history of medical and psychiatric disorder, and any additional information regarding possible physical precipitants, concomitants, and so on of the current disorder; (2) the *psychosocial* axis, including information on the individual's adjustment to all aspects of his/her social environment (wherein symptoms are viewed as individual adaptations to the context of family and the larger social world; and (3) the *intrapsychic* axis, including indexes of ego strength and weakness, primary modes of defense, and current intrapsychic conflicts and their relationship to symptom formation.

Finally, assessment of marital/family disorder proceeds according to a similarly broad-based approach involving: (1) assessment of each family member on the biological, psychosocial, and intrapsychic dimensions identified above; and (2) assessment of family structure, dynamics and interpersonal functioning, including attention to the adaptive and maladaptive patterns of (*a*) communication (e.g., depression/suppression of anger), (*b*) activity, and (*c*) coping with the depressive disorder of the identified patient.

When dealing with individuals who have suspected depression, the clinician must assess the severity and subtype of depression in order to properly plan treatment interventions. This requires some in-depth questioning of an individual regarding subjective and behavioral experience. This type of focus on the individual is something that some marital and family therapists are either theoretically against doing or are not accustomed to doing during family sessions. Nonetheless, it is our contention that an assessment of the individual is an essential component of family/marital treatment in which one member of the family presents with a depressive disorder. Individual assessment can be done either with the identified patient during an individual session or in the presence of family members as during a family session; it is, however, our experience that it can best be done in a family session where one can explore the internal experience of the individual and then relate that *internal* experience to the *interpersonal* experience as it unfolds during the family interaction. Such in-depth attention to one individual's experience and pain from depression does not disrupt the system's point of view but rather is a necessary feature of assessment of problem areas and can be integrated into an overall treatment approach (Gurman & Kniskern, 1981).

A multidimensional assessment of depressive symptomatology is ideally designed to evaluate the severity of the depressive disorder along each of the following major dimensions of symptomatology: mood, somatic symptoms, cognition, motivation, and interpersonal behavior. In addition to interview data and behavioral observations, a broad-based battery of self-assessment measures is recommended. This multidimensional assessment battery includes the Depression Adjective Checklist (DACL) with several alternate forms providing a quick, *repeatable* measure of *mood* (Lubin, 1967); the Hamilton Rating Scale (Hamilton, 1960), a 17-item interviewer-assisted measure of symptom severity, tapping a heterogeneous group of symptoms but with an emphasis on *somatic* and *behavioral* symptoms; the Beck Depression Inventory (Beck, Ward, Mendelsohn, Mock, & Erbaugh, 1961), a 21-item interviewer-assisted self-rating inventory which serves as a particularly useful measure of *cognitive* state (including mood, pessimism, guilt, self-hate, irritability); the self-report version of the Social Adjustment Scale ([SAS-SR]; Weissman & Bothwell, 1976) which provides a measure of *interpersonal functioning,* including family and marital relations, parental role-functioning (and shows sensitivity to change in depressed patients) and the Pleasant Events Schedule (MacPhillamy & Lewinsohn, 1972), an index of activity level, reinforcement potential and obtained reinforcement (Glazer, Clarkin, & Hunt, 1981) which is particularly useful for behavioral intervention and the daily logging of behavior.

Measures of family and/or marital functioning are recommended as a means of assessing the depressed patient's family/marital adjustment, mode of adaptation and family/marital environment. Moos and Moos (1976) have developed a self-report measure tapping quality of the patient's family environment, a measure which can be used to inferentially assess the possible contribution of family environment variables to the depressive disorder. In addition, the self-report measure of family cohesion and family adaptability, developed by Olson, Bell, and Portner (1978), provides an index of family structure and adaptability. This instrument has particular utility for research purposes, constructed, as it is, on an empirical basis, and tapping dimensions (family *structure* and *function*) which have been shown to bear an empirical relationship to clinical manifestations of psychopathology (Moos & Fuhr, 1982).

Finally, in order to assess marital role-functioning and adjustment, the authors recommend the use of the Dyadic Adjustment Scale (Spanier, 1976), a

31-item self-report measure which is intended to assess the quality of marital or dyadic relations, tapping the specific dimensions described as "satisfaction," "cohesion," "consensus," and "affectional expression." A more extensive, however lengthy (280-item), self-report instrument, the Marital Satisfaction Inventory, developed by Snyder (1979), includes nine subscale measures of specific dimensions of marital interaction, and two forms of the inventory—one for couples with children, and one for childless couples. This scale is notable for its inclusion of a measure of social desirability, or the tendency to adjust responses to accommodate to the perceived demands of the social situation. Both scales represent improvements over the most frequently used 15-item instrument, the Locke-Wallace Marital Adjustment Test, which has been criticized for its sensitivity to social desirability effects, and the relatively low correlations obtained between scores for the two partners (Spanier, 1972).

During the initial phase of treatment, family/marital assessment involves primarily history-gathering, the use of standardized measures (e.g., self-report inventories, structured interview rating instruments), and the concurrent observation of ongoing family interaction processes manifest in the interview/inventory process. A more detailed assessment of the general characteristics of family structure, dynamics and interpersonal functioning is deferred to the second phase of treatment which is more directly geared to modification of maladaptive coping strategies and patterns of communication among family members. It is during this second phase of treatment that the more formal techniques and strategies of traditional family therapies are employed; hence, it is during this phase that process-oriented assessment methods are implemented (e.g., videotape monitoring and assessment of specific intervention strategies and techniques). Finally, assessment of treatment outcome involves posttreatment and follow-up administration of measures used previously during the pretreatment assessment process. Consistent with the principles of good research design, the inclusion of repeated measures permits some degree of standardization and control over method variance, or the extent to which the method of assessment contributes to variation in outcome.

Treatment Goals and Strategies

The overall goals for family/marital treatment of a depressive disorder can be conceptualized in terms of: (1) reduction or removal of the depressive symptoms in the identified patient; and (2) modification of maladaptive interpersonal behavior patterns and attitudes (of the identified patient and/or family members) which tend to exacerbate or reinforce other components of the depressive disorder.

Somatic Therapies.   The presence of an endogenous depression in one or more family members raises consideration of somatic treatments of the depressive symptomatology (e.g., electroconvulsive therapy (ECT) or psychopharmacotherapy). It is the opinion of the authors that the person suffering from endogenous depression should be treated with proper medication. Furthermore, Glick and Clarkin (1981) recommended *early* treatment of the symptom component, initiated prior to, or concurrent with, the introduction of interpersonal psychotherapeutic treatment, such as marital or family therapy.

The underlying rationale for this approach is based on the premise that the symptoms of depression can prevent, or retard, interpersonal behavior change. Glick and Clarkin (1981) note that the dysphoria, anhedonia, anergia, and reduced motivation which characterize the depressive state, can have deleterious effects on family relations. These authors emphasize that a rapid amelioration of some symptoms via initiation of chemotherapy early in the course of treatment can reduce the secondary sources of interpersonal conflict and enhance the therapist's efficacy in the eyes of both patient and family. The clinician needs to be aware of the heterogeneous nature of depressive disorders and the diverse etiologies involving various combinations of biochemical, intrapsychic, and interpersonal factors. This diversity in the nature and causes of the depressive disorders calls for particular flexibility in perspective and approach to treatment (Bernstein, 1982; Glick & Clarkin, 1981; Mayo, 1979). The clinician is urged to use a combination of both somatic and interpersonal treatments which maximize treatment response by intervening at several levels of the depressive process, paying particular attention to the timing of these interventions.

Considerations in Combining Psychosocial and Somatic Therapies.   Some family and marital therapists may speculate that such combination procedures will compromise the family treatment in at least two ways: (1) the focus on the identified patient (IP) with depression may put too much emphasis on the *IP* as opposed to the family/marital *system,* thus shifting "blame" and responsibility for change onto the individual person and his/her biology; and (2) it may be feared that a decrease in the depression of the identified patient may reduce motivation for change and thereby forestall needed long-term changes within the family system. (Here it is suggested that a decrease in depression would simply foster short-term solutions, thus encouraging the couple to leave treatment prematurely.)

It is the author's observation that neither of the two dangers *necessarily* occurs and, in most cases, when the pharmacotherapy is handled strategically, these danger situations do not arise. Nevertheless, as a precaution, it can be made clear to the couple/family that the symptoms of depression that respond to medication are those of: early morning awakening, reduced or lack of libido, decreased concentration, and depressed mood. It can also be made clear that certain components of the depression do not respond to medication alone and require needed family/couple interactional change (e.g., "target" problems, negative feedback among family members, lowered self-esteem, and lack of intimacy). With this distinction clearly communicated to family members, the decrease in depression due to chemotherapy provides not a danger but an opportunity to proceed further and carry out the more long-range work of interpersonal interactional change. Without such normalization of mood in the identified patient as can be achieved with the help of ECT or chemotherapy, the second phase of family/marital treatment cannot be approached.

Specific Models of Family/Marital Therapy for Treatment of Depression. Drawing on the treatment research of Goldstein, Rodnick, Evans, May, and Steinberg (1978) and the treatment model developed by Anderson, Hogarty, and Reiss (1980) for the outpatient treatment of schizophrenics and their families, Glick et al. (1983) have designed a general treatment program for brief family/marital intervention in the treatment of acute exacerbations of schizophrenia and affective disorder. The goals, strategies, and techniques for focused family intervention in a hospital setting are outlined in the *Training Manual for Inpatient Family Intervention* (Clarkin, Newman, DeMane, Haas, Spencer, & Glick, 1982), available from the authors upon request.

Inpatient family intervention (IFI) represents an eclectic approach to family/marital intervention in the treatment of an acute illness, requiring hospitalization. Many of the principles of IFI parallel those identified by Jacobson and McKinney (1982) in their discussion of family treatment of affective disorders. As indicated earlier, the initial phase of treatment is primarily educative and supportive, dedicated to educating the family regarding the nature of the disorder, alleviating family guilt about the causes of the disorder, and aiding the family in developing a cognitive schema for understanding and planning for future coping with the disorder. It is only during the latter phase of treatment that interventions aimed at modifying family structure and interactional processes are initiated. The general goals and strategies of inpatient family intervention (see Table 2) give some overview of the approach used in the inpatient treatment of families with a family member identified as having a major affective disorder.

Typical Issues in Family/Marital Treatment of Depressive Disorders

We will briefly address here four general issues that typically arise during the course of family/marital treatment when one or more members are depressed. First, when one or more family members are assessed as having an endogenous depression (either unipolar or bipolar), requiring some form of somatic treatment, it is important to provide all family members information concerning the cause, course, and treatment of the depressive disorder. The value of a psychoeducational intervention is that it offers the family a basis for developing a more realistic understanding of the nature and causes of the depression. Such understanding usually acts to reduce family members' sense of responsibility and guilt for the episode; it also provides intellectual tools which aid in coping with the current and potential future depressive episodes.

Related to the issue of use of medication is the general issue of the "diagnosis" that the family members attribute to the depressed member. This

TABLE 2
Goals and strategies of inpatient family intervention

Goals	Strategies
1. Acceptance of the reality of the illness and development of an understanding of the current episode.	Form an alliance with the family; identify and empathize with family's previous attempts at coping; provide factual information about the illness; trace with the family the emergence of psychotic symtoms in the interpersonal context; educate the family about the course of depressive symptoms and prognosis.
2. Identification of possible precipitating stresses relevant to the current episode.	Identify and rank-order current stresses; discuss how the family deals with these stresses.
3. Identification of likely future stresses both within and outside the family.	Anticipate future stresses and family coping behaviors.
4. Elucidation of the interaction sequence within the family that produces stress on the identified patient.	Inform the family that current family interactions do not cause the depression but are likely to trigger reoccurrence of symptoms; identify family interactive sequence that precede patient's depressive behaviors; empathize with the family's frustration and anger towards the patient's depression.
5. Planning of a strategy for managing and/or minimizing future stresses.	Lead discussion of possible return of depressive symptoms and the means of coping with them; educate the family in adjusting expectations of the patient; anticipate the potential stresses of the patient's reentry into the community.
6. Acceptance of the need for continued treatment following discharge from the hospital.	Educate the family about the needs for management of depression.

family assessment of the problem is important, both for role-inducing the family into the most appropriate treatment and for how the family and patient interact on a daily basis. Family/spouse attributions of the depressed member vary from "currently depressed," "depressed and overcome with stress," to "stubborn," "just trying to manipulate us," and "lazy." The clinician's functional analysis of the depressive behaviors, family contexts, and history and phenomenology of the depression will guide him in treatment planning, strategies of intervention, and instructions to the family on how to interact with the identified patient. A spouse who is clearly in an endogenous depressive episode can be declared by the therapist as in a sick role (Klerman, Weissman, Rounsaville, & Chevron, 1984) with the implication of diminished functioning for a *temporary* period. On the other hand, when the depression is nonendogenomorphic and involves much secondary gain family members may be instructed to use extinction techniques on various depressive behaviors (Lieberman, 1970).

Second, family/marital interventions frequently focus on skills develop-ment (specifically, skills for problem solving and coping with major depres-sive episodes). Based on the family therapy dictum that leverage for change resides more directly with the more healthy, rather than the more sympto-matic, family member, it follows that the therapist should utilize the coping strengths of everyone in the family in order to deal with the present and future depressive episodes of the identified patient. Coping skills include the informed family's increased capacity to (*a*) detect the early stages of a depres-sive episode, (*b*) understand and effectively handle an exacerbation of the disorder, should it recur, (*c*) locate appropriate sources of care when depres-sive symptoms arise; and (*d*) put aside blame and feelings of personal re-sponsibility when depressive symptoms recur. When coping skills such as these are effectively utilized, the disruptive impact of a depressive episode is minimized and the patient and family come to view such episodes not as disasters that occur randomly but as events over which the patient and family can exert some active influence or control. The sense of personal control over the depressive process can be a powerful factor in reducing or prevent-ing feelings of helplessness considered central to depressive conditions (Se-ligman, 1974); thus, the family's active coping behavior may reduce the poten-tial for secondary depressive reactions among family members living with the depressed patient.

A third principle in marital/family treatment of depression pivots on the relationship between lowered self-esteem in the depressed individual and the interactional sequences that tend to either maintain, or to alter levels of self-esteem among all members of the family. As indicated earlier, there is evidence to suggest that hostility and overinvolvement (e.g., emotional over-reactivity, overly controlling behavior) of family members tends to increase the likelihood of relapse and rehospitalization for depressed patients (Vaughn & Leff, 1976). Thus, one of the major objectives of family/marital therapy is to reduce aversive interaction which decreases self-esteem. Such an effort involves instruction and/or modeling of communication skills, as learning how to express anger constructively in a family or marital setting, in a manner that family members can effectively communicate dissatisfaction without damaging the self-esteem of another.

A fourth principle of marital/family treatment for depression relates to the therapist's role as a stimulus to the development of closeness and inti-macy with spouse and/or family members. Brown and Harris (1978b) main-tain that individuals who lack an intimate relationship are more likely to develop a depressive disorder than are those who have such supports in their familial and social environment. Furthermore, a majority of women who request treatment of depression have marital conflicts; such marital problems appear to prevent the development of emotional intimacy (Weissman & Pay-kel, 1974). The removal or diminution of hostile interaction does not, how-ever, necessarily lead to increased intimacy in couples and families; intimacy can be conceived of as a developed capacity and skill which needs nourish-ment in and of itself. Marital/family sessions can be helpful in developing intimacy once hostile interaction has been reduced; they provide a forum in which each individual can share parts of himself or herself in the presence of the other spouse, thus deepening the awareness of the other with the therapist modeling acceptance.

Case Illustrations

Four case illustrations of the use of family/marital intervention in the treatment of depressive disorders will be presented. These cases have been selected as prototypic examples of the kinds of families that present with depression: (1) a family struggling with a depressed and suicidal teenage daughter; (2) a couple dealing with the stress of marital conflict and separation, and subsequent development of depression in the husband; (3) a couple whose efforts to cope with the symptoms of an endogenous depression in the wife are met with concomitant marital stress and problems; and (4) a couple who experience constriction of the marital relationship as a result of a characterological depressive disorder in the male.

Depressed and Suicidal Teenager. A 17-year-old female, high school senior was referred for evaluation following her attempted suicide with an overdose of pills. Earlier on the night of the suicide attempt, the girl had been involved in an angry fight with her mother over her request for pizza. The patient remembers the mother saying that she was a "spoiled brat" and asking if she would be "happier living elsewhere." The patient recalls that, feeling rejected and despondent, she went to her room, wrote a note saying that she had had a mental breakdown and was going to a friend's house, and then went upstairs to her room and left another note stating that she loved her parents but that she could not talk with them. She added a request that her favorite glass animals be given to a particular friend of hers. The parents returned home later that evening, found their daughter comatose, and took her to a hospital emergency room.

Upon evaluation, it was apparent that this adolescent teenager, the second of three children of upper middle-class, and very intelligent, parents, was struggling with a view of herself as less bright, clever, and attractive than her two siblings. She felt ignored and essentially rejected by her hard-working, professional father, and in hostile conflict with her well-organized and omnipresent mother. The daughter was having difficulty developing a sense of separation from her mother and a sense of her individual identity. She experienced her mother's directives as intrusive interference with her efforts to express her autonomy and independence. Clinical evaluation following the suicide attempt revealed that this depressed youngster was quite concerned about her mother's own emotional well-being. The mother, it was learned, had a history of mild to moderate depression, following the family's move from a major midwestern city to the East Coast one year earlier. During a family session, the daughter, with a worried, pained expression on her face, spoke of her perceptions of the mother as having changed since the family had moved. In her own way, the girl proceeded to describe the mother's depression. According to her, the mother had not been herself since the move, she had seemed aloof and preoccupied; it was noted that she had not been dressing neatly, nor attractively, nor had she seemed at all concerned about her physical appearance. At this point during the family session, the mother became tearful and began to describe a chronic state of depression dating back to the move. She described herself as having been unable to adjust to the change. She indicated that she felt that her husband's career was moving ahead and that she was being left behind without friends and without any opportunity for her own professional advancement. At the same time, she expressed a sense of unwillingness, and inability, to ask for professional help with her depression; this was something that she had never considered to be a legitimate alternative for herself, believing, as she did, that people should pull themselves up by their own bootstraps.

In this case, family treatment proceeded for six sessions; this period enabled the family to talk about the suicide attempt of the daughter and to explore the meaning of this event. The daughter's yearnings for closeness to the father and for some expanded communication and time with her were expressed and most willingly accepted by the father. The mother was able to express her own sense of disappointment and loss following the move; this communication enabled her to begin to explore some alternatives for her own enjoyment. As psychotherapy proceeded, it was concluded that neither daughter nor mother were in need of psychotropic medication for the depression. The daughter's growing autonomy permitted her to begin a course of individual treatment which further helped her to separate and individuate in her relationship with her mother. Brief marital treatment was initiated; enhancement of the marital relationship via increased intimacy and communication of mutual support enabled the mother to make further gains in her own adjustment to the new surroundings; depressive symptoms remitted.

Situational Depression Accompanying Divorce. The J. couple were in their 40s, working in professional careers, and rearing two children, an 11-year-old boy and a 9-year-old girl. The wife was convinced that she wanted a divorce. Exploration in marital therapy during the first six sessions revealed that the marital relationship had been emotionally distant prior to the husband's extramarital affair. The wife expressed a sense of desire for a life without her husband. As she made it increasingly clear that she was not simply reacting to his affair but that for other reasons as well, she wanted a divorce, he became more and more despondent and suffered some sleep disturbance. Both spouses began to fear that he would become depressed, nonfunctional, and suicidal as had happened some 15 years earlier. Although he showed some mild vegetative signs, the symptom picture was not of sufficient severity to indicate a need for psychotropic medication. Despite the husband's depression, the wife continued to affirm her desire for divorce. In a logical, clear fashion, she proposed a reasonable time frame for divorce proceedings; he began to plan for the time of divorce and the many changes it would bring; he also proceeded to gather information concerning financial planning. Gradually, as he actively prepared for the divorce, his mood and attitude began to shift toward greater acceptance of the divorce; he was then able to proceed with the announcement of the divorce to the children and the finalization of plans for divorce proceedings.

Depressed Wife and Marital Problems.   The B. couple were in their late 30s with two sons, ages four and six, when Mrs. B.'s mother died of a massive heart attack. During the following year, the wife became depressed, reportedly troubled by early morning awakening, decreased libido, impairment of concentration, crying spells, and preoccupation with the loss of her mother to whom she had been deeply attached. During this time, the husband secluded himself, convinced that things would not improve until his wife pulled herself together and out of her depression. Without hope of relief, the wife decided to consult a psychiatrist. This occurred approximately one year following her mother's death. The psychiatrist who evaluated her condition concluded that she was experiencing a form of endogenous depression and elected to treat her with amitriptyline. The dysphoria, concentration deficit, and sleeping difficulties cleared. Individual therapy proceeded with exploration of the wife's feelings of intense closeness to her mother, coupled with a growing awareness of her anger toward her husband whose emotional distancing provoked feelings of abandonment and resentment over being left to assume the primary responsibility for parenting the growing boys. A marital evaluation was recommended, and with great reluctance, the husband appeared for the interview, during which he suggested that the major problem was his wife's depression. She angrily admitted having been depressed since the mother's death but felt that he had totally withdrawn from her; she wanted more from a marital relationship then was available to her. After several sessions, the husband began to realize that his aloofness was contributing to her sense of isolation; with some glimmer of insight into his contribution to the problems, he came to see his own difficulty with emotional intimacy in general, and, in particular, in his relationship with his wife. As the therapy progressed and family dynamics became more clearly defined, it was revealed that there was a history of alcoholism and depression in the families of the two spouses. The influence of these family histories was, it appeared, contributing to the couple's marital difficulties. The wife was terrified of anger as expressed by a male; for her, it called to mind and signified the violence of her alcoholic father who verbally and physically abused members of the family. The woman's husband had a volatile temper; during momentary flare-ups, the wife would withdraw, feeling terrified of her husband. He began to realize that these moments were destructive to the marital relationship; with motivation for each to seek change, the marital therapy proceeded with more active involvement of both partners, and communication improved between the two of them.

Characterological Depressive Disorder.   Mr. C. was a 63-year-old married male with a recent (four-year) history of "recurrent major depression, without psychotic features" and with a background of chronic depressive adjustment, characterized by mild social withdrawal, low self-esteem, and a generally pessimistic outlook. His 40-year marriage was described as a chronically unhappy relationship in which Mr. C. displayed a clinging, childlike dependency and suppressed the expression of anger toward his wife. Mrs. C. had, over the years, assumed increasing responsibility for all home management/budget functions. In general, Mrs. C. had assumed a more directive, parental role in relation to her highly passive, easily discouraged husband.

After 40 years of marriage and 11 years of employment at his then current job, Mr. C. complained of increased boredom and restlessness both at home and at work. A rapidly deteriorating course of depression led to his being hospitalized for one month at which time he reported having broken up with a woman with whom he had had an affair over the previous 12 months (the most recent of a series of similar involvements over the previous 12 to 15 years).

Mr. C. underwent two subsequent courses of brief hospital treatment for exacerbations of his depressive condition, one an ineffective trial of Monamine oxidose inhibitors (MAOI) and another showing only partial response to a course of ECT, both ending with poor resolution of the depression symptomotology. Following discharge, Mr. C. attended a prevocational planning program on a three-day-per-week basis. His time at home was spent largely in bed, sleeping. Mrs. C., a dominating and opinionated woman, tended to "lay down the law" at home. Her directiveness left little room for Mr. C. to take initiative. Mr. C. reported feeling "more depressed." Mrs. C., seeing her husband become increasingly lethargic and avoidant of structured activity, coaxed him out of bed routinely and urged him to tackle household repairs in order to keep him occupied. Three months following his third hospitalization, Mr. C. had, with much ambivalence, decided to retire from his job. He started several part-time jobs for brief periods (one to two weeks), ultimately quitting each time due to anxiety and fears of failure.

Whereas Mr. C. reported diminishing satisfaction with his marriage, Mrs. C. reported that the relationship had "never been better." She admitted that she had to persistently encourage her husband "to keep busy," providing him activities to keep him occupied. She indicated that she was more directive with him than ever previously, but said this with a smile, as if pleased with this aspect of the marriage. At this time, Mr. and Mrs. C. were spending considerably more time together. Mr. C. noted that he felt increasingly despondent in his wife's presence.

Due to Mrs. C.'s minimal response to individual psychotherapy and chemotherapy, the C.'s were referred for marital therapy by his outpatient psychiatrist. During the initial six sessions of marital therapy, it appeared that the wife's controlling, directive style was complementary to Mr. C's extreme passive-dependency. Although admittedly resentful of his wife's directives (given that they seemed to promote Mr. C.'s feelings of inadequacy), and apparently more dysphoric in her presence, he stated that he generally "welcomed" her efforts to mobilize him; he explained that he was certain that without such directives, he would become increasingly anergic and isolative. In summary, Mr. C. experienced considerable ambivalence toward his wife, their relationship offered him little pleasure; he found himself seeking out relationships with other women as a means of compensating for this lack. Mr. and Mrs. C.'s relationship had achieved some homeostatic balance of conflict-free needs-gratification for the two partners. Neither partner complained of "marital problems"; it was only as a result of an exacerbation of Mr. C.'s depression that marital dysfunction was noted and the couple was referred for marital therapy.

Family/Marital Treatment in the Prevention of Family Psychiatric Disorder

Empirical Rationale for Preventive Intervention with Families of Patients with Affective Disorder.   Family stress in response to the depressive disorder of the identified patient may result in an exacerbation of the target disorder (Vaughn & Leff, 1976), the precipitation of associated psychopathology in other family members, and/or the eventuation of psychiatric disorder in offspring. Empirical evidence of an association between adult psychopathology and depression among offspring (Beardslee, Bemporad, Keller, & Klerman, 1983; Mednick, Schulsinger, & Garfinkel, 1975; Orvaschel, Weissman, & Kidd, 1980; Rutter, Tizard, & Whitmore, 1970), longitudinal studies of children at risk for psychopathology (Garmezy, 1974; Grunebaum, Cohler, & Kauffman, 1978; Robins, 1966), and children of divorced parents (Hetherington, Cox, & Cox, 1978), as well as retrospective reports of marital/family discord or parental rejection in the childhood histories of depressed adults, provide a logical rationale for employing early family intervention strategies as a preventative measure in the treatment of parental/family pathology. Although there are no prospective, controlled studies of the effects of early family/marital intervention on the psychosocial adjustment/psychopathology of offspring, the association of parental psychopathology with psychopathology among offspring suggests that this is an area which merits further study. Furthermore, in vivo studies of depressed adults reveal that the parenting functions of these patients (and, in particular, female patients) tend to be disturbed, characterized by patterns of disaffection, friction, and disengagement from offspring (Weissman, Paykel, & Klerman, 1972).

Clinical observations on treatment of adults with major depressive disorders has led several clinicians to conclude that the major depressive disorders are more harmful to the development of the child than are the schizophrenic disorders (Anthony, 1969; Grunebaum et al. 1978; Philips, 1983; Weissman et al., 1972). Philips, in his review of the research on children at risk for psychiatric disorder, makes a convincing argument for preventive intervention efforts with this population (Philips, 1983). In a review of the research literature on the specific maladaptive effects of adult affective disorder on the psychosocial adjustment of offspring, Philips (1983) notes the need for greater emphasis on preventive intervention, including: (1) early diagnosis and education for prevention; (2) effective treatment of current cases; and (3) appropriate follow-up services and medical supervision to the chronic patient, aimed at reducing the severity of symptoms and preventing relapse and rehospitalization.

Value of Family/Marital Intervention as a Method of Preventive Intervention.

From the perspective of the categories of preventive intervention conceptualized by Caplan (1964), family/marital intervention approaches offer particular promise; in view of the empirical evidence of significant risk for psychopathology in the offspring of patients with affective disorder, adults who present with affective disorders constitute a prime target population for marital/family intervention. A multimodal model of family/marital intervention for treatment of the target affective disorder represents an effective integration of preventive strategies at all levels of Caplan's (1964) preventive intervention model: primary, secondary, and tertiary.

In terms of primary prevention (i.e., prevention efforts directed to reducing the *incidence* of disorder), the *educative component* of family intervention strategies alerts patient and family to the intrafamilial and extrafamilial conditions, events and forces which may precipitate a depressive episode. Interventions directed toward modification of maladaptive family interaction patterns and coping strategies also serve some prophylactic function, enhancing family "resistance" to stress, and thus, potentially reducing the risk of psychiatric disorder among offspring. There is a great need for well-designed prospective studies in the sphere of primary prevention of depression. Research in this area would serve both important practical functions as well as contribute to our understanding of the etiology and course of depressive disorders.

The secondary preventive functions of intervention (i.e., those aimed at reducing the *prevalence* of the disorder, are directly served by interventions which effectively reduce the frequence of relapse and/or the length of the target episode of the psychiatric disorder. These include family/marital intervention strategies aimed at disrupting and modifying intrafamilial interaction patterns which support and maintain the affective disorder.

Finally, the tertiary preventive functions are represented by those interventions intended to reduce residual deficits and their impact upon the quality of life of the identified patient, family members, and the larger social network. These are represented by family/marital strategies designed to remediate social skills deficits and maladaptive interaction patterns involving the patient and the family or the larger social group. Here, too, educative interventions play an important role, in terms of: (1) modifying family/patient expectations for the patient's resumption of functioning in the family and community; (2) educating patient and family to the rationale for the treatment of choice; and (3) enlisting family support for patient compliance with the recommended treatment regimen.

References

Abramson, L. Y., Seligman, M. P., & Teasdale, J. D. (1978). Learned helplessness in humans: Critique and reformulation. *Journal of Abnormal Psychology, 87,* 49–74.

Akiskal, H. S. (1983). Dysthymic disorder: Psychopathology of proposed chronic depressive subtypes. *American Journal of Psychiatry, 140,* 11–21.

Akiskal, H. S., Bitar, A. H., Puzantian, V. R., Rosenthal, T. L., & Walker, P. W. (1978). The nosological status of neurotic depressions: A prospective three- to four-year follow-up examination in the light of the primary-secondary and the unipolar-bipolar dichotomies. *Archives of General Psychiatry, 35,* 756–766.

Akiskal, H. S., Hirschfeld, M. A., & Yerevanian, B. I. (1983). The relationship of personality to affective disorders: A critical review. *Archives of General Psychiatry, 40,* 801–810.

Anderson, C. M., Hogarty, G. E., & Reiss, D. J. (1980). Family treatment of adult schizophrenic patients: A psychoeducational approach. *Schizophrenia Bulletin, 6,* 490–505.

Anthony, E. J. (1969). A clinical evaluation of children with psychotic parents. *American Journal of Psychiatry, 126,* 177–184.

Baldwin, J. (1971). Five-year incidence of reported psychiatric disorder. In J. Baldwin (Ed.), *Aspects of the epidemiology of mental illness.* Boston: Little, Brown.

Baron, M., Mendlewicz, J., Gruen, R., Asnis, L., & Fieve, R. R. (1981). Assortative mating in affective disorders. *Journal of Affective Disorders, 3,* 167–171.

Bateson, G. (1972). *Steps to an ecology of mind.* New York: Ballantine Books.

Beardslee, W. R., Bemporad, J., Keller, M. B., & Klerman, G. L. (1983). Children of parents with affective disorder: A review. *American Journal of Psychiatry, 140,* 825–831.

Beck, A. T. (1967). *Depression: Clinical, experimental and theoretical aspects.* New York: Harper & Row.

Beck, A. T., Rush, A. J., Shaw, B. F., & Emery, G. (1978). *Cognitive therapy of depression: A treatment manual.* Unpublished manuscript, University of Pennsylvania, Philadelphia.

Beck, A. T., Ward, C. H., Mendelsohn, M., Mock, J., & Erbaugh, J. (1961). An inventory for measuring depression. *Archives of General Psychiatry, 4,* 561–571.

Bernstein, N. R. (1982). Affective disorders and the life cycle. In E. R. Val, F. M. Gaviria, & J. A. Flaherty (Eds.), *Affective disorders: Psychopathology and treatment.* Chicago: Year Book Medical Publishers.

Birchler, G. R. (1972). *Differential patterns of instrumental affiliative behavior as a function of degree of marital distress and level of intimacy.* Unpublished doctoral dissertation. University of Oregon.

Birchler, G. R., & Webb, L. (1975, April). *A social learning formulation of discriminating interaction behaviors in happy and unhappy marriages.* Paper presented at the annual meeting of the Southwest Psychological Association, Houston.

Birtchnell, J. (1981). Some familial and clinical characteristics of female suicidal psychiatric patients. *British Journal of Psychiatry, 138,* 381–390.

Birtchnell, J., & Kennard, J. (1982). Some marital and childbearing characteristics of early mother-bereaved women. *British Journal of Medical Psychology, 55,* 177–186.

Birtchnell, J., & Kennard, J. (1983a). Does marital maladjustment lead to mental illness? *Social Psychiatry, 18,* 79–88.

Birtchnell, J., & Kennard, J. (1983b) Marriage and mental illness. *British Journal of Psychiatry, 142,* 193–198.

Bowen, M. (1966). The use of family theory in clinical practice. *Comprehensive Psychiatry, 7,* 345–374.

Briscoe, C. W., & Smith, J. B. (1969). Depression and marital turmoil. *Archives of General Psychiatry, 28,* 811–817.

Briscoe, C. W., Smith, J. B., Robins, E., Marten, S., & Gaskin, F. (1973). Divorce and psychiatric disease. *Archives of General Psychiatry, 29,* 119–125.

Brown, C., Bhrolchain, M., & Harris, T. (1975). Social class and psychiatric disturbance among women in an urban population. *Sociology, 9,* 225–254.

Brown, G. W., Birley, J. L. T., & Wing, J. K. (1972). Influence of family life on the course of schizophrenic disorders: A replication. *British Journal of Psychiatry, 121,* 241–258.

Brown, G. W., & Harris, T. (1978a). Social origins of depression: A reply. *Psychological Medicine, 8,* 577–588.

Brown, G. W., & Harris, T. (1978b). *Social origins of depression: A study of psychiatric disorders in women.* New York: Free Press.

Brown, G. W., Harris, T., & Copeland, J. R. (1977). Depression and loss. *British Journal of Psychiatry, 130,* 1–18.

Bullock, R. C., Siegel, R., Weissman, M., & Paykel, E. S. (1972). The weeping wife: Marital relations of depressed women. *Journal of Marriage and the Family, 34,* 488–495.

Bunney, W. E., Jr., Murphy, D. L., Goodwin, F. K., & Borge, G. F. (1972). The "switch process" in manic-depressive illness. *Archives of General Psychiatry, 27,* 295–302.

Cammer, L. (1971). Family feedback in depressive illness. *Psychosomatics, 12,* 127–132.

Caplan, G. (1964). *Principles of preventive psychiatry.* London: Tavistock Publications.

Cassano, G. B., Maggini, C., & Akiskal, H. S. (1983). Short-term subchronic and chronic sequelae of affective disorders. *Psychiatric Clinics of North America, 6*(1), 55–67.

Clarkin, J. F., Newman, J., DeMane, N., Haas, G. L., Spencer, J. H., & Glick, I. D. (1982). *Training manual for inpatient family intervention.* Unpublished manuscript.

Coleman, R. E., & Miller, A. G. (1975). The relationship between depression and marital maladjustment in a clinical population: A multitrait-multimethod study. *Journal of Consulting and Clinical Psychology, 43,* 647–651.

Coyne, J. C. (1976). Depression and the response of others. *Journal of Abnormal Psychology, 85,* 186–193.

Crow, J. F., & Felsenstein, J. (1968). The effect of assortative mating on the genetic composition of a population. *Eugenics Quarterly 15,* 85–97.

Davenport, Y. B., Adland, M. L., & Gold, P. W. (1979). Manic-depressive illness: Psychodynamic features of multigenerational families. *American Journal of Orthopsychiatry, 49,* 24–35.

Demers, R. G., & Davis, L. S. (1971). The influence of prophylactic lithium treatment on the marital adjustment of manic-depressives and their spouses. *Comprehensive Psychiatry, 12,* 348–355.

DiMascio, A., Weissman, M. M., Prusoff, B. A., Neu, C., Swilling, M., & Klerman, G. L. (1979). Differential symptom reduction by drugs and psychotherapy in acute depression. *Archives of General Psychiatry, 36,* 1450–1456.

Ellis, A., & Harper, R. A. (1961). *A guide to rational living.* Hollywood, CA.: Wilshire Book.

Feldman, L. B. (1976). Depression and marital interaction. *Family Process, 15,* 389–395.

Filippo, J. R., & Lewinsohn, P. M. (1971). Effects of failure on the self-esteem of depressed and nondepressed subjects. *Journal of Consulting and Clinical Psychology, 36,* 151.

Fitzgerald, R. G. (1972). Mania as a message: Treatment with family therapy and lithium carbonate. *American Journal of Psychotherapy, 26,* 547–555.

Frank, E., Targum, S. D., Gershon, E. S., Anderson, C., Stewart, B. D., Davenport, Y., Ketchum, K. L., & Kupfer, D. J. (1981). A comparison of nonpatient and bipolar patient-well spouse couples. *American Journal of Psychiatry, 138,* 764–768.

Friedman, A. S. (1975). Interaction of drug therapy with marital therapy in depressive patients. *Archives of General Psychiatry, 32,* 619–637.

Garmezy, N. (1974). Children at risk: The search for the antecedents of schizophrenia. II. Ongoing research programs, issues, and intervention. *Schizophrenia Bulletin, 9,* 55–125.

Glazer, H. I., Clarkin, J. F., & Hunt, H. F. (1981). Assessment of depression. In J. F. Clarkin & H. Glazer (Eds.), *Depression: Behavioral and directive treatment strategies.* New York: Garland Publishing.

Glick, I. D., & Clarkin, J. F. (1981). Family therapy when an affective disorder is diagnosed. In A. S. Gurman (Ed.), *Questions and answers in the practice of family therapy.* New York: Brunner/Mazel.

Glick, I. D., Haas, G. L., Spencer, J. H., Clarkin, J. F., Lewis, A., Newman, J., DeMane, N., Good-Ellis, M., & Harris, E. (1983). *Inpatient family intervention: A controlled evaluation of practice.* Paper presented at the annual meeting of the American Psychiatric Association, New York City.

Goldstein, M. J., Rodnick, E. H., Evans, J. R., May, P. R. A., & Steinberg, M. R. (1978). Drug and family therapy in the aftercare of acute schizophrenics. *Archives of General Psychiatry, 35,* 1169–1177.

Greene, B. L., Lustig, N., & Lee, R. R. (1976). Marital therapy when one spouse has a primary affective disorder. *American Journal of Psychiatry, 133,* 827–830.

Grunebaum, H., Cohler, B. J., & Kauffman, C. (1978). Children of depressed and schizophrenic mothers. *Child Psychiatry and Human Development, 8,* 219–228.

Gurman, A. S. (1981). Integrative marital therapy: Toward the development of an interpersonal approach. In S. H. Budman (Ed.), *Forms of brief therapy.* New York: Guilford Press.

Gurman, A. S., & Kniskern, D. P. (1978). Research on marital and family therapy: Progress, perspective, and prospect. In S. L. Garfield & A. E. Bergin (Eds.), *Handbook of psychotherapy and behavior change.* New York: John Wiley & Sons.

Gurman, A. S., & Kniskern, D. P. (1981). Family therapy outcome research: Knowns and unknowns. In A. Gurman & D. Kniskern (Eds.), *Handbook of family therapy.* New York: Brunner/Mazel.

Haley, J. (1963). Marriage therapy. *Archives of General Psychiatry, 8,* 213–234.

Hamilton, M. (1960). A rating scale for depression. *Journal of Neurology, Neurosurgery and Psychiatry, 23,* 56–61.

Henderson, S., Byrne, D. G., & Duncan-Jones, P. (1981). Neurosis and the social environment. Academic Press: Sydney.

Henderson, S., Duncan-Jones, P., McAuley, H., & Ritchie, K. (1978). The patient's primary group. *British Journal of Psychiatry, 132,* 74–86.

Hetherington, E. M., Cox, M., & Cox, R. (1978). The aftermath of divorce. In J. H. Stevens & M. Matthews (Eds.), *Mother-child/father-child relationship.* Washington, DC: National Association for the Education of Young Children.

Hinchcliffe, M., Hooper, D., Roberts, F. J., & Vaughan, P. W. (1975). A study of the interaction between depressed patients and their spouses. *British Journal of Psychiatry, 126,* 164–172.

Hinchcliffe, M. K., Roberts, F. J., Hooper, D., & Vaughan, P. W. (1977). The melancholy marriage: An inquiry into the interaction of depression. II. Expressiveness. *British Journal of Medical Psychology, 50,* 125–142.

Hoffman, L. (1981). *Foundations of family therapy: A conceptual framework for systems change.* New York: Basic Books.

Hogan, P., & Hogan, B. K. (1975). The family treatment of depression. In F. F. Flach & S. C. Draghi (Eds.), *The nature and treatment of depression.* New York: John Wiley & Sons.

Hooper, D., Roberts, F. J., Hinchcliffe, M. K., & Vaughan, P. W. (1977). The melancholy marriage: An inquiry into the the interaction of depression. I. Introduction. *British Journal of Medical Psychology, 50,* 113–124.

Horowitz, H. M., Weckler, D. A., & Doren, R. (1983). Interpersonal problems and symptoms of depression: A cognitive approach. In P. C. Kendall (Ed.), *Advances in cognitive-behavioral research and treatment* (Vol. II). New York: Academic Press.

Ilfeld, F. W. (1977). Current social stressors and symptoms of depression. *American Journal of Psychiatry, 134,* 161–166.

Ineichen, B. (1976). Marriage and neurosis in a modern residential suburb: An application of the Ryle Marital Patterns test. *British Journal of Psychiatry, 129,* 248–251.

Jacobson, A., & McKinney, W. T. (1982). Affective disorders. In J. H. Greist, J. W. Jefferson, & R. L. Spitzer (Eds.), *Treatment of mental disorders.* New York: Oxford University Press.

Jacobson, N. S., Follette, W. C., & McDonald, D. W. (1982). Reactivity to positive and negative behavior in distressed and nondistressed married couples. *Journal of Consulting and Clinical Psychology, 50,* 706–714.

Jacobson, N. S., & Moore, D. (1981). Spouses as observers of the events in their relationship. *Journal of Consulting and Clinical Psychology, 49,* 269–277.

Klein, D. (1974). Endogenomorphic depressions: Toward a terminologic revision. *Archives of General Psychiatry, 31,* 447–454.

Klerman, G. L., DiMascio, A., Weissman, M., Prusoff, B., & Paykel, E. S. (1974). Treatment of depression by drugs and psychotherapy. *American Journal of Psychiatry, 131,* 186–191.

Klerman, G. L., Weissman, M., Rounsaville, B., & Chevron, E. (1984). *Interpersonal psychotherapy of depression.* New York: Basic Books.

Klaepelin, E. (1921). *Manic-depressive illness and paranoia.* Edinburgh: E & S Livingstone, Ltd.

Kreitman, N. (1964). The patient's spouse. *British Journal of Psychiatry, 110,* 159–173.

Lewinsohn, P. M., & Hoberman, H. M. (1982). Depression. In A. S. Bellack, M. Hersen, & A. E. Kazdin (Eds.), *International handbook of behavior modification and therapy.* New York: Plenum Publishing.

Lewinsohn, P. M., & Shaffer, M. (1971). Use of home observations as an integral part of the treatment of depression: Preliminary report and case studies. *Journal of Consulting and Clinical Psychology, 37,* 87–94.

Lewinsohn, P. M., Weinstein, M., & Alper, T. (1970). A behavioral approach to the group treatment of depressed persons: A methodological contribution. *Journal of Clinical Psychology, 26,* 525–532.

Libet, J., & Lewinsohn, P. M. (1973). The concept of social skill with special reference to the behavior of depressive persons. *Journal of Consulting and Clinical Psychology, 40,* 304–312.

Lidz, T. A. R., Cornelison, S. F., & Terry, D. (1960). Schism and skew in the families of schizophrenics. In R. Bell & E. F. Vogel (Eds.), *A modern introduction to the family.* New York: Free Press.

Lieberman, R. (1970). Behavioral approaches to family and group therapy. *American Journal of Orthopsychiatry, 40,* 106–119.

Lubin, B. (1967). *Manual for depression adjective checklists.* San Diego: Educational and Industrial Testing Service.

Ludwig, A. M., & Ables, M. F. (1974). Mania and marriage: The relationship between biological and behavioral variables. *Comprehensive Psychiatry, 15,* 411–421.

MacPhillamy, D. S., & Lewinsohn, P. M. (1972). *The measurement of reinforcing events.* Paper presented at the 80th annual convention of the American Psychological Association, Honolulu.

Matussek, P., & Feil, W. B. (1983). Personality attributes of depressive patients: Results of group comparisons. *Archives of General Psychiatry, 40,* 783–790.

Matussek, P., & Neuner, R. (1981). Loss events preceding endogenous and neurotic depressions. *Acta Psychiatrica Scandinavica, 64,* 340–350.

Mayo, J. A. (1979). Marital therapy with manic-depressive patients treated with lithium. *Comprehensive Psychiatry, 20,* 419–426.

Mayo, J. A., O'Connell, R. A., & O'Brien, J. (1978, May). *Families of manic depressives: Effect of treatment.* Presented at the APA Convention, Atlanta.

McLean, P. D., Ogston, K., & Grauer, L. (1973). A behavioral approach to the treatment of depression. *Journal of Behavior Therapy and Experimental Psychiatry, 4,* 323–330.

Mednick, S. A., Schulsinger, R., & Garfinkel, R. (1975). Children at high risk for schizophrenia: Predisposing factors and intervention. In M. L. Keitzman, S. Sutton, & J. Zubin (Eds.), *Experimental approaches to psychopathology.* New York: Academic Press.

Merikangas, K. R., Bromet, E. J., & Spiker, D. G. (1983). Assortative mating, social adjustment, and course of illness in primary affective disorder. *Archives of General Psychiatry, 40,* 795–800.

Merikangas, K. R., & Spiker, D. (1982). Assortative mating among inpatients with primary affective disorder. *Psychological Medicine, 12,* 753–764.

Minuchin, S. (1974). *Families and family therapy.* Cambridge, MA: Harvard University Press.

Moos, R. H., & Fuhr, R. (1982). Personal communication.

Moos, R. H., & Moos, B. S. (1976). A typology of family social environments. *Family Process, 15,* 357–371.

Murphy, G. E., Woodruff, R. A., Jr., Herjanic, K., & Super, G. (1974). Variability of the clinical course of primary affective disorder. *Archives of General Psychiatry, 30,* 757–761.

Negri, F., Melica, A. M., Zuliani, R., Gasperini, M., Macciardi, F., & Smeraldi, E. (1981). Genetic implications in assortative mating of affective disorders. *British Journal of Psychiatry, 138,* 236–239.

Olson, D. H., Bell, R., & Portner, J. (1978). FACES: Family Adaptability and Cohesion Evaluation Scales. Mimeograph, University of Minnesota.

Orvaschel, H., Weissman, M. M., & Kidd, K. K. (1980). Children and depression. *Journal of Affective Disorders, 2,* 1–16.

Paykel, E. S. (Ed.). (1982). *Handbook of affective disorders.* New York: Guilford Press.

Paykel, E. S., Myers, J. K., Dienelt, M. N., Klerman, G. L., Lindethal, J. J., & Pepper, M. P. (1969). Life events and depression: A controlled study. *Archives of General Psychiatry, 21,* 753–760.

Paykel, E. S., & Weissman, M. M. (1973). Social adjustment and depression. *Archives of General Psychiatry, 28,* 659–663.

Pearlin, L. I., & Lieberman, M. A. (1977). Social sources of emotional distress. In R. Simmons (Ed.), *Research in community mental health.* Greenwich, CT.: JAI Press.

Philips, I. (1983). Opportunities for prevention in the practice of psychiatry. *American Journal of Psychiatry, 140,* 389–395.

Rehm, L. P. (1977). A self-control model of depression. *Behavior Therapy, 8,* 787–804.

Reid, J. B. (1967). *Reciprocity in family interaction.* Unpublished doctoral dissertation. University of Oregon.

Robins, L. N. (1966). Deviant children grown up. Baltimore: Williams & Wilkins.

Rounsaville, B. J., Klerman, G. L., & Weissman, M. M. (1981). Do psychotherapy and pharmacotherapy for depression conflict? *Archives of General Psychiatry, 38,* 24–29.

Rounsaville, B. J., Weissman, M. M., Prusoff, B. A., & Herceg-Baron, R. L. (1979). Marital disputes and treatment outcome in depressed women. *Comprehensive Psychiatry, 20,* 483–490.

Rubinstein, D. & Timmins, J. F. (1978). Depressive dyadic and triadic relationships. *Journal of Marriage and Family Counseling, 4,* 13–23.

Russell, A., Russell, L., & Waring, E. M. (1980). Cognitive family therapy: A preliminary report. *Canadian Psychiatric Association Journal, 15,* 64–67.

Rutter, M., & Quinton, D. (1977). Psychiatric disorder: Ecological factors and concepts of causation. In H. McGurk (Ed.), *Ecological factors in human development.* Amsterdam, Neth.: North Holland.

Rutter, M., Tizard, J., & Whitmore, K. (1970). *Education, health and behavior.* London: Longmans.

Sager, C. J . (1976). *Marriage contracts and couple therapy.* New York: Brunner/Mazel.

Satir, V. (1967). *Conjoint family therapy: A guide to theory and technique.* Palo Alto, CA.: Science & Behavior books.

Seligman, M. E. P. (1974). Depression and learned helplessness. In R. J. Friedman & M. M. Katz (Eds.), *The psychology of depression: Contemporary theory and research.* New York: John Wiley & Sons.

Seligman, E. M. (1975). *Helplessness.* San Francisco: W. H . Freeman.

Snyder, D. K. (1979). Multidimensional assessment of marital satisfaction. *Journal of Marriage and the Family, 41,* 813–823.

Spanier, G. B. (1972). Further evidence on methodological weaknesses in the Locke-Wallace Marital Adjustment Scale and other measures of adjustment. *Journal of Marriage and the Family, 34,* 403–404.

Spanier, G. B. (1976). Measuring dyadic adjustment: New scales for assessing the quality of marriage and similar dyads. *Journal of Marriage and the Family, 38,* 15–28.

Stuart, R. B. (1969). Token reinforcement in marital treatment. In R. D. Rubin & G. M. Franks (Eds.), *Advances in behavior therapy, 1968.* New York: Academic Press.

Targum, S. D., Dibble, E. D., Davenport, Y. B., & Gershon, E. S. (1981). The family attitudes questionnaire: Patients' and spouses' views of bipolar illness. *Archives of General Psychiatry, 38,* 562–568.

Vaughn, C. E., & Leff, J. P. (1976). The influence of family and social factors on the course of psychiatric illness: A comparison of schizophrenic and depressed neurotic patients. *British Journal of Psychiatry, 129,* 125–137.

Wadeson, H. S., & Fitzgerald, R. G. (1971). Marital relationship in manic-depressive illness. *Journal of Nervous and Mental Disease, 153,* 180–196.

Waring, E. M., & Russell, L. (1982). Cognitive family therapy. In F. W. Kaslow (Ed.), *The international book of family therapy.* New York: Brunner/Mazel.

Watzlawick, P., & Coyne, J. C. (1980). Depression following stroke: Brief problem-focused family treatment. *Family Process, 19,* 13–18.

Watzlawick, P. D., Jackson, D. D., & Beavin, J. (1967). *Pragmatics of human communication.* New York: W. W. Norton.

Watzlawick, P., Weakland, J., & Fisch, R. (1974). *Change: Principles of problem formation and problem resolution.* New York: W. W. Norton.

Weintraub, M., Segal, R. M., & Beck, A. T. (1974). An investigation of cognition and affect in the depressive experience of normal men. *Journal of Consulting and Clinical Psychology, 42,* 911.

Weiss, R. L. (1978). The conceptualization of marriage and marriage disorders from a behavioral perspective. In T. J. Paolino & B. S. McCrady (Eds.), *Marriage and marital therapy: Psychoanalytic, behavioral, and systems theory perspectives.* New York: Brunner/Mazel.

Weiss, R. L., Hops, H., & Patterson, G. R. (1973). A framework for conceptualizing marital conflict, a technology for altering it, some data from evaluating it. In L. A.

Hamerlynck, L. C. Handy, & E. J. Mash (Eds.), *Behavior change: Methodology, concepts and practice*. Champaign, IL: Research Press.

Weissman, M. M., & Bothwell, S. (1976). The assessment of social adjustment by patient self-report. *Archives of General Psychiatry, 33,* 1111–1115.

Weissman, M. M., Klerman, G. L., & Paykel, E. S. (1974). Treatment effects on the social adjustment of depressed patients. *Archives of General Psychiatry, 30,* 771–778.

Weissman, M. M., & Paykel, E. S. (1974). *The depressed woman: A study of social relationships*. Chicago: University of Chicago Press.

Weissman, M. M., Paykel, E. S., & Klerman, G. L. (1972). The depressed woman as a mother. *Social Psychiatry, 7,* 98–108.

Weissman, M. M., Prusoff, B. A., DiMascio, A., Neu, C., & Klerman, G. L. (1979). Research directions on comparisons of drugs and psychotherapy in depression. *Psychopharmacology Bulletin, 15,* 19–21.

Weissman, M. M., Rounsaville, B. J., Prusoff, B. A., & Chevron, E. (1983). Personal communication.

Wills, T. A., Weiss, R. L., & Patterson, G. R. (1974). A behavioral analysis of the determinants of marital satisfaction. *Journal of Consulting and Clinical Psychology, 42,* 802–811.

Wynne, L. (1961). Intrafamilial splits and alignments in exploratory family therapy. In N. Ackerman (Ed.), *Exploring the base for family therapy*. New York: Family Service Association of America.

Youngren, M. A., & Lewinsohn, P. M. (1980). The functional relationship between depression and problematic interpersonal behavior. *Journal of Abnormal Psychology, 89,* 333–341.

Chapter 7

Alternate Psychotherapies for Depression: Transactional Analysis, Gestalt Therapy, and Reality Therapy

Gregory W. Lester

The decades of the 1960s and 1970s gave birth to a great deal of interest in psychology and human behavior, and spawned a popularization of psychology which came to be known as the "human potential movement." During this time a variety of new theories regarding human behavior, emotional dysfunction, and treatment of emotional problems were developed. Predictably, these new psychological theories were greeted with mixed reactions from the professional community. To some they represented important progress in our ability to understand ourselves and our emotional functioning. To others they were simply old wine in new bottles, offering new terminology and mass appeal in the place of genuine scientific advancement.

While the debate concerning the quality of scientific advancement offered by the theories of the 1960s and 1970s continues into the 1980s, the conceptualizations and treatment techniques offered by the new theories have found wide use and acceptance by many mental health professionals. Transactional Analysis, Gestalt Therapy, and Reality Therapy are three of the best known theories from this era, and are the focus of the present chapter. Each theory's conceptualization of and treatment approach for depression will be presented and discussed.

TRANSACTIONAL ANALYSIS

Background

Transactional Analysis (TA) was developed during the 1960s by Dr. Eric Berne and his associates of the San Francisco Social Psychiatry Seminars (later the International Transactional Analysis Association). TA may be the best known and most widely used of the psychological theories from the human potential movement, as it has been popularized in several best-selling books (Berne, 1964; Harris, 1969; James & Jongeward, 1971). Paradoxically, the mass acceptance of TA has led some professionals to view the approach as oversimplified and superficial. Nevertheless, the TA approach has found its way into many therapists' conceptualizations and therapy techniques, and offers a specific formulation of and treatment techniques for the problem of depression.

TA Personality Theory

TA defines personality as consisting of three separate, distinct parts known as ego-states. An ego-state is a cohesive and internally consistent set of feelings, thoughts, and behaviors. The "Child" ego-state (ego-states are always capitalized) is an intact recording of the thoughts, feelings, and behaviors which an individual experienced during childhood. When a person's consciousness is "in" Child, the person acts, thinks, and feels in exactly the same manner that he or she did as a child. The "Parent" ego-state is an intact recording of the thoughts, feelings, and behaviors of parental figures from childhood. The "Adult" ego-state is the rational, logical, problem-sovling part of the personality. When a person's consciousness is "in" Adult, the individual is task oriented and problem-solving oriented, and is relatively unemotional.

According to TA theory, as an individual's consciousness shifts from one ego-state to another there are observable alterations in voice tone, vocabulary, behavior, and speech content. Internally, there are corresponding shifts in thought, mood, attitude, and perceptions. Thus, personality operates to a large extent as if there were three separate individuals within each person.

Each ego-state contains a particular set of information about oneself and the world. This information varies from one individual to another, depending upon the pesonalities of the parental figures incorporated into the Parent ego-state, the individual's childhood temperament and early experience recorded in the Child ego-state, and the intellectual capacity available in the Adult ego-state. The information in one ego-state can also contradict the information in another ego-state. For example, an individual whose parents insisted that eating liver was good for children might have a "Liver is good, eat liver" message recorded in his or her Parent ego-state. As a child the person may have despised liver, and so may have a Child ego-state recording that "Liver is yukky, I don't want to eat liver." When this person goes to the grocery store, there may be an internal battle between the Parent message "You should eat liver" and the Child's "I hate liver, I won't eat liver." Because the function of the Adult ego-state is planning and problem solving, if the individual has a well-functioning Adult ego-state a third internal voice may be present and help to solve the conflict ("Liver is healthy because of the nutrients, and I can find other foods with those nutrients that I enjoy eating more than liver.")

The Role of Parent Ego-State Injunctions in Depression

Because young children do not have well-functioning Adult ego-states to help them deal with the world on a logical and rational basis, they absorb principles, rules, and ideas about themselves and life from parental figures. This information is incorporated into the personality and becomes the Parent ego-state. One particular aspect of Parent information which TA calls "injunctions" are the prohibitions which parents present to their children. Some of these prohibitions are practical safety messages such as "Don't take candy from strangers" or "Don't play in the street." Parents also, usually without being aware of doing so, pass on prohibitions in the emotional realm ("Boys don't cry, good girls don't get mad"). According to TA theory, the first step in predisposing an individual to depression occurs when a message is sent by the parents to the child that the child should not exist or is somehow flawed and is therefore unacceptable. TA calls this message a "Don't Exist" injunction (Goulding & Goulding, 1979). "Don't Exist" injunctions can be transmitted in a variety of ways including directly telling the child that he or she is not wanted, abusing the child, blaming the child for marital and family problems, or exiling the child to relatives, boarding schools, or the street. "Don't Exist" injunctions can also be transmitted in a subtle manner through nonverbal communication or implication; other children can be favored over the child, or stories about how difficult the child's birth was can be told and retold.

When the child perceives that the parental figures believe the child is unworthy or should not exist, the "Don't Exist" injunction is received by the child and is incorporated into the child's developing Parent ego-state. Thus, this child becomes an individual who carries an "I should not exist" belief around in his or her mind along with the other messages sent by the parents and contained in the Parent ego-state. Usually the awareness that a "Don't Exist" message exists in one's mind fades over time. Many adult psychother-apy patients do not have direct access to the message from their parents that they were unwanted. Instead, adults who have "Don't Exist" injunctions often experience a vague feeling that they do not belong or are somehow unde-serving of success, or simply that "something is wrong" and they feel like they are "bad."

The Role of Child Ego-State Decisions in Depression

TA theory states that at a very early age children make decisions about what kind of person they are and how their life should go (Goulding & Goulding, 1979). These decisions are the basis of a plan for the individual's life and are recorded in the Child ego-state of the personality. While the decisions are originally made consciously by the child, over time the decisions themselves usually fade from consciousness while the life course set by the decisions remains. For example, a child who is abandoned by a beloved parent might decide "Getting close to someone hurts too much and I'll never let anyone close enough to hurt me again." As an adult, the individual may not be aware that he or she made this decision as a child, even though he or she is living a life which prevents emotional closeness with others.

Because much of the information about life which children receive comes from parent figures, early Child ego-state decisions are often made on the basis of parental messages (Berne, 1972). Thus, the second step in predisposing an individual to depression (after the receipt of the "Don't Exist" injunction) is the decision by the child that the "Don't Exist" injunction is accurate and should be acted upon. TA calls this a "depressive early decision." In this decision the child decides that he or she is bad and should not exist. Because the Child ego-state is the area of the personality in which a plan for life is formulated, a child who agrees with the "Don't Exist" injunction will base his or her plan on these beliefs. The specific manner in which the depressive decision is carried out varies, depending upon the particular individual. Some may decide "When things get too bad, I'll solve the problem by killing myself," while others may decide "I'll just keep to myself and not be a bother to anyone," and still others may decide that they will get someone else to kill them (Goulding & Goulding, 1979). In any case, these individuals suffer the double impact of a Parent ego-state message which tells them not to exist, and a Child ego-state decision which indicates that the Parent message is correct and should be acted upon.

Given that children differ in their inborn temperament, some children who are sent a "Don't Exist" injunction are unwilling to agree that the message is correct. These children may decide "If you don't love me I will look until I find someone who does," and will spend their lives looking for people who will love them. Such individuals will likely have a vague internal discomfort (the "Don't Exist" injunction in the Parent ego-state), but because they have decided that their needs are important and they act to meet the needs, they often avoid depression.

Life Positions and Depression

TA theory states that the early Child ego-state decision which defines an individual's life plan is intended to answer the question: "What am I like and what are other people like?" (Berne, 1972). TA theory defines the four possible responses to this question (Harris, 1969):

1. I'm an OK person, and so are you.
2. I'm an OK person, but you are not-OK.
3. I'm not an OK person, but you are OK.
4. I'm not an OK person, and neither are you.

An early decision which agrees with a "Don't Exist" injunction has as one of its primary elements the perception that "I'm not-OK." This belief places a sense of being not-OK (bad, inadequate, and so on) at the core of the individual's world view and life plan. TA calls the "I'm not-OK" decision a "depressive life position." The feeling of being not-OK is often one of the most obvious elements in depression. Individuals suffering from depression often have a strong sense of being bad, of personal failure and inadequacy, and of hopelessness and helplessness. While the decision that "I'm not-OK" is common to all depressions, the position as to the "OKness" of other people can vary. Some individuals suffering from depression believe that other people are OK, and thus better than they are, while others believe that other people are not-OK and thus are not in any better shape than they are and cannot help them.

Stroking Patterns and Depression

TA theory states that interpersonal attention is absolutely essential in maintaining psychological and emotional health. In early childhood this attention usually takes the form of physical touching and holding, and in later years it generally becomes more verbal and symbolic. TA uses the term *strokes* or *stroking* to describe interpersonal attention.

There are two general categories of strokes: positive and negative. As the names imply, positive strokes feel pleasurable and negative strokes feel painful. Despite their differing comfort value, both types of strokes offer the interpersonal stimulation required for emotional survival. Because survival is the primary need of humans, the pleasure or pain value of strokes is less important than the question of whether or not some kind of stroking is received.

Individuals suffering from depression tend to be unable to seek and receive strokes, and thus suffer a stroking "deficit" (Steiner, 1974). This deficit keeps the individual feeling isolated and alone, thus intensifying the sense of aloneness and not allowing the receipt of positive messages which could contradict the early depressive decision. Nevertheless, some strokes are usually received by individuals suffering from depression, and these strokes tend to be negative. While these strokes may serve to keep the individual functioning to some extent, the strokes are also painful and thus serve to continue the unpleasant sensations involved in depression.

The stroking deficit experienced by individuals suffering from depression as well as the receipt of negative strokes is usually a pattern which was developed during childhood. Often the child felt that positive strokes were unavailable or undeserved, and thus sought out the only strokes available, which were negative strokes. As an adult, then, receiving negative strokes may feel "normal" to the individual. These strokes serve to support and confirm the early decision that the individual is not-OK.

Psychological Games and Depression

Psychological games are one of the most widely known concepts in TA theory. A psychological game (Berne, 1964) is a repetitive pattern of interactions which appears to be plausible and logical but which is secretly designed to produce evidence which supports an individual's Parent injunctions and early decisions. To an outsider a game may appear to be an innocent, or at least accidental, occurrence which ends up with the individuals involved experiencing painful feelings. The clue which reveals that a game is not simply a chance occurrence but is actually an unconscious plan to create painful feelings is that the individual playing the game plays it repeatedly. If the interaction were a chance occurrence, the person would decide that he or she did not want to feel badly in that manner again and would take steps to see that the interaction was not repeated. This would require Adult functioning and planning, and because games are played without Adult awareness, no such alteration of the game pattern is available to the individual.

Individuals suffering from depression play games which are designed to continue to "prove" that they are not-OK individuals and to gather the negative strokes which they have come to accept as normal. They may surround themselves with others who are unwilling to provide positive strokes and who are willing to provide negative strokes. TA defines a variety of such depressive games (Berne, 1964; Stuntz, 1971). One example of a depressive game, "Kick Me" (Berne, 1964) is outlined below:

Spouse 1: You don't love me anymore, do you?

Spouse 2: Of course I still love you.

Spouse 1: How come you don't show it?

Spouse 2: What do you mean? I show it.

Spouse 1: You just never do nice things for me.

Spouse 2: That's not true!

Spouse 1: Yes, it is! You don't love me!

Spouse 2: Look, I do the best I can, and I don't know why you can't accept anything I do for you. Why can't you be a little appreciative? What in the world is wrong with you?

Spouse 1: [*Crying*] See? You think something's wrong with me. You don't love me.

On the surface, this interaction seems to simply be a request by Spouse 1 for reassurance which, for some reason, goes badly. The quality which reveals that the request is really the first step in a psychological game is that the manner in which Spouse 1 asks for reassurance is an attack. Spouse 2, who is more than willing to be defensive about the matter, provides the negative strokes desired by Spouse 1. Through this interaction Spouse 1 repeats the experience of the original Parent injunction ("There's something wrong with you") and feels rejected, punished, and not-OK, which is a reliving of the original depressive Child decision. Spouse 2, of course, is unconsciously a willing partner in the game and is living out his or her own life plan through the game.

Racket Feelings and Depression

TA separates feelings into two categories: Natural feelings, and Racket feelings (Berne, 1972). Natural feelings are those which an individual experiences as a result of inborn temperament. They are the feelings which are appropriate to the situation. Racket feelings are feelings which, during childhood, were encouraged and allowed by parents so that a child would not experience or express feelings which the parents themselves were not comfortable feeling and expressing. In one family, for example, the parents may fear expressions of anger, so the children are encouraged to express only sadness. In another family sadness may not have been allowed, so sad feelings were covered up with guilt. The feelings which were allowed and which hide other feelings are the "Racket" feelings. Racket feelings come to feel "normal," and are the feelings which are collected through playing psychological games.

TA theory states that depression itself is not a feeling, but rather a condition where an individual shows a variety of symptoms. There are a variety of feelings which are experienced as part of being depressed including sadness, anger, frustration, and guilt. TA calls these feelings, which are experienced as part of depression, Racket feelings.

It seems common for individuals who suffer from depression to have been prohibited from experiencing and expressing anger as children. Instead, feelings connected with a sense of being not-OK including guilt, sadness, fear, helplessness, and hopelessness were allowed and elicited. These become the individual's Racket feelings, and the depressive psychological games played by the individual are designed to avoid experiencing anger and to reexperience the "allowable" depressive feelings.

Racket feelings also serve as a form of emotional blackmail and justification. The child who has received a "Don't Exist" injunction may decide that if he or she just feels bad enough, love can be won from the parent figures. Later in life, then, the person may use being depressed to try to elicit nurturing. Unfortunately, the idea that being sufficiently unhappy will result in increasing nurturing usually turns out to be a fantasy, and most often brings an undesired result. Others become tired of giving nurturing and the depressive position is ultimately reinforced as the person plays games which result in the receipt of negative strokes and the reexperiencing of the original injunction rather than receiving the desired nurturing.

Racket feelings are collected like trading stamps. When enough of the painful feelings have been collected, the depressed person feels justified in taking some sort of self-destructive action. These feelings are then "traded in" on a crying spell, running away, a drinking binge, or suicide. The internal rational is "Anybody who feels this bad would. . . ."

The Adult Ego-State and Depression

The elements which predispose an individual to depression, the "Don't Exist" injunction and the early depressive decision, occur at a time when an individual's Adult ego-state has not developed sufficiently to be able to rationally figure out a solution to the problem presented by the unpleasant circumstance in which the child has found him or herself. As a result, the depression is played out without awareness of its origins by the Adult ego-state. The person's Adult may function quite well in other areas (thus the "successful businessperson" who quite unexpectedly commits suicide) but because he or she was not around to see the original elements of the depression, the individual is unaware of the source of the painful feelings. Thus, individuals suffering from depression may give themselves Parent orders ("Quit being a crybaby, get going!"), but are unable to rationally analyze their own depression.

Depressive Life Scripts

A life script is an individual's plan for life which is designed by the early decisions of the young child. It is the overall life course which is played out through the principles outlined to this point. An overview of a depressive life script might look like this:

Act I: Introduction to Life. A child is born. The parental figures unwittingly communicate the child's unwanted status to the child, who records a "Don't Exist" injunction into his or her Parent ego-state. The child decides that the parental figures know what they are talking about and that indeed the child is flawed and unworthy. The child decides that "I am not-OK, I'll probably never be happy, and if things get bad enough I'll kill myself."

Act II: The Script Is Played Out. The child grows older and forgets that he or she decided to feel not-OK. However, the decision is firmly implanted in the child's world view and is constantly reexperienced and "proven" to be accurate as the person plays depressive psychological games which repeatedly result in receiving negative strokes and few positive strokes. Racket feelings of sadness, guilt, hopelessness, and helplessness are reexperienced and collected through these games. Life seems to be painful, things seem to always go wrong, and he or she has a deep sense of inadequacy. Because the Adult ego-state did not begin to function adequately until after the injunction and early decision were made, the individual can make no sense out of why this is happening and why there seems to be no way of feeling better.

Act III: The Curtain Falls and the Show Closes. After a number of years of playing the games and collecting negative strokes and reexperiencing painful feelings, adequate evidence has been collected that, indeed, the person is not-OK. The Racket feelings are then cashed in for the unhappy ending of suicide, or some other destructive course. The suicide may be violent and sudden, or it may be long term, subtle, and slow. Thus, the Parent injunction is proven "correct."

TA Treatment of Depression

TA treatment of depression is designed to alter the three basic elements in depression: (1) lack of Adult awareness of the injunction, early decision, stroking patterns, games, and life script which make up the depression; (2) the presence of the "Don't Exist" injunction; and (3) the presence of the early depressive decision. There are three different "schools" (Barnes, 1977) of TA treatment, each of which offers a specific treatment strategy for depression. Each approach focuses primarily on one element of the depression, and while each of these approaches will be described separately, they are not usually practiced in separate, "pure" forms. There is much overlap between the approaches, and a combination of them is generally used by experienced TA therapists.

Increasing Adult Awareness

One of the primary characteristics of all life scripts is that they are played out without awareness of the Adult ego-state. For practical purposes, then, a depressive life script is unconscious. An individual suffering from depression is not aware that he or she is setting up situations in order to collect negative strokes and Racket feelings so that an unhappy ending can be caused and the early decision and injunction can be lived out. By bringing these factors into Adult awareness, the individual has increased control over his or her behavior and feelings and can choose to behave in ways which are more rewarding. Once the person has become aware of the foundation and process of the depression, new behaviors can be planned and practiced which are designed to induce more positive feelings and experiences of personal OKness. In addition, the person's awareness that the "I am not-OK" belief is a relic of childhood rather than some cosmic truth releases him or her from much of the power of the message.

As with most TA therapies, increasing Adult awareness of depressive life scripts is usually accomplished in a group therapy setting. The therapist can use the interactions of the group members to point out psychological games and unconscious requests for negative strokes which the group members demonstrating. When the behavioral patterns are made clear, plans for new behaviors can be made, and they can be practiced in the group where they will be reinforced. In addition, some TA therapists use the group setting as a context for teaching TA theory, which also increases Adult functioning (Berne, 1966).

Changing the "Don't Exist" Injunction

Because a Parent ego-state "Don't Exist" injunction forms the initial basis for depression, a second approach to treating depression is to eliminate this message and to replace it with a nondepressive message in the Parent ego-state. This therapy process is often called "reparenting" (Schiff, 1970) because the content of the Parent ego-state is changed. While the actual techniques used in reparenting vary, the basis of the process is encouraging a regression to a childlike state (activating the young Child ego-state while blocking out the Parent and Adult ego-states) to the time when the original "Don't Exist" injunction was given. While the person reexperiences this early state of dependency and vulnerability, the therapist and/or group members present new positive and nurturing Parent messages to the person. In this way, a new set of messages is recorded in the person's Parent ego-state, and the "Don't Exist" injunction is contradicted and eliminated. Without the "Don't Exist" injunction the person no longer has a reason to decide that he or she is not-OK, and the need for the depression is eliminated. The amount of regression encouraged during reparenting varies with the severity of the depression and the setting of the therapy. Full regressions are usually only encouraged in inpatient settings and with psychotic level disorders (Schiff, 1975). Reparenting has been performed on an outpatient basis, usually utilizing partial regressions and disorders which are not psychotic in nature (Weiss & Weiss, 1977).

Changing the Early Depressive Decision

The "Don't Exist" injunction presents the original stimulus which encourages the child to decide that he or she is not-OK. Putting this injunction into action and actually living out a life script which is designed to prove that "I am not-OK" is a result of the depressive decision in the Child ego-state. The third TA treatment approach is designed to change this early depressive decision. This treatment, which is often called Redecision Therapy (Goulding & Goulding, 1979), involves a process of activating an early scene where the individual made the decision that he or she was not-OK. The scene is brought into the here-and-now through a Gestalt style empty-chair or psychodrama technique. During the reliving of the scene the therapist and/or group members encourage the individual to disagree with the parental injunction and to make a new decision that no matter what the Parent ego-state messages are, the person will believe that he or she is OK and deserves to exist and to be happy.

The Role of Strokes in Treating Depression

Steiner (1974) has noted that stroking patterns have repeatedly appeared as significant in the life scripts of individuals suffering from depression. Steiner defines a set of informal cultural rules regarding the exchange of strokes which he calls the "stroke economy." These are rules which restrict the giving and receiving of strokes, and result in stroking deficits for individuals who follow the rules. Included in such rules are prohibitions from giving strokes when they are asked for, asking for strokes, accepting strokes, rejecting strokes, and stroking oneself.

In addition to the attention given to particular etiological factors in depression, all of the TA approaches to treating depression alter stroking patterns. The Adult-oriented approach alters stroking patterns by having individuals become aware of their lack of positive strokes and to initiate new behaviors which will provide strokes. These behaviors are then practiced. The reparenting approach offers the individual increased positive stroking through the new nurturing Parent messages which are available in the restructured Parent ego-state. The reparenting process itself also offers strokes and presents a model of stroke exchange. Redecision Therapy encourages individuals to self-stroke, to reject negative strokes, and to stroke others.

GESTALT THERAPY

Background

Gestalt Therapy was developed during the 1960s by Frederick S. Perls. Although Perls developed the theory over nearly a decade, Gestalt Therapy only became well known during the late 1960s when Perls resided at California's Esalen Institute. During this time Perls and Esalen became one of the primary centers of the human potential movement.

The Cycle of Needs

Gestalt Therapy conceptualizes life as being an ongoing cycle of: (1) experiencing a need; (2) performing actions which meet and satisfy that need; and (3) with that need satisfied, another need becoming dominant. This need/satisfaction cycle begins at birth and continues throughout life (Perls, 1973). An effectively functioning individual operates smoothly within the cycle by experiencing needs, meeting them, and moving on to new needs.

Gestalt Therapy calls experiencing a need "opening a gestalt." A gestalt is the particular pattern of perceptions and experience which becomes dominant and stands out from all other perceptions because of the need which is dominant at that time. Thus, when an individual experiences a particular need, the bodily experiences and elements of the environment which are connected to that need form the open gestalt. If, for example, an individual is hungry, the open gestalt of hunger consists of the sensation of having an empty stomach; growling noises from the stomach; a heightened sense of smell; increased sensitivity to food, kitchen, restaurants; fantasies of eating appealing food; and frustration that one is having to wait for food. When appropriate action is taken and food is obtained, prepared, and consumed, the need is satisfied and the perceptions involving food and eating recede into the background. Perceptions regarding food and eating are less important, and the gestalt is "closed." Space in the perceptual and experiential field is then created for a new gestalt to be opened.

For example, after eating, the individual may become aware that he or she is tired. A new gestalt of fatigue, with sensations of tired muscles, closing eyes, and fantasies regarding comfortable sleeping quarters becomes important. In order to close this new gestalt, rest must be obtained. As long as an individual operates smoothly within the cycle of opening and closing gestalts by becoming aware of needs, meeting them, and allowing new needs to appear, the person's life will work smoothly.

One characteristic of individuals suffering from depression is that their functioning in the need/satisfaction cycle is ineffective, and they have difficulty meeting their current needs. They cannot sleep when they are tired, or they sleep even though they are not tired. They overeat or undereat. When they are with people they are uncomfortable and sad, and when they are alone they feel lonely and have the desire to be with people. Their ability to open and close gestalts is impaired, thus making it difficult for them to meet their own needs.

Awareness and the Need/Satisfaction Cycle

The basis for being able to experience a need (open a gestalt) is the ability to be aware of oneself (Perls, 1969b). Needs are not experienced simply on an intellectual level, but rather are perceived on a total organismic level. A need to urinate, for example, is sensed as both a bodily sensation and a set of thoughts and perceptions designed to locate an appropriate place to urinate. The need to cry may consist of sad thoughts, painful emotions, shortened breathing, and a sensation of heat around the eyes. Thus, for an individual to be able to be aware of needs, he or she must have a clear awareness of his or her internal state. He or she must be "in touch" with the internal world.

Individuals suffering from depression are characterized by limited awareness of their internal state. It is not unusual for them to report feeling "numbness" "nothingness," or "emptiness." There seems to be an inability to experience the full intensity of thinking, feeling, or bodily sensations. As a result, individuals suffering from depression do not become aware of needs (open gestalts) and thus cannot meet needs and make room for new needs (close gestalts).

Mechanisms which Interfere with Gestalt Formation

According to Gestalt Therapy, there are four basis mechanisms which get an individual "off track" from the needs/satisfaction cycle, (Perls, Hefferling, & Goodman, 1951) and an individual acquires these mechanisms from the manner in which he or she was treated as a child. Perls called these mechanisms introjection, projection, confluence, and retroflection.

Introjection. Introjection occurs when an individual "swallows whole" external principles, rules, thoughts, or beliefs. Because the unquestioning adoption of external beliefs and feelings does not integrate these psychological entities into the personality, they do not function as part of the person and do not operate in the best interest of the individual. For example, if a boy unquestioningly adopts his father's attitude that "men don't cry," he has introjected this belief. The boy's ability to express sadness when he needs to do so thus becomes impaired. Over time, the introject may also begin to dull his awareness of feeling sadness itself. Thus, when the boy needs to experience sadness and to cry, he cannot do so. People who use introjection may have been provided with harsh rules, regulations, and commands as children. They felt compelled to adopt these rules in order to survive in their environment.

Projection. Projection is the process of attributing an internal personality characteristic to the external environment. Projection is usually the result of having first introjected a belief, attitude, or feeling and then trying to eject the foreign matter. For example, the boy who introjected his father's "men don't cry" belief may deny that he thinks crying is bad, but may feel that "other people" think it is bad and will ridicule him for crying. Thus he is not only prevented from expressing sadness, but the projection of the belief prevents him from being aware that he has adopted the belief that "men don't cry." Thus, individuals who use projection experienced a background of introjecting in order to survive, but also tried to maintain some sense of sovereignty by expelling the unwanted psychological entity into the environment.

Confluence. Confluence is the name Perls gave to the inability to experience independence from the environment. Confluent individuals become overadapted to the environment and lose touch with their sovereignty and ability to take care of themselves. Infants are confluent in their early relationship with their mothers, and indeed during this time mother is responsible for much of the functioning of their needs/satisfaction cycle. With a lack of independence in later life, however, the person does not clearly experience his or her needs separately from others. This occurs in individuals who are prevented from experiencing independence from their primary caretakers. An example of such confluence is the mother or father who says to a child "I'm cold, put your sweater on."

Retroflection. Retroflection is the process of treating oneself as if the self were the environment. Retroflection occurs when actions designed to alter the environment in order to meet needs are prevented or interfered with. Thus, if a boy is angry with his father but is also taught that "you don't talk back to your father," he is prevented from expressing his anger toward his father. But because he still has a need to express anger, the boy may turn the anger toward himself and become self-destructive or self-abusive. He is thus "retroflecting" his anger away from its intended target (the environment) and toward himself.

Unfinished Business

An individual's ability to become aware of a need (open a gestalt) is based on having an uncluttered perceptual and experiential field. Only with a clear background will an open gestalt (a present need) stand out clearly and distinctly. If the field is cluttered with several open gestalts (unmet needs), the identity of the dominant need and the appropriate actions and environmental manipulations required to meet the need become confused. According to Gestalt Therapy, the result of utilizing introjection, projection, confluence, and retroflection is that the individual is prevented from meeting needs. A backlog of unmet needs then clutters the perceptual field which makes present needs increasingly difficult to perceive and meet. Old needs which were never met and thus are still open gestalts are known as "unfinished business."

Let us suppose that an individual comes home tired from a long day at work. The dominant need (open gestalt) is fatigue. Suppose, however, that the individual skipped lunch in order to complete some work and thus is also very hungry when he or she arrives home. The fatigue which the individual experiences is very unpleasant and is a need which requests action. However, being hungry is also unpleasant. Now there are two competing gestalts in the foreground, and each open gestalt is interfering with the resolution of the other. The person cannot eat because he or she is too tired to cook, but cannot sleep because the unpleasant sensations of hunger keep him or her awake.

Perls conceptualized all "neurotics" as carrying around large amounts of unfinished emotional business, or unclosed gestalts (Perls, 1973). These unresolved issues from the past continue to clutter the perceptual and experiential field and prevent the person from effectively being aware of and meeting needs in present-day life. Old angers, pains, indecisions, unexpressed resentments, and uncried tears haunt the emotional functioning of the person and drain energy and attention away from present needs.

Individuals who suffer from depression are those persons whose unfinished business has been developed largely through the use of retroflection. Retroflection results in a self-punishing style, which can be contrasted with the result of other mechanisms, such as projection, which results in a paranoid style. Often individuals who suffer from depression were punished for experiencing and expressing anger as children, and thus have learned to retroflect anger toward themselves. This results in the depressive sensations of feeling bad about oneself, having low self-esteem, and being self-destructive.

Gestalt Treatment of Depression

Gestalt treatment of depression is designed to close the archaic open gestalts and thus resolve the unfinished business which clutters the perceptual and experiential field, stop retroflections, and increase the ability to be aware of and to meet needs. Because gestalts are opened and closed only in the realm of immediate physical, cognitive, and emotional experience, Gestalt Therapy does not consider "talking about" issues or analyzing their origin to be therapeutic. Only by working on issues in the "here and now," or as if the problem were actually occurring at that moment in therapy, will the person's total experience of the problem (and thus the open gestalts) be available for therapeutic intervention. In order to allow individuals to reexperience problems within the therapy session, Gestalt therapists use psychodrama-type techniques which involve an actual reexperiencing of the issue in the therapy room. Perls favored a one-person psychodrama called the "empty chair," which is a technique involving one person creating a dialogue with him or herself by switching between two chairs. Perls felt that allowing one individual to take both parts of the dialogue keeps other people's projections out of the therapy and thus allows for a clearer delineation of the unfinished business problem and solution.

When a depressed person works on an issue during Gestalt Therapy, he or she is asked to bring the issue into the here and now and to act it out as if it were happening at the present moment. The Gestalt therapist will then look for the unclosed gestalts, the unfinished business, and the retroflections. For example, for an individual who is depressed and states that he or she "feels like a terrible person," a Gestalt therapist might conceptualize this as a retroflection of the desire to tell someone else (likely someone from the past) that he or she is a terrible person. The individual might be asked to tell "him or herself" in the empty chair that he or she is a terrible person. The person would then be asked to switch chairs and to respond to the accusation that he or she is a terrible person. In this way a dialogue is formed in which the retroflected aggression is directed outward (to the empty chair) instead of inward. The individual's experience of directing aggression outward rather than inward might be further reinforced by being encouraged to fantasize different people from the past in the empty chair and to tell each one of them that he or she is a terrible person.

In addition to working on issues which the depressed individual brings to the session from his or her outside life, behaviors which occur during the therapy session are often carefully monitored and addressed by the therapist. Increased awareness of and expressions of meaningful behaviors is then encouraged. For example, an individual who refuses to make eye contact with the therapist might be asked to repeat the phrase "I will not look at you." An angry tone of voice may then be noticed by the therapist who has the person switch to "I am angry with you." The angry tone may increase and the person may be asked to fantasize someone in the empty chair and to tell the person "I hate you." Thus, the lack of eye contact has been used to uncover aggression which has been retroflected and not expressed outwardly.

REALITY THERAPY

Background

Reality Therapy was developed during the 1960s by William Glasser. Working primarily with juvenile law offenders in a state youth facility, Glasser decided to break with his analytic background and to develop a more efficient, direct, change-oriented form of treatment.

Human Needs and Responsible Behavior

Reality Therapy's basic premise is that people who repeatedly engage in self-defeating behaviors are ignoring or distorting some aspect of reality. If the person were fully facing up to reality, he or she would see that the behaviors in question do not result in a favorable outcome and would take steps to change the behaviors. A major focus of reality therapy, then, is to help people face the reality that their lives are not going well at the present time.

Reality Therapy defines two basic human needs which all people inherently strive to meet. The first need is to love and to be loved. The second need is to feel worthwhile. The key to meeting these needs is to behave responsibly. Responsible behavior is defined as behavior which effectively meets needs, and irresponsible behavior is that which does not meet needs (Glasser, 1965). Reality Therapy states that emotional or behavioral "symptoms" appear when a person is behaving irresponsibly and his or her basic needs are not being met. Reality therapists do not concern themselves with why one person shows one type of psychological symptom and another shows a different symptom. Instead, their focus is on the underlying symptom of all emotional problems: the person's failure to behave responsibly and thus to love and be loved and to feel worthwhile.

Depression, then, is not important as a distinct category to the reality therapist. Depression is seen simply as one of the many possible symptoms resulting from a failure to meet one's needs. Depression is not treated as a particular disorder which requires different and specific treatment techniques, but rather as an indication that the individual is behaving irresponsibly and his or her needs are not being met. It is the irresponsible behavior which is the focus of treatment.

Reality Therapy and the Treatment of Depression

Reality Therapy stresses personal involvement of the therapist with the person seeking help. Specific therapeutic techniques are seen as less important than the willingness of the therapist to be actively involved with the individual during the therapy sessions. The therapist is active, directive, and willing to self-disclose and to be "genuine" with the individual. A passive, withdrawn, analytic stance is actively avoided.

Reality therapists avoid talking about the person's past, as a discussion of the past will only result in the focus of therapy deviating from the person's current life problems. Change is seen as being possible by simply dealing with the behaviors which are not working well at the present time.

Reality therapists evaluate the responsibility or irresponsibility of the individual's current behavior. They readily label behaviors which are not effective in meeting needs as "bad" or "immoral." In treating a depressed individual, the Reality therapist does not offer sympathy or "unconditional positive regard" (Glasser, 1975). Instead, the therapist will actively push the depressed person to behave more responsibly by becoming increasingly involved in getting his or her needs met. Passive and withdrawn behaviors will be labeled "wrong" and "bad," as they are unhelpful in improving the person's life. Even if the depressed person feels that he or she is only "going through the motions," he or she will be encouraged to be active socially and at work. The assumption in this approach is that whether or not the depressed person enjoys the activities, simply engaging in the behaviors will begin to result in needs being met and the depression (the sign that needs are not being met) being alleviated. If an individual states that he or she is very depressed and cannot get out of bed to be active at work or socially, a reality therapist might state that staying in bed is a bad thing to do. He or she may label the behavior as being lazy or wrong. The therapist will tell the individual to get out of bed, even if he or she does not want to do so. The person will be pushed by the therapist to become increasingly active in life even if he or she feels resistive.

DISCUSSION

As is the case in much of the mental health field, research is lacking in the area of TA, Gestalt Therapy, and Reality Therapy and depression. Most of the research involving these theories has been general in nature (Smith & Glass, 1977) rather than focusing on depression. There have, however, been a few preliminary studies regarding TA and depression.

Golub and Guerriero (1981) presented a TA-training program to a group of learning disabled boys and found that self-esteem among the boys significantly improved as a result of the program. While the population addressed in this study makes the applicability of the results to depression indirect, the study does provide a possible future direction for research where TA training could be designed to raise self-esteem in depressed individuals.

Pinsker and Russell (1978) developed a set of positive verbal strokes which were presented to subjects while the temperature of the subjects' fingertips were measured. Results showed that fingertip temperature significantly increased when the positive strokes were given. These results suggest that positive verbal strokes have an impact on individuals which is sufficiently substantial to be measured by physiological changes. Again, the importance of these results for depression is by implication. The data from the study provides indications that strokes are important to individuals, as they can be measured by physiological changes.

Because Pinsker and Russell's study demonstrated a physiological impact of verbal strokes and several clinical articles have noted observations that stroking patterns seem related to depression (Erskine, 1980; Leibl & Dedauw, 1979; Loomis & Landsman, 1980), Fetsch and Sprinkle (1982) presented a stroking seminar to eight individuals who had sought counseling at a university counseling center. The participants were defined as experiencing reactive depressions and obtained scores greater than 13 on the Beck Depression Inventory. Each participant was tested for depression level, Natural Child ego-state energy level, Nurturing Parent ego-state energy level, frequency of giving positive verbal strokes, and frequency of receiving positive verbal strokes. The participants were given four, two-hour group sessions at one-week intervals. The first session taught the participants to give positive verbal strokes. The second session taught them to ask for strokes. The third session taught the participants to stroke themselves with positive self-statements. The final session focused on increasing physical stroking.

Results indicated that the depression level of the participants decreased significantly, from a mean Beck Depression Inventory score of 19 to a score of

11.63. Increases in Natural Child and Nurturing Parent energy were also reported. Measures of receiving verbal strokes increased, while giving verbal strokes did not increase. The results of this study suggest that altering depressed individuals' stroking patterns may be useful in treating depression. The findings are preliminary, as no control or no-treatment group was used, and the sample size of eight participants is very small. Nevertheless, the study does suggest that further investigation of training in increasing positive stroking in depression is appropriate.

The lack of well-controlled studies regarding depression and TA, Gestalt, and Reality Therapy makes evaluating their contribution to conceptualizing and treating depression difficult. With a greater move toward specifying particular treatments for particular disorders, hopefully research in this area will increase.

An observational analysis of the approaches suggests that each approach has positive elements to offer in the conceptualization and treatment of depression. TA, for example, presents a cohesive theory regarding the etiology of depression and TA treatment approaches offer behavioral, cognitive, and emotional interventions. The presence of a feeling that the individual is not worthy (the depressive decision in the Child ego-state) and a sense of not belonging (the "Don't Exist" injunction) are often obvious symptoms of depression. The TA formulation remains a theoretical structure, however, and research regarding the presence of such parental messages and conscious, early childhood decisions would be essential in examining the accuracy of the model to clinical depressions.

Gestalt, like TA, offers a reasonably comprehensive formulation of depression. The self-punishing nature of depression (retroflection) and diminished capacity to meet one's needs because of other concerns (unfinished business) are both often readily observable in depression. Gestalt treatment focuses on widening the individual's capacity to experience and to resolve distracting emotional issues. Both factors address major symptom areas of depression. In a manner similar to TA, research regarding the importance of unresolved past experiences and retroflection are important in testing the accuracy of the Gestalt theoretical formulation to clinical depression. Reality Therapy offers a formulation of depression which intentionally focuses on the here-and-now problems of living. This focus seems to be beneficial in that encouragement to become active and involved with life seems appropriate to depressed individuals, who are often passive and withdrawn. Nevertheless, Reality Therapy's conceptualization that a depressed individual's behavior does not meet needs does not address the issue of why depression is the symptom displayed by one individual while another individual's unmet needs present another symptom. It seems important to isolate the factors involved in specific symptom formulation, and Reality Therapy does not address this issue satisfactorily. Perhaps research directed toward defining how each symptom is a particular type of unsuccessful attempt to meet the needs to love and be loved and to feel worthwhile would be useful.

Overall, then, TA, Gestalt, and Reality Therapy offer generally helpful conceptualizations regarding depression, and many different avenues of investigation and research are opened up by the theories. Research regarding these approaches and the conceptualization and treatment of depression is in its infancy, and will hopefully continue and expand. Because the people responsible for the development of these theories and their use have traditionally been practitioners, research has not been a major focus. In order to validate the applicability of the theories to depression, increased quantity and quality of research will be necessary.

References

Barnes, G. (1977). *Transactional analysis After Eric Berne.* New York: Harper & Row.

Berne, E. (1961). *Transactional analysis in Psychotherapy.* New York: Grove Press.

Berne, E. (1964). *Games people play.* New York: Random House.

Berne, E. (1966). *Principles of group treatment.* New York: Grove Press.

Berne, E. (1972). *What do you say after you say hello?.* New York: Grove Press.

Birnbaum, J. (1973) *Cry anger, a cure for depression.* Ontario: General Publishing Co.

Dusay, J. M. (1977). *Egograms.* New York: Bantam Books.

Erskine, R. G. (1980). Identification and cure of stroke ripoff. *Transactional Analysis Journal, 10,* 74–76.

Fetsch, R. J., & Sprinkle, R. L. (1982). Stroking treatment effects on depressed mood. *Transactional Analysis Journal, 12,* 213–217.

Glasser, W. S. (1960). *Mental health or mental illness.* New York: Harper & Row.

Glasser, W. S. (1965). *Reality therapy.* New York: Harper & Row.

Glasser, W. S. (1975). *The identity society.* New York: Harper & Row.

Golub, S., & Guerriero, L. A. (1981). The effects of a transactional analysis training program on self-esteem in learning disabled boys. *Transactional Analysis Journal, 11,* 244–246.

Goulding, M. M., & Goulding, R. L. (1979). *Changing lives through redecision therapy.* New York: Brunner/Mazel.

Goulding, R. L., & Goulding, M. M. (1978). *The power is in the patient.* San Francisco: Transactional Analysis Press.

Harris, T. A. (1969). *I'm OK—You're OK.* New York: Harper & Row.

Helmering, D. W. (1976). *Group therapy, who needs it.* Millbrae, CA: Celestial Arts Publishing.

James, M., & Jongeward, D. (1971). *Born to win.* Reading, MA: Addison-Wesley Publishing.

James, M. (Ed.). (1977). *Techniques in transactional analysis.* Reading, MA: Addison-Wesley Publishing.

Latner, J. (1973). *The gestalt therapy book.* New York: Julian Press.

Leibl, R. D., & Dedauw, G. (1979). The self-statements of success. *Transactional Analysis Journal, 9,* 110–112.

Loomis, M. E., & Landsman, S. G. (1980). Manic-depressive structure: Assessment and development. *Transactional Analysis Journal, 10,* 284–290.

Perls, F. S. (1969a). *Gestalt therapy verbatim.* Moab, UT: Real People Press.

Perls, F. S. (1969b). *In and out the garbage pail.* Moab, UT: Real People Press.

Perls, F. S. (1973). *The gestalt approach and eyewitness to therapy.* Palo Alto, CA: Science & Behavior Books.

Perls, F. S., Hefferling, R. F., & Goodman, P. (1951). *Gestalt therapy.* New York: Crown Publishers.

Pinsker, E. J., & Russell, H. L. (1978). The effect of positive verbal strokes on fingertip skin temperature. *Transactional Analysis Journal, 8,* 306–309.

Polster, E., & Polster, M. (1973). *Gestalt therapy integrated.* New York: Brunner/Mazel.

Schiff, J. L. (1970). *All my children.* New York: Pyramid Books.

Schiff, J. L. (1975). *Cathexis reader.* New York: Harper & Row.

Smith, M. L., & Glass, G. V. (1977). Meta-analysis of psychotherapy outcome studies. *American Psychologist, 32,* 752–760.

Steiner, C. M. (1974). *Scripts people live.* New York: Bantam Books.

Stuntz, E. C. (1971). *Review of games 1962–1970.* San Francisco: Transactional Analysis Press.

Weiss, J., & Weiss, L. (1977). Corrective parenting in private practice. In G. Barnes (Ed.), *Transactional analysis after Eric Berne,* New York: Harper & Row.

Woolams, S., & Brown, M. (1979). *TA: The total handbook of transactional analysis.* Englewood Cliffs: Prentice-Hall.

Zunin, L. (1972). *Contact: The first four minutes.* New York: Ballantine Books.

Chapter 8

Psychotherapy Research in Depression: An Overview

Alan S. Bellack
The Medical College of Pennsylvania at EPPI

Depression is one of the core human emotions, and as such, has long been a popular topic in literature and philosophy. However, until recently it had not received great attention by mental health experts. In some respects, it was a poor stepsister to schizophrenia and anxiety. That situation has changed dramatically in the last 10 years. If depression has not become the most widely debated and studied topic in the mental health literature, it is certainly competing for that honor. One can expect to find one or more articles about some aspect of depression in just about every issue of each of the major psychology and psychiatry journals. The study of depression has become so specialized that no one can be expert on every aspect of the literature.

In part reflecting this complexity, the term *depression* has been relegated to a secondary status in favor of the more encompassing term *affective disorders*. The simplistic diagnostic dichotomies that were popular up to 10 years ago (e.g., psychotic-neurotic, endogenous-exogenous) have similarly been displaced by multidimensional schemas (e.g., *Diagnostic and Statistical Manual of Mental Disorders [DSM-III]*), and the adequacy of even these more complex systems is hotly debated (Overall & Zisook, 1980; Winokur, 1979; Yerevanian & Akiskal, 1979). The 1950s emphasis on the phenomenology of depression has been replaced by family, genetic, and biological studies (De Pue, 1979). In keeping with the current emphasis on the psychobiology of the affective disorders, there have been great strides in the development and sophisticated application of pharmacological agents, including lithium, tricyclic antidepressants, and *monoamine oxidase inhibitors* (MAOIs). While current pharmacological treatments have numerous limitations (e.g., high rates of noncompliance, treatment refusal, unpleasant side effects, and recidivism upon termination), they are sufficiently effective to serve as a benchmark for new and alternative interventions (Klerman, 1983).

Research on psychosocial factors in depression and psychological treatments has kept apace with the biological literature. The importance of life events and social support networks in the onset of depressive episodes is now well documented (Brown, 1979; Monroe, Bellack, Hersen, & Himmelhoch, 1983). There is also an extensive literature implicating maladaptive cognitive patterns (Beck, 1976), lack of adequate positive reinforcement in the environment (Lewisohn, Youngren, & Grosscup, 1979), and social skill deficits (Bellack, Hersen, & Himmelhoch, 1980). The specific etiology of affective disorders is uncertain, but there is little question that these various psychosocial factors play a major role in the course of the disorder among vulnerable individuals (Akiskal, 1979).

This fact, together with the limitations of pharmacological interventions (as well as philosophical questions about the use of drugs), have stimulated a resurgence of interest in the use of psychotherapies for depression. As evidenced by the chapters in Part 1 of this book, several new therapies have been developed over the last 10 years, and older therapies have been modified or reconceptualized in light of recent data. There is now a large and impressive body of literature documenting the effectiveness of psychosocial interventions (Steinbrueck, Maxwell, & Howard, 1983: Weissman, 1979). In fact, psychotherapies have frequently proven to be as effective or more effective then pharmacotherapy. Unfortunately, despite the size and quality of the literature, more questions remain to be answered than have been answered to date. We still know relatively little about how psychotherapies work, for which patients they are appropriate, how they should be conducted, how they compare to one another, and so on. The previous chapters in this part have described the respective treatments and their underlying theories, have reviewed the relevant literatures, and have raised questions pertinent to the particular intervention. The purpose of this chapter is to provide a critical overview of psychosocial strategies in general. As such, this chapter will not attempt to systematically evaluate each approach. Rather, issues will be abstracted which are germaine to several different treatments and, where possible, attempts made to raise questions and to draw conclusions which cut across specific theoretical and conceptual boundaries. The intent here is to step back and look at the literature as a whole, rather than to microscopically evaluate each strategy or to conduct a comparative analysis. Moreover, no attempt will be made to systematically analyze the research literature. There are numerous excellent reviews currently available (Klerman, 1983; Kovacs, 1980; Rush, 1982). Instead, I will deal with what I regard to be more general issues, and problems which seem to plague the literature as a whole.

SPECIFIC ISSUES WITH GENERAL RELEVANCE

There are idiosyncratic conceptual and procedural problems associated with each of the specific approaches. However, there are also a number of issues which have broader relevance even though they are most apparent and/or clearly discussed in the context of one or the other particular strategies. This section will focus on the latter. The broader significance of some of the issues will be identified when they are first addressed. The relevance of other issues will become more apparent as they recur in subsequent sections.

Interpersonal Psychotherapy

Interpersonal psychotherapy (IPT) is one of the most highly regarded of the new psychotherapies for depression. It has yielded impressive results in two extensive clinical trials (Klerman, DiMascio, Weissman, Prusoff, & Paykel, 1974; Weissman, Prusoff, DiMascio, Neu, Goklaney, & Klerman, 1979). These studies are especially noteworthy in that they included extensive clinical assessments on a carefully diagnosed sample of clinically depressed patients. As will be discussed later, assessment and diagnostic inconsistencies have been a bane of the literature. Many other studies have been uninterpretable due to the use of subclinical populations or idiosyncratic measures. IPT procedures are described in a well-prepared treatment manual. In addition to serving as an excellent resource for clinicians, manuals are now regarded as a necessity for the experimental evaluation of psychotherapies. Only when procedures are carefully detailed in a manual can the reviewer determine precisely what was done, how erstwhile different treatments actually differ, and whether a subsequent study (especially one conducted by a different research group) actually involved a faithful replication. As a function of the sophistication of the investigators and the methodology employed, the results of these two studies on IPT are probably most responsible for the current widespread belief that psychotherapies can be as effective as pharmacotherapy.

In reading the literature one gets the impression that the effectiveness of IPT is unquestioned. Its inclusion in the *National Institute of Mental Health* (NIMH) Treatment of Depression Collaborative Research Program enhances this image of IPT as a well-established intervention. However promising IPT may be, this tacit assumption of effectiveness is really not justified by the existing empirical literature. First, a data base of only two studies is simply not sufficient to draw universal conclusions, regardless of how impressive the methodology or results. In the case of IPT, the results are impressive, but clearly not definitive. For example, in the second (and more extensive) of the two studies the primary reported differences are reflected in survival curves, rather than in specific, objective measures of improvement. That is, IPT delayed symptomatic failure as well as pharmacotherapy. But, it is unclear how efficient either intervention was at producing specific, positive changes.

A second concern about the existing data base pertains to the replicability of the treatment. To this point, the positive results for IPT have all been reported by one research group. Needless to say, the findings must be viewed with great caution until they are replicated by an independent group that does not have a commitment to the approach. There are really two aspects to this issue of replicability. First, are the results due to the specific therapeutic operations rather than the enthusiasm and general clinical skill of the people who developed the procedure? It is not uncommon for new procedures to achieve great success in the hands of the originator, only to prove ineffective when applied by less enthusiastic or more critical practitioners. Second, is the technique specific enough that someone other than the originator can learn and apply it? The existence of a detailed treatment manual does not necessarily ensure this second aspect of replicability. In fact, the IPT manual is more specific about treatment content and what should not be done than about precisely how it should be conducted. For the most part, it employs "standard" psychotherapeutic techniques: procedures which are difficult to define or teach. One recent study documented that naive raters listening to audiotapes could distinguish IPT sessions from cognitive therapy sessions (DeRubeis, Hollon, Evans, & Bemis, 1982). But, the differentiation seemed to be based more on the occurrence/nonoccurrence of specific cognitive therapy techniques than on identifiable IPT techniques. In any case, the NIMH Collaborative Research Program will provide answers to both of these major questions in the next few years.

One final concern about IPT also deserves mention. Curiously, the treatment seems to have been developed more as an ethical, credible control condition than in response to a well-developed conceptual model of the disorder it is meant to treat. As detailed throughout this book, there is an impressive body of literature documenting the central role of interpersonal difficulties in the course of the affective disorders. As such, IPT clearly has face validity. However, IPT is not tied to a model which explains how and why interpersonal problems contribute to affective disorders. Given the multifaceted nature of affective disorders, this etiological conservatism is probably quite judicious. More importantly, IPT does not provide a conceptual/theoretical model for understanding how the treatment works, or why specific techniques are employed. It ascribes to a loose psychodynamic model, but is explicitly not psychoanalytic and does not seem to promote insight. It seeks to improve role functioning and interpersonal relationships, but does not systematically teach interpersonal skills or promote in vivo behavior change in the manner of the behavioral therapies. I am not implying that an atheoretical intervention cannot be effective, or that IPT advocates should retrospectively develop a theory to explain their success. Yet, the absence of a conceptual model severely limits the future evaluation or development of the approach. It seems unlikely that the current (and original) IPT procedure is the penultimate version, never to be improved upon. But without a model upon which to base and evaluate variations, advancement can only come by clinical bootstraps (e.g., "Based on my experience I think x will work better than y, and z is really superfluous"). Better understanding of the disorder and its treatment require a more systematic and integrated approach.

Cognitive Therapy

The development and status of cognitive therapy parallels that of IPT in many respects. Cognitive therapy has also produced impressive results in a few well-conducted clinical trials. The procedures are described in an excellent treatment manual. The treatment is regarded by many as equal or superior to pharmacotherapy, and it is included as one of the core interventions in the NIMH Collaborative Program. As with IPT, positive results for cognitive therapy have been reported primarily by strong adherents of the approach. More "impartial" evaluations are needed. However, as indicated above, cognitive therapy procedures appear to be more specific and operationalized, making replication more feasible. Moreover, cognitive therapy has already been successfully employed at several research sites in addition to Beck's Center for Cognitive Therapy (Murphy, Simons, Wetzel, & Lustman, 1984; Rush & Watkins, 1981; Shaw, 1977).

In contrast to IPT, cognitive therapy is based upon a well-developed theoretical model. Beck and his colleagues have conceptualized depression as primarily the result of a series of cognitive distortions. Improvement is hypothesized to require cognitive change, and the treatment procedures are designed specifically to rectify the problem by teaching the patient new and more effective ways to think. Thus, etiology, maintaining factors, and change are all conceived of in a conceptually integrated manner. This model lends itself to research, and it has stimulated an extensive literature.

Unfortunately, recent data have raised serious questions about its validity. It has not (yet) been possible to verify the occurrence of the specific cognitive distortions hypothesized by Beck. If they occur at all, they apparently are not characteristic of all depressed patients (Hamilton & Abramson, 1983). Furthermore, those cognitive distortions that have been identified seem to be symptoms of the disorder, rather than etiological or maintaining factors (Lewinsohn, Steinmetz, Larson, & Franklin, 1981). This is a most important distinction which has important implications for our evaluation of cognitive therapy, as well as our understanding of the disorder. For example, several studies have found that pharmacotherapy reduces maladaptive cognitions as rapidly and extensively as cognitive therapy (Silverman, Silverman, & Lustman, 1984; Simons, Garfield, & Murphy, 1984). These findings imply that the specific procedures employed in cognitive therapy may not be critical, and that the active therapeutic agent is some other, as yet undetermined, factor. Or, at the very least, that the major procedures do not work by altering cognitions in the manner specified by the theory. Can cognitive therapy then be made more effective if the true active factor is discovered and highlighted? We will discuss this issue further below, as it applies to other interventions as well.

Behavior Therapy

The title "behavior therapy" as applied to the treatment of depression is really something of a misnomer, as there is no one behavioral treatment for the disorder. In fact, cognitive therapy is regarded by many as a behavior therapy, and might just as well be included in this section as discussed separately. For the most part, the various "behavioral" therapies are linked by a common approach to the study and conceptualization of human behavior more than by shared treatment procedures. There is an emphasis on: (1) operational measurement and observable (or at least objectifiable) phenomena rather than on inferential variables and intrapsychic processes; (2) factors currently maintaining the targeted behavior rather than on historical antecedants; and (3) active, direct, and educational interventions rather than on conversation, self-exploration, and insight.

Within these broad parameters, behavioral conceptualizations of depres
sion have variously emphasized relative rates of positive reinforcement and
punishment, styles of self-evaluation and self-reinforcement, and social skills
deficits. Accordingly, behavioral strategies have included programs to increase activity levels and rates of positive reinforcement, cognitively oriented
strategies to modify self-control behaviors, marital therapy, social skills training, and so on. Frequently, various specific behavioral techniques have been
combined into treatment packages. This latter phenomenon makes it difficult
to evaluate many of the behavioral strategies. For example, McLean and Hakstian (1979) reported positive results for a 10-week behavior therapy program that included marital therapy, coping skills training, social skills training, and some cognitive therapy. Conversely, Shaw (1977) reported negative
results for a behavioral program, but his treatment lasted only four weeks,
focused on increasing pleasant events by scheduling positive activities and
providing some social skills training, and did not include a marital component.

The Shaw study illustrates another problem which characterizes much of
the behavioral literature: research conducted on subclinical populations and/
or with subclinical interventions. The former problem has already been
widely discussed in the literature and will not be addressed here (Hersen,
Bellack, & Himelhoch, 1981; Kazdin, 1981). The use of subclinical interventions does warrant comment. As with drugs, psychotherapies have minimum
and optimal "dosage" requirements. There is always some quantitative or
qualitative "amount" of therapy which is necessary in order to produce
change. Simply labeling a brief intervention "therapy *x*" and nominally providing some of the procedures associated with that form of therapy does not
guarantee that a sufficient "dose" was provided.

This issue is well illustrated in the area of social skills training. As indicated above, Shaw included some social skills training as part of his four-
week program. Rehm, Fuchs, Roth, Kornblith, and Romano (1979) subsequently evaluated a six-week program of group assertion training. The skills
training programs of both Shaw (1977) and Rehm et al. (1979) were found to
be ineffective, and are widely cited as demonstration that social skills training
is not effective in the treatment of depression. However, neither of those
programs provided enough intensive or extensive treatment, or targeted the
full range of skill deficits which characterize depressed patients. For the most
part, depressed patients have long histories of maladaptive interpersonal
response styles. They either have never been able to develop close personal
relationships with others, or have alienated friends and relatives during the
course of their illness. If they are married, they almost invariably have conflicted marital relationships. If unmarried, they generally have serious difficulties developing and maintaining heterosocial relationships. The extent and
long history of these maladaptive response styles make them resistant to
change. Considerable instruction and practice are required. A handful of
sessions is simply not sufficient.

Social skills training can be an extremely effective intervention when applied to the relevant target areas with sufficient intensity. My colleagues and I have recently completed a major investigation of this approach and found it to be superior to amitriptyline (Bellack, Hersen, & Himmelhoch, 1983; Hersen, Bellack, Himmelhoch, & Thase, 1984). One hundred twenty-five nonpsychotic, unipolar depressed women were assigned to one of four treatment conditions, including social skills training with and without amitriptyline, amitriptyline alone, and psychotherapy. Highly experienced therapists conducted 12 weeks of initial treatment followed by six months of booster sessions. Social skills training was applied according to a structured treatment manual, but it was tailored to the needs of the individual patient. Training covered a variety of interpersonal problem areas, including relationships at work, with friends, relatives, and spouse, or in dating situations. Within these areas, it taught a variety of specific skills, including expressing affection and approval, standing up for one's rights, and developing intimate relationships.

Social skills training proved to be highly effective. It had the lowest dropout rates, and yielded the highest number of patients who were significantly improved. These results were maintained during the booster phase. Our form of social skills training shares some techniques with the Shaw and Rehm et al. versions, but there really is little comparability. Given our understanding of the nature and severity of skills deficits in depression, it is not at all surprising that our program was effective while the others were not. However, interpretation of the literature as a whole is complicated by the fact that the same title is applied to these diverse programs with different applicability and probability of success.

Other Psychotherapies

In contrast to the three approaches discussed above, the other therapies described in this section of the book do not have a solid research base. As such, they are more difficult to evaluate. Any critical commentary would be more polemical than substantive. It is clear that a large proportion of practicing psychotherapists employ a psychodynamic model in treating depression. For the most part, they are convinced that their techniques are effective, even in the absence of well-controlled research. My own position is that unsystematic clinical observation and uncontrolled case reports are not sufficient to validate a procedure, no matter how fervent the testament. Ultimately, it is encumbent upon adherents of these alternative approaches to document their techniques with sound empirical data. The pressure to provide such documentation is probably greater than ever before, due to the development of highly effective alternatives (e.g., IPT, cognitive therapy, social skills training). The scientific community, the public, and third-party fee payers all need to know the justification for unproven, expensive treatments, when relatively inexpensive and well-documented alternatives are available.

Marital therapy and short-term psychodynamic therapy seem to be the most promising of the strategies covered in this series of chapters. As previously indicated, interpersonal problems, especially marital conflict, are almost universal components of depression. It is most unusual to find a married depressed patient who does not have marital difficulty of some sort. Consequently, marital therapy is a clearly face valid approach. There is an extensive literature supporting the efficacy of marital therapy in the reduction of such conflict across diagnostic groups (Jacobson & Bussod, 1983). Much less is known about the utility of conjoint treatment for the primary disorder of one member of the couple. It should also be underscored that various approaches to marital therapy differ among themselves as much as the various approaches to individual psychotherapy. The critical research question is, thus, what type of marital therapy, if any, is effective for treating the depression of the primary patient? My own bias is that behavioral marital therapies hold the most promise (e.g., Weiss & Wieder, 1982). They focus on improving communication skills, decreasing conflict, and increasing the amount of positive interchange, all elements of other successful treatments. If the marital situation plays a central role in the disorder, marital therapy may well be more effective than individual therapies. Conversely, if the patient has interpersonal problems that extend beyond the home, or if the depression is not tied to marital conflict, marital therapy may not be sufficient.

Short-term psychodynamic therapy shares many elements with other successful therapies. The duration of treatment, the focus on current issues more than historical exploration, an active therapist orientation, and a supportive therapeutic relationship are as common to IPT, cognitive therapy, and the various behavior therapies as they are to psychodynamic therapy. As will be discussed below, these elements may be as, or more, important than the theoretically specific features on which the techniques differ. Moreover, my colleagues and I found a short-term dynamic therapy to be quite effective in the clinical trial described above (Bellack et al., 1983: Hersen et al., 1984). One of the four treatment groups received 12 weeks of individual dynamic psychotherapy and a pill placebo. This group improved as much, on average, as either of the two social skill groups or the amitriptyline-only group. Only when we examined the proportion of patients significantly improved did the social skill condition prove to be superior, and even under this more restrictive criterion the psychotherapy condition was as effective as the medication. Curiously, we had originally included this group as a control condition, and had not developed a treatment manual or precisely outlined the nature of the treatment. Rather, we simply employed experienced and committed therapists, and asked them to conduct their preferred treatment within general guidelines (e.g., no specific homework or focus on interpersonal skills, no extensive historical exploration). Further research, in which the psychotherapy is objectified in a treatment manual, is certainly warranted.

GENERAL ISSUES

Diagnosis

The diagnosis and categorization of the affective disorders has been a controversial issue for some time. Numerous schemas have been developed, only to be eventually discounted after proving to be unsatisfactory. These ongoing diagnostic controversies have serious impact on any attempted evaluation of psychotherapy research. Different researchers have tended to use different diagnostic systems and/or to accept patients into protocols, based upon their own clinical or conceptual predilections. In other cases, the erstwhile same systems have been applied differentially due to differences in interpretation or criteria (e.g., How much sleep disturbance qualifies as "very disturbed?"). Some behavioral researchers have eschewed traditional diagnosis altogether in favor of a phenomenological or behavioral analysis. As a result, different research groups have tended to study somewhat (or entirely) different populations, making interstudy comparisons functionally impossible.

DSM-III is a marked improvement over previous diagnostic systems in both reliability and specificity. It has decreased much of the controversy in the field, and increased the chances for comparability across studies. It is now encumbent on any current or future research to provide *DSM-III* diagnoses of all subjects. It should also be documented that the diagnoses were made by an experienced clinician and subjected to a reliability check. Of course, not all researchers agree that *DSM-III* is appropriate or adequate. But, it is sufficiently well accepted that it serves as a minimal standard of comparability, and should be included regardless of any additional system that is employed.

The *DSM-III* categories to which psychotherapies are generally applied, and therefore most relevant for our discussion, are major depression and dysthymic disorder. It is widely presumed, although not widely written, that many studies have included a significant proportion of patients whose true diagnosis was adjustment disorder with depressed mood. This latter disorder is short lived by definition, and frequently remits with a minimum of therapeutic support and/or the mere passage of time. Any study which included a substantial proportion of such patients would likely appear to have had very positive results. However, the "success" would not be specific to the treatment procedures and would not be generalizable to more chronic disorders. Conversely, such spontaneous remissions make it difficult to find true differences in the effectiveness of different treatments (i.e., both minimal and powerful interventions produce change).

Major depression and dysthymic disorder are more enduring and severe, but they are relatively heterogeneous categories and do not afford sufficient specificity. For example, major depression includes both psychotic and nonpsychotic patients, so-called endogenous patients as well as nonendogenous, those that require hospitalization and those well enough to function as outpatients. Dysthymic disorder includes "characterological" depressions, as well as patients who experience a prolonged, single episode and some who have recurrent episodes surrounding periods of good remission. Moreover, these categories primarily reflect severity of disturbance on several symptomatic dimensions. They do not differentiate patients on the basis of many other important dimensions, such as phenomenology, social skill levels, cognitive response styles, social support networks, and life events (i.e., dimensions that are thought to be important by the various models described in this section of the book).

It is widely assumed by clinicians that psychotic and endogenous depressions are not responsive to psychosocial interventions. The various psychotherapies described in this volume are thus, to some extent, competing over the nonpsychotic and nonendogenous patients. But it is my experience, and one shared by colleagues as well as several of the contributors to this volume (e.g., Hoberman & Lewinsohn, Chapter 2, Rounsaville et al., Chapter 5), that nonpsychotic and nonendogenous depressions are quite heterogeneous, and are not all responsive to the same intervention. A large percentage of the patients in my social skills protocol had clear-cut interpersonal problems, but some did not. Some seemed clearly to be characterized by the cognitive distortions described by Beck, but many did not. I am a consultant on a large clinical trial of social skills training and nortriptyline for the treatment of dysthymic disorder being conducted by Robert Becker at Medical College of Pennsylvania at EPPI and Richard Heimberg at State University of New York (SUNY), Albany. In contrast to our major depression patients in Pittsburgh, Becker and Heimberg's patients seem much more prone to negative life events. They seem to move from one crisis to another.

If patients really differ on dimensions such as those described above, they probably require different interventions. Thus, cognitive therapy may be appropriate for patients suffering from cognitive distortions, IPT may be appropriate for patients with restricted social networks or excessive grief reactions, social skills training may be appropriate for patients with specific skill deficits, and so on. Conversely, various interventions might be explicitly inappropriate for some patients by failing to target critical factors. If this hypothesis is accurate, it might explain the similar degree of success reported for the diverse treatments, as well as the relatively high dropout rates. By assigning patients to treatment at random, there are likely to be an unspecified proportion for whom the treatment is definitely appropriate, another proportion for whom it is adequate albeit not the most suitable, and a third group for whom it is clearly inappropriate. Patients in the first two groups would be expected to do very well and moderately well, respectively, while those in the third group would do poorly and/or drop out.

Most of the major clinical trials have experienced this general pattern of results. But, it has not yet proven possible to predict treatment outcome on the basis of pretreatment subject characteristics. Unfortunately, there currently are no empirical data to support any subclassification of depressed patients beyond the *DSM-III* categories. This is probably the most pressing research need in the entire area. We must be able to match patients to treatment based upon a systematic analysis of the patient's needs and the goals and capabilities of the intervention. This requires: (1) an empirically validated subclassification system: and (2) an empirical evaluation of precisely how the various successful interventions work, what types of changes they effect, and, by implication, what types of patients they are appropriate for.

Assessment of Outcome

I have previously referred to interstudy variation in diagnosis, patient population, and the manner in which identically labeled treatments are administered. Assessment strategies and outcome criteria are equally variable. It is virtually impossible to find two studies that have employed the same set of measures. Even when there is adequate overlap, methods of analyzing and reporting the data vary so much as to make interstudy comparisons virtually impossible. There appears to be a general consensus that outcome is multidimensional, and that one must employ an assessment battery that taps different sources of data (e.g., independent clinical evaluator, self-report, significant other, therapist) (Hersen, 1981; Rehm, 1981). There also seems to be a tacit agreement that such a battery should include the Raskin Eligibility Depression Scale as a screening device, and the Hamilton Depression Rating Scale and Beck Depression Inventory as primary outcome measures. However, greater consistency is needed.

Prior to selecting specific assessment instruments, we must have agreement on which dimensions of outcome to measure. DeRubeis and Hollon (1981) have identified several critical factors, including: universality of treatment (what proportion of patients improve), acceptability of treatment (e.g., refusal and dropout rates), magnitude of effects, stability (e.g., relapse prevention) and safety. I would add two other factors: proportion of patients achieving remission or marked improvement, and speed of symptom improvement. All studies should present data on each of these dimensions in order to facilitate a comprehensive evaluation of effects. Moreover, the results should be presented in as straightforward a manner as possible: for example, means, standard deviations, and basic univariate statistical analyses. At times, multivariate statistics, factor scores, life table analysis, and other derived or overall analyses are appropriate and informative. However, such analyses tend to be idiosyncratic to individual studies, and often make it impossible for the reader to interpret the full range of findings (e.g., factor scores completely mask raw data and do not permit an evaluation of real change on dependent measures or direct comparison to other studies). When the investigator believes such analyses are desirable, they should be supplemented by basic descriptive statistics.

In keeping with the prior discussion of treatment specificity, it is also essential for advocates of different techniques to develop measures to evaluate the treatment-specific effects of the intervention. For example, does cognitive therapy produce changes in specific styles of thinking when it is effective and fail to produce such changes in cases for which it is not effective? Does social skills training improve specific aspects of interpersonal performance, and do changes on those dimensions correlate with symptom reduction? There really are two questions to be answered. First, does the treatment produce the specific changes it proposes to make? Second, do those changes relate to symptomatic improvement? The former question bears on the validity of the treatment technique: Does it do what it is supposed to? The latter relates to the validity of the theory on which the treatment is based: Does the patient improve if (and only if) the hypothesized critical changes occur? As stated previously, it is not sufficient simply to demonstrate that a particular treatment works. We must know how, why, and for whom it works.

Do Current Treatments Really Differ?

In the discussion above, I have drawn the inference that each of the various empirically supported treatments may work for subgroups of depressed patients which have somewhat different problems. However, that is not really the most parsimonious explanation of the literature as a whole. Some years ago Luborsky, Singer, and Luborsky (1975) reviewed the literature on psychotherapy in general. To loosely paraphrase their conclusion, "all approaches had won and all deserved prizes." Just about every type of therapy subjected to empirical evaluation had proven to be effective, and there was little to choose among them. In a recent meta-analysis of the psychotherapy literature as applied to depression, Steinmetz et al. (1983) reached essentially the same conclusion. While there are specific methodological critiques associated with every major clinical trial, an overview of the literature suggests that each approach has achieved a similar magnitude of success with a similar proportion of patients in a similar time frame and with similar durability during follow-up. This phenomenon is most surprising, given that the diverse treatments are based on quite different theoretical models and employ seemingly different procedures. There are four possible explanations:

1. The treatments achieve the same ends by different means. This explanation would be valid if improvement depended upon one or several particular changes, and there were any number of different ways in which those changes could be accomplished. For example, IPT, cognitive therapy, social skills training, and other behavioral therapies all urge the patient to engage in more activities, especially social activities. Increased social activity is likely to result in an improved social network and, possibly, increased social support. If, as Brown (1979) suggests, social support is the key factor, each of the interventions would be successful for a reason coincidental to the specific strategies employed. Those strategies and the associated procedures might provide a useful package with which to increase the social network, but they would not be theoretically valid or clinically necessary.

2. The treatments achieve different ends, each of which is important. This explanation would be valid if depression was characterized by a number of problems, each of which required some attention. Each of the major treatments would operate on a different subset of the problem areas, resulting in moderate improvement. For example, the depressed patient might have some cognitive distortions, insufficient response contingent social reinforcement, insufficient social support, and specific social skills deficits. Change in any one of those areas would help to alleviate distress, but would not lead to full remission and/or would leave the patient with a high chance of relapse.

3. Different treatments achieve different ends which are relevant for different patients. As discussed in a previous section, this possibility would be valid if there were different functional or etiological subcategories of depression (e.g., depression resulting from cognitive distortions *or* interpersonal problems). Thus, each of the major treatments would be suitable for different subgroups of patients. The implication of this possibility is that all treatments look good on average, as they help some patients a lot, some a little, and some not at all.

4. All treatments achieve the same ends by the same means. This alternative would be the least appealing to theorists and researchers in the area, but is the most parsimonious. It implies that all treatments have some nonspecific commonality, which is really all that is needed to produce change. A likely candidate for the commonality is the relationship with a warm, supportive therapist. There are ample data documenting that good therapists, regardless of orientation, are indistinguishable in regard to provision of warmth, empathy, and a positive therapeutic environment (Greenwald, Kornblith, Hersen, Bellack, & Himmelhoch, 1981; Sloane, Staples, Cristol, Yorkston, & Whipple, 1975). Referring again to Brown, that might be all that depressed patients need. They come for therapy feeling hopeless, helpless, and alone in the world. The therapist changes all of that. He/she builds hope by providing an explanation for the disorder and a way to eliminate it. By simply coming for therapy the patient is taking some action to help him/herself, thus decreasing feelings of helplessness. This is accentuated as the therapist encourages the patient to do more things and engage more people. Finally, the therapist is a source of social support, someone who cares, who will listen, and who can be relied upon.

The outcome data provide considerable support for this hypothesis. All major therapies have achieved substantial improvement in four to six weeks (Hersen et al., 1984; Rush & Watkins, 1981; Shaw, 1977; Weissman, Prusoff, DiMascio, Neu, Goklaney, & Klerman, 1979). Examination of improvement curves suggests that the greatest proportion of change in longer studies has been achieved in this brief time span. This is too short a period for the changes deemed critical by the various models to occur. That is, gross skill deficits, major disturbances in cognitive style, severely restricted social networks, and so on cannot be substantially changed in four, five, or six weeks. If the various theories are accurate, change should occur gradually, over months rather than weeks. Furthermore, follow-up data suggest that surprisingly big proportions of successfully treated patients seek further treatment, despite continued high rates of symptom remission (Kovacs, Rush, Beck, & Hollon, 1981; Weissman, Klerman, Prusoff, Shalomskas, & Padian, 1981). These treatment-seekers may have had brief relapses and then improved prior to the follow-up assessment. More likely, they liked therapy and saw the need for continued support. It should also be emphasized that this hypothesis is consistent with the nature of the disorder. Depression is a notoriously cyclical disorder. A significant proportion of patients experience single or repeated episodes of a few months' duration. Thus, treatment might simply provide the essential support and encouragement needed to help patients through the rough spots while their depression remits naturally. Or, it could help speed up the ongoing process, making the episode shorter by stimulating patients to be more active and help themselves.

All of the possibilities described above are consistent with some of the data. None can safely be ruled out at this time. As pointed out, the fourth alternative is the most parsimonious and is probably the most logical given our current knowledge about the disorder and the outcome literature. Obviously further research is vitally needed. Treatment advances are apt to be limited until we learn more about the disorder. At this time, it makes less sense to have a horse race and try to *prove* which treatment is really best, than to try to better categorize the disorder and learn the etiology and maintaining factors of each identified category. Of course, treatment research can contribute to this process by providing convergent validation for various theories (e.g., do patients with social skills deficits improve more with skills training than other treatment?). But, the focus should be on the disorder and the way therapy works rather than simply on comparative outcome evaluations.

References

Akiskal, H. S. (1979). A biobehavioral approach to depression. In R. A. Depue (Ed.), *The psychobiology of the depressive disorders: Implications for the effects of stress* (pp. 409–437). New York: Academic Press.

Beck, A. T. (1976). *Cognitive therapies and the emotional disorders.* New York: International Universities Press.

Bellack, A. S., Hersen, M., & Himmelhoch, J. M. (1980). Social skills training for depression: A treatment manual. *Journal Supplement Abstract Service Catalog of Selected Documents in Psychology, 10,* 92. (Ms. No. 2156).

Bellack, A. S., Hersen, M., & Himmelhoch, J. M. (1983). A comparison of social skills training, pharmacotherapy, and psychotherapy for depression. *Behaviour Research and Therapy, 21,* 101–107.

Brown, G. W. (1979). The social etiology of depression—London studies. In R. A. Depue (Ed.), *The psychobiology of the depressive disorders: Implications for the effects of stress* (pp. 263–289). New York: Academic Press.

DePue, R. A. (1979). *The psychobiology of the depressive disorders: Implications for the effects of stress.* New York: Academic Press.

DeRubeis, R. J., & Hollon, S. D. (1981). Behavioral treatment of affective disorders. In L. Michelson, M. Hersen, & S. M. Turner (Eds.), *Future perspectives in behavior therapy.* New York: Plenum Publishing.

DeRubies, R. J., Hollon, S. D., Evans, M. D., & Bemis, K. M. (1982). Can psychotherapies for depression be discriminated? A systematic investigation of cognitive therapy and interpersonal therapy. *Journal of Consulting and Clinical Psychology, 50,* 744–756.

Greenwald, D. P., Kornblith, S. J., Hersen, M., Bellack, A. S., & Himmelhoch, J. M. (1981). Differences between social skill therapists and psychotherapists in treating depression. *Journal of Consulting and Clinical Psychology, 49,* 757–759.

Hamilton, E. W., & Abramson, L. Y. (1983). Cognitive patterns and major depressive disorder. A longitudinal study in a hospital setting. *Journal of Abnormal Psychology, 92,* 173–184.

Hersen, M. (1981). The assessment of deficits and outcomes. In L. P. Rehm (Ed.), *Behavior therapy for depression: Present status and future directions* (pp. 301–316). New York: Academic Press.

Hersen, M., Bellack, A. S., & Himmelhoch, J. M. (1981). A comparison of solicited and nonsolicited female unipolar depressives for treatment outcome research. *Journal of Consulting and Clinical Psychology, 49,* 611–613.

Hersen, M., Bellack, A. S., Himmelhoch, J. M., & Thase, M. E. (1984). Effects of social skill training, amitriptyline, and psychotherapy in unipolar depressed women. *Behavior Therapy, 15,* 21–40.

Jacobson, N. S., & Bussod, N. (1983). Mental and family therapy. In M. Hersen, A. E. Kazdin, & A. S. Bellack (Eds.), *The clinical psychology handbook.* Elmsford, NY: Pergamon Press.

Kazdin, A. E. (1981). Outcome evaluation strategies. In L. P. Rehm (Ed.), *Behavior therapy for depression: Present status and future directions* (pp. 317–336). New York: Academic Press.

Klerman, G. L. (1983). Psychotherapies and somatic therapies in affective disorders. *Psychiatric Clinics of North America, 6,* 85–103.

Klerman, G. L., DiMascio, A., Weissman, M. M., Prusoff, B., & Paykel, E. S. (1974). Treatment of depression by drugs and psychotherapy. *American Journal of Psychiatry, 131,* 186–191.

Kovacs, M. (1980). The efficacy of cognitive and behavior therapies for depression. *American Journal of Psychiatry, 137,* 1495–1501.

Kovacs, M., Rush, A. J., Beck, A. T., & Hollon, S. D. (1981). Depressed outpatients treated with cognitive therapy or pharmacotherapy. *Archives of General Psychiatry, 38,* 33–39.

Lewinsohn, P. M., Steinmetz, J. L., Larson, D. W., & Franklin, J. (1981). Depression-related cognitions: Antecedent or consequence? *Journal of Abnormal Psychology, 90,* 213–219.

Lewinsohn, P. M., Youngren, M. A., & Grosscup, S. L. (1979). Reinforcement and depression. In R. A. DePue (Ed.), *The psychobiology of the depressive disorders: Implications for the effects of stress.* New York: Academic Press.

Luborsky, L., Singer, B., & Luborsky, L. (1975). A comparative study of psychotherapies: Is it true that "everyone has won and all deserve prizes"? *Archives of General Psychiatry, 32,* 995–1008.

McLean, P. D., & Hakstian, A. R. (1979). Clinical depression: Comparative efficacy of outpatient treatments. *Journal of Consulting and Clinical Psychology, 47,* 818–836.

Monroe, S. M., Bellack, A. S., Hersen, M., & Himmelhoch, J. M. (1983). Life events, symptom course, and treatment outcome in unipolar depressed women. *Journal of Consulting and Clinical Psychology, 51,* 604–615.

Murphy, G. E., Simons, A. D., Wetzel, R. D., & Lustman, P. J. (1984). Cognitive therapy and pharmacotherapy. *Archives of General Psychiatry, 41,* 33–41.

Overall, J. E., & Zisook, S. (1980). Diagnosis and the phenomenology of depressive disorders. *Journal of Consulting and Clinical Psychology. 48,* 626–634.

Rehm, L. P. (1981). Future directions. In L. P. Rehm (Ed.), *Behavior therapy for depression: Present status and future directions* (pp. 365–373). New York: Academic Press.

Rehm, L. P., Fuchs, C. Z., Roth, D. M., Kornblith, S. J., & Romano, J. M. (1979). A comparison of self-control and assertion skills treatments of depression. *Behavior Therapy, 10,* 429–442.

Rush, A. J. (Ed.), (1982). Short-term psychotherapies for depression. New York: Guilford Press.

Rush, A. J., & Watkins, J. T. (1981). Group versus individual cognitive therapy: A pilot study. *Cognitive Therapy and Research, 5,* 95–103.

Shaw, B. F. (1977). Comparison of cognitive therapy and behavior therapy in the treatment of depression. *Journal of Consulting and Clinical Psychology, 45,* 543–551.

Silverman, J. S., Silverman, J. A., & Lustman, P. J. (1984). Do maladaptive attitudes cause depression? *Archives of General Psychiatry, 41,* 28–30.

Simons, A. D., Garfield, S. L., & Murphy, G. E. (1984) The process of change in cognitive therapy and pharmacotherapy for depression. *Archives of General Psychiatry. 41,* 45–54.

Sloane, R. B., Staples, F. R., Cristol, A. H., Yorkston, N. J., & Whipple, K. (1975). *Psychotherapy versus behavior therapy.* Cambridge, MA: Harvard University Press.

Steinbrueck, S. M., Maxwell, S. E., & Howard, G. S. (1983). A meta-analysis of psychotherapy and drug therapy in the treatment of unipolar depression with adults. *Journal of Consulting and Clinical Psychology, 51,* 856–863.

Steinmetz, J. L., Lewinsohn, P. M., & Antonuccio, D. O. (1983). Prediction of individual outcome in a group intervention for depression. *Journal of Consulting and Clinical Psychology, 51,* 331–337.

Weiss, R. L., & Wieder, G. B. (1982). Marital distress. In A. S. Bellack, M. Hersen, & A. E. Kazdin (Eds.), *International handbook of behavior modification and therapy* (pp. 767–809). New York: Plenum Publishing.

Weissman, M. M. (1979). The psychological treatment of depression: Evidence for the efficacy of psychotherapy alone in comparison with an in combination with pharmacotherapy. *Archives of General Psychiatry, 36,* 1261–1289.

Weissman, M. W., Klerman, G. L., Prusoff, B. A., Sholomskas, D., & Padian, N. (1981). Depressed outpatients: Results one year after treatment with drugs and/or interpersonal psychotherapy. *Archives of General Psychiatry, 38,* 51–55.

Weissman, M. M., Prusoff, B. A., DiMascio, A., Neu, C., Goklaney, M., & Klerman, G. L. (1979). The efficacy of drugs and psychotherapy in the treatment of acute depressive episodes. *American Journal of Psychiatry, 136,* 555–558.

Winokur, G. (1979). Unipolar depression. *Archives of General Psychiatry, 36,* 47–52.

Yerevanian, B. I., & Akiskal, H. S. (1979). "Neurotic," characterological and dysthymic depressions. *Psychiatric Clinics of North America. 2,* 595–617.

Chapter 9

Medication and Somatic Therapies in the Treatment of Depression

Katherine M. Noll
Elmhurst College
Illinois State Psychiatric Institute, Chicago, Illinois

John M. Davis
Illinois State Psychiatric Institute, Chicago, Illinois

Frank DeLeon-Jones
West Side Veterans Administration Medical Center, Chicago, Illinois

INTRODUCTION

The virtually invariant presenting symptoms of severe depression, not only across cultures (Andrews, Kiloh, & Neilson, 1973; Master & Zung, 1977; Venkoba Rao & Nammalvar, 1977; Zung, 1977) but also through history (Altschule, 1976), suggests that some process other than normal reaction to experience is at work. Various theorists have proposed explanations for the failure of severely depressed patients to respond well to psychologically directed therapies, but the most parsimonious explanation would appear to be the operation of a biologically based mechanism which leads to a disorder of mood or affect. This explanation has evolved from attempts to elucidate the mechanism of action of antidepressant agents. Perhaps it would have been more elegant had medical treatments for depression derived from the study of nervous system chemistry in individuals showing the symptoms of depression. The truth is that most medical treatments for depression have been discovered accidentally, and understanding of the biological processes underlying depression has, to a large extent, come from the study of the manner in which nervous system chemistry is altered by the use of antidepressant treatments. That most cases of serious or prolonged depression have a biochemical basis in the nervous system currently is doubted by few professionals involved in their treatment, although it certainly should not be overlooked that many of the abnormalities observed in the brain chemistry of depressed patients could result from prolonged stress (Anisman & Zacharko, 1982). In most individuals, at least initially, relief from stress reverses the biochemical abnormality. Some people, however, seem not to show spontaneous recovery from depression (or presumably from the underlying biochemical abnormalities) after stress; and in many of these the process repeats itself after a period of time, or after exposure to new stress. Eventually, especially in those who have periods of excitement or exaltation between episodes of depression, the process seems to become autonomous and the mood cycle then recurs without additional stress.

It is in the treatment of these individuals with "autonomous" depression that medical approaches have their greatest impact. This chapter will concentrate on how these treatments were discovered, their current patterns of use, the evidence for their success in relieving depression, current evidence of how they achieve their effect on depression, and what problems may be encountered in their use.

HISTORY

Prior to the 20th century there were no recorded cases of successful somatic treatment of depression. It is somewhat ironic that two of the most effective treatments for depression, which are still in use, originated in the 20th century in the process of a search for a cure for schizophrenia.

The earliest demonstrably effective treatment for depression was convulsive therapy, although it was not recognized at its inception that it was most effective in treating depression. According to Max Fink's (1979) comprehensive review of convulsive therapies, its inception occurred following Laszlo Meduna's observation in the 1920s that the glia (cells in the nervous system that supply supportive functions to nerve cells, both structurally and metabolically) of autopsied epileptic patients showed changes opposite to the glial changes found in autopsied schizophrenic brain. Although his attempts to "infect" epileptic patients with schizophrenia were unsuccessful, Meduna observed that "schizophrenic" patients who had seizures recovered from catatonia. He then instituted a search for a safe agent to induce seizures therapeutically. Sakel (1956) had already induced convulsions (accidentally) in patients he was treating for morphine dependence with insulin. Meduna experimented with camphor and finally pentylenetetrazol (Metrazol), and observed a number of improved cases. That those who improved significantly were actually cases of affective disorders seems probable now, as true, chronic schizophrenia when accurately diagnosed appears to evidence little or no response to convulsive therapy. At that time, however, the idea was current that "even a little bit of schizophrenia is schizophrenia" (Lewis & Piotrowski, 1954) and so all patients who showed any evidence of psychotic perception, delusions, or thought disorganization were so diagnosed. By 1935 Ugo Cerletti had experimented with the induction of seizures in animals with electric currents (1956) as his studies had led him to feel that electrically induced seizures did not have some of the problems associated with the other methods. His first patient, while showing a number of supposedly schizophrenic symptoms, had shown some response earlier to pentylene-tetrazol. This patient also responded well to electrically induced convulsions. This mode of inducing seizures did seem to be safer than the chemical methods, and its use spread rapidly. It was accepted in the United States by 1939 (Kalinowski, 1970). Since that time its specificity for affective disorders has been essentially confirmed, and a number of further improvements in its use which have improved efficacy and reduced side effects have been introduced. These will be described in the discussion of electroconvulsive therapy.

In 1949, in *The Medical Journal of Australia,* Cade published the results of studies he had been doing with lithium salts. Initially he had observed that urea, injected into guinea pigs, produced a toxic excitement which bore some resemblance to manic excitement. Attempting to find a substance which would form a salt with urea and inactivate its toxic effects, he tried lithium carbonate. He noted that after a delay of a couple of hours, the animals became lethargic and unresponsive for a period of time and then returned to their normal behavior. Hypothesizing apparently that urea might be the toxic agent in mania, Cade then used lithium citrate (more readily soluble than lithium carbonate) to treat 10 manic patients. The success of the treatment was spectacular. Cade had either been very lucky or had chosen the patients very carefully, as all 10 showed relief from their manic symptoms within two weeks (though two proved to have residual symptoms of dementia and schizophrenia); discontinuation of the lithium was followed by rapid relapse, and reinstatement of lithium by symptom remission. Unfortunately, few clinicians working with manic patients apparently read *The Medical Journal of Australia*; Cade's results were not reported to have been replicated outside Australia until 1954 (Schou, Juel-Neilson, Stromgren, & Voldby, 1954). As a result of deaths from lithium toxicity in cardiac patients given lithium salts as a salt substitute (in the absence of sodium the kidney conserves all other salts), the FDA had banned lithium from the U.S. Pharmacopoeia at approximately this time. Its use was not approved in the United States until 1970, when it could be demonstrated conclusively that it could be administered and monitored safely.

Chlorpromazine, one of the earliest successful antipsychotic drugs, had originally been developed as an antihistamine (and has significant antihista-minic properties, as do virtually all psychotropic medications). It was observed to produce a significant reduction in activity level in laboratory animals without any apparent loss of alertness or responsivity. When, because of this property, it was given to agitated psychotic patients, it proved to have a desirable effect on them (though the fact that it actually reduced the psychosis itself was not immediately recognized). The potential of this drug for producing profits *was* immediately recognized, however, and pharmaceutical houses embarked on a search for an unpatented compound with similar properties. One of these, virtually identical structurally with chlorpromazine, proved not to have significant antipsychotic properties, but to be a remarkably effective mood elevator in depressed patients (without altering mood in nondepressed persons and so having little abuse potential; Kuhn, 1958). This drug was imipramine, the first of the tricyclic antidepressants (so-called because of the three-carbon ring structure which forms the basis of the molecule).

At approximately the same time that imipramine's antidepressant properties were being recognized, iproniazid, a compound which among other actions inhibits the enzyme monoamine oxidase (Zeller, Barsky, Fouts, Kirchheimer, & Van Orden, 1952), was also being tested as an antidepressant. It is the stereoisomer (mirror-image compound) of isoniazid, a drug effective in the treatment of tuberculosis. It had been given to tubercular patients, who were then observed to have a noticeable mood elevation (Bloch, Dooneief, Buchberg & Spellman, 1954; Selikoff, Robitzek, & Ornstein, 1952). Tubercular patients frequently show symptoms of depression, which are generally assumed to be a normal psychological response to having a devastating and perhaps fatal illness. Tests on clinically depressed nontubercular populations quickly demonstrated its effectiveness in relieving depression not secondary to tuberculosis as well (Crane, 1957; Kline, 1958; Loomer, Saunders, & Kline, 1957).

Thus by the end of the 1950s, serendipitous findings had provided psychiatry with a variety of treatment modes in addition to psychotherapy to approach the treatment of depression. A number of newer treatments have followed, but the majority derive from this original group of electroconvulsive therapy (ECT), lithium, tricyclic antidepressants (TCAs), and monoamine oxidase inhibitors (MAOIs). Study of the effects of these treatments on experimental animals, as well as studies of the biochemistry of depressed patients that are ethically and scientifically reasonable, have contributed to advancing the understanding of what it is that has gone awry in the brains of severely depressed patients. One important goal of these studies is that of improving treatment accuracy and speed; most of these treatments require a significant amount of time to become fully effective, and not all treatments are effective with all depressed patients. Some depressions have proved to be very resistant to being relieved by somatic or pharmacological treatment. It was the custom in the past, when a patient had failed to respond to one or two medical treatments, to assume this to be evidence that their depression was reactive or characterological. However, refinements in prediction of what treatments will be most effective with which patients have reduced this resistant minority more and more, suggesting that virtually all depressions which do not remit spontaneously with the relief of the individual from immediate stress (a relief which may be provided through psychotherapy) will ultimately prove to be medically treatable. As this would not only alleviate unnecessary suffering but also relieve the patient from "taking the blame" for their misery, it is a goal to be approached as rapidly as possible.

DIFFERENTIAL DIAGNOSIS AND THE ISSUE OF "DEPRESSIVE EQUIVALENTS" OR "MASKED DEPRESSION"

Diagnosis is an activity which has several appropriate purposes. Ideally, accurate classification of disorders results not only in some understanding of the etiology of a disorder, but in addition predicts the expectable course of the illness, indicates the appropriate treatment, and describes what symptoms will be found in individuals having that disorder. When a diagnosis, accurately made, provides all of this information, it is an exceedingly valuable aid to both patient and helping professional. However, it is frequently the case that a diagnosis fails to do one or more of these things. In this case its value is diminished in proportion to how much needed information it fails to provide. Failure of a diagnosis to suggest appropriate treatment may be the most important failure, but this could arise from a successful treatment not yet having been discovered, as well as from the diagnosis being inaccurate. Individual differences may provide differences in symptoms and course of illness, even when diagnosis is accurate; etiology may be unknown even when all other aspects of diagnosis are satisfied. If, however, a particular diagnosis fails to provide any of the needed knowledge about the patient, it may be worse than useless, as it may result in the patient's acquiring a label which will prejudice others against him or her or result in his/her failing to be given an appropriate available treatment.

It was the frequent failure of psychiatric diagnosis to satisfy any of the purposes of diagnosis that resulted in a reaction of many in the helping professions against the entire concept of classification of mental disorders in the 1950s and 1960s. Even with the advent of successful medical treatments not only for depression but also for psychoses of various kinds, it did not become immediately evident that diagnosis had become more likely to result in appropriate treatment than had been the case in the past. However, as research began to clarify more and more which patients, with which clusters of symptoms, would respond most rapidly and completely to which treatments, the importance of accurate diagnosis became increasingly apparent. For example, while antipsychotic medications will frequently reduce manic excitement substantially, they rarely provide a remission as satisfactory as that seen in patients treated with lithium (and recently, carbamazepine). The manic patient taking antipsychotic drugs is uncomfortable, the symptoms are often incompletely controlled, and the patient appears to stand a greater risk of developing tardive dyskinesia (especially when depressed) than do genuinely schizophrenic patients similarly treated. Thus it has become very important to distinguish manic from schizophrenic patients as early in the course of the illness as possible. However, this often proves more difficult to accomplish in practice than in theory, since even though in textbooks the symptoms of mania appear to be significantly different from those of schizophrenia, in actual patients the difference is often not so evident. As mentioned earlier, until recently the majority of mental health professionals agreed with Bleuler

(1911/1950) that a diagnosis of affective disorder should be made only if all possibility of schizophrenia had been ruled out. Thus, the majority of psychotic patients ended up diagnosed as schizophrenic, and particularly when hospitalized were treated with antipsychotic drugs once these became available.

It has been demonstrated conclusively that lithium is not a particularly effective treatment for schizophrenic patients with a chronic symptom pattern and no evidence of elevated or depressed affect. However, Hirschowitz, Casper, Garver, and Chang (1980) studied a group of patients admitted with schizophrenic or schizo-affective symptoms, and found that 80 percent of those with a good prognosis (by the criteria of McCabe, Fowler, Cadoret, & Winokur, 1971) showed substantial remission of symptoms, even schizophrenic symptoms, in a two-week trial on lithium alone. Edelstein, Schultz, Hirschowitz, Kanter, and Garver (1981) found that a good response to lithium in apparently schizophrenic patients could be predicted if the patient showed a reduction of thought disorder in response to intravenously infused physostigmine (a drug which potentiates the action of the neurotransmitter acetylcholine by inhibiting the enzyme that normally breaks it down). In addition, Van Kammen, Docherty, Marder, & Bunney (1981) found that good antidepressant and antipsychotic responses to lithium could be predicted by *worsening* of thought disorder in response to amphetamine. Finally, these "good prognosis" patients were also those who were more likely to show symptom improvement without drugs over a 30-day period, and to improve when *removed* from antipsychotic medication (Marder, Van Kammen, Docherty, Rayner, & Bunney, 1979). While it probably should not be concluded without question that this evidence "proves" that these patients are actually affective disorder patients rather than schizophrenic patients, it does introduce some question into their inclusion with the classic schizophrenic group. If a diagnosis of affective disorder would mean that these patients would receive more effective treatment with fewer side effects, however, that possibility should be considered.

Depression is frequently seen in apparently schizophrenic patients, both accompanying the psychotic symptoms and especially following resolution of the psychosis with antipsychotic drugs. While most clinicians recognize that serious depression preceding the onset of psychosis is usually an indicator of an affective disorder, there is relatively little agreement as to whether or not the patient is actually schizophrenic as well, nor of the most effective treatment approach to these patients, who can be quite difficult to treat. Depression during or following psychosis has been hypothesized to result either directly from the antipsychotic drugs or psychologically from the recovering patient's recognition of the devastating effects a diagnosis of schizophrenia will have on his or her life. Thus it may be directly treated in neither case, since in the former it will be argued that the antipsychotic is necessary to establish and maintain remission, and in the latter that the depression is realistic, and therefore not appropriately treated medically. Given the evidence in the preceding paragraph, however, it seems as though it may be quite important to make further efforts to discover which patients will respond more effectively to treatment for an affective disorder, since not only is the prognosis more hopeful, but the treatment has fewer long-term risks.

In an effort to improve reliability of diagnosis, effectiveness of treatment, and homogeneity of patient groups for research purposes, a group of researchers at Washington University in St. Louis developed a set of diagnostic groups with specific inclusion and exclusion criteria (Feighner, Robins, Guze, Woodruff, Winokur, & Muñoz, 1972). These were developed into the Research Diagnostic Criteria (Spitzer, Endicott, & Robins, 1978), and were ultimately adopted by the American Psychiatric Association's third edition of the *Diagnostic and Statistical Manual* (*[DSM-III]*; 1980). To the extent that the existing categories are neither overinclusive nor overexclusive, these criteria have proved to be very useful. However, considerable evidence exists that some categories still are not perfectly accurate. More and more research suggests that "schizophrenia" is a composite of a number of etiologically and/ or biochemically distinct disorders (e.g., Noll & Davis, 1983), and that affective disorders are underdiagnosed.

Traditionally, the defining symptom of depression has been the depressed mood itself, a tradition followed by *DSM-III*. However, the discovery in the 1960s, which has continued to the present, that antidepressant drugs are highly effective in treating a number of disorders not usually thought even to be related to the affective disorders, has inevitably brought up the question of whether those antidepressant-responsive disorders are actually affective disorders in disguise—so-called depressive equivalents or masked depression. In some cases the relationship is fairly evident on close examination. Because it is still considered shameful in this culture to suffer from a mental disorder, it frequently happens that an individual with some of the somatic symptoms of depression will present him/herself to a physician for treatment of the physical rather than the emotional symptom. One of the most common symptoms of depression is insomnia. A large proportion of patients ultimately referred to a sleep clinic for a diagnostic work-up prove to have a readily measured depressed mood (Coble, Foster, & Kupfer, 1976; Kales, Caldwell, Preston, Healey, & Kales, 1976) and a pattern of sleep stages resembling that found in depression (Gillin, Duncan, Pettigrew, Frankel, & Snyder, 1979; Kupfer, 1977; Kupfer & Foster, 1975). Another frequent concomitant of depression is hypersensitivity to pain or the development of a chronic pain syndrome (Kramlinger, Swanson, & Maruta, 1983; Lesse, 1974; Ward & Bloom, 1979; Ward, Bloom, & Friedel, 1979). There is not perfect overlap of these groups; some depressed patients do not complain of pain and some chronic pain patients are not depressed (Kramlinger et al., 1983; Pilowsky & Bassett, 1982; Reich, Tupin & Abramowitz, 1983), but the relationship of depression and pain is substantial (Kramlinger et al., 1983; Reich et al., 1983; Ward & Bloom, 1979; Ward et al., 1979), and adequate treatment for the depression frequently results in relief from pain as well (Lesse, 1974; Ward & Bloom, 1979; Ward et al., 1979). A more extended discussion of diagnosis and the relationship of depression to other disorders can be found in other chapters of this volume.

A number of disorders without obvious depression among the presenting symptoms have been found, often accidently, to respond well to treatment with antidepressant agents. A controversy has arisen over whether these antidepressant-responsive disorders are actually alternate manifestations of the same biochemical condition underlying depression, or whether they are different disorders which perhaps respond to a different property of these drugs. The list is remarkably broad, but the careful reader should recognize the appearance of some common themes. These disorders (as described by the authors of the studies), with the agent to which they have been found to respond, include:

1. Neurotic illness
   a. TCA amitriptylene: Johnstone, Owens, Frith, McPherson, Dowie, Riley, & Gold, 1980.
2. Anxiety
   a. TCA imipramine: Klein, 1980.
   b. Amitriptylene: Davidson, Linnoila, Raft, & Turnbull, 1981.
3. Anxiety attacks
   a. Imipramine and amitriptylene: Jobson, Linnoila, Gillam, & Sullivan, 1978.
4. Agoraphobia
   a. Imipramine: Klein, 1967; Matuzas & Glass, 1983; Mavissakalian, Perel, & Michelson, 1984; Sheehan Ballenger, & Jacobsen, 1980; Zitrin, Klein, & Woerner, 1978; Zitrin, Klein, & Woerner, 1980.
   b. MAOI phenelzine: Mountjoy, Roth, Garside, & Leitch, 1977; Sheehan et al., 1980; Solyom, Heseltine, McClure, Solyom, Ledwidge, & Steinberg, 1973; Tyrer, Candy, & Kelly, 1973; Tyrer & Steinberg, 1975.
   c. MAOI iproniazid: Lipsedge, Hajioft, Huggins, Napier, Pierce, Pike, & Rich, 1973.
5. Panic attacks
   a. Imipramine: Garakani, Zitrin, & Klein, 1984; Gorman, Fyer, Gliklich, King, & Klein, 1981; Nurnberg & Coccaro, 1982.
   b. Imipramine or TCA desipramine: Rifkin, Klein, Dillon, & Levitt, 1981.
   c. TCA chlorimipramine: Gloger, Grunhaus, Birmacher, & Troudart, 1981; Grunhaus, Gloger, & Birmacher, 1984.
6. School phobia
   a. Imipramine: Gittelman-Klein & Klein, 1973.
7. Other phobias
   a. Imipramine: Zitrin et al., 1978.
8. Obsessive neurosis, obsessional disorder, and obsessive-compulsive disorder

   a. TCA doxepin and imipramine: Turner, Hersen, Bellak, Andrasik, & Capparell, 1980. Phenelzine: Isberg, 1981.
   b. MAOI tranylcypromine: Jenike, 1981.
   c. Imipramine and chlorimipramine: Mavissakalian & Michelson, 1983.
   d. Chlorimipramine: Ananth, Pecknold, Van den Steen, & Engelsmann, 1981; Insel, Murphy, & Alterman, 1983; Thoren, Asberg, Bertilsson, Mellstrom, Siogvist, & Traskman, 1980; Thoren, Asberg, Cronholm, Jornestedt, & Traskman, 1980.
 9. Briquet's syndrome
   a. Imipramine: Maany, 1981.
10. Anorexia nervosa
   a. Amitriptylene: Moore, 1977; Needleman & Weber, 1977.
   b. Imipramine: White & Schaultz, 1977.
11. Bulimia
   a. Imipramine: Pope, Hudson, Jonas, & Yurgelun-Todd, 1983.
   b. Phenelzine and tranylcypromine: Walsh, Stewart, Wright, Harrison, Roose, & Glassman, 1982.
   c. TCAs, MAOIs, and new antidepressants: Brotman, Herzog, & Woods, 1984. Lithium: Gross Ebert, Faden, Goldberg, Nee, & Kaye, 1981.
12. Cataplexy
   a. Imipramine: Linnoila, Simpson, & Skinner, 1980.
13. Catatonia
   a. Lithium and/or ECT: Abrams & Taylor, 1977.
14. Traumatic war neurosis
   a. Phenelzine: Hogben & Cornfield, 1981.
15. Hyperactivity and attention deficit disorder
   a. Imipramine: Cox, 1982; Linnoila, Gualtieri, Jobson, & Staye, 1979; Werry, Aman, & Diamond, 1980.
   b. Amitriptylene: Kupietz & Balka, 1976.
16. Childhood enuresis
   a. Imipramine and desipramine: Rapoport, Mikkelsen, Zavadil, Nee, Gruenau, Mendelson, & Gillin, 1980.
17. Borderline personality disorder
   a. Imipramine: Klein, 1964, 1968, 1977; Petti & Unis, 1981.
18. Aggressive behavior in convicts
   a. Lithium: Marini & Sheard, 1977; Sheard, Marini, Bridges, & Wagner, 1976.

Most drugs, and psychotropic drugs as much as any others, have a large number of effects on the body's chemistry. The property or properties of these treatments that are therapeutic in depression may or may not be the same properties that are therapeutic in these other conditions. It would be interesting, however, if many of the disorders traditionally subsumed under the designation "neurosis" prove to be alternate manifestations of depression instead.

MEDICATION IN THE TREATMENT OF DEPRESSION

There are a variety of classification systems into which the medications used in treating depression could be organized. In addition, some of the groups can be further broken down in terms either of the structure or the apparent functions of the drugs; sometimes both are taken into account in some classification systems. The breakdown used in this paper is dictated to some extent by tradition—TCAs and MAOIs are distinguished both by structure and by the mechanism by which each was originally proposed to have its therapeutic effect (although now there is some question as to whether their modes of action really are different), while "second-generation" antidepressants are distinguished from the others to some extent by the time at which they were developed, as well as the fact that in most cases they differ significantly in structure from the TCAs and MAOIs.

TRICYCLIC ANTIDEPRESSANTS

The tricyclic antidepressants are a group of drugs which were originally developed in the course of the search for unpatented compounds with the properties of chlorpromazine. The structure of chlorpromazine is that of two benzene rings separated by bonds to a sulfur and a nitrogen atom, forming a third intermediate ring. From the nitrogen atom a three-carbon side chain is attached, ending in another nitrogen and two methyl groups; a chloride ion is bonded to one of the benzene rings.

The difference between chlorpromazine and imipramine, the first of the tricyclic antidepressants, is the absence of the chloride ion and the substitution of two carbon atoms (an "ethylene bridge") for the sulfur in the center ring. This has the effect of flattening the ring structure somewhat, and appears to be to some extent responsible for the differences in the two drugs' properties (see Figure 1). Other TCAs are very similar to imipramine, all having a three-ring structure with a three-carbon side chain. Of the commonly used TCAs, amitriptylene, the next to appear, differs from imipramine by the substitution of a carbon for the nitrogen in the center ring; desipramine and nortriptylene differ, respectively, from imipramine and amitriptylene by the substitution of a hydrogen for one of the methyl groups on the side chain; doxepin substitutes an oxygen for one of the carbons in the ethylene bridge (Figure 1). These changes produce slight differences in the drugs' properties and side effects, and many patients will show a good antidepressant response to one of the compounds and not to the others. In general, however, all show a high level of effectiveness in relieving symptoms of depression.

Effectiveness

The proportion of patients showing a therapeutic response to TCA treatment reported in the literature varies from roughly 60 percent to nearly 95 percent

FIGURE 1
Chemical structures of tricyclic antidepressants currently available (with trade names).

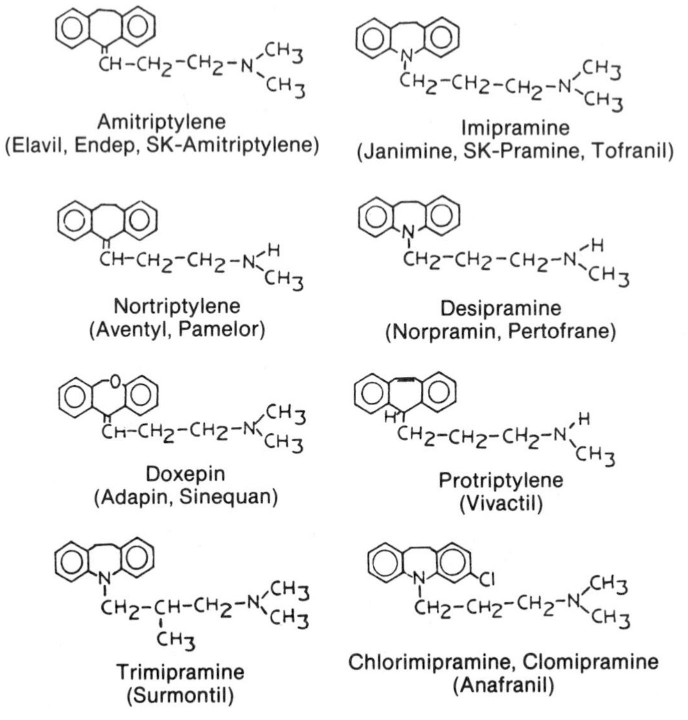

Amitriptylene
(Elavil, Endep, SK-Amitriptylene)

Imipramine
(Janimine, SK-Pramine, Tofranil)

Nortriptylene
(Aventyl, Pamelor)

Desipramine
(Norpramin, Pertofrane)

Doxepin
(Adapin, Sinequan)

Protriptylene
(Vivactil)

Trimipramine
(Surmontil)

Chlorimipramine, Clomipramine
(Anafranil)

of patients studied (Barranco, Thrash, Hackett, Frey, Ward, & Norris, 1979; Cutler & Heiser, 1978; Morris & Beck, 1974; Stewart, Quitkin, Fyer, Rifkin, McGrath, Liebowitz, Rosnick, & Klein, 1980; Stewart, Quitkin, Liebowitz, McGrath, Harrison, & Klein, 1983). A variety of factors may account for the observed differences in effectiveness reported in different studies. In early studies it was not yet recognized that therapeutic response generally is not a graded response but more of an all-or-none phenomenon: if the dose of medication is too low, the patient will show no response at all, even though they might respond very well at a higher dose. Individual metabolic factors impact substantially on the amount of active drug that is available in the nervous system, so that it may be difficult to predict the appropriate oral dose for a given patient. In addition, some patients are more likely to show a good response than others; those with symptoms of "endogenous" depression are far more likely to respond well to treatment with TCAs than patients with symptoms more classically "neurotic" or characterological (Bielski & Friedel, 1976; Friedel, 1983). For these and other reasons, while early studies usually showed an advantage of drug over placebo treatment, their response rates are likely lower than would be found now with better methods for predicting treatment response. Table 1 presents a summary of controlled double-blind studies of the effectiveness of TCAs.

Drug efficacies are usually expressed in one of two ways. Some researchers report the percentages of patients improved on the drug and on placebo; others use a rating scale and give the mean change in the population as a whole. Each of these methods has advantages and disadvantages. The rating scale method tends to obscure the differences between responding and non-responding patients, but provides an indication of the extent of changes usually observed (keeping in mind that there is a difference between a clinically and a statistically significant difference). The percent improved method does not permit within-group comparisons and establishes an arbitrary cutoff which may be more or less rigorous depending on a number of factors. In the studies reported here, 30 compared percent improvement on imipramine with percent improvement on placebo; 65 percent of the patients treated with imipramine improved compared with 30 percent on placebo. There were no studies in which placebo clearly produced a better result than imipramine, a finding with an extremely low probability of occurring by chance—about 10^{-31} (Fleiss, 1973).

Research has been continuing on the issue of prediction of response to TCAs. While the endogenous-reactive or endogenous-neurotic distinction was once thought to predict response to antidepressant treatment, this has generally not been supported by research. Not only have "neurotic" patients with no clear evidence of depression responded well to some of the TCAs, but the presence of a psychologically important precipitating stressor as an indicator of nonendogenous depressions has failed to have predictive value (Leff, Roatch, & Bunney, 1970). Bielski and Friedel (1976), reviewing a large number of prospective double-blind studies found that response to both imipramine and amitriptylene was predicted by high socioeconomic status, slow onset of symptoms, loss of appetite, loss of weight, middle and late insomnia (early waking), and psychomotor agitation or retardation. Predictors of poor response were "neurotic," hypochondriacal, and hysterical traits, multiple prior episodes, and delusions. A number of researchers have ob-

TABLE 1
Summary of double-blind studies of tricyclic antidepressant effectiveness

Drug		Number of studies in which the effect of treatment was				
Generic name	Trade name*	Greater than placebo	Equal to placebo	Greater than imipramine	Equal to imipramine	Less than imipramine
Imipramine	Tofranil	30	14	—	—	—
Amitriptylene	Elavil	9	2	2	5	0
Desipramine	Norpramin	3	2	2	6	1
Nortriptylene	Pamelor	4	0	0	0	0
Protriptylene	Vivactil	2	0	0	2	0
Trimipramine	Surmontil	1	0	2	0	0

Note. These figures represent controlled studies only. A TCA was not considered better than placebo or imipramine unless a statistically significant difference existed between the two drugs in their relative effectiveness.
* Most commonly prescribed brand listed for brevity.

served the difficulty of treating delusional depressed patients (Ananth, 1978; Bielski & Friedel, 1976; Glassman, Perel, Shostak, Kantor, & Fleiss, 1977), but Quitkin, Rifkin, & Klein (1978) reported that these patients responded when given much higher doses than those needed to produce remission in nondelusional patients. A 40-year follow-up of delusional and nondelusional patients with primary unipolar depression showed no significant differences between them in long-term outcome, in either depressive symptoms or social adjustment, even though the delusional patients had had poorer short-term responses to treatment (Coryell & Tsuang, 1982).

Many researchers have turned to biological markers to try to predict response to treatment. Mood response to d-amphetamine has been reported to predict a therapeutic response to TCAs (Fawcett & Siomopoulos, 1971; U'Prichard, Greenberg, Sheehan, & Snyder, 1978; Van Kammen & Murphy, 1978), as has improvement in mood in response to sleep deprivation (Wirz-Justice, Puhringer, & Hole, 1979). Low urinary levels of the catecholamine metabolite 3-methoxy, 4-hydroxy phenylethylene glycol (MHPG) have been associated with good response to TCAs (Bielski & Freidel, 1976; Rosenbaum, Sehatzberg, Maruta, Orsulak, Cole, Grab, & Schildkraut, 1980). Beckman and Goodwin (1975) and Cobbin, Requin-Blow, Williams, & Williams (1979) found that patients with low pretreatment urinary MHPG were more likely to respond to imipramine, while those with high pretreatment urinary MHPG were more likely to respond to amitriptylene; but Spiker, Edwards, Hanin, Neil, and Kupfer (1980) failed to find pretreatment MHPG predicted response to amitriptylene.

Another biological marker it was hoped would predict treatment response was response to the dexamethasone suppression test. Severely endogenously depressed patients frequently fail to suppress cortisol production normally in response to a dose of dexamethasone. It was hoped that this marker would not only provide a diagnostic tool for recognizing depression, but would also predict response to treatment, especially with TCAs (Fraser, 1983; Nelson, Orr, Stevenson, & Shane, 1982). While some of the initial findings were hopeful, ultimately the "dex test" (or DST) was shown to miss many treatment-responsive patients as well as not being a test specific for depression (Davis, Dysken, Matuzas, & Nasr, 1983; Feiger, 1983; Munro, Hardiker, & Leonard, 1984; Prabhu & el-Guebaly, 1983).

Thus to date no completely satisfactory predictors of response to antidepressant treatments have been found, either in symptoms or biological markers. The problem of prediction of treatment response is such an important one, however, because of its promise of reducing the duration of suffering, that it can be expected that the search for these markers will continue. In the meantime, treatment decisions will continue to be made somewhat haphazardly, perhaps by combining predictors.

It should be noted that therapeutic response to antidepressant drugs usually shows some delay after the initiation of treatment. While a change is seen in the patient's sleep pattern almost immediately after beginning treatment if the treatment will be effective (Kupfer, Foster, Reich, Thompson, &

Weiss, 1976; Kupfer, Hanin, Spiker, Neil, & Coble, 1979), obvious changes in mood take longer. Some mood response will usually be observable within the first three weeks of treatment, but full response may take four weeks or longer.

Mode of Use

Dosage. Dosage is a particularly important consideration in the use of TCAs. The evidence has demonstrated quite conclusively that below a certain minimum dose these drugs are ineffective in most cases; above a certain level they are highly toxic and even fatal. Table 2 presents the dose range found to be effective and nontoxic in most patients.

Traditionally, treatment has been initiated at a relatively small dose (such as 25 mg of imipramine or amitriptylene three times a day) and increased within a few days if the patient tolerates the dose well. The dose is usually raised gradually toward the higher end of the dose range until either the patient begins to show clear evidence of improvement or side effects become intolerable (Hollister, 1976). In the young, healthy adult the entire dose is usually taken h.s. (at bedtime); most studies have found this once-a-day dosage as effective as giving the drug in divided doses, and one study found this schedule more effective than divided doses (Weise, Stein, Pereira-Ogan, Csanalosi, & Rickels, 1980). One virtue of the h.s. dose schedule is that if the patient has difficulty tolerating side effects produced by the peak levels of the drug in the bloodstream, particularly the sedation produced by a number of these compounds, these effects will be highest during sleep and will probably have diminished by the time the patient awakens and is aware of them. It has often been observed that for most outpatients, compliance is significantly better when medication does not have to be taken a number of times during the day when the individual's normal daily activities may interfere with adherence to the medication schedule.

Kinetics and Plasma Concentration. There is substantial variation among patients in the rate of intestinal absorption and metabolism of

TABLE 2
Tricyclic antidepressant drugs and their approximate effective dose ranges

Generic name	Trade names	Effective dose range (mg/day)
Amitriptylene	Amitril, Elavil, Endep, SK-Amitriptylene	150–250
Desipramine	Norpramin, Pertofrane	75–200
Doxepin	Adapin, Sinequan	75–300
Imipramine	Antipress, Imavate, Janimine Presamate, SK-Pramine, Tofranil	150–300
Nortriptylene	Aventyl, Pamelor	30–100
Protriptylene	Vivactil	15–40
Trimipramine	Surmontil	50–300

TCAs, and there are differences in the volume of body "compartments" (such as fatty tissue, bone, plasma, extracellular fluid, and cell cytoplasm—each of which has different properties) into which the drug is distributed (Muscettola, Goodwin, Potter, Claeys, & Markey, 1978; Sathananthan, Gershon, Almeida, Spector, & Spector, 1976). In the past, physicians tended to be rather conservative in using antidepressants at least in part because of their toxicity, and to some extent in an effort to reduce side effects. At one time, 150 mg/day of imipramine was believed to be an adequate therapeutic dose for most patients, and indeed at that level many patients did show a response. However, when assays were developed to measure the amount of imipramine and its active metabolite desipramine actually present in the patient's plasma, it was found that there were vast individual differences in the plasma drug concentration resulting from a given oral dose of the medication. Glassman et al. (1977) calculated patients' dose on the basis of body weight, a calculation which resulted in an average dose of about 200 mg/day. However, even at that dose a number of the patients proved to have low plasma levels of drug and there was a high relationship between plasma concentration and symptom improvement. In their study, nondelusional patients with plasma concentrations of 180 ng/ml or more of imipramine and desipramine combined showed a high probability of therapeutic response to treatment while patients with lower concentrations had a low probability of response. When the oral dose of the patients with plasma concentrations below 180 ng/ml was raised to bring their plasma levels above 200 ng/ml, more than half of these patients responded. More recently, Peselow, Deutsch, and Fieve (1983) have replicated these findings and Nelson, Jatlow, Quinlan, and Bowers (1982) have reported a similar finding for desipramine alone (with the critical plasma concentration in this case 125 ng/ml). This suggests that many treatment failures with TCAs may result from undermedication and that physicians should feel more comfortable about raising a patient's dose of TCAs if they fail to show a therapeutic response at a normal dose level and are not experiencing intolerable side effects.

A possible problem with this method may arise when nortriptylene, the less-sedating metabolite of amitriptylene, is being used. Nortriptylene appears to exhibit a "therapeutic window" phenomenon (Asberg, Cronholm, Sjokvist, & Tuck, 1971; Zeigler, Co, & Biggs, 1977), in that there appears to be an upper as well as a lower limit to the therapeutic plasma concentration, and above this therapeutic range there is a decline in therapeutic effects; the therapeutic concentration apparently lies between 50 and 150 ng/ml of plasma. Ward, Friedel and Bloom (1978) have reported a similar finding for doxepin, with an optimal range from 128–364 ng/ml. This finding received support when receptor binding was studied by Smith, Misra, Leelavathi, Shelat, Allen, Schoolar, & Gordon (1981); however, the authors of this study also reported significant variability in results of concentration assays using different methods and cautioned that this needs further study.

Kocsis, Bowden, Chang, Casper, Frazer, & Stoll (1983) failed to find a window effect with either imipramine and amitriptylene or their metabolites.

This study also found that plasma levels tended to increase with age at the same dose level. This relationship between age and plasma concentration was also observed by Nies, Robinson, Friedman, Green, Cooper, Ravaris, & Ives (1977), and Musa (1979) verified age and sex differences in plasma levels reported by Gram, Sondergard, Christiansen, Petersen, Bech, Reisdy, Ibsen, Ortman, Nagy, Rencker, Jacobsen, & Krautwald (1977) and showed that increased plasma levels in older female patients were found primarily in patients with more "endogenous" symptoms. Musa (1981, 1983) also found that plasma steady state levels at the same dose were significantly lower in bipolar than in unipolar patients for amitriptylene and nortriptylene and for desipramine but not imipramine. Recent reviews of the literature on the relationship between plasma concentrations of TCAs and their metabolites, and the relationship of these to treatment response, have emphasized the fact that the impact of these individual physiological differences on plasma concentration and therapeutic response have made response prediction from plasma levels complicated (Friedel, 1982; Simpson, Pi, & White, 1983). In addition to factors such as age, sex, and the ability of the liver to metabolize the drugs, patients may be engaging in activities affecting their drug absorption which are not taken into account. Linnoila, George, Guthrie, and Leventhal (1981) noted that cigarette smoking appeared to result in a significant reduction in plasma concentrations of amitriptylene and nortriptylene, and the tendency of affective patients to smoke heavily is often noted. However, it may be possible to predict ultimate plasma concentrations of TCAs at a particular dose in individual patients on the basis of an assay of absorption of a single dose; Fankhauser, Scheiber, Perrier, Finley, and Potter (1983) and Potter, Zavadil, Kopin, and Goodwin (1980) have reported a high correlation between the plasma concentration of drug reached by a single dose and the ultimate amount of the drug a patient will absorb into plasma at normal dose levels.

Proposed Mechanisms of Action

Early Theories. When the antidepressant effects of imipramine and of the MAOI iproniazid were first observed, the mechanism by which they exerted their antidepressant action was essentially unknown. At that time none of the putative neurotransmitters had been positively identified as such, and their action was not yet well understood. However, following the observation of Glowinski and Axelrod (1964) that the TCAs prevented reuptake of norepinephrine into nerve terminals, attention was directed toward the possible role of the monoamine neurotransmitters in depression. Since the effect of preventing removal of the transmitters from the synapse by blocking their reuptake into the presynaptic neuron would be to prolong their action, it was reasoned that a deficiency of these substances might be the factor underlying the appearance of symptoms of depression. This led to an examination of known actions of these neurotransmitters, and it was found that there was a relationship between the observed symptoms of depression and the functional effects of reducing their availability. This was then worked into the

Catecholamine Hypothesis of depression, which stated that depression results from a functional deficiency of catecholamines in brain areas concerned with emotion (Bunney & Davis, 1965; Schildkraut, 1965); and the Indoleamine Hypothesis, that there is a functional deficiency of serotinin (Coppen, 1967; Lapin & Oxenkrug, 1969). While much of the data available from animal research into neurotransmitter function supported these hypotheses (which were initially believed to be in conflict with each other), one problem remained with the theory that the antidepressants worked by increasing the postsynaptic availability of these transmitters. Reuptake blockade occurs virtually immediately following TCA administration, as is observed with cocaine and amphetamines, but observation of patients taking them showed that while some symptom improvement might be evident within a week of beginning treatment, full remission of depression symptoms required three weeks or longer. Thus the acceptance of transmitter reuptake blockade as the single explanation of the therapeutic action of TCAs has largely been rejected, and more current research efforts have focused on changes that follow the same time course as the therapeutic effects of these drugs.

A number of candidate effects have been observed. Those receiving the most attention currently are those which involve the drugs' effects on receptors rather than the amount or location of the transmitters themselves (Costa, 1981; Enna & Kendall, 1981; Murphy, Siever, Cohen, Roy, & Pickar, 1983; Sulser, 1983). This is logically reasonable, as it is now believed that it is the *receptor* which ultimately determines a neurotransmitter's postsynaptic action. This newer view of the means by which transmitters effects are enacted may account for the fact that some transmitters appear to have an excitatory effect at some synapses (making the next neuron more likely to "fire") and an inhibitory effect (making the next neuron less likely to "fire") at others.

Effects on Catecholamine Receptors.   The observation that tritium-labeled (^{3}H) TCAs bind with high affinity to alpha-adrenergic receptors, one of the identifiable types of receptor responsive to norepinephrine (U'Prichard et al., 1978) was rapidly followed by evidence that over the 21-day period required for significant therapeutic benefit of TCAs these alpha-receptors became subsensitive (Crews & Smith, 1978) and norepinephrine release was stabilized relative to an earlier fluctuation and somewhat reduced from the levels initially observed (Svensson & Usdin, 1978). Subsequent studies have indicated that in the majority of patients with major depressive disorders the number of alpha-receptors (especially presynaptic alpha$_2$-receptors) is actually increased (Garcia-Sevilla, Zis, Hollingsworth, Greden, & Smith, 1981; Kafka, Siever, Targum, Lake, & Van Kammen, 1983; Siever & Lewy, 1983; Smith, Hollingsworth, & Zis, 1983), although they may be abnormally unresponsive (Garcia-Sevilla et al., 1981; Kafka et al., 1983; Siever, Kafka, Targum, Lake, & Murphy, 1983; Siever & Lewy, 1983). Chronic treatment with TCAs has also been reported to increase the alpha-adrenergic response of individual nerve cells to norepinephrine (Menkes, Aghajanian, & McCall, 1980), but to reduce alpha-receptor sensitivity overall (Siever, Cohen & Murphy, 1981).

The evidence concerning beta-adrenergic receptors is somewhat less complex. Chronic treatment with TCAs uniformly has been reported to reduce both the availability and sensitivity of these receptors, and action called "down-regulation" (Aghajanian, 1981; Extein, Tallman, Smith, & Goodwin, 1983; Frazer, 1981; Pandey & Davis, 1981; Sulser, 1983; Svensson, 1980). As beta-receptors are important in anxiety as well as in cardiac function, this could help to explain the antianxiety effects of TCAs in other disorders with anxiety as a symptom in addition to its anxiolytic effect in depression. This antianxiety effect could be a direct result of reuptake blockade, as presence of an overabundance of transmitter has often been observed to result, eventually, in a reduction in receptor number or sensitivity that balances the effect of excessive neurotransmitter. That this is the explanation of the antidepressant effects of TCAs seems unlikely, however, since this would predict an antidepressant effect for propranolol (Inderal), a medication often given to cardiac patients. Not only has it not been reported to be an antidepressant in these patients, but has sometimes been associated with the onset of depressive symptoms.

Effects on Serotonin Receptors.   Like norepinephrine, serotonin also appears to act at two different receptors: (1) postsynaptic receptors which mediate its interneuronal effects, and (2) presynaptic "autoreceptors" which regulate its intracellular metabolism. The density or affinity of the presynaptic receptors (5-HT_1 receptors) for serotonin can be studied with tritiated imipramine (^3H IMI), which binds to them with high affinity, while postsynaptic receptors (5-HT_2) are studied by the binding of tritiated spiroperidol (^3H SP) (Snyder & Peroutka, 1983; Stanley, Mann, & Gershon, 1983). A number of studies have shown that in depressed patients the binding of ^3H IMI is significantly below normal on blood platelets (Asarch, Shih, & Kulcsar, 1980; Briley, Langer, Raisman, Sechter, & Zarifan, 1980; Langer, Zarifan, Briley, Raisman, & Sechter, 1982; Paul, Rehavi, Skolnick, & Goodwin, 1981; Suranyi-Cadotte, Nair, Wood, & Schwartz, 1983), which ordinarily have large numbers of serotonin receptors, although their function is not clearly understood (Tuomisto, 1974). In addition, the study of postmortem brain specimens from suicide victims also shows a decrease in ^3H IMI binding sites and an increase in the density of postsynaptic 5-HT_2 receptors (Stanley et al., 1983; Mann, Stanley, & McBride, 1983). The increase in 5-HT_2 receptors is generally interpreted as a "denervation supersensitivity"; that is, an indicator of reduced availability of the neurotransmitter in the synapse for which the postsynaptic neuron attempts to compensate by increasing the density of receptors. Therefore, the finding that the density of 5-HT_2 receptors is reduced after chronic TCA treatment (Peroutka & Snyder, 1980) is consistent with the observations described above, and with the finding that serotonin turnover is increased (Sherman, 1979) and that 5-HT_2 sensitivity is increased (Aghajanian, 1981; de

Montigny & Aghajanian, 1978; Enna & Kendall, 1981; Friedman & Dallob, 1979; Friedman, Cooper, & Dallob, 1983) after long-term TCA treatment. The overall effect appears to be to increase the effects of serotonin in the brain after long-term treatment with TCAs.

Anticholinergic Effects.   All drugs with known antidepressant effects appear to have anticholinergic effects as well (Biel, 1970a,b; Biel, Nuhfer, Hoya, Leiser, & Abood, 1962), although these effects are usually considered to be a side effect rather than a therapeutic effect. That this effect is actually one of the therapeutic effects could be concluded from a number of lines of evidence implicating acetylcholine neurotransmission in the main symptoms of depression. This was first illustrated by the demonstration that manic patients given the acetylcholinesterase inhibitor physostigmine showed a rapid onset of symptoms of depression (Davis, Berger, Hollister, & Defraites, 1978; Janowsky, El-Yousef, Davis, & Sekerke, 1973a, 1973b), so severe that in one study the patients refused to volunteer for a subsequent attempt to produce a cholinergic effect with choline chloride (Davis & Berger, 1978). In addition, Sitaram and his colleagues (Gillin & Sitaram, 1980; Sitaram, Moore, & Gillin, 1978; Sitaram, Nurnberger, Gershon, & Gillin, 1980) demonstrated that the rapid onset of dream sleep found in depressed patients could also be demonstrated by injecting physostigmine intravenously into both symptomatic and recovered patients during sleep. This suggested that even in a recovered state, persons with a history of depression are supersensitive to the effects of acetylcholine. The therapeutic effects of antidepressants had not been observed to correlate highly with their observed peripheral anticholinergic effects, but Weinstock and Cohen (1976) demonstrated that the *central* anticholinergic potency of antidepressants was strongly correlated with the drugs' therapeutic efficacy even when they were not highly related to their peripheral anticholinergic properties. Therefore it seems likely that the anticholinergic activity of antidepressants may not be an accidental side effect, but an important part of the drugs' therapeutic benefits.

Antihistaminic Effects.   The apparent high correlation of depression with symptoms of allergy has been observed at various times (Nasr, Altman, & Meltzer, 1981). Thus the discovery that TCAs are also potent antihistamines (Green & Maayani, 1977; Kanof & Greengard, 1978; Richelson, 1980, 1981, 1982) may be no accident (chlorpromazine was initially synthesized as an antihistamine candidate). In addition to blocking histamine receptors as an immediate effect, TCAs used over a long term produce a reduction in histamine receptor sensitivity (Pandey, Krueger, Sudershan & Davis, 1982). While drugs developed and used specifically as antihistamines have not been demonstrated to be effective antidepressants, antihistamines have been shown to have antidepressant or anti-learned-helplessness effects in animal studies (Wallach & Hedley, 1979). Thus, like these compounds' beta-receptor down-regulating properties, the antihistaminic effect is unlikely to be the sole source of their therapeutic effect, but may be an important aspect of it.

Other Properties of TCAs.   One of the effects of TCAs on the nervous system which seems likely to relate to their therapeutic effects is their effect on membranes. Of particular importance is their effect on the blood-brain barrier, where they increase its permeability to substances such as ethanol and water (Preskorn & Hartman, 1979). As this effect can be demonstrated to occur with other antidepressant treatments of various kinds as well (Preskorn, Irwin, Simpson, Friesen, Rinne, & Jerkovich, 1981), it seems likely that this effect also is not accidental. It may be mediated by antidepressants' effects on catecholamine systems, which are known to have central vasoregulatory effects (Preskorn et al., 1981).

Side Effects and Adverse Effects of TCA Treatment

As with most medications with a substantial impact on the function of the body, TCAs have a number of effects in addition to the intended ones. These are generally considered to be "side" effects, and as some are generally considered undesirable, adverse effects. There appears to be little, if any, significant difference in the overall therapeutic efficacy of the TCAs (Morris & Beck, 1974), and so the choice of which of these compounds to use for a given patient may be based on these other effects.

Therapeutic Use of Side Effects.   It has been observed that TCAs can be divided into two basic groups on the basis of the presence of activating or sedating side effects (Goodwin, Cowdry, & Webster, 1978; Lewi & Colpaert, 1976). The most sedating of the TCAs is usually considered to be amitriptylene; the removal of a methyl group from the side chain of the TCA molecule apparently removes this effect and so the desmethylated TCAs are usually more activating; among these are nortriptylene, desipramine, and protriptylene. Thus if the patient is very agitated and complains of severe insomnia, amitriptylene may be an appropriate choice of treatment; while imipramine may be a good choice if the patient is neither agitated nor retarded, and if activation is desirable, desipramine and at the extreme protriptylene should have this effect (Cutler & Heiser, 1978). The tricyclic drugs can also be classified as to whether they potentiate primarily serotonergic or adrenergic function. The sedating TCAs are thought to be more serotonergic, while the activating TCAs appear to promote catecholaminergic functions. Chlorimipramine, which in mid-1984 was available in the United States only on a research basis, is believed to have the most potent serotonergic properties (Kessler, 1978), but its metabolite desmethylchlorimipramine has noradrenergic properties. Amitriptylene is also strongly serotonergic, but again its metabolite nortriptylene is noradrenergic. Doxepin has been investigated particularly for its anxiety-relieving properties (Davis, 1975; Rickels, Hutchinson, Weise, Csanalosi, Chung, & Case, 1972).

Cardiovascular Effects.   The TCAs have been observed to have a number of significant effects on the cardiovascular system. They generally tend to reduce blood pressure, especially systolic blood pressure (Reed, Smith, Schoolar, Hu, Leelavathi, Mann, & Lippman, 1980), and in patients with a tendency to hypertension this can be a beneficial effect. However, in some patients the postural hypotension can be so great as to produce loss of consciousness on standing; injuries resulting from this are the most significant adverse effect of these drugs in terms of frequency (A. Glassman, personal communication, November 1983). The TCAs also induce tachycardia and conduction delay in many patients (Reed et al., 1980). There have been a number of reports of deaths believed to result from the cardiovascular effects of TCAs when taken as an overdose. Caution is indicated in patients with certain preexisting cardiac disorders, such as conduction defects. In contrast to these reports, however, Avery and Winokur (1976) have reported excess mortality from heart disease in patients *not* adequately treated for depression with TCAs (dosage less than 300 mg/day of imipramine or equivalent) or ECT. Thus treatment with TCAs in adequate doses reduces total mortality in affective patients both by reducing suicidality with the relief of depression, and by reducing risk from cardiac disease. TCAs have antiarrhythmic effects (Bigger, Kantor, Glassman, & Perel, 1978), and Reed et al. (1980), studying the effects of nortriptylene in geriatric patients, found that while these patients showed a mild hypotension (postural drop of 15.2/1.9 mm Hg), mild conduction delay (10 msec), and nonsignificant tachycardia (increase of 3.5 beats/min), even those patients with preexisting cardiovascular disease showed no evidence of cardiotoxicity when careful choice of dose was made and plasma levels were monitored.

Anticholinergic Effects.   The anticholinergic properties of TCAs are responsible for many of what are considered to be their side effects, from autonomic effects to central anticholinergic syndrome (Van der Kolk, Shader, & Greenblatt, 1978). These can include dry mouth, sweating, blurring of vision, constipation, and urinary retention, most of which abate over time. As is true of any drug with anticholinergic properties, TCAs have also been theoretically associated with increased intraocular pressure in patients with narrow-angle glaucoma, where their effects are proportional to their influence on pupil dilation. This effect does not apply to open-angle glaucoma (the more common type), as in the latter case excessive resistance to outflow is caused by changes in the outflow channels themselves, and is independent of the size of the pupil (Van der Kolk et al., 1978). For this reason, a physician prescribing TCAs should take a careful patient history, including information about any family history of glaucoma or blindness. When this information is not available or not known, an ophthalmological examination might be recommended.

Elderly patients have been observed to be more susceptible to the anticholinergic effects of TCAs than are younger patients (Weinberger, 1977), perhaps because of the decline in intact cholinergic receptors with age. Snyder and Yamamura (1977) have suggested that these patients might be treated with TCAs with the least potent antimuscarinic anticholinergic effects (e.g., desipramine). It is also wise to evaluate other medications being used by elderly patients for their anticholinergic properties; cardiovascular medications such as furosemide (Lasix) may contribute substantially to the total anticholinergic action of the patient's combined medications, and the result can range from the nuisance of urinary retention to the confusion or even psychosis of the central anticholinergic syndrome. As this may in many cases mimic dementia from organic deterioration, the source of the patient's difficulties may be attributed to the aging process rather than correctly to drug side effects, and the patient may suffer needlessly.

Suicide and Overdose Potential. TCAs are toxic in large doses, and such ingestion can lead to death from cardiovascular toxicity (Mielke, 1976). The dose resulting in death in a large proportion of cases is relatively low; little more than one week's dose at therapeutic levels. In addition, the risk of suicide attempts appears to be the highest soon after the patient begins to recover from the worst of the depression. For this reason, TCAs should not be prescribed in large quantities for outpatients who might be considering suicide without careful supervision of the medication by someone other than the patient. When an overdose has been taken, treatment is usually supportive; but when indicated, there may be benefit from stimulating cholinergic mechanisms by the administration of intravenous physostigmine (Wood, Brown, Coleman, & Evans, 1976).

Effects in Pregnancy. Evidence regarding possible teratogenicity of TCAs has been minimal, which is significant given the excess of women of childbearing age using these medications. A report in 1972 (McBride, 1972) of an apparent association of maternal use of imipramine during pregnancy with congenital limb deformities similar to those resulting from the use of thalidomide produced a flurry of studies of the use of TCAs in pregnancy. However, carefully controlled studies failed to find an increase in congenital malformations or other birth defects in children born to women taking TCAs at any stage of pregnancy, and it was concluded that ". . . Available information does not support the contention that tricyclic antidepressants are a cause of limb reduction deformities" (Goldberg & DiMascio, 1978). As with all drugs, use during pregnancy or in patients not using regular birth control should be limited where possible.

It is well known that while depression during pregnancy does not appear to occur with especially high frequency, depression following childbirth is quite common, particularly in women with bipolar affective disorders. It should be noted that TCAs taken by lactating mothers do appear in breast milk (Bader & Newman, 1980), so a nursing mother probably should not be treated with TCAs without consideration of this fact. If the treatment is essential, the mother might be advised to switch to bottle-feeding her infant. There is no data on the long-term effects of TCAs on infants, and there may be some risk associated with unnecessary exposure to psychoactive drugs during an important period of neuronal development.

Weight Gain.   A commonly reported side effect of TCA treatment is weight gain, particularly in amitriptylene therapy (Paykel, Mueller, & De la Vergne, 1973). While this effect may be utilized therapeutically in some anorexic patients, not all patients will consider this to be a benefit. Study of this effect of TCAs is complicated by the fact that weight loss is a common symptom of depression. Thus it is somewhat unclear whether the weight gain is directly related to the drug or more indirectly a result of improvement in the symptoms of depression. Patients in one study (Paykel et al., 1973) who continued on a maintenance dose of amitriptylene after symptomatic recovery continued to gain weight while those who discontinued medication after three months of treatment did not. In addition, those maintained on the drug reported significantly more craving for carbohydrates than did those not taking it. No differences were observed between those on open withdrawal and patients on placebo control, so this does not appear to result from the patients' expectations. The importance of this effect on patients' self-esteem should not be ignored, as at least one patient in this study had a relapse of depressive symptoms apparently related to distress over inability to control her weight.

Exotic Side Effects.   A number of other symptoms and effects have been reported in the literature which appear to have been related to TCA therapy. These have included blood abnormalities, nephrogenic diabetes insipidus, and cerebellar dysfunction (Mielke, 1976). Most of these appear to be relatively rare if in fact they are a TCA effect; many of them may be chance associations with TCA therapy. One side effect not often reported in the literature but often complained of by patients is speech difficulty. This usually takes the form of a dysphasia in which the patient has difficulty "finding" words, especially those not in common usage, or will find difficulty finishing a thought. Word substitution also occurs, in which a word is substituted for another similar-sounding word, or words from unspoken thoughts intrude into what the individual is saying, a sort of "Freudian slip." In its most extreme form this can result in complete speech blockage (Schatzberg, Cole, & Blumer, 1978; Sholomskas, 1978). This can be relieved by removal from the medication, and may not reappear if the patient is switched to a different TCA. Another frequently encountered but infrequently reported side effect is tinnitus, which also is relieved by withdrawal of the medication (Evans & Golden, 1981; Racy & Ward-Racy, 1980). Patients also have complained of vivid hypnagogic and hypnopompic hallucinations (Hemmingsen & Rafaelsen, 1980). The authors of this report suggest that even though most patients will probably not experience this, it would probably be appropriate to inform patients of this possibility and to note that if it occurs they should not be concerned.

Withdrawal Effects.   In addition to the reported side effects of the use of TCAs, another problem sometimes encountered is that of symptoms accompanying withdrawal, particularly sudden withdrawal. While TCAs do not appear to be addictive in the classical sense, and while patients do not appear to develop tolerance to their main therapeutic effects, patients do tend to become tolerant of some of the side effects and anticholinergic effects. Tolerance to the side effects is usually considered beneficial to continued treatment, since many cases of noncompliance with treatment result from patients' distress over anticholinergic symptoms. However, in many cases, if the drugs are withdrawn abruptly, a number of symptoms will appear within a day or two. These range from anxiety (Gawin & Markoff, 1981; Law, Petti, & Kazdin, 1981) to generalized malaise, sleep disturbance and vivid dreams, gastrointestinal symptons, and movement disorders (Mirin, Schatzberg, & Creasey, 1981). The sudden appearance of symptoms of hypomania and mania have also been reported to follow withdrawal (Dilsaver, Kronfol, Sackellares, & Greden, 1983). These symptoms may also be produced by cholinomimetic agents and can usually be successfully treated with anticholinergic drugs; in most cases they will gradually disappear even without treatment (Mirin et al., 1981). In a review of these studies, Dilsaver and his associates (1983) have argued for a "cholinergic overdrive" hypothesis to explain not only these TCA-withdrawal effects, but to some extent the affective disorder itself. This is in agreement with the conceptualization of affective disorder as a disorder of adrenergic-cholinergic equilibrium as originally proposed by Janowsky and Davis (1979). However, as most patients who have been TCA treated for an adequate period of time will remain in remission from depression for some time after TCA withdrawal, it seems likely that cholinergic overdrive is inadequate to explain the entire affective syndrome.

"SECOND-GENERATION" ANTIDEPRESSANTS

The search for new antidepressants continues to occupy a significant part of pharmaceutical companies' research efforts. Depression is a very common disorder, the high prevalence of which is being more and more recognized, and so the market for antidepressants is by no means exhausted. Despite the wide variety of treatments currently available, there are still unsolved problems. Some patients seem to be resistant to many or all of the currently available drugs, and so the search continues for medications which will be effective with these difficult patients. Some patients suffer excessively from the side effects of current treatments, or can't tolerate them because of complicating medical illnesses such as glaucoma or heart disease; therefore the search continues for compounds with good antidepressant properties but few side effects. The length of time required for antidepressant drugs to be completely effective is considered by many to be an important problem; an antidepressant with a short latency of therapeutic effect would have a large market. While it is most common for the search for new compounds to center around the existing ones, some of the drugs which have been promoted in recent years as antidepressants have had structures significantly different from those of the original TCAs and MAOIs.

The development of some of these was based on their demonstrating properties in preliminary tests which are believed to produce the therapeutic effects of the current antidepressants. In particular, effects resulting in the increased availability of the monoamine neurotransmitters have marked experimental drugs for tests as antidepressants. However, a number of compounds which have shown these properties in preclinical research have failed to work in clinical trials, casting some doubt on whether the original hypotheses of the antidepressants' effectiveness were correct (Kelwala, Stanley, & Gershon, 1983). In some cases, observed mood elevation in patients being treated with the drug for some other condition led to clinical tests as antidepressants. Thus there are currently a number of proposed antidepressant compounds available or in the testing stage which differ in some significant ways from the standard TCAs and MAOIs. These have often been referred to as the "second generation" of antidepressants (Shopsin, 1980). The structures of some of the currently available drugs of this group are shown in Figure 2.

FIGURE 2
Chemical structures of "second-generation" antidepressants currently in use or under study (with trade names when available).

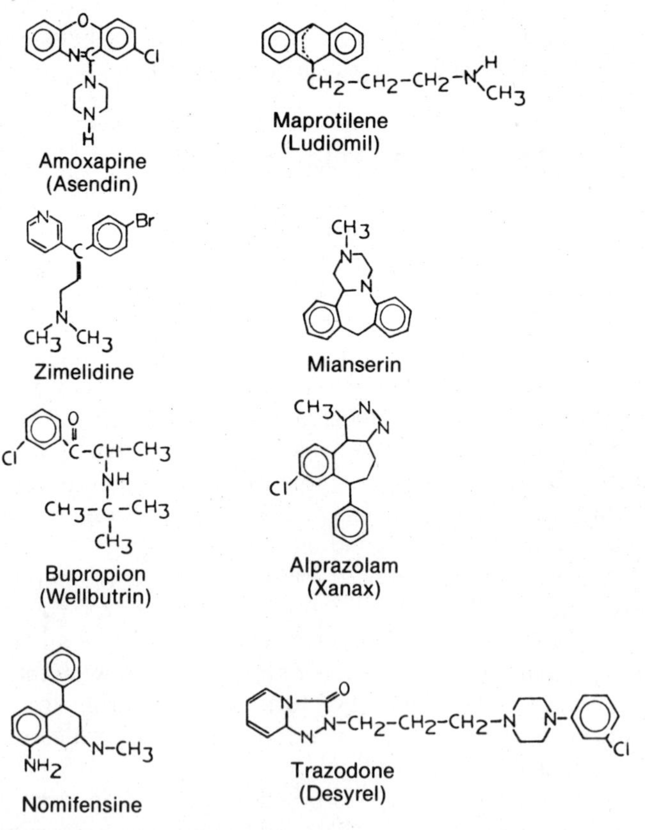

Amoxapine
(Asendin)

Maprotilene
(Ludiomil)

Zimelidine

Mianserin

Bupropion
(Wellbutrin)

Alprazolam
(Xanax)

Nomifensine

Trazodone
(Desyrel)

Effectiveness

As there are a number of effective antidepressant treatments of the standard variety currently available, and because these are now generally believed to be effective for the majority of patients, studies of the effectiveness of new antidepressants tend to use a "standard" TCA treatment as the control group to which the experimental treatment is compared. Generally a new treatment must show either a greater treatment effect than the standard treatment, or fewer or less severe side effects, to be a good candidate for marketing. Table 3 summarizes a number of studies comparing new antidepressants to standard treatment or to placebo when available (Davis, Fredman, & Linden, 1983; Zung, 1983).

Dosage

As was noted in the discussion of TCAs, a great deal of experience with a drug may be necessary before it becomes clear what factors establish the dose range which will be both safe and effective for the majority of patients who will respond to treatment with the drug. Thus the guidelines presented in Table 4 are somewhat tentative. In most cases, dose range for new antidepressants is similar to that for standard TCAs (which also show a wide range).

Special Issues in the Use of New Antidepressants

Side Effects and Adverse Effects. As noted before, the search has continued for new antidepressants which either have therapeutic benefit for

TABLE 3
Summary of studies of the effectiveness of the new antidepressants

Drug		Number of studies	Number of patients	Percent improved		
Generic name	U.S. trade name			New drug	Standard drug	Placebo
Alprazolam	Xanax	2	664	73	74	53
Amoxapine	Asendin	6	186	81	—	57
		19	784	79	73	—
Bupropion	*	3	186	59	—	19
Clomipramine	*	6	350	61	62	—
Lofepramine	*	4	160	55	60	—
Maprotiline	Ludiomil	20	1,638	73	73	—
Mianserin	*	9	574	54	64	—
		3	156	67	—	25
Nomifensine	*	8	220	54	55	—
		3	155	80	—	24
Trazodone	Desyrel	12	705	61	—	29
		18	913	62	58	—
Trimipramine	Surmontil	5	199	60	42	—
Viloxazine	*	9	399	64	62	—

NOTE: Figures derived from Davis, Fredman, and Linden, 1983; and Fabre, Brodie, Garver, and Zung, 1983.

* Available in the United States only on an experimental basis.

TABLE 4
New antidepressants and their approximate effective dose ranges

Drug		Effective dose range (mg/day)
Generic name	Trade name	
Alprazolam	Xanax	0.5–4.0
Amoxapine	Asendin	100–400
Bupropion	†	300–700*
Clomipramine	†	30–300
Maprotiline	Ludiomil	50–300
Mianserin	†	30–150
Nomifensine	†	50–200
Trazodone	Desyrel	150–600
Trimipramine	Surmontil	50–300
Zimelidine	†	150–300

* Should be taken in divided doses.

† Available in the United States only on an experimental basis.

patients who showed poor responses to existing treatments, or which do not have the side effects associated with current treatments which make them problematic for some patients. Some of the new antidepressants have been recommended for special populations for one of these reasons. Unfortunately, some of them have proved to have new problems or side effects as well.

The new antidepressant which has appeared to generate the most literature in this regard is amoxapine (Asendin). Amoxapine is closely related structurally to loxapine, and antipsychotic drug, and one of its metabolites has potent neurolepticlike activity (Cohen, Harris, Altesman, & Cole, 1982). This has suggested it as a special possibility for patients with psychotic depression, who in the past been considered particularly difficult to treat adequately; and in fact it has been reported to have been used successfully in several cases (Anton & Sexauer, 1983). However, along with its neuroleptic-like activity it appears to have the potential to produce neuroleptics' undesirable side effects as well, to which affective patients appear to be especially sensitive. Effects so far reported have included Parkinsonian-like extrapyramidal symptoms (Sunderland, Orsulak & Cohen, 1983; Thornton & Stahl, 1984); akinesia, a "deficit in the initiation of voluntary behaviors" (Gammon & Hansen, 1984); akathisia, a feeling of intense physical restlessness (Ross, Walker, & Peterson, 1983); increased serum prolactin and galactorrhea, the secretion of milk from the breasts (Gelenberg, Cooper, Doller, & Maloof, 1979); and tardive dyskinesia, a group of unattractive involuntary movements of the face and upper torso (Ereshefsky, 1983; Lapierre & Anderson, 1983, Lesser, 1983). In addition, though amoxapine is frequently recommended for its apparent lack of anticholinergic side effects, some cases of apparently anticholinergic effects have been reported for it, such as impotence, inhibition of ejaculation, or painful ejaculation in men; and inability to reach orgasm in women (Gross, 1982; Kulik & Wilbur, 1982; Schwarcz, 1982; Shen, 1982).

Another new antidepressant with some reports of unexpected side effects is trazodone (Desyrel). It has been reported in some cases to cause psychosis (Kraft, 1983) and cardiac arrhythmia (Lippmann, Bedford, Manshadi, & Mather, 1983); but the most unusual side effect reported for this drug is priapism, a prolonged and usually painful erection in men which may require surgical intervention and have long-term dysfunctional effects (Scher, Krieger, & Juergens, 1983). A number of cases of this have been reported to be associated with trazodone use, and it is suspected that prolonged clitoral erection may occur in women (who complain of urethral problems), but this has not been proven. As surgical intervention frequently results in permanent impotence in men, this condition has quite serious implications. A patient reporting an increase in frequency and/or duration of erections should be suspected of having impending priapism and should be removed from the drug at once (Scher et al., 1983). In addition, trazodone has been reported to induce delirium in some bulemic patients (Damlouji & Ferguson, 1984); the authors of this last report suggest that the serotonergic system, which is believed to be strongly affected by trazodone (Ayd & Settle, 1982), may already be abnormal in these patients. One study reported a failure of trazodone to exhibit significant antidepressant properties (with a response rate of 10 percent, as compared to 80 percent with imipramine), and also reported that most of the patients, whether or not they showed therapeutic response, developed a subtle but unmistakable toxic confusional state (Shopsin, 1980). This included drowsiness, fatigue, lightheadedness, dizziness, ataxia, and inability to think clearly. Other studies have found trazodone significantly superior to placebo (Davis & Vogel, 1981); and one even reported it superior to imipramine (Fabre & Feighner, 1983), though 48 percent of patients studied complained of drowsiness as a side effect.

Maprotiline (Ludiomil) use has been reported to have been associated with seizures in several different settings (Kim, 1982; Ramirez, 1983; Schwartz & Swaminathan, 1982). It is unclear whether the drug was solely responsible for the initiation of the seizures or whether it simply potentiated a preexisting predisposition; in any case it would appear that maprotiline is contraindicated in any patient for whom there is any history of seizures or seizure-related phenomena. Another problem reported with maprotiline has been the development of atrial flutter in a patient with preexisting first-degree heart block (Tollefson, Lesar, & Herzog, 1984).

Unexpected Effects. The use of alprazolam (Xanax) as an antidepressant presents an interesting issue. Alprazolam is a benzodiazepine, a drug of the same class as Valium and Librium. While anxiety, even to a debilitating degree, is a frequent concomitant of depression, it has generally been found that benzodiazepines are ineffective in relieving the anxiety of depression and may even in some patients contribute to worsening of the depression (Aden, 1983). However, a study employing a large number of patients has found alprazolam to have significant antidepressant properties approximately equivalent to standard tricyclic drug treatment (Feighner, 1982, 1983). It has also appeared to have an earlier onset of action compared to standard treatment. It is particularly indicated for the elderly, for whom side effects are so often a serious complication of antidepressant treatment; mild sedation so far seems to be the only side effect (Pitts, Fann, Sajadi, & Snyder, 1983). It may be important to monitor alprazolam plasma levels in elderly patients, as some of them, men in particular, may metabolize the drug more slowly than do younger patients (Greenblatt, Divoll, Abernethy, Moschitto, Smith, & Shader, 1983). The only major side effect currently reported for alprazolam is one which may characterize many of the benzodiazepines (Hall & Zisook, 1981), the appearance of a significant increase in hostility, reported to occur in 10 percent of the subjects in one study (Rosenbaum, Woods, Groves, & Klerman, 1984). The effect appears very early in treatment, and discontinuation of the drug relieves it. It is unclear whether the drug released previously suppressed, preexisting hostility or whether this represents a pathological reaction to benzodiazepines.

Proposed Mechanisms of Action of New Antidepressants

As is the case with the tricyclic antidepressants, efforts to discover the antidepressant mechanism of action of the new antidepressants has moved away from reuptake blockade of neurotransmitters to other effects, especially those which parallel the time course of the drugs' therapeutic action. Many of the new antidepressants have proved to have little or no direct effect on neurotransmitters, at least on the neurotransmitters traditionally studied in regard to the action of antidepressants. Receptor effects in particular are currently the focus of scrutiny, and the number of different types of receptors studied and the number of neurotransmitters and neuromodulators whose receptors are being observed has multiplied rapidly in the last few years.

While the early theories of antidepressant drug action were undoubtedly overly simplistic, it still seems likely that neurotransmitters and their postsynaptic effects are centrally involved in depression and in the therapeutic action of antidepressant treatments. However, pharmaceutical company researchers must have some starting points from which to work in developing new antidepressant agents, and these starting points are likely to be the transmitter-related properties that are currently believed to be involved in depression. If these properties are used as a screening device for agents to be tested as antidepressants, then virtually all drugs found to be antidepressants will have them, even if they are actually unrelated to the drugs' real therapeutic action. Given this warning, it still seems probable that the "simple" neurotransmitters (5-HT, NE, DA, ACh, and histamine, along with all of their various pre- and postsynaptic receptors, and membrane and "second-messenger" effects) have a great deal to do with the therapeutic actions of the new antidepressants. Research on both animals and to a lesser extent humans has found these agents to have pervasive effects on many aspects of emotion, motivation, and behavior. But it should be realized, while discussing the current hypotheses of treatment action, that a number of other candidates are waiting in the wings—hormones, prostaglandins, and neuromodulators like the opioid peptides.

The blockade of the neuronal reuptake of the monoamine neurotransmitters (NE, DA, and 5-HT) initially observed by Axelrod and his colleagues (Axelrod, Whitby, & Hertting, 1961), and believed for some time to be the primary mode of action of the tricyclic antidepressants, has, as noted earlier, a number of problems. The extent of reuptake blockade varies considerably not only from treatment to treatment but also among neurotransmitters, and it is unrelated to the therapeutic potency of the drug (Baldessarini, 1983). In addition, drugs have been developed which provide the classic profile of reuptake blockade, but prove to have no antidepressant properties (Kelwala et al., 1983). Several of the new antidepressant compounds, such as mianserin, bupropion, and iprindole, appear to have no discernable effects on the monoamines at all (Mendlewicz, Pinder, Stulemeijer, & Van Orth, 1982; Shopsin, 1980; Shur, Checkley, & Delgado, 1983), thus leaving open the possibility that their antidepressant effect may lie entirely elsewhere. As with the TCAs, acetylcholine and histamine are also under study, and even tyramine (a dietary amino acid affecting catecholamine metabolism) and phenylethylamine (a catecholamine breakdown product with amphetamine-like properties) are being investigated (Shopsin, 1980).

Thus the study of the pharmacological and therapeutic effects of the new antidepressants fails to add significant clarification to the mechanism(s) by which these and other antidepressants relieve depression. It seems nearly certain that no single biochemical or neurophysiological hypothesis can account for the clinical action of all antidepressants (Baldessarini, 1983), particularly since the affective disorders are almost certainly biologically heterogeneous. But as the properties of more and more antidepressants are studied, patterns should appear which lead toward an understanding of affective disorder and its treatment.

MONOAMINE OXIDASE INHIBITORS

As described at the beginning of the chapter, the MAO inhibitor antidepressants (MAOIs) were first studied as antitubercular drugs, and only as antidepressants when that effect was noted in tubercular patients. The first of these was iproniazid, but when it was discovered that this drug can produce a rare but troublesome liver toxicity, other MAO inhibitors were developed that also had antidepressant actions. Figure 3 illustrates the chemical structures of the MAOIs currently available in the United States.

Effectiveness

Some evidence has suggested that, in general, the MAOIs are less effective overall than the TCAs. However, these observations may have been con-

FIGURE 3
Chemical structures of monoamine
oxidase inhibitors currently available (with
trade names).

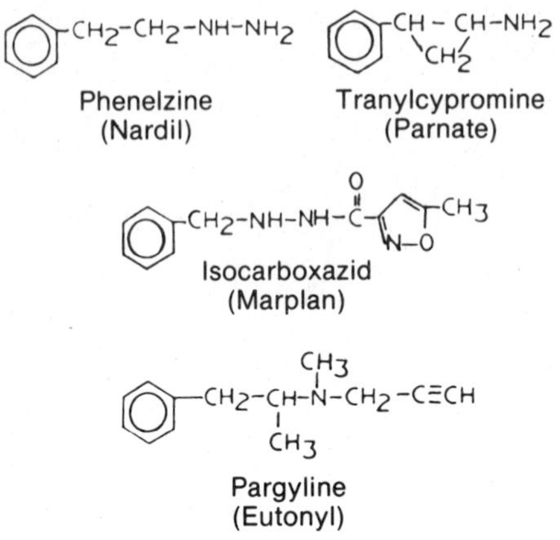

Phenelzine
(Nardil)

Tranylcypromine
(Parnate)

Isocarboxazid
(Marplan)

Pargyline
(Eutonyl)

founded by a number of factors, particularly in older studies when the doses used may in some cases have been too low to be effective. In addition, a number of studies have suggested that MAOIs, or perhaps some of the MAOIs, are most effective when used with specific patient populations (which will be discussed later). Table 5 summarizes a series of double-blind studies of MAOIs currently available in the United States.

Pargyline (Eutonyl) is currently approved by the FDA for use as an antihypertensive drug. However, it is to some extent selective in its MAO inhibition, and recent research has suggested that this may become a relevant issue; MAO exists in two forms, designated MAO-A and MAO-B (Murphy, Cohen, Siever, & Roy, 1983; Neff & Fuentes, 1976). MAO-A deaminates norepinehrine, serotonin, and dopamine, while MAO-B deaminates only dopamine in some species (Neff & Fuentes, 1976), though it may also affect norepinephrine in humans (Murphy et al., 1981). When only MAO-B is inhib-

TABLE 5
Effectiveness of monoamine oxidase inhibitors as antidepressants

Drug		Number of studies in which the effect of treatment was				
Generic name	Trade name	Greater than placebo	Equal to placebo	Greater than imipramine	Equal to imipramine	Less than imipramine
Isocarboxazid	Marplan	2	4	0	2	2
Pargyline	Eutonyl	2	0	0	0	0
Phenelzine	Nardil	11	4	0	4	3
Tranylcypromine	Parnate	2	1	0	3	0

NOTE: These figures represent controlled studies only. An MAO inhibitor was not considered better than placebo or imipramine unless a statistically significant difference existed between the two drugs in their relative effectiveness.

ited, brain stores of dopamine are greatly increased following the injection of a dopamine precursor in rats, while serotonin stores are increased only moderately after a dose of its precursor (Maitre, Delini-Stula, & Waldmeier, 1976). Thus inhibition of one of these enzymes selectively might have different therapeutic effects than inhibition of the other alone.

Mode of Use

Dosage.   In contrast to other antidepressant drugs, MAOIs appear to be approximately equivalent in strength, so that their effective dose ranges are fairly similar (see Table 6).

Early in the use of MAOIs it was discovered that tubercular patients taking these drugs who ingested foods rich in the amino acid tyramine, such as aged or ripened cheeses, red wines, and certain kinds of broad beans, among other things, sometimes developed a hypertensive crisis leading in a few cases to death from intracranial bleeding. This led to considerable conservatism in prescribing MAOIs, and many patients were probably given doses too low to be effective. The hypertensive crisis, often called the "cheese effect," is still a matter of concern in the use of these agents. Combined with the report that they were not as effective as TCAs in the treatment of depression, this led to the virtual abandonment of the use of MAOIs as a major agent in treating depression for some length of time. More recently, however, it has become evident that some patients are particularly likely to respond well to MAOIs, and many of these patients will fail to respond to any other treatment. While both phenelzine and tranylcypromine have been observed to be effective in treating patients with the classic symptoms of endogenous depression, designated as "melancholia" in *DSM-III* (McGrath, Quitkin, Harrison, & Stewart, 1984; Paykel, Rowan, Parker, & Bhat, 1982; Rees & Davies, 1961), the group of patients most likely to benefit from MAOIs appear to be those with the more "neurotic" pattern of symptoms. This is the very group of patients who have classically been seen as having a depression that is "reactive"—that is, simply a pathological degree or prolongation of more-or-less normal emotional responses to rejection, loss of self-esteem, or loss of a loved person (especially if "ambivalently loved"). These patients have usually responded poorly or not at all to tricyclics or ECT, and it has often been concluded that their depression is therefore "psychological" or "characterological," and thus not treat-

TABLE 6

Monoamine oxidase inhibitors and their
approximate effective dose range

Drug		Effective dose range (mg/day)
Generic name	Trade name	
Isocarboxazid	Marplan	20–60
Pargyline	Eutonyl	25–75
Phenelzine	Nardil	60–90
Tranylcypromine	Parnate	20–60

able by biochemical means. However, the patients who have been loosely grouped this way have been found in a number of studies to be particularly responsive to MAOIs (Davidson, Weiss, Sullivan, Turnbull, & Linnoila, 1981; Liebowitz, Quitkin, Stewart, McGrath, Harrison, Rabkin, Tricamo, Markowitz, & Klein, 1984; Pare, 1976; Paykel et al., 1982; Ravaris, Robinson, Ives, Nies, & Bartlett, 1980).

In general, the differential diagnosis of these patients from other depressed patients has been somewhat vague, with the most commonly reported distinguishing feature of the MAOI responders being high levels of anxiety, often including panic attacks. As anxious, agitated patients are less incapacitated than patients with psychomotor retardation, they tend to have been more likely to be outpatients than inpatients (Pare, 1976). The poor showing of MAOIs in some studies may be related to this factor as large-scale studies are usually hospital based, and so the patients are more likely to have the classic pattern of melancholia. As evidence has accumulated, a more precise picture of the MAOI responder seems to be emerging. In addition to the presence of mixed depression and anxiety, these patients frequently have preserved the ability to respond to pleasurable events while they are taking place, do not lose weight, and may have a history of "rejection sensitivity" and/or "hysteroid dysphoria" (Davidson & Turnbull, 1983; Liebowitz et al., 1983; Quitkin et al., 1983; Ravaris et al., 1980; Stern, Rush, & Mendels, 1980). Nevertheless, the absence of these traits in a patient should in no way preclude a trial of MAOIs if the patient fails to respond to other treatments, as many patients with classic endogenous features respond only to MAOIs (Pare, 1976).

Kinetics and Degree of Inhibition.   Following the discovery that iproniazid increases intracellular concentrations of the monoamine neurotransmitters by inhibiting the action of MAO, the enzyme responsible for the intracellular metabolism of these compounds (Griesemer, Barsky, Dragstedt, Wells, & Zeller, 1953; Zeller & Barsky, 1952), the therapeutic action of MAO inhibitors has been believed to be related to the extent to which they inhibit MAO. This has been estimated by measuring the extent of inhibition of blood platelet MAO in most cases, and while studies of dose-response relationships have tended to support a relationship between MAO inhibition and therapeutic response, it has not been as clear cut as might be desired. Good clinical response has been related to high levels of MAO inhibition early in treatment (Robinson, Nies, Ravaris, Ives, & Bartlett, 1978), with a mean effective dose of 1 mg/kg of body weight; phenelzine appeared to have to reduce platelet MAO activity by at least 60 percent for a therapeutic response to appear (Davidson, McLeod, & White, 1978). However, other studies have found the relationship of platelet MAO inhibition to clinical response less apparent, especially with other drugs such as isocarboxazid (Davidson et al., 1981; Lader & Savage, 1981).

A number of studies have supported the observation that higher doses are related to better clinical response (Pare, 1976; Stern et al., 1980; Tyrer,

Gardner, Lambourn, & Whitford, 1981). As with the TCAs, a good policy would appear to be that of increasing the dose at a moderate rate until either a good clinical response appears or side effects become undesirably severe. Like TCAs, therapeutic response to MAOIs may require as long as six weeks to become unmistakable, so treatment should not be abandoned for lack of response after a shorter period.

Special Issues in the Use of MAO Inhibitors

Acetylation Rate. Many drugs of the hydrazine class, which includes phenelzine and isocarboxazid (but not tranylcypromine), undergo acetylation in the liver by an acetyltransferase which is genetically regulated (Price Evans & White, 1964). As this removes the drug from its active state before it can interact with MAO, the rate at which this reaction takes place could affect the dose or therapeutic response of patients; and indeed the more severe side effects of phenelzine were observed fairly early to be associated with slow acetylation rates (Price Evans, Davison, & Pratt, 1963). Using the rate of acetylation of sulfadimidine as a measure of rate of acetylation, Johnstone and Marsh (1973) found that slow acetylators of this test substance responded better to phenelzine than did rapid acetylators. This finding was replicated by some researchers (Johnstone, 1976; Paykel, West, Rowan, & Parker, 1982) but not by others (Davidson, McLeod, & Blum, 1978; Robinson et al., 1978; Tyrer et al., 1981). Acetylation rate is believed to be genetically controlled, but Paykel et al. (1983) found faster acetylation in patients with a history of increased alcohol intake, and Olsen and Morland (1978) report that alcohol consumption increases acetylation rate. Paykel and his colleagues (1983) concur in the recommendation that the acetylation problem be attacked by increasing any patient's dose as high as possible without incurring intolerable side effects.

MAO-A versus MAO-B Inhibition. The most commonly used MAOIs, phenelzine, isocarboxazid, and tranylcypromine, appear to inhibit all forms of MAO unselectively. Recently, however, considerable interest has been expressed in the selective inhibition of MAO-A or MAO-B. The only selective inhibitor currently available in the United States is pargyline, an MAO-B inhibitor, but it is not completely selective, nor is it FDA approved for use other than as an antihypertensive drug. As noted earlier, MAO-A oxidizes NE, DA, and 5-HT, while MAO-B oxidizes catecholamines selectively. In addition, these two forms of MAO are distributed differently in the nervous system.

The two drugs which have been studied for their selective MAO inhibition are available in the United States only on a research basis. These are clorgyline, an inhibitor of MAO-A, and deprenyl (or 1-deprenyl), an MAO-B inhibitor more specific than pargyline.

Clorgyline has shown promise in a number of tests. Its most interesting indication appears to be as a treatment for an otherwise extremely difficult disorder to treat, rapid-cycling bipolar illness (usually defined as more than four episodes per year, though some patients have been observed to go through complete cycles every few days). One reason this disorder is especially problematic is that its onset has frequently appeared to be iatrogenic, occurring in response to an effort to treat depression with a TCA (Bunney, 1978; Dunner, Vijayalakshmy, & Fieve, 1977; Extein, Potter, Wehr, & Goodwin, 1979; Wehr & Goodwin, 1979) or even one of the unselective MAOIs (Mattsson & Seltzer, 1981). Unfortunately, these patients are also extremely resistant to lithium therapy, and in at least half, the best that can be done is to attenuate the manias with lithium while leaving severe, suicidal depressions unrelieved (Potter, Murphy, Wehr, Linnoila, & Goodwin, 1982). Thus the finding of a treatment for this disorder could be expected to be greeted with some enthusiasm. Clorgyline shows promise for treating rapid cycling, either alone or in combination with lithium (Linnoila, Karoum, & Potter, 1982; Potter et al., 1982; Ross, Hauger, Scheinin, Linnoila, & Potter, 1983) as well as showing good response as a general antidepressant (Murphy et al., 1983; Murphy, Lipper, Pickar, Jimerson, Cohen, Garrick, Alterman, & Campbell, 1981). While it might appear to act by increasing the availability of the catecholamine neurotransmitters, this would not be consistent with a reduction in bipolar symptoms; research at the National Institute of Mental Health (NIMH) has suggested that it probably acts by reducing the number or sensitivity of brain norepinephrine receptors (Murphy et al., 1983).

The other selective MAOI, deprenyl, has been studied particularly because of its apparent reduction in risk for the major undesirable side effect of MAOI therapy, the "cheese effect." However, while deprenyl does appear to be effective in roughly the same patient group for whom the MAOIs are especially recommended (Mann, Aarons, Frances, Brown & Kocsis, 1983; Mann, Francis, Kaplan, Kocsis, & Peselow, 1982) and has shown apparently little evidence of "cheese effect" in patients treated with it for Parkinson's disease (Elsworth, Glover, Reynolds, Sandler, Lees, Phupradit, Shaw, Stern, & Kumar, 1978; Knoll, 1981), it is not certain that patients with affective disorders escape the problem. Some researchers have argued that deprenyl does not carry a risk of tyramine-induced hypertensive crisis (Quitkin, Liebowitz, McGrath, Harrison, & Rabkin, 1983), but others have observed a hypertensive response to a tyramine challenge in affective patients treated with deprenyl even at a relatively low dose (Simpson, White, Pi, Razani, & Sloane, 1983). Sandler (1981) argues that the "cheese effect" may be a result of the same property of the drugs which reduces depression, and is therefore likely to accompany any effective MAOI.

Side Effects. In addition to the best known of the side effects of MAOIs, the "cheese effect" already discussed, and the liver toxicity which caused iproniazid to be withdrawn from use in the United States, MAO inhibitors appear to have side effects very similar to those of the TCAs (Quitkin et al., 1983; Ravaris et al., 1980). Orthostatic hypotension (a sudden drop in blood pressure when the person sits up or stands up, especially if they do so quickly) is mentioned by many researchers, along with sedation, dry mouth, and other apparently anticholinergic effects. Decreased sexual drive (Quitkin et al., 1983) and anorgasmia (Lesko, 1982; Pohl, 1983; Wyatt, Fram, Buchbinder, & Snyder, 1971) have been observed, particularly in women; the anorgasmia was accompanied by increased appetite and weight gain (Pohl, 1983). Cardiovascular effects reported have included hypertension as well as hypotension, and sometimes peripheral edema—swelling of hands and feet (Quitkin et al., 1983). In addition, some cases have been reported of peripheral neuropathy (damage or injury to nerves outside the central nervous system), including the carpal tunnel syndrome of paresthesias, numbness, and pain in the hand produced by pressure on the median nerve (Harrison, Stewart, Lovelace, & Quitkin, 1983). This may be caused by a pyridoxine (vitamin B6) deficiency due to interaction between the drug and the vitamin. To avoid this potentially dangerous side effect, the authors of this report suggest that MAOI patients be given pyridoxine supplements.

One commonly reported adverse effect of phenelzine treatment is the appearance of a behavioral disturbance including apparently manic symptoms (Pickar, Murphy, Cohen, Campbell, & Lipper, 1982). The patient may show an initial good response to the drug, but after several weeks of apparently normal mood a syndrome develops resembling an irritable mania. The patient becomes explosively angry with little provocation, and has severely reduced sleep. These symptoms can frequently be relieved by discontinuing the drug until the symptoms subside and then resuming treatment at a lower dose. However, in some patients these symptoms will reappear each time the drug is reinstated and will ultimately require treatment with MAOIs to be withdrawn.

Mechanisms of MAOI Antidepressant Action

As stated earlier, the mechanism of action of the MAO inhibitor antidepressants has long been believed to be that of increasing the availability of the monoamine neurotransmitters by decreasing the rate at which they were broken down. Recent evidence has tended to put this hypothesis in jeopardy, since it has become more and more apparent that particularly in the group of patients suffering from severe anxiety, part of the antidepressant effect is the *reduction* of catecholamine postsynaptic action rather than its increase. With the TCAs, this long-term effect which more closely parallels the timing of the therapeutic benefits of treatment appears to be accomplished by a reduction in postsynaptic sensitivity to catecholamines, especially NE. Davidson et al. (1981) have reasoned that "typical" depression may be characterized by hyper-reactive beta-adrenergic receptors, while "atypical" depression is characterized by hyper-responsive alpha-adrenergic receptors. Thus a drug effect which reduced either the availability of NE (and perhaps DA) or receptor sensitivity to it would be therapeutic. Waldmeier, Felner, and Maitre (1981) observed an increase in NE and 5-HT levels in rat brain with clorgyline, with a consequent decrease in synthesis; DA synthesis was strongly reduced. Beta-adrenergic receptors have been noted to be reduced by both pargyline and deprenyl, with deprenyl also increasing binding of tritiated imipramine, suggesting increased 5-HT sensitivity (Zsilla, Barbaccia, Gandolfi, Knoll, & Costa, 1983). An increase in serotonin sensitivity would make sense as an important therapeutic effect of MAOIs, as Shopsin (1980) reports that serotonergic facilitation is the most commonly found effect of antidepressants. In addition, inhibition of 5-HT synthesis reliably produced return of depression symptoms in patients who had responded therapeutically to either imipramine or tranylcypromine (Shopsin, Friedman, & Gershon, 1976). Mendlewicz and Youdim (1980, 1981) have reported that the antidepressant effects of deprenyl and 5-HTP (a serotonin precursor) are potentiated when the two drugs are administered together.

Thus it seems probable that at least some of the MAOIs' antidepressant effects are mediated by changes in monoamine neurotransmission. These drugs also have clearly documented anticholinergic effects, and cholinergic supersensitivity has also been implicated in depression (see TCA discussion). It is possible that histamine receptors are also impacted by MAO inhibitors, though this has not been reported; other psychoactive brain compounds such as phenylethylamine are almost certainly affected by these drugs. Ultimately it seems likely that their biochemical effects will be shown to be similar to those of the TCAs and new antidepressants.

LITHIUM

Effectiveness

Since Cade's initial report (1949) of lithium's effectiveness as an antimanic agent, virtually every study of its use has confirmed its value for this purpose, with highly favorable results regardless of whether the study was open, single-blind, or double-blind (Schou, 1968). At the time of Schou's review (1968), only one study had been published which showed equivocal results, and that had been a report of two patients given quite low doses. With lithium, as with other treatments for affective disorders, it appears to be necessary to reach a certain minimum level of treatment for any measurable therapeutic benefit to be observed, and response is to some extent all-or-none. Thus, conservatism in prescribing lithium in order to avoid its potential toxic effects may result in an apparent treatment failure in a patient who would respond well at an adequate dose. In addition, when response to lithium occurs, it tends to be a complete response; as with the majority of Cade's original 10 cases, the individual even if symptomatic for years is essentially restored to premorbid personality and functioning. By the time of the publication of the *Archives of General Psychiatry's* special issue on the lithium ion (Goodwin, 1979), research interest had shifted from earlier placebo-controlled studies to comparisons of lithium with antipsychotic drugs in the treatment of mania (Goodwin & Zis, 1979). Placebo-controlled double-blind studies of lithium available at that time had shown response rates to lithium ranging from 63 percent to 90 percent, with higher rates occurring among patients with the more classic pattern of mania of elation, increased activity, grandiosity, decreased need for sleep, resistance to fatigue, and so on (Murphy & Beigel, 1974; Taylor & Abrams, 1975).

In his review, Schou (1968) observed that he and his colleagues considered the indication for the use of lithium to be a diagnosis of manic-depressive disorder, which in Denmark was synonymous with endogenous affective disorder, and included cases with a history of depressions only. The most important distinguishing feature of the depressions experienced by these individuals was the autonomous quality of mood, with little or no response to environmental variation; other symptoms of the sort currently designated as "melancholia" in *DSM-III* were also considered to be part of the syndrome. However, Schou noted the ambiguity of evidence of lithium's therapeutic effects in the treatment of depression. While there were some reports in the literature of depression remitting following lithium administration, in most of those cases (which constituted a minority of the cases in which it was attempted) withdrawal of lithium was *not* followed by relapse, suggesting the possibility that remission had been spontaneous rather than a result of lithium. However, it was clear then that a patient who had shown a good remission from mania on lithium would remain in remission, in most cases, and as long as lithium was continued would be protected against depressions as well as against the recurrence of mania. Schou felt, however, that the issue had not been adequately addressed, and recommended further studies of lithium as an antidepressant.

Two more recent reviews (Mendels, 1982; Mendels, Ramsey, Dyson, & Frazer, 1979) have proven more optimistic. Mendels et al. (1979) reported that of 12 double-blind studies, 9 had observed a significant antidepressant effect of lithium; Mendels (1982) reported on 11 positive double-blind studies. Though in some studies lithium appeared to be as effective as other standard treatments (i.e., Mendels, Secunda, & Dyson, 1972; Watanabe, Ishino, & Otsuki, 1975; Worrall, Moody, Peet, Dick, Smith, Chambers, Adams, & Naylor, 1979), many of the studies found that certain patients were significantly more likely to respond to lithium as an antidepressant than were others. The predictor of lithium response in depression most likely to be noted was evidence that the patient's affective disorder was bipolar in character (i.e., Baron, Gershon, Rudy, Jonas, & Buchsbaum, 1975). However, Watanabe et al. (1975) had an 81.8 percent good response rate in 26 patients by the fifth week of treatment, even though only two were clearly bipolar at the beginning of the study. In a study in which the majority of the patients were considered to be manic-depressive (bipolar) at the outset of the study (Worrall et al., 1979), lithium appeared to be a more effective antidepressant than imipramine. However, most of the studies have reported that some clearly bipolar patients failed to respond (as had occurred in the earlier negative studies of lithium as an antidepressant).

Other predictors of lithium response than a history of mania have been sought, since truly bipolar patients may not yet have had a manic episode, and not all bipolar patients respond to lithium as an antidepressant. One approach has been the use of personality tests. Donnelly, Goodwin, Waldman, and Murphy (1978) reported two scales (one for males and one for females) derived from the Minnesota Multiphasic Personality Inventory, using one group of patients, which discriminated lithium antidepressant responders from nonresponders with 100 percent accuracy in a second group of patients. Unfortunately, Campbell and Kimball (1984) were unable to replicate the earlier findings; in fact, the scales appeared to have done little better than chance in predicting response among their patients.

One possible predictor of response to lithium has been a pretreatment blood calcium: magnesium ratio greater than 2.62 (Carman, Post, Teplitz & Goodwin, 1974), a ratio significantly higher than the normal ratio of 1.6 (Faragella, 1975). This ratio appears to be abnormal in depressed patients, as Faragella observed it to range between 2.0 and 3.4 in his sample. This may be accounted for to some extent by an extremely low magnesium level in the tissues of depressed patients (Harris & Beauchemin, 1959). In addition, response to lithium is predicted by an increase in plasma magnesium and calcium in the first few days of lithium administration (Bennie, 1975; Carman et al., 1974; Crammer, 1975), an effect which also predicts successful response to ECT (Faragella & Flach, 1970; Flach & Faragella, 1970) and to imipramine (Flach & Faragella, 1970). This effect is frequently accompanied by a *decrease* in calcium excretion in urine (Bjorum, Hornum, Mellerup, Plenge, & Rafaelsen, 1975; Faragella & Flach, 1970; Flach & Faragella, 1970) and an increase in calcium storage in bone (Flach & Faragella, 1970). All of these factors may be related to lithium transport into and out of cells, which is genetically controlled and appears to be abnormal in many patients with affective disorders, especially bipolar patients (Dorus, Pandey, Shaughnessy, Gavira, Val, Ericksen, & Davis, 1979; Dorus, Cox, Gibbons, Shaughnessy, Pandey, & Cloninger, 1983; Goodnick, Meltzer, Fieve, & Dunner, 1982; Pandey, Dorus, Davis, & Tosteson, 1979; Ramsey, Frazer, Mendels & Dyson, 1979).

Mode of Use

Dosage and Kinetics.   The major issue in lithium dosage appears to be the daily oral dose required to arrive at an intracellular concentration which is below the toxic level but within the therapeutic range. Cade (1949) chose the doses he used with his initial cases on the basis of the recommendations of the British Pharmacopoeia and of Culbreth in the 1927 *Materia Medica and Pharmacology*. Cade found that many patients could tolerate up to twice as much as these sources recommended, but that many would show toxic symptoms in one to three weeks on this dose. However, apparently recognizing that too low a dose would fail to result in therapeutic benefit, he recommended that a patient be kept on this high a dose "whilst he continues to improve." Once normal emotional tone was attained, the dose was to be progressively reduced to one third of the original therapeutic dose.

More recently, other considerations have entered into the decision concerning dose. In Cade's day antipsychotic drugs were not available and so did not complicate lithium administration; now, many or even most patients, because of behavioral unmanageability, will receive antipsychotic drugs at least while the lithium has not yet taken effect. This can be problematic, because antipsychotics appear to drive lithium into cells unusually rapidly (cf., Cohen & Cohen, 1974; Siris, Cooper, Rifkin, Brenner, & Lieberman, 1982), which may result in the rapid onset of symptoms of lithium toxicity. Lithium toxicity is dangerous not only because it may prove ultimately fatal if not checked, but also because a history of toxic symptoms of lithium has been associated with kidney damage. Such damage may not necessarily result from lithium treatment, though, since many affective disorder patients show some evidence of kidney function abnormalities even when they have never taken lithium. In addition, not all patients respond to lithium, and so it would be expected that these patients would be particularly likely to develop symptoms of toxicity before they had improved at all.

Currently, lithium dosage is usually calculated in milligrams rather than in grains, and most preparations are available in 300-mg tablets or capsules. As another aspect of the effort to avoid toxic plasma levels of lithium, the total daily dose is usually divided into two or more separate doses to be taken at intervals during a 24-hour period. This, however, introduces a problem in terms of patient medication compliance once the patient has left the hospital (or in patients treated without hospitalization), since most studies have demonstrated that the more times a medication must be taken, the less likely patients are to follow the regimen accurately. Recently there have been a number of efforts to produce a satisfactory sustained-release lithium preparation, and at least two of these are currently available in the United States (Eskalith CR, 450 mg, and Lithobid, 300 mg). They possess the additional advantage of increasing the likelihood of survival after an accidental or intentional overdose. However, there have been some problems with such preparations (Grof, 1979), and it remains to be seen whether these will eliminate the problems of multiple daily doses.

As there are enormous differences among patients in absorption of lithium from the digestive tract, it has proved necessary to find some method for monitoring the amount of lithium in a patient's system. Since this must be done, in most cases, on a fairly routine basis, a method both easy and inexpensive has been needed which also provides a reasonable estimate of the patient's therapeutic standing. The method that has received the widest acceptance is the measurement of concentration of lithium in blood plasma, usually calculated in milliequivalents per liter (mEq/l). Standardization of this procedure has proved to be necessary for the sake of accuracy, and the exploration of the best conditions for accuracy of measurement has been done by Amdisen (1967, 1975, 1977). For the best standardization of this procedure, Amdisen (1975) has recommended determination of the lithium concentration by drawing a blood sample 12 hours after the evening dose of lithium, in a patient who has been receiving the same divided daily dosage for at least one week and has complied fully with the treatment. On the basis of this determination, concentrations of lithium in blood plasma of 0.6 to 1.2 mEq/l have been associated with low relapse rates (Grof, 1979). Earlier work had suggested a therapeutic range up to 2.0 mEq/l, but many patients show some signs of toxicity at this higher level.

A number of factors affect plasma levels of lithium. As mentioned previously, the ratio of plasma lithium to intracellular lithium is somewhat pertinent, and appears to be genetically controlled, with bipolar patients generally having higher intracellular lithium concentrations relative to the concentration in plasma. Renal lithium clearance over time varies from person to person even under normal conditions. In addition, the patient's intake of table salt (NaCl) appears to be quite important; the mortalities in the 1950s occurred in individuals on a restricted salt intake, since in the presence of low sodium levels in the blood the kidney conserves and concentrates other salts, including lithium. This can result in toxic plasma lithium levels even on a dose the patient has done well on previously. Therefore the lithium patient should never be put on a sodium-restricted diet unless plasma lithium can be constantly monitored. By the same token, other factors which might reduce plasma sodium or total body fluids could be expected to result in increased lithium concentrations, such as heavy perspiration in the summer or when working hard. Other factors which have been reported to increase plasma lithium concentrations are antiprostaglandins such as indomethacin (Frohlich, Leftwich, Ragheb, Oates, Reiman, & Buchanan, 1978; Reimann, Diener, & Frohlich, 1983), ibuprofen, which is now available over the counter in the United States (Ragheb, Ban, Buchanan, & Frohlich, 1980), diclofenac (Reimann & Frohlich, 1980), and even aspirin (Bendz & Feinberg, 1984). Thus patients (and other physicians treating them) probably need to be aware of the possibility that these substances could interact with their lithium dose and produce toxicity.

The most common practice in psychiatry is to arrive at a maintenance dose level by trial and error. Patients are usually started on 600–1,200 mg/day depending on weight and age, and plasma level determinations are made periodically and dose adjusted accordingly. Unfortunately this practice has a number of problems, not the least of which is the assumption that the patient is completely compliant and has taken the most recent dose exactly 12 hours prior to blood drawing. Therefore for some time efforts have been made to establish a procedure which would predict the appropriate dose for a given patient. The most common strategy has been that of administering a single "loading" dose of lithium to the patient and then estimating absorption and excretion by drawing successive blood samples (Amdisen, 1977; Bergner, Berniker, & Cooper, 1973; Caldwell, Westlake, & Connor, 1971; Poust, Mallinger, & Mallinger, 1976).

A simpler but fairly accurate method has been developed by Cooper and his associates (Cooper & Simpson, 1976; Cooper, Bergner, & Simpson, 1973). They reported that a therapeutic lithium dose could be predicted from plasma concentration of lithium taken exactly 24 hours after a single 600-mg dose. On the basis of this concentration a therapeutic dose could be calculated from a nomogram they published. Their findings have been replicated in several other settings (i.e., Chang, Pandey, & Kinard, 1978; Fava, Molnar, Block, Lee, & Perini, 1984; Seifert, Bremkamp, & Junge, 1975) and have been reported to provide an appropriate dose with fewer blood drawings than the trial-and-error method (Fava et al., 1984).

Special Issues in the Use of Lithium

Toxicity and Side Effects. The most important problem in lithium use is, of course, the fact that there is little distance between the dose which is therapeutically effective and the dose which is ultimately lethal. However, in most cases if the patient is allowed free access to table salt (Baer, Kassir, & Fieve, 1970), toxicity is unlikely to set in so rapidly that it cannot be alleviated by discontinuing lithium until the symptoms subside and then reinstating it at a lower dose.

Symptoms of lithium poisoning were described by Cade (1949) as referable mainly to the alimentary and nervous systems; primary symptoms are abdominal pain, loss of appetite, nausea, and ultimately vomiting sometimes accompanied by diarrhea. The patient may also feel giddy and have a gross tremor, uneven gait, slurred speech, muscle twitching, feelings of weakness and depression; they usually *look* ill as well—"pinched, gray, drawn, and cold." These symptoms are readily recognized by the patient as well as by those around him or her. It is wise to instruct the patient carefully to recognize these symptoms should they occur (preferably with a written list, as the patient may not be in good condition to remember instructions at the time lithium is initiated), then to discontinue lithium, and notify the physician.

Lithium interacts with many, perhaps most, proteins in the body, and could therefore be expected to have a large number of effects and side effects, some beneficial and many not. About 90 percent of the patients in one large sample (Vestergaard, Amdisen, & Schou, 1980) complained of some side effect from lithium, though only 25 percent complained of three or more. A full discussion of lithium's side effects is beyond the scope of this paper, but a few of the more prominent will be described.

An effect of lithium observed fairly early in its use (Schou, 1958) was the appearance in many patients of a relatively benign diabetes insipidus. The patient develops an increase in thirst with an increase in most cases of fluid intake (polydipsia); these are presumably the result of a significant increase in urinary output (polyuria). In some cases this may be sufficiently severe as to threaten the patient's electrolyte balance, though in most cases little harm seems to accrue to the patient if they can tolerate psychologically the need to be near adequate fluid supplies and toilet facilities most of the time; the greatest annoyance appears to occur if the patient is awakened several times in the night by the need to empty the bladder. If this side effect appears to require treatment, the patient can be given a thiazide diuretic. Thiazides have the paradoxical effect in treating diabetes insipidus of causing a reduction in urine volume. However, it will be necessary to adjust the patient's lithium dose, since thiazides also cause lithium retention (Jefferson & Greist, 1981). The observation of this effect of lithium in some patients led to a number of studies of renal function in lithium patients, and renal abnormalities have appeared to be very common (Hansen & Amdisen, 1978; Hestbech, Hansen, Amdisen, & Olsen, 1977; Jenner, 1979). However, there is little evidence of serious impairment of normal kidney function even in patients showing apparently lithium-induced changes (Coppen, Bishop, Bailey, Cattell, & Price, 1980), and the occurrence of chronic renal failure appears not to be increased in lithium patients over its rate of occurrence in the general population (Goodwin, 1979; Jenner, 1979).

A number of central nervous system effects appear to be associated with lithium use, although there is some disagreement concerning the extent to which these are directly attributable to the lithium itself (Ghadirian & Lehmann, 1980; Reisberg & Gershon, 1979). Most often reported are changes in EEG patterns, and these may signal developing toxicity in lithium patients (Shopsin, Johnson, & Gershon, 1970). Organic brain syndromes, seizures, and neurolepticlike extrapyramidal symptoms are found less frequently. Tardive dyskinesia may appear in patients with a history of treatment with neuroleptics; these appear particularly when the patient shows symptoms of depression and may in fact indicate a dangerous *reduction* in lithium levels. These effects have been reviewed by Ghadirian and Lehmann (1980) and by Reisberg and Gershon (1979).

Another commonly observed side effect of lithium is hand tremor. This is usually a fine tremor, reported by about half of lithium patients (Reisberg & Gershon, 1979; Vestergaard et al., 1980), and it is usually not disruptive of the patient's normal functioning. If it becomes a problem, however, it can be relieved with propranolol (Inderal), suggesting that it is produced by some kind of beta-adrenergic activity (Kirk, Baastrup & Schou, 1972).

Other side effects observed with lithium have included increases in white blood cell counts, EKG changes (flattening or inversion of T-waves), changes in glucose tolerance, decreases in thyroid hormones, and possible increases in birth defects in babies born to mothers taking lithium during pregnancy, though this last has been disputed. It has been recommended that pregnant women for whom discontinuing lithium would be inadvisable should be monitored very carefully and an effort made to avoid wide fluctuations in lithium plasma levels (Reisberg & Gershon, 1979).

One somewhat unexpected side effect of lithium observed recently, in this case a beneficial one, is the occurrence of improvement in asthma during lithium treatment (Christodoulou & Vareltzides, 1978; Nasr & Atkins, 1977; Putnam, 1978) along with relief from other allergic reactions. This suggests that the powerful antihistaminic properties observed with TCAs may in some way be a part of lithium's action as well (Bracha, Ebstein, & Belmaker, 1979).

Proposed Mechanism of Lithium Action

Perhaps more than any other treatment for affective disorders, and probably because of its simplicity as a single atom in ionized form, lithium has generated efforts to understand how it relieves and protects against depression and mania. The hope has been that with understanding would come an understanding of the ultimate "cause(s)" of the affective disorders. However, despite 35 years of use and study, the answer does not appear to be much closer than it has ever been, although new research and new discoveries about lithium continue to run parallel to the increases in understanding of the brain and its functions. As observed earlier, lithium appears to impact on nearly every body system. Changes brought about in nervous system function by lithium tend to resemble those produced by other affective disorder treatments—changes in serotonin (cf., Coppen, Swade, & Wood, 1980), changes in acetylcholinesterase and cholinergic function (Fieve, Milstoc, Kumbaraci, & Dunner, 1976; Janowsky, Abrams, McCunney, Groom, & Judd, 1979; Russell, Pechnick, & Jope, 1981; Tollefson & Senogles, 1982), effects on catecholamines (Bunney, Pert, Rosenblatt, Pert, & Gallaper, 1979), effects on peptide neurotransmitters (Byck, 1976), effects on sleep (Mendels & Chernik, 1973), effects on circadian rhythms of neurotransmitters and receptors (Kafka, Wirz-Justice, Naber, Marangos, O'Donohve, & Wehr, 1982). Some of the most interesting theories have been those dealing with lithium's effect on serotonergic systems (Mandell & Knapp, 1977) and its stabilizing effect on subsensitivity-supersensitivity receptor changes with catecholamines (Bunney & Garland, 1982). No theory, however, has yet been sufficiently elaborated to account for all of the abnormalities observed in affective disorder patients. That is not to say that any of the existing theories are necessarily wrong; it is even possible that several are simultaneously correct, perhaps in different combinations in different forms of the affective disorders. In any case, the study of lithium has seemed to many to be one of the most fruitful areas for attempting to understand the affective disorders, and it seems likely that these efforts will advance along with the study of the nervous system and its actions.

OTHER MEDICATIONS

Stimulants

Some clinicians have suggested that a considerable proportion of the illegal use of stimulants—amphetamines and cocaine, for example—is by individuals experiencing subclinical levels of depression and desperately seeking some means of relieving their chronically dysphoric feelings. Unfortunately for these people, this class of drugs has generally failed to produce remissions from depression of the kind provided by the other treatments described in this paper, and in some cases stimulants make depression worse, providing the kind of postdrug "crash" so familiar to "speed freaks" of the the 1960s and 1970s. In addition, amphetamines have frequently been observed to produce a paranoid psychosis, and while in normal volunteers this has usually occurred after relatively large doses, in some individuals even small doses can precipitate these episodes. Patients with affective disorders, especially bipolar patients, may be at special risk for the development of this problem.

Amphetamine was found to be less effective than placebo in treating depressed outpatients according to a study by the British General Practitioners Research Group (1964); another British study found it less effective than phenelzine and no better than placebo (Hare, Dominian, & Sharpe, 1962); and an American Veterans Administrative research team also found it no better than placebo (Overall, Hollister, Pokorny, Casey, & Katz, 1962).

As noted in the discussion of TCAs, one role which stimulants may play is in diagnosis: a mood response to a single dose may be a good predictor of a therapeutic response to TCAs (cf., Van Kammen & Murphy, 1978).

The one case in which stimulants such as amphetamines and methylphenidate may be helpful in treating depression is where an individual has a history of hyperkinetic behavior in childhood or minimal brain dysfunction syndrome. In childhood, stimulants have a paradoxical calming effect on such patients. However, even if treated in childhood these patients continue to have problems, often on into adulthood (Thorley, 1984); and one of the most common problems they have later is depression (Borland & Heckman, 1976). If it is assumed that their depression in adulthood is actually a continuation of their childhood disorder, it would seem reasonable that it might respond to treatment with the same drugs that relieve the symptoms of the disorder in childhood. Stimulants are sometimes effective in treating depression secondary to diffuse brain damage, such as that seen in carbon monoxide poisoning or brain damage from general anesthesias.

Endocrine Treatments

Thyroid Hormones.   It is not at all uncommon for hypothyroid patients to show depression as one of the symptoms of their disorder, and frequently depression is diagnosed before the thyroid disorder is noted. Conversely, hyperthyroid conditions are often mistaken for mania and vice versa. Thus it should not be surprising that thyroid hormones have been used both to treat depression and to potentiate other treatments for depression. Initially noted by Prange, Wilson, Rabon, and Lipton (1969), the best investigated and validated of these is the use of L-triiodothyronine (T_3) to enhance response to TCAs in patients who respond to them but to do so slowly or incompletely; these patients may have appeared to be refractory to treatment. This effect has been repeatedly replicated by the original researchers (Goodwin, Prange, Post, Muscettola, & Lipton, 1982; Prange, Wilson, Knox, McClane, & Lipton, 1970; Wilson, Prange, McClane, Rabon, & Lipton, 1970; summarized in Prange & Loosen, 1982) and by others (cf., Extein, 1982; Targum, Greenberg, Harmon, Kessler, Salenian, & Fram, 1984). Moreover, thyrotropin releasing hormone (TRH), a factor which normally stimulates pituitary release of thyroid stimulating hormone (TSH), has been observed to act as an antidepressant itself, both when given orally (cf., Itil, Patterson, Polvan, Bigelow, & Bergey, 1975; Prange & Wilson, 1972; Van der Vis-Melsen & Wiener, 1972) and intravenously (cf., Kastin, Ehrensing, Schalch, & Anderson, 1972; Pecknold & Ban, 1977; Prange & Wilson, 1972; Van den Burg, Van

Praag, Bos, Piers, Van Zanton, & Doorenbos, 1975, 1976), though other researchers have failed to verify the finding. In any case, the remission of depression was short lived, lasting about one week in most cases, and even the original researchers have concluded that the results are equivocal (Prange & Loosen, 1982).

Another group of researchers noted unusually high levels of the isomer (mirror-image) form of T_3 in depressed patients (Cowdry, Wehr, Zis, & Goodwin, 1983; Kirkegaard & Faber, 1981; Linnoila, Cowdry, Lamberg, Makinen, & Rubinow, 1983); this form would be biologically inactive and might represent either a failure of the thyroid gland to form the correct hormone in adequate amounts or abnormal metabolism of another thyroid hormone, thyroxine (T_4), to a metabolically inactive form (Linnoila et al., 1983). In any case, a defect in the catecholamine system, particularly reduced beta-adrenergic response, could account for all of the thyroid hormone findings in depressed patients (Linnoila et al., 1983; Targum et al., 1984). Replacement of the normal hormones or stimulation of additional hormone release would correct these effects.

L-thyroxine (levothyroxine, or T_4) has also been used successfully in treating affective disorders (Stancer & Persad, 1982; Targum et al., 1984), and appears to be especially effective in treating rapid-cycling bipolar disorder (Stancer & Persad, 1982) which, as noted before, is particularly resistant to treatment.

Other Hormones and Neuropeptides. Prange and Loosen (1982) have written an excellent review of the existing evidence for antidepressant effects various neuropeptides, chains of amino acids with hormone effects on neural cells. In addition to T_3, T_4, and TRH, other hormones that have been investigated as antidepressants have included melanocyte-stimulating hormone release-inhibiting factor (MIF-I), luteinizing hormone releasing hormone (LHRH), thyroid stimulating hormone (TSH), insulin, glutathione, and a variety of naturally occurring nervous system opiatelike compounds. MIF-I has been reported to have antidepressant effects in small doses (Ehrensing & Kastin, 1974, 1978). Prange et al. (1970) found TSH to potentiate the effects of other antidepressant drugs, but reasoned that it did so by increasing thyroid release of T_3, already demonstrated to have that effect.

The issue is somewhat tricky for the use of opiates. While these compounds, some of which are found naturally occurring in the nervous system, were apparently an accepted mode of treatment for depression before the advent of other antidepressant drugs (Verebey, Volavka, & Clouet, 1978), there appear to date to have been no well-controlled studies of their use, and the problem of potential addiction (or tolerance, so that the dose of the drug initially effective no longer works) is sufficiently serious that it can't be brushed off. There was some hope that the endogenous opiates (endorphins) manufactured in the nervous system would somehow escape these problems, but so far they have not appeared to do so. The initially hopeful report of Kline et al. (Kline, Li, Lehman, Lajtha, Laski, & Cooper, 1977) of relief of chronic, intractable depression, at least briefly, with beta-endorphin, could not be replicated. However, the close relationship of endogenous opiates with serotonin in the control of pain sensitivity still suggests that opiates may be involved in depression at least in some patients. There has recently been a renewal of interest in the treatment of depression with a combination of dexedrine, an amphetamine, and demerol, an opiate, which was reported to relieve depression previously but did not appear to gain much note at the time (Lehmann, Ananth, & Geagea, 1971).

Anticonvulsants

While it has long been recognized that there is considerable similarity between some kinds of schizophrenia and some kinds of epilepsy, particularly temporal lobe epilepsy, there has been a notable lack of hypotheses suggesting affective disorders as epileptiform, especially given the effectiveness of induced seizures in *relieving* the symptoms of depression. Thus the assertion of Jack Dreyfus, the founder of the financial Dreyfus Fund, that diphenylhidantoin (Dilantin) was not only an effective antidepressant but the only one which had worked for him has been greeted with considerable scepticism (Sun, 1982). After developing debilitating depression which failed to respond to treatment over several years, Dreyfus got the idea that his mood swings and "turned-on mind" might be caused by faulty electrical activity, and persuaded his physician to prescribe Dilantin for him. His dramatic response to this treatment led him to devote years to promoting the treatment and writing a book, *A Remarkable Medicine Has Been Overlooked* (1981). Nevertheless, perhaps partly because of Dreyfus's nonmedical background or because of his crusader stance, the medical community largely turned a deaf ear to his urgings that Dilantin be widely investigated as a treatment for affective disorders.

Thus there has been some surprise over the success in the treatment of bipolar affective disorders, particularly those refractory to treatment with lithium, with carbamazepine (Tegretol). Carbamazepine is an anticonvulsant which has been used for some time to treat a number of neural disorders from neuralgia and pain syndromes to temporal lobe seizures. It was especially effective in relieving the psychiatric symptoms associated with *complex partial seizures,* in which it may not be at all apparent that the patient is experiencing seizure activity (Dalby, 1975). The therapeutic benefit of this drug on the often manic-depressivelike symptoms of these patients led to several trials of carbamazepine in treatment of bipolar affective disorders, both in Japan (Okuma, Inanga, & Otsuki, 1979, 1981; Takezabi & Hanaoka, 1971) and in the United States (Ballenger & Post, 1978, 1980). The Japanese study (1981) and the American study (1980) were large, double-blind studies, and found carbamazepine as effective as lithium in treating mania; however, it was also effective in 50 percent of the patients whose mania had not responded to lithium. These findings have been replicated (Folks, King, Dowdy, Petrie, Jack, Koomen, Swenson, & Edwards, 1982; Nelson, 1984; Post, Udhe, Ballenger, Chatterji, Greene, & Bunney, 1983a; Post, Uhde, Ballenger & Squillace, 1983b), and it has been demonstrated not only to be safe in combination with lithium (Keisling, 1983; Lipinsky & Pope, 1982; Nolen, 1983), but possibly to act in a synergistic fashion with lithium, as the combination may be effective when neither drug is effective alone (Keisling, 1983; Lipinsky & Pope, 1982). As is the case with lithium, it is less effective as an antidepressant, but does work for some patients; the degree of antidepressant response appears to be correlated with plasma levels not of carbamazepine itself but with one of its metabolites (carbamazepine-10,11,-epoxide—Post et al., 1983a). The normal dose level appears to be between 600–1,600 mg/day. In the study by Post et al. (1983a), the dose was arrived at by starting at an initial dosage of 200–400 mg/day and increasing slowly until clinical response was noted, side effects supervened, 1,600 mg/day was reached, or plasma levels above 12 mg/ml were achieved. The only serious side effect noted for this drug in the many years it has been in use as an anticonvulsant has been a very few cases of agranulocytosis, a fatal blood disorder. The incidence of this disorder has been estimated at 1/10,000 patients taking the drug.

Transmitter Precursors

The formulation of the early Catecholamine and Indoleamine Hypotheses of the biochemical "cause" of depression led to the obvious suggestion that if these neurotransmitters were deficient in depressed patients, one strategy for treating depression could be to try to replace them or increase their availability. These are very simple molecules, and easily synthesized in the laboratory; however, the transmitters themselves do not cross the blood-brain barrier, and so administering them orally or even intravenously or by injection will not increase their concentration in the central nervous system. They are normally manufactured in the CNS from elements either available in the diet or from dietary elements that have been transformed in digestion and then taken up into the brain. The final enzymatic change making them into transmitters takes place in the brain itself. The strategy that was ultimately developed then was that of increasing the availability of the dietary precursors of the transmitters, in hopes that this would ultimately increase their concentration in the brain. This strategy (called the "precursor load" strategy) had proved very effective in treating patients with Parkinson's disease, in whom destruction of dopamine-containing neurons in the nigrostriatal tract of the brain had resulted in the loss of control of movement. The precursor of dopamine given to these patients, which will cross the blood-brain barrier, was L-dopa, the immediate precursor of dopamine. The Catecholamine Hypothesis of depression at that time reasoned that norepinephrine was the transmitter deficient in depressed patients; however, norepinephrine is synthesized from dopamine the the CNS, and dopamine itself does not cross the blood-brain barrier. Thus L-dopa was the nearest precursor that could be administered.

Early efforts to treat depression by administering L-dopa to depressed patients were unsuccessful; many of these patients became agitated and irritable, and some developed overt psychosis. A small number seemed to derive some benefit from the treatment, but this was unpredictable, and as existing treatments were more predictable and had fewer adverse reactions, the use of L-dopa as an antidepressant was largely abandoned.

Somewhat better success was achieved by administering serotonin precursors. The immediate precursor of serotonin, 5-hydroxytryptophan, does cross the blood-brain barrier. Unfortunately, this drug also causes severe diarrhea, like that seen in patients with serotonin-secreting carcinoid tumors of the digestive tract; and in its initial trials it did not appear to have much value as an antidepressant (Schildkraut & Kety, 1967). Other investigators tried administering a precursor one step farther back in the metabolic chain of serotonin, L-tryptophan, a dietary amino acid which is a component of most proteins and which, in moderate doses, does not appear to produce the unpleasant side effects of 5-hydroxytryptophan. These efforts met with mixed to moderate success at first (cf., Farkas, Dunner, & Fieve, 1976; Lopez-Ibor Alino, Ayuso Gutierrez, & Montejo Iglesias, 1973; Murphy, Baker, Kotin, & Bunney, 1973). However, Lapin and Oxenkrug (1969) had pointed out that the presence of large amounts of tryptophan in the bloodstream had the effect of mobilizing the liver enzyme tryptophan pyrrolase, with the result that most of the tryptophan would be shunted away from the CNS into what is called the "kynurenine pathway." Studies in which tryptophan was administered with a pyrrolase inhibitor (allopurinol and niacinamide are both effective) have had a better rate of success (cf., Badawy & Evans, 1974; Chouinard, Young, Annable & Sourkes, 1977; MacSweeney, 1975; Shopsin, 1978). Others have administered pyridoxine (vitamin B_6) supplements (the decarboxylase which converts 5-hydroxytryptophan to serotonin used B_6 as a cofactor, an element necessary for the enzyme to function) along with the tryptophan with some success (cf., Cocheme, 1970; Rao & Broadhurst, 1976). In addition, as with some other antidepressants, the dose appears to be important, and Chouinard, Young, Annable, and Sourkes (1978) have given guidelines for its most effective use. Tryptophan's effectiveness has been particularly noted when it is given in combination with other antidepressants (cf., Walinder, Skott, Carlsson, Nagy, & Ross, 1976), and Chouinard et al. (1978) suggest that in this case the dose for unipolar patients should probably be reduced to half of what would be given if it were administered alone.

Probably the most thorough study of the role of serotonin in depression and the use of serotonin precursors as antidepressants has been done by H. M. van Praag. He has also spelled out the symptoms which identify the patients most likely to benefit from these treatments, and his reviews of this work (cf., Van Praag 1981, 1982) are excellent in clarifying the conditions for the use of this strategy and the possible sources of failure when the treatment does not work.

Methylation

Physicians have been aware for some time that many patients with a deficiency of dietary folic acid show a number of psychiatric symptoms, the most common of which is depression (Botcz & Botez, 1982; Ghadirian, Ananth, & Englesmann, 1980; Reynolds, Preese, Bailey, & Coppen, 1970; Reynolds & Stramentinoli, 1983; Trimble, Corbett, & Donaldson, 1980). In addition, lithium patients with low plasma folate (the ionized form of folic acid) are the most likely to relapse (Coppen & Abou-Saleh, 1982). Supplements of folic acid have been demonstrated in many cases to relieve depression (Botez, Botez, Leveille, Bielman, & Cadotte, 1979; Reynolds, Chanarin, Milner, & Matthews, 1966). In fact, if large doses are given for a prolonged time, it may lead to symptoms resembling mania (Prakash & Petrie, 1982).

In studies of the "transmethylation hypothesis" of schizophrenia, researchers using S-adenosylmethione (SAMe) as a donor of methyl groups (compounds containing one carbon and three hydrogen atoms, important in many metabolic functions) noted inadvertently that this drug, while it increased psychosis in schizophrenics, appeared to reduce symptoms of depression (Fazio, Andreoli, Agnoli, Casacchia, Cerbo, & Pinzello, 1974). This was verified in double-blind studies (Agnoli, Andreoli, Casacchia, & Cerbo, 1976; Kufferle & Grunberger, 1982; Miccoli, Porro, & Bertolino, 1978; Muscettola, Galzenati, & Balbi, 1982) and by studies in Great Britain (Carney, Martin, Bottiglieri, Reynolds, Nissenbaum, Toone, & Sheffield, 1983) and the United States (Lipinsky, Cohen, Frankenburg, Tohen, Waternaux, Altesman, Jones, & Harris, 1984). The U.S. study also noted, as had been the case with folic acid, that some bipolar patients experienced induction of mania when given SAMe, as is frequently the case when they are given other antidepressants (Lipinsky et al., 1984).

Another methyl donor with apparent antidepressant properties is methylene blue (Narsapur & Naylor, 1983). The patients in this study were patients whose affective disorders (both unipolar and bipolar) had been resistant to other treatments; 14 of 19 showed definite improvement. This study was not double-blind, as one effect of methylene blue is bright blue urine, making a blind condition difficult. However, the length of the trials (up to 19 months) makes placebo effect unlikely. Nevertheless, since virtually all of these patients were taking other drugs as well, it is difficult to determine whether the treatment acted alone or synergistically with the other treatments.

Reynolds and Stramentinoli (1983) connect all of these findings into a more unified framework. Nervous system folic acid produces SAMe as one of its metabolites; SAMe then is a major source of methyl groups to methylate other biological substances. Hirata and Axelrod (1980) have argued that methylation of cell membrane fats is the initial step in the cellular effects of the neurotransmitter-receptor interaction. Thus a deficiency of folic acid, for either dietary or metabolic reasons, would affect neurotransmitter function, receptor sensitivity, and endocrine function, among other things. Intervening at a later point in the system, by giving SAMe, would then restore these functions to normal; as would giving other methyl donors or folic acid itself, if the problem were not at a point between folic acid and the methylation of organic compounds.

Other Drug Treatments with Reported Antidepressant Effects

Although it has frequently been observed that antipsychotic drugs have rarely been effective as antidepressants, and have (perhaps most noticeably in bipolar patients) often had side effects for depressed patients that were more severe or more distressing even than these effects in schizophrenic patients, there have been over the years a number of reports of some of these drugs having antidepressant benefits for some patients. This evidence has been reviewed by Robertson and Trimble (1982), who conclude that there is indeed evidence for beneficial effect of some drugs of this class, especially in patients with mixed anxiety and depression. Early work concentrated mainly on thioridazine (Mellaril), but more recently drugs of the thioxanthine class (represented in the United States by thiothixine, Navane) have generated considerable interest. The advantages of these drugs has appeared to be, in addition to their antimanic and antiagitation properties, that they have fewer anticholinergic side effects (though they are to some extent anticholinergic) and more rapid onset of action than TCAs.

Another drug for which antidepressant properties have been reported is bromocriptine (Colonna, Petit, & Lepine, 1979; Jouvent, Abensour, Bonnet, Widlocher, Agid, & Lhermitte, 1983; Schubert, Fleischhacker, & Demel, 1982). Exactly how this drug acts is unclear. While it is believed to be a drug which mimics the action of dopamine at dopamine receptors, in the doses usually used clinically it actually seems to be antidopaminergic. It is currently believed that it has this effect by stimulating receptors outside the synapse itself, on the *pre*synaptic neuron, thus stimulating a feedback system designed ultimately to reduce that neuron's output of dopamine. Because of this property it is currently being investigated as an antipsychotic drug, and it appears to be especially effective in patients resistent to the antipsychotic properties of other neuroleptic drugs. Dose is very important in this case; if the dose is high enough for the drug actually to get into the synapse and stimulate postsynaptic receptors, the psychosis is made worse rather than better. Thus it is unclear whether its antidepressant properties are generated by its prodopaminergic or its antidopaminergic effects.

Other drugs with reported antidepressant properties have included cyproheptadine (Periactin), an antihistaminic and possibly antiserotonergic drug used in some studies to induce weight gain in patients with anorexia nervosa (Halmi, Eckert, & Falk, 1983); buprenorphine, an opiate believed to have a low potential for addition (Emrich, Vogt, Herz, & Kissling, 1982); rubidium, an element closely related to lithium in its biochemical properties (Fieve & Jamison, 1982); salbutamol, a stimulator of beta-adrenergic receptors (Simon, Lecrubier, Puech, & Widlocher, 1983); tetrahydrobiopterin, a cofactor of the first enzyme in the metabolic pathways of both serotonin and the catecholamines, and therefore a critical regulator of the availability of those neurotransmitters (Curtius, Niederweiser, Levine, Lovenberg, Woggon, & Angst, 1983); captopril, and inhibitor of angiotensin-converting enzyme and enkephalinase which might increase CNS endogenous opiates (Zubenko & Nixon, 1984); and enalapril, another antihypertensive drug similar to captopril which appeared to induce a euphorialike state in both hypertensive patients and medical-student controls (Cohen, Anderson, White, Griffing, & Melby, 1984).

At this time there seems to be little question that medication is useful and effective in the treatment of depression. While not all individuals find relief from depression in medication, and psychotherapy is very important in treating many types of depression (discussed at length in many other chapters of this volume), it seems likely that medication will continue to be important, especially in the treatment of patients whose mood shows little or no response either to their cognitions or to environmental events, and who appear to have an inherited biochemical defect in the processes governing mood and emotion. It may be helpful for other patients in psychotherapy, enabling them to derive greater benefit from it.

No single medication yet investigated is either universally effective or without undesirable side effects. Most relieve depression only slowly or after a period of time. As biochemical research becomes more refined, it seems likely that the dysfunctions underlying depression will eventually be untangled. Research to find better antidepressants, or to improve the probability of choosing the right treatment, will no doubt continue.

SOMATIC THERAPIES FOR DEPRESSION

Electroconvulsive Therapy

In the years following Cerletti's discovery of the therapeutic benefit of inducing seizures by means of electric current passed through the brain this treatment was tried on a great variety of patients. It was a fairly terrifying treatment; neither the anesthesia nor the muscle-relaxing drugs used today to soften the psychological impact of the treatment were in use then; patients were often lined up outside the treatment room and watched other patients being wheeled out in a semiconscious, confused state after treatment. Muscles and tendons were often torn during the convulsion; teeth and bones sometimes broke under the stress of muscle contraction. When patients regained consciousness they frequently had a virtually total retrograde amnesia. Their past would return to them slowly, but often incompletely even after years, and many believed that they experienced an irreversible loss of ability to learn and remember new things as well as an inability to reconstruct their personal history. It is no wonder, then, that many felt as described by the Canadian artist, William Kurelek, that they were being executed, not once but many times. Kurelek made a moving film of his experiences, *The Maze,* which is available through many college and university audiovisual services.

It is not too surprising then that many resented this treatment deeply. Even those whose depression was relieved by these treatments often wondered if it were worth the price, and since the treatments at that time were believed to benefit primarily schizophrenia (which then included any disorder with any evidence of psychotic thought processes), many patients were subjected to long series of treatments which failed to help them and may in fact have contributed to the deterioration of the chronic schizophrenic patients. This fear has been to some extent communicated to the general public, whose fear of being subjected to such harsh "help" against their will was reflected in the passage of a law recently prohibiting the use of the ECT in Berkeley, California.

It seems somewhat ironic that the passage of that statute occurred at a time when diagnostic and treatment refinements have made ECT not only safer and less disturbing than at any time before, but also more likely to work. It is now recognized that depression, particularly that with classical endogenous symptoms (*DSM-III,* melancholia), is the primary indication for ECT, though it can be of benefit in many cases in the treatment of mania when other treatments fail to work. To relieve the psychological impact of the treatment on patients, they are anesthetized briefly before and during the treatment; muscle-relaxing drugs prevent convulsion damage to bones and muscles; oxygen loading of the blood before the seizure reduces brain damage from seizure anoxia to near zero. The recent discovery that the treatment was as effective or nearly as effective if the current is passed through the nondominant brain hemisphere only, has proven to relieve complaints of memory loss almost entirely. Patients awakening after one of these "unilateral" seizures are as alert and in contact with their past as any patient awakening from brief general anesthesia, and these patients do not complain of memory defects later. In addition, ECT is the most rapidly effective treatment for depression currently available, with most patients showing significant improvement in about one week. There have even been a number of reports of patients showing complete recovery after a single treatment (Rich, 1984).

This, then, is in striking contrast to the evidence that the use of ECT has declined dramatically in the last decade (cf., Mills, Pearsall, Yesavage, & Salzman, 1984). Many physicians who have years of experience in the use of both ECT and other treatments for depression believe that ECT is not only more effective than other treatments, but that it is safer as well, with actually fewer documented cases of undesirable cardiac and anticholinergic effects. Why, then, especially in public hospitals, is it disappearing from use?

Effectiveness

A major review of the outcome literature for ECT was published by Scovern and Kilmann in the *Psychological Bulletin* in 1980. They discussed the findings of 60 studies which compared the therapeutic efficacy of ECT with control procedures or other treatments. They found most of the studies to be methodologically flawed and comparison of findings somewhat difficult due to variations in procedure, measurement, follow-up time, patient population, methods of inducing and monitoring seizures, and so on. They noted that few recent studies have compared ECT with placebo or no treatment, and that most recent studies have been concerned not with the effectiveness of ECT per se but with comparisons of various methods. Diagnostic distinctions appear to have been somewhat fuzzy, especially in some of the older studies. However, they felt that despite these criticisms the evidence warranted the conclusion that for depressed patients with the classic endogenous symptom pattern, ECT is not only an effective treatment but more effective than other, pharmacological treatments—especially if the depression is severe or accompanied by delusions. Because of its rapid action they also felt that it was especially warranted when the patient is suicidal (though other authors have argued that if the patient is appropriately supervised this need not be an issue). Scovern and Kilmann concluded that patients other than those with endogenous depression are poor candidates for ECT. However, some other authors have found that elements of "neurotic" or "reactive" symptoms do not necessarily predict a failure to do well with ECT (Davidson, McLeod, Law-Yone, & Linnoila, 1978; Paul, Extein, Calil, Potter, Chodoff, & Goodwin, 1981; Rich, Spiker, Jewell, & Neil, 1984). These authors again note that there is a relationship of ECT effectiveness to severity of the depressive symptoms, and Paul et al. (1981) report excellent results in patients who had been refractory to a number of other treatments (eight of nine patients referred to NIMH after multiple treatment failures elsewhere).

In a review of 24 double-blind studies of ECT effectiveness from 1956 through 1981, Janicak, Davis, Gibbons, Ericksen, Chang, and Gallagher (in press) compared studies using placebo controls, simulated ECT treatment controls, and comparisons with TCAs and MAOIs. They used a procedure called "meta-analysis" to get a central indication of how patients were affected by any of the treatments, so that these studies could be compared. Across all studies, the following effectiveness rates were found:

Real ECT	77.8%
Simulated ECT	27.8
Placebo	37.6
TCAs	64.3
MAO inhibitors	32.0

No apparent explanation appears for the unusually good showing of "placebo" in these studies, nor the poor showing of the MAO inhibitors (unless patient selection procedures had eliminated any "atypical" cases). If placebo works via the belief of the patient that he/she is being given adequate treatment, it would be expected that simulated ECT would have at least as powerful an effect as a pill placebo.

Other predictors of response to ECT have been proposed. Double-blind studies conducted at Northwick Park Hospital in Great Britain by the Clinical Research Centre of the Division of Psychiatry (1984) found that only the presence of delusions predicted a good response to ECT, which was consistent with Perry, Morgan, Smith, and Tsuang's (1982) finding that 86 percent of ECT-treated delusional depressed patients responded well, as compared with 42 percent treated with a combination antidepressant-antipsychotic. Coryell and Zimmerman (1984) found that Winokur's Familial Pure Depressive Disease and Sporadic Depressive Disease subtypes showed a much better response to ECT than did individuals from families with Depressive Spectrum Disease (see Winokur et al., 1978, for a discussion of this distinction). Early escape from dexamethasone suppression of cortisol release also predicted a good response to ECT, but the presence or absence of symptoms of melancholia did not.

One of the most interesting discussions of predictors of ECT response is that of Max Hamilton (1982). After noting that the Funkenstein and Shagass tests of autonomic reactivity do not add much to the prediction of ECT response, he discusses personality measures which have been proposed to distinguish ECT-responsive from nonresponsive patients. MMPI and Rorschach-derived scales appeared to be more measures of depression than a significant addition to the existing distinctions. The most entertaining finding was that good response to treatment was correlated with a high score on the California F scale, originally designed to measure bigotry and authoritarianism. These high scores were thought to reflect high stereotypy and rigidity, and low critical ability and imagination. These scores were also positively correlated with age, which was itself positively correlated with ECT response. Apparently experience does not increase open-mindedness. The final profile of a good ECT responder was one with traits commonly described as "obsessional," a personality style frequently seen in depressive patients.

Mode of Use

Over the years a great number of methods have been employed for the administration of ECT. There are variations in intensity of current, duration, waveform, frequency, and so on. In this discussion the description of technique will be based on the recommendations of two of the researchers who have done the greatest amount of work with ECT, Max Fink (1979) and Richard Abrams (1982).

In addition to a preliminary discussion of selection of ECT patients, Fink (1979), in his chapter "A Manual for Convulsive Therapy," recommends that the physician put a special effort into gaining the trust and confidence of the patient, and that this should help to reduce the patient's anxiety or fear about the procedure. The patient should always be adequately informed about the treatment so that genuine consent can be obtained. Fink feels that if a voluntary, competent patient refuses the treatment, an alternate treatment (and perhaps therapist) should be provided. He feels that the therapist is presented with a substantial dilemma if the patient who refuses treatment cannot be considered either competent or voluntary; the consent of family, authorities, other psychiatrists, or consultants is not an acceptable substitute. He gives an example of a good consent form, and recommends that treatment should be administered with palpable compassion for the patient's experience.

Both Fink and Abrams recommend substantial pretreatment physical evaluation of the patients, with a complete medical history and routine laboratory screening tests. The condition of the patient's bone structure is especially important, as is some measure of the patient's ability to metabolize the muscle relaxant drug succinylcholine (Anectine) rapidly (in rare individuals with deficient pseudocholinesterase, the enzyme which breaks down this drug, prolonged inability to breathe voluntarily after the treatment can present a serious hazard).

If the patient is to be treated in the morning, Fink recommends that the patient take nothing (even water) by mouth after 10 P.M. the previous evening; Abrams recommends nothing after midnight. This is to prevent the risk of inhaling stomach contents vomited as a reaction to the anesthesia and is a standard preanesthesia precaution. Both recommend injection of an anticholinergic drug to reduce excess secretions of the mouth and digestive tract and to avoid severe reduction in heart rate from excess stimulation of the vagus nerve during the seizure. Fink also recommends giving patients a small dose of amobarbital or a benzodiazepine antianxiety drug if they are anxious; it should be noted, however, that this may elevate the patient's seizure threshhold.

Only two ECT treatment machines are currently manufactured in the United States, Medcraft and MECTA. These two machines use different waveforms; a discussion of the significance of this is provided by Weaver and Williams (1982). Both machines are designed to control the application of the stimulus within therapeutic and safe limits, though certain adjustments can be made to meet the needs of the particular patient. The lowest possible dosage of energy which will produce a complete seizure will be the safest for the patient and have the fewest undesirable aftereffects; electrode placement is one of the most important factors affecting the amount of energy required and will be discussed. Equipment for administering anesthesia and oxygen should be present, and the physician should be skilled in emergency resuscitation procedures and have the necessary drugs and equipment available for this.

Whether the presence of an anesthesiologist is necessary is a matter of debate; Fink at least recommends that the person responsible for the anesthesia have special training in the type of rapid, light anesthesia necessary in ECT treatment. Both authors recommend forced ventilation with oxygen as soon as the intravenous anesthesia takes effect. Electrodes and the patient's skin should be clean and free of residues; a commercial electrode jelly or paste will provide a good contact and reduce resistance and the risk of burns.

Both authors recommend monitoring the seizure, preferably with an EEG, since "missed" seizures are particularly likely with the use of muscle relaxants, and this may be a cause of response delay or failure. Sometimes the application of a tourniquet to an extremity before the administration of the muscle relaxant is used, so the convulsive movements of the extremity can be observed, since the relaxant will not have affected that extremity. However, this method is not highly reliable, and it is important to ascertain that a seizure has actually occurred. The most reliable method is to monitor brain activity with an EEG.

Historically, it has been observed that in most cases if treatments are stopped as soon as the patient has shown a recognizable mood response, the patient has a high probability of subsequent relapse (cf., Rich, 1984). Thus the rule of thumb among many physicians using ECT has been to treat until a positive mood response appears and then give two more treatments. Treatments are usually given two or three times a week; improvement is usually seen after the third or fourth seizure. Fink notes that one author suggests that between 210 and 600 seconds of total seizure time may be optimal for patients with a depressive psychosis. More work is being done on this, and a "therapeutic window," such as that noted for some medications for depression, may yet be developed.

Special Issues in the Use of ECT

Cognitive and Memory Impairment. When chronic schizophrenic patients were treated with ECT, it was usually clear that they did not show a complete return to normal even when they did become less depressed or even in some cases less psychotic. These patients have usually been deteriorating over time from a highest level of functioning reached fairly early in life, and it may be difficult to ascertain what part of their residual symptomatology reflects the schizophrenic process and what part is secondary to the treatment. Patients with affective disorders, however, usually return to relatively or even completely normal function following successful treatment, and these patients may be acutely aware of residual deficits and vocal in their complaints about them. Thus it became clear early in the use of ECT in depression that recovered patients complained bitterly about memory loss; not only, they said, did they fail to recover all of what they once knew, but they also could no longer store and retrieve new information as well as they had previously.

At one time this forgetting was thought to be part of the therapeutic effect of ECT; "forgetting their troubles," as it were. However, it was soon demonstrated that the extent of memory impairment was not correlated with clinical improvement. Immediately following a series of ECT treatments administered in the traditional way, temple-to-temple, retrograde amnesia is virtually total, and some anterograde amnesia (inability to remember new experiences) is also present. Anterograde amnesia usually resolves very shortly after treatments are terminated, and it has generally been believed that complete recovery of memory functions takes place within a few weeks, despite patients' complaints, since no significant residual deficit can be shown on standard memory tests. However, most memory tests measure relatively immediate memory, and few studies have used retention periods longer than 30 minutes (Squire & Chace, 1975). Squire and Chace (1975) found that although no evidence for persisting memory deficits could be found in their sample of patients six to nine months after ECT using six different tests of recent and remote memory, those who had had bilateral ECT rated their memory impaired significantly more often than the other subjects of this study. While depressed patients generally show memory defects before receiving treatment (cf., Malloy, Small, Miller, Milstein, & Stout, 1982), a replication by Squire, Wetzel, and Slater (1979) showed that the nature of postbilateral-ECT memory complaints differed quantitatively and qualitatively from those before treatment. While these complaints had diminished six months later, they remained the same in nature as those one week after treatments. Another study (Daniel, Crovitz, Weiner, & Rogers, 1982) showed that the post-ECT memory deficit resembles that seen in Korsakoff's syndrome or bilateral hippocampal damage in that the patients show a deficit in free but not cued recall, suggesting that what is affected is not memory storage but memory retrieval. That these memory defects are not simply imagined gains credibility from two sources: first, depressed elderly patients with a history of ECT have shown more deterioration in cognitive functioning on psychological tests than depressed elderly patients with no past ECT (Pettinati & Bonner, 1984); and second, depressed patients successfully treated with ECT involving the cortex on the nondominant (usually the right) side only do not complain of nor show these memory problems (cf., Squire, 1977).

Unilateral versus Bilateral ECT. Fink (1979) believes that it is the action of the seizure in the diencephalon of the brain—structures underlying the cortex—that produces the therapeutic benefit of the seizure. If the seizure could be confined to those structures, and not affect the cortex at all, theoretically it should be possible to obtain the therapeutic benefit of the treatment with fewer of its hazards. However, it appears that this would require a procedure so invasive that it would have additional risks of its own. Thus the search was begun some time ago for a means to induce these diencephalic seizures with as little impact as possible on the cortex through which the current must pass. The most satisfactory solution appears to be that of passing the current through half of the cerebral cortex, as it appears to be possible in most cases to initiate a subcortical seizure by this means. If the patient's dominant hand, eye, and foot are determined (by asking the patient to pretend to throw something, kick something, and sight through a paper tube—two out of three wins) and the electrodes placed on the ipsilateral, nondominant side, the patient will recover from the anesthesia with little or no confusion or memory loss; while if the placement is contralateral—passing the current through the dominant hemisphere—the aftereffects appear to be virtually the same as with bilateral ECT except that the antidepressant effect is poorer. Early research on unilateral ECT suggested that it was not as effective as bilateral ECT (cf., Abrams, Fink, Dornbush, Feldstein, Volavka, & Roubicek, 1972). Taylor and Abrams continue to publish evidence that fewer treatments are required with bilateral ECT, but relatively few others agree with them (some of the controversy has appeared in articles and letters to the editor of the 1984 issues of the *American Journal of Psychiatry*). Many users of ECT believe that the apparent inferiority of unilateral ECT is an artifact of the fact that it is slightly more difficult to initiate a complete seizure by this means; they recommend EEG monitoring to be certain that the seizure has actually taken place.

It should be recognized, though, that there is some evidence that while verbal memory is much less affected by unilateral nondominant ECT than by bilateral ECT, some other functions may indeed be altered. Visuospatial, musical, and artistic abilities appear to involve the right hemisphere in most people. These may be altered by ECT, although two reviews of studies of nonverbal memory effects of unilateral nondominant ECT (Daniel & Crovitz, 1983; Fromm-Auch, 1982) have failed to find evidence that these functions are impaired long term.

A number of different placements of the electrodes for unilateral ECT have been suggested; Fink (1979) shows seven possibilities (p. 228). Generally, one electrode is placed just above an imaginary line from the canthus of the ear to the corner of the eye, and the other approximately 8–10 cm away. The important consideration is the placement which will induce a complete subcortical seizure with the least current. Some researchers have argued that the d'Elia placement (the second electrode at the vertex of the skull) is optimal for this purpose (cf., d'Elia, Ottosson, & Stromgren, 1983; Erman, Welch, & Mandel, 1979). The paper by d'Elia et al. (1983) presents an excellent brief discussion of the current issues involved in the use of ECT.

Proposed Mechanisms of Action of ECT

As with the other antidepressant treatments, a number of possible mechanisms of action have been proposed over the years. The majority of these are reviewed by Fink (1979), who concludes with his own well-elaborated hypotheses.

Some of the older hypotheses are entertaining, particularly the psychological theories. While some careful researchers were already postulating hypothalamic and other brain stem localities as the likely site of action, psychological theories tended to focus either on the meaning of the experience of the seizures themselves to the patient or the psychological sequelae of the seizures. One widely held view was that the patient's overwhelming sense of guilt and self-blame were relieved by receiving a punishment massive enough to equal the weight of their imagined accumulation of sin. Another hypothesis held that the apparent regression induced by the (bilateral) ECT allowed the patient to develop more denial, as a healthier means of coping with whatever defense failings had allowed them to be overwhelmed by depression. A third theory held simply that the most powerfully emotion-laden memories were erased by ECT, allowing the patient essentially to return to an earlier, more psychologically happy time. None of these theories has been supported by experimental evidence.

There has been more support for hypotheses concerning the effects of

ECT, especially the long-term effects, on the brain itself. Some of these have been neurophysiologic and others biochemical; over time they have converged with the theories of action of the other successful antidepressant treatments. Fink's own theory is that

> Hypothalamic dysfunction is a core process in endogenous depressive psychosis. Convulsive therapy alters hypothalamic activity both by direct stimulation of hypothalamic cells and by increasing the functional neurotransmitter activity in the brain, thereby releasing substances, probably peptide hormones, that alter the vegetative functions of the body and the endocrine glands. Specific substances are released that modify mood and the behaviors associated with mood disturbances. The biochemical events that precede and accompany the seizure are the trigger for increased neurohumoral activity. In ECT, the direct stimulation of electric currents augment but are not necessary for the effects on hypothalamic functions (1979, p. 173).

As with the other antidepressants, the most current hypotheses have to do with ECT-induced changes in neurotransmitter receptors (cf., Chiodo & Antelman, 1980; Deakin, Owen, Cross, & Dashwood, 1981; Lerer, Stanley, & Gershon, 1983) and the effects on endogenous opiates (cf., Alexopoulos, Inturrisi, Lipman, Frances, Haycox, Dougherty, & Rossier, 1983; Belensky, Blatt, Hitzemann, Tortella, & Holaday, 1983). As is true of other antidepressant treatments, these hypotheses seem to be converging on, but have not reached, some central unifying understanding of their action.

SLEEP, LIGHT AND CIRCADIAN RHYTHM MANIPULATIONS

When patients who have been treated for major affective disorders are followed up for more than a year or two, it becomes apparent that in the vast majority of cases (80–100 percent) their disorder is recurrent and cyclic (Corfman, 1979; Zis & Goodwin 1979). Because of this, a number of those who study affective disorders have concluded that the cycles of affective change in these individuals vary in a rhythmic manner that is similar to the rhythmic cyclic changes accompanying many biological processes (cf., Corfman, 1979). These rhythms are usually described as circadian—that is, a cycle repeating every 24 hours (like the sleep-wake cycle, body temperature cycle, and a number of hormone cycles); ultradian—taking place over less than a 24-hour period (such as the hunger-eating-digestion cycle or some 90-minute cycles of alertness and sleep rhythms); or infradian—cycles longer than 24 hours (such as the yearly hormonal cycles thought to control the onset of puberty, or women's monthly hormonal cycles regulating fertility). Many of these cycles appear to be "entrained"—that is, kept synchronized with other cycles—by the daily light-dark cycles that usually accompany sunrise and sunset and are associated with sleeping and waking. This entrainment is mediated biochemically, probably at least to some extent by the production of melatonin from serotonin in the pineal gland. An enzyme which is part of the metabolic process which converts serotonin to melatonin is activated by the *absence* of light stimulation of the retina (via several other processes). In rats, total brain serotonin is substantially reduced by 12 hours of darkness.

It has been recognized for some time that the normal biological rhythms of patients with affective disorders are grossly disturbed (cf., Elithorn, Bridges, Lobban, & Tredre, 1966). There is considerable variation among individuals in the stability of their biological rhythms, and as long ago as 1939, Kleitman observed that the biological rhythms of individuals with personalities and body builds of the type usually associated with manic-depressive disease (Elithorn et al., 1966) had the most labile body rhythms. Other evidence of abnormal biological rhythms in affective patients has included abnormal sleep EEG (cf., Kupfer, Spiker, Coble, Neil, Ulrich, & Shaw, 1981), abnormal cycles of serotonin uptake by blood platelets (Oxenkrug, Prakhje, & Mikhalenko, 1978), abnormal urinary melatonin secretion rhythms (Mendlewicz, Linkowski, Branchey, Weinberg, Weitzman, & Branchey, 1979; Wetterberg, Beck-Friis, Aperia, & Petterson, 1979), abnormal cortisol fluctuations (cf., Arato & Rihmer, 1979; Wetterberg et al., 1979, and papers dealing with the dexamethasone suppression test), abnormal pulse and blood pressure rhythms (Rudolf, Bischofs, Blaszkiewicz, Bremer, & Tolle, 1976), and so on (for a summary, see for example Wehr, Wirz-Justice, & Goodwin, 1983).

The connection between circadian rhythms and the sleep-wake cycle is perhaps the most obvious, and one of the cardinal symptoms of endogenous depression is that the patient feels markedly worse in the morning on wakening. Thus it would seem reasonable to attempt to manipulate the circadian rhythms by artificially manipulating sleep, with the hope that this might have a beneficial impact on depression symptoms. The first researchers to report studying this systematically appear to be Pflug and Tolle (1971), who studied endogenous and "neurotic" depressed patients and healthy volunteers. The study was single blind, in that the subjects were told they were being kept awake in the interests of some other tests which were in fact performed. The patients with the endogenous symptom pattern appeared to have benefited the most, with a few experiencing remission of symptoms beginning at that point; some with neurotic symptoms also benefited, but less evidently. In most of the endogenously depressed patients, however, symptoms of depression returned as soon as the patients had again had a "good night's sleep." Healthy subjects reported having difficulty staying awake during the night without sleep and about half complained of a generalized malaise by morning. Pflug and Tolle recommended the use of this treatment as a way of initiating a remission, perhaps with antidepressant drugs as an adjunct.

The technique does not appear to have caught on rapidly, possibly because of the apparently transient nature of the effect. Two Danish studies (Larsen, Lindberg, & Skovgaard, 1976; Svendsen, 1976) attempted to prolong the effect by repeating the sleep deprivation. Some patients appeared to do quite well with this treatment regimen, but as the studies were uncontrolled it is difficult to conclude that the treatment was really more successful than a placebo treatment; in any case, Svendsen noted that it appeared to have no side effects.

More studies have been done, however, and it seems reasonable to conclude at this point that sleep deprivation has at least a temporary significant mood-elevating effect in many patients with affective disorders (King, 1980), and in many ways the effect resembles the physiological and biochemical effects of standard antidepressants (Amin, 1978; Buchsbaum, Gerner, & Post, 1981; Elsenga & Van den Hoofdakker, 1983; Wirz-Justice et al., 1979). It may predict (Wirz-Justice et al., 1979) or potentiate (Elsenga & Van den Hoofdakker, 1983) response to other antidepressant drugs. However, some researchers have observed sleep deprivation, whether forced or spontaneous, to be followed in some patients by a switch to mania (Wehr, Goodwin, Wirz-Justice, Breitmaier, & Craig, 1982; Zimanova & Vojtechovsky, 1974).

One problem of course has been the limit to the length of time a patient may be sleep deprived. One solution has been to repeat the night without sleep once or twice a week; another has been to reduce total sleep by depriving patients of part of night's sleep—the morning hours. This method has also been reported to be successful (Schilgen, Bischofs, Blaszkiewicz, Bremer, Rudolf, & Tolle, 1976; Van Bemmel & Van den Hoofdakker, 1981). The apparent reason for depriving patients of morning sleep, rather than evening sleep, has been to deprive them selectively of more REM sleep, which occurs in greater quantity toward morning. However, another interesting confound is present, as best can be determined, in all of the sleep deprivation studies—it is extremely difficult to keep people awake in the dark; an individual can most successfully be kept awake all night in a brightly-lit room with activities which will hold his or her attention.

Residents of Sweden, especially northern Sweden, where the days are extremely short in winter, have long been aware of the emotional darkness which seems for many to accompany the long, dark nights. There is a special name for this feeling, *grubbla,* which is probably most nearly rendered in English as "brooding." There is a matching giddy light-headedness and lightness of mood that often appears during the midsummer days when the sun sets only very briefly and it is never completely dark. These mood changes are only slightly related to the amount of actual sleeping people do. Seasonal variations in depression, mania, and suicide have been observed in other places also. The observation of physician Peter Mueller of clear seasonal variations in the affective state of one of his patients, with winter depression and hypomania setting in in spring, which was also strongly latitude related, led him to try aborting one of her depressions with early morning light therapy (from about 5 A.M. to sunrise). When this treatment was successful, a larger study was undertaken at NIMH. A large number of patients with clearly seasonal affective disorders were located through a newspaper article soliciting people with major affective disorders (by RDC criteria) with these same seasonal changes. As described by Rosenthal et al. (1983), these patients have tended to be women in their mid-30s, with onset of their illness in their mid-20s, and depression every winter since the onset. Their depressions are characterized by retardation, hypersomnia, overeating, carbohydrate craving, and weight gain; 80 percent of these patients were diagnosed as having bipolar II-type disorder (severe depressions with some periods of hypomania but no true manias), 15 percent as having bipolar I disorder (classic manic-depressive disorder), and only 5 percent as having unipolar disorder. Hypothesizing that these symptoms might be related to melatonin secretion, and noting that bright light suppresses melatonin secretion, these researchers treated patients with either bright, white full-spectrum light or dim yellow light in a crossover design for three hours after dusk and three hours before dawn. Bright white light had a clearly antidepressant effect, and relapse occurred when patients switched to dim yellow light even though they were blind to the hypotheses of the study (Rosenthal, Sack, Parry, Mendelson, Davenport, Lewy, Gillin, & Wehr, 1983; Rosenthal, Sack, Gillin, Lewy, Goodwin, Davenport, Mueller, Newsome, & Wehr, 1984). Kripke, Risch and Janowsky (1983) produced greater reductions in depression by exposing patients to only one hour of bright white light (5:00–6:00 A.M.) than by exposing them to dim red light for the same time period; these researchers replicated their finding with another 12 patients, in whom additional awakenings with dim red light (1:00–2:00 A.M.) were found to have no effect.

It is not yet clear how these treatments have their effect, but some researchers have argued that many affective disorders are actually disorders of circadian rhythm (cf., Wehr et al., 1979; Wehr & Wirz-Justice, 1982). This would suggest that sleep deprivation and/or treatment with bright light somehow reset these individuals' biological clocks to a more normal function, though the transience of the effect of single treatments of this type suggests that these patients are extremely sensitive to ambient conditions producing depression in them. Not all depressed patients appear to be clearly "rhythm disordered" or responsive to these treatments, but for those who are, the treatment is both extremely inexpensive and remarkably safe. It is to be hoped that further evidence on this will soon be forthcoming.

There have been many cases of patients who have shown a remarkable response to a treatment after many treatments have failed to work. In these cases, during the time when no treatment seems to help, there is always a temptation to wonder if the patient is not somehow resisting treatment voluntarily; to speculate that the "secondary gain" the patient receives from the sick role is enough to maintain their symptoms. Most depressed patients, however, would insist that no secondary gain would be adequate to make a depression even endurable, let alone desirable. So long as there is any chance of finding a means to help relieve these individuals' suffering, the effort should not be abandoned. Given the number of treatments for depression outlined in this chapter, the failure of a patient to respond even after several have been tried should not be taken as an indication that the patient's depression is "characterological" (a term often used by frustrated medical staff to mean not only untreatable, but also in some way the patient's own fault). If standard treatments have failed to help a patient, it might be appropriate to try some of the more unusual treatments, or combinations of treatments (some of which succeed where no single treatment has done so).

Advances are rapidly being made in this field. It is greatly to be hoped that prolonged, intractable depression may soon become a historical disorder.

References

Abrams, R. (1982). Technique of electroconvulsive therapy. In R. Abrams & W. B. Essman (Eds.), *Electroconvulsive therapy: Biological foundations and clinical applications* (pp. 41–55). New York: Spectrum Publications.

Abrams, R., Fink, M., Dornbush, R. L., Feldstein, S., Volavka, J., & Roubicek, J. (1972). Unilateral and bilateral electroconvulsive therapy: Effects on depression, memory, and the electroencephalogram. *Archives of General Psychiatry, 27,* 88–91.

Abrams, R., & Taylor, M. A. (1977). Catatonia: Prediction of response to somatic treatments. *American Journal of Psychiatry, 134,* 78–80.

Aden, G. C. (1983). Alprazolam in clinically anxious patients with depressed mood. *Journal of Clinical Psychiatry, 44,* 22–24.

Aghajanian, G. K. (1981). Tricyclic antidepressants and single-cell responses to serotonin and norepinephrine: A review of chronic studies. In E. Usdin, W. E. Bunney, & J. M. Davis (Eds.), *Neuroreceptors—Basic and clinical aspects* (pp. 27–35). New York: John Wiley & Sons.

Agnoli, A., Andreoli, V., Casacchia, M., & Cerbo, R. (1976). Effect of S-adenosyl-L-methionine (SAMe) upon depressive symptoms. *Journal of Psychiatric Research, 13,* 43–54.

Alexopoulos, G. S., Inturrisi, C. E., Lipman, R., Frances, R., Haycox, J., Dougherty, J. H., & Rossier, J. (1983). Plasma immunoreactive beta-endorphin levels in depression: Effect of electroconvulsive therapy. *Archives of General Psychiatry, 40,* 181–183.

Altschule, M. D. (1976). *The development of traditional psychopathology.* New York: John Wiley & Sons.

Amdisen, A. (1967). Serum lithium determinations for clinical use. *Scandinavian Journal of Clinical and Laboratory Investigations, 20,* 104–108.

Amdisen, A. (1975). Monitoring of lithium treatment through determination of the serum lithium concentration. *Danish Medical Bulletin, 22,* 277–291.

Amdisen, A. (1977). Serum level monitoring and clinical pharmacokinetics of lithium. *Clinical Pharmacokinetics, 2,* 73–92.

American Psychiatric Association. (1980). *Diagnostic and statistical manual of mental disorders* (3rd ed.). Washington, DC: Author.

Amin, M. (1978). Response to sleep deprivation and therapeutic results with antidepressants. *Lancet, 2,* 165.

Ananth, J. (1978). Clinical prediction of antidepressant response. *International Pharmacopsychiatry, 13,* 69–93.

Ananth, J., Pecknold, J. C., Van den Steen, N., & Engelsmann, F. (1981). Double-blind comparative study of clomipramine and amitriptylene in obsessive neurosis. *Progress in Neuro-Psychopharmacology, 5,* 257–262.

Andrews, G., Kiloh, L. G., & Neilson, M. (1973). Patterns of depressive illness. *Archives of General Psychiatry, 29,* 670–673.

Anisman, H., & Zacharko, R. M. (1982). Depression: The predisposing influence of stress. *The Behavioral and Brain Sciences, 5,* 89–99.

Anton, R. F., & Sexauer, J. D. (1983). Efficacy of amoxapine in psychotic depression. *American Journal of Psychiatry, 140,* 1344–1347.

Arato, M., & Rihmer, Z. (1982). Sleep deprivation and cortisol secretion. *American Journal of Psychiatry, 139,* 135.

Asarch, K. B., Shih, J. C., & Kulcsar, A. (1980). Decreased 3H-imipramine binding in depressed males and females. *Communications in Psychopharmacology, 4,* 425–432.

Asberg, M., Cronholm, B., Sjokvist, F., & Tuck, D. (1971). Relationship between plasma level and therapeutic effects of nortriptylene. *British Medical Journal 3,* 331–334.

Asberg, M., Thoren, P., Traskman, L., Bertilsson, L., & Ringberger, V. (1976). "Serotonin depression"—A biochemical subgroup within the affective disorders. *Science, 191,* 478–480.

Avery, D., & Winokur, G. (1976). Mortality in depressed patients treated with electroconvulsive therapy and antidepressants. *Archives of General Psychiatry, 33,* 1029–1037.

Axelrod, J., Whitby, L.G., & Hertting, G. (1961). Effect of psychotropic drugs on the uptake of H3-norepinephrine by tissues. *Science, 133,* 83–84.

Ayd, F. J., Jr., & Settle, E. C., Jr. (1982). Trazodone: A novel, broad-spectrum antidepressant. *Modern Problems in Pharmacopsychiatry, 18,* 49–69.

Badawy, A. A-B., & Evans, M. (1974). Tryptophan plus a pyrrolase inhibitor for depression? *Lancet, 2,* 1209–1210.

Bader, T. F., & Newman, K. (1980). Amitriptylene in human breast milk and the nursing infant's serum. *American Journal of Psychiatry, 137,* 855–856.

Baer, L., Kassir, S., & Fieve, R. (1970). Lithium-induced changes in electrolyte balance and tissue electrolyte concentration. *Psychopharmacologia, 47,* 216–224.

Baldessarini, R. J. (1983). How do antidepressants work? In J. M. Davis & J. W. Maas (Eds.), *The affective disorders* (pp. 243–260). Washington, DC: American Psychiatric Press.

Ballenger, J.C., & Post, R. M. (1978). Therapeutic effects of carbamazepine in affective illness: A preliminary report. *Communications in Psychopharmacology, 2,* 159–175.

Ballenger, J. C., & Post, R. M. (1980). Carbamazepine in manic-depressive illness: A new treatment. *American Journal of Psychiatry, 137,* 782–790.

Baron, M., Gershon, E. S., Rudy, V., Jonas, W. Z., & Buchsbaum, M. (1975). Lithium carbonate response in depression. *Archives of General Psychiatry, 32,* 1107–1111.

Barranco, S. F., Thrash, M. L., Hackett, E., Frey, J., Ward, J., & Norris, E. (1979). Early onset of response to doxepin treatment. *Journal of Clinical Psychiatry, 40,* 265–269.

Beckman, H., & Goodwin, F. K. (1975). Antidepressant response to tricyclics and urinary MHPG in unipolar patients. *Archives of General Psychiatry, 32,* 17–21.

Belensky, G. L., Blatt, S., Hitzemann, R., Tortella, F. C., & Holaday, J. W. (1983, May). *Electroconvulsive shock and endogenous opioids.* Paper presented at the meeting of the American Psychiatric Association, New York.

Bendz, H., & Feinberg, M. (1984). Aspirin increases serum lithium ion levels. *Archives of General Psychiatry, 41,* 310–311.

Bennie, E. H. (1975). Lithium in depression. *Lancet, 1,* 216.

Bergner, P-E. E., Berniker, K., & Cooper, T. B. (1973). Lithium kinetics in man: Effect of variation in dosage pattern. *British Journal of Pharmacology, 49,* 328–339.

Biel, J. H. (1970a). Non-monoamine oxidase inhibitor antidepressants: Structure-activity relationships. In W. G. Clark & J. del Giudice (Eds.), *Principles of psychopharmacology* pp. 269–278). New York: Academic Press.

Biel, J. H. (1970b). Monoamine oxidase inhibitor antidepressants: Structure-activity relationships. In W. G. Clark and J. del Giudice (Eds.), *Principles of psychopharmacology* (pp. 289–302). New York: Academic Press.

Biel, J. H., Nuhfer, P. A., Hoya, W. K., Leiser, L. A., & Abood, L. G. (1962). Cholinergic blockade as an approach to the development of new psychotropic agents. *Annals of the New York Academy of Sciences, 96,* 251–262.

Bielski, R. J., & Friedel, R. O. (1976). Prediction of tricyclic antidepressant response. *Archives of General Psychiatry, 33,* 1479–1489.

Bigger, J. T., Jr., Kantor, S. J., Glassman, A. H., & Perel, J. M. (1978). Cardiovascular effects of tricyclic drugs. In M. A. Lipton. A. DiMascio, & K. F. Killam (Eds.), *Psychopharmacology: A generation of progress* (pp. 1033–1046). New York: Raven Press.

Bjorum, N., Hornum, I., Mellerup, E. T., Plenge, P. K., & Rafaelsen, O. J. (1975). Lithium, calcium, and phosphate. *Lancet, 1,* 1243.

Bleuler, E. (1950). *Dementia praecox oder Gruppe der Schizophrenien.* Leipzig: F. Deuticke. (Original work published 1911).

Bloch, R. G., Dooneief, A. S., Buchberg, A. S., & Spellman, S. (1954). The clinical effects of isoniazid in the treatment of pulmonary tuberculosis. *Annals of Internal Medicine, 40,* 881–900.

Borland, B. L., & Heckman, H. K. (1976). Hyperactive boys and their brothers: A 25-year follow-up study. *Archives of General Psychiatry, 33,* 669–675.

Botez, M. I., & Botez, T. (1982). Folic acid deficiency and depression. *Psychosomatics, 23,* 63.

Botez, M. I., Botez, T., Leveille, J., Bielman, P., & Cadotte, M. (1979). Neuropsychological correlates of folic acid deficiency: Facts and hypotheses. In M. I. Botez & E. H. Reynolds (Eds.), *Folic acid in neurology, psychiatry, and medicine* (pp. 435–461). New York: Raven Press.

Bracha, H., Ebstein, R., & Belmaker, R. H. (1979). Possible mechanism of lithium's effect in bronchial asthma. *American Journal of Psychiatry, 136,* 734.

Briley, M. S., Langer, S. Z., Raisman, R., Sechter, D., & Zarifan, E. (1980). Tritiated imipramine binding sites are decreased in platelets of untreated depressed patients. *Science, 209,* 303–305.

Brotman, A. W., Herzog, D. B., & Woods, S. W. (1984). Antidepressant treatment of bulemia: The relationship between bingeing and depressive symptomatology. *Journal of Clinical Psychiatry, 45,* 7–9.

Buchsbaum, M. S., Gerner, R., & Post, R. M. (1981). The effects of sleep deprivation on average evoked responses in depressed patients and in normals. *Biological Psychiatry, 16,* 351–363.

Bunney, W. E., Jr. (1978). Psychopharmacology of the switch process in affective disorders. In M. A. Lipton, A. DiMascio, & K. F. Killam (Eds.), *Psychopharmacology: A generation of progress* (pp. 1249–1259). New York: Raven Press.

Bunney, W. E., Jr., & Davis, J. M. (1965). Norepinephrine in depressive reactions. *Archives of General Psychiatry, 13,* 483–494.

Bunney, W. E., Jr., & Garland, B. L. (1982). A second generation catecholamine hypothesis. *Pharmacopsychiatry, 15,* 111–115.

Bunney, W. E., Jr., Pert, A., Rosenblatt, J., Pert, C. B., & Gallaper, D. (1979). Mode of action of lithium: Some biological considerations. *Archives of General Psychiatry, 36,* 898–901.

Byck, R. (1976). Peptide transmitters: A unifying hypothesis for euphoria, respiration, sleep, and the action of lithium. *Lancet, 2,* 72–73.

Cade, J. F. J. (1949). Lithium salts in the treatment of psychotic excitement. *The Medical Journal of Australia, 2,* 349–352.

Caldwell, H. C., Westlake, W. J., & Connor, S. M. (1971). A pharmacokinetic analysis of lithium carbonate absorption from several formulations in man. *Journal of Clinical Pharmacology, 11,* 349–356.

Campbell, D. R., & Kimball, R. R. (1984). Replication of "Prediction of antidepressant response to lithium": Problems in generalizing to a clinical setting. *American Journal of Psychiatry, 141,* 706–707.

Carman, J. S., Post, R. M., Teplitz, T. A., & Goodwin, F. K. (1974). Divalent cations in predicting antidepressant response to lithium. *Lancet, 2,* 1454.

Carney, M. W. P., Martin, R. Bottiglieri, T., Reynolds, E. H., Nissenbaum, H., Toone, B. K., & Sheffield, B. F. (1983). Switch mechanism in affective illness and S-adenosylmethionine. *Lancet, 1,* 820–821.

Cerletti, U. (1956). Electroshock therapy. In F. Marti-Ibanez, A. M. Sackler, M. D. Sackler, & R. R. Sackler (Eds.), *The great physiodynamic therapies in psychiatry* (pp. 91–120). New York: Hoeber-Harper.

Chang, S. S., Pandey, G. N., & Kinard, K. (1978). Predicting the optimal lithium dosage. Abstract No. 140 in *Syllabus and Scientific Proceedings for 1978* (p. 68). Washington, DC: American Psychiatric Association.

Chiodo, L. A., & Antelman, S. M. (1980). Electroconvulsive shock: Progressive dopamine autoreceptor subsensitivity independent of repeated treatment. *Science, 210,* 799–801.

Chouinard, G., Young, S. N., Annable, L., & Sourkes, T. L. (1977). Tryptophan-nicotinamide combination in depression. *Lancet, 1,* 249.

Chouinard, G., Young, S. N., Annable, L., & Sourkes, T. L. (1978). Tryptophan dosage critical for its antidepressant effect. *British Medical Journal, 1,* 1422.

Christodoulou, G. N., & Vareltzides, A. G. (1978). Possitive side effects of lithium? *American Journal of Psychiatry, 135,* 1249.

Clinical Research Centre, Division of Psychiatry. (1984). The Northwick Park ECT trial predictors of response to real and simulated ECT. *British Journal of Psychiatry, 144,* 227–237.

Cobbin, D. M., Requin-Blow, B., Williams, L. R., & Williams, W. O. (1979). Urinary MHPG levels and tricyclic antidepressant drug selection. *Archives of General Psychiatry, 36,* 1111–1115.

Coble, P., Foster, G., & Kupfer, D. J. (1976). Electroencephalographic sleep diagnosis of primary depression. *Archives of General Psychiatry, 33,* 1124–1127.

Cocheme, M. (1970). L-tryptophan versus ECT *Lancet, 1,* 1392.

Cohen, B. M., Harris, P. Q., Altesman, R. J., & Cole, J. O. (1982). Amoxapine: Neuroleptic as well as antidepressant? *American Journal of Psychiatry, 139,* 1165–1167.

Cohen, L. M., Anderson, G., White, R. H., Griffing, G., & Melby, J. (1984). Enalapril and hypertension. *American Journal of Psychiatry, 141,* 1012–1013.

Cohen, W. J., & Cohen, N. H. (1974). Lithium carbonate, haloperidol, and irreversible brain damage. *Journal of the American Medical Association, 230,* 1283–1287.

Colonna, L., Petit, M., & Lepine, J. P. (1979). Bromocriptine in affective disorders. *Journal of Affective Disorders, 1,* 173–177.

Cooper, T. B., Bergner, P-E. E., & Simpson, G. M. (1973). The 24-hour serum lithium level as a prognosticator of dosage requirements. *American Journal of Psychiatry, 130,* 601–603.

Cooper, T. B., & Simpson, G. M. (1976). The 24-hour lithium level as a prognosticator of dosage requirements: A two-year follow-up study. *American Journal of Psychiatry, 133,* 440–443.

Coppen, A. (1967). The biochemistry of affective disorders. *British Journal of Psychiatry, 113,* 1237–1264.

Coppen, A., & Abou-Saleh, M. T. (1982). Plasma folate and effective morbidity during long-time lithium therapy. *British Journal of Psychiatry, 141,* 87–89.

Coppen, A., Bishop, M. E., Bailey, J. E., Cattell, W. R., & Price, R. G. (1980). Renal function in lithium and non-lithium treated patients with affective disorders. *Acta Psychiatrica Scandinavica, 62,* 343–355.

Coppen, A., Ghose, K., Montgomery, S., Rama Rao, V. A., Bailey, J., & Jorgensen, A. (1978). Continuation therapy with amitriptylene in depression. *British Journal of Psychiatry, 133,* 28–33.

Coppen, A., Swade, C., & Wood, K. (1980). Lithium restores abnormal platelet 5-HT transport in patients with affective disorders. *British Journal of Psychiatry, 136,* 235–238.

Corfman, E. (1979). *Depression, manic-depressive illness, and biological rhythms* (DHHS Publication No. (ADM) 81-889). Washington, DC: Department of Health and Human Services.

Coryell, W., & Tsuang, M. T. (1982). Primary unipolar depression and the prognostic importance of delusions. *Archives of General Psychiatry, 39,* 1181–1184.

Coryell, W., & Zimmerman, M. (1984). Outcome following ECT for primary unipolar depression: A test of newly proposed response predictors. *American Journal of Psychiatry, 141,* 862–867.

Costa, E. (1981). The modulation of postsynaptic receptors by neuropeptide cotransmitters: A possible site of action for a new generation of psychotropic drugs. In E. Usdin, W. E. Bunney, & J. M. Davis (Eds.), *Neuroreceptors—Basic and clinical aspects* (pp. 15–25). New York: John Wiley & Sons.

Coursey, R. D. (1975). Personality measures and evoked responses in chronic insomniacs. *Journal of Abnormal Psychology, 84,* 239–249.

Cowdry, R. W., Wehr, T. A., Zis, A. P., & Goodwin, F. K. (1983). Thyroid abnormalities associated with rapid cycling bipolar illness. *Archives of General Psychiatry, 40,* 414–420.

Cox, W. H., Jr. (1982). An indication for the use of imipramine in attention deficit disorder. *American Journal of Psychiatry, 139,* 1059–1060.

Crammer, J. (1975). Lithium, calcium, and mental illness. *Lancet 1,* 215–216.

Crane, G. E. (1957). Isoniazid (Marsilid) phosphate, a therapeutic agent for mental disorders and debilitating disease. *Psychiatric Research Reports, 8,* 142–152.

Crews, F. T., & Smith, C. B. (1978). Presynaptic alpha-receptor subsensitivity after long-term antidepressant treatment. *Science, 202,* 322–324.

Culbreth, D. M. R. (1927). *Materia medica and pharmacology* (7th ed.), p. 743. Cited in Cade, 1949.

Curtius, H-Ch., Niederweiser, A., Levine, R. A., Lovenberg, W., Woggon, B., & Angst, J. (1983). Successful treatment of depression with tetrahydrobiopterin. *Lancet, 1,* 657–658.

Cutler, N. R., & Heiser, J. F. (1978). The tricyclic antidepressants. *Journal of the American Medical Association, 240,* 2264–2266.

Dalby, M. A. (1975). Behavioral effects of carbamazepine. In J. K. Penny & D. D. Daly (Eds.), *Complex partial seizures,* vol. 2 (pp. 331–342). New York: Raven Press.

Damlouji, N. F., & Ferguson, J. M. (1984). Trazodone-induced delirium in bulemic patients. *American Journal of Psychiatry, 141,* 434–435.

Daniel, W. F., & Crovitz, H. F. (1983). Acute memory impairment following electroconvulsive therapy: 2. Effects of electrode placement. *Acta Psychiatrica Scandinavica, 67,* 57–68.

Daniel, W. F., Crovitz, H. F., Weiner, R. D., & Rogers, H. J. (1982). The effects of ECT modifications on autobiographical and verbal memory. *Biological Psychiatry, 17,* 919–924.

Davidson, J., Linnoila, M., Raft, D., & Turnbull, C. D. (1981). MAO inhibition and control of anxiety following amitriptylene therapy. *Acta Psychiatrica Scandinavica, 63,* 147–152.

Davidson, J., McLeod, M. N., & Blum, M. R. (1978). Acetylation phenotype, platelet monoamine oxidase inhibition, and the effectiveness of phenelzine in depression. *American Journal of Psychiatry, 135,* 467–469.

Davidson, J., McLeod, M. N., Law-Yone, B., & Linnoila, M. (1978). A comparison of electroconvulsive therapy and combined perphenazine-amitriptylene in refractory depression. *Archives of General Psychiatry, 35,* 639–642.

Davidson, J., McLeod, M. N., & White, H. L. (1978). Inhibition of platelet monoamine oxidase in depressed subjects treated with phenelzine. *American Journal of Psychiatry, 135,* 470–472.

Davidson, J., & Turnbull, C. (1983). Isocarboxazid: Efficacy and tolerance. *Journal of Affective Disorders, 5,* 183–189.

Davidson, J., Weiss, J., Sullivan, J., Turnbull, C., & Linnoila, M. (1981). A placebo controlled evaluation of isocarboxazid in outpatients. In M. B. H. Youdim & E. S. Paykel (Eds.), *Monoamine oxidase inhibitors—The state of the art* (pp. 115–124). New York: John Wiley & Sons.

Davis, J. M. (1975). Tricyclic antidepressants. In L. L. Simpson (Ed.), *Drug treatment of mental disorders* (pp. 127–146). New York: Plenum Publishing.

Davis, J. M., Dysken, M. W., Matuzas, W. M., & Nasr, S. J. (1983). Some conceptual aspects of laboratory tests in depression. *Journal of Clinical Psychiatry, 44* [Sec. 2], 21–26.

Davis, J. M., Fredman, D. J., & Linden, R. D. (1983). A review of the new antidepressant medication. In J. M. Davis & J. W. Maas (Eds.), *The affective disorders* (pp. 1–29). Washington, DC: American Psychiatric Press.

Davis, J. M., & Vogel, C. (1981). Efficacy of trazodone: Data from European and United States Studies. *Journal of Clinical Psychopharmacology, 1* (No. 6 Suppl.), 27S–34S.

Davis, K. L., & Berger, P. A. (1978). Pharmacological investigations of the cholinergic imbalance hypotheses of movement disorders and psychosis. *Biological Psychiatry, 13,* 23–49.

Davis, K. L., Berger, P. A., Hollister, L. E., & Defraites, E. (1978). Physostigmine in mania. *Archives of General Psychiatry, 35,* 119–122.

Deakin, J. F. W., Owen, F., Cross, A. J., & Dashwood, M. J. (1981). Studies on possible mechanisms of action of electroconvulsive therapy; Effects of repeated electrically induced seizures on rat brain receptors for monoamines and other neurotransmitters. *Psychopharmacology, 73,* 345–349.

d'Elia, G., Ottosson, J-O., & Stromgren, L. S. (1983). Present practice of electroconvulsive therapy in Scandinavia. *Archives of General Psychiatry, 40,* 577–581.

de Montigny, C., & Aghajanian, G. K. (1978). Tricyclic antidepressants: Long-term treatment increases responsivity of rat forebrain neurons to serotonin. *Science, 202,* 1303–1306.

Dilsaver, S. C., Kronfol, Z., Sackellares, J. C., & Greden, J. F. (1983). Antidepressant withdrawal syndromes: Evidence supporting the cholinergic overdrive hypothesis. *Journal of Clinical Psychopharmacology, 3,* 157–164.

Donnelly, E. F., Goodwin, F. K., Waldman, I. N., & Murphy, D. L. (1978). Prediction of antidepressant responses to lithium. *American Journal of Psychiatry, 135,* 552–556.

Dorus, E., Cox, N. J., Gibbons, R. D., Shaughnessy, R., Pandey, G. N., & Cloninger, R. (1983). Lithium ion transport and affective disorders within families of bipolar patients. *Archives of General Psychiatry, 40,* 545–552.

Dorus, E., Pandey, G. N., Shaughnessy, R., Gavira, M., Val, E., Ericksen, S., & Davis, J. M. (1979). Lithium transport across red cell membrane: A cell membrane abnormality in manic-depressive illness. *Science, 205,* 932–933.

Dreyfus, J. (1981). *A remarkable medicine has been overlooked.* New York: Simon and Schuster.

Dunner, D. L., Vijayalakshmy, P., & Fieve, R. R. (1977). Rapid cycling manic depressive patients. *Comprehensive Psychiatry, 18,* 561–566.

Edelstein, P., Schultz, J. R., Hirschowitz, J., Kanter, D. R., & Garver, D. L. (1981). Physostigmine and lithium response in the schizophrenias. *American Journal of Psychiatry, 138,* 1078–1081.

Ehrensing, R. H., & Kastin, A. J. (1974). Melanocyte-stimulating hormone release inhibiting hormone as an antidepressant. *Archives of General Psychiatry, 30,* 63–65.

Ehrensing, R. H., & Kastin, A. J. (1978). Dose-related biphasic effect of prolyl-leucyl-glycinamide (MIF-I) in depression. *American Journal of Psychiatry, 135,* 562–566.

Elithorn, A., Bridges, P. K., Lobban, M. C. & Tredre, B. E. (1966). Observations on some diurnal rhythms in depressive illness. *British Medical Journal 2,* 1620–1623.

Elsinga, S., & Van den Hoofdakker, R. H. (1983). Clinical effects of sleep deprivation and clomipramine in endogenous depression. *Journal of Psychiatric Research, 17,* 361–374.

Elsworth, J. D., Glover, V., Reynolds, G. P., Sandler, M., Lees, A. J., Phupradit, P., Shaw, K. M., Stern, G. M., & Kumar, P. (1978). Deprenyl administration in man: A selective monoamine oxidase B inhibitor without the "cheese effect." *Psychopharmacology, 57,* 33–38.

Emrich, H. M., Vogt, P., Herz, A., & Kissling, W. (1982). Antidepressant effects of buprenorphine. *Lancet 2,* 709.

Enna, S. J., & Kendall, D. A. (1981). Interaction of antidepressants with brain neurotransmitter receptors. *Journal of Clinical Psychopharmacology, 1*(suppl.), 12S–16S.

Ereshefsky, L. (1983). Toxicities of amoxapine. *Clinical Pharmacy, 2,* 106–108.

Erman, M. K., Welch, C. A., & Mandel, M. R. (1979). A comparison of two unilateral ECT electrode placements: Efficacy and electrical energy considerations. *American Journal of Psychiatry, 136,* 1317–1319.

Evans, D. L., & Golden, R. N. (1981). Protriptylene and tinnitus. *Journal of Clinical Psychiatry, 1,* 404–406.

Extein, I. (1982). Case reports of L-triiodothyronine potentiation. *American Journal of Psychiatry, 138,* 966–967.

Extein, I., Potter, W. Z., Wehr, T. A., & Goodwin, F. K. (1979). Rapid mood cycles following a "noradrenergic" but not a "serotonergic" antidepressants. *American Journal of Psychiatry, 136,* 1602–1603.

Extein, I. L., Tallman, J., Smith, C. C., & Goodwin, F. K. (1983, May). *Lymphocyte beta receptors in affective disorders.* Paper presented at the meeting of the American Psychiatric Association, New York.

Fabre, L. F., Brodie, K. H., Garver, D., & Zung, W. W. K. (1983). A multicenter evaluation of bupropion versus placebo in hospitalized depressed patients. *Journal of Clinical Psychiatry, 44,* 88–94.

Fabre, L. F., & Feighner, J. P. (1983). Long-term therapy for depression with trazodone. *Journal of Clinical Psychiatry, 44,* 17–21.

Fankhauser, M. P., Scheiber, S. C., Perrier, D., Finley, P. R., & Potter, R. L. (1983, May). *Single dose prediction methods for antidepressants.* Paper presented at the meeting of the American Psychiatric Association, New York.

Faragella, F. F., & Flach, F. F. (1970). Studies of mineral metabolism in mental depression: I. The effects of imipramine and electric convulsive therapy on calcium balance and kinetics. *Journal of Nervous and Mental Disease, 151,* 120–129.

Faragella, F. F. (1975). Mineral metabolism. In F. F. Flach & S. C. Draghi (Eds.), *The nature and treatment of depression* (pp. 387–395). New York: John Wiley & Sons.

Farkas, T., Dunner, D. L., & Fieve, R. R. (1976). L-tryptophan in depression. *Biological Psychiatry, 11,* 295–302.

Fava, G. A., Molnar, G., Block, B., Lee, J. S., & Perini, G. I. (1984). The lithium loading dose method in a clinical setting. *American Journal of Psychiatry, 141,* 812–813.

Fawcett, J., & Siomopoulos, V. (1971). Dextroamphetamine response as a possible predictor of improvement with tricyclic therapy in depression. *Archives of General Psychiatry, 25,* 247–255.

Fazio, C., Andreoli, V., Agnoli, A., Casacchia, M., Cerbo, R., & Pinzello, A. (1974). Therapy of schizophrenia and depressive disorders with *S*-adenosyl-*L*-methionine. *IRCS Medical Science-Nervous System, 2,* 1015.

Feiger, A. (1983). *Biological testing in psychiatry.* The Upjohn Company, Kalamazoo, MI.

Feighner, J. P. (1982). Benzodiazepines as antidepressants: A triazolobenzodiazepine used to treat depression. *Modern Problems in Pharmacopsychiatry, 18,* 196–212.

Feighner, J. P. (1983). The new generation of antidepressants. *Journal of Clinical Psychiatry, 44* (5, Sec. 2), 49–55.

Feighner, J. P., Robins, E., Guze, S. B., Woodruff, R. A., Winokur, G., & Múnoz, R. (1972). Diagnostic criteria for use in psychiatric research. *Archives of General Psychiatry, 26,* 57–63.

Fieve, R. R., & Jamison, K. R. (1982). Rubidium: Overview and clinical perspectives. *Modern Problems in Pharmacopsychiatry, 18,* 145–163.

Fieve, R. R., Milstoc, M., Kumbaraci, T., & Dunner, D. L. (1976). The effect of lithium on red blood cell cholinesterase activity in patients with affective disorders. *Diseases of the Nervous System, 37,* 240–243.

Fink, M. (1979). *Convulsive therapy: Theory and practice.* New York: Raven Press.

Flach, F. F., & Faragella, F. F. (1970). The effects of imipramine and electric convulsive therapy on the excretion of various minerals in depressed patients. *British Journal of Psychiatry, 116,* 437–438.

Fleiss, J. L. (1973). *Statistical methods for rates and proportions.* New York: John Wiley & Sons.

Folks, D. G., King, L. D., Dowdy, S. B., Petrie, W. M., Jack, R. A., Koomen, J. C., Swenson, B. R., & Edwards, P. (1982). Carbamazepine treatment of selected affectively disordered patients. *American Journal of Psychiatry, 139,* 115–117.

Fraser, A. R. (1983). Choice of antidepressant based on the dexamethasone suppression test. *American Journal of Psychiatry, 140,* 786–787.

Frazer, A. (1981). Antidepressant drugs: Effect on adrenergic responsiveness and monoamine receptors. In E. Usdin, W. E. Bunney, & J. M. Davis (Eds.), *Neuroreceptors—Basic and clinical aspects* (pp. 85–98). New York: John Wiley, & Sons.

Friedel, R. O. (1982). The relationship of therapeutic response to antidepressant plasma levels: An update. *Journal of Clinical Psychiatry, 43,* 37–42.

Friedel, R. O. (1983). Clinical predictors of treatment response. In J. M. Davis and J. W. Maas (Eds.), *The affective disorders* (pp. 379–384). Washington, DC: American Psychiatric Press.

Friedman, E., Cooper, T. B., & Dallob, A. (1983). Effects of chronic antidepressant treatment on serotonin receptor activity in mice. *European Journal of Pharmacology, 89,* 69–76.

Friedman, E., & Dallob, A. (1979). Enhanced serotonin receptor activity after chronic treatment with imipramine or amitriptylene. *Communications in Psychopharmacology, 3,* 89–92.

Friedman, M. J., & Lipowski, Z. J. (1981). Pseudodementia in a young Ph.D. *American Journal of Psychiatry, 138,* 318–382.

Frohlich, J. C., Leftwich, R., Ragheb, M., Oates, J. A., Reiman, M., Oates, J. A., Reiman, I., & Buchanan, D. (1979). Indomethacin increases plasma lithium. *British Medical Journal 1,* 1115–1116.

Fromm-Auch, D. (1982). Comparison of unilateral and bilateral ECT: Evidence for selective memory impairment. *British Journal of Psychiatry, 141,* 608–613.

Gammon, G. D., & Hansen, C. (1984). A case of akinesia induced by amoxapine. *American Journal of Psychiatry, 141,* 283–284.

Garakani, H., Zitrin, C. M., & Klein, D. F. (1984). Treatment of panic disorder with imipramine alone. *American Journal of Psychiatry, 141,* 446–448.

Garcia-Sevilla, J. A., Zis, A. P., Hollingsworth, P. J., Greden, J. F., & Smith, C. B. (1981). Platelet alpha$_2$-adrenergic receptors in major depressive disorder. *Archives of General Psychiatry, 38,* 1327–1333.

Gawin, F. H., & Markoff, R. A. (1981). Panic anxiety after abrupt discontinuation of amitriptylene. *American Journal of Psychiatry, 138,* 117–118.

Gelenberg, A. J., Cooper, D. S., Doller, J. C., & Maloof, F. (1979). Galactorrhea and hyperprolactinemia associated with amoxapine therapy. *Journal of the American Medical Association, 242,* 1900–1901.

General Practitioners Research Group. (1964). Report Number 51: Dexamphetamine compared with an inactive placebo in depression. *Practitioner, 192,* 151.

Ghadirian, A. M., Ananth, J., & Engelsmann, F. (1980). Folic acid deficiency and depression. *Psychosomatics, 21,* 926–929.

Ghadirian, A. M., & Lehmann, H. E. (1980). Neurological side effects of lithium: Organic brain syndrome, seizures, extrapyramidal side effects, and EEG changes. *Comprehensive Psychiatry, 21,* 327–335.

Gillin, J. C., Duncan, W., Pettigrew, K. D., Frankel, B. L., & Snyder, F. (1979). Successful separation of depressed, normal, and insomniac subjects by EEG sleep data. *Archives of General Psychiatry, 36,* 85–90.

Gillin, J. C., & Sitaram, N. (1980). Acetylcholine and norepinephrine: Sleep and mood.

Continuing medical education syllabus and scientific proceedings in summary form: The 133rd annual meeting of the American Psychiatric Association (p. 31). Washington DC: American Psychiatric Association.

Gittelman-Klein, R., & Klein, D. F. (1973). School phobia: Diagnostic considerations in the light of imipramine effects. *The Journal of Nervous and Mental Disorder, 156,* 199–215.

Glassman, A. H., Perel, J. M., Shostak, M., Kantor, S. J., & Fleiss, J. L. (1977). Clinical implications of imipramine plasma levels for depressive illness. *Archives of General Psychiatry, 34,* 197–204.

Gloger, S., Grunhaus, L., Birmacher, B., & Troudart, T. (1981). Treatment of spontaneous panic attacks with chlomipramine. *American Journal of Psychiatry, 138,* 1215–1217.

Glowinski, J., & Alexrod, J. (1964). Inhibition of uptake of tritiated noradrenaline in the intact rat brain by imipramine and structurally related compounds. *Nature, 204,* 1318–1319.

Goldberg, H. L., & DiMascio, A. (1978). Psychotropic drugs in pregnancy. In M. A. Lipton, A. DiMascio, & K. F. Killam (Eds.), *Psychopharmacology: A generation of progress* (pp. 1047–1055). New York: Raven Press.

Goodnick, P. J., Meltzer, H. L., Fieve, R. R., & Dunner, D. L. (1982). Differences in lithium kinetics between bipolar and unipolar patients. *Journal of Clinical Psychopharmacology, 2,* 48–50.

Goodwin, F. K. (Ed.). (1979). The lithium ion [Special issue]. *Archives of General Psychiatry, 38*(8).

Goodwin, F. K., Cowdry, R. W., & Webster, M. H. (1978). Predictors of drug response in the affective disorders: Toward and integrated approach. In M. A. Lipton, A. DiMascio, & K. F. Killam (Eds.), *Psychopharmacology: A generation of progress* (pp. 1277–1278). New York: Raven Press.

Goodwin, F. K., Prange, A. J., Post, R. M., Muscettola, G., & Lipton, M. A. (1982). Potentiation of antidepressant effects by *L*-triiodothyronine in tricyclic nonresponders. *American Journal of Psychiatry, 139,* 34–38.

Goodwin, F. K., & Zis, A. P. (1979). Lithium in the treatment of mania: Comparisons with neuroleptics. *Archives of General Psychiatry, 36,* 840–844.

Gorman, J. M., Fyer, A. F., Gliklich, J., King, D., & Klein, D. F. (1981). Effect of imipramine on prolapsed mitral valves of patients with panic disorder. *American Journal of Psychiatry, 138,* 977–978.

Gram, L. F., Sondergard, I., Christiansen, J., Petersen, G. O., Bech, P., Reisdy, N., Ibsen, I., Ortman, J., Nagy, A., Dencker, S. J., Jacobsen, O., & Krautwald, O. (1977). Steadystate kinetics of imipramine in patients. *Psychopharmacology, 54,* 255–261.

Green, J. P., & Maayani, S. (1977). Tricyclic antidepressant drugs block histamine H2 receptor in brain. *Nature, 269,* 163–165.

Greenblatt, D. J., Divoll, M., Abernethy, D. R., Moschitto, L. J., Smith, R. B., & Shader, R. I. (1983). Alprazolam kinetics in the elderly: Relation to antipyrine disposition. *Archives of General Psychiatry, 40,* 287–290.

Griesemer, E. C., Barsky, J., Dragstedt, C. A., Wells, J. A., & Zeller, E. A. (1953). Potentiating effect of iproniazid on the pharmacological action of sympathomimetic amines. *Proceedings of the Society for Experimental Biology and Medicine, 83,* 699–701.

Grof, P. (1979). Some practical aspects of lithium treatment: Blood levels, dosage prediction, and slow-release preparations. *Archives of General Psychiatry, 36,* 891–893.

Gross, H. A., Ebert, M. H., Faden, V. B., Goldberg, S. C., Nee, L. E., & Kaye, W. H. (1981). A double-blind controlled trial of lithium carbonate in primary anorexia nervosa. *Journal of Clinical Psychopharmacology, 1,* 376–381.

Gross, M. D. (1982). Reversal by bethanechol of sexual dysfunction caused by anticholinergic antidepressants. *American Journal of Psychiatry, 139,* 1193–1194.

Grunhaus, L., Gloger, S., & Birmacher, B. (1984). Clomipramine treatment for panic attacks in patients with mitral valve prolapse. *Journal of Clinical Psychiatry, 45,* 25–27.

Grunhaus, L., Gloger, S., & Weisstub, E. (1981). Panic attacks: A review of treatments and pathogenesis. *The Journal of Nervous and Mental Disease, 169,* 608–613.

Hall, R. C. W., & Zisook, S. (1981). Paradoxical reactions to benzodiazepines. *British Journal of Clinical Pharmacology, 11,* 99S–104S.

Halmi, K. A., Eckert, E., & Falk, J. R. (1983). Cyproheptadine, an antidepressant and weight-inducing drug for anorexia nervosa. *Psychopharmacology Bulletin, 19,* 103–105.

Hamilton, M. (1982). Prediction of the response of depressions to ECT. In R. Abrams and W. B. Essman (Eds.), *Electroconvulsive therapy: Biological foundations and clinical applications* (pp. 113–127). New York: Spectrum Publications.

Hansen, H. E., & Amdisen, A. (1978). Lithium intoxication. *Quarterly Journal of Medicine, 47,* 123–144.

Hare, E. H., Dominian, J., & Sharpe, L. (1962). Phenelzine and dexamphetamine in depressive illness: A comparative trial. *British Medical Journal 1,* 9.

Harrison, W., Stewart, J., Lovelace, R., & Quitkin, F. (1983). Case report of carpal tunnel syndrome associated with tranylcypromine. *American Journal of Psychiatry, 140,* 1229–1230.

Harkness, L., Giller, E. L., Bialos, D., & Waldo, M. C. (1982). Chronic depression: Response to amitriptylene after discontinuation. *Biological Psychiatry, 17,* 913–917.

Harris, W. H., & Beauchemin, J. A. (1959). Cerebrospinal fluid calcium, magnesium, and their ratio in psychosis of organic and functional origin. *Yale Journal of Biological Medicine, 29,* 117–123.

Hemmingsen, R., & Rafaelsen, O. J. (1980). Hypnagogic and hypnopompic hallucinations during amitriptylene treatment. *Acta Psychiatrica Scandinavica. 62,* 364–368.

Hestbech, J., Hansen, H. E., Amdisen, A., & Olsen, S. (1977). Chronic renal lesions following long-term treatment with lithium. *Kidney International, 12,* 205–213.

Hirata, F., & Axelrod, J. (1980). Phospholipid methylation and biological signal transmission. *Science, 209,* 1082–1090.

Hirschowitz, J., Casper, R., Garver, D. L., & Chang, S. (1980). Lithium response in good prognosis schizophrenia. *American Journal of Psychiatry, 137,* 916–920.

Hogben, G. L., & Cornfield, R. B. (1981). Treatment of traumatic war neurosis with phenelzine. *Archives of General Psychiatry, 38,* 440–445.

Hollister, L. E. (1976). Clinical use of tricyclic antidepressants. *Diseases of the Nervous System, 37* [Sec. 2], 17–21.

Imlah, N. W., Ryan, E., & Harrington, J. A. (1965). The influence of antidepressant drugs on the response to electronconvulsive therapy and on subsequent relapse rates. *Neuro-Psychopharmacology, 4,* 438–442.

Insel, T. R., Murphy, D. L., & Alterman, I. S. (1983, May). *Obsessional disorder: Pharmacologic approaches.* Paper presented at the meeting of the American Psychiatric Association, New York.

Isberg, R. S. (1981). A comparison of phenelzine and imipramine in an obsessive-compulsive patient. *American Journal of Psychiatry, 138,* 1250–1251.

Itil, T. M., Patterson, C. D., Polvan, N., Bigelow, A., & Bergey, B. (1975). Clinical and CNS aspects of oral and i.v. thryotropin-releasing hormone in depressed patients. *Diseases of the Nervous System, 36,* 529–536.

Janicak, P. G., Davis, J. M., Gibbons, R. D., Erickson, S., Chang, S., & Gallagher, P. (in press). Efficacy of electro-convulsive therapy (ECT): A meta-analysis. *American Journal of Psychiatry.*

Janowsky, D. S., Abrams, A., McCunney, S., Groom, G., & Judd, L. L. (1979). Lithium and acetylcholine interactions. In K. L. Davis & P. A. Berger (Eds.), *Brain Acetylcholine and Neuropsychiatric Disease* (pp. 45–51). New York: Plenum Publishing.

Janowsky, D. S., & Davis, J. M. (1979). Psychological effects of cholinomimetic agents. In K. L. Davis & P. A. Berger (Eds.), *Brain acetylcholine and neuropsychiatric disease* (pp. 3–14). New York: Plenum Publishing.

Janowsky, D. S., El-Yousef, M. K., Davis, J. M., & Sekerke, H. J. (1972). A cholinergic-adrenergic hypothesis of mania and depression. *The Lancet, 2,* 632–635.

Janowsky, D. S., El-Yousef, M. K., Davis, J. M., & Sekerke, H. J. (1973a). Parasympathetic suppression of manic symptoms by physostigmine. *Archives of General Psychiatry, 28,* 542–547.

Janowsky, D. S., El-Yousef, M. K., Davis, J. M., & Sekerke, H. J. (1973b). Antagonistic effects of physostigmine and methylphenidate in man. *American Journal of Psychiatry, 130,* 1370–1376.

Jefferson, J. W., & Greist, J. H. (1981). Some hazards of lithium use. *American Journal of Psychiatry, 138,* 93–94.

Jenike, M. A. (1981). Rapid response of severe obsessive-compulsive disorder to tranylcypromine. *American Journal of Psychiatry, 138,* 1249–1250.

Jenner, F. A. (1979). Lithium and the question of kidney damage. *Archives of General Psychiatry, 36,* 888–890.

Jobson, K., Linnoila, M., Gillam, J., & Sullivan, J. L. (1978). Successful treatment of severe anxiety attacks with tricyclic antidepressants: A potential mechanism of action. *American Journal of Psychiatry, 135,* 863–864.

Johnstone, E. C. (1976). The relationship between acetylator status and inhibition of monoamine oxidase, excretion of free drug and antidepressant response in depressed patients on phenelzine. *Psychopharmacologia* (Berlin), *46,* 289–294.

Johnstone, E. C., & Marsh, W. (1973). Acetylator status and response to phenelzine in depressed patients. *Lancet, 1,* 567–570.

Johnstone, E. C., Owens, D. G. C., Frith, C. D., McPherson, K., Dowie, C., Riley, G., & Gold, A. (1980). Neurotic illness and its response to anxiolytic and antidepressant treatment. *Psychological Medicine, 10,* 321–328.

Jouvent, R., Abensour, P., Bonnet, A. M., Widlocher, D., Agid, Y., & Lhermitte, F. (1983). Antiparkinsonian and antidepressant effects of high doses of bromocriptine. *Journal of Affective Disorders, 5,* 141–145.

Kafka, M. S., Siever, L. J., Targum, S. D., Lake, C. R., & Van Kammen, D. P. (1983, May). *Alpha-receptor function in some psychiatric disorders.* Paper presented at the meeting of the American Psychiatric Association, New York.

Kafka, M. S., Wirz-Justice, A., Naber, D., Marangos, P. J. O'Donohue, T. L., & Wehr, T. A. (1982). Effect of lithium on circadian neurotransmitter receptor rhythms. *Neuropsychobiology, 8,* 41–50.

Kales, A., Caldwell, A. B., Preston, T. A., Healey, S., & Kales, J. D. (1976). Personality patterns in insomnia. *Archives of General Psychiatry, 33,* 1128–1134.

Kalinowski, L. (1970). Biological psychiatric treatments preceeding pharmacotherapy. In F. Ayd & B. Blackwell (Eds.), *Discoveries in Biological Psychiatry* (pp. 59–67). Philadelphia: J. B. Lippincott.

Kanof, P. D., & Greengard, P. (1978). Brain histamine receptors as targets for antidepressant drugs. *Nature, 272,* 329–333.

Kastin, A. J., Ehrensing, R. H., Schalch, D. S., & Anderson, M. S. (1972). Improvement in mental depression with decreased thyrotropin response after administration of thyrotropin-releasing hormone. *Lancet, 2,* 740–742.

Kay, D. W. K., Fahy, T., & Garside, R. F. (1970). A seven-month double-blind trial of amitriptylene and diazepam in ECT-treated depressed patients. *British Journal of Psychiatry, 117,* 667–671.

Keisling, R. (1983). Carbamazepine and lithium carbonate in the treatment of refractory affective disorders. *Archives of General Psychiatry, 40,* 223.

Kelwala, S., Stanley, M., & Gerson, S. (1983). History of antidepressants: Successes and failures. *Journal of Clinical Psychiatry, 44* (5, Sec. 2), 40–48.

Kessler, K. A. (1978). Tricyclic antidepressants: Mode of action and clinical use. In M. A. Lipton, A. DiMascio, & K. F. Killam (Eds.), *Psychopharmacology: A generation of progress* (pp. 1289–1302). New York: Raven Press.

Kim, W. Y. (1982). Seizures associated with maprotiline. *American Journal of Psychiatry, 139,* 845–846.

King, D. (1980). Sleep deprivation therapy in depression syndromes. *Psychosomatics, 21,* 404–407.

Kirk, L., Baastrup, P. C., & Schou, M. (1972). Propranolol and lithium-induced tremor. *Lancet, 1,* 839.

Kirkegaard, C., & Faber, J. (1981). Altered serum levels of thyroxine, triiodothyronines and diiodothyronines in endogenous depression. *Acta Endocrinologica, 96,* 199–207.

Klein, D. F. (1964). Delineation of two drug-responsive anxiety syndromes. *Psychopharmacologia, 5,* 397–408.

Klein, D. F. (1967). The importance of psychiatric diagnosis in prediction of clinical drug effects. *Archives of General Psychiatry, 16,* 118–126.

Klein, D. F. (1968). Psychiatric diagnosis and a typology of clinical drug effects. *Psychopharmacologia, 13,* 237–254.

Klein, D. F. (1977). Psychopharmacological treatment and the delineation of borderline disorders. In P. Hartocollis (Ed.), *Borderline personality disorders: The concept, the syndrome, the patient* (pp. 365–383). New York: International Universities Press.

Klein, D. F. (1980). Anxiety reconceptualized. *Comprehensive Psychiatry, 21,* 411–427.

Kleitman, N. (1939). *Sleep and Wakefulness.* Chicago: University of Chicago Press.

Klerman, G. L., DiMascio, A., Weissman, M. M., Prussof, B., & Paykel, E. S. (1978). Treatment of depression by drugs and psychotherapy. *American Journal of Psychiatry, 131,* 186–191.

Kline, N. S. (1958). Clinical experience with iproniazid, *Journal of Clinical and Experimental Psychopathology, 19*(Suppl. 1), 72–78.

Kline, N. S., Li, C. H., Lehman, H. E., Lajtha, A., Laski, E., & Cooper, T. (1977). Beta-endorphin-induced changes in schizophrenic and depressed patients. *Archives of General Psychiatry, 34,* 1111–1113.

Knoll, J. (1981). The pharmacology of selective MAO inhibitors. In M. B. H. Youdim and E. S. Paykel (Eds.), *Monoamine Oxidase Inhibitors—The State of the Art* (pp. 45–61). New York: John Wiley & Sons.

Kocsis, J., Bowden, C. L., Chang, S., Casper, R. C., Frazer, A., & Stoll, P. (1983, May). *Tricyclic plasma levels and clinical response.* Paper presented at the meeting of the American Psychiatric Association, New York.

Kraft, T. B. (1983). Psychosis following trazodone administration. *American Journal of Psychiatry, 140,* 1383–1384.

Kramlinger, K. G., Swanson, D. W., & Maruta, T. (1983). Are patients with chronic pain depressed? *American Journal of Psychiatry, 140,* 747–749.

Kripke, D. F., Risch, S. C., & Janowsky, D. S. (1983, May). *One hour of bright light reduces depression.* Paper presented at the meeting of the American Psychiatric Association, New York.

Kufferle, B., & Grunberger, J. (1982). Early clinical double-blind study with *S*-adenosyl-*L*-methionine: A new potential antidepressant. In E. Costa & G. Racagni (Eds.), *Typical and Atypical Antidepressants: Clinical Practice* (pp. 175–180). New York: Raven Press.

Kuhn, R. (1958). The treatment of depressive states with G 22355 (imipramine hydrochloride). *American Journal of Psychiatry, 115,* 459–464.

Kulik, F. A., & Wilbur, R. (1982). Case report of painful ejaculation as a side effect of amoxapine. *American Journal of Psychiatry, 119,* 233–234.

Kupfer, D. J. (1977). EEG sleep correlates of depression in man. In I. Hanin & E. Usdin (Eds.), *Animal models in psychiatry and neurology* (pp. 181–188). Elmsford, NY: Pergamon Press.

Kupfer, D. J., & Foster, F. G. (1975). The sleep of psychotic patients: Does it all look alike? In D. X. Freedman (Ed.), *Biology of the major psychoses* (pp. 143–159). New York: Raven Press.

Kupfer, D. J., Hanin, I., Spiker, D. G., Neil, J., & Coble, P. (1979). EEG sleep and tricyclic plasma levels in primary depression. *Communications in Psychopharmacology, 3,* 73–80.

Kupfer, D. J., Foster, F. G., Reich, L., Thompson, K. S., & Weiss, B. (1976). EEG sleep changes as predictors in depression. *American Journal of Psychiatry, 133,* 622–626.

Kupfer, D. J., Spiker, D. G., Coble, P. A., Neil, J. F., Ulrich, R., & Shaw, D. H. (1981). Sleep and treatment prediction in endogenous depression. *American Journal of Psychiatry, 138,* 429–434.

Kupietz, S. S., & Balka, E. B. (1976). Alterations of the vigilance performance of children receiving amitriptylene and methylphenidate pharmacotherapy. *Psychopharmacology, 50,* 29–33.

Kurelek, W. (1970). *The maze.* From the Houghton Mifflin film series, "The Frontiers of Psychological Inquiry."

Lader, M., & Savage, I. (1981). Clinical and biochemical effects of combined antidepressant therapy. In M. B. H. Youdim & E. S. Paykel (Eds.), *Monoamine oxidase inhibition—The state of the art* (pp. 163–176). New York: John Wiley & Sons.

Langer, S. Z., Zarifan, E., Briley, M., Raisman, R., & Sechter, D. (1982). High-affinity 3H-imipramine binding: A new biological marker in depression. *Pharmacopysychiatry, 13,* 4–10.

Lapierre, Y. D., & Anderson, K. (1983). Dyskinesia associated with amoxapine antidepressant therapy: A case report. *American Journal of Psychiatry, 140,* 493–494.

Lapin, I. P., & Oxenkrug, G. F. (1969). Intensification of the central serotonergic processes as a possible determinant of the thymoleptic effect. *Lancet, 2,* 132–136.

Larsen, J. K., Lindberg, M. L., & Skovgaard, B. (1976). Sleep deprivation as a treatment for endogenous depression. *Acta Psychiatrica Scandinavica, 54,* 167–173.

Law, W. III, Petti, T. A., & Kazdin, A. E. (1981). Withdrawal symptoms after graduated cessation of imipramine in children. *American Journal of Psychiatry, 138,* 647–649.

Leff, M. J., Roatch, J. F., & Bunney, W. R., Jr. (1970). Environmental factors preceding the onset of severe depressions. *Psychiatry, 33,* 298–311.

Lehmann, H. E., Ananth, J., & Geagea, K. C. (1971). Treatment of depression with dexedrine and demerol. *Current Therapy and Research, 13,* 42–49.

Lerer, B., Stanley, M., & Gershon, S. (1983, May). *Cholinergic receptor subsensitivity— A neurochemical basis for ECT-induced amnesia?* Paper presented at the meeting of the American Psychiatric Association, New York.

Lesko, L. M. (1982). Three cases of female anorgasmia associated with MAOIs. *American Journal of Psychiatry, 139,* 1353–1354.

Lesse, S. (1974). Atypical facial pain of psychogenic origin: A masked depression syndrome. In S. Lesse (Ed.), *Masked depression* (pp. 302–317). New York; Jason Aronson.

Lesser, I. (1983). Case report of withdrawal dyskinesia associated with amoxapine. *American Journal of Psychiatry, 140,* 1358–1359.

Lewis, N. D. C., & Piotrowski, Z. A. (1954). Clinical diagnosis of manic-depressive psychosis. In P. Hoch & J. Zubin (Eds.), *Depression.* New York: Grune & Stratton.

Lewi, P. J., & Colpaert, F. C. (1976). On the classification of antidepressant drugs. *Psychopharmacology, 49,* 219–224.

Liebowitz, M. R., Quitkin, F. M., Stewart, J. W., McGrath, P. J., Harrison, W., Rabkin, J. G., Tricamo, E., & Klein, D. F. (1983, May). *Phenelzine vs imipramine in atypical depression*. Paper presented at the meeting of the American Psychiatric Association, New York.

Liebowitz, M. R., Quitkin, F. M., Stewart, J. W., McGrath, P. J., Harrison, W., Rabkin, J., Tricamo, E., Markowitz, J. S., & Klein, D. F. (1984). Phenelzine v imipramine in atypical depression. *Archives of General Psychiatry, 41,* 669–677.

Linnoila, M., Cowdry, R., Lamberg, B-A., Makinen, T., & Rubinow, D. (1983). CSF triiodothyronine (rT3) levels in patients with affective disorders. *Biological Psychiatry, 18,* 1489–1492.

Linnoila, M., George, L., Guthrie, S., & Leventhal, B. (1981). Effect of alcohol consumption and cigarette, smoking on antidepressant levels of depressed patients. *American Journal of Psychiatry, 138,* 841–842.

Linnoila, M., Gualtieri, C. T., Jobson, K., & Staye, J. (1979). Characteristics of the therapeutic response to imipramine in hyperactive children. *American Journal of Psychiatry, 136,* 1201–1203.

Linnoila, M., Karoum, F., & Potter, W. Z. (1982). Effect of low-dose clorgyline on 24-hour urinary monoamine excretion in patients with rapidly cycling bipolar affective disorder. *Archives of General Psychiatry, 39,* 513–516.

Linnoila, M., Simpson, D., & Skinner, T. (1980). Characteristics of therapeutic response to imipramine in cataplectic men. *American Journal of Psychiatry, 137,* 237–238.

Lippman, S., Bedford, P., Manshadi, M., & Mather, S. (1983). Trazodone cardiotoxicity. *American Journal of Psychiatry, 140,* 1383.

Lipsedge, M. S., Hajioft, J., Huggins, P., Napier, L., Pierce, J., Pike, D. J., & Rich, M. (1973). The management of severe agoraphobia: A comparison of iproniazid and systematic desensitization. *Psychopharmacologia, 32,* 67–80.

Lipinsky, J. F., Cohen, B. M., Frankenburg, F., Tohen, M., Waternaux, C., Altesman, R., Jones, B., & Harris, P. (1984). Open trial of *S*-adenosylmethionine for treatment of depression. *American Journal of Psychiatry, 141,* 448–450.

Lipinsky, J. F., & Pope, H. G. (1982). Possible synergistic action between carbamazepine and lithium carbonate in the treatment of three acutely manic patients. *American Journal of Psychiatry, 139,* 948–949.

Lipton, M. A., & Goodwin, F. K. (1975). A controlled study of thyrotropin releasing hormone in hospitalized depressed patients. *Psychopharmacology Bulletin, 11,* 28–29.

Loomer, H. P., Saunders, J. C., & Kline, N. S. (1957). A clinical and pharmacodynamic evaluation of iproniazid as a psychic energizer. *Psychiatric Research of the American Psychiatric Association, 8,* 129–141.

Lopez-Ibor Alino, J. J., Ayuso Gutierrez, J. L., & Montejo Iglesias, M. L. (1973). Tryptophan and amitriptylene in the treatment of depression: A double-blind study. *International Pharmacopsychiatry, 8,* 145–151.

Maany, I. (1981). Treatment of depression associated with Briquet's syndrome. *American Journal of Psychiatry, 138,* 373–376.

MacSweeney, D. A. (1975). Treatment of unipolar depression. *Lancet, 2,* 910–911.

Maitre, L., Delini-Stula, A., & Waldmeier, P. C. (1976). Relations between the degree of monoamine oxidase inhibition and some psychopharmacological responses to monoamine oxidase inhibitors in rats. In Ciba Foundation Symposium 39, *Monoamine Oxidase and its Inhibition* (pp. 247–270). New York: Elsevier-North Holland Publishing.

Malloy, F. W., Small, I. F., Miller, M. J., Milstein, V., & Stout, J. R. (1982). Changes in neuropsychological test performance after electroconvulsive therapy. *Biological Psychiatry, 17,* 61–67.

Mandell, A. J., & Knapp, S. (1977). A neurobiological theory of action of lithium in the treatment of manic-depressive psychosis. In J. M. R. Delgado & F. V. DeFeudis (Eds.), *Behavioral neurochemistry* (pp. 223–249). New York: Spectrum Publications.

Mann, J. J., Aarons, S., Frances, A., Brown, R., & Kocsis, J. (1983, May). *Predictors of antidepressant response to deprenyl.* Paper presented at the meeting of the American Psychiatric Association, New York.

Mann, J. J., Frances, A., Kaplan, R. D., Kocsis, J., & Peselow, E. D. (1982). The relative efficacy of 1-deprenyl, an selective monoamine oxidase type B inhibitor, in endogenous and nonendogenous depression. *Journal of Clinical Psychopharmacology, 2,* 54–57.

Mann, J. J., Stanley, M., & McBride, P. A. (1983, May). *Suicide and a specific serotonin receptor lesion.* Paper presented at the meeting of the American Psychiatric Association, New York.

Marder, S. R., Van Kammen, D. P., Docherty, J. P., Rayner, J., & Bunney, W. E., Jr. (1979). Predicting drug-free improvement in schizophrenic psychosis. *Archives of General Psychiatry, 36,* 1080–1085.

Marini, J. L., & Sheard, M. H. (1977). Antiaggressive effect of lithium ion in man. *Acta Psychiatrica Scandinavica, 55,* 269–286.

Master, R. S., & Zung, W. W. K. (1977). Depressive symptoms in patients and normal subjects in India. *Archives of General Psychiatry, 34,* 972–974.

Mattsson, A., & Seltzer, R. L. (1981). MAOI-induced rapid cycling bipolar affective disorder in an adolescent. *American Journal of Psychiatry, 135,* 677–678.

Matuzas, W., & Glass, R. M. (1983). Treatment of agoraphobia and panic attacks. *Archives of General Psychiatry, 40,* 220–222.

Mavissakalian, M., & Michelson, L. (1983). Tricyclic antidepressants in obsessive-compulsive disorder. *The Journal of Nervous and Mental Disease, 171,* 301–306.

Mavissakalian, M., Perel, J. M., & Michelson, L. (1984). The relationship of plasma imipramine and N-desmethylimipramine to improvement in agoraphobia. *Journal of Clinical Psychopharmacology, 4,* 36–40.

McBride, W. G. (1972). Limb deformities associated with iminodibenzyl hydrochloride. *The Medical Journal of Australia, 1,* 492.

McCabe, M. S., Fowler, R. C., Cadoret, R. J., & Winokur, G. (1971). Familial differences in schizophrenia with good and poor prognosis. *Psychological Medicine, 1,* 326–332.

McGrath, P. J., Quitkin, F. M., Harrison, W., & Stewart, J. W. (1984). Treatment of melancholia with tranylcypromine. *American Journal of Psychiatry, 141,* 288–289.

Mendels, J. (1982). Role of lithium as an antidepressant. *Modern Problems of Pharmacopsychiatry, 18,* 138–144.

Mendels, J., & Chernik, D. A. (1973). The effect of lithium carbonate on the sleep of depressed patients. *International Pharmacopsychiatry, 8,* 184–192.

Mendels, J., Ramsey, A., Dyson, W. L., & Frazer, A. (1979). Lithium as an antidepressant. *Archives of General Psychiatry, 36,* 845–846.

Mendels, J., Secunda, S. K., & Dyson, W. L. (1972). A controlled study of the antidepressant effects of lithium carbonate. *Archives of General Psychiatry, 26,* 154–157.

Mendlewicz, J., Linkowski, P., Branchey, L., Weinberg, U., Weitzman, E. D., & Branchey, M. (1979). Abnormal 24-hour pattern of melatonin secretion in depression. *Lancet, 2,* 1362.

Mendlewicz, J., Pinder, R. M., Stulemeijer, S. M., & Van Orth, R. (1982). Monoamine metabolites in cerebrospinal fluid of depressed patients during treatment with mianserin or amitriptyline. *Journal of Affective Disorders, 4,* 219–226.

Mendlewicz, J., & Youdim, M. B. H. (1980). Antidepressant potentiation of 5-hydroxytryptophan by L-deprenil in affective illness. *Journal of Affective Disorders, 2,* 137–146.

Mendlewicz, J., & Youdim, M. B. H. (1981). A selective MAO-B Inhibitor (L-deprenil) and 5-HTP as antidepressant therapy. In M. B. H. Youdim & E. S. Paykel (Eds.), *Monoamine oxidase inhibitors—The state of the art* (pp. 177–188). New York: John Wiley & Sons.

Menkes, D. B., Aghajanian, G. K., & McCall, R. B. (1980). Chronic antidepressant treatment enhances alpha-adrenergic and serotonergic responses in the facial nucleus. *Life Sciences, 27,* 45–55.

Miccoli, L., Porro, V., & Bertolino, A. (1978). Comparison between the antidepressant activity of S-adenosylmethionine (SAMe) and that of some tricyclic drugs. *Acta Neurologica, 33,* 243–255.

Mielke, D. H. (1976). Adverse reactions of thymoleptics. In D. M. Gallant and G. M. Simpson (Eds.), *Depression: Behavioral, biochemical, diagnostic and treatment concepts* (pp. 273–307). New York: Spectrum Publications.

Mills, M. J., Pearsall, D. T., Yesavage, J. A., & Salzman, C. (1984). Electroconvulsive therapy in Massachusetts. *American Journal of Psychiatry, 141,* 534–538.

Mindham, R. H. S., Howland, C., & Shepherd, M. (1973). An evaluation of continuation therapy with tricyclic antidepressants in depressive illness. *Psychological Medicine, 3,* 5–17.

Mirin, S. M., Schatzberg, A. F., & Creasey, D. E. (1981). Hypomania and mania after withdrawal of tricyclic antidepressants. *American Journal of Psychiatry, 138,* 87–89.

Moore, D. C. (1977). Amitriptylene therapy in anorexia nervosa. *American Journal of Psychiatry, 134,* 1303–1304.

Morris, J. B., & Beck, A. T. (1974). The efficacy of antidepressant drugs: A review of research (1958–1972). *Archives of General Psychiatry, 30,* 667–674.

Mountjoy, C. Q., Roth, M., Garside, R. F., & Leitch, L. (1977). A clinical trial of phenelzine in anxiety depressive and phobic neurosis. *British Journal of Psychiatry, 131,* 486–492.

Munro, J. G., Hardiker, T. M., & Leonard, D. P. (1984). The dexamethasone suppression test in residual schizophrenia with depression. *American Journal of Psychiatry, 141,* 250–252.

Murphy, D. L., Baker, M., Kotin, J., & Bunney, W. E., Jr. (1973). Behavioral and metabolic effects of L-tryptophan in unipolar depressed patients. In J. Barchas & E. Usdin (Eds.), *Serotonin and behavior* (pp. 529–534). New York: Academic Press.

Murphy, D. L., & Beigel, A. (1974). Depression, elation, and lithium carbonate responses in manic patient subgroups. *Archives of General Psychiatry, 31,* 643–684.

Murphy, D. L., Cohen, R. M., Siever, L. J., & Roy, B. F. (1983, May). *Mode of antidepressant action of selective MAOI.* Paper presented at the meeting of the American Psychiatric Association, New York.

Murphy, D. L., Lipper, S., Pickar, D., Jimerson, D., Cohen, R. M., Garrick, N. A., Alterman, I. S., & Campbell, I. C. (1981). Selective inhibition of monoamine oxidase type A: Clinical antidepressant effects and metabolic changes in man. In M. B. H. Youdim & E. S. Paykel (Eds.), *Monoamine oxidase inhibitors—The state of the art* (pp. 189–205). New York: John Wiley & Sons.

Murphy, D. L., Siever, L. J., Cohen, R. M., Roy, B. F., & Pickar, D. (1983). Some clinical evidence supporting the possible involvement of neurotransmitter receptor sensitivity changes in the action of antidepressant drugs during long-term treatment. In J. M. Davis & J. W. Maas (Eds.), *The affective disorders* (pp. 317–332). Washington, DC: American Psychiatric Press.

Musa, M. N. (1979). Imipramine plasma level differences in depression types. *Research Communications in Psychology, Psychiatry and Behavior, 4,* 109–114.

Musa, M. N. (1981). Depression sub-types affect the steady-state plasma levels and therapeutic efficacy of amitriptylene and nortriptylene. *Research Communications in Psychology, Psychiatry and Behavior, 6,* 1–8.

Musa, M. N. (1983). Variability of steady-state plasma concentration of desipramine among depression types. *Research Communications in Psychology, Psychiatry and Behavior, 8,* 55–60.

Muscettola, G., Galzenati, M., & Balbi, A. (1982). SAMe versus placebo: A double-blind comparison in major depressive disorders. In E. Costa and G. Racagni (Eds.), *Typical and atypical antidepressants: Clinical practice* (pp. 151–156). New York: Raven Press.

Muscettola, G., Goodwin, F. K., Potter, W. Z., Claeys, M. M., & Markey, S. P. (1978). Imipramine and desipramine in plasma and spinal fluid: Relationship to clinical response and serotonin metabolism. *Archives of General Psychiatry, 35,* 621–625.

Narsapur, S. L., & Naylor, G. J. (1983). Methylene blue: A possible treatment for manic depressive psychosis. *Journal of Affective Disorders, 5,* 155–161.

Nasr, S., Altman, E. G., & Meltzer, H. Y. (1981). Concordance of atopic and affective disorders. *Journal of the Affective Disorders, 3,* 291–296.

Nasr, S. J., & Atkins, R. W. (1977). Coincidental improvement in asthma during lithium treatment. *American Journal of Psychiatry, 134,* 1042–1043.

Needleman, H. L., & Weber, D. (1977). The use of amitriptylene in anorexia nervosa. In R. A. Vigersky (Ed.), *Anorexia nervosa* (pp. 357–362). New York: Raven Press.

Neff, N. H., & Fuentes, J. A. (1976). The use of selective monoamine oxidase inhibitor drugs for evaluating pharmacological and physiological mechanisms. In Ciba Foundation Symposium 39, *Monoamine oxidase and its inhibition* (pp. 163–179). New York: Elsevier-North Holland Publishing.

Nelson, H. B. (1984). Cost effectiveness of carbamazepine in refractory bipolar illness. *American Journal of Psychiatry, 141,* 465.

Nelson, J. C., Jatlow, P., Quinlan, D. M., & Bowers, M. B., Jr. (1982). Desipramine plasma concentration and antidepressant response. *Archives of General Psychiatry, 39,* 1419–1422.

Nelson, W. H., Orr, W. W., Stevenson, J. M., & Shane, S. R. (1982). Hypothalamic-pituitary-adrenal axis activity and tricyclic response in major depression. *Archives of General Psychiatry, 39,* 1033–1036.

Nies, A., Robinson, D. S., Friedman, M. J., Green, R., Cooper, T. B., Ravaris, C. L., & Ives, J. O. (1977). Relationship between age and tricyclic antidepressant plasma levels. *American Journal of Psychiatry, 134,* 790–793.

Nolen, W. A. (1983). Carbamazepine, a possible adjunct or alternative to lithium in bipolar disorder. *Acta Psychiatrica Scandinavica, 67,* 218–225.

Noll, K. M., & Davis, J. M. (1983). Biological theories in schizophrenia. In A. Rifkin (Ed.), *Schizophrenia and affective disorders: Biology and drug treatment* (pp. 139–204). Boston: John Wright-PSG.

Nurnberg, H. G., & Coccaro, E. F. (1982). Response of panic disorder and resistance of depression to imipramine. *American Journal of Psychiatry, 139,* 1060–1062.

Okuma, T., Inanga, K., & Otsuki, S. (1979). Comparison of the antimanic efficacy of carbamazepine and chlorpromazine: A double-blind controlled study. *Psychopharmacology, 66,* 211–217.

Okuma, T., Inanga, K., Otsuki, S. (1981). A preliminary double-blind study on the efficacy of carbamazepine in the prophylaxis of manic-depressive illness. *Psychopharmacology, 73,* 95–96.

Olsen, H., & Morland, J. (1978). Ethanol-induced increase in drug acetylation in man and isolated rat liver cells. *British Medical Journal 2,* 1260–1262.

Overall, J. E., Hollister, L. E., Pokorny, A. D., Casey, J. F., & Katz, G. (1962). Drug therapy in depressions: Controlled evaluation of imipramine, isocarboxazid, dextroamphetamine, amobarbital, and placebo. *Clinical and Pharmacological Therapy, 3,* 16.

Oxenkrug, G. H., Prakhje, I., & Mikhalenko, I. N. (1978). Disturbed circadian rhythm of 5HT uptake by blood platelets in depressive psychosis. *Activitas Nervosa Superior, 20,* 66–67.

Pandey, G. N., & Davis, J. M. (1981). Treatment with antidepressants, sensitivity of beta-adrenergic receptors and affective illness. In E. Usdin, W. E. Bunney, & J. M. Davis (Eds.), *Neuroreceptors—Basic and clinical aspects* (pp. 99–120). New York: John Wiley & Sons.

Pandey, G. N., Dorus, E., Davis, J. M., & Tosteson, D. C. (1979). Lithium transport in human red blood cells. *Archives of General Psychiatry, 36,* 902–908.

Pandey, G. N., Krueger, A., Sudershan, P., & Davis, J. M. (1982). Treatment with antidepressants and histamine receptor mediated 3H-cyclic AMP formation in guinea pig cortex. *Life Sciences, 30,* 921–927.

Pare, C. M. B. (1976). Introduction to clinical aspects of monoamine oxidase inhibitors in the treatment of depression. In Ciba Foundation Symposium 39, *Monoamine oxidase and its inhibition* (pp. 271–280). New York: Elsevier-North Holland Publishing.

Paul, S. M., Extein, I., Calil, H. M., Potter, W. Z., Chodoff, P., & Goodwin, F. K. (1981). Use of ECT with treatment-resistant depressed patients at the National Institute of Mental Health. *American Journal of Psychiatry, 138,* 486–489.

Paul, S. M., Rehavi, M., Skolnick, P., & Goodwin, F. K. (1981). High affinity binding sites for [3H] imipramine in human brain and platelet: Clinical implications. *Advances in the Biosciences, 31,* 187–194.

Paykel, E. S., Mueller, P. S., & De la Vergne, P. M. (1973). Amitriptylene, weight gain, and carbohydrate craving: A side effect. *British Journal of Psychiatry, 123,* 501–507.

Paykel, E. S., Rowan, P. R., Parker, R. R., & Bhat, A. V. (1982). Response to phenelzine and amitriptylene in subtypes of outpatient depression. *Archives of General Psychiatry, 39,* 1041–1049.

Paykel, E. S., West, P. S., Rowan, P. R., & Parker, R. R. (1982). Influence of acetylator phenotype on antidepressant effects of phenelzine. *British Journal of Psychiatry, 141,* 243–248.

Pecknold, L. C., & Ban, T. A. (1977). TRH in depressive illness. *Pharmacopsychiatry, 12,* 166–173.

Penry, J. K., & Daly, D. D. (Eds.). (1975). *Complex partial seizures: Neurology* (Vol. 2). New York: Raven Press.

Peroutka, S. J., & Snyder, S. H. (1980). Long-term antidepressant treatment decreases spiropridol-labeled serotonin receptor binding. *Science, 210,* 88–90.

Perry, P. J., Morgan, D. E., Smith, R. E., & Tsuang, M. T. (1982). Treatment of unipolar depression accompanied by delusions. *Journal of Affective Disorders, 4,* 195–200.

Peselow, E. D., Deutsch, S. I., & Fieve, R. R. (1983). Imipramine plasma levels and clinical response in depressed outpatients. *Research Communications in Psychology, Psychiatry, and Behavior, 8,* 75–83.

Petti, T. A., & Unis, A. (1981). Imipramine treatment of borderline children: Case reports with a controlled study. *American Journal of Psychiatry, 138,* 515–518.

Pettinati, H. M., & Bonner, K. M. (1984). Cognitive functioning in depressed geriatric patients with a history of ECT. *American Journal of Psychiatry, 141,* 49–52.

Pflug, B., & Tolle, R. (1971). Disturbance of the 24-hour rhythm in endogenous depression and the treatment of endogenous depression by sleep deprivation. *International Pharmacopsychiatry, 6,* 187–196.

Pickar, D., Murphy, D. L., Cohen, R. M., Campbell, I. C., & Lipper, S. (1982). Selective and nonselective monoamine oxidase inhibitors: Behavioral disturbances during their administration to depressed patients. *Archives of General Psychiatry, 39,* 535–540.

Pilowsky, I., & Bassett, D. L. (1982). Pain and depression. *British Journal of Psychiatry, 141,* 30–36.

Pitts, W. M., Fann, W. E., Sajadi, C., & Snyder, S. (1983). Alprazolam in older depressed inpatients. *Journal of Clinical Psychiatry, 44,* 213–215.

Pohl, R. (1983). Anorgasmia caused by MAOIs. *American Journal of Psychiatry, 140,* 510.

Pope, H. G., Jr., Hudson, J. I., Jonas, J. M., & Yurgelun-Todd, D. (1983). Bulimia treated with imipramine: A placebo-controlled, double-blind study. *American Journal of Psychiatry, 140,* 554–558.

Post, R. M., Udhe, T. W., Ballenger, J. C., Chatterji, D. C., Greene, R. F., & Bunney, W. E., Jr. (1983a). Carbamazepine and its -10,11-epoxide metabolite in plasma and CSF. *Archives of General Psychiatry, 40,* 673–676.

Post, R. M., Uhde, T. W., Ballenger, J. C., & Squillace, K. M. (1983b). Prophylactic efficacy of carbamazepine in manic-depressive illness. *American Journal of Psychiatry, 140,* 1602–1604.

Potter, W. Z., Murphy, D. L., Wehr, T. A., Linnoila, M., & Goodwin, F. K. (1982). Clorgyline: A new treatment for patients with rapid-cycling disorder. *Archives of General Psychiatry, 39,* 505–510.

Potter, W. Z., Zavadil, A. P., Kopin, I. J., & Goodwin, F. K. (1980). Single-dose kinetics predict steady-state concentrations of imipramine and desipramine. *Archives of General Psychiatry, 37,* 314–320.

Poust, R. J., Mallinger, A. G., & Mallinger, J. (1976). Pharmacokinetics of lithium in human plasma and erythrocytes. *Psychopharmacological Communications, 2,* 91–103.

Prabhu, V., & el-Guebaly, N. (1983). Cortisol secretion and DST in affective disorders—Methodological concerns. *Canadian Journal of Psychiatry, 28,* 602–611.

Prakash, R., & Petrie, W. M. (1982). Psychiatric changes associated with an excess of folic acid. *American Journal of Psychiatry, 139,* 1192–1193.

Prange, A. J., Jr., & Loosen, P. T. (1982). Neuropeptides as novel antidepressants. *Modern Problems in Pharmacopsychiatry, 18,* 164–177.

Prange, A. J., Jr., & Wilson, I. C. (1972). Thyrotropin releasing hormone (TRH) for the immediate relief of depression: A preliminary report. *Psychopharmacologia, 26,* 82.

Prange, A. J., Jr., Wilson, I. C. Knox, A., McClane, T. K., & Lipton, M. A. (1970). Enhancement of imipramine by thyroid stimulating hormone: Clinical and theoretical implications. *American Journal of Psychiatry, 127,* 191–199.

Prange, A. J., Jr., Wilson, I. C., Lara, P. P., Alltop, L. B., & Breese, G. R. (1972). Effects of thyrotropin-releasing hormone in depression. *Lacet, 2,* 999–1002.

Prange, A. J., Jr., Wilson, I. C., Rabon, A. M., & Lipton, M. A. (1969). Enhancement of imipramine antidepressant activity by thyroid hormone. *American Journal of Psychiatry, 126,* 457–469.

Preskorn, S. H., & Hartman, B. (1979). The effect of tricyclic antidepressants on cerebral fluid dynamics. *Biological Psychiatry, 14,* 235–250.

Preskorn, S. H., Irwin, G. H., Simpson, S., Friesen, D., Rinne, J., & Jerkovich, G. (1981). Medical therapies for mood disorders alter the blood-brain barrier. *Science, 213,* 469–471.

Price Evans, D. A., Davison, K., & Pratt, R. T. C. (1963). The influence of acetylator phenotype on the effects of treating depression with phenelzine. *Clinical Pharmacology and Therapeutics, 6,* 430–435.

Price Evans, D. A., & White, T. A. (1964). Human acetylation polymorphism. *Journal of Laboratory and Clinical Medicine, 63,* 394–403.

Prien, R. F., Caffey, E. M., & Klett, C. J. (1973). Lithium carbonate and imipramine in prevention of depressive episodes. *Archives of General Psychiatry, 29,* 420–425.

Putnam, P. L. (1978). Possible positive "side effects" of lithium. *American Journal of Psychiatry, 135,* 388.

Quitkin, F. M., Liebowitz, M. R., McGrath, P. J., Harrison, W., & Rabkin, J. G. (1983, May). *A trial of deprenyl in atypical depression.* Paper presented at the meeting of the American Psychiatric Association, New York.

Quitkin, F., Rifkin, A., Kane, J., Ramos-Lorenzi, J. R., & Klein, D. F. (1978). Prophylactic effect of lithium and imipramine in unipolar and bipolar II patients. *American Journal of Psychiatry, 135,* 570–572.

Quitkin, F., Rifkin, A., & Klein, D. F. (1978). Imipramine response in deluded depressive patients. *American Journal of Psychiatry, 135,* 806–811.

Racy, J., & Ward-Racy, E. A. (1980). Tinnitus in imipramine therapy. *American Journal of Psychiatry, 137,* 854–855.

Ragheb, M., Ban, T. A., Buchanan, D., & Frohlich, J. C. (1980). Interaction of indomethacin and ibuprofen with lithium in manic patients under a steady-state lithium level. *Journal of Clinical Psychiatry, 41,* 397–398.

Ramirez, A. L. (1983). Seizures associated with maprotiline. *American Journal of Psychiatry, 140,* 509–510.

Ramsey, T. A., Frazer, A., Mendels, J., & Dyson, W. L. (1979). The erythrocyte lithium-plasma lithium ratio in patients with primary affective disorder. *Archives of General Psychiatry, 36,* 457–461.

Rao, B., & Broadhurst, A. D., (1976). Tryptophan and depression. *British Medical Journal, 1,* 460.

Rapoport, J. L., Mikkelsen, E. J., Zavadil, A., Nee, L., Gruenau, C., Mendelson, W., & Gillin, J. C. (1980). Childhood enuresis: II. Psychopathology, tricyclic concentration in plasma, and antienuretic effect. *Archives of General Psychiatry, 37,* 1146–1152.

Ravaris, C. L., Robinson, D. S., Ives. J. O., Nies, A., & Bartlett, D. (1980). Phenelzine and amitriptylene in the treatment of depression: A comparison of present and past studies. *Archives of General Psychiatry, 37,* 1075–1080.

Reed, K., Smith, R. C., Schoolar, J. C., Hu, R., Leelavathi, D. E., Mann, E., & Lippman, L. (1980). Cardiovascular effects of nortriptylene in geriatric patients. *American Journal of Psychiatry, 137,* 986–989.

Rees, L., & Davies, B. (1961). A controlled trial of phenelzine (Nardil) in the treatment of severe depressive illness. *Journal of Mental Science, 107,* 560.

Reimann, I. W., Diener, U., & Frohlich, J. C., (1983). Indomethacin but not aspirin increases plasma lithium ion levels. *Archives of General Psychiatry, 40,* 283–286.

Reimann, I. W., Frohlich, J. C. (1980). Effects of diclofenac on lithium kinetics. *Clinical Pharmacology and Therapy, 30,* 348–352.

Reich, J., Tupin, J., & Abramowitz, S. I., (1983). Psychiatric diagnosis of chronic pain patients. *American Journal of Psychiatry, 140,* 1495–1498.

Reisberg, B., & Gershon, S. (1979). Side effects associated with lithium therapy. *Archives of General Psychiatry, 36,* 879–887.

Reynolds, E. H., Chanarin, I., Milner, G., & Matthews, D. M. (1966). Anticonvulsant therapy, folic acid and vitamin B12 metabolism and mental symptoms. *Epilepsia, 7,* 261–270.

Reynolds, E. H., Preece, J. M., Bailey, J., & Coppen, A. (1970). Folate deficiency in depressive illness. *British Journal of Psychiatry, 117,* 287–292.

Reynolds, E. H., & Stramentinoli, G. (1983). Folic acid, *S*-adenosylmethionine and affectve disorder. *Psychological Medicine, 13,* 705–710.

Rich, C. L. (1984) Recovery from depression after one ECT. *American Journal of Psychiatry, 141,* 1010–1011.

Rich, C. L., Spiker, D. G., Jewell, S. W., & Neil, J. F. (1984). *DSM-III,* RDC, and ECT: Depressive subtypes and immediate response. *Journal of Clinical Psychiatry, 45,* 14–18.

Richelson, E. (1980). Psychotrophic drugs and histamine II_1-receptors of cultured mouse neuroblastoma cells. *Psychopharmacology Bulletin, 16,* 38–40.

Richelson, E. (1981). Tricyclic antidepressants: Interactions with histamine and muscarinic acetylcholine receptors. In S. J. Enna, J. B. Malick, & E. Richelson (Eds.), *Antidepressants: Neurochemical, behavioral, and clinical perspectives,* (pp. 53–73). New York: Raven Press.

Richelson, E. (1982). Pharmacology of antidepressants in use in the United States. *Journal of Clinical Psychiatry, 43* [Sec. 2], 4–11.

Rickels, K., Hutchinson, J. C., Weise, C. C., Csanalosi, I., Chung, H. R., & Case W. G. (1972). Doxepin and amitriptylene-perphenazine in mixed anxious-depressed neurotic outpatients: A collaborative controlled study. *Psychopharmacologia, 23,* 305–318.

Rifkin, A., Klein, D. F., Dillon, D., & Levitt, M. (1981). Blockade by imipramine or desipramine of panic induced by sodium lactate. *American Journal of Psychiatry, 138,* 676–677.

Robertson, M. M., & Trimble, M. R. (1982). Major tranquilizers used as antidepressants. *Journal of Affective Disorders, 4,* 173–193.

Robinson, D. S., Nies, A., Ravaris, C. L., Ives, J. O., & Bartlett, D. (1978). Clinical pharmacology of phenelzine. *Archives of General Psychiatry, 35,* 629–635.

Rosenbaum, A. H., Schatzberg, A. F., Maruta, T., Orsulak, P. J., Cole, J. O., Grab, E. L., & Schildkraut, J. J. (1980). MHPG as a predictor of antidepressant response to imipramine and maprotiline. *American Journal of Psychiatry, 137,* 1091–1092.

Rosenbaum, J. F., Woods, S. W., Groves, J. E., & Klerman, G. L. (1984). Emergence of hostility during alprazolam treatment. *American Journal of Psychiatry, 141,* 792–793.

Rosenthal, N. E., Sack, D. A., Gillin, J. C., Lewy, A. J., Goodwin, F. K., Davenport, Y., Mueller, P. S., Newsome, D. A., & Wehr, T. A. (1984). Seasonal affective disorder. *Archives of General Psychiatry, 41,* 72–80.

Rosenthal, N. E., Sack, D. A., Parry, B. L., Mendelson, W., Davenport, Y., Lewy, A. J., Gillin, J. C., & Wehr, T. A. (1983, May). *Seasonal affective disorder and phototherapy.* Paper presented at the meeting of the American Psychiatric Association, New York.

Ross, D. R., Walker, J. I., & Peterson, J. (1983). Akathisia induced by amoxapine. *American Journal of Psychiatry, 140,* 115–116.

Ross, R. J., Hauger, R., Scheinin, M., Linnoila, M., & Potter, W. Z. (1983, May). *Mechanism of action of clorgyline.* Paper presented at the meeting of the American Psychiatric Association, New York.

Rudolf, von G. A. E., Bischofs, W., Blaszkiewicz, F., Bremer, W., & Tolle, R. (1976). Kreislauffunctionen im unbeeinflussten und modifizierten zirkadianen rhythmus bei depressionen. [Circulatory function in natural and modified circadian rhythm in depression.] *Drug Research, 26,* 1174–1177.

Russell, R. W., Pechnick, R., & Jope, R. S. (1981). Effects of lithium on behavioral reactivity: Relation to increases in brain cholinergic activity. *Psychopharmacology, 73,* 120–125.

Sakel, M. (1956). The classical Sakel shock treatment: A reappraisal. In F. Marti-Ibanez, A. M. Sackler, M. D. Sackler, & R. R. Sackler (Eds.), *The great physiodynamic therapies in psychiatry* (pp. 13–75). New York: Hoeber-Harper.

Sandler, M. (1981). Deprenyl, monoamine oxidase inhibition and the "cheese effect": Some outstanding problems. In M. B. H. Youdim & E. S. Paykel (Eds.), *Monoamine oxidase inhibitor—The state of the art* (pp. 207–212). New York: John Wiley & Sons.

Sathananthan, G. L., Gershon, S., Almeida, M., Spector, N., & Spector, S. (1976). Correlation between plasma and cerebrospinal fluid levels of imipramine. *Archives of General Psychiatry, 33,* 1109–1110.

Schatzberg, A. F., Cole, J. O., & Blumer, D. P. (1978). Speech blockage: A tricyclic side effect. *American Journal of Psychiatry, 135,* 600–601.

Scher, M., Krieger, J. N., & Juergens, S. (1983). Trazodone and priapism. *American Journal of Psychiatry, 140,* 1362–1363.

Schildkraut, J. J. (1965). The catecholamine hypothesis of affective disorders: A review of supporting evidence. *American Journal of Psychiatry, 122,* 509–522.

Schildkraut, J. J., & Kety, S. S. (1967). Biogenic amines and emotion. *Science, 156,* 21–30.

Schilgen, von B., Bischofs, W., Blaszkiewicz, F., Bremer, W., Rudolf, G. A. E., & Tolle, R. (1976). Totaler and partieller schlafentzug in der behandlung von depressionen. [Total and partial sleep deprivation in the treatment of depression]. *Drug Research, 26,* 1171–1173.

Schou, M. (1958). Lithium studies: I. Renal elimination. *Acta Pharmacologica et Toxicologica, 15,* 85–98.

Schou, M. (1968). Lithium in psychiatric therapy and prophylaxis. *Journal of Psychiatric Research, 6,* 67–95.

Schou, M., Baastrup, P. C., Gros, P. (1970). Pharmacological and clinical problems of lithium prophylaxis. *British Journal of Psychiatry, 116,* 615–619.

Schou, M., Juel-Neilson, N., Stromgren, E., & Voldby, H. (1954). The treatment of manic psychoses by the administration of lithium salts. *Journal of Neurology, Neurosurgery and Psychiatry, 17,* 250–260.

Schubert, H., Fleischhacker, W. W., & Demel, I. (1982). Bromocriptin bei organischen depressionen. [Bromocriptine in organic depression]. *Pharmacopsychiatry, 15,* 103–106.

Schwarcz, G. (1982). Case report of inhibition of ejaculation and retrograde ejaculation as side effects of amoxapine. *American Journal of Psychiatry, 139,* 233–234.

Schwartz, L., & Swaminathan, S. (1982). Maprotiline hydrochloride and convulsions. *American Journal of Psychiatry, 139,* 244–245.

Scovern, A. W., & Kilmann, P. R. (1980). Status of electroconvulsive therapy: Review of the outcome literature. *Psychological Bulletin, 87,* 260–303.

Seager, C. P., & Bird, R. L., (1962). Imipramine with electrical treatment in depression—A controlled trial. *Journal of Mental Science, 108,* 704–707.

Seifert, R., Bremkamp, H., & Junge, C. (1975). Vereinfachte lithiumeinstellung durch belastungstest. [Simplified lithium adjustment by means of a loading-dose test]. *Psychopharmacologia, 43,* 285–286.

Selikoff, T. J., Robitzek, E. H., & Ornstein, G. C. (1952). Toxicity of hydrazine derivatives of isonicotinic acid in the chemotherapy of human tuberculosis. *Quarterly Bulletin of Sea View Hospital, 13,* 17.

Sheard, M. H., Marini, J. L., Bridges, C. I., & Wagner, E. (1976). The effect of lithium on impulsive aggressive behavior in man. *American Journal of Psychiatry, 133,* 1409–1413.

Sheehan, D. U., Ballenger, J., & Jacobsen, G. (1980). Treatment of endogenous anxiety with phobic, hysterical and hypochondriacal symptoms. *Archives of General Psychiatry, 36,* 51–59.

Shen, W. W. (1982). Female orgasmic inhibition by amoxapine. *American Journal of Psychiatry, 139,* 1220–1221.

Sherman, A. (1979). Time course of the effects of antidepressants on serotonin in rat neocortex. *Communications in Psychopharmacology, 3,* 1–5.

Sholomskas, A. J. (1978). Speech blockage in young patients taking tricyclics. *American Journal of Psychiatry, 135,* 1572–1573.

Shopsin, B. (1978). Enhancement of the antidepressant response to *L*-tryptophan by a liver pyrrolase inhibitor: A rational treatment approach. *Neuropsychobiology, 4,* 188–192.

Shopsin, B. (1980). Second generation antidepressants. *Journal of Clinical Psychiatry, 41* (12, Sec. 2), 45–56.

Shopsin, B., Friedman, E., & Gershon, S. (1976). Parachlorophenylalanine reversal of tranylcypromine effects in depressed patients. *Archives of General Psychiatry, 33,* 811–819.

Shopsin, B., Johnson, G., & Gershon, S. (1970). Neurotoxicity with lithium: Differential drug responsiveness. *International Pharmacopsychiatry, 5,* 170–182.

Shur, E., Checkley, S., & Delgado, I. (1983). Failure of mianserin to affect autonomic function in the pupils of depressed patients. *Acta Psychiatrica Scandinavica, 67,* 50–55.

Siever, L. J., Cohen, R. M., & Murphy, D. L. (1981). Antidepressants and alpha$_2$-adrenergic autoreceptor desensitization. *American Journal of Psychiatry, 138,* 681–682.

Siever, L. J., Kafka, M. S., Targum, S. D., Lake, C. R., & Murphy, D. L. (1983, May). *Platelet alpha$_2$-adrenergic receptor number and function in depression.* Paper presented at the meeting of the Association for Biological Psychiatry, New York.

Siever, L. J., & Lewy, A. (1983, May). *Adrenergic metabolism and alpha$_2$-adrenergic receptors.* Paper presented at the meeting of the American Psychiatric Association, New York.

Simon, P., Lecrubier, Y., Puech, A., & Widlocher, D. (1983). Beta-adrenergic stimulants and depressive states. In J. M. Davis & J. W. Maas (Eds.), *The affective disorders* (pp. 273–281). Washington, DC: American Psychiatric Press.

Simpson, G. M., Pi, E. H., & White, K. (1983). Plasma drug levels and clinical response to antidepressants. *Journal of Clinical Psychiatry, 44,* 27–34.

Simpson, G., White, K., Pi., E. H., Razani, J., & Sloane, R. B. (1983, May). *Tyramine sensitivity in deprenyl-treated patients.* Paper presented at the meeting of the American Psychiatric Association, New York.

Siris, S. G., Cooper, T. B., Rifkin, A. E., Brenner, R., & Lieberman, J. A. (1982). Plasma imipramine concentrations in patients receiving concomitant fluphenazine decanoate. *American Journal of Psychiatry, 139,* 104–106.

Sitaram, N., Moore, A. J., & Gillin, J. C. (1978). The effect of physostigmine on normal human sleep and dreaming. *Archives of General Psychiatry, 35,* 1239–1243.

Sitaram, N., Nurnberger, J. I., Jr., Gershon, E. S., & Gillin, J. C. (1980). Faster cholinergic REM sleep induction in euthymic patients with primary affective illness. *Science, 208,* 200–202.

Smith, C. B., Hollingsworth, P. J., & Zis, A. P. (1983, May). *Platelet alpha₂ receptors in psychiatric patients.* Paper presented at the meeting of the American Psychiatric Association, New York.

Smith, R. C., Misra, C. H., Leelavathi, D. E., Shelat, H., Allen, R., Schoolar, J., & Gordon, J. (1981). Receptor studies of the effects and blood levels of neuroleptic and antidepressant drugs. In E. Usdin, W. E. Bunney, & J. M. Davis (Eds.), *Neuroreceptors—Basic and clinical aspects* (pp. 215–230). New York: John Wiley & Sons.

Snyder, S. H., & Peroutka, S. J. (1983). A possible role of serotonin receptors in antidepressant drug action. *Pharmacopsychiatry, 15,* 131–134.

Snyder, S. H., & Yamamura, H. I. (1977). Antidepressants and the muscarinic acetylcholine receptor. *Archives of General Psychiatry, 34,* 236–238.

Solyom, L., Heseltine, G. F. D., McClure, D. J., Solyom, C., Ledwidge, B., & Steinberg, G. (1973). Behaviour therapy vs. drug therapy in the treatment of phobic neurosis. *Journal of the Canadian Psychiatric Association, 18,* 25–32.

Spiker, D. G., Edwards, D., Hanin, I., Neil, J. F., & Kupfer, D. J. (1980). Urinary MHPG and clinical response to amitriptylene in depressed patients. *American Journal of Psychiatry, 137,* 1183–1187.

Spitzer, R. L., Endicott, J., & Robins, E. (1978). Research diagnostic criteria: Rationale and reliability. *Archives of General Psychiatry, 35,* 773–782.

Squire, L. R. (1977). ECT and memory loss. *American Journal of Psychiatry, 134,* 997–1001.

Squire, L. R., & Chace, P. M. (1975). Memory functions six to nine months after electroconvulsive therapy. *Archives of General Psychiatry, 32,* 1557–1564.

Squire, L. R., Wetzel, C. D., & Slater, P. C. (1979). Memory complaint after electroconvulsive therapy: Assessment with a new self-rating instrument. *Biological Psychiatry, 14,* 791–801.

Stancer, H. C., & Persad, E. (1982). Treatment of intractable manic-depressive disorder with levothyroxine. *Archives of General Psychiatry, 39,* 311–312.

Stanley, M., Mann, J. J., & Gershon, S. (1983, May). *Serotonergic receptor alterations in the brains of suicide victims.* Paper presented at the meeting of the Society for Biological Psychiatry, New York.

Stern, S. L., Rush, A. J., & Mendels, J. (1980). Toward a rational pharmacotherapy of depression. *American Journal of Psychiatry, 137,* 545–552.

Stewart, J. W., Quitkin, F., Fyer, A., Rifkin, A., McGrath, P., Liebowitz, M., Rosnick, L., & Klein, D. F. (1980). Efficacy of desipramine in endogenomorphically depressed patients. *Journal of Affective Disorders, 2,* 165–176.

Stewart, J. W., Quitkin, F. M., Liebowitz, M. R., McGrath, P. J., Harrison, W. M., & Klein, D. F. (1983). Efficacy of desipramine in depressed outpatients. *Archives of General Psychiatry, 40,* 202–207.

Sulser, F. (1983). Antidepressant treatments: Regulation and adaptation of functional receptor systems. In J. M. Davis & J. W. Mass (Eds.), *The affective disorders* (pp. 261–272). Washington, DC: American Psychiatric Press.

Sun, M. (1982). Book touts Dilantin for depression. *Science, 215,* 951–952.

Sunderland, T., Orsulak, P. J., & Cohen, B. M. (1983). Amoxapine and neuroleptic side effects: A case report. *American Journal of Psychiatry, 140,* 1233–1235.

Suranyi-Cadotte, B., Nair, N. P. V., Wood, P. L., & Schwartz, G. (1983, May). *Platelet 3H-imipramine binding: Clinical implications.* Paper presented at the meeting of the American Psychiatric Association, New York.

Svendsen, K. (1976). Sleep deprivation therapy in depression. *Acta Psychiatrica Scandinavica, 54,* 184–192.

Svensson, T. H. (1980). Effect of chronic treatment with tricyclic antidepressant drugs on identified brain noradrenergic and serotonergic neurons [Monograph]. *Acta Psychiatrica Scandinavica, 61,* (suppl. 280), 121–131.

Svensson, T. H., & Usdin, T. (1978). Feedback inhibition of brain noradrenaline neurons by tricyclic antidepressants: alpha-receptor mediation. *Science, 202,* 1089–1091.

Takezabi, H., & Hanaoka, M. (1971). The use of carbamazepine in the control of manic-depressive psychosis and other manic-depressive states. *Journal of Clinical Psychiatry, 13,* 173–183.

Targum, S. D., Greenberg, R. D., Harmon, R. L., Kessler, K., Salerian, A. J., & Fram, D. H. (1984). The TRH test and thyroid hormone in refractory depression. *American Journal of Psychiatry, 141,* 463.

Taylor, M. A., & Abrams, R. (1975). Acute manic—Clinical and genetic study of responders and nonresponders to treatments. *Archives of General Psychiatry, 32,* 863–865.

Thoren, P., Asberg, M., Bertilsson, L., Mellstrom, B., Sjoqvist, F., & Traskman, L. (1980). Clomipramine treatment of obsessive-compulsive disorder: II. Biochemical aspects. *Archives of General Psychiatry, 37,* 1289–1294.

Thoren, P., Asberg, M., Cronholm., B., Jornestedt, L., & Traskman, L. (1980). Clomipramine treatment of obsessive-compulsive disorder: I. A controlled clinical trial. *Archives of General Psychiatry, 37,* 1281–1285.

Thorley, G. (1984). Review of follow-up and follow-back studies of childhood hyperactivity. *Psychological Bulletin, 96,* 116–132.

Thornton, J. E., & Stahl, S. M. (1984). Case report of tardive dyskinesia and Parkinsonism associated with amoxapine therapy. *American Journal of Psychiatry, 141,* 704–705.

Tollefson, G., Lesar, T., & Herzog, C. (1984). Atrial flutter and maprotiline. *Journal of Clinical Psychiatry, 45,* 31–33.

Tollefson, G. D., & Senogles, S. (1982). A cholinergic role in the mechanism of lithium in mania. *Biological Psychiatry, 18,* 467–479.

Trimble, M. R., Corbett, J. A., & Donaldson, D. (1980). Folic acid and mental symptoms in children with epilepsy. *Journal of Neurology, Neurosurgery, and Psychiatry, 43,* 1030–1034.

Tuomisto, J. (1974). A new modification for studying 5-HT uptake by blood platelets: A reevaluation of tricyclic antidepressants as uptake inhibitors. *Journal of Pharmacy and Pharmacology, 26,* 92–100.

Turner, S. M., Hersen, M., Bellack, A. S., Andrasik, F., & Capparell, H. V. (1980).

Behavioral and pharmacological treatment of obsessive-compulsive disorders. *The Journal of Nervous and Mental Disease, 168,* 651–657.

Tyrer, P., Candy, J., & Kelly, J. (1973). Phenelzine in phobic anxiety: A controlled trial. *Psychological Medicine, 3,* 120–124.

Tyrer, P., Gardner, M., Lambourn, J., & Whitford, M. (1981). Dosage and acetylator status in clinical response to phenelzine. In M. B. H. Youdim & E. S. Paykel (Eds.), *Monoamine oxidase inhibitors—The state of the art* (pp. 149–161). New York: John Wiley & Sons.

Tyrer, P., & Steinberg, D. (1975). Symptomatic treatment of agoraphobia and social phobias: A follow-up study. *British Journal of Psychiatry, 127,* 163–168.

U'Prichard, D. C., Greenberg, D. A., Sheehan, P. P., & Snyder, S. H. (1978). Tricyclic antidepressants: Therapeutic properties and affinity for alpha-noradrenergic receptor binding sites in the brain. *Science, 199,* 197–198.

Van Bemmel, A. L., & Van den Hoofdakker, R. H. (1981). Maintenance of therapeutic effects of total sleep deprivation by limitation of subsequent sleep. *Acta Psychiatrica Scandinavica, 63,* 453–462.

Van den Burg, W., van Praag, H. M., Bos, E. R. H., Piers, D. A., van Zanton, A. K., & Doorenbos, H. (1975). TRH as a possible quick-acting but short-lasting antidepressant. *Psychological Medicine, 5,* 404–412.

Van den Burg, W., van Praag, H. M., Bos, E. R. H., Piers, D. A., van Zanton, A. K., & Doorenbos, H. (1976). TRH by slow continuous infusion: An antidepressant? *Psychological Medicine, 6,* 393–397.

Van der Kolk, B. A., Shader, R. I., & Greenblatt, D. J. (1978). Autonomic effects of psychotropic drugs. In M. A. Lipton, A. DiMascio, & K. F. Killam (Eds.), *Psychopharmacology: A generation of progress* (pp. 1009–1020). New York: Raven Press.

Van der Vis-Melsen, M. J. E., & Weiner, J. D. (1972). Improvement in mental depression with decreased thyrotropin response after administration of thyrotropin-releasing hormone. *Lancet, 2,* 1415.

Van Kammen, D. P., Docherty, J. P., Marder, S. R., & Bunney, W. E., Jr. (1981). Acute amphetamine response predicts antidepressant and antipsychotic responses to lithium carbonate in schizophrenic patients. *Psychiatry Research, 4,* 313–325.

Van Kammen, D. P., & Murphy, D. L. (1978). Prediction of imipramine antidepressant response by a one-day *d*-amphetamine trial. *American Journal of Psychiatry, 135,* 1179–1184.

Van Praag, H. M. (1981). Management of depression with serotonin precursors. *Biological Psychiatry, 16,* 291–310.

Van Praag, H. M. (1982). Significance of serotonin precursors as antidepressants. *Modern Problems in Pharmacopsychiatry, 18,* 117–138.

Venkoba Rao, A., & Nammalvar, N. (1977). The course and outcome in depressive illness: A follow-up study of 122 cases in Madurai, India. *British Journal of Psychiatry, 130,* 392–396.

Verebey, K., Volovka, J., & Clovet, D. (1978). Endorphins in psychiatry. *Archives of General Psychiatry, 35,* 877–888.

Vestergaard, P., Amdisen, A., & Schou, M. (1980). Clinically significant side effects of lithium treatment. *Acta Psychiatrica Scandinavica, 62,* 193–200.

Waldmeier, P. C., Felner, A. E., & Maitre, L. (1981). Long-term effects of selective MAO inhibitors on MAO activity and amine metabolism, In M. B. H. Youdim & E. S. Paykel (Eds.), *Monoamine Oxidase Inhibitors—The State of the Art.* New York: John Wiley & Sons Ltd.

Walinder, J., Skott, A., Carlsson, A., Nagy, A., & Roos, B-E. (1976). Potentiation of the antidepressant action of clomipramine by tryptophan. *Archives of General Psychiatry, 33,* 1384–1389.

Wallach, M. B., & Hedley, L. R. (1979). The effects of antihistamines in a modified bahavioral despair test. *Communications in Psychopharmacology, 3,* 35–39.

Walsh, B. T., Stewart, J. W., Wright, L., Harrison, W., Roose, S. P., & Glassman, A. H. (1982). Treatment of bulemia with monoamine oxidase inhibitors. *American Journal of Psychiatry, 139,* 1629–1630.

Ward, N. G., & Bloom, V. (1979). Treatment of patients with pain and depression. In *Somatic depression: Special insights for primary care physicians.* (Postgraduate Medicine Communications, Special Report, March 1979). New York: Pfizer Laboratories Division, Pfizer, Inc.

Ward, N. G., Bloom, V. L., & Friedel, R. O. (1979). The effectiveness of tricyclic antidepressants in the treatment of coexisting pain and depression. *Pain, 7,* 331–341.

Ward, N. G., Friedel, R. O., & Bloom, V. L. (1978, September). *The relationship of tricyclic plasma levels to antidepressant response.* Paper presented at the meeting of the American Psychiatric Association 30th Institute on Hospital and Community Psychiatry, Kansas City, MO.

Watanabe, S., Ishino, H., & Otsuki, S. (1975). Double-blind comparison of lithium carbonate and imipramine in treatment of depression. *Archives of General Psychiatry, 32,* 659–668.

Weaver, L., & Williams, R. W. (1982). The electroconvulsive therapy stimulus. In R. Abrams & W. B. Essman (Eds.), *Electroconvulsive therapy: Biological foundations and clinical applications* (pp. 129–156). New York: Spectrum Publications.

Wehr, T. A., & Goodwin, F. K. (1979). Rapid cycling in manic depressives induced by tricyclic antidepressants. *Archives of General Psychiatry, 36,* 555–559.

Wehr, T. A., Goodwin, F. K., Wirz-Justice, A., Breitmaier, J., & Craig, C. (1982). 48-hour sleep-wake cycles in manic-depressive illness. *Archives of General Psychiatry, 39,* 559–565.

Wehr, T. A., & Wirz-Justice, A. (1982). Circadian rhythm mechanisms in affective illness and in antidepressant drug action. *Pharmacopsychiatry, 15,* 31–39.

Wehr, T. A., Wirz-Justice, A., & Goodwin, F. K. (1983). Circadian rhythm disturbances in affective illness and their modification by antidepressant drugs. In J. M. Davis & J. W. Maas (Eds.), *The affective disorders* (pp. 333–346). Washington; DC: American Psychiatric Press.

Wehr, T. A., Wirz-Justice, A., Goodwin, F. K., Duncan, W., & Gillin, J. C. (1979). Phase advance of the circadian sleep-wake cycle as an antidepressant. *Science, 206,* 710–713.

Weinberger, D. R. (1977). Tricyclic choice for ill elderly patients. *American Journal of Psychiatry, 134,* 1048.

Weinstock, M., & Cohen, D. (1976). Tricyclic antidepressant drugs as antagonists of muscarinic receptors in sympathetic ganglia. *European Journal of Pharmacology, 40,* 321–328.

Weise, C. C., Stein, M. K., Pereira-Ogan, J., Csanalosi, I., & Rickels, K. (1980). Amitriptyline once daily versus three times daily in depressed outpatients. *Archives of General Psychiatry, 37,* 555–560.

Werry, J. S., Aman, M. G., & Diamond, E. (1980). Imipramine and methylphenidate in hyperactive children. *Journal of Child Psychology and Psychiatry, 21,* 27–35.

Wetterberg, L., Beck-Friis, J., Aperia, B., & Petterson, U. (1979). Melatonin/cortisol ratio in depression. *Lancet, 2,* 1361.

White, J. H., & Schnaultz, N. L. (1977). Successful treatment of anorexia nervosa with imipramine. *Diseases of the Nervous System, 38,* 567–568.

Wilson, I. C., Prange, A. J., Jr., McClane, T. K., Rabon, A. M., & Lipton, M. A. (1970). Thyroid-hormone enhancement of imipramine in non-retarded depression. *New England Journal of Medicine, 282,* 1063–1067.

Winokur, G., Behar, D., Van Valkenburg, C., & Lowry, M. (1978). Is a familial definition of depression both feasible and valid? *Journal of Nervous and Mental Disorder, 166,* 764–768.

Wirz-Justice, A., Puhringer, W., & Hole, G. (1979). Response to sleep deprivation as a predictor of therapeutic results with antidepressant drugs. *American Journal of Psychiatry, 136,* 1222–1223.

Wood, C. A., Brown, J. R., Coleman, J. H., & Evans, W. E. (1976). Management of tricyclic toxicities. *Diseases of the Nervous System, 37,* 459–461.

Worrall, E. P., Moody, J. P., Peet, M., Dick, P., Smith, A., Chambers, C., Adams, M., & Naylor, G. J. (1979). Controlled studies of the acute antidepressant effects of lithium. *British Journal of Psychiatry, 135,* 255–262.

Wyatt, R. J., Fram, D. H., Buchbinder, R., & Snyder, F. (1971). Treatment of intractable narcolepsy with monoamine oxidase inhibitor. *New England Journal of Medicine, 285,* 987–991.

Zeigler, V. E., Co, B. T., & Biggs., J. T. (1977). Plasma nortriptylene levels and ECG findings. *American Journal of Psychiatry, 134,* 441–443.

Zeller, E. A., & Barsky, J. (1952). In vivo inhibition of liver and brain monoamine oxidase by 1-isonicotinyl-2-isopropyl hydrazine. *Proceedings of the Society for Experimental Biology and Medicine, 81,* 459–461.

Zeller, E. A., Barsky, J., Fouts, J. R., Kirchheimer, W. F., & Van Orden, L. S. (1952). Influence of isonicotinic acid hydrazide (INH) and 1-isonicotinyl-2-isopropyl hydrazide (IIH) on bacterial and mammalian enzymes. *Experientia, 8,* 349–350.

Zimanova, J., & Vojtechovsky, M. (1974). Sleep deprivation as a potentiation of antidepressive pharmacotherapy? *Activitas Nervosa Superior, 16,* 188–189.

Zis, A. P., & Goodwin, F. K. (1979). Major affective disorder as a recurrent illness. *Archives of General Psychiatry, 36,* 835–839.

Zitrin, C. M., Klein, D. F., & Woerner, M. G. (1978). Behavior therapy, supportive psychotherapy, imipramine, and phobias. *Archives of General Psychiatry, 35,* 307–316.

Zitrin, C. M., Klein, D. F., & Woerner, M. G. (1980). Treatment of agoraphobia with group exposure in vivo and imipramine. *Archives of General Psychiatry, 37*, 63–72.

Zsilla, G., Barbaccia, M. L., Gandolfi, O., Knoll, J., & Costa, E. (1983). (-)-Deprenyl a selective MAO "B" inhibitor increases [3H] imipramine binding and decreases beta-adrenergic receptor function. *European Journal of Pharmacology, 89*, 111–117.

Zubenko, G. S., & Nixon, R. A. (1984). Mood-elevating effect of captopril in depressed patients. *American Journal of Psychiatry, 141*, 110–111.

Zung, W. W. K. (1977). Operational diagnosis and diagnostic categories of depressive disorders. In W. E. Fann, I Karacan, A. D. Pokorny, & R. L. Williams (Eds.), *Phenomenology and treatment of depression* (pp. 217–234). New York: Spectrum Publications.

Zung, W. W. K. (1983). Review of placebo-controlled studies with bupropion. *Journal of Clinical Psychiatry, 44* (5, sec. 2), 104–114.

Chapter 10

The Comparative Efficacy of Psychotherapy and Pharmacotherapy for Depression

Ernest Edward Beckham
William R. Leber
Department of Psychiatry and Behavioral Sciences; University of Oklahoma Health Sciences Center

The question of whether medication or psychotherapy is more effective in the treatment of unipolar depression has become an important theoretical and practical issue. Theoretically, it has implications for understanding the nature of depression. On a practical level, it is important for clinicians to know which treatment or combination of treatments will alleviate depression most quickly and lastingly. Professional issues also arise because of the considerable competition today between groups providing mental health care. Decisions regarding whether patients need psychotherapy or medication structure the relationships between physicians and nonphysicians in community mental health centers, hospitals, and private practice.

There is now considerable experimental evidence that both psychotherapy and pharmacotherapy can be powerful treatments for outpatients with unipolar depression. Interestingly, some of the most rigorous evidence for the efficacy of psychotherapy in treating depression has come from studies where it was compared with pharmacotherapy. Psychotherapy research on depression benefited from the comparative studies because, among other things, many of the studies used clinically depressed subjects diagnosed by strict diagnostic inclusion criteria and employed ratings by blind clinical evaluators instead of relying solely on self-report instruments. Such methodological improvements have since been increasingly incorporated in psychotherapy research.

This chapter will attempt to do three things: (1) review the existing studies; (2) discuss the research issues in this area; and (3) point out the clinical implications of research findings to date.

Preparation of this manuscript was supported in part by Grant MH33760 from the National Institute of Mental Health.

SUMMARY OF STUDIES COMPARING MEDICATION AND PSYCHOTHERAPY

Early Studies

The three earliest studies to examine the relative merits of psychotherapy and pharmacotherapy for depression were done by Covi, Lipman, Derogatis, Smith, and Pattison (1974); Friedman (1975); and Klerman, DiMascio, Weissman, Prusoff, and Paykel (1974). Covi et al. (1974) compared the effects of imipramine, diazepam, and placebo for a sample of women between the ages of 20 and 50. Patients in each of the medication treatments received either 20 minutes contact every two weeks (the psychotherapy control group), or 90 minutes a week of intensive dynamic group psychotherapy. Results showed imipramine to be clearly more effective than diazepam and placebo. Amount of psychotherapy contact had no effect on depressive symptoms for the sample as a whole; however, persons with low initial levels of interpersonal sensitivity (irritability, feelings of inadequacy, criticalness) were more likely to benefit from being assigned to the intensive group therapy rather than to the minimal supportive therapy (Covi, Lipman, Alarcon, & Smith, 1976). For further information on this study, the reader is referred to Lipman and Covi (1976).

Friedman (1975) compared the effects of amitriptyline and placebo administered over 12 weeks. Patients in each drug condition received either high psychotherapeutic contact in the form of marital therapy or low psychotherapeutic contact (one-half hour every two weeks). The patients receiving the combination of active medication and marital therapy showed the greatest improvement on most outcome measures. Compared to marital therapy, the effects of drug therapy appeared faster, showing a greater amount of relief from symptoms after four weeks of treatment. However, after 12 weeks of treatment there was no difference in the amount of symptom relief between drug therapy and marital therapy. Marital therapy was superior to amitriptyline in its improvement of patient participation and performance of family-role tasks, and in its bringing about of a positive perception of marital relationships.

Neither of the above studies directly compared patients receiving no pill at all (all patients received at least a placebo) with patients receiving medication alone. It is conceivable that patients receiving psychotherapy alone might respond somewhat differently from those receiving a placebo with their psychotherapy. The first study to make such a comparison was done by Klerman et al. (1974). Klerman et al. compared the effectiveness of amitriptyline and short-term psychotherapy for the maintenance of depressives who had already recovered on a regimen of amitriptyline. Their design crossed medication (amitriptyline, placebo, and no pill) with amount of psychotherapy contact (an hour a week of interpersonal psychotherapy with a social worker, or 15 minutes monthly contact during medication visits). Patients receiving amitriptyline were less likely to relapse than those taking placebo and no pill. Weekly psychotherapy was not more effective in preventing symptomatic relapse compared to the minimal contact. However, patients receiving weekly psychotherapy had better social adjustment at eight months than patients not receiving it (Weissman, Klerman, Paykel, Prusoff, & Hanson, 1974). Overall, the combination of treatments was the most efficacious since patients in it had both a lower relapse rate and higher social functioning. A limitation of this study was that all patients had already been treated with amitriptyline. Thus, patients may have regarded psychotherapy as a second-class therapy. New treatment alliances had to be formed with therapists by patients in the psychotherapy condition. Obviously, patients who did not respond to medication in the acute phase of treatment were not included in the study since this was a maintenance study. A later study by the same research group (Weissman, Prusoff, DiMascio, Neu, Goklaney, & Klerman, 1979) used subjects who had not yet received treatment at the research site.

Treatment of Acute Depression with Interpersonal Therapy

Weissman et al. (1979) compared the effects of short-term interpersonal psychotherapy (IPT) and no psychotherapy, in conjunction with subjects being treated by pharmacotherapy or receiving no pill at all. A description of interpersonal psychotherapy can be found elsewhere in this book and in the published treatment manual (Klerman, Weissman, Rounsaville, & Chevron, 1984). Both the psychotherapy alone and the amitriptyline alone were more effective than the nonscheduled control treatment, and the combination of pharmacotherapy and psychotherapy was more effective than either treatment alone. Overall, the individual treatments were approximately equal in effectiveness. However, after random treatment assignment more persons refused psychotherapy (32 percent) than pharmacotherapy (17 percent), combined treatment (4 percent), or even nonscheduled treatment (9 percent). Once in treatment, only 40 percent of patients completed the pharmacotherapy alone treatment, whereas 70 percent completed treatment in the psychotherapy and combined treatment conditions (Herceg-Baron, Prusoff, Weissman, DiMascio, Neu, & Klerman, 1979). Pharmacotherapy quickly improved vegetative symptoms such as sleep and appetite disturbance, while psychotherapy was superior in having a rapid effect on depressive mood, suicidal ideation, work adjustment, and improvement in interests (DiMascio, Weissman, Prusoff, Neu, Zwelling, & Klerman, 1979). The additive effect of the combined treatment condition was hypothesized to result from its having the advantages of each of the individual treatments.

The Research Diagnostic Criteria subtypes of situational depression and endogenous depression proved predictive of differential treatment response (Prusoff, Weissman, Klerman, & Rounsaville, 1980). Endogenous depression responded poorly to the interpersonal psychotherapy alone, but responded well to the combination treatment, whereas nonendogenous depression responded best to the interpersonal psychotherapy and did not benefit from the addition of amitriptyline to the IPT treatment. Whether or not depression was diagnosed as situational was also predictive of treatment response. Situational depressions responded well to all treatments, whereas nonsituational depressions responded best to combined treatment only. Differential treatment response was not predicted by personality characteristics (Zuckerman, Prusoff, Weissman, & Padian, 1980). However, Zuckerman et al. did find that persons low in neuroticism and high in extroversion, as measured by the Maudsley Personality Inventory, had the best social adjustment at the one-year follow-up, no matter what treatment they received.

After one year, the significant differences in depressive symptoms among treatment groups had disappeared, and most patients were asymptomatic. The only remaining difference in treatment effects was that patients treated with IPT were functioning better socially (Weissman, Klerman, Prusoff, Sholomskas, & Padian, 1981).

Further studies comparing IPT and medication are being done at the University of Pittsburgh and the University of Southern California (Klerman, et al., 1984, p. 21). The University of Pittsburgh will test various combinations of IPT, imipramine, and placebo with outpatients with recurrent depression. The USC study will examine the efficacy of nortriptyline, placebo, and IPT for ambulatory depressed elderly.

Comparisons of Cognitive Therapy with Pharmacotherapy

The first study to directly compare medication against psychotherapy alone without a pill of any sort was done by Rush, Beck, Kovacs, and Hollon (1977). The study was simple in design, yet significant in its impact because it was the first to suggest that psychotherapy might be more effective than medication for outpatient depression. Seventy-nine percent of patients receiving cognitive/behavioral therapy showed marked improvement, that is, had final Beck Depression Inventory (BDI) scores less than 10. However, only 22 percent of patients receiving imipramine showed marked improvement. In addition, fewer patients assigned to cognitive/behavioral therapy terminated prematurely. Pharmacotherapy significantly reduced the level of depression in subjects receiving it. However, cognitive/behavioral therapy was more effective as judged not only by BDI scores, but also by Hamilton and Raskin scores. The multiplicity of types of outcome scores is important because the Beck Depression Inventory heavily weights cognitive symptoms of depression which might be expected to improve as a direct result of cognitive therapy. Cognitive therapy also resulted in significantly greater improvement in self-concept and hopelessness (Rush, Beck, Kovacs, Weissenburger, & Hollon, 1982). No clear differential treatment effectiveness was found between patients with endogenous and nonendogenous depressions (Kovacs, Rush, Beck, & Hollon, 1981). However, Research Diagnostic Criteria subtypes were not diagnosed and the endogenicity measure was based on Hamilton items, which may be an inadequate method of assessing endogenous depression. At a 12-month follow-up, cognitive-behavioral patients still had lower BDI scores, but no difference was apparent between groups in Hamilton and Raskin scores. Patients in the pharmacotherapy condition relapsed at twice the rate of the psychotherapy patients; however, this difference was not statistically significant. While the 12-month follow-up revealed no major differences between patient groups, this does not necessarily mean that the treatments were essentially equal. First, it has been pointed out by some psychotherapy researchers that the goal of psychotherapy may be to hasten the remission of symptoms, since many symptoms (including depression) will often eventually remit without treatment. Cognitive/behavioral therapy did apparently produce remission more rapidly than medication in this study. Second, it is impossible to prevent patients who do not improve from seeking further help. Patients who are still depressed at the end of a study are likely to seek further help, and one would expect that without rigorous control of patient contacts with professional and nonprofessional helpers, treatment differences will be minimized in follow-up evaluations.

Another study at Philadelphia (Beck, Hollon, Young, & Bedrosian, 1979) examined the comparative efficacy of cognitive behavioral therapy (CBT) versus CBT plus amitriptyline. Both treatment conditions resulted in significant decreases in depressive symptomatology. There was no difference in results between treatments, except that a greater percentage of patients receiving the cognitive therapy alone had "marked" or "complete" improvement. There was a trend for patients receiving the combination treatment to have less symptomatology at the one-year follow-up, but this may have been due to the fact that those patients received more follow-up treatment than the cognitive therapy alone group.

Blackburn, Bishop, Glen, Whalley, and Christie (1981) tested the efficacy of cognitive therapy alone, medication alone (amitriptyline or clomipramine), and a combination treatment of both. Subjects were hospital and general practice outpatients. For the hospital outpatient group the combination treatment was more effective than either of the individual treatments on six out of seven measures. However, in the general practice outpatient group, cognitive therapy was as effective as the combination treatment on all seven measures. Medication alone ranked third in effectiveness in the hospital outpatient group and a poor third in general practice outpatients. An attempt was made to separate endogenous from nonendogenous patients using items from the Hamilton Rating Scale for Depression. However, no interaction was found between this measure and type of treatment. This study has been criticized on the grounds that the response to pharmacotherapy of the general practice outpatients was unusually poor and was based on a small number of subjects (Goldberg, 1982).

Teasdale, Fennell, Hibbert, and Amies (1984) compared "treatment as usual" (TAU) delivered by general practice physicians against the same treatment plus cognitive therapy. The cognitive therapy was administered by a clinical psychologist. "Treatment as usual" consisted of visits to general practitioners where the physicians were told to "treat patients as they would normally." Of 17 patients in this condition, 10 were taking antidepressant medication within the recommended dose range. Thus, treatment as usual included medication as a major part of the therapy. The combined treatment group achieved significantly better posttreatment scores on all measures of depression. However, there were no differences between groups at a three-month follow-up.

A recent study by Hollon and colleagues at the University of Minnesota examined the efficacy of cognitive therapy, cognitive therapy in combination with imipramine, imipramine alone, and acute imipramine treatment followed by maintenance imipramine therapy until the end of the follow-up period of one year (DeRubeis, 1983). At the end of 12 weeks, the combined treatment was significantly more effective than imipramine alone. The advantage of combined therapy over cognitive therapy did not reach statistical significance. At the end of the six-month follow-up period, persons who had received cognitive therapy with or without medication were less likely to have relapsed or to have sought further treatment than persons receiving the acute imipramine therapy (no maintenance). In general, the treatments including cognitive therapy were more likely to bring about sustained remission than the medication only conditions, though these differences did not attain significance. A final important observation is that there were two successful suicides and two unsuccessful attempts in this study. All of them used the study medication as the means of their attempt. Three of the patients were receiving drug only treatment; one was in the combined treatment but had not yet received the first session of cognitive therapy. As mentioned later in this chapter, in discussing the relative efficacy of treatments, suicidal patients may require special consideration.

Murphy, Simons, Wetzel, and Lustman (1984) compared cognitive therapy, nortriptyline, a combination of cognitive therapy and nortriptyline, and cognitive therapy plus active placebo. Seventy of 87 patients assigned to treatment completed the protocol. All treatment groups were significantly improved, and there was no differential effectiveness among treatments in reducing depressive symptoms. However, there were differences in dropout rates. Patients receiving medication alone were most likely to drop out, and patients receiving cognitive therapy in conjunction with either medication or placebo were least likely to drop out (Simons, Levine, Lustman, & Murphy, 1984). Patients high in learned resourcefulness, as measured by the Rosenbaum Self-Control Schedule ([SCS]; Rosenbaum, 1980), were more likely to respond to cognitive therapy, and patients low on the SCS were more likely to respond to pharmacotherapy (Simons, Lustman, Wetzel, & Murphy, in press). Cognitive distortions (as measured by the Dysfunctional Attitude Scale, the Automatic Thoughts Questionnaire, and the Cognitive Response Test) did not improve more rapidly with cognitive therapy than with pharmacotherapy (Simons, Garfield, & Murphy, 1984). The results of the study are at variance with Rush et al. (1977), which this study was intended to replicate, where cognitive therapy was found to be superior to imipramine. On the basis of their own study and the existing literature Murphy et al. (1984) concluded that cognitive therapy and pharmacotherapy were "moderately effective but

. . . neither additive nor interfering in their effects." Persons with very low Beck Depression Inventory (BDI) scores (close to zero) were less likely to relapse than patients considered improved but with depression scores still showing residual symptomatology (BDI less than 10). Finally, the results suggested that dysfunctional attitudes and social adjustment at termination were important in predicting relapse. Persons high in dysfunctional attitudes and low in social adjustment were more likely to relapse (Simons, Murphy, Levine, & Wetzel, 1984). Methodologically, this study is the only one which has provided a description of the therapeutic interaction between pharmacotherapists and patients. Some effort was apparently made to limit the scope of this interaction so that only minimal supportive intervention was allowed.

A comparison of group cognitive behavioral therapy, psychodynamic group therapy, imipramine, doxepin, and placebo in treating elderly depressed patients showed superior effectiveness for the medications over the group psychotherapies (Jarvik, Mintz, Steuer, & Gerner, 1982). Forty-five percent of patients receiving medication had full remissions, whereas only 12 percent receiving group psychotherapy did. There was no significant difference in effectiveness between the psychotherapies. Two possible confounds are mentioned by the authors. First, patients who could not be taken off of their prestudy medication or who had medical contraindications for tricyclics were not assigned to pharmacotherapy but were sometimes assigned to receive psychotherapy. Thus, patients receiving psychotherapy may have experienced greater health problems—a major concern of the elderly. Second, they point out that Hamilton scores were rated by therapists of the patients receiving medication, but they were rated by independent evaluators for psychotherapy patients. Treatment results in the group cognitive behavioral therapy were not as good as those reported by Gallagher and Thompson (1982) for individual cognitive therapy for the elderly. In fact, the patients treated with individual cognitive therapy by Gallagher and Thompson had levels of improvement almost identical to the patients receiving medication in Jarvik et al. (1982).

The only other study which has been done thus far examining the effects of group cognitive therapy in the context of medication was a pilot study by Rush and Watkins (1981). It compared group cognitive therapy, individual cognitive therapy, and individual cognitive therapy plus antidepressant medication. No additive effect was found for the combination treatment over individual therapy alone. There was a trend for persons in group cognitive therapy to do more poorly than persons in either of the individual treatments. Final BDI scores averaged 16.2 for group members, 8.6 for persons in individual cognitive therapy, and 5.9 for persons receiving individual cognitive therapy plus medication. Another study with the elderly comparing group cognitive therapy with medication (in this case alprazolam) is currently being conducted at the University of Arizona by Larry Beutler. More work needs to be done studying the effects of group cognitive therapy both alone and in combination with medication, since it provides a more cost effective means of delivering treatment and would be more affordable to many patients than individual treatment.

In summary, studies comparing individual cognitive therapy with medication for depression have shown cognitive therapy to be a powerful treatment. In every instance, individual cognitive therapy has been as effective or more effective than medication alone. However, studies of group cognitive therapy suggest that it may be a less powerful treatment; in at least one instance it was shown to be less effective than medication.

Studies Comparing Behavior Therapy and Pharmacotherapy

McLean and Hakstian (1979) were the first to compare a primarily behavioral treatment for depression with medication. There were four treatment conditions altogether: (1) behavior therapy, (2) amitriptyline, (3) short-term analytic psychotherapy, and (4) relaxation training. The behavior therapy condition used graduated practice and modeling techniques as well as focusing on goal attainment in the patient's communication, behavioral productivity, social interaction, assertiveness, decision making, problem solving, and cognitive self-control. Clients in the behavior therapy condition were seen with their spouses when possible. The short-term psychotherapy treatment was modeled on the work of Marmor (1973, 1975) and Wolberg (1967) and was designed to develop insight into psychodynamic forces and the recognition of personality problems as related to past experiences. Relaxation training was highly structured, and the participating spouses in it were treated in the same manner as the clients. Dropout rates were lowest in the behavior therapy condition, where only 5 percent dropped out before scheduled termination. On the other hand, 30 percent of the psychotherapy patients dropped out, and 36 percent of the drug therapy patients dropped out. Short-term psychoanalytic psychotherapy had the poorest results of all four treatments on 6 out of 10 outcome measures. On the other hand, the behavioral treatment was most effective on a wide variety of types of self-report measures.

Bellack, Hersen, and Himmelhoch (1981) compared the effectiveness of social skills training combined with amitriptyline, social skills training combined with placebo, amitriptyline alone, and psychotherapy combined with placebo. The social skills training involved 12 weekly one-hour sessions of role-playing procedures. As in the McLean and Hakstian study (1979), patients receiving amitriptyline alone had the highest premature termination rate (55 percent). Patients receiving social skills training plus amitriptyline and psychotherapy plus placebo had lower dropout rates (29 percent and 23 percent, respectively). However, the lowest premature termination rate occurred in the group receiving social skills training plus placebo (15 percent). Patients with milder depressions were more likely to drop out of the conditions including amitriptyline than from the social skills training or psychotherapy conditions that did not include medication. As a result, conditions with active medication carried more severely depressed patients to termination, and analyses examining only patients completing the study showed social skills training without medication to be the most effective treatment. When treatment dropouts were included in an endpoint analysis, however, this difference disappeared, and all four treatments were about equally as powerful (Thase, Hersen, Himmelhoch, & Bellack, 1984).

A reanalysis of the data examined treatment response among melancholic and nonmelancholic subtypes (Thase, Himmelhoch, Hersen, & Bellack, 1984). A statistically and clinically significant difference was found in treatment responsiveness and dropout rates. Melancholic patients (19 percent of the overall sample) responded better to amitriptyline than to the psychosocial interventions, while nonmelancholic patients responded better to the psychosocial interventions (psychotherapy and social skills training). Similarly, dropout rates were significantly higher for melancholic patients receiving psychosocial interventions without amitriptyline and for nonmelancholic patients who were receiving amitriptyline. Melancholic patients receiving the combination of amitriptyline and social skills training did significantly worse than those receiving amitriptyline alone. While session notes indicate that the patients receiving combined treatment were receiving dosages of medication in the target range, they were still prescribed about 50 mg/day less medication than patients receiving amitriptyline alone (Thase et al., 1984). Thus, it appears that the prescribing psychiatrists reduced the dosage for some reason—either because they felt that patients in the combined treatment did not need as much medication or because the patients did not want as much and using their newly acquired assertive skills convinced the pharmacotherapist to prescribe less.

Social skills training is now being compared with nortriptyline to determine their relative efficacy in treating dysthymic disorder. The study, which is being conducted by Robert Becker (Albany Medical College) and Richard Heimberg (SUNY-Albany), crosses medication (nortriptyline or placebo) with type of psychotherapy contact (social skills training or supportive therapy). Initial results suggest that all treatments appear to provide rapid relief, but it is unknown if they will differ in prophylactic effectiveness for symptomatic relapse during the follow-up period (R. Heimberg, personal communication, July 9, 1984).

Wilson (1982) compared the efficacy of a modification of Lewinsohn's technique of pleasant events task assignment; relaxation training; and minimal contact (two one-hour sessions). In addition, all patients were administered either amitriptyline or a placebo for the two-month period of treatment. The task assignment treatment consisted of seven sessions of therapy designed to increase the number and the quality of patients' activities. At the four-week assessment, subjects receiving amitriptyline were significantly less depressed than those receiving placebo medication. However, by the end of treatment, no significant difference in depression was found between subjects receiving amitriptyline and those receiving placebo. Behavior therapy plus amitriptyline or placebo was significantly more effective than minimal contact plus amitriptyline or placebo at the mid-therapy evaluation but not at termination. Wilson noted that two findings cast doubt on the validity of Lewinsohn's behavioral theory of depression: first, the task assignment treatment did not reduce depressive symptoms significantly more than relaxation; second, there was no increase in the Pleasant Events Schedule cross-product scores (frequency of pleasant events × enjoyability of events) as depression improved. The study did confirm that combining some form of structured interpersonal contact with an antidepressant, such as amitriptyline, hastened improvement over no contact and placebo treatment. However, overall, the results are difficult to understand given the considerable data from other studies for the effectiveness of amitriptyline.

Roth, Bielski, Jones, Parker, & Osborn (1982) compared Rehm's (1977) self-control treatment for depression with a combination of self-control therapy plus antidepressant medication (desipramine). Patients met weekly in groups for two-hour treatment sessions over a three-month period. Both treatments produced significant symptom improvement as measured by both the Beck Depression Inventory and the Hamilton Rating Scale for Depression. As found by Wilson (1982), at four weeks those receiving pharmacotherapy with the behavioral intervention were significantly more improved than those receiving behavior therapy alone. By the end of treatment, however, there was no significant difference between conditions. Two important problems with this study were the relatively small sample size (26 total subjects) and a lack of a measure of endogenicity.

Comparisons of Short-Term Analytic Therapy with Medication

Four of the studies reviewed above included short-term psychotherapy treatments which were dynamically oriented. Jarvik et al. (1982) found a moderate beneficial effect for group psychodynamic therapy, but Covi et al. (1974) found no main effect for dynamic group therapy in alleviating depressive symptoms. Bellack et al. (1981) found that individual short-term dynamic therapy performed as well overall as amitriptyline and social skills training, but McLean and Hakstian (1979) found individual dynamic therapy to be decidedly inferior to all of the other treatments they compared: behavior therapy, relaxation, and medication. The studies examining Interpersonal Psychotherapy have shown it to have considerable promise; however, because of its focus on current concerns rather than on unconscious conflicts, transference phenomena, and so on, results from those studies are probably best not grouped under the heading of "dynamic" therapies. Thus, there is a decided lack of clarity about the effectiveness of short-term psychodynamic therapy in treating depression. This is not too surprising, however, since psychodynamic theory is not one single entity but is actually composed of many schools. Now that treatment manuals are beginning to be developed in this area, these will need to be compared to understand to what degree different "dynamic" treatments are actually comparable.

Meta-Analysis of Comparative Efficacy

A meta-analysis of psychotherapy and drug therapy for unipolar depression was conducted by Steinbrueck, Maxwell, and Howard (1983). They surveyed those studies using adults which either contrasted psychotherapy with a control group or with medication alone. There were too few studies examining combined treatments of psychotherapy and medication to include them in the meta-analysis. Psychological interventions included behavior, interpersonal, cognitive, and marital therapies. Imipramine and amitriptyline were the medications most often used as the pharmacotherapies in the studies. The average effect size of the drug therapies was .61, while for psychotherapy, the average effect size was 1.22, a statistically significant difference. (An effect size is the difference between two means, such as between the mean outcome for a treatment condition versus mean outcome for a control or placebo condition, divided by their common standard deviation). There were no statistically significant differences among psychotherapies in effect size. While this finding of superiority of psychotherapy over medication has not been found in most of the comparative studies reviewed above, it is consistent with the fact that some of the comparative studies found psychotherapy to be superior to medication, but outside of the three earliest studies, none of them found medication to be superior to psychotherapy.

The NIMH Treatment of Depression Collaborative Research Program

In the mid-1980s the National Institute of Mental Health Treatment of Depression Collaborative Research Program (Waskow, Parloff, Hadley, & Autry, in press) is being conducted at three treatment sites across the country, including the University of Oklahoma Health Sciences Center, George Washington University, and Western Psychiatric Institute. The purpose of the study is to compare in a rigorously controlled manner the efficacy of two psychotherapies—interpersonal psychotherapy and cognitive psychotherapy—against a reference treatment of imipramine plus clinical management. Imipramine was chosen because of the considerable research demonstrating its efficacy for depression. A placebo plus clinical management condition was included to establish the efficacy of the medication for patient populations at the research sites. The design tests these treatments directly against each other, without using a combination of psychotherapy plus medication. The study embodies many methodological advances in the field including:

1. The use of blind clinical evaluators.
2. Rigorous independent evaluation of treatments to ensure that they conform to treatment manuals.
3. Use of explicit diagnostic criteria for depression (primarily the Research Diagnostic Criteria).
4. Use of specially trained, experienced psychiatrists and psychologists as therapists to ensure competence in the therapy they deliver.
5. Rigorous control of all concurrent treatments patients might otherwise be receiving.

6. Medical screening to exclude patients whose depression might be organically based.

7. Adequate length of treatment and number of sessions for each treatment (approximately 16 weeks, 16–20 sessions of psychotherapy).

8. Adequate sample size (240 subjects).

One limitation of the collaborative study design is that no biological diagnostic procedures for depression were included, such as the Dexamethasone Suppression Test, Thyroid Challenge Test, or sleep studies. Thus, the diagnosis of endogenous subtype will be done by clinical symptomatology alone. The study will also not address whether a combination treatment of psychotherapy and pharmacotherapy is more helpful than the individual treatments alone. Finally, the study shares the limitation of other studies that only one antidepressant is being used and that patients who do not respond to it are not switched to other available medications such as other tricyclics, monoamine oxidase inhibitors (MAOI), and lithium.

Summary of Outcome Studies

In the studies reviewed here, psychotherapy (including behavior therapy) yielded superior results over medication in three instances (Blackburn et al., 1981; McLean & Hakstian, 1979 [behavior therapy over amitriptyline]; Rush et al., 1977). If the Klerman et al. (1974) maintenance study is excluded on the grounds that all of the patients in it had already responded to medication, psychotherapy yielded inferior results compared to medication in three studies (Covi et al., 1974; Jarvik et al., 1982; McLean & Hakstian, 1979 [amitriptyline over dynamic therapy]). All three of these instances used an analytic treatment, and two of them used a group mode of treatment. Cognitive therapy was also used in Jarvik et al., but in a group format. In six comparisons, there was no significant difference in effect (Bellack et al., 1981; Friedman, 1975; DeRubeis, 1983; Murphy et al., 1984; Weissman et al., 1979; Wilson, 1982). This tallying of the results of comparative studies does not agree with the results of the meta-analysis of Steinbrueck et al. (1983) who found a clear superiority for psychotherapy over medication. This may be due to the use of different patient populations in psychotherapy studies and in pharmacotherapy studies. Psychotherapy studies have tended to use outpatient populations whereas pharmacotherapy studies have tended to use inpatients. In studies which have directly compared psychotherapy versus pharmacotherapy using the same populations, there is no clear superiority of one type of treatment over another. The strongest conclusion that can be drawn in favor of psychotherapy is that some individual forms of therapy which have been specifically targeted toward depression (including behavioral, cognitive, and interpersonal interventions) have consistently performed as well as or better than tricyclic medication for outpatient depression.

Combined treatment of psychotherapy and pharmacotherapy was more effective than pharmacotherapy alone in five studies (Blackburn et al., 1981;

Friedman, 1975; Weissman et al., 1979; DeRubeis, 1983; Teasdale et al., 1984; Weissman et al., 1979). Combined treatment was equally as effective as pharmacotherapy in three (Bellack et al., 1981; Murphy et al., 1984; Wilson, 1982). Combined treatment was more effective than psychotherapy alone in three instances (Blackburn et al., 1981 [hospital outpatients only]; Friedman, 1975; Weissman et al., 1979) and equally as effective as psychotherapy in seven cases (Beck et al., 1979; Bellack et al., 1981; Blackburn et al., 1981 [general practice outpatients only]; DeRubeis, 1983; Murphy et al., 1984; Roth et al., 1982; Wilson, 1982).

The fact that combined treatment is superior to individual treatments in some studies but not others is puzzling. One answer to this puzzle, as found by Thase et al. (1984) in their reanalysis, is that pharmacotherapists may tend to underprescribe medication when their patients are also receiving psychotherapy. Another possible explanation is that since in most studies, improvement was rather rapid, patients were not able to improve beyond a certain rate—that there are certain biological, psychological, or environmental constraints upon the rate at which patients may remit from their depression. DeRubeis (1983) has pointed out that many of the standard outcome measures (such as the BDI) have skewed distributions and significant floor effects. It is precisely when one wants to look at the effectiveness of a treatment that may be very strong over a moderately strong treatment that such floor effects could become most bothersome. He recommends the use of the MMPI-D scale as an outcome measure with a more normalized distribution to overcome this problem.

The above results suggest that there is currently no evidence to support strict adherence to either a psychotherapeutic or pharmacological model of treating outpatient depression. Each type of treatment has demonstrated its ability to alleviate symptoms of depression. Each appears to have particular strengths: pharmacotherapy with endogenous depressions and vegetative symptoms, psychotherapy with social adjustment. It is time for researchers and clinicians to abandon any remaining vestiges of an artificial mind/body dichotomy in theorizing about and treating depression. Such a dichotomy is an impediment to theory and practice. Clearly, clinicians need to be sensitive to the possibility that medication may well be the treatment of choice for depressions diagnosable as endogenous or melancholic (Thase et al., 1984; Weissman et al., 1979). In addition, while not all depressions will necessarily involve disturbances of monoamine functioning or other neurochemical changes in a causative manner, most major depressions involve vegetative changes which may benefit from medication. At the same time, there is now very strong evidence that a majority of major depressions seen on an outpatient basis can be treated fairly well by individual psychotherapy (the effectiveness of group psychotherapy seems more doubtful). Even depressions which may be considered biological in origin may cause problems in the patient's personality or social environment which then require some form of readjustment counseling.

LIMITATIONS ON THE GENERALIZABILITY OF RESEARCH FINDINGS

It must be kept in mind that the above studies do not exhaustively compare psychotherapy and pharmacotherapy as such but rather contrast specific types of each delivered in strict regimens. Neither psychotherapists nor pharmacotherapists in these studies were allowed to treat depression with all the means available to them. For pharmacotherapists this has meant that they have not been allowed to switch from serotonergic-acting to noradrenergic-acting TCAs, or from a tricyclic to an MAO inhibitor or lithium. There is evidence that atypical depressions (depressions with hyperphagia, hypersomnia, and weight gain) respond better to MAO inhibitors than to tricyclics (Liebowitz et al., 1984). Moreover, comparative studies have not determined medication dosages for patients by their blood serum levels but have used the typical practice of prescribing without benefit of this knowledge. Thus, the demonstrated response to medication has really been a demonstrated response to a strict treatment regimen with one or two tricyclic antidepressants in each study. Finally, it should be noted that these treatment results apply only to current tricyclic antidepressants and current psychotherapies and not to future treatments which may be developed.

The results of most of the above studies were derived from fairly homogeneous populations of nonbipolar adult outpatients who did not have major complicating psychiatric disorders, such as alcoholism and drug abuse. Where these other disorders coexist with depression, treatment is likely to require special modifications and may differ substantially from treatment of uncomplicated depression. Investigators have begun to examine the effects of various forms of antidepressant treatments for retarded persons (Matson, 1982), and for persons with different levels of socioeconomic status (Padfield, 1976). In addition, suicidal patients may also require special considerations in determining type of treatment (DeRubeis, 1983). These and other factors may well tip the balance in favor of psychotherapy or pharmacotherapy for a specific population.

Future research needs to include persons with bipolar disorder—both in its severe and mild forms. While lithium has generally become the treatment of choice for bipolar depressions, psychotherapy may still be beneficial. Psychotherapy might be effective either by reducing the perceived stressfulness of environmental situations (which may be triggering a latent genetic predisposition) or through alteration of depressive behaviors which may tend to perpetuate a depressive environment (Coyne, 1982).

ISSUES IN RESEARCH

The methodological criteria for sound comparative outcome research have been increasingly clarified. Luborsky, Singer, and Luborsky (1975) succinctly outlined their methodological requirements for outcome studies comparing psychotherapies:

1. Controlled assignment of patients to treatment groups, through randomization or matching.
2. Use of real patients.
3. Equal competence of therapists for each group.
4. Use of experienced therapists.
5. Presentation of treatments as equally valued to patients.
6. Outcome measures which take into account target goals of each treatment.
7. Treatment outcomes that are evaluated by independent (nontherapist) measures.
8. Obtaining of information regarding other concurrent treatments.
9. Inspection of treatments delivered to ensure that they fit the treatment designated in the design.
10. Comparability of treatments in amounts of frequency.
11. Adequate amounts given of each treatment.
12. Adequate sample size.

In designing studies comparing psychotherapy with pharmacotherapy there are special difficulties which arise for which there are no perfect solutions. For example, it is difficult to decide how to provide "equal amounts" of psychotherapy and pharmacotherapy. Should this be measured by total duration of treatment, by number of sessions, or by total time spent in sessions? Moreover, a researcher must decide whether or not to compare the two treatments as actually practiced, in which case supportive counseling techniques could be used freely by pharmacotherapists, or to compare the treatments in such a way as to prevent any counseling from "contaminating" the pure effects of the medication. However, to prevent the physician from providing a normal degree of support creates an artificial situation and can alienate patients. This, in turn, may cause poor medication compliance. Thus, there is another necessary piece of information which should be reported in comparative studies of psychotherapy and pharmacotherapy: the nature of the communication from physicians to patients in a "medication alone" treatment. It is important to allow physicians to establish a normal supportive relationship with patients. On the other hand, where a treatment condition is meant to demonstrate the effects of medication alone, the experimenter needs to ensure that active psychotherapeutic interventions have not occurred beyond "nonspecific" factors such as support and empathy.

Weissman (1979) pointed out a variety of possible problems which may arise in studies comparing psychotherapy and pharmacotherapy. Among other things, she suggested that studies should use treatments which have been developed specifically for depression (rather than generic treatment such as "psychoanalytic therapy") and that research reports should discuss whether findings were clinically significant as well as whether they were statistically significant. Luborsky et al. (1975) also included a category for "specific defects" in judging the validity of studies. We would suggest that given current knowledge of depression, it must be considered a grave defect for studies not to investigate the interaction between treatments and endogenicity, since there is very strong evidence that certain depressions (termed *endogenous* or *melancholic*) have a biological basis. (Melancholia is a *DSM-III* subtype of major depression that includes a smaller, more exclusively defined group than the Research Diagnostic Criteria "endogenous subtype"). A variety of pharmacological treatment studies have supported the idea that endogenous patients are more medication responsive than other types of depressed patients (e.g., Guy, Ban, & Schaffer, 1983; Raskin & Crook, 1976). Thus, studies which include a broad mixture of nonendogenous, endogenous, and melancholic patients may show no differential effectiveness by treatment type until the interaction of treatment by endogenicity subtype is analyzed. One caveat needs to be offered, however. Degree of endogenicity is correlated with severity. Analyses of treatment response by degree of endogenicity must make sure that any findings are not simply a reflection that mild and severe depression respond differentially to treatments.

There is also a need for greater use of biological process measures. Measures of theoretically important psychological processes such as self-control, participation in pleasant events, and dysfunctional attitudes, have been increasingly used. However, as yet there has been little data published relating measures of biological processes such as monoamine metabolite levels, DST response, and sleep processes to psychotherapy response. Important questions to be answered include how pretreatment differences on these measures may predict differential treatment responsiveness and what, if any, changes occur in these physiological systems during psychotherapy versus pharmacotherapy. Just as interpersonal psychotherapy and marital therapy were found to have specific process effects upon social adjustment, it is possible that medication may prove superior in restoring biological homeostatic mechanisms.

Just as the presence of melancholia in a patient may predict differential treatment response, there may also be psychological individual differences which predict how individuals will respond to treatment. For example, Simons et al. (in press) found that persons with high scores on the Self-Control Schedule (Rosenbaum, 1980) responded better to cognitive therapy than to medication. The broad implications of this may lie in two directions: first, it may be that no matter what the type of psychological treatment, persons who tend to take active charge of their own lives will respond better to psychotherapy than to medication. Alternatively, it may be that some patients have coping styles congruent with a particular type of psychotherapy and are likely to do very well in that type of therapy. Beckham and Adams (1984) developed the Coping Strategies Scales specifically to measure coping styles in depression. Persons scoring high on "active" coping styles such as problem solving or cognitive restructuring might well respond better to psychotherapy than to medication.

An important methodological issue is that studies need to have sufficient numbers of subjects in each condition if differences in treatment effectiveness are to be detected. This requires more subjects when two effective treatments are being compared where the outcome differences between groups may be small than where an active treatment and a control group are compared and there is likely to be a greater disparity in outcome. Studies upholding the null hypothesis—that there is no difference in effectiveness between treatments—need to be examined for their statistical power. When results are reported, it would be helpful for investigators to state the power of the design for small, medium, and large effect sizes, or alternatively, for a difference in treatment effects that would be clinically significant and meaningful to the reader (e.g., power [to detect a difference in treatment outcomes of 5 or greater on the Hamilton Scale] = .7).

Kupfer and Rush (1983) outlined methodological issues for pharmacological and biological studies. Most relevant here is their suggestion that the process of how patients are selected and the criteria for inclusion and exclusion should be clearly stated, since these will determine the population for which the results apply. Along this same line, we would suggest that studies specify dropout rates for all treatments, whether dropouts were replaced, and whether they were included in the outcome analyses. It also needs to be made clear at what point in the process of intake, screening, randomization, and treatment the dropouts occurred. For treatments that sometimes have high dropout rates (as medication alone did in Bellack et al., 1981), the results can be heavily dependent upon whether an attempt is made to assess symptomatology of dropouts at the end of the aborted treatment period, or whether final outcome analyses are performed without any data on the dropouts being incorporated. A related issue regards whether persons are counted as dropouts if they refuse to enter the treatment to which they are randomly assigned. Some patients will withdraw if they receive a treatment assignment counter to their expectations, even if they were aware from their initial contact with the research study that they would be randomly assigned to either medication or psychotherapy.

Another way in which reporting of results might be improved would be by outlining effectiveness of treatments along several dimensions rather than by overall effect size only. Hollon (1981) has listed four measures of treatment effect:

1. **Magnitude.** How much symptom change occurs in the average patient? This is the statistic most typically published.
2. **Generality.** How many of the target symptoms are significantly reduced by a treatment? For example, how many of the *DSM-III* symptoms of major depression are reduced by psychotherapy and by medication in a study?
3. **Universality.** How many persons demonstrate significant benefit? It is conceivable that two treatments could demonstrate equal magnitude of change with one producing great change in a few subjects and the other producing a small amount of change in most subjects.

4. Stability.   Are changes in symptomatology from a treatment maintained over time? Studies have increasingly taken this into account by performing follow-up evaluations.

All of these provide important information which may or may not be reflected in the typical statistic of magnitude. Hollon also lists two other factors which need to be known in interpreting treatment results: safety of each treatment (side effects, suicidal risk) and acceptability of each treatment (dropout rates, and so on).

Finally, there are serious methodological problems still to be overcome in obtaining useful follow-up information. Measures of symptoms may be misleading because patients who are not improved at termination may be the ones who are most likely to seek further treatment and may improve for that reason. Some studies have attempted to alleviate this problem by examining whether patients return to treatment during the follow-up period. This is a helpful analysis but is confounded by the fact that patients may return to psychotherapy for general growth rather than because they actually need treatment for depression. Moreover, such analyses are not very powerful because they typically use a nonparametric statistic (i.e., the patient either does or does not return to treatment). This might become a more powerful method if studies also examined how quickly patients in different conditions reentered treatment.

Despite these problems, there has been obvious improvement in the methodology of comparative psychotherapy and pharmacotherapy studies. Introduction of blind raters has been a major advance, as has been the use of experimental designs where psychotherapy alone (without placebo) can be directly compared with placebo or with medication. Other improvements have included development of treatment manuals both for psychotherapy (e.g., Beck, Rush, Shaw, & Emery, 1979; Klerman et al., 1984) and for pharmacotherapy (e.g., Fawcett, 1980), use of treatments designed specifically for depression, and increased use of a variety of independent outcome measures such as the Beck Depression Inventory, the Hamilton Rating Scale for Depression, and social adjustment scales.

Certain areas of methodology still need to become more uniform, however. These include ensuring that treatments are initially presented as equally valuable to patients; using independent blind clinical evaluators; sampling treatments to ensure that therapists proceed according to their treatment manual and that pharmacotherapists provide only "mild" supportive psychotherapy; ensuring that each treatment is given for a reasonable length of time—probably a minimum of three months; and using a measure of endogenicity such as the RDC endogenous criteria and/or the *DSM-III* measure for melancholia. Until it is clear that the addition of placebo to psychotherapy does not diminish or enhance the effectiveness of a psychological intervention, it is important that studies include one cell where psychotherapy is given without a pill. Klerman (1983) has discussed this issue and has called for a six-cell design which crosses medication, placebo, and no pill with psychotherapy and no psychotherapy. This allows for unconfounded interpretation of results. Murphy et al. (1984) compared psychotherapy alone with psychotherapy plus placebo and found no significant difference in results. However, further research still needs to be done before psychotherapy plus placebo can be equated with psychotherapy without taking a pill. If nothing else, there may be a difference in attrition rates between the two, since some persons dislike the idea of taking a pill and other patients do not see how it is possible to improve without one.

FUTURE RESEARCH DIRECTIONS

Much remains to be learned about how different treatments bring about change in the depressive syndrome. There are a variety of factors which may cause, exacerbate, maintain, or diminish depressive symptoms in everyday life (Billings & Moos, 1982). These include such things as major stressors, daily hassles, social support availability, individual internal resources (e.g., self-esteem), and individual coping responses. Changes in any of these may directly affect depressive symptoms or may affect other factors which then affect the individual's depression. Each type of therapy may exert its effect on particular areas of functioning and through it have an impact on the overall syndrome of depressive symptoms. It may be, for example, that antidepressants improve vegetative functioning directly while cognitive therapy affects vegetative symptoms via cognitions of the patient. Antidepressants may affect negative cognitions directly, or such improvement may be a result of an improvement in sleep, energy, and a generally improved sense of well-being. The picture regarding such a chain of events is unclear. There is some evidence that antidepressants may actually cause improvement in cognitive functioning (i.e., memory) even before there is apparent clinical improvement in other areas (Glass, Ithlenhuth, Hartel, Matuzas, & Fischman, 1981).

Second, thus far there has been very little research into the question of how effective psychotherapy will be with medication nonresponders and how effective medication may be with psychotherapy nonresponders. Fennell and Teasdale (1982) examined the efficacy of cognitive therapy for five drug-refractory depressed patients and found only modest changes in BDI scores (30.8 to 21.4). Only one of the five patients markedly improved to a BDI score of less than 10. It would be logical that endogenous patients might be psychotherapy resistant but responders to medication and that nonendogenous patients might have the opposite type of response. However, there may also be some patients who are not responsive to either type of treatment.

Third, while cost effectiveness research is not considered by some to be a proper subject of pure psychotherapy research, it is nevertheless an important area of knowledge to our society. None of the studies reviewed attempted to delineate the relative cost in professional manpower of each treatment relative to benefit or the dollar cost to consumers for treatment relative to the benefit provided.

CLINICAL IMPLICATIONS

The lack of clear superiority of one type of treatment for depression over another suggests that there is a need for close cooperation among the mental health professions in providing quality care for depressed patients. Purely psychological or purely pharmacological interventions may be sufficient for some persons; however, treating all patients alike with the armamentarium a particular mental health professional happens to possess (whether psychotherapy or pharmacotherapy) will result in less than adequate care for many patients. The likelihood is that some patients in need of medication will not get it and will fruitlessly pursue counseling in an attempt to overcome an endogenous depression. On the other hand, some patients treated by medication alone may well fail to achieve the level of social adjustment they previously had, even after the major depressive symptoms have remitted.

Various objections that have been lodged against combining medication with psychotherapy do not seem to be supported by the evidence. Rounsaville, Klerman, & Weissman (1981) examined six different hypotheses regarding whether psychotherapy and pharmacotherapy conflict when used together to treat depression. These hypotheses were (1) that use of medication would create antitherapeutic attitudes in the therapist and patient, that is, that a directive subject/object relationship would be created rather than a presumably more therapeutic subject/subject relationship (an issue raised by Docherty et al., 1977); (2) that reduction of symptoms through pharmacotherapy would reduce the patient's felt need for continuing psychotherapy; (3) that pharmacotherapy would undercut the defenses of patients by removing symptoms without also removing underlying psychic conflict; (4) that the use of medication would impart a message to the patient that he is unlikely to resolve his problems without a pharmacological crutch. They also tested two hypotheses concerning whether psychotherapy might have an adverse effect on pharmacotherapy: (1) that psychotherapy encourages the patient to focus on conflict-laden issues and thereby tends to counteract the pharmacotherapy effect, and (2) that psychotherapy could be disruptive by encouraging patients who actually have a biochemical disorder to interrupt their biological treatment to seek psychotherapy.

Rounsaville et al. (1981) did not find that therapists administering the combination treatment tended to treat their subjects with more "directive" techniques and fewer "facilitating" techniques than in the psychotherapy alone condition. Nor did they find that patients in the combined treatment spent less time discussing interpersonal issues or were less reflective than persons receiving psychotherapy alone. While the addition of medication to psychotherapy did improve the symptom picture of patients more quickly than psychotherapy alone, the psychotherapy alone group did not have a lower dropout rate due to higher "motivation from symptoms" but in fact had a higher dropout rate. Moreover, the combined treatment patients did not differ from the psychotherapy patients in the mean number of sessions attended. There was also no evidence for symptom substitution or symptom recurrence in patients receiving the combined treatment as might be expected if pharmacotherapy prevented patients from working on their inner conflicts. Nor was there evidence that patients in the combined treatment began to devalue psychotherapy. Patients in the psychotherapy alone and combined treatment group did not differ in their utilization of psychotherapy after termination from the research treatment although patients receiving the combined treatment did seek pharmacotherapy more frequently after leaving the study. Finally, Rounsaville et al. (1981) found no evidence that the addition of psychotherapy diminished the efficacy of pharmacotherapy by encouraging patients to focus on upsetting and disruptive material or by discouraging them from seeking out further pharmacotherapy. In fact, the combination treatment was more effective than pharmacotherapy alone. Only Thase et al. (1984) found a negative interaction between psychosocial treatment and medication. This applied only to their melancholic patients and appears to have been due to the fact that their therapists were prescribing less medication in these cases—in essence a negative interaction effect on therapist behavior!

CONCLUSION

Research on the comparative efficacy of psychotherapy and pharmacotherapy for depression is expanding. Psychotherapy is becoming empirically established as a viable treatment for outpatient depression alongside of antidepressant medications. The evidence thus far suggests that neither psychotherapy nor pharmacotherapy has any clear superiority in treating outpatient depression. There are indications that medications may be a necessary component of treatment for melancholic depressions, and that patients receiving psychotherapy tend to have better social adjustment. There is still much to learn about which patients will benefit from medication alone, from psychotherapy alone and from combined treatment.

References

Beck, A. T., Hollon, S. D., Young, J. E., & Bedrosian, R. C. (1979, July). *Treatment of depression with cognitive therapy and amitriptyline.* Paper presented at the meeting of the Society for Psychotherapy Research, Oxford, England.

Beck, A. T., Rush, A. J., Shaw, B. F., & Emery, G. (1979). *Cognitive therapy of depression.* New York: The Guilford Press.

Beckham, E. E., & Adams, R. L. (1984). Coping behavior in depression: Report on a new scale. *Behavior Research and Therapy, 22,* 71–75.

Bellack, A. S., Hersen, M., & Himmelhoch, J. (1981). Social skills training compared with pharmacotherapy and psychotherapy in the treatment of unipolar depression. *American Journal of Psychiatry, 138,* 1562–1567.

Billings, A. G., & Moos, R. (1982). Psychosocial theory and research: An integrative framework and review. *Clinical Psychology Review, 2,* 213–237.

Blackburn, I. M., Bishop, S., Glen, A. I. M., Whalley, L. J., & Christie, J. E. (1981). The efficacy of cognitive therapy in depression: A treatment trial using cognitive therapy and pharmacotherapy, each alone and in combination. *British Journal of Psychiatry, 139,* 181–189.

Covi, L., Lipman, R. S., Alarcon, R. D., & Smith, V. K. (1976). Drug and psychotherapy interactions in depression. *American Journal of Psychiatry, 133,* 502–508.

Covi, L., Lipman, R. S., Derogatis, L. R., Smith, J. E., & Pattison, J. H. (1974). Drugs and group psychotherapy in neurotic depression. *American Journal of Psychiatry, 131,* 191–198.

Coyne, J. C. (1982). A critique of cognitions as causal entities with particular reference to depression. *Cognitive Therapy and Research, 6,* 3–13.

DeRubeis, R. J. (1983, December). *The cognitive-pharmacotherapy project: Study design, outcome, and clinical followup.* Paper presented at the American Association of Behavior Therapy, Washington, DC.

DiMascio, A., Weissman, M. M., Prusoff, B. A., Neu, C., Zwelling, M., & Klerman, G. L. (1979). Differential symptom reduction by drugs and psychotherapy in acute depression. *Archives of General Psychiatry, 36,* 1450–1456.

Docherty, J. P., Marder, S. R., Van Kammen, D. P., & Siris, S. G. (1977). Psychotherapy and pharmacotherapy: Conceptual issues. *American Journal of Psychiatry, 134,* 529–533.

Fawcett, J. (1980). *Clinical management—imipramine—placebo administration manual: For the NIMH Psychotherapy of Depression Collaborative Program.* Mimeographed.

Fennell, M. J., & Teasdale, J. D. (1982). Cognitive therapy with chronic, drug-refractory depressed outpatients: A note of caution. *Cognitive Therapy and Research, 6,* 455–460.

Friedman, A. S. (1975). Interaction of drug therapy with marital therapy in depressive patients. *Archives of General Psychiatry, 32,* 619–637.

Gallagher, D. E., & Thompson, L. W. (1982). Treatment of major depressive disorder in older adult outpatients with brief psychotherapies. *Psychotherapy: Theory, Research, and Practice, 19,* 482–490.

Glass, R. M., Ithlenhuth, E. H., Hartel, F. W., Matuzas, W., & Fischman, M. W. (1981). Cognitive dysfunction and imipramine in outpatient depressives. *Archives of General Psychiatry, 38,* 1048–1051.

Goldberg, D. (1982). Cognitive therapy for depression. *British Medical Journal, 284,* 143–144.

Guy, W., Ban, T. A., & Schaffer, J. D. (1983). Differential treatment responsiveness among mildly depressed patients. In P. J. Clayton & J. E. Barrett (Eds.), *Treatment of depression: Old controversies and new approaches.* New York: Raven Press.

Herceg-Baron, R. L., Prusoff, B. A., Weissman, M. M., DiMascio, A., Neu, C., & Klerman, G. L. (1979). Pharmacotherapy and psychotherapy in acutely depressed patients: A study of attrition patterns in a clinical trial. *Comprehensive Psychiatry, 20,* 315–325.

Hollon, S. D. (1981). Comparisons and combinations with alternative approaches. In L. P. Rehm (Ed.), *Behavior therapy for depression: Present status and future directions.* New York: Academic Press.

Jarvik, L. F., Mintz, J., Steuer, J., & Gerner, R. (1982). Treating geriatric depression: A 26-week interim analysis. *Journal of the American Geriatrics Society, 30,* 713–717.

Klerman, G. L. (1983). Psychotherapies and somatic therapies in affective disorders. *Psychiatric Clinics of North America, 6,* 85–103.

Klerman, G. L., DiMascio, A., Weissman, M., Prusoff, B., & Paykel, E. S. (1974). Treatment of depression by drugs and psychotherapy. *American Journal of Psychiatry, 131,* 186–191.

Klerman, G. L., Weissman, M. M., Rounsaville, B. J., & Chevron, E. S. (1984). *Interpersonal psychotherapy of depression.* New York: Basic Books.

Kovacs, M. (1983). Psychotherapy versus drug therapy of depression. In J. Korf & L. Pepplinkhuizen (Eds.), *Depression: Molecular and psychologically based therapies.* Drachten, The Netherlands: TGO Foundation.

Kovacs, M., Rush, A. J., Beck, A. T., & Hollon, S. (1981). Depressed outpatients treated with cognitive therapy or pharmacotherapy: A one-year follow-up. *Archives of General Psychiatry, 38,* 33–39.

Kupfer, D. J., & Rush, A. J. (1983). Recommendations for publication on depression. *Journal of Consulting and Clinical Psychology, 51,* 807–808.

Liebowitz, M. R., Quitkin, F. M., Stewart, J. W., McGrath, P. J., Harrison, W., Rabkin, J., Tricamo, E., Markowitz, J. S., & Klein, D. F. (1984). Phenelzine v. imipramine in atypical depression. *Archives of General Psychiatry, 41,* 669–677.

Lipman, R. S., & Covi, L. (1976). Outpatient treatment of neurotic depression: Medication and group psychotherapy. In R. L. Spitzer and D. F. Klein (Eds.), *Evaluation of psychological therapies: Psychotherapies, behavior therapies, drug therapies, and their interactions.* Baltimore: The Johns Hopkins Press.

Luborsky, L., Singer, B., & Luborsky, L. (1975). Comparative studies of psychotherapies: Is it true that "everyone has won and all must have prizes"? *Archives of General Psychiatry, 32,* 995–1007.

Marmor, J. (1973). *Psychiatry in transition.* New York: Brunner/Mazel.

Marmor, J. (1975). Academic lecture: The nature of the psychotherapeutic process revisited. *Canadian Psychiatric Association Journal, 20,* 557–565.

Matson, J. L. (1982). The treatment of behavioral characteristics of depression in the mentally retarded. *Behavior Therapy, 13,* 209–218.

McLean, P. D., & Hakstian, A. R. (1979). Clinical depression: Comparative efficacy of outpatient treatments. *Journal of Consulting and Clinical Psychology, 47,* 818–836.

Murphy, G. E., Simons, A. D., Wetzel, R. D. & Lustman, P. J. (1984). Cognitive therapy and pharmacotherapy: Singly and together in the treatment of depression. *Archives of General Psychiatry, 41,* 33–41.

Padfield, M. (1976). The comparative efficacy of two counseling approaches on the intensity of depression among rural women of low socioeconomic status. *Journal of Counseling Psychology, 23,* 209–214.

Prusoff, B. A., Weissman, M. M., Klerman, G. L., & Rounsaville, B. J. (1980). Research Diagnostic Criteria subtypes of depression: Their role as predictors of differential response to psychotherapy and drug treatment. *Archives of General Psychiatry, 37,* 796–801.

Raskin, A., & Crook, T. H. (1976). The endogenous-neurotic distinction as a predictor of response to antidepressant drugs. *Psychological Medicine, 6,* 59–70.

Rehm, L. P. (1977). A self-control model of depression. *Behavior Therapy, 8,* 787–804.

Rosenbaum, M. (1980). A schedule for assessing self-control behaviors: Preliminary findings. *Behavior Therapy, 11,* 109–121.

Roth, D., Bielski, R., Jones, M., Parker, W., & Osborn, G. (1982). A comparison of self-control therapy and combined self-control therapy and antidepressant medication in the treatment of depression. *Behavior Therapy, 13,* 133–144.

Rounsaville, B. J., Klerman, G. L., & Weissman, M. M. (1981). Do psychotherapy and pharmacotherapy for depression conflict? Empirical evidence from a clinical trial. *Archives of General Psychiatry, 38,* 24–29.

Rush, A. J., Beck, A. T., Kovacs, M., & Hollon, S. (1977). Comparative efficacy of cognitive therapy and pharmacotherapy in the treatment of depressed outpatients. *Cognitive Therapy and Research, 1,* 17–37.

Rush, A. J., Beck, A. T., Kovacs, M., Weissenburger, J., & Hollon, S. D. (1982). Comparison of the effects of cognitive therapy and pharmacotherapy on hopelessness and self-concept. *American Journal of Psychiatry, 139,* 862–866.

Rush, A. J., & Watkins, J. T. (1981). Group versus individual cognitive therapy: A pilot study. *Cognitive Therapy and Research, 5,* 95–103.

Simons, A. D., Garfield, S. L., & Murphy, G. E. (1984). The process of change in cognitive therapy and pharmacotherapy for depression: Changes in mood and cognition. *Archives of General Psychiatry, 41,* 45–51.

Simons, A. D., Levine, J. L. Lustman, P. J., and Murphy, G. E. (1984). Patient attrition in a comparative outcome study of depression: A follow-up report. *Journal of Affective Disorders, 6,* 163–173.

Simons, A. D., Lustman, P. J., Wetzel, R. D., & Murphy, G. E. (in press). Predicting response to cognitive therapy of depression: The role of learned resourcefulness. *Cognitive Therapy and Research.*

Simons, A. D., Murphy, G. E., Levine, J. L., & Wetzel, R. D. (1984, June). *Sustained improvement one year after cognitive and/or pharmacotherapy of depression.* Paper presented at the meeting of the Society for Psychotherapy Research, Lake Louise, Alberta, Canada.

Steinbrueck, S. M., Maxwell, S. E., & Howard, G. S. (1983). A meta-analysis of psychotherapy and drug therapy in the treatment of unipolar depression with adults. *Journal of Consulting and Clinical Psychology, 51,* 856–863.

Teasdale, J. D., Fennell, M. J. V., Hibbert, G. A., & Amies, P. L. (1984). Cognitive therapy for major depressive disorder in primary care. *British Journal of Psychiatry, 144,* 400–406.

Thase, M. E., Hersen, M., Himmelhoch, J. M., & Bellack, A. S. (1984, June). *Social skills training for non-bipolar depression: A re-appraisal.* Paper presented at the meeting of the Society for Psychotherapy Research, Lake Louise, Alberta, Canada.

Thase, M. E., Himmelhoch, J. M., Hersen, M., & Bellack, A. S. (1984, May). *Poor response to psychotherapies in melancholia.* Paper presented at the meeting of the American Psychiatric Association, Los Angeles, California.

Waskow, I. E., Parloff, M. B., Hadley, S. W., & Autry, J. H. (in press). The NIMH

Treatment of Depression Collaborative Research Program: Background and research plan. *Archives of General Psychiatry.*

Weissman, M. M. (1979). The psychological treatment of depression: Evidence for the efficacy of psychotherapy alone, in comparison with, and in combination with pharmacotherapy. *Archives of General Psychiatry, 36,* 1261–1269.

Weissman, M. M., Klerman, G. L., Paykel, E. S., Prusoff, B., & Hanson, B. (1974). Treatment effects on the social adjustment of depressed patients. *Archives of General Psychiatry, 30,* 771–778.

Weissman, M. M., Klerman, G. L., Prusoff, B. A., Sholomskas, D., & Padian, N. (1981). Depressed outpatients: Results one year after treatment with drugs and/or interpersonal psychotherapy. *Archives of General Psychiatry, 38,* 51–55.

Weissman, M. M., Prusoff, B. A., DiMascio, A., Neu, C., Goklaney, M., & Klerman, G. L. (1979). The efficacy of drugs and psychotherapy in the treatment of acute depressive episodes. *American Journal of Psychiatry, 136,* 555–558.

Wilson, P. H. (1982). Combined pharmacological and behavioral treatment of depression. *Behaviour Research and Therapy, 20,* 173–184.

Wolberg, L. R. (1967). *Short-term psychotherapy.* New York: Grune & Stratton.

Zuckerman, D. M., Prusoff, B. A., Weissman, M. M., & Padian, N. S. (1980). Personality as a predictor of psychotherapy and pharmacotherapy outcome for depressed outpatients. *Journal of Consulting and Clinical Psychology, 48,* 730–735.

PART 2

Assessment

Chapter 11

Diagnostic Criteria for Depression

William R. Leber
Ernest Edward Beckham
Pamela Danker-Brown
Department of Psychiatry and Behavioral Sciences; University of
Oklahoma Health Sciences Center

INTRODUCTION

The understanding of mood disorders has been the focus of a variety of
philosophers, clinicians, and researchers for centuries. Over time, depression
has come to be classified as one among a variety of types of mental disorders.
During the 20th century, the sophistication and complexity of proposed classification systems for depression has increased. The dichotomizing by
Kraepelin of mental illness into manic-depressive disorder and dementia
praecox was followed by a succession of systems delineating a variety of
subtypes of depression. The current prevalent diagnostic system in America,
the *Diagnostic and Statistical Manual of Mental Disorders* ([*DSM-III*]; American Psychiatric Association, 1980), lists seven separate depressive and manic
disorders under Affective Disorders in addition to two "atypical" categories.
In addition, *DSM-III* provides additional categories for normal grief reaction
(Uncomplicated Bereavement); for the mild depressive reaction of a normal
individual to a significant stressful event (Adjustment Disorder with Depressed Mood); and for depression resulting from specific medical disorders
(Organic Affective Disorder).

This chapter will first review the rationale for diagnosis as a treatment
and research tool for mental disorders. It will then examine some of the
current major diagnostic distinctions and systems which have been proposed
for depression. An appendix is also included to assist clinicians in obtaining
diagnostic information.

Preparation of this manuscript was supported in part by Grant MH33760, from the
National Institute of Mental Health.

ISSUES IN THE CLASSIFICATION OF DEPRESSION AND OTHER MENTAL DISORDERS

Many of the problems involved in the diagnosis of depression are linked to the difficulties and controversies inherent in the field of psychiatric diagnosis in general. These range from the basic question of whether diagnosis has any value at all to attempting to find agreement regarding the nature of mental disorders and the assumptions which should underlie diagnostic systems.

Szasz (1957) and others have questioned whether diagnosis of mental disorders is a useful or appropriate activity. He has asserted that depression and other mental disorders are not illnesses but patterns of behavior that deviate from prevailing legal, moral, or social norms. In his view, diagnosis obscures the individual's responsibility for his/her behavior by placing the patient in a passive role, making resolution of the problem unlikely. With regard to depression, the authors reject Szasz's argument on several grounds:

1. The purpose of diagnosis should not be confused with its misuse. Current research demonstrates that there are subtypes of depression (e.g., unipolar and bipolar) which vary in etiology, course, treatment response, and so on. While such diagnoses can be used to communicate to patients that their role is to be the passive recipient of treatment, this would be a misuse of the categories.

2. While the depressed person is somewhat disruptive to his social environment, treatment is most often initiated by the depressed person him/herself, not by relatives. The pain of depression is generally most bothersome to the individual experiencing it.

3. There is considerable evidence that some forms of depression (bipolar disorder, schizoaffective disorder, and melancholic unipolar depression) are illnesses resulting from genetic and biological dysfunction.

4. Distinctions between depression and schizophrenia, unipolar and bipolar depression, psychotic and nonpsychotic depression, have made resolution of these conditions more likely rather than less likely because they have led to increased specificity and effectiveness of treatment.

DEFINITIONS AND ASSUMPTIONS

Classification is a process of ordering complex phenomena into categories by a specified set of criteria. This superficially simple task encounters numerous complexities when applied to depression and other mental disorders. One must begin with the question of what is to be classified—types of depressed persons, patterns of depressive behavior, or etiologies of depression? Second, are psychiatric/psychological problems, such as depression, best seen as diseases, disorders, dysfunctions, or some other construct? Decisions on nomenclature strongly imply certain views regarding etiology and treatment. The term *mental disorder* is the currently agreed-upon term, but there has been considerable disagreement over its definition. Stengel (1959) noted that to define mental disorder one would also have to define mental health and concluded that "there is no prospect of agreement on these concepts today" (p. 613). More recently, Klein (1978) and Spitzer and Endicott (1978) offered proposals for defining the term *mental disorder*, which were carefully examined by the Task Force on Nomenclature and Statistics of the American Psychiatric Association for inclusion in *DSM-III*. Neither definition was included because "no definition would be satisfactory and therefore any attempt to formulate one was doomed to failure" (Spitzer & Williams, 1980). Spitzer and Williams articulated what they believed to be the basic assumptions "necessarily implicit in a classification of mental disorders":

1. That one can identify behavioral signs or symptoms that do not occur randomly but occur in meaningful patterns that can be identified as syndromes.
2. That these patterns of behavior are undesirable because they are associated with distress or disability.
3. That underlying these patterns is a dysfunction *within the individual* [emphasis ours].
4. That these patterns of behavior are systematically related to other variables, such as etiology, prognosis, and treatment response.
5. That inclusion of certain nonbehavioral correlates of syndromes, such as information about etiology, in the definition of the syndrome provides more useful information than behavioral description alone.
6. That diagnostic classes can be organized into a hierarchy such that a disorder high in the hierarchy may include all of the characteristics found in disorders lower in the hierarchy but the reverse is not true.

These assumptions generally appear valid regarding classification of depression, although it is not at all clear that the total locus of depression or other disorders is "within the individual." For example, family therapists generally locate the dynamics of depressive behavior within the family system. It is also not clear that all depressions can be assigned a fixed place in a hierarchy.

Any discussion of the diagnosis of depression must take into account the controversy regarding the "medical model" of diagnosis. Traditionally, mental disorders were viewed as a subset of all medical disorders and thus as having an organic etiology. This assumption has been frequently criticized (Schacht & Nathan, 1977; Szasz, 1957; Ullman & Krasner, 1965; Zubin, 1977–78). Spitzer and colleagues (Spitzer & Williams, 1980; Spitzer & Wilson, 1975) have argued that these criticisms are based on a misunderstanding of the medical model and that the model asserts that the basis for mental disorders is an organismic dysfunction which may be behavioral, psychological, or physical in nature. Any model that intends to incorporate current research must recognize the role of genetics and biology on the one hand, and developmental psychology, cognitive processes, environmental contingencies, and social processes on the other.

The field of psychopathology has not yet reached a level of knowledge that would allow identification of the best system of classification for depression. Some authors have even argued that classification systems are no more than convenient creations which have been constructed for our own purposes, and that they do not necessarily have any true basis in reality. According to Zigler and Phillips (1961), "a diagnostic system cannot be described as true or false, but only as useful or not useful in attaining prescribed goals." A more balanced view, however, is that classification systems can be either natural or artificial (Brill, 1974). A natural classification system reflects "some deeper underlying pattern or reality" while an artificial system "is purely arbitrary and synthetic and is developed for utilitarian purposes." For example, the authors of this chapter would view the diagnosis of "major depression," as it currently exists, to reflect the presence of an actual disorder (or a group of related disorders) present in many patients. The reality of the disorder is reflected in its having distinct genetic history, biology, course, symptom cluster, and response to treatment. On the other hand, the level of severity which it designates could be made more or less stringent, and the label of major depression would still serve a useful purpose. In this sense, it is synthetic. The diagnosis of melancholia is less arbitrary in that it most likely reflects the presence of certain biochemical processes not present in nonmelancholic depressions.

THE PURPOSE OF DIAGNOSIS

Most authors appear to agree that the fundamental purposes of diagnosis are to provide: (1) a common language that facilitates communication about mental disorders; (2) information useful to clinicians in making decisions regarding treatment and prevention; and (3) descriptive systems for classifying persons for the purpose of conducting research on the causes and correlates of mental disorder (Blashfield & Draguns, 1976a; Caveny, Wittson, Hunt & Herrman, 1955; Goodwin & Guze, 1984; Spitzer & Williams, 1980).

Communication.   The most fundamental purpose of diagnosis is to be a basis for communication. Stengel (1959) noted that without a common international classification system, exchange of information and thus progress in the understanding of mental disorders is hindered. This can be clearly seen in the field of depression where estimates of worldwide incidence and prevalence have been hindered by use of different terminology and diagnostic criteria (Boyd & Weissman, 1981).

Research Classification.   Diagnosis serves a simplifying function by allowing a complex set of symptoms to be characterized as one concept and promoting research on correlates of such syndromes. This makes possible the study of extremely complex psychological phenomena. The main alternative—examining correlates of individual symptoms—is not only impractical but generally fails to lead to knowledge about etiology and treatment response.

Clinical Prediction.   This goal is often cited by clinical practitioners as the most important reason for classification. Clinicians make diagnoses of depression primarily because of the belief that those diagnoses will help predict treatment response and other clinically relevant information, such as which patients will respond to tricyclic medication or be most susceptible to depressive relapse.

With these theoretical aspects regarding diagnosis in mind, some of the major approaches to diagnosis of depression will now be examined.

CLASSIFICATIONS OF DEPRESSION

Emile Kraepelin included the manifestations of what is now called depression within the overall rubic of "manic-depressive illness." This broad category included "certain slight and slightest colorings of mood, some of them periodic, some of them continually morbid, which on the one hand are to be regarded as the rudiment of more severe disorders, on the other hand passing over without sharp boundary into the domain of personal predisposition" (Kraepelin, 1913). The array of affective manifestations included in this description encompasses the full range of affective disorders from major depression and mania to depressive personality.

Kraepelin's thinking about manic-depressive insanity contained a harbinger of one of the main theoretical issues which confronts the field today— that of the biological basis of depression. He believed that the basic causes of manic-depressive insanity were to be found in "permanent, internal changes which very often, perhaps always, are innate" (Kraepelin, 1913). In addition to the likelihood of a biologically based etiology, Kraepelin also believed that manic-depressive insanity was characterized by a good short-term prognosis with a high likelihood of recurrence, and that the manic and depressive manifestations of the disorder were but opposite poles of the same underlying process. As alternatives to this unitary concept, a number of suggested subtypes of depressive disorders have been advanced. Certain dichotomies in classification have found widespread acceptance because of their clinical utility. Among these are the neurotic-psychotic, the reactive-endogenous, the primary-secondary, and the unipolar-bipolar distinctions.

The Neurotic-Psychotic Distinction

The neurotic-psychotic dichotomy has been one of the most widely used and most confusing classifications of depression. *Psychotic depression* has been used to mean endogenous depression, severe depression, or depression accompanied by hallucinations or delusions. *Neurotic depression* has been a synonym for reactive depression, characterological depression, chronic depression, nonendogenous depression, mild depression, depression secondary to characterological disorders, and depression unaccompanied by hallucinations or delusions. Due to this multiplicity of meanings, Klerman, Endicott, Spitzer, and Hirschfeld (1979) suggested that the term neurotic depression was too vague to have any further clinical usefulness. Neurotic depression continues to be part of ICD-9 (World Health Organization, 1978), but was essentially deleted from *DSM-III*. Depressive neurosis is listed as a synonym for Dysthymic Disorder in *DSM-III*. However, its meaning is specifically restricted to signify chronic, mild depression. Recent research suggests that a neurotic or characterological process is not necessarily involved and that biological abnormalities occur in some of these depressions (see Chapter 17). For that reason, it is misleading to label dysthymic disorder as a neurotic disorder.

DSM-III, as well as ICD-9, clearly preserves the diagnosis of psychotic depression. Within the diagnosis of major depression, "psychotic features" may be noted when hallucinations or delusions occur. This, of course, only refers to one of the traditional meanings of the term, but this refinement of the definition should actually make the category a more useful one.

The distinction between depressions with and without accompanying psychotic symptomatology is a dichotomy particularly attractive to clinicians because of the dramatic differences in presentation and because of the important implications for treatment. Psychotic depressions are generally thought to necessitate treatment by medication and/or electroconvulsive therapy (ECT). Delusional depressions (one type of psychotic depression) have been found to respond less well to tricyclics alone than nondelusional depression (Glassman & Roose, 1981) and often to require treatment with neuroleptics and ECT (Nelson & Bowers, 1978). In addition, delusional patients are much less likely to spontaneously remit (Glassman & Roose, 1981) and tend to have a poor short-term outcome regardless of treatment received (Coryell & Tsuang, 1982).

The Reactive-Endogenous Distinction

Another significant attempt to dichotomize depressive disorders has been the reactive-endogenous distinction. Theoretically, endogenous depressions have been distinguished from reactive depressions by presumed biological etiology and independence from precipitating life events (an "autonomous" quality). In recent years, the term *endogenous depression* has been increasingly limited to describing a particular cluster of symptoms; that is, loss of weight, terminal insomnia, psychomotor retardation, guilt, and so on, without consideration of whether precipitating events appear to have triggered the depression (cf., Research Diagnostic Criteria [RDC]; Spitzer, Endicott, & Robins, 1978).

There is considerable evidence for the validity of an endogenous depressive syndrome. In his review, Kendell (1976) noted that one of the few areas of agreement in the classification of depression is the concept of an "endogenous/psychotic" depression. He based this conclusion on the fact that numerous cluster analytic and factor analytic studies using different types of data have almost uniformly identified an endogenous syndrome. Mendels and Cochrane (1968) examined a number of factor analytic studies and concluded that a factor is typically found which corresponds to the endogenous-reactive dimension. This factor has usually been a statistically bipolar one, and it has been pointed out that the majority of the items which load on this factor define the endogenous pole, with usually only one or two items relating to the presence of a significant precipitating event, and loading on the reactive pole of the factor (Lewinsohn, Zeiss, Zeiss, & Haller, 1977). Lewinsohn et al. suggest that the failure to identify a separate factor representing reactive depression may be simply a methodological problem—that an insufficient number of items measuring the reactive pole are included in most measures, making it unlikely that a separate factor tapping this concept could be defined.

Nelson and Charney (1981) reviewed factor, cluster, and discriminant analysis studies of the symptomatology, physiology, and treatment response of depressed patients and identified a recurring concept of "major depressive illness characterized by a depressive syndrome unaffected by environmental change, associated with alterations of neurochemistry and requiring biological treatment" (p. 1). They labeled this type of depression *autonomous*. The most frequent symptoms associated with autonomous depression were psychomotor retardation and agitation, severe depressed mood, and lack of reactivity. Sleep changes and appetite or weight changes were found to occur so often in nonautonomous depressions that they may be of questionable utility in differential diagnosis of endogenous depression. Nelson and Charney (1981) also suggested that there was evidence for two types of endogenous depression: retarded anhedonic depression, which was most responsive to tricyclic medication, and agitated delusional depression, which appeared to respond best to a combination of antipsychotic and tricyclic medications. A review of all of the studies documenting the existence of an endogenous type of depression is beyond the scope of this chapter. However, further evidence for the concept of endogenous depression continues to be generated in new studies using factor analytic, cluster analytic, and discriminant analytic techniques (e.g., Andreasen & Grove, 1982; Davidson, Turnbull, Strickland, & Belyea, 1984; Feinberg & Carroll, 1982, 1983; Matussek, Söldner, & Nagel, 1981). The concept is represented in current diagnostic systems as the endogenous subtype of major depression in the RDC and the melancholic subtype of major depression in *DSM-III*.

Reactive depression has generally denoted a depression that follows an environmental event which would be stressful for most persons or which is particularly stressful for reasons idiosyncratic to a particular patient. The appearance of this distinction in the early part of the century (Gillespie, 1929) was consistent with the increase in attention being paid to the environment and its effects on behavior. The label has enjoyed a certain amount of face validity, since clinicians frequently feel they are able to identify events which precipitated their patients' depressions.

Despite the face validity of the concept of reactive depression, considerable disagreement has arisen as to the sufficiency of an environmental event to cause a major affective disorder. Paykel (1974) found that nearly all depressive episodes were preceded by "stressful events," and that there was no consistent relationship between the severity of the stress and the severity of the depression. Moreover, when the statistical relationship between stressors and depression has been studied, only about 10 percent of the variance of depression can be accounted for by environmental events (Warheit, 1979). On the other hand, studies have shown that stressful events are clearly more common among depressed persons than nondepressed persons (Billings, Cronkite, & Moos, 1983; Brown & Harris, 1982; Costello, 1982). The issue is further complicated by the finding that in addition to discrete stressful events, chronic strain (e.g., an ongoing financial or marital problem) is associated with depressive symptoms (Pearlin & Schooler, 1978).

In a study of the diagnosis of *situational depression,* Hirschfeld (1981) found mixed evidence for the validity of the construct. On the one hand, persons with situational depression were more likely to recover in six months than persons with nonsituational depression. Symptomatically, situational depressives had more depressed mood, more suicidal ideation and behavior, more anger and self-pity, and more alcohol and drug abuse. But surprisingly, there was no overall difference between "situational" and "nonsituational" groups in their amount of recent stress, their endogenous factor scores, or their personality scores. Benjaminsen (1981) studied endogenous and nonendogenous primary depressives and found no significant differences between groups in the number of stressful events preceeding the episode. Thus, it remains unclear whether the reactive versus nonreactive distinction has sufficient reliability and validity to be useful for either clinicians or researchers.

The concept of reactive depression was prominent until the development of *DSM-III.* In *DSM-II* (American Psychiatric Association, 1968), reactive depression might be classified under Depressive Neurosis, Psychotic Depressive Reaction, or Adjustment Reaction of Adult Life, depending on the concomitant symptomatology. The concept of a psychosocial precipitant triggering depression was also incorporated in the Research Diagnostic Criteria, which includes a situational subtype of major depressive disorder. However, it has not been included in *DSM-III* except to the degree that it is reflected on Axis IV (severity of psychosocial stressors).

Although reactive and endogenous subtypes were thought to be somewhat different in their symptomatology, studies over the past 20 years attempting to show differences among patients categorized into endogenous and reactive groups have shown mixed results. Significantly different scores on a retarded depression factor of the Hamilton Rating Scale were reported by Hamilton and White (1959) between endogenous and reactive groups of patients, but not by Rose (1963). Prusoff, Weissman, Klerman, and Rounsaville (1980) found that situational depressions were less likely to have endogenous symptomatology then nonsituational depressions. Thus, it remains unclear whether reactive and endogenous depressions are opposites or represent two orthogonal dimensions. The evidence for the validity of the concept of reactive depression is weak; the endogenous subtype clearly has more evidence for its validity at the current time.

The Primary-Secondary Distinction

One of the more recent diagnostic distinctions to be suggested is that between primary and secondary depression (Robins & Guze, 1972). Primary depression was originally characterized as a full depressive syndrome meeting the criteria for major depression and a lack of any preexisting, nonaffective psychiatric disorder or life-threatening or incapacitating medical illnesses (Feighner, Robins, Guze, Woodruff, Winokur, & Muñoz, 1972). More recently, serious medical illness has not been included in the list of exclusionary diagnoses. Secondary depression, on the other hand, refers to depressive symptomatology which occurs subsequent to any of the nonaffective psychiatric disorders, including anxiety disorders, schizophrenia, alcoholism, drug dependency, antisocial personality, sexual deviations, mental retardation, and organic brain syndrome. The rationale behind the distinction was that depression which resulted as a reaction to another illness would follow a course similar to the initial illness (Andreasen, 1982). Some support for the validity of the distinction has been found in the stability of the diagnoses over time. Murphy, Woodruff, Herjanic, and Fischer (1974) presented a prospective five-year follow-up study which indicated that the diagnosis of primary depression tended to remain stable over time; that is, that persons with a diagnosis of primary depression at the beginning of that time tended to have the same diagnosis at the end of the study. Similarly, Faravelli and Poli (1982) found that approximately 81 percent of patients diagnosed as primary depressives met the same criteria after four years.

The utility of the primary-secondary distinction has thus far been primarily in its research applications. Research carried out using only patients with primary depression has the advantage of a more homogeneous population unaffected by the wide variety of psychiatric symptoms and possible biological dysfunctions which may accompany the other psychiatric disorders. This conclusion is supported by research showing that secondary depression is common in patients with other psychiatric disorders and that the demographic characteristics of secondary depressives can differ considerably from those of primary depressives (Weissman, Pottenger, Kleber, Ruben, Williams, & Thompson, 1977). There is some evidence that the primary-secondary distinction may be clinically useful. Reveley and Reveley (1981) studied both types of depressives during the course of inpatient treatment and found that primary depressives showed a greater degree of recovery as reflected in scores on the Hamilton Rating Scale for Depression (HRSD) and the Zung Self-Rating Depression Scale (SDS), even though both groups received comparable treatment.

One difficulty with the distinction is in determining which preexisting conditions should define the differentiation. Andreasen (1982) points out that in the original formulation of the distinction only certain preexisting psychiatric disorders led to a diagnosis of secondary depression—notably alcoholism, anxiety states, hysteria, and antisocial personality. The more recent trend has been to classify as secondary those depressions preceded by any nonaffective psychiatric disorder. This classification leads to such a heterogenous group of patients that the utility of the diagnosis is likely to be limited. Future research might profitably be aimed at further subtyping of secondary depressions. Such research could study depressions occurring after more narrowly defined groups of preexisting conditions in order to maximize the homogeneity of samples of secondary depressives.

The primary-secondary distinction cuts across the reactive-endogenous distinction. For example, Nelson and Charney (1980) reported that 92 percent of their patients with endogenous depression, and 45 percent of patients with reactive depression were diagnosed as having primary depression. Bipolar depressions are considered to be primary, and the incidence of other psychiatric disorders prior to bipolar disorder onset has not been found to be above chance levels (Akiskal, Walker, Puzantian, King, Rosenthal, & Dranon, 1983).

There is currently no conclusive evidence to suggest that primary and secondary depression predict differences in treatment responsiveness or etiology. If future evidence should consistently support differences between the groups in genetic history, biology, treatment response, or course of illness, then this distinction may become a useful addition to the nosology.

The Unipolar-Bipolar Distinction

Leonhard (1957) proposed that depressions with and without manic periods should be viewed as two different types of depression. Since then, researchers have vigorously pursued this thesis with a variety of types of studies. The question has not been one of whether bipolar disorder is different from unipolar disorder, since the phenomenology of the two disorders is remarkably different. Manic periods involve clear elation or excessive irritability, heightened energy and activity, expansive self-esteem which may even reach delusions of grandeur, talkativeness and/or racing thoughts, distractability, decreased need for sleep, and impulsive behavior. The issue has been whether the depressive phase of bipolar disorder is distinguishable from unipolar depression. Research into the distinction has been in six different areas: genetic history, demographic characteristics, course of illness, biological processes, symptomatology, and treatment responsiveness.

Genetic Transmission.   Studies have left no doubt that bipolar disorder is strongly determined by genetic factors. The evidence is also clear for unipolar depression, but the effect appears to be less strong (see Chapter 24). Whether a diagnostic distinction should be made between the two disorders rests to some degree on whether different genotypes behind each can be identified.

A variety of studies (e.g., Winokur, Clayton, & Reich, 1969; Trzebiatowska-Trzeciak, 1977) have found an elevated incidence of bipolar relatives in the pedigrees of bipolar patients. However, relatives of strictly diagnosed unipolar patients do not show such an increased incidence of bipolar disorder (Angst, 1966; Perris, 1966). This suggests that two different genotypes may be present. On the other hand, relatives of bipolar patients show crossover between the two diagnoses in that there is a significant incidence of unipolar disorder among them (approximately 10 percent; Angst, 1966; Perris, 1966).

Another type of evidence which would support a distinction between bipolar disorder and unipolar disorder would be if identical twins tended to be concordant for bipolar disorder or unipolar disorder rather than each twin manifesting a different disorder. Zerbin-Rudin (1969) found that monozygotic twins had a 71 percent concordance rate for affective disorder and that out of those who were concordant, 81 percent were also concordant for the type of disorder. This tendency toward concordance of type of affective disorder has been confirmed by Bertelsen, Harvald, and Hauge (1977).

Several investigators (e.g., Baron, Klotz, Mendlewicz, & Rainer, 1981; Gershon, Baron, & Leckman, 1975) have proposed that bipolar and unipolar disorders may be a result of a single continuum of genetic liability with bipolar disorder resulting when there is a greater genetic deviance. In their review, Depue and Monroe (1978) concluded that the evidence suggested distinct types of genetic transmission between the two disorders, with at least a subgroup of bipolar disorders having a dominant X-linked inheritance and unipolar disorders having a polygenic mode of transmission. Perris (1982) in his review concluded that bipolar disorder was most likely heterogeneous and that X-linked transmission was probably involved in some but not all bipolar depression. If bipolar depression does prove to be heterogeneous, as unipolar depression has, then the task of genetically differentiating the two types of disorder becomes more complex.

Demographic and Social Characteristics.   Both Angst (1966) and Perris (1966) have found that the sex distribution in bipolar disorders is approximately equal between males and females. In unipolar depression, women typically outnumber men by approximately a 2 : 1 ratio (Weissman & Klerman, 1977).

Course of Illness.   Age of onset of bipolar depression is typically in the late 20s while the mean age of onset for unipolar depression as been found to be in the early 40s (Angst, 1966; Carlsson, Kotin, Davenport, & Adland, 1974; Perris, 1966; Winokur et al., 1969). Angst et al. (1973) found a tendency for the number of episodes of bipolar disorder to be self-limiting so that patients who had been under observation for 40 years did not have a significantly higher number of episodes than patients observed for 15 years. The apparent overall limit for bipolar patients was about nine episodes, whereas for unipolar depressives it was found to be only four to six episodes.

Biological Processes.   Perris (1982) reviewed the biological studies regarding the two disorders and found that there were inconclusive results as to whether there was any distinct difference in their biochemistry. Studies are continuing to explore possible differences in metabolites of neurotransmitters, neuroendocrine response, EEG, and other biological measures.

Symptomatic Differences.   There is accumulating evidence that bipolar and unipolar depressions differ in minor ways in their symptomatology. Compared to unipolar depressives, bipolar patients are more likely to have hypersomnia rather than insomnia (Akiskal et al., 1983; Detre, Himmelhoch, Swartzburg, Anderson, Byck, & Kupfer, 1972). Bipolar patients are more likely to have somatic complaints (Beigel & Murphy, 1971; Katz, Robins, Croughan, Secunda, & Swann, 1982) and less likely to experience subjective anxiety (Beigel & Murphy, 1971; Katz et al., 1982).

Response to Treatment.   Both bipolar and unipolar patients often show a beneficial response to lithium, although there is some evidence that depressed bipolar patients respond better than persons with unipolar depression (see review by Coppen, Metcalfe, & Wood, 1982). Katz et al. (1982) found that depressed bipolar patients responded somewhat more poorly to tricyclics than unipolar depressives. Unipolar patients tended to improve in the area of agitation whereas bipolar patients tended to deteriorate on that symptom. Similarly, anxiety improved among unipolar patients as a response to tricyclic medication but became worse in the bipolar group.

Conclusion.   The above studies suggest that there are some distinct differences between unipolar and bipolar depression. However, the two disorders also have a great many similarities. It is not yet clear that bipolar depression is anything more than a severe genotypic variant of unipolar depression. When bipolar depression has been compared with endogenous unipolar depression rather than with all unipolar depression, some of the differences have become less striking (Abrams & Taylor, 1980). More research is needed to delineate the differences and similarities between the two types of disorder.

The Winokur-Iowa Classification System

Winokur has proposed that there are three types of unipolar major depression: those where there is a first-degree relative with depression (pure depressive disease); those where there is a first-degree relative with alcoholism or sociopathy (depression spectrum disease); and those where there is no family history of psychiatric disorder (sporadic depressive disease) (Winokur, 1979; Winokur, Cadoret, Dorzab, Baker 1971). According to Winokur, these familial guidelines classify distinct patient groups with different sociodemographic characteristics. The typical patient with depression spectrum illness among Winokur's sample was a woman with onset of depression before age 40, with more depression in female relatives than male relatives, and with alcoholism and sociopathy in male relatives. On the other hand, the typical patient with pure depressive disease was a male with onset of the disorder after age 40, with equal amounts of depression in male and female relatives, and negligible findings of alcoholism and sociopathy in his history. Patients with depressive spectrum disease had a more variable course to their depression and were less likely to become chronic, whereas persons with pure depressive disease were both more likely to have an acute onset and to develop chronic depression. Pure depressive disease is viewed as a more severe illness, while depression spectrum disease is seen as less severe and arising out of a chaotic lifestyle (Coryell & Winokur, 1982).

Van Valkenburg, Lowery, Winokur, and Cadoret (1977) found few of these predicted symptomatic differences between pure depressive probands and patients with spectrum depression. They did find that persons with depression spectrum disease were less likely to have been previously depressed, and that persons with pure depressive disease were more prone to relapse. Cross-validation research from the NIMH Collaborative Program on the Psychobiology of Depression found only partial confirmation of differences in the two types of depressions (Andreasen & Winokur, 1979). Patients with pure depressive disease and nonfamilial depression had more restless sleep and engaged in more self-blame than depression-spectrum patients, while the latter were more suspicious, nervous, helpless, bizarre, and psychotic. However, differences were not found on several predicted dimensions including sex ratio, age of onset, duration of hospitalization, or personality traits (e.g., "hysterical traits").

One study which clearly supported the Winokur system found that 76 percent of patients with pure depression disease responded to dexamethasone challenge with abnormally high cortisol levels, whereas only 7 percent of patients with depression spectrum disease did so (Schlesser, Winokur, & Sherman, 1980). This supported the hypothesis that persons with pure depressive disease have a genetic-biological etiology to their depression. This work awaits replication. In general, considerable validation work remains to be done with Winokur's diagnostic categories.

The Akiskal Classification of Dysthymia

Akiskal and his research group at the University of Tennessee have developed a classification system for chronic depressions (Chapter 17). Based on sleep measures (e.g., REM latency), family history, course of illness, and medication responsivity, Akiskal (1983) has proposed four types of chronic depression. He found that some patients with what appeared to be "characterological" depression responded to tricyclic medications and also had shortened REM latency, both characteristics of endogenous depression (Akiskal, Rosenthal, Haykal, Lemmi, Rosenthal, & Scott-Strauss, 1980). He termed this type of depression *subaffective dysthymia,* signifying that it was of the same biological nature as the full affective syndromes, but manifested at less than complete syndromal intensity. Other persons with early onset chronic depression did not have biological characteristics of depression. The latter group had more evidence of personality traits of impulsivity, immaturity, and manipulativeness. Their depressions were apparently of characterological origin. Hence, this condition was termed *character spectrum disorder*. Alcoholism and/or sociopathy were often present in the relative of these patients. Two other categories of chronic depression included unremitted major depression with onset in adult life, and dysphoric mood secondary to an incapacitating medical disorder or chronic psychiatric disorder. Akiskal's categories hold considerable promise for making more informed, intelligent treatment decisions for chronic depressives in the future. However, validation research at other sites is needed.

Endogenomorphic Depression and Hysteroid Dysphoria

Klein (1974) has proposed that depressions can be classified as *endogenomorphic, acute dysphoria,* or *chronic overreactive dysphoria. Endogenomorphic* depressions are hypothesized to result from a biological defect that inhibits the experience of pleasure. *Acute dysphoria* is the term applied to reactive depression, defined as "a sudden dysphoric reaction of frustration in a normal personality." The *chronic overreactive dysphorias* refer to "chronic overreactions to disappointment and demoralization." Klein hypothesizes that the capacity for pleasure is maintained in the dysphoric disorders.

A special diagnostic subgroup proposed by Klein within chronic overreactive dysphoria is hysteroid dysphoria. Patients in this category are characterized as very responsive to external praise and support and as very susceptible to depression when disappointed in romantic relationships. They have been described by Klein and Davis (1969) as egocentric, emotional, romantically centered, and possessive. Symptoms of the syndrome are thought to be "atypical"; that is, to include oversleeping and over eating. Klein postulates that the etiology of this disorder lies in a biological dysfunction in the regulation of affect. Monoamine oxidase inhibitors (MAOIs) are suggested as the treatment of choice (Liebowitz & Klein, 1981). Controlled data on therapeutic response of these patients to MAOIs would validate this specific form of atypical depression but have thus far been lacking (Spitzer & Williams, 1982). However, Liebowitz et al. (1984) have presented preliminary data which suggest that phenelzine (an MAOI) may be superior to imipramine for atypical depressions that meet criteria for hysteroid dysphoria or that are accompanied by panic attacks.

Current American Classifications of Depression—RDC and DSM-III.

The two predominant current classification systems used in the United States have their roots in the research criteria for primary affective disorder developed by the Washington University (St. Louis) group (Feighner et al., 1972). The work of the St. Louis group was further refined by Spitzer et al. (1978) in their development of the Research Diagnostic Criteria (RDC). The development of the RDC was motivated by a need for a "consistent set of criteria for the description or selection of samples of subjects with functional psychiatric illnesses" (Spitzer et al., 1978).

The RDC, in turn, became the skeleton for a major part of the *DSM-III* which was adopted by the American Psychiatric Association and published in 1980. The intent of the task force charged with the development of *DSM-III* was to produce an atheoretical diagnostic system (American Psychiatric Association, 1980, p. 7). The rationale for this goal was that the diagnostic system would presumably be used by clinicians from a variety of theoretical orientations, and that for most disorders there was not yet conclusive evidence regarding etiology.

The concept of major depression is central to both the RDC and *DSM-III* categorization of affective disorders. Feighner et al. (1972) cited a series of 11 articles as the basis for the St. Louis criteria for depression. However, the exact rationale behind the selection of each of the specific criteria has never been fully set forth for any of the three systems. It is reasonable to wonder how the particular set of symptoms was selected, and why certain other frequent symptoms associated with depression, such as feelings of hopelessness, or social withdrawal were not included. Additionally, it is reasonable to ask on what basis the RDC requires five symptoms (*DSM-III*, four symptoms) rather than some other number, for diagnosis of definite major depression. A third question has to do with the rationale behind the duration requirement for the diagnosis of major depression. *DSM-III* and the RDC require two weeks, whereas Feighner et al. (1972) require four weeks. Finally, other questions regard clinically significant levels of each symptoms. For example, why was a criterion of two pounds per week chosen by Feighner et al. (1972) as the clinically significant level for weight loss?

One way to approach the above questions would be to study false positives and negatives, and true positives and negatives, for different combinations of the above criteria. Unfortunately, such research requires an external criterion for major depression, which currently does not exist. There are several possible criteria, none of which is entirely satisfactory. Research on criteria for major depression might be carried out by studying medication responsive versus nonresponsive patients; hospitalized depressives versus nonhospitalized depressives; or DST suppressors versus nonsuppressors. The diagnosis of major depression, as currently defined by *DSM-III*, is a heterogeneous category and is not meant to include only medication responsive or biologically based depressions (although these qualities are thought to be true for the melancholic subtype). As it currently exists, the category of major depression has rather arbitrary boundaries.

Despite the lack of a published rationale for individual symptoms and criteria, the concept of major depression as it is variously defined in the criteria of the St. Louis group, the RDC, and the *DSM-III*, is a step forward because it allows for the reliable selection of relatively homogeneous samples of patients for research. The use of distinct guidelines for rating symptomatology such as those offered in the SADS (Schedule for Affective Disorders and Schizophrenia) for the RDC has been an important step in the refinement of criteria. Suggestions for rating individual symptoms of major depression are included in the appendix of this chapter.

Current Issues with DSM-III

Even though the *DSM-III* is a milestone in the development of an empirical diagnostic system, it requires further refinement. One troublesome area is the diagnosis of Dysthymic Disorder. As it is currently formulated, this diagnosis covers a broad range of chronic depressive symptomatology which may be significant but not severe enough in degree to merit a diagnosis of major depression. Akiskal (see Chapter 17) has presented evidence that this category represents a heterogenous group of disorders, and has proposed an alternative classification system.

A second area which has not been addressed well enough in *DSM-III* is the differentiation of grief and depression. Normal grief experienced when a loved one dies is categorized under the nondiagnostic "V" codes as Uncomplicated Bereavement. Clayton, Halikas and Maurice (1972) reported that 35 percent of a sample of widowed subjects experienced symptomatology sufficient in severity and quality to meet criteria for major depression in the month following the spouse's death. Accordingly, *DSM-III* notes that normal bereavement may include all of the symptomatology which accompanies major depressive disorder, except for marked psychomotor retardation, suicidal thoughts, or feelings of worthlessness (American Psychiatric Association, 1980). Thus, it is the occurrence of a death which mainly differentiates major depression and uncomplicated bereavement. The ironic result of this is that if a woman's husband dies and she experiences depression, it is not considered a disorder; but if her husband leaves her and she never sees him again, the same symptomatology could qualify as major depression. While the events are quite similar in their effects, that is, loss of a major part of the social support system, they lead to much different diagnoses.

A third problem is that Adjustment Disorder with Depressed Mood is classified outside of the affective disorders. This diagnosis would include some depressions of moderate severity, not quite meeting criteria for major depression, which appear to be triggered by an external stress. Some of the depressions classified in this category would have more in common with affective disorders than with the other adjustment disorders.

A final limitation of the *DSM-III* diagnostic categories for depression is their relative lack of demonstrated predictive validity for psychological intervention. Currently, research has not been published that indicates that the *DSM-III* categories of depression provide for differential prediction of treatment success. It has been proposed that a sixth axis is necessary for *DSM-III*, one that could be labeled "psychodynamic evaluation" (Karasu & Skodal, 1980). The purpose of this axis would be to provide additional information in the diagnosis which would be useful in formulating psychotherapeutic intervention. Any attempt to develop such an axis, however, would certainly run into difficulty since it would require aggreement on a theoretical system. Still, the fact remains that the atheoretical approach of *DSM-III* oftentimes provides little direction regarding appropriate psychological intervention.

FUTURE DIRECTIONS

A Biological Classification of Depression?

In the past ten years, advances in criterion based diagnosis and the discovery of measurable biological abnormalities have occurred (Rush, 1985). Therefore, an approach different from the above descriptive diagnostic systems using of laboratory diagnostic procedures to distinguish biologically based depressions from nonbiologically based depressions may eventually be possible. Such a diagnostic procedure would likely have advantages in predicting relative treatment response to psychotherapy and somatic therapies. The classification systems already discussed attempt to achieve this using descriptive criteria, terming biological depression *primary, endogenous, pure depressive, melancholic, endogenomorphic,* or *subaffective dysthymia.* A biological classification based on laboratory data might well prove to be more valid.

One problem with attempting to achieve a firm biological versus nonbiological distinction is that it assumes that biological depression is clearly separable from nonbiological depression, whereas in fact, the data are ambiguous on this point. Most biological measures show a continuous distribution, suggesting that there may be degrees of biological involvement in depression. A second problem is that some biological processes found in depression may well be epiphenomenal rather than etiological (see Chapter 25). A third problem is that even where etiological processes are identified, rules must be established pertaining to how laboratory data are to be integrated into a decision model. For example, how might DST, REM, and TRH/TSH measures be integrated to make a decision about the presence of melancholia? Moreover, how are they to be integrated with data from the clinical interview, which is still the primary tool of the mental health professional in assessing depression?

None of the above problems is insurmountable. Further research will most likely establish which biological processes are etiologic and which are epiphenomenal. Decision rules employing laboratory data, clinical symptomatology, and psychosocial processes can then be developed—complex though they may be. However, much remains to be learned before such a sophisticated diagnostic system can be put in place.

Classification Based on Psychosocial Processes

Another important dimension for diagnostic classification which has yet to be utilized is the nature of the psychological factors which may precipitate or maintain depression. Study of depressed patients might reveal subgroups with different psychological dynamics—each amenable to a particular type of psychotherapeutic intervention. The beginning of such a diagnostic classification is present in the formulation of interpersonal psychotherapy (IPT; see Chapter 5). Klerman, Weissman, Rounsaville, and Chevron (1984) conceptualized depression as arising from one of four sources: unresolved grief, interpersonal role disputes, interpersonal deficits, and role transitions. Specific strategies of IPT are employed to deal with each of these problem areas.

Other psychological categories for defining "subtypes" of depression might include loss of positive social reinforcers, uncontrollable environmental stress, or chronic characterological features (e.g., chronic guilt, chronic anger). Depressions conceptualized as arising from each of these sources might be approached in a different psychotherapeutic manner. The development of a diagnostic system which allowed for the specification of such factors would greatly assist clinicians in quickly identifying differential treatments for various depressions. The major obstacle to such a system is the lack of a widely held, common theoretical understanding of the etiology of depression. However, within specific theoretical systems, such categories could be readily developed, as has been done with IPT. Commonalities among the categories of various theoretical systems might allow for the eventual development of a unified classification system.

CRITERIA FOR EVALUATING CLASSIFICATION SYSTEMS

There are at least three criteria by which diagnostic systems may be evaluated: reliability, validity, and feasibility.

Reliability. Reliability refers to the likelihood that a person will be given the same diagnosis by different persons, or by the same person at different times. Lack of reliability was a major criticism of the first and second editions of the *Diagnostic and Statistical Manual of Mental Disorders* (Blashfield & Draguns, 1976b; Zigler & Phillips, 1961). Low reliability necessarily means that a system will have poor validity (although high reliability does not necessarily mean that a system will have high validity). There are several possible sources of variance in descriptive diagnoses, including differences in level of training of diagnosticians; poorly operationalized diagnostic categories; intradiagnostician inconsistency; use of different sources of information (self-report, behavioral observation, information from significant others); and most importantly, use of different diagnostic systems. Research with the *DSM-III* and with descriptive diagnostic systems upon which *DSM-III* was based suggests that reliability has been improved by the including of operational definitions of disorders with specific inclusion and exclusion criteria (Helzer, Clayton, Pambakian, Reich, Woodruff, & Reveley, 1977; Helzer, Robins, Taibleson, Woodruff, Reich, & Wish, 1977; Spitzer & Williams,

1980). Reliability statistics for major affective disorders in the two *DSM-III* field trials were Kappa = .68 and .80 (American Psychiatric Association, 1980). These findings suggest that adequate agreement among raters is possible with this system.

Validity. Classification systems may be examined with regard to several types of validity. Face validity is simply the extent to which clinicians agree upon the description of a class of diagnostic categories. This is sometimes, but not always, the easiest type of validity to demonstrate.

Descriptive validity refers to the degree of homogeneity among individuals within a given class. There are two problems with measurement of this type of validity. First, there are no symptoms (not even sad mood) which are found in all depressed patients, although there are symptoms found in most depressives. Second, homogeneity is a relative concept and there is no agreed-upon statistical test for homogeneity, although Wilk's lambda has been cited by Blashfield and Draguns (1976b) as perhaps the most useful statistic for describing homogeneity.

Predictive validity means that a diagnosis predicts characteristics other than those included in the definition of the class. Studies which assess family background, treatment response, complications and course of different diagnostic subtypes address issues of predictive validity.

Construct validity signifies a network of consistent empirical relationships between the diagnosis on the one hand, and other diagnoses and other aspects of depression on the other. Because of this "nomological net" the construct can be inferred to have some basis in reality. For example, for "endogenous depression" to have validity as a construct it must be shown to explain certain experimental results. A finding that "endogenous" depressions and "nonendogenous" depressions differ in symptoms, genetic background, and personality characteristics would support the construct validity of the two subtypes.

Feighner et al. (1972) described several criteria for establishing diagnostic validity for mental disorders:

1. The development of an accurate description of the clinical features associated with the disorder.
2. The conduct of chemical, physiological, and other laboratory studies in order to describe the biological aspects of classification.
3. The development of exclusionary criteria which may be used reliably to differentiate one disorder from another.
4. The conduct of follow-up studies in order to determine whether or not patients originally diagnosed with a particular disorder will subsequently be found to show a clinical course consistent with that disorder.
5. The conduct of family studies in order to determine the degree of genetic contribution to the occurrence of a disorder and to further delineate the biological aspects of the disorder.

Feasibility.   Even a very reliable system that has good validity will not be put to use if it is not practical. A system which requires elaborate training, time-consuming procedures, or expensive equipment may be useful for research but not for clinicians. For that reason, a biological classification requiring a battery of tests, such as the DST, thyroid challenge, and sleep studies, may not gain wide acceptance as a standard system of diagnosis.

Reliability, Validity, and Feasibility of **DSM-III.**   As stated above, inter-rater reliability of *DSM-III* criteria for major depression appears adequate. However, statistics from reliability studies may overestimate the actual reliability of an instrument in clinical use, because of the more stringent controls applied in such studies.

There is no ultimate criterion by which to judge the validity of *DSM-III* criteria for major depression since the term *major* is relative in meaning. However, if the issue is not the validity of major depression versus some other type of depression (e.g., RDC minor depression), then there is considerable data which supports the validity of the diagnosis as representing a construct distinct from other types of psychopathology (e.g., schizophrenia, anxiety disorders). However, a review of such studies would be beyond the scope of this chapter. Since *DSM-III* relies primarily on information obtainable in interviews, it is a system which is feasible for use in most settings.

CONCLUSION

Descriptive diagnosis of depressive disorders has advanced considerably since Kraepelin, and its evolution is continuing. There are no signs that agreement on any "ultimate" nosology for depression is near. The next two decades are likely to see the introduction of laboratory tests as auxiliary or even primary diagnostic procedures. Improvement in diagnostic procedures will hopefully bring with it better prediction of responsiveness to somatic therapies, as well as to psychosocial interventions, although the latter seems a more distant goal.

Appendix

Practical Diagnostic Interviewing

This appendix is included to assist professionals in interviewing depressed patients and to point out practical issues in the diagnosis of major depression.

There are no universally accepted interview questions to elicit information regarding depressive symptoms. One interview format which is widely used by researchers, however, is the Schedule for Affective Disorders and Schizophrenia ([SADS]; Endicott & Spitzer, 1978). Questions from the SADS that probe for symptoms of major depression and for symptoms of melancholia are provided in Appendix 2 of this book.

An episode of major depression is not diagnosed by a patient's current symptoms, but by his/her symptoms during the worst part of the current episode. One must determine the presence or absence of a syndrome (clustering of symptoms) which includes the required number of symptoms of major depression. Thus, if a patient has not met criteria in the past week or two, but clearly did a month prior to the interview, the person may still be within the overall episode of major depression. It is possible for patients with moderately severe depression to have periods of a half or even a whole day every few weeks where several of the symptoms, including depressive mood, may remit. These temporary remissions sometimes occur when the patient has scheduled an appointment for help and gains a sense of hope and relief. This can mislead an interviewer who does not probe beyond the current symptoms.

The dysphoric mood must be relatively pervasive throughout most of every day during the worst point of the depression. The disturbance must be prominent; that is, it should not be the mild dysphoria of which chronic depressives often complain. Patients may characterize their depressive mood by a variety of descriptors. They may say that they feel "depressed, sad, blue, hopeless, low, down in the dumps, or irritable." *DSM-III* allows for the possibility that some patients will not show persistent mood disturbance but will show pervasive or near pervasive decreases in interest in their usual activities (see paragraph 4 below). Concurrent with the persistent dysphoric mood, *DSM-III* requires that patients must have at least four out of eight other symptoms. These must also occur nearly every day for at least two weeks.

1. Poor appetite and/or weight loss have long been considered a hallmark of depressive illness. There has been less consensus regarding whether increased appetite and weight gain should also be counted as symptoms. Feighner et al. (1972) in the original St. Louis research criteria did not include hyperphagia and weight gain as symptoms of major depression while *DSM-III* and RDC have included these. For most patients the judgment of whether appetite is disturbed or weight is fluctuating is not problematic and is very straightforward. However, this can be a difficult symptom to assess in some patients for the following reasons:

A. A patient may have a medical illness or be on medication which may affect their appetite or weight.

B. Patients may experience fluctuating appetite with consistent, alternating low-level weight gains and losses. If this is different from their normal self it should probably be counted as a symptom.

C. Patients may report an increased appetite for sweets or chocolate, but a decreased appetite for their normal foods.

D. Patients may report that they are dieting, but that in contrast to their past diets, they are now losing weight effortlessly because they are not hungry.

E. Patients may report that they get no pleasure from eating but are nevertheless eating more than usual.

When the clinician encounters ambiguous symptoms such as these, it is probably best to decide if the symptom is present by using the following two guidelines: (1) Is it different from their normal self? (2) Does it seem to be a problem for them? That is, are they bothered by the symptoms? If the answer to both of these is yes, then it is probably best to count it as a clinical symptom.

The Research Diagnostic Criteria (RDC) provide guidelines for what constitutes significant weight gain and significant weight loss. They define these as a change of 1 pound a week over several weeks or 10 pounds a year when not dieting.

2. A second concomitant symptom of major depression is sleep disturbance: either insomnia or hypersomnia. Again, insomnia has long been considered a symptom of depression. Hypersomnia has only recently begun to be accepted as a symptom of major depression. In judging whether or not insomnia is present in a patient, the evaluator must consider initial, middle, and terminal insomnia. Initial insomnia occurs when a patient has difficulty going to sleep. The Hamilton Rating Scale for Depression rates this as present if a patient takes more than a half an hour to go to sleep, and this would seem to be a reasonable guideline. Middle insomnia describes the phenomenon of awakening during the night. This symptom is not rated for patients who awaken merely because of a need to void, to feed a baby, and so on, unless they have significant difficulty going back to sleep. Finally, terminal insomnia is present when patients awaken one to three hours prior to their usual time of arising. They may go back to sleep, have some difficulty returning to sleep, or not be able to sleep again at all. The SADS suggests that terminal insomnia be rated if a patient is unable to achieve more than five hours of sleep.

Hypersomnia occurs when a patient sleeps more than usual (not simply rests in bed more than usual). The SADS rates hypersomnia as present if the patient is sleeping at least one hour more than usual.

Problems which may arise in the judgment of whether insomnia or hypersomnia are present include:

A. Patients who work night shifts or swing shifts may have their sleep cycle disrupted because of having to conform to the pace of daily activities of others, or they may have their sleep disrupted by the changes in their work hours. Here it is useful to inquire as to what the person's sleep habits were like prior to the depression.

B. Patients may be on antidepressant medication or other medications causing an improvement of their sleep. The SADS suggests that patients be rated for what patients think their sleep would be like were they not on medication.

C. Some patients may report a mixture of hypersomnia and insomnia. That is, they may report sleeping excessively during the day and having difficulty sleeping at night.

D. Some patients will report staying up late at night until they fall asleep.

E. Patients may awaken due to pain from a physical illness.

Again, it can be helpful in ambiguous cases to decide if the sleep behavior is different from normal and whether it is perceived as a problem for the patient.

3. A third concurrent symptom of major depression is psychomotor disturbance—either in the form of agitation or retardation. This is more than a subjective sense of anxiety or fatigue, but must be relatively persistent overt behavioral change. The SADS suggests that psychomotor retardation should occur most of the time for seven or more consecutive days to be rated. Thus, for a person to be rated as having this symptom, he/she would need to be demonstrating clearly slowed speech or movements for most of every day for an entire week. In addition to slowed speech and slowed movements, patients may exhibit difficulty in initiating speech (increased pauses), or markedly reduced amounts of speech. Sometimes psychomotor retardation is clearly visible within the diagnostic interview. Even in such cases, however, the patient must still be asked about their behavior in this area since a person may not have exhibited it persistently throughout the week. It can be helpful to ask whether or not family or friends have commented that the patient is moving or talking more slowly.

Psychomotor agitation involves restlessness, pacing, and an inability to sit still. It may also involve constant talking or even yelling or shouting at times. Patients may exhibit this in the office by rubbing their hands together or pulling at their hair while remaining seated. In a more extreme form, a patient may actually get up out of his/her chair and walk around the room during the interview. The SADS suggests that for agitation to be rated as present, it must persist most of the time for at least several days. Difficulties in diagnosing this symptom sometimes arise when it is possible that psychomotor slowing has resulted from age, physical illness, or medication.

4. The fourth symptom of major depression is loss of interest or pleasure in the patient's usual activities. This may include a decrease in sexual drive. Patients often report that the things they normally do are not as pleasurable as usual for them. It is not necessary that the patients have *no* interest in their usual activities, but they must have *less* interest or derive less pleasure from several of the activities they are normally interested in.

5. Patients may also complain of a loss of energy or fatigue. Again, according to *DSM-III* criteria, this should be something which they experience every day. Sometimes the clinician will have to help the patient distinguish between loss of energy and loss of interest. Some patients report fatigue and loss of energy but upon reflection decide that it is actually their interest in things which has decreased.

6. Feelings of worthlessness, self-reproach, or excessive or inappropriate guilt are common in depression and are a sixth symptom of major depression. While *DSM-III* does not specify that self-reproach should be excessive or inappropriate, there are some actions for which it is appropriate to feel a reasonable degree of remorse. For example, someone who has deliberately harmed someone else might be experiencing appropriate self-reproach and appropriate guilt. At the same time it can be very difficult to decide when guilt is appropriate, and such a decision is laden with the cultural and moral values of the diagnostician. The general requirement that symptoms be present everyday or almost everyday for two weeks helps to determine when guilt is excessive, although it is conceivable that in some situations, the duration criterion could be met, and the guilt would still be appropriate.

7. While difficulty concentrating and slowed thinking are aspects of psychomotor retardation, complaints or evidence of diminished ability to think or concentrate such as slowed thinking or indecisiveness, are considered a separate symptom of major depression, perhaps because they may be present when psychomotor retardation is not. Patients may be asked about their ability to focus their attention on conversations, television programs, their work, and so on. Again, it is important to distinguish for the patient between loss of interest and inability to concentrate. In addition to the SADS probe questions, the patient may be asked, "Are there some things which you are interested in, but you still can't seem to keep your mind on them?"

8. Finally, any recurrent thoughts of one's own death, suicidal ideation, wishes to be dead, or suicide attempts are to be regarded as a symptom of major depression. It would seem reasonable that any suicide attempt within the two-week period would be judged as fulfilling this *DSM-III* criterion, although *DSM-III* is not clear on this point. Because patients in major depression do not necessarily experience thoughts of death or suicidal ideation every day, we feel that persistent suicidal ideation should be counted as a symptom even if it does not occur daily.

USING THE DSM-III IN DIAGNOSING DEPRESSION

Once organicity and psychosis have been ruled out, the most important step in applying *DSM-III* criteria is to determine whether or not an individual meets criteria for a Major Depressive Episode (criteria for this diagnosis are listed in Appendix 1 of this book). For persons meeting the criteria, the major depression may be superimposed on a chronic form of affective disorder (e.g., dysthymic and cyclothymic disorders), or it may be part of an overall bipolar disorder. If the person meets criteria for major depression, it may be diagnosed as "with psychotic features" or "with melancholia."

If there was not a two-week period during the episode where the person met criteria for major depression but they have experienced depression "most or all of the time" for the last two years, then they may meet criteria for Dysthymic Disorder (also in Appendix 1 of the book). If instead, there were numerous periods of hypomania and mild depression during the last two years, they may meet criteria for Cyclothymic Disorder. When one of these milder, chronic forms of depression preexisted the major depression by two years, then both the diagnosis of major depression and of the milder, chronic affective disorder is to be made.

If the depression is of shorter duration than two years and is of less than full syndromal intensity (i.e., does not meet criteria for Major Depressive Episode), then it may be diagnosed as Adjustment Disorder with Depressed Mood or Atypical Depression. A diagnosis of Adjustment Disorder requires, among other things, that there be an identifiable stressor, that the reaction be excessive or cause impairment and that it is not simply one instance of a pattern of overreaction as might be seen in personality disorders. Mild depression of less than two years' duration without an identifiable stressor would be diagnosed as Atypical Depression or might not be diagnosed as depression at all if the dysphoria were explainable by another psychiatric condition.

References

Abrams, R., & Taylor, M. A. (1980). A comparison of unipolar and bipolar depressive illness. *American Journal of Psychiatry, 137,* 1084–1087.

Akiskal, H. S. (1983). Dysthymic disorder: Psychopathology of proposed chronic depressive subtypes. *American Journal of Psychiatry, 140,* 11–20.

Akiskal, H. S., Rosenthal, T. L., Haykal, R. F., Lemmi, H., Rosenthal, R. H., & Scott-Strauss, A. (1980). Characterological depressions: Clinical and sleep EEG findings separating "subaffective" dysthymias from "character spectrum" disorders. *Archives of General Psychiatry, 37,* 777–783.

Akiskal, H. S., Walker, P., Puzantian, V. R., King, D., Rosenthal, T. L., & Dranon, M. (1983). Bipolar outcome in the course of depressive illness: Phenomenologic, familial, and pharmacologic predictors. *Journal of Affective Disorders, 5,* 115–128.

American Psychiatric Association. (1968). *Diagnostic and statistical manual of mental disorders* (2nd ed.). Washington, DC: Author.

American Psychiatric Association. (1980). *Diagnostic and statistical manual of mental disorders* (3rd ed.). Washington, DC: Author.

Andreasen, N. C. (1982). Concepts, diagnosis and classification. In E. S. Paykel (Ed.), *Handbook of affective disorders.* New York: Guilford Press.

Andreasen, N. C., & Grove, W. M. (1982). The classification of depression: Traditional versus mathematical approaches. *American Journal of Psychiatry, 139,* 45–52.

Andreasen, N. C., & Winokur, G. (1979). Newer experimental methods for classifying depression: A report from the NIMH Collaborative Pilot Study. *Archives of General Psychiatry, 36,* 447–452.

Angst, J. (1966). Zur Atiologie and Nosologie endogener depressiver Psychosen. *Monographien aus dem Gesamtgebiete der Neurologie and Psychiatrie.* Berlin: Springer.

Angst, J., Baastrup, P., Grof, P., Hippius, H., Poldinger, W., & Weis, P. (1973). The course of monopolar depression and bipolar psychoses. *Psychiatrica, Neurologica, et Neurochirurgia, 76,* 489–500.

Baron, M., Klotz, J., Mendlewicz, J., & Rainer, J. (1981). Multiple threshold transmission of affective disorders. *Archives of General Psychiatry, 38,* 79–84.

Beigel, A., & Murphy, D. L. (1971). Unipolar and bipolar affective illness: Differences in clinical characteristics accompanying depression. *Archives of General Psychiatry, 24,* 215–220.

Benjaminsen, S. (1981). Primary nonendogenous depression and features attributed to reactive depression. *Journal of Affective Disorders, 3,* 245–259.

Bertelson, A., Harvald, B., & Hauge, M. (1977). A Danish twin study of manic-depressive disorders. *British Journal of Psychiatry, 130,* 330–351.

Billings, A. G., Cronkite, R. C., & Moos, R. H. (1983). Social-environmental factors in unipolar depression: Comparisons of depressed patients and nondepressed controls. *Journal of Abnormal Psychology, 92,* 119–133.

Blashfield, R. K., & Draguns, J. G. (1976a). Evaluation criteria for psychiatric classification. *Journal of Abnormal Psychology, 85,* 151–155.

Blashfield, R. K., & Draguns, J. G. (1976b). Toward a taxonomy of psychopathology: The purpose of psychiatric classification. *British Journal of Psychiatry, 129,* 574–583.

Boyd, J. H., & Weissman, M. M. (1981). Epidemiology of affective disorders. *Archives of General Psychiatry, 38,* 1039–1046.

Brill, H. (1974). Classification and nomenclature of psychiatric conditions. In S. Arieti (Ed.), *American handbook of psychiatry.* New York: Basic Books.

Brown, G. W., & Harris, T. O. (1978). *Social origins of depression: A study of psychiatric disorder in women.* New York: Free Press.

Carlsson, G. A., Kotin, J., Davenport, Y. B., & Adland, M. (1974). Follow-up of 53 bipolar manic depressive patients. *British Journal of Psychiatry, 124,* 134–139.

Caveny, E. L., Wittson, C. L., Hunt, W. A., & Herrman, R. S. (1955). Psychiatric diagnosis: Its nature and function. *Journal of Nervous and Mental Disease, 121,* 367–373.

Clayton, P. J., Halikas, J. A., & Maurice, W. L. (1972). The depression of widowhood. *British Journal of Psychiatry, 120,* 71–78.

Coppen, A., Metcalfe, M., & Wood, K. (1982). Lithium. In E. S. Paykel (Ed.), *Handbook of affective disorders.* New York: Guilford Press.

Coryell, W., & Tsuang, M. T. (1982). Primary unipolar depression and the prognostic importance of delusions. *Archives of General Psychiatry, 39,* 1181–1184.

Coryell, W., & Winokur, G. (1982). Course and outcome. In E. S. Paykel (Ed.), *Handbook of affective disorders.* New York: Guilford Press.

Costello, C. G. (1982). Social factors associated with depression: A retrospective community study. *Psychological Medicine, 12,* 329–339.

Davidson, J., Turnbull, C., Strickland, R., Belyea, M. (1984). Comparative diagnostic criteria for melancholia and endogenous depression. *Archives of General Psychiatry, 4,* 506–511.

Depue, R. A., & Monroe, S. M. (1978). The unipolar-bipolar distinction in the depressive disorders. *Psychological Bulletin, 85,* 1001–1029.

Detre, T., Himmelhoch, J., Swartzburg, M., Anderson, C. M., Byck, R., & Kupfer, D. J. (1972). Hypersomnia and manic-depressive disease. *American Journal of Psychiatry, 128,* 1303–1305.

Endicott, J., & Spitzer, R. L. (1978). A diagnostic interview: The Schedule for Affective Disorders and Schizophrenia. *Archives of General Psychiatry, 35,* 837–844.

Engel, G. L. (1977). The need for a new medical model: A challenge for biomedicine. *Science, 196,* 129–136.

Faravelli, C., & Poli, E. (1982). Stability of the diagnosis of primary affective disorder: A four-year follow-up study. *Journal of Affective Disorders, 4,* 35–39.

Feighner, J. P., Robins, E., Guze, S. B., Woodruff, R. A., Winokur, G., & Muñoz, R. (1972). Diagnostic criteria for use in psychiatric research. *Archives of General Psychiatry, 26,* 57–63.

Feinberg, M., & Carroll, B. J. (1982). Separation of subtypes of depression using discriminant analysis: I. Separation of unipolar endogenous depression from nonendogenous depression. *British Journal of Psychiatry, 140,* 384–391.

Feinberg, M., & Caroll, B. J. (1983). Separation of subtypes of depression using discriminant analysis: Separation of bipolar endogenous depression from nonendogenous ("neurotic") depression. *Journal of Affective Disorders, 5,* 129–139.

Gershon, E. S., Baron, M., & Leckman, J. F. (1975). Genetic models of the transmission of affective disorders. *Journal of Psychiatry Research, 12,* 301–317.

Gillespie, R. D. (1929). Clinical differentiation of types of depression. *Guy Hospital Reprints, 79,* 306–344.

Glassman, A. H., & Roose, S. P. (1981). Delusional depression: A distinct entity? *Archives of General Psychiatry, 38,* 424–427.

Goodwin, D. W., & Guze, S. B. (1984). *Psychiatric diagnosis.* New York: Oxford University Press.

Hamilton, M., & White, J. (1959). Clinical syndromes in depressive states. *Journal of Mental Disorders, 105,* 485–498.

Helzer, J. E., Clayton, P. J., Pambakian, R., Reich, T., Woodruff, R. A., & Reveley, M. A. (1977). Reliability of psychiatric diagnosis. II: The test/retest reliability of diagnostic classifications. *Archives of General Psychiatry, 34,* 136–141.

Helzer, J. E., Robins, L. N., Taibleson, M., Woodruff, R. A., Reich, T., & Wish, E. D. (1977). Reliability of psychiatric diagnosis. I: A methodological review. *Archives of General Psychiatry, 34,* 129–133.

Hirschfeld, R. M. A. (1981). Situational depression: Validity of the concept. *British Journal of Psychiatry, 139,* 297–305.

Karasu, T. B., & Skokol, A. E. (1980). VIth Axis for DSM-III: Psychodynamic evaluation. *American Journal of Psychiatry, 137,* 607–610.

Katz, M. M., Robins, E., Croughan, J., Secunda, S., & Swann, A. (1982). Behavioural measurement and drug response characteristics of unipolar and bipolar depression. *Psychological Medicine, 12,* 25–36.

Kendell, R. E. (1975). The concept of disease and its implications for psychiatry. *British Journal of Psychiatry, 127,* 305–315.

Kendell, R. E. (1976). The classification of depressions: A review of contemporary confusion. *British Journal of Psychiatry, 129,* 15–28.

Klein, D. F. (1974). Endogenomorphic depression: A conceptual and terminological revision. *Archives of General Psychiatry, 31,* 447–454.

Klein, D. F. (1978). A proposed definition of mental illness. In R. L. Spitzer & D. F. Klein (Eds.), *Critical issues in psychiatric diagnosis.* New York: Raven Press.

Klein, D. F., & Davis, J. M. (1969). *Diagnosis and drug treatment of psychiatric disorders.* Baltimore: Williams & Wilkins.

Klerman, G. L., Endicott, J., Spitzer, R., & Hirschfeld, R. M. A. (1979). Neurotic depressions: A systematic analysis of multiple criteria and meanings. *American Journal of Psychiatry, 136,* 57–61.

Klerman, G. L., Weissman, M. M., Rounsaville, B. J., & Chevron, E. S. (1984). *Interpersonal psychotherapy of depression.* New York: Basic Books.

Kraepelin, E. (1913). *Manic-depressive insanity and paranoia,* in *Textbook of psychiatry* (R. M. Barclay, trans.). Edinburgh: E & S Livingstone.

Leonhard, K. (1957). *Aufteilung der Endogenen Psychosen.* Berlin: Akademieverlag.

Lewinsohn, P. M., Zeiss, A. M., Zeiss, M. A., & Haller, R. (1977). Endogenicity and reactivity as orthogonal dimensions in depression. *Journal of Nervous and Mental Disorders, 164,* 327–332.

Liebowitz, M. R., & Klein, D. (1981). Interrelationship of hysteroid dysphoria and borderline personality disorder. *Psychiatric Clinics of North America, 4,* 67–87.

Liebowitz, M. R., Quitkin, F. M., Stewart, J. W., McGrath, P. J., Harrison, W., Rabkin, J., Tricamo, E., Markowitz, J. S., & Klein, D. F. (1984). Phenelzine versus Imipramine in atypical depression: A preliminary report. *Archives of General Psychiatry, 41,* 669–677.

Matussek, P., Söldner, M., & Nagel, D. (1981). Identification of the endogenous depressive syndrome based on the symptoms and the characteristics of the course. *British Journal of Psychiatry, 138,* 361–372.

Mendels, J., & Cochrane, C. (1968). The nosology of depression: The endogenous-reactive concept. *American Journal of Psychiatry, 124,* 1–11.

Mendlewicz, J., & Baron, M. (1981). Morbidity risks in subtypes of unipolar depressive illness: Differences between early and late onset forms. *British Journal of Psychiatry, 139,* 463–466.

Menninger, K., Mayman, M., & Pruyser, P. (1963). *The vital balance; The life process in mental health and illness.* New York: Viking Press.

Murphy, G. E., Woodruff, R. A., Herjanic, M., & Fischer, J. R. (1974). Validity of the diagnosis of primary affective disorder: A prospective study with a five-year follow-up. *Archives of General Psychiatry, 30,* 751–756.

Nelson, J. C., & Bowers, M. B., Jr. (1978). Delusional unipolar depression: Description and drug response. *Archives of General Psychiatry, 35,* 1321–1328.

Nelson, J. C., & Charney, D. S. (1980). Primary affective disorder criteria and the endogenous-reactive distinction. *Archives of General Psychiatry, 37,* 787–793.

Nelson, J. C., & Charney, D. S. (1981). The symptoms of major depressive illness. *American Journal of Psychiatry, 138,* 1–13.

Paykel, E. S. (1974). Recent life events and clinical depression. In E. K. Gunderson & R. H. Rahe (Eds.), *Life stress and illness,* Springfield, IL: Charles C Thomas.

Pearlin, L. I., & Schooler, C. (1978). The structure of coping. *Journal of Health and Social Behavioral, 19,* 2–21.

Perris, C. (1966). A study of bipolar and unipolar recurrent depressive psychoses. *Acta Psychiatrica Scandinavica, 42*(Suppl. 194): 1.

Perris, C. (1982). The distinction between bipolar manic-depressive and unipolar affective disorders. In E. S. Paykel (Ed.), *Handbook of affective disorders.* New York: Guilford Press.

Prusoff, B. A., Weissman, M. M., Klerman, G. L., & Rounsaville, B. J. (1980). Research Diagnostic Criteria subtypes of depression: Their role as predictors of differential response to psychotherapy and drug treatment. *Archives of General Psychiatry, 37,* 796–801.

Reveley, A. M., & Reveley, M. A. (1981). The distinction of primary and secondary affective disorders: Clinical implications. *Journal of Affective Disorders, 3,* 273–279.

Robins, E., & Guze, S. B. (1972). Classification of affective disorders: The primary-secondary, the endogenous-reactive, and the neurotic-psychotic concept. In T. A. Williams, M. M. Katz, & J. A. Shield (Eds.), *Recent Advances in the Psychobiology of the Depressive Illnesses.* DHEW Publication No. (HSM) 79–9053, US Government Printing Office.

Rose, J. T. (1963). Reactive and endogenous depression response to E.C.T. *British Journal of Psychiatry, 109,* 213–217.

Rosenthal, T. L., Akiskal, H. S., Scott-Strauss, A., Rosenthal, R. H., & David, M. (1981). Familial and developmental factors in characterological depressions. *Journal of Affective Disorders, 3,* 183–192.

Rush, A. J. (1985). Diagnosis of affective disorders. In A. J. Rush & K. Z. Altshuler (Eds.). *Recent advances in the diagnosis and treatment of depression.* New York: Guilford Press.

Schacht, T., and Nathan, P. E. (1977). But is it good for the psychologists? *American Psychologist, 32,* 1017–1025.

Schlesser, M. A., Winokur, W., & Sherman, B. M. (1980). Hypothalamic-pituitary-adrenal axis activity in depressive illness. *Archives of General Psychiatry, 37,* 737–743.

Spitzer, R. L., & Endicott, J. (1978). Medical and mental disorder: Proposed definition. In R. L. Spitzer & D. F. Klein (Eds.), *Critical issues in psychiatry diagnosis.* New York: Raven Press.

Spitzer, R. L., Endicott, J., & Robins, E. (1978). Research Diagnostic Criteria: Rationale and reliability. *Archives of General Psychiatry, 35,* 773–782.

Spitzer, R. L., & Williams, J. B. W. (1980). Classification of mental disorders and *DSM-III.* In H. I. Kaplan, A. M. Freedman, & B. J. Sadock (Eds.), *Comprehensive textbook of psychiatry* (3rd ed.; Vol. 1). Baltimore: Williams & Wilkins.

Spitzer, R. L., & Williams, J. B. W. (1982). *Hysteroid dysphoria:* An unsuccessful attempt to demonstrate its syndromal validity. *American Journal of Psychiatry, 139,* 1286–1291.

Spitzer, R. L., & Wilson, P. T. (1975). Nosology and the official psychiatric nomenclature. In A. M. Freedman, H. I. Kaplan, & B. J. Sadock (Eds.), *Comprehensive textbook of psychiatry* (2nd ed.; Vol. I). Baltimore: Williams & Wilkins.

Stengel, E. (1959). Classification of mental disorders. *Bulletin of the World Health Organization, 21,* 601–621.

Szasz, T. S. (1957). The problem of psychiatric nosology. *American Journal of Psychiatry, 114,* 405–413.

Szasz, T. S. (1961). *The myth of mental illness.* New York: Harper & Row.

Trzebiatowska-Trzeciak, O. (1977). Genetical analysis of unipolar and bipolar endogenous affective psychoses. *British Journal of Psychiatry, 131,* 478–485.

Ullmann, L. P., & Krasner, L. (1965). Introduction. In L. P. Ullman & L. Krasner (Eds.), *Case studies in behavior modification.* New York: Holt, Rinehart, & Winston.

Van Valkenburg, C., Lowry, M., Winokur, G., & Cadoret, R. (1977). Depression spectrum disease versus pure depressive disease: Clinical, personality, and course differences. *Journal of Nervous and Mental Disease, 16,* 341–347.

Warheit, G. J. (1979). Life events, coping, stress, and depressive symptomatology. *American Journal of Psychiatry, 136,* 502–507.

Weissman, M. M., & Klerman, G. L. (1977). Sex differences in the epidemiology of depression. *Archives of General Psychiatry, 34,* 98–111.

Weissman, M. M., Pottenger, M., Kleber, H., Ruben, H. L., Williams, D. & Thompson, W. D. (1977). Symptom patterns in primary and secondary depression. *Archives of General Psychiatry, 34,* 854–862.

Winokur, G. (1979). Unipolar depression: Is it divisible into autonomous subtypes? *Archives of General Psychiatry, 36,* 47–52.

Winokur, G., Cadoret, R., Dorzab, J., & Baker, M. (1971). Depressive disease: A genetic study. *Archives of General Psychiatry, 24,* 135–144.

Winokur, G., Clayton, P., & Reich, T. (1969). *Manic-depressive illness.* St. Louis, MO: C. V. Mosby.

World Health Organization. (1978). Mental disorders: Glossary and guide to their classification in accordance with the ninth revision of the *International Classification of Diseases.* Geneva: Author.

Zerbin-Rudin, E. (1969). Zur Genetik depressiver Erkrankungen. In Hippius & Selbach (Eds.), *Das Depressive Syndrom* (pp. 37–56). München, Berlin: Urban and Schwarzenberg.

Zigler, E., & Phillips, L. (1961). Psychiatric diagnosis: A critique. *Journal of Abnormal and Social Psychology, 63,* 607–618.

Zubin, J. (1977–78). But is it good for science? *Clinical Psychologist, 31,* 5–7.

Chapter 12

The Assessment of the Severity and Symptom Patterns in Depression

Brian F. Shaw
T. Michael Vallis
Scott B. McCabe
University of Toronto and The Clarke Institute of Psychiatry

INTRODUCTION

This chapter is concerned with the assessment of psychological variables related to depression (specifically major depressive disorders [MDD]). Depression involves psychological (e.g., self-criticism, anhedonia), biological (e.g., weight loss, insomnia), and social (e.g., avoidance, passivity) symptoms that impair an individual's ability to function normally. The emphasis of this review will be on methods to assess the severity and symptom pattern of depression with particular attention to the reliability, validity, and clinical utility of the measures.

Reliability and validity are important in the assessment of depression (or any construct) for at least three reasons. First, in order to design an appropriate intervention strategy an accurate descriptive classification or diagnostic system needs to be established. As the number of psychological interventions for depression increases the question of the efficacy of specific treatments with specific types of individuals will receive more attention. For instance, traditional clinical thinking posits that pharmacological or physiological interventions are particularly effective with certain subtypes of depression (e.g., tricyclic antidepressants for patients with endogenous depression without hypochondriasis), whereas almost by exclusion psychological interventions are frequently considered more effective for individuals not exhibiting these features. These treatment decisions place a heavy emphasis on accurate assessment and subtyping. Second, without a reliable and valid assessment it becomes very difficult to select appropriate targets for intervention for a given individual's treatment. Some depressed patients, for example, exhibit pervasive anhedonia and require careful planning of daily activities. Others exhibit social skills deficits and benefit from skill acquisition programs. Third, in order to evaluate the effectiveness of therapy some metric of symptom severity is required. If this metric lacks adequate reliability and/or validity, evaluation is impaired, if not prevented.

In our evaluation of the major psychological methods for assessing depression, we will consider both interview methods and self-report methods of assessment. This review will include some measures still in the development stage. The review is not intended to be exhaustive. Instead, it is designed for relatively easy use as a reference by the clinician. Assessment techniques can be categorized into those that screen for the *presence of depression* (i.e., diagnostic assessments concerned with the inclusion and exclusion criteria) and those that assess the *severity of the depression* (not directly relevant for diagnostic purposes). It is important not to confuse the information provided by these two types of tests.

When considering the assessment of depression the clinician must always remain aware of the fact that depression is a multifaceted condition. Despite numerous efforts, work on subtyping this disorder has generally been unrewarding. Nevertheless, we can expect that in time research will provide clinically meaningful classifications (see Skinner & Blashfield, 1982). At present, one surprising error that can still be observed involves confusing the syndrome of depression with one of its symptoms (most frequently mood; Beck, 1967). Thus, when an individual's mood changes there is a tendency to think that all other symptoms will also change. A positive change in mood that sometimes precedes a suicide attempt is but one example of erroneous thinking underscoring the importance of not equating symptoms and the syndrome. Adequate assessment of depression should not be restricted to a single dimension, such as mood, but should sample the range of relevant factors including psychological, biological, and social functioning.

Before we begin our discussion of the psychological assessment of depression a further word about subtypes of depression is in order. As a result of recent research (e.g., Depue & Monroe, 1979) as well as the advent of the Research Diagnostic Criteria ([RDC]; Spitzer, Endicott, & Robins, 1978) and the *Diagnostic and Statistical Manual—III* ([*DSM-III*]; American Psychiatric Association, 1980), renewed attention to the value of classifying the depressions has developed. Techniques reviewed in this chapter are most frequently used with *DSM-III* categories of major depressive disorder, bipolar disorder, (bipolar I, II, and III), dysthymic disorder, intermittent depressive disorder, and minor depressive disorder. One might question how psychological assessment fits with such categorization. Do all of the assessment measures apply to all categories, or only to certain subtypes? Our position is that regardless of the type of depression it is essential to assess the severity and pattern of the depressive symptomatology. By classifying we anticipate descriptive and prognostic differences between groups. An empirical emphasis on assessment will help determine the relevant differences. Please note that this chapter deals with the severity and symptom pattern of a depressive episode, not the differential diagnoses of depression, which is dealt with in Chapter 11 by Leber, Beckham, and Danker-Brown. Also, we focus mainly on the depressive aspect of affective disorders. For completeness, however, we review two selected measures of mania in the appendix of this chapter.

INTERVIEWING THE DEPRESSED PATIENT

Among the most frequent interview methods are the Hamilton Rating Scale for Depression ([HRSD]; Hamilton, 1960; Hamilton & White, 1959), the depression subsection of the Schedule for Affective Disorders and Schizophrenia ([SADS]; Endicott & Spitzer, 1978), and the depression subsection of the Present State Examination ([PSE]; Wing, Birley, Cooper, Graham, & Isaacs, 1967). Prior to reviewing these methods, however, we consider some of the more practical issues involved in interviewing a depressed patient. These issues (common to all interviews) include the interviewer's knowledge of the disorder, of the behavioral correlates of depression, and the interviewer's clinical demeanor.

The task of interviewing a depressed patient can be a difficult and frustrating one frequently accompanied by irritability and negative affect on the part of the interviewer (Beck, 1967). Depressed individuals may experience marked difficulties maintaining an interpersonal interaction, particularly when they are under pressure to produce information. They may be unresponsive, have difficulty following questions, or be nondisclosing, all of which can contribute to the interviewer's frustration.

Before beginning an interview several factors need to be considered. It is assumed that the interviewer is familiar with the range of depressed symptomatology. Despite problems and objections to the system (e.g., Smith & Kraft, 1983) familiarity with the *Diagnostic and Statistical Manual* (*DSM-III*) is recommended. Interviewers should also be aware of the paradoxical reports of depressed patients. Beck (1967) discusses some of these paradoxes. For example, a successful business woman may portray her level of functioning as inefficient when she has in fact experienced only a small change in an otherwise highly efficient manner. The reports of depressed patients are often stated in absolutes or extremes. It is important for the interviewer to have the necessary skills (i.e., warmth, empathy, ability to reflect content, feeling, or process) to be sensitive to the patient's verbal and nonverbal communication. These skills understandably increase the completeness and validity of the information obtained by increasing self-disclosure. For example, a patient may be seriously considering suicide and yet be reluctant on first contact to tell this information to the interviewer. The probability of disclosure is increased if the clinician is perceived as understanding, warm, and concerned. Instructional texts, such as Evans, Hearn, Uhlemann and Ivey (1984) are useful to develop these interviewing and counseling skills.

In terms of the actual content of the information obtained the interviewer should obtain a relevant and complete history. This history should definitely include information about the current episode, past episodes, significant medical history, and family history. It is often useful to have the patient make an initial report on a Life History Questionnaire (Lazarus, 1971). Any additional relevant information on known markers or risk factors for depression (e.g., a history of bipolar disorder in a first-degree relative) should also be obtained. Kupfer and Rush (1983) have outlined the specific factors relevant to depression that should be included in scientific reports. This outline can also serve as a guide to the types of information clinicians should obtain from depressed patients.

When interviewing a depressed individual it is important to work toward an understanding of the patient's phenomenology (i.e., the situation *from his/her perspective*). While a patient's descriptions may seem implausible or exaggerated to the interviewer (e.g., "I am hollow inside," "I think I might be the devil I'm so evil") they are understandable in that they may be based on a negative view of the self, the world, and the future (Beck, 1967). Discussion of a diagnosis is reassuring to most patients who are confused about their symptomatology. However, diagnostic formulations should not be presented without a clear opportunity to answer questions. Avoid using the term *depressive* to describe the patient as there is an implication of a trait that may reinforce a notion that the patient will remain depressed. Most patients experience episodes of depression and, while they may remain vulnerable to depression, few are chronically depressed (see Chapter 17 by Akiskal and Simmons for a discussion of dysthymic disorder). Clinicians should also be aware that discussing diagnosis might increase a patient's sadness as a result of the labeling process (i.e., "I'm depressed because I'm depressed"). For these reasons, it is important to obtain feedback from patients as to their reactions to the interview and interviewer. Depressed patients may misinterpret an interviewer's comments in a negative way. For example, if an interviewer interrupts the patient in an attempt to structure the interview the patient may interpret this behavior as an indication that the interviewer doesn't respect him/her, or is not really interested in what he/she has to say. Thus, it is useful to explain the constraints of the interview with respect to limited time, necessary information to be gathered, and the importance of direction at the onset of the interview before such negative reactions can occur. Patients may be informed that their task is to let the interviewer see the full extent of their current feeling, thinking, and behavior. Some patients react self-critically if they cry and a supportive encouraging response is required. The clinician should avoid perjorative labeling of the patient and an attitude that the patient may *want* to be depressed. (Like defense lawyers, clinicians would be wise to assume that their patients want to be free, of depression.)

The clinician must always be sensitive to possible suicidal ideation or behavior when interviewing a depressed individual. While a few novice clinicians may endorse the myth that questioning about suicide might increase its likelihood, this belief has *not* been supported by research or experience. An open, frank, and matter-of-fact discussion of suicide is essential for an accurate assessment of suicidal potential (Linehan, 1981). Several suicide scales may be useful guides to the clinician's questioning: the Suicide Ideation Scale

(Beck & Kovacs, 1979); the Reasons for Living Questionnaire (Linehan & Chiles, 1983; also see Chapter 18 of this book on predictors of suicidal behavior by Boyer and Guthrie).

In addition to the content of the patient's reports, nonverbal characteristics may be useful indicators of depression. Speech rate and quality of voice are often associated with depressed affect. Depressed individuals will often speak in a slowed manner and their voice is frequently monotone. A change in activity level is another nonverbal behavior associated with depression. Depressed individuals may be slowed in their physical movements as well as their speech rate (psychomotor retardation). Conversely, agitation (increased activity noted by such things as pacing, wringing of the hands, shifting in chair) may be a feature of the depressed individual's presentation. The posture of a depressed individual may also give clues to depression. Depressed individuals commonly sit with their heads down and their shoulders slumped forward, avoid eye contact, and smile rarely (see work on nonverbal behavior by Fisch, Frey & Hirsbrunner, 1983; Ekman & Friesen, 1974; Waxer, 1974).

It must be stressed that the above verbal and nonverbal indicants are not always differentially diagnostic of depression. These behaviors are frequently observed in psychiatric conditions other than depression (e.g., anxiety states, schizophrenia). It is important, nonetheless, to be sensitive to the above features, as they are readily observable and are clear signs of disordered functioning and equally important improvements in the patient's condition.

More formal techniques to assess the overt behavior and speech qualities of depressed individuals have been developed, and are worthy of mention. Williams, Barlow and Agras (1972) have developed the Ward Behavior Checklist for use with hospitalized patients. This scale has been demonstrated to have excellent inter-rater reliability and has been shown to relate to other measures of depression. Lewinsohn (1976) and Howes and Hokanson (1979) assessed the verbal behavior of depressives as it relates to the construct of social skill and have developed an elaborate coding scheme for speech content. Assessment techniques such as those developed by Williams et al. (1972), Lewinsohn (1976), and Howes and Hokanson (1978) have not been widely employed when assessing depression in the clinic. Also, the extent to which these assessment systems are appropriate for nonhospitalized patients (or to patients with less severe depressions) is not clear. Nonetheless, these techniques are available and can be developed.

INTERVIEW METHODS OF ASSESSING DEPRESSION

In this section we review the Schedule for Affective Disorders and Schizophrenia, the Hamilton Rating Scale for Depression, and the Present State Examination. We realize this review is not exhaustive. We chose to consider in detail several of the most common methods rather than presenting limited reviews of numerous methods.

Schedule for Affective Disorders and Schizophrenia

To facilitate the reliability of interviews used to establish Research Diagnostic Criteria (RDC) diagnoses, Endicott and Spitzer (1978) designed the Schedule for Affective Disorders and Schizophrenia (SADS). The SADS was developed in an attempt to reduce the variance between interviewers in the type and amount of information available from which to make a diagnosis. To reduce the variance in the criteria (both inclusion and exclusion criteria) required to make a diagnosis the Research Diagnostic Criteria were also specified by this group (Spitzer et al. 1978). Alternatively, the *DSM-III* classification system which was developed after the RDC may be used but there are some differences between RDC and *DSM-III* diagnostic criteria. It is noteworthy that the SADS is not restricted to the assessment of depression, but covers a wide variety of psychiatric categories, including major depressive disorder, dysthymic disorder, schizophrenia, anxiety disorders and personality disorders.

Three versions of the SADS interview are available: the regular version, the lifetime version, and the change version. The regular version is composed of two parts. Part I assesses the symptomatology (and severity) of the current episode. The current episode is evaluated both at its worst point and over the week prior to the interview. Part II assesses past psychiatric disturbances and relevant historical information (e.g., schooling, adolescent social patterns). The lifetime version of the SADS is similar to Part II of the regular version, except the current episode is included within the time frame of the interview (i.e., historical information up to and including the present). As a result, less consistent and detailed information is provided about the current episode in the lifetime version. Also, the lifetime version does not allow for assessment of the severity of the current episode. The change version of the SADS involves those questions from Part I of the regular version which assess severity. By obtaining severity judgments over time (e.g., before and after treatment) a measure of change is obtained.

The SADS interview is highly structured and involves the use of a detailed guide. The interviewer progresses through a series of specific questions that cover a variety of psychiatric conditions. Depending on the answers to the questions the interviewer can explore in greater detail specific symptoms and characteristics related to a particular disorder (e.g., if a patient has had a period of at least one week where the predominant mood was sadness then the specific relevant symptomatology of a major depression are explored in detail). Interviewers are encouraged to use all sources of information available in making their decisions. It is recommended that the SADS be employed only by highly trained individuals with extensive clinical knowledge. In our experience the average interview requires two hours to complete.

In addition to diagnostic decisions, the SADS interview allows the calculation of summary scale scores. These summary scales were developed on the basis of clinical knowledge and on factor analyses of types of psychopathology. Summary scales for depression include depressive mood and ideation, endogenous features, depressive-associative features, and suicidal ideation and behavior.

Reliability estimates for the depression section of the SADS are impressive. Endicott and Spitzer (1978) report inter-rater reliability coefficients (intraclass coefficients) of at least .95 for the depression summary scales. These data were based on 150 interviews. As well, the internal consistency of the summary scales was high (at least .95), and the scales were moderately intercorrelated (.40 to .90). Finally, the summary scales were shown to correlate moderately (.42 to .68) with the depression scales of the Katz Adjustment Scale (Katz & Lyerly, 1963) and the Symptom Checklist ([SCL-90]; Derogatis, Lipman, & Covi, 1973).

In terms of the reliability of diagnoses made through SADS interviews, Spitzer et al. (1978) report a kappa of .90 for the diagnosis of major depressive disorder and .81 for minor depressive disorder (the RDC criteria were used). Clearly, these data indicate that the RDC and the SADS interview can be employed in a highly reliable manner. In addition to having high reliability, the SADS reduces the variance in information obtained by different interviewers and can be adapted to *DSM-III* diagnoses. This latter point suggests that the SADS can be a widely applicable method for clinicians.

Perhaps the weakest feature of the SADS is that it is time consuming, and therefore costly, to administer. It requires the efforts of a skilled clinician familiar with psychopathology. This requirement may restrict its use since there are numerous settings where experienced clinicians do not have sufficient time to administer a two-hour interview. A related concern has to do with the fact that the SADS addresses the issue of establishing a diagnosis more than it does the issue of formulating the most appropriate treatment plan. A clinician with limited time might choose to perform a functional assessment (e.g., Hersen & Bellack, 1976) that would yield information with more direct treatment implications, although in time it is hoped that specific descriptive diagnoses will be more useful to the prediction of treatment response. More recently two other structured interview formats that yield *DSM-III* diagnoses have been developed for use by unskilled interviewers (the Diagnostic Interview Schedule [DIS], Robins, Helzer, Croughan, & Ratcliff, 1981; and the Structured Clinical Interview for Diagnosis [SCID]; Williams & Spitzer, 1984).

The Diagnostic Interview Schedule (DIS), for instance, has been developed for use by laypersons. As with the SADS, the DIS assesses a wide variety of psychiatric conditions in addition to depression. Interviewers proceed through the highly structured interview guide, recording answers to closed-ended questions. Probes are required for some questions, and these are indicated in the guide. The actual probes to be used are specified in the guide. Thus, very little is left to the discretion of the interviewer. Questions are designed to yield decisions both on a lifetime basis as well as more currently (last two weeks, last month, last six months, last year). As well, the information generated is consistent with both RDC and *DSM-III* criteria. Robins et al. (1981) compared interviews by laypeople with one week of training to those by psychiatrists, with favorable results. For instance, kappas of .63 and .64 resulted for *DSM-III* and RDC diagnoses of depression respectively. Further, laypersons identified 80 percent of depression cases and 84 percent of noncases (no depression diagnosis) that were identified by psychiatrists. Thus, the possibility of using nonclincian evaluation for the assessment of depression (and other psychiatric disorders) is very real indeed.

The Hamilton Rating Scale for Depression

The Hamilton Rating Scale for Depression (HRSD) is historically the most common interview measure of depression. It was devised by Hamilton (1960) to improve on other measures available at the time. According to Hamilton (1960) the major disadvantages with depression measures existing in the 50s included the following: the measures were often developed with a normal population and therefore were not sensitive to qualitative and quantitative differences from clinical depression, self-report measures had low reliability and were of limited use with semiliterate patients; and general psychopathology measures did not assess depression with sufficient precision.

Hamilton's original scale involved 21 items, 17 of which were scored. The remaining four (diurnal variation, depersonalization, paranoia, obsessive-compulsiveness) were considered either unrelated to the severity of depression or were too infrequent to be included in the scoring. The HRSD was intended to be used as an index of severity with individuals already diagnosed as suffering from depression (i.e., it is not a diagnostic measure). The scale is completed following a clinical interview (Hamilton estimated 30-minute interviews as typical). While some rough interview guidelines were presented by Hamilton, there is often considerable variability in the type and amount of information obtained by different interviewers (see Sotsky & Glass, 1983). Hamilton acknowledged that ". . . its value depends entirely on the skill of the interviewer in eliciting the necessary information. . ." (1960, p. 56). Interviewers are encouraged to use all sources of information available to them, in addition to the actual interview.

There have been two modifications to the HRSD since the original version. First, specific descriptive anchor points were developed for each of the values for each item. This was intended to objectify the ratings. Second, the "cognitive" items, assessing hopelessness, helplessness, and worthlessness, have been added. The 24-item scale is currently being used in the NIMH Treatment of Depression Collaborative Research Program (see Elkin, Parloff, Hadley, & Autry, 1985). Even though there are up to 24 items in the scale, most researchers score only the assigned 17 items. Thus, the value of the additional items is questionable (i.e., if they are not included in the total score for the severity of the disorder, they serve only as descriptors). Of the 17 scorable items, 9 are rated on 5-point (0–4) scales, and 8 on 3-point (0–2) scales (total scores range from 0 to 52). The 0–2 items are limited to judgments of whether the symptom is present or absent with a score of 1 reserved for judgments that the symptom is trivial or doubtful. No evaluation is made as to the degree of severity on these items (Hamilton, personal communication, 1984). The 0–4 items reflect a symptom that is either absent or present to a trivial, mild, moderate, or severe degree (scores of 1, 2, 3, or 4, respectively). Hamilton (personal communication, 1984) states that "the rater should not hesitate to record if the symptom is severe, even though he recognizes that other patients are even worse." This introduces ambiguity into the ratings, since a given rating may represent different things for two different patients. It was originally suggested that two raters complete the HRSD for each interview and their scores be summed. This procedure enhances the reliability of ratings (see Epstein, 1979). In lieu of two raters, Hamilton (1960) recommended that the score of a single rater be doubled. While this method makes the score comparable to when two raters are involved it in no way enhances reliability. It would avoid confusion if the number of raters is clearly reported in clinical or scientific documents.

Scores on the HRSD (based on a single rater) of 6 or below are considered to reflect normal, nondepressed functioning; scores of 7–17 are considered to reflect mild depression; scores of 18–24 are considered to reflect moderate depression; and scores of 25 or more are considered to reflect severe depression. In several major multisite collaborative psychotherapy studies (e.g., the NIMH Treatment of Depression Collaborative Research Program), a score of 14 or greater is required for outpatients to be entered into the study (Sotsky & Glass, 1983). A cutoff score of 17 has frequently been used as the criterion for entry into many drug outcome studies (see Endicott, Cohen, Nee, Fleiss, & Sarantakos, 1981).

The HRSD is perhaps the most frequently used severity measure of depression, particularly with inpatients and in drug outcome studies. There has been some variation in the scoring of the scale (e.g., some investigators score the helplessness, hopelessness, and worthlessness items; see Hedlund & Vieweg, 1979). While these modifications have not markedly influenced the reliability and validity coefficients of the HRSD (Hedlund & Vieweg, 1979; Sotsky & Glass, 1983) they do impair the comparability of the HRSD to the original 17-item version. If summary scores are used it is important to note whether any modifications have been made to the original scale. To minimize misinterpretation of data, it would be possible for clinicians who use some modification of the scale to also report the 17-item score.

Very little data is available on the internal consistency of the HRSD. Schwab, Bialow, and Holzer (1967) report item-total correlations ranging from .45 to .78 for medical patients. Bech, Bolwig, Kramp, and Rafaelsen (1979) reported item-total correlations ranging from −.02 to .81 (median = .47). Thus, the scale demonstrates only moderate homogeneity. For a scale to assess the range of depressive symptomatology adequately, however, low to moderate internal consistency may not be a major problem, a point considered more fully below.

Data on the inter-rater reliability of the HRSD are impressive. Hedlund and Vieweg (1979) reviewed nine studies which report inter-rater reliability coefficients of .84 or above (the exception was one study which reported a coefficient of .52) It is important to note that these investigators conducted a systematic search of all available research reports on the HRSD from 1967 to 1979. Therefore, the high reliabilities reported above are not likely a function of selective reporting.

The HRSD is most frequently used by experienced clinicians and as such, it may be expensive, particularly if Hamilton's recommendations are followed and two raters are used. Notably, O'Hara and Rehm (1983) found that with only five hours of training undergraduates could reach acceptable inter-rater reliability ($r = .76$). Each of the three trained undergraduate students' ratings correlated at least .82 with the mean rating of four expert judges. Ziegler, Meyer, Rosen, and Biggs (1978) examined the reliability of the HRSD when ratings were made from a videotape of an interview. Ratings made by psychiatric residents (via videotape) correlated .97 with ratings made by two experienced psychiatrists (via actual interview). Together, these data are encouraging in that they suggest that experienced professionals may not be required for the HRSD to be employed in a reliable manner. Nonetheless, caution should be used when interpreting data from inexperienced raters. Reliability of nonprofessional raters must be documented, it cannot be assumed.

High inter-rater reliability of the HRSD may be partly a function of the shared background, experience, and attitude that exist when raters from the same setting are used (Sotsky & Glass, 1983). Different raters from different settings are less likely to be similar on these factors and may therefore attenuate reliability. Further, Sotsky and Glass (1983) suggest that the range of scores might be restricted when the HRSD is employed with moderately depressed outpatients. This possibility relates to the heavy loading of somatic items on the HRSD, relative to mood or cognitive items. Outpatients may experience less somatic symptoms than inpatients. Restriction of range of scores would be expected to lower the reliability coefficient. Sotsky and Glass's (1983) position is bolstered by data from their pilot study that revealed only moderate inter-rater reliability (.52) when raters were from different sites and moderately depressed outpatients were evaluated.

Based on the data from the pilot study, Sotsky and Glass (1983) propose specific guidelines for scoring HRSD items. These guidelines are more highly operationalized than those provided by Hamilton. They focus on the following dimensions: severity, frequency, objectivity, specificity, and activity. Once raters had been trained in the use of these guidelines inter-rater reliability increased to .78. Clearly, further interest in the use of these guidelines is warranted. Increased specificity in the scoring criteria will facilitate the use of this scale. This development is particularly exciting given that the HRSD can be used reliably by relatively nonexperienced raters.

In terms of validity, the HRSD has been shown to differentiate depressed individuals from normals, and to differentiate depressed individuals from nondepressed psychiatric patients (Hedlund & Vieweg, 1979). As well, HRSD scores are related to global severity ratings by clinicians, and moderately related to other measures of depression such as the BDI, the SDS, and the MMPI (e.g., based on a survey of a wide variety of studies, Hedlund & Vieweg

[1979] reported median correlations between the HRSD and the BDI, SDS, and MMPI as follows: .58, .45, and .44, respectively).

While concurrent validity estimates are acceptable, data on discriminant validity are less available. Sotsky and Glass (1983) report a study by Giser which found that HRSD scores were as highly correlated to the depression scale of the SCL-90 (Derogatis et al., 1973) as they were to the anxiety and obsessive-compulsive scales of the SCL-90, which calls into question the discriminative validity of the scale.

In addition to being correlated with other scales the HRSD has repeatedly been shown to be sensitive to change in the severity of depression, as measured by global ratings and other tests. Several factor analyses have been conducted on the HRSD. While numerous factors (up to six) have been extracted only two consistent factors emerge across studies. One factor taps the general severity of depression, on which all items tend to load positively. The second factor can be labeled agitated-retarded in that symptoms of anxiety and retardation load highly (and in opposite direction) on this factor.

Endicott et al. (1981) report a procedure for deriving HRSD ratings from the SADS interview. They present a specific algorithm whereby SADS scores on specific items can be converted to HRSD scores on corresponding items. In a few cases several items from the HRSD are collapsed into one item in the SADS. When raters completed the HRSD and SADS on 48 depressed inpatients, the correlation between extracted HRSD (extracted from the SADS) and actual HRSD scores was .92. Endicott et al. (1981) point out that agreement between extracted and actual HRSD scores is about the same as the agreement between actual HRSD scores from more than one rater.

In conclusion, the HRSD is an interview measure that appears to be reliable, demonstrates moderate associations with other depression measures, and is sensitive to change. Data suggest that specific steps can be taken to increase reliability and that there is potential for the scale to be used by trained but relatively nonexperienced individuals (e.g., undergraduates). The HRSD can also be extracted reliably from the SADS interview. While the scale is generally useful, there are some additional problems with the scale that should be noted. First, the anchor points for some items are unclear. For instance, the anchor points for the psychic anxiety item mix objective observation (scale value 3—apprehensive attitude apparent in face or speech) with self-reported concern not necessarily limited to the present (e.g., scale value 2—worrying about minor matters). This raises a second problem with the scale: ratings include two time periods, the immediate situation and the past week. There are no guidelines for resolving discrepancies which occur between these two time frames. Finally, it should be noted that one item, insight, is rarely scored in an outpatient setting. Such a low-frequency item would contribute little to the scale. Future work with this scale should address these issues. Also, future research should focus on the use of the HRSD with moderately depressed outpatients as well as focus on the discriminative validity of the HRSD.

The Present State Examination

Another interview method used to assess depression, and psychopathology in general, is the Present State Examination ([PSE]; Wing et al., 1967). This measure is a semistructured interview designed to assess the presence of a variety of psychopathological conditions present over the preceding month. The interview was designed as a clinician rating scale and not simply a verbal questionnaire. The interviewer asks questions that probe various areas of psychopathology. Once an area of pathology is suspected the interviewer begins a process that Wing et al. (1967) label as "cross-examination." The task is to obtain sufficient information on which to make specific decisions about the presence, absence, or severity of a particular symptom. The interviewer decides if a particular symptom is present; the patient's responses are not accepted uncritically. Nine editions of this interview have been constructed. Reliabilities for the depression subsection have ranged from .72 to .90 in several studies. Based on PSE information only, two independent examiners reached agreement 80 percent of the time on diagnoses of psychotic depression and nonpsychotic depression (Wing, Cooper, & Sartorias, 1974). Reliability of ratings of the presence of specific symptoms of depression were also acceptable. In contrast to the data on reliability little data pertaining to validity are available.

The PSE appears to be a reliable instrument. It has not been used all that frequently (particularly in North America) and thus, accumulated experience with this scale is not great. The interviewer focuses on only the past month and this format is a limiting factor, since historical information is essential for diagnoses such as bipolar disorder and dysthymic disorder. Finally, as discussed by Wing et al. (1967), the use of the PSE by a wide variety of interviewers has not been systematically examined. Thus, at the present time, the PSE interview is less useful than either the HRSD or the SADS interview.

SELF-REPORT METHODS OF ASSESSMENT

In this section we will describe and evaluate the following self-report tests: the Beck Depression Inventory (BDI), the Minnesota Multiphasic Personality Inventory-Depression Scale (MMPI-D), the Carroll Rating Scale for Depression (CRS), the Zung Self-Rating Depression Scale (SDS), the Center for Epidemiologic Studies-Depression Scale (CES-D), the Lubin Depression Adjective Checklist (DACL), and the Visual Analogue Scale (VAS). Note that with the exception of the MMPI-D none of these scales were originally designed to diagnose depression but rather were meant to measure depressive symptomatology or severity. Even though diagnosis was the original aim of the MMPI-D this goal has not been attained.

Beck Depression Inventory

The Beck Depression Inventory ([BDI]; Beck, Ward, Mendelson, Mock, & Erbaugh, 1961) is the most frequently used self-report method of assessing severity of depression. The scale is essentially clinically derived and designed to measure both "attitudes and symptoms which appeared to be specific for depression and those which were consistent with descriptions in the psychiatric literature. . ." while not intending "to reflect any theory regarding the etiology of depression" (Beck & Beamesderfer, 1974, p. 155). This 21-item scale was originally intended to be interviewer assisted, but common practice at present is to have the patient complete the test in an unassisted self-report manner. Each item in the inventory consists of four self-evaluative statements scored 0 to 3, with increasing scores indicating greater severity of depression. Responses are added to yield a total score, ranging from 0 to 63. One item that assesses weight loss is not scored if the individual indicates that he/she has been attempting to lose weight. BDI scores are generally categorized into levels of depression in the following manner: 0–9 indicates a normal nondepressed state, 10–15 reflects mild depression, 16–23 reflects moderate depression, and 24–63 reflects severe depression. In many clinical settings posttreatment scores between 0–9 are considered to indicate depression in remission, scores between 10–15 to indicate partial remission, and scores between 16–63 to indicate that the individual remains symptomatic. Easy administration facilitates the use of the scale in clinical applications. Repeated administration allows assessment of between session change and quick evaluation of suicidal ideation.

Extensive examination of the internal consistency of the scale has been reported in the literature. Split-half reliability coefficients have been reported in the range of .58 to .93 (Beck & Beamesderfer, 1974; Gallagher, Nies, & Thompson, 1982; Reynolds & Gould, 1981; Strober, Green, & Carlson, 1981). Item-total correlations ranged from .22 to .86 with the average being .68 (Strober et al., 1981). Test-retest reliability, although suggested to be a poor evaluative criterion due to the expected fluctuation of symptom severity during a depressive episode, ranged from .69 to .90 (Gallagher et al., 1982; Strober, et al., 1981).

In terms of concurrent validity the BDI has correlated with clinician's ratings of depth of depression in the range of .62 to .77 (Beck et al., 1961; Bumberry, Oliver, & McClure, 1978; Metcalfe & Goldman, 1965; Nussbaum, Wittig, Hanlon, & Kurland, 1963; Salkind, 1969; Strober et al., 1981). As well, correlations with HRSD, MMPI-D, SDS, and MACL have been moderate to good (Bloom & Brady, 1968; Burkhart, Gynther, & Fromuth, 1980; Nielson, Secunda, Friedman, & Williams, 1972; Nussbaum et al., 1963; Schwab et al., 1967; Williams et al., 1972; Zung, 1969).

The BDI is a useful instrument as it has also been demonstrated to be applicable across a variety of cultures. Cross-cultural applicability has been tested in subjects from Switzerland, France, Finland, and Czechoslovakia (Blaser, Low, & Schaublin, 1968; Delay, Picot, Lemperiere, & Mirouze, 1963; Stenback, Rimon, & Turunen, 1967; Vinar & Grof, 1969). As well, various forms of the BDI, including an abridged version (13 items, Beck & Beck, 1972) and a modified version (the scoring key was removed to avoid possible response bias due to the numbers beside each of the self-evaluative statements; statements were randomized; and respondents were instructed to pick the most representative statement) have been used and demonstrated to be adequately reliable and valid (Beck & Beamesderfer, 1974; May, Urquart, & Taran, 1969; Reynolds & Gould, 1981; Scott, Hannum, & Ghrist, 1982). The abridged version has also been shown to be an effective tool for clinicians requiring a quickly administered device to screen for depression (Beck & Beck, 1972), although the 21-item BDI takes only 10 to 15 minutes to complete.

The BDI has been criticized as being a measure of a social undesirability response set and not a measure of depression (Langevin & Stancer, 1979). Although Beck and Beamesderfer (1974) have addressed this issue and suggest that social undesirability might in itself be diagnostic of depression, Langevin and Stancer (1979) viewed this explanation as unacceptable. They maintained that depression is a "unitary concept" and as such, should have only one factor in a factor analytic study. In fact, more than one factor is usually identified. However, depression has always been identified as a varied, diverse problem with affective, physiological, behavioral, and cognitive symptoms associated with it. Thus, on a scale designed to measure many aspects of depressive symptomatology it is predictable that more than one factor would be extracted in a factor analysis. In fact, social desirability, as measured by the Marlowe-Crowne social desirability scale (Crowne & Marlowe, 1960), has only been weakly correlated to the BDI ($r = -.26$; Reynolds & Gould, 1981). As other researchers (e.g., Nevid, 1983) have pointed out in a similar controversy involving the Hopelessness Scale (Beck, Weissman, Lester, & Trexler, 1974), a scales covariation with social desirability should not make it invalid as long as the covariation is consistent with theory, and overlap between the two constructs is not completely redundant. Similarly, although many factors are extracted in factor analytic studies of the BDI (e.g., Weckowicz, Muir, & Cropley, 1967) as long as they are in line with depressive symptomatology and/or theory, the scales should not be viewed as useless or simply measuring another concept. The position that there is only one factor in depression runs counter not only to the use of the BDI but to a multidimensional notion of depression. The fact that many depression scales, including the BDI, are designed to assess the variety of factors involved in depression has implications for the internal consistency estimates. Low estimates might not reflect a poor scale, they might suggest a multifactored scale. Factor analyses of the BDI clearly support this notion.

Another criticism of the BDI has been reported in a study of 170 undergraduate psychology students reported by Meites, Lovallo, and Pishkin (1980). These authors found the correlation between the BDI and the Taylor Manifest Anxiety Inventory ($r = .64$) greater than the correlation between the BDI and the SDS ($r = .60$). Thus the BDI may be as highly related to anxiety measures as depression measures. Future work on the discriminant validity of the BDI is required, particularly with clinical samples including anxiety disorders.

Minnesota Multiphasic Personality Inventory

The MMPI (Hathaway & McKinley, 1943) was originally designed to be an objective pencil and paper method of deriving psychodiagnostic labels for individuals. Due to the unreliability of the nosological system (see Hersen, 1976) and high intercorrelations between scales, however, this purpose has largely failed. Current procedures for interpretation include descriptions of the person's likely behaviors and attitudes based on a profile analysis rather than on the interpretation of individual scale scores. Overlap between scale items makes such a profile interpretation of questionable validity.

The MMPI is an empirically derived scale whose items were selected, not necessarily on face, or construct validity principles, but on their ability to discriminate between normal and patient groups. Thus the validity of the scales is dependent on the validity of the diagnosis of the criterion group. The resultant scale contains 566 self-referent items, including 4 validity scales and 10 clinical scales. Other scales have been developed in addition to these but are not typically used in standard clinical practice. Items of the MMPI are answered in a forced choice true/false format and scale scores are standardized (T-scores, mean = 50, standard deviation = 10). T-scores greater than 70 are interpreted as clinically significant and, as noted earlier, the pattern of the scale elevations is an important consideration.

The MMPI-D scale consists of 60 items and was originally designed to measure symptomatic depression. The items include aspects of depression such as low self-worth, psychomotor retardation, withdrawal, lack of interest, and physical complaints. Although high scores (above 80 T) may suggest clinical depression, more moderate scores tend to be indicative of low morale and lack of involvement (Graham, 1977). Since the depression scale is a good indicant of distress, high scores (above 70 T) may suggest a need for psychotherapy or counseling (Graham, 1977).

In terms of internal consistency, split-half reliability coefficients have been reported in the range of .58 to .84 (Gilliland & Colgin, 1951; Winfield, 1952). Test-retest reliability coefficients with a delay of one day to two weeks have been reported in the range of .69 to .96 in college students (Butcher & Dahlstrom, 1964; Faschingbauer, 1972; Windle, 1955) and .72 to .89 in psychiatric patients (Eichman, 1973; Jurjevich, 1966; Newmark, 1971, 1973).

The MMPI-D scale has also been shown to have acceptable concurrent validity. Correlation coefficients with other self-report measures (e.g., BDI, SDS) fall in the moderate to good range (r = .56 to .80: Biggs, Wylie, & Ziegler, 1978; Brown & Zung, 1972; Nussbaum et al., 1963; Zung, 1967, 1968, 1969; Zung, Richards, & Short, 1965). Also, comparisons between clinician's ratings of depression and MMPI-D scores have shown moderate correspondence (r = .51: Endicott & Jortner, 1966).

Factor analytic studies of the internal structure of the MMPI-D have consistently shown multiple factors, many that are not consistent with depression (Comrey, 1957; O'Conner, Stefic, & Gresock, 1957). Both Comrey (1957) and O'Conner et al. (1957) have suggested that rather than one score for depression, the scale should be interpreted in component parts based on their factor analytic studies. Dempsey (1964) shortened the 60-item scale to 30 items (D–30) in an attempt to increase its homogeneity. Using contextual analysis (Dempsey & Baumoff, 1963), he calculated a coefficient of dimensionality for each item. Only those items best correlating to a depressive dimension were retained. This resulted in a significant improvement in the split-half reliability of the test despite shortening it by 30 items. Dempsey (1964) proposed that the 30 items more accurately measure depression and that the 30 excluded items actually contributed more to error variance than to depression score variance.

Another study attempting to refine the MMPI-D scale was reported by Burkhart, Gynther and Fromuth (1980). These authors categorized MMPI-D items as obvious, neutral, and subtle in their relationship to depression. They found that the correlation between the MMPI-D obvious items (D–O) and the BDI was greater ($r = .60$) than between the BDI and the full-scale correlation ($r = .49$). As well, it was seen that the subtle items were *negatively* correlated to BDI scores ($r = -.22$). Burkhart et al. (1980) suggest that "practitioners may want to give more weight to D–O [obvious, face valid item scores] than to the standard D scores because the former predict the criterion [BDI scores] more powerfully than the latter" (p. 751, bracket added).

The fact that it was developed for diagnostic purposes clearly limits the applicability of the MMPI-D scale. Nevertheless, it is frequently used to index severity, and these two purposes should not be equated. High D-scale scores may not necessarily reflect the severity of depression since the MMPI scales are highly correlated. Thus, elevations on the other scales (e.g., psychoasthenia or hypochondriasis) might account for elevations in the D-scale (due to item overlap). This problem, in conjunction with the difficulty in criterion validation of the MMPI (i.e., scale items chosen not necessarily to tap relevant aspects of depression but simply to differentiate depressed from nondepressed groups) leads us to not recommend this test. Other instruments described in this chapter have more to recommend them as measures of depressive symptomatology.

The Carroll Rating Scale for Depression

Carroll et al. (Carroll, Feinberg, Smouse, Rawson, & Greden, 1981) developed the Carroll Rating Scale for Depression (CRS) to obtain a self-report instrument closely following the item content of the HRSD. Because the BDI is concerned mostly with psychological and cognitive features whereas the HRSD is more concerned with behavioral and somatic features, the BDI in itself was not seen as an adequate self-report inventory (Carroll et al., 1981).

The CRS consists of 52 statements with each written in a self-descriptive format (e.g., "I feel in good spirits"). Individuals respond to each question in a forced choice yes/no format based on their feelings over the past few days. To partially control for possible acquiescent response sets, 40 statements are keyed yes while the remaining 12 statements are indicative of depression if answered no.

The CRS translates the HRSD to a self-report format, and like the HRSD, has a total score range of 0 to 52. HRSD items scored 0 to 4 are represented by four statements in the CRS, while items scored 0 to 2 on the HRSD are represented in the CRS by two statements. The cutoff indicating clinically significant depression is a score of 10.

Internal consistency has been reported by Carroll et al. (1981) in the form of split-half correlations coefficients (r = .87) and item total correlations, (median r = .55, range = .05 to .78). A correlation matrix involving items of the CRS and the HRSD indicated that corresponding item correlations ranged from −.06 to .73 (median .60). This would indicate that a direct match between CRS and HRSD items was not obtained, although the diagonal of the matrix showed that 13 of 17 CRS items were correlated most strongly with their HRSD counterpart. Items measuring retardation, agitation, somatic anxiety, and loss of insight were correlated most strongly to other HRDS items rather then their intended counterparts.

In terms of concurrent validity, total score correlations between the HRSD and the CRS range from .71 to .80 (Carroll et al., 1981; Feinberg et al., 1981); the BDI and the CRS correlated r = .86; and the CRS was correlated with a clinician's four-point global rating of depression .67. The CRS has also been correlated with patients global self-ratings on a Visual Analogue Scale (to be described later) .68 (Feinberg, Carroll, Smouse, & Rawson, 1981).

The CRS was able to distinguish severity of depression at a level comparable to the HRSD for a low-severity group. As severity of depression increases the CRS scores no longer match the HRSD scores (scores on the CRS are greater than scores on the HRSD with increased severity; Feinberg et al., 1981).

Thus the CRS relates well to the HRSD. There may be some tendency for the CRS scores to be inflated as severity of depression increases. As well, there seems to be a tendency for nonendogeneous patients (these patients who had a primary diagnosis of neurotic depression) to overrate the severity of their symptoms. Overall, the utility of this measure is good in that it is comparable to the HRSD while not requiring the clinician to interview the patient.

Zung Self-Rating Depression Scale (SDS)

Zung (1965) developed a self-rating scale that was intended to be a short, comprehensive, and reliable instrument that measured severity of depression. Items were developed to tap features of depression that had been identified in previous factor analytic studies (e.g., Friedman, Cowitz, Cohen, & Granick, 1963; Grinker, Miller, Sabshin, Nunn, & Nunnally, 1961; Overall, 1962). Twenty items were generated following this method. Items assess mood (e.g., feeling downhearted and blue, crying spells), psychological factors (e.g., hopelessness, irritability, suicidal, ideation) and psychomotor factors (e.g., agitation, retardation). Each item is rated on a four-pointed continuous scale, with scale anchors ranging from, "a little of the time," to "most of the time." Half of the 20 items are worded in a depressed tone (e.g., "I feel down-hearted and blue") and half are worded in a nondepressed tone (e.g., "I feel that I'm useful and needed").

The scale is presented in easy-to-administer booklets and requires minimal time (10–15 minutes) to complete. Each item is assigned a weight from 1 to 4, with 4 refering to the most depressed alternative. A depression index is then generated by summing the item scores and dividing by 80. This index yields a value from .25 to 1.00, with 1.00 being the maximum.

Very little work has been conducted to investigate the reliability of this scale. We are unaware of data that address the stability of the SDS (i.e., test-retest reliability) or the internal consistency of the scale (i.e., split-half and item-total coefficients), although Knight, Waal-Manning, and Spears (1983) report an alpha coefficient of .79 for the SDS. While one might argue that a scale designed to measure the severity of depression does not require test-retest reliability (see discussion in BDI section) the paucity of other reliability studies is notable.

On the other hand, more effort has been devoted to issues of validity. Zung et al. (1965), Zung (1969), and Zung and Wonnacott (1970) have demonstrated that the SDS discriminates depressed from nondepressed psychiatric patients and normal subjects (nondepressed patients had diagnoses such as anxiety reactions, personality disorders, and psychological disturbances).

While the SDS appears to differentiate depressed from nondepressed individuals, its ability to discriminate severity of depression is less clear. Carroll, Fielding, and Blashki (1973) found that the SDS did not discriminate severity of depression among patients while Biggs et al. (1978) reported that SDS scores differed significantly among four groups of depressed outpatients classified in terms of severity by clinician's global ratings. Zung and Wonnacott (1970) attempted to establish whether the SDS could discriminate responders to electroconvulsive therapy (ECT) or pharmacotherapy. This was done in an attempt to predict treatment response based on SDS scores. This study was poorly designed for this purpose, however, and instead attempted to discriminate the ECT group from the drug-treated group on specific SDS items.

Accumulated data on concurrent validity indicates that the SDS correlates moderately to highly with the HRSD, the MMPI-D scale, the BDI, and clinicians' estimates of the severity of depression (Biggs et al., 1978; Brown & Zung, 1972; Zung, 1967, 1969; Zung et al., 1965). Raft, Spencer, Toomey, and Brogan (1977) found that general medical outpatients who were diagnosed as having "masked depression" (individuals whose primary complaint was somatic illness) were not identified by the SDS. These authors conclude that the SDS should not be used in a general medical setting due to this possible misclassification. Finally, Zung (1967) demonstrated that the SDS is not influenced by a variety of demographic factors, including age, sex, marital status, education, financial status, and intellectual level.

One of the useful features of the SDS is that is has been translated into 10 different languages. Zung (1969) demonstrated that the scale discriminated diagnostic groups (depressed from nondepressed and normal) for most of these translated version. The availability of translated versions clearly facilitates the use of this scale with a variety of populations.

In summary, the SDS is an easy to administer and widely applicable scale. It is lacking however in data on psychometric qualities (particularly reliability). The test was initially constructed to measure the severity of depression but the available validity data provide only weak evidence that this goal has been achieved. The scale appears more useful for the identification of depressed individuals than it does for the accurate assessment of the severity of depression. Also there is some evidence that it is not adequate for use in a general medical setting. It should be noted, however, that the SDS has been shown to be responsive to decreased depression as a function of successful treatment (Zung, 1965, 1968).

Center for Epidemiologic Studies Depression Scale

The Center for Epidemiologic Studies Depression scale (CES-D) was developed to measure depressive symptomatology in the general population (Radloff, 1977). The scale consists of 20 items obtained from other previously validated scales ([MMPI-D], [BDI], [SDS]; Gardner, 1968; Raskin, Schulterbrandt, Reatig, & McKeon, 1969). Items were selected from areas of depressive symptomatology previously described and validated. The items tap areas of depressed mood, feelings of guilt and worthlessness, feelings of helplessness and hopelessness, psychomotor retardation, loss of appetite, and sleep disturbance. Although previous scales have been designed to assess severity, the CES-D was intended to assess depressive symptomatology with emphasis on the affective component, depressed mood (Radloff, 1977). This goal was partially accomplished, as a factor analysis of the CES-D revealed four factors with the largest factor being depressed mood. This factor accounted for only 16 percent of the variance, however.

Individuals respond to each item based on the frequency of occurrence during the past week (0—rarely or none of the time [less than one day] to 3—most or all of the time [five to seven days]). Four of the items are worded in a positive manner to partially control for response bias. The range of the scores on the CES-D is 0 to 60 with higher scores indicating more symptom presence, weighted by frequency of occurrence. A suggested cutoff score of 16 is indicative of significant depressive symptomatology (Craig & VanNatta, 1978). Husaini et al. (Husaini, Neff, Harrington, Hughes, Stone, 1980) suggest cutoffs of 17 and 23 for "possible" and "probable" depression. The scale has been used in interviewer-assisted and self-report formats (Boyd, Weissman, Thompson, & Myers, 1982; Radloff, 1977).

Internal consistency of the CES-D is good. Split-half correlations were .85 for patient groups and .77 for normal groups. Coefficient alpha and Spearman-Brown coefficients were .90 and .92 for patients groups, .85 and .87 for normal groups. Test-retest (time interval—six months), with no intervening life events to disrupt scores, was .54 (Radloff, 1977).

In terms of concurrent validity, the CES-D has correlated moderately with other measures of depression (e.g., HRSD and Raskin scales). The CES-D and the DACL correlated .37 to .51 in normal groups while a correlation of .70 was found in patient groups (Radloff, 1977). Correlations with the BDI of .81 and .90 with the SDS have been reported for recovered depressed patients (Weissman, Prussoff, & Newberry, 1975). Interviewer ratings of depression and the CES-D correlated moderately at .46 to .53 (Radloff, 1977). As well it was demonstrated that the CES-D was responsive to change in patients severity of depression. Low negative correlations with social desirability as measured by the Marlowe-Crowne scale also lends to the scales usefulness.

Even though a factor analysis revealed four factors (depressed affect, positive affect, somatic and retarded activity, and interpersonal factors), they were all consistent with depresssion. For this reason, as well as the high internal consistency across groups, Radloff (1977) suggests that only a total score should be calculated. Boyd et al. (1982) found that of the persons who had scores of 16 or more only one third were diagnosed by the RDC as depressed, while 36 percent of those people diagnosed as having major depressive disorders had scores of less than 16. Boyd et al. suggest that these errors could be explained by nay saying response sets, or exclusion criteria of the RDC, or by the presence of other medical illnesses. They suggest methods of overcoming these problems, such as changing cutoff scores, incorporation of the test in an interview format, screening for other psychiatric or medical illness, and defining the construct "role impairment" in the RDC diagnostic criteria. In a similar study, Lewinsohn and Teri (1982) compared the CES-D to the SADS interview. Only 34 percent of those scoring above a cutoff score of 17 met criteria for depression in the SADS. The authors attribute the discrepancy to the fact that scales such as the CES-D represent tabulations of symptoms or complaints (regardless of etiology), rather than assessment of an independant syndrome. Together, these data suggest that the scale should not be used as a clinical diagnostic instrument (e.g., Boyd et al., 1982; Myers & Weissman, 1980), although these authors suggest that by lowering the cutoff scores, thereby reducing false negatives, this scale could be used as a rough screening instrument. The scale should also prove to be useful in nonpsychiatric settings.

Depression Adjective Checklist

The Depression Adjective Checklist (DACL) were designed to measure "transient depressed mood, feeling, or emotion" as the BDI and MMPI-D were "available for the measurement of more chronic enduring depression" (Lubin, 1965, p. 57). The author decided on a checklist format due to ease of administration and high face validity. Seven lists (four of 32 adjectives and three of 34) were developed. The four lists of 32 adjectives contained 22 positive adjectives (those adjectives checked more often by depressed patients) and 10 negative adjectives (those adjectives checked more often by normal subjects). The remaining three lists contain 34 adjectives, 22 positive and 12 negative. Responses are scored such that higher scores indicate greater depressed mood. Internal consistency of the lists is high, with split-half correlations ranging from .82 to .93 for the seven lists and correlations between the seven lists ranging from .80 to .93 (Lubin, 1965). Unfortunately, validity coefficients are rather disappointing. Concurrent validity coefficients with the MMPI-D are low to moderate (.25 to .53), although correlations with the BDI were somewhat better, in the range of .38 to .66 (Christenfeld, Lubin, & Satin, 1978; Lubin, 1965). Zung's Self-Rating Depression Scale correlated .41 with the DACL form E in one study (Christenfeld, Lubin, & Satin, 1978) and in the range of .51 to .64 in another study (Marone & Lubin, 1968). These latter authors also reported a correlation between clinician's global ratings and the DACL. Social desirability effects seem negligible in that Christenfeld, Lubin, and Satin (1978) found a correlation of .08 between the DACL and the Marlowe-Crowne Social Desirability Scale (Christenfeld, Lubin, & Satin, 1978). The DACL also seems responsive to changes in severity of depression. Lubin, Hornstra, and Love (1974) found that patients scores lowered from a pretreatment interview to a posttreatment three-month follow-up.

Clinical utility of the DACL is good in reference to administration time (two to three minutes) *but* the ability to discriminate between diagnostic groups has been shown to be less than adequate (Lubin, 1965). Also, issues of sex differences between lists has not been addressed. Users are informed of differences and are told to choose lists for use with reference to these differences (Lubin, 1965). A possible explanation for low concurrent validity coefficients with other instruments is that the DACL was designed to measure only a depressed mood compared with the syndrome of depression. Depression is a complex state involving cognitive, motivational, behavioral, and affective components. Thus, while the DACL is easy to administer it would not be recommended for clinical use unless a sophisticated method of measuring change was developed.

Visual Analogue Scale (VAS)

The Visual Analogue Mood Scale (VAMS), a modification of the scale proposed by Aitken (1969), is simply a 100-mm line. Individuals are asked to respond to the question "How is your mood right now?" by making a mark at some point on the line that best describes their mood. Anchors at the left edge are "worst" and at the right edge "best." The score is the distance in millimeters from the left edge of the line. Thus, higher scores indicate better mood. As a result, it would be likely that the correlations with measures of depression would be negative. In fact, negative correlations of −.61 to −.67 between VAMS and the SDS have been reported (Folstein & Luria, 1973; 1975). In comparing the Clyde Mood Scale (Clyde, 1950) to the VAMS it was found that the VAMS consistently reflected depression but not other moods such as aggression. Test-retest correlations have been reported in the range of .61 to .73 (Folstein & Luria, 1973). The Visual Analogue Scale for Depression (Aitken, 1969) has been compared to the HRSD, BDI, and SDS and correlations of .51 to .88 have been reported by Davies, Burrows and Poynton (1975).

The VAMS is reasonably related to depressed mood as indicated above but it is not suggested for uses other than obtaining only a rough estimate of *depressed mood*. The Visual Analogue Scales (VAS) seem reasonably related to depression and other depression measures but they are seriously lacking in the amount of information that they offer. As well, it is virtually impossible to compare two respondents' scores, as they may use different criteria to place themselves at various points on the line.

Comparative Value of Self-Report and Interview Measures

Given the multifaceted nature of depression, consideration of the advantages and disadvantages of self-report versus interviewer rater scales is in order. The characteristics of the self-report and interviewer rater measures reviewed in this chapter are presented in Table. 1. Interviewer rating scales are thought to have higher validity than self-report scales because of the extent of information available to the interviewer from both the patient and other sources. Kazdin (1981, p. 361) in a review of the measures to assess childhood depression states, "the interview not only allows the child to report on his or her perceptions of the problem but also permits the clinician to draw conclusions about areas the patient may not explicitly address. Thus, the sources of data available in an interview include, but also suppress, the information available from self-report measures."

The advantage of higher validity is potentially offset by the lower reliability of the interview-based measure. Test-retest reliability of the instruments is generally seen as impractical because of the changing nature (particularly the severity) of the disorder. Inter-rater reliability may be reduced by the varied ways of applying the rating scale. As we have seen *with training* many of these interview-based scales have good inter-rater reliability but the emphasis is on the training, and many clinicians have not had this type of training.

Self-report scales, on the other hand, may suffer from problems with validity despite strong reliability. Most of the scales have high face validity and, therefore, responses can be easily distorted by individuals who are operating with a social undesirability set for reasons other than depression. Individuals who want to fake good will also have little challenge. For this reason, these tests, like any psychometrics, require careful interpretation. With use, clinicians will begin to see patterns that will guide their interpretations. We still know very little about the validity of the test when we subject them to repeated applications (e.g., weekly testing with the BDI). Nonetheless, from a clinical position, it is most important to look for discrepancies in the endorsement of specific items from week to week. If a treatment is targeted to a specific aspect of the syndrome then these items deserve special scrutiny. For example, if a cognitive therapist intervenes on the patient's sense of failure he/she can check for changes in the patient's written as well as verbal self-report.

TABLE 1

Test	Type	Administration time	Reliability	Validity	Special qualities/limitations
Beck Depression Inventory (BDI)	Self-report	10–15 minutes 21 questions	Test-retest: $r = .69$ to .90 Split half: $r = .58$ to .93	Concurrent: $r = .62$ to .77 (clinicians ratings)	Translated versions available
Minnesota Multiphasic Personality Inventory-Depression Scale (MMPI-D)	Self-report	90–120 minutes* 60 items	Test-retest: $r = .69$ to .96 Split half: $r = .58$ to .84	Concurrent: $r = .56$ to .80 with other self-report scales $r = .51$ with clinicians 5 pt. ratings	Part of larger test which severely depressed patients may have trouble completing
Carroll Rating Scale for Depression (CRS)	Self-report	10–20 minutes 52 items	Split half: $r = .87$	Concurrent: $r = .71$ to .86 with other self-report scales $r = .67$ with clinicians ratings	
Zung Self-Rating Depression Scale (SDS)	Self-report	10–15 minutes 20 items	Not aware of any relevant data	Concurrent: $r = .56$ to .80 with other self-report scales $r = .69$ with clinicians estimates discriminant—acceptable	Translated into at least 10 languages
Center for Epidemiologic Studies Depression Scale (CES-D)	Self-report or interview	10–15 minutes 20 items	Test-retest: $r = .54$ Split half: $r - .77$ to .85	Concurrent: $r = .37$ to .90 with other self-report measures $r = .46$ to .53 with clinicians ratings	Difficult to assess utility in present form with suggested cutoffs

Instrument	Administration	Time	Reliability	Validity	Comments
Depression Adjective Checklists (DACL)	Self-report	2–3 minutes	Split half: $r = .82$ to $.93$	Concurrent: $r = .25$ to $.53$ discriminant poor	Poor discriminant validity only designed to measure mood
Visual Analogue Mood Scale (VAMS)	Self-report	1 minute	Test-retest: $r = .61$ to $.73$	Concurrent: $r = .51$ to $.88$	Rough estimate of depressed mood. Very little information given
Schedule for Affective Disorder and Schizophrenia (SADS) Depressive Subscales	Interviewer rated	15–30 minutes †	Inter-rater: .95 reliability of diagnosis: kappa = .80 – .90	Concurrent: $r = .40$ to $.68$	Time consuming to administer full scale
Hamilton Rating Scale for Depression (HRSD)	Interviewer rated	30 minutes	Inter-rater: $r = .52$ to $.98$ item-total: $r = .02$ to $.81$	Concurrent: $r = .44$ to $.58$	Questionnable discriminant validity
Present State Examination Depression Section (PSE)	Interviewer rated	15–30 minutes	Inter-rater: $r = .72 – .90$ reliability of diagnosis: 80 percent	Little to no available data	Restricted to past month not widely used in North America

* Entire MMPI requires this time. D scale could be completed in 10–15 minutes.
† Entire interview takes much longer to administer.

Special Considerations

Two issues in the assessment of the severity and symptom patterns of depression have direct clinical relevance and deserve special consideration: relevant subtypes, and conditions that may interfere with or cloud our judgments of depression.

Depression is an ubiquitous term. The concept has been used in a variety of ways over the years. The general public speaks of being depressed when they are referring to their sad moods. For most clinicians, however, the term is reserved for a syndrome or disorder that in turn can be divided into various subtypes. We have earlier commented on our preference at this time to follow the *DSM-III* categorization. While the system has some difficulties (e.g., its recent development precludes many statements about the differential treatment response or prognosis of groups, such as major depressive disorder and dysthymic disorder) it is based on relatively clear criteria that serve as a good foundation for future work.

The introduction of dysthymic disorder (previously categorized as neurotic depression) is one hallmark of the *DSM-III* as a descriptive nosology. Akiskal (1981; Akiskal, Rosenthal, Haykal, Lemmi, Rosenthal, & Scott-Strauss, 1980) has reported relevant research with these patients. He subdivides dysthymic patients into those with "character spectrum disease" (individuals who have characterological depression; early onset of symptoms) and those with "subaffective" disorder (those patients who have never really recovered from an episode of Major depression; typically later onset of symptoms). Further research is required to evaluate the prognostic value on preferred treatments of these conditions.

The differentiation of anxiety disorders from depression and a subtyping of anxious depressed patients (see Fowles & Gersh, 1981; Gersh & Fowles, 1981) remains uncertain and deserves comment. Whenever one is assessing depression it is useful to obtain a concomitant assessment of anxiety. Anxiety states are clinically important in that a number of depressed patients report concomitant anxiety, particularly as the severity of the depression lessens. Riskind and Beck (1983) reported using the Hamilton Rating Scale for Anxiety (Hamilton, 1959) to distinguish between generalized anxiety disorder, major depressive disorder, and "mixed" disorder (an amalgam of anxiety and depression symptoms). They found that clusters of symptoms rather than total scores were effective in discriminating the groups. This study is but one example of a line of research using multivariate statistical methods to discriminate diagnostic groups. The emphasis is on the grouping of symptoms from standard assessment instruments and the procedure emphasizes the importance of a careful selection of measures used to subtype patients.

Another subtyping distinction within depression is the endogenous-nonendogenous distinction. Endogeneous symptoms have been described by a number of investigators (e.g., Klein, 1974; Carroll, Feinberg, Greden, Haskett, James, Steiner, & Tarika, 1980). The previous endogenous-reactive or endogenous-exogenous categorizations that were dependent upon judgments of etiology (e.g., Kiloh & Garside, 1963) are no longer viewed as useful. Nevertheless, the new endogenous classifications are thought to be predictive, with recent research pointing to their value when using antidepressants. Notably studies using some forms of psychological interventions such as cognitive-behavior therapy (Beck, Rush, Shaw, & Emery, 1979) have not found the endogenous-nonendogenous classification to be useful in the prediction of treatment response (e.g., Blackburn, Bishop, Glen, Whalley, & Christie, 1981). Other subtypings such as hysteroid dysphoria (Klein, 1974; Williams & Spitzer, 1984) may prove to be useful in the future but at present there is little support for their value.

There are other subtypes of depression that deserve further consideration. Paykel (1971) reported on four categories of depressed patients (psychotic, anxious, and hostile depressed patients, and young depressed patients with personality disorder). Similarly, Overall and colleagues (e.g., Overall & Zisook, 1980) have also reported on a phenomenological classification system using the Brief Psychiatric Rating Scale (Overall & Gorham, 1962) and other scales to classify patients into four subtypes: anxious, hostile, retarded, or agitated. With the advent of microprocessors clinicians may be able to make better use of the complex information available to the field. In particular, the prediction of which types of patients will respond to which therapeutic interventions may require an assessment of subtypes. Following on the initial assessment to detect depression, to measure its severity, and to determine the appropriate subtype, the clinician will be in a better position to plan treatment. At present, clinicians tend not to use statistically derived subtypes (e.g., factor scores) due in part to technological limitations, and yet many of the measures previously reported may require factor or cluster analysis to derive treatment relevant predictions.

From a clinical perspective it is important to differentiate conditions where the symptoms of depression are concomitants of another disorder rather than a primary diagnosis. In fact, depression as a symptom is widely found in a number of disorders. Even more confusing is the tendency of some investigators to speak of depressive equivalents or masked depression. Depression may appear as a symptom in many disorders ranging from schizophrenia to phobic disorders. The term *secondary depression* was coined to describe individuals who have a primary medical or psychiatric diagnosis other than MDD and yet who also exhibit signs and symptoms of depression. At this time, it is difficult to assess differential treatment responses of primary versus secondary depressions and we can simply make note of the distinction and its potential usefulness. A number of medical disorders are accompanied by symptoms of depression (see Chapter 22 in this volume by Kathol) and these disorders should be ruled out.

Two conditions will be mentioned in this context as examples. Patients dependent upon alcohol or drugs *during withdrawal* frequently experience physiologically based symptoms of sleep disturbance, appetite loss, decreased libido, and a general apathy. These symptomatic changes are a function of the state of withdrawal rather than depression (Steer, Shaw, Beck &

Fine, 1977). Similarly, patients with anorexia nervosa who are under conditions of starvation may also experience symptoms of depression. Of course, some drug dependent and some patients with anorexia nervosa meet the criteria for a depressive disorder (Garner & Bemis, 1984).

Conclusion

This chapter reviewed the commonly used methods of detecting the syndrome of depression and measuring both its severity and symptom patterns. The major emphasis has been on the psychometric properties and the clinical utility of the measures. Advances in our field are often preceded by (and dependent upon) advances in the measurement of our constructs. In the past 20 years the assessment of depression has progressed and it is hoped that this chapter will serve as an encouragement to clinicians to employ these readily available, well-researched instruments while continuing to investigate the variations in this most interesting disorder.

SUMMARY

In this chapter we have reviewed the psychological assessment of depression. A large number of specific psychometric scales have been included. The number of methodological criteria, in combination with the number of measures examined, makes the task of integrating the information difficult. In an attempt to facilitate integration, Table 1 summarizes our evaluation of the various psychometric measures. The following criteria are evaluated: interrater reliability, internal consistency, concurrent validity, and a discriminant validity. As well, we distinguish the type of scale (self-report or interviewer rated) and include relevant comments where appropriate.

On the basis of our experience in working with depressed patients we have developed what we consider a useful assessment battery. Although some of these measures were not covered in the present chapter, readers might

TABLE 2
Recommended assessment battery

Session	Recommended measures
First Session	SADS Interview
	Hamilton Rating Scale (HRSD) extracted from the SADS Interview
	Beck Depression Inventory (BDI)
	Symptom Checklist-90 (SCL-90)
	Hopelessness Scale (HS)
Weekly	Beck Depression Inventory
Monthly	Hamilton Rating Scale for Depression (HRSD)
Termination	SADS-C
	Hamilton Rating Scale for Depression (HRSD)
	Beck Depression Inventory (BDI)
	Symptom Checklist-90 (SCL-90)
	Hopelessness Scale (HS)

find this information useful. Table 2 outlines our recommended assessment battery.

Brief Review of Selected Mania Measures

Although we focus selectively on assessment of depression in this chapter, it is instructive to briefly consider measures of mania. This is particularly relevant for cases of bipolar disorder. We include in this appendix a representative self-report and observer-rated scale, in that order.

MMPI—MA SCALE

The MMPI mania scale (Ma) is a 46-item, self-report scale developed to identify hypomanic symptomatology in psychiatric patients (McKinley & Hathaway, 1944). Common characteristics of mania include overactivity, elevated (but unstable) mood, and flight of ideas. Although the scale items are very heterogenous the more face valid items reflect these areas. Example items include: "I have periods of such great restlessness that I cannot sit long in a chair"; "At time I have fits of laughing and crying I cannot control"; and "At times my thoughts have raced ahead faster than I could speak them." The scale was developed using a criterion group of psychiatric patients suffering from hypomania and mild acute mania. Patients suffering from severe symptoms of mania are typically unable to concentrate sufficiently to complete this measure and were, therefore, left out.

Scores of the Ma scale are related to age and race. Young subjects often score in the range of 55 to 65T while it is not uncommon for older subjects to score below 50T. Black subjects typically score higher (range of 60 to 70T) than white subjects. Scores above 90T are clinically significant and may suggest the patient is in the manic phase of a manic-depressive disorder (Graham, 1977).

Internal reliability estimates reported in Dahlstrom, Welsh and Dahlstrom (1975) indicate that split-half reliability estimates range from .55 to .64. Test-retest reliability coefficients (psychiatric patients, interval one day to two weeks) range from .71 to .81.

Thus the Ma scale of the MMPI appears acceptably reliable. No comment on the validity of this scale can be made as we are unaware of any relevant data. Finally, it is important to note that acute manic patients would likely be unable to complete this self-report scale. Therefore, it is suggested that a more appropriate observer rated scale be used as discussed in the following section.

THE MANIC-STATE RATING SCALE

In response to the increase in interest in mania that accompanied the use and availability of lithium carbonate, Beigel, Murphy and Bunney (1971; see also Beigel &

Murphy, 1971) constructed an observer-rated scale. The rating scale contains 26 items that were derived from interviews with five nurses who had considerable experience working with manic inpatients. Interviews were structured around 16 comprehensive issues that were considered relevant to mania. From the transcripts of the interviews items judged to reflect the affect, behavior, and cognition of mania were selected. Nurses own words were used as much as possible since they were the intended raters. The resulting 26 items included items such as the following: looks depressed (item 1), moves from one place to another (item 3), is irritable (item 11), has diminished impulse control (item 20), and jumps from one object to another (item 26). It is important to note that items do not appear to be independent in their content (e.g., is sexually preoccupied [item 25] and talks about sex [item 37]).

Beigel et al. (1971) had nurses complete the rating scale following an eight-hour period of observation. It is not stated whether this was a continuous observation period. Differential observation time across raters might be a source of error variance. Raters evaluated each item on two dimensions; frequency and intensity. Both ratings are made on a 5-point Likert scale and the product of the two raters (range 0–25) is used as the item score. Beigel et al. (1971) report on the reliability of the scale. Twelve nurses rated a group of 13 patients (seven were unipolar depressives, six bipolar depressives). At least two raters evaluated each patient and different raters were used for different patients. Since raters weren't consistent from patient to patient the intraclass correlation coefficient might be biased if it was based on a single analysis of variance for a crossed design, rather than the appropriate balanced incomplete block design. No information is provided in the study to clarify this, however. Despite this methodological question, Biegel et al. report extremely high item reliability coefficients (ranging from. 86 to .99). Reliability was equally high when the small sample of manic patients was considered alone. Thus, the scale appears to have high reliability, when used by experienced nurses, trained in the use of the scale and allowed an extended observation period.

In addition to reliability Beigel et al. also report on the concurrent validity of the scale. They correlated the nurses' ratings with a global mania rating (15-point scale) made by staff psychiatrists. The validity coefficients for 22 of the 26 items were highly significant (ranging from .86 to .93). Beigel et al. also report on the correlation between the Manic-State Rating Scale and a checklist of manic symptoms completed by the nurse raters. However, each item in the checklist corresponds to one or more items in the ratings scale. Since there is almost total item overlap and the same raters completed both scales, information on the correlation between scales is of little meaning and therefore will not be reported.

Thus, the Manic-State Rating Scale has been developed specifically for use with bipolar depressives and has demonstrated adequate reliability and concurrent validity. The scale has been used as an outcome measure to evaluate change (e.g., Beigel & Murphy, 1971; Janowsky, Judd, Huey, Rochman, Parker, & Segal, 1978) and is worthy of future examination. Additional evaluation of the scale would be worthwhile.

References

Aitken, R. C. B. (1969). Measurement feelings using visual analogue scales. *Proceedings of the Royal Society of Medicine, 62,* 989–993.

Akiskal, H. (1981). Subaffective disorders: Dysthymic, cyclothymic and bipolar II disorders in the "borderline" realm. *Psychiatric Clinics of North America, 4,* 25–46.

Akiskal, H., Rosenthal, T., Haykal, R., Lemmi, H., Rosenthal, R., & Scott-Strauss, A. (1980). Characterological depressions. Clinical and sleep EEG findings separating "subaffective dysthymias" from "character spectrum disorders." *Archives of General Psychiatry, 33,* 777–783.

American Psychiatric Association (1980). *Diagnostic and statistical manual of mental disorders (DSM-III).* Washington, DC: Author.

Bech, P., Bolwig, T., Kramp, P., & Rafaelsen, O. (1979). The Beck-Rafaelsen Mania Scale and the Hamilton Depression Scale. *Acta Psychiatrica Scandinavia, 59,* 420–430.

Beck, A. T. (1967). *Depression: Clinical, experimental and therapeutic aspects.* New York: Harper & Row.

Beck, A. T. (1972). *Depression: Causes and treatment.* Philadelphia: University of Pennsylvania Press.

Beck, A. T., & Beamesderfer, A. (1974). Assessment of depression: The depression inventory. In P. Pichot (Ed.), *Psychological measurement in psychopharmacology. Modern problems in pharmacopsychiatry,* (Vol. 7). Basel, Switz.: Karger.

Beck, A. T., & Beck, R. W. (1972). Screening depressed patient in family practice. A rapid technique. *Postgraduate Medicine, 52,* 81–85.

Beck, A., & Kovacs, M. (1979). Assessment of Suicidal Intention: The scale for suicide ideation. *Journal of Consulting and Clinical Psychology, 47,* 343–352.

Beck, A., Rush, A., Shaw, B., & Emery, G. (1979). *Cognitive therapy of depression.* New York: Guilford Press.

Beck, A. T., Ward, C. H., Mendelson, M., Mock, J., & Erbaugh, J. (1961). An inventory for measuring depression. *Archives of General Psychiatry, 4,* 561–571.

Beck, A. T., Weissman, A., Lester, D., & Texler, L. (1974). Measurement of pessimism: The hopelessness scale. *Journal of Consulting and Clinical Psychology, 42,* 861–865.

Beigel, A., & Murphy, D. (1971). Assessing clinical characteristics of the manic state. *American Journal of Psychiatry, 128,* 44–50.

Beigel, A., Murphy, D., & Bunney, W. (1971). The manic state rating scale: Scale construct, reliability, and validity. *Archives of General Psychiatry, 25,* 256–262.

Biggs, J. T., Wylie, L. T., & Ziegler, V. E. (1978). Validity of the Zung Self-Rating Depression Scale. *British Journal of Psychiatry, 132,* 381–385.

Blackburn, I., Bishop, S., Glen, A., Whalley, L., & Christie, J. (1981). The efficacy of cognitive therapy in depression: A treatment trial using cognitive therapy and pharmacotherapy each alone and in combination. *British Journal of Psychiatry, 131,* 181–189.

Blaser, R., Low, D., & Schaublin, A. (1968). Die Messung der depressionstiefe mit einmen Fragebogen. *Psychiat. Clin., 1,* 299–319.

Blashfield, R., & Skinner, H. (1982). Increasing the inpact of cluster analysis research. The case of psychiatric classification. *Journal of Consulting and Clinical Psychology, 50,* 727–735.

Bloom, P. M., & Brady, J. P. (1968). An ipsative validation of the Multiple Affect Adjective Checklist. *Journal of Clinical Psychology, 24,* 45–46.

Boyd, J. H., Weissman, M. M., Thompson, W. D., & Myers, J. K. (1982). Screening for depression in a community sample. Understanding the discrepancies between depression symptom and diagnostic scales. *Archives of General Psychiatry, 39,* 1195–1200.

Brown, G. L., & Zung, W. W. K. (1972). Depression scales: Self-physician-rating? A validation of certain clinically observable phenomena. *Comprehensive Psychiatry, 13,* 361–367.

Bumberry, W., Oliver, J. M., & McClure, J. N. (1978). Validation of the Beck Depression Inventory in a university population using psychiatric estimate as the criterion. *Journal of Consulting and Clinical Psychology, 46,* 150–155.

Burkhart, B. R., Gynther, M. D., & Fromuth, M. E. (1980). The relative predictive validity of subtle versus obvious items on the MMPI depression scale. *Journal of Clinical Psychology, 36,* 748–751.

Butcher, J. N., & Dahlstrom, W. G. (1964). *Comparability of the taped and booklet versions of the MMPI.* Unpublished paper, University of North Carolina.

Carroll, B. J., Feinberg, M., Greden, J. F., Haskett, R. F., James, N., Steiner, M., & Tarika, J. (1980). Diagnosis of endogenous depression: Comparison of clinical, research and neuroendocrine criteria. *Journal of Affective Disorders, 2,* 177–194.

Carroll, B. J., Feinberg, M., Smouse, P. E., Rawson, S. G., & Greden, J. F. (1981). The Carroll Rating Scale for Depression I.

Carroll, B. J., Fielding, J. M., & Blashki, T. G. (1973). Depression ratings scales. A critical review. *Archives of General Psychiatry, 28,* 361–366.

Christenfeld, R., Lubin, B., & Satin, M. (1978). Concurrent validity of the depression adjective checklist in a normal population. *American Journal of Psychiatry, 135,* 582–584.

Clyde, D. (1950). *Construction and validation of an emotional association test.* Unpublished Ph.D. thesis, Pennsylvania State College.

Comrey, A. (1957). A factor analysis of items on the MMPI depression scale. *Educational Psychological Measurement, 17,* 578–585.

Craig, T., & Van Natta, P. (1978). Current medication use and symptoms of depression in a general population. *American Journal of Psychiatry, 135,* 1036–1039.

Crowne, D., & Marlowe, D. (1960). A new scale of social desirability independent of psychopathology. *Journal of Consulting Psychology, 24,* 349–354.

Dahlstrom, W., Welsh, G., & Dahlstrom, L. (1975). *An MMPI Handbook: Volume II: Research Applications.* Minneapolis: University of Minnesota Press.

Davies, B., Burrows, G., & Poynton, C. (1975). A comparative study of four depression rating scales. *Australian and New Zealand Journal of Psychiatry, 9,* 21–24.

Delay, J., Pichot, P., Lemperiere, T., & Mirouze, R. (1963). La nosologie des états depressifs. Rapports entre l'étiologie et la semiologie II. Résultats du questionnaire de Beck. *Encephale, 52,* 497–505.

Dempsey, P. (1964). A unidimensional depression scale for the MMPI. *Journal of Consulting Psychology, 28,* 364–370.

Dempsey, P., & Baumoff, M. (1963). The statistical use of artifact distributions to establish chronological sequence. *American Antiquities, 28,* 496–509.

Depue, R. A., & Monroe, S. M. (1979). The unipolar-bipolar distinction in the depressive disorders. *Psychological Bulletin, 85,* 1001–1029.

Derogatis, L. R., Lipman, R. S., & Covi, L. (1973). SCL-90: An outpatient psychiatric rating scale—preliminary report. *Psychopharmacology Bulletin, 9,* 13–25.

Eichman, W. J. (1973). *A short-term retest study of female psychiatric cases.* Unpublished manuscript, University of North Carolina.

Ekman, P., & Friesen, W. (1974). Nonverbal behavior and psychopathology. In R. Friedman & M. Katz (Eds.), *The psychology of depression: Contemporary theory and research.* Washington, DC: Winston.

Elkin, I., Parloff, M., Hadley, S., & Autry, I. (1985). The NIMH treatment of depression collaborative research program. *Archives of General Psychiatry, 42,* 305–316.

Endicott, J., Cohen, J., Nee, J., Fleiss, J., & Sarantakos, S. (1981). Hamilton Depression Rating Scale, extracted from regular and change versions of the Schedule for Affective Disorders and Schizophrenia. *Archives of General Psychiatry, 38,* 98–103.

Endicott, J., & Spitzer, R. (1978). A diagnostic interview: The Schedule for Affective Disorders and Schizophrenia. *Archives of General Psychiatry, 35,* 837–844.

Endicott, N. A., & Jortner, S. (1966). Objective meaasures of depression. *Archives of General Psychiatry, 15,* 249–255.

Epstein, S. (1979). The stability of behavior: I. On predicting most of the people much of the time. *Journal of Personality and Social Psychology, 37,* 1097–1126.

Evans, D., Hearn, M., Uhlemann, M., & Ivey, A. (1984). *Essential interviewing: A programmed approach to effective communication* (2nd ed.). Monterey, CA: Brooks/Cole Publishing.

Faschingbauer, T. R. (1972). *A short written form of the group MMPI.* Unpublished doctoral dissertation, University of North Carolina.

Feinberg, M., Carroll, B. J., Smouse, P. E., & Rawson, S. G. (1981). The Carroll Rating Scale for Depression III. Comparison with other rating instruments. *British Journal of Psychiatry, 138,* 205–209.

Fisch, J., Frey, S., & Hirsbrunner, H. (1983). Analyzing nonverbal behavior in depression. *Journal of Abnormal Psychology, 92,* 307–318.

Folstein, M. F., & Luria, R. E. (1973). Reliability, validity and clinical application of the Visual Analogue Mood Scale. *Psychological Medicine, 3,* 479–486.

Fowles, D. C., & Gersh, F. (1979). Neurotic depression: The endogeneous-neurotic distinction. In R. A. Depue (Ed.), *The psychology of depressive disorders: Implications for the effects of stress* (pp. 55–80). New York: Academic Press.

Friedman, A. S., Cowitz, B., Cohen, H. W., & Granick, S. (1963). Syndromes and themes of psychotic depression. *Archives of General Psychiatry, 9,* 504–509.

Gallagher, D., Nies, G., & Thompson, L. W. (1982). Reliability of the Beck Depression Inventory with older adults. *Journal of Consulting and Clinical Psychology, 50,* 152–153.

Gardner, E. (1968). *Development of a symptom check list for the measurement of depression in the population.* Unpublished.

Garner, D., & Bemis, K. (1984). Cognitive therapy for anorexia nervosa. In D. Garner & P. Garfinkel (Eds.), *A Handbook for the treatment of anorexia nervosa and bulimia.* New York: Guilford Press.

Gersh, F. S., & Fowles, D. C. (1979). Neurotic depression: The concept of anxious depression: In R. A. Depue (Ed.), *The psychology of depressive disorders: Implications for the effects of stress* (pp. 81–104). New York: Academic Press.

Gilliland, A. R., & Colgin, R. (1951). Norms, reliability and forms of the MMPI. *Journal of Consulting Psychology, 15,* 435–438.

Graham, J. R. (1977). *The MMPI: A practical guide.* New York: Oxford University Press.

Grinker, R. R., Miller, J., Sabshin, M., Nunn, R., & Nunally, J. C. (1961). *Phenomena of depressions.* New York: Harper & Row.

Hamilton, M. (1959). The assessment of anxiety states by rating. *British Journal of Medical Psychology, 32,* 30–55.

Hamilton, M. (1960). A rating scale for depression. *Journal of Neurology, Neurosurgery and Psychiatry, 12,* 56–62.

Hamilton, M. (1984). Personal communication to Dr. E. Beckham, February, 1984.

Hamilton, M., & White, J. (1959). Clinical syndromes in depressive states. *Journal of Mental Science, 105,* 985–987.

Hathaway, S. R., & McKinley, J. C. (1943). *The Minnesota Multiphasic Personality Schedule* (rev. ed.), Minneapolis: University of Minnesota Press, 1942.

Hedlund, J., & Vieweg, B. (1979). The Hamilton Rating Scale for Depression: A comprehensive review. *Journal of Operational Psychiatry, 10,* 149–162.

Hersen, M. (1976). Historical perspectives in behavioral assessment. In M. Hersen & A. Bellack (Eds.), *Behavioral assessment: A practical handbook.* Elmsford, NY: Pergamon Press.

Howes, M., & Hokanson, J. (1979). Conversational and social responses to depressive interpersonal behavior. *Journal of Abnormal Psychology, 88,* 625–634.

Husaini, B. A., Neff, J. A., Harrington, J. B., Hughes, M. D., & Stone, R. H. (1980). Depression in rural communities: Validating the CES-D scale. *Journal of Community Psychology, 8,* 20–27.

Janowsky, D., Judd, L., Huey, L., Rochman, N., Parker, D., & Segal, D. (1978). Naloxone effects on manic symptoms and growth-hormone levels. *The Lancet* 320.

Jurjevich, R. M. (1966). Short interval test-retest stability of MMPI, CPI, Cornell Index, and Symptom Check List, *Journal of General Psychology, 74,* 201–206.

Katz, M. M., & Lyerly, S. B. (1963). Methods for measuring adjustment and social behavior in the community: Rationale, description, discriminative validity and scale development. *Psychological Reports, 13,* 503–535.

Kazdin, A. E. (1981). Assessment techniques for childhood depression: A critical appraisal. *Journal of American Academic Child Psychiatry, 22,* 157–164.

Kiloh, L. G., & Garside, R. F. (1963). The independence of neurotic depression and endogenous depression. *British Journal of Psychiatry, 109,* 451–463.

Klein, D. F. (1974). Endogenomorphic depression. *Archives of General Psychiatry, 31,* 447–454.

Knight, R. G., Waal-Manning, H. J., & Spears, G. F. (1983). Some norms and reliability data for the State-Trait Anxiety Inventory and the Zung Self-Rating Depression Scale. *British Journal of Clinical Psychology, 22,* 245–249.

Kupfer, D., & Rush, A. J. (1983). Recommendations for scientific reports on depression. *American Journal of Psychiatry, 140,* 1327–1328.

Langevin, R., & Stancer, H. (1979). Evidence that depression rating scales primarily measure a social undesirability response set. *Acta Psychiatrica Scandinavica, 59,* 70–79.

Lazarus, A. (1971). *Behavior therapy and beyond.* New York: McGraw-Hill.

Lazarus, R. (1982). Thoughts on the relations between emotion and cognition. *American Psychologist, 37,* 1019–1024.

Lewinsohn, P. (1976). Manual of instruction for behavior ratings used for observation of interpersonal behavior. In E. Mash & L. Terdal (Eds.), *Behavior therapy assessment.* New York: Springer Publishing.

Lewinsohn, P., & Teri, L. (1982). Selection of depressed and nondepressed subjects on the basis of self-report data. *Journal of Consulting and Clinical Psychology, 50,* 590–591.

Linehan, M. (1981). A social-behavioral analysis of suicide and parasuicide: Implications for clinical assessment and treatment. In J. Clarkin & H. Glazer (Eds.), *Depression, behavioral and directive intervention strategies.* New York: Garland STPM Press.

Linehan, M., & Chiles, J. (1983). Reasons for staying alive when you are thinking of killing yourself: The Reasons for Living Inventory. *Journal of Consulting and Clinical Psychology, 51,* 276–286.

Lubin, B. (1965). Adjective checklists for measurement of depression. *Archives of General Psychiatry, 12,* 57–62.

Lubin, B., Hornstra, R. K., & Love, A. (1974). Course of depressive mood in a psychiatric population upon application for service and at 3- and 12-month reinterview. *Psychological Reports, 34,* 424–426.

Luria, R. E. (1975). The validity and reliability of the Visual Analogue Mood Scale. *Journal of Psychiatric Research, 12,* 51–57.

Marone, J., & Lubin, B. (1968). Relationship between set 2 of the Depression Adjective Check Lists (DACL) and Zung Self-Rating Depression Scale (SDS). *Psychological Reports, 22,* 333–334.

May, A. E., Urquart, A., & Taran, J. (1969). Self-evaluation of depression in various diagnostic and therapeutic groups. *Archives of General Psychiatry, 21,* 191–194.

McKinley, J., & Hathaway, S. (1944). The MMPI: V. Hysteria, hypomania, and psychopathic deviate. *Journal of Applied Psychology, 28,* 153–174.

Meites, K., Lovallo, W., Pishkin, V. (1980). A comparison of four scales for anxiety, depression, and neuroticism. *Journal of Clinical Psychology, 36,* 427–432.

Metcalfe, M., & Goldman, E. (1965). Validation of an inventory for measuring depression. *British Journal of Psychiatry, 111,* 240–242.

Myers, J. K., & Weissman, M. M. (1980). Use of a self-report symptom scale to detect depression in a community sample. *American Journal of Psychiatry, 137,* 1081–1084.

Nevid, J. S. (1983). Hopelessness, social desirability and construct validity. *Journal of Consulting and Clinical Psychology, 51,* 139–140.

Newmark, C. S. (1971). MMPI: Comparison of the oral form presented by a live examiner and booklet form. *Psychological Reports. 29,* 797–798.

Newmark, C. S. (1973). *Brief retest stability with female psychiatric cases.* Unpublished materials, University of North Carolina.

Nielson, A., Secunda, S., Friedman, R., & Williams, T. (1972). Prevalence and recognition of depression among ambulatory patients in a group medical practice. Proceeding at meeting of American Psychiatric Association, Dallas.

Nussbaum, K., Wittig, B. A., Hanlon, T. E., & Kurland, A. A. (1963). Intravenous nialamide in the treatment of depressed female patients. *Comprehensive Psychiatry, 4,* 105–116.

O'Conner, J., Stefic, E., & Gresock, C. (1957). Some patterns of depression. *Journal of Clinical Psychology, 13,* 122–125.

O'Hara, M., & Rehm, L. (1983). Hamilton rating scale for depression: Reliability and validity of judgements of novice rates. *Journal of Consulting and Clinical Psychology, 51,* 318–319.

Overall, J. E. (1962). Dimensions of manifest depression. *Psychiatric Research, 1,* 239–245.

Overall, J. E., & Gorham, D. R. (1962). The brief psychiatric rating scale. *Psychological Reports, 10,* 799–812.

Overall, J., & Zisook, S. (1980). Diagnosis and the phenomenology of depressive disorders. *Journal of Consulting and Clinical Psychology, 48,* 626–634.

Paykel, E. S. (1971). Classification of depressed patients: A cluster analysis derived grouping. *British Journal of Psychiatry, 118,* 275–288.

Radloff, L. S. (1977). The CES-D scale: A self-report depression scale for research in the general population. *Applied Psychological Measurement, 1,* 385–401.

Raft, D., Spencer, R. F., Toomey, T., & Brogan, D. (1977). Depression in medical outpatients; Use of the Zung scale. *Diseases of the Nervous System, 38,* 999–1004.

Raskin, A., Schulterbrandt, J., Reatig, N., & McKeon, J. (1969). Replication of factors of psychopathology in interview, ward behavior, and self-report ratings of hospitalized depressives. *Journal of Nervous and Mental Disease, 148,* 87–96.

Reynolds, W. M., & Gould, J. W. (1981). A psychometric investigation of the standard and short form Beck Depression Inventory. *Journal of Consulting and Clinical Psychology, 49,* 306–307.

Riskind, J., & Beck, A. (1983). *Phenomenology of emotional disorder: Symptoms that differentiate between generalized anxiety disorder, major depressive disorder, and mixed disorder.* Paper presented at the World Congress on Behavior Therapy. Washington, DC.

Robins, L. N., Helzer, J. E., Croughan, J., & Ratcliff, K. S. (1981). National Institute of Mental Health Diagnostic Interview Schedule: Its history, characteristics and validity. *Archives of General Psychiatry, 38,* 381–389.

Salkind, M. R. (1969). Beck Depression Inventory in general practice. *Journal of the Royal College of General Practice. 18,* 267.

Schwab, J., Bialow, M., & Holzer, C. (1967). A comparison of two rating scales for depression. *Journal of Clinical Psychology, 23,* 94–96.

Scott, N. A., Hannum, T. E., & Ghrist, S. L. (1982). Assessment of depression among incarcerated females. *Journal of Personality Assessment, 46,* 372–379.

Skinner, H., & Blashfield, R. (1982). Increasing the impact of cluster analysis research: The case of psychotic classification. *Journal of Consulting and Clinical Psychology, 50,* 727–735.

Smith, D., & Kraft, W. (1983). *DSM-III*: Do psychologists really want an alternative? *American Psychologist, 38,* 777–785.

Sotsky, S., & Glass, D. (1983). *The Hamilton Rating Scale. A critical appraisal and modification for psychotherapy research.* Paper presented at the Annual Convention of the Society for Psychotherapy Research, Sheffield, England.

Spitzer, R., Endicott, J., & Robins, E. (1978). Research diagnostic criteria: Rationale and reliability. *Archives of General Psychiatry, 35,* 773–782.

Steer, R. A., Shaw, B. F., Beck, A. T., & Fine, E. W. (1977). Structure of depression in black alcoholic men. *Psychological Reports, 41,* 1235–1241.

Stenbeck, A., Rimon, R., & Turunen, M. (1967). Validitet av Taylor Manifest Anxiety Scale. *Nord. Psykiat., 21,* 79–85.

Strober, M., Green, J., & Carlson, G. (1981). Utility of the Beck Depression Inventory with psychiatrically hospitalized adolescents. *Journal of Consulting and Clinical Psychology, 49,* 482–483.

Vinar, O., & Grof, P. (1968). Die depressive symptomatologie in Lichte des Beckschen Fragebogens; in *Hippus das depressive Syndrom* Berlin:

Waxer, P. (1974). Nonverbal cues for depression. *Journal of Abnormal Psychology, 53,* 318–322.

Weckowicz, T. E., Muir, W., & Cropley, A. J. (1967). A factor analysis of the Beck Inventory of Depression. *Journal of Consulting Psychology, 31,* 23–28.

Weissman, M. M., Prusoff, B., & Newberry, P. B. (1975). *Comparison of CES-D, Zung, Beck Self-Report Depression Scales.* Technical report ADM 42-47-83. Rockville, Md., Center for Epidemiologic Studies, National Institute of Mental Health.

Williams, J., Barlow, D., & Agras, W. (1972). Behavioral assessment of severe depression. *Archives of General Psychiatry, 72,* 303–337.

Williams, J., & Spitzer, R. (Eds.), (1984). *Psychotherapy research: Where are we and where should we go?* New York: Guilford Press.

Windle, C. (1955). Further studies of test-retest effect on personality questionnaires. *Educational and Psychological Measurement, 15,* 246–253.

Winfield, D. L. (1952). An investigation of the relationship between intelligence and the statistical reliability of the MMPI. *Journal of Clinical Psychology, 8,* 146–148.

Wing, J., Birley, J., Cooper, J., Graham, P., & Isaacs, A. (1967). Reliability of a procedure for measuring and classifying "Present Psychiatric State." *British Journal of Psychiatry, 113,* 499–515.

Wing, J. K., Cooper, J. F., & Sartorias, N. (1974). *Measurement and classification of psychiatric symptoms: An instructional manual for the PSE and Catego Program.* New York: Cambridge University Press.

Ziegler, V., Meyer, D., Rosen, S., & Biggs, J. (1978). Reliability of video taped Hamilton ratings. *Biological Psychiatry, 13,* 119–122.

Zung, W. W. K. (1965). A Self-Rating Depression Scale. *Archives of General Psychiatry, 12,* 63–70.

Zung, W. W. K. (1967). Factors influencing the self-rating depression scale. *Archives of General Psychiatry, 16,* 543–547.

Zung, W. W. K. (1968). Evaluating treatment methods for depressive disorders. *American Journal of Psychiatry, 124,* 40–48.

Zung, W. W. K. (1969). A cross-cultural survey of symptoms of depression. *American Journal of Psychiatry, 126,* 154–159.

Zung, W. W. K., Richards, C. B., & Short, M. J. (1965). Self-rating depression scale in an outpatient clinic. *Archives of General Psychiatry, 13,* 508–515.

Zung, W. W. K., & Wonnacott, T. H. (1970). Treatment prediction in depression using a self-rating scale. *Biological Psychiatry, 2,* 321–329.

Chapter 13

Measures of Psychological Processes in Depression

Constance Hammen
University of California, Los Angeles

Susan E. Krantz
VA Medical Center, Palo Alto, California

Each psychological theory of depression specifies different variables that are presumed to play a primary role in the development and maintenance of depression. The evaluation of the validity and utility of these theories requires the development of measures of such variables. Measures which meet rigorous psychometric standards can then be used to test the important aspects of the theory, including the ways in which depressed and nondepressed persons differ, the relationships between the primary factor and other factors specified by the theory, and the covariation between the factor and changes in mood.

This chapter will describe the crucial mechanisms specified by each of several major psychological theories of depression and the measures which have been developed to test the role of these factors. The major purpose of this chapter is to examine whether the psychometric properties of the measures allow valid conclusions to be drawn from their use in tests of the theories.

Brief summaries of the major cognitive and behavioral theories are presented, followed by descriptions and psychometric reviews of their major assessment procedures. Whenever such procedures are available, greatest attention is given to those procedures whose psychometric properties have been examined by both the originators of the measure and independent investigators. A separate section discusses the issues associated with assessing depressive cognitions. In the final section, there is a brief critique of the assumptions of the theories and measures in order to provide a framework for drawing appropriate conclusions from the various uses of the measures.

COGNITIVE APPROACHES TO DEPRESSION

Cognitive Distortion Model of Depression

Beck (1967, 1976) has asserted that depression is the result of negative and distorted views regarding the self, the world, and the future. Depressed people typically view the self as inadequate and worthless. Interacting with one's world is construed as a difficult task fraught with insurmountable barriers and demands which cannot be met. The future is approached with pessimism. These beliefs are manifested both in automatic thoughts which occur in specific situations and in general themes and underlying assumptions that give rise to the automatic thoughts.

A core assumption of Beck's model is that these negative cognitions are distorted or biased representations of the available information. Common errors include a focus on one aspect of a situation taken out of context while ignoring more salient aspects (selective abstraction), overgeneralizations from a single event to a wide range of events, inferences made arbitrarily and in the absence of supportive evidence (arbitrary inference), exaggerations of undesirable outcomes (magnification), and the minimization of desirable outcomes. For example, a lecturer may focus on the single critical comment from the audience and ignore more positive comments. A woman may conclude that she is being rejected if a Valentine's Day card is not accompanied by a gift.

A number of measures are used to assess these cognitive biases. The measures which have undergone more extensive validation procedures are the Cognitive Bias Questionnaire (Hammen & Krantz, 1976; Krantz & Hammen, 1979), the Automatic Thoughts Questionnaire (Hollon & Kendall, 1980), the Dysfunctional Attitude Scale (Weissman & Beck, 1978), and the Irrational Beliefs Test (Jones, 1969).

The Cognitive Bias Questionnaire (CBQ). The CBQ is a questionnaire procedure to assess depressive negative thinking and to evaluate negative bias independently of dysphoric tone. The measure consists of six problematic situations common to college students (Hammen & Krantz, 1976) or psychiatric inpatients (Krantz & Hammen, 1979). Three of the situations have interpersonal themes; three have achievement themes. Four multiple-choice questions (with the exception of one story with three questions) pertaining to the protagonists' thoughts and feelings follow each story. These 23 response options were constructed to capture two crossed dimensions: distorted versus nondistorted and depressed versus nondepressed. The distorted versus nondistorted dimension denoted the presence or absence of inferences that are unwarranted in light of the available information. The depressed versus nondepressed dimension referred to the presence or absence of dysphoria (and not to the presence or absence of the syndrome of depression). The depressed-distorted options are all examples of Beck's typology of logical errors including magnification, selective abstraction, overgeneralization, and arbitrary inference, but independent judges were unable to reliably distinguish between the different types of errors. Items were included only if at least 8 out of 10 clinical psychology graduate student judges agreed as to whether the item was depressive or nondepressive and distorted or nondistorted. For example, one vignette described Shelly, a college sophomore living in the dorms, who is one of the few women remaining on her floor on a Friday evening. The other residents were out for the evening or away for the weekend. The respondent is asked to imagine as vividly as possible what Shelly might think and feel about "being alone on a Friday night." The four response options were:

1. Doesn't bother me because I figure I'll have a date next weekend for sure (nondepressed-distorted).
2. Upsets me and makes me feel lonely (depressed-nondistorted).
3. Upsets me and makes me start to imagine endless days and nights by myself (depressed-distorted).
4. Doesn't bother me because one Friday night alone isn't that important; probably everybody has spent one night alone (nondepressed-nondistorted).

Krantz and Hammen (1979) reported data on the internal consistency and the test-retest reliability of the CBQ. Coefficients of internal consistency were only moderate (alpha = .62 and .69 in two of the student samples). The lack of a strong degree of consistency appears to be due to the heterogeneity in the construct of cognitive bias, which, as noted above, includes an array of different types of beliefs. The test-retest correlations over periods of four to eight weeks indicated satisfactory stability over time (r = .48 and .60, p < .001, in two student samples). It should be noted, however, that the low scores that characterized the majority of subjects in these normal student samples may be more stable than the higher scores in a depressed population, since the likelihood of decreases in depressive mood and cognitions among initially depressed subjects is probably greater than the likelihood of increases in depressed mood and cognition among initially nondepressed subjects. Thus, it remains to be seen whether these satisfactory test-retest correlations will be replicated in depressed samples.

Krantz and Hammen (1979) reported data on the validity of the CBQ from one sample of clinically depressed outpatients, one sample of depressed and nondepressed psychiatric inpatients, and four independent samples of students. In the depressed outpatient sample, Glass (1978; cited in Krantz & Hammen, 1979) reported significant correlations between depressed-distorted scores and Beck Depression Inventory (BDI) scores, and found that the scores were sensitive to a treatment for depression. In all other samples, depressed subjects gave significantly more depressive-distorted responses than nondepressed subjects. These results subsequently have been replicated by several investigators. Norman, Miller, and Klee (1983) found significant differences in the depressive-distorted CBQ scores when comparing two depressed samples (depression was the primary diagnosis in one sample and the secondary diagnosis in the other) with a nondepressed schizophrenic inpatient sample. Blaney, Behar, and Head (1980) found that depressive-distorted scores were significantly correlated with the intensity of depressive symptoms in two independent student samples (r = .26 in Sample 1 and .44 in Sample 2, both ps < .001). Frost and MacInnis (1983) found significant correlations with BDI scores obtained 3 to 10 weeks before and two days after the CBQ was administered ($r = .43$ and $r = .51$, both $ps < .005$) and with the depression scale of the Multiple Adjective Affect Checklist at the latter testing ($r = .35, p < .05$) among depressed college women, despite the restricted range of depression scores. Going one step further than the typical correlations between self-report measures, they also showed that depressive-distortion scores were significantly correlated with depressive speech tone in a self-description dictated into a tape recorder ($r = .50, p < .05$).

The results from these correlational studies are consistent with the data from experimental manipulations of mood states. Using a modified version of the CBQ, Goodwin and Williams (1982) found that depressive mood inductions significantly increased the depressive-distortion scores, although the effect differed somewhat by the type of mood induction (self-referent or somatic). Similarly, Riskind and Rholes (in press) found that a depressive mood induction procedure led to a significant elevation in CBQ scores in a self-devaluative mood induction condition but not in a somatic induction condition.

One question which arises is the degree to which the correlations with depression scores are due to the dysphoric content of the depressive-distortion score versus the distorted quality (Beckham & Leber, 1984). Although these two constructs are inextricably intertwined, this question may be examined by comparisons of the correlations of the depressed-distorted and depressed-nondistorted scores (i.e., dysphoria with or without distortion) with depression scores. In both the Blaney et al. (1980) and Frost and MacInnis (1983) studies, the correlations of the depressive-nondistorted score with measures of depression were consistently lower than the correlations obtained with the depressive-distorted scale (rs between the depressive-nondistorted scale and depression scores ranged from .10 to .30). Unreported data from one of the Krantz and Hammen (1979) samples, however, indicate that the correlations of the depressive-distortion scores with depression are no greater than those of the depressive-nondistorted scores. Thus, it is unclear whether the distorted quality of this scale adds to its relationship with depression beyond that provided by the dysphoric aspect of this CBQ scale.

Tests of the specificity of the measure to depression, however, yielded mixed results. Krantz and Hammen (1979) found significant correlations of the depressive-distortion score with the anxiety-tension, anger, confusion, fatigue, and vigor scores of the Profile of Mood States, but only the depression and vigor scales remained significant after controlling for the other mood states. Frost and MacInnis (1983), however, replicated the finding that anxiety was not related to the depressive-distortion score after controlling for depression, but did find that hostility correlated with the depressive-distortion score even after controlling for the variance shared with depression ($r = .29$, $p < .05$).

Several cautions regarding the CBQ are in order. The concept of cognitive bias is an extremely complex one, as discussed below, and the authors have voiced concern that items on the CBQ represent considerable heterogeneity of interpretations, attributions, predictions, and the like (Krantz & Hammen, 1979). Although the instrument appears to be sensitive to variations in depressed mood level, depressive distortions assessed in this fashion are infrequent, typically less than 6 out of 23 for depressed persons. In addition, a potential practical limitation is that the measure is tied to specific socioenvironmental contexts and populations. The two existing versions were designed for and validated on student or psychiatric populations, and so its use may be limited to these groups. Finally it should be noted that although the biased quality of the depressive-distortion score appears to correlate somewhat more highly with depression scores than do depressive-nondistortions, the dysphoric aspect of the depressive-distortion scale undoubtedly contributes to its association with depression inventories.

Automatic Thoughts Questionnaire (ATQ).   While the CBQ was designed to tap the theoretical categories describing depressive thought processes, the ATQ was derived empirically. To identify common depressive thoughts, Hollon and Kendall (1980) asked students to recall a depressing situation and to list their thoughts in that situation. Redundant or incomprehensible items were eliminated, and the remaining 100 items were submitted to an independent group of students. The students were asked to rate how often each statement had "popped into their head" in the last week on a five-point scale ranging from "not at all" to "all the time." The 100 items, together with the Beck Depression Inventory (BDI), were submitted to a new group of students in order to identify these items which discriminate between the mildly to moderately depressed and the nondepressed students. The final scale consisted of 30 items. Sample items are "I'm worthless," "I can't get started," and "My future is bleak."

Estimates of the internal reliability of the ATQ are quite strong. The split-half reliability coefficient was .97; the coefficient alpha was .96 (both $ps <$ .001). This finding was replicated with students by Dobson and Breiter (1983) and with mental health center and medical outpatients by Harrell and Ryon (1983). Test-retest reliability was not reported.

The construct validity of the ATQ is indicated by Hollon and Kendall's (1980) findings of the expected differences between depressed and nondepressed students in their ATQ scores. Similarly, Dobson and Breiter (1983) found strong correlations between the ATQ and the severity of depressive symptoms among students ($r = .62$ for females and .64 for males, both $ps <$ .001). These correlations between the ATQ and depression were significantly stronger than the correlations with depression evidenced by two other measures of depressive cognitions, including the Dysfunctional Attitude Scale (Weissman & Beck, 1978), to be discussed in the next section. Harrell and Ryon (1983) reported that depressed outpatients scored significantly higher on the ATQ than did nondepressed psychiatric outpatients and medical patient controls. Eaves and Rush (1984) similarly found significant differences during an initial testing between depressed inpatients and community controls. When the depression remitted following pharmacotherapy, psychotherapy (cognitive therapy was not used) or both, the ATQ scores of the formerly depressed patients approached those of control subjects and the earlier differences between the groups were no longer apparent.

A factor analysis of the ATQ (Hollon & Kendall, 1980) revealed four factors reflecting (1) personal maladjustment and desire for change, (e.g., "What's wrong with me?"), (2) negative self-concept and expectations, (e.g., "My future is bleak"), (3) low self-esteem, (e.g., "I'm worthless"), and (4) giving up and helplessness (e.g., "I can't finish anything"). Although Hollon and Kendall make no assumptions about the biased versus accurate nature of these automatic thoughts, it is evident that these factors are similar to many of the cognitive distortions described by Beck.

The ATQ shows promise as a brief and easily administered measure of dysfunctional thoughts. Coyne and Gotlib (1983), however, have raised the question of whether or not subjects can reliably estimate how often automatic negative thoughts occur to them in a week, given Beck's (Beck, Rush, Shaw, & Emery, 1979) belief that specific training in "thought-catching" is required.

Dysfunctional Attitude Scale (DAS).   The DAS (Weissman, 1978; Weissman & Beck, 1978) consists of two parallel 40-item forms that draw upon Ellis's views of general irrational themes in thinking as well as Beck's notions about thoughts specific to depression (see Appendix 7). Respondents indicate the extent of their agreement with each item on a seven-point scale. The items include attributions about causes, expectancies of control, predictions about the likelihood of desired outcomes, perfectionistic performance standards, rigid ideas about the events which should occur, and concern about the judgments of others. A sample item from the DAS is "If I fail at my work then I'm a failure as a person."

The DAS shows good internal consistency and stability over time. Weissman's (1979) report of alpha coefficients ranging from .89 to .92 and a test-retest correlation of .84 over an eight-week period were replicated by Hamilton and Abramson (1983), O'Hara, Rehm, and Campbell (1982), and Riskind, Beck and Smucker (1983). Minor deviations from these figures are the slightly lower test-retest correlation of .71 over the same time span reported by Hamilton and Abramson (1983) and a correlation of .62 over a 12-week period reported by Riskind et al. (1983).

Evidence of the construct validity of the DAS can be inferred from its use with both clinical and nonclinical populations. Weissman and Beck (1978) reported correlations ranging from .36 to .47 ($ps < .001$) with the BDI and the depression subscale of the Profile of Mood States in a student population. Hamilton and Abramson (1983) found that DAS scores were significantly elevated among depressed inpatients shortly after admission in comparison to nondepressed psychiatric patients and nondepressed community volunteers. By discharge, the DAS scores had dropped significantly and so the earlier differences between groups had dissipated. Eaves and Rush (1984) also found both the differences in the DAS scores between depressed inpatients and community controls and the improvement in the DAS. However, their results differ from those of Hamilton and Abramson (1983) in that the differences between depressives and controls remained significant following treatment. O'Hara et al. (1982), in a study of predictors of postpartum depression, found that DAS scores correlated with BDI scores during the second trimester ($r = .28, p < .001$) but did not add significantly to the prediction of postpartum BDI scores beyond that provided by the second trimester BDI scores. Dobson and Breiter (1983) reported similar correlations between DAS and BDI scores among students ($r = .30$ for females and $.36$ for males, both ps $< .001$). Riskind et al. (1983) reported a somewhat higher correlation with the BDI in a depressed outpatient sample ($r = .44, p < .001$). Significant correlations of the DAS with measures of anxiety disappeared when BDI scores were held constant. The DAS also predicted the outcome of a cognitive therapy treatment even after controlling for the pretreatment BDI scores (Keller, 1983) and was sensitive to changes resulting from a coping skills treatment for depression (Fleming & Thornton, 1980). Finally, the DAS has been shown to correlate $.52$ with the depressive-distortion scale of the CBQ (Weissman, 1978).

Although the DAS was intended to be a measure of stable depressogenic attitudes and test-retest reliability was high, scores appeared to be highly affected by current mood, as reported both by Weissman (1979) and Hamilton and Abramson (1983). Thus, the utility of the measure as a stable test of depressive cognitions is questionable.

Irrational Beliefs Test (IBT).

The IBT (Jones, 1969) was designed to tap the irrational beliefs which Ellis links to a variety of psychological disturbances including, but not limited to, depression. Ellis's more broadband irrational beliefs overlap considerably with the distortions specific to depression identified by Beck, and so the utility of the IBT as a measure of depressive cognitive biases will be considered.

The IBT consists of 100 items; respondents rate the extent of their agreement with each item on a five-point Likert scale. The 10 subscales are: demand for approval; high self-expectations; blame proneness; frustration reactivity (becoming terribly upset with undesirable outcomes); emotional irresponsibility (the belief that unhappiness is caused by factors outside one's control); anxious overconcern (obsessive worry about potential difficulties in the future); avoidance; dependency; helplessness (the belief that it is impossible to surmount the influence of past history); and perfectionism. These subscales were created by means of a factor analysis performed on students' responses to items originally generated on intuitive grounds and validated by the consensus of independent judges. Except for minor differences, this factor structure was subsequently replicated by Lohr and Bonge (1980).

The internal homogeneity of the subscales, based upon item-total correlations, ranged from .66 and .80 with a mean of .74. Reports of test-retest reliability for the total score range from .92 over a 24-hour period (Jones, 1969) to .79 over eight weeks (Lohr & Bonge, 1980), with an additional report of .88 over an unspecified period (Trexler & Karst, 1972).

The original validation procedures were conducted with a general psychiatric inpatient sample, but more recent studies of depression suggest that the IBT is also associated with depressive symptomatology among students. Nelson (1977) reported that the correlation coefficient between the total IBT score and the BDI was .53 in a student sample. LaPointe and Crandell (1980) found significant differences between depressed students and nondepressed, nonneurotic students (as assessed by the neuroticism subscale of the Maudsley Personality Inventory) on all IBT subscales. They also found that even though Ellis did not intend the RET constructs to be specific to depression, the depressed group scored higher on the total IBT score in comparison to a group of subjects with high neuroticism scores but low depression scores. Thus, there is some evidence that the measure taps beliefs that are particularly characteristic of depression. The IBT has also been shown to be sensitive to changes in a depression treatment study (Fleming & Thornton, 1980). Interpretations of the IBT, however, may be confounded by its inverse correlations with intelligence and education level and the highly significant sex difference reported by Jones (1969) and partially replicated by Nelson (1977).

Thus, the psychometric properties of the IBT are satisfactory and there is preliminary evidence that the beliefs it assesses are somewhat specific to depression. However, the presumption that the IBT assesses enduring, traitlike beliefs requires tests in longitudinal studies that have not yet been performed. In addition, the work to date with student populations precludes conclusions about its research or clinical utility with clinically depressed patients.

Attributional Model of Depression

The attributional reformulation of the learned helplessness model of depression asserts that depressive mood is a function of the kinds of causal attributions people make for a lack of control over outcomes (Abramson, Seligman, & Teasdale, 1978; Seligman, Abramson, Semmel, & Von Baeyer, 1979). Depressive symptoms are expected when the cause is seen as a factor located inside the self (internal locus of causality), that is expected to persist over time (stable), and will have widespread effects (global). For example, it is predicted that depression in a therapist will result from the therapist's view that a client's premature termination results from the therapist's own mistakes (an internal factor), that are associated with enduring personality traits (stable), and which affect other interpersonal relationships (global). By contrast, it is expected that depression will not occur if the client's premature termination is perceived by the therapist to be the result of a poor client-therapist match (external) which occurs only sporadically (unstable) and does not affect other spheres of one's life (specific).

It was originally suggested that attributions made in a given situation reflect a stable tendency or style of the individual. More recently, Metalsky and Abramson (1981) added that attributions are a joint function of both the individual's stable, generalized beliefs and the information inherent in the specific situation which points to a particular attribution. The relative influence of individual and situational factors varies across different situations.

There are two major classes of procedures for the assessment of causal attributions. These two classes differ in the level of abstraction required from the respondent. First-order attribution measures ask that the respondent rate the degree to which each of several causes, described in a specific and concrete manner, influence a given outcome. For example, a measure of this type inquires about the influence of low ability in producing a failure. The investigator uses these responses to make inferences about the locus of causality, stability and (less frequently) the globality dimensions based on a priori assumptions about the dimensional properties of the specific causes. To illustrate, the subject who attributes the failure largely to low ability is said to have made an internal, stable attribution. Second-order measures, by contrast, ask the subject to rate the more abstract, dimensional properties of the causes rather than the causes themselves. For example, the subject is asked to rate the degree to which cause is something internal versus external to the self. Although some second-order measures ask the subject to first specify the concrete cause (e.g., low ability) which is subsequently rated on the internality dimension, this specification of a cause is not used in the scoring procedures. A major impetus for these second-order measures was the recognition that laypeople may not construe the attributional properties of the specific causes in the same way as do scientists. Indeed, Krantz and Rude (1984) found that the agreement between lay persons and scientists on the dimensional properties of specific causes is poor and that the correlations between attributions obtained from first- and second-order methods are not impressive. They suggested that the mixed results on the relationship between attribution and depression may be due in part to the use of different measures that show poor concurrent validity when compared with each other.

The current discussion will focus upon the Attributional Style Questionnaire ([ASQ]; Peterson, Semmel, Von Baeyer, Abramson, Metalsky, & Seligman, 1982), since it is virtually the only procedure for assessing attributions that is standardized and accompanied by information on its psychometric properties.

Attributional Style Questionnaire (ASQ).   The ASQ consists of 12 hypothetical situations. Six of the situations describe good outcomes; six describe bad outcomes. The six good and six bad outcomes are each comprised of three situations with affiliation themes and three with achievement themes. The subject is asked to imagine the self in that situation and to describe briefly the major cause of each event. The subject then rates: (1) the extent to which the cause is due to something about the respondent or something about other people or circumstances (internal versus external); (2) whether the cause will again be present in similar situations in the future (stable versus unstable); and (3) whether the cause influences only situations similar to the one being discussed or also influences other areas of the person's life (global versus specific).

Several studies have examined the internal consistency and test-retest reliability of the ASQ. The alphas for the internality, stability, and globality dimensions taken individually are disappointing: they range from .44 to .58 for the six good outcomes and from .46 to .69 for the six bad outcomes (Peterson et al., 1982). More adequate internal consistency is achieved by combining the internality, stability, and globality dimensions following the good outcomes into a composite good outcome score; the same procedure is used to form a composite bad outcome score (alphas = .75 and .72, for the good and bad outcomes, respectively). Similar internal consistency figures on the individual dimensions and on the composites were reported by Golin, Sweeney, and Shaeffer (1981) and Manly, McMahon, Bradley, and Davidson (1982). Unfortunately neither the individual dimension scores nor the composite scores permit adequate tests of predictions concerning the individual dimensions. Furthermore, the meaning of the composite score has not been clearly explicated.

An examination of the alpha coefficients of the good and bad affiliative versus achievement situations yields more unacceptable figures: Peterson et al. (1982) reported that these coefficients ranged from .21 to .53. Since there were no differences between affiliation and achievement situations, however, the two types of situations may be combined, thereby circumventing the problem of low reliability at this level of analysis. In any event, the researcher and clinician are cautioned to avoid individual dimension subscales and the affiliative versus achievement subscales until successful modifications of the scale are accomplished.

Test-retest correlations over a five-week period yielded moderate evidence of the stability of the scores over time (Peterson et al., 1982). The coefficients for the good and bad composite scores were .70 and .64, respectively; the coefficients for the three dimensions within each of the good and bad outcomes ranged from .58 to .69 with a mean of .62. A replication of these findings over a four-week period by Golin et al. (1981) produced similar test-retest correlations for the good and bad composites ($r = .67$ for both) and coefficients for the three dimensions of good and bad outcomes (mean $r = .57$, range from .47 to .66) that were only slightly lower than those reported by Peterson et al. (1982).

A number of studies have examined the relationship between the ASQ and depressed mood (Blaney et al. 1980; Cutrona, 1983; Eaves & Rush, 1984; Golin, et al., 1981; Manly et al., 1982; Miller, Klee, & Norman, 1982; Mukherji, Abramson, & Martin, 1982; O'Hara et al., 1982; Peterson et al., 1982; Raps, Peterson, Reinhard, Abramson, & Seligman, 1982; Seligman et al., 1979). Two consistent patterns emerge. First, attributions for the bad outcomes are somewhat more strongly related to depressed mood than are the attributions for good outcomes, thereby supporting the common therapeutic strategy of focusing reattribution training more on negative outcomes than on positive outcomes. Second, the composite scores tend to be more strongly related to depression than are the individual dimensions. This latter finding is not at all surprising given the low internal consistency of the individual dimensions in comparison to the moderate internal consistency of the composite scales.

The findings on the degree to which ASQ scores are related to depressed mood, however, are much less consistent across the 10 studies cited above. The magnitude of the associations reported by Seligman and colleagues (Raps et al., 1982; Seligman et al., 1979) was not replicated by the eight other studies (which include nine independent samples), with the exception of the Eaves and Rush (1984) study. Although the data from the independent investigators were usually in the predicted direction and often attained significance, the magnitude of the correlations was, in virtually all cases, more modest. For example, when considering the correlations between depressive mood and the strongest of the ASQ variables, the composite score for negative outcomes, Seligman's et al. (1979) report of a correlation of .48 seems discrepant from the other reported coefficients which ranged from $-.03$ to .35 with a mean of .21. Similar discrepancies in reports on the magnitude of the correlations were apparent for the positive outcome composite: Seligman's et al. report of a correlation of $-.22$ with the BDI is higher than most other reports which ranged from .05 to $-.20$ with a mean correlation coefficient of .10.

Although the ASQ has been of great heuristic value as demonstrated by the number of studies of normal and clinical populations using this measure since its recent introduction, its promise appears to be limited by the fact that the replications of the original works tended to yield rather weak associations between the ASQ and depressive mood. Furthermore, the seeming clarity in the definition of the three attribution dimensions was not matched by satisfactory coefficients of internal consistency, although the alpha coefficients for the composite score combining the three dimensions is adequate. The construct validity of the ASQ is also threatened by the finding that subjects do not show the same attributional pattern on the ASQ as they do in their attributions for stressful life events or for laboratory tasks (Miller et al., 1982). Finally, evaluations of the assumption that the ASQ measures an enduring, traitlike style has produced mixed results: Hamilton and Abramson (1983) observed that the depressive attributional style evident among depressed inpatients upon admission had disappeared by the time of discharge, while Eaves and Rush (1984) found mixed evidence on changes over time in the attributional style of depressed inpatients.

Self-Control Model of Depression

Rehm (1977) proposes that depression is the result of deficits in self-control behaviors. The self-control model of depression draws heavily upon Kanfer's (1971) more general self-control model which posits that individuals use three sequential processes—self-monitoring, self-evaluation, and self-reinforcement—to acquire and maintain the behaviors necessary to meet their goals. Rehm claims that the depressed person exhibits deficits in each of these phases in the self-control process. At the self-monitoring phase, the depressed individual selectively attends to negative events and to immediate versus delayed outcomes. At the self-evaluation phase, the self-monitored behaviors are compared to an internal criterion or standard. The perfectionistic standards of depressed persons may set the stage for perceived failures and discourage continued efforts toward unattainable goals. Finally, any discrepancy between observed behavior and performance standards during the self-evaluation phase leads to self-punishment. The self-punishment serves to discourage future goal-directed behaviors and may account for the psychomotor retardation, inhibition, and low response rates that are typical of depression.

The measurement of self-control processes is considerably less well developed and less frequently used in comparison to the processes basic to the previously discussed theories. Only two self-control assessment procedures could be located: the Self-Control Questionnaire (Rehm, Kornblith, O'Hara, Lamparski, Romano, & Volkin, 1981) and the Self-Control Schedule (Rosenbaum, 1980).

Self-Control Questionnaire (SCQ). The 41-item SCQ was designed to assess attitudes and beliefs about self-control behavior. Items include statements such as "It's no use trying to change the things that make me miserable," "When I do something right, I take time to enjoy the feeling," and "My mood is related to my behavior." It is clear from these items that the SCQ draws upon a more broadly defined model of self-control than that limited to the early model consisting of self-monitoring, self-evaluation, and self-reinforcement.

The internal consistency and test-retest reliability of the SCQ appear satisfactory from preliminary reports. The homogeneity of SCQ items is indicated by O'Hara's et al. (1982) report of an alpha coefficient of .82 and by Rude's (1983) replication of this finding (alpha = .88). Test-retest reliability is also satisfactory: O'Hara (1978, cited by O'Hara et al., 1982) claimed that the test-retest correlation coefficient after a five-week period was .86.

The few studies which allow inferences about the construct validity of the SCQ yield mixed results. O'Hara et al. (1982) reported that the SCQ scores obtained from women during the second trimester of pregnancy correlated with BDI scores that were obtained, on the average, almost 12 weeks after delivery ($r = .31, p < .001$). Rude's (1983) data on the concurrent administration of the SCQ and two measures of depression to depressed outpatients were less promising ($r = .05$ with the BDI and .11 with the D-30 subscale of the MMPI-D scale, both ps N.S.). It should be noted, though, that the restricted range of scores among this clinically depressed sample probably reduced the correlation between the SCQ and the measures of depression that may emerge in a more heterogenous population. The data on the sensitivity of the SCQ to self-control interventions are mixed: SCQ scores were sensitive to treatment in a study by Rehm, Kornblith, O'Hara, Lamparski, Romano, & Volkin (1981) but not in a later study by Kornblith, Rehm, O'Hara, and Lamparski (1983). In addition, Rehm, Kaslow, Rabin, and Willard (1981) found no evidence that the prediction of posttreatment depression was enhanced by pretreatment SCQ scores. It is clear that definitive conclusions on the construct validity of this measure await further research.

One caution should be noted regarding the interpretation of the SCQ: the SCQ measures "attitudes and beliefs" about self-control; it does not measure actual self-control behaviors and cognitions themselves. Since it is the self-control processes and not the attitudes about self-control that are thought to be the crucial processes in depression, and since the relationship between these two constructs has not been investigated, a more direct measure of self-control process is needed.

Self-Control Schedule (SCS).   The SCS (Rosenbaum, 1980) is a 36-item questionnaire designed to assess: (*a*) the use of cognitions to control emotional and physical responses including depression, anxiety, anger, boredom, hunger, and pain (e.g., "When I am feeling depressed, I try to think about pleasant events"); (*b*) the application of problem-solving procedures to common problems, such as being short of money or tackling an unpleasant task (e.g., "When I plan to work, I remove all the things that are not relevant to my work"); (*c*) the ability to delay gratification (e.g., "Faced with the need to make a decision, I usually find out all the possible alternatives instead of deciding quickly and spontaneously"); and (*d*) perceptions of self-efficacy (e.g., "I need outside help to get rid of some of my bad habits"). The SCS is reproduced in Appendix 6. Like the Irrational Beliefs Test (Jones, 1969), the intended scope of this measure is not limited to depression but the processes it taps are thought to be central to depression. Although its use in depression research has been quite limited, it will be described here because it is the only existing measure which purports to measure self-control behaviors rather than attitudes about self-control.

The development of the SCS proceeded in several stages. First, two experienced psychologists were asked to judge 60 items describing self-control behaviors or self-efficacy perceptions. The items on self-control behaviors were judged on whether the situation is likely to be experienced by a wide range of people and whether the item reflects an effective use of a self-control strategy. Second, the 44 items agreed upon by both judges were given to a sample of students. The final questionnaire consists of the 36 items which elicited a wide range of responses and which contributed to the internal consistency of the scale.

Rosenbaum (1980) conducted the psychometric studies on four samples of Israeli students, one sample of U.S. students, and one sample of Israeli men. Based on the strong similarity of the means and standard deviations of the U.S. and Israeli samples, Rosenbaum argues that the two nationalities are comparable.

The internal reliability of the SCS was computed from data on five of the six samples. The alpha coefficients ranged from .78 to .84 with a mean of .81. An independent replication by Rude (1983) yielded a slightly higher alpha coefficient (.88). Test-retest reliability over a period of four weeks (Rosenbaum, 1980) indicated that the SCS scores are quite stable ($r = .86 \, p < .01$). Thus, these estimates of the reliability of the SCS are encouraging.

Very little information is available on the validity of the SCS for the measurement of the self-control processes involved in depression, but the existing evidence does not support the construct validity of this measure. Rehm, Kaslow, Rabin, and Willard (1981) found that SCS scores, like the previously reported SCQ scores, were not among the more important predictors of the outcomes of self-control interventions. Rude (1983) was unable to find evidence of an association with depression ($r = -.08$ for the BDI and $-.28$ for the D-30, both N.S.). It should be remembered, however, that the magnitude of the correlations was likely to have been reduced by the restricted range of scores in Rude's clinically depressed population. Nonetheless, support of the concurrent validity of the SCS is indicated by its correlation of .54 ($p < .01$) with the SCQ.

Additional Measures of Depressive Cognition. Several additional fixed-format self-report procedures exist which will be noted only briefly because they have not apparently been used beyond their original development or because only minimal psychometric information is available. Weintraub, Segal, and Beck (1974) developed a story completion measure of negative cognitions that were correlated with depressed mood in college males. Lefebvre (1981) also developed a Cognitive Error Questionnaire, patterned after the Hammen and Krantz CBQ, consisting of 24 short vignettes followed by a dysphoric cognition representing a cognitive error that the subjects rate according to whether they would think in that way. Lefebvre found that raters could not reliably distinguish between the various types of cognitive distortions described by Beck, Rush, Shaw, & Emery (1979), but overall higher distortion scores were found in depressed inpatients than normal controls. Lefebvre also reports reliability data which indicate adequate psychometric properties. Finally, Lewinsohn and colleagues reported efforts to develop depression treatment outcome measures based on various cognitive approaches. They developed a Subjective Probability Questionnaire, a Personal Beliefs Inventory, and a Cognitive Events Schedule; psychometric data are reported by Muñoz (1977). Lewinsohn, Muñoz, and Larson (1978) found, in general, that negative cognitions about the self were more discriminating of depressives than cognitions about "the world." In a later study, Lewinsohn, Steinmetz, Larson, and Franklin (1981) report data from a longitudinal study indicating that scores on these measures and other cognitions were associated with current depressed mood, but appear to be neither antecedents nor sequelae of depression. Thus, they appeared not to measure a stable trait independent of present mood, but higher scores were associated with persistence of depression.

All the major instruments to assess depressogenic cognitions reported thus far employ fixed-choice procedures in which the investigator has determined the content of items. These procedures assess cognitions about hypothetical events or assess cross-situational beliefs and attitudes. One procedure which attempts to assess instantaneous "automatic thoughts" that occur in response to vignettes of various situations is the Cognitive Response Test, developed by Watkins and Rush (1983). Fifty vignettes based on various areas of social functioning are presented, and the open-ended response is scored according to a manual developed by the authors. Responses are coded as rational or irrational, and depressed or not. Preliminary data indicate that depressed outpatients scored more irrational-depressed responses than did controls. The scoring system is reported to be reliable, but further information about the characteristics of the procedure is not available.

Another procedure recently developed by Davison, Robins, and Johnson (1983) for naturalistic assessment of cognitions is termed the Articulated Thoughts during Simulated Situations (ATSS) procedure. The ATSS presents specific simulated stressful and neutral situations to the subject and then permits open-ended verbal responding rather than response to investigator-determined choices. The verbalizations of the participant may be subjected to various types of scoring. Thus far there have not been published reports of use with depressed persons, but the ATSS may hold promise as an alternative to questionnaires—although like the latter it presents hypothetical situations.

BEHAVIORAL APPROACHES TO DEPRESSION

Level of Reinforcement

Since the late 1960s Peter Lewinsohn has been identified with the best developed behavioral approach to depression. It is a multifactorial approach with several facets, but the essential postulate is that depression is a consequence of reduction in response-contingent positive reinforcement. Lewinsohn (1974) elaborated the theory to suggest that there are three ways such a reduction might occur: events may not be reinforcing or lose reinforcer effectiveness; reinforcing events may become unavailable; or they may be available but the person lacks the skills to elicit them. He has also postulated that depressed individuals are relatively more sensitive to aversiveness and that experienced aversiveness leads to a variety of consequences that reduce the experience of positive reinforcement. An important step in testing such hypotheses and in developing clinical interventions based on such a model has been the development of the Pleasant Events Schedule (MacPhillamy & Lewinsohn, 1972) and its corollary, the Unpleasant Events Schedule (Lewinsohn & Talkington, 1979). These self-report measures are intended to index the frequency and enjoyability of events with reinforcing properties (or aversiveness), and are described below. These scales have been used in theoretical research on depression and activity, as well as being used as tools to design interventions or evaluate therapy outcome.

Pleasant Events Schedule (PES).   The PES (MacPhillamy & Lewinsohn, 1972) was developed to provide self-reported frequency and enjoyability of engagement in common pleasurable activities (see Appendix 8). The scores are presumed to be an index of reinforcement. Developed by having a diverse group of individuals list pleasurable events, a final list of 320 items includes a broad range of relatively common social and solitary events. Examples include "wearing new clothes," "playing baseball," "going naked," "having a lively talk." Individuals rate all items on a three-point scale of frequency and a three-point scale of enjoyability. A third possible score is a multiplicative score of frequency times enjoyability, termed *obtained pleasure*. The scale may be subdivided into several content subscales: a rationally derived bipolar SN scale (128 items) that distinguishes social from nonsocial items, and several principal component-derived scales. Among the latter are a bipolar MF scale identifying masculine and feminine role-related activities, a bipolar IE scale identifying a dimension of extraverted stimulus seeking versus love of solitude and quiet, and Scale RB which identifies enjoyment of crafts and outdoors. There is also an empirically derived scale MR that identifies 49 items most universally and strongly correlated with mood ratings (Lewinsohn & Graf, 1973). This subscale has been further factor analyzed into five interpretable content factors (Lewinsohn, Youngren, & Grosscup, 1979).

Psychometric properties of the scale, including major subscales, are reported by MacPhillamy & Lewinsohn (1982). Test-retest reliability of the subscales appears to be adequate, based on stability over testings one month, two months, and three months apart, ranging from .69 to .88 at one month and .50 to .72 at three months. As expected, the traitlike scales (e.g., sex role preference, introversion/extraversion) tend to be more stable than mood-related items. Various validity studies are reported indicating good concurrent validity (self-ratings compared with peer ratings and with trained observers' ratings) and good predictive validity. Construct validity has been assessed in various ways. Several studies have found significant correlations between positive moods and engagement in pleasant events or negative moods and relatively low levels of pleasant events (Lewinsohn et al., 1979; Lewinsohn & Libet, 1972). The general PES scale and MR subscale discriminate between depressed persons and controls (e.g., Lewinsohn & Amenson, 1978), and among depressed patients who show different levels of improvement in behaviorally oriented therapies (Lewinsohn et al., 1979). Rehm, Fuchs, Roth, Kornblith, and Romano (1979) found that subjects in a self-control therapy program reported more mood-related (MR) items on the PES than did other groups, and also showed significant reductions in depressive symptoms. In a later study, however, Kornblith et al. (1983) found no effects of treatment on the reported rate of pleasant events.

MacPhillamy and Lewinsohn (1982) raise the possibility of a yea-saying response bias moderator variable in the PES, and constructed a K-scale to assess this possibility. Changes in intercorrelations between moderated and unmoderated scale scores with depression scores suggested that the K-scale may be a useful addition (p. 374). However, across clinical groups the predicted PES patterns appear to obtain regardless of whether moderated or unmoderated scores are used.

The PES has proved clinically useful in describing activity patterns in older adults (Lewinsohn & MacPhillamy, 1974), and in generating individualized activity schedules in behavioral and cognitive-behavioral therapies for depression. MacPhillamy and Lewinsohn (1982) have also reported norms for white adults in the Pacific Northwest.

Despite the care taken to evaluate the psychometric adequacy of the PES, several criticisms of the instrument have been raised. At the theoretical level, the concept of "reinforcement" as indexed by the PES might be questioned. The construct of reinforcement is circular, dependent upon the behavioral effects with which it is associated, and a functional relationship between mood and pleasant activity, as mediated by reinforcement, can only be inferred. Engagement in pleasurable activities may have its positive effects on depression because of alternative factors besides reinforcement as such (e.g., distraction from negative feelings and thoughts, sense of mastery, and so on). Hammen and Glass (1975), for instance, argued that the effects of engagement in positive activities are cognitively mediated—an approach which suggests that traditional concepts such as reinforcement as a sheer function of event occurrence may be overly simplistic.

Hollon and Bemis (1981) have also argued that we cannot be sure if events actually occurred or whether reports were influenced by memory or reporting bias (e.g., current depression might reduce recall or reporting of actual positive experiences). Although the concurrent validation studies reported by MacPhillamy and Lewinsohn (1982) suggest relatively good agreement between normal subjects' self-report and others' reports, that agreement indeed was lowest for the general PES score and the Mood Related items score—the two scales that are of particular interest to depression researchers. Also, the observer study was based on only 13 subjects, and overall the validation work on accuracy of reporting has not been done for depressed persons. Considerable evidence has accumulated for mood-dependent memory bias in the recall of personal events (e.g., Bower, 1981; Lloyd & Lishman, 1975; Teasdale & Fogarty, 1979). Therefore, it is conceivable that depressed persons will inaccurately report the frequency or enjoyability of events they have experienced (Buchwald, 1977). Thus, the meaning of scale scores in terms of their validity for depicting depressives' actual experiences may be questionable. Despite these limitations, however, the PES as a descriptive tool may be extremely useful in planning and tracking engagement in positive activities in the treatment of depression (Beck et al., 1979; Lewinsohn et al., 1979).

Unpleasant Events Schedule (UES).   The UES was developed in the same fashion as the PES, and also consists of 320 aversive items scored in the same way. The psychometric properties of the UES have been reported by Lewinsohn and Talkington (1979) and indicate good internal consistency (alpha = .96 for total score), and good test-retest reliability (.52–.62 from one to three months). It has been shown to have the predicted relationship with depression (Grosscup & Lewinsohn, 1980) and discriminated between depressives, psychiatric controls, and normals (Lewinsohn et al., 1979). However, the total score differences in the latter research appeared to be accounted for not by a higher frequency of negative events among depressives but by greater perceived aversiveness of the items, a cognitive element whose causal relationship with depression is unclear. Furthermore, it has been noted that the UES consists of a mixture of items typically considered to be episodic stressful life events, chronic or ongoing stressors, and "daily hassles." Kanner, Coyne, Schaefer, and Lazarus (1981) suggest that these conceptually distinct negative items should be kept separate, because the "daily hassles" are better predictors of concurrent and subsequent depression than are episodic major life events. If it is indeed important to separately assess the three types of negative experiences, other instruments are now available, developed apart from a behavioral perspective on depression.

Social Skill Assessment

Lewinsohn's hypothesis that depressed persons may lack requisite social skills to obtain reinforcers has never actually defined precisely which skills are important or which ones are uniquely dysfunctional in depressives. Similarly, others have discussed impaired social role functioning (Weissman, & Paykel, 1974), social reactions to dysphoria (Coyne, 1976; Hammen & Peters, 1978), or reduced social competence (Fisher-Beckfield & McFall, 1982), but to date there is no theory of social skill impairment which details the nature of interpersonal behaviors in depression. Instead, there are numerous empirical investigations of specific behaviors, employing a variety of methods.

The simplest behavioral observation studies of depression have been perhaps the least satisfactory. There have been reports of nonverbal differences with depressives displaying diminished eye contact, slower speech rate, and other behavior (Hinchliffe, Lancashire, & Roberts, 1971a, 1971b; Waxer, 1974). Youngren & Lewinsohn (1980), however, note that most studies of nonverbal behaviors in depression have been on hospitalized inpatients typically interacting with an experimenter or staff member, thereby limiting the generalizability of obtained results. Youngren and Lewinsohn (1980) did not find such simple nonverbal differences in their own studies using outpatients interacting with peers.

A second approach has focused on verbal content. Hokanson, Sacco, Blumberg, and Landrum (1980), for instance, found that under certain experimental conditions, depressed students communicated more self-devaluation and other negative behaviors. Rehm et al. (1979) found significant reductions in negative self-references in the speech of depressives following a self-control treatment program, but there was no control group of nondepressives as a comparison. Jacobson and Anderson (1982) found that relatively depressed students differed only slightly from the nondepressed in categories of speech content, such as negative self-statements, questions, self-disclosures, and other behaviors, but did observe that depressed persons delivered significantly more negative self-statements than did the nondepressed. Even more important, however, was the timing of the content. Jacobson and Anderson employed methods for analyzing the sequence of conversational exchange, and found that depressives emitted more unsolicited self-disclosures than did the nondepresssed. Thus, the timing of their own conversation, rather than content as such, appeared to display social skill dysfunction. The authors interpret the result in terms of depressives' self-preoccupation, but their main emphasis is the need for examination of the sequence, and not simply content of interaction, in future studies interpersonal behavior.

Perhaps the area of greatest consistency in results on the overt interpersonal behavior of depressives has been in the responses of others to the depressed person. Two types of research have been conducted: one uses trained observers to make global ratings of depressed persons' behaviors, and the other elicits the reactions of peers who have just interacted with the depressed individual. Youngren and Lewinsohn (1980) had raters observe depressed outpatients interacting in dyads and small groups with psychiatric and normal control subjects. The author developed ratings of "interpersonal style," consisting of descriptors rated on seven-point scales by observers, including a Social Skill subscale of 15 items (e.g., "friendly," "assertive"). The Social Skill scale distinguished between depressives and controls in the group condition. Thus, there was some evidence of the hypothesized social skill deficit in depressives; however, it occurred only in the group but not dyadic interactions, and the specific components of the problematic behavior as judged by observers were not specified. The authors urge more sophisticated content analyses and examination of observers' judgment process to clarify depressives' negative impact on others. In an additional major study of social skill in depressed outpatients (Lewinsohn, Mischel, Chaplin, & Barton, 1980), observers rated 17 positive attributes (e.g., friendly, assertive, warm). The observers rated depressives lower on these dimensions than the controls. Thus, it appeared that while depressives may indeed negatively judge themselves, external observers also found them to be less skilled on social skill qualities.

Although acceptable levels of interjudge agreement were found for the social skill ratings, it is unclear whether and under what conditions these ratings could be used by other investigators to capture unique depressive behaviors. The trait terms are rather general, and also the degree to which specific behaviors were actually dysfunctional rather than merely rated lower by judges responding to some global negative reaction remains to be clarified.

Studies using peer reactions rather than trained observers have also shown that interactions with depressed others led to rejection and other negative interpersonal responses (e.g., Coyne, 1976; Hammen & Peters, 1977, 1978; Howes & Hokanson, 1979; Marks & Hammen, 1982; Strack & Coyne, 1983), and many of the interaction studies have also found that interacting with a depressed other makes one depressed, anxious, and hostile. Coyne and colleagues argue that depression elicits negative reactions, and that these reactions are quite accurately perceived by the depressed persons, possibly leading to withdrawal or to a sense of failure which heightens depression. However, the precise nature of the depressive's offending behaviors is not known; what it is that depressives do that leads to the negative reactions of others is a problem for further research. Assessment procedures for such dysfunctions have not been developed.

Finally, the procedures which have been associated with the clearest interpersonal dysfunctions are self-report measures. An Interpersonal Events Schedule (Lewinsohn et al., 1979; Youngren & Lewinsohn, 1980) is reported to assess engagement in and impact of interpersonal events or cognitions about them, and contains eight rationally derived subscales. Test-retest reliability results indicate good stability over one to three months (rs in the .60s), but other psychometric properties are not known. The Interpersonal Events Schedule generally has provided evidence confirming Lewinsohn's hypothesis that depressives report greater interpersonal dysfunction than normals. Whether the scale identifies actual deficits or only depressives' negative cognitions about most facets of themselves, however, remains ambiguous on the basis of the relatively mixed findings of verbal and nonverbal behavioral differences between groups.

A final method for measuring social skill deficits in depression concerns assessment of social competence. A role-play procedure has recently been developed by Fisher-Beckfield and McFall (1982), and is presented in the section on problem solving and coping. Other role-play methods might prove useful as assessment procedures for the hypothesized interpersonal or social skills problems of depressives once theory has detailed the nature of alleged skill deficits. As indicated, however, empirical data from studies in this area have yet to pinpoint particular "depressive" behaviors.

Coping and Depression

There is no major theory of depression that hypothesizes that the essential dysfunction leading to depression is inadequate coping skills. Nevertheless, several researchers have suggested the need for a multifactorial model of depression which includes stressful life events as well as cognitions and resources for appraising and dealing with them. Thus, we may ask whether depressed persons have diminished skills in coping with stressors that may contribute to their depression. An extended discussion of coping is well beyond the scope of this chapter. However, we will attempt to review several approaches to the assessment of coping and its relation to depression.

At the outset, it is important to note the heterogeneity of usages of the term *coping,* and complexities in the assessment of coping. Definitions typically include both cognition and behavior, and instruments are generally self-report questionnaires, some administered in traitlike terms ("in general how likely are you to . . .)"), and others relating to specific situations. Thus, all methods reported need to be weighed in terms of the validity considerations raised previously with regard to the assessment of cognitions.

Ways of Coping Checklist.   As part of their efforts to study transactive aspects of psychopathology and to understand depressives' "ecological niche," Coyne and Lazarus have attempted to study depressives' ways of coping with everyday stresses (Coyne & Lazarus, 1980; Coyne, Aldwin, & Lazarus, 1981). Appraisal and coping processes are seen as mediating the reciprocal relationship between person and environment; coping efforts serve two main functions in this view: problem solving and emotional regulation. A 68-item Ways of Coping Checklist was developed by Folkman and Lazarus (1980) to cover cognitive and behavioral coping from the following domains: defensive coping (such as avoidance, intellectualization), problem solving, information-seeking, inhibition of action, direct action, and magical thinking. Individuals are requested to recall their most recent stressful event and then complete the checklist with that event in mind. Items are scored in terms of contribution to problem-focused or emotion-focused coping. Initial research indicated that coping responses were affected by the type of stressful event and by the appraisal of the event as changeable or requiring acceptance. Subsequently, factor analyses yielded seven interpretable subscales with a mean coefficient alpha of .84. These are problem-focused, wishful thinking, help seeking/avoidance, growth, minimization of threat, emotional support, and self-blame (Aldwin, Folkman, Schaefer, Coyne, & Lazarus, 1980). Test-retest reliability data are not reported. As applied to community residents defined as depressed or not on the Hopkins Symptom Checklist, Coyne et al. (1981) found that depressed persons differed overall, but specifically on two of the subscales: they engaged in more wishful thinking and more seeking of emotional support. They did not differ on problem-focused coping or other scales. Also, the authors report significant differences on 8 of the 68 individual items. Coyne et al. also found that depressives felt that they needed more information as they appraised the events. The authors interpret the findings to suggest that depressed persons feel uncertain—they seek advice, support, and more information—rather than feeling helpless to affect a situation. Of course, as Coyne et al. note, the procedure does not permit assessment of the effectiveness of coping. Although provocative interpretations of results are offered, the results need to be replicated on larger samples (there were only 15 depressed subjects in the Coyne et al. study) and with clinically depressed persons.

Billings and Moos Coping Responses.   A questionnaire containing 32 items rated on a four-point scale of frequency of usage was developed by Billings and Moos (1982) to represent items from their taxonomy of coping. The three domains of the taxonomy are appraisal-focused coping, problem-focused coping, and emotion-focused coping. Appraisal-focused coping includes "logical analysis" of the stressor and consequences, and contains four items with coefficient alpha of .53 for depressed patients (Billings, Cronkite, & Moos, 1983). Problem-focused coping includes seven items tapping "seeking information" (alpha = .63 for patients), and five items on "problem-solving" (alpha = .66). Emotion-focused coping includes six items concerning "affective regulation" (alpha = .63), and "emotional discharge" with six items (alpha = .41). Subjects complete the questionnaire with reference to a personal, recent, stressful event. Additional reliability data are not available.

The construct validity of this procedure is demonstrated by the finding that several domains significantly discriminated between depressed patients and community controls (Billings et al., 1983). Depressed persons reported significantly more information-seeking but less problem solving, and more emotional discharge. The groups did not differ on affective regulation or logical analysis coping responses. The authors interpret these differences as consistent with their hypothesis, derived from cognitive theories, that depressed persons have greater difficulty making decisions and taking action, similar to results reported by Coyne et al. (1981). They also suggest that depressives may overrely on emotional discharge coping, a strategy they consider relatively unefficacious (see also Beckham & Buck, 1983).

Coping Strategies Scales. A measure specific to depression was recently developed and reported by Beckham and Adams (1984). Based on a very broad definition of coping, the COSTS instrument consists of 139 items derived from the general literature on coping with depression, stress, and illness. These were grouped into 10 content scales according to judges' assignments. Subjects are asked to rate whether or not they performed each response in the past two weeks, and whether they then felt worse, the same or better.

One-hundred sixty-four patients in treatment for nonpsychotic depression served as initial subjects. It was determined that 9 of the 10 scales had coefficients of internal reliability greater than .70. A factor analysis procedure subsequently yielded three stable factors with high levels of internal consistency; these are termed: individual coping (engaging in activities), containment/passivity, and emotional expression/social support (which attempts to elicit support through emotional expression). In terms of construct validity, as might be predicted, BDI scores correlated negatively with general activity coping, and positively with passivity and emotional expression. On individual items, patients indicated that extremes of emotional regulation (containment or expression) made them feel worse, while a variety of strategies were seen as making them feel better. There was no control group for comparing depressed and nondepressed persons' effective strategies, but the authors suggest that the measure has potential for identifying therapy goals and evaluating treatment outcome.

Other research on coping in depressives has been sparse, but has generally failed to find significant overall differences in coping between depressed and nondepressed persons. For instance, in using standardized checklists of coping thoughts and behaviors, Rippere (1976) and Fremouw, Cormier, Rapp, Steinfeld, and Cormier (1979) found no significant differences; Padesky and Hammen (1978) found that depressed and nondepressed students were equally effective in generating coping options to hypothetical problems; that is, they "knew" how to cope. Astor-Dubin and Hammen (1984) reported that moderately depressed and nondepressed students did not differ in their coping behaviors and their reported effectiveness when open-ended interview data on coping were categorized according to a 2 × 2 taxonomy similar to that proposed by Lazarus and Launier (1978): cognitive and behavioral, problem-focused and palliative. In view of the conflicting results on depressive coping behaviors, it will be important in the future to try to distinguish what depressed persons *do* from what they *report* they do and to ascertain whether there may be skill differences or emotional reaction differences at the source of any observed differences on questionnaires.

A tentative answer to this question has recently been proposed by Parker and Brown (1982). They reported the construction of an Antidepressive Behavior Measure, which yielded 22 items for the final version, containing 6 content domains following principal-components analysis (recklessness, socialization, distraction, problem solving, passivity, and self-consolation). The scale was administered to diagnosed depressed outpatients and controls, and readministered to the depressed patients when they were no longer depressed. The depressed saw themselves as significantly less likely to socialize and seek distraction and more likely to be passive. However, when no longer depressed, the only difference that remained was on the passivity scale, which in turn seemed to be accounted for solely by the item indicating greater use of sleeping pills. The authors discuss the common problem of symptoms confounded with coping behaviors, and conclude that apparent coping decrements are state dependent and probably due to depressed mood influencing reports of behavior. Therefore, across the various studies there does not emerge a clear sense of skill decrements which contribute to depression onset or maintenance.

Problem Inventory for College Students (PICS). A new instrument has recently been developed by Fisher-Beckfield and McFall (1982) to measure competence in college men. Although general lack of competence as such has not been hypothesized to be a cause of depression, the instrument may yield information on social skill and on problem-solving ability in the context of typical college concerns. Seventy-three items representing common problem situations for male students in the social and academic domains emerged from an elaborate behavioral-analytic method. Item selection involved task analysis and item sampling, item evaluation, response enumeration, and response evaluation as detailed in the behavior analytic method of Goldfried and D'Zurilla (1969). The final product involved 31 items concerning problems in social interaction and 21 concerning academic problems that could be scored with a raters' manual for level of competence. Each item is administered by audiotape, requiring a role-played solution or description of what to do. The PICS achieved high interjudge reliabilities (mean $r = .75$), and the coefficient alpha was .85 for interpersonal items and .79 for academic items. The authors found that depression scores accounted for 11.5 percent of the variance in interpersonal competence scores (and 5.9 percent for academic competence). Eight interpersonal competence items were especially associated with depression, but unfortunately their content was not reported. It remains to be determined whether lack of competence in solving such problems is a depressogenic factor, or a symptom of depression which may decrease when depression decreases.

ISSUES IN THE ASSESSMENT OF COGNITIONS

Having presented the most widely used instruments for assessing depressogenic cognitions, it is important to evaluate them in general in terms of considerations unique to cognitive assessment. There are several important issues that arise in interpreting the validity of any of the various procedures reviewed—issues that pose both procedural and conceptual challenges to cognitive formulations.

What Is Being Measured? The fundamental issue in the cognitive assessment enterprise is the question: What is being measured? There are various facets of this problem, some conceptual and some methodological. Obviously, internal events cannot be directly observed. We have only indirect methods requiring high levels of inference, limited by individuals' ability to report on their cognitions, subject to various inaccuracies and reactive to the methods employed to assess them.

Perhaps the first question that arises is: What is cognition? The term is typically used to describe both the processes involving thinking and perceiving, and the content or product of such a process. The process versus content distinction has not been clearly drawn in most depression research, often with the result that demonstrated differences between the content of cognitions given by depressed and nondepressed persons has implicitly been taken as evidence of differences in the process of their thinking. All of the instruments available and reported in this chapter pertain to the content of cognition only. For instance, instruments may show that depressed persons select more negative interpretations, predictions, or causal ascriptions, but they do not show that the inference process itself or the mode of reaching conclusions differs from that of nondepressed persons.

The extent to which individuals can accurately report on their cognitive content and processes has been the subject of considerable controversy. Regarding the accuracy of reports on the cognitive content, we must question whether self-report captures actual content or simply the person's implicit theories about their thoughts and beliefs. These theories about cognitive content may have been established prior to the measurement situation or may be structured by cues in the measurement situation. Also, responses may be influenced by all the biases that affect any measurement situation, such as experimenter demand and self-presentational tendencies. Similar issues arise regarding the accuracy of reports on cognitive processes. Nisbett and Wilson (1977), for instance, have argued that people are not good reporters of their cognitive processes, often unable to report on factors that actually affect their inferences, but relying instead on a priori causal theories about what affected their responses. Thus, there must be caution about taking self-report data to be veridical samples of individuals' actual cognitions.

The question of accuracy of reports is further related to the matter of levels of assessment. Hollon and Bemis (1981) have discussed "surface" versus "deep" structures applied to cognitive assessment. They have suggested that individuals probably are more able to be aware of and to report "surface" cognitions than "deep" ones which may be the underlying assumptions (or irrational beliefs) which produce depressive "surface" cognitions. The instruments reported in this chapter represent a mixture of both situation-specific self-statements (surface cognitions) and beliefs or assumptions (deep structures), commonly without specifying which or indicating the different implications of each.

A final question about what is being assessed is the question: What is cognitive bias? Coyne and Gotlib (1983) have pointed out that the critical theoretical terms *bias, distortion,* and *error* are commonly used interchangeably. They note that *error* or *distortion* require persistence of beliefs in the face of strong evidence to the contrary. Yet this condition is not met when hypothetical stories omit evidence contrary to negative beliefs or when experimenters carefully conceal the bogus nature of the feedback. The question of depressive "bias," moreover, is complicated by recent research which suggests that observed differences between depressed and nondepressed persons may reflect not depressive bias, but rather the biases of nondepressives or of both groups. Alloy and Abramson (1979) and Lewinsohn, Mischel, Chaplin, and Barton (1980), for instance, have cited evidence that nondepressed persons appear to bask in an illusory glow of emphasizing or exaggerating self-enhancing information, while minimizing the negative, compared to objective standards or external judges' opinions (see also review by Coyne & Gotlib, 1983). The cognitions of depressed persons in these situations, on the other hand, even though more negativistic, were more accurate. Thus, cognitive patterns of responding by depressed persons on questionnaires and in laboratory tasks raise significant interpretive questions. Do they represent depressive bias? Do they represent underlying beliefs and propositions or relatively fleeting, surface self-statements? Are they accurate representations of actual mental content, or are they persons' theories about their mental content? Do they describe and elaborate depressive process or merely content? These questions are further affected by various methodological considerations which are discussed next.

Methodological Concerns in Assessing Cognition. The issues raised above concerning what is being assessed pertain to the validity of cognitive assessment procedures for measuring the constructs they purport to measure. In addition to the theoretical issues of whether people have access to cognitions and what level of cognitions is reported, additional threats to the validity of cognitive assessment procedures stem from nature of the procedures themselves. Fixed-format, self-report procedures, however much they may simplify assessment, constrain the respondent's choices, and may have been drawn (either rationally or empirically) from a universe of experiences which do not match the subjects' own. This seems especially critical for cognitive assessment where idiosyncratic ways of thinking are of interest. Most of the instruments discussed above share this characteristic. In vivo thought-sampling of spontaneous cognitions has not been systematically applied to depression, except in conjunction with cognitive-behavioral therapy for depression (Beck et al., 1979). Two open-ended response format methods, ATSS (Davison et al., 1983) and PICS (Fisher-Beckfield & McFall, 1982) were briefly described above, but to date neither has been extensively used to assess depressive cognitive processes. Another problem is that the cueing situations themselves (experimenter-presented hypothetical events) necessarily introduce artificiality. Moreover, open-ended techniques might also elicit global response tendencies, stereotypes, or other responses which are not veridical samples of subjects' actual or typical spontaneous cognition—a problem shared with laboratory paradigms and self-report procedures.

Thus, the method of assessment, whether fixed or free format, invariably introduces to some degree an artificiality which undermines our confidence that respondents' reports reflect their actual personal cognitive experience. Nonetheless, selection of the appropriate methodology may increase the likelihood of valid sampling of cognition. Hollon and Bemis (1981), for instance, have urged specifying the level of cognition desired, and then selecting a format relatively more compatible with that level. Thus, "deeper" structures might be tapped with the "endorsement" method rather than spontaneous, free-form methods. That is, individuals might be willing to indicate level of agreement with experimenter-provided attitudes and assumptions, but relatively better able to produce more "surface" self-statements in open-ended assessment procedures. The investigator must be aware, however, that endorsement methods may more readily indicate respondents' acceptance of content validity than the fact that they have actually occurred to the respondent (Hollon & Bemis, 1981, p. 138).

These authors also raise two additional threats to the validity of cognitive assessment procedures as a function of methods employed: the assumptions of temporal stability and situational stability. The first refers to the common assumption of "cognitive intransience" (Hollon & Kendall, 1980) that cognitive contents and processes do not change across time. As will be seen, there is ample evidence for rejecting this assumption, especially for mood-related cognitions. Event-related cognitions may also covary over time with changes in the environment. Moreover, reliance on retrospective methods, as most cognitive appraisal procedures involve, may not only falsely assume that past cognitions have remained stable but may also falsely assume accurate retrieval of past cognitions. These assumptions are questionable; errors occur which are due not only to forgetting but also to selective recall due to the effects of current mood on what is retrieved from memory (e.g., Bower, 1981; Teasdale, 1983).

The question of situational stability is one which has been raised repeatedly in the assessment domain (e.g., Mischel, 1973). Cognitions, like personality traits, are likely to be highly affected by the characteristics of the situation rather than being static across diverse circumstances. Yet most procedures aimed at assessing cognitions commonly employ no situational domain of content, or else sample only a few situations. Depressive cognitive bias, for instance, might differ in the domains of achievement and interpersonal events for different individuals.

Finally, we may also question the implicit assumption in our measurement procedures that cognition is a monolithic and unitary phenomenon. Davis (1979; Davis & Unruh, 1981) suggests that the cognitive self-schema of the recently depressed individual is weak and processes information in a disorganized manner. It may be speculated that inconsistent, disorganized processing will at times yield inconsistent or even contradictory thoughts about a given topic. The possibility of contradictions in even relatively well-organized schemas should also be entertained. The multiple-choice or true/false formats of most current assessment methods, however, do not allow for the possibility that cognition may not always be internally consistent. Indeed, the criterion of high internal consistency in all our measurement procedures may need to be reevaluated if the phenomenon we are attempting to measure is itself not internally consistent.

The multiplicity of concerns raised about cognitive assessment procedures may seem disheartening to those who wish to use or develop such instruments. However, a more positive way to look at it is that problematic instruments have exposed problematic theories about cognitions. It is to be hoped that developments in theories about cognition and cognitive processes will help to lay the groundwork for improved methods of assessment and vice versa.

Methodological Concerns regarding the Depression-Cognition Link. It is clear that at least modest associations between depression and depressive cognitions are found using most measures of cognition. Interpretations of these associations, however, must be made with caution since the widely used self-report measures of depressive mood themselves tap cognition. Thus, the obtained associations may partially reflect the overlap in the content of the measures of depression and cognitions (Beckham & Leber, personal communication, 1984). The use of assessment procedures without a significant cognitive component is needed to determine the extent to which depressive cognition is related to the noncognitive components of depression.

IMPLICATIONS FOR APPROPRIATE RESEARCH AND CLINICAL USE OF MEASURES

Each of the measures reviewed was originally developed with the intention of assessing a psychological process considered to contribute to the cause or maintenance of the depression syndrome. Moreover, implicit in the theoretical underpinnings of each measure is a further set of assumptions: it is assumed that the target behavior is specific to depression and that the behaviors are stable, at least insofar as they contribute to an ongoing vulnerability to depression. The psychometric adequacy of each instrument has been reviewed, but the assumptions about the use of these measures require brief comment.

The Causality/Vulnerability Issue. A full consideration of the validity of any psychological theory of depression is beyond the scope of this chapter. However, it needs to be made clear that the instruments reviewed were conceived to be measures of "depressogenic" processes, with the corollary that high scores on such instruments identify the causal problem or vulnerability factor for the individual which marks a deficit or dysfunction leading to depression. Two recent lines of research cast doubt on the validity of this assumption. First, an emerging body of data challenges the assumption that the presumed depressive cognitive bias processes prominent in the theories of Beck and Seligman actually occur or are unique to depression. Alloy and Abramson (1979), for instance, have argued that it is nondepressed persons who display a characteristic bias, while depressives are actually accurate, or "sadder but wiser." Lewinsohn et al. (1980) reached a similar conclusion after demonstrating that observers and depressed persons agreed in their negative judgments of the latters' interpersonal behavior but nondepressives overestimated their skills compared to observers' ratings. Coyne and Gotlib (1983) have reviewed some of the logical and methodological problems inherent in the literature on depressive cognitive bias, and conclude that the issue is far from resolved. At the very least, it should be recognized that the presumed depressogenic processes have been called into question. In interpreting elevated scores on cognitive measures, the meaning of low scores also may be raised, and the processes which underlie the performances of both depressed and nondepressed persons is very much an open question being vigorously pursued.

A second body of research addresses the fundamental assumption that the depressogenic behaviors are stable and mark a vulnerability process. Recent research employing crucial longitudinal designs has cast considerable doubt on this assumption. Lewinsohn et al. (1981) showed that persons who became depressed during the course of their investigation did not differ initially from persons who did not become depressed on a variety of measures of depressive cognitions corresponding to Beck and Seligman's theories. Hamilton and Abramson (1983) showed that the Dysfunctional Attitude Scale and the Attribution Style Questionnaire were highly unstable in an inpatient depressed population, showing a reduction to normal levels when depressive symptoms remitted. Eaves and Rush (1984) also found a significant decrease in the DAS scores of an inpatient population following remission, although the scores of the remitted patients remained significantly higher than those of community controls. Parker and Brown (1982) also demonstrated that reported coping behaviors mirrored the depressed state, so that when the depression diminished, coping behaviors were nearly indistinguishable from those of nondepressed persons. Other research not specifically germane to the measures discussed in this chapter also strongly supports the idea of mood state dependent cognitions rather than stable depressive cognitions (e.g., Clark & Teasdale, 1982; Hammen, Miklowitz, & Dyck, 1985). This growing body of research challenges the presumption that dysfunctional cognitions lead to depression in a simple linear model of causality, and suggest instead that depressed mood causes depressive cognitions, or that the two are interactive in a fashion that confounds simplistic causal theories.

In fairness, it must be considered that the instruments currently in use do not tap sufficiently "deep" processes that may be more enduring vulnerability factors. Indeed, Beck, Epstein, and Harrison (1982) raise the possibility of different levels of cognitive phenomena, with cognitions about stimuli seen as relatively transient, and beliefs and assumptions about the self and the world seen as relatively more stable. Unfortunately, however, the DAS measure of such beliefs has not been shown to be stable (Hamilton & Abramson, 1983). It is possible that further developments in schema research will verify Beck's proposition, but to date research generally has not supported it.

The causality/vulnerability discussion has centered on measures of cognition and coping, with neglect of social skills assessment. Such research needs to be done. However, the same cautions in interpreting scores are warranted: restraint in assuming that high (dysfunctional) scores indicate a causal process, and consideration of the likelihood that social behaviors which are deficient during the depressive period may improve when the depression remits.

The Specificity Issue. As discussed in the review of measures, the question of the specificity of the behavior to depression must not be assumed. Many studies have not investigated the issue at all, merely presuming a deficit specific to depression rather than a general disturbance in personal functioning. Few studies have included appropriate control groups to test the question. For instance, Krantz and Hammen (1979) and Norman et al. (1983) found the CBQ depressive bias scores to be higher in depressed than nondepressed inpatients, and Hamilton and Abramson (1983) also found DAS scores to be higher in depressed inpatients then psychiatric and normal controls. LaPointe and Crandell (1980) found IBT scores to be higher among depressed than "neurotic" students (although, interestingly, Ellis does not consider the RET constructs measured by the IBT to be specific to depression).

On the other hand, Hollon and Kendall (1980) reported that the ATQ and a measure of trait anxiety were highly associated with each other. It has also been shown that the DAS is strongly correlated with mood states other than depression (Riskind et al, 1983; Weissman & Beck, 1978) and with deficits in assertiveness (Hammen, Jacobs, Mayol, & Cochran, 1980). Hammen et al. also found that an assertion training program for subjects with assertiveness deficits improved the subjects' DAS scores. Because of the coexistence of depression with these other difficulties (i.e., Gotlib [1984] notes that anxious or unassertive individuals are often depressed), it is not clear whether the associations of measures of depressive cognition with affective and behavioral states other than depression are related to these other disturbances themselves or to their overlap with depression.

The degree to which measures of depressive cognitions have a unique relationship with depression is obfuscated by the high intercorrelations between depressed, anxious, and hostile mood states. This issue has been examined by removing the variance common to the various mood states. For instance, Krantz and Hammen (1979), Weissman (1979), Frost and MacInnis (1983), and Riskind et. al (1983) used various ways of partialling out mood scores on inventories of depressed mood from measures of depressive cognitive bias. These procedures yielded somewhat mixed results. Perhaps the best conclusion to be drawn at this point is that specificity to depression should not be assumed until considerably more research addresses this important question.

Despite these gloomy conclusions about the limitations of current measures of "depressogenic" behaviors, there remain two significant and highly appropriate usages of the procedures. For researchers, the instruments are clearly necessary to test theoretical models, and the soundest of the instruments enable more valid tests of hypotheses. For clinicans, the instruments may prove highly useful in developing individualized treatments.

Differential Selection and Evaluation of Treatment Approaches.   Identification of dysfunctional social skills, negativistic beliefs, reduced pleasant activities, or deficient coping strategies may all provide targets for effective intervention in depression. The identification of different deficits may provide a basis for choosing to use the particular psychotherapeutic techniques developed for those deficits. Of course, the prevailing assumption that treatment should be aimed at remedying deficits must be tested; an alternative possibility is that treatments will be more effective when they capitalize on existing strengths.

It is important to avoid the treatment-etiology fallacy that significant reductions in depression following such specific interventions attest to the etiological significance of the treated depressive process. This logic is misleading because processes that cause the disorder are not necessarily the same processes that if altered, would effectively reverse the disorder. Given that the treatment-etiology fallacy is avoided, the measures may help in explicating the processes which change in therapy, and whether such processes are associated with particular interventions.

References

Abramson, L. Y., Seligman, M. E. P., & Teasdale, J. D. (1978). Learned helplessness in humans: Critique and reformulation. *Journal of Abnormal Psychology, 87,* 49–94.

Aldwin, C., Folkman, S., Schaefer, C., Coyne, J. C., & Lazarus, R. S. (1980). *Ways of coping: A process measure.* Paper presented at the annual convention of the American Psychological Association, Montreal, Canada.

Alloy, L., & Abramson, L. (1979). Judgment of contingency in depressed and nondepressed students: Sadder but wiser? *Journal of Experimental Psychology: General, 108,* 441–485.

Astor-Dubin, L., & Hammen, C. L. (1984). Cognitive-behavioral coping responses of men and women. *Cognitive Therapy and Research, 8,* 85–90.

Beck, A. T. (1967). *Depression: Clinical, experimental, and theoretical aspects.* Philadelphia: University of Pennsylvania Press.

Beck, A. T. (1976). *Cognitive therapy and the emotional disorders.* New York: International Universities Press.

Beck, A. T., Epstein, N., & Harrison, R. (1982). *Cognitions, attitudes, and personality dimensions in depression.* Paper presented at the annual meeting of the Society for Psychotherapy Research, Smuggler's Notch, Vermont.

Beck, A. T., Rush, A. J., Shaw, B., & Emery, G. (1979). *Cognitive therapy of depression.* New York: Guilford Press.

Beckham, E. E., & Adams, R. L. (1984). Coping behavior in depression: Report on a new scale. *Behavior Research and Therapy, 22,* 71–75.

Beckham, E. E., & Buck, P. (1983, August). *Clinician and patient views of coping behaviors in depression.* Paper presented at the meeting of the American Psychological Association, Anaheim, CA.

Beckham, E. E., & Leber, W. (1984). Personal communication.

Billings, A., & Moos, R. (1982). Stressful life events and symptoms: A longitudinal model. *Health Psychology, 1,* 99–117.

Billings, A. G., Cronkite, R. C., & Moos, R. H. (1983). Social-environmental factors in unipolar depression: Comparisons of depressed patients and nondepressed controls. *Journal of Abnormal Psychology, 92,* 119–133.

Blaney, P. H., Behar, V., & Head, R. (1980). Two measures of depressive cognitions: Their association with depression and with each other. *Journal of Abnormal Psychology, 89,* 678–682.

Bower, G. (1981). Mood and memory. *American Psychologist, 36,* 129–148.

Buchwald, A. (1977). Depressive mood and estimates of reinforcement frequency. *Journal of Abnormal Psychology, 86,* 443–446.

Clark, D. M., & Teasdale, J. D. (1982). Diurnal variation in clinical depression and accessibility of memories of positive and negative experiences. *Journal of Abnormal Psychology, 91,* 87–95.

Coyne, J. C. (1976). Toward on interactional description of depression. *Psychiatry, 39,* 28–40.

Coyne, J. C., Aldwin, C., & Lazarus, R. (1981). Depression and coping in stressful episodes. *Journal of Abnormal Psychology, 90,* 439–441.

Coyne, J. C., & Gotlib, I. H. (1983). The role of cognition in depression: A critical appraisal. *Psychological Bulletin, 94,* 472–505.

Coyne, J. C., & Lazarus, R. (1980). Cognition, stress, and coping: A transactional perspective. In I. L. Kutosh and L. B. Schlesinger (Eds.), *Handbook on stress and anxiety.* San Francisco: Jossey–Bass.

Cutrona, C. (1983). Causal attributions and perinatal depression. *Journal of Abnormal Psychology, 92,* 161–172.

Davis, H. (1979). Self-reference and the encoding of personal information in depression. *Cognitive Therapy and Research, 3,* 97–110.

Davis, H., & Unruh, W. (1981). The development of the self-schema in adult depression. *Journal of Abnormal Psychology, 90,* 125–133.

Davison, G. C., Robins, C., & Johnson, K. (1983). Articulated Thoughts during Simulated Situations: A paradigm for studying cognition in emotion and behavior. *Cognitive Therapy and Research, 7,* 17–40.

Dobson, K. S., & Breiter, H. J. (1983). Cognitive assessment of depression: Reliability and validity of three measures. *Journal of Abnormal Psychology, 92,* 107–109.

Eaves, G., & Rush, A. J. (1984). Cognitive patterns in symptomatic and remitted unipolar major depression. *Journal of Abnormal Psychology, 93,* 31–40.

Fisher-Beckfield, D., & McFall, R. M. (1982). Development of a competence inventory for college men and evaluation of relationships between competence and depression. *Journal of Consulting and Clinical Psychology, 50,* 697–705.

Fleming, B. M., & Thornton, D. W. (1980). Coping skills training as a component in the short-term treatment of depression. *Journal of Consulting and Clinical Psychology, 48,* 652–654.

Folkman, S., & Lazarus, R. S. (1980). An analysis of coping in a middle-aged community sample. *Journal of Health and Social Behavior, 21,* 219–239.

Fremouw, W., Cormier, W., Rapp, S., Steinfield, B., & Cormier, S. (1979). *Cognitive and behavioral coping styles of college students for depression.* Unpublished manuscript.

Frost, R. O., & MacInnis, D. J. (1983). The Cognitive Bias Questionnaire: Further evidence. *Journal of Personality Assessment, 47,* 173–177.

Glass, D. R. (1978). *An evaluation of a brief treatment for depression based on the learned helplessness model.* Unpublished doctoral dissertation, University of California, Los Angeles.

Goldfried, M., & D'Zurilla, T. (1969). A behavioral-analytic model for assessing competence. In C. Spielberger, (Ed.), *Current topics in clinical and community psychology, 1,* 151–196.

Goldried, M., & D'Zurilla, T. (1969). A behavioral-analytic model for assessing competence. In C. Spielberger, (Ed.), *Current topics in clinical and community psychology, 1,* 151–196.

Golin, S., Sweeney, P. D., & Shaeffer, D. E. (1981). The causality of causal attributions in depression: A cross-lagged panel correlation analysis. *Journal of Abnormal Psychology, 90,* 14–22.

Goodwin, A. M., & Williams, J. M. G. (1982). Mood induction research: Its implications for clinical depression. *Behavior Research and Therapy, 20,* 373–382.

Gotlib, I. H. (1984). Depression and general psychopathology in university students. *Journal of Abnormal Psychology, 93,* 19–30.

Grosscup, S. J., & Lewinsohn, P. M. (1980). Unpleasant and pleasant events, and mood. *Journal of Clinical Psychology, 36,* 252–259.

Hamilton, E. W., & Abramson, L. Y. (1983). Cognitive patterns and major depressive disorders: A longitudinal study in a hospital setting. *Journal of Abnormal Psychology, 92,* 173–184.

Hammen, C. (1981, August). *Issues in cognitive research on depression: Attributional models.* Paper presented at the meeting of the American Psychological Association, Los Angeles, CA.

Hammen, C., Miklowitz, D., & Dyck, D. (1985). Stability and severity parameters of depressive self-schema responding. *Journal of Social and Clinical Psychology,* in press.

Hammen, C., Jacobs, M., Mayol, A., & Cochran, S. (1980). Dysfunctional cognitions and the effectiveness of skills and cognitive behavioral assertion training. *Journal of Consulting and Clinical Psychology, 48,* 685–695.

Hammen, C. L., & Glass, D. R. (1975). Depression, activity, and evaluation of reinforcement. *Journal of Abnormal Psychology, 84,* 718–721.

Hammen, C. L., & Krantz, S. E. (1976). Effects of success and failure on depressive cognitions. *Journal of Abnormal Psychology, 85,* 577–586.

Hammen, C. L., & Peters, S. D. (1977). Differential responses to male and female depressive reactions. *Journal of Consulting and Clinical Psychology, 45,* 994–1001.

Hammen, C. L., & Peters, S. D. (1978). Interpersonal consequences of depression. Responses to men and women enacting a depressed role. *Journal of Abnormal Psychology, 87,* 322–332.

Harrell, T. H., & Ryon, N. B. (1983). Cognitive-behavioral assessment of depression: Clinical validation of the Automatic Thoughts Questionnaire. *Journal of Consulting and Clinical Psychology, 51,* 721–725.

Hinchliffe, M. K., Lancashire, M., & Roberts, F. J. A. (1971a). Depression: Defense mechanisms in speech. *British Journal of Psychiatry, 118,* 471–472.

Hinchliffe, M. K., Lancashire, M., & Roberts, F. J. A. (1971b). Study of eye-contact in depressed and recovered psychiatric patients. *British Journal of Psychiatry, 119,* 213–215.

Hokanson, J. E., Sacco, W. P., Blumberg, S. R., & Landrum, G. C. (1980). Interpersonal behavior of depressive individuals in a mixed-motive game. *Journal of Abnormal Psychology, 89,* 320–332.

Hollon, S. D., & Bemis, K. M. (1981). Self-report and the assessment of cognitive functions. In M. Hersen & A. S. Bellack (Eds.), *Behavioral assessment: A practical handbook* (pp. 125–174). New York: Pergamon Press.

Hollon, S., & Kendall, P. (1980). Cognitive self-statements in depression: Development of an automatic thoughts questionnaire. *Cognitive Therapy and Research, 4,* 383–396.

Howes, M. J., & Hokanson, J. E. (1979). Conversational and social responses to depressive interpersonal behavior. *Journal of Abnormal Psychology, 88,* 625–634.

Jacobson, N., & Anderson, E. (1982). Interpersonal skill and depression in college students: An analysis of the timing of self-disclosures. *Behavior Therapy, 13,* 271–282.

Jones, R. G. (1969). A factored measure of Ellis' irrational belief system, with personality and maladjustment correlates. *Dissertation Abstracts International, 29,* 11–13.

Kanfer, F. H. (1971). The maintenance of behavior by self-generated stimuli and reinforcement. In A. Jacobs & L. B. Sachs (Eds.), *The psychology of private events,* New York: Academic Press.

Kanner, A. D., Coyne, J. C., Schaefer, C., & Lazarus, R. (1981). Comparison of two modes of stress measurement: Daily hassles and uplifts versus major life events. *Journal of Behavioral Medicine, 4,* 1–39.

Keller, K. E. (1983). Dysfunctional attitudes and cognitive therapy for depression. *Cognitive Therapy and Research, 7,* 437–444.

Kornblith, S. J., Rehm, L. P., O'Hara, M. W., & Lamparski, D. M. (1983). The contribution of self-reinforcement training and behavioral assignments to the efficacy of self-control therapy for depression. *Cognitive Therapy and Research, 7,* 499–528.

Krantz, S. E., & Hammen, C. L. (1979). Assessment of cognitive bias in depression. *Journal of Abnormal Psychology, 88,* 611–619.

Krantz, S. E., & Rude, S. S. (1984). The selection of different causes or the assignment of different dimensional meanings? *Journal of Personality and Social Psychology, 47,* 193–203.

LaPointe, K. A., & Crandell, C. J. (1980). Relationships of irrational beliefs to self-reported depression. *Cognitive Therapy and Research, 4,* 247–250.

Lazarus, R., & Launier, R. (1978). Stress-related transactions between person and environment. In L. Pervin and M. Lewis, (Eds.), *Internal and external determinants of behavior.* New York: Plenum Publishing.

Lefebvre, Mark F. (1981). Cognitive distortion and cognitive errors in depressed psychiatric and low back pain patients. *Journal of Consulting and Clinical Psychology, 49,* 517–525.

Lewinsohn, P. M. (1974). A behavioral approach to depression. In R. J. Friedman & M. M. Katz (Eds.), *The psychology of depression: Contemporary theory and research* (pp. 157–185). New York: Halstead Press.

Lewinsohn, P. M., & Amenson, C. (1978). Some relations between pleasant and un-pleasant mood-related events and depression. *Journal of Abnormal Psychology, 87,* 644–654.

Lewinsohn, P. M., & Graf, M. (1973). Pleasant activities and depression. *Journal of Consulting and Clinical Psychology, 41,* 261–268.

Lewinsohn, P. M., Larson, D. W., & Muñoz, R. F. (1982). The measurement of expectancies and other cognitions in depressed individuals. *Cognitive Therapy and Research, 6,* 437–446.

Lewinsohn, P. M., & Libet, J. (1972). Pleasant events, activity schedules, and depression. *Journal of Abnormal Psychology, 79,* 291–295.

Lewinsohn, P. M., & MacPhillamy, D. J. (1974). The relationship between age and engagement in pleasant activities. *Journal of Gerontology, 29,* 290–274.

Lewinsohn, P., Mischel, W. Chaplin, W., & Barton, R. (1980). Social competence and depression: The role of illusory self-perceptions. *Journal of Abnormal Psychology, 89,* 203–212.

Lewinsohn, P., Muñoz, R., & Larson, D. (1978). *Measurement of expectations and cognitions in depressed patients.* Paper presented at the meeting of the Association for the Advancement of Behavior Therapy, Chicago, IL.

Lewinsohn, P., Steinmetz, J., Larson, D., & Franklin, J. (1981). Depression related cognitions: Antecedent or consequence? *Journal of Abnormal Psychology, 90,* 213–219.

Lewinsohn, P., & Talkington, J. (1979). Studies on the measurement of unpleasant events and relations with depression. *Applied Psychological Measurement, 3,* 83–101.

Lewinsohn, P., Youngren, M. A., & Grosscup. S. (1979). Reinforcement and depression. In R. A. Depue (Ed.), *The psychobiology of the depressive disorders: Implications for the effects of stress* (pp. 291–316). New York: Academic Press.

Lloyd, G. G., & Lishman, W. A. (1975). Effect of depression on the speed of recall of pleasant and unpleasant experiences. *Psychological Medicine, 5,* 173–180.

Lohr, J. M., & Bonge, D. (1980). Retest reliability of the Irrational Beliefs Test. *Psychological Reports, 47,* 1314.

MacPhillamy, D. J., & Lewinsohn, P. M. (1972). *The Pleasant Events Schedule.* Unpublished manuscript.

MacPhillamy, D. J., & Lewinsohn, P. M. (1974). Depression as a function of levels of desired and obtained pleasure. *Journal of Abnormal Psychology, 83,* 651–657.

MacPhillamy, D. J., & Lewinsohn, P. M. (1982). The Pleasant Events Schedule: Studies on reliability, validity and scale intercorrelation. *Journal of Consulting and Clinical Psychology, 50,* 363–380.

Manly, P. C., McMahon, R. J., Bradley, C. F., & Davidson, P. O. (1982). Depressive attributional style and depression following childbirth. *Journal of Abnormal Psychology, 91,* 245–254.

Marks, T., & Hammen, C. L. (1982). Interpersonal mood induction: Situational and individual determinants. *Motivation and Emotion, 6,* 387–399.

Metalsky, G. I., & Abramson, L. Y. (1981). Attributional styles: Toward a framework for conceptualization and assessment. In P. C. Kendall and S. D. Hollon (Eds.), *Assessment strategies for cognitive behavioral interventions* (pp. 13–58). New York: Academic Press.

Miller, I. W., Klee, S. H., & Norman, W. H. (1982). Depressed and nondepressed inpatients' cognitions of hypothetical events, experimental tasks and stressful life events. *Journal of Abnormal Psychology, 91,* 78–81.

Mischel, W. (1973). Toward a cognitive social-learning reconceptualization of personality. *Psychological Review, 80,* 252–283.

Mukherji, B. R., Abramson, L. Y., & Martin, D. J. (1982). Induced depressive mood and attributional patterns. *Cognitive Therapy and Research, 6,* 15–22.

Muñoz, R. F. (1977). *A cognitive approach to the assessment and treatment of depression.* Doctoral dissertation, University of Oregon, Eugene, OR.

Nelson, R. E. (1977). Irrational beliefs in depression. *Journal of Consulting and Clinical Psychology, 45,* 1190–1191.

Nisbett, R. E., & Wilson, T. D. (1977). Telling more than we can know: Verbal reports on mental process. *Psychological Review, 84,* 231–259.

Norman, W. H., Miller, I. W., & Klee, S. H. (1983). Assessment of cognitive distortion in a clinically depressed population. *Cognitive Therapy and Research, 7,* 133–140.

O'Hara, M. W., Rehm, L. P., & Campbell, S. B. (1982). Predicting depressive symptomatology: Cognitive-behavioral models and postpartum depression. *Journal of Abnormal Psychology, 91,* 457–461.

Padesky, C., & Hammen, C. L. (1978, April). *Knowing and doing: Coping response patterns in depressed and non-depressed college students.* Paper presented at the meeting of the Western Psychological Association, San Francisco, CA.

Parker, G. B., & Brown, L. B. (1982). Coping behaviors that mediate between life events and depression. *Archives of General Psychiatry, 39,* 1386–1391.

Peterson, C., Semmel, A., Von Baeyer, C., Abramson, L. Y., Metalsky, G. I., & Seligman, M. E. P. (1982). The Attributional Style Questionnaire. *Cognitive Therapy and Research, 6,* 287–300.

Raps, C. S., Peterson, C., Reinhard, K. E., Abramson, L. Y., & Seligman, M. E. P. (1982). Attributional style among depressed patients. *Journal of Abnormal Psychology, 91,* 102–108.

Rehm, L. P. (1977). Self-control model of depression. *Behavior Therapy, 8,* 787–804.

Rehm, L. P., Fuchs, C., Roth, D., Kornblith, S., & Romano, J. (1979). A comparison of self-control and assertion skill treatments of depression. *Behavior Therapy, 10,* 429–442.

Rehm, L. P., Kaslow, N. J., Rabin, A. C., & Willard, R., (1981). *Prediction of outcome in a self-control behavior-therapy program for depression.* Paper presented at the annual meeting of the American Psychological Association, Los Angeles, CA.

Rehm, L. P., Kornblith, S. J., O'Hara, M. W., Lamparski, D. M., Romano, J. M., & Volkin, J. I. (1981). An evaluation of major components in a self-control therapy program for depression. *Behavior Modification, 5,* 459–489.

Rippere, V. (1976). Antidepressive behavior: A preliminary report. *Behavior Research and Therapy, 14,* 289–299.

Riskind, J. H., Beck, A. T., & Smucker, M. R. (1983). *Psychometric properties of the Dysfunctional Attitudes Scale in a clinical population.* Paper presented at the meeting of the World Congress on Behavior Therapy, Washington, DC.

Riskind, J. H., & Rholes, W. S. (in press). Somatic vs. self-evaluative statements in the Velton Mood Induction Procedure: Effects on negativistic interpretation and depressed mood. *Journal of Social and Clinical Psychology.*

Rosenbaum, M. (1980). A schedule for assessing self-control behaviors: Preliminary findings. *Behavior Therapy, 11,* 109–121.

Rude, S. S. (1983). *An investigation of differential response to two treatments of depression.* Doctoral dissertation, Stanford University.

Seligman, M. E. P., Abramson, L. Y., Semmel, A., & Von Baeyer, C. (1979). Depressive attributional style. *Journal of Abnormal Psychology, 88,* 242–248.

Strack, S., & Coyne, J. C. (1983). Social confirmation of dysphoria: Shared and private reactions. *Journal of Personality and Social Psychology, 44,* 798–806.

Teasdale, J. (1983). Negative thinking in depression: Cause, effect, or reciprocal relationship? *Advances in Behaviour Research and Therapy, 5,* 3–25.

Teasdale, J., & Fogarty, S. (1979). Differential effects of induced mood on retrieval of pleasant and unpleasant memories from episodic memory. *Journal of Abnormal Psychology, 88,* 248–257.

Trexler, L. D., & Karst, T. O. (1972). Rational Emotive Therapy, placebo, and no treatment effects of public speaking anxiety. *Journal of Abnormal Psychology, 79,* 60–67.

Watkins, J. T., & Rush, A. J. (1983). Cognitive Response Test. *Cognitive Therapy and Research, 7,* 425–436.

Waxer, P. (1974). Nonverbal cues for depression. *Journal of Abnormal Psychology, 53,* 319–322.

Weintraub, M., Segal, R. M., & Beck. A. T. (1974). An investigation of cognition and affect in the depressive experiences of normal men. *Journal of Consulting and Clinical Psychology, 42,* 911.

Weissman, A. N. (1978, November). *Development and validation of the Dysfunctional Attitude Scale (DAS).* Paper presented at the meeting of the Association for the Advancement of Behavior Therapy, Chicago, IL.

Weissman, A. N. (1979). *The Dysfunctional Attitude Scale: A validation study.* Doctoral dissertation. University of Pennsylvania.

Weissman, A. N., & Beck, A. T. (1978). *Development and validation of the Dysfunctional Attitude Scale: A preliminary investigation.* Paper presented at the meeting of the American Educational Research Association, Toronto, Canada.

Weissman, M. M., & Paykel, E. S. (1974). *The depressed woman.* Chicago: University of Chicago Press.

Wortman, C., & Dintzer, L. (1978). Is an attributional analysis of the learned helplessness phenomenon viable?: A critique of the Abramson-Seligman-Teasdale Reformulation. *Journal of Abnormal Psychology, 87,* 75–90.

Youngren, M. A., & Lewinsohn, P. M. (1980). The functional relationship between depression and problematic interpersonal behavior. *Journal of Abnormal Psychology, 89,* 333–341.

Chapter 14

New Medical Diagnostic Procedures for Depression

Jan Fawcett
Professor and Chairman
Department of Psychiatry
Rush-Presbyterian-St. Luke's Medical Center
Chicago, Illinois

Howard M. Kravitz
Assistant Professor
Departments of Psychiatry and Psychology & Social Sciences
Medical Director, Sleep Disorder Service and Research Center
Rush-Presbyterian-St. Luke's Medical Center
Chicago, Illinois

INTRODUCTION

When one of the authors (JF) was initially considering the offer of chairmanship of the department of psychiatry at Rush-Presbyterian-St. Luke's Medical Center in the early 1970s, an unusual request was made—acceptance of the position would be contigent upon, among other things, the establishment of a psychobiology laboratory under the auspices of the department of psychiatry. This, indeed, was innovative in its day, and it was thought odd that a psychiatrist would want a laboratory, of all things (maybe that was where heads were shrunk!). However, the request was granted and, as we look back over the evolution of "biological psychiatry" and see how it has expanded and extended beyond biochemistry and pharmacology and into neuroendocrinology and even radiology, we cannot say that we are surprised. After all, the understanding of the bases of mental illness involves more than just psychodynamic and psychosocial foundations, but an understanding of the total functioning of man, biomedical and psychosocial, or as described by Engel, the biopsychosocial model (Engel, 1977, 1980). In this chapter we will focus on the biomedical challenge, and how psychiatry and the rest of the social sciences may benefit from its application toward the diagnosis and treatment of the depressive disorders.

The advent of the clinical laboratory and the introduction of state-related laboratory tests, useful for both screening for disease and monitoring treatment progress, have changed the course of medical practice. Recently there has been growing interest in the application of various biomedical procedures to psychiatric evaluation. Good state-related markers have similar characteristics regardless of the clinical problem to which they are applied, including sensitivity and specificity for the illness in question, reliability and validity of the procedure itself, risk benefit as concerns the patient, and cost effectiveness. In addition, it should be known whether the finding is the result of a pathophysiologic *state,* in which case serial testing should be possible in order to correlate with clinical status and predict remission and relapse, or whether a *trait* is being measured, in which case it can be used as a screening test in susceptible or vulnerable populations.

The development of batteries of diagnostic studies is the current focus of research in biological aspects of affective disorders, particularly the depressive disorders. Diagnostic testing has three major functions. The first is to assist the clinician in categorizing the disorders with which he/she is confronted. The second is to assist in the selection of the most specific and efficacious treatment for the disorder. The third is to monitor the course of the disorder and determine the prognosis for recovery based on normalization of the test result, as well as to predict future susceptibility or vulnerability to relapse.

However, it should be remembered that these procedures should supplement clinical skills demonstrated at the bedside, and are not substitutes for clinical interviewing. The astute clinician acquires an understanding of the laboratory procedures and knowledge of their limitations, and integrates the information derived from these results into a treatment plan.

In this chapter, we will review the current state-of-the-art of diagnosis and treatment of depression as seen through the eyes of the "psychobiologist" and the psychobiology laboratory. These diagnostic procedures currently serve us in two general ways in depressive disorders: (1) as a research tool with which to help us subclassify depressive disorders, and (2) to help the practicing clinician choose and monitor a treatment modality. We will review these procedures from both of these perspectives, and describe the advance of these procedures from the research setting to clinical practice.

IN THE BEGINNING: BIOGENIC AMINES—PAST, PRESENT, AND (?) FUTURE

Monoamine Hypotheses

The biogenic amine hypothesis, which postulates that altered function of one or more neuroamines acting as synaptic neurotransmitters or modulatory neurohormones at nerve terminals in the central nervous system (CNS) is linked to disturbed affective behavior, has been the most prominent theory of affective disorders advanced over the past two decades. In its simplest form, all of the amine hypotheses of depressive illness postulate that clinical depression is associated with a functional deficit of one or more CNS monoamines at receptor sites. The predominant focus has been on the role of two of these neuroamines: norepinephrine (NE), a catecholamine (CA), and serotonin (5-HT), an indoleamine (IA), and their metabolites, 3-methoxy-4-hydroxyphenylglycol (MHPG) (from NE), and 5-hydroxyindoleacetic acid (5-HIAA) (from 5-HT). Homovanillic acid (HVA), the metabolite of dopamine (DA), another CA, and acetylcholine (ACh), a quaternary alkyl amine, have also been examined. In addition, the brain has also been found to contain and form other adrenergic amines, such as phenylethylamine (PEA). One or more of these amines may act as co-transmitters, modulators, or regulators of synaptic transmission mediated by a chemically related neurotransmitter. Thus, tryptamine, an IA, may be a modulator of serotonergic synapses, and PEA may similarly modulate CA synapses. The concept of one neuron-one neurotransmitter (Dale, 1935) is too simplistic. In fact, investigations by Sabelli and co-workers (Sabelli, Mosnaim, Vasquez, Giardina, Borison, & Pedemonte, 1976) extended Dale's principle to account for the production of more than one family of transmitters in a neuron and for the release of these metabolically related co-transmitters from the same neuron. Hokfelt and associates (Hokfelt, Johansson, Ljungdahl, Lundberg, & Schultzberg, 1980) reported on the coexistence of peptides and monoamines within the same neuron; these peptides also can act as neurotransmitters (or neuromodulators). Therefore, one biogenic amine may affect the metabolism or levels of another, and there may be complex interactions between monoaminergic systems and other neurotransmitter or neuromodulator systems.

Early formulations of the hypothesis suggesting that the pathophysiology of affective disorders involves alterations in central neuroamines arose from observations that tricyclic antidepressants (TCA), monoamine oxidase inhibitors (MAOI), and stimulants activate brain monoamine synapses, while drugs such as reserpine reduce neuroamine transmission and induce depression (Everett & Toman, 1959). However, to date, a specific biochemical basis for affective disorders has not been established and the exact mechanism(s) by which efficacious medications alleviate symptoms have not been fully elucidated. Many of these hypotheses focus on a single amine and assume that the clinical problem rests with some abnormaility in this amine.

Data for these hypotheses have evolved from two sources: (1) behavioral (including mood) responses obtained from pharmacological studies, and (2) the measurement of the concentration of amine metabolites in body fluids or tissues, with or without (or before and after) a pharmacological challenge. These pharmacological studies (which will not be individually reviewed here) initially suggested the biogenic amine hypothesis, but yielded contradictory reports in further attempts to test this hypothesis, and led to more direct efforts to detect alterations in biogenic amine metabolism in affective disorders (Charney, Menkes, Heninger, 1981; Davis, 1970; Everett & Toman, 1959; Goodwin & Bunney, 1971; Kuhn, 1957, 1958; Mendels & Frazer, 1974). In the second type of study, the assumption has been made that the concentration of amine metabolites in body fluids and tissues reflects the functional status of central monoaminergic systems. Problems arising from the interpretation of these indirect findings have led to techniques which may allow more direct investigation of central amine function by measuring levels of amine metabolites in various readily available tissues and body fluids of humans. To date, the most direct method of investigating these amines has been the study of their metabolites in cerebrospinal fluid (CSF), blood, urine, and postmortem brain tissue (not reviewed here). Changes in the urinary, plasma, and CSF metabolites are thought to reliably reflect and parallel amine metabolism changes in brain, but we will discuss some of the difficulties associated with these methods.

Catecholamine Measures

The CA hypothesis has been the source of numerous reviews (Baldessarini, 1975; Davis, 1977; Garver, & Davis, 1979; Prange, 1964; Schildkraut, 1969; Shopsin, Wilk, Sathananthan, Gershon, & Davis, 1974). It predicts that some if not all depressions are associated with an absolute or relative decrease in CA, particularly NE, available at central adrenergic receptor sites. Thus, the amount, distribution, or metabolism of NE in the brain may be altered in both depression and mania, and certain drugs which alter the affective state in humans also significantly affect CA disposition and metabolites in brain. Schildkraut (1965) and Bunney and Davis (1965) proposed that some depressive disorders may be associated with an absolute or relative CA deficiency, particularly NE, at functionally important adrenergic receptor sites in brain. However, they acknowledged the potential reductionistic oversimplification involved in postulating a purely biochemical etiology and ignoring other potential physiological, psychological, and sociocultural factors. This CA depletion hypothesis of depression led to further measurements of NE metabolites in the hopes of demonstrating some disturbance of CA metabolism in depressives which would be referable to CNS dysfunction (Maas, Fawcett, & Dekirmenjian, 1968).

Considerable experimental evidence, based primarily on correlations between changes in NE metabolism and affective states, has been accumulated both in support of and at variance with this hypothesis. Because these investigations suggested that MHPG was the major measurable brain NE metabolite indicative of CNS turnover, the focus of CA research has been primarily on this substance (Axelrod, Kopin, & Mann, 1959; Dekirmenjian & Maas, 1970; Ebert & Kopin, 1975; Gitlow, Mendlowitz, Bertani, Wilk, & Wilk, 1971; Goodall & Rosen, 1963; Maas, Dekirmenjian, & Jones, 1973; Maas et al., 1968; Maas, Hattox, Greene, & Landis, 1979; Maas & Landis, 1965, 1971; Schanberg, Breese, Schildkraut, Gordon, & Kopin, 1968; Schanberg, Schildkraut, Breese, & Kopin, 1968; Schildkraut, 1973a; Schildkraut, Green, Gordon, & Durell, 1966; Schildkraut, Keeler, Grab, Kantrowich, & Hartmann, 1973; Schildkraut, Keeler, Paporisek, & Hartmann, 1973; Schildkraut, Orsulak, Schatzberg, Gudeman, Cole, Rohde, & La Brie, 1978; Schildkraut, Watson, Draskoczy, &

Hartmann, 1971). It is important to distinguish MHPG from vanillylmandelic acid (VMA), the major NE metabolite measured in urine, which along with normetanephrine and metanephrine originates mainly in CA pools outside the CNS. Studies indicate that 20 percent (Blombery, Kopin, Gordon, Markey, & Ebert, 1980; Kopin, 1978; Mardh, Sjoquist, & Anggard, 1981) to 70 percent (Maas, et. al., 1979) of urinary MHPG is of central origin, but there exists a wide range of MHPG content measurable in the urines of normal controls (900 to 3,500 mcg/24 hours) (Fawcett, Maas, & Dekirmenjian, 1972; Goodwin & Potter, 1979; Hollister, Davis, Overall, & Anderson, 1978; Maas, et al., 1968; Schatzberg, Rosenbaum, Orsulak, Rohde, Maruta, Kruger, Cole, & Schildkraut, 1981) which overlaps the "reduced" range found in depressives (less than 1,400 mcg/24 hours) (Maas, et. al., 1968). Further complicating matters, MHPG may be converted to VMA in the periphery (Blombery et al., 1980). Investigators from the NIMH multicenter Collaborative Program on the Psychobiology of Depression (Koslow, Maas, Bowden, Davis, Hanin, & Javaid, 1983) have shown that urinary MHPG levels alone do not reveal a depression-associated change, but that measurement of total body CA output reflects whole body NE turnover better than any one CA or CA metabolite.

Studies of urinary MHPG support the view that a CA deficit may play a role in some but not all depressions. Maas and associates (1968) reported on pilot data demonstrating a significant reduction in urinary MHPG in a heterogeneous group of depressives compared with healthy controls regardless of sex. A review by Goodwin and Potter (1979) revealed that depressives as a group excreted 25 percent less MHPG than healthy controls, though overall many of them excreted normal or above normal amounts of MHPG. Looking at depressive subtypes, bipolars excreted less than normals and unipolars (DeLeon-Jones, Maas, & Dekirmenjian, 1975; Schildkraut, Keeler, Grab, Kantrowich, & Hartmann, 1973; Schildkraut, Keeler, Paporisek, & Hartmann, 1973) but although some endogenous depressives excreted MHPG in the range of bipolars, generally no endogenous-nonendogenous dichotomy has been evident among unipolars (Schildkraut, 1978; Schildkraut et al., 1978).

The results of investigations of CSF MHPG in depressives compared with controls have been mixed, showing reduced levels in some (Post, Gordon, Goodwin, & Bunney, 1973; Subrahmanyan, 1975) but not all studies (Shaw, O'Keefe, MacSweeney, Brooksbank, Noguera, & Coppen, 1973; Shopsin et al., 1973; Wilk, Shopsin, Gershon, & Suhl, 1972). Comparisons of urinary and CSF MHPG have demonstrated a correlation in some studies (Agren, 1982; Maas, Kocsis, Bowden, Davis, Redmond, Hanin, & Robins, 1982) but further replication is pending. The physiological significance of this is questionable, as a 24-hour urine collection is an integrated measure, while CSF represents only a single point in time and may be susceptible to diurnal variation in turnover rate.

Similarly, plasma MHPG measurements also represent a research tool (Charney, Heninger, Sternberg, Redmond, Leckman, Maas, & Roth, 1981; Charney, Heninger, Sternberg, & Roth, 1981; Halaris, 1978; Halaris & DeMet, 1979; Jimerson, Ballenger, Lake, Post, Goodwin, & Kopin, 1981; Kopin, Gordan, Jimerson, & Polinsky, 1983; Leckman, Maas, Redmond, & Heninger, 1980; Markianos & Beckmann, 1976; Sweeney, Leckman, Maas Hattox, & Heninger, 1980). Contrary to what would be predicted by the CA hypothesis of affective disorders, there is presently no supportive evidence for lower plasma MHPG levels in depressives. Further, the relationship between 24-hour urinary MHPG and plasma-free MHPG is difficult to interpret due to questions about free MHPG metabolism and the proportion of urinary MHPG originating centrally. Once again, diurnal variation needs to be accounted for in the case of one-time plasma levels. It is premature to comment further on its potential clinical use, though it would certainly eliminate concerns for compliance with a 24-hour urine collection and the resistances encountered in any endeavor to routinely perform spinal taps for CSF contents.

HVA, the deaminated o-methylated metabolite of DA, is the most abundant metabolite of this comparatively neglected CA (Goodall & Alton, 1968). (Another is dihydroxyphenylacetic acid, DOPAC.) Most of the studies of DA in depression involve CSF studies of HVA, as urinary HVA is of little value because of the question of central versus peripheral origin. Previous reviews (DeLeon-Jones, 1982; Goodwin & Post, 1975; Randrup, Munkvad, Fog, Gerlach, Molander, Kjellberg, & Sheel-Kruger, 1975; Zis & Goodwin, 1982) revealed that baseline CSF HVA was reduced in depressives in some studies. Similar results were obtained with probenecid-induced HVA accumulation (Berger, Faull, Kilkowski, Anderson, Kraemer, Davis, & Barchas, 1980; Bowers, 1974b; Goodwin, Post, Dunner, & Gordon, 1973; Korf & Van Praag, 1971; Sjostrom, 1973; Van Praag & Korf, 1975; Van Praag, Korf, & Puite, 1970) in depressives as compared with controls. These data need to be regarded with caution because of the potential for activity-induced artifact.

Indoleamine Measures

The IA hypothesis of depression postulates that functional levels of brain 5-HT are reduced and may directly contribute to or predispose to depressive psychopathology. This hypothesis is based on research involving: (1) tryptophan (precursor) metabolism and therapy, (2) CSF studies, (3) postmortem brain studies, and (4) 5-HT and hypothalamic-pituitary-adrenal (HPA) function. Early studies found abnormally low blood tryptophan levels and decreased urinary tryptophan excretion in depressives (Coppen, 1967; Coppen, Shaw, & Malleson, 1965; Coppen, Shaw, Malleson, Eccleston, & Grundy, 1965; Rodnight, 1961). Serotonin precursors (L-tryptophan and L-5-hydroxytryptophan) have been used to treat depression, with or without antidepressants, and have produced good responses, especially in depressives with low CSF 5-HIAA (Davis, 1970; Pare & Sandler, 1959; Van Praag, 1981; Wirz-Justice, 1977; Zarcone, Berger, Brodie, Sack, & Barchas, 1977), the principle metabolite of 5-HT centrally and peripherally (Lovenberg & Engelman, 1971). They may potentiate the effects of antidepressants. Measures of urinary 5-HT and tryptamine, and their metabolites, are not useful because of a large peripheral contribution (Bueno & Himwich, 1967; Coppen, 1967; Lovenberg &

Engelman, 1971) while plasma and CSF tryptophan and blood 5-HT levels and 5-HT uptake measurements are equivocally useful (Murphy, Campbell, & Costa, 1978). CSF 5-HIAA in depressives, as compared with controls, has been reviewed elsewhere, and has provided mixed results, though it is reduced by about 30 percent in at least a subgroup of depressives (DeLeon-Jones, 1982; Goodwin & Post, 1975; Murphy et al., 1978; Zis & Goodwin, 1982) but never significantly higher (Murphy et al., 1978). Asberg and her associates (Asberg, Bertilsson, Tuck, Cronholm, & Sjoqvist, 1973; Asberg, Thoren, Traskman, Bertilsson, & Ringberger, 1976) have demonstrated a bimodal distribution, suggesting a low 5-HIAA subgroup, but this may represent an artifactual distribution due to an overrepresentation of males in the low 5-HIAA group (Asberg, Thoren, Traskman, Bertilsson, & Ringberger, 1976), or it may be due to a bimodal distribution in the 24-hour 5-HT rhythm without alteration in total 24-hour 5-HT turnover (Kripke, 1976). Although a reduced CSF 5-HIAA may reflect the hypothesized 5-HT reduction in brain, we still do not clearly understand the mechanism resulting in depression. Further, a subgroup of manics as well as depressives may have a 5-HT deficit (Coppen, Prange, Whybrow, & Noguera, 1972; Prange, Wilson, Lynn, Alltop, & Stikeleather, 1974), further muddling the hypothesis.

Investigation of suicide attempters has uncovered a subgroup of depressives with low CSF 5-HIAA (Asberg, Traskman, & Thoren, 1976). Attempts in this group were significantly more common and of a "more active, determined type" compared with other depressives. Follow-up (Traskman, Asberg, Bertilsson, & Sjostrand, 1981) expanded these findings. CSF 5-HIAA was significantly lower in their sample of suicide attempters, particularly those who were depressed and those who used more violent means (both depressed and nondepressed subjects) compared with controls. CSF 5-HIAA was lower, though not significantly so, in nondepressed suicide attempters as a group. Most important, at one-year postlumbar puncture follow-up there was a 20 percent mortality by suicide in those patients with CSF 5-HIAA below the median. CSF 5-HIAA levels were also examined in the context of HPA dysfunction in suicidal patients (Carroll, Greden, & Feinberg, 1981; Traskman, Tybring, Asberg, Bertilsson, Lantto, Schalling, 1980).

Although the data for a 5-HT theory of depression at best are only equivocally supportive, it is certainly tempting and intriguing to consider CSF 5-HIAA as a possible biological marker of suicidality and potential lethality. Further study needs to be done. Suicide is the most serious consequence of depressive illness, and our current clinical predictors are suboptimal indicators because of low sensitivity and specificity as well as low base rate of the behavior (Pokorny, 1983; Roy, 1982).

PEA Measures

The PEA hypothesis of affective behavior (Sabelli & Mosnaim, 1974) states that PEA is a neuromodulator responsible for sustaining attention and mood, possibly via modulation of brain CA synapses. A deficit in its brain content and/or a decrease in the turnover of endogenous PEA may play a major pathophysiological role in certain forms of endogenous depression, while an increase in brain PEA levels or activation of specific PEA receptors in brain neurons may underlie manic episodes and may contribute to the actions of antidepressant and stimulant (amphetamines) drugs. PEA, formed from a dietary amino acid, phenylalanine, is pharmacologically, structurally, and metabolically related to CA and to amphetamine, and its biological actions are partly mediated by CA release and partly due to other mechanisms (Fuxe, Grobecker, & Jonsson, 1967; Sabelli & Borison, 1976). It is unique among the endogenous neuroamines in producing amphetamine-like behavioral and electrophysiological effects (Nakajima, Kakimoto, & Sano, 1964).

Several investigators (Fischer, Heller, & Miro, 1968; Mosnaim, Inwang, Sugerman, DeMartini, & Sabelli, 1973) using nonspecific methods for measuring this neuroamine reported that urinary PEA excretion was reduced in a subgroup of depressives. However, PEA excretion is quite low and highly variable. Using a more sensitive method (Javaid & Davis, 1981) our group has found PEA excretion significantly reduced in many depressives (unipolar and bipolar) compared with controls. Further, the measurement of urinary PEA may be a poor indicator of its central metabolism because most of it is rapidly metabolized to phenylacetic acid (PAA).

Since PEA is mainly metabolized by monoamine oxidase (MAO) type B to form PAA, we are now studying the 24-hour excretion of this latter acid in subjects with *DSM-III* diagnosed unipolar and bipolar affective disorders. It is excreted in much greater quantities than other neuroamine metabolites, in milligram rather than microgram amounts, and is thus easier to measure. We have found (Sabelli, Fawcett, Gusovsky, Edwards, Jeffriess, & Javaid, 1983; Sabelli, Fawcett, Gusovsky, Javaid, Edwards, & Jeffriess, 1983) that the urinary excretion of PAA is markedly decreased in about 60 percent of depressives and increased in 44 percent of manics (normal range 70 to 175 mg/24 hours in 70 percent of controls). Further, PAA urinary content returns to normal with resolution of illness.

These changes in PAA excretion are sufficiently marked and consistent, and thus may provide a state marker to assist in the diagnosis and monitoring of affective disorders. Because we have found no great differences between untreated depressives and those treated ineffectively, we suspect that the urinary PAA test might serve in the monitoring of depressives illness regardless of treatment, much like blood glucose levels serve to monitor diabetes and measure its degree of control.

Further support for the usefulness of PAA measurements come from the investigations of Sandler and associates (Sandler, Ruthven, Goodwin, & Coppen, 1979), who found CSF PAA levels were lower in patients with "primary depressive illness" compared with controls. B. M. Davis and associates (Davis, Durden, & Boulton, 1982) reported that depressives excrete two other substances (urinary p-hydroxymandelic and p-hydroxyphenylacetic acids), the major metabolites of octopamine and tyramine, two other "trace amines" probably synthesized in vivo from PEA (Boulton, Dyck, & Durden, 1974; Tallman, Saavedra, & Axelrod, 1976).

Although the measurement of urinary PAA excretion is a simple, reliable and rapid test, two basic issues need to be addressed before it can be heralded as the next "gold standard" of biological markers. First, from a theoretical standpoint, relating PAA excretion to PEA metabolism in brain implies an assumption not supported by empirical studies; there are actually no data regarding the different proportions in which brain and peripheral tissue contribute to urinary PAA. However, this question is less significant for PAA metabolites than other neuroamine metabolites because PEA readily crosses the blood brain barrier, and the brain accumulates blood-borne PEA against a concentration gradient (Borison, Mosnaim, & Sabelli, 1974; Nakajima et al., 1964); thus, peripheral concentrations are, by necessity, in dynamic equilibrium (Borison, Sabelli, & Ho, 1975). Second, from a clinical standpoint, the test is nonspecific. It does not differentiate bipolar from unipolar depressives nor other depressive subtypes, and low excretion has been noted in a subgroup of manics (Sabelli, Fawcett, Gusovsky, Edwards, Jeffriess, & Javaid, 1983) and in chronic schizophrenics (Potkin, Wyatt, & Karoum, 1980). There are no normative data from other psychiatric or medical disorders.

Thus, PAA excretion seems to be a fairly sensitive test for depressive disorders since the differences noted are so marked that they are reflected not only in average group values but also in individual cases. Using the 70 mg/24-hour lower limit, there are 15 percent false positives among controls and 29–48 percent false negatives among depressives requiring hospitalization. Further, an excretion rate above the upper limit of 175 mg/24-hour identifies about 40 percent of manics. These results support the PEA theory of affect to the extent that PAA has been found to be: (1) reduced in all groups of depressives in comparison with normal control subjects, and high in a significant number of manics, (2) increased (with recovery to normal levels) by antidepressant drugs which result in successful treatment, yet still significantly low in those unsuccessfully treated, and (3) reduced by antimanic treatment roughly in parallel with clinical recovery. Further, this excretion is not affected by sex or normal mood variation, but is lower in the elderly.

In order to develop a more convenient clinical test, we are presently studying plasma PAA in control subjects.

Central Cholinergic Factors

The concept of depression resulting from hyperactive or overactive central cholinergic synapses developed from the idea of a cholinergic-adrenergic balance, and a hypothesis related to classical autonomic nervous system function (Janowsky, El-Yousef, & Davis, 1974; Janowsky, El-Yousef, Davis, & Sekerke, 1972; Risch, Kalin, & Janowsky, 1981; Sitaram & Gillin, 1980). These theories developed from the observations of behavioral effects from poisoning by organophosphate insecticides; part of the clinical picture in these individuals was the production of a depressive state (Gershon & Shaw, 1961). Unfortunately, there is no measurable central metabolite of ACh. Studies involving ACh have involved the administration of physostigmine, arecoline, atropine or other atropine-like drugs, or ACh precursors (Janowsky, El-Yousef, Davis, & Sekerke, 1972). Pharmacological challenge studies such as these have indirectly and qualitatively measured neurotransmitter interactions through measurements in other systems (e.g., neuroendocrine and sleep studies).

Conclusions

The pharmacological literature suggests that treatments that deplete monoamines, inhibit their synthesis, or block their actions may induce depression. Further, it has been postulated that the effects of increasing or decreasing actions of 5-HT or ACh tend to be opposite those involving NE or DA; that is, the actions are reciprocal. This contradicts data suggesting that depression involves deficits in both NE and 5-HT (such as the "permissive hypothesis" (Kety, 1971; Mendels & Frazer, 1975; Prange et al., 1974)), and the hypothesis remains to be proven (Zis & Goodwin, 1982). However, the effects of long-term administration of a variety of antidepressant treatments on NE and 5-HT turnover are highly variable (Asberg et al., 1973; Beckman & Goodwin, 1975, 1980; Beckmann & Murphy, 1977; Beckmann, St. Laurent, & Goodwin, 1975; Bertilsson, Asberg, & Thoren, 1974; Bowers, 1974a; Cobbin, Requin-Blow, Williams, & Williams, 1979; Coppen, Rama Rao, Ruthven, Goodwin, & Sandler, 1979; Fawcett, Maas, & Dekirmenjian, 1972; Gaertner, Krueter, Scharek, Wiatr, & Breyer-Pfaff, 1982; Goodwin, Cowdry, & Webster, 1978; Greenspan, Schildkraut, Gordon, Baer, Aronoff, & Durell, 1970; Hollister, Davis, & Berger, 1980; Maas et al., 1982; Maas, Fawcett, & Dekirmenjian, 1972; Maitre, Waldmeier, Greengrass, Jackel, Sedlucek, & Delini-Stula, 1975; Modai, Apter, Gulomb, & Wijsenbeek, 1979; Pickar, Sweeney, Maas, & Heninger, 1978; Post & Goodwin, 1974; Potter, Calil, Extein, Gold, Wehr, & Goodwin, 1981; Potter, Calil, Extein, Muscettola, & Goodwin, 1981; Prange, Wilson, Knox, McClane, Breese, Martin, Alltop, & Lipton, 1972; Ridges, Bishop, Goldberg, Corner, Gringras, Hamlet, Heyes, Miller, Parrack, & Sleeman, 1980; Rosenbaum, Schatzberg, Maruta, Orsulak, Cole, Grab, & Schildkraut, 1980; Sacchetti, Allaria, Negri, Biondi, Smeraldi, & Cazzulo, 1979; Sacchetti, Smeraldi, Cagnasso, Biondi, & Bellodi, 1976; Schatzberg, Orsulak, Rosenbaum, Maruta, Kruger, Cole, & Schildkraut, 1980; Schatzberg, Orsulak, Rosenbaum, Maruta, Kruger, Cole, & Schildkraut, 1982; Schatzberg, Rosenbaum, Orsulak, Rohde, Maruta, Kruger, Cole, & Schildkraut, 1981; Schildkraut, 1973b; Schildkraut et al., 1978; Schildkraut, Orsulak, Schatzberg, Cole, & Rosenbaum, 1981; Shopsin et al., 1973; Shopsin et al., 1974; Siwers, Ringberger, Tuck, & Sjoqvist, 1977; Spiker, Edwards, Hanin, Neil, & Kupfer, 1980; Steiner, Radwan, Elizur, Blum, Atsman, & Davidson, 1979; Traskman, Asberg, Bertilsson, Cronholm, Mellstrom, Neckers, Sjoqvist, Thoren, & Tybring, 1979; Van Praag, 1977a, 1977b; Veith, Bielski, Bloom, Fawcett, Narasimhachari, & Friedcl, 1983; Waldmeier, Baumann, Greengrass, & Maitre, 1976). No single common effect is identifiable at present, and studies of turnover of the various metabolites, most notably MHPG and 5-HIAA, have not demonstrated consistent correlations between changes in these metabolites and clinical response. In fact, both MHPG and 5-HIAA have been measured in the same patients in few studies. (Koslow et al., 1983; Maas et al., 1982; Ridges et al., 1980).

Maas (1975) attempted to introduce some order into our understanding of the persistent chaos in this area of investigation. Based on available data, he postulated that Type A depressives have an alteration in central noradrenergic (but not dopaminergic) systems, while Type B patients do not have a NE system deficit but that "serotonin appears to be a worthwhile candidate for investigation."

Sabelli and associates (Sabelli, Fawcett, Javaid, & Bagri, 1983) described Type I and Type II depressions; the former may involve a deficit in *various* amine systems but has as its final common pathway a responsiveness to imipramine (IMI)-like antidepressants, while there is currently little evidence for monoamine depletion in the latter, which are responsive to amitriptyline (AMI)-like and nortriptyline (NT)-like antidepressants.

Thus, we should be skeptical of any single amine hypothesis purporting to account for depression; it must be oversimplified. Similarly, even two-disease (e.g., Type A and Type B) and interactive or permissive hypotheses have their drawbacks. Overall, the evidence favoring these hypotheses is weak. The importance of the contribution of the various biogenic amines still remain to be determined (Baldessarini, 1975; Veith et al., 1983). Pharmacologically, it is difficult to selectively affect a single system. We have become cognizant of the effects of antidepressant drugs on multiple neurotransmitter systems. Adding to the complexity of this problem, the active metabolites of the available antidepressants may affect various neurotransmitters differentially. Similarly, it has yet to be proven whether any amine deficiency in the brain is either a necessary or sufficient basis for predisposing to or triggering depressive illness. There are many possible interactions between these neurotransmitters as well as between these transmitters and the neuroendocrine system (Carroll, Greden, Haskett, Feinberg, Albala, Martin, Rubin, Heath, Sharp, McLeod, & McLeod, 1980; K. L. Davis, Hollister, Mathe, Davis, Rothpearl, Faull, Hsieh, Barchas, & Berger, 1981) and the endogenous opioid (endorphin/enkephalin) system (Pickar, Cohen, Naber, & Cohen, 1982). Depressive illness may also be responsible for changes in neuronal receptor sensitivities. Down modulation of supersensitive receptors may be the mechanism of antidepressant action by which the balance between various amine systems is adjusted (Charney, Menkes, & Heninger, 1981).

Summary

In the 1980s measures of monoamine metabolites have not been established as clinically valid, either for the diagnosis of depression or for the prediction of antidepressant treatment response. However, enough positive data exists to support continued investigation of monoamine profiles in affective disorders, and further evidence may render one monoamine or a combination of them clinically useful. Though their clinical value as predictors of therapeutic response or for subclassifying depressive disorders remains unclear, they may yet prove to have heuristic value in providing a framework for advancing our knowledge of functional CNS neurochemistry and neurophysiology.

PSYCHONEUROENDOCRINE STUDIES OF DEPRESSIVE DISORDERS

Introduction

Whereas measures of monoamine metabolites have thus far proved of limited usefulness, psychoneuroendocrine investigations may provide us with a "window on the brain," an indirect yet potential clinically useful view of brain function. First, the monoamine neurotransmitters we have just discussed regulate the secretion from hypothalamic neuroendocrine cells (Carroll, Greden, Haskett et al., 1980b; Checkley, 1980; Frohman & Stachura, 1975), so deficiencies may be mirrored in altered hormonal responses. Second, depressive mood as well as vegetative symptoms, such as disturbances in sleep, appetite, libido, and diurnal variation, and autonomic symptoms suggest hypothalamic dysfunction.

Modifications of these endocrinological test procedures and in the data interpretation enabled their adaptation to the study of psychiatric disorders. They now give indication of being able to detect subtle neuroendocrine defects or deficits which accompany depressive states. Whether these are of etiological significance or are just an indirect indicator of dysfunction remains to be determined. Preliminary reports justify their use on at least an adjunctive basis, though further study is clearly indicated prior to their routine use, and certainly before they supplant clinical skills. These biological markers of depression may allow identification of particular subgroups presently unrecognized among the heterogenous group of related disorders identified as "depressions," as well as suggest treatment.

Cortisol and the Dexamethasone Suppression Test (DST)

Basic Research into Cortisol and the Hypothalamic-Pituitary-Adrenal (HPA) Axis. With curiosity piqued by Selye's suggestion that pituitary-adrenal cortical system function could be triggered or regulated by psychological stimuli, numerous investigators sought to confirm or refute his "General Adaptation Theory" (Selye, 1959). Early investigators reported increased 24-hour urinary cortisol excretion and basal plasma cortisol levels in depressives. Fawcett and Bunney (1967) and Rubin and Mandell (1966) recognized the association of adrenal cortical overactivity and consequent hyper-

FIGURE 1
Adenohypophyseal hormones

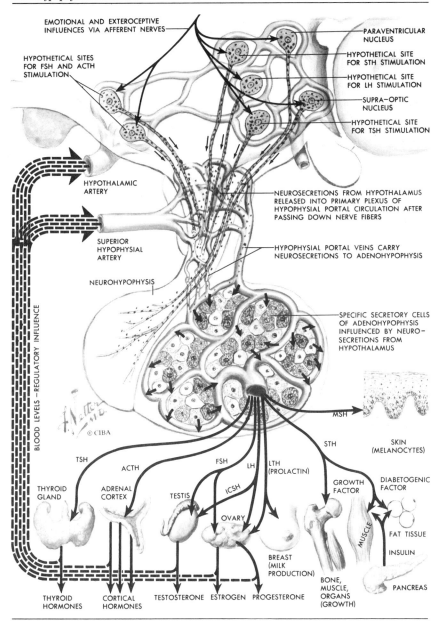

secretion of cortisol and its metabolites with severe depressive psychopathology. Rubin and Mandell (1966) proposed this increased activity to be the endocrinological correlate of a "loss of ego defense strength," which was earlier described by Sachar and associates (Sacher, Mason, Kolmer, & Artiss, 1963) as "ego disintegration." They further suggested that this pituitary-adrenal hyperfunction and depression may be linked through the limbic system and hypothalamus, which regulate both depressed mood and adrenocorticotropic hormone (ACTH) release. Fawcett and Bunney (1967) suggested that there was an interrelationship between pituitary-adrenal function and biogenic amines. They also found extremely high urinary 17-hydroxycorticosteroid (17-OHCS) excretion in suicide attempters, especially in those at increased risk of lethal suicide attempts (Bunney & Fawcett, 1965).

Krieger and associates (Krieger, Allen, Rizzo, & Krieger, 1971) described the circadian periodicity of ACTH release and adrenal corticosteroid secretion in hospitalized and nonhospitalized controls. They found that age, sex, and hospitalization had no effect on this periodicity. Normally, plasma cortisol concentrations reach a peak of up to 25 mcg percent between 6 and 9 A.M., and fall to a nadir of less than 8 mcg percent between midnight and 2 A.M. This periodicity was absent in patients with Cushing's syndrome, implying an absence of the postulated neural feedback mechanism. Sachar and associates (Sachar, Hellman, Roffwarg, Halpern, Fukushima, & Gallagher, 1973) demonstrated disrupted diurnal cortisol secretion patterns in severe (psychotic) depressives; depressives exhibited 11–13 pulses during a 24-hour period, whereas normally cortisol is secreted in bursts of about nine episodes per day, more intensely during early morning hours. This suggested abnormal disinhibition of the centers normally regulating ACTH release, and implicated limbic system dysfunction.

Liddle (1960) reported on the use of dexamethasone, a potent synthetic glucocorticoid, to artificially elevate total circulating corticosteroids. This now-standard technique, called the Dexamethasone Suppression Test (DST), was originally used to test the suppressibility of the HPA and to assist in the diagnosis of Cushing's syndrome. The site of action of this drug is within the central nervous system, at the median eminence of the hypothalamus and within the limbic system areas involved in the regulation of corticotropin releasing factor (CRF) and ACTH release. Normally, ACTH secretion from the pituitary is suppressed by normal cortisol hormonal levels; this negative feedback system is disrupted in adrenocortical hyperfunction. In the DST, the HPA system normally is inhibited promptly; gradations of response, from complete nonsuppressibility to "early escape" are seen in Cushing's as well as in depressive disorder (see later). Krieger and associates (1971) found that the dose and time of dexamethasone administration were important factors in determining the duration of its effect in abolishing subsequent maximal peaks. They suggested that there may be only one "critical period" of ACTH release within the 24-hour cycle.

Fawcett and Bunney (1967) reported that some of their agitated psychotic depressives failed to suppress 17-OHCS urinary excretion normally following

FIGURE 2
Hypothalamic-pituitary-adrenal axis

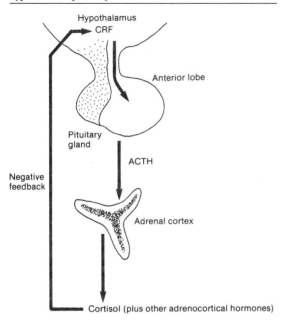

dexamethasone. Butler and Besser (1968) reported similar nonsuppression of plasma cortisol in patients with severe primary affective disorder. Carroll and associates (Carroll, Martin, & Davies, 1968) noted nonsuppression of plasma 11-OHCS in severe depressives, with reversibility upon recovery, distinguishing these patients from those with Cushing's syndrome. Stokes and associates (Stokes, Pick, Stoll, & Nunn, 1975) reported plasma cortisol resistance to dexamethasone suppression using 1, 2, and 8 mg dexamethasone doses. On the other hand, Shopsin and Gershon (1971) and Verghese and associates (Verghese, Matthews, & Mathia, 1979) were unable to replicate these findings and concluded that the adrenocortical overactivity theory of depression could not be supported.

Carroll (1976) refuted that "ego defense breakdown" hypothesis of hyperadrenocortisolism in his report of dexamethasone suppression and cortisol measurements in severely ill depressives and in schizophrenics with secondary depression; both groups demonstrated a high level of ego defense breakdown by Sachar's criteria. The persistent elevation of plasma (and CSF) cortisol and urine-free cortisol post-dexamethasone suppression in the primary depressives but not in the schizophrenics with secondary depression indicated that the HPA activation and DST nonsuppression were associated with the process of a primary depressive illness, not depressive symptoms alone. Further studies have also indicated that the source of the elevated plasma cortisol and urinary corticosteroid metabolite excretion is excessive

ACTH release rather than adrenal hyperactivity (Carroll, 1978). This provides further evidence for a suprahypophyseal (or, limbic system-hypothalamic) origin of the dysfunction in depression.

The Standardization of the DST.   One factor lacking in the early studies was standardization of the procedure, which would take into account both the temporal patterns of cortisol release (and thus indicate when to give the dexamethasone) and the optimal dexamethasone dose. It is important to understand that depressives can be distinguished from Cushing's patients. True Cushing's patients do not suppress even at higher dexamethasone doses, whereas depressives should. In other words, the HPA disturbance is more subtle in depression. A subgroup of depressives demonstrated an abnormal early escape from suppression, indicating disinhibition of the normal CNS regulatory influences within the limbic system and HPA axis for ACTH-cortisol release in primary depressive illness (Carroll, Curtis, & Mendels, 1976a, 1976b). Thus, rather than inducing absolute suppression of HPA activity with dexamethasone for at least 24 hours, there is an "early escape," indicating at least partial resistance to this suppression. Many other depressives demonstrated normal suppression of early morning (8 A.M.) plasma cortisol concentrations, but "escaped" suppression later in the day (4 P.M. or 11 P.M.). Although it had been reported that an earlier escape from suppression indicated that both the depression and the HPA dysfunction were more severe (Carroll et al., 1976a), further study has shown that the severity of illness itself may not be a factor in the DST (Carroll, Feinberg, Greden, Tarika, Albala, Haskett, James, Kronfol, Lohr, Steiner, deVigne, & Young, 1981). Nonsuppression seems to be a more specific finding in melancholia, thereby indicating a categorical distinction between endogenous (melancholia) and nonendogenous depression. The post-DST cortisol levels may be higher in psychotic depressives (Schatzberg, Rothschild, Stahl, Bond, Rosenbaum, Lofgren, MacLaughlin, Sullivan, & Cole, 1983). An elevated cortisol level (nonsuppression) at any sampling time indicates abnormal HPA disinhibition and a positive test.

The neural basis for this disinhibition has been the subject of investigation, but remains uncertain. Defects or deficits in alpha (and/or beta) receptors, as well as disturbances in central monoamine neurotransmitter activity or cholinergic-adrenergic balance have been suggested. Other alternatives include nonspecific factors which influence adrenocortical function and produce an override of both circadian and feedback systems. There is no data indicating that this disinhibition is an etiological factor in the development of depressive disorders, though it is temporally associated with its occurrence. The HPA overactivity may only reflect limbic system dysfunction.

Better understanding of HPA physiology, especially of ACTH release and cortisol secretion, and their circadian periodicity, has led to refinement of the DST procedure (Carroll, 1982; Carroll, Feinberg, et al., 1981). The procedure presently recommended is as follows:

Day 1: 1.0 mg (0.5 mg for children) of dexamethasone taken orally at 11 P.M. or 11:30 P.M. Lowering of the dose from 2 mg to 1 mg did not significantly change the specificity of the test while the sensitivity increased twofold (Carroll, 1982; Carroll, Feinberg, et al., 1981).

Day 2: Blood samples drawn for plasma cortisol determinations at 8 A.M., 4 P.M., and 11 P.M. For outpatients, 4 P.M. samples only are obtained for reasons of convenience and practicality. The plasma cortisol criterion of greater than 5 mcg/dl by competitive protein binding, or greater than 4 mcg/dl by radioimmunoassay (RIA) in any post-dexamethasone blood sample is abnormal. Sources of variation in these assays have been reviewed by Meltzer and Fang (1983). Seventy-eight percent of all positive tests were obtained with the 4 P.M. test alone, and 98 percent by obtaining both 4 P.M. and 11 P.M. collections.

A further option includes drawing baseline plasma cortisol levels on day 1 prior to dexamethasone administration, but in our experience this adds little to the interpretation of test results. Testing should not be repeated at less than five-day intervals.

Clinical studies of the efficacy of this test in depressive disorders, particularly "melancholia" (American Psychiatric Association, 1980; Carroll, Feinberg, Greden, Haskett, James, Steiner, & Tarika, 1980) have been reviewed by others (Baldessarini, 1983; Carroll, 1982; Gwirtsman, Gerner, & Sternbach, 1982; Kalin, Risch, Janowsky, & Murphy, 1981). Overall, the sensitivity (rate of true positive test results in patients with a clinical diagnosis of depression) for the combined group of inpatients and outpatients (only 4:00 P.M. cortisols available for most outpatients) has been about 50 percent, and the specificity (rate of true negative test results in those without depression) has been about 95 percent; this latter value indicates a low rate of false positives. Most positive results have been in endogenous depressives, or melancholics. As would be expected from the higher base rate of melancholic depressives in inpatients, the sensitivity of the DST has been higher in inpatients. The diagnostic confidence (predictive value, or proportion of abnormal results which are true-positive for the diagnosis in question) of an abnormal (positive) DST, has been about 90 percent for melancholia.

Various causes of false positive and false negative results have been reported as the test continues to be evaluated in various clinical settings. Medical conditions contributing to false positive results include: pregnancy; Cushing's disease or syndrome; obesity or malnutrition, severe weight loss or anorexia nervosa (to less than 80 percent of ideal body weight); hepatic enzyme induction (usually from drugs such as barbiturates); uncontrolled diabetes mellitus; temporal lobe epilepsy; alcoholism (both during active use and in the acute withdrawal period); renovascular hypertension; chronic hemodialysis; malignancies with ectopic ACTH secretion; and major physical illnesses in general. False negative results may occur with Addison's disease, hypopituitarism, and possibly other endocrine diseases, as well as with about 50 percent of melancholics. Various medications may also alter the results (Carroll, Feinberg, et. al., 1981; Nuller & Ostroumova, 1980). Those which produce false positive results include high-dose estrogens, reserpine, phenytoin, barbiturates, meprobamate, narcotics, and carbamazepine (Privitera, Greden, Gardner, Ritchie, & Carroll, 1982) while (high-dose) benzodiazepines, corticosteroids (including topical and nasal formulations), dextroamphetamine, cyproheptadine, and possibly L-tryptophan and spironolactone may produce false negative results. Other psychotropics drugs, including antidepressants, antipsychotics, and lithium, do not appear to affect the results of the test.

As with any other laboratory test, its usefulness is measured in its clinical applicability. Its major drawback is the limited sensitivity, which restricts its value as a general screening test for diagnosing depression (as we explain to our nonpsychiatrist colleagues, "you'll still have to examine the patient"). A negative test does not exclude the diagnosis of a major depressives disorder; a positive test may confirm the clinical diagnosis. It may be of some benefit in difficult differential diagnostic issues, such as "pseudodementia," especially in apathetic elderly patients, for whom a positive test would justify more aggressive therapeutic intervention (although a potential effect of age in producing a false positive DST has been reported [Spar & Gerner, 1982]). Further nosological applications have been studied. Its use in determining genetic subtypes of depression have been reported (Schlesser, Winokur, & Sherman, 1979; 1980) but not confirmed (Carroll, Greden, Feinberg, James, Haskett, Steiner, & Tarika, 1980; Mendlewicz, Charles, & Franckson, 1982). Evaluations of clinical subtypes of depression in relation to the DST have also been undertaken and continue to be investigated (Carroll, Feinberg, et al., 1980; Evans & Nemeroff, 1983; Feinberg & Carroll, 1982).

Therapeutically, nonsuppression is regarded as a biological state marker of depression, which normalizes with remission (Albala, Greden, Tarika, & Carroll, 1981; Goldberg, 1980a, 1980b; Greden, Albala, Haskett, James, Goodman, Steiner, & Carroll, 1980; Greden, Gardner, King, Grunhaus, Carroll, & Kronfol, 1983; Holsboer, Liebl, & Hofschuster, 1982; Nuller & Ostroumova, 1980). It is unresolved whether a positive DST result predicts response to treatment (W. A. Brown, Johnston, & Mayfield, 1979; Carroll, 1981). W. A. Brown and others (W. A. Brown, 1980; W. A. Brown, Haier, & Qualls, 1980, 1981) and Fraser (1983) have suggested that the DST may predict response to specific antidepressants. Nonsuppressors in their samples responded better to IMI-like drugs, whereas suppressors responded preferentially to AMI-like drugs. Data from Amsterdam and associates (Amsterdam, Winokur, Bryant, Larkin, & Rickels, 1983) however supported the converse. More recent studies by Greden (Greden, Kronfol, Gardner, Feinberg, Mukhopadhyay, Albala, & Carroll, 1981), Nelson (Nelson, Orr, Stevenson, & Shane, 1982), and Peselow and Fieve (1982) reported no such correlations between DST results and treatment response.

Lastly, although the DST is a safe test, a recent report by Sovner (1983) described an "amphetamine-like behavioral reaction" to dexamethasone. Two previous reports (Asberg, Varpila-Hannson, Tomba, Aminoff, Martensson, Thoren, Traskman-Bendz, Eneroth, & Astrom, 1981; Beck-Friis, Aperia, Kjellman, Ljunggren, Petterson, Sara, Sjolin, Unden, & Wetterberg, 1981) reported four suicide attempts (one completed) following dexamethasone administration (low dose) for the DST. The cause of these reactions remains speculative.

To summarize, it is apparent that the DST may be a state-dependent marker, indirectly reflecting limbic-HPA disinhibition. Presently, its specific value appears to be in confirming the diagnosis of melancholia, for which it is quite specific, but is limited by its sensitivity rate of only 50 percent. Nonsuppressors tend to normalize with remission, and thus it is potentially useful as an indicator for terminating antidepressant treatment. Similarly, an abnormal result in a patient who is clinically symptom free may herald a relapse. Though it is a relatively simple test to perform, and yields potentially clinically useful data, caution must be advised against its indiscriminant use. It should be used in the context of a comprehensive psychiatric and medical evaluation. Certainly more field testing in addition to basic research is required to elucidate its meaning and future value.

OTHER TESTS OF LIMBIC SYSTEM-HYPOTHALAMIC-PITUITARY FUNCTION

Thyroid-Releasing Hormone (TRH) Stimulation Test

Perhaps the best studied of the other neuroendocrine tests evaluated in depressive populations is the TRH stimulation test. Investigations of the relationship between depressive disorders and the hypothalamic-pituitary-thyroid (HPT) axis arose from observations of the effects of various diseases of the thyroid gland on mood states. Prange and associates (Prange, Wilson, Lara, Alltop, & Breese, 1972) reported a diminished (blunted) thyroid stimulating hormone (TSH) response to intravenous administration of a commercially available synthetic tripeptide, protirelin (TRH) in 3 of 10 depressed women who had normal baseline thyroid hormone levels. Ten years later, Loosen and Prange (1982) reviewed 47 studies involving 963 patients; of these, all but five studies involving only 36 patients reported findings consistent with the initial results.

Normally, TSH levels demonstate diurnal variation, with a nocturnal rise. It is modulated by TRH, which facilitates TSH release, and by thyroid hormones (thyroxine, T_4 and triiodothyronine, T_3), which provide feedback inhibition to TSH release. The pituitary is quite responsive to small thyroid hormone changes within the physiological (normal) range. The anterior pituitary receives feedback peripherally as well as via the portal venous system, the latter through hormones secreted by hypothalamic neurons regulated by

FIGURE 3
Hypothalamic-pituitary-thyroid axis

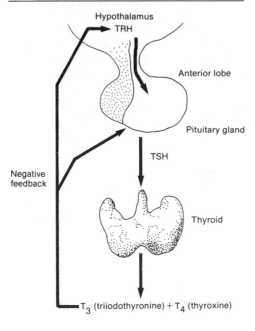

Thyroid hormones

other brain neuronal systems involving various monoamines. Several of these monoamines are thought to play a role in the TSH response to TRH: NE appears to stimulate TRH cells and the subsequent hypothalamic TRH release; 5-HT has mainly an inhibitory role; DA, while demonstrating some stimulatory effect, is inactive when its conversion to NE is blocked (Martin, Reichlin, & Brown, 1977). Beyond this, the normal neurophysiological control of TRH release and TSH secretion is not well understood. Therefore, any hypothesis purporting to explain the pathophysiological significance of changes in monoamine neurotransmitters, receptors, and the thyroid and its hormones, all occurring within the context of depressive disorders, must remain only speculative, and further consideration of these hypotheses is beyond the scope of this chapter, though the reader may refer elsewhere (Loosen & Prange, 1982; Whybrow & Prange, 1981).

In general psychiatric practice, the TRH test is performed by giving an intravenous infusion of 500 mcg of TRH over 30 to 60 seconds at 8 or 9 A.M. to a patient who has fasted overnight, is recumbent (or at rest), and preferably is drug free for seven days in order to eliminate potential drug effects which may complicate the interpretation of results. (This latter restriction may not be necessary as Kirkegaarde and associates (Kirkegaarde, Bjorum, Cohn, Faber, Lauridsen, & Nerup, 1977) presented evidence that the TSH response is unaffected by alpha- or beta-adrenergic antagonists and agonists, 5-hydroxy-tryptophan, IMI, diazepam, and low doses of chlorpromazine, although high doses increased the response, as did chronic lithium (Gold, Goodwin, Wehr, & Rebar, 1977). An indwelling catheter is usually used, and inserted 30 minutes prior to infusion, in order to minimize any possible nonspecific stress effect. A baseline TSH level is drawn at this time, and repeated at time 0, the time of infusion. Oral TRH administration is discouraged because of potential differential absorption and in order to provide time-limited pituitary stimulation. Different TRH doses and rates of administration have been used. The dose-response curve is linear up to a maximum TRH dose of 500 mcg; above 500 mcg the TSH response reaches a plateau (Hollister, Davis, & Berger, 1976). In addition, this dose, being slightly supramaximal, may facilitate simultaneous study of behavioral changes. Consonant with this, early studies reported an antidepressant effect from TRH as well as demonstration of an abnormal pituitary response (Kastin, Ehrensing, Schalch, & Anderson, 1972; Prange, Wilson, Lara, Alltop, & Breese, 1972), but usually this behavioral response is only an occasional brief euphoria.

Although detailed studies have involved repeated measurements of serum TSH concentration (usually by radioimmunoassay) over a three-hour period, the peak TSH response generally occurs at 30 minutes, and a single assay at this time may yield nearly as much clinically significant and relevant information (Loosen & Prange, 1982). A blunted, or abnormal, response is determined by the delta TSH (ΔTSH) or baseline value subtracted from the peak value. This is the crucial as well as the most controversial issue of the test. Loosen and Prange (1982) have "arbitrarily defined" this maximal ΔTSH as less than 5.0 microU/ml, while others have reported cutoff values as low as 2.5 (Karlberg, Kjellman, & Kagedol, 1978) and as high as less than 7.0 microU/ml (Extein, Pottash, Gold, Cadet, Sweeney, Davies, & Martin, 1980; Extein, Pottash, Gold, & Cowdry, 1982; Gold, Pottash, Extein, Martin, Howard, Mueller, & Sweeney, 1981). Depending upon the criterion value chosen, blunted responses have been reported in 25 to 50 percent of patients with major depressive disorders, in contrast to few nondepressive, minor depressive, or schizophrenic patients or normal volunteers (Baldessarini, 1983; Targum, 1983). The response may be more blunted in unipolar than bipolar depressives (Gold, Pottash, Ryan, Sweeney, Davies, & Martin, 1980). An association with severity of illness does not appear likely. Specificity has ranged from 90 to 100 percent (Baldessarini, 1983). False-positive blunted responses have been reported to be due to increasing age; male sex; acutely reduced caloric intake (anorexics demonstrate delayed peak responses); chronic renal failure; Klinefelter's syndrome; alcoholism; previously administered somatostatin, neurotensin, dopamine, thyroid hormone, or glucocorticoids; and possibly various endocrinopathies, including hyper- and hypothyroidism, Cushing's, acromegaly, and primary pituitary dysfunction. Repetitive TRH administration may also cause a false positive blunting, and therefore performance of this test should be limited to once weekly at most.

What is the clinical utility of this as yet unstandardized test? The functional significance of a blunted response is still incompletely understood. Apparently it is sometimes a trait marker and sometimes a state marker, but in neither case does it necessarily seem to be related to the cause of the depression, which is also unknown (Loosen & Prange, 1982). Kirkegaarde (1981) described the "double delta" value for predicting outcome: those patients whose maximal TSH response between admission and discharge increased by 2 microU/ml tended to maintain their clinical remission. However, the prognostic value of a persistently abnormal TSH despite clinical remission is unclear, but it may be related to a high vulnerability to depression (Loosen & Prange, 1982). Further, the test may also be useful in unmasking subclinical hypo- and hyperthyroidism, long recognized as causes of affective and behavioral disorders (Whybrow & Prange, 1981). Clinically, Loosen and Prange (1982) emphasized that in psychiatric patients with diminished TSH response to TRH stimulation there has been no clinical evidence for pituitary or thyroid disease, and baseline thyroid function tests have been normal for the majority of those patients studied.

Last is the question of sequential use of the DST and TRH stimulation test. That they have different bases for the abnormality is demonstrated by the fact that only a minority of patients with major depressive disorder have both abnormalities (Targum, Sullivan, & Byrnes, 1982). It has been established that serum cortisol elevations reduce the TSH response, and this correlation was reported in earlier studies (Loosen, Prange, & Wilson, 1978a, 1978b). However, Extein and associates (Extein, Pottash, & Gold, 1981) found only 30 percent of depressives were abnormal on both tests, which suggests that there may be no significant association between the two tests. Thus, Loosen and Prange (1982) concluded that it is extremely doubtful that adrenal activation accounts for the TSH blunting which occurs during depression. Although the DST is the better standardized test, and thus may yield more understandable data, if the two are to be used sequentially, the TRH test should be done first, as the glucocorticoid dexamethasone may cause blunting of the TRH test results (Targum et al., 1982).

The TRH stimulation test is a safe and relatively simple test to perform, but yields more uncertain data. Certainly there is evidence that a significant number of major depressives have abnormalities in the HPT axis. This is further evidence of a biological link with affective disorders, and this is another area which requires further investigation. Once again, this is not a test which should be used blindly without concomitant detailed clinical evaluation.

Growth Hormone

The hypothalamic-pituitary-growth hormone (GH) system has not been studied as well as the HPA or HPT. Neural control of GH release from the anterior pituitary is under hypothalamic control via somatostatin (GH inhibitory factor) and GH-releasing factor, as well as from extrahypothalamic limbic system connections. GH may also be released by alpha-adrenergic, dopaminergic, and serotonergic agonists and beta-adrenergic antagonists (Blackard & Heidingsfelder, 1968). GH is secreted episodically, and the daily maximal surge in blood level occurs repetitively each night, at 24-hour intervals, within the first two hours after sleep onset, and coincides with the first appearance of slow wave sleep (Stages 3 and 4) (Boyar, 1978).

GH is frequently considered a "stress-responsive" hormone, and levels may rapidly rise in response to physical and psychological stress (and can occur independent of adrenal activation and cortisol secretion), such as physical exercise and hypoglycemia, while hyperglycemia or increased free fatty acids will decrease its secretion. This stress response is mediated through limbic connections (G. M. Brown, Seggie, Chambers, & Ettigi, 1978). Various other metabolic, pharmacologic, and neural factors may affect its secretion (G. M. Brown & Reichlin, 1972; Martin, 1973). Fasting plasma GH levels are normally quite low, less than 2 ng/ml (by RIA), and basal levels remain in this range in depressives, despite the distress of illness (Carroll & Mendels, 1976). Marked loss of body weight alone in nondepressed individuals may produce elevated GH levels (Landon, Greenwood, Stamp, & Wynn, 1966).

Abnormalities of GH secretion in depressive disorders include diminished (less than 5 ng/ml) response to insulin-induced hypoglycemia and to CA (noradrenergic) agonists (including amphetamine, dopa, clonidine, desipramine), abnormal release following TRH administration, and altered sleep-induced release. The response to some but not all adrenergic agonists has been reported to be low. Initial reports of reduced GH response to L-dopa and apomorphine in depressives (especially unipolar depressives) proved instead to be related mainly to the variables of age and estrogen status, which had not been controlled (Casper, Davis, Pandey, Garver, & Dekirmenjian, 1977; Sachar, Altman, Gruen, Glassman, Halpern, & Sassin, 1975; Sachar, Frantz, Altman, & Sassin, 1973; Sachar, Mushrush, Perlow, Weitzman, & Sassin, 1972). No consistent abnormalities have been found when these variables have been controlled. One study by Gold and associates (Gold, Goodwin, Wehr, Rebar, & Sack, 1976) reported unipolar-bipolar differences in response to L-dopa. No such differences in response to either L-dopa or apomorphine were reported by Maany and associates (Maany, Mendels, Frazer, & Brunswick, 1979); this was interpreted as consistent with normal dopaminergic function in depressives.

The GH response to dextroamphetamine may be a primarily noradrenergic-mediated response, although there is evidence that dopaminergic systems are also involved (W. A. Brown, 1977; W. A. Brown, Corriveau, & Ebert, 1978; W. A. Brown & Williams, 1976). Langer and associates (Langer, Heinze, Reim, & Matussek, 1976) reported that intravenous dextroamphetamine administration led to a significantly lower GH response in endogenous depressives as compared with reactive depressives, other psychiatric control groups, and normal controls, but age and estrogen status (menopausal status) were not controlled, and may override differences attributed to diagnostic categories. Halbreich and associates (Halbreich, Sachar, Asnis,

Quitkin, Nathan, Halpern, & Klein, 1982) refuted these findings. They found that the GH response to dextroamphetamine neither differentiated between endogenous depressive and age- and sex-matched normal controls, nor between different types of depression. Thus the positive predictive value of a diminished GH appears low, although a normal or augmented response may rule out an endogenous primary depressive disorder. Checkley (1979; Checkley & Crammer, 1977) similarly found no differences using methylamphetamine.

Study of GH secretion has also been linked to models aimed at understanding the role of CNS aminergic receptors in the amine hypothesis of depressive disorders. Clonidine, an alpha-adrenergic receptor agonist, stimulates pre- and postsynaptic alpha receptors as well as GH secretion. This response to clonidine has been reported to be significantly reduced in endogenous depressives, suggesting subsensitivity of the postsynaptic alpha-1 receptors (Matussek, Ackenheil, Hippius, Muller, Schroder, Schultes, & Wasilewski, 1980; Matussek & Laakman, 1981). (Receptor sites studies, including platelet 5-HT uptake and tritiated-IMI binding studies, as well as investigations of the endogenous opioid system, will not be reviewed in this chapter; Meltzer, Arora, Baber, & Tricou, 1981; Paul, Rehavi, Skolnick, Ballenger, & Goodwin, 1981; Pickar, Cohen, Naber, & Cohen, 1982). The GH response to clonidine and desipramine (DMI, a tricyclic antidepressant, TCA), is also undergoing study. As with amphetamine and clonidine, endogenous depressives had diminished GH response to desipramine; normals and neurotic depressives did not (Matussek & Laakman, 1981). This and studies by Checkley and associates (Checkley, Slade, & Shur, 1981; Checkley, Slade, Shur, & Dawling, 1981) have indicated that DMI has effects on alpha adrenoreceptor function in depressives. Thus, GH response to pharmacologic challenge may provide a means by which we may understand antidepressant mechanism of action.

It had been considered established that the GH response to insulin-induced hypoglycemia is diminished in major endogenous depression (W. A. Brown et al., 1978; Endo, Endo, Nishikubo, Yamaguchi, & Hatotani, 1974; Gregoire, Brauman, deBuck, & Corvilain, 1977; Gruen, Sachar, Altman, & Sassin, 1975; Mueller, Heninger, & McDonald, 1969a, 1969b; Sachar, Finkelstein, & Hellman, 1971; Sachar, Frantz, Altman, & Sassin, 1973). Casper and associates (Casper, Davis, Pandey, Garver, & Dekirmenjian, 1977) found similar elevations in baseline GH in patients with major affective disorders and in healthy controls, consistent with a preserved stress response, but significantly lower rises in GH after insulin-induced hypoglycemia in both the manics and depressives compared with the normal subjects. Estrogen status has not affected the outcome of this challenge test (Gruen et al., 1975), but the response was impaired or absent in diencephalic Cushing's (Cushing's disease) (Krieger, 1973). Carroll (1972) found no relationship between this GH response and the DST in the same patients. Thus, the release of GH by ACTH is independent of the cortisol response to ACTH.

Preliminary data from the Collaborative Program on the Psychobiology of Depression (Koslow, Stokes, Mendels, Ramsey, & Casper, 1982) has demonstrated contrary findings, and offer no support for the view that the hypothalamic-pituitary-GH system is altered in depressives. Unipolar depressives demonstrated significantly greater resistance to insulin-induced hypoglycemia, similar to an earlier report by Carroll (1969). However, the mean peak GH concentrations were not significantly different between unipolar and bipolar depressives and/or normal controls, even though greater range and variability in this peak response was noted in bipolar depressives. They cited methodological differences such as controlling for weight deviation from the ideal body weight (should be within 20 percent), estrogen status (they studied only postmenopausal females), and minimum fall in plasma glucose from the baseline, which were indiscriminantly controlled in previous studies, as the basis for the discrepant findings. Thus, a blunted plasma glucose rather than GH response to insulin-induced hypoglycemia may be a more sensitive test for defining a subset of depressives, and the blunted GH response may indicate a primary dysfunction of insulin-resistance.

This decreased sensitivity to exogenous insulin is mediated by both 5-HT and NE; thus this evidence for deficient GH response in depressives is consistent with diminished functional activity of one or both of these transmitters (Bivens, Lebovitz, & Feldman, 1973; Garver, Pandey, Dekirmenjian, & DeLeon-Jones, 1975; Takahashi, Kondo, Yoshimura, & Ochi, 1974). Evidence for its value as a state-dependent marker of depression, especially primary endogenous depression rather than secondary or neurotic subtypes, is the observation that this altered response reverts to normal upon clinical recovery (Endo et al., 1974; Gregoire et al., 1977).

TRH administration may produce an increased GH release in depressives, which is ordinarily only seen in patients with acromegaly (Martin, 1973). Preliminary evidence suggests that this abnormal TRH response and the reduced GH response to insulin hypoglycemia indicate a common underlying mechanism, either at the pituitary level, as in acromegaly, or at the hypothalamic level, indicating a neurotransmitter defect or deficiency.

Data on the GH release during the slow wave sleep of depressives is sparse (Schilkrut, Chandra, Osswald, Ruther, Baarfusser, & Matussek, 1975). Mendelson and associates (Mendelson, Jacobs, Gillin, & Wyatt, 1979) provided evidence that different neurotransmitter pathways may mediate sleep-regulated GH secretion than those involved in insulin-induced GH secretion, and postulated a role for the cholinergic system in facilitation of the former.

Studies involving growth hormone may offer another view of altered brain function in depression. The major flaws in these studies are lack of careful control of the major variables which may affect the interpretation of the results, that is, age, sex, menopausal (estrogen) and weight status, and any other variable that may influence the hormonal response, including a GH response to catheter insertion and sleep-related GH secretion if the patient falls asleep during the procedure (Carroll, 1980). Any explanation of the so-called abnormal results by necessity must await definition of a true abnormal result from rigorously defined criteria established in a population of normal controls. For now, the clinical usefulness of these various challenge tests involving GH response is limited.

Prolactin

Studies of disturbed prolactin secretion in depression are few in number. Prolactin is secreted during physiological and psychological stress, and is regulated by an inhibitory factor thought to be dopamine, and its secretion may be increased by 5-HT agonists (Ettigi & Brown, 1977). Bipolar depressives may have somewhat lower basal plasma levels and blunted sleep-related release (Mendlewicz, Van Cauter, Linkowski, L'Hermite, & Robyn, 1980), prolactin's predominant release time.

Gonadotropins

Gonadotropins include follicle-stimulating hormone (FSH) and luteinizing hormone (LH). Information regarding neuroendocrine control or the neural basis of their secretion and function in depression is speculative at best, and will not be further reviewed here (Checkley, 1980; Ettigi & Brown, 1977).

Summary and Conclusions

One of the major problems of modern psychiatry is the tendency to jump at an opportunity for objectifying clinical bedside and phenomenological data with screening procedures (laboratory and pharmacological challenges) before we understand the mechanism or implications of such data. Most of these data serve heuristically to help form testable hypotheses which can be used to further solve the riddle of depression and its treatment; but the clinician may be misled without a proper understanding of their applicability. Combined studies and neuroendocrine batteries have been investigated (Amsterdam, Winokur, Lucki, Caroff, Snyder, & Rickels, 1983; A. Winokur, Amsterdam, Caroff, Snyder, & Brunswick, 1982). To date, the most clinically useful neuroendocrine tests in depression are the DST and the TRH stimulation test, but the sensitivity for either of these tests alone is about 50 percent, and only 11 to 30 percent of depressives manifest both abnormalities (Extein et al., 1981; Targum et al., 1982). Therefore, good clinical diagnosis, supplemented by thoughtful use of these tests in carefully selected patients is the prudent advice offered here regarding both initial diagnosis and serial testing. These tests should be used to answer questions regarding diagnosis, treatment and prognosis, not add to the already existing confusion.

THE STIMULANT CHALLENGE TEST AND DEPRESSION

Despite the widespread use (and usefulness) of antidepressant drugs, prediction of individual therapeutic response to specific agents remains an important unsolved problem. As emphasized above, attempts to diagnose and subtype depression, and predict treatment response on the basis of various putative biological markers and neurochemical and endocrinological challenge tests may still be premature. However, these same investigations suggest that there are several subtypes of symptomatologically similar depressive disorders which can be distinguished by the differential response to stimulant agents and antidepressants as well as by the pattern of associated neuroamine and neuroendocrine changes (Maas, 1975; Sabelli, Fawcett, Javaid, & Bagri, 1983). In an attempt to develop research approaches to both the problems of the prediction of antidepressant drug response and the investigation of the CA depletion hypothesis of depression, Fawcett and associates found dextroamphetamine (D-AMPH) to be a potentially useful research drug for behavioral-biochemical interventions (Fawcett & Siomopoulos, 1971; Fawcett et al., 1972). D-AMPH is known to exert rapid mood effects, despite its generally limited use as a true antidepressant. As anyone who has needed to stay awake and alert for any protracted period of time knows, D-AMPH as well as its congeners, such as methylphenidate (Ritalin®), are powerful stimulants. They are also known to produce increased confidence as well as elation, increased energy and motor activity, and agitation in humans. The rapid and rather dramatic, though relatively short-lived, mood effects of these stimulants provide an interesting contrast with the delayed and gradual but lasting effects of the antidepressants in clinically depressed patients. Early trials with D-AMPH revealed that some patients demonstrated rapid and sometimes dramatic improvement in mood while others showed little or no behavioral changes. There is a wide range of individual differences in response to stimulants. These behavioral effects are primarily mediated by the catecholamine NE (Hanson, 1967; Sulser, Owens, Norvich, & Dingell, 1968; Weissman, Koe, & Tenen, 1966) in a manner similar to the postulated mechanism by which (some) antidepressants (e.g., IMI-like TCA) exert a therapeutic effect in clinical depression (i.e., through the inhibition of reuptake of free NE). This led to the hypothesis that a test dose of D-AMPH might predict a therapeutic response to the TCA. Relief of depressive symptoms and fatigue with acute stimulant administration, and a subsequent potential depressogenic effect with chronic administration, presumably related to brain neuroamine depletion (Schildkraut, Watson, Draskoczy, & Hartmann, 1971; Watson, Hartmann, & Schildkraut, 1972) provide an empirical basis for the neuroamine hypothesis of depression. However, other research has demonstrated potential roles for DA and noncatecholic phenylethylamines (Borison et al., 1974; Borison, Mosnaim, & Sabelli, 1975; Moore, 1977) as well as 5-HT (Innes, 1963) and ACh systems (Deffenu Bartolini, & Pepeu, 1970). Since all of these neurotransmitter systems are important in the brain, it is illogical to attribute these behavioral effects to the action of this drug on any one system. Further, the effect may vary with individual stimulants: for example, methylphenidate is thought to preferentially affect central DA systems (Costall & Naylor, 1974; Ferris & Tang, 1979; Ferris, Tang, & Maxwell, 1972).

Reports by Fawcett and colleagues (Fawcett & Siomopoulos, 1971; Fawcett et al., 1972; Fawcett, Sabelli, Gusovsky, Epstein, Javaid, & Jeffriess, 1983;

Maas et al., 1972; Sabelli, Fawcett, Javaid, & Bagri, 1983) and others (Van Kammen & Murphy, 1975; 1978; 1979) suggested that patients can be differentiated on the basis of behavioral responses to moderately high oral doses (10–15 mg twice a day) of D-AMPH or methylphenidate (30 mg twice a day); patients who had a positive response to either of these stimulants subsequently tended to benefit from treatment with a NE reuptake-blocking TCA, such as IMI or DMI. Despite the fact that it has been relatively untested in published clinical trials, the authors and others have found it to be a simple, rapid, noninvasive and safe procedure which may distinguish biochemically different types of depression. Its primary value lies in its clinical usefulness in predicting specific TCA response in each individual patient. This is contrasted with neuroamine metabolite levels, which demonstrate overlap between depressive subtypes and the "normal range," and thus are not useful clinical indicators in individual cases. Although there is a continuum of responses, subjects can be classified as responders and nonresponders on the basis of subjective and objective mood ratings. In our clinical experience, the delayed and overall effects of D-AMPH and methylphenidate following oral administration over a period of at least two days is more indicative of prediction of TCA response to treatment than the short-lasting mood changes; this important distinction between the immediate and transient euphoric effects and the delayed and more sustained antidepressant effects have been reported by Checkley (1978) as well as observed by the authors (unpublished data). We give either stimulant for one to three days, and use the patient's self-report of presence or absence of mood elevation to choose a specific TCA treatment. We are currently investigating the usefulness of various mood scales and appropriate times to administer them, both for inpatients and outpatients. We do not have adequate data regarding prediction of response to MAOI, but our clinical experience suggests MAOI responders show partial, small mood elevation to stimulant challenge. Amphetamines and methylphenidate may precipitate or exacerbate psychotic symptoms in schizophrenics, but this does not appear to be a problem in affective disorder patients, although we have observed the precipitation of manic episodes in bipolar depressives (Angrist, Rotrosen, & Gershon, 1980; Janowsky & Davis, 1976; Janowsky, El-Yousef, Davis, & Sekerke, 1973; Segal & Janowsky, 1978). Although clinically we find little difference between the two stimulants as predictors, some patients do preferentially respond to one of the two drugs, and in the case of patients who do not respond to one agent at maximal dose over three days, we repeat the trial with the other. Further, pharmacological studies suggest potential important differences, and comparative studies are needed to test this possibility. When we use amphetamine-like stimulants as a challenge test in depressives, we consider mood elevation as well as precipitation of manic-like episodes to be positive responses, whereas lack of mood change, increased energy or motor activity alone, or the triggering or exacerbation of dysphoric anxiety or agitation are negative responses.

In a naturalistic, nondouble-blinded study, Sabelli and associates (Sabelli, Fawcett, Javaid, & Bagri, 1983) found that patients who responded favorably to methylphenidate responded to IMI or DMI, but not to nortriptyline (NT) or amitriptyline (AMI), and that methylphenidate-negative patients responsive to AMI maintained their therapeutic response following substitution of NT or AMI. (Adequate plasma levels were achieved for all TCA.) This latter point is worth noting because it has been accepted that both DMI and NT are "NE reuptake blockers," while AMI is a "5-HT reuptake blocker" (Maas, 1975). Our findings suggest that NT may actually be more similar to AMI than to IMI or DMI in its pharmacological and biochemical activity profile.

On the basis of these findings of differential responsiveness to methylphenidate challenge and of differential therapeutic efficacy of DMI and NT, a new model for subtyping depressive disorders was postulated. While Maas's model (1975) was based on hypothetical differences in monoaminergic mechanisms, Sabelli and coworkers (Sabelli, Fawcett, Javaid, & Bagri, 1983) speculated that Type I depressions, responsive to methylphenidate and IMI-like antidepressants, may be associated with a deficit in various brain monoamines (NE, 5-HT, PEA) and that Type II depressions, responsive to AMI and NT, may also be associated with a PEA deficit at times, but there is little evidence for NE or 5-HT depletion.

Presently, the Stimulant Challenge Test depends upon subjective reports and behavioral observations, which may be discrepant (Fawcett & Siomopoulos, 1971). An objective biochemical or physiological response would render this test more objective. Earlier studies by Fawcett and associates (Fawcett et al., 1972; Maas et al., 1972) have demonstrated an association between D-AMPH response, subsequent DMI response, and low pretreatment MHPG urinary excretion, which increased with clinical improvement, suggesting a relationship between altered noradrenergic function and D-AMPH-DMI response; this requires further investigation. Pharmacological data indicate D-AMPH, methylphenidate, and TCA affect brain PEA levels (Fawcett, Sabelli, Javaid, Epstein, Maiorano, & Fawcett, 1981; Mosnaim, Inwang, & Sabelli, 1974; Spatz & Spatz, 1978), while our clinical studies show increased PEA and PAA excretion. We are currently studying the correlation between behavioral responses to the stimulants, urinary PAA excretion, and stimulant-induced change in PAA excretion, in order to attempt to discern the biochemical basis for the mood elevating effects of these stimulants. These effects may be related to PEA-like actions rather than CA release, which mediates other CNS actions of amphetamines (Fischer, Ludmer, & Sabelli, 1967; Sabelli, Borison, Diamond, Havdala, & Narasimhachari, 1978).

Attempts have been made to correlate the psychopharmacological response to these stimulants with various neuroendocrinological changes, especially in HPA and hypothalamic-pituitary-growth hormone systems, in order to clarify neurochemical disturbances occurring in depressive disorders. These challenge studies have been reviewed elsewhere and will not be described here (Risch, Kalin, & Murphy, 1982; Siever, Insel, & Uhde, 1982).

Attempts have also been made to correlate methylphenidate responsiveness and the DST (Brawley, 1979; P. Brown & Brawley, 1983; Sternbach, Gwirtzman, & Gerner, 1981). Significant negative correlations were found between the responses to the two tests; dexamethasone suppressors had a positive mood change, while nonsuppressors (cortisol hypersecretors) had negative stimulant responses in most cases. These responses are contrary to the hypothesis that DST nonsuppression indicates a central noradrenergic deficit state (Carroll, Feinberg, Greden, Tarika, Albala, Haskett, James, Kronfol, Lohr, Steiner, deVigne, & Young, 1981; Sachar, Asnis, Nathan, Halbreich, Tabrizi, & Halpern, 1980; Sachar, Halbreich, Asnis, Nathan, Halpern, & Ostrow, 1981) as methylphenidate responsiveness predicts TCA response to IMI-like antidepressants ("NE reuptake blockers"). In these studies, nonsuppressors were *negative* methylphenidate responders, but in support of Fawcett's original data (Fawcett et al., 1972; Fawcett & Siomopoulos, 1971; Maas et al., 1972) 16 of 17 methylphenidate responders improved significantly with IMI, while 23 of 24 nonresponders demonstrated a significant response to AMI. It was postulated (P. Brown & Brawley, 1983) that serotonergic mediation of cortisol hypersecretion may be the important underlying regulatory neuroamine mechanism. However, aside from the interrelationship between the stimulant challenge and DST response, it is important to note that the Stimulant Challenge Test itself did indicate future antidepressant responsiveness.

Ettigi and associates (Ettigi, Hayes, Narasimhachari, Hamer, Goldberg, & Secord, 1983) gave a DST and a stimulant challenge test to 18 unipolar depressives, and then treated them with DMI. They found that 10 of 13 amphetamine responders were DMI treatment responders while 2 of 5 amphetamine nonresponders were DMI nonresponders (no statistically significant difference between DMI responders and nonresponders based on the response to oral amphetamine). Importantly, however, overall the amphetamine test correctly predicted 67 percent (12 of 18) of the DMI treatment responses. These studies indicate the need for replication with double-blind stimulant administration as well as with standardized criteria for defining response and instruments for measuring stimulant response. As mentioned earlier, since methylphenidate may preferentially affect DA systems (and GH secretion) at the doses tested (W. A., Brown, 1977; W. A. Brown et al., 1978); future studies should also involve D-AMPH, which additionally affects cortisol secretion and noradrenergic systems. Thus, study of endocrine (cortisol, GH) response to stimulant challenge may be useful for objectifying the Stimulant Challenge Test for predicting antidepressant response.

Finally, there is the question of whether the stimulant challenge assesses state or trait responsiveness. In clinical practice we have found it valuable to obtain a detailed drug history from each patient, as we can predict responsiveness to TCA at a better-than-chance level just by determining which patients have abused stimulants under stressful situations or during dysphoric states with favorable improvement (lessening of dysphoric tension states, improved mood or relaxed and calm feelings). We have also noted a number of patients with a positive stimulant response who improved with IMI-like TCA during one depressive episode but demonstrated no stimulant response and instead improved with AMI-like TCA during a subsequent episode, as well as patients who have switched back and forth in pharmacological responsiveness. Thus the "state-trait" issue remains unresolved.

Summary and Conclusions

Current findings support the potential usefulness of the Stimulant Challenge Test as a simple, rapid, and safe procedure which may predict specific antidepressant response in individual patients as well as provide a tool for distinguishing between biochemically heterogenous depressions. This response may be either a biological trait marker or a state marker. Confirmation of this test is still required in a larger group of carefully diagnosed patients studied under standard double-blind conditions and employing more objective indexes of responsiveness, such as biochemical or endocrinological measures, as well as measures of mood and behavior. Extant behavioral ratings alone may be suboptimal, and partial responses are difficult to interpret. Further confirmation of response requires antidepressant blood level monitoring, to be sure a therapeutic medication dose was prescribed in order to confirm or refute the ability to prognosticate clinical course. Correlation with other diagnostic and biochemical procedures such as we have described in this chapter may help us develop a battery of diagnostic techniques to enhance our diagnostic skills and provide indications for various treatment modalities. We also need to clarify state versus trait issues, including intraindividual changes in response to a stimulant challenge occurring over time and at different stages of a depressive episode. This may reflect covariance in the dynamic state of other biological as well as clinical features.

LITHIUM TRANSPORT

Early studies suggested that certain forms of depressive illness were associated with electrolyte shift across neuronal membranes, such as increase in intracellular sodium and altered calcium excretion (Coppen, 1972). However, investigation was limited by the techniques available for in vivo study. More recent study has uncovered another potential "marker" with possible clinical relevance, lithium transport. It has been demonstrated that while the red blood cell (RBC)/plasma lithium concentration (Li^+ ratio) is relatively constant over time for each individual (Mendels & Frazer, 1973; Trevisan, Ostrow, Cooper, Liu, Sparks, & Stamler, 1981), there is substantial interindividual variability in this ratio, determined by variability in the phloretin-sensitive Li^+-Na^+ counterflow (Li^+ efflux) (Ostrow, Pandey, Davis, Hurt, & Tosteson, 1978). The RBC Li^+ ion concentration is usually approximately one third that of the plasma concentration under steady state conditions (Mendels & Frazer, 1973). Since the report of a Li^+-Na^+ ion countertransport in human RBCs by Haas and associates (Haas, Schooler, & Tosteson, 1975), various pathways for lithium transport in human RBC have been described (Bunney, Pert, Rosenblatt, Pert, & Gallaper, 1979; Ehrlich & Diamond, 1980; Pandey,

Dorus, Davis, & Tosteson, 1979; Pandey, Sarkadi, Haas, Gunn, Davis, & Tosteson, 1978). Ostrow and associates (1978) demonstrated that the in vivo Li^+ is determined by the dynamic balance between phloretin-sensitive Li^+-Na^+ counterflow and Li^+ leakage pathways, and that approximately 25 percent of the manic-depressive (but not controls, schizophrenics, or unipolar depressives) that they examined had a marked *reduction* in the countertransport mechanism mediated by Li^+-Na^+ exchange, which effects a $1:1$ exchange of Na and Li ions, resulting in markedly *increased* in vivo and in vitro Li^+ ratios. This defect is an intrinsic property of the RBC membrane. However, although the rate of Na-dependent Li^+ efflux and the Li^+ ratio correlates significantly with each other, other factors may be involved in determining the latter (Ostrow, Trevisan, Okonek, Gibbons, Cooper, & Davis, 1982). The interindividual variability of this Li^+ ratio is largely determined by variability in the counterflow mechanism. The specificity of these measurements may be affected by race and blood pressure (Canessa, Adragna, Solomon, Connolly, & Tosteson, 1980; Ostrow et al., 1982). Thus, the pre-lithium treatment counterflow may be predictive of the in vivo Li^+ ratio, and increased lithium ratios may be predictive of a clinical response to lithium treatment.

The potential genetic basis for this defect among bipolars in regards to its potential clinical application cannot be minimized, as the incidence of bipolar disease in first-degree relatives is 10 to 25 percent (Ehrlich & Diamond, 1980). In vivo and in vitro studies in control populations have demonstrated that genetic factors contribute to interindividual differences in this ratio (Dorus, Pandey, & Davis, 1975; Dorus, Pandey, Frazer, & Mendels, 1974). Subsequent study has indicated a significantly higher ratio in affectively ill first-degree relatives of manic-depressive probands independent of whether the ill relative had a unipolar or bipolar illness (Dorus, Pandey, Shaughnessy, Gaviria, Val, Ericksen, & Davis, 1979). A family history of schizophrenic illness was not found among subjects with low rates of Li^+ efflux (high Li^+ ratio), while low Li^+ efflux rates (high Li^+ ratio) correlated with familial forms of major affective disorders (Ostrow et al., 1982).

Dorus and associates (Dorus, Cox, Gibbons, Shaughnessy, Pandey, & Cloninger, 1983) have identified genetic polymorphism (i.e., the existence in the general population of different alleles at a particular gene locus) at a single autosomal gene locus which is involved in control of the lithium ion ratio and is associated with vulnerability to bipolar and related affective disorders. Thus, in relatives of bipolar patients, the same major gene locus is involved in genetic transmission both of the variability in the lithium ratio and of affective disorders. In normal families the genetic transmission of variability in the lithium ratio is determined by this genes locus, whose expression is modified by multifactorial variability. High lithium ratios have been found in normals, demonstrating that this finding may be associated with observable behavioral differences. A subgroup of normal women with high ratios was found to differ on personality scales from those with low ratios, suggesting the need for longitudinal studies to determine whether they eventually develop overt psychiatric illness (Dorus et al., 1983).

Although the results of ongoing studies and further investigations will be required to answer questions regarding diagnostic specificity and clinical utility, lithium transport studies give early indication of being an exciting new tool for investigating affective disorders. The lithium ratio appears to be a trait marker (totally independent of mood states, with exceptions noted in rapid cycling bipolars and women with premenstrual syndrome (Ostrow et al., 1982)), which may point out susceptible populations and indicate potential lithium responsiveness. Certainly these findings indicate the importance of obtaining a good family history as well as obtaining collateral history from family members in the diagnostic and pretreatment evaluation of any patient with a major psychiatric disorder.

NEUROPHYSIOLOGICAL STUDIES

Sleep Markers in Depression

Sleep is one of the neurovegetative functions which may become disturbed as a consequence of the limbic system-hypothalamic dysfunction which occurs in depressive disorders. Disturbed sleep as an accompaniment of depressive illness was described by Hippocrates. Years later, Freud became interested in dream content, which became an integral part of his psychoanalytic theory. Aserinksy and Kleitman (1953) and Dement and Kleitman (1957) electrophysiologically defined dreams as rapid eye movement (REM) sleep and opened the brain to neurophysiological study, allowing dreams to be studied from a biological perspective. Kupfer and Foster (1978), early investigators in this "modern era" of the use of the sleep laboratory in depressive illness, reviewed the pre-1976 literature of EEG sleep and depression beginning with the work of Diaz-Guerrero and associates (Diaz-Guerrero, Gottlieb, & Knott, 1946). Significant methodological difficulties limited the usefulness of the findings from all but 6 of 18 of these early studies of the sleep of the depressed (involving only 119 patients, excluding single case studies) (Kupfer & Foster, 1978). These problems included deficiencies in controls for drug-free status and concomitant physical illness, nonstandardized diagnostic criteria, and lack of standardized sleep laboratory protocols and scoring criteria.

Particularly notable findings which were replicated by Kupfer and his group (Coble, Gordon, & Kupfer, 1976; Foster, Kupfer, Coble, & McPartland, 1976; Kupfer, 1976) were shortening of the first REM latency (REML) to 60 minutes or less after sleep onset, and increased first REM density (REMD). REML is the number of minutes of sleep until the first REM period, normally 70 to 110 minutes after sleep onset; REMD is a measure of ocular activity per minute of REM sleep, and is thereby independent of the amount of time spent asleep and of the continuity of sleep. A third REM abnormality detected is the predominance of REM in the first half of the night (two thirds of REM time normally occurs in the second half) (Vogel, Vogel, McAbee, & Thurmond, 1980). This altered REM temporal distribution may represent a phase-advance of the circadian mechanism which controls REM sleep, and may suggest a mechanism for understanding these REM changes (see later). Actual REM time has not been demonstrated to significantly differ between drug-free depressives and controls (Gillin, Duncan, Pettigrew, Frankel, & Snyder, 1979), although the first REM period is often longer in depressives.

The REM sleep of the depressed can therefore be characterized as (1) too early (decreased REML), (2) too active (increased REMD), and (3) too long (associated with altered REM temporal distribution). These REM sleep alterations, especially the REML and REMD components, have emerged as the most prominent and specific polysomnographic findings associated with depressive disorders. The shortened first REML of the depressed patient has been the most replicated finding (Kupfer & Foster, 1972), and has been observed in various subtypes of endogenomorphic depression (Kupfer & Thase, 1983), including endogenous, melancholic, and autonomous; unipolar and bipolar; psychotic (delusional) and schizoaffective; but not neurotic or reactive depressions. Akiskal has reported this finding in "subaffective dysthymias" (Akiskal, 1983; Akiskal, Rosenthal, Haykal, Lemmi, Rosenthal, & Scott-Strauss, 1980) as well as in hypomanic individuals (Akiskal & Lemmi, 1982), though patients with manic disorders have been difficult to evaluate, for obvious reasons (Kupfer & Foster, 1975). In comparison with the normal range of REML, two independent groups (Coble, Kupfer, & Shaw, 1981; Schulz, Lund, Cordina, & Dirlich, 1979) reported a bimodal distribution in depressives of very short latencies (20 minutes or shorter) and short REML (40 to 60 minutes), with a trough between 20 and 40 minutes after sleep onset. The more severe depressives, especially inpatients, tended to have shorter REML (Reynolds, Newton, Shaw, Coble, & Kupfer, 1982; Spiker, Coble, Cofsky, Foster, Kupfer, 1979).

Using the shortened first REML and increased first REMD criteria, it has been possible to distinguish primary from secondary depressives (including depression associated with other psychiatric illness and secondary depressives with and without medical disorders) with 80–85 percent accuracy (by methods of discriminant analysis), and dementia from depressive pseudodementia, but not primary unipolar from bipolar depressives (Coble et al., 1976; Duncan, Pettigrew, & Gillin, 1979; Foster et al., 1976; King, Akiskal, Lemmi, Wilson, Belluomini, & Yerevanian, 1981; Kupfer, 1976; Kupfer, Foster, Coble, McPartland, & Ulrich, 1978; Reynolds, Spiker, Hanin, & Kupfer, 1983). Recently, Reynolds and associates (Reynolds, Shaw, Newton, Coble, & Kupfer, 1983) also separated primary depressives from those with generalized anxiety disorder by REML, REM percent, and REM activity measurements. Delusional depressives and schizoaffective depressives demonstrated more severe REM aberrations, as well as more impairment of sleep continuity, while unipolarity or bipolarity had no significant additional effect on these parameters (Kupfer, Broudy, Coble, & Spiker, 1980; Kupfer, Broudy, Spiker, Neil, & Coble, 1979).

Other more nonspecific changes involve the more general parameters of sleep architecture and non-REM (especially delta) sleep. Depressives are usually hyposomnic. Sleep is lighter (less stages 3 and 4, or delta, sleep) and continuity is disrupted (they take longer to fall asleep, have more nocturnal wakenings and stage shifts, and have early morning wakening). Overall, sleep is shorter, as reflected in reduced total sleep time and sleep efficiency. On the other hand, about 15 to 20 percent of depressives, usually (but not always) bipolars, are hypersomnic (Detre, Himmelhoch, Swartzburg, Anderson, Byck, & Kupfer, 1972; Kupfer, Himmelhoch, Swartzburg, Anderson, Byck, & Detre, 1972; Reynolds, Coble, Kupfer, & Shaw, 1982); it is important to distinguish this from fatigue due to insomnia or hyposomnia, which results in poor sleep even during attempts to nap during the day (Kupfer, Gillin, Coble, Spiker, Shaw, & Holzer, 1981).

Carroll (1980) and Kupfer and Thase (1983) reviewed a number of polysomnographic studies of depressives published since 1977 (Akiskal, Lemmi, Yerevanian, King, & Belluomini, 1982; Feinberg, Gillin, Carroll, Greden, & Zis, 1982; Fink, Foster, Kupfer, & Spiker, 1977; Gillin et al., 1979; Kupfer, Foster, Coble, McPartland, & Ulrich, 1978; Reynolds, Shaw, Newton, Coble, & Kupfer, 1983; Reynolds, Spiker, Hanin, & Kupfer, 1983; Rush, Giles, Roffwarg, & Parker, 1982) to assess the diagnostic accuracy (number of true positives correctly identified divided by the total number of abnormal test results) of the procedure. Sensitivity ranged from 61 to 90 percent and specificity from 74 to 100 percent, with an overall diagnostic confidence ranging from 78 to 100 percent for REML and REM activity (density) data for primary, endogenous, or melancholic depressives. In this regard it compares quite favorably with, and actually is more sensitive than, the DST (Feinberg, Gillin, Carroll, Greden, & Zis, 1981; Rush, et al., 1982; Rush, Roffwarg, Giles, & Parker, 1981), and the sequential use of these two tests may enhance the potential for diagnosing endogenous depressions, with a high degree of specificity and sensitivity. However, once again methodological differences hamper further comparisons of data. Differences in diagnostic criteria and lack of standardization (definitions and criterion values) of polysomnographic indexes, especially REML (Knowles, MacLean, & Cairns, 1982b) continue to provide sources of variance.

There have also been questions about the importance of an adaptational, or first-night effect (Coble, McPartland, Silva, & Kupfer, 1974; Kupfer, Weiss, Detre, & Foster, 1974; Mendels & Hawkins, 1976b). Reynolds, Shaw, et al., (1983), comparing patients with primary depressive and generalized anxiety disorders, observed that the anxious patients showed few significant changes between the first and second nights, while the depressives showed increases in several REM measurements except for REML, which was stable in both groups. Though it may not always be a confounding factor, two or three study nights are usually performed for research purposes. However, because of practical and financial considerations only one night is performed for clinical purposes at some centers.

Despite these reports, the specificity of these REM-related changes for affective disorders, particularly depression, have been questioned. A number of polysomnographic changes, especially REML and sleep continuity, accompany aging (Gillin, Duncan, Murphy, Post, Wehr, Goodwin, Wyatt, & Bunney,

1981; Reynolds, Spiker, et al., 1983; Ulrich, Shaw, & Kupfer, 1980) as well as medical and neurological disorders (Freeman, 1978; Tamura & Karacan, 1981; Williams, 1978). Other causes of the more specific finding of decreased REML include narcolepsy and acute withdrawal from REM-suppressing drugs, which includes most psychoactive drugs. Alternatively, current psychotropic drug use, especially antidepressants, suppress REM and preclude polysomnographic measurement of REM parameters. Thus, a two-week drug "washout" is required. Other sleep disorders associated with hypersomnolence (e.g., sleep apnea) and disorders of the sleep-wake cycle (e.g., shift work, sleep and/or REM deprivation, and circadian rhythm disturbances) may be associated with a shortened first REML. Although a reduced REML is generally not found in normal controls or insomniacs (Gillin et al., 1979), schizophrenics (Mendelson, Gillin, & Wyatt, 1977), or transient dysphoric states in normal subjects (Cohen, 1979), it has been reported in individuals with stress-related (Cartwright, 1983; Greenberg, Perlman, & Gampel, 1972) and obsessive-compulsive disorders (Insel, Gillin, Moore, Mendelson, Loewenstein, & Murphy, 1982). The applicability of these findings to the studies of depressed children is currently being studied (Puig-Antich, Goetz, Hanlon, Davies, Thompson, Chambers, Tabrizi, & Wcitzman, 1982; Puig-Antich, Goetz, Hanlon, Tabrizi, Davies, & Weitzman, 1983; Young, Knowles, MacLean, Boag, & McConville, 1982).

The evidence presented here, as well as a large body of data we have not cited due to space considerations, indicate that these REM-related sleep findings in depressives represent state-dependent psychobiologic markers. Still unclear and as yet unresolved is the question of whether these measures are also trait markers associated with a genetic predispostion to the development of depressive disorders. Longitudinal studies of patients (especially drug-free) as well as studies of asymptomatic first-degree relatives of depressive probands are required to determine whether abnormal REML or REMD exists to the manifestation of overt depressive illness (indicating a risk factor), and/or whether these markers continue into remission (indicating a vulnerability or susceptibility to recrudescence). Particularly important in these studies would be the definition of "recovered" or "asymptomatic," and their measurements.

The little data available is inconclusive (Avery, Wildschiodtz, & Rafaelsen, 1982; Cartwright, 1983; Hauri, Chernick, Hawkins, & Mendels, 1974; Hauri & Hawkins, 1971; Knowles, Cairns, Waldron, Delva, Letemendia, & MacLean, 1980; Kupfer, 1982b; Kupfer, & Foster, 1972, 1973; Mendels & Chernick, 1972, 1975; Mendels & Hawkins, 1967a; Schulz & Trojan, 1979), but suggests that for some individuals this marker has potential as an indicator of trait-related vulnerability. Another possibility is that normalization of this biological indicator of depression lags behind clinical improvement. Untreated, these sleep measures may be quite persistent (Coble, Kupfer, Spiker, Neil, & McPartland, 1979). Kupfer and associates (Kupfer, Targ, & Stack, 1982) found no difference in baseline sleep measures or clinical response to AMI between familial pure depressive disorders and sporadic depressive disorders (Winokur,

1974), but a 50 mg challenge dose of AMI following two drug-free weeks produced a significantly greater degree of immediate REM suppression in the familial group.

Changes in REM parameters, particularly decreased REM percent and prolongation of the first REML, following a two-day test dose of an antidepressant may predict subsequent treatment response to a course of antidepressant treatment (Gillin, Wyatt, Fram, & Snyder, 1978; Kupfer, 1982a; Kupfer, Foster, Reich, Thompson, & Weiss, 1976; Kupfer, Spiker, Coble, Neil, Ulrich, & Shaw, 1980, 1981; Svendsen & Christensen, 1981). Delusional depressives with markedly shortened REML as well as atypical depressives and a group of major depressives with normal or long first REML seem to be particularly resistant to the REM-suppressing effects of TCA, and respond poorly to subsequent treatment (Akiskal, 1982; Kupfer, Spiker, Rossi, Coble, Ulrich, & Shaw, 1983; Quitkin, Schwartz, Liebowitz, McGrath, Halpern, Puig-Antich, Tricamo, Sachar, & Klein, 1982). The clinical significance of this information is obviously to minimize the amount of time spent awaiting a treatment response which is destined not to be forthcoming with a particular antidepressant.

Kupfer and associates (Kupfer, Hanin, Coble, Spiker, Sorisio, & Grau, 1982) studied the acute and chronic (one to two years) effects of AMI (plus NT) steady state plasma levels on sleep measures. Total TCA levels were significantly and consistently correlated with *continued suppression* of REM percent and REML. Thus, tolerance to the REM-suppressing effects of AMI did not develop during long-term treatment. This would seem to squelch any hypothesis that the efficacy of TCA are related to nonspecific sedative effects of antidepressants on the symptom of insomnia. Further, it points to a potential psychobiologic relationship between sleep, depression, neurotransmitters, and drug therapy, and provides a rationale for applying this biologic measure to subtype depressions on the basis of drug responsiveness.

More interesting is the fact that there appears to be a differential effect of TCA on REML and REMD. REML, a tonic component of REM, is prolonged and REM sleep time is consistently and persistently reduced by TCA, while REMD and activity, phasic components of REM sleep, are only transiently decreased, and thus demonstrate more tolerance to the drug effect (Kupfer, Spiker, Coble, & McPartland, 1978; Kupfer, Spiker, Rossi, Coble, Shaw, & Ulrich, 1982). This then may suggest potential state and trait markers of depression: the REML (tonic component) indicates present state, and may either remain short with incomplete treatment or become short once again despite continued therapy if a relapse supervenes, while increased REMD (phasic component) indicates continued vulnerability in the proband or susceptibility in an unaffected family member (Cartwright, 1983).

Vogel postulated that the antidepressant effect of pharmacotherapy and of selective REM sleep deprivation (SRSD) is related to their REM suppressant property, and that antidepressant drugs may be identified by their capacity for producing large and sustained REM sleep reduction (Vogel, 1981; Vogel et al., 1980; Vogel, Thurmond, Gibbons, Sloan, Boyd, & Walker, 1975). (Lack of this effect on REM may explain the relatively short-lived efficacy of ECT.) Further, the abnormal temporal distribution of REM was normalized by the REM suppressant effect of both REM suppressing treatments. SRSD produced a delay in REM on the first recovery night; REM was *temporally* inhibited in the first half of the night and increased in the second half ("REM rebound") (Vogel et al., 1980). This degree of subsequent "REM pressure" which develops following REM deprivation may be an indicator of the potential antidepressant efficacy of REM suppression (Vogel, McAbee, Barker, & Thurmond, 1977). However, these findings require replication.

These REM findings implicate a dysfunctional sleep cycle "oscillator," leading to a circadian rhythm disturbance in depression. Wehr and Goodwin (1981) have suggested a "phase-advance" chronobiological model to account for the change in the REM temporal distribution and the shortened first REML. In other words, physiological, biochemical, and endocrinological changes which normally occur as a function of time of day have been shifted earlier relative to the external clock time, and REM changes occur concomitantly. Treatment with either partial sleep deprivation during the second half of the night, SRSD, or total sleep deprivation results in (transient) depressive remission (Gillin, 1983). Wehr and associates (Wehr, Wirz-Justice, Goodwin, Duncan, & Gillin, 1979) demonstrated that a six-hour phase advance of sleep could induce clinical remission, similar to the effect of antidepressant pharmacotherapy, and speculated that this occurs by preventing sleep during a critical sleep-sensitive phase of the circadian temperature rhythm. Clinically, switches into and out of depression tend to occur in the early morning, near this critical phase (Wehr & Goodwin, 1981). They described a similar phase advance in MHPG excretion, body temperature, and motor activity (Wehr, Muscettola, & Goodwin, 1980) in 10 bipolar patients. Jarrett and associates (Jarrett, Coble, & Kupfer, 1983) described cortisol hypersecretion with a nocturnal rise significantly closer to sleep onset, which is also associated with a decreased REML (Asnis, Halbreich, Sachar, Nathan, Ostrow, Novacenko, Davis, Endicott, & Puig-Antich, 1983; Jarrett et al., 1983). Nasrallah and associates (Nasrallah & Coryell, 1982; Nasrallah, Kuperman, & Coryell, 1980) reported that DST nonsuppression predicted an antidepressant response to sleep deprivation, with subsequent suppression on retest, but they only obtained 8 A.M. cortisol levels. Alteration in processes governing nonREM sleep may also be involved (Knowles, MacLean, & Cairns, 1982a).

Neurophysiological and neurochemical data gleaned from polysomnographic studies of normal and depressed subjects have led to the development of other techniques to study neurotransmitter changes underlying normal sleep as well as to better understand changes in neuroamines and their receptors occurring in affective illness. Sitaram and associates (Sitaram, Wyatt, Dawson, & Gillin, 1976) demonstrated the effect of the centrally active anticholinesterase agent physostigmine in reducing REML, but it did not affect REM length, REMD, or nonREM sleep. To further test the hypothesis of cholinergic (muscarinic) receptor supersensitivity in affective illness, Sitaram and coworkers developed the "cholinergic REM-induction test" (Sitaram,

Nurnberger, Gershon, & Gillin, 1980, 1982). An intravenous infusion of arecholine (a direct muscarinic agonist) given 25 minutes after the end of the first REM period resulted in a shortening of the second REML. This induction of the REML occurred significantly more rapidly in a group of remitted bipolar patients as well as in a group of volunteers with a history of affective disorder in themselves or in first-degree relatives, as compared with normal controls. Scopolamine, a centrally active cholinergic muscarinic receptor antagonist, blocked this effect (Sitaram, Moore, & Gillin, 1978). A third manipulation of the cholinergic system involved the morning injection of scopolamine into normal subjects (Sitaram & Gillin, 1980). Interruption of cholinergic transmission lasts about six hours and wears off by bedtime. After three consecutive mornings of scopolamine injections, cholinergic supersensitivity resulted, and decreased first REML and increased REMD developed. Further comment should be made of the findings of the increased first REMD, which differentiated the remitted drug-free patients from normal controls. This suggests that the cholinergic supersensitivity is more than a state marker; it may be a persistent trait marker uncovered through sleep EEG studies.

Taken together, these findings provide support for an adrenergic (or serotonergic)-cholinergic balance in the modulation of affect (Janowsky et al., 1972), and further evidence against the "one neurotransmitter-one disease" hypotheses of manic-depressive illness. The relative dominance of one of these neurotransmitter systems may play an etiopathogenetic role in these disorders. Thus, a disturbance of the homeostatic regulation of the central autonomic nervous system may tip the balance toward affective illness. The "reciprocal inhibition" model of the REM-nonREM sleep cycle (McCarley, 1982) is congruent with Sitaram and Gillin's findings. Alterations in REML and REMD appear to be related to cholinergic-monoaminergic imbalance. This also may provide some understanding of why anticholinergic agents alone do not relieve depression. Obviously, more than one neurotransmitter system is involved. Further, the role of altered receptor sensitivities needs to be further evaluated with other pharmacological challenges.

To summarize, clearly there are practical and research roles for the sleep laboratory in affective illness. Its present drawbacks are the need for a drug-free state for at least two weeks, the requirement of two nights of evaluation (and the accompanying financial considerations), and the need to further standardize criterion values and measurements. Generally, patients are quite accepting of the procedure and it provides useful information for diagnostic and treatment applications. Of equal importance is its use as a research tool to further delineate the biological underpinnings of affective illness, especially as both state (REML) and trait (REMD) markers have been identified. Further investigation needs to be undertaken to determine its specificity, especially in regard to its ability to distinguish depression from stress reactions, as well as to determine the role of polysomnographic studies as part of a "depressive battery" and its hierarchical status in sequential laboratory testing.

OTHER ELECTROPHYSIOLOGICAL AND NEURORADIOLOGIC STUDIES

Brain Imaging: A Glimpse at Things to Come

Advances in electrophysiological, radiological, and computer technology have led to newer brain-imaging procedures with potential applications in the evaluation of the "functional" disorders of the brain, psychiatric disorders. Up until now, the procedures described have provided at best only indirect measurement of neurochemical and neurophysiological activity in the CNS, either via assays of body fluids or analysis of the effect(s) of pharmacological agents on biobehavioral indexes. Electroencephalographic data (including polysomnographic recordings) alone only give indication of patterns of electrical and cortical activity in the brain arising spontaneously and in response to various stimuli. Conventional brain imaging techniques, such as cerebral angiography and radioisotope brain scans, provide images of the brain but demonstrate limited capability to correlate actual function with structure. These techniques are not adept at allowing study of discrete areas with any significant degree of specificity.

The first major advance in safe and noninvasive imaging of the brain was computerized axial tomography ([CT scans]; Pearlson, Veroff, & McHugh, 1981; Rieder, Mann, Weinberger, Van Kammen, & Post, 1983). The CT scan is limited by its ability to discern structure alone, though at much greater resolution than previously existing radiographic procedures. The usefulness of CT scanning for diagnosing depressive illness has been limited.

With the newer techniques, involving elaborations of and advances over the older, we are moving toward the capability of quantifying activity within particular anatomic structures. For example, as conventional EEG provides no qualitative data and inconsistent quantitative data in psychiatric disorders, Shagass and coworkers (Shagass, Roemer, & Straumanis, 1982) have utilized a computational model (amplitude time series analysis) to classify various diagnostic groups according to level of EEG activation. Average evoked response, a pattern of electrical manifestations of the brain in response to various external sensory stimuli (auditory, visual, somatosensory) of increasing intensity (Chiappa & Ropper, 1982), may distinguish bipolar and unipolar depressives (Buchsbaum, Landau, Murphy, & Goodwin, 1973) by detecting alterations in reactivity to external stimulation. These evoked potentials are extracted from background activity by computer signal averaging, and represent another advance of EEG and electrophysiological technology.

Newer computerized spectral analysis techniques have allowed EEG data segments and evoked potentials to be mapped, thus allowing EEG and evoked potentials to become imaging instruments. A further extension of this topographic approach is brain electrical activity mapping ([BEAM]; Duffy, Bartels, & Burchfiel, 1981; Duffy, Burchfiel, & Lombroso, 1979), which maps EEG and evoked potential data as two-dimensional colored images. Thus, differences in both quantitative and topographic EEG frequency distributions may enhance and refine our ability to classify psychiatric disorders as well as observe "normalization" of responses with various therapeutic modalities.

Newer advances allow us to do more than just visualize the brain (i.e., structure); metabolic measures provide us with a more direct in vivo indicator of regional brain activity (i.e., function) while subjects respond to stimulations both from the surrounding environment as well as from within (e.g., hallucinations). Present emphasis is on the three-dimensional quantitative measurements of biological activities (biochemical and physiological function) in the brain through noninvasive procedures involving less radiation exposure. The most recently introduced techniques are positron emission (transaxial) tomography (PETT, or PET scan) and nuclear magnetic resonance imaging ([NMR]; Brownell, Budinger, Lauterbur, & McGreer, 1982; James, Price, Rollo, Patton, Erickson, Coulam, & Partain, 1982). The potential applicability of these procedures to the study of affective disorders remains to be determined.

Once again, the questions of trait versus state changes as well as clinical applicability are raised. The tools to answer the questions, and our ability to understand and integrate the information, are being developed relatively rapidly, as seen over the past decade. These technological wonders have not yet reached the status of routine clinical tests or part of routine diagnostic batteries. In some ways, our technology to develop new instruments is more advanced than our ability to take full advantage of them. In the future, they may aid our understanding of the basic mechanisms of depression.

The brain remains one of the last frontiers, but with our new tools we are becoming more confident explorers. The most exciting aspect is the potential to study the human functioning brain in vivo. This may certainly give us new insights into the underpinnings of the biologically and phenomenologically heterogenous groups of psychiatric disorders, or as we have been concerned with here, the depressive disorders. Imagine the benefits of nonhazardous, noninvasive techniques to study the brain and to help us understand why suicide is the best alternative some of our patients can choose, or how our antidepressants really work.

CONCLUSIONS

We think it is clear from the data presented here that psychiatry, far from being a stagnant and passé field, whose eulogies are being written, is at the forefront of leading a multidisciplinary approach to solve the many mysteries of what has been called the "myth of mental illness." Depressive illness, to its sufferers, is far from a myth. New medical techniques will increasingly aid the clinician in the diagnosis and prediction of treatment and provide new and more sophisticated probing techniques for the researcher. Our new technology has led to the creation of a "new breed," the "psychobiologist," a clinical investigator who is able to integrate psychosocial data and clinical phenomenology with the technology of biomedicine.

In the beginning, measures of biogenic amines, the neurotransmitters and neuromodulators of the brain, were explored as an adjunctive diagnostic tool. With increased awareness of the contribution from other metabolic systems, neuroendocrine data was integrated into evaluation procedures. Currently, the DST and TRH stimulation tests appear to provide the most useful information for subtyping depressives, but lack of conclusive evidence about specificity for depression, as well as possibly limited sensitivity may restrict their use. They do not provide the whole answer. Further, specific questions relating to prediction of treatment response remain unanswered. The use of pharmacological probes, such as the Stimulant Challenge Test, may further enhance our ability to predict treatment response as well as study particular neurotransmitter systems. (This includes evaluation of the endogenous opioid system, not covered in this chapter.) The more recent advances may provide more direct information about structure and function of the brain. These include visual imaging techniques, as well as the electrophysiological study of sleep and study of circardian rhythms.

Though much clinical investigation still needs to be done, some recommendations can be offered. Clinically, the most readily available tests are the DST and TRH stimulation test. If test results are inconclusive, polysomnographic studies, if available, would be the next most valuable in aiding diagnosis. In centers where available, and if the patient has been unmedicated for two weeks, sleep studies may be the study of choice. The Stimulant Challenge Test is recommended for predicting treatment response. The Stimulant Challenge Test is readily adaptable to outpatient use, and in fact we frequently use this test and bypass the others in the clinical management of our outpatients. The clinician is advised to use these techniques carefully in conjunction with good clinical history taking and diagnostic skills.

References

Agren, H. (1982). Depressive symptom patterns and urinary MHPG excretion. *Psychiatry Research, 6,* 185–196.

Akiskal, H. S. (1982). Factors associated with incomplete recovery in primary depressive illness. *Journal of Clinical Psychiatry, 43,* 255–271.

Akiskal, H. S. (1983). Dysthymic disorders: Psychopathology of proposed chronic depressive subtypes. *American Journal of Psychiatry, 140,* 11–20.

Akiskal, H. S., & Lemmi, H. (1982). Hypomanic personality: Clinical and sleep EEG study. In *New Research Abstracts of the 135th Annual Meeting of the American Psychiatric Association.* Toronto, Canada.

Akiskal, H. S., Lemmi, H., Yerevanian, B., King, D., & Belluomini, J. (1982). The utility of the REM latency tests in psychiatric diagnosis: A study of 81 depressed outpatients. *Psychiatry Research, 7,* 101–110.

Akiskal, H. S., Rosenthal, T. L., Haykal, R. F., Lemmi, H., Rosenthal, R. H., & Scott-Strauss, A. (1980). Characterological depressions: Clinical and sleep EEG findings separating "subaffective dysthymias" from "character spectrum disorders." *Archives of General Psychiatry, 37,* 777–783.

Albala, A. A., Greden, J. F., Tarika, J., & Carroll, B. J. (1981). Changes in serial dexamethasone suppression tests among unipolar depressives receiving electroconvulsive treatment. *Biological Psychiatry, 16,* 551–560.

American Psychiatric Association. (1980). *Diagnostic and statistical manual of mental disorders* (3rd ed.). Washington, DC: Author.

Amsterdam, J. D., Winokur, A., Bryant, S., Larkin, J., & Rickels, K. (1983). The dexamethasone suppression test as a predictor of antidepressant response. *Psychopharmacology, 80,* 43–45.

Amsterdam, J. D., Winokur, A., Lucki, I., Caroff, S., Snyder, P., & Rickels, K. (1983). A neuroendocrine test battery in bipolar patients and healthy subjects. *Archives of General Psychiatry, 40,* 515–521.

Angrist, B., Rotrosen, J., & Gershon, S. (1980). Responses to apomorphine, amphetamine, and neuroleptics in schizophrenic subjects. *Psychopharmacology, 67,* 31–38.

Asberg, M., Bertilsson, L., Tuck, D., Cronholm, B., & Sjoqvist, F. (1973). Indoleamine metabolites in the cerebrospinal fluid of depressed patients before and during treatment with nortriptyline. *Clinical Pharmacology and Therapeutics, 14,* 277–286.

Asberg, M., Thoren, P., Traskman, L., Bertilsson, L., & Ringberger, V. (1976). "Serotonin depression"—A biochemical subgroup within the affective disorders? *Science, 191,* 478–480.

Asberg, M., Traskman, L., & Thoren, P. (1976). 5-HIAA in the cerebrospinal fluid: A biochemical suicide predictor? *Archives of General Psychiatry, 33,* 1193–1197.

Asberg, M., Varpila-Hannson, R., Tomba, P., Aminoff, A-K., Martensson, B., Thoren, P., Traskman-Bendz, L., Eneroth, P., & Astrom, G. (1981). Suicidal behavior and the dexamethasone suppression test. *American Journal of Psychiatry, 138,* 994–995.

Aserinsky, E., & Kleitman, N. (1953). Regularly occurring periods of eye motility, and concomitant phenomena during sleep. *Science, 118,* 273–274.

Asnis, G. M., Halbreich, U., Sachar, E. J., Nathan, R. S., Ostrow, L. C., Novacenko, H., Davis, M., Endicott, J., & Puig-Antich, J. (1983). Plasma cortisol secretion and REM period latency in adult endogenous depression. *American Journal of Psychiatry, 140,* 750–753.

Avery, D., Wildshiodtz, G., & Rafaelsen, O. (1982). REM latency and temperature in affective disorder before and after treatment. *Biological Psychiatry, 17,* 463–470.

Axelrod, J., Kopin, I. J., & Mann, J. D. (1959). 3-methoxy-4-hydroxyphenylglycol sulfate: A new metabolite of epinephrine and norepinephrine. *Biochimica et Biophysica Acta, 36,* 576–577.

Baldessarini, R. J. (1975). The basis for amine hypotheses in affective disorders: A critical evaluation. *Archives of General Psychiatry, 32,* 1087–1093.

Baldessarini, R. J. (1983). *Biomedical aspects of depression and its treatment.* Washington, DC: American Psychiatric Press.

Beck-Friis, J., Aperia, B., Kjellman, B., Ljunggren, J. G., Petterson, U., Sara, V., Sjolin, A., Unden, F., & Wetterberg, L. (1981). Suicidal behavior and the dexamethasone suppression test. *American Journal of Psychiatry, 138,* 993–994.

Beckmann, H., & Goodwin, F. K. (1975). Antidepressant response to tricyclics and urinary MHPG in unipolar patients: Clinical response to imipramine or amitriptyline. *Archives of General Psychiatry, 32,* 17–21.

Beckmann, H., & Goodwin, F. K. (1980). Urinary MHPG in subgroups of depressed patients and normal controls. *Neuropsychobiology, 6,* 91–100.

Beckmann, H., & Murphy, D. L. (1977). Phenelzine in depressed patients: Effects on urinary MHPG excretion in relation to clinical response. *Neuropsychobiology 3,* 49–55.

Beckmann, H., St. Laurent, J., & Goodwin, F. K. (1975). The effect of lithium on urinary MHPG in unipolar and bipolar depressed patients. *Psychopharmacologia, 42,* 277–282.

Berger, P. A., Faull, K. F., Kilkowski, J., Anderson, P. J., Kraemer, H., Davis, K. L., & Barchas, J. D. (1980). CSF monoamine metabolites in depression and schizophrenia. *American Journal of Psychiatry, 137,* 174–180.

Bertilsson, L., Asberg, M., & Thoren, P. (1974). Differential effect of chlorimipramine and nortriptyline on cerebrospinal fluid metabolites of serotonin and noradrenalin in depression. *European Journal of Clinical Pharmacology, 7,* 365–368.

Bivens, C. H., Lebovitz, H. E., & Feldman, J. M. (1973). Inhibition of hypoglycemia-induced growth hormone secretion by the serotonin antagonists cyproheptadine and methysergide. *New England Journal of Medicine, 289,* 236–239.

Blackard, W. G., & Heidingsfelder, S. A. (1968). Adrenergic receptor control mechanism for growth hormone secretion. *Journal of Clinical Investigation, 47,* 1407–1414.

Blombery, P. A., Kopin, I. J., Gordon, E. K., Markey, S. P., & Ebert, M. H. (1980). Conversion of MHPG to vanillylmandelic acid. *Archives of General Psychiatry, 37,* 1095–1098.

Borison, R. L., Mosnaim, A. D., & Sabelli, H. C. (1974). Biosynthesis of brain 2-phenylethylamine: Influence of decarboxylase inhibitors and D-amphetamine. *Life Sciences, 15,* 1837–1848.

Borison, R. L., Mosnaim, A. D., & Sabelli, H. C. (1975). Brain 2-phenylethylamine as a mediator for the central actions of amphetamine and methylphenidate. *Life Sciences, 17,* 1331–1344.

Borison, R. L., Sabelli, H. C., & Ho, B. (1975). Influence of a peripheral monoamine oxidase inhibitor (MAOI) upon the central nervous system levels and pharmacological effects of 2-phenylethylamine (PEA). *Pharmacologist, 17,* 258.

Boulton, B. A., Dyck, L. E., & Durden, D. A. (1974). Hydroxylation of B-phenylethylamine in the rat. *Life Sciences, 15,* 1673–1683.

Bowers, M. B. (1974a). Amitriptyline in man: Decreased formation of central 5-hydroxyindole-acetic acid. *Clinical Pharmacology and Therapeutics, 15,* 167–170.

Bowers, M. B. (1974b). Lumbar CSF 5-hydroxyindoleacetic acid and homovanillic acid in affective syndromes. *The Journal of Nervous and Mental Disease, 158,* 325–330.

Boyar, R. (1978). Sleep-related endocrine rhythms. In S. Reichlin, R. Baldessarini, & J. Martin (Eds.), *The hypothalamus.* New York: Raven Press.

Brawley, P. (1979). Dexamethasone, methylphenidate, and depression. In *Abstracts of the Scientific Proceedings of the 132nd Annual Meeting of the American Psychiatric Association.* Washington, DC: American Psychiatric Association.

Brown, G. M., & Reichlin, S. (1972). Psychologic and neural regulation of growth hormone secretion. *Psychosomatic Medicine, 34,* 45–61.

Brown, G. M., Seggie, J. H., Chambers, J. W., & Ettigi, P. G. (1978). Psychoendocrinology and growth hormone: A review. *Psychoneuroendocrinology, 3,* 131–153.

Brown, P., & Brawley, P. (1983). Dexamethasone suppression test and mood response to methylphenidate in primary depression. *American Journal of Psychiatry, 140,* 990–993.

Brown, W. A. (1977). Psychologic and neuroendocrine response to methylphenidate. *Archives of General Psychiatry, 34,* 1103–1108.

Brown, W. A. (1980). Studies of response to dexamethasone in psychiatric patients. *Psychopharmacology Bulletin, 16,* 44–45.

Brown, W. A., Corriveau, D. P., & Ebert, M. H. (1978). Acute psychologic and neuroendocrine effects of dextroamphetamine and methylphenidate. *Psychopharmacology, 58,* 189–199.

Brown, W. A., Haier, R. J., & Qualls, C. B. (1980). Dexamethasone suppression test identifies subtypes of depression which respond to different antidepressants. *Lancet, 1,* 928–929.

Brown, W. A., Haier, R. J., & Qualls, C. B. (1981). The dexamethasone suppression test in the identification (of) subtypes of depression differentially responsive to antidepressants. *Psychopharmacology Bulletin, 17,* 88–89.

Brown, W. A., Johnston, R., & Mayfield, D. (1979). The 24-hour dexamethasone suppression test in a clinical setting: Relationship to diagnosis, symptoms, and response to treatment. *American Journal of Psychiatry, 136,* 543–547.

Brown, W. A., & Williams, B. W. (1976). Methylphenidate increases serum growth hormone concentrations. *Journal of Clinical Endocrinology and Metabolism, 43,* 937–939.

Brownell, G. L., Budinger, T. F., Lauterbur, P. C., & McGeer, P. L. (1982). Positron tomography and nuclear magnetic resonance imaging. *Science, 215,* 619–626.

Buchsbaum, M., Landau, S., Murphy, D., & Goodwin, F. (1973). Average evoked response in bipolar and unipolar affective disorders: Relationship to sex, age of onset, and monoamine oxidase. *Biological Psychiatry, 7,* 199–212.

Bueno, J. R., Himwich, H. E. (1967). A dualistic approach to some biochemical problems in endogenous depression. *Psychosomatics, 8,* 82–94.

Bunney, W. E., & Davis, J. M. (1965). Norepinephrine in depressive reactions: A review. *Archives of General Psychiatry, 13,* 483–494.

Bunney, W. E., & Fawcett, J. A. (1965). Possibility of a biochemical test for suicide potential. An analysis of endocrine findings prior to three suicides. *Archives of General Psychiatry, 13,* 232–239.

Bunney, W. E., Pert, A., Rosenblatt, J., Pert, C. B., & Gallaper, D. (1979). Mode of action of lithium: Some biological considerations. *Archives of General Psychiatry, 36,* 898–901.

Butler, P. W. P., & Besser, G. M. (1968). Pituitary-adrenal function in severe depressive illness. *Lancet, 1,* 1234–1236.

Canessa, M., Adragna, N., Solomon, H. S., Connolly, T. M., & Tosteson, D. C. (1980). Increased sodium-lithium countertransport in red cells of patients with essential hypertension. *New England Journal of Medicine, 302,* 772–776.

Carroll, B. J. (1969). Hypothalamic-pituitary function in depression illness: Insensitivity to hypoglycemia. *British Medical Journal, 3,* 27–28.

Carroll, B. J. (1972). The hypothalamic-pituitary-adrenal axis in depression. In B. Davis, B. J. Carroll, R. M. Mowbray (Eds.), *Depressive illness: Some research studies.* Springfield, IL: Charles C Thomas.

Carroll, B. J. (1976). Limbic system-adrenal cortex regulation in depression and schizophrenia. *Psychosomatic Medicine, 38,* 106–121.

Carroll, B. J. (1978). Neuroendocrine function in psychiatric disorders. In M. A. Lipton, A. DiMascio, & K. F. Killam (Eds.), *Psychopharmacology: A generation of progress.* New York: Raven Press.

Carroll, B. J. (1980). Implications of biological research for the diagnosis of depression. In J. Mendlewicz (Ed.), *New advances in the diagnosis and treatment of depressive illness.* Amsterdam, The Netherlands: Excerpta Medica.

Carroll, B. J. (1981). Clinical applications of the dexamethasone suppression test. *International Drug Therapy Newsletter, 16,* 1–4.

Carroll, B. J. (1982). The dexamethasone suppression test for melancholia. *British Journal of Psychiatry, 140,* 292–304.

Carroll, B. J., Curtis, G. C., & Mendels, J. (1976a). Neuroendocrine regulation in depression. I. Limbic system-adrenocortical dysfunction. *Archives of General Psychiatry, 33,* 1039–1044.

Carroll, B. J., Curtis, G. C., & Mendels, J. (1976b). Neuroregulation in depression. II. Discrimination of depressed from nondepressed patients. *Archives of General Psychiatry, 33,* 1051–1058.

Carroll, B. J., Feinberg, M., Greden, J. F., Haskett, R. F., James, N. McI., Steiner, M., & Tarika, J. (1980). Diagnosis of endogenous depression: Comparison of clinical, research and neuroendocrine criteria. *Journal of Affective Disorders, 2,* 177–194.

Carroll, B. J., Feinberg, M., Greden, J. F., Tarika, J., Albala, A. A., Haskett, R. F., James, N. McI., Kronfol, Z., Lohr, N., Steiner, M., deVigne, J. P., & Young, E. (1981). A specific laboratory test for the diagnosis of melancholia: Standardization, validation, and clinical utility. *Archives of General Psychiatry, 38,* 15–22.

Carroll, B. J., Greden, J. F., & Feinberg, M. (1981). Suicide, neuroendocrine dysfunction and CSF 5-HIAA concentration in depression. In B. Angrist, G. D. Burrows, & M. Lader (Eds.), *Recent advances in neuropsychopharmacology.* Elmsford, NY: Pergamon Press.

Carroll, B. J., Greden, J. F., Feinberg, M., James, N. McI., Haskett, R. F., Steiner, J., & Tarika, J. (1980). Neuroendocrine dysfunction in genetic subtypes of primary unipolar depression. *Psychiatry Research, 2,* 251–258.

Carroll, B. J., Greden, J. F., Haskett, R., Feinberg, M., Albala, A. A., Martin, F. I. R., Rubin, R. T., Heath, B., Sharp, P. T., McLeod, W. L., & McLeod, M. F. (1980). Neurotransmitter studies of neuroendocrine pathology in depression. *Acta Psychiatrica Scandinavica, 61* (Suppl. 280), 183–199.

Carroll, B. J., Martin, F. I. R., & Davies, B. (1968). Resistance to suppression by dexamethasone of plasma 11-OHCS levels in severe depressive illness. *British Medical Journal, 3,* 285–287.

Carroll, B. J., & Mendels, J. (1976). Neuroendocrine regulation in affective disorders. In E. J. Sacher (Ed.), *Hormones, behavior, and psychopathology.* New York: Raven Press.

Cartwright, R. D. (1983). Rapid eye movement sleep characteristics during and after mood-disturbing events. *Archives of General Psychiatry, 40,* 197–201.

Casper, R. C., Davis, J. M., Pandey, G. N., Garver, D. L., & Dekirmenjian, H. (1977). Neuroendocrine and amine studies in affective illness. *Psychneuroendocrinology, 1,* 105–113.

Charney, D. S., Heninger, G. R., Sternberg, D. E., Redmond, D. E., Leckman, J. F., Maas, J. W., & Roth, R. W. (1981). Presynaptic adrenergic-receptor sensitivity in depression: The effect of long-term desipramine treatment. *Archives of General Psychiatry, 38,* 1334–1340.

Charney, D. S., Heninger, G. R., Sternberg, D. E., & Roth, R. H. (1981). Plasma MHPG in depression: Effects of acute and chronic desipramine treatment. *Psychiatry Research, 5,* 217–229.

Charney, D. S., Menkes, D. B., & Heninger, G. R. (1981). Receptor sensitivity and the mechanism of action of antidepressant treatment: Implications for the etiology and therapy of depression. *Archives of General Psychiatry, 38,* 1160–1180.

Checkley, S. A. (1978). A new distinction between the euphoric and the antidepressant effects of methylamphetamine. *British Journal of Psychiatry, 133,* 416–423.

Checkley, S. A. (1979). Corticosteroid and growth hormone responses to methylamphetamine in depressive illness. *Psychological Medicine, 9,* 107–115.

Checkley, S. A. (1980). Neuroendocrine tests of monoamine function in man: A review of basic theory and its application to the study of depressive illness. *Psychological Medicine, 10,* 35–53.

Checkley, S. A., & Crammer, J. L. (1977). Hormone response to methylamphetamine in depression: A new approach to the noradrenaline depletion hypothesis. *British Journal of Psychiatry, 131,* 582–586.

Checkley, S. A., Slade, A. P., & Shur, E. (1981). Growth hormone and other responses to clonidine in patients with endogenous depression. *British Journal of Psychiatry, 138,* 51–55.

Checkley, S. A., Slade, A. P., Shur, E., & Dawling, S. (1981). A pilot study of the mechanism of action of desipramine. *British Journal of Psychiatry, 138,* 248–251.

Chiappa, K. H., & Ropper, A. H. (1982). Evoked potentials in clinical medicine. *New England Journal of Medicine, 306,* 1140–1150, 1205–1211.

Cobbin, D., Requin-Blow, B., Williams, L. R., & Williams, W. O. (1979). Urinary MHPG levels and tricyclic antidepressant selection. *Archives of General Psychiatry, 36,* 1111–1115.

Coble, P., Gordon, F. G., & Kupfer, D. J. (1976). Electroencephalographic sleep diagnosis of primary depression. *Archives of General Psychiatry, 33,* 1124–1127.

Coble, P. A., Kupfer, D. J., & Shaw, D. H. (1981). Distribution of REM latency in depression. *Biological Psychiatry, 16,* 453–466.

Coble, P. A., Kupfer, D. J., Spiker, D. G., Neil, J. F., & McPartland, R. J. (1979). EEG sleep in primary depression: A longitudinal placebo study. *Journal of Affective Disorders, 1,* 131–138.

Coble, P. A., McPartland, R. J., Silva, W. J., & Kupfer, D. J. (1974). Is there a first night effect? (A revisit). *Biological Psychiatry, 9,* 215–219.

Cohen, D. B. (1979). Dysphoric affect and REM sleep. *Journal of Abnormal Psychology, 88,* 73–77.

Coppen, A. (1967). The biochemistry of affective disorders. *British Journal of Psychiatry, 113,* 1237–1264.

Coppen, A. (1972). Mineral metabolism in affective disorders. *British Journal of Psychiatry, 111,* 1133–1142.

Coppen, A., Prange, A. J., Whybrow, P. C., & Noguera, R. (1972). Abnormalities of indoleamines in affective disorders. *Archives of General Psychiatry, 26,* 474–478.

Coppen, A., Rama Rao, V. A., Ruthven, C. R. J., Goodwin, B. L., & Sandler, M. (1979). Urinary 4-hydroxy-3-methoxyphenylglycol is not a predictor for clinical response to amitriptyline in depressive illness. *Psychopharmacology, 64,* 94–97.

Coppen, A., Shaw, D. M., & Malleson, A. (1965). Changes in 5-hydroxytryptophan metabolism in depression. *British Journal of Psychiatry, 111,* 105–107.

Coppen, A., Shaw, D. M., Malleson, A., Eccleston, E., & Grundy, G. (1965). Tryptamine metabolism in depression. *British Journal of Psychiatry, 111,* 993–998.

Costall, B., & Naylor, R. J. (1974). The involvement of dopaminergic systems with the stereotyped behavior patterns induced by methylphenidate. *Journal of Pharmacy and Pharmacology, 26,* 20–33.

Dale, H. H. (1935). Pharmacology and nerve endings. *Proceedings of the Royal Society of Medicine, 28,* 319–332.

Davis, B. M., Durden, D. A., & Boulton, A. A. (1982). Plasma concentrations of p- and m-hydroxyphenylacetic acid and phenylacetic acid in humans: Gas chromatographic-high resolution mass spectrometric analysis. *Journal of Chromatography, 230,* 219–230.

Davis, J. M. (1970). Theories of biological etiology of affective disorders. *International Review of Neurobiology, 12,* 145–175.

Davis, J. M. (1977). Central biogenic amines and theories of depression and mania. In W. E. Fann, I. Karacan, & A. D. Pokorny (Eds.), *Phenomenology and treatment of depression.* New York: Spectrum Publications.

Davis, K. L., Hollister, L. E., Mathe, A. A., Davis, B. M., Rothpearl, A. B., Faull, K. F., Hsieh, J. Y. K., Barchas, J. D., & Berger, P. A. (1981). Neuroendocrine and neurochemical measurements in depression. *American Journal of Psychiatry, 138,* 1555–1562.

Deffenu, G., Bartolini, A., & Pepeu, G. (1970). Effects of amphetamine on cholinergic systems of the cerebral cortex of the cat. In E. Costa & S. Garattini (Eds.), *Amphetamines and related compounds.* New York: Raven Press.

Dekirmenjian, H., & Maas, J. W. (1970). An improved procedure of 3-methyl-4-hydrophenylethylene glycol determined by gas-liquid chromatography. *Analytical Biochemistry, 35,* 113–122.

DeLeon-Jones, F. A. (1982). Biochemical aspects of affective disorders. In E. R. Val, F. M. Gaviria, & J. A. Flaherty (Eds.), *Affective disorders: Psychopathology and treatment.* Chicago: Year Book Medical Publishers.

DeLeon-Jones, F., Maas, J. W., & Dekirmenjian, H. (1975). Diagnostic subtypes of affective disorders and their urinary excretion of catecholamine metabolites. *American Journal of Psychiatry, 132,* 1141–1148.

Dement, W., & Kleitman, N. (1957). The relation of eye movements during sleep to dream activity: An objective method for the study of dreaming. *Journal of Experimental Psychology, 53,* 339–346.

Detre, T., Himmelhoch, J., Swartzburg, M., Anderson, C. M., Byck, R., & Kupfer, D. J. (1972). Hypersomnia and manic-depressive disease. *American Journal of Psychiatry, 128,* 1303–1305.

Diaz-Guerrero, R., Gottlieb, J. S., & Knott, J. R. (1946). The sleep of patients with manic-depressive psychosis, depressive type: An electroencephalographic study. *Psychosomatic Medicine, 8,* 399–404.

Dorus, E., Cox, N. J., Gibbons, R. D., Shaughnessy, R., Pandey, G. N., & Cloninger, C. R. (1983). Lithium ion transport and affective disorders within families of bipolar patients: Identification of a major gene locus. *Archives of General Psychiatry, 40,* 545–552.

Dorus, E., Pandey, G. N., & Davis, J. M. (1975). Genetic determinant of lithium ion distribution: An in vitro and in vivo monozygotic-dizygotic twin study. *Archives of General Psychiatry, 32,* 1097–1102.

Dorus, E., Pandey, G. N., Frazer, A., & Mendels, J. (1974). Genetic determinant of lithium ion distribution: I. An in vitro monozygotic-dizygotic twin study. *Archives of General Psychiatry, 31,* 463–465.

Dorus, E., Pandey, G. N., Shaughnessy, R., Gaviria, M., Val, E., Ericksen, S., & Davis, J. M. (1979). Lithium transport across red cell membrane: A cell membrane abnormality in manic-depressive illness. *Science, 205,* 932–934.

Duffy, F. H., Bartels, P. H., & Burchfiel, J. (1981). Significance probability mapping: An aid in the topographic analysis of brain electrical activity. *Electroencephalography and Clinical Neurophysiology, 51,* 455–462.

Duffy, F. H., Burchfiel, J. L., & Lombroso, C. T. (1979). Brain electrical activity mapping (BEAM): A method for extending the clinical utility of EEG and evoked potential data. *Annals of Neurology, 5,* 309–332.

Duncan, W. C., Pettigrew, K. D., & Gillin, J. C. (1979). REM architecture changes in bipolar and unipolar depression. *American Journal of Psychiatry, 136,* 1424–1427.

Ebert, M. H., & Kopin, I. J. (1975). Differential labelling of origins of urinary catecholamine metabolites by dopamine-C^{14}. *Transactions of the Association of American Physicians, 88,* 256–264.

Ehrlich, B. E., & Diamond, J. M. (1980). Lithium, membranes, and manic-depressive illness. *Journal of Membrane Biology, 52,* 187–200.

Endo, M., Endo, J., Nishikubo, M., Yamaguchi, T., & Hatotani, N. (1974). Endocrine studies in depression. In N. Hatotani (Ed.), *Psychoneuroendocrinology. Proceedings of the Workshop Conference of the International Society for Psychoneuroendocrinology, Mieken, September 3–5, 1973.* Basel: S. Karger AG.

Engel, G. L. (1977). The need for a new medical model: A challenge for biomedicine. *Science, 196,* 129–136.

Engel, G. L. (1980). The clinical application of the biopsychosocial model. *American Journal of Psychiatry, 137,* 535–544.

Ettigi, P. G., & Brown, G. M. (1977). Psychoneuroendocrinology of affective disorder: An overview. *American Journal of Psychiatry, 134,* 493–501.

Ettigi, P. G., Hayes, P. E., Narasimhachari, N., Hamer, R. M., Goldberg, S., & Secord, G. J. (1983). d-Amphetamine response and dexamethasone suppression test as predictors of treatment outcome in unipolar depression. *Biological Psychiatry, 18,* 499–504.

Evans, D. L., & Nemeroff, C. B. (1983). Use of the dexamethasone suppression test using *DSM-III* criteria on an inpatient psychiatric unit. *Biological Psychiatry, 18,* 505–511.

Everett, G. M., & Toman, J. E. P. (1959). Mode of action of Rauwolfia alkaloids and motor activity. In J. Masserman (Ed.), *Biological Psychiatry,* New York: Grune & Stratton.

Extein, I., Pottash, A. L. C., & Gold, M. S. (1981). Relationship of TRH test and dexamethasone suppression test abnormalities in unipolar depression. *Psychiatry Research, 4,* 49–53.

Extein, I., Pottash, A. L. C., Gold, M. S., Cadet, J., Sweeney, D. R., Davies, R. K., & Martin, D. M. (1980). The thyroid stimulating hormone response to thyrotropin releasing hormone in mania and bipolar depression. *Psychiatry Research, 2,* 199–204.

Extein, I., Pottash, A. L. C., Gold, M. S., & Cowdry, R. W. (1982). Using the protirelin test to distinguish mania from schizophrenia. *Archives of General Psychiatry, 39,* 77–81.

Fawcett, J. A., & Bunney, W. E. (1967). Pituitary adrenal function and depression: An outline for research. *Archives of General Psychiatry, 16,* 517–535.

Fawcett, J., Maas, J., & Dekirmenjian, H. (1972). Depression and MHPG excretion: Response to dextroamphetamine and tricyclic antidepressants. *Archives of General Psychiatry, 26,* 246–251.

Fawcett, J., Sabelli, H., Gusovsky, F., Epstein, P., Javaid, J., & Jeffriess, H. (1983). Phenylethylaminic mechanisms in maprotiline antidepressant effect. *Federation Proceedings, 42,* 1164.

Fawcett, J., Sabelli, H. C., Javaid, J. I., Epstein, P., Maiorano, M., & Fawcett, R. (1981, October 30–November 3). *Urinary Phenylethylamine in affective disorders.* Presented at the World Psychiatric Association Regional Meeting, New York City.

Fawcett, J., & Siomopoulos, V. (1971). Dextroamphetamine response as a possible predictor of improvement with tricyclic therapy in depression. *Archives of General Psychiatry, 25,* 247–255.

Feighner, J. P., Robins, E., Guze, S. B., Woodruff, R. A., Winokur, G., & Muñoz, R. (1972). Diagnostic criteria for use in psychiatric research. *Archives of General Psychiatry, 26,* 57–63.

Feinberg, M., & Carroll, B. J. (1982). Separation of subtypes of depression using discriminant analysis. I. Separation of unipolar endogenous depression from nonendogenous depression. *British Journal of Psychiatry, 140,* 384–391.

Feinberg, M., Gillin, J. C., Carroll, B. J., Greden, J. F., & Zis, A. P. (1981). EEG studies of sleep and the dexamethasone suppression test in the diagnosis of depression. *Psychopharmacology Bulletin, 17,* 20–22.

Feinberg, M., Gillin, J. C., Carroll, B. J., Greden, J. F., & Zis, A. P. (1982). EEG studies of sleep in the diagnosis of depression. *Biological Psychiatry, 17,* 305–316.

Ferris, R., & Tang, F. L. M. (1979). Comparison of the effects of the isomers of amphetamine, methylphenidate and deoxypipradol on the uptake of l-(^{3}H)norepinephrine and (^{3}H)dopamine by synaptic vesicles from rat whole brain, striatum and hypothalamus. *Journal of Pharmacology and Experimental Therapeutics, 210,* 422–428.

Ferris, R., Tang, F., & Maxwell, R. (1972). A comparison of the capacities of isomers of amphetamine, deoxypipradol and methylphenidate to inhibit the uptake of tritiated catecholamines into rat cerebral cortex, hypothalamus and striatum and into adrenergic nerves of rabbit aorta. *Journal of Pharmacology and Experimental Therapeutics, 181,* 407–416.

Fink, M., Foster, F. G., Kupfer, D. J., & Spiker, D. G. (1977). EEG sleep diagnosis of medical disease in depression. *Neuropsychobiology, 3,* 167–178.

Fischer, E., Heller, B., & Miro, A. N. (1968). B-phenylethylamine in human urine. *Arzneimittel Forschung, 18,* 1486.

Fischer, E., Ludmer, L. I., & Sabelli, H. C. (1967). The antagonism of phenylethylamine to catecholamines on mouse motor activity. *Acta Physiology Latinoamerica, 17,* 15–21.

Foster, F. G., Kupfer, D. J., Coble, P., & McPartland, R. J. (1976). Rapid eye movement sleep density: An objective indicator in severe medical-depressive syndromes. *Archives of General Psychiatry, 33,* 1119–1123.

Fraser, A. (1983). Choice of antidepressant based on the dexamethasone suppression test. *American Journal of Psychiatry, 140,* 786–787.

Freeman, F. R. (1978). Sleep in patients with organic diseases of the nervous system. In R. L. Williams & I. Karacan (Eds.), *Sleep disorders: Diagnosis and treatment.* New York: John Wiley & Sons.

Frohman, L. A., & Stachura, M. E. (1975). Neuropharmacologic control of neuroendocrine function in man. *Metabolism, 24,* 211–234.

Fuxe, K., Grobecker, H., & Jonsson, J. (1967). The effect of B-phenylethylamine on central and peripheral monoamine-containing neurons. *European Journal of Pharmacology, 2,* 202–207.

Gaertner, J. H., Krueter, J., Scharek, G., Wiatr, G., & Breyer-Pfaff, V. (1982). Do urinary MHPG and plasma drug levels correlate with response to amitriptyline therapy? *Psychopharmacology, 76,* 236–239.

Garver, D. L., & Davis, J. M. (1979). Minireview: Biogenic amine hypotheses of affective disorders. *Life Sciences, 24,* 383–394.

Garver, D. L., Pandey, G. N., Dekirmenjian, H., & DeLeon-Jones, F. (1975). Growth hormone and catecholamines in affective disease. *American Journal of Psychiatry, 132,* 1149–1154.

Gershon, S., & Shaw, F. H. (1961). Psychiatric sequelae of chronic exposure to organophosphorus insecticides. *Lancet, 1,* 1371–1384.

Gillin, J. C. (1983). The sleep therapies of depression. *Neuro-Psychopharmacology and Biological Psychiatry, 7,* 351–364.

Gillin, J. C., Duncan, W. C., Murphy, D. L., Post, R. M., Wehr, T. A., Goodwin, F. K., Wyatt, R. J., & Bunney, W. E. (1981). Age-related changes in sleep in depressed and normal subjects. *Psychiatry Research, 4,* 73–78.

Gillin, J. C., Duncan, W., Pettigrew, K. D., Frankel, B. L., & Snyder, F. (1979). Successful separation of depressed, normal, and insomniac subjects by EEG sleep data. *Archives of General Psychiatry, 36,* 85–90.

Gillin, J. C., Wyatt, R. J., Fram, D., & Snyder, F. (1978). The relationship between changes in REM sleep and clinical improvement in depressed patients treated with amitriptyline. *Psychopharmacology, 59,* 267–272.

Gitlow, S. E., Mendlowitz, M., Bertani, L. M., Wilk, S., & Wilk, E. K. (1971). Human norepinephrine metabolism—Its evaluation by administration of tritiated nor-epinephrine. *Journal of Clinical Investigation, 50,* 859–865.

Gold, M. S., Pottash, A. L. C., Extein, I., Martin, D. M., Howard, E., Mueller, E. A., & Sweeney, D. R. (1981). The TRH test in the diagnosis of major and minor depression. *Psychoneuroendocrinology, 6,* 159–169.

Gold, M. S., Pottash, A. L. C., Ryan, N., Sweeney, D. R., Davies, R. K., & Martin, D. M. (1980). TRH-induced TSH response in unipolar, bipolar, and secondary depressions: Possible utility in clinical assessment and differential diagnosis. *Psychoneuroendocrinology, 5,* 147–155.

Gold, P. W., Goodwin, F. K., Wehr, T., & Rebar, T. (1977). Pituitary thyrotropin response to thyrotropin-releasing hormone in affective illness: Relationship to spinal fluid amine metabolites. *American Journal of Psychiatry, 134,* 1028–1031.

Gold, P. W., Goodwin, F. K., Wehr, T., Rebar, R., & Sack, R. (1976). Growth-hormone and prolactin response to levodopa in affective illness. *Lancet, 2,* 1308–1309.

Goldberg, I. K. (1980a). Dexamethasone suppression test as an indicator of safe withdrawal of antidepressant theory. *Lancet, 1,* 376.

Goldberg, I. K. (1980b). Dexamethasone suppression tests in depression and response to treatment. *Lancet, 2,* 92.

Goodall, McC., & Alton, H. (1968). Metabolism of 3-hydroxytryptamine (dopamine) in human subjects. *Biochemical Pharmacology, 17,* 905–914.

Goodall, McC., & Rosen, L. (1963). Urinary excretion of noradrenalin and its metabolites at ten-minute intervals after intravenous injection of dl-noradrenalin-2-C^{14}. *Journal of Clinical Investigation, 42,* 1578–1588.

Goodwin, F. K., & Bunney, W. E. (1971). Depression following reserpine: A reevaluation. *Seminars in Psychiatry, 3,* 435–448.

Goodwin, F. K., Cowdry, R. W., & Webster, M. H. (1978). Predictors of drug response in the affective disorders: Toward an integrated approach. In M. A. Lipton, A. DiMascio, & K. F. Killam (Eds.), *Psychopharmacology: A generation of progress.* New York: Raven Press.

Goodwin, F. K., & Post, R. M. (1975). Studies of amine metabolites in affective illness and in schizophrenia: A comparative analysis. In D. X. Freedman (Ed.), *Biology of the major psychoses.* New York: Raven Press.

Goodwin, F. K., Post, R. M., Dunner, D. L., & Gordon, E. K. (1973). Cerebrospinal fluid amine metabolites in affective illness: The probenecid technique. *American Journal of Psychiatry, 130,* 73–79.

Goodwin, F. K., & Potter, W. Z. (1979). Norepinephrine metabolite studies in affective illness. In E. Usdin, I. J. Kopin, & J. Barchas (Eds.), *Catecholamines: Basic and clinical frontiers, Vol. 2. Proceedings of the Fourth International Catecholamine Symposium.* Elmsford NY: Pergamon Press.

Greden, J. F., Albala, A. A., Haskett, R. F., James, N. McI., Goodman, L., Steiner, M., & Carroll, B. J. (1980). Normalization of dexamethasone suppression test: A laboratory index of recovery from endogenous depression. *Biological Psychiatry, 15,* 449–458.

Greden, J. F., Gardner, R., King, D., Grunhaus, L., Carroll, B. J., & Kronfol, Z. (1983). Dexamethasone suppression tests in antidepressant treatment of melancholia: The process of normalization and test-retest reproducibility. *Archives of General Psychiatry, 40,* 493–500.

Greden, J. F., Kronfol, Z., Gardner, R., Feinberg, M., Mukhopadhyay, S., Albala, A. A., & Carroll, B. J. (1981). Dexamethasone suppression test and selection of antidepressant medications. *Journal of Affective Disorders, 3,* 389–396.

Greenberg, R., Pearlman, C. A., & Gampel, D. (1972). War neuroses and the adaptive function of REM sleep. *British Journal of Medical Psychology, 45,* 27–33.

Greenspan, K., Schildkraut, J. J., Gordon, E. K., Baer, L., Aronoff, M. S., & Durell, J. (1970). Catecholamine metabolism in affective disorders—III. MHPG and other catecholamine metabolites in patients treated with lithium carbonate. *Journal of Psychiatric Research, 7,* 171–183.

Gregoire, F., Brauman, H., deBuck, R., & Corvilain, J. (1977). Hormone release in depressed patients before and after recovery. *Psychoneuroendocrinology, 2,* 303–312.

Gruen, P. H., Sachar, E. J., Altman, N., & Sassin, J. (1975). Growth hormone responses to hypoglycemia in postmenopausal depressed women. *Archives of General Psychiatry, 32,* 31–33.

Gwirtsman, H., Gerner, R. H., & Sternbach, H. (1982). The overnight dexamethasone suppression test: Clinical and theoretical review. *Journal of Clinical Psychiatry, 43,* 321–327.

Haas, M., Schooler, J., & Tosteson, D. C. (1975). Coupling of lithium to sodium transport in human red cells, *Nature, 258,* 425–427.

Halaris, A. E. (1978). Plasma 3-methoxy-4-hydroxyphenylglycol in manic psychosis. *American Journal of Psychiatry, 135,* 493–494.

Halaris, A. E., & DeMet, E. M. (1979). Studies of norepinephrine metabolism in manic and depressive states. In E. Usdin, I. J. Kopin, & J. Barchas (Eds.), *Catecholamines: Basic and Clinical Frontiers, Vol. 2. Proceedings of the Fourth International Catecholamine Symposium.* New York: Pergamon Press.

Halbreich, U., Sachar, E. J., Asnis, G. M., Quitkin, F., Nathan, R. S., Halpern, F. S., & Klein, D. F. (1982). Growth hormone response to dextroamphetamine in depressed patients and normal subjects. *Archives of General Psychiatry, 39,* 189–192.

Hanson, L. C. F. (1967). Evidence that the central action of (+)-amphetamine is mediated via catecholamine. *Psychopharmacologia, 10,* 289–297.

Hauri, P., Chernik, D. A., Hawkins, D. R., & Mendels, J. (1974). Sleep of depressed patients in remission. *Archives of General Psychiatry, 31,* 386–391.

Hauri, P., & Hawkins, D. (1971). Phasic REM, depression, and the relationship between sleeping and waking. *Archives of General Psychiatry, 25,* 56–63.

Hokfelt, T., Johansson, O., Ljungdahl, A., Lundberg, J. M., & Schultzberg, M. (1980). Peptidergic neurones. *Nature, 284,* 515–521.

Hollister, L. E., Davis, K. L., & Berger, P. A. (1976). Pituitary response to thyrotropin-releasing hormone in depression. *American Journal of Psychiatry, 33,* 1393–1396.

Hollister, L. E., Davis, K. L., & Berger, P. A. (1980). Subtypes of depression based on excretion of MHPG and response to nortriptyline. *Archives of General Psychiatry, 37,* 1107–1110.

Hollister, L. E., Davis, K. L., Overall, L. E., & Anderson, T. (1978). Evaluation of MHPG in normal subjects. *Archives of General Psychiatry, 35,* 1410–1415.

Holsboer, F., Liebl, R., & Hofschuster, E. (1982). Repeated dexamethasone suppression test during depressive illness: Normalization of test result compared with clinical improvement. *Journal of Affective Disorders, 4,* 93–101.

Innes, I. R. (1963). Actions of dexamphetamine on 5-hydroxytryptamine receptors. *British Journal of Pharmacology, 21,* 427–435.

Insel, T. R., Gillin, J. C., Moore, A., Mendelson, W. B., Loewenstein, R. J., & Murphy, D. L. (1982). The sleep of patients with obsessive-compulsive disorder. *Archives of General Psychiatry, 29,* 1372–1377.

James, A. E., Price, R. R., Rollo, F. D., Patton, J. A., Erickson, J. J., Coulam, C. M., & Partain, C. L. (1982). Nuclear magnetic resonance imaging: A promising technique. *Journal of the American Medical Association, 247,* 1331–1334.

Janowsky, D. S., & Davis, J. M. (1976). Methylphenidate, dextroamphetamine and levamfetamine: Effects on schizophrenic symptoms. *Archives of General Psychiatry, 33,* 304–308.

Janowsky, D. S., El-Yousef, M. K., & Davis, J. M. (1974). Acetylcholine and depression. *Psychosomatic Medicine, 36,* 248–257.

Janowsky, D. S., El-Yousef, M. K., Davis, J. M., & Sekerke, H. J. (1972). A cholinergic-adrenergic hypothesis of mania and depression. *Lancet, 2,* 632–635.

Janowsky, D. S., El-Yousef, M. K., Davis, J. M., & Sekerke, H. J. (1973). Provocation of schizophrenic symptoms by intravenous administration of methylphenidate. *Archives of General Psychiatry, 28,* 185–191.

Jarrett, D. B., Coble, P. A., & Kupfer, D. J. (1983). Reduced cortisol latency in depressive illness. *Archives of General Psychiatry, 40,* 506–511.

Javaid, J. I., & Davis, J. M. (1981). GLC analysis of phenylalkyl primary amines using nitrogen detector. *Journal of Pharmacologic Science, 70,* 813–815.

Jimerson, D. C., Ballenger, J. C., Lake, C. R., Post, R. M., Goodwin, F. K., & Kopin, I. J., (1981). Plasma and CSF MHPG in normals. *Psychopharmacology Bulletin, 17,* 86–87.

Kalin, N. H., Risch, S. C., Janowsky, D. S., & Murphy, D. L. (1981). Use of the dexamethasone suppression test in clinical psychiatry. *Journal of Clinical Psychopharmacology, 1,* 64–69.

Karlberg, B. E., Kjellman, B. F., & Kagedol, B. (1978). Treatment of endogenous depression with oral thyrotropin. *Acta Psychiatrica Scandinavica, 58,* 389–400.

Kastin, A. J., Ehrensing, R. H., Schalch, D. S., & Anderson, M. S. (1972). Improvement in mental depression with decreased thyrotropin response after administration of thyrotropin-releasing hormone. *Lancet, 2,* 740–742.

Kety, S. S. (1971). Brain amines and affective disorders. In B. T. Ho & W. M. McIsaac (Eds.), *Brain chemistry and mental disease.* New York: Plenum Publishing.

King, D., Akiskal, H. S., Lemmi, H., Wilson, W., Belluomini, J., & Yerevanian, B. I. (1981). REM density in the differential diagnosis of psychiatric from medical-neurologic disorders: A replication. *Psychiatry Research, 5,* 267–276.

Kirkegaarde, C. (1981). The thyrotropin response to thyrotropin-releasing hormone in endogenous depression. *Psychoneuroendocrinology, 6,* 189–212.

Kirkegaarde, C., Bjorum, N., Cohn, D., Faber, J., Lauridsen, U. B., & Nerup, J. (1977). Studies on the influence of biogenic amines and psychoactive drugs on the prognostic value of the TRH stimulation test in endogenous depression. *Psychoneuroendocrinology, 2,* 131–136.

Knowles, J. B., Cairns, J., Waldron, J., Delva, N., Letemendia, F. J., & MacLean, A. W. (1980). Sleep disturbances: A characteristic of primary depression or of primary depressives? *Sleep Research, 9,* 172.

Knowles, J. B., MacLean, A. W., & Cairns, J. (1982a). REM sleep abnormalities in depression: A test of the phase-advance hypothesis. *Biological Psychiatry, 17,* 605–609.

Knowles, J. B., MacLean, A. W., & Cairns, J. (1982b). Definitions of REM latency. Some comparisons with particular reference to depression. *Biological Psychiatry, 17,* 993–1002.

Kopin, I. J. (1978). Measuring turnover of neurotransmitters in human brain. In M. A. Lipton, A. DiMascio, & K. F. Killam (Eds.), *Psychopharmacology: A generation of progress.* New York: Raven Press.

Kopin, I. J., Gordon, E. K., Jimerson, D. C., & Polinsky, R. J. (1983). Relation between plasma and cerebrospinal fluid levels of 3-methoxy-4-hydroxyphenylglycol. *Science, 219,* 73–75.

Korf, J., & Van Praag, H. M. (1971). Amine metabolism in human brain: Further evaluation of the probenecid test. *Brain Research, 35,* 221–230.

Koslow, S. H., Maas, J. W., Bowden, C. L., Davis, J. M., Hanin, I., & Javaid, J. (1983). CSF and urinary biogenic amines and metabolites in depression and mania. A controlled, univariate analysis. *Archives of General Psychiatry, 40,* 999–1010.

Koslow, S. H., Stokes, P. E., Mendels, J., Ramsey, A., & Casper, R. (1982). Insulin tolerance test: Human growth hormone response and insulin resistance in primary unipolar depressed, bipolar depressed and control subjects. *Psychological Medicine, 12,* 45–55.

Krieger, D. T. (1973). Lack of responsiveness to L-DOPA in Cushing's disease. *Journal of Clinical Endocrinology and Metabolism, 36,* 277–284.

Krieger, D. T., Allen, W., Rizzo, F., & Krieger, H. P. (1971). Characterization of the normal temporal pattern of plasma corticosteroid levels. *Journal of Clinical Endocrinology and Metabolism, 32,* 266–284.

Kripke, D. F. (1976). Serotonin depression. *Science, 194,* 214.

Kuhn, R. (1957). Uber die behandlung depressive zustande mit einem iminodibenzylderivat (G22355). *Schweizerische Medizinische Wochenschrift, 87,* 1135.

Kuhn, R. (1958). The treatment of depressive states with G22355 (imipramine hydrochloride). *American Journal of Psychiatry, 115,* 459–464.

Kupfer, D. J. (1976). REM latency: A psychobiologic marker for primary depressive disease. *Biological Psychiatry, 11,* 159–174.

Kupfer, D. J. (1982a). Interaction of sleep, antidepressants, and affective disease. *Journal of Clinical Psychiatry, 43* (Sect. 2), 30–35.

Kupfer, D. J. (1982b). EEG sleep as a biological marker in depression. In E. Usdin & I. Hanin (Eds.), *Biological markers in psychiatry and neurology.* Elmsford, NY: Pergamon Press.

Kupfer, D. J., Broudy, D., Coble, P. A., & Spiker, D. G. (1980). EEG sleep and affective psychoses. *Journal of Affective Disorder, 2,* 17–25.

Kupfer, D. J., Broudy, D., Spiker, D. G., Neil, J. F., & Coble, P. A. (1979). EEG sleep and affective disorders: I. Schizoaffective disorders. *Psychiatry Research, 1,* 173–178.

Kupfer, D. J., & Foster, F. G. (1972). Interval between onset of sleep and rapid eye movement sleep as an indicator of depression. *Lancet, 2,* 684–686.

Kupfer, D. J., & Foster, F. G. (1973). Sleep and activity in a psychotic depression. *The Journal of Nervous and Mental Disease, 156,* 341–348.

Kupfer, D. J., & Foster, F. G. (1975). The sleep of psychotic patients: Does it all look alike? In D. X. Freedman (Ed.), *Biology of the major psychoses.* New York: Raven Press.

Kupfer, D. J., & Foster, F. G. (1978). EEG sleep and depression. In R. W. Williams & I. Karacan (Eds.), *Sleep disorders: Diagnosis and treatment.* New York: John Wiley & Sons.

Kupfer, D. J., Foster, F. G., Coble, P., McPartland, R. J., & Ulrich, R. F. (1978). The application of EEG sleep for the differential diagnosis of affective disorders. *American Journal of Psychiatry, 135,* 69–74.

Kupfer, D. J., Foster, F. G., Reich, L., Thompson, K. S., & Weiss, B. (1976). EEG sleep changes as predictors in depression. *American Journal of Psychiatry, 133,* 622–626.

Kupfer, D. J., Gillin, J. C., Coble, P. A., Spiker, D. G., Shaw, D., & Holzer, B. (1981). REM sleep, naps, and depression. *Psychiatry Research, 5,* 195–203.

Kupfer, D. J., Hanin, I., Coble, P. A., Spiker, D. G., Sorisio, D., & Grau, T. G. (1982). EEG sleep and tricyclic blood levels: Acute and chronic administration in depression. *Journal of Clinical Psychopharmacology, 2,* 8–13.

Kupfer, D. J., Himmelhoch, J. M., Swartzburg, M., Anderson, C., Byck, R., & Detre, T. P. (1972). Hypersomnia in manic-depressive disease (A preliminary report). *Diseases of the Nervous System, 33,* 720–724.

Kupfer, D. J., Spiker, D. G., Coble, P., & McPartland, R. J. (1978). Amitriptyline and EEG sleep in depressed patients: I. Drug effect. *Sleep, 1,* 149–159.

Kupfer, D. J., Spiker, D. G., Coble, P. A., Neil, J. F., Ulrich, R., & Shaw, D. H. (1980). Depression, EEG sleep and clinical response. *Comprehensive Psychiatry, 21,* 212–220.

Kupfer, D. J., Spiker, D. G., Coble, P. A., Neil, J. F., Ulrich, R., & Shaw, D. H. (1981). Sleep and treatment prediction in endogenous depression. *American Journal of Psychiatry, 138,* 429–434.

Kupfer, D. J., Spiker, D. G., Rossi, A., Coble, P. A., Shaw, D., & Ulrich, R. (1982). Nortriptyline and EEG sleep in depressed patients. *Biological Psychiatry, 17,* 535–546.

Kupfer, D. J., Spiker, D. G., Rossi, A., Coble, P. A., Ulrich, R., & Shaw, D. (1983). Recent diagnostic and treatment advances in REM sleep and depression. In P. Clayton & J. Barrett (Eds.), *Treatment of depression: Old controversies and new approaches.* New York: Raven Press.

Kupfer, D. J., Targ, E., & Stack, J. (1982). Electroencephalographic sleep in unipolar depressive subtypes: Support for a biological and familial classification. *The Journal of Nervous and Mental Disease, 170,* 494–498.

Kupfer, D. J., & Thase, M. E. (1983). The use of the sleep laboratory in the diagnosis of affective disorders. *Psychiatric Clinics of North American, 6,* 3–25.

Kupfer, D. J., Weiss, B. L., Detre, T. P., & Foster, F. G. (1974). First night effect revisited: A clinical note. *The Journal of Nervous and Mental Disease, 159,* 205–209.

Landon, J., Greenwood, F. C., Stamp, T. C. B., & Wynn, V. (1966). The plasma sugar, free fatty acid, cortisol and growth hormone response to insulin and the comparison of this procedure with other tests of pituitary and adrenal function. II. In patients with hypothalamic or pituitary dysfunction or anorexia nervosa. *Journal of Clinical Investigation, 45,* 437–449.

Langer, G., Heinze, G., Reim, B., & Matussek, N. (1976). Reduced growth hormone responses to amphetamine in "endogenous" depression patients: Studies in normal, "reactive" and "endogenous" depressive, schizophrenic, and chronic alcoholic subjects. *Archives of General Psychiatry, 33,* 1471–1475.

Leckman, J. F., Maas, J. W., Redmond, D. E., & Heninger, G. R. (1980). Effects of oral clonidine on plasma 3-methoxy-4-hydroxyphenylglycol (MHPG) in man: Preliminary report. *Life Sciences, 26,* 2179–2185.

Liddle, G. (1960). Tests of pituitary-adrenal suppressibility in the diagnosis of Cushing's syndrome. *The Journal of Clinical Endocrinology and Metabolism, 20,* 1539–1560.

Loosen, P. T., & Prange, A. J. (1982). Serum thyrotropin response to the thyrotropin-releasing hormone in psychiatric patients: A review. *American Journal of Psychiatry, 139,* 405–416.

Loosen, P. T., Prange, A. J., & Wilson, I. C. (1978a). Influence of cortisol on TRH-induced TSH response in depression. *American Journal of Psychiatry, 135,* 244–246.

Loosen, P. T., Prange, A. J., & Wilson, I. C. (1978b). The thyrotropin response to thyrotropin-releasing hormone in psychiatric patients: Relation to serum cortisol. *Progress in Neuropsychopharmacology, 2,* 479–486.

Lovenberg, W., & Engelman, K. (1971). Assay of serotonin, related metabolites and enzymes. *Methods of Biochemical Analysis, 19 (Suppl.),* 1–34.

Maany, I., Mendels, J., Frazer, A., & Brunswick, D. (1979). A study of growth hormone release in depression. *Neuropsychobiology, 5,* 282–289.

Maas, J. W. (1975). Biogenic amines and depression: Biochemical and pharmacological separation of two types of depression. *Archives of General Psychiatry, 32,* 1357–1361.

Maas, J. W., Dekirmenjian, H., & Jones, F. (1973). Identification of depressed patients who have a disorder of norepinephrine metabolism and/or disposition. In E. Usdin & S. Snyder (Eds.), *Frontiers in catecholamine research—Proceedings of the Third International Catecholamine Symposium.* New York: Pergamon Press.

Maas, J. W., Fawcett, J. A., & Dekirmenjian, H. (1968). 3-methoxy-4-hydroxyphenylglycol (MHPG) excretion in depressive states: A pilot study. *Archives of General Psychiatry, 19,* 129–134.

Maas, J. W., Fawcett, J. A., Dekirmenjian, H. (1972). Catecholamine metabolism, depressive illness, and drug response. *Archives of General Psychiatry, 26,* 252–262.

Maas, J. W., Hattox, S. E., Greene, N. M., & Landis, D. H. (1979). 3-methoxy-4-hydroxyphenyleneglycol production by human brain in vivo. *Science, 205,* 1025–1027.

Maas, J. W., Kocsis, J. H., Bowden, C. L., Davis, J. M., Redmond, D. E., Hanin, I., & Robins, E. (1982). Pretreatment neurotransmitter metabolites and response to imipramine or amitriptyline treatment. *Psychological Medicine, 12,* 37–43.

Maas, J. W., & Landis, D. H. (1965). In vivo studies of the metabolism of norepinephrine in the central nervous system. *Journal of Pharmacology and Experimental Therapeutics, 163,* 147–162.

Maas, J. W., & Landis, D. H. (1971). The metabolism of circulating norepinephrine in human subjects. *Journal of Pharmacology and Experimental Therapeutics, 177,* 600–612.

Maitre, L., Waldmeier, P. C., Greengrass, P. M., Jackel, J., Sedlucek, S., & Delini-Stula, A. (1975). Maprotiline—Its position as an antidepressant in the light of recent neuropharmacological and neurobiochemical findings. *The Journal of International Medical Research, 3* (Supple. 2), 2–15.

Mardh, G., Sjoquist, B., & Anggard, E. (1981). Norepinephrine metabolism in man using deuterium labelling: The conversion of 4-hydroxy-3-methoxyphenylglycol to 4-hydroxy-3-methoxymandelic acid. *Journal of Neurochemistry, 36,* 1181–1185.

Markianos, E., & Beckmann, H. (1976). Diurnal changes in dopamine-B-hydroxylase, homovanillic acid and 3-methoxy-4-hydroxyphenylglycol in serum of man. *Journal of Neural Transmission, 39,* 79–93.

Martin, J. B. (1973). Neural regulation of growth hormone secretion. *The New England Journal of Medicine, 288,* 1384–1393.

Martin, J. B., Reichlin, S., & Brown, G. M. (1977). *Clinical neuroendocrinology.* Philadelphia: F. A. Davis.

Matussek, N., Ackenheil, M., Hippius, H., Muller, F., Schroder, H-Th., Schultes, H., & Wasilewski, B. (1980). Effect of clonidine on growth hormone release in psychiatric patients and controls. *Psychiatry Research, 2,* 25–36.

Matussek, N., & Laakman, G. (1981). Growth hormone response in patients with depression. *Acta Psychiatrica Scandinavica, 63* (Supple. 290), 122–126.

McCarley, R. W. (1982). REM sleep and depression: Common neurobiological control mechanisms. *American Journal of Psychiatry, 139,* 565–576.

Meltzer, H. Y., Arora, R. C., Baber, R., & Tricou, B. J. (1981). Serotonin uptake in blood platelets of psychiatric patients. *Archives of General Psychiatry, 38,* 1322–1326.

Meltzer, H. Y., & Fang, V. S. (1983). Cortisol determination and the dexamethasone suppression test: A review. *Archives of General Psychiatry, 40,* 501–505.

Mendels, J., & Chernik, D. A. (1972). A follow-up study of the sleep patterns of three unipolar depressed patients. *Sleep Research, 1,* 142.

Mendels, J., & Chernik, D. A. (1975). Sleep changes in affective illness. In F. F. Flach & S. C. Draghi (Eds.), *The nature and treatment of depression.* New York: John Wiley & Sons.

Mendels, J., & Frazer, A. (1973). Intracellular lithium concentration and clinical response: Towards a membrane theory of depression. *Journal of Psychiatric Research, 10,* 9–18.

Mendels, J., & Frazer, A. (1974). Brain biogenic amine depletion and mood. *Archives of General Psychiatry, 30,* 447–451.

Mendels, J., & Frazer, A. (1975). Reduced central serotonergic activity in mania: Implications for the relationship between depression and mania. *British Journal of Psychiatry, 126,* 241–248.

Mendels, J., & Hawkins, D. (1967a). Sleep and depression: A follow-up study. *Archives of General Psychiatry, 16,* 536–542.

Mendels, J., & Hawkins, D. R. (1967b). Sleep laboratory adaptation in normal subjects and depressed patients ("first night effect"). *Electroencephalography and Clinical Neurophysiology, 22,* 556–558.

Mendelson, W. B., Gillin, J. C., & Wyatt, R. J. (1977). *Human sleep and its disorders.* New York: Plenum Publishing.

Mendelson, W. B., Jacobs, L. S., Gillin, J. C., & Wyatt, R. J. (1979). The regulation of insulin-induced and sleep-related human growth hormone secretion: A review. *Psychoneuroendocrinology, 4,* 341–349.

Mendlewicz, J., Charles, G., & Franckson, J. M. (1982). The dexamethasone suppression test in affective disorder: Relationship to clinical and genetic subgroups. *British Journal of Psychiatry, 141,* 464–470.

Mendlewicz, J., Van Cauter, E., Linkowski, P., L'Hermite, M., & Robyn, C. (1980). The 24-hour profile of prolactin in depression. *Life Sciences, 27,* 2015–2024.

Modai, I., Apter, A., Gulomb, M., & Wijsenbeek, H. (1979). Response to amitriptyline and urinary MHPG in bipolar depressive patients. *Neuropyschobiology, 5,* 181–184.

Moore, K. E. (1977). The actions of amphetamines on neurotransmitters: A brief review: *Biological Psychiatry, 12,* 451–462.

Mosnaim, A. D., Inwang, E. E., & Sabelli, H. C. (1974). The influence of psychotropic drugs on the levels of endogenous 2-phenylethylamine in rabbit brain. *Biological Psychiatry, 8,* 227–234.

Mosnaim, A. D., Inwang, E. E., Sugerman, J. H., DeMartini, W. J., & Sabelli, H. C. (1973). Ultraviolet spectrophotometric determination of 2-phenylethylamine in biological samples and its possible correlation with depression. *Biological Psychiatry, 6,* 235–257.

Mueller, P. S., Heninger, G. R., & McDonald, R. K. (1969a). Intravenous glucose tolerance test in depression. *Archives of General Psychiatry, 21,* 470–477.

Mueller, P. S., Heninger, G. R., & McDonald, R. K. (1969b). Insulin tolerance test in depression. *Archives of General Psychiatry, 21,* 587–594.

Murphy, D. L., Campbell, I., & Costa, J. L. (1978). Current status of the indoleamine hypothesis of affective disorders. In M. A. Lipton, A. DiMascio, & K. F. Killam (Eds.), *Psychopharmacology: A generation of progress.* New York: Raven Press.

Nakajima, T., Kakimoto, Y., & Sano, I. (1964). Formation of B-phenylethylamine in mammalian tissues and its effects on motor activity in the mouse. *Journal of Pharmacology and Experimental Therapeutics, 143,* 319–325.

Nasrallah, H. A., & Coryell, W. H. (1982). Dexamethasone nonsuppression predicts the antidepressant effects of sleep deprivation. *Psychiatry Research, 6,* 61–64.

Nasrallah, H. A., Kuperman, S., & Coryell, W. (1980). Reversal of dexamethasone nonsuppression with sleep deprivation in primary depression. *American Journal of Psychiatry, 137,* 1463–1464.

Nelson, W. H., Orr, W. W., Stevenson, J. M., & Shane, S. R. (1982). Hypothalamic-pituitary-adrenal axis activity and tricyclic response in major depression. *Archives of General Psychiatry, 39,* 1033–1036.

Nuller, J. L., & Ostroumova, M. N. (1980). Resistance to inhibiting effect of dexamethasone in patients with endogenous depression. *Acta Psychiatrica Scandinavica, 61,* 169–177.

Ostrow, D. G., Pandey, G. N., Davis, J. M., Hurt, S. W., & Tosteson, D. C. (1978). A heritable disorder of lithium transport in erythrocytes of a subpopulation of manic-depressive patients. *American Journal of Psychiatry, 135,* 1070–1078.

Ostrow, D. G., Trevisan, M., Okonek, A., Gibbons, R., Cooper, R., & Davis, J. M. (1982). Sodium dependent membrane processes in major affective disorders. In E. Usdin & I. Hanin (Eds.), *Biological markers in psychiatry and neurology.* Elmsford, NY: Pergamon Press.

Pandey, G. N., Dorus, E., Davis, J. M., & Tosteson, D. C. (1979). Lithium transport in human red blood cells: Genetic and clinical aspects. *Archives of General Psychiatry, 36,* 902–908.

Pandey, G. N., Sarkadi, B., Haas, J., Gunn, R. B., Davis, J. M., & Tosteson, D. C. (1978). Lithium transport pathways in human red blood cells. *Journal of General Physiology, 72,* 233–247.

Pare, C. M. B., & Sandler, M. (1959). A clinical and biochemical study of a trial of iproniazid in the treatment of depression. *Journal of Neurology, Neurosurgery, and Psychiatry, 22,* 247–251.

Paul, S. M., Rehavi, M., Skolnick, P., Ballenger, J. C., & Goodwin, F. K. (1981). Depressed patients have decreased binding of tritiated imipramine to platelet serotonin "transporter." *Archives of General Psychiatry, 38,* 1315–1317.

Pearlson, G. A., Veroff, A. E., & McHugh, P. R. (1981). The use of computed tomography in psychiatry: Recent application to schizophrenia, manic-depressive illness, and dementia syndromes. *Johns Hopkins Medical Journal, 149,* 194–202.

Peselow, E. D., & Fieve, R. R. (1982). Dexamethasone suppression test and response to antidepressants in depressed outpatients. *The New England Journal of Medicine, 307,* 1216–1217.

Pickar, D., Cohen, M. R., Naber, D., & Cohen, R. M. (1982). Clinical studies of the endogenous opioid system. *Biological Psychiatry, 17,* 1243–1276.

Pickar, D., Sweeney, D. R., Maas, J. W., & Heninger, G. R. (1978). Primary affective disorder, clinical state change, and MHPG excretion: A longitudinal study. *Archives of General Psychiatry, 35,* 1378–1383.

Pokorny, A. D. (1983). Prediction of suicide in psychiatric patients. *Archives of General Psychiatry, 40,* 249–257.

Post, R. M., & Goodwin, F. K. (1974). Effects of amitriptyline and imipramine on amine metabolites in the cerebrospinal fluid of depressed patients. *Archives of General Psychiatry, 30,* 234–239.

Post, R. M., Gordon, E. K., Goodwin, F. K., & Bunney, W. E. (1973). Central norepinephrine metabolism in affective illness: MHPG in the cerebrospinal fluid. *Science, 179,* 1002–1003.

Potkin, S. G., Wyatt, R. J., & Karoum, F. (1980). Phenylethylamine (PEA) and phenylacetic acid (PAA) in the urine of chronic schizophrenic patients and controls. *Psychopharmacology Bulletin, 16,* 52–54.

Potter, W. Z., Calil, H. M., Extein, I., Gold, P. W., Wehr, T. A., & Goodwin, F. K. (1981). Specific norepinephrine and serotonin uptake inhibitors in man: A crossover study with pharmacokinetic, biochemical, neuroendocrine and behavioral parameters. *Acta Psychiatrica Scandinavica, 63*(Supple. 290), 152–170.

Potter, W. Z., Calil, H. M., Extein, I., Muscettola, G., & Goodwin, F. K. (1981). Crossover study of zimelidine and desipramine in depression: Evidence for amine specificity. *Psychopharmacology Bulletin, 17,* 26–29.

Prange, A. J. (1964). The pharmacology and biochemistry of depression. *Diseases of the Nervous System, 25,* 217–221.

Prange, A. J., Wilson, I. C., Knox, A. E., McClane, T. K., Breese, G. R., Martin, B. R., Alltop, L. B., & Lipton, M. A. (1972). Thyroid-imipramine clinical and chemical interaction: Evidence for a receptor deficit in depression. *Journal of Psychiatric Research, 9,* 187–205.

Prange, A. J., Wilson, I, C., Lara, P. P., Alltop, L. B., & Breese, G. R. (1972). Effects of thyrotropin-releasing hormone in depression. *Lancet, 2,* 999–1002.

Prange, A. J., Wilson, I, C., Lynn, C. W., Alltop, L. B., & Stikeleather, R. A. (1974). L-trytophan in mania: Contribution to a permissive hypothesis of affective disorders. *Archives of General Psychiatry, 30,* 56–62.

Privitera, M. R., Greden, J. F., Gardner, R. W., Ritchie, J. C., & Carroll, B. J. (1982). Interference by carbamazepine with the dexamethasone suppression test. *Biological Psychiatry, 17,* 611–620.

Puig-Antich, J., Goetz, R., Hanlon, C., Davies, M., Thompson, J., Chambers, W. J., Tabrizi, M. A., & Weitzman, E. D. (1982). Sleep architecture and REM sleep measures in prepubertal children with major depression: A controlled study. *Archives of General Psychiatry, 39,* 932–939.

Puig-Antich, J., Goetz, R., Hanlon, C., Tabrizi, M. A., Davies, M., & Weitzman, E. D. (1983). Sleep architecture and REM sleep measures in prepubertal major depressives: Studies during recovery from the depressive episode in a drug-free stage. *Archives of General Psychiatry, 40,* 187–192.

Quitkin, F. M., Schwartz, D., Liebowitz, M. R., McGrath, P. J., Halpern, F., Puig-Antich, J., Tricamo, E., Sachar, E. J., & Klein, D. F. (1982). Atypical depressives: A preliminary report of antidepressant response and sleep patterns. *Psychopharmacology Bulletin, 18,* 78–80.

Randrup, A., Munkvad, I., Fog, R., Gerlach, J., Molander, L., Kjellberg, B., & Scheel-Kruger, J. (1975). Mania, depression, and brain dopamine. In W. B. Essman & L. Valzelli (Eds.), *Current developments in psychopharmacology* (Vol. 2). New York: Spectrum Publications.

Reynolds, C. F., Coble, P. A., Kupfer, D. J., & Shaw, D. H. (1982). Depressive patients and the sleep laboratory. In C. Guilleminault (Ed.), *Sleeping and waking disorders: Indications and techniques.* Reading, MA: Addison-Wesley Publishing.

Reynolds, C. F., Newton, T. F., Shaw, D. H., Coble, P. A., & Kupfer, D. J. (1982). Electroencephalographic sleep findings in depressed outpatients. *Psychiatry Research, 6,* 65–75.

Reynolds, C. F., Shaw, D. H., Newton, T. F., Coble, P. A., & Kupfer, D. J. (1983). EEG sleep in outpatients with generalized anxiety: A preliminary comparison with depressed outpatients. *Psychiatry Research, 8,* 81–89.

Reynolds, C. F., Spiker, D. J., Hanin, I., & Kupfer, D. J. (1983). Electroencephalographic sleep, aging, and psychopathology: New data and state of the art. *Biological Psychiatry, 18,* 139–155.

Ridges, A. P., Bishop, F. M., Goldberg, I. J. L., Corner, T., Gringras, M., Hamlet, G., Heyes, J., Miller, P., Parrack, S., & Sleeman, M. (1980). A combined biochemical and general practice study: II. Biochemical aspects. *The Journal of International Medical Research, 8*(Suppl. 3), 37–44.

Rieder, R. O., Mann, L. S., Weinberger, D. R., van Kammen, D. P., & Post, R. M. (1983). Computed tomographic scans in patients with schizophrenia, schizoaffective, and bipolar affective disorder. *Archives of General Psychiatry, 40,* 735–739.

Risch, S. C., Kalin, N. G., & Janowsky, D. S. (1981). Cholinergic challenges in affective illness: Behavioral and neuroendocrine correlates. *Journal of Clinical Psychopharmacology, 1,* 186–192.

Risch, S. C., Kalin, N. H., & Murphy, D. L. (1982). Neurochemical mechanisms in the affective disorders and neuroendocrine correlates. *Journal of Clinical Psychopharmacology, 1,* 180–185.

Rodnight, R. (1961). Body fluid indoles in mental illness. *International Review of Neurobiology, 3,* 251–292.

Rosenbaum, A. H., Schatzberg, A. F., Maruta, T., Orsulak, P. J., Cole, J. O., Grab, E. L., & Schildkraut, J. J. (1980). MHPG as a predictor of antidepressant response to imipramine and maprotiline. *American Journal of Psychiatry, 137,* 1090–1092.

Roy, A. (1982). Risk factors for suicide in psychiatric patients. *Archives of General Psychiatry, 39,* 1089–1095.

Rubin, R. T., & Mandell, A. J. (1966). Adrenal cortical activity in pathological emotional states: A review. *American Journal of Psychiatry, 123,* 387–400.

Rush, A. J., Giles, D. E., Roffwarg, H. P., & Parker, C. R. (1982). Sleep EEG and dexamethasone suppression test findings in outpatients with unipolar major depressive disorders. *Biological Psychiatry, 17,* 327–341.

Rush, A. J., Roffwarg, H. P., Giles, D. E., & Parker, C. R. (1981). Sleep EEG and dexamethasone suppression test findings in unipolar depressions. *Psychopharmacology Bulletin, 17,* 22–23.

Sabelli, H. C., & Borison, R. L. (1976). Non-catecholamine adrenergic modulators. *Advances in Biochemical Psychopharmacology, 15,* 69–74.

Sabelli, H. C., Borison, R. L., Diamond, B. I., Havdala, H. S., & Narasimhachari, N. (1978). Phenylethylamine and brain function. *Biochemical Pharmacology, 27,* 1707–1711.

Sabelli, H. C., Fawcett, J., Gusovsky, F., Edwards, J., Jeffriess, H., & Javaid, J. (1983). Phenylacetic acid as an indicator in bipolar affective disorders. *Journal of Clinical Psychopharmacology, 3,* 268–270.

Sabelli, H. C., Fawcett, J., Gusovsky, F., Javaid, J., Edwards, J., & Jeffriess, H. (1983). Urinary phenyl acetate: A diagnostic test for depression? *Science, 220,* 1187–1188.

Sabelli, H. C., Fawcett, J., Javaid, J., & Bagri, S. (1983). The methylphenidate test for differentiating desipramine-responsive from nortriptyline-responsive depression. *American Journal of Psychiatry, 140,* 212–214.

Sabelli, H. C., & Mosnaim, A. D. (1974). Phenylethylamine hypothesis of affective behavior. *American Journal of Psychiatry, 131,* 695–699.

Sabelli, H. C., Mosnaim, A. D., Vasquez, A. J., Giardina, W. J., Borison, R. L., & Pedemonte, W. A. (1976). Biochemical plasticity of synaptic transmission. A critical review of Dale's Principle. *Biological Psychiatry, 11,* 481–524.

Sacchetti, E., Allaria, E., Negi, F., Biondi, P. A., Smeraldi, E., & Cazzulo, C. O. (1979). 3-methoxy-4-hydroxyphenylglycol and primary depression: Clinical and pharmacological considerations. *Biological Psychiatry, 14,* 473–484.

Sacchetti, E., Smeraldi, E., Cagnasso, P., Biondi, P. A., & Bellodi, L. (1976). MHPG, amitriptyline and affective disorders: A longitudinal study. *International Pharmacopsychiatry, 11,* 157–162.

Sachar, E. J., Altman, N., Gruen, P. H., Glassman, A., Halpern, F. S., & Sassin, J. (1975). Human growth hormone responses to L-DOPA: Relation to menopause, depression, and plasma DOPA concentration. *Archives of General Psychiatry, 32,* 502–503.

Sachar, E. J., Asnis, G., Nathan, R. S., Halbreich, U., Tabrizi, M. A., & Halpern, F. S. (1980). Dextroamphetamine and cortisol in depression: Morning plasma cortisol levels suppressed. *Archives of General Psychiatry, 37,* 755–757.

Sachar, E. J., Finkelstein, J., & Hellman, L. (1971). Growth hormone responses in depressive illness. I. Response to insulin tolerance test. *Archives of General Psychiatry, 25,* 263–269.

Sachar, E. J., Frantz, A. G., Altman, N., & Sassin, J. (1973). Growth hormone and prolactin in unipolar and bipolar depressed patients: Response to hypoglycemia and L-DOPA. *American Journal of Psychiatry, 130,* 1362–1367.

Sachar, E. J., Halbreich, U., Asnis, G. M., Nathan, R. S., Halpern, F. S., & Ostrow, L. (1981). Paradoxical cortisol responses to dextroamphetamine in endogenous depression. *Archives of General Psychiatry, 38,* 1113–1117.

Sachar, E. J., Hellman, L., Roffwarg, H., Halpern, F. S., Fukushima, D. K., & Gallagher, T. F. (1973). Disrupted 24-hour patterns of cortisol secretion in psychotic depression. *Archives of General Psychiatry, 28,* 19–24.

Sachar, E. J., Mason, J. W., Kolmer, H. S., & Artiss, K. L. (1963). Psychoendocrine aspects of acute schizophrenic reactions. *Psychosomatic Medicine, 25,* 510–537.

Sachar, E. J., Mushrush, J., Perlow, M., Weitzman, E. D., & Sassin, J. (1972). Growth hormone responses to L-DOPA in depressed patients. *Science, 178,* 1304–1305.

Sandler, M., Ruthven, C. R. J., Goodwin, B. L., & Coppen, A. (1979). Decreased cerebrospinal fluid concentration of free phenylacetic acid in depressive illness. *Clinica Chimica Acta, 93,* 169–171.

Schanberg, S. M., Breese, G. R., Schildkraut, J. J., Gordon, E. K., & Kopin, I. J. (1968). 3-methoxy-4-hydroxyphenylglycol sulfate in brain and cerebrospinal fluid. *Biochemical Pharmacology, 17,* 2006–2008.

Schanberg, S. M., Schildkraut, J. J., Breese, G. R., & Kopin, I. J. (1968). Metabolism of normetanephrine H[3] in rat brain—Identification of conjugated 3-methoxy-4-hydroxyphenylglycol as major metabolite. *Biochemical Pharmacology, 11,* 247–254.

Schatzberg, A. F., Orsulak, P. J., Rosenbaum, A. H., Maruta, T., Kruger, E. R., Cole, J. O., & Schildkraut, J. J. (1980). Toward a biochemical classification of depressive disorders: IV. Pretreatment urinary MHPG levels as predictors of antidepressant response to imipramine. *Communications in Psychopharmacology, 4,* 441–445.

Schatzberg, A. F., Orsulak, P. J., Rosenbaum, A. H., Maruta, T., Kruger, E. R., Cole, J. O., & Schildkraut, J. J. (1982). Toward a biochemical classification of depressive disorders: V: Heterogeneity of unipolar depressions. *American Journal of Psychiatry,* *139,* 471–475.

Schatzberg, A. F., Rosenbaum, A. H., Orsulak, P. J., Rohde, W. A., Maruta, T., Kruger, E. R., Cole, J. O., & Schildkraut, J. J. (1981). Toward a biochemical classification of depressive disorders. III. Pretreatment urinary MHPG levels as predictors of response to treatment with maprotiline. *Psychopharmacology, 75,* 34–38.

Schatzberg, A. F., Rothschild, A. J., Stahl, J. B., Bond, T. C., Rosenbaum, A. H., Lofgren, S. B., MacLaughlin, R. A., Sullivan, M. A., & Cole, J. O. (1983). The dexamethasone suppression test: Identification of subtypes of depression. *American Journal of Psychiatry, 140,* 88–91.

Schildkraut, J. J. (1965). The catecholamine hypothesis of affective disorders: A review of supporting evidence. *American Journal of Psychiatry, 122,* 509–522.

Schildkraut, J. J. (1969). Neuropharmacology and the affective disorders. *The New England Journal of Medicine, 28,* 197–201, 248–255, 302–308.

Schildkraut, J. J. (1973a). Catecholamine metabolism and affective disorders: Studies of MHPG excretion. In E. Usdin & S. Snyder (Eds.), *Frontiers in Catecholamine Research—Proceedings of the Third International Catecholamine Symposium.* Elmsford, NY: Pergamon Press.

Schildkraut, J. J. (1973b). Norepinephrine metabolites and biochemical criteria for classifying depressive disorders and predicting response to treatment. *American Journal of Psychiatry, 130,* 695–699.

Schildkraut, J. J. (1978). Current status of the catecholamine hypothesis of affective disorders. In M. A. Lipton, A. DiMascio, & K. F. Killam (Eds.), *Psychopharmacology: A generation of progress.* New York: Raven Press.

Schildkraut, J. J., Green, R., Gordon, E. K., & Durell, J. (1966). Normetanephrine excretion and affective states in depressive patients treated with imipramine. *American Journal of Psychiatry, 123,* 690–700.

Schildkraut, J. J., Keeler, B. A., Grab, E. L., Kantrowich, J., & Hartmann, E. (1973). MHPG excretion and clinical classification of depressive disorders. *Lancet, 1,* 1251–1252.

Schildkraut, J. J., Keeler, B. A., Paporisek, M., & Hartmann, E. (1973). MHPG excretion in depressive disorders: Relations to clinical subtypes and desynchronized sleep. *Science, 181,* 762–764.

Schildkraut, J. J., Orsulak, P. J., Schatzberg, A. F., Cole, J. O., & Rosenbaum, A. H. (1981). Possible pathophysiological mechanisms in subtypes of unipolar depressive disorders based on differences in urinary MHPG levels. *Psychopharmacology Bulletin, 17,* 90–91.

Schildkraut, J. J., Orsulak, P. J., Schatzberg, A. F., Gudeman, J. E., Cole, J. O., Rohde, W. A., & LaBrie, R. A. (1978). Toward a biochemical classification of depressive disorders: I: Differences in urinary excretion of MHPG and other catecholamine metabolites in clinically defined subtypes of depression. *Archives of General Psychiatry, 35,* 1427–1433.

Schildkraut, J. J., Watson, R., Draskoczy, P. R., & Hartmann, E. (1971). Amphetamine withdrawal: Depression and MHPG excretion. *Lancet, 2,* 485–486.

Schilkrut, R., Chandra, O., Osswald, M., Ruther, E., Baarfusser, B., & Matussek, N. (1975). Growth hormone release during sleep and with thermal stimulation in depressed patients. *Neuropsychobiology, 1,* 70–79.

Schlesser, M. A., Winokur, G., & Sherman, B. M. (1979). Genetic subtypes of unipolar primary depressive illness distinguished by hypothalamic-pituitary-adrenal axis activity. *Lancet, 1,* 739–741.

Schlesser, M. A., Winokur, G., & Sherman, B. M. (1980). Hypothalamic-pituitary-adrenal axis activity in depressive illness: Its relationship to classification. *Archives of General Psychiatry, 37,* 737–743.

Schulz, H., Lund, R., Cording, C., & Dirlich, G. (1979). Bimodal distribution of REM sleep latencies. *Biological Psychiatry, 14,* 595–600.

Schulz, H., & Trojan, B. (1979). A comparison of eye movement density in normal subjects and in depressed patients before and after remission. *Sleep Research, 8,* 49.

Segal, D. S., & Janowsky, D. S. (1978). Psychostimulant-induced behavioral effects: Possible models of schizophrenia. In M. A. Lipton, A. DiMascio, & K. F. Killam (Eds.), *Psychopharmacology: A generation of progress.* New York: Raven Press.

Selye, H. (1959). Stress and the general adaptation syndrome. *British Medical Journal, 1,* 1383–1392.

Shagass, C., Roemer, R. A., & Straumanis, J. J. (1982). Relationships between psychiatric diagnosis and some quantitative EEG variables. *Archives of General Psychiatry, 39,* 1423–1435.

Shaw, D. M., O'Keefe, R., MacSweeney, D. A., Brooksbank, B. W. L., Noguera, R., & Coppen, A. (1973). 3-methoxy-4-hydroxyphenylglycol in depression. *Psychological Medicine, 3,* 333–336.

Shopsin, B., & Gershon, S. (1971). Plasma cortisol response to dexamethasone suppression in depressed and control patients. *Archives of General Psychiatry, 24,* 320–326.

Shopsin, B., Wilk, S., & Gershon, S. (1973). Collaborative psychopharmacologic studies exploring catecholamine metabolism in psychiatric disorders. In E. Usdin & S. Snyder (Eds.), *Frontiers in catecholamine research—Proceedings of the Third International Catecholamine Symposium.* Elmsford, NY: Pergamon Press.

Shopsin, B., Wilk, S., Gershon, S., Davis, K., & Suhl, M. (1973). Cerebrospinal fluid MHPG: An assessment of norepinephrine metabolism in affective disorders. *Archives of General Psychiatry, 28,* 230–233.

Shopsin, B., Wilk, S., Sathananthan, G., Gershon, S., & Davis, K. (1974). Catecholamines and affective disorders revisited: A critical assessment. *The Journal of Nervous and Mental Disease, 158,* 369–383.

Siever, L., Insel, T., & Uhde, T. (1982). Noradrenergic challenges in the affective disorders. *Journal of Clinical Psychopharmacology, 1,* 193–206.

Sitaram, N., & Gillin, J. C. (1980). Development and use of pharmacological probes of the CNS in man: Evidence of cholinergic abnormality in primary affective illness. *Biological Psychiatry, 15,* 925–955.

Sitaram, N., Moore, A. M., & Gillin, J. C. (1978). Induction and resetting of REM sleep rhythm in normal man by arecholine: Blockade by scopolamine. *Sleep, 1,* 83–90.

Sitaram, N., Nurnberger, J. I., Gershon, E. S., & Gillin, J. C. (1980). Faster cholinergic REM sleep induction in euthymic patients with primary affective illness. *Science, 208,* 200–202.

Sitaram, N., Nurnberger, J. I., Gershon, E. S., & Gillin, J. C. (1982). Cholinergic regulation of mood and REM sleep: Potential model and marker of vulnerability to affective disorder. *American Journal of Psychiatry, 139,* 571–576.

Sitaram, N., Wyatt, R. J., Dawson, S., & Gillin, J. C. (1976). REM sleep induction by physostigmine infusion during sleep. *Science, 191,* 1281–1283.

Siwers, B., Ringberger, V. A., Tuck, J. R., & Sjoqvist, F. (1977). Initial clinical trial based on biochemical methodology of zimelidine (a serotonin uptake inhibitor) in depressed patients. *Clinical Pharmacology and Therapeutics, 21,* 194–200.

Sjostrom, R. (1973). 5-hydroxyindoleacetic acid and homovanillic acid in cerebrospinal fluid in manic-depressive psychosis and the effect of probenecid treatment. *European Journal of Clinical Pharmacology, 6,* 75–80.

Sovner, R. (1983). An amphetamine-like reaction to the dexamethasone suppression test in depressed patients. *Journal of Clinical Psychopharmacology, 3,* 236–238.

Spar, J. E., & Gerner, R. (1982). Does the dexamethasone suppression test distinguish dementia from depression? *American Journal of Psychiatry, 139,* 238–240.

Spatz, H., & Spatz, N. (1978). Urinary and brain phenylethylamine levels under normal and pathological conditions. In A. D. Mosnaim & M. E. Wolf (Eds.), *Non-catecholic phenylethylamines: Part I: Phenylethylamine: Biological mechanisms and clinical aspects.* New York: Marcel Dekker, Inc.

Spiker, D. G., Coble, P., Cofsky, J., Foster, F. G., & Kupfer, D. J. (1979). EEG sleep and severity of depression. *Biological Psychiatry, 13,* 485–488.

Spiker, D. G., Edwards, D., Hanin, I., Neil, J. F., & Kupfer, D. J. (1980). Urinary MHPG and clinical response to amitriptyline in depressed patients. *American Journal of Psychiatry, 137,* 1183–1187.

Steiner, M., Radwan, M., Elizur, A., Blum, I., Atsman, A., & Davidson, S. (1979). Urinary 3-methoxy-4-hydroxyphenylglycol (MHPG) excretion in depression. *Japanese Journal of Experimental Medicine, 49,* 95–99.

Sternbach, H., Gwirtzman, H., & Gerner, R. H. (1981). The dexamethasone suppression test and response to methylphenidate in depression. *American Journal of Psychiatry, 138,* 1629–1631.

Stokes, P. E., Pick, G. R., Stoll, P. M., Nunn, W. D. (1975). Pituitary-adrenal function in depressed patients: Resistance to dexamethasone suppression. *Journal of Psychiatric Research, 12,* 271–281.

Subrahmanyan, S. (1975). Role of biogenic amines in certain pathological conditions. *Brain Research, 87,* 355–362.

Sulser, F., Owens, M. L., Norvich, M. R., & Dingell, J. V. (1968). The relative role of storage and synthesis of brain norepinephrine in psychomotor stimulation evoked by amphetamine or by desipramine and tetrabenazine. *Psychopharmacologia, 12,* 322–332.

Svendsen, K., & Christensen, P. G. (1981). Duration of REM sleep latency as a predictor of effect of antidepressant therapy: A preliminary report. *Acta Psychiatrica Scandinavica, 64,* 238–243.

Sweeney, D. R., Leckman, J. F., Maas, J. W., Hattox, S. E., & Heninger, G. R. (1980). Plasma free and conjugated MHPG in psychiatric patients: A pilot study. *Archives of General Psychiatry, 37,* 1100–1103.

Takahashi, S., Kondo, H., Yoshimura, M., & Ochi, Y. (1974). Growth hormone re sponses to administration of L-5-hydroxytryptophan (L-5-HTP) in manic-depressive psychosis. In N. Hatotani (Ed.), *Psychoneuroendocrinology. Proceedings of the Workshop Conference of the International Society for Psychoneuroendocrinology, Mieken, September 3–5, 1973.* Basel: S. Karger AG.

Tallman, J. F., Saavedra, J. M., & Axelrod, J. (1976). Biosynthesis and metabolism of endogenous tyramine and its normal presence in sympathetic nerves. *Journal of Pharmacology and Experimental Therapeutics, 199,* 216–221.

Tamura, K., & Karacan, I. (1981). Sleep in neurological diseases. *Psychiatric Annals, 11,* 35–48.

Targum, S. D. (1983). Neuroendocrine challenge studies in clinical psychiatry. *Psychiatric Annals, 13,* 385–395.

Targum, S. D., Sullivan, A. C., & Byrnes, S. M. (1982). Neuroendocrine interrelationships in major depressive disorders. *American Journal of Psychiatry, 139,* 282–286.

Traskman, L., Asberg, M., Bertilsson, L., Cronholm, B., Mellstrom, B., Neckers, L. M., Sjoqvist, F., Thoren, P., & Tybring, G. (1979). Plasma levels of chlorimipramine and its desmethyl metabolite during treatment of depression. *Clinical Pharmacology and Therapeutics, 26,* 600–610.

Traskman, L., Asberg, M., Bertilsson, L., & Sjostrand, L. (1981). Monoamine metabolites in CSF and suicidal behavior. *Archives of General Psychiatry, 38,* 631–636.

Traskman, L., Tybring, G., Asberg, M., Bertilsson, L., Lantto, O., & Schalling, D. (1980). Cortisol in the CSF of depressed and suicidal patients. *Archives of General Psychiatry, 37,* 761–767.

Trevisan, M., Ostrow, D., Cooper, R., Liu, K., Sparks, S., & Stamler, J. (1981). Methodological assessment of assays for red cell sodium concentration and sodium-dependent lithium efflux. *Clinica Chimica Acta, 116,* 319–329.

Ulrich, R. F., Shaw, D. H., & Kupfer, D. J. (1980). Effects of aging on EEG sleep in depression. *Sleep, 3,* 31–40.

Van Kammen, D. P., & Murphy, D. L. (1975). Attenuation of the euphoriant and activating effects of d- and l-amphetamine by lithium carbonate treatment. *Psychopharmacologia, 44,* 215–224.

Van Kammen, D. P., & Murphy, D. L. (1978). Prediction of imipramine antidepressant response by a one-day d-amphetamine trial. *American Journal of Psychiatry, 135,* 1179–1184.

Van Kammen, D. P., & Murphy, D. L. (1979). Prediction of antidepressant response to lithium carbonate by a 1-day administration of d-amphetamine in unipolar depressed women. *Neuropsychobiology, 5,* 266–273.

Van Praag, H. M. (1977a). New evidence of serotonin-deficient depressions. *Neuropsychobiology, 3,* 56–63.

Van Praag, H. M. (1977b). Significance of biochemical parameters in the diagnosis, treatment, and prevention of depressive disorders. *Biological Psychiatry, 12,* 101–131.

Van Praag, H. M. (1981). Management of depression with serotonin precursors. *Biological Psychiatry, 16,* 291–310.

Van Praag, H. M., & Korf, J. (1975). Neuroleptics, catecholamines, and psychoses: A study of their interrelations. *American Journal of Psychiatry, 132,* 593–597.

Van Praag, H. M., & Korf, J., Puite, J. (1970). 5-hydroxyindoleacetic acid levels in the cerebrospinal fluid of depressive patients treated with probenecid. *Nature, 225,* 1259–1260.

Veith, R. C., Bielski, R. J., Bloom, V., Fawcett, J. A., Narasimhachari, N., & Friedel, R. O. (1983). Urinary MHPG excretion and treatment with desipramine or amitriptyline: Prediction of response, effect of treatment, and methodological hazards. *Journal of Clinical Psychopharmacology, 3,* 18–27.

Verghese, A., Matthews, J., & Mathia, G. (1979). Plasma cortisol in depressive illness. *Indian Journal of Psychiatry, 15,* 72–79.

Vogel, G. W. (1981). The relationship between endogenous depression and REM sleep. *Psychiatric Annals, 11,* 423–428.

Vogel, G. W., McAbee, R., Barker, K., & Thurmond, A. (1977). Endogenous depression improvement and REM pressure. *Archives of General Psychiatry, 34,* 96–97.

Vogel, G. W., Thurmond, A., Gibbons, P., Sloan, K., Boyd, M., & Walker, M. (1975). REM sleep reduction effects on depressive syndromes. *Archives of General Psychiatry, 32,* 765–777.

Vogel, G. W., Vogel, F., McAbee, R. S., & Thurmond, A. J. (1980). Improvement of depression by REM sleep deprivation: New findings and a theory. *Archives of General Psychiatry, 37,* 247–253.

Waldmeier, P. C., Baumann, P., Greengrass, P. M., & Maitre, L. (1976). Effects of clomipramine and other tricyclic antidepressants on biogenic amine uptake and turnover. *Postgraduate Medical Journal, 52*(Suppl. 3), 33–39.

Watson, R., Hartmann, E., & Schildkraut, J. J. (1972). Amphetamine withdrawal: Affective state, sleep patterns, and MHPG excretion. *American Journal of Psychiatry, 129,* 263–269.

Wehr, T. A., & Goodwin, F. K. (1981). Biological rhythms and psychiatry. In S. Arieti & H. K. H. Brodie (Eds.), *American handbook of psychiatry: Advances and new directions* (2nd ed.; Vol. 7). New York: Basic Books.

Wehr, T. A., Muscettola, G., & Goodwin, F. K. (1980). Urinary 3-methoxy-4-hydroxy-phenyglycol circadian rhythm: Early timing (phase-advance) in manic-depressive compared with normal subjects. *Archives of General Psychiatry, 37,* 257–263.

Wehr, T. A., Wirz-Justice, A., Goodwin, F. K., Duncan, W., & Gillin, J. C. (1979). Phase advance of the circadian sleep-wake cycle as an antidepressant. *Science, 206,* 710–713.

Weissman, A., Koe, B. K., & Tenen, S. S. (1966). Antiamphetamine effects following inhibition of tyrosine hydroxylase. *Journal of Pharmacology and Experimental Therapeutics, 151,* 339–352.

Whybrow, P. C., & Prange, A. J. (1981). A hypothesis of thyroid-catecholamine-receptor interaction: Its relevance to affective illness. *Archives of General Psychiatry, 38,* 106–113.

Wilk, S., Shopsin, B., Gershon, S., & Suhl, M. (1972). Cerebrospinal fluid levels of MHPG in affective disorders. *Nature, 235,* 440–441.

Williams, R. L. (1978). Sleep disturbances in various medical and surgical conditions.

In R. L. Williams and I. Karacan (Eds.), *Sleep disorders: Diagnosis and treatment.* New York: John Wiley & Sons.

Winokur, A., Amsterdam, J., Caroff, S., Snyder, P. J., & Brunswick, D. (1982). Variability of hormonal responses to a series of neuroendocrine challenges in depressed patients. *American Journal of Psychiatry, 139,* 39–44.

Winokur, G. (1974). The division of depressive illness into depressive spectrum disease and pure depressive disease. *International Pharmacopsychiatry, 9,* 5–13.

Wirz-Justice, A. (1977). Theoretical and therapeutic potential of indoleamine precursors in affective disorders. *Neuropsychobiology, 3,* 199–233.

Young, W., Knowles, J. B., MacLean, A. W., Boag, L., & McConville, B. J. (1982). The sleep of childhood depressives: Comparison with age-matched controls. *Biological Psychiatry, 17,* 1163–1168.

Zarcone, V. P., Berger, P. A., Brodie, H. K. H., Sack, R., & Barchas, J. D. (1977). The idoleamine hypothesis of depression: An overview and pilot study. *Journal of Clinical Psychiatry, 38,* 646–653.

Zis, A. P., & Goodwin, F. K. (1982). The amine hypothesis. In E. S. Paykel (Ed.), *Handbook of affective disorders.* New York: Guilford Press.

PART 3

Special Topics

Chapter 15

Depression in Children and Adolescents

Kay Kline Hodges
University of Missouri School of Medicine

Lawrence J. Siegel
University of Texas Medical Branch

Information about the etiological factors of depression in adults as well as effective treatment approaches for adult depressive disorders has increased significantly over the past two decades. However, the material presented in this chapter reflects a more recent interest in the study of depressive disorders in children and adolescents. It is only within the last decade that systematic investigations have begun to explore the basic features of depressive disorders in individuals under the age of 18. Research on depression with adults has progressed to the stage where the focus is primarily on identifying specific subgroups within the affective disorders. In contrast, research with children continues to focus on whether depressive symptoms can be differentiated from other behavior disorders in this population (Lefkowitz & Burton, 1978).

While there is little disagreement that children can become sad or unhappy, there continues to be considerable debate as to whether children can manifest depressive disorders in a manner similar to those identified in adults (Cantwell & Carson, 1979; Schulterbrant & Raskin, 1977). Several perspectives on the nature of a depressive disorder or syndrome in children can be identified in the literature. One view is that while children may show sad affect, they cannot become depressed (Anthony, 1975; Rie, 1966). This perspective is shared primarily by researchers and clinicians with a psychodynamic orientation who suggest that adequate superego development is necessary for depression to occur. Accordingly, a child's superego is not sufficiently developed to permit a child to become depressed.

A second view is that the primary features of adult depression do not

Acknowledgements: The authors wish to acknowledge the help of Daniel Burbach who served as a research assistant.

exist in children, but that depressive equivalents are manifested as other behavioral symptoms such as delinquent behavior, learning problems, phobias, and so on (Glaser, 1968). This concept, often called "masked" depression, has been criticized by a number of authors who note that every symptom that has been proposed as an overt manifestation of some underlying depression, also represents symptoms that reflect the total range of behavior disorders in children. As a result, this concept offers little in the way of providing guidelines for a differential diagnosis of depression in children versus other forms of behavior disorders.

Another perspective in the literature is that children can manifest depressive disorders in a manner similar to adult depression including the affective, cognitive, motivational, vegetative, and psychomotor components. In addition to these primary clinical features, this view also suggests that other developmentally associated symptoms such as enuresis, school phobia, and aggressive behavior may be exhibited concurrently with the primary depressive behaviors (Brumback, Dietz-Schmidt, & Weinberg, 1977; McConville, Boag, & Purohit, 1973).

Finally, some authors have proposed that while children may exhibit depressive symptoms that parallel those seen in adults, these depressive behaviors often are transitory in nature and, therefore, do not persist as they do in adults. Furthermore, this perspective suggests that since many of these symptoms are observed in normal children at various developmental periods, the notion that these behaviors are pathological or dysfunctional in nature is questionable (Gittleman-Klein, 1977; Lefkowitz & Burton, 1978).

A fundamental distinction between children and adults, which introduces considerable complexity into the research process on affective disorders in children, is the developmental changes which children experience (Kashani, Husain, Shekim, Hodges, Cytryn, & McKnew, 1981; Strober & Werry, in press). Children are constantly changing. These changes are reflected in cognitive and affective development which, in turn, may have important influences on the expression of depressive symptoms at any particular stage in the child's development. As a result of these developmental shifts, the researcher in this area is faced with the unique problem of establishing the extent to which children's behavior at different age-groups reflect normal developmental processes or deviations from those processes (Rutter, in press). Such developmental considerations dictate that diagnostic criteria or normative behaviors be investigated for each age- or stage-related group. These issues do not confront the clinician or researcher in the area of adult depression.

This chapter will provide an overview of the theoretical and empirical literature on depression in children and adolescents. Issues in the diagnosis and assessment of depression in this population are addressed including the influence of developmental factors. Research related to the epidemiology, etiology, and associated features of childhood depression, including suicide, are reviewed. Finally, this chapter discusses various approaches to the treatment of depression in children and adolescents.

ISSUES OF DIAGNOSIS/CLASSIFICATION

In discussing diagnosis, issues related to the criteria in the *Diagnostic and Statistical Manual* of *Mental Disorders* (*DSM-III*) (American Psychiatric Association, 1980) should probably first be mentioned since it is the major reference for making diagnostic decisions in the United States. In *DSM-III*, children may be given any diagnosis unless they meet an exclusionary criteria regarding age. The Task Force on Nomenclature and Statistics for *DSM-III* decided against including any diagnostic categories for affective disorders in childhood (Spitzer, 1976). The diagnostic criteria for childhood depression are basically the same as for adults.

According to the *DSM-III* criteria, for children age six or over, the familiar criteria for major depressive episode for adults is needed: dysphoric mood, or loss of interest or pleasure in all or almost all usual activities and pastimes, as well as four out of eight possible symptoms, have to be present nearly every day for a period of at least two weeks. The symptoms are: poor appetite, sleep difficulties, psychomotor agitation or retardation, loss of interest or pleasure in usual activities, fatigue, feelings of worthlessness, complaints or evidence of diminished ability to think or concentrate, and/or recurrent thoughts of death or suicide ideation.

In addition, the diagnostic criteria for major depressive episode specifies that for children under six years, dysphoric mood may have to be inferred from a "persistently sad facial expression." Also, it specifies that for these children under six years, at least three of the first four listed symptoms must be met; that is, the child must have at least three of the following symptoms: poor appetite, sleeping difficulties, psychomotor agitation or retardation, and/or loss of interest or pleasure in usual activities. It is noteworthy that for the criteria, "loss of interest or pleasure in usual activities," children under six years can meet the criteria with "signs of apathy" (American Psychiatric Association, 1980, p. 214). In the narrative comments about the esssential features of major depressive episode, it is mentioned that in the case of children, failure to make expected weight gains might be seen instead of significant weight loss, and that hypoactivity rather than psychomotor retardation may be observed in addition to psychomotor agitation. Thus, the essential features of major depressive episode are seen as basically similar for infants, children, adolescents, and adults.

In *DSM-III*, a distinction is made between the essential features, which are required in order to make the diagnosis, and associated features, which are not part of the diagnostic criteria. These associated features are often thought to be present, but not invariably so. For major depressive episode, "age specific associated features" are discussed. It is noted that in prepubertal children, intense anxiety symptoms may be noted. In adolescent males, the following associated features were listed: negativistic or frankly antisocial behavior, feelings of wanting to leave home or not being understood or approved of, restlessness, grouchiness, aggression, sulkiness, a reluctance to cooperate in family ventures, withdrawal from social activities, school difficulties, inattention to personal appearance, increased emotionality (with particular sensitivity to rejection of loved ones), and substance abuse (American Psychiatric Association, 1980, pp. 211–212).

A second diagnosis which may be given when depression is observed is dysthymic disorder, also referred to as depressive neurosis. This diagnosis is given when there is a chronic disturbance of mood involving dysphoric mood or loss of interest, but it is not of sufficient severity and duration to meet the criteria for major depressive episode. The essential characteristics for adults are the same as for children and adolescents. The only variation is the time duration required. For adults, a two-year duration of chronic disturbance of mood is required, in contrast to children and adolescents for whom a one-year duration of chronic disturbance of mood is sufficient. The age-specific associated features for dysthmic disorder are the same as those given for major depressive episode.

While *DSM-III* provides descriptions of the diagnostic categories which hopefully enable clinicians to communicate about the same set of patients, there is a paucity of information available about the reliability of these categories, and even less available about their validity. The National Institute of Mental Health (NIMH) sponsored two sets of field trials to study inter-rater reliability (American Psychiatric Association, 1980, pp. 467–472). The kappa coefficients of agreement for all affective disorders (major affective disorder, dysthymic disorder, and all others listed in this general category) for children was .53 for Phase I of the field trials ($n = 71$) and .30 for the second phase ($n = 55$). The individual kappa coefficients for major affective disorder was .36 for Phase I and $-.02$ for Phase II. In Phase I, 16.9 percent of the children were diagnosed as having an affective disorder, whereas, in Phase II, 9.1 percent were so diagnosed. These results are less than fair and overall do not provide sufficient evidence that affective disorders can be reliably diagnosed in children and adolescents. In contrast, the kappa statistics for adults were .69 for all affective disorders in Phase I and .83 in Phase II, suggesting good inter-rater reliability for adults. Other studies assessing reliability of *DSM-III* criteria for depressive disorders in children have been similarly disappointing (Cantwell, Russell, Mattison, & Will, 1979a, 1979b). Unfortunately, a recent study of inter-rater reliability of *DSM-III* in children (Werry, Methven, Fitzpatrick, & Dixon, 1983) provided no data on affective disorders. Of the 195 children in the study, only one child had such a diagnosis, and that was a case of bipolar disorder which had to be excluded from the study for reasons related to clinical care.

On the issue of validity, no evidence is given in the *DSM-III Manual.* In fact, in making a decision about childhood depression, there was "controversy regarding the presence of clinical depression in children and, if it exists, whether or not it is fundamentally different from depression in adults" (Spitzer, 1976, p. 455).

Over the last 10 to 15 years there has been a marked change in what are considered areas of consensus and controversy within the area of childhood depression. Former areas of controversy, which no longer seem to have much credibility, are the theoretical positions that depression does not exist in childhood and that depression in childhood is primarily manifested in a "masked" form. It is generally accepted now that depression does exist in children, and that there are a subset of children who manifest symptoms indicating overt depression. In fact, even persons who have formally defended the notion of masked depression in children came to retract this position (Cytryn, McKnew, & Bunney, 1980). The general consensus now is that a thorough interview with the child and parent should reveal the presence of depression, if it exists, even if other symptoms are emphasized in the initial presentation (Carlson & Cantwell, 1980; Paykel & Norton, 1982). Puig-Antich (1982) has made an interesting observation that those persons who initially proposed the notion of masked depression may have been clinically astute in their identification of depressive symptoms, through play interviews, before more direct and sophisticated assessment procedures and interviews for children were developed.

Currently the major controversy in research in the area of diagnosis of childhood depression is whether the essential characteristics of depression are the same for adults as for children and adolescents. Puig-Antich's (1982) position is characteristic of the group of researchers who argue that childhood depression does not differ significantly from depression in adults. While Puig-Antich states that there may be developmental changes in the expression of affective symptoms, he concludes that an assessment of the current data available suggests that no major changes occur after age six or seven years. He proposes that the diagnostic criteria should be essentially the same for children and adults, although the process of assessment differs. For example, school-age children have poor chronological sense of time and have concrete language. For adolescents, developing a personal rapport is an area of difficulty. Puig-Antich (1982) emphasizes developing effective assessment procedures before assuming that the diagnostic criteria are different.

In contrast, other researchers and clinicians argue that there is insufficient data on which to base a conclusion about whether depression in childhood and/or adolescence is parallel to adult depression. In general, this group of researchers considers the developmental aspects of children and adolescents so great as to raise the question of whether essential (or associated) features differ for age or developmental level (reviewed by Cantwell, 1982). In addition, given that children have unique developmental characteristics, it may be that the clinical picture for children contains some unique features not typically observed in adults. As of yet, there is no consensus among the major researchers and clinicians as to: (1) the essential features of childhood depression and how they compare to adult depression, and (2) the associated features of childhood depression and whether there are age-specific differences.

Other diagnostic schemata have also been offered for childhood depression. They will be reviewed here because they serve as a possible reference source for future studies addressing the issue of essential and associated features of childhood and adolescent depression. Some of the first attempts to define the clinical characteristics of depressed children were done by Ling, Oftedal, and Weinberg (1970), and Poznanski and Zrull (1970). Ling et al. (1970) considered a child depressed if 4 of the following 10 characteristics were present:

1. Significant mood changes.
2. Social withdrawal.
3. Increasingly poor performance in school.
4. Sleep disturbances.
5. Aggressive behavior not previously present.
6. Self-deprecation.
7. Lack of energy.
8. Somatic complaints other than headache.
9. School phobia.
10. Weight loss.

Poznanski and Zrull (1970) described clinical characteristics of overtly depressed children, whom they depicted as in a state of "chronic unhappiness or sadness." They included negative self-image and problems in handling aggression. Negative self-image was typically a very predominant and pervasive feature. In a more recent article, Poznanski (1982) indicated that she gave the diagnosis of depressive syndrome when children with depressed affect had five of the following symptoms: anhedonia, lowered self-esteem, impairment of school work, sleep difficulty, excessive fatigue, psychomotor retardation, social withdrawal, and morbid or suicidal ideation. She noted that for children difficulty in concentrating is often experienced in school work. Also, poor self-esteem is more likely to be expressed concretely by children, such as through comments about their own bodies. She noted that vegetative symptoms are less common in children than in adults.

In 1973 Weinberg, Rutman, Sullivan, Penick, and Dietz described very specific diagnostic criteria which have become a foundation for much of the work which followed. The Weinberg criteria, as they have come to be known, were derived from the Feighner criteria used for adults (Feighner, Robins, Guze, Woodruff, Winokur, & Muñoz, 1972). They contain the same 10 characteristics as those listed in Ling et al. (1970) except that school phobia was changed to "change in attitude towards school," with school phobia and "does not enjoy school activities" being included under this heading. Also, it was further specified that the child must have dysphoric mood and self-deprecatory ideation as well as two or more of the remaining eight symptoms.

It is noteworthy that there are several differences between the Weinberg and *DSM-III* criteria, besides the specific symptoms mentioned. One, of course, is that for Weinberg the dysphoric mood *and* low self-esteem are essential characteristics. In the *DSM-III* criteria for major depressive disorder, dysphoric mood *or* loss of interest or pleasure in almost all usual activities or pastimes must be present. Second, in the list of remaining symptoms, Weinberg requires only two out of the remaining eight, while *DSM-III* requires four of the additional eight symptoms. Third, the Weinberg criteria require that the symptoms have to represent a change in the child's usual behavior, while the *DSM-III* diagnosis does not require that. Fourth, for the Weinberg criteria the symptoms must be present for more than one month, whereas in *DSM-III* the symptoms must be present for at least two weeks. Fifth, the Weinberg criteria do not contain exclusionary criteria for schizophrenia or other disorders. Sixth, the Weinberg criteria are stated in terms which are typically used for children, such as school performance. Also, the term *aggression* is used, which is sometimes considered to be the equivalent of irritability and psychomotor agitation in adults. Seventh, in the Weinberg criteria, for each of the major 10 symptoms several characteristic behaviors are listed for each symptom. In determining the diagnosis, a symptom is accepted as positive if at least one of the characteristic behaviors listed for the category is considered by the parent and/or child to be a concern and is a change from the usual self. Petti (1978) developed a scoring system for the Weinberg criteria which permitted rating of symptoms on severity from zero to three. Petti's scoring system was referred to as the Bellevue Index of Depression and involved a semistructured interview.

A comparison of the Weinberg and *DSM-III* criteria was conducted by Carlson and Cantwell (1982b) with 102 psychiatrically referred children. Their results suggest that the Weinberg criteria are overinclusive. However, since the two sets of criteria differ in many respects, these findings do not necessarily mean that a modified use of the symptom list targeted by the Weinberg criteria would result in overinclusion. Also, in conducting research in this area, it is important to heed the warning made by Carlson and Cantwell (1980) that there is a meaningful distinction between symptoms (a single component providing evidence of a disease), syndromes (groupings of symptoms), and disorders (a set of symptoms representing abnormality in functioning). Their research comparing children's responses obtained with a psychiatric interview revealed that depressive symptoms and syndromes were far more frequently observed than affective disorders (Carlson & Cantwell, 1980).

The question of what is the most valid set of diagnostic criteria for childhood depression remains unanswered. The research task involved is made more difficult by the fact that there are no independent criteria, such as biological markers, available to use in validation of the criteria. In order to determine the most appropriate criteria, the following appears essential:

1. Phenomenological studies to determine if there is variation in symptoms with age.
2. Determination of which sets of symptoms occur together across the various ages.
3. Determination of which sets of symptoms (or syndromes) represent an abnormality in functioning (referred to as a disorder).

4. Studies of the biological correlates of the disorders, their natural history, and their response to different interventions.
5. Determination of whether each disorder or set of symptoms can be reliably diagnosed.
6. Determination of the stability of symptoms to determine whether their duration is more than transient.
7. Studies of how these sets of symptoms or disorders may be subclassified so as to better design treatment approaches, as has been done with adult disorders.

There are some existing studies which present preliminary research efforts in these areas. For example, several phenomenological studies have collected data on the incidence of various symptoms, although age-specific variations have not been systematically examined (Brumback, Dietz-Schmidt, & Weinberg, 1977; Inamdar, Siomopoulos, Osborn, & Bianchi, 1979; Schoenbach, Kaplan, Grimson, & Wagner, 1982). Factor analytic studies provide information about how symptoms cluster; however, it is difficult to collect the large set of protocols needed for depressed children meeting diagnostic criteria. In a study by Hodges, Siegel, Mullins, and Griffin (1983), a factor analysis of responses on the Children's Depression Inventory is presented. Achenbach and Edelbrock's (1983) work with the Child Behavior Checklist, which consists of empirically derived subscales, yields some information relevant to the clustering of depressive symptoms in the general population. While there are a number of articles discussing classification schemata (e.g., Cytryn & McKnew, 1972, 1974; Malmquist, 1971), only the work by McConville et al. (1973) is based on any empirical efforts. The question of stability of depressive symptoms had been questioned in the major review article by Lefkowitz and Burton (1978). However, recent work by Tesiny and Lefkowitz (1982a) supports the stability of symptoms over a six-month period, while the work of Kovacs and her colleagues (Kovacs, Feinberg, Crouse-Novak, Paulauskas, & Finkelstein, 1984) and Cytryn, McKnew and their colleagues (Apter, Borengasser, Hamovit, Bartko, Cytryn, & McKnew, 1982; Cytryn, McKnew, Zahn-Waxler, & Gershon, in press) provide evidence of the stability of depressive disorders over longer periods of time (i.e., four- to five-year follow-ups).

PREVALENCE AND EPIDEMIOLOGY

The incidence of depression in children and adolescents is difficult to evaluate because of the lack of generally accepted methods of assessment and diagnostic criteria. Prevalence rates have been found to vary considerably depending on a number of factors including the population studied (i.e., prepubescent children or adolescents, psychiatric, or medical patients) and the diagnostic criteria and evaluation procedures used (Carlson & Cantwell, 1979). For example, in a review of 11 epidemiological studies, Kashani, Husain, et al. (1981) note that rates of depression in children have been found to range from 0.14 percent to 59 percent.

In a general population of children on the Isle of Wight, Rutter, Tizard, and Whitmore (1970) found an incidence of depression less than 0.2 percent in 10- and 11-year-old children, while at age 14 and 15 the rate was 0.45 percent. Similarly, Lefkowitz and Tesiny (1982) in a large sample of normal elementary school children found that 5.2 percent exhibited depressive symptoms. There were no differences in the rate of these symptoms in males or females. Finally, in a randomly selected sample of children in the general population, Kashani and Simonds (1979) found that 1.9 percent met *DSM-III* criteria for a major affective disorder.

Among children attending an outpatient psychiatric clinic, Pearce (1977) found that approximately 10 percent of prepubertal children showed depressive symptoms, whereas 23 percent of adolescents exhibited such symptoms. Twice as many males as females were depressed in the prepubertal group. However, in the adolescent sample, twice as many girls as boys showed depressive symptoms. In a similar sample, however, Poznanski and Zrull (1970) found that only about 1 percent of the children met their criteria for depression. These children were reevaluated approximately seven years later and 50 percent of them remained clinically depressed (Poznanski, Cook, & Carroll, 1979).

Carlson and Cantwell (1979) investigated 210 children between 7 and 17 years old who were seen either in an outpatient clinic or an inpatient service of a psychiatric facility. The study found that 60 percent of the children had depressive symptoms and 49 percent scored in the moderately depressive range on a self-report measure. However, when the children were assessed with a diagnostic interview, only 28 percent were judged to meet *DSM-III* criteria for a depressive disorder. In addition, when the sample was divided into outpatient and inpatient groups, 16 percent and 36 percent, respectively, were diagnosed as depressed. Petti (1978) reported that 59 percent of children hospitalized on a psychiatric unit were diagnosed as depressed.

The incidence of depression in children with medical disorders and other clinical problems has also been investigated. Kashani, Barbero, and Bolander (1981) studied 100 children, 7 to 12 years old, who were hospitalized for various medical illnesses and surgery in a pediatric hospital ward. Seven percent were diagnosed as depressed, while 38 percent exhibited dysphoric mood. In a sample of children and adolescents 6 to 17 years old who were being treated for various malignant diseases, 17 percent met *DSM-III* criteria for a major depressive disorder (Kashani & Hakami, 1982).

Weinberg et al. (1973) found that 57 percent of children ages 6 to 12, who were referred to an educational diagnostic clinic for children with learning or behavior problems in the classroom, met their criteria for a depressive disorder. Similarly, Brumback, Jackoway, and Weinberg (1980) found that 62 percent of children referred to an educational diagnostic center exhibited depressive symptoms.

Although it is difficult to draw definitive conclusions from the literature at this time, it does appear that the incidence of depressive disorders in the general population of children and adolescents is relatively low. However, the rate of depression appears to be greater in clinical populations. Furthermore, the prevalence of depression in children hospitalized in psychiatric settings increases steadily with age (Carlson & Strober, 1979).

DEVELOPMENTAL ISSUES

Now that there is a growing consensus that childhood depression exists, the question of whether childhood and adult depression are phenomenologically similar has become a dominant focus in the literature. This question is currently being explored by cross-sectional studies in which symptoms of depression as well as hypothesized correlate characteristics (e.g., self-esteem, locus of control expectations) are assessed for children of various age-groups (e.g., Albert & Beck, 1975; Kaslow, Rehm & Siegel, in press). However, the nature of this inquiry and the methodology being utilized assumes a simplistic notion of developmental issues.

Developmental aspects of childhood depression have been largely ignored. In fact, major review papers of the topic have failed to even highlight the potential importance of the issue. In only a few empirical studies has a developmental perspective been considered. Furthermore, no theory of childhood depression, which would certainly have to address developmental issues, has emerged. In theoretical discussions numerous authors have stated that a developmental view is important (e.g., Cytryn & McKnew, 1974; Klerman, 1976; McConville et al., 1973; Rie, 1966; Rutter, in press; Siomopoulos & Inamdar, 1979). A few such discussions have offered a very general framework for conceptualizing some developmental aspects of childhood depression (e.g., Anthony, 1975; Bemporad, 1982; Philips, 1979). However, all of the authors utilized the psychoanalytical developmental phases/tasks as a basic framework, with the role of cognitive level, the effect of family, and environmental influences also included. For example, Bemporad (1982) differentiated four age-groupings: younger than five years, early latency (5–8 years), latency to preadolescence (9–12 years), and adolescence. He purports that preschool children do not tend to sustain depressive moods and that they react quite rapidly to positive or protective environmental influences. In contrast, early latency age children do express sadness, withdrawal, and general inhibition. They have more immature reasoning skills, are less able to verbalize their feelings, and are very vulnerable to environmental influences. However, for the older children, negative self-esteem is described as a critical causal factor. Their greater cognitive maturity tends to permit more self-appraisal and more internalization of others' expectations and views of them. Adolescents are distinct from the other younger groups due to their more sophisticated sense of time. Adolescents can experience "dread of the future," and can be prone to undue pessimism because they lack the "moderation gained from experience." Based on these notions, Bemporad (1982) does not recommend direct work with the child until age nine or so. Discussions by Philips (1979) and Anthony (1975) are quite similar, with Anthony emphasizing the "regulation" of self-esteem as a critical factor.

The relationship between developmental issues and childhood depression is obviously multifaceted. In the discussion which follows, the issue will be explored from three major perspectives: (1) symptomatology as a function of age or developmental level; (2) the effect of age-related phenomenon upon the development of depressive symptoms; and (3) the effect of depressive symptoms (or processes postulated as responsible for the etiology of depression) upon the personality development of the child.

The issue of the relationship between symptom presentation and age probably represents the least complex way of approaching the developmental issues. For example, the results of a study by McConville et al. (1973) suggest developmental trends in manifestations of depressive symptoms. Children 6 to 8 years old tended to express sadness and helplessness; negative self-esteem was generally expressed by children older than 9 years; whereas excessive guilt and thoughts of self-destruction were reported only in the oldest children (over 11 years). Typically, research on childhood psychopathology relates symptoms to chronological age, with the tacit assumption being made that age is equivalent to developmental level (Achenbach, 1978). However, in the area of childhood depression, symptoms may vary with developmental level of the child's cognitive ability (e.g., Piagetian stages), psychosocial functioning (e.g., psychodynamic stages); affective/emotional awareness; and psychosexual maturity (e.g., puberty). For example, Rutter (in press) reports on a study by Pearce in which sexual maturity was used as the independent variable, rather than age. The results indicated that for prepubertal children, depression was twice as frequent in boys, whereas for the postpubertal children, it was twice as frequent in girls. It is important to note that age would have been an unsatisfactory indicator of developmental level for sexual maturity since onset of puberty varies across individuals and because of the later onset of puberty for boys than girls.

A more complex level of studying developmental issues involves the influence of age-related processes upon the development/maintenance of depressive symptoms. In this regard, there are at least two content areas worthy of investigation. First is the question of whether there are developmentally related abilities which must be present for certain types of depressive experiences. For example, an understanding of time perspective has been postulated as essential for the development of feelings of hopelessness (Bemporad, 1982; Siomopoulos & Inamdar, 1979). Also, an ability to have intrapsychic self-representation is thought to be necessary in order for certain evaluative experiences, resulting in low self-esteem, to take place (Anthony, 1975; Rie, 1966). Thus, various symptom presentations may be dependent upon the acquisition of specific age-related abilities.

Second, the development of various depressive symptoms may be influenced by age-related stresses. Possible types of life stresses include developmental transitions which involve time to adjust (e.g., puberty onset, entering high school) and "life strains" (Hoeper & Pierce, 1984). In the literature, the term *life strains* has been defined as the stress involved in ongoing personal relationships with others, who have various social roles relative to the self (Hoeper & Pierce, 1984). Such social stressors usually necessitate a change in the individual's life, which can have a negative or positive effect on functioning, depending on the individual's coping skills and social support system. For example, the increase in frequency and change in sex ratio of depressive disorders at the time of puberty may be etiologically related to the type of social stressors associated with dating for males versus females (Rutter, in press).

Another aspect of developmental issues as they relate to depression involves the impact of pathological influences on the ongoing development of the child. The presence of childhood depression could affect the child's current functioning as well as interfere with the child's/adolescent's future development. One major difference between adults and children is that the child is involved in a constant process of growth—cognitively, physically, socially, and emotionally. A depressive disorder could affect the child's future adjustment through failure to learn various skills or through a narrowing of the child's repertoire of skills, which had previously been available to the child. Thus, childhood depression may have a pervasive and more generalized effect on the child's personality, which would extend considerably beyond the acute symptoms. For example, various processes have been postulated as the mechanisms underlying the development of depression. If originating in the childhood or adolescent years, these various socialization processes may critically impact on the child's ongoing personality development. The various socialization deficits which have been studied in the literature include: cognitive distortions (e.g., Beck, 1972); learned helplessness (e.g., Abramson, Seligman, & Teasdale, 1978); poor social skills resulting in a failure to obtain reinforcements from the environment (Lewinsohn, Teri, & Hoberman, 1983); and deficits in self-control behavior involved in self-monitoring, self-evaluating, and self-reinforcement (Rehm, 1977). These theoretical models are reviewed by Kashani, Husain, et al. (1981), Kaslow and Rehm (1983, in press).

In order to study these significant issues related to developmental influences, the current research efforts will need to extend beyond cross-sectional studies in which chronological age is used as the independent variable. Developmental level, assessed for the variables of interest, would be the preferable independent variable. In addition, methodological designs which permit the observation of developmental processes need to be used. Longitudinal, follow-up, and modified cross-sectional designs are needed. Studying several cohort groups also helps distinguish between historical trends versus developmental trends, both of which could account for observed age differences. Only a few studies which meet some of these criteria have yet been completed (Cytryn, McKnew, Zahn-Waxler, & Gershon, in press; Kovacs et al., 1984; Rutter, in press).

Rutter, Graham, Chadwick, and Yule (1976) conducted a four-year follow-up study of the Isle of Wight general population of 10 and 11 year olds. At follow-up depressive feelings were much more prevalent, with over two fifths of the adolescents reporting depressed moods compared to 13 percent expressing depressive feelings at age 10. There was also a sharp increase in depressive disorders as they became adolescents, although diagnosable disorders were still less prevalent than depressive feelings.

Kovacs and her colleagues (Kovacs et al., 1984) have studied children with confirmed depressive disorders (major depressive episode, dysthymic disorder, and adjustment disorder with depressed mood). This is a longitudinal project in which the course of the illness is being studied (e.g., age of onset and pattern of recovery). Cytryn, McKnew, and their colleagues are conducting longitudinal studies of children with parents who have major affective disorders (Cytryn et al., in press; Cytryn, McKnew, Zahn-Waxler, Radke-Yarrow, Gaensbauer, Harmon, & Lamour, in press). In this work the parents have confirmed diagnoses, while the potential illness of the child is one of the questions being investigated. Such children are at high risk for developing affective illnesses. This presents an opportunity to study the issue of continuity versus discontinuity of affective disorders. The results of their follow-up studies with latency age children and infants suggest that depression in children is not transient, but quite persistent. They also observed that disturbances in the child's affect regulation and social interactions could be identified early with a "gradual coalescence of prodromal symptoms" into an affective illness identifiable with increasing age. They concluded that a diagnosable depressive presentation usually did not emerge until six or seven years of age, with the clinical picture of the illness changing with the developmental processes.

ASSESSMENT

Assessing depression is generally perceived to be a complex task because it involves reporting subjective experience and relies less on direct observation, compared to other disorders. In addition, assessment of affective states in children and adolescents is even more complicated because of their developmentally related cognitive limitations. Despite these problems, numerous measures to assess depression in children have been generated in the last 10 years. As a consequence of the recency of the interest in this area, most of these measures are still in the preliminary stages of development. As such, the data relevant to psychometric properties is for the most part incomplete. In this section, the major assessment instruments currently in use today are reviewed, including self-rating scales, clinician-rated scales, diagnostic interviews, and peer inventories. Emphasis is placed on summarizing the psychometric data which is available and highlighting future research needs. In the discussion of the various instruments, they are presented in the order corresponding to their appearance in the literature. Comprehensive reviews of this area are presented by Kazdin and Petti (1982) and Strober and Werry (in press).

Self-Rating Scales

Five self-rating scales have been used with children and adolescents. All of them except the Beck Depression Inventory ([BDI]; Beck, 1972) were specifically developed for children. The BDI is included because there is some evidence that it can be used validly with adolescents. Two of the scales, the Children's Depression Inventory (Kovacs & Beck, 1977) and the Children's Depression Adjective Checklist (Brewer & Lubin, 1983) are modified versions of adult measures. The remaining two scales, the Self-Rating Scale (Birleson, 1981) and the Children's Depression Scale (Lang & Tisher, 1978) were derived by generating a pool of items based on a review of the relevant literature. All of these self-rating scales are still relatively new and in the process of being developed. Reliability and validity with these self-report measures have not been adequately demonstrated to permit clinical or diagnostic use, and in some cases perhaps research usage may be premature, especially for some age-groups.

The Children's Depression Inventory (CDI) was the first of these scales to be developed. While reliability has been established with nonclinic children aged 10 years and older, data relevant to reliability (especially test-retest) is yet to be published for clinic children (Kovacs, 1980–81). The CDI has good content validity, if the diagnostic criteria for major depressive disorder (MDD) is used as the appropriate content domain to be assessed. All the diagnostic criteria are inquired about, except perhaps for psychomotor agitation or retardation. It is apparent that the authors tried to include items which corresponded to these symptoms as manifested by children. However, some symptoms which are irrelevant to the diagnosis of MDD are asked about in the CDI, such as noncompliance and somatic concerns. While there is evidence of construct and criterion-related validity, there is insufficient evidence of discriminant validity (e.g., that the CDI identified "depression," as opposed to any other psychiatric problem). Also, more research needs to be done to determine any age differentiation.

The Children's Depression Scale (CDS) has a child version and adult companion form for significant others. In the manual for the CDS, there is no report on test-retest reliability. However, Tisher and Lang (1983) reported on a study by Tonkin and Hudson in which adequate reliability was found for nonclinic children, ages 9 to 13 years only. In terms of content validity, the CDS includes many items not relevant to the diagnosis of MDD, such as family relationships, mother's health, dreams, and fear of harming parents. This appears to be secondary to the fact that the authors used children manifesting school refusal as their "depressed" group. Also, several criteria in MDD are not included, such as appetite and diminished ability to think. The validation data presented in the manual are limited. The major validity study is a contrasted groups design, with a small sample size and use of school refusal as the depressed group. There is no evidence of discriminant validity (i.e., syndrome specificity). Also, the normative data provided is not age-relevant and is apparently based on data from 37 nonclinic children, aged 9 to 16 years. While several other ongoing and recent studies are cited by Tisher and Lang (1983), no other significant evidence of the validation of the CDS is presented. However, data suggesting age differences are reported, further emphasizing the need for age appropriate norms. Also, there is no evidence of validity for the six CDS subscales.

The Beck Depression Inventory (BDI) has been studied with adolescent populations by Chiles, Miller, and Cox (1980), who modified the wording but not the content of three items of the BDI, and by Strober, Green, and Carlson (1981) and Teri (1982), who used an unmodified version of the BDI. The results of the Chiles et al., (1980) study failed to provide any evidence of reliability or validity for the BDI with adolescents. However, the Strober, Green, and Carlson study yielded evidence of reliability, including test-retest, and of validity with a psychiatric adolescent sample. Patients with a diagnosis of MDD could be differentiated from nondepressed patients, based on the BDI score. In terms of content validity, the BDI contains items which roughly correspond with the diagnostic criteria for MDD, with few items which do not directly correspond to the criteria for MDD.

The Weinberg criteria were used as the original point of reference in developing the Self-Rating Scale (SRS). Test-retest and internal consistency reliability have been demonstrated with a very small sample of emotionally disturbed children. However, the time interval for the test-retest reliability was not reported. No data relevant to validity were provided; however, reference is made to a factor analysis. The SRS has items corresponding to most of the diagnostic criteria, however, it differs from the MDD diagnosis in: (1) the duration requirement is one week rather than two weeks; (2) three criteria are not sufficiently inquired about (i.e., psychomotor agitation or retardation, diminished ability to think, and guilt); and (3) several items irrelevant to the diagnosis of MDD are included (e.g., "horrible" dreams, somatic complaints, ability to talk to someone, and feeling like running away).

One of the most recently developed measures is the Children's Depression Adjective Checklist (C-DACL). This instrument differs from the other measures in several fundamental ways. It assesses dysphoric mood only, with none of the other symptoms in MDD (except perhaps fatigue) being inquired about. Also, the time duration is restricted to the present state (i.e., "how you feel today"). The reliability data suggest good internal consistency across several different sample types. The test-retest reliability scores were considered to be inadequate, which the authors regard as not problematic given that it is designed to be a "state" measure. There are data supporting the validity of the C-DACL for preadolescent children; however, there is no evidence of discriminant validity (except a negative correlation to self-ratings of elation). The data for adolescents (13 years and older) was not supportive, leaving Brewer and Lubin (1983) to conclude that the scale was only appropriate for use with preadolescents (8–12 years). Another study, by Sokoloff and Lubin

(1983), provided some data supportive for use with adolescents; however, the case for using the C-DACL with adolescents still appears to be quite weak at this time.

Clinician-Rated Scales

The Bellevue Index of Depression ([BID]; Petti, 1978) is a modified version of a scale originally devised by Ling et al. (1970) and revised by Weinberg et al. (1973). Unfortunately, there are little data available on the BID. No evidence of test-retest, internal consistency, or interscorer agreement is provided. The items on the BID include all the diagnostic criteria in MDD, as well as a few symptoms not included in the criteria (e.g., belief of persecution, somatic complaints, aggressive behavior). The empirical evidence for validity is restricted to one study which demonstrated agreement between the BID criteria for depression and an independent clinician's classification of the child as depressed or nondepressed. Given that some interviewing appears to be involved in using this measure and that judgments about severity of symptoms are made, the issue of interscorer agreement is particularly important. Also, discriminant validation data are lacking.

The Children's Depression Rating Scale (CRDS), developed by Poznanski and her colleagues (Poznanski et al., 1979), was designed to be a modified version of the Hamilton Depression Rating Scale which would be appropriate for children. In 1983 Poznanski introduced a revised version of the scale (CDRS-R). The revised CDRS includes a set of questions to ask the child and permits a seven-point, rather than five-point, rating system for each response item. Compared to other measures, the CDRS and CDRS-R have a considerable amount of data suggesting good reliability with clinic samples aged 6 to 12 years, including test-retest, internal consistency, and inter-rater reliability (Poznanski, Grossman, Buchsbaum, Banegas, Freeman, & Gibbons, 1984). However, it would be preferable if the agreement on the inter-rater reliability was completed on an item-by-item basis, rather than for total score. The diagnostic criteria for MDD are inquired about, except perhaps for diminished ability to think. The only symptom on the CDRS-R which is not included in MDD or dysthymic disorder is physical complaints. The validation studies have included three different clinical samples: psychiatric inpatients, psychiatric outpatients, and pediatric inpatients. While the findings support the validity of the CDRS-R, the fact that the same clinicians apparently gave the child a global rating for depression as well as scored the CDRS-R raises the question of possible halo effects (Strober & Werry, in press).

Diagnostic Interviews

Five diagnostic interviews have been used to assess depression in children and adolescents. Two of these interviews, the Interview Schedule for Children (Kovacs, 1983) and the Kiddie-Schedule for Affective Disorders and Schizophrenia (Puig-Antich & Chambers, 1978), were originally developed for the purpose of assessing depression in children. The remaining three were designed to assess the entire spectrum of disorders observed in children, including depression. Since all these interviews can be used, and have been used, to diagnose depression in children and adolescents, they are reviewed here.

The Interview Schedule for Children (ISC) was first developed in 1974 and later refined in 1977 (Kovacs, 1983). There is evidence of good inter-rater reliability based on item-by-item agreement. The procedure involved one clinician interviewing the patient in the presence of another observing clinician. The two clinicians independently scored the ISC. Kovacs, (1983) recognized that the nature of the probes asked by the interviewing clinician and vigilance on the part of the observer may artificially enhance agreement. As anticipated, it was noted that the ratings for behavioral observations made by the clinicians were less reliable than the ratings of the symptoms which are inquired about from the child. As of yet, there are little data available about the validity of the ISC.

The Schedule for Affective Disorders and Schizophrenia for School Age Children (K-SADS) was developed by Puig-Antich and his colleagues (Chambers, Puig-Antich, & Tabrizi, 1978). The K-SADS was derived from the adult scale developed by Endicott and Spitzer (1978). There are two versions—one to assess current psychopathology (i.e., present episode version) and the other to assess past and current episodes (i.e., epidemiologic version).

It is difficult to discuss the reliability of data relevant to the K-SADS because it is not easily accessible. The information is apparently contained in unpublished papers which were presented at professional meetings. References have been made to adequate inter-rater reliability (Chambers et al., 1978) as well as to adequate test-retest reliability (Hirsch, Paez, & Chambers, 1980, as cited in Puig-Antich, Goetz, Hanlon, Davies, Thompson, Chambers, Tabrizi & Weitzman, 1982). The only published report of data refers to a kappa value of .77 for test-retest reliability for K-SADS-P, although it is not clear what diagnoses (depression and/or nondepressive disorders) were included (Puig-Antich et al., 1982). In their review, Strober and Werry (in press) report that all but two items assessing depression (i.e., excessive guilt and impaired concentration) have acceptable inter-rater reliability (citing personal communication with Puig-Antich). To their credit, the authors have provided a discussion of the subtle issues involved in inquiring about and scoring the various depressive symptoms (Puig-Antich, Chambers, & Tabrizi, 1983). Use of such should facilitate establishing reliability. The validation studies with regard to Kiddie-SADS have been conducted almost exclusively with children who had been diagnosed as having major depressive disorder or who were referred to the prepubertal depression clinic administered by Puig-Antich and his colleagues. These are primarily psychobiological studies in which it has been found that children identified as depressed have characteristics similar to those observed in depressed adults (e.g., Puig-Antich, Chambers, Halpern, Hanlon, & Sachar, 1979; Puig-Antich, Goetz, Hanlon, Tabrizi, Davies, & Weitzman, 1983; Puig-Antich, Perel, Lupatkin, Chambers,

Shea, Tabrizi, & Stiller, 1979). While the K-SADS appears to be reliable and valid when applied to known depressed children, there is no evidence to suggest that these findings are generalizable to other samples of children (i.e., normal, less severely disturbed children, or children with other psychiatric disorders) or to other contexts for administration (i.e., other clinicians beyond those trained by Puig-Antich, other testing situations outside of an intensive study protocol).

The Diagnostic Interview for Children and Adolescents (DICA) was developed by Herjanic and her colleagues to assess a broad range of psychiatric symptoms through a structured interview (Herjanic, Herjanic, Brown, & Wheatt, 1975). The DICA has since been revised considerably, with questions added to obtain information on timing, duration, and severity of symptoms. In the only report of inter-rater reliability, good agreement was cited; however, methodology was not described (Herjanic et. al., 1975). These same data were cited in a 1982 article (Herjanic & Reich), and it was clarified that 10 interviewers watched and independently rated one of two taped child interviews. No data are available on reliability for the depressive symptoms. The evidence for validity of the DICA is derived from one contrasted group study, conducted before the revisions to the interview and done without blind procedures (Herjanic & Campbell, 1977). In future validation studies, it would be important to specifically assess the items relevant to depressive symptoms if it is to be used in studying childhood depression. The kappas for depressive symptoms were disappointingly low in a concordance study between mother and child report (Herjanic & Reich, 1982). However, these results should not be considered indicative of a unique weakness of the DICA, given the current literature on poor reliability in assessing more subjectively experienced symptoms.

The Child Assessment Schedule (CAS) was developed in 1978 by Hodges in collaboration with McKnew and Cytryn (Hodges, Kline, Stern, Cytryn, & McKnew, 1982). It differs from the other interviews in that the primary purpose in developing the CAS was to design an instrument which would be optimally appropriate for use with children, both in terms of the content of the questions and the interviewing process. The CAS has undergone revision, specifically in the area of obtaining additional information about onset and duration of symptoms. Two independent studies have assessed inter-rater reliability and found it to be quite acceptable (Hodges, Kline, Stern, Cytryn, & McKnew, 1982; Hodges, McKnew, Cytryn, Stern, & Kline, 1982). In addition, these results were found with various samples of subjects, including psychiatric outpatients, psychiatric inpatients, nonpsychiatric controls, and children of affectively disturbed and normal mothers. The results of the validation study were very supportive and involved three types of procedures, including comparisons among contrasted groups, correspondence with maternal report, and correspondence with child self-report (Hodges, Kline, et. al., 1982). For all three analyses, the data specifically relevant to depressive symptoms indicated adequate validity. To aid researchers, the authors have written guidelines to assist in establishing reliability (Hodges, 1983) and have conducted a concordance study between the CAS and K-SADS (Hodges, McKnew, Burbach, & Roebuck, 1984).

The most recently developed interview is the Diagnostic Interview Schedule for Children (DISC). Even though there are no data available yet on reliability or validity, it is being mentioned here because it is anticipated that the DISC may be used for epidemiological research in the future. The interview is being developed under the auspices of the National Institute of Mental Health for the specific purpose of generating an interview to use in collecting epidemiological data about prevalence of psychiatric disorders.

Peer Inventories

The Peer Nomination Inventory of Depression (PNID) was developed by Lefkowitz and Tesiny (1980). It is an innovative approach which yields information about peers' judgments, and, as such, provides data from an important significant other in the child's life. The set of studies conducted on the PNID is impressive in terms of the large sample size and the various types of reliability and validity which have been assessed. There are considerable data supporting test-retest reliability, internal consistency, and inter-rater agreement (i.e., agreement among peers) for the PNID (Lefkowitz & Tesiny, 1980, 1982). If *DSM-III* diagnostic categories are used to assess content validity, the PNID would not fair well. In fact, only four of the criteria appear to even be inquired about. These include: dysphoric mood, sleep difficulty (as manifested only by sleeping in class), loss of interest or pleasure in usual activities including social contact, and feelings of worthlessness. In fact, 6 of the 14 depression items appear to exclusively tap loss of interest in social activities. The PNID certainly could not be regarded as yielding sufficient information to reflect on a diagnosis of depression. The validation studies have been extensive, and include correlation with: (1) ratings by self, teachers, and parents, (2) indexes of various types of functioning, (3) personality variables, and (4) demographic characteristics (Tesiny & Lefkowitz, 1980, 1982; Lefkowitz, Tesiny, & Gordon, 1980). While the data are very supportive, some of the correlations are also relatively low, questioning somewhat the strength of the convergent validity. Also, there are other unexpected high correlations which raise issues about discriminant validity and about the nature of the variable being assessed by the PNID (Tesiny & Lefkowitz, 1982). However, overlap among such constructs is not an issue which is unique to the PNID.

Parent Scales

Many of the scales described above have parallel forms for parents or other significant informants, such as teachers. In addition, there are other scales which can yield information about depressive symptoms, such as the Child Behavior Checklist (Achenbach & Edelbrock, 1983) and the Personality Inventory for Children (Wirt, Lachar, Klinedinst, & Seat, 1977). However, a review of these measures is beyond the scope of the chapter.

Future Research Needs

From the above review, it is apparent that much work still needs to be conducted with most of the measures. The areas of most concern include:

1. Establishing test-retest reliability.
2. Establishing inter-rater reliability.
3. Establishing validity, especially discriminant validity.
4. Studying (and/or controlling) sources of bias.
5. Exploring effects of various testing conditions, contexts, or procedures.
6. Investigating possible age differences, and where needed, establishing age-relevant norms.
7. Conducting reliability and validity studies with various types of persons (i.e., subject samples) to whom research results will be applied (e.g., psychiatric, nonpsychiatric, medical).
8. Exploring the effect of disorder severity and type on the reliability and validity of measures.

Also, researchers will need to study several other issues which need to be addressed, regardless of the specific measure being used. Two major concerns include: (1) how to integrate and/or utilize information from various informants, given that there are known areas of poor concordance between parents and children, and (2) how to classify depressive phenomenon (e.g., distinguishing between depressive disorder, symptoms associated with depressive disorder, and general unhappiness). In the interim, researchers will need to choose measures most suitable for their purposes, also taking into consideration the current psychometric data available and the resources as well as limitations of their specific study.

COGNITIVE FEATURES OF CHILDHOOD DEPRESSION

Findings from the adult literature on depression have guided much of the research in the area of childhood depression. In taking this approach, a number of variables known to be related to depression in adults have been evaluated for their relevance to childhood depression. One of the areas in which parallels between adult and childhood depression has been investigated is the relationship between depressive symptoms and several cognitive variables including general intellectual functioning, problem-solving skills, and attributional style.

In a sample of children ages 5 to 12 who were seen at an educational diagnostic clinic, Brumback et al. (1980) found no differences on depressed and nondepressed children's performances on standardized tests of intellectual functioning and academic achievement. On the other hand, Lefkowitz and Tesiny (1980) and Tesiny, Lefkowitz, and Gordon (1980) report a negative relationship between self-rated depression and both intellectual functioning and academic achievement (standardized reading and math scores) in a large group of public elementary school children.

Kaslow (1981) found that depressed children in the first and fourth grades showed impaired performance on the Block Design, Coding, and Digit Span subtests from the WISC-R but did not differ from nondepressed children on the Vocabulary subtest or the Trail Making Test from the Halsted Reitan Battery. There was, however, no relationship between self-reported depression and the performance of children in the eighth grade on any of these tasks.

Problem-solving skills on impersonal tasks (i.e., block designs and anagrams) was investigated by Kaslow, Tanenbaum, Abramson, Peterson, and Seligman (1983) in a sample of school children 9 to 11 years old. Moderate inverse correlations were found between performance on these problem-solving tasks and children's scores on the Children's Depression Inventory. Similarly, Mullins, Siegel, and Hodges (in press) found that higher levels of self-reported depression were associated with lower performance on an anagram task in a group of elementary school children. Finally, Schwartz, Friedman, Lindsay, and Narrol (1982) found that children who endorsed greater numbers of depressive symptoms on a self-report measure had longer latencies and made more errors on the Matching Familiar Figures Test even when controlling for differences in intellectual abilities.

The relationship between depressive symptoms and cognitive interpersonal problem-solving abilities as measured by the children's Social Means-Ends Problem Solving Procedure developed by Shure and Spivack (1972) was investigated by Mullins et al. (in press) in children 9 to 12 years old attending a public elementary school. No consistent relationship was found between depression and interpersonal problem-solving skills as reflected in the number of means stated toward a given story goal and the number of obstacles that were reported on the way to that goal. Similar findings are reported by Griffin and Siegel (in press) in a sample of adolescents ages 13 to 18.

Locus of control has been investigated in a number of studies of depressed children and adolescents. Using a sample of fifth and sixth graders, Moyal (1977) found a strong positive correlation between external locus of control and depression scores. External locus of control was also found to be negatively related to self-esteem. In a study by Lefkowitz et al. (1980), external locus of control was associated with high levels of depression and internal locus of control with lower levels of depression in prepubertal school children. Depressed children attributed positive events to external causes and negative events to internal causes significantly more than nondepressed children in a study by Leon, Kendall, and Garber (1980). Tesiny and Lefkowitz (1982b) found that high depression scores, as measured by peer nominations, were associated with high external locus of control. Furthermore, these findings were stable over a six-month interval. Finally, Griffin and Siegel (in press) found that high levels of self-reported depression were associated with greater external locus of control in a group of adolescents. In addition, locus of control accounted for the greatest amount of variance in the adolescents' scores on the Beck Depression Inventory.

Recently, several studies have investigated attributional styles in depressed children and adolescents. Generally, the findings suggest that depressed children have a "depressogenic" attributional style similar to that seen in depressed adults (Kaslow & Rehm, 1983). In a sample of first-, fourth-, and eighth-grade school children, Kaslow (1981) found that depressed children made more internal, stable, and global attributions for failure and more external, unstable, and specific attributions for success as compared to non-depressed children. These findings have been replicated by Seligman, Kaslow, Tanenbaum, Abramson, and Alloy (1981) and Griffin and Siegel (in press). Furthermore, this depressogenic style was found to predict depressive symptoms six months later (Seligman et al., 1981).

SUICIDAL BEHAVIOR AND DEPRESSION

In adults a high incidence of affective disorders, as well as alcoholism, has been found among persons committing or attempting suicide (e.g., Barraclough, Bunch, Nelson, & Sainsbury, 1974). Since this has been a consistent finding in the adult literature, the question of whether the same association exists for children and adolescents has been raised. In examining this question, it is necessary to consider children and adolescents separately because they show very different patterns in suicidal behavior. For the purposes of this discussion, "children" will refer to those younger than 15 years old, while "adolescents" will be defined as 15 to 19 years old. The reason for using these age ranges is that they are used by the National Center for Health Statistics and the World Health Organization in determining suicide rates (Shaffer & Fisher, 1981). Various degrees of suicidal behavior will be reviewed, including successful suicides, suicide attempts, as well as suicidal threats and reported ideation.

Suicides

Statistics on suicide rates reveal that suicide among children is rare. Using the 1978 statistics, Shaffer and Fisher (1981) demonstrated that while children under the age of 15 constituted 23 percent of the total population, childhood suicides represented less than 1 percent of the suicides in 1978. In addition, this low suicide rate for children has been observed across various cultures and has been relatively stable over time, as evidenced in the United States for the 15 years prior to 1978, and in statistics for the United Kingdom for the past 40 years (Shaffer & Fisher, 1981). In addition, after reviewing various possible sources of underestimating suicide deaths (i.e., erroneously categorizing a suicide death as "undetermined"), Shaffer and Fisher (1981) concluded that the true rate of childhood suicide would still be quite low, even if all questionable and undetermined deaths were included.

In contrast, suicide rates for adolescents are much higher than for children. In 1978, 5.88 percent of suicides were committed by adolescents compared to less than 1 percent by children. Also, in contrast to the stable trend observed for children, the suicide rate for adolescents has tripled from 1956 to 1975, and at present is the highest level ever recorded (Holinger & Offer, 1982). In fact, suicide is now the third leading cause of adolescent deaths following accidents and homocides (Holinger, 1979). While the accident rate has not changed in the last 15 years, the suicide and homocide rates have doubled for adolescents, suggesting an increase in these types of violent deaths. While this increase is of great concern, it is noteworthy that the percentage of adolescents who commit suicide is less than the total percentage of adolescents in the population, which was 9.63 percent in 1978. In addition, Shaffer and Fisher (1981) would estimate that if all "undetermined" deaths were included in these computations, the percentage of adolescent deaths which could be suicides would still not exceed 7 percent of the total number of suicides.

For both children and adolescents, suicide rates are higher for males than females, with the ratio decreasing with age. Also, the rate is higher in whites than nonwhites for both age groupings. However, within the adolescent group, the suicide rate has increased at a higher rate for males and for whites with the rate for white males having increased the most over the past 20 years (Holinger & Offer, 1981). In both children and adolescents, violent/active means of executing suicide are the most common (Shaffer & Fisher, 1981).

Suicide Attempts

While data is available for successful suicides, much less information is available for attempted suicide and suicide threats. There are no requirements for reporting suicide attempts with the information in the literature generated by studies from various medical settings. Like suicides, suicide attempts are relatively rare in children. In contrast, for adolescents the patterns for suicide and attempted suicide are quite different. Rutter (in press) discussed three major ways in which they differ: (1) suicide attempts decrease progressively after adolescence, whereas suicides increase progressively with age; (2) females attempt suicide more than do males, which is the opposite direction from the observed for successful suicides, and (3) attempted suicide is less commonly associated with an affective disorder than completed suicide. Little is known about why adolescents attempt suicide, but it appears that the dynamics of suicide attempters are different from those of completers. However, there is also obvious overlap between the two groups since it is estimated that 10 percent to 15 percent of suicide attempters are eventually successful in committing suicide. Approximately a quarter of successful suicides had made previous attempts (as reviewed by Carlson, 1983). It is estimated that the ratio of suicides to suicide attempts is 1 : 100 for adolescents, compared to a 1 : 10 ratio for adults (Jacobziner, 1965).

Suicide Ideation and Threats

In contrast to the low rate of childhood suicide and known suicide attempts, suicidal threats as well as ideation appear to be quite common. Lourie (1967) reported that 70 percent of a school-age sample of children with emotional problems reported thoughts of killing themselves and 54 percent of a sample of "normal" school-age children had such thoughts. In a study of psychiatric inpatients, aged 8 to 13 years, Carlson and Orbach (1982) found that 55 percent said that they had thought about killing themselves, with half of these children reporting past suicide attempts. In a study of 6- to 12-year-old outpatients, Pfeffer, Conte, Plutchik, and Jerrett (1980) found that 13 percent of the sample reported suicide ideation and 8 percent had made suicidal threats. The same authors (Pfeffer, Conte, Plutchik, and Jerrett, 1979) studied inpatients in a child psychiatric unit and found that 19 percent of them had suicidal ideation, while 26 percent had made suicidal threats. A total of 72 percent of the inpatients and 33 percent of the outpatients had suicidal ideation or demonstrated some type of suicidal behavior such as a suicide attempt. Unfortunately, comparable data are not available for adolescents.

This set of data about various types of suicidal behavior indicate that: (1) in childhood, suicide and suicide attempts are relatively rare, although threats, and especially thoughts about suicide, are much more common; and (2) in adolescence, rates for suicide and suicide attempts are much higher. At a cursory examination, these data are consistent with what is currently known about depression from the epidemiological literature (e.g., Kashani, McGee, Clarkson, Anderson, Walton, Williams, Silva, Robins, Cytryn, & McKnew, 1983; Rutter, in press). Specifically, the prevalence of depression is low in childhood, with a marked increase at puberty and a continuing increase through adolescence. However, a closer scrutiny of available studies raises questions about whether depression, or the lack of it, is an essential variable in suicidal behavior, or the absence of it. In the discussion which follows, relevant empirical studies will be reviewed for children and then adolescents.

In Shaffer's (1974) classic study, he collected data about all the children who successfully committed suicide over a seven-year period in the United Kingdom ($n = 31$). This was a retrospective study in which various records (i.e., coroner, educational, medical, psychiatric, and social services) were reviewed and interviews conducted with school personnel. While no information was given about type of psychiatric disorder, 30 percent of the sample were either seeing a psychiatrist or on a waiting list. The presence of various psychiatric symptoms was also assessed, with approximately 40 percent of the children being characterized by "depressed mood or tearfulness." Suicide had been discussed, threatened, or attempted by 46 percent of the children. A history of depression in the parents or siblings, before the child's death, was present for 20 percent of the cases, and family members had attempted suicide in 13 percent of the cases. In addition, for 30 percent of the cases, at least one of the parents was characterized as a "heavy drinker." While these findings suggest that depression was present in the lives of many of the families, it is not clear that the pattern of symptoms found would be different from, for example, psychiatrically ill children who do not commit suicide. Also, based upon the data that could be collected, it would have to be assumed that 60 percent of the children did not have "depressed mood."

A study by Carlson and Cantwell (1982a) represents one of the few efforts to explicitly study the relationship between suicidal behavior and depression. Their sample was 102 children seen for evaluation in an outpatient setting, age 7 to 17. Thus, their study spanned both age-groups of childhood and adolescence. They did not find differences between these two age-groups for intensity or frequency of suicide ideation or for diagnosis of depression. However, they comment that this may have been due to the severity of their referred clinic population. They assessed suicide ideation with an item from the Children's Depression Inventory (CDI) and from the child's response during a psychiatric interview. The association between suicide ideation and a diagnosis of major affective disorder was strong. The percent of children with depressive disorders in each of the response groups was as follows: suicide ideation denied (on at least one measure), 11 percent; thoughts of suicide, but "would not do it," 34 percent; and clear suicide ideation and would do it if they had an opportunity, 83 percent. In contrast, there was much less evidence of a direct relationship between being diagnosed as depressed and suicide attempt. Of those children who attempted suicide, only 45 percent were diagnosed as depressed. Thus, while suicide ideation is probably an indicator of intensity of depression, it is puzzling why many children who attempt suicide do not admit to symptoms indicating depressive disorder, and why many children with suicide ideation are not diagnosed as depressed nor choose to act on the feelings. The authors conclude that other variables besides depression are needed to explain suicidal ideation and attempts. They also suggest that it is probably unwise for clinicians to be less concerned with attempters who do not report significant depression.

There are several other studies which have yielded information about the degree of association between depression and suicidal behavior in children, even though exploring that relationship was not their primary objective. Only those studies which included a nonsuicidal comparison group were considered worthy of review here. In the only psychiatric outpatient study, Pfeffer et al. (1980) found that suicidal and nonsuicidal children did not differ significantly in acute or chronic symptoms of depressive affect. In a similar study of psychiatric inpatients by the same authors (Pfeffer et al., 1980), a significant difference was found between the suicidal and nonsuicidal groups for acute depressive symptoms (i.e., displayed within last six months) but not for chronic depressive symptoms. Nor did the two groups differ in percentage of children given a diagnosis of depression (24 percent in each group). In a replication study with psychiatric inpatients from a higher socioeconomic status, Pfeffer and her colleagues found more of an association between suicide potential and depressive disorder (Pfeffer, Solomon, Plutchik, Mizruchi, & Weiner, 1982). However, the authors conclude that "the amount of variance accounted for by these correlations was relatively small so that the ability to predict suicidal behavior from diagnoses appears to be limited" (p. 568).

Similar results have been found in other studies with psychiatric inpatients. Kosky (1983) found that 25 percent of Australian children admitted to a unit for suicide attempts had a diagnosis of depressive neurosis, whereas 28 percent of the nonsuicidal children had depressive illnesses. Carlson and Orbach (1982) reported that depressed and nondepressed inpatient children did not differ in suicidal ideation. Also, suicidal children did not differ from nonsuicidal children in ratings on depression given by the child or the staff; nor did they differ in percentage diagnosed as depressed. Cohen-Sandler, Berman, and King (1982) found that 65 percent of the suicidal children had an affective disorder, whereas 38 percent of the children with a depressive disorder evidenced suicidal behavior.

Comparable studies with adolescents (i.e., 15- to 19-year-old age-group) which yield data about the relationship between depression and suicide are notably scarce in the literature. While there are at least three studies about adolescent suicide attempts in which a nonsuicidal comparison group was included in the research design, none of these studies assessed depressive disorders or symptoms (Teicher & Jacobs, 1966; Tishler & McKenry, 1982; Topol & Reznikoff, 1982). In her review, Carlson (1983) reported on a study by Hudgens (1974) in which one third of adolescent suicide attempters in a hospitalized sample "met criteria for a depressive syndrome."

While the studies reviewed above certainly suggest that there is overlap between depressive symptoms/disorders and suicidal behavior, it is equally apparent that the relationship is probably complex and involves other critical variables. The extent to which depressive features are typically observed (e.g., ranging from misery to vegetative symptoms) is unclear, and the extent to which suicidal behavior results from an interaction between depressive symptoms and other factors (e.g., family situation) is not known. The task of identifying the multiple determinants of suicidal behavior, and the relationship among these variables, will most likely be complex. In addition, the factors which tend to protect children from suicide and the factors which place adolescents at greater risk need to be identified.

Numerous variables have been identified in the empirical literature as discriminating between suicidal and nonsuicidal children. These variables, some of which appear to be inherently related to a diagnosis of depression, include the following:

1. Hopelessness (Kazdin, French, Unis, Esveldt-Dawson, & Sherick, 1983; Pfeffer et al., 1979).
2. Attitudes toward life (i.e., wish to live) and death (i.e., wish to die) (Orbach, Feshbach, Carlson, Glaubman, & Gross, 1983; Pfeffer et al., 1979).
3. Parental depression, suicidal behavior, and/or alcoholism (Carlson & Cantwell, 1982a; Garfinkel, Froese, & Hood, 1982; Kosky, 1983; Pfeffer et al., 1979, 1980; Pfeffer, Plutchik, & Mizruchi, 1983).

4. Family disorganization or chaos (Cohen-Sandler et al., 1982; Mattson, Seese, & Hawkins, 1969).
5. Intrafamilial aggression, including physical abuse of the child (Kosky, 1983; Pfeffer et al., 1983).
6. Aggressive threats by suicidal child (Cohen-Sandler et al., 1982; Pfeffer et al., 1983).
7. Pattern of progressively stressful life events (Cohen-Sandler et al., 1982).
8. Recent and multiple losses (Cohen-Sandler et al., 1982; Kosky, 1983).
9. Intellectual and physical precociousness (Pfeffer et al., 1982; Shaffer, 1974).
10. Increased psychomotor activity (Pfeffer et al., 1980).
11. Beliefs about death such as reversibility (Carlson & Orbach, 1982; McIntire, Angle, & Struempler, 1972; Orbach & Glaubman, 1979; Pfeffer et al., 1979).

The last factor regarding the child's beliefs about death differs from the others in that it could better explain a high rate of suicidal behavior, rather than the low rate of suicide in children. It has been shown that the level of sophistication of a child's understanding of death corresponds to his level of cognitive development, as defined by the Piagetian stages (Koocher, 1973). While there is considerable individual variation, a study of normal children by Childers and Wimmer (1971) found that while the universality of death was understood by all the children by age 9, the concept of the irreversibility of death was still not understood by 37 percent of the children at age 10. Thus, young children in general tend to believe that the state of death is reversible. Furthermore, deviations from the typical developmental pattern in concept formation regarding death have been observed for children with suicidal behavior. Compared to controls, a greater percentage of children with suicidal behavior believe that death is temporary (McIntire et al., 1972; Orbach & Glaubman, 1979; Pfeffer, et al., 1979). In addition, these children have a greater tendency to view their personal death as reversible, but others' deaths as irreversible (Carlson & Orbach, 1982; Orbach & Glaubman, 1979).

Other factors have been suggested as explanatory variables, although they were not mentioned above because no empirical data have been generated about them. They are: (1) the practical issue of the child's limited access to self-destructive means, (2) the child's cognitive immaturity, and the resultant difficulty in successfully planning and implementing a suicidal act, (3) the support and/or protection from social isolation provided by the family, and (4) the children's lack of real desire to kill themselves, despite their suicidal behavior (Carlson & Orbach, 1982; Shaffer & Fisher, 1981).

Although much has been written about factors which contribute to suicidal behavior in adolescents (e.g., Glaser, 1978; Toolan, 1978), there is again little empirical data. A study by Teicher and Jacobs (1966) suggested that suicidal adolescents experienced more chronic problems combined with an escalation of recent problems, and increased social isolation, compared to nonsuicidal adolescents. Other factors which have been found to differentiate suicidal and nonsuicidal adolescents include: feelings of hopelessness, external locus of control, extent of peer problems, and degree of family problems (Topol & Reznikoff, 1982). Corder, Shorr, and Corder (1974) compared suicidal and nonsuicidal disadvantaged adolescents on variables which have been identified as predictors of suicidal behavior in the adult literature. There were significant differences for the following: (1) hopelessness, (2) lack of control over their environment, (3) absence of warm adult parental figure, (4) conflict with parent, (5) high activity level, (6) little school involvement, and (7) poor impulse control. Although Holinger and Offer (1981) did not provide relevant empirical data, they propose that the increasing rate of suicide among white male adolescents may be secondary to the "action-oriented style" and "pressure for performance" placed on them.

Much additional research obviously needs to be done to better identify the multiple determinants of suicidal behavior, and how they are related to depression. The existing empirical data suggest that the relationship between depression and suicide in children and adolescents probably differs considerably from that for adults. In the literature on adults, there is much stronger evidence that suicidal behavior takes place within the context of a psychiatric illness, most commonly depression, and less typically alcoholism (Carlson, 1983). This observation has clinical implications in that a different set of guidelines for making treatment decisions regarding children and adolescents is probably needed. From the available data, it is clear that depression should not be viewed as essential in order for suicidal behavior, especially an attempt, to be regarded as serious. Furthermore, the suicides and attempts made by both children and adolescents are quite serious; they typically involve lethal means and constitute deliberate actions. Also, the data on repeat attempts suggest that the repeat rate is high, and that these children are at considerable risk of dying as a result of a successful suicide (Carlson, 1983; Ladame & Jeanneret, 1982). Despite these facts, clinicians are apparently using the presence of a depressive disorder as a necessary feature for hospitalizing child and adolescent suicide attempters (Carlson & Cantwell, 1982a). The existing body of literature is more consistent with Lourie's (1967) advice that any attempt should be regarded as serious and that it is important to impress upon children, adolescents, and "their families that we consider suicide attempts as danger signals, even if they do not" (p. 6).

TREATMENT OF CHILDHOOD DEPRESSION

The literature on the treatment of depression in children is quite limited owing in large part to the very recent developments in the diagnosis and assessment of depressive disorders in children and adolescents and to the recent general acceptance that depression as a clinical entity is observable in children. As Cantwell (1982) has aptly noted, there are as many different treatment approaches that have been suggested and used with depressed children as there are etiological theories for this disorder. Much of the literature in this area is based on anecdotal evidence, clinical observation, and is significantly influenced by the theoretical biases of the authors. There are few well-controlled investigations of the therapeutic efficacy of the various treatment modalities for childhood depression, particularly for psychological and traditional psychotherapy approaches. There does, however, appear to be a growing consensus that the treatment of depression in children and adolescents should be multimodal, involving several intervention strategies that are based on information obtained from a comprehensive assessment of the child and his or her family (Cantwell, 1982; Glaser, 1978; Kashani, Husain, et al., 1981).

Guidelines and case reports of traditional psychotherapy and the psychoanalytic treatment of depression in children have been presented by a number of authors (e.g., Bemporad, 1978; Boverman & French, 1979; Gilpin, 1976). To date, there have been no adequate investigations demonstrating the efficacy of this approach with depressed children and adolescents.

A detailed case report of a chronically depressed, multiproblem 10-year-old girl using multiple-treatment approaches is reported by Petti, Bornstein, Delamater, and Connors (1980). The treatment program included the concurrent use of psychodynamically oriented psychotherapy, psychiatric hospitalization and the use of antidepressant medication, group and family therapy, and a behavioral intervention for the purpose of teaching her appropriate social skills with children and adults.

Glaser (1978) outlines the use of an "eclectic" approach to the treatment of depression in adolescents. He notes several issues that he believes are important to address in therapy with depressed adolescents including feelings of loss and abandonment and a distorted self-image. Because of the multiple determinants of depression in adolescents, he suggests that the sequential or concurrent use of varied treatment approaches is essential. Furthermore, he cautions that antidepressant medication should only be used with psychotherapy and not by itself.

A behavioral treatment program for the treatment of depression in a 10-year-old male is reported in a case study by Frame, Matson, Sonis, Fialkov, and Kazdin (1982). Several behaviors that were considered to reflect his depression were targeted for treatment including lack of eye contact, bland affect, and inappropriate body position. Treatment was conducted on an inpatient basis and consisted of a skills training approach including instructions, modeling, role-playing, and feedback about the quality of his performance. Each behavior was sequentially treated using a multiple-baseline design over 28 daily sessions. A 12-week follow-up assessment indicated that improvements in the target behaviors had been maintained following his discharge from the hospital. As yet, there have not been any systematic investigations of the use of cognitive-behavioral treatment approaches for depression in children, although the use of these techniques for the treatment of specific target behaviors which characterize depression in this population has been suggested (Kaslow & Rehm, 1983).

There has been a growing interest in the use of psychopharmacological interventions in the treatment of depression in children and adolescents (Elkins & Rapoport, 1983; Puig-Antich, in press: Rapoport, 1977). There have been a number of studies, reporting the use of antidepressant medications with this population (e.g., Frommer, 1967; Kuhn & Kuhn, 1972; Kupfer, Coble, Kane, Petti, & Conners, 1979; Puig-Antich, Blau, Marx, Greenhill, & Chambers, 1978; Weinberg et al., 1973). However, in contrast to the literature on the use of the major antidepressant drugs (i.e., monoamine oxidase inhibitors and tricyclics) in the treatment of depression in adults, there have been almost no methodologically adequate investigations of the use of these drugs with depressed children and adolescents (Cantwell, 1982; Cantwell & Carlson, 1979). In her review of this area, Rapoport (1977) concluded that "no clear positive antidepressant drug effect or symptoms specific for children selected for dysphoria has been demonstrated" (p. 96). In a more recent review, Elkins and Rapoport (1983) still came to essentially the same conclusion. Numerous methodological problems exist in the studies that have been reported with children including the lack of clearly specified diagnostic criteria for subject selection, failure to use appropriate control groups and double-blind research designs, and the use of procedures for assessing treatment outcome that are unreliable and/or do not have adequately established validity. Although there appear to be some promising findings in this area, further well-designed studies are needed as well as the assessment of potential side effects of antidepressants when used with children (Werry, 1982).

References

Abramson, L. Y., Seligman, M. E. P., & Teasdale, J. (1978). Learned helplessness in humans: Critique and reformulation. *Journal of Abnormal Psychology, 87,* 49–74.

Achenbach, T. M. (1978). Psychopathology of childhood: Research problems and issues. *Journal of Consulting and Clinical Psychology, 46,* 759–776.

Achenbach, T. M., & Edelbrock, C. (1983). *Manual for the Child Behavior Checklist and Revised Child Behavior Profile.* Burlington, VT: Queen City Printers.

Albert, N., & Beck, A. T. (1975). Incidence of depression in early adolescence: A preliminary study. *Journal of Youth and Adolescence, 4,* 301–307.

American Psychiatric Association. (1980). *Diagnostic and statistical manual of mental disorders (DSM-III)* (3rd ed.). Washington, DC: Author.

Anthony, E. J. (1975). Childhood depression. In E. J. Anthony & T. Benedek (Eds.), *Depression and human existence.* Boston: Little, Brown.

Apter, A., Borengasser, M. A., Hamovit, J., Bartko, J., Cytryn, L., & McKnew, D. H. (1982). A four-year follow-up of depressed children. *Journal of Preventive Psychiatry, 1,* 331–335.

Barraclough, B., Bunch, J., Nelson, B., & Sainsbury, P. (1974). A hundred cases of suicide: Clinical aspects. *British Journal of Psychiatry, 125,* 355–373.

Beck, A. T. (1972). *Depression.* Philadelphia: University of Pennsylvania Press.

Bemporad, J. R. (1978). Psychotherapy of depression in children and adolescents. In S.

Arieti & J. Bemporad (Eds.), *Severe and mild depression: A psychotherapeutic approach.* New York: Basic Books.

Bemporad, J. R. (1982). Management of childhood depression: Developmental considerations. *Psychosomatics, 23,* 272–279.

Birleson, P. (1981). The validity of depressive disorder in childhood and the development of a self-rating scale: A research report. *Journal of Child Psychology and Psychiatry, 22,* 73–88.

Boverman, H., & French, A. P. (1979). Treatment of the depressed child. In A. P. French & I. N. Berlin (Eds.), *Depression in children and adolescents.* New York: Human Sciences Press.

Brewer, D., & Lubin, B. (1983). *Adjective checklists for the measurement of depressive mood in children and adolescents.* Unpublished manuscript.

Brumback, R. A., Dietz-Schmidt, S. G., & Weinberg, W. A. (1977). Depression in children referred to an educational diagnostic center: Diagnosis and treatment and analysis of criteria and literature review. *Diseases of the Nervous System, 38,* 529–535.

Brumback, R. A., Jackoway, M. K., & Weinberg, W. A. (1980). Relation of intelligence to childhood depression in children referred to an educational diagnostic center. *Perceptual and Motor Skills, 50,* 11–17.

Cantwell, D. P. (1982). Childhood depression: A review of current research. In B. B. Lahey & A. E. Kazdin (Eds.), *Advances in clinical child psychology (Vol. 1).* New York: Plenum Publishing.

Cantwell, D. P., & Carlson, G. (1979). Problems and prospects in the study of childhood depression. *Journal of Nervous and Mental Disease, 167,* 522–529.

Cantwell, D. P., Russell, A. T., Mattison, R., & Will, L. (1979a). A comparison of *DSM-II* and *DMS-III* in the diagnosis of childhood psychiatric disorders. I. Agreement with expected diagnosis. *Archives of General Psychiatry, 36,* 1208–1213.

Cantwell, D. P., Russell, A. T., Mattison, R., & Will, L. (1979b). A comparison of *DSM-II* and *DSM-III* in the diagnosis of childhood psychiatric disorders. IV. Difficulties in use, global comparisons and conclusions. *Archives of General Psychiatry, 36,* 1227–1228.

Carlson, G. A. (1983). Depression and suicidal behavior in children and adolescents. In D. P. Cantwell & G. A. Carlson (Eds.), *Affective disorders in childhood and adolescence: An update.* New York: Spectrum Publications.

Carlson, G. A., & Cantwell, D. P. (1979). A survey of depressive symptoms in a child and adolescent psychiatric population. *Journal of the American Academy of Child Psychiatry, 18,* 587–599.

Carlson, G. A., & Cantwell, D. P. (1980). A survey of depressive symptoms, syndrome, and disorder in a child psychiatric population. *Journal of Child Psychology and Psychiatry, 21,* 19–25.

Carlson, G. A., & Cantwell, D. P. (1982a). Suicidal behavior and depression in children and adolescents. *Journal of the American Academy of Child Psychiatry, 21,* 361–368.

Carlson, G. A., & Cantwell, D. P. (1982b). Diagnosis of childhood depression: A comparison of the Weinberg and *DSM-III* criteria. *Journal of the American Academy of Child Psychiatry, 21,* 247–250.

Carlson, G. A., & Orbach, I. (1982, October). *Depression and children's attitudes toward death and suicide.* Paper presented at the American Academy of Child Psychiatry meetings, Washington, DC.

Carlson, G., & Strober, M. (1979). Affective disorders in adolescence. *Psychiatric Clinics of North America, 2,* 511–526.

Chambers, W., Puig-Antich, J., & Tabrizi, M. A. (1978). *The ongoing development of the Kiddie-SADS (Schedule for Affective Disorders and Schizophrenia for School-age Children).* Presented at the annual meeting of the American Academy of Child Psychiatry, San Diego, CA.

Childers, P., & Wimmer, M. (1971). The concept of death in early childhood. *Child Development, 42,* 1299–1301.

Chiles, J. A., Miller, M. L., & Cox, G. B. (1980). Depression in an adolescent delinquent population. *Archives of General Psychiatry, 87,* 1179–1184.

Cohen-Sandler, R., Berman, A. L., & King, R. A. (1982). Life stress and symptomatology: Determinants of suicidal behavior in children. *Journal of the American Academy of Child Psychiatry, 21,* 178–186.

Corder, B. F., Shorr, W., & Corder, R. F. (1974). A study of social and psychological characteristics of adolescent suicide attempters in an urban, disadvantaged area. *Adolescence, 9,* 1–6.

Cytryn, L., & McKnew, D. H. (1972). Proposed classification of childhood depression. *American Journal of Psychiatry, 129,* 63–69.

Cytryn, L., & McKnew, D. H. (1974). Factors influencing the changing clinical expression of the depressive process in children. *American Journal of Psychiatry, 131,* 879–881.

Cytryn, L., McKnew, D. H., & Bunney, W. E. (1980). Diagnosis of depression in children: A reassessment. *American Journal of Psychiatry, 137,* 22–25.

Cytryn, L., McKnew, D. H., Zahn-Waxler, C., & Gershon, E. S. (in press). Developmental issues in risk research: The offspring of affectively ill parents. In M. Rutter, C. E. Izard, & P. B. Read (Eds.), *Depression in children: Developmental perspectives.*

Cytryn, L., McKnew, D. H., Zahn-Waxler, C., Radke-Yarrow, M., Gaensbauer, T. J., Harmon, R. J., & Lamour, M. (in press). Affective disturbances in the offspring of affectively ill parents—A developmental view. *American Journal of Psychiatry.*

Elkins, R., & Rapoport, J. L. (1983). Psychopharmacology of adult and childhood depression: An overview. In D. P. Cantwell & G. A. Carlson (Eds.), *Affective disorders in childhood and adolescence: An update.* New York: Spectrum Publications.

Endicott, J., & Spitzer, R. L. (1978). A diagnostic interview: The schedule for affective disorders and schizophrenia. *Archives of General Psychiatry, 35,* 837–844.

Feighner, J. P., Robins, E., Guze, S. B., Woodruff, R. A., Winokur, G., & Muñoz, R. (1972). Diagnostic criteria for use in psychiatric research. *Archives of General Psychiatry, 26,* 57–63.

Frame, C., Matson, J. L., Sonis, W. A., Fialkov, M. J., and Kazdin, A. E. (1982). Behavioral treatment of depression in a prepubertal child. *Journal of Behavior Therapy and Experimental Psychiatry, 13,* 239–243.

Frommer, E. A. (1967). Treatment of childhood depression with antidepressant drugs. *British Medical Journal, 1,* 729–732.

Garfinkel, B. D., Froese, A., & Hood, J. (1982). Suicide attempts in children and adolescents. *American Journal of Psychiatry, 139,* 1257–1261.

Gilpin, D. C. (1976). Psychotherapy of the depressed child. In E. J. Anthony & D. C. Gilpin (Eds.), *Three clinical faces of childhood.* New York: Spectrum Publications.

Gittleman-Klein, R. (1977). Definitional and methodological issues concerning depressive illness in children. In J. Schulterbrandt & A. Raskin (Eds.), *Depression in childhood: Diagnosis, treatment, and conceptual models.* New York: Raven Press.

Glaser, K. (1968). Masked depression in children and adolescents. *American Journal of Psychotherapy, 21,* 565–574.

Glaser, K. (1978). The treatment of depressed and suicidal adolescents. *American Journal of Psychotherapy, 32,* 252–269.

Griffin, N. J., & Siegel, L. J. (in press). Correlates of depressive symptoms in adolescence. *Journal of Youth and Adolescence.*

Herjanic, B., & Campbell, W. Differentiating psychiatrically disturbed children on the basis of a structured interview. *Journal of Abnormal Child Psychology, 5,* 127–134.

Herjanic, B., Herjanic, M., Brown, F., & Wheatt, T. (1975). Are children reliable reporters? *Journal of Abnormal Child Psychology, 3,* 41–48.

Herjanic, B., & Reich, W. (1982). Development of a structured psychiatric interview for children: Agreement between child and parent on individual symptoms. *Journal of Abnormal Child Psychology, 10,* 307–324.

Hodges, K. (1983). *Guidelines to aid in establishing inter-rater reliability with the Child Assessment Schedule.* Unpublished manuscript.

Hodges, K., Kline, J., Stern, L., Cytryn, L., & McKnew, D. (1982). The development of a child assessment interview for research and clinical use. *Journal of Abnormal Child Psychology, 10,* 173–189.

Hodges, K., McKnew, D., Burbach, D. J., & Roebuck, L. (1984). *Diagnostic concordance between two structured interviews for children: The Child Assessment Schedule and the Kiddie-SADS.* Presented at the annual meeting of the American Psychological Association, Tornoto, Canada.

Hodges, K., McKnew, D., Cytryn, L., Stern, L., & Kline, J. (1982). The Child Assessment Schedule (CAS) diagnostic interview: A report on reliability and validity. *Journal of the American Academy of Child Psychiatry, 21,* 468–473.

Hodges, K. K., Siegel, L. J., Mullins, L., & Griffin, H. (1983). Factor analysis of the Children's Depression Inventory. *Psychological Reports, 53,* 759–763.

Hoeper, E. W., & Pierce, W. E. (1984). *The complex epidemiology of psychiatric symptomatology.* Unpublished manuscript.

Holinger, P. C. (1979). Violent deaths among the young: Recent trends in suicide, homicide, and accidents. *American Journal of Psychiatry, 136,* 1144–1147.

Holinger, P. C., & Offer, D. (1981). Perspectives on suicide in adolescence. *Research in Community and Mental Health, 2,* 139–157.

Hollinger, P. C., & Offer, D. (1982). Prediction of adolescent suicide: A population model. *American Journal of Psychiatry, 139,* 302–307.

Hugdens, R. W. (1974). *Psychiatric disorders in adolescents.* Baltimore: Williams & Wilkins.

Inamdar, S. C., Siomopoulos, G., Osborn, M., & Bianchi, E. C. (1979). Phenomenology associated with depressed moods in adolescents. *American Journal of Psychiatry, 136,* 156–159.

Jacobziner, H. (1965). Attempted suicides in adolescence. *Journal of the American Medical Association, 191,* 101–105.

Kashani, J. H., Barbero, G. J., & Bolander, F. D. (1981). Depression in hospitalized pediatric patients. *Journal of the American Academy of Child Psychiatry, 20,* 123–134.

Kashani, J., & Hakami, N. (1982). Depression in children and adolescents with malignancy. *Canadian Journal of Psychiatry, 27,* 474–476.

Kashani, J. H., Husain, A., Shekim, W. O., Hodges, K. K., Cytryn, L., & McKnew, D. H. (1981). Current perspectives on childhood depression: An overview. *American Journal of Psychiatry, 138,* 143–153.

Kashani, J. H., McGee, R. O., Clarkson, S. E., Anderson, J. C., Walton, L. A., Williams, S., Silva, P. A., Robins, A. J., Cytryn, L., & McKnew, D. H. (1983). Depression in a sample of 9-year-old children: Prevalence and associated characteristics. *Archives of General Psychiatry, 40,* 1217–1223.

Kashani, J., & Simonds, J. F. (1979). The incidence of depression in children. *American Journal of Psychiatry, 136,* 1203–1205.

Kaslow, N. J. (1981, August). *Social and cognitive correlates of depression in children from a developmental perspective.* Paper presented at the American Psychological Association, Los Angeles, CA.

Kaslow, N. J., & Rehm, L. P. (1983). Childhood depression. In. R. J. Morris & T. R. Kratochwill (Eds.), *The practice of child therapy: A textbook of methods.* New York: Pergamon Press.

Kaslow, N. J., & Rehm, L. P. (in press). Conceptualization, assessment, and treatment of depression in children. In A. E. Kazdin & P. Bornstein (Eds.), *Handbook of clinical behavior therapy with children.* Homewood, IL: Dorsey Press.

Kaslow, N. J., Tanenbaum, R. C., Abramson, L. Y., Peterson, C., & Seligman, M. E. P. (1983). Problem-solving deficits and depressive symptoms among children. *Journal of Abnormal Child Psychology, 11,* 497–502.

Kaslow, N. J., Rehm, L. P., & Siegel, A. W. (in press). Social and cognitive correlates of depression in children: A developmental perspective. *Journal of Abnormal Child Psychology.*

Kazdin, A. E., French, N. H., Unis, A. S., Esveldt-Dawson, K., & Sherick, R. B. (1983). Hopelessness, depression, and suicidal intent among psychiatrically disturbed inpatient children. *Journal of Consulting and Clinical Psychology, 51,* 504–510.

Kazdin, A. E., & Petti, T. A. (1982). Self-report and interview measures on childhood and adolescent depression. *Journal of Child Psychology and Psychiatry, 23,* 437–457.

Klerman, G. L. (1976). Age and clinical depression: Today's youth in the twenty-first century. *Journal of Gerontology, 31,* 318–323.

Koocher, G. P. (1973). Childhood, death, and cognitive development. *Developmental psychology, 9,* 369–375.

Kosky, R. (1983). Childhood suicidal behavior. *Journal of Child Psychology and Psychiatry, 24,* 457–468.

Kovacs, M. (1980–81). Rating scales to assess depression in school-aged children. *Acta Paedopsychiatrica, 46,* 305–315.

Kovacs, M. (1983). *The Interview Schedule for Children (ISC): Interrater and parent-child agreement.* Unpublished manuscript.

Kovacs, M., & Beck, A. T. (1977). An empirical-clinical approach toward a definition of childhood depression. In J. G. Schulterbrandt & A. Raskin (Eds.), *Depression in childhood: Diagnosis, treatment, and conceptual models.* New York: Raven Press.

Kovacs, M., Feinberg, T. C., Crouse-Novak, M. A., Paulauskas, S. L., & Finkelstein, R. (1984). Depressive disorders in childhood. I. A longitudinal prospective study of characteristics and recovery. *Archives of General Psychiatry, 41,* 229–237.

Kuhn, V., & Kuhn, R. (1972). Drug therapy for depression in children: Indications and methods. In A. L. Annell (Ed.), *Depressive states in childhood and adolescence.* Stockholm: Almquist & Wiksell.

Kupfer, D., Coble, P., Kane, J., Petti, T., & Conners, C. K. (1979). Imipramine and EEG sleep in children with depressive symptoms. *Psychopharmacology, 60,* 117–123.

Ladame, F., & Jeanneret, O. (1982). Suicide in adolescence: Some comments on epidemiology and prevention. *Journal of Adolescence, 5,* 355–366.

Lang, M., & Tisher, M. (1978). *Children's Depression Scale.* Victoria, Australia: The Australian Council for Educational Research.

Lefkowitz, M. M., & Burton, N. (1978). Childhood depression: A critique of the concept. *Psychological Bulletin, 85,* 716–726.

Lefkowitz, M. M., & Tesiny, E. P. (1980). Assessment of childhood depression. *Journal of Consulting and Clinical Psychology, 48,* 43–50.

Lefkowitz, M. M., & Tesiny, E. P. (1982, August). *Depressive symptoms in children: Prevalence and correlates.* Presented at the annual meeting of the American Psychological Association, Washington, DC.

Lefkowitz, M. M., Tesiny, E. P., & Gordon, N. H. (1980). Childhood depression, family income, and locus of control. *Journal of Nervous and Mental Disease, 168,* 732–735.

Leon, G. R., Kendall, P. C., & Garber, J. (1980). Depression in children: Parent, teacher, and child perspectives, *Journal of Abnormal Child Psychology, 8,* 221–235.

Lewinsohn, P., Teri, L., & Hoberman, H. M. (1983). Depression: A perspective on etiology, treatment, and life span issues. In M. Rosenbaum, C. Franks, & Y. Jaffe (Eds.), *Perspectives on behavior therapy in the eighties.* New York: Springer Publishing.

Ling, W., Oftedal, G., & Weinberg, W. (1970). Depressive illness in childhood presenting as severe headache. *American Journal of the Disabled Child, 120,* 122–124.

Lourie, R. S. (1967). Suicide and attempted suicide in children and adolescents. *Texas Medicine, 63,* 58–63.

Malmquist, C. P. (1971). Depression in childhood and adolescence. *The New England Journal of Medicine, 284,* 887–893.

Mattsson, A., Seese, L. R., & Hawkins, J. W. (1969). Suicidal behavior as a child psychiatric emergency. *Archives of General Psychiatry, 20,* 100–109.

McConville, B. J., Boag, L. C., & Purohit, A. P. (1973). Three types of childhood depression. *Canadian Psychiatric Association Journal, 18,* 133–138.

McIntire, M. S., Angle, C. R., & Streumpler, L. J. (1972). The concept of death in midwestern children and youth. *American Journal of Diseases of Children, 123,* 527–532.

Moyal, B. R. (1977). Locus of control, self-esteem, stimulus appraisal, and depressive symptoms in children. *Journal of Consulting and Clinical Psychology, 45, 951– 952.*

Mullins, L. L., Siegel, L. J., & Hodges, K. K. (in press). Cognitive problem-solving and life event correlates of depressive symptoms in children. *Journal of Abnormal Child Psychology.*

Orbach, I., Feshbach, S., Carlson, G., Glaubman, H., & Gross, V. (1983). Attraction and repulsion by life and death in suicidal and in normal children. *Journal of Consulting and Clinical Psychology, 51,* 661–670.

Orbach, I., & Glaubman, H. (1979). The concept of death and suicidal behavior in young children. *Journal of the American Academy of Child Psychiatry, 88,* 671– 674.

Paykel, E. S., & Norton, K. R. W. (1982). Diagnoses not to be missed; Masked depression. *British Journal of Hospital Medicine, 28,* 151–157.

Pearce, J. (1977). Depressive disorder in childhood. *Journal of Child Psychology and Psychiatry, 18,* 79–82.

Petti, T. A. (1978). Depression in hospitalized child psychiatry patients: Approaches to measuring depression. *Journal of the American Academy of Child Psychiatry, 17,* 49–59.

Petti, T. A., Bornstein, M., Delamater, A., & Conners, C. K. (1980). Evaluation and multimodality treatment of a depressed prepubertal girl. *Journal of the American Academy of Child Psychiatry, 19,* 690–702.

Pfeffer, C. R., Conte, H. R., Plutchik, R. & Jerrett, I. (1979). Suicidal behavior in latency-age children: An empirical study. *Journal of the American Academy of Child Psychiatry, 18,* 679–692.

Pfeffer, C. R., Conte, H. R., Plutchik, R., & Jerrett, I. (1980). Suicidal behavior in latency-age children: An outpatient population. *Journal of the American Academy of Child Psychiatry, 19,* 703–710.

Pfeffer, C. R., Plutchik, R., & Mizruchi, M. S. (1983). Suicidal and assaultive behavior in children: Classification, measurement, and interrelations. *American Journal of Psychiatry, 140,* 154–157.

Pfeffer, C. R., Solomon, G., Plutchik, R., Mizruchi, M. S., & Weiner, A. (1982). Suicidal behavior in latency-age psychiatric inpatient: A replication and cross validation. *Journal of the American Academy of Child Psychiatry, 21,* 564–569.

Philips, I. (1979). Childhood depression: Interpersonal interactions and depressive phenomena. *American Journal of Psychiatry, 136,* 511–515.

Poznanski, E. O. (1982). The clinical phenomenology of childhood depression. *American Journal of Orthopsychiatry, 52,* 308–313.

Poznanski, E. O., Cook, S. C., & Carroll, B. J. (1979). A depression rating scale for children. *Pediatrics, 64,* 442–450.

Poznanski, E. O., Grossman, J. A., Buchsbaum, Y., Banegas, M., Freeman, L., & Gibbons, R. (1984). Preliminary studies of the reliability and validity of the children's depression rating scale. *Journal of the American Academy of Child Psychiatry, 23,* 191–197.

Poznanski, E., & Zrull, J. P. (1970). Childhood depression: Clinical characteristics of overtly depressed children. *Archives of General Psychiatry, 23,* 8–15.

Puig-Antich, J. (1982). The use of RDC criteria for major depressive disorder in children and adolescents. *Journal of the American Academy of Child Psychiatry, 21,* 291–293.

Puig-Antich, J. (in press). Antidepressant treatment in children: Current state of the evidences. In E. Friedman, S. Gershon, & J. Mann (Eds.), *Depression and antidepressants: Implications for cause and treatment.* New York: Raven Press.

Puig-Antich, J., Blau, S., Marx, N., Greenhill, L. L., & Chambers, W. (1978). Prepubertal major depression disorder. *Journal of the American Academy of Child Psychiatry, 17,* 695–707.

Puig-Antich, J., & Chambers, W. J. (1978). *Schedule for Affective Disorders and Schizophrenia for School-Age Children (6–16 years)-Kiddie-SADS.* Unpublished manuscript, New York State Psychiatric Institute, New York.

Puig-Antich, J., Chambers, W. J., Halpern, F., Hanlon, C., & Sachar, E. J. (1979). Cortisol hypersecretion in prepubertal depressive illness. *Psychoneuroendocrinology, 4,* 191–197.

Puig-Antich, J., Chambers, W. J., & Tabrizi, M. (1983). The clinical assessment of current depressive episodes in children and adolescents: Interviews with parents and children. In D. P. Cantwell & G. A. Carlson (Eds.), *Affective disorders in childhood and adolescence: An update.* New York: Spectrum Publications.

Puig-Antich, J., Goetz, R., Hanlon, C., Davies, M., Thompson, J., Chambers, W. J., Tabrizi, M. A., & Weitzman, E. D. (1982). Sleep architecture and REM sleep measures in prepubertal children with major depression: A controlled study. *Archives of General Psychiatry, 39,* 932–939.

Puig-Antich, J., Goetz, R., Hanlon, C., Tabrizi, M. A., Davies, M., & Weitzman, E. D. (1983). Sleep architecture and REM sleep measures in prepubertal depressives: Studies during recovery from the depressive episode in a drug free state. *Archives of General Psychiatry, 40,* 187–192.

Puig-Antich, J., Perel, J. M., Lupatkin, W., Chambers, W. J., Shea, C., Tabrizi, M. A., & Stiller, R. L. (1979). Plasma levels of imipramine (IMI) and desmethyl-imipramine (DMI) and clinical response in prepubertal major depressive disorder: A preliminary report. *Journal of the American Academy of Child Psychiatry, 18,* 616–627.

Rapoport, J. L. (1977). Pediatric psychopharmacology and childhood depression. In J. G. Schulterbrandt & A. Raskin (Eds.), *Depression in childhood: Diagnosis, treatment and conceptual models,* New York: Raven Press.

Rehm, L. P. (1977). A self-control model of depression. *Behavior Therapy, 8,* 787–804.

Rie, H. E. (1966). Depression in childhood: A survey of some pertinent contributions. *Journal of the Academy of Child Psychiatry, 5,* 653–685.

Rutter, M. (in press). The developmental psychopathology of depression: Issues and perspectives. In M. Rutter, C. E. Izard, & P. B. Read (Eds.), *Depression in childhood: Developmental perspectives.* New York: Guilford Press.

Rutter, M., Graham, P., Chadwick, O., & Yule, W. (1976). Adolescent turmoil: Fact or fiction? *Journal of Child Psychology and Psychiatry, 17,* 35–56.

Rutter, M., Tizard, J., & Whitmore, K. (Eds.). (1970). *Education, health, and behavior.* London: Longmans.

Schoenbach, V. J., Kaplan, B. H., Grimson, R. C., & Wagner, E. H. (1982). Use of a symptom scale to study the prevalence of a depressive syndrome in young adolescents. *American Journal of Epidemiology, 116,* 791–800.

Schulterbrandt, J. G., & Raskin, A. (1977). *Depression in childhood: Diagnosis, treatment, and conceptual models.* New York, Raven Press.

Schwartz, M., Friedman, R., Lindsay, R., & Narrol, H. (1982). The relationship between conceptual tempo and depression in children. *Journal of Consulting and Clinical Psychology, 50,* 488–490.

Seligman, M. E. P., Kaslow, N. J., Tannenbaum, R. L., Abramson, L. Y., & Alloy, L. (1981). *Depressive symptoms, attributional style, and helplessness deficits in children.* Unpublished manuscript.

Shaffer, D. (1974). Suicide in childhood and early adolescence. *Journal of Child Psychology and Psychiatry, 15,* 275–291.

Shaffer, D., & Fisher, P. (1981). The epidemiology of suicide in children and young adolescents. *Journal of the American Academy of Child Psychiatry, 20,* 545–565.

Shure, M., & Spivack, G. (1972). Means ends thinking, adjustment and social class among elementary school-aged children. *Journal of Consulting and Clinical Psychology, 38,* 348–353.

Siomopoulos, G., & Inamdar, S. C. (1979). Developmental aspects of hopelessness. *Adolescence, 14,* 233–238.

Sokoloff, R. M., & Lubin, B. (1983). Depressive mood in adolescent, emotionally disturbed females: Reliability and validity of an adolescent checklist (C-DACL). *Journal of Abnormal Child Psychology, 11,* 531–536.

Spitzer, R. L. (1976). Depressive disorder in childhood. *American Journal of Psychiatry, 133,* 455–456.

Strober, M., Green, J., & Carlson, G. (1981). Utility of the Beck Depression Inventory with psychiatrically hospitalized adolescents. *Journal of Consulting and Clinical Psychology, 49,* 482–483.

Strober, M., & Werry, J. S. (in press). The assessment of depression in children and adolescents. In N. Sartorius & T. A. Ban (Eds.). *Assessment of depression.* Geneva: World Health Organization.

Teicher, J. D., & Jacobs, J. (1966). Adolescents who attempt suicide: Preliminary findings. *American Journal of Psychiatry, 122,* 1248–1257.

Teri, L. (1982). Depression in adolescence: Its relationship to assertion and various aspects of self-image. *Journal of Clinical Child Psychology, 11,* 101–106.

Tesiny, E. P., & Lefkowitz, M. M. (1982a). Childhood depression. A 6-month follow-up study. *Journal of Consulting and Clinical Psychology, 50,* 778–780.

Tesiny, E. P., & Lefkowitz, M. M. (1982b, August). *Assessing childhood depression: Cumulative data.* Presented at the annual meeting of the American Psychological Association, Washington, DC.

Tesiny, E. P., & Lefkowitz, M. M., & Gordon, N. H. (1980). Childhood depression, locus of control, and school achievement. *Journal of Educational Psychology, 72,* 506–510.

Tisher, M., & Lang, M. (1983). The children's depression scale: Review and further developments. In D. P. Cantwell & G. A. Carlson (Eds.), *Affective disorders in childhood and adolescence: An update:* New York: Spectrum Publications.

Tishler, C. L., & McKenry, P. C. (1982). Parental negative self and adolescent suicide attempts. *Journal of the American Academy of Child Psychiatry, 21,* 404–408.

Toolan, J. M. (1978). Therapy of depressed and suicidal children. *American Journal of Psychotherapy, 32,* 243–251.

Topol, P., & Reznikoff, M. (1982). Perceived peer and family relationships, hopelessness and locus of control as factors in adolescent suicide attempts. *Suicide and Life-Threatening Behavior, 12,* 141–150.

Weinberg, W. A., Rutman, J., Sullivan, L., Penick, E. C., & Dietz, S. G. (1973). Depression in children referred to an educational diagnostic center: Diagnosis and treatment. *Journal of Pediatrics, 83,* 1065–1072.

Werry, J. S. (1982). Pharmacotherapy. In B. B. Lahey & A. E. Kazdin (Eds.), *Advances in clinical child psychology* (Vol. 5). New York: Plenum Publishing.

Werry, J. S., Methven, R. J., Fitzpatrick, J., & Dixon, H. (1983). The interrater reliability of *DSM-III* in children. *Journal of Abnormal Child Psychology, 11,* 341–354.

Wirt, R. D., Lachar, D., Klinedinst, J. K., & Seat, P. D. (1977). *Multidimensional description of child personality: A manual for the Personality Inventory for Children.* Los Angeles: Western Psychological Services.

Chapter 16

Depression in the Elderly

Alan Stoudemire
Assistant Professor of Psychiatry
Emory University School of Medicine
Atlanta, Georgia

Dan G. Blazer
Associate Professor of Psychiatry
Head, Division of Social and Community Psychiatry
Duke University Medical Center
Durham, NC

INTRODUCTION

There are a number of biological, psychological, and sociological reasons why the phenomenon of depression in the elderly should be given special consideration. Therefore, a "biopsychosocial" model of illness is most appropriate for understanding the interacting causes for depression in the elderly population. From the *biological* standpoint, biochemical changes in the elderly may contribute to development of depression, such as rising levels of the enzyme monoamine oxidase, neuroendocrine changes, and decreases in brain norepinephrine. Physiological changes in the elderly also can be critically important in the pharmacologic management of depression because of enhanced susceptibility to side effects of antidepressants.

The *psychology* of aging also deserves special attention, since the success with which the elderly individual adapts to the developmental tasks and stresses of aging will determine susceptibility to depression. Psychological aspects of aging also have important implications in psychotherapeutic treatment planning; for example, the elderly may have learned to incorporate certain negative cognitive distortions about the aging process that may predispose them to depression. Because multiple losses are often encountered as one ages, grief-oriented therapy may often be indicated. Family therapy to shore up support networks is often of special importance.

From the sociological perspective, stresses such as financial strain, distant families, diminished social contacts, retirement, and cultural prejudices against the elderly may contribute to the development of depression. Social interventions are often of extreme importance for treatment planning and therapeutic outcome.

This chapter will discuss depression in the elderly from each of these perspectives: biological, psychological, and sociological. In addition, special considerations in the differential diagnosis, psychotherapy, pharmacologic treatment of depression in late life will also be examined.

THE EPIDEMIOLOGY OF LATE LIFE DEPRESSION

Depending on the methodological approach to the identification of individuals suffering from depression in late life, prevalence rates will vary. If one considers only significant depressive symptoms (which may be associated with normal grief or as a reaction to illness) prevalence rates are generally much higher reaching 15 percent in the community (Blazer & Williams, 1980). In contrast, if one uses specific diagnostic criteria for making a diagnosis of depressive illness (such as Research Diagnostic Criteria), the rates are closer to 5 percent (Weissman & Myers, 1978). There is no evidence that major depressive disorders increase with age, and in fact, the rates may be somewhat lower among the elderly than they are during the middle of the life cycle (Weissman & Myers, 1978). Females continue, according to more recent studies, to have a proportionately increased rate of depression when compared to males in late life, as they do at other stages of the life cycle (Myers, Weissman, Tishler, Holzer, Leaf, Orvaschel, Anthony, Boyd, Burke, Kramer, & Stoltzman, 1984).

The clinician, however, must not interpret these rates as evidence for decreased concern about the burden of late life depression in our society. For example, suicide rates increase almost linearly with age, this increase being explained predominately by an age-related increase in suicide rates among white males. Though many are concerned about the rate of suicide among adolescents, as this is a most tragic and frequently publicized event, the rate of suicide among those 85 and older is almost four times as great. In addition, the overall dysfunction resulting from depression in the elderly is significant. For example, 28 percent of those suffering from a major depressive illness were found to be suffering from an impairment in social functioning and 28 percent were economically impaired (Blazer & Williams, 1980).

BIOLOGICAL ASPECTS OF AGING IN THE ELDERLY

A number of biological factors associated with aging are pertinent to the topic of depression since biological phenomena associated with aging may influence the development of affective illness. Most age-dependent neurotransmitter studies have been in animals. These studies generally show decline of whole brain levels of norepinephrine and acetylcholine with norepinephrine being the most affected (Samorajski, Rolsten, & Ordy, 1971). Dopamine and norepinephrine have been shown to be generally lower in older animals in the corpus striatum and hypothalamus (Finch, 1973). Human studies with norepinephrine have indicated small declines in the rhombencephalon (Robinson, Nies, Davis, Bunney, Davis, Colburn, Bourne, Shaw, & Coopen, 1972). No clear trends of changes in serotonin levels have been observed with increasing age.

Studies of enzymes involved in metabolism of neurotransmitters demonstrate that levels of monoamine oxidase (MAO) increased with age in human brain, platelets, and plasma (Robinson et al., 1972), with women having higher average platelet and plasma MAO activity than men. Since estrogen serves as a partial MAO inhibitor, this may account for rising MAO activity in postmenopausal women.

Catechol-o-methyltransferase (COMT), the second major metabolic enzyme of norepinephrine and dopamine has not been demonstrated to change with age (Robinson, Sourkes, Nies, Harris, Spector, Bartlett, & Kate, 1977). These results suggest that oxidative amination rather than methylation is the primary form of biogenic amine metabolism associated with aging in the central nervous system ([CNS]; Samorajski & Hartford, 1980).

Endocrine changes associated with aging also may be important. Women experience dramatic changes in endocrine function, primarily related to ovarian estrogen and progesterone with the menopause. To what extent these changes contribute to susceptibility to depression is not known, but they may at least partially account for the increase in MAO activity in the elderly. In men, advanced age is associated with declining function of testicular Leydig cells which produce testosterone in response to gonadotropin stimulation.

Hyperphysiologic levels of cortisol can induce depression in patients with hyperadrenalism or by iatrogenic steroid replacement. Recent research with the use of the Dexamethasone Suppression Test (DST) as a possible biological marker of depression is based on the concept of deranged neuroendocrine functioning in depression (see Chapter 14; Carroll, 1982) and relates to catecholamine theories of depression since central catecholamines may regulate hypothalmic functioning. Several researchers have noted *normal* diurnal patterns of cortisol in elderly individuals (Grad, Rosenberg, Liberman, Trachtenberg, & Kral, 1971) although there may be some decline in the responsiveness of the adrenal cortex to ACTH with aging (Bowman & Wolf, 1969; Grad et al., 1971).

Tourigny-Rivard et al. (Tourigny-Rivard, Raskind, & Rivard, 1981) compared the DST in 10 healthy young (mean age 29.9) versus 10 healthy elderly subjects and found that age alone did not affect the overnight DST result (Jenike, 1983). Another study using the DST in a depressed elderly population largely confirms these findings (Spar & LaRue, 1983). Use of DST is somewhat problematic in the elderly, since almost any stressful medical illness can confound DST results (i.e., false-positive results may result from hypertension, uncontrolled congestive heart failure, renal failure, cancer, infections, recent surgery, fever, nausea, diabetes, Cushing's syndrome, weight loss, alcoholism). Numerous medications also confound test results by accelerating dexamethasone metabolism; namely, phenytoin, barbiturates, meprobamate, glutethimide, methyprylon, methaqualone, and carbamaze-pine (Carroll, 1982). In addition, the laboratory technique used in cortisol assay is critical, with much more reliable results being obtained with the competitive protein binding assay than with the much more commonly used radioimmunoassay kits ([RIA]; Meltzer & Fang, 1983).

Thyrotropin-releasing hormone (TRH) induced thyroid-stimulating hor-mone (TSH) response in older rats is decreased as compared to younger animals (Meites, Huang, & Reigle, 1976). The TRH-stimulation test has also recently been tested as a biological marker for depression in humans (see Chapter 14). This test also varies with age, particularly in men (Snyder & Utiger, 1972; Winokur, Amsterdam, Oler, Mendels, Snyder, Caroff, & Bruns-wick, 1983).

Sleep parameters are also a possible marker of depressive illness, since shortened REM latency appears frequently in depressed subjects. A shift to-ward normalization of REM latency after administration of tricyclics appears to be a potential predictor of a positive response to treatment (Kupfer, Spiker, Coble, Neil, Ulrich, & Shaw, 1981).

In the normal elderly individual, the most dramatic change in their sleep pattern as compared to younger adults is the marked reduction in slow wave sleep, primarily Stage 4 sleep, and increases in nighttime awakenings and Stage 1 sleep (Ulrich, Shaw, & Kupfer, 1980). There is also some indication of a possible decline in total REM sleep with age. Some research suggests that REM latency decreases with normal aging although this is not a consistent finding (Dement, Laughton, & Carskadon, 1982). In depressed patients, how-ever, REM latency shows a distinct decrease between ages 18 and 60 years which is an effect not well demonstrated in normal nondepressed adults (Ulrich et al., 1980).

In a study of depressed patients over age 60 (Kupfer, Spiker, Coble, & Shaw, 1978), the patients showed considerable shortening of REM latency, reduced efficiency of sleep, and increased nocturnal arousals as compared to published norms for the elderly. When compared with data on depressed patients who are younger, shortened REM effects were similar but with more marked decreases in delta sleep.

As noted earlier, total REM sleep may decline slightly with age, but rela-tive amount of REM sleep compared to total sleep time are maintained until extremely old age (where some decline does apparently occur; Dement et al., 1982). When a decline in the proportion of REM sleep is noted, it tends to correlate with cerebral dysfunction (Feinberg, Koresko, & Heller, 1967; Fein-berg, Koresko, & Shaffner, 1965). Given the suggestive data about possible reduced REM latencies with aging and the well-confirmed marked decrease in Stage 4 sleep in the elderly, it is critical that age matched healthy controls be used in future studies in order to develop the EEG studies as a diagnostic instrument for depression in the elderly.

The sleep EEG may also be a useful marker for diagnosing dementia. At least one study found that 11 patients with primary degenerative dementia have less Stage 3 sleep, no Stage 4 sleep, little REM sleep, increased fragmentation of sleep, and disrupted sleep/wake diurnal cycles as compared to 10 elderly healthy men (Prinz, Peskind, Vitaliano, Raskind, Eisdorfer, Zemcuznikov, & Gerber, 1982). These patients were not evaluated for the presence of depression.

Sleep disturbances in the elderly therefore may indicate the presence of either dementia or depression. The fact that elderly patients seem to sleep more "poorly" (i.e., increased number of nocturnal awakenings) should not mislead one to overlook unusual sleep disturbance as a sign of depression in the elderly.

Physiological changes occur in the elderly that are not directly related to the etiology of depression but which are important for pharmacological treatment (Salzman, 1982). There is little to no significant change in the absorption of most psychotropic drugs that accompanies the aging process, although antacids, milk of magnesia, and anticholinergics delay absorption—all of which are commonly used by the elderly. Since the percentage of total body fat increases with age, higher serum concentrations of water-soluble drugs (that is, those that are not distributed in fatty tissue) are usually achieved per given dose in the elderly. All psychotropics, however (except lithium), are lipid soluble. The half-life of psychotropics, however, tends to increase with age primarily due to reduced clearance capacities of metabolic organs. Cardiac output and splanchnic blood flow also decrease with aging and most psychotropic drugs (except lithium) ae metabolized via hepatic microsomal enzymes. The prolonged half-lives of psychotropic drugs due to decreased clearance capacity partially accounts for the elderly patients' sensitivity to side effects and overmedication.

Decreased hepatic metabolism which decreases demethylation of imipramine and amitriptyline coupled with decreased hepatic hydroxylation leads to higher levels of nortriptyline. Decreased hepatic activity also would generally contribute to prolonged steady-state blood levels as well (Nies, Robinson, Friedman, Green, Cooper, Ravaris, & Ives, 1977). In terms of neurotoxicity, decreased hepatic metabolism definitely increases the potential for minor tranquilizer toxicity, but these drugs are not usually indicated in the treatment of depression.

Since there are age-related decreases in renal blood flow, glomerular filtration rate, reabsorptive and excretory capacity (even though serum BUN/creatinine remain stable) the pharmacokinetics of lithium metabolism also are affected. Lithium is excreted through renal mechanisms, therefore, the half-life of lithium in the elderly increases (Schou, 1968). For that reason, a reduction in dosage of lithium in the range of 50 percent is often necessary and "loading" doses should be decreased. Elderly patients are also much more susceptible to the neurotoxic side effects of lithium, especially mental confusion, tremors, or other signs of central nervous system dysfunction. Sodium-depleting diuretics, also used commonly in the elderly, raise lithium levels and may cause toxicity requiring blood levels to be frequently monitored. Methyldopa and indomethacin also reduce renal lithium clearance (Ayd, 1977). Lithium can interfere with thyroid functioning and induce hypothyroidism calling for surveillance of thyroid function before and during treatment.

The elderly patient with heart disease, especially those with cardiac conduction delays, are vulnerable to the quinidine-like effects of most tricyclic antidepressants. The elderly also are prone to orthostatic hypotension induced by tricyclics. In addition, many medical conditions associated with aging may be worsened by the anticholinergic side effects of tricyclics, such as narrow angle glaucoma, prostatic hypertrophy, and constipation leading to fecal impaction. The occurrence of orthostatic hypotension in patients with cerebrovascular disease or severe coronary artery disease can cause sudden shifts of blood flow potentially increasing the risk of dizziness, fainting, falling, or even stroke and myocardial infarction. Anticholinergic side effects include dry mouth, blurred vision, rapid heart rate, and even confusion and delirium. In general, all of these physiological factors indicate conservative medication of elderly patients and careful monitoring for toxic side effects due to the elderly patient's special vulnerabilities.

Indications for the use of these medications in the elderly will be discussed later in addition to details of psychopharmacologic management of depression. Additional emphasis will be placed on monitoring and managing side effects of these medications in light of the elderly patient's special physical vulnerabilities.

PSYCHOLOGICAL ASPECTS OF AGING AND DEPRESSION

A number of psychological factors can influence the development of depression in the elderly. Themes that tend to emerge in the literature center on how the aging person handles loss, copes psychologically with the social aspects of aging, and maintains self-esteem in the face of retirement and other role changes.

In the psychoanalytic literature loss is discussed as in important etiologic factor in the emergence of depression, an observation relevant to the elderly since they are at risk for multiple losses as they grow older. Yet the psychoanalytic tradition for many years was partially influenced by Freud's pessimism regarding the elderly's capacity for psychotherapeutic work. For example, Zetzel (1965) viewed the psychological task of aging as involving passive acceptance of loss and resignation that was to be accomplished without bitterness. Successful adaptation to aging involved the ability to accept these losses with an attitude of passive resignation.

Freud differentiated mourning (grief) from melancholia (depression) and observed that in depression, the "loss" that is experienced may be a result of an intrapsychic process as contrasted with the interpersonal loss associated with grief that occurred through death (Freud, 1917/1950). Depression, as opposed to grief, often involved intense feelings of self-reproach, guilt, and decreased self-esteem that derive from hostility that the patient unconsciously directed toward the lost object with the anger ultimately being directed against the patient's own ego.

Cath (1965) postulated that seeking appropriate emotional and interpersonal restitution for the losses incurred in late life was a major adaptive task in the elderly. Failure to reconstitute or adapt to losses could lead to depression.

Some authors have argued that depression in the elderly is more related to loss of self-esteem from an inability to successfully provide oneself with gratification of needs and drives, or because one feels especially vulnerable to threats to basic security (Busse, Barnes, Silverman, Shy, Thaler, Frost, 1954). The importance of regulation of self-esteem has been emphasized by other authors, particularly Bibring (1953), who viewed depression as a particular ego state. While self-esteem can be traumatized by childhood experiences and the frustration for love; depression may also result from frustration of narcissistic aspirations to be good and to maintain a satisfactory self-image. Bibring viewed depression basically as resulting from conflicts within the ego, and indicative of feelings of helplessness, powerlessness, and the failure to regulate self-esteem. Jacobson (1953) also believed that loss of self-esteem was the basic cause of depression.

The concept of "learned helplessness" (discussed in Chapter 26) is particularly germane to understanding depression in the elderly (Seligman, 1974). Older persons are at higher risk for being placed in situations in which they are relatively helpless, whether it be due to physical, social, or financial circumstances. They may view themselves as out of control of progressive physical illnesses; they may also find themselves unable to predict financial demands, and often feel themselves "being left" through death of their peers, spouses, or through relocation of their families. Unable to change or control these situations, they may literally "give up," leading to emotional withdrawal, apathy, and depression. Understanding this sense of helplessness as it relates to the phenomena of depression in the elderly has important implications for diagnostic assessment and treatment planning for the elderly population.

While a complete review of psychological theories of aging is not possible in this chapter (a good overview can be found in Chapter V of Blazer's *Depression in Late Life,* 1982), several aspects from the theories briefly presented here can be summarized as applicable to diagnosis and treatment of the elderly. In particular, the role of loss is usually evident, whether it is in the form of a loved one, health, employment, or professional or social position. Loss in the form of separations can occur, such as by family relocation or the elderly being "placed" in a nursing home. Self-esteem may be particularly vulnerable to damage with aging, as the elderly must confront societal prejudices regarding their expected usefulness, functioning, and activity. Perceptions of helplessness, powerlessness, and futility are often associated with aging. While none of these problems are unique to the elderly, aging does seem to increase the likelihood of encountering such stressors and can contribute to precipitating, perpetuating, or exacerbating affective illness in the elderly. Age-related decline in cognitive functioning and memory also often leaves the elderly patient with fewer resources to manage stress.

Sociological Aspects of Aging

From the sociological perspective, the older adult is subject to special stresses that may contribute to the development of depression, such as increasing numbers of interpersonal losses (spouses, siblings, friends, and sometimes the premature death of children). Losses may also take the form of separations, such as the dispersal of children and other family members to distant cities in a highly mobile society that often leaves the elderly behind. Declining health can also force older adults to leave their homes and neighborhoods to relocate in nursing homes and retirement communities eroding previously well-established social support systems.

Retirement may bring with it the perception that one has lost a meaningful role in society. Individuals whose self-esteem is highly dependent on either the status of their work or productivity can find this event emotionally devastating. Formerly highly independent individuals may find themselves forced into stereotypically determined roles which regard the elderly as dependent, roleless, forgetful, petulant, and even asexual—a constellation of societal prejudices known as "ageism" (Butler, 1975).

Other stresses for the elderly include the fear of financial deprivation which is often exacerbated by unpredictable economic forces such as inflation, changing tax rates, rising health care costs, and periodic fuel cost increases. The elderly individual may correctly perceive that they have no control of these external economic forces and be forced to struggle with economic realities on a fixed income. Elderly citizens who have not had the advantage of financial planning from early life, or have not participated in pension plans may find themselves destitute. Astronomical increases in health care costs with lagging insurance reimbursements also exacerbate the financial stress associated with aging.

The physical consequences of aging may limit social activities. Not only does aging increase the susceptibility to almost every physical illness, deteriorating sensory functioning may make enjoying leisure activities more difficult (such as music, movies) and physical limitations may limit recreation (tennis, golf). Access to cultural and social events may be a problem if driving privileges are curtailed.

DIAGNOSIS OF DEPRESSION IN THE ELDERLY

The diagnosis of depression in the elderly is marked by a number of special difficulties. "True" clinical depression in the elderly must be differentiated from the mild dysphoria or demoralization that may be caused by increased physical, social, and economic stresses to which the aged may be subjected (Blazer & Williams, 1980). In addition, the expected amount of depressive affect that accompanies bereavement must be differentiated from profound depression that can accompany pathological grief reactions (Brown & Stoudemire, 1983). Demoralization, defined as a state in which a person feels helpless and trapped by overwhelming life circumstances, is also seen in the elderly and must be differentiated from depression which may require intensive medical and psychiatric evaluation. On the other hand, dysphoric and demoralized feelings in the elderly should not be accepted as an inevitable part of growing older—beneath these feelings may be more profound affective disturbances or medical problems causing such complaints. ·

Many symptoms of the elderly which may be associated with increasing physical disability or deterioration are also associated with depression. Sleep disturbances (especially increased numbers of nighttime awakenings), easy fatigability, decreased appetite, constipation, and multiple "pains" can be associated with a number of the physical disorders or even the side effects of medication. Elderly patients may also find themselves withdrawing from previously held social or recreational interests as physical limitations accrue or interpersonal losses are suffered.

Demoralization, emotional depletion, and dysphoria may also accompany retirement or losing the sense of one being an active and productive member of society and family. Financial pressures and loneliness leading to dysphoric pessimism must also be differentiated from severe affective disorders. Making such clinical differentiations is often not easy under any circumstances but is only exacerbated by some of the dysphorigenic aspects of late life stress.

Numerous authors have also noted that late life depressions are qualitatively different from depressions in earlier life. The frequency of psychotic or delusional depressions appear to be more common as age increases (Kiloh & Garside, 1963). On the other hand, guilt-ridden depressions appear to be less frequent in the elderly (Busse et al., 1954). Other authors have noted increased numbers of so-called masked depressions that tend to be characterized by hypochondriacal fixations or somatic complaints (De Alarcon, 1964). With respect to bipolar affective disorder (manic-depressive illness), manic episodes tend to be atypical (Langley, 1975). Overactivity is usually not as pronounced, mania may be mistaken for "agitated" depression and manic and depressive symptoms may be mixed at any given time. Speech may take on a more circumstantial, obsessional quality in contrast to the pressured flight of ideas seen in younger patients. Paranoid delusions also are more common. A manic episode in the elderly can also be mistaken for a delirium, especially if coexisting dementia exists.

Many physical illnesses can induce depression or mimic its symptoms. Metabolic disturbances, such as hypothyroidism, hypercalcemia, hyper- or hypoadrenalism, diabetes mellitus, uremia, anemia, and occult carcinoma (especially pancreatic carcinomas and lymphoma) can be present with depressive symptomatology. (A partial list of physical illnesses associated with depression is presented in Table 1 and discussed more extensively in Chapter 22.)

TABLE 1
Medical conditions that may cause
symptoms of depression

Endocrine:
    Adrenal insufficiency (Addison's disease)
    Hyperadrenalism (Cushing's syndrome)
    Hypothyroidism
    Hyperthyroidism
    Hypoparathyroidism
    Hyperparathyroidism
    Hypoglycemia
    Diabetes mellitus
Vitamin deficiency:
    B_{12} (pernicious anemia)
    Iron deficiency anemia
Neurologic:
    Multiple sclerosis
    Dementia
    Parkinson's disease
Collagen vascular diseases:
    Rheumatoid arthritis
    Systemic lupus erythematosus
Malignancies:
    Lymphoma
    Pancreatic carcinoma
    Brain tumors
Cardiovascular:
    Cerebral ischemia
    Congestive heart failure
Metabolic:
    Uremia
    Liver failure (usually hepatitis)
Infections:
    Postviral depression

Patients with Parkinson's disease are also often affected by severe depressions that probably are partially biologically determined (Mayeux, Stern, Rosen, & Leventhal, 1981). A number of medications (such as reserpine and methyldopa) apparently can induce depression (see Table 2). Certain types of brain damage may make the diagnosis difficult, especially in patients who have difficulty with comprehension or expression of speech from stroke-related aphasias or difficulties with the expression of verbalization of mood (see below). Patients with dementia may also become depressed, and severe depression may mimic dementia (depressive pseudodementia as discussed later).

Given such complex and confounding factors, depression in the elderly presents special difficulties for the clinician. Not only is the psychological construct of what actually determines a "case" of depression difficult to define, the diagnosis is complicated by sorting out a number of physical conditions that may induce or mimic depression as well. Accurate diagnosis, how-

TABLE 2
Medications that may cause
depressive symptoms
_____

Antihypertensives:
  Reserpine
  Alpha-methyldopa
  Propranolol (high doses)
Anti-Parkinsonian agents:
  L-dopa
  Carbidopa
Hormones:
  Corticosteroids
Anti-glaucoma:
  Carbonic anhydrase inhibitors
Psychiatric drugs:
  Sedative hypnotics
  Minor tranquilizers (benzodiazepines)
_____

ever, is critical if the most effective treatment plan is to be developed. For example, the therapeutic management of lonely demoralization due primarily to lack of meaningful social contacts would be quite different from a major depression with somatic delusions; dysphoria over financial stress would be managed differently from persistent grief over the loss of a spouse.

DIFFERENTIAL DIAGNOSIS

Despite these complicating factors, diagnostic criteria now exist that are helpful in differentiating the various types of affective disorders encountered in the elderly population (American Psychiatric Association, 1980). The differential diagnosis of affective (mood) disorders in the elderly includes: major depression, bipolar disorder (manic-depressive illness), adjustment disorder, schizoaffective disorder, hypochondriasis, uncomplicated bereavement, and organic affective disorders. While a complete discussion of psychiatric differential diagnosis is not possible here, the reader is referred to other chapters on other psychological disorders associated with depression (Chapters 20 and 21).

The persistence, depth, and extent of symptoms encountered in a major depression differentiate this disorder from other forms of depression. (See Appendix 1 for *DSM-III* criteria for major depression.) Somatic, endogenous, or "vegetative" signs are usually present to some degree, such as sleep disturbance (often early morning awakening), poor appetite, weight loss, psychomotor agitation or retardation, anhedonia, fatigue (often worse in the morning), slowed thinking, memory impairments, and difficulty concentrating. All of these symptoms, however, can be caused by underlying physical illness or medications. Paranoid ideation, auditory hallucinations, profound guilt, suicidal thoughts, somatic delusions, and a preoccupation with personal failings

TABLE 3
Differential diagnosis of depressive symptoms in the elderly

   I. Organic mental disorder
     A. Primary degenerative dementia, senile onset with depression.
     B. Multi-infarct dementia.
     C. Substance-induced organic mental disorder with depression (alcoholism, barbiturates, benzodiazepines, antihypertensives).
     D. Organic affective syndrome (see Table 1).
  II. Paranoid disorder
 III. Schizoaffective disorder (rare in the elderly)
 IV. Affective disorder
     A. Bipolar disorder
        1. Mixed.
        2. Depressed.
        3. Manic.
     B. Major depression, with or without melancholia
        1. Single episode.
        2. Recurrent.
     C. Cyclothymic disorder.
     D. Dysthymic disorder (depressive neurosis).
   V. Anxiety disorder (depression may be associated with or superimposed on an acute or chronic anxiety disorder)
  VI. Somatoform disorder
     A. Hypochondriasis.
     B. Psychogenic pain disorder.
 VII. Adjustment disorder with depressed mood
VIII. Other
     A. Uncomplicated bereavement.
     B. Marital problems.
     C. Phase of life problem or other life circumstance problem.
     D. Parent-child problem.
  IX. Sleep disorder

and inadequacies can complicate the clinical picture as well. The presence of psychotic symptoms and their congruence with the depressive mood also subtype the depressive episode according to *DSM-III* criteria. If the mood disorder is particularly profound and vegetative-biological signs markedly disruptive, the depression can also be subtyped as "with melancholia." Exclusions for the diagnosis of a major depression include schizophrenia, organic factors causing depression (physical illness, toxins, or medications) and uncomplicated bereavement.

The history obtained from the patient is also important in addition to the diagnostic criteria. Important data include previous episodes of depression, suicide attempts, previous treatments received (medication, electroconvulsive therapy [ECT], hospitalization), medical history, and family history of depression. A thorough evaluation of recent psychosocial stressors that may have induced the depression (separations, family crises, deaths, financial problems) is critical to the diagnostic assessment. Depressed elderly patients frequently identify their problems as physical and focus on various types of somatic distress in an effort to seek help. Pain complaints may also be prominent. Depression which is verbally denied by the patient or "hidden" by somatization is referred to as "masked" depression.

Dysthymic disorder is the term used in *DSM-III* for chronic depressive neurosis or characterological depression. (*DSM-III* Criteria for dysthymic disorder are contained in Appendix 1.) Patients with this disorder tend to have long-standing depressions that seem to be inextricably woven into their character structure. Dysthymic disorders usually date from childhood or early adulthood. Oftentimes traumatic experiences may be identified (such as separations, deaths, abandonments, abuses, or emotional deprivations) from which the patient never fully recovered. Patients with dysthymic disorder, however, may also suffer periodic major depressions and the two diagnoses are not mutually exclusive.

Adjustment disorders may be accompanied by depression and/or anxiety. An adjustment disorder is a "maladaptive" response to a life stress impairing the individual's capacity to cope socially and occupationally. These disorders tend to be self-limiting as the external stressor is removed or the patient adapts to the life difficulty.

Hypochondriasis is an unrealistic preoccupation with a somatic symptom as representing some disease or disorder. Real physical symptoms or conditions may exist, but the patient may develop an obsessive fear that the symptom represents something terribly serious and even life threatening. Such patients can be passively dependent on their physicians or be angry, demanding and manipulative for more medication, more tests, or more reassurance. These patients tend to respond poorly to advice and simple reassurances. Patients who are depressed may also have prominent somatic symptoms and interpret them unrealistically, or have exacerbations of previously stable symptoms, but the mood disturbance forms the underlying cause of their distress, and the somatic concerns tend to diminish as mood improves with treatment. Some depressed patients may have limited cognitive, psychological, verbal, and intellectual skills with which to express their subjective experience of distress when they are depressed, and their mood disorder may be communicated through physical complaints. Other patients, especially those with rigid, obsessive-compulsive defensive structures and a need to deny their feelings, may tend to somatize and even deny being depressed when it is readily apparent to the clinician.

Patients with dementia may also suffer major depression. Dementia (of whatever etiology) is characterized by a pervasive loss of intellectual skills primarily related to dysfunction of higher cortical centers, including impairments in memory, abstract thinking, motor performance, social skills, motivation, judgment, perceptual performance, and personality. Depression may occur with dementia, especially in its early phases or shortly after diagnosis. A problem often encountered, however, is in differentiating patients who are primarily depressed but have memory and other cognitive symptoms associated with their depression (depressive pseudodementia) for those with "true" dementia (primary degenerative dementia, multi-infarct dementia, and so on).

Criteria that help differentiate depressive pseudodementia originally developed by Wells (1979) have been widely published. For example, patients with depressive pseudodementia had a more precise date of onset of their symptoms, they usually had a previous psychiatric history, their symptoms progressed more rapidly, they tended to complain more stridently of their cognitive losses, they used "I don't know" answers more, and a pervasive mood disturbance was evident. While these criteria might be somewhat helpful, it is almost impossible during the initial evaluation to differentiate the cognitive changes associated with depression and those associated with dementia. Cognitive impairments may occur with depression which are at times indistinguishable from those encountered in organic mental disorders (McAllister, 1983). To some extent, the term *pseudodementia* is a misnomer since it implies that the cognitive deficits somehow are not "real" as opposed to the "organic" pathology in a true dementia. Some form of underlying cerebral dysfunction that causes the mood disturbance may also simultaneously induce memory disturbance (such as disturbed monoamine neurotransmitter dysfunction). As mood improves with treatment in depressed "pseudodemented" patients, memory usually improves as well.

From the diagnostic point of view, given the difficulty in differentiating dementia from pseudodementia on clinical grounds, the use of ancillary diagnostic procedures has been suggested. Several authors have invoked the use of the EEG as a diagnostic instrument in this clinical situation with a normal EEG being associated with the depressed patient (Kiloh, 1961; Post, 1975; Wells, 1979). Most clinicians, however, have found that this laboratory test is neither sensitive nor specific for dementia.

More recently, hope has been placed in the dexamethasone suppression test as a helpful laboratory aid to differentiate pseudodementia from dementia. If the DST was normal in dementia and abnormal in depression, this would reflect in the diagnostic assessment. Unfortunately, such a trend has not been found. A recent report found that the DST was positive (abnormal) in over half of a group of demented patients who showed no evidence of depression (Spar & Gerner, 1982). Other studies also find large numbers of patients with primary degenerative dementia with positive DST results (Raskind, Peskind, Rivard, Veith, & Barnes, 1982).

The TRH-stimulation test, a similar neuroendocrine research instrument used in depression, shows abnormal TSH responses in approximately 25 percent of depressed patients and blunted TSH responses increase with advancing age (Winokur et al., 1983). This test has not been used extensively as yet in addressing the problem of differentiating dementia from pseudodementia.

Although relatively expensive and time-consuming, EEG sleep studies (discussed earlier) might be of some benefit in the diagnosis of dementia and depression. In one study of 18 patients over age 60 who were depressed, reduced sleep time, shortened REM latency, and high REM density were found similar to EEG findings of depressed patients under age 60. The "depressed sleep EEG" as compared to normative age-matched controls in the elderly population was also abnormal with relative shortening of REM latency, reduced sleep efficiency and increased awakenings (Kupfer, et al., 1978). Sleep EEG differences have also been noted between nondemented and demented elderly subjects with demented patients having even less Stage 3 sleep, no Stage 4 sleep, and more fragmentation of sleep than would be expected in this age-group (Prinz et al., 1982). Sleep studies, therefore, also may give some guidelines in the diagnosis of depression and dementia but adequate standardization is not available yet for widespread application. Even if standardization was possible, financial restraints and practical considerations might limit their application.

The clinician, evaluating a patient with depression and cognitive deficits is thus faced with a dilemma. A treatable cause of dementia could be overlooked if one does not perform a thorough medical, neurological, and laboratory evaluation. On the other hand, if one undertakes a "rule out dementia" approach first, controversy exists as to the necessary extent to which the laboratory work-up should proceed in a patient who is relatively stable and has no focal neurological findings (specifically in regards to the necessity of CT-scanning, EEG, and lumbar puncture). The greatest danger, however, is in misdiagnosing a patient with depression with secondary cognitive deficits as being primarily demented. It is indeed a tragedy when such patients are sent to nursing homes and institutions when effective treatment could reverse both their mood and cognitive disorder.

A general guideline in these situations is that every patient with evidence of a major depression needs a thorough medical evaluation. For elderly patients this is even more imperative. If significant cognitive deficits are found on psychological testing or mental status examination, consultation is usually recommended before antidepressant medication or ECT is instituted. An alternative approach is to begin antidepressants or ECT empirically after a screening medical evaluation and to watch for parallel improvements in mood and cognition. Failure of either parameter to improve after a reasonable trial of treatment are grounds for more extensive evaluation. If the patient's memory improves with mood, the diagnosis of pseudodementia tends to be confirmed. If mood improves, but cognition remains impaired, more intensive investigation may be necessary to rule out a treatable dementia. If neither mood nor cognition improve, then an underlying medical or neurological condition may be present that has been overlooked, also calling for more intensive examination.

The Aprosodias: A Possible Complication in the Evaluation of Brain Damaged Depressed Patients

Recent reports from the neuropsychiatric literature have described patients, primarily with right cerebral hemispheric lesions, who have peculiar difficulties in comprehending auditory and visual expressions of affect and who also have difficulty in expressing affect. Such disorders have been termed *aprosodias* (Ross, 1981). Patients with aprosodias may have deficits in the expression and comprehension of affect. For example, dependent to some extent on the location of the lesion, patients with right hemispheric lesions may have difficulty in interpreting affect-laden gesturing and speech and an inability to display affect through gesturing or verbal communication. Although these seeming disorders of affective comprehension and expression have been described in limited numbers of patients, these observations can be clinically important. For example, patients with some right-sided lesions may be "depressed," but may have lost the ability to effectively communicate their depressed feelings. They may also have difficulty in comprehending the clinician's questions regarding mood. The absence of depressive affect in such patients therefore may not rule out depression—other vegetative-endogenous features can be used as parameters of affective illness as well as objective observations of the patient's behavior.

Right cerebral brain damaged patients can also show affective disregulation, such as in apathetic-indifferent reactions, indifferent-euphoric reactions, or joking or social disinhibition. Left brain damaged patients, in contrast, may develop aphasias (receptive or expressive) that complicate the diagnosis of depression and are more likely to show their affect in the form of anger, despair, hopelessness, and depression (Sackheim, Greenberg, Weiman, Gur, Hungerbuhler, & Geschwind, 1982). All of these considerations must be taken into account when examining patients with possible affective illness who have suffered brain damage (usually from cerebrovascular accidents).

NORMAL AND PATHOLOGICAL GRIEF

Normal grief reactions in general are self-limiting (six months to one year) but poor adaptation after the loss of a spouse may lead to a form of chronic dysphoria. Pathological grief or unresolved grief can merge into incapacitating depression.

Normal grief is an expected reaction to loss which is usually accompanied by crying, feelings of emptiness, somatic sensations (throat tightness, shortness of breath, sighing), anorexia, insomnia, preoccupation with the deceased, and often social withdrawal. The survivor may also take on certain aspects of the deceased or develop symptoms similar to those of the deceased. Some degree of remorse or guilt regarding past relationships with the deceased may occur. Anger over the loss, at physicians, God, even the deceased themselves (for having "left" them behind) are common reactions. Under most circumstances, these symptoms begin to remit after one year as the loss is mourned, the lost person is psychologically relinquished, and new adaptations are made. Symptoms may recur on significant anniversaries, such as birthdays, holidays, or date of death.

Occasionally, however, the usual depressive symptoms that accompany the grief process can merge into a profound and serious depression, often with prominent somatic features. Such a syndrome is well labeled a pathological grief reaction (Brown & Stoudemire, 1983; Stoudemire & Brown, 1984).

Pathological grief can be either delayed or distorted. Grief may be delayed because either the body of the deceased is lost, destroyed, or never viewed causing the death to seem unreal; or the survivor may rigidly repress the grief-related affect, show no emotion, or largely deny the loss. Multiple losses can be overwhelming leaving the individual in a perpetual state of "shock" with the grief process arrested in that phase.

Grief can also be distorted by problematic aspects of the survivor's relationship with the deceased prior to death, such as unresolved anger. The survivor may therefore actually be relieved about the death but subsequently feel guilty about these feelings and become depressed. Guilt may be specially intense if some perceived lapse in the survivor's behavior contributed to the death of the loved one.

Signs of pathological grief include persistent overactivity without a sense of loss, prolonged acquisition of symptoms of the deceased, deterioration in health, severe anniversary reactions, refusal to relinquish clothing or other belongings of the deceased after a reasonable period of time, panic attacks, and severe depression. Pathological grief reactions usually require intensive psychotherapy for their resolution. They must not be benignly accepted by a therapist and be expected to resolve spontaneously.

TREATMENT OF DEPRESSION

Evaluation

Every patient suspected of having a major depression should have a medical evaluation; this clinical rule is even more important for the elderly since they are at higher risk for physical illnesses and medication side effects that induce organic affective syndromes. Because of the possibility of medication-induced side effects, it is also important to have basic laboratory tests that evaluate baseline physiological functioning that will identify any metabolic abnormalities predisposing to toxicity; that is, renal failure, liver failure, or congestive heart failure. An electrocardiogram is also critical since antidepressants may cause conduction disturbances and tachycardia. Hypothroidism can induce depression; pernicious anemia (B_{12} deficiency) can cause dementia and other mental status changes that can be mistaken for depression.

If significant cognitive deficits exist with the depression, or if focal neurological findings exist, then a dementia evaluation is indicated (Stoudemire & Thompson, 1981). The differentiation of depressive pseudodementia from dementia has been discussed earlier as well as the dilemma as to what extent these patients should be evaluated neurologically. The TRH-stimulation test, dexamethasone suppression test, and sleep studies remain largely research instruments due to their lack of diagnostic sensitivity.

Psychopharmacologic Considerations

Tricyclic or tetracyclic antidepressant medication (TCA) in association with supportive psychotherapy is indicated in the treatment of major depression. If melancholia, suicidal ideation, or preexisting medical conditions are present or if inadequate social support exists, hospitalization is usually indicated. In the elderly the "threshold" for hospitalization is low because of the possibility of medication-induced side effects, such as orthostatic hypotension (leading to falls) associated with these drugs, plus the risk of suicide. Patients who are profoundly melancholic, imminently suicidal, severely agitated and obsessional, psychotic, paranoid, or have severe pseudodementia respond much more rapidly and effectively to electroconvulsive therapy ([ECT] discussed below). In many elderly patients ECT is a much safer form of treatment than pharmacologic therapy.

Antidepressants may have significant cardiovascular effects. On the electrocardiogram (EKG) they tend to increase the P-R interval, QRS duration, QTc time and flatten the T-wave (Kantor, Glassman, Bigger, Perel, & Giardina, 1978; Giardina, Bigger, Glassman, Perel, & Kantor, 1979; Burckhardt, Raeder, Müller, Imhof, & Neubauer, 1978). The primary effect of tricyclics of clinical concern on the EKG is their quinidinelike effect; that is, their propensity to increase conduction time. This may precipitate higher degrees of heart block when preexisting bundle-branch block exists. Serial EKGs and cardiological consultation are usually mandatory in patients who have significant preexisting heart block to monitor for worsening of this condition under antidepressant therapy until they are stable. A benefit of the "quinidinelike" effect, however, is the antiarrhythmic effects of the tricyclics. In some patients, ventricular arrhythmias may markedly improve while on antidepressant medication.

Orthostatic hypotension is a potentially serious side effect of tricyclics and is probably due to adrenergic receptor blockade. In clinical practice, tertiary amines (amitriptyline, imipramine) tend to cause more severe hypotensive effects than secondary amines (nortriptyline, desipramine) (Roose, Glassman, Siris, Walsh, Bruno, & Wright, 1981). Possibly the best clinical predictor of the development of drug-induced orthostatic hypotension is a predrug postural hypotensive drop in blood pressure.

Recent evidence suggests that antidepressants (at least imipramine and doxepin) have minimal effects on left ventricular function and can usually be safely used in patients which chronic heart disease unless severe impairment is present (Veith, Raskind, Caldwell, Barnes, Gumbrecht, & Ritchie, 1982). Doxepin is often mentioned as the "safest" antidepressant to use in the cardiac patient, but the original studies that this information was based upon used drug levels that were probably subtherapeutic (Vohra, Burrows, & Sloman, 1975).

Anticholinergic side effects of TCA, as noted earlier, can cause tachycardia in addition to prostatic obstruction, urinary retention, severe constipation, visual blurring, nausea, dry mouth, decreased sweating, confusion, and delirium.

In patients being treated for hypertension, antidepressants block the effects of quanethidine, clonidine, and methyldopa and potentiate the hypotensive effect of prazosin.

New antidepressants have recently been marketed with varying degrees of claims for reduced toxicities. These include amoxapine (Asendin), maprotiline (the "tetracyclic" Ludiomil) and trazodone (Desyrel). Amoxapine is metabolized to loxapine, an antipsychotic, and potentially may be of greater use with psychotic depressions, although its use in this manner is largely speculative. Amoxapine purportedly is more "activating" and has a more rapid onset of action than other antidepressants, but the data for this is anecdotal. Unfortunately, there is also the potential for the development of extrapyramidal side effects and tardive dyskinesia with this medication, in contrast to other antidepressants. Trazodone is a "low potency" antidepressant (average therapeutic dose of about 300 mg/day) which has low anticholinergic effects, but its antihistaminic effects can mimic some anticholinergic effects; it is sedating and it is therefore not devoid of side effects. Trazodone also may cause severe priapism (intractable penile erection). Maprotiline has lower anticholinergic properties than amitriptyline and imipramine. A recent summary of the adrenergic, cholinergic and histaminic receptor blocking effects of these medications provide some rationale for predicting their relative side effects (Richelson, 1982).

The choice of antidepressants in the elderly is often a matter of choosing the drug with the least side effects. Amitriptyline is the most sedating, has the most anticholinergic effects, and may also cause more orthostatic hypotension. For this reason, amitriptyline is often poorly tolerated in the elderly. Medications with the least anticholinergic potential are tolerated best, such as desipramine, maprotiline, and trazodone. Low anticholinergic effects also will decrease the chances of tachycardia. Based on adrenergic blockade data (Richelson, 1982), maprotiline, protriptyline, imipramine, and desipramine should cause less orthostatic hypotension, although it is difficult to correlate these findings from laboratory receptor studies with clinical observations. The more sedating antidepressants (i.e., amitriptyline and doxepin) are useful in agitated depressions or where sleep disturbance is prominent. Doxepin is particularly useful where pain complaints are a factor, and it has fewer anticholinergic effects than amitriptyline.

Given these observations, antidepressants with low anticholinergic and lower alpha-adrenergic blockade are probably first-line drugs for the elderly. Patients should begin on lower doses than in healthy middle-aged adults (perhaps 50 percent), and titrated slowly upward while monitoring for side effects such as precipitation of narrow angle glaucoma, confusion, urinary retention, intestinal obstruction (through fecal impaction), delirium or confusion, severe orthostatic hypotension, tachycardia, or cardiac conduction delays. Drug levels may be obtained if evidence of toxicity develops, patients fail to respond, or if compliance is questioned. The full daily dose can be given at bedtime to foster compliance.

Antipsychotic medications (neuroleptics) are sometimes used as adjuncts in the treatment of severely agitated or delusional depressions. The elderly tend to be prone to the Parkinsonianlike side effects of these agents and are more prone to develop tardive dyskinesia. Lower potency phenothiazines, such as chlorpromazine, also cause orthostatic hypotension and are anticholinergic. Higher potency neuroleptics, such as haloperidol and thiothixene, cause few orthostatic changes but are higher in extrapyramidal actions. Thiothixene tends to have fewer extrapyramidal side effects than haloperidol. Thioridazine is sedating and has some "built-in" antimuscarinic potential which decreases extrapyramidal and Parkinsonian side effects. In general, neuroleptics should be used in low doses, for short periods of time, and only as adjuncts in the treatment of agitated or psychotic depression in the elderly, and be tapered and discontinued as soon as possible.

Benzodiazepines are not recommended in the treatment of depression. They may cause confusion especially in patients with elements of underlying dementia. A possible exception is alprazolam, a new triazolobenzodiazepine. In at least one study, alprazolam was shown to be equivalent to imipramine and superior to placebo in the treatment of depression in the dose range of 2–3 mg (Feighner, Aden, Fabre, Rickels, Smith, 1983).

Psychostimulants such as methylphenidate occasionally have been recommended for patients who cannot tolerate tricyclics, MAO inhibitors, or refuse electrotherapy. As such, these medications are "fourth-line" choices. Doses that have been recommended for methylphenidate are 10 mg. twice a day (Katon & Raskind, 1980). These drugs, however, may cause agitation, restlessness, insomnia, anorexia, and rebound depression when they are stopped. They are probably most useful when used with heavy doses of narcotics to prevent excessive sedation in certain types of terminally ill patients with intractable pain.

MAO Inhibitors

Since monoamine oxidase tends to increase in the platelets and brain with aging (therefore increasing rates of catecholamine metabolism) some rationale exists for the use of these medications in the elderly. The MAO inhibitor phenelzine and tranylcypromine have been used with reasonably good results in the elderly (Ashford & Ford, 1979). Use of these drugs, however, involves a high degree of patient cooperation to avoid use of sympathomimetic drugs (such as ephedrine, methylphenidate, phenylephrine) that may induce profound hypertensive crises in patients on MAO inhibitors. Tyramine-containing foods also may precipitate hypertensive crises and must be avoided as well (beer, red wine, certain cheeses, fava beans). For these reasons, MAO inhibitors are not generally recommended and must be used with caution and with careful supervision.

Lithium Carbonate

Lithium carbonate is indicated for patients suffering from bipolar affective disorders for the treatment of mania and prevention of recurrent attacks of both mania and depression. Conclusive evidence that lithium is effective in recurrent unipolar depression is lacking.

Since lithium is excreted by the kidney, renal function (blood urea nitrogen [BUN], creatinine clearance) should be measured before treatment is started as well as obtaining serum electrolyte levels, electrocardiogram, and thyroid function tests. Lithium can possibly cause renal interstitial fibrosis with long-term use and also may induce nephrogenic diabetes. The elderly are also more susceptible to the neurotoxic effects of lithium, such as confusion, lethargy, ataxia, and tremor. Concurrent sodium-depleting diuretics raise lithium levels. Gastrointestinal side effects include nausea, vomiting, abdominal pain, and diarrhea.

Because the rate of renal lithium excretion decreases with age, lower doses of lithium are usually required in the elderly. Lithium toxicity may appear at "normal" levels (which are usually standardized with healthy younger adult populations, 0.8–1.2 mEq/ml in most centers). Lithium-induced EKG changes include inversion and flattening of the T-wave which are usually benign in therapeutic serum levels. Lithium levels must be monitored more frequently in the elderly and used with great care if sodium-depleting diuretics are concurrently taken.

The Use of Electrotherapy in the Elderly

Despite its negative public image, electrotherapy or electroconvulsive therapy is probably the safest, most rapid, and effective treatment for psychotic and profound melancholic depressions of the elderly, especially if medical conditions exist that make the anticholinergic, cardiac, and hypotensive effects of antidepressants poorly tolerated. The use of anesthesia, muscle relaxants, barbiturates, unilateral nondominant electrode placement, and low-energy stimulus wave forms have decreased the risks and side effects of electrotherapy.

Electrotherapy is definitely indicated for imminently suicidal patients for whom it would be dangerous to wait for the two–four-week "lag time" of the antidepressants to take full effect. Psychotic, severely agitated and pseudodemented patients respond more promptly as well. Patients who fail to respond to medication (given the fact that the medication has been given for a sufficient length of time, compliance has been assured, and therapeutic drug levels have been maintained) are also candidates since 80–85 percent of depressed drug "nonresponders" will respond to electrotherapy (Avery & Lubrano, 1979). Unilateral electrode placement seems to be as effective as bilateral placement in most patients and tends to decrease postictal confusion.

A few special circumstances call for caution in the use of electrotherapy. These include recent myocardial infarction and severe hypertension. Space occupying central nervous system (CNS) lesions, such as brain tumors, are generally considered an absolute contraindication. Patients with succinylcholinesterase deficiency cannot have succinylcholine as a muscle relaxant. The elderly also at times require more high electrical stimulus intensity than younger patients (Weiner, 1982). The presence of dementia with depression does not prevent electrotherapy from improving associated depression, although postictal confusion and memory disturbances may be increased. Elderly patients receiving electrotherapy should always have an anesthesiologist during the course of their treatments. Dramatic and remarkable results are often obtained with electrotherapy, especially in the most severe forms of affective illness.

PSYCHOTHERAPY

Themes that may emerge in psychotherapy of the elderly include issues involving coping with deteriorating health, financial difficulties, loss of self-esteem through relinquishing previously held productive roles, feelings of abandonment and neglect by children, and grief reactions. Butler (1975) notes that common themes in psychotherapy include grief, physical dysfunction, independence-dependence problems, concerns about the passage of time, and stereotypical issues regarding the elderly. Loneliness and isolation also occur frequently in the elderly.

Despite these more or less common themes, the elderly also may be suffering from the same types of neurotic conflicts that younger adults suffer. Aging does not in itself "dissolve" previous existing conflicts or personality characteristics, even those of a problematic nature; neurotic conflicts may stabilize with age or become exacerbated with the stress of aging. For these reasons, it should not be assumed that elderly patients are not candidates for insight-oriented treatment. Elderly patients are still subject to the same range of conflicts seen in younger patients but their severity may be exacerbated by dwindling financial resources, marginal social and family supports, and deteriorating health. Psychotherapy in the elderly must actively focus not only on what is the apparent intrapsychic conflict for the patient but also actively address alleviating the stress of social problems as well.

Busse and Pfeiffer (1977) recommended that in working with older individuals, the therapist should take an active role in identifying and clarifying the patient's current difficulty. They recommended a form of short-term treatment that was based upon the establishment of defined goals, support for adaptation to life changes, acceptance of greater dependency, and supportive interventions to continue involvement in interpersonal activities. Busse and Pfeiffer also strongly encouraged the use of "social conversation" during part of the session to facilitate the patient's feeling of being part of a meaningful therapeutic relationship.

Psychotherapeutic management of bereaved older adults involves permitting patients to verbalize their feelings of pain and sorrow and allowing them freedom to cry. Often times, grief-oriented psychotherapy calls for encouraging the patient to carefully review their relationship with the deceased. All aspects of the emotional involvement with the deceased should be encouraged including feelings of love, guilt, anger, ambivalence, and hostility. The full and free expression of the range of affects should be encouraged, including anger, which the bereaved may feel guilty about expressing. Using the analogy of grief being a "wound" that must heal with time is often a helpful cognitive image for the bereaved to use in understanding their experience. As such, they can symbolically conceptualize their feelings and have some assurance that the pain will remit with time. As the psychotherapy with the bereaved proceeds, the therapy should take the role of encouraging social contacts in the development of new interpersonal relationships as patients gradually turn to their future and adapt to their loss.

Cognitively oriented therapies may have special significance for the elderly particularly since depression in this age-group may be secondary to disturbed ways of perceiving oneself and perceiving one's place in society. Cognitive therapy (Beck, Rush, Shaw & Emery, 1979) rests on the theory that an individual's affective state is largely dependent upon the way in which experience is perceived and cognitively structured. Cognitive thought distortions of one's self-image, life experiences, and the future are held to precede and precipitate depressed affect. Cognitive psychotherapeutic techniques focus on restructuring and correcting cognitive distortions that cause and perpetuate depression.

The theoretical cognitive model proposed by Beck et al. (1979) consists of three major components: (1) the "negative triad" (see below), (2) "underlying beliefs" or "schema," and (3) cognitive errors (i.e., information processing). The "negative triad" referred to consists of negative views of *oneself, experiences,* and *the future.* Depressed patients usually have low self-esteem and see themselves as inadequate, defective, helpless, worthless, and unlovable. The depressed patient also views life itself and the external world as basically hostile, negative, threatening, and overwhelming. The future may be perceived as hopeless, empty, and offering only the possibility of more frustration, failure, and disappointment.

The components of the "negative triad" (self, experience, future) interact to form a "schema" or framework for the evaluation of new information and experience. The schema may lead to unrealistic expectations and devaluation of oneself with subsequent depressed mood.

Cognitive errors, the third major component of Beck's cognitive model, describes errors of logic and fault information processing (Gallagher & Thompson, 1983). Thinking may be disturbed *stylistically* (exaggeration of negative and minimization of positives), *semantically* (inexact labeling of events), and *formally* (automatic, involuntary prepetuation of negative thoughts despite evidence to the contrary).

The task of the cognitive therapist is to correct negatively distorted perceptions of reality by:

1. Enabling patients to *monitor* negative thoughts as they occur.
2. Helping the patient recognize connections between these thoughts and depressed affect.

3. Facilitating critical examination of the evidence for and against automatic negative thoughts.
4. Helping the patient develop reality-oriented perceptions of oneself and experiences.
5. Promoting the correction of dysfunctional beliefs that predispose to the development of negative thoughts and subsequent depressed affect (Gallagher & Thompson, 1983).

The concept of negative cognitive schema is particularly germane to the elderly and relates to the concept of "ageism"; that is, culturally determined prejudicial views that regard older individuals as inferior, weak, unproductive, passive, dependent, and sexually restricted. As individuals grow older they may adopt these negative views and integrate them into their self-concepts. These internalized concepts also will negatively affect how one views oneself in relation to family and society. Internalization of these concepts may lead to a negative cognitive schema that makes one highly vulnerable to the development of depression. Thus one's perception of what it means to age and to be elderly may predispose one to developing negative cognitions and depressive affect. One's perception of growing older may, in effect, overide other biological and social determinants involved in the aging process (Thomae, 1970). If one perceives retirement as a negative event, the likelihood of a negative adjustment (possibly with depression) increases (Emery, 1981).

Cognitive therapy with elderly would therefore attempt to identify negative cognitions that are associated with distorted views of aging that the individual may have learned to apply to oneself and experiences. Such cognitive distortions might involve those that have led the patient to devalue their self-worth, productivity, sexuality, physical, and social capabilities. Readers are referred to Chapter 1 by Sacco and Beck for a more detailed description of the techniques of cognitive therapy.

An assessment of the "family situation" is often an important part of the psychotherapeutic assessment of the older patient. The family assessment would include: (1) identification of who the available family members are and their accessibility for providing support, (2) determination of the quality of the relationship with the elderly patient, (3) identification of sources of conflict within the family, and (4) determination of the attitude of the family toward the patient's depressive illness.

The onset of depression or other types of illness in the elderly patient that requires intervention by children who may have been previously separated from their parents for years provides a setting for the revitalization of old latent parent-child conflicts (Blazer, 1982). The ability of middle-aged children to resolve conflicts with their parents has been called "filial maturity" and will determine to what extent the children are able to overcome past resentments to aid the elderly parent in distress. If the parent has previously been dominant in an authoritarian manner in the family which has led to repressed anger the situation may even be more tense and laden with conflict for parent and child alike. On a more positive note, illness or crisis in the elderly patient can serve as a means to bring families together and to heal or at least look beyond previous unresolved conflicts.

Psychotherapy Outcome Research with the Depressed Elderly

In recent years studies have begun to test the efficacy of cognitive, behavioral, and short-term dynamic therapies for the depressed elderly. These studies are typically on the order of pilot studies but nevertheless represent an important beginning.

In the only study examining the efficacy of individual treatment, Gallagher and Thompson (1982, 1983) compared cognitive therapy, behavior therapy, and brief dynamic therapy. Depressive symptoms were significantly reduced in all treatment conditions. Cognitive and behavioral treatments were more effective than insight therapy when symptoms were assessed at six weeks following treatment but not at termination. One advantage of cognitive therapy over behavior therapy was that fewer patients in cognitive therapy dropped out of treatment (20 percent versus 50 percent). Endogeneity (according to RDC criteria) was a major factor in improvement of patients in all of the psychotherapies. Nonendogenous patients responded better to the psychotherapies than did the endogenous patients.

Gallagher (1981) examined the comparative efficacy of behavioral group therapy and supportive group therapy for elderly depressed persons. The behavioral treatment was aimed at improving social skills and increasing pleasant activities, based on the model of Lewinsohn. The supportive treatment centered on helping patients "to clarify their statements about their feelings and what influenced their moods, to express their feelings, and to develop an atmosphere of group support." Both treatments resulted in improvement on self-report measures of depression and social behaviors and on observer ratings of interpersonal skill. Differential treatment effects between the two groups were noted only for positive verbal interactions in group, which improved most in the behavioral treatment. Behavioral subjects also reported greater improvement in "life satisfaction" and in "overall level of functioning."

Thompson, Gallagher, Nies, and Epstein (1983) applied a similar behavioral intervention to the one used above with patients who were generally mildly depressed or nondepressed (average BDI = 12). Both professional and nonprofessional instructors were used in this group psychoeducational approach which taught behavioral coping skills. Level of depression was reduced at a statistically significant level but not at a clinically significant level (BDI = 12.05 to 9.4). Life satisfaction and frequency and enjoyability of pleasant events were also increased. No differences in outcome were observed between groups led by professionals and nonprofessionals.

A comparison of cognitive-behavioral group therapy and psychodynamic group therapy (Steuer, Mintz, Hammen, Hill, Jarvik, McCarley, Motoike, &

Rosen, 1984) found that both groups of patients had significantly reduced depressive symptomatology at the end of treatment. There was a statistically significant difference favoring cognitive behavioral treatment over psychodynamic treatment on the Beck Depression Inventory, but there was no difference between groups in treatment effectiveness on the Hamilton Rating Scale for Depression.

Thus, initial studies suggest that the depressed elderly can benefit from psychotherapy. These studies have been limited to outpatient depression, however, and there is no evidence as to what their effectiveness would be with more severe depressions (such as patients with melancholia or who are suicidal or psychotic).

CONCLUSION: PSYCHOTHERAPY WITH THE ELDERLY

In summary, psychotherapy with older patients does not significantly differ from therapy with younger individuals although the therapist is usually more vigorous in identifying practical stresses operating and social interventions may be more active. Involvement of the family is of prime importance in shoring up the patient's support system and martialing other resources. Core psychodynamic issues may revolve around struggling with dependency issues and grief resolution. Cognitive-behavioral therapies may be especially important to help the patient overcome learned distortions about aging that have led patients to devalue themselves and their potential at this stage of life. An eclectic treatment plan that emphasizes elements of all of these approaches— including a thorough medical evaluation and antidepressant medication if necessary—will maximize therapeutic outcome. This eclectic orientation is the essence of the biopsychosocial approach presented at the outset of this discussion as a conceptual model for assessing and treating depression in late life.

References

Ashford, J. W., & Ford, C. V. (1979). Use of MAO inhibitors in elderly patients. *American Journal of Psychiatry, 136,* 1466–1467.

American Psychiatric Association. (1980). *Diagnostic and statistical manual of mental disorders* (3rd ed.). Washington, DC: Author.

Avery, D., & Lubrano, A. (1979). Depression treated with imipramine and ECT: The DeCarolis study reconsidered. *American Journal of Psychiatry, 136,* 559–562.

Ayd, F. (1977). Broadening the clinical uses of lithium: Coadministering lithium and thiazide diuretics. *International Drug Therapy Newsletter, 12,* 25–27.

Beck, A. T., Rush, A. J., Shaw, B. F., & Emery, G. (1979). *Cognitive therapy of depression.* New York: Guilford Press.

Bibring, E. (1953). The mechanism of depression In P. Greenacre (Ed.), *Affective disorders* (pp. 13–48). New York: International Universities Press.

Blazer, D. G. (1982). *Depression in late life.* St. Louis, MO: C. V. Mosby.

Blazer, D. G., & Williams, C. D. (1980). Epidemiology of dysphoria and depression in an elderly population. *American Journal of Psychiatry, 137,* 439–444.

Bowman, R. E., & Wolf, R. C. (1969). Plasma 17-hydroxy-corticosteroid response to ACTH. *Proceedings of the Society for Experimental Biology and Medicine, 130,* 61–64.

Brown, J. T., & Stoudemire, A. (1983). Normal and pathological grief. *Journal of American Medical Association, 239,* 213–216.

Burckhardt, D., Raeder, E., Müller, V., Imhof, P., & Neubauer, H. (1978). Cardiovascular effects of tricyclic and tetracyclic antidepressants. *Journal of American Medical Association, 239,* 213–216.

Busse, E. W., Barnes, R. H., Silverman, A. J., Shy, G. M., Thaler, M., & Frost, L. L. (1954). Studies of the processes of aging: Factors that influence the psyche of elderly persons. *American Journal of Psychiatry, 110,* 897–903.

Busse, E. W., Barnes, R. H., Silverman, A. J., Thaler, M., & Frost, L. L. (1955). Studies of the process of aging. X. The strengths and weaknesses of psychic functioning in the aging. *American Journal of Psychiatry, 111,* 896–901.

Busse, E. W., & Pfeiffer, E. (1977). *Behavior and adaptation in late life* (2nd ed.) Boston: Little, Brown.

Butler, R. N. (1975). Psychotherapy in old age. In S. Arieti (Ed.), *American handbook of psychiatry* (2nd ed., Vol. 5, pp. 807–828). New York: Basic Books.

Carroll, B. J. (1982). Use of the dexamethasone suppression test in depression. *Journal of Clinical Psychiatry, 43,* 44–48.

Cassell, J. (1976). The contribution of the social environment to host resistance. *American Journal of Epidemiology, 104,* 107–123.

Cath, S. (1965). Discussion notes. In M. A. Berezin & S. Cath (Eds.), *Geriatric psychiatry* (pp. 128, 129). New York: International Universities Press.

De Alarcon, R. (1964). Hypochondriasis and depression in the aged. *Gerontology Clinic, 6,* 266–277.

Dement, W. C., Laughton, E. M., & Carskadon, M. A. (1982). "White paper" on sleep and aging. *Journal of the American Geriatrics Society, 30,* 25–50.

Emery, G. (1981). Cognitive therapy with the elderly. In G. Emery, S. D. Hollon, & R. C. Bedrosian (Eds.), *New directions in cognitive therapy* (pp. 84–98). New York: Guilford Press.

Feighner, J. P., Aden, G. C., Fabre, L. F., Rickels, K., & Smith, W. T. (1983). Comparison of alprazolam, imipramine, and placebo in the treatment of depression. *Journal of the American Medical Association, 249,* 3057–3064.

Feinberg, I., Koresko, R., & Heller, N. (1967). EEG sleep patterns as a function of normal and pathological aging in man. *Journal of Psychiatric Research, 5,* 107–144.

Feinberg, I., Koresko, R., & Shaffner, I. (1965). Sleep electroencephalographic and eye movement patterns in patients with chronic brain syndrome. *Journal of Psychiatric Research, 3,* 11–26.

Finch, C. E. (1973). Catecholamine metabolism in the brains of aging male mice. *Brain Research, 52,* 261–276.

Freud, S. (1950). Mourning and melancholia. In *Collected papers* (Vol. 4, pp. 152–172). London: Hogarth Press. (Original work published 1917)

Gallagher, D. (1981). Behavioral group therapy with elderly depressives: An experimental study. In D. Upper & S. M. Ross (Eds.), *Behavioral group therapy, 1981: An annual review.* Champaign, IL: Research Press Co.

Gallagher, D., & Thompson, L. W. (1982). Treatment of major depressive disorder in older adult outpatients with brief psychotherapies. *Psychotherapy: Theory, research, and practice, 19,* 482–490.

Gallagher, D., & Thompson, L. W. (1983). Cognitive therapy for depression in the elderly: A promising model for treatment and research. In L. D. Breslau and M. R. Haug (Eds.), *Depression and aging: Causes, care, and consequences* (pp. 168–192). New York: Springer Publishing Co.

Georgotas, A. (1983). Affective disorders in the elderly: Diagnostic and research considerations. *Age and Aging* 12, 1–10.

Giardina, E-G. V., Bigger, J. T., Jr., Glassman, A. H., Perel, J. M., & Kantor, S. J. (1979). The electrocardiographic and antiarrythmic effects of imipramine hydrochloride at therapeutic plasma concentrations. *Circulation, 60,* 1045–1052.

Grad, B., Rosenberg, G. N., Liberman, H., Trachtenberg, J., & Kral, V. A. (1971). Diurnal variation of the serum cortisol level of geriatric subjects. *Journal of Gerontology, 26,* 351–357.

Greden, J. F., Gardner, R., King, D., Grunhaus, L., Carroll, B. J., & Kronfol, Z. (1983). Dexamethasone suppression test in antidepressant treatment of melancholia. *Archives of General Psychiatry, 40,* 493–500.

Jacobson, E. (1953). Contributions to the metapsychology of cyclothymic depression. In P. Greenacre (Ed.), *Affective disorders* (pp. 49–83). New York: International Universities Press.

Jenike, M. A. (1983). Dexamethasone suppression test as a clinical aid in elderly depressed patients. *Journal of the American Geriatric Society, 31,* 45–48.

Kantor, S. J., Glassman, A. H., Bigger, J. T., Jr., Perel, J. M., & Giardina, E. V. (1978). The cardiac effects of therapeutic plasma concentrations of imipramine. *American Journal of Psychiatry, 135,* 534–538.

Katon, W., Raskind, M. (1980). Treatment of depression in the medically ill elderly with methylphenidate. *American Journal of Psychiatry, 137,* 963–965.

Kiloh, L. G. (1961). Pseudo-dementia. *Acta Psychiatrica Scandinavica, 37,* 336–351.

Kiloh, L. G., & Garside, R. F. (1963). The independence of neurotic depression and endogenous depression. *British Journal Psychiatry, 109,* 451–463.

Kupfer, D. J., Spiker, D. G., Coble, P. A., Neil, J. F., Ulrich, R., & Shaw, D. H. (1981). Sleep and treatment prediction in endogenous depression. *American Journal of Psychiatry, 138,* 429–434.

Kupfer, D. J., Spiker, D. G., Coble, P. A., & Shaw, D. H. (1978). Electroencephalographic sleep recordings and depression in the elderly. *Journal of the American Geriatric Society, 26,* 53–57.

Langley, G. E. (1975). Functional psychoses. In J. G. Howells (Ed.), *Modern perspectives in the psychiatry of old age* (pp. 326–355). New York: Brunner/Mazel.

Mayeux, R., Stern, Y., Rosen, J., & Leventhal, J. (1981). Depression, intellectual impairment, and Parkinson disease. *Neurology, 31,* 645–650.

McAllister, T. W. (1983). Overview: Pseudodementia. *American Journal Psychiatry, 140,* 528–532.

Meites, J., Huang, H., & Reigle, G. D. (1976). Relation of the hypothalamo-pituitary-gonadal system to decline of reproductive functions in aging female rats. In F. Labrie, J. Meites, and G. Pelletier (Eds.), *Hypothalamus and endocrine functions* (pp. 3–20). New York: Plenum Publishing.

Meltzer, H. Y., & Fang, V. S. (1983). Cortisol determination and the dexamethasone suppression test. *Archives of General Psychiatry, 40,* 501–505.

Myers, J. K., Weissman, M. M., Tishler, G. L., Holzer, C. E., Leaf, P. J., Orvaschel, H., Anthony, J. C., Boyd, J. H., Burke, J. D., Jr., Kramer, M., & Stoltzman, R. (1984). Six-month prevalence of psychiatric disorders in three communities: 1980–1982. *Archives of General Psychiatry, 41,* 959–967.

Nies, A., Robinson, D. S., Friedman, M. J., Green, R., Cooper, T. B., Ravaris, C. L., & Ives, J. O. (1977). Relationship between age and tricyclic antidepressant plasma levels. *American Journal of Psychiatry, 134,* 790–793.

Post, F. (1975). Dementia, depression, and pseudodementia. In D. F. Benson and D. Blumer (Eds.), *Psychiatric aspects of neurologic disease* (pp. 99–120). New York: Grune & Stratton.

Prinz, P. N., Peskind, E. R., Vitaliano, P. O., Raskind, M. A., Eisdorfer, C., Zemcuznikov, N., & Gerber, C. J. (1982). Changes in the sleep and waking EEG's of nondemented and demented elderly subjects. *Journal of the American Geriatric Society, 30,* 86–93.

Raskind, M., Peskind, E., Rivard, M-F., Veith, R., & Barnes, R. (1982). Dexamethasone suppression test and cortisol circadian rhythm in primary degenerative dementia. *American Journal of Psychiatry, 139,* 1468–1471.

Richelson, E. (1982, November 23-26). Management of the depressed patient: The art and science of compliance. Part V: A psychopharmacologic perspective. *Journal of Clinical Psychiatry Monograph.*

Robinson, D. S., Nies, A., Davis, J. N., Bunney, W. E., Davis, J. M., Colburn R. W., Bourne, H. R., Shaw, D. M., & Coopen, A. J. (1972). Aging, monoamines, and monoamine oxidase. *Lancet, 1,* 290–291.

Robinson, D. S., Sourkes, T. L., Nies, A., Harris, L. S., Spector, S., Bartlett, D. L., & Kaye, I. S. (1977). Monoamine metabolism in human brain. *Archives of General Psychiatry, 34,* 89–92.

Roose, S. P., Glassman, A. H., Siris, S. G., Walsh, B. T., Bruno, R. L., & Wright, L. B. (1981). Comparison of imipramine- and nortriptyline-induced orthostatic hypotension: A meaningful difference. *Journal of Clinical Psychopharmacology, 1,* 316–319.

Ross, E. D. (1981). The aprosodias: Functional-anatomic organization of the affective components of language in the right hemisphere. *Archives of Neurology, 38,* 561–569.

Ross, E. D., & Rush, A. J. (1981). Diagnosis and neuroanatomical correlates of depression in brain-damaged patients. *Archives of General Psychiatry, 38,* 1344–1354.

Sackeim, H. A., Greenburg, M. S., Weiman, A. L., Gur, R. C., Hungerbuhler, J. P., & Geschwind, N. (1982). Hemispheric asymmetry in the expression of positive and negative emotions. *Archives of Neurology, 39,* 210–218.

Salzman, C. (1982). A primer on geriatric psychopharmacology. *American Journal of Psychiatry, 139,* 67–74.

Samorajski, T., & Hartford, J. M. (1980). Brain physiology of aging. In E. W. Busse & D. G. Blazer (Eds.), *Handbook of geriatric psychiatry* (pp. 46–82). New York: Van Nostrand Reinhold.

Samorajski, T., Rolsten, C., & Ordy, J. M. (1971). Changes in behavior, brain, and neuroendocrine chemistry with age and stress in C57BL/6J male mice. *Journal of Gerontology, 26,* 168–175.

Schou, M. (1968). Lithium in psychiatric therapy and prophylaxis. *Journal of Psychiatry Research, 6,* 67–95.

Seligman, M. E. P. (1974). Depression and learned helplessness. In R. J. Friedman & M. M. Katz, (Eds.), *The psychology of depression: Contemporary theory and research* (pp. 83–125). Washington, DC: V. H. Winston & Sons.

Snyder, P. J., & Utiger, R. D. (1972). Response to thyrotropin releasing hormone (TRH) in normal man. *Journal of Clinical Endocrinology Metabolism, 34,* 380–385.

Spar, J. E., & Gerner, R. (1982). Does the dexamethasone suppression test distinguish dementia from depression? *American Journal of Psychiatry, 139,* 238–240.

Spar, J. E., & LaRue, A. (1983). Major depression in the elderly: *DSM-III* criteria and the dexamethasone suppression test as predictors of treatment response. *American Journal of Psychiatry, 140,* 844–847.

Steuer, J., & Austin, E. (1980). Family abuse of the elderly. *Journal of the American Geriatrics Society, 28,* 372–380.

Steuer, J. L., Mintz, J., Hammen, C. L., Hill, M. A., Jarvik, L. F., McCarley, T., Motoike, P., & Rosen, R. (1984). Cognitive-behavioral and psychodynamic group psychotherapy in treatment of geriatric depression. *Journal of Consulting and Clinical Psychology, 52,* 180–189.

Stoudemire, A. (in press). Depression in the medically ill. In J. L. Houpt and H. K. H. Brodie (Eds.), *Consultation—Liaison psychiatry and behavioral medicine.* New York: J. B. Lippincott Co.

Stoudemire, A., & Brown J. T. (1984). Delayed and distorted grief: Pathological patterns of bereavement. *Trauma, 26,* 1–20.

Stoudemire, A., & Thompson T. L. (1981). Recognizing and treating dementia. *Geriatrics, 36,* 112–120.

Thomae, H. (1970). Theory of aging on cognitive theory of personality. *Human Development, 13,* 1–16.

Thompson, L. W., Gallagher, D., Nies, G., & Epstein, D. (1983). Evaluation of the effectiveness of professionals and nonprofessionals as instructors of "Coping with Depression" classes for elders. *The Gerontologist, 23,* 390–396.

Tourigny-Rivard, M. F., Raskind, M., & Rivard, D. (1981). The dexamethasone suppression test in an elderly population. *Biological Psychiatry, 16,* 1177–1184.

Ulrich, R. F., Shaw, D. H., & Kupfer, D. J. (1980). Effects of aging on EEG sleep in depression. *Sleep, 3,* 31–40.

Veith, R. C., Raskind, M. A., Caldwell, J. H., Barnes, R. F., Gumbrecht, G., & Ritchie, J. L. (1982). Cardiovascular effects of tricyclic antidepressants in depressed patients with chronic heart disease. *The New England Journal of Medicine, 306,* 954–959.

Vohra, J., Burrows, G. D., & Sloman, G. (1975). Assessment of cardiovascular side effects of therapeutic doses of tricyclic antidepressant drugs. *Australia-New Zealand Medicine, 5,* 7–11.

Weiner, R. (1982). The role of electroconvulsive therapy in the treatment of depression in the elderly. *Journal of the American Geriatric Society, 30,* 710–712.

Weissman, M. M., & Myers, J. K. (1978). Affective disorders in a U.S. urban community. *Archives of General Psychiatry, 35,* 1304–1311.

Wells, C. E. (1979). Pseudodementia. *American Journal of Psychiatry, 136,* 895–900.

Winokur, A., Amsterdam, J. D., Oler, J., Mendels, J., Snyder, P. J., Caroff, S. N., & Brunswick, D. J. (1983). Multiple hormonal responses to protirelin (TRH) in depressed patients. *Archives of General Psychiatry, 40,* 525–531.

Zetzel, E. (1965). Metapsychology of aging. In M. A. Berezin & S. Cath (Eds.), *Geriatric psychiatry* (pp. 109–118). New York: International Universities Press.

Chapter 17

Chronic and Refractory Depressions: Evaluation and Management

Hagop S. Akiskal

Professor, Department of Psychiatry, University of Tennessee College of Medicine, Memphis

Rebecca C. Simmons

Resident, Department of Psychiatry, University of Tennessee College of Medicine, Memphis

INTRODUCTION

Chronic depressions present one of the greatest challenges facing mental health practitioners today. While great strides have been made in the field of affective disorders (Whybrow, Akiskal, & McKinney, 1984), our knowledge of the etiology, classification, and treatment of *chronic* depressive conditions is still quite primitive. Yet this group of disorders—characterized by low-grade, protracted depressive manifestations—accounts for approximately 10–15 percent of all depressive disorders (Akiskal, Bitar, Puzantian, Rosenthal, & Walker, 1978; Kielholz, Terzani, & Gaspar, 1979; Robins & Guze, 1972). It was in recognition of the clinical importance of these prevalent forms of depressive suffering that the diagnostic rubric of *dysthymic disorder* was included in the *DSM-III* (American Psychiatric Association, 1980). Unfortunately, this term embraces too broad and heterogeneous a group of chronic dysphoric conditions, thus contributing little to our understanding of the nature and course of chronic depressive disorders. However, the operational definition of dysthymai is the initial step in the development of clinical research in this area.

This chapter will review current diagnostic, nosologic, and treatment approaches to chronic depressive disorders. Because of the paucity of systematic research in this area—and the absence of well-designed controlled studies on treatment—we shall summarize the existing research literature and outline promising research leads rather than engaging in extensive clinical discourse. Finally, we shall emphasize that delineating specific subtypes of chronic depression with relatively unique clinical and etiologic correlates is key to developing rational treatment approaches.

DEFINITIONAL ISSUES

Before *DSM-III*, it was unclear how chronic depressions should be categorized. Neurotic depression, the *DSM-III* precursor of dysthymic disorder, was a broad concept embracing all depressions that did not fit into endogenous, psychotic, and manic-depressive categories. Two independent studies demonstrated that this rubric—referring to precipitated, mild depressions with significant neurotic and characterologic pathology—lacked operational clarity and longitudinal validity (Akiskal, Bitar, Puzantian, Rosenthal, & Walker, 1978; Klerman, Endicott, Spitzer, & Hirschfeld, 1979). Many of these patients had concurrent nonaffective diagnoses; others seemed to remit, with or without future recurrences; and a third group developed psychotic depressive, or hypomanic and manic breakdowns. As chronicity and long-standing characterologic pathology seemed to characterize some of these subgroups, this aspect of neurotic depressive suffering was viewed as the most useful connotation to retain in the third edition of the American Psychiatric Association's *Diagnostic Statistical Manual of Mental Disorders* (1980).

Work involved in the development of the Research Diagnostic Criteria ([RDC]; Spitzer, Endicott, & Robins, 1978) led to the delineation of two types of low-grade protracted depressions: chronic minor depressive disorder, and intermittent depressive disorder. The latter concept replaced the diagnosis of depressive personality in earlier versions of the RDC. These rubrics, representing the precursors of the *DSM-III* concept of dysthymic disorder, refer to depressive suffering milder in intensity over time with relatively short, symptom-free intervals, if any. The concept of dysthymic disorder, emphasizing fluctuating course and intermittent chronicity, emerged from these definitions.

The essential characteristics of dysthymia, as delineated in *DSM-III*, include: (1) chronicity, defined as either persistent or intermittent depressive symptoms of at least two years' duration; (2) subsyndromal intensity; that is, fewer symptoms than those required for the diagnosis of an acute major depression; (3) absence of affective delusions and hallucinations; and (4) absence of manic or hypomanic manifestations. Onset is insidious, or follows a definable depressive episode. Although dysthymia as such is classified within the large class of affective disorders, *DSM-III* (American Psychiatric Association, 1980) states that "often the affective features of this disorder are viewed as secondary to an underlying Personality Disorder." Thus, *DSM-III* is equivocal in pronouncing dysthymia as a primary affective disorder. This creates dilemmas for the clinical characterization of chronic depressions.

Most clinicians are accustomed to thinking of affective disorders as characterized by an acute and episodic course. This conceptualization may bias the clinician, on semantic grounds alone, against making a diagnosis of "chronic depression." Moreover, the personality traits of these patients are often such that attention is rapidly diverted from the affective pathology to their more enduring personality styles (Price, 1978). Chronic, low-grade depressions are often intricately intertwined with a lifestyle of maladjustment, gloom, and despair, or narcissistic demands, as well as never-ending demands placed on their family and associates, culminating in marked interpersonal dissonance. These patients are often shunned by others, including the health care professional to whom they turn for relief (Berblinger, 1970). Frequently, they have been seen for multiple, vague, somatic complaints, with anxiety and/or other autonomic nervous system disturbances overshadowing any other depressive symptoms (Akiskal, 1983; Weissman & Klerman, 1977). Indeed they are commonly diagnosed as "hypochondriacal," or merely as "crocks," after little evidence is found to suggest an underlying medical disease. Trials of anxiolytics and sedative-hypnotics do not allay their complaints. After repeated treatment failures, even the most experienced clinicians are likely to change the patient's diagnosis to one of primary characterologic disorder, thereby limiting the range of treatment indications and the likelihood of therapeutic benefits.

Another problem for the clinicians is the heterogeneity of the conditions subsumed under the dysthymic rubric. The age of onset, the nature of the affective symptoms, type of characterologic pathology, and concurrent nonaffective disorders are variable, suggesting the need for delineating subtypes within this category. As discussed in subsequent sections of this chapter, these subtypes call for different treatment approaches. Because predictive validity relating to treatment response is among the most important characteristics of a clinical diagnostic manual, we believe that subsequent revisions of *DSM-III* should incorporate subclassifications of dysthymic disorders that reflect such treatment implications.

CLASSIFICATION

The term *double depression* has been coined to refer to the superimposition of acute (major) and protracted low-grade (dysthymic) depressions (Keller & Shapiro, 1982). Data from our mood clinic have indicated the occurrence of such "double depressions" in two thirds of a chronic depressive population (Akiskal, 1983). Thus, admixtures of syndromal and subsyndromal manifestations occur in the majority of chronic depressions (Rounsaville, Sholomskas, & Prusoff, 1980). Likewise, a clinical population chosen on the basis of chronic depression will typically consist of only a small number of "pure" dysthymics by *DSM-III* criteria (Akiskal, King, Rosenthal, Robinson, & Scott-Strauss, 1981). It is not yet known why some patients progress from a chronic subsyndromal level of affective disturbance to a major syndromal depressive episode. In some instances, hypomanic episodes may also be superimposed. Familial-genetic, characterologic, and stressful life events or biologic insults appear relevant. These considerations underscore the importance of delineating distinct subtypes of chronic depressive disorders in order to advance the overall body of knowledge and the quality of patient care.

Studies conducted at the University of Tennessee (Akiskal, 1983; Akiskal et al, 1981; Akiskal, Rosenthal, Haykal, Lemmi, Rosenthal, & Scott-Strauss,

1980; Rosenthal, Akiskal, Scott-Strauss, Rosenthal, & David, 1981) have provided the framework for a classificatory schema of chronic depressive conditions based on age of onset, familial and developmental variables, treatment response, and laboratory findings (Figure 1). A basic distinction is made between chronic depressive patterns which are the residuum of incompletely remitted primary major unipolar episodes—typically having their onset in adult life—and dysthymic patterns that begin insidiously in late childhood or adolescence in the absence of a major episode. In the early onset group, depressive attitudes have become so ingrained as to appear part of the character structure, conforming to the clinical colloquialism of "characterologic depression"; our work has shown that this group itself is divisible into subaffective dysthymic and character-spectrum subgroups. The subaffective subgroup, while not presenting a fully affective syndrome, nevertheless responded to tricyclic antidepressants and/or lithium carbonate; the character-spectrum subgroup did not respond to such medication. Finally, chronic depressions secondary to validated preexisting nonaffective disorders we chose to consider dysphoric reactions to underlying conditions such as panic, obsessive-compulsive, or schizophrenic disorder, or the early phase of dementia. A special subgroup within the chronic secondary dysphorias is represented by those individuals with disabling medical diseases of childhood onset—for example, severe asthma, hemophilia, and polycystic disease—and who develop chronic depressive attitudes closely interwoven with the course of their medical disorder.

Our classificatory schema for the heterogeneous group of chronic depressive disorders grew in part from our experience in treating patients referred to our mood clinic by clinicians who regarded them as "refractory" to the usual modalities deemed effective in affective disorders. Many had been ill—either persistently or intermittently—for more than two years, thereby meeting the *DSM-III* duration criterion for dysthymic disorders.

FIGURE 1
*Chronic depressions**

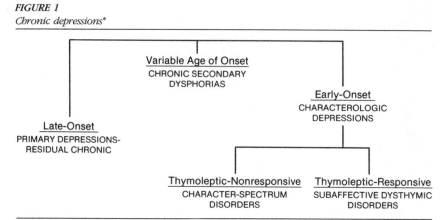

* Proposed classification of chronic depressions based on Akiskal (1983). Reproduced with permission.

However, syndromal and subsyndromal admixtures of depression (e.g., "double depression") were the most common clinical picture. Although only 10 percent could be considered "pure" dysthymics with subsyndromal level of depression, low-grade depression was the *predominant* pattern in most patients. This is probably best explained by the fact that syndromal depressions tend to respond to treatment (especially pharmacotherapy), and may even remit spontaneously without specific treatment. Furthermore, severe chronic depression of syndromal proportion is poorly tolerated and may lead to self-destruction. It is the low-grade dysthymic level of depression, often woven into the personality structure and not easily distinguished from it, that provides the greatest diagnostic and therapeutic challenge to the clinician.

The heterogeneity of these chronic depressive disorders suggested that they were the final common pathway of many different affective and nonaffective processes and that rational treatment approaches would very much depend on subdivisions based on these diverse processes.

TREATMENT IMPLICATIONS OF PROPOSED CHRONIC DEPRESSIVE SUBTYPES

Although controlled treatment trials have not been undertaken in the chronic depressive subtypes to be described, we present treatment implications for each of these subtypes based on etiologic and psychopathologic findings revealed in our studies.

Chronic Residual Phase of Unipolar Depression

According to current estimates, 10–15 percent of all patients with a primary affective disorder fail to recover fully (Akiskal et al., 1978; Kielholz et al., 1979; Robins & Guze, 1972; Weissman & Klerman, 1977). Such an outcome may develop after one or more episodes of acute major depression (Akiskal et al., 1981). This type of chronic depression is usually late in onset (over 50 years), typically without a previous history of low-grade depression or of other validated psychiatric disorders. In the Tennessee study almost all were unipolar, and premorbid personalities of patients were generally unremarkable (Akiskal, 1982). Forty percent had endogenomorphic features. REM latency findings in these patients were indistinguishable from those of patients in an acute major depressive episode, suggesting that affective processes were relevant to these chronic depressive residuals.

One previous study had concluded that the tendency to chronicity in these patients might be due to inadequate treatment (Weissman & Klerman, 1977). This is an unlikely explanation, given the fact that the natural history of unipolar depression is remission after several months of illness, even in the absence of specific treatment. Our research has shown that these chronic residuals are best understood as the convergence of multiple interacting factors, both psychological and biological (Akiskal, 1982):

1. Familial affective loading for unipolar depression.
2. Multiple deaths of family members.
3. Disabled spouses or other family members.
4. Secondary drug dependence.
5. Use of depressant antihypertensive agents.
6. Incapacitating concurrent medical disease.

These factors were significantly less frequent in a control group of episodic unipolar depressives who had shown full recovery without low-grade residuals (Table 1).

Continuing pharmacotherapy and psychotherapy are indicated for this group of patients. Heterocyclic antidepressants are useful in reversing vegetative and psychomotor disturbances, as well as suicidal ideation, and controlled trials have indicated high rates of relapse on placebo (Ayd, 1975; Ward, Bloom & Friedel, 1979). Interpersonal psychotherapy, while not specifically tested in chronic depression, may attenuate the interpersonal and role conflicts experienced by depressed individuals (Weissman & Akiskal, 1984). Furthermore, supportive measures may strengthen the patient's coping skills when faced with new adaptive demands (Akiskal, 1982; Weissman & Akiskal, 1984). Most resistant to treatment in these cases are the postdepressive attitudes of passivity, dependence, and resignation. Although it would appear that a cognitive approach might be of help in reversing such attitudes, uncontrolled experience suggests that cognitive therapy is generally disappointing with chronic depressives (Rush, 1983).

TABLE 1

Comparison of chronic primary depressives with episodic primary depressive controls*

Variable	Chronic (percent)	Episodic (percent)	P
Personality			
"Unstable" (histrionic-sociopathic)	21	15	ns
Depressive (Schneider)	44	28	ns
Stressors†			
Multiple deaths in family	21	3	< .05
Disabled family member	21	3	< .05
Superimposed medical illness	47	10	< .001
Use of depressant antihypertensives	21	3	< .05
Secondary sedativism and alcoholism	34	17	< .05
Development			
Psychiatric illness in both parents	16	13	ns
Loss of parent < age 15	21	18	ns
Family history			
Depression only	42	20	< .05
Bipolar illness	5	3	ns

* Summarized from Akiskal (1982).

† Given the possibility that this type of stressors could be correlates of age, the episodic group was limited to 30 age- and sex-matched subjects.

Chronic Secondary Dysphorias

Discouragement, decreased confidence and self-esteem, varying degrees of social withdrawal, intermittent morose mood, and fleeting suicidal ideation are common accompaniments of disabling, disfiguring, and progressive medical or psychiatric illness (Clayton & Lewis, 1981). These dysphorias are understandable psychologic reactions to chronic neurologic, rheumatologic, somatization, obsessive-compulsive, phobic, and panic disorders (Akiskal, 1983). The joint presence of both medical and psychiatric disorder is especially potent in producing refractory dysphorias (Akiskal et al., 1981). These dysphoric reactions tend to parallel the vicissitudes of the underlying disorder (Clayton & Lewis, 1981), and therefore are best viewed as secondary demoralization responses (Klein, 1974). If the illness begins early in life, the melancholy attitude is typically woven into the character structure of the patient. Whether occurring in the setting of psychiatric or medical illness, onset is rarely with a major depressive episode, and family history is negative for affective disorders (Akiskal et al., 1981). Finally, dexamethasone suppression test (DST) and REM latency findings are usually within the nonaffective range (Akiskal & Lemmi, 1983; Akiskal & Tashjian, 1983; Akiskal, Lemmi, Dickson, King, Yerevanian, & VanValkenburg, 1984). As argued elsewhere, these findings converge in providing compelling evidence that the dysthymic rubric should not be invoked for these conditions (Akiskal, 1983). Chronic medical and neurotic disorders are *depressing* by their very nature, and low-grade dysphoric manifestations do not constitute a psychopathologic process distinct from the underlying disorder.

Although patients suffering from secondary dysphorias are typically treated with soporific heterocyclic antidepressants, no controlled drug trials have been conducted to document their efficacy. Group therapy, to address concerns common to dysphoric patients suffering from disabling medical disorders, would be a reasonable alternative or adjunct but, again, the efficacy of the approach is not supported by controlled studies. When an anxiety disorder forms the substrate for the dysphoric reaction, monoamine oxidase inhibitors (MAOI) are generally believed to be effective. Such patients, often referred to as "mixed anxiety depressives" (Kendell, 1976; Paykel, 1971), have been the subject of several controlled drug trials. The superiority of MAOIs over tricyclic drugs has been upheld in some, but not all, studies (Davidson, 1983; Davidson, Miller, Turnbull, & Sullivan, 1982; Liebowitz, Quitkin, Stewart, McGrath, Harrison, Rabkin, Tricamo, Markowitz, & Klein, 1984; Tyrer, 1979).

Characterologic Depressions

Characterologic depressions represent a spectrum of low-grade depressions with onset in late childhood or adolescence and an intermittent, presumably lifelong course (Akiskal et al., 1980; Rosenthal et al., 1981). Onset is usually insidious, with full manifestations apparent before age 25. If a major depressive episode is superimposed, it tends to be short lived and symptoms return to the premorbid low-grade depressive baseline. This group of patients is most representative of the *DSM-III* dysthymic disorder category. Indeed, in proposed revisions of *DSM-III*, the nosologic territory of dysthymia would be restricted to this early onset group (Akiskal, in press a).

The term *characterologic* implies early onset and intertwining of character and depression such that depression has become a prominent part of the patient's personality. The rubric of "hysteroid dysphoria" (Liebowitz & Klein, 1979) denoting low self-esteem, an exquisite sensitivity to loss of romantic attachments, passive-dependent and histrionic personality traits, a low threshold for alcohol and other sedative hypnotic drugs, and a persistent tendency toward dysphoria and manipulative suicidal gestures, has also been invoked for some of these patients. The patient's mood is typically geared toward and reactive to environmental praise. So-called atypical depressions (Davidson et al., 1982) are closely related to this clinical picture, with symptoms of hypersomnia, overeating, and reverse diurnal variation, and with "neurotic" symptoms (somatic, phobic anxiety, and hysterical features) often predominating over depressive manifestations.

In our recent research on these early onset characterologic depressions, we carefully excluded all patients whose chronic dysphoric symptoms were superimposed on a preexisting anxiety disorder (who, in our schema, belong to the secondary dysphoric category). As summarized in Table 2, our work

TABLE 2
*Significant differences between subtypes of characterologic depressions**

	Subaffective Dysthymic disorder (N = 20)	Character-spectrum disorder (N = 30)
Thymoleptic response (defining characteristic)	Yes	No
Pharmacologic hypomania (percent)	35	0
Female (percent)	55	83
Personality	Introverted-obsessive	Unstable-hysteroid-antisocial
Developmental object loss (percent)	25	60
Family history (percent):		
Unipolar	30	3.3
Bipolar	35	3.3
Alcoholism	10	53
Assortative mating	10	47
REM latency†	< 70 min.	70–110 min.
Hypersomnia (percent)	55	10
Superimposed major depressive episodes (percent)	55	13
Unfavorable social outcome (percent)	3	30

* Summarized from Akiskal et al. (1980) and Rosenthal et al. (1981).
† Measured during habitual dysthymic condition.

suggested the existence of at least two subtypes of low-grade, early onset chronic depression conforming to the character-spectrum and subaffective dysthymic patterns.

Character-Spectrum Disorders. This pattern is primarily manifested in characterological pathology, including dependent, histrionic-sociopathic, and schizoid traits, reminiscent of the RDC categories of intermittent depressive and labile personality disorders. Two thirds of the characterologic depressives in our studies were assigned to this group, based in part on failure to respond to systematic trials of tricyclics and lithium carbonate (Akiskal et al., 1980; Rosenthal et al., 1981). Furthermore, REM latency values were within the normal range, and there were high rates of familial alcoholism but not of familial affective disorders. Broken homes and childhood parental losses seemed to supply the developmental roots for these character disturbances. This subtype was conceptualized as developmentally based, with chronic dysphoria representing the adverse consequences of parental alcoholism, sociopathy, and related disorders.

Subaffective Dysthymia. In this subtype, the personality disturbances are milder and appear to be secondary to frequent episodes of low-grade endogenous depression, approximating the minor episodic depression of the RDC terminology. In 35 percent, family history is positive for bipolar affective disorder, which explains the high rate of pharmacologically occasioned hypomania in this subtype (Akiskal et al., 1980; Rosenthal et al., 1981). REM latencies are within the range for patients with primary affective disorders, and patients are responsive to noradrenergic tricyclics, lithium, or both. In addition, these patients, unlike the character-spectrum subgroup, seem to conform to Schneider's (1958) depressive typology, providing independent validation for the distinction between the personality patterns of the two subgroups. All of these findings converge in suggesting that these predominantly subsyndromal depressions of early onset represent *formes frustes* of primary affective disorders—hence the designation *subaffective* dysthymia.

It is generally believed that the response of characterologic depressions to pharmacotherapy is unrewarding, and response to psychotherapy seems equally disappointing. However, our experience suggests that energetic and systematic pharmacotherapy, coupled with psychotherapy, may benefit a significant minority—about a third—of these patients (Akiskal et al., 1980). Pharmacologic interventions seem to alleviate the intermittent retarded depressive substrate characterized by psychomotor inertia, hypersomnia, and anhedonia. However, the gains made with pharmacotherapy are typically short lived, unless supplemented with psychotherapy; that is, social skills and related behavioral approaches to provide these patients with appropriate social behaviors in which they are deficient. Conversely, retarded patients who lack hedonic drive and oversleep, seem unable to benefit from these psychotherapeutic approaches given in the absence of competent pharmacotherapy.

Puig-Antich's (1982) work on childhood depression has shown that conduct disorder is a common concomitant. He has, therefore, hypothesized that untreated childhood depression is the precursor of several classes of adult characterologic difficulties. Our experience with characterologic depressions provides partial support for this formulation, especially among the subaffective dysthymic subgroup. In these patients—suffering from early onset, intermittent subsyndromal depressions with hypersomnic-retarded clinical picture, unfounded lowering of self-esteem, guilt, and anhedonia—the diathesis seems, at least in part, to be hereditary. The chronic intermittent tendency to experience these disabling symptoms probably prevents optimum ego maturation and the development of appropriate social skills (Akiskal, 1981b). History for familial bipolar disorder and the mobilization of brief hypomania upon tricyclic challenge can be considered as a marker for bipolarity and suggests the use of lithium carbonate (with or without tricyclics, as indicated by clinical course).

At this point we are uncertain of the nosologic nature of the character-spectrum subgroup, although our results suggest some affinity to sociopathy, somatization disorder, and alcoholism. There is no known satisfactory treatment approach for this subgroup. This is in part definitional, as these patients were identified because of failure to respond. This failure can be explained in part by poor compliance in that patients seek help at times of crisis and demand symptom relief. These patients tend to have low thresholds for side effects of thymoleptic medications, and the treating physician may be inclined to change drugs before a trial of adequate dosage and duration can be given. Trying to engage these patients in any formal psychotherapy is a difficult task. It is conceivable that the distress of at least some of these patients—and their inability to form satisfactory transference—is due to residual attention deficit disorder (Andrulonis, Glueck, Stroebel, Vogel, Shopiro, & Aldridge, 1981). Therefore, drugs such as magnesium pemoline or methylphenidate, coupled with an educational approach (rather than formal psychotherapy) might be of benefit in some cases of what we have described here as character-spectrum disorders. Others may benefit from a trial with phenelzine (Liebowitz & Klein, 1979).

The etiologic and therapeutic challenge of characterologic depressions is a complex task for the future. The relationship of character pathology to depressive disorder has been conceptualized elsewhere (Akiskal, Hirschfeld, & Yerevanian, 1983). The foregoing discussion is provided as a general framework for clinicians and researchers struggling with these very "difficult" and "intractable" patients.

THE QUESTION OF INTRACTABLE DEPRESSIONS

Terminologic Aspects

The terms *intractable, treatment-resistant,* and *refractory* depression refer to increasing degrees of difficulty in treating depression. *Intractability* is the more general term and connotes a depression that is difficult to treat. Treatment resistance implies relative refractoriness to first-line interventions deemed effective for depressive illness; this definition obviously depends on what clinicians in a given setting consider to be the "standard" treatments. Probably most clinicians would consider the use of two different tricyclics given in adequate doses and duration as a minimum standard. The designation refractory depression can be applied to patients who, having failed to respond to first-line interventions, remain unresponsive to additional trials such as a MAOI or electroconvulsive therapy (ECT).

It is important to remember that treatment resistance and refractoriness are not synonymous with chronicity, because spontaneous recovery sometimes occurs in depressions that were initially considered unresponsive. Nor should one consider chronic depression to be refractory. Findings summarized in this chapter suggest the value of combined pharmacologic-psychotherapeutic approaches in several subtypes of chronic depressions.

Although many reviews (Ananth & Ruskin, 1974; Gerner, 1983; Shaw, 1977; Stern & Mendels, 1981) have been devoted to the subject of intractable depressions, no controlled data are available. Nevertheless, many creative attempts have been made to alleviate the suffering of these patients. Accordingly, we shall first summarize what appear to be the common denominators in many of these attempts, and then review our own experience at the University of Tennessee Mood Clinic.

Recommendations in the Literature

It is generally agreed that one must first make sure that the patient received at least two suitable tricyclics from different classes and the MAOI phenelzine in sufficient dose and duration, and that patient compliance with drug regimens was satisfactory. If this is not the case, one must repeat this step using plasma tricyclic level determinations whenever available. It may be especially useful to try some of the new heterocyclic antidepressants (Ayd, 1983) or an MAOI not given previously. Other somatic therapies that may prove beneficial include lithium carbonate, alone or in combination with either a tricyclic or an MAOI such a tranylcypromine, for 8–12 weeks. There are now several reports in the literature of lithium augmentation of both MAOI and tricyclic antidepressants (de Montigny, Grunberg, Mayer, & Deschenes, 1981; Himmelhoch, Detre, Kupfer, Swartzburg, & Byck, 1972; Nelson & Byck, 1982; Price, Conwell, & Nelson, 1983). MAOIs are often better tolerated than tricyclic antidepressants despite dietary restrictions, and they are usually preferred over the latter whenever anxiety symptoms are prominent (Pare, Rees, & Sainsbury, 1962; West & Dally, 1959). Some authors have used carbamazepine in lieu of lithium, especially in those depressions suspected of having underlying limbic lobe pathology (Okuma, 1983) whether revealed through sleep-deprived EEG or neuropsychologic testing. Finally some advocate the combination of a tertiary tricyclic antidepressant (always given first or concurrently) and phenelzine (Ananth & Luchins, 1977; Winston, 1971), a combination now considered to be safe—even safer than an MAOI given alone (Pare, Kline, Hallstrom, & Cooper, 1982)—although not proven superior to either drug alone.

L-triiodothyronine (T_3) in low, single morning doses of 25–50 mcg is believed by some to be effective either alone or as an adjunct to previously ineffective tricyclic antidepressants (Extein, 1982). This may be especially true for women who may have subtle degrees of thyroid failure—not shown by routine thyroid indexes—but revealed by an exaggerated thyroid-stimulating hormone (TSH) response to thyrotropin-releasing hormone (TRH) stimulation or upon measurement of antithyroid antibodies. Methylphenidate may also briefly enhance the efficacy of tricyclic antidepressants (Drummer, Girlin, & Givirtsman, 1983). The serotonin precursor L-tryptophan is also being tried for refractory depressions, insomnia, and bipolar affective illness (Beitman & Dunner, 1982). It has been given with MAOIs, tricyclic antidepressants, and allopurinol. Other unorthodox approaches include combining tricyclics with reserpine dextroamphetamines, sinemet, bromocriptine, or steroids (Stern & Mendels, 1981).

This review would be incomplete without mention of an approach to treatment-resistant depressions developed by Kielholz in Basel, Switzerland (Kielholz et al., 1979). The setting is an inpatient unit solely for the intensive therapy of endogenous depressions that have remained "therapy-resistant" after trials with two "correctly selected" antidepressants, given on an outpatient basis. The patient is placed in the hospital for seven days initially "to relax" with the aid of a major tranquilizer, given intramuscularly. Beginning the second week, an oral tranquilizer is used, along with an intravenous drip infusion, containing clomipramine[1] and maprotiline, one to three ampoules of each per 90-minute infusion, administered daily for another two to three weeks. Pharmacotherapy is "invariably combined with psychotherapy and autogenous training, coupled with massage of the nuchal region" and followed by group gymnastics. When the depression begins to lift, the patient is shifted to oral antidepressant therapy throughout the hospital course. It is claimed that this treatment brings about full remission in 70 percent of patients.

Cingulotomy remains a highly controversial treatment, usually undertaken as a last resort for highly distressed refractory patients who fail to show an appreciable response to full therapeutic doses of the somatic treatments outlined above (Price, 1978; Bartlett, Bridges, & Kelly, 1981).

The University of Tennessee Approach

We have developed a systematic approach for evaluating patients with intractable depression referred to our clinic (Akiskal, in press b). Although many

---

[1] Not marketed in the United States, but available in Canada and many European countries.

such patients had previously been deemed "refractory" prematurely (i.e., after brief psychotherapy or substandard and/or inadequate tricyclic trials), we are currently seeing referrals after the failure of a much more sophisticated spectrum of therapeutic trials. This is due both to the feedback to regional clinicians provided from our clinic and to the overall improved level of information disseminated nationally concerning affective disorders. Although there is an obvious need for individualized approaches to patients in this area, the following outline provides our general approach to patients considered "intractable."

Full Psychiatric Evaluation.   A comprehensive semistructured interview is the necessary first step in such an evaluation. It may last up to 90 minutes or more, and should cover all aspects of the major psychiatric disorders, both cross-sectionally and longitudinally, as well as details of the patient's developmental, social, personal, and medical history. Past medical and psychiatric records should also be studied carefully. This evaluation serves several important purposes. It assures the patient of the completeness of the evaluation, thereby engendering hope and encouraging future compliance and cooperation with the procedures to follow, described below. Additionally, it may reveal unsuspected diagnostic possibilities such as a subtle bipolar disorder, underlying schizoid or anxiety disorders, or contributing factors from medical illness and/or medical (e.g., antihypertensive) or nonmedical (e.g., alcohol) drug use.

Drug-Free Baseline.   In general, a drug-free baseline should be established by observing the patient off all psychoactive medications before reinstating or initiating any treatment trial. To accomplish this, it may be necessary to withdraw current medications gradually to avoid withdrawal symptoms, which may even occur when tricyclic antidepressants are discontinued abruptly. Moreover, some patients may require brief hospitalization for detoxification from drugs such as sedative-hypnotics or ethanol, which may contribute to the chronicity seen in some depressed patients.

DST, TRH, and Sleep EEG Procedures.   The drug-free baseline period also allows the clinician to conduct a dexamethasone suppression test (DST), thyroid function tests, and a sleep EEG in cases where such procedures are deemed appropriate (Akiskal & Lemmi, 1983; Carroll, 1982; Kupfer & Thase, 1983; Loosen and Prange, 1982).

When interpreted in the context of clinical findings, the DST may corroborate the presence of a subtle melancholic process requiring vigorous chemotherapeutic intervention. Also, persistent nonsuppression indicates the need for continued energetic treatment.

The protirelin (or thyrotropin) test measures the response of the thyroid-stimulating hormone (TSH) to stimulation by thyrotropin-releasing hormone (TRH), and can be useful in differentiating depressions secondary to thyroid dysfunction from primary depressive illnesses. A blunted TSH response is suggestive of a chronic unipolar depressive disorder, while the response is usually exaggerated in the presence of depression that is secondary to thyroid failure. Indeed, subtle degrees of hypothyroidism—sometimes responsible for anergic depressions in women (Gold, Pottash, Mueller, & Extein, 1981)— are primarily detectable by TRH challenge.

A sleep EEG recording may aid the clinician in diagnosing underlying primary affective illness, anxiety disorders, and organic disease—either systemic or involving the central nervous system. In primary affective disorders, latency to the first REM period is considerably shortened from a mean of 90 minutes. This measure can be especially helpful when patients present with confusing mixtures of chronic depressive as well as borderline personality traits. Recordings from patients with anxiety disorders will often show normal to decreased REM percentages (Akiskal et al., 1984). As for organic affective syndromes, REM density is decreased to low levels (King, Akiskal, Lemmi, Wilson, Belluomini, & Yerevanian, 1981); in primary depression this measure is either normal or elevated.

Medical Evaluation.   Physical examination, blood chemistry, a complete blood count, and urinalysis are the first steps in evaluating underlying medical illnesses in intractable depressions. Further procedures depend on the clinicians' index of suspicion based on psychiatric and medical history as well as REM density findings. Despite their rarity as etiological factors in intractable depressions, occult malignancies, such as abdominal lymphomas and carcinoma of the head of the pancreas, are especially treacherous entities in this regard (Fras, Littin, & Pearson, 1967). Another rare, but treatable cause of chronic depression is an epileptic disorder without a seizure component (Blumer, 1982).

Treatment Recommendations.   Our recommendations derive from the nosologic and etiologic considerations discussed above. Pharmacologic management should of course be provided in the context of a supportive psychotherapeutic relationship (Akiskal, 1981a). In general, because of the ease of administration, it is best to begin with two chemically dissimilar tricyclics, given consecutively, unless past personal or family history of pharmacologic response suggests otherwise; when plasma monitoring of tricyclics is available, and cardiac consultation does not contraindicate it, it may prove useful to go beyond the "FDA dose." It is also worthwhile to give adequate trials with dissimilar MAOIs, for example, phenelzine (up to 75 mg/day) or tranylcypromine (up to 60 mg/day); the former is most likely to work in anxious and, the latter in anergic, depressions. Anergic depressions may also be secondary to subclinical hypothyroidism and this is where thyroid replacement is most likely to be therapeutically beneficial. Antianxiety agents are not generally effective as primary treatment of chronic depressions except for those with an anxiety disorder substrate; alprazolam is of promise for such patients, having the advantage over MAOIs, that it can be given without regard to dietary restrictions. In our experience, lithium carbonate is most effective—singly or in combination with a tricyclic such as desipramine or a MAOI such as tranylcypromine—in the presence of familial bipolar history. Such history is not uncommon in recurrent unipolar and dysthymic depressions which, as discussed elsewhere (Akiskal, in press a), belong to a bipolar spectrum. The antiepileptic carbamazepine is not only effective in rapid-cycling bipolar patients, but also in intermittent and protracted dysphorias emanating from abnormal limbic discharges. Finally, antipsychotic neuroleptics in modest doses (e.g., Stelazine, 5–10 mg/day) may sometimes prove beneficial for depressions seen in schizotypal individuals, or may enhance tricyclic antidepressants in partially remitted psychotic depressives; because of the risk of tardive dyskinesia, such neuroleptic use should be for short periods of time. Sufficient data on the safety and usefulness of other pharmacologic combinations is not currently available. For this reason, when the foregoing measures fail, we recommend a full course of ECT which, more often than not, proves effective in chronic depressives with an endogenous substrate.

SUMMARY

Recent clinical and epidemiologic studies have revealed the existence of a large number of individuals with low-grade depressions which run an intermittently chronic course. This is a heterogenous group of disorders that overlaps considerably with personality, anxiety, and medical disorders. The classification and treatment of these disorders represent major challenges for psychiatric research. Drawing heavily on our own research in this area, we have presented a systematic approach to chronic depressions and issues regarding intractability have been addressed. Our treatment approach to these conditions is based on nosologic and etiologic considerations. The clinician should make sure that all possible factors involved in chronicity, such as concurrent nonaffective psychiatric disorders, disabling medical disease, and life stressors, have been identified. Past personal and family history of response to tricyclics, MAOIs, or lithium are often useful guides in choosing the proper medication in intractable depressions. Full psychiatric evaluation, selective medical work-up, and laboratory procedures may reveal subtle factors (e.g., an unsuspected bipolar II disorder, mild autoimmune thyroiditis, or an anxiety disorder with depressive clinical presentation), that would dictate different treatment strategies. In brief, in intractable depressions the original diagnosis must be reassessed as if the patient were presenting as a new case. Finally, supportive and practical psychotherapeutic approaches which focus on social skills, marital, and vocational aspects appear generally more useful than those that delve extensively into developmental vicissitudes.

References

Akiskal, H. S. (1981a). Clinical overview of depressive disorders and their pharmacological management. In G. C. Palmer (Ed.), *Neuropharmacology of central and behavioral disorders* (pp. 37–72). New York: Academic Press.

Akiskal, H. S. (1981b). Subaffective disorders: Dysthymic, cyclothymic and bipolar II disorders in the "borderline" realm. *Psychiatric Clinics of North America, 4,* 25–46.

Akiskal, H. S. (1983). Dysthymic disorder: Psychopathology of proposed chronic depressive subtypes. *American Journal of Psychiatry, 140,* 11–20.

Akiskal, H. S. (1982). Factors associated with incomplete recovery in primary depressive illness. *Journal of Clinical Psychiatry, 43,* 266–271.

Akiskal, H. S. (in press, a). The boundaries of affective disorders: Implications for defining temperamental variants, atypical subtypes, and schizoaffective disorders. In G. Tischler (Ed.), *DSM-III: An interim appraisal.* Washington, DC: American Psychiatric Press.

Akiskal, H. S. (in press, b). The challenge of chronic depressions: Diagnostic, etiologic and therapeutic aspects. In A. Dean, (Ed.), *Depression in multidisciplinary perspective.* New York: Brunner/Mazel.

Akiskal, H. S., Bitar, A. H., Puzantian, V. R., Rosenthal, T. L., & Walker, P. W. (1978). The nosological status of neurotic depression: A prospective 3–4 year follow-up examination in light of the primary-secondary and the unipolar-bipolar dichotomies. *Archives of General Psychiatry, 40,* 801–810.

Akiskal, H. S., Hirschfeld R., & Yerevanian, B. I. (1983). The relationship of personality to affective disorders—A critical review. *Archives of General Psychiatry, 40,* 801–810.

Akiskal, H. S., King, D., Rosenthal, T. L., Robinson, D., & Scott-Strauss, A. (1981). Chronic depressions. Part 1. Clinical and familial characteristics in 137 probands. *Journal of Affective Disorders, 3,* 297–315.

Akiskal, H. S., & Lemmi, H. (1983). Clinical, neuroendocrine, and sleep EEG diagnosis of "unusual" affective presentations: A practical review. *Psychiatric Clinics of North America, 6,* 69–83.

Akiskal, H. S., Lemmi, H., Dickson, H., King D., Yerevanian, B., & VanValkenburg, C. (1984). Chronic depressions. Part 2. Sleep EEG differentiation of primary dysthymic disorders from anxious depressions. *Journal of Affective Disorders, 6,* 287–295.

Akiskal, H. S., Rosenthal, T. L., Haykal, R. F., Lemmi, H., Rosenthal, R. H., & Scott-Strauss, A. (1980). Characterological depressions: Clinical and sleep EEG findings separating "subaffective" dysthymias from "characterspectrum" disorders. *Archives of General Psychiatry, 37,* 777–783.

Akiskal, H. S., & Tashjian, R. (1983). Affective disorders: Part II. Recent advances in laboratory and pathogenetic approaches. *Hospital and Community Psychiatry, 34,* 822–830.

American Psychiatric Association (1980). *Diagnostic and statistical manual of mental disorders* (3rd ed.). Washington, DC: Author.

Ananth, J., & Luchins, D. (1977). A review of combined tricyclic and MAOI therapy. *Psychiatry, 18,* 221–280.

Ananth, J., & Ruskin, R. (1974). Treatment of intractable depression. *International Pharmacopsychiatry, 9,* 218–229.

Andrulonis, P. A., Glueck, B. C., Stroebel, C. F., Vogel, N. G., Shapiro, A. L., & Aldridge, D. M. (1981). Organic brain dysfunction and the borderline syndrome. *Psychiatric Clinics of North America, 4,* 47–66.

Ayd, F. J. (1975). Maintenance doxepin (sinequan) therapy for depressive illness. *Diseases of the Nervous System, 36,* 109–114.

Ayd, F. J. (1983). Continuation and maintenance antidepressant therapy. In F. J. Ayd, I. J. Taylor, & B. T. Taylor, B. T. (Eds.), *Affective disorders reassessed* (pp. 73–99). Baltimore: Ayd Medical Communications.

Bartlett, J., Bridges, P., & Kelly, D. (1981). Contemporary indications for psychosurgery. *British Journal of Psychiatry, 138,* 507–511.

Beitman, B. D., & Dunner, D. L. (1982). L-tryptophan in the maintenance treatment of bipolar II MDI. *American Journal of Psychiatry, 139,* 1498–1499.

Berblinger, K. W. (1970). Loneliness and the depressive perspective: The chronically depressed patient. In A. J. Enelow, (Ed.), *Depression in medical practice* (pp. 157–168). Rahway, NJ: Merck & Co.

Blumer, D. (1982). Specific psychiatric complications in certain forms of epilepsy and their treatment. In H. Sands (Ed.), *Epilepsy: A handbook for the mental health professional* (pp. 97–110). New York: Brunner/Mazel.

Carroll, B. J. (1982). The dexamethasone suppression test for melancholia. *British Journal of Psychiatry, 140,* 292–304.

Clayton, P. J., & Lewis, C. E. (1981). The significance of secondary depression. *Journal of Affective Disorders, 3,* 25–35.

Davidson, J. (1983). MAO inhibitors: A clinical perspective. In F. J. Ayd, I. J. Taylor, & B. T. Taylor (Eds.), *Affective disorders reassessed: 1983* (pp. 41–55). Baltimore: Ayd Medical Communications.

Davidson, J. R. T., Miller, R. D., Turnbull, C. D., & Sullivan, J. L. (1982). Atypical depression. *Archives of General Psychiatry, 39,* 527–534.

de Montigny, C., Grunberg, F., Mayer, A., & Deschenes, J. P. (1981). Lithium induces rapid relief of depression in tricyclic antidepressant drug nonresponders. *British Journal of Psychiatry, 138,* 252–256.

Drummer, E. J., Girlin, M. J., & Givirtsman, H. E. (1983). Desipramine and methylphenidate combination treatment for depression: Case report. *American Journal of Psychiatry, 140,* 241–242.

Extein, I. (1982). Case reports of L-triiodothyronine potentiation of responsiveness to tricyclic antidepressants. *American Journal of Psychiatry, 17,* 29–30.

Fras, I., Littin, E. M., & Pearson, J. S. (1967). Comparison of psychiatric symptoms in carcinoma of the pancreas with those in some other intra-abdominal neoplasms. *American Journal of Psychiatry, 123,* 1553–1562.

Gerner, R. H. (1983). Systematic treatment approach to depression and treatment resistant depression. *Psychiatric Annals, 13,* 40–49.

Gold, M. S., Pottash, A. C., Mueller, E. A., & Extein, I. (1981). Grades of thyroid failure in 100 depressed and anergic psychiatric inpatients. *American Journal of Psychiatry, 138,* 253–255.

Himmelhoch, J. M., Detre, T. P., Kupfer, D. J., Swartzburg, M., & Byck, T. C. (1972). Treatment of previously intractable depressions with tranylcypromine and lithium. *Journal of Nervous and Mental Disorders, 155,* 216–220.

Keller, M. B., & Shapiro, R. W. (1982). "Double depression": Superimposition of acute depressive episodes on chronic depressive disorders. *American Journal of Psychiatry, 139,* 438–442.

Kendell, R. E. (1976). The classification of depression: A contemporary confusion. *British Journal of Psychiatry, 129,* 15–28.

Kielholz, P., Terzani, S., & Gasper, M. (1979). Treatment for therapy resistant depressions. *International Pharmacopsychiatry, 14,* 94–100.

King, D., Akiskal, H. S., Lemmi, H., Wilson, W., Belluomini, J., & Yerevanian, B. I. (1981). REM density in the differential diagnosis of psychiatric from medical-neurological disorders: A replication. *Psychiatry Research, 4,* 267–276.

Klein, D. F. (1974). Endogenomorphic depression: A conceptual and terminologic revision. *Archives of General Psychiatry, 31,* 447–454.

Klerman, G. L., Endicott, J., Spitzer, R., & Hirschfeld, R. M. A. (1979). Neurotic depressions: A systematic analysis of multiple criteria and meanings. *American Journal of Psychiatry, 136,* 57–61.

Kupfer, D. J., & Thase, M. E. (1983). The use of the sleep laboratory in the diagnosis of affective disorders. *Psychiatric Clinics of North America, 6,* 3–25.

Liebowitz, M. R., & Klein, D. F. (1979). Hysteroid dysphoria. *Psychiatric Clinics of North America 2,* 555–575.

Liebowitz, M. R., Quitkin, F. M., Stewart, J. W., McGrath, P. J., Harrison, W., Rabkin, J., Tricamo, E., Markowitz, J. S., & Klein, D. F. (1984). Phenelzine vs. imipramine in atypical depression. *Archives of General Psychiatry, 41,* 669–677.

Loosen, P. T., & Prange, A. J. (1982). Serum thyrotropin response to thyrotropin-releasing hormone in psychiatric patients: A review. *American Journal of Psychiatry, 139,* 405–416.

Nelson, J. C., & Byck, B. (1982). Rapid response to lithium in phenelzine nonresponders. *British Journal of Psychiatry, 141,* 85–86.

Okuma, T. (1983). Therapeutic and prophylactic effects of carbamazepine in bipolar disorder. *Psychiatric Clinics of North America, 6,* 157–174.

Pare, C. M. B., Kline, N., Hallstrom, C., & Cooper, T. B. (1982). Will amitryptiline prevent the "cheese" reaction of monoamine oxidase inhibitor? *Lancet, 2,* 1983–186.

Pare, C. M. B., Rees, L., & Sainsbury, M. J. (1962). Differentiation of two genetically specific types of depression by the response to antidepressants. *Lancet, 2,* 1340–1343.

Paykel, E. S. (1971). Classification of depressed patients: A cluster analysis derived grouping. *British Journal of Psychiatry, 118,* 275–288.

Price, J. S. (1978). Chronic depressive illness. *British Medical Journal, 2,* 1200–1201.

Price, L. H., Conwell, Y., & Nelson, J. C. (1983). Lithium augmentation of combined neuroleptic-tricyclic treatment in delusional depression. *American Journal of Psychiatry, 140,* 318–322.

Puig-Antich, J. (1982). Major depression and conduct disorders in prepuberty. *Journal of the American Academy of Child Psychiatry, 21,* 118–128.

Robins, E., & Guze, S. B. (1972). Classification of affective disorders: The primary-secondary, the endogenous-reactive and the neurotic-psychotic concepts. In T. A. Williams, M. M. Katz, & J. A. Shields (Eds.): *Recent advances in the psychobiology of the depressive illnesses.* Washington, DC: U.S. Government Printing Office.

Rosenthal, T. L., Akiskal, H. S., Scott-Strauss, A., Rosenthal, R. H., & David, M. (1981).

Familial and developmental factors in characterological depressions. *Journal of Affective Disorders, 3,* 183–192.

Rounsaville, B. J., Sholomskas, P., & Prusoff, B. A. (1980). Chronic mood disorders in depressed outpatients: Diagnosis and response to pharmacotherapy. *Journal of Affective Disorders, 2,* 73–88.

Rush, A. J. (1983). Cognitive therapy of depression: Rationale, techniques, and efficacy. *Psychiatric Clinics of North America, 6,* 105–127.

Schneider, K. (1958). *Psychopathic personalities.* In M. W. Hamilton, (Trans.). London: Cassel Ltd.

Shaw, D. M. (1977). The practical management of affective disorders. *British Journal of Psychiatry, 130,* 432–451.

Spitzer, R. L., Endicott, J., & Robins, E. (1978). *Research diagnostic criteria for a selected group of functional disorders* (3rd ed.). New York: New York Psychiatric Institute, Biometrics Research Division.

Stern, S. L., & Mendels, J. (1981). Drug combinations in the treatment of refractory depression: A review. *Journal of Clinical Psychiatry, 42,* 368–373.

Tyrer, P. (1979). Clinical use of monoamine oxidase inhibitors. In E. S. Paykel, & A. Cooper (Eds.): *Psychopharmacology of affective disorders* (pp. 159–178). Oxford: Oxford University Press.

Ward, N. G., Bloom, V. L., & Friedel, R. O. (1979). The effectiveness of tricyclic antidepressants in chronic depression. *Journal of Clinical Psychiatry, 40,* 49–52.

Weissman, M. M., & Akiskal, H. S., (1984). The role of psychotherapy in chronic depressions: A proposal. *Comprehensive Psychiatry, 25,* 23–31.

Weissman, M. M., & Klerman, G. L. (1977). The chronic depressive in the community: Unrecognized and poorly treated. *Comprehensive Psychiatry, 18,* 523–532.

West, E. M., & Dally, P. J. (1959). Effects of ipionazid in depressive syndromes. *British Medical Journal, 1,* 1491–1494.

Whybrow, P. C., Akiskal, H. S., & McKinney, W. T. (1984). *Mood disorders: Toward a new psychobiology.* New York: Plenum Publishing.

Winston, F. (1971). Combined antidepressant therapy. *British Journal of Psychiatry, 118,* 301–304.

Chapter 18

Assessment and Treatment
of the Suicidal Patient

Jenny L. Boyer
Lesley Guthrie

INTRODUCTION

As the 10th leading cause of death in the United States, suicide is a serious national problem. The national suicide rate in 1982, as estimated by the U.S. Public Health Services, National Center for Health Statistics, was 11.7 per 100,000 people. The number of attempts has risen since the mid-1950s and continues to increase (Liberman & Eckman, 1981). Moreover, it has been estimated in a review of the literature that there are two to eight times as many attempts as completed suicides (Linehan, Goodstein, Nielson, & Chiles, 1983). Attempted suicides also take a considerable toll on our society, emotionally and economically. For example, suicidal behavior has a considerable impact on hospital resources. In the United Kingdom, suicide attempts account for 20 percent of all acute medical admissions (Hirsch, Walsh, & Draper, 1982). In the United States, 15 percent of psychiatric visits to a general hospital emergency room are made by individuals who have a moderate degree of suicidal ideation and/or have made a recent attempt. At facilities which accept police referrals and have ambulance service, the percentage may be as high as 40 percent (Jacobs, 1982).

Since many suicides occur in people who are experiencing depression, it is paramount that persons treating depression understand the risk factors associated with suicide and ways of treating suicidal patients. This chapter will review the current state of assessment and treatment of suicidal behavior. Additionally, some ethical and legal issues will be covered. A brief discussion of suicidal behavior in children is also provided.

ASSESSMENT OF SUICIDAL RISK

This section will address a number of aspects of assessment. First, suicidal risk factors will be reviewed. Second, some psychological assessment instru-

Preparation of this chapter was supported in part by NIMH grant MH33760.

ments for evaluating patients will be described. Third, a brief review of biochemical assessment will also be included. Finally, a clinical checklist of risk factors for suicidal behavior will be included in the appendix to the chapter.

Risk Factors

In a clinical setting, the interview is the most typical means of assessing potential suicidal behavior. If the interview is to be maximally effective it is important that the clinician has an extensive knowledge of the major risk factors for suicidal behavior.

Sex.   The rate of completed suicides is three times greater for men as compared to women; the ratio for attempted suicides is reversed, women being three times more likely than men to make attempts (Linehan, Goodstein, Nielson, & Chiles, 1983). However, there is evidence that the number of completed suicides in women is increasing as women begin to choose more violent means. It has been hypothesized that the lower completion rate in females is due, at least in part, to the use of less lethal methods.

Birth Cohorts and Age.   Older males, over 45, are more at risk for completed suicides than are younger males. Although in the United States there has been a gradual increase in the completed suicide rate for males between ages 15 and 34, the relative risk for this age-group is still below that for males in their sixth and seventh decades. For females, the risk rises steadily to the postmenopausal period and then declines. For parasuicide (unsuccessful suicide attempts), both males and females are more likely to be below age 30.

A cross-sectional analysis of age of suicides at any one particular time will not show the increasing rate of suicide with age because such an analysis compares persons of different generations. For example, Hellon and Solomon (1980) found a bimodal distribution of suicide risk for persons in Alberta in 1976 with males being at highest risk in the 20–24 and 50–54 age-groups. However, a longitudinal analysis of cohorts continued to demonstrate that as a cohort (five-year age span) continued to age, its suicide rate also continued to climb (Solomon & Hellon, 1980). Murphy and Wetzel (1980) found that in the U.S. population, successive birth cohorts started with a higher rate of suicide and that the rate continued to increase with age. It is startling that for the last 25 years in the United States, each successive cohort has been more at risk for suicide than the previous generation at the same age. As the cohorts age, the total number of suicides for the United States should dramatically increase.

Family History.   Persons who attempt or complete suicide are more likely to have a high family incidence of attempted or completed suicide (Rogers, Sheldon, Barwick, Letofsky, & Lancee, 1982). Further, suicidal persons often have a positive family history for psychiatric illness, especially depression. The most vulnerable person has a family history for both suicidal behavior and depression (Murphy & Wetzel, 1982).

A family history interview might include an inquiry about early parental loss, (death, divorce, or permanent separation). If family life stabilized after a loss, suicidal trends have been reported to be minimal; but if loss resulted in long-term disruption of family life, suicidal behavior has been reported to be more likely (Adam, Lohrenz, Harper, & Streiner, 1982). Further, a long-term history of an unstable, chaotic, family environment is correlated with an increased risk for suicidal behavior (Adam, Bouckous & Streiner, 1982).

Environmental Stressors

Current, as well as previous, environmental stressors seem to be related to increased suicidal risk. Suicide attempters reported four times as many stressful life events as the general population and one and a half times as many as a group of depressed patients (Paykel, 1979). Examples of stressful life events were a new person living in the home, a serious illness in a family member, a serious personal physical illness, a court appearance for criminal offense, and, most importantly, an argument with a significant other. Unemployment, economic distress, and recent lifestyle changes are also theorized to be linked with increased risk for suicidal behavior (Linehan & Laffaw, 1982; Slater & Depue, 1981). Slater and Depue (1981) theorized that loss of social support, especially if perceived by the patient as a total loss, is an important risk factor to be noted by the interviewing clinician. Roy (1982) also noted that living alone, bereavement, separation, divorce, and widowhood were risk factors for suicidality.

Medical History

Fawcett (1972) reported that 70 percent of patients who committed suicide had in fact one or more active illnesses. Examples of disorders found to have a high association with suicide were rheumatoid arthritis, peptic ulcer, hypertension, severe dyspnea, and chronic renal failure being treated with dialysis. For malignant or incurable diseases such as carcinoma, critical periods seem to be while the diagnosis and prognosis are still at issue and during the phase of realization as to the seriousness of the condition. Visits to a physician in the week preceding the attempt, appear to be of importance according to Isherwood, Adam, and Hornblow (1982). In a study of 150 suicidal attempts, Isherwood et al. found that 5 percent had received outpatient medical attention in the week prior to the attempt. The reason for this high rate of suicide attempts among medical patients remains to be elucidated.

Psychiatric History

A history of previous psychiatric treatment is also a positive risk indicator. Roy (1982) found that 58 percent of completed outpatient suicides had seen a psychiatrist within the week before the act. Of these successful suicides, 81 percent had been psychiatrically admitted as inpatients at the last professional contact, and of those patients, 44 percent committed suicide within a month of discharge. Although the period immediately following psychiatric inpatient and outpatient treatment is an extremely vulnerable one, the risk for suicide remains relatively high for 6 to 12 months after discharge.

Psychiatric inpatients in general have a three to four times higher suicide rate than the general population and are probably most vulnerable during the first week of admission (Copas & Robin, 1982). A suicide attempt concurrent with treatment—either inpatient or outpatient—usually is especially serious because it indicates that the patient has little faith in the beneficial effects of the treatment. Additionally, individuals who refuse continuing psychiatric contact after an attempt are especially high risk (Hirsch et al., 1982).

Clinical Change. An abrupt clinical change, either a sudden improvement or a rapid deterioration, requires reassessment of risk for suicidal behavior (Fawcett & Susman, 1975). This is consistent with clinical observation of the need for increased vigilance in depressed patients as their depression begins to lift. Fawcett and Susman also mention the importance of recent dreams involving symbolic peaceful scenes of death, especially where death is viewed as exciting or euphoric.

Previous Attempts. One of the major indicators of future suicidal behavior is a history of previous attempts. Past suicidal ideation as well as previous attempts have been significantly correlated with subsequent attempts (Hankoff, 1982; Myers, 1982; Roy, 1982). Pokorny (1983) also notes that suicide attempts, threats, and ideas are strong indicators of future completed suicides and are stronger indicators than psychiatric diagnostic groupings. Hirsch et al. (1982) found that of individuals who have attempted suicide, 2 percent will successfully commit suicide within one year and 10–39 percent will make a second unsuccessful attempt.

Diagnosis

Depression is the diagnostic category most often associated with an increased risk for suicidal behavior (Copas & Robin, 1982; Evenson, Wood, Nuttall, & Cho, 1982; Isherwood, Adam, & Hornblow, 1982). Weissman (1974) found that depression was diagnosed in 35–79 percent of subjects who attempted suicide, and later investigations (Goldney, Adam, O'Brien, & Termansen, 1981) reported percentages at the higher end of that range. However, Motto (1974) cautions that suicidal behavior can be generated in the presence of practically any diagnostic entity and, at times, in the absence of pathological states.

Although it has been generally considered that depression is the diagnostic entity associated with the greatest risk for suicidal behavior, Montgomery and Montgomery (1982) believe that the majority of patients admitted to hospitals following an episode of suicidal behavior may be best categorized as personality disorders. They indicate that suicidal acts in this group tend to be impulsive and are often associated with transient mood disturbances which should not be diagnosed as depressive illness. The patients are described as typically impulsive, hostile, unpredictable, and angry. Copas and Robin (1982), however, in considering actual suicides, note that personality disorders have lower rates of completion than the affective group of disorders. Thus, it may be that persons with personality disorders are more likely to be attempters, while completers are more likely to have recurrent affective disorders without personality disorders.

Substance abuse is also a risk factor for suicidal behavior. Hankoff (1982) found substance abuse to be present in 30 percent of suicide attempters, in contrast to a 20 percent incidence in psychiatric clinic populations. Morrison (1982) found that primary alcoholism was not strongly associated with suicide; when alcoholism was secondary to another psychiatric disorder (e.g., depression), the risk for suicide increased to twice that of the general psychiatric population. Acute alcoholism has also been reported by Jacobs (1982) to be associated with higher suicidality. It may be that patients who attempt suicide are impulsive in many areas of their life including suicidal behavior, the failure to maintain long-term relationships, and so on. Or it may be that they are not impulsive except when abusing substances.

A careful assessment of psychosis should always be made by the clinician when assessing suicidal intent and lethality. Schizophrenia is associated with increased risk (Morrison, 1982; Roy, 1982), and clinicians should be especially sensitive to paranoid schizophrenia since social support is often minimal or perceived as such by persons with this diagnosis. Patients with psychotic depression are also of special concern since they may not be realistically aware of any reasons to live.

Personality Factors

In addition to personality disorders per se, a number of general personality factors have been associated with an increased risk of suicidal behavior. Dependency has been theorized to be a risk factor by some authors (Fawcett & Susman, 1975; Shneidman, 1979). Helplessness and hopelessness have been cited by others (Jacobs, 1982; Kovacs, Beck, and Weissman, 1975). Kovaks, Beck, & Weissman (1975) reported hopelessness to be a better predictor of suicide than depression in a sample of hospitalized suicide attempters. The Hopelessness Scale is discussed in the "Psychological Assessment Instruments" section of this chapter. External locus of control has also been correlated with hopelessness (Goldney, 1982). Other personality factors that have been noted to increase the risk for suicidal behavior are the inability to accept help (Jacobs, 1982), an impaired capacity for interpersonal relationships, (Fawcett, Leff & Bunney, 1969; Fawcett & Susman, 1975), and poor problem solving under high stress (Schotte & Clum, 1982).

Braucht (1979) found that suicide attempters do not have the requisite personality resources to socialize well in their neighborhoods and that there is a "mismatch" between the individuals and their ecological niches which is in some way related to the desire to end life. Thus, some personality characteristics may lead directly to higher suicidal risk while others, such as poor social skills, may lead to environmental stress which in turn increases suicidal risk.

Intent and Lethality. The concepts of intent and lethality are frequently mentioned in the literature. Intent is defined by Jacobs (1982) as the patient's subjective expectation that a particular self-destructive act will or will not end in death. Lethality, on the other hand, is the degree of danger to life that the act might have, or has had. In practice, the avenues of inquiry for assessment of intent and lethality overlap, so in discussing these two aspects of suicidal behavior, it is difficult to make a clear delineation.

Waters, Sendbuehler, Kincel, Boodoosingh, and Marchenko (1982) concluded in their review that despite an abundance of research, the best indicator of risk is still a statement of suicidal intent by the patient, whether it be direct or indirect. The seriousness of intent to commit suicide is generally associated with the degree of planning of the attempt, and a detailed, deliberate strategy indicates greater risk than a vague plan. The clinician should ask what method the individual anticipates using and whether the means is readily accessible. The clinician should also note if the plan is such that the individual is unlikely to be discovered and if preparations have been made for death, such as making a recent will. In addition to the apparent seriousness of the method used, it is also important to clarify what the person actually knows about the lethality of a particular method. It is prudent to inquire whether the person has prepared a suicide note or imagined writing one. Shneidman (1979) estimated 2–20 percent of suicidal individuals leave notes. Hankoff (1982) delineated a number of factors which are associated with serious intent and lethality: deliberate planning, the presence of a suicide note, an attempt done early in the morning, use of more than one method at a time, efforts made not to be discovered, and being in treatment at the time of the act.

Prediction. It might be assumed that the individual indicators taken together could result in a good prediction of suicidal behavior. However, Pokorny (1983), collected test and demographic data on 4,800 patients who were consecutively admitted to the inpatient psychiatric service of a Veterans Administration hospital. He developed a set of rating instruments using items from established rating scales and incorporating most of the items that have been shown to predict higher suicide rates. These predictors resulted in too many false positives, with one quarter of the total group predicted as being "future suicides" when in fact only 1–5 percent were. Although attempts to identify individual suicides were unsuccessful, many items were found to have substantial correlations with suicide and attempted suicide. He concluded that "identification of particular persons who will commit suicide is not currently feasible, because of the low sensitivity and specificity of available identification procedures and the low base rate of the behavior." Thus, it is currently not possible for clinicians to make accurate predictions about suicidal behavior.

PSYCHOLOGICAL ASSESSMENT INSTRUMENTS

Reviewers of the literature regarding assessment of suicide risk (T. R. Brown & Sheran, 1972; Farberow, 1981; Lester, 1970, 1974) conclude that standard psychological tests such as the MMPI, the TAT, and the Rorschach are less accurate predictors of suicidality than are specially constructed scales which focus directly on suicidal ideation and behavioral planning.

Aaron T. Beck and his associates have developed three scales specifically for the purpose of assessing suicide: The Suicide Intent Scale (SIS), the Hopelessness Scale (HS), and the Scale for Suicidal Ideation (SSI). The Suicide Intent Scale obtains information about suicide attempts which have been made and about preparation for the act, method, and expectation for rescue (Beck, Schuyler, & Herman, 1974). Beck, Weissman, Lester, and Trexler (1976) factor analyzed this scale and identified the following factors: attitudes toward the attempt, communication with others, planning, and precautions against discovery. They concluded that both cognitive and behavioral factors were critical in prediction of suicide.

The Beck Hopelessness Scale (Beck, Weissman, Lester, & Trexler, 1974) was developed when the Beck Depression Inventory (Beck, Ward, & Mendelson, 1961) was factor analyzed and suicidal wishes were found to correlate highly with hopelessness. Kovacs, Beck, and Weissman (1975) reported hopelessness as measured by the scale to be a better predictor than a depression inventory in a sample of hospitalized suicide attempters. Hopelessness was reported in the same study to be highly correlated with patients' self-ratings of their wish to die, even when the predictive effects of overall severity of depression were statistically removed. The Beck Hopelessness Inventory has been critiqued by Linehan and Nielson (1981) as being too highly correlated with social desirability. Specifically, they reported a significant negative correlation between the Hopelessness Scale and the Edwards Social Desirability Scale (Edwards, 1970), a measure of social desirability. The social desirability issue has been further elaborated by Nevid (1983) and Linehan and Nielson (1983). The primary concern of Linehan and Nielson (1981, 1983) is that there may be too many false negatives on the Hopelessness Scale because it is socially desirable to present oneself as optimistic.

Beck, Kovaks, and Weissman (1979) developed the Scale for Suicidal Ideation. The instrument was designed to quantify the intensity of "current conscious intent by scaling various dimensions of self-destructive thoughts or wishes in persons who have not made a recent suicide attempt." A factor analysis of the SSI revealed three factors: (1) active suicidal desire, (2) preparation, and (3) passive suicidal desire. Beck et al. believed this instrument would prove to be useful for researchers and clinicians alike. Certain behavioral items (e.g., suicide note), which were of too low a frequency to be predictive were retained so that the instrument would be clinically useful. In general, Beck and his associates have emphasized assessing both ideational and behavioral correlates of suicide in their instruments. There are other authors who put more emphasis on the importance of behavioral indicators

(Dopat & Boswell, 1963; Resnik & Hawthorne, 1972; Tuckman & Youngman, 1968).

Most of the research on suicidality, to date, has focused on identifying negative personal and social characteristics of suicide attempters and completers (e.g., Beck, Resnick, & Lettieri, 1974; Kreitman, 1977; Neuringer, 1974b). Comparatively little attention has been directed toward identification of adaptive personality factors which suicidal persons lack. Recently some authors of specific scales have attempted to assess such adaptive characteristics rather than concentrating only on the maladaptive ones. The Hope Index Scale (Obayuwana, Collins, Carter, Mamidanna, Mahura, & Wilson, 1982) correlates negatively with the Beck Hopelessness Inventory and predicts suicidality better than an index of depression alone.

The Reasons for Living Inventory ([RFL]; Linehan, Goodstein, Nielsen, & Chiles, 1983) asks subjects to rate how important various reasons for living would be if they contemplated suicide. Factor analysis of the scale indicated six primary reasons for living: survival and coping beliefs, responsibility to family, child-related concerns, fear of suicide, fear of social disapproval, and moral objections. In two samples (shoppers and psychiatric inpatients) the RFL differentiated suicidal from nonsuicidal individuals. In the shopping center sample, the fear of suicide subscale differentiated between previous ideators and previous parasuicides. Previous parasuicides were found to have significantly less fear of death than persons with ideation only. In the psychiatric inpatient sample, the child-related concerns differentiated between current ideators and current parasuicides. The authors noted that persons scoring high on reasons for living in the areas of survival and coping, responsibility to family, and child-related concern scales were less likely to attempt suicide. This was true for both the shopping center and psychiatric samples.

The SAD PERSONS Scale developed by Patterson, Dohn, Bird, and Patterson (1983) is based on 10 major risk factors. It is an example of a clinical checklist rather than a research scale. A group of medical students who were taught the SAD PERSONS Scale demonstrated a significantly greater ability to differentiate a low-risk from a high-risk patient, using as a criterion the judgment of three experienced psychiatrists. A control group of students who did not receive instruction on the use of the scale rated significantly more patients at high risk for suicide. The 10 factors in this scale are represented in the name of the scale as an acronym: sex, age, depression, previous attempt, ethanol abuse, rational thinking loss, social supports lacking, organized plan, no spouse, and sickness.

BIOCHEMICAL ASSESSMENT

Several reports have focused on the role of the monoamine neurotransmitter systems in suicidal behavior. The results suggest that 5-hydroxy-indoleacetic acid (5-HIAA), a metabolite of serotonin, might have potential as an additional diagnostic tool in the identification of individuals who are at risk for suicide attempts. Studies using both depressed patients and patients with personality disorders suggest that regardless of diagnosis, suicide attempters had significantly lower cerebrospinal fluid (CSF) levels of 5-HIAA as compared to normal controls (Brown, Goodwin, & Bunney, 1982; VanPraag, 1982). Brown, Goodwin, and Bunney (1982) found that in a group of patients with personality disorders, a history of suicidal behavior was associated with a life history characterized by higher levels of aggression. Both behavior patterns were associated with decreased levels of CSF 5-HIAA. Suicide attempts made by depressed patients with low CSF 5-HIAA levels were found to be more frequent and of a more aggressive nature (Asberg, Träskman, & Thoren, 1976). Comparing a group of suicide attempters of mixed diagnostic categories with normal controls, differences in CSF 5-HIAA levels were most marked in depressed patients who had made a violent suicide attempt. This suggests that CSF levels of 5-HIAA might be especially useful for identifying depressed patients who are at high risk for successful suicides (Agren, 1980).

Some researchers have investigated plasma and urinary cortisol levels with regard to suicidality. Farberow (1981) reviewed studies suggesting that high cortisol levels are positively correlated with a higher risk for suicide. He recommended increased protective precautions for patients with such cortisol levels. Ostroff, Giller, Bonese, Ebersole, Harkness, and Mason (1982) found that elevated 24-hour urinary cortisol level taken in isolation was not highly specific for suicidal patients; however, its predictive value was enhanced in their sample by combination with 24-hour urinary norepinephrine-epinephrine ratios which were found to be lower in suicidal as compared to nonsuicidal patients.

In summary, current knowledge on the assessment of sucidality focused on three major areas. First, there is continuing research on specific risk factors, such as sex, age, family history, environmental stressors, psychiatric history, or previous attempts. Second, psychological assessment instruments are being designed for the assessment of suicidality, such as the Beck scales and the Reasons for Living Inventory. Third, biochemical assessment methods, such as those based on the monoamine transmitter systems, are being developed.

A clinical checklist of risk factors is included in the appendix at the end of chapter. The list is specifically designed to be helpful to clinicians interviewing suicidal patients and is, therefore, more inclusive than exclusive with regard to risk factors for suicidality.

TREATMENT OF SUICIDE

Outcome Studies

Much of the literature on treatment of the suicidal individual is nonempirical. The paucity of research data to guide the professional in selecting the treatment of choice for the suicidal client is documented in a recent review article by Hirsch, Walsh, and Draper (1982) who identified only 11 trials of medical or social intervention for patients following parasuicide. This section will briefly summarize this research and also provide an introduction to some of the proposed treatment approaches.

Investigators have studied the effectiveness of early intervention programs, comparing the suicide rates in regions with and without a crisis center (Bridge, 1977; Jennings & Barraclough, 1978). No statistically significant decrease in the suicide rate in towns with these centers was demonstrated. Other studies have addressed the efficacy of domiciliary (home visit) intervention (Gibbons, 1979; Hawton, 1979). Although significant improvement in mood and social adjustment and a reduction in the use of psychiatric services was noted, there was no effect of treatment on parasuicide rates. Liberman and Eckman (1981) compared a behavior therapy package (which included social skills and anxiety management training and contracting with family members) with an insight-oriented therapy program in an inpatient psychiatric setting. Comparing suicide repeat rates before and after treatment, the results showed that for both groups there was a significant reduction in suicide attempts at the two-year follow-up period.

Retrospective follow-up studies of patients self-selected for treatment suggest that patients who attend treatment have a lower repeat rate of parasuicide (Greer & Bagley, 1971; Kennedy, 1972). Such findings do not necessarily confirm the effectiveness of treatment, as it might be that those patients who choose to attend treatment have an inherently lower risk rate. On the other hand, Montgomery and Montgomery (1982) looked at the effects of a depot neuroleptic (flupenthixol) as compared to placebo, on a group of patients with personality disorders who had made at least three previous suicide attempts. The authors also looked at the effect of orally administered antidepressant (mianserin) compared with placebo on the same population. Results indicated that there was a significant reduction in the number of suicide attempts in the experimental as compared to the control group for the depot neuroleptic only. Part of the success of the depot neuroleptic treatment could be attributed to excellent compliance.

Hirsch, Walsh, and Draper (1982) concluded that no one current intervention strategy is better than others for preventing repeat parasuicides. Although the study by Liberman and Eckman (1981) did demonstrate a significant treatment effect, Hirsch, Walsh, and Draper (1982) pointed out that the study left unanswered the question of whether the critical element was close weekly follow-ups or the behavioral and insight-oriented treatments. They concluded, therefore, that the only clear and unchallenged treatment effect was that of the depot neuroleptic, found by Montgomery and Montgomery (1982).

TREATMENT APPROACHES

In considering the treatment of parasuicide, it is useful to begin with the concept of prevention: both the prevention of the occurrence of any suicidal behavior and the prevention of the repetition of an attempt. Hankoff (1982) divides the prevention of suicidal behavior into primary, secondary, and tertiary prevention. Primary prevention strategies are defined as those which are used prior to the development of any symptoms. Hankoff states that primary prevention of suicide in terms of broad social or political change is not practical. Others, however, hold out hope for such change. Jeger (1979) states that there is an "urgent need for developing alternative perspectives and approaches to suicide prevention" through behavioral-ecological change.

Secondary prevention involves direct emergency treatment, outreach efforts such as telephone hotlines, and early detection programs (Hankoff, 1982). Hinson (1982) outlined some possible strategies for suicide intervention by telephone hotline volunteers. However, only a small percentage of suicidal individuals use such services (Greer & Anderson, 1979). For many suicidal persons, the emergency room is their first contact with treatment personnel. Jacobs (1982) outlines a comprehensive approach to the evaluation and care of suicidal behavior in emergency settings. Frederick (1981) provides a useful set of guidelines for emergency room staff in dealing with suicidal patients. Briefly, he suggests:

1. Listening.
2. Assessing thoughts and emotions.
3. Accepting each complaint and feeling.
4. Asking about the suicide directly.
5. Watching out for quick recoveries.
6. Becoming an advocate for the patient.
7. Utilizing available resources.
8. Acting specifically.
9. Being prepared to seek assistance and consultation.
10. Never rejecting or attempting to deny suicidal thoughts.
11. Never attempting to shock the person out of the suicidal act.

After the assessment phase, a treatment phase (tertiary prevention) can be implemented. Generally these tertiary treatment interventions are somewhat different than traditional psychotherapy approaches. For example, the therapeutic neutrality of psychoanalytic psychotherapy may have to be abandoned (Bellack & Faithhorn, 1981).

The treatment approaches can be classified under two main categories: support and control strategies. The support strategies address the absence of perceived social support. The control strategies address dyscontrol experienced by the suicidal individual as helplessness, impulsivity, anger, and problem-solving deficits.

Support Strategies

Giving the client support and helping increase the support base with others not only decreases social isolation but also begins to address dependency needs. In practical terms, the therapist can support the client by increasing the number of therapy sessions and by having a call-in system between sessions to monitor the client's stability. For clients of high lethality, 24-hour availability seems to be important. In involving relatives and friends, every effort should be made to obtain consent from the client; but for safety as well as for support, confidentiality may need to be broken in order to inform close family members of the client's suicidal potential. Family and friends can be asked to support the client between sessions or in conjoint sessions. It is essential that the therapist be aware of interactions of the patient with rejecting relatives. An even wider network can be provided for the client through education about crisis telephone lines and, where appropriate, a church or a community agency.

A contract between therapist and client is frequently initiated by the clinician, stating that the client will call the therapist, or present at the emergency room rather than act on suicidal impulses. In forming a contract with the client, the therapist is conveying a willingness to be available to provide support. However, implicit in the contract is the assumption that the client is responsible for the control of suicidality. If a client will not agree to a contract or is very reluctant to do so, this is a strong indicator for hospitalization. Frederick (1981) considers that contracts may be more effective with highly verbal persons with above-average education. However, many writers continue to recommend contract formation as an integral part of the treatment of parasuicide.

In creating activity around the suicidal individual, in being available, and in giving advice where necessary, the therapist is conveying to the client that he or she is supported and cared for and that something can and is being "done." However, this is merely a first step, and later phases of therapy need to help clients develop ways to support and care for themselves. If social isolation is due to a social skill deficit, then social skills training can be appropriate to help a client develop and maintain an adequate support base. If the client has chronic difficulty maintaining relationships, the way that the client alienates others can be discussed and the therapeutic interaction may be used as a model of the client's pathological interactions (Kiev, 1981). In attempting to provide support the therapist is, at least in part, also meeting some of the client's dependency needs. Again, encouragement of dependency is probably therapeutic in the early phase of therapy, but the issue of dependency and how it relates to the client's suicidal behavior will need to be examined in the later phase of therapy if chronic dependency patterns are to be ended. A. Hendin (1981) states, "In the treatment of suicidal individuals one is struck with how often the word *management* is used synonymously with therapy. . . . Since many suicidal patients are themselves preoccupied with management and control, therapy can become a contest with the suicidal patient. . . ." The therapist is cautioned not to enter into a power struggle with the client. Support and encouragement must be given in such a way that the client does not feel controlled or manipulated.

Support and contracts will be ineffective if the therapist cannot engage and maintain the client's commitment to therapy (Beck, Rush, Shaw, and

Emery, 1979). The therapist can build bridges between therapy sessions by saying that an issue the client raises is interesting and can be dealt with in the next session. Asking the client to make some notes and bring them in next time for discussion can reinforce the commitment to attend and participate in the next therapy session.

Control Strategies

Feelings of dyscontrol, helplessness, hopelessness, and despair are pervasive for most suicidal individuals. The most immediate intervention for dyscontrol is to decrease the availability of the method, such as taking away pills or guns. The second step is to encourage the client to acknowledge such feelings, and to assess how realistic such feelings are. The treatment approaches subsequently used to aid the client in controlling his/her suicidal ideation will depend on the type of client and the dynamics accompanying the suicidal impulse. Beck et al. (1979) suggest that if the client's sense of hopelessness is based partly on pervasive negative expectations, then cognitive interventions aimed at the patient's pessimism would be helpful. Beck et al. also suggest working specifically on the client's view of life and death, by eliciting from the client reasons for living and reasons for dying, and attempting to shift the client from an emphasis on death to one on life. To produce the reasons for living column it is sometimes necessary to take the client back to a happier period in his or her life. Beck et al. caution that it is important that the therapist not try to talk the client out of his/her suicidal behavior by suggesting the positive factors but should instead facilitate production by the client. If there is a sound reality base to his or her helplessness, such as illness or extreme social isolation, the intervention might involve a different approach, such as the mobilization of a social network.

Given the often impulsive nature of suicidal behavior and the sense that suicidal individuals have that they cannot control their suicidal ideation, treatments for disorders of impulse control may well be applicable. Clients need to be encouraged to tolerate their distressing feelings. The therapist can provide them with behavioral assignments to assist them in learning tolerance of emotional pain. If clients can recognize that they do indeed have control over their thoughts and feelings, they can gain a sense of internal control. A cognitive approach outlined by Watkins (1983) helps patients recognize that their impulses are not uncontrollable. They are asked to monitor and recall the exact instance in which they became aware of their urges and what thoughts were occurring at the moment. One of the most frequent self-statements made by impulse control patients as well as by suicidal patients is "I can't stand it." Clients are taught to realize that they can stand just about anything, even though it does not feel good. The clients can then begin to use new, coping self-statements such as: "I can handle it;" "Remember to think;" "Put it out of your mind;" "Keep on going." Guided imagery and role-playing can be used to help the client to relive the previous crisis situation that led to the precipitation of suicidal impulses. The client then practices coping strategies that could have been applied in order to handle the situation successfully. The client is prepared to deal with future stresses through cognitive rehearsal of control strategies and generation of appropriate alternative behaviors. It is useful as a further preventive measure to warn clients that suicidal impulses are likely to fluctuate during the course of therapy and that reoccurrence of suicidal thoughts should not be interpreted as an absence of progress. The therapist can, at the time of reoccurrence, review with the client the strategies to be used to cope with such an increase in suicidal ideation.

Generation of alternatives is an especially important aspect of the treatment of disorders of impulse control and of the treatment of suicidal behavior. This decreases the client's sense of futility by widening the range of possible thoughts, fantasies, and actions from the dichotomous, "either I can go on in misery, or I can kill myself" to a variety of problem-solving behaviors. It might be necessary to remind the client that life is often a choice between undesirable alternatives and that the key is to choose the most desirable one that is practicably attainable (Shneidman, 1980). Since suicide may be seen by clients as the only way out of an insoluble problem, conveying that there are other ways of looking at the situation and at the future is a significant initial step. The client can then be aided in generating choices other than the suicidal behavior. Kiev (1981) suggests that alternatives of suicidal behavior might be elicited by inquiring about the client's past interests and achievements. For example, a client can choose to call a friend, have a cup of coffee in a restaurant, and so on, as a means of handling the immediate impulse. Although clients may see these as undesirable alternatives, they can be reminded that they still have the option of killing themselves in the future. In later sessions, once the client has convinced himself or herself that anything can be tolerated and that control is possible in the worst of circumstances since alternatives are available, then it is time for the therapist to mention the larger decision of living or dying. The therapist can now make it clear to the client that the decision to live or die is now a matter of real choice given that the client can realistically examine alternatives and maintain self-control.

In addition to helping the client generate personal and unique alternatives to suicide, it is also helpful for the therapist to teach more general ways of coping with problems. Many of these may help clients increase their sense of control and defuse the increase in tension that clients feel they cannot stand. Examples of this are relaxation training, systematic desensitization, and physical activity (Jeger, 1979). Encouraging clients to seek company during a crisis not only acts as an alternative to suicidal behavior but also begins to reintroduce an adequate schedule of positive reinforcement. Many suicidal individuals do not know how to ask for help in appropriate ways in times of increased stress and teaching them appropriate ways to do so adds another alternative response to suicidal behavior. A further technique to be considered is assertiveness training. This may be helpful by providing a greater sense of self-efficacy and thus may provide a greater sense of hope.

Finally, group therapy can provide support and comfort because other members have often experienced similar suicidal feelings. Additionally a group offers a place in which dependency needs can be initially shared and later replaced with more appropriate self-sufficiency. For chronically suicidal clients the group gives an accessible and ongoing place where recurring crises can be handled. It is important in such groups, however, to have some members who are not suicidal in order to provide therapeutic perspective.

Therapist Reactions

The reactions of the therapist to the suicidal patient are crucial factors in the successful outcome of treatment. Hendin (1981) suggests that therapists should consult with colleagues, not just about dispositional and treatment decisions, but also about their own feelings and thoughts. The therapist needs to accept the fact that no treatment can guarantee that a suicide will not occur. If the therapist can adopt such an attitude it can help guard against seeing the "success" of therapy as an issue of self-esteem. Since suicidal patients may manipulate others through the anxiety which they can arouse by the threat of suicide, they may test the therapist to see if he/she will respond in a similar way. Being free from anxiety allows the therapist to make more accurate decisions about which requests from the client are unreasonable.

Medication

Another aspect to be considered in the treatment of the suicidal individual is the use of medication, but that is beyond the scope of this chapter. Medication may be helpful by improving the overall depression, improving sleep, decreasing anxiety, and providing new hope that the patient's distress will be controlled.

Conclusion

Suicide is itself an action which can be conceptualized as an effort by the individual to stop unbearable pain by "doing something." Thus, one of the hallmarks of intervention for suicidal behavior is an action orientation. An active orientation by the therapist conveys to the patient that something is being done by others and that he or she can do something himself/herself as an alternative to thinking about and attempting to commit suicide. In addition to the active therapeutic orientation, it is important that others provide social and personal support while the client is helped to develop an increased sense of control and thus decrease the sense of helplessness and hopelessness.

SUICIDE IN CHILDREN AND ADOLESCENTS

Children and adolescents who attempt or complete suicide are a heterogeneous group. Like adults they differ in their problems and backgrounds. Researchers who have attempted to classify suicidal children and adolescents have concluded that most suicidal behavior is related to depression (Carlson & Cantwell, 1982; Crumly, 1982). However, there is a subset of children and adolescents who are not depressed, but who are still suicidal. This section will primarily cover nondepressed suicidal youth rather than depressed suicidal youth (see Chapter 15, "Depression in Children and Adolescents").

Pfeffer, Plutchik, and Mizruchi (1983) were able to delineate two clearly distinct types of suicidal children from ages 6–12. One group was characterized by good reality testing, minimal aggression, neurosis, and depression. The second group was characterized be deficits in reality testing, intense expression of aggression, multiple acting-out behaviors, and relatively little depression. Shaffer (1974) also described two subgroups of suicidal children. One was isolated, withdrawn, and depressed, and the other was impetuous and violent. Thus, there seems to be a subgroup of suicidal children who are not predominantly depressed but who are aggressive and possibly psychotic.

Inander, Lewis, Siomopoulas, Shanok, and Lamela (1982) studied psychotic inpatients adolescents who were both violent and suicidal. The authors noted that the combination of violence and suicidality was "especially characteristic" of psychotic adolescents. The findings of Inander et al. (1982) are consistent with Pfeffer et al. (1983) who concluded that "deficits in reality testing" (psychotic processes) were more likely in youth who were suicidal, aggressive, and relatively nondepressed as compared to youth who were clearly depressed.

Carlson and Cantwell (1982) used the Children's Depression Inventory (CDI) and semistructured interview to study 102 psychiatrically referred children and adolescents. In their sample, 71 percent of subjects with suicidal ideation and high depression scores on CDI met the criteria for depressive disorders. The majority of those with suicidal ideation but low depression scores had behavior disorder diagnoses. Carlson and Cantwell (1982) also reported that nondepressed suicidal children were much less likely to be psychiatrically hospitalized than depressed suicidal children. Other researchers (McIntire, Angle, Wikoff, & Schict, 1977; Toolan, 1975) have noted that while depression is the most common motivation for child and adolescent suicide, that hostility, aggression, and escape from intolerable situations are the next most common motivations.

Whether suicidality in children and adolescents is always evidence of emotional illness is a less controversial issue than it is with adults. Crumley (1982) believes that suicidality is always evidence of emotional illness and that it is most usually found in depression with underlying personality disorders. His opinion is that the presence of personality, with or without depression, in indicative of potential suicidality.

LEGAL ISSUES

Involuntary Commitment

The most common state statutory standard for involuntary commitment or emergency detention is that a person must be judged to be mentally ill by a physician and that that person must also be judged to be dangerous to himself or others or unable to adequately care for himself (e.g., Oklahoma Statutes Ann.). Although statutes vary depending on the particular state, there are some rather typical procedures in civil commitment. A police officer, a family member, or a mental health professional usually initiates involuntary detention by alleging that a person has threatened his or her own life. a physician (or sometimes a psychologist) examines the person and signs an affidavit that the person is mentally ill. The person is then detained on an emergency basis for a few days (e.g., 72 hours in the District of Columbia Ann.). Formal commitment begins when a petition is filed, either by a concerned person or by the district attorney, depending on the state. A hearing is then held where the petitioner must prove that the person is currently mentally ill *and* currently dangerous to him/herself (e.g., suicidal). If the dangerousness to self standard is not judged to be met at the time of the hearing, even if it has been met a few days earlier, there is no basis for the person to be committed. Thus, only if a patient admits current serious suicidal ideation at the time he or she is being examined *and* reports serious psychiatric symptomology may the patient be committed. It is significant that involuntary commitment is impossible unless mental illness is present, even a person is actively suicidal. It can be agreed that it is possible for a person to intend his or her own death without the presence of mental illness. An example of such intent might be a situation where living was so physically painful that death was preferred.

Malpractice

Most of the literature regarding suicide and the law is in the area of malpractice. Malpractice law is case law rather than statutory law primarily because mental health professionals usually determine an appropriate standard of performance for themselves rather than a legislature determining it for them. Case law is continuously evolving yet is a firm precedent for similar cases. Cases in the malpractice literature typically deal with whether a particular clinician met the standards of his or her profession. Occasionally courts will declare a professional standard inappropriate and create a new duty that the profession did not recognize on its own. An example of that occurred in the *Tarasoff* decision (*Tarasoff* v. *The Regents of the University of California*, 1976). In that case the professional duty to warn a potential homicidal victim was first recognized.

Malpractice law is a specific area within the general law of negligence. If one has committed an act of malpractice, one is also negligent. The law of negligence is generally civil case law, although criminal statutes provide for a few types of criminal negligence. It is possible to be both civilly and criminally negligent if one violates both the civil and criminal law with an act of malpractice.

Negligence is found only if, according to expert testimony, deviant behavior of the clinician were judged "unreasonable." It is assumed that there is a professional standard of conduct against which a court can measure the allegedly negligent behavior. In the area of clinical management of suicidal patients it is not always clear what constitutes appropriate care. There are some obvious guidelines for appropriate care, however. These would be protecting the patient from self-harm and ensuring appropriate confidentiality.

Involuntary hospitalization is the mechanism whereby suicidal patients may be protected from themselves despite their desire to die. Voluntary hospitalization has much the same function, but suicidal patients must, of course, be willing, at least at the time of hospitalization, to agree to it. Courts will scrutinize the reasoning behind involuntary detention at the commitment hearing or during a malpractice suit. As long as the clinician documents the reason for detention, showing that it was a "good faith" action based on reasonable inference of suicidal potential, there will not be liability. To the extent the clinician attempts to detain involuntarily for reasons other than that outlined in the involuntary commitment statutes, then the clinician would be vulnerable to charges of false imprisonment. Reasonable inference of suicidal potentiality might be based on suicidal verbalization or recent attempts of self-destruction.

Most malpractice liability in this area regards inpatient hospital practice where courts have scrutinized the security on inpatient units. Questions such as whether the staff could have anticipated the result (legal foreseeability) and whether they failed to provide a reasonable measure of security are typical. Courts may examine all records on the unit to determine whether negligence has occurred. Usually an expert witness is asked by the court to review all records and provide an opinion about such questions.

There have been some cases where court judgments that suicide was foreseeable were somewhat unreasonable from the authors' point of view. For example, in *Boyce* v. *California* (1970) clinicians were held liable because a patient killed himself 36 hours after discharge from an inpatient unit in a state hospital. While the patient's diagnosis was paranoid schizophrenia and alcoholism, and while he had attempted suicide several times previously, clinicians stated that he had shown marked improvement, was legally competent on discharge, and that they could not foresee suicide. On the basis of such case law, it is advisable to document in the chart the presence or absence of suicidal ideation in patients when considering discharge. If such ideation exists, it is advisable to document that it was the recommendation of the clinician that the patient remain hospitalized indefinitely, despite the patient's not meeting the involuntary civil commitment standard. If adequate documentation exists, a reviewing court will be aware that the clinician did everything legally possible to protect the patient. There have also been cases where courts have clearly recognized the difficulty of foreseeability of suicide. For example, in a New York State case (*Hirsh* v. *State of New York,* 1960), an inpatient in a state hospital obtained enough pills to successfully complete suicide, and the court said that it was not possible to watch the patient's every move. Thus, the court recognized a balance of interests between strict confinement and a therapeutic environment.

Another area where potentiality for suicidal behavior exists is when the clinician mishandles the transference relationship. Courts might look for unprofessional involvement by clinicians with patients which subsequently results in harm to patients. Thus, if a patient were to commit suicide following a love affair with a clinician, the court might rule that the clinician is legally liable for the consequences of unprofessional behavior.

Confidentiality

In suicide cases there is reason to break confidentiality when disclosure is necessary to prevent suicide. An example of breaking confidentiality might be attempting to commit the patient involuntarily or warning relatives of the patient's suicidality. There is a legal duty on the part of a clinician to attempt to commit any patient involuntarily who is overtly suicidal (e.g., state civil commitment statutes). But there is not a legal requirement to break confidentiality in order to warn relatives and friends of the patient's suicidality (*Bellah* v. *Greenson,* 1977; *Tarasoff,* 1976). In homicidality, however, there is a requirement, at least in California, to warn potential victims of a patient's serious homicidal threats (*Tarasoff,* 1976).

A concrete example might be when a patient admits serious suicidal ideation, but is not planning immediate suicide. The patient will not meet involuntary commitment standards, but may eventually commit suicide. The clinician should recommend hospitalization to the patient for protection from potential suicidal behavior. But should the relatives be warned? Ethically they may be warned if the clinician judges that it is in the best interest of the client, but it is not required by law. There is a balancing of the interests between therapeutic confidentiality and physical protection of the patient.

Release of confidential information for implementation of treatment without prior informed consent or a court order might result in malpractice liability for a clinician. For example, if unauthorized release of confidential records of the suicidal patient by the clinician or the clinician's employee which subsequently results in loss of job for the patient could be demonstrated in court, there would be civil liability for the clinician. Further, if treatment for a suicidal patient could result in harm to the patient (e.g., electroshock therapy), there would be liability for a clinician if prior informed consent (preferably written) could not be demonstrated.

The statute of limitations for malpractice lawsuits is two years. This means that a suit must be filed within two years from the time the patient or family notice the damage. In the case of suicide, the suit would probably have to be brought within two years after the patient's death.

If a patient does commit suicide despite efforts to prevent him or her from doing so, there are some steps that a prudent clinician should take to protect himself or herself from malpractice claims. For example, the clinician should consult an attorney immediately and ask him or her to be present when there are legal inquiries from the relatives or from an insurance company. Further, disclosure of confidential material should not be made without a consultation to one's professional society so that the rights to confidentiality of the deceased person are not violated.

ETHICS

There is no doubt that the psychological and psychiatric literature shows a relationship between suicide and mental illness; however, it would be difficult to maintain that all suicide attempts are a result of mental illness. If mental illness were a necessary condition for a suicide attempt, then it would follow that no life situation exists in which a person with good judgment would choose to end life. Moskop and Engelhardt (1979) provide some guidelines for assessment of whether mental illness exists when suicidal intent exists. They suggest that the decision to commit suicide should not be equated with insanity or mental disease. An example of a rational suicide might be when a person with a painful, degenerative disease deliberately chooses death rather than choosing a severe reduction in quality of life. An irrational suicide might be judged to occur when a person with a history of a mental disorder and who has no painful, degenerative disease, unrealistically believes that the life situation is intolerable and unalterable. The latter example might be a case for involuntary commitment; whereas, in the former one, the clinician might respect the patient's wish to die. Of course, there is the viewpoint of persons like Thomas Szasz (1974) who believe that both involuntary commitment and suicide prevention violate the individual's absolute right to free choice.

With regard to ethical or legal issues, a clinician should refer to his or her professional society's standards of ethics. When it is not obvious what is appropriate behavior after one has read the standard of ethics and pertinent case illustrations, one should consult licensed colleagues within the profession or the governing board of one's profession. In this regard, it is preferable to have written rather than oral consultation so that efforts of the clinician to act in an ethical manner are documented.

Appendix

The Clinical Checklist of Suicidality

(All the questions are phrased so that a yes answer increases the likelihood or seriousness of a suicide attempt.)

A. Age and sex.
   1. Factors increasing the likelihood of a successful suicide.
      a. Is the person male?

  b. Is the person over 45?

  c. Is the person single?

  d. Does the person have experience with or access to a deadly weapon?

2. Factors increasing the likelihood of a suicide attempt.

  a. Is the person female?

  b. Is the person under 30?

  c. Does the person have access to drugs?

B. Intent and lethality.

1. Does the person report thinking about suicide or death?

2. Does the person state an intention to commit suicide to the clinician or relative? If not, has the person made a veiled threat?

3. Does the person have a plan to commit suicide?

  a. If so, how detailed and specific is the plan?

  b. How lethal is the plan?

  c. Is the plan one that would make it unlikely that someone would intervene?

4. Has the person made preparation for death (e.g., made a will, written a suicide note)?

5. Is the person calm even though expressing suicidal thoughts?

6. Is the person unafraid of death?

7. Does the person see no reason to live?

8. Does the person see no hope for the future?

9. Does the person see no alternative to suicide?

10. Has the person had dreams of death or suicide?

11. Does the person believe he or she is a failure?

C. Information about previous attempts.

1. If the person has made an attempt in the past:

  a. Was a method used that was likely to be lethal?

  b. Was more than one method used?

  c. Was the person harmed by the attempt?

  d. Was a note left?

  e. Was a plan used that made rescue unlikely?

  f. If the person has made multiple attempts, has lethality increased over time?

  g. Was the person in treatment at the time of the previous attempt?

  h. Was the attempt early in the morning?

D. Environmental support and stressors.

1. Is the person separated, divorced, widowed, or living alone?

2. If the person is in a permanent relationship, is there likelihood of divorce?

3. Does the person see the spouse as hostile, competitive, or nonsupportive?

4. Does the person have a desire for revenge?

5. Is the person fairly recently bereaved?

6. Is there a recent loss (within the last few weeks) or an anticipation of loss (person, job, position)?

7. Is the person socially isolated? Are they becoming more isolated?

8. Is the person showing intense dependency in relationships?

9. Is the time of assessment near an anniversary date of a significant other's suicide?

10. Is there a history of early parental loss (death, divorce, permanent separation) which resulted in long-term disruption of family life, or history of unstable, chaotic, long-term family environment?

11. Has there been an increase in life events that are perceived as moderately to

severely negative and as relatively uncontrollable in the last six months, especially in the last month?

    a. Serious arguments, especially with spouse?

    b. Serious illness of family member?

    c. Having a new person in the home?

    d. Having to appear in court for an offense?

  12. Is economic distress present?

  13. Is the person unemployed?

  14. Have there been recent major lifestyle changes?

E. Physical factors.

  1. Is the person medically ill or have they had an accident (especially if elderly)?

  2. Has the person sought medical care within the last six months?

F. Treatment.

  1. Has the person had previous psychiatric treatment?

  2. Has there been recent psychiatric contact?

  3. If the person is currently in treatment, are they dissatisfied with their treatment?

G. Psychopathology.

  1. Does the person have a positive psychiatric history for depression, a personality disorder, schizophrenia, chronic alcoholism or drug addiction?

  2. Does the person currently present with severe depression, paranoia, psychosis, panic, or agitation?

  3. Has there been a recent failure of paranoid or obsessive-compulsive defenses, so that they seem less paranoid or obsessive-compulsive?

  4. Does the person's depression seem to be considerably worse in the morning?

  5. Does the person have strong perfectionistic tendencies and tend toward rigid thinking?

  6. Does the person have a history of violent impulsive behavior toward self or others?

  7. If there are feelings of hopelessness and helplessness, has there been an abrupt change for better or worse?

  8. Does the person report a sense of loss of control?

  9. Does the person seem unable to accept help or to reject help?

References

Adam, K. S., Bouckous, A., & Streiner, D. (1982). Parental loss and family stability in attempted suicide. *Archives of General Psychiatry, 39,* 1081–1085.

Adams, K. S., Lohrenz, J. G., Harper, D., & Streiner, D. (1982). Early parental loss and suicidal ideation in university students. *Canadian Journal of Psychiatry, 27,* 275–281.

Agren, H. (1980). Symptom patterns in unipolar and bipolar depression correlating with monoamine metabolites in the cerebrospinal fluid: II. Suicide. *Psychiatry Research, 3,* 225–236.

Asberg, M., Träskman, L., & Thorén, P. (1976). 5-HIAA in the cerebrospinal fluid—A biochemical suicide predictor? *Archives of General Psychiatry, 33,* 1193–1197.

Beck, A. T., Kovacs, M., & Weissman, A. (1979). Assessment of suicidal intent: The scale for suicidal ideation. *Journal of Consulting and Clinical Psychology, 47,* 343–352.

Beck, A. T., Resnik, H. L. P., & Lettieri, D. J. (Eds.). (1974). *The prediction of suicide,* Bowie, MD: Charles Press Pubs.

Beck, A. T., Rush, A. J., Shaw, F. B., & Emery, G. (1979). *Cognitive therapy of depression.* New York: Guilford Press.

Beck, A. T., Schuyler, D., & Herman, I. (1974). Development of Suicidal Intent Scales. In A. T. Beck, H. L. P. Resnik, & D. J. Lettieri (Eds.), *The prediction of suicide.* Bowie, MD: Charles Press Pubs.

Beck, A. T., Ward, C. H., & Mendelson, M. (1961). An inventory for measuring depression. *Archives of General Psychiatry, 4,* 561–571.

Beck, A. T., Weissman, A., Lester, D., & Trexler, L. (1974). Measurement of pessimism: The hopelessness scale. *Journal of Consulting and Clinical Psychology, 42,* 861–865.

Beck, A. T., Weissman, A., Lester, D., & Trexler, L. (1976). Classification of suicidal behaviors. II: Dimensions of suicidal intent. *Archives of General Psychiatry, 33* (7), 835–837.

Bellack, L., & Faithorn, P. (1981). Crises and special problems in psychoanalysis and psychotherapy. New York: Brunner/Mazel.

Bellah v. Greenson, C. V. No. 39770 (Cal. Oct. 5, 1977).

Boyce v. California, Docket No. C11077 (Cal. Super. Ct., L. A. County 1970).

Braucht, G. (1979). Interactional analysis of suicidal behavior. *Journal of Consulting and Clinical Psychology, 47,* 653–669.

Bridge, T. P. (1977). Suicide prevention centers: Ecological study of effectiveness. *Journal of Nervous and Mental Disorders, 164,* 18–24.

Brown, G. L., Goodwin, F. K., & Bunney, W. E. (1982). Human aggression and suicide: Their relationship to neuropsychiatric diagnoses and serotonin metabolism. In B. T. Ho, J. C. Schoolar, & E. Usdin (Eds.), *Serotonin in biological psychiatry: Advances in biochemical psychopharmacology* (Vol 34). New York: Raven Press.

Brown, T. R., & Sheran, T. J. (1982). Suicide prediction: A review. *Life Threatening Behavior, 2,* 67–98.

Carlson, G. A., & Cantwell, D. P. (1982). Suicidal behavior and depression in children and adolescents. *Journal of the American Academy of Child Psychiatry, 21,* 361–368.

Copas, J. B., & Robin, A. (1982). Suicide in psychiatric inpatients. *The British Journal of Psychiatry, 141,* 503–511.

Crumley, F. E. (1982). The adolescent suicide attempt: A cardinal symptom of a serious psychiatric disorder. *American Journal of Psychotherapy, 36,* 158–163.

Dopat, T. L., & Boswell, J. W. (1963). An evaluation of suicidal intent in suicide attempts. *Comprehensive Psychiatry, 4,* 117–125.

Edwards, A. L. (1970). *The measurement of personality traits by scales and inventories.* New York: Holt, Rinehart & Winston.

Evenson, R. C., Wood, J. B., Nuttall, E. A., & Cho, D. W. (1982). Suicide rates among public mental health patients. *Acta Psychiatrica Scandinavica, 66,* 254–264.

Farberow, N. L. (1981). Assessment of suicide. In. P. McReynolds (Ed.) (1981). *Advances in psychological assessment* (pp. 124–190). San Francisco: Jossey-Bass.

Fawcett, J. (1972). Suicidal depression and physical illness. *The Journal of the American Medical Association, 219,* 1303–1306.

Fawcett, J., Leff, M., & Bunney, W. E. (1969). Suicide: Clues from interpersonal communication. *Archives of General Psychiatry, 21,* 129–137.

Fawcett, J., & Susman, P. (1975). The clinical assessment of acute suicidal potential: A review. *Rush-Presbyterian-St. Luke's Medical Bulletin, 14,* 86–104.

Frederick, C. J. (1981). Suicide prevention and crisis intervention in mental health emergencies. In C. E. Walker (Ed.), *Clinical practice of psychology* (pp. 189–213). New York: Pergamon Press.

Furst, S. S., & Ostow, M. (1979). The psychodynamics of suicide. In L. D. Hankoff, & B. Einsider (Eds.), *Suicide: Theory and clinical aspects.* Littleton, MA: PSG Publishing Co.

Gibbons, J. S., (1979). Management of self-poisoning: Social work intervention. In R. Farmer, & S. Hirsch (Eds.), *The suicide syndrome* (pp. 237–245). London: Croom Helm.

Goldney, R. D. (1981). Attempted suicide in young women: Correlates of lethality. *British Journal of Psychiatry, 139,* 382–390.

Goldney, R. D. (1982). Attempted suicide and death anxiety. *Journal of Clinical Psychiatry, 43,* 159.

Goldney, R. D., Adam, K. S., O'Brien, J. C., & Termansen, P. (1981). Depression in young women who have attempted suicide: An international replication study. *Journal of Affective Disorders, 3,* 327–337.

Greer, S., & Anderson, M. (1979). Samaritan contact among 325 patients. *British Journal of Psychiatry, 135,* 263–268.

Greer, S., & Bagley, C. R. (1971). Effect of psychiatric intervention in attempted suicide: A controlled study. *British Medical Journal, I,* 310–312.

Halperin, D. A. (1979). Psychodynamic strategies with outpatients. In L. D. Hankoff & B. Einsidler (Eds.), *Suicide: Theory and clinical aspects* (pp. 363–372). Littleton, MA: PSG Publishing Co.

Hankoff, L. D. (1982). Suicide and attempted suicide. In F. S. Paykel (Ed.), *Handbook of affective disorders* (pp. 416–428). New York: Guilford Press.

Hawton, K. (1979). Domiciliary and outpatient treatment following deliberate self-poisoning. In R. Farmer & S. Hirsch (Eds.) *The suicide syndrome.* London: Croom Helm.

Hellon, C. P., & Solomon, M. I. (1980). Suicide and age in Alberta, Canada, 1951 to 1977. *Archives of General Psychiatry, 37,* 505–510.

Henderson, S. (1981). Social relationships, adversity, and neurosis: An analysis of prospective observations. *British Journal of Psychiatry, 138,* 391–398.

Hendin, A. (1981). Psychotherapy and suicide. *American Journal of Psychotherapy, 35,* 469–480.

Hendin, H. (1978). Suicide: The psychosocial dimension. *Suicide and Life-Threatening Behavior, 8,* 99–117.

Hinson, J. (1982). Strategies for suicide intervention by telephone. *Suicide and Life-Threatening Behavior, 12,* 176–184.

Hirsch, S. R., Walsh, C., & Draper, R. (1982). Parasuicide: A review of treatment intervention. *Journal of Affective Disorders, 4,* 299–311.

Hirsh v. State of New York, 8 N.Y. 2d 125; 282 N.Y.S. 2d 29b; 168 N.E. 2d 372 (1960).

Inander, S. C., Lewis, D. O., Siomopoulos, G., Shanok, S. S., & Lamela, M. (1982). Violent and suicidal behavior in psychotic adolescents. *American Journal of Psychiatry, 139,* 932–935.

Isherwood, J., Adam, K. S., & Hornblow, A. R. (1982). Life event stress, psychosocial factors, suicide attempt, and auto accident proclivity. *Journal of Psychosomatic Research, 26,* 371–384.

Jacobs, D. (1982). Evaluation and care of suicidal behavior in emergency settings. *The International Journal of Psychiatry in Medicine, 12,* 295–310.

Jeger, A. M. (1979). Behavior theories and their application. In L. D. Hankoff & B. Einsidler (Eds.), *Suicide: Theory and clinical aspects* (pp. 179–199). Littleton, MA: PSG Publishing Co.

Jennings, C., & Barraclough, B. M. (1978). Have the Samaritans lowered the suicide rate?—A controlled study. *Psychological Medicine, 8,* 413–422.

Kennedy, P. (1972). Efficacy of a regional poison treatment center. *British Medical Journal, IV,* 255–257.

Kiev, A. (1981). The management of suicidal patients. *Current Psychiatric Therapies, 20,* 183–187.

Kovacs, M., Beck, A. T., & Weissman, A. (1975). Hopelessness: An indicator of suicide risk. *Suicide, 5,* 98–103.

Kreitman, N. (1977). *Parasuicide.* New York: John Wiley & Sons.

Lester, D. (1970). Attempts to predict suicide using psychological tests. *Psychological Bulletin, 74,* 1–17.

Lester, D. (1974). Demographic versus clinical prediction of suicidal behaviors: A look at some issues. In A. T. Beck, H. L. P. Resnik, & D. J. Lettieri (Eds.), *The prediction of Suicide.* Bowie, MD: Charles Press Pubs.

Lettieri, D. J. (1974). Research issues in developing prediction scales. In C. Neuringer (Ed.), *Psychological assessment of suicidal risk.* Springfield, IL: Charles C Thomas.

Liberman, P. R., & Eckman, T. (1981). Behavior therapy v. insight-oriented therapy for repeat suicide attempters. *Archives of General Psychiatry, 38,* 1126–1130.

Linehan, M. M., Goodstein, J. L., Neilson, S. L., & Chiles, J. A. (1983). Reasons for staying alive when you are thinking of killing yourself: The Reasons for Living Inventory. *Journal of Consulting and Clinical Psychology, 51,* 276–286.

Linehan, M. M., & Laffaw, J. A. (1982). Suicidal behavior among clients at an outpatient psychology clinic versus the general population. *Suicide and Life-Threatening Behavior, 12,* 234–239.

Linehan, M. M., & Nielson, S. L. (1981). Assessment of suicide ideation and parasuicide: Hopelessness and social desirability. *Journal of Consulting and Clinical Psychology, 49,* 773–775.

Linehan, M. M., & Nielson, S. L. (1983). Social desirability: Its relevance to the measurement of hopelessness in a suicidal behavior. *Journal of Consulting and Clinical Psychology, 51,* 141–143.

McIntire, M. S., Angle, C. R., Wikoff, R. L., & Schict, M. L. (1977). Recurrent adolescent suicidal behavior. *Pediatrics, 60,* 605–608.

Montgomery, S. A., & Montgomery D. (1982). Pharmacological prevention of suicidal behavior. *Journal of Affective Disorders, 4,* 291–298.

Morrison, J. R. (1982). Suicide in a psychiatric practice population. *The Journal of Clinical Psychiatry, 9,* 348–352.

Moskop, J., & Engelhardt, H. T. (1979). The ethics of suicide: A secular view. In L. D. Hankoff & B. Einsidler, (Eds.), *Suicide: Theory and clinical aspects.* Littleton, MA: PSG Publishing Co.

Motto, J. A. (1974). Refinement of variables on assessing suicidal risk. In A. T. Beck, H. L. P. Resnik, & D. J. Lettieri (Eds.), *The prediction of suicide.* Bowie, MD: Charles Press Pubs.

Murphy, G. E., & Wetzel, R. D. (1980). Suicide risk by birth cohort in the United States, 1949 to 1974. *Archives of General Psychiatry, 37,* 519–523.

Murphy, G. E., & Wetzel, R. D. (1982). Family history of suicidal behavior among suicide attempters. *Journal of Nervous Disease, 170,* 86–90.

Myers, E. D. (1982). Subsequent deliberate self-harm in patients referred to a psychiatrist: A prospective study. *The British Journal of Psychiatry, 140,* 132–137.

Neuringer, C. (1974a). Problems of Assessing Suicidal Risk. In C. Neuringer (Ed.), *Psychological assessment of suicidal risk.* Springfield, IL.: Charles C Thomas.

Neuringer, C. (Ed.) (1974b). Psychological assessment of suicidal risk. Springfield, IL: Charles C Thomas.

Neuringer, C. (1979). Relationship between life and death among individuals of varying levels of suicidality. *Journal of Consulting and Clinical Psychology, 47,* 407–408.

Nevid, J. S. (1983). Hopelessness, social desirability, and construct validity. *Journal of Consulting and Clinical Psychology, 51,* 139–140.

Obayuwana, A. D., Collins, J. L., Carter, A. L., Mamidanna, S. R., Mahura, C. C., & Wilson, S. B. (1982). Hope Index Scale: An instrument for the objective assessment of hope. *Journal of the National Medical Association, 74,* 766–781.

Oklahoma Statutes Ann. tit. 43A gg3, 54.1 (Supp. 1977).

Ostroff, R., Giller, E., Bonese, K., Ebersole, E., Harkness, L., & Mason, J. (1982). Neuroendocrine risk factors of suicidal behavior. *American Journal of Psychiatry, 139,* 1323–1325.

Patterson, W. M., Dohn, H. H., Bird, J., & Patterson, G. A. (1983). Evaluation of suicidal patients: The SAD PERSONS Scale. *Psychosomatics, 24,* 343–349.

Paykel, E. S. (1979). Life stress. In L. D. Hankoff, & B. Einsidler (Eds.) *Suicide: Theory and clinical aspects* (pp. 225–234). Littleton, MA: PSG Publishing Co.

Pfeffer, C. R., Plutchik, L. P., & Mizruchi, M. S. (1983). Suicidal and assaultive behavior in children: Classification, measurement, and interrelations. *American Journal of Psychiatry, 140,* 154–157.

Pokorny, A. D. (1983). Prediction of suicide in psychiatric patients. *Archives of General Psychiatry, 40,* 249–257.

Poser, E. G. (1970). Toward a theory of behavioral prophylaxis. *Journal of Behavior Therapy and Experimental Psychiatry, 1,* 39–45.

Resnik, H. L. P., & Hawthorne, B. C. (Eds.). (1972). Suicidal prevention in the 70s. (DHEW Publication No. HSM 72-9054). Washington, DC: U.S. Government Printing Office.

Rogers, J., Sheldon, A., Barwick, C., Letofsky, K., & Lancee, W. (1982). Help for families of suicide: Survivors support program. *Canadian Journal of Psychiatry, 27,* 444–449.

Roy A. (1982). Risk factors for suicide in psychiatric patients. *Archives of General Psychiatry, 39,* 1089–1095.

Rush, A. J., Beck, A. T., Kovacs, M., Weissenburger, J., & Hollon, S. D. (1982). Comparison of the effects of cognitive therapy and pharmacotherapy on hopelessness and self-concept. *American Journal of Psychiatry, 139,* 862–865.

Rydin, E., Schalling, D., & Asberg, M. (1982). Rorschach ratings in depressed and suicidal patients with low levels of 5-hydroxyindolacetic acid in cerebrospinal fluid. *Psychiatry Research, 7,* 229–243.

Schotte, D. E., & Clum, G. A. (1982). Suicide ideation in a college population: A test of a model. *Journal of Consulting and Clinical Psychology, 50,* 690–696.

Schutz, B. M. (1982). Legal liability in psychotherapy. San Francisco: Jossey-Bass.

Shaffer, D. (1974). Suicide in childhood and early adolescence. *Journal of Child Psychology and Psychiatry 15,* 285–291.

Shneidman, E. S. (1979). An overview: Personality, motivation, and behavior theories. In L. D. Hankoff & B. Einsidler (Eds.), *Suicide: Theory and clinical aspects* (pp. 143–163). Littleton, MA: PSG Publishing Co.

Shneidman, E. S. (1980). Psychotherapy with suicidal patients. In T. B. Karasu & L. Bellack (Eds.), *Specialized techniques in individual psychotherapy.* New York: Brunner/Mazel.

Siegal, K. (1982). Rational suicide: Considerations for the clinician. *Psychiatric Quarterly, 54,* 77–84.

Slater, J., & Depue, R. A. (1981). The contribution of environmental events and social support to serious suicide attempts in primary depressive disorders. *Journal of Abnormal Psychology, 90,* 275–285.

Solomon, M. I., & Hellon, C. P. (1980). Suicide and age in Alberta, Canada, 1951–1979. *Archives of General Psychiatry, 37,* 551–513.

Szasz, T. S. (1974). *The myth of mental illness: Foundation of a theory of personal conduct* (rev. ed.). New York: Harper & Row.

Tarasoff v. The Regents of the University of California, 131 Cal. Rptr. 16, 551 P. 2d 334 (1976).

Toolan, J. M. (1975). Suicide in children and adolescents. *American Journal of Psychotherapy, 29,* 334–344.

Tuckman, I., & Youngman, W. F. (1968). A scale for assessing suicidal risk of attempted suicide. *Journal of Clinical Psychology, 24,* 17–19.

VanPraag, H. M. (1982). Depression, suicide and the metabolism of serotonin in the brain. *Journal of Affective Disorders, 4,* 275–290.

Warren, H. M. (1979). Pastoral counseling. In C. D. Hankoff, & B. Einsidler (Eds.), *Suicide: Theory and clinical aspects* (pp. 383–389). Littleton, MA: PSG Publishing Co.

Waters, B. G. H., Sendbuehler, J. M., Kincel, R. L., Boodoosingh, L. A., & Marchenko, I. (1982). The use of the MMPI for the differentiation of suicidal and nonsuicidal depressions. *Canadian Journal of Psychiatry, 27,* 663–667.

Watkins, J. T. (1983). Treatment of disorders of impulse control, In C. E. Walker (Ed.), *The handbook of clinical psychology: Theory, research, and practice* Vol. II; pp. 590–632). Homewood, IL: Dow Jones-Irwin Press.

Weissman, M. M. (1974). The epidemiology of suicide attempts, 1960 to 1971. *Archives of General Psychiatry, 30,* 737–736.

Yufit, R. I., Benzies, B., Fonk, M. E., & Fawcett, J. A. (1970). Suicide potential and time perspective. *Archives of General Psychiatry, 23,* 158–163.

Chapter 19

The Role of Self-Help Assignments in the Treatment of Depression

David D. Burns
Presbyterian-University of Pennsylvania Medical Center

Russell L. Adams
University of Oklahoma

Arthur D. Anastopoulos
University of Iowa

Self-help assignments are therapeutic activities conducted by patients outside of regularly scheduled therapy sessions. Although clinical use of self-help assignments has existed for many years, it is only in recent times that they have been regarded as an integral part of the therapy process. Along with this recognition there has been an increasing tendency for clinicians to utilize self-help assignments in a systematic fashion throughout the course of therapy. Such a tendency is readily apparent in many applications of behavior therapy, as well as among contemporary cognitive-behavioral approaches to the treatment of depression (Beck, Rush, Shaw, & Emery, 1979; Rehm, 1977).

Despite the fact that clinical use of self-help assignments has become more visible in recent times, it has not received a great deal of systematic attention in the literature. To date, the work of Shelton and his associates (Shelton & Ackerman, 1974; Shelton & Levy, 1981) represents the only comprehensive treatment of this topic. Working primarily from a behavioral perspective, Shelton and his colleagues have addressed a broad range of self-help issues, including reasons for using self-help assignments, ways in which self-help assignments may be applied to the treatment of various psychological problems, and types of patients for whom self-help assignments may not be indicated. In addition, these investigators have reported findings that lend empirical support to their utilization of self-help assignments within various behavioral treatment contexts (Chesney & Shelton, 1976; Shelton, 1975; Shelton & Ackerman, 1974).

In contrast with Shelton's contributions, this chapter will focus relatively greater attention upon the role played by self-help assignments within contemporary cognitive and behavioral approaches to the treatment of depression. Initial attention will be directed toward a brief delineation of the historical context out of which current usage of self-help assignments has emerged. Recent estimates of the prevalence of this intervention strategy will be discussed next. Subsequent attention will be focused upon a variety of practical and theoretical considerations that provide a rationale for incorporating self-help assignments into treatment. This will be followed by a review of available empirical evidence that addresses the impact of self-help assignments upon treatment outcome. The final portion of the chapter will encompass several matters of practical importance. In particular, descriptions of various self-help assignments, illustrations of commonly encountered resistance, and suggestions for dealing with such resistance will be discussed.

HISTORICAL OVERVIEW

Clinical use of self-help assignments is neither a new phenomenon nor one that is exclusive to any particular brand of psychotherapy. Dunlap (1936) and Herzberg (1941) were perhaps the first to cite some reliance upon self-help assignments as an aid to psychotherapy. Subsequent utilization of self-help assignments was reported in the context of Karpman's (1949) psychoanalytically oriented objective therapy and in Salter's (1949) behaviorally oriented conditioned reflex therapy. Although each of these investigators was beginning to acknowledge certain advantages to having patients engage in therapeutic activities outside of scheduled sessions, it was not until much later that self-help assignments began to emerge as an integral part of the therapy process. Kelly's (1955) systematic utilization of self-help assignments in the context of his fixed role therapy marked the beginning of this new era. Ellis's (1962) systematic incorporation of self-help assignments within his rational-emotive therapy approach provided further impetus to this movement. Kanfer and Phillips's (1966) development of instigation therapy elevated this clinical procedure to a new level of importance, in that systematic use of self-help became the focus of treatment. More recent examples of how self-help assignments have been incorporated into psychotherapy may be found in Master's and Johnson's (1970) sexual dysfunction therapy, in Lange and Jakubowski's (1976) assertiveness training program, and in Beck's (Beck et al., 1979) and Rehm's (1977) approaches to the treatment of depression.

PREVALENCE

In spite of the numerous references attesting to the use of self-help assignments, relatively little is known about the actual degree to which these procedures have been incorporated into clinical practice. Prevalence estimates, such as those that might be derived from surveys of practicing clinicians, have not appeared in the literature. To the extent that the research literature is representative of clinical therapy trends, it has been possible on a limited basis to obtain indirect prevalence estimates. In a review of 500 clinical outcome studies that appeared in eight behavior therapy journals from 1973 to 1980, Shelton and Levy (1981) found that 68 percent included some type of self-help assignment as part of the treatment package. Of the 20 studies that dealt specifically with the treatment of depression, 50 percent cited some reliance upon self-help assignments as a therapeutic tool. Analogous estimates for more recent behavior therapy trends, as well as for other therapy approaches, have not been reported.

RATIONALE

Although limited by the absence of accurate prevalence estimates, it would appear to be the case that certain forms of therapy (e.g., cognitive and behavior therapies) emphasize the use of self-help assignments more so than others (e.g., psychodynamic therapy). In light of the degree to which self-help assignments have been incorporated into these clinical approaches, an important question arises: On what basis is there justification for including self-help assignments as part of the treatment package?

Several practical advantages may be cited. The first of these involves a consideration of the fact that self-help assignments serve as a vehicle for dealing systematically with aspects of patients' lives (e.g., sexual dysfunction) that are not directly accessible within the therapy setting. Of additional importance is that systematic use of self-help assignments greatly increases the amount of time and effort that patients spend in therapeutically related activities. Not only does this serve to reinforce what patients have learned in therapy; it also makes it possible for patients to develop a greater sense of therapeutic continuity from session to session. In addition to these advantages, self-help assignments may be used to increase therapeutic efficiency throughout the course of treatment. This may be accomplished by allowing patients to consider certain topics and/or to engage in certain activities (e.g., reading assignments) at times when it is most convenient and beneficial for them to do so.

Theoretical justification for using self-help assignments may be derived from a variety of sources. Though not exclusive to depression treatment, one way to defend this clinical strategy is on the basis of the behavioral principle of generalization. According to this principle, behavioral responses may be expected to generalize from the context in which they were originally learned (e.g., therapy) to other contexts (e.g., real-life) primarily as a function of the degree to which available discriminative stimuli and reinforcement contingencies are similar across contexts. By virtue of the fact that most therapy settings are dissimilar from real-life settings, patients may not display therapeutically learned behaviors in extratherapy settings. To increase the likelihood that treatment gains will generalize to situations in patients' natural environments, therapists may choose to encourage them to engage in self-help assignments that involve practicing therapeutically learned behavior patterns in real-life settings. As patients practice such assignments, therapeutically learned patterns of behavior become more closely associated with naturally occurring discriminative stimuli and reinforcement contingencies. As a result, the likelihood that such behaviors will be exhibited in real-life settings is greatly enhanced.

Another argument for using therapeutic self-help assignments may be derived from a consideration of the behavioral distinction between massed versus spaced practice. Implicit in this distinction is the notion that certain types of learning may be facilitated by having such learning take place in sessions spaced closely together rather than far apart in time. Given that many forms of therapy are scheduled on what seems to be a spaced practice basis (e.g., weekly), it is not surprising that some patients lose track of therapeutic lessons from session to session. Although it is possible to rectify this situation by means of increasing the number of weekly therapy sessions that patients attend, such a solution tends to be rather inconvenient and costly. A more practical and efficient way of accomplishing this same goal is by encouraging patients to engage in therapeutic self-help assignments that require relatively constant attention and effort between therapy sessions.

Further theoretical support for employing self-help procedures stems from a consideration of models in which attention is directed toward patients' perceptions of self-control. For example, Bandura (1977) has proposed that individuals' expectations of personal efficacy (i.e., self-efficacy) are the primary determinants of whether or not they will initiate and/or maintain efforts to cope with problematic situations. In a similar vein, Kopel and Arkowitz (1975) have argued that self-attributed behavior change tends to endure across situations and time more so than changes attributed to external agents (e.g., therapists). Because it is not uncommon for some patients to adopt a relatively passive and submissive role when in therapy, they may be inclined to attribute therapeutic gains to their therapists' efforts rather than to their own. To increase the likelihood that patients will perceive themselves as effective problem solvers, therapists may advise them to engage in self-help activities in which they are likely to experience success. As perceptions of effective self-control increase, so does the likelihood that patients will become motivated to initiate and/or to maintain therapeutic change.

In addition to these general considerations, it is possible to justify the therapeutic use of self-help assignments in depression treatment specifically on the basis of inferences drawn from contemporary models of depression. For example, Beck and his associates (Beck et al., 1979) have placed a great deal of emphasis upon the ways in which distorted cognitions contribute to the maintenance of depressive affect and behavior. As part of Beck's approach to the treatment of depression, patients must learn to identify common patterns of unrealistic negative thinking and to challenge such thinking by examining available objective evidence. Because objective evidence that may be used to disconfirm faulty thinking usually is not found within the therapy setting, it becomes necessary to shift therapeutic attention to situations in patients' everyday lives. A particularly convenient and effective way of doing this is by having them perform self-help assignments that provide practice in collecting objective evidence under real-life conditions.

In contrast with Beck's cognitive emphasis, Lewinsohn (1974) has suggested a model of depression in which relatively greater emphasis is placed upon behavioral considerations. According to Lewinsohn, depression may be viewed as a type of extinction phenomenon in which there is either a loss or lack of response contingent positive reinforcement. In Lewinsohn's approach to treating depression, patients must learn to locate potential reinforcers in their environment and to develop appropriate strategies for attaining such reinforcers. As might be expected, such treatment goals lend themselves especially well to becoming the focus of ongoing therapeutic self-help assignments.

In Rehm's (1977) model of depression, theoretical attention is directed toward cognitive and behavioral factors. Expanding upon Kanfer's (1970) three-stage model of self-regulation, Rehm has conceptualized depression in terms of deficiencies in self-monitoring, self-evaluation, and/or self-reinforcement abilities. For Rehm, an important element of depression treatment involves strengthening patients' skills in one or more of these self-regulation areas. Implicit in this approach is the notion that the major responsibility for therapeutic change rests with the patient rather than with the therapist. As a way of assisting patients in assuming this responsibility, therapists may wish to encourage them to engage in self-help activities that provide real-life opportunities for improving self-monitoring, self-evalution, and self-reinforcement skills.

EMPIRICAL SUPPORT

While it should be apparent that there is ample practical and theoretical justification for using self-help assignments in depression treatment, it is important to relize that such information does not provide a sufficient basis for concluding that these procedures are clinically useful. To reach this conclusion, it becomes necessary to have supportive empirical evidence.

Unfortunately, inconsistent findings have emerged from the relatively small number of studies that have examined the clinical utility of self-help assignments in depression treatment. As part of a series of investigations that have addressed various facets of Rehm's (1977) depression treatment program, Kornblith and his associates (Kornblith, Rehm, O'Hara, & Lamparski, in press) compared treatment groups in which depressed females received either a combination of didactic training (i.e., reviewing the treatment rationale, weekly group discussions, in-session exercises) and behaviorally oriented self-help assignments (i.e., practice in developing self-control skills) or didactic training alone. Contrary to the authors' expectations, the results of this study clearly indicated that the addition of self-help procedures did not enhance therapeutic effectiveness beyond that of didactic training alone. In a related investigation, Harmon and her associates (Harmon, Nelson, & Hayes,

1980) provided depressed clients either with a combination of weekly nondirective group therapy and two types of daily self-monitoring assignments or with nondirective group therapy alone. On the basis of between subject and within subject comparisons, Harmon et al. found that daily participation in self-monitoring activities was related both to increases in self-reported pleasant activities and to decreases in depressed mood.

Apart from the above studies that were conducted in the context of depression treatment, there have been investigations that have addressed the therapeutic role of self-help assignments in other clinical areas. For example, Shelton (1975) reported that it was advantageous to include self-help assignments as part of clinical efforts to reduce stuttering. Similar therapeutic benefits were noted by Chesney and Shelton (1976) in the context of a biofeedback program for reducing headaches. In an investigation of 87 psychiatric outpatients who received a combination of rational-emotive therapy and systematic written homework, Maultsby (1971) found a significantly greater degree of self-reported compliance and/or satisfaction with self-help activities among patients who displayed relatively greater therapeutic gains following treatment. Although limited by methodological considerations, these results were interpreted as evidence attesting to the therapeutic value of self-help procedures. In a methodologically more direct fashion, Kazdin and Mascitelli (1982) reported that patients who engaged in ongoing self-help assignments were more likely to display posttreatment and follow-up gains in assertiveness skills as compared to patients who were not instructed to use such procedures.

While the overall pattern of these findings would appear to be supportive, it may be somewhat premature to conclude that self-help assignments are clinically useful. The relatively small number and breadth of pertinent studies, the presence of questionable methodology in some of these studies, and the absence of support in a study (Kornblith et al., in press) that maintained relatively high standards of methodology rigor are reasons for interpreting currently available evidence in a cautious manner. Circumstances such as these would seem to indicate a need for further research directed toward clarifying the therapeutic role played by self-help assignments.

In conducting this type of research, investigators need to be aware of several methodological factors that may confound interpretations of obtained results. For example, it is not appropriate to assume that patients who are assigned to treatment conditions that include self-help assignments actually employ these procedures. It is also possible that some control group patients, who do not receive instructions to engage in self-help activities, do so on their own initiative.

In experimental designs in which comparisons are made between such groups, it is critical that some attempt be made to assess the degree to which all patients participate in therapeutic activities outside of the clinical setting. The most convenient way of obtaining such compliance estimates is based upon patients' self-reporting. Unfortunately, patients' self-reporting may be susceptible to numerous types of intentional or unintentional inaccuracies, such as incomplete reporting and reporting based upon a desire to please therapists. This may help to explain why compliance figures were reported in only 5 percent of the 500 clinical outcome studies reviewed by Shelton and Levy (1981). For this reason it becomes necessary to incorporate ways of monitoring the accuracy of self-reporting. When the self-help exercises involve written procedures, such as keeping a daily log of thoughts, feelings, or behaviors, these assignments can be accurately monitored simply by reviewing them at the beginning of each therapy session. Among the other options that exist is the possibility of having patients rate items that provide some estimate of demand characteristics or recruiting the assistance of significant others in monitoring patients' activities between sessions.

In addition to addressing patient compliance considerations, investigators should attend to various characteristics of the self-help procedures themselves. It would be of clinical and methodological significance to know about the frequency and duration of self-help activities, the settings in which these activities occur, and their impact on a patient's mood. It seems likely that certain types of self-help assignments will be more therapeutic than others. While some degree of differentiation may be based upon theoretical considerations (e.g., cognitive versus behavioral), it may be more useful to design self-help procedures that take the problems and needs of individual patients into account. In view of the vast number and variety of self-help assignments that may be employed, investigators may want to reconsider the appropriateness of asking whether or not self-help assignments enhance therapeutic effectiveness. Instead, it may be more useful to concentrate empirical attention upon how best to tailor self-help assignments to a wide variety of clinical problems.

HOW TO INTRODUCE THE CONCEPT OF SELF-HELP TO THE PATIENT

Many patients expect nothing more from psychotherapy than to be listened to by a supportive, caring therapist. They may not be committed to the idea of doing systematic self-help assignments between sessions. Since the effectiveness of cognitive and behavioral therapies can depend on the patient's participation in self-help assignments it is important to negotiate this issue as early in therapy as possible.

One way to introduce the concept is to give patients a memo called "The Concept of Self-Help" to read and review at home between the first and second therapy sessions. This memo (see appendix at end of chapter) emphasizes the importance of self-help, describes several types of self-help techniques, and asks patients to indicate how much time they are willing to devote to self-help work between sessions. The memo concludes with a list of 27 reasons why patients sometimes resist helping themselves. Patients identify any attitudes and feelings that may describe the way they feel by putting checks in the appropriate boxes as they read the memo. When problems with

TABLE 1
Ten characteristics of good self-help assignments

1. Clear instructions.   The purpose and rationale of each assignment must be clearly spelled out to the patient. It can be helpful for the patient and therapist to make a list of the next week's self-help assignments at the end of each session.
2. Practical and relevant.   The work must be relevant to problems that are of immediate concern to the patient, and the patient must be able to see that the proposed assignment will help solve these problems.
3. Systematic progression and continuity.   The self-help assignments start out at a simple, basic level and gradually become more challenging and sophisticated. Patients might simply be asked to read a pamphlet on depression, to record their daily activities, or to list some upsetting events or feelings during the first week of treatment. In subsequent weeks, the therapist guides the patient through a systematic, step-by-step training program designed to correct distorted thinking patterns and self-defeating attitudes and behavior patterns.
4. Collaboration.   The patient and therapist work together as co-equals on a team pursuing mutually negotiated goals. If the patient becomes angry, loses trust, or indicates a reluctance to work between sessions, the therapist explores these feelings using active listing skills to pinpoint the specific reasons for the resistance.
5. Flexibility.   The therapist strikes a balance between focused cognitive-behavioral interventions and interpersonal support. This balance must be constantly reevaluated and will differ for each patient. Patients with a borderline personality disorder may require a slower, more empathic style because of their fear of being controlled and their tendency to react in a rebellious, oppositional manner to their therapists' requests to do self-help assignments. In contrast, patients with previous psychoanalytic therapy may require more structure and direction from the therapist to counteract their excessive tendency to ventilate painful feelings without defining and resolving specific problems.
6. Feedback.   The therapist reviews each patient's self-help work at the beginning of each session and provides specific, constructive feedback. Failure to review the self-help assignments is a serious therapeutic mistake. This conveys the impression that the assignments are not an important part of the treatment. In contrast, the therapist's genuine and consistent interest in the patient's work can be a potent motivating force.
7. Fail-safe mechanism.   Some self-help assignments will involve the risk of a negative outcome. For example, a shy man may be given the assignment of smiling at strangers or asking a woman for a date. It is important to help him identify and talk back to the negative thoughts he might have in the event of failure or rejection ahead of time. Then the assignment can be viewed as a "can't lose" proposition. Either he will get a date and have a success experience or he will be turned down and have the opportunity to work on overcoming his fears of rejection.
8. Creativity and persistence.   Often a patient will have a fixed negative belief or a refractory problem which has persisted for many years. Numerous therapeutic interventions may fail to make any dent in these attitudes and feelings. The therapist will need numerous creative strategies to attack the problem persistently with a variety of methods. Having a preceptor or a consultant available can be enormously helpful. This can provide fresh strategies and provide emotional support so the therapist does not get overwhelmed or burned out or begin to buy into the patient's feelings of hopelessness.
9. Increasing autonomy.   Over a period of time, patients will develop more effective problem-solving skills so they can eventually function as their own therapists and terminate therapy. However, they can be encouraged to come back for tune-ups following the completion of therapy whenever they experiences relapses or need help with a personal problem.
10. Sensitivity.   Therapists should be sensitive to each patient's level of intelligence and social and religious background so they can develop self-help assignments that will be helpful for a wide variety of patients.

adherence to the self-help aspect of treatment develop in the course of treatment, the therapist and patient can review the memo, identify possible reasons for the resistance and develop a plan to correct the problem.

Patients who fill out the "Concept of Self-Help" memo sometimes indicate their willingness to do self-help assignments seven days per week for one or two hours per day. In the authors' experience, this is an unrealistically high expectation. Patients who try to do too much at first may become frustrated if they don't get immediate results. Fifteen to 30 minutes per day of self-help work four or five days per week is a more realistic goal for most patients.

The 10 characteristics of good self-help assignments are listed in Table 1. Therapists can begin with simple assignments that become increasingly challenging as the therapy progresses. Patients should be advised that the rate at which they master the techniques and begin to experience relief varies greatly, and that at least 5 to 15 sessions are usually required before patients begin to improve. Patients should also be forewarned that after their first positive mood switch there is almost always a temporary relapse and that they may feel disillusioned and hopeless and want to give up at this time. Persistence with the therapy and the self-help work in spite of these feelings is crucial. Patients should be reassured that these relapses are normal and can even be beneficial. When they are resolved patients usually have a far greater understanding of the factors that trigger their negative moods and a better ability to apply the techniques that are the most helpful for them.

Therapeutic interventions should be tailored to each patient's specific problems, intelligence level, and cultural and religious background. Dr. Ivy Blackburn and her associates (Blackburn, Bishop, Glen, Whalley, & Christie, 1981) at the University of Edinburgh in Scotland reported that cognitive behavior therapy was effective in treating depressed blue-collar, working-class people that would not ordinarily be considered highly intellectual or psychologically sophisticated. These findings indicate that cognitive-behavior therapy can be effective for patients from a wide range of social and intellectual levels when the therapist takes into account the needs, feelings, and personal values of each individual patient.

SELF-HELP METHODS

The following techniques are illustrations of several of the most useful self-help methods used in cognitive-behavioral therapy. The successful application of these methods requires considerable expertise, and this section is not intended as a treatment manual. Readers interested in the actual application of cognitive-behavioral therapy should consult references describing these methods in greater detail (Beck et al., 1979; Burns, 1980; Burns, in press).

Taping Sessions.   Patients can be encouraged to tape all their sessions (with the exception of the initial history taking and diagnostic evaluation) and to listen to these tapes between sessions. This has many advantages:

(1) Patients who monopolize the therapeutic hour by talking excessively about their problems without developing plans for change are often more collaborative after hearing how they come across on tape. (2) When patients have an especially helpful session, reviewing the tape can help them understand and remember key insights and concepts. Many patients report that listening to the tapes can be far more helpful than the actual sessions because they feel more relaxed and able to absorb new ideas. Some patients will report listening to a particularly useful session numerous times. (3) The patient may become more aware of something the therapist said that was annoying, unclear, or incorrect and share this feedback at the beginning of the subsequent session.

Bibliotherapy. Many patients can benefit by reading self-help books that are relevant to their problems. Books on assertiveness training can be quite helpful to patients with interpersonal problems. *Feeling Good: The New Mood Therapy* (Burns, 1980) is a treatment manual designed specifically for depressed patients who are receiving cognitive and behavioral therapies.

When reading assignments are given it is important to encourage patients to raise questions about what they read and to provide negative and positive reactions to the concepts and techniques that are described. Then the therapist can clarify any misunderstandings and help the patient apply the methods that are most relevant to his or her problem.

Pleasure Predicting Sheet. Since a lack of motivation is a common symptom of depression, techniques that can help a patient become more productive will often lead to an improvement in mood. Patients who are depressed sometimes stop engaging in previously rewarding activities because they feel defeated and assume that anything they attempt will be unsuccessful or unrewarding. If patients have experienced any important losses, such as divorce or the loss of a job, they may give up on life because of feelings of hopelessness and the belief that they can never again feel happy because of the loss.

As a way of helping patients break out of this cycle, a therapist can encourage them to schedule activities with the potential for pleasure, learning, or personal growth in the "Activity" column of the Pleasure Predicting Sheet (Burns, 1980) as illustrated in Figure 1. Potential activities could include shopping, cleaning one's desk, reading a good book, applying for a job, cooking a gourmet meal, and so on. If patients object that they can't think of anything that would be satisfying or enjoyable, it can sometimes help to ask them about activities which used to be enjoyable, such as playing a musical instrument, playing squash or attending a chess club.

In the "Companion" column, patients record with whom they plan to do each activity. Some of the activities should be done alone and some of them should be done with others. It is important that the activities patients schedule when they are alone be as creative and interesting as those done with other people. Otherwise they may fall into the trap of scheduling rewarding and challenging activities with others, and dull or self-destructive activities

FIGURE 1

Pleasure predicting sheet

Hypothesis: I can't feel happy and fulfilled when I'm alone.

Activity (Schedule activities with a potential for pleasure or personal growth)	Companion (If alone, specify self)	Satisfaction	
		Predicted (record this before each activity) (0–100)	*Actual (record this after each activity) (0–100)*
Clean my desk	Self	20	80
Jog	Self	85	85
Go to movie with boyfriend	Ted	95	50 (we argued all night)
Go to lunch	Alice	60	70
Go shopping	Mother	60	80

Source: Adapted from D. D. Burns, *Feeling Good: The New Mood Therapy* (New York: William Morrow, 1980). Copyright © David D. Burns, M.D.

when alone. This might reinforce a dependent patient's belief that being alone is necessarily an unpleasant experience.

In the "Predicted Satisfaction" column, the patient estimates how satisfying or pleasurable each activity will be using a 0 (for the least) to 100 (for the most) rating system. These predictions must be recorded *before* each activity is begun. The patient is instructed to complete the listed activities at home between sessions. After each activity has been completed the patient records how satisfying it actually turned out to be using the same 0 to 100 rating system in the "Actual Satisfaction" column.

Patients are encouraged to bring these Pleasure Predicting Sheets to sessions to review with the therapist. Comparing the "Predicted" and "Actual" satisfaction columns can be especially useful. Depressed patients often discover that certain activities turn out to be more satisfying than they predicted. This can help passive, lethargic patients become more productively involved because it makes them more aware of how unrealistic their negative expectations can be. Patients may also discover that the activities they do by themselves can be as satisfying as the activities with other people, and sometimes more so. This often comes as a surprise to dependent patients. Learning that other people are neither necessary nor sufficient for happiness can lead to increased self-esteem and help patients function in a more independent and self-reliant manner.

Some patients will report that a number of the activities they planned are, in fact, quite dissatisfying and unrewarding. Then the therapist can ask about any negative thoughts, feelings, and attitudes that may have spoiled the experience. Perfectionistic patients may find that they get excessively self-critical and disappointed if they don't perform in an outstanding manner in every situation. Dependent patients may find that when they do activities alone, such as going to a movie or eating at a restaurant, they upset themselves with negative thoughts, such as: "It's a couples' world"; "I'm out of place here"; "I have no one to be close to"; "There must be something wrong with me." Cognitive restructuring techniques can be used to help patients modify these self-defeating attitudes so they can develop greater self-esteem and an increased capacity to enjoy various activities.

Daily Mood Log. Most therapists are quite aware that depressed patients tend to think about themselves and their experience in a very negative and somewhat illogical manner (Beck, 1967). While there is a considerable controversy whether these negative cognitions are the cause (Beck, 1963, 1964) or the result (Zajonc, 1980) of the depression or both (Teasdale & Fogarty, 1979); a number of investigators have reported that as patients learn to think about themselves in a more positive and realistic way, an improvement in mood is frequently observed (Blackburn et al., 1981; Kovacs, 1980; Murphy, Simons, Wetzel, & Lustman, 1984; Rush, Beck, Kovacs, & Hollon, 1977; Shaw, 1977).

One helpful technique is to have patients keep a journal of their negative thoughts and feelings using the Daily Mood Log, as illustrated in Figure 2. The

FIGURE 2

The daily mood log

Upsetting Event.   Briefly describe the upsetting situation: **My roommate asks me to clean up the apartment after the party.**

Feelings.   Specify sad, anxious, guilty, etc. and rate each feeling on scale from 1 (the least) to 99 (the worst): **Hurt–80 40 percent; Sad–80 50 percent; Guilty–80 50 percent**

Automatic thought	Rational response
Write down each negative thought and rate how much you believe it on a scale of 0 (the least) to 100 (the most).	Identify the distortion(s) in each automatic thought and substitute a more realistic and positive one. Rate how much you believe it between 0 (the least) and 100 (the most).
1. Everyone knows how disorganized and selfish I am. 100 50	1. Mind reading; overgeneralization: I'm disorganized at times and I'm organized at times. Everybody doesn't think about me the same way. 75
2. I'm completely self-centered and thoughtless. I'm just no good. 100 25	2. All-or-nothing thinking: I'm thoughtless at times, and at times I can be quite thoughtful. I probably do act overly self-centered at times. I can work on this. I may be imperfect but I'm not "no good!" 75
3. My roommate probably hates me. I have no real friends. 100 25	3. Mind reading; all-or-nothing thinking: My friendships are just as real as anyone's. At times I take criticism as rejection of *me,* Gail, the person. But others are usually not rejecting me. They're just expressing dislike for what I *did* (or said)—and they still accept me afterward. 75

OUTCOME: After reviewing your rational responses, rate how much you believe each of the automatic thoughts on a scale 0 to 100. Cross out your original rating and put in your revised estimate. Then re-rate your negative feelings on a scale of 0 to 99 so you can evaluate how much you have improved.

Source: Figure 2 was adapted from David D. Burns, *Feeling Good: The New Mood Therapy* (New York: William Morrow, 1980), with the permission of David D. Burns. © 1980 by David D. Burns, M.D.

patient first writes down a brief description of an upsetting event along with his or her negative feelings. Then the patient records the "automatic thoughts" associated with these feelings and identifies the distortions in these thoughts using Table 2 as a guide. Finally, the patient substitutes more positive and realistic thoughts in the "Rational Response" column of the form.

At the beginning of therapy patients will need considerable guidance in how to identify and modify their negative thoughts. As therapy progresses, most patients will develop increased skill so they can begin to use the Daily Mood Log on their own. Patients are encouraged to continue using this technique throughout their lives whenever they feel upset and have difficulty dealing with a personal problem.

The Cost-Benefit Analysis.   Some patients feel ambivalent about giving up negative feelings, such as depression, anger, anxiety, or guilt, because they may believe these feelings are healthy and helpful to them. In some cases the patient may be right, since negative emotions can serve a constructive purpose. Often, however, patients will cling to negative feelings that are quite destructive. One patient who felt guilty when she learned her child was having difficulties at school found it difficult to talk back to her self-critical

TABLE 2
Definitions of cognitive distortions

1. All-or-nothing thinking.   The patient looks at things in absolute, black and white categories. This is also called dichotomous thinking.
2. Overgeneralization.   The patient views a negative event as a never-ending pattern of defeat.
3. Mental filter.   The patient dwells on the negative aspects of a situation and ignores the positives.
4. Discounting the positive.   The patient insists that his or her positive qualities or accomplishments "don't count."
5. Jumping to conclusions.   The patient develops a belief that isn't clearly justified by the facts.
   a. Mind reading: The patient assumes that people are reacting negatively to him or her when there's no definite evidence for this.
   b. Fortune-telling: The patient arbitrarily predicts that things can't change or will turn out badly.
6. Magnification or minimization.   The patient blows things up out of proportion or shrinks their importance inappropriately.
7. Emotional reasoning.   The patient reasons from how he or she feels: "I feel like a failure; therefore I must really be one."
8. Should statements.   The patient tries to motivate himself or herself with of "shoulds," "shouldn'ts," "must's," "ought's," and "have to's."
9. Labeling.   Patients may identify with their mistakes and label themselves as "*a* fool" or "*a* loser" instead of trying to pinpoint the cause of the problem so they can learn from it.
10. Personalization and blame.   Patients may blame themselves for a negative event they weren't entirely responsible for (such as getting an illness or getting divorced). Conversely, they may blame other people, external events, or fate and overlook ways that they might have contributed to a problem.

This table was adapted from D. Burns, *Feeling Good: The New Mood Therapy* (New York: William Morrow & Co., 1980). For further information, see Chapter Three, "You Feel the Way You Think."

thoughts because she felt convinced that she was a "bad mother" and thought it was appropriate to feel guilty. Another patient was still consumed by bitterness and resentment toward her former husband years after her divorce. She told her therapist that she was reluctant to try to modify her angry feelings. She explained that, "it's my husband's fault that I feel so miserable. He never gave our marriage a chance. Why should *I* have to be the one to change?"

Anxious patients may be equally reluctant to give up their negative feelings because they think their fears will *help* them in some way. A psychologist receiving treatment for panic attacks felt so incapacitated by the fear that she might flunk her certification exam that she couldn't study. She didn't want to fill out the Daily Mood Log between sessions because she was afraid that any reduction in her anxiety would make her too complacent to study.

The Cost-Benefit Analysis (Burns, 1980; Burns, 1984) can be an effective way of dealing with a patient's ambivalence about giving up negative feelings. The therapist suggests that the patient make a list of the advantages and disadvantages of continuing to feel anxious (or angry or guilty) along with a second list of the advantages and disadvantages of feeling better. The woman whose Cost-Benefit Analysis is illustrated in Figure 3 was afraid of overcoming her depression and suicidal impulses because she felt these feelings gave her an excuse to divorce her husband. She was afraid that if she overcame her depression she'd lose her motivation to change and end up stuck in a bad marriage. The Cost-Benefit Analysis helped her see that she would still be free to decide whether or not to stay in her marriage once she overcame her depression. This insight helped her make a greater commitment to therapy and she began to improve more rapidly.

FIGURE 3
The cost-benefit analysis

Advantages of being depressed and angry	Disadvantages of being depressed and angry
1. I don't have to appear to be happy.	1. I won't feel fulfilled and satisfied.
2. I can spite people who expect me to be happy all the time.	2. I'll still have all my problems and I won't try to solve them.
3. I can be lazy.	3. I'll probably stay with my husband no matter how I feel.
4. I don't have to be nice to people.	4. I may kill myself and that wouldn't help anything.
5. I can fail.	

Advantages of being happy and joyful	Disadvantages of being happy and joyful
1. I'll be able to be wrong without getting so upset and defensive.	1. I won't have excuses when I don't do the things I should.
2. I'll be able to make decisions and feel good about them.	2. I won't be able to feel sad and upset all the time.
3. I'll feel more fulfilled and satisfied	3. I may lose the urge to leave my husband.
4. I won't worry as much.	
5. I won't want to commit suicide.	
6. I can get on with my life.	

The Cost-Benefit Analysis has a number of other therapeutic applications. If the patient has a difficult decision to make, such as whether to get engaged or to stay single and date a variety of people, he or she can be encouraged to make a list of the advantages and disadvantages of both options at home between sessions. Then the therapist and patient can discuss the consequences of these options and balance the advantages against the disadvantages of each. For a more detailed discussion of this technique, see Burns (in press).

Finally, patients can use the Cost-Benefit Analysis to evaluate the consequences of certain dysfunctional attitudes that may be contributing to their mood swings (Burns, 1980). These dysfunctional attitudes may involve the need to be perfect, the need to get everyone's approval, the need to be loved, and so on. Analyzing the costs and benefits of these attitudes can often lead to the development of a more realistic and adaptive personal value system.

SIGNS OF THERAPEUTIC RESISTANCE

The failure to complete self-help assignments is often a symptom of therapeutic resistance. While some patients will express their negative feelings to the therapist quite openly, others may be quite inassertive and afraid of dealing with any conflict directly. They may tend to deny their feelings and express them indirectly. The following signs suggest that a patient may be developing negative feelings that need to be explored:

1. The patient continually "forgets" to follow through on self-help assignments between sessions.
2. The patient acts argumentative, oppositional, or sarcastic during therapy sessions.
3. The patient comes late to sessions or cancels sessions at the last minute.
4. The patient neglects to pay for therapy sessions.
5. The patient complains excessively during sessions, jumping from grievance to grievance without working systematically on any one problem.
6. The patient protests that the therapist doesn't understand his or her feelings.
7. The patient asks about some new kind of therapy or consults with another therapist without first reviewing this with the primary therapist.
8. The patient appears desperate, helpless, and overwhelmed and asks the therapist what to do. When the therapist tries to make a helpful suggestion, the patient responds by saying "that wouldn't help me" or "I've already tried that." Then the patient becomes more agitated and demanding.
9. The patient appears upset but insists he/she doesn't *feel* like talking or doesn't *have* to talk.

10. The patient comes to therapy intoxicated on drugs or alcohol or dressed inappropriately.

WAYS OF MOTIVATING RESISTANT PATIENTS

It can be quite important to find out specifically why a particular patient resists doing self-help assignments. Therapists can ask patients to write down the negative thoughts that come to mind whenever they think about doing them. Since resistant patients are unlikely to do this on their own between sessions, the therapist and patient can do it together during a therapy session using the Daily Mood Log. Susan, the woman whose Daily Mood Log is illustrated in Figure 4 was annoyed with a girlfriend who had abruptly broken off their relationship without any explanation. Although Susan had written her friend two letters asking what the problem was, she did not receive any reply. Susan felt depressed and angry about this and hadn't done any self-help assignments. You can see by examining her automatic thoughts that she was telling herself that she didn't have enough time to do any self-help assignments, that it would be just as effective to think the problem through in her

FIGURE 4

The daily mood log

Upsetting Event.   Briefly describe the upsetting situation: **Between sessions I avoid writing down my negative thoughts about a friend who refuses to talk to me.**

Feelings.   Specify sad, anxious, guilty, etc. and rate each feeling on a scale from 1 (the least) to 99 (the worst): **Angry–~~90~~ 70 percent; Frustrated–~~90~~ 70 percent; Sad–~~90~~ 50 percent**

Automatic thoughts	Rational responses
Write down each negative thought and rate how much you believe it on a scale of 0 (the least) to 100 (the most).	Identify the distortion(s) in each automatic thought and substitute a more realistic and positive one. Rate how much you believe it between 0 (the least) and 100 (the most).
1. I don't have enough time to do the homework. ~~90~~ 0	1. Jumping to conclusions: I could take 15 to 30 minutes to write down my negative thoughts instead of watching TV. 100
2. It's not going to matter anyway. ~~90~~ 50	2. Fortune-telling: I know it does matter because I can often see how silly my negative thoughts are once they're written down. 100
3. I can do it better in my head so I don't need to write my negative thoughts down. ~~90~~ 50	3. Jumping to conclusions: I can't do it better in my head. The negative thoughts just keep spinning through my mind. 90
4. She's the one who isn't talking to me and I haven't done anything wrong, so I have every right to be angry about this. ~~100~~ 50	4. Blaming: Being angry isn't going to change the situation. Why go on feeling angry about a situation when there's nothing I can do about it? 75

OUTCOME: After reviewing your rational responses, rate how much you believe each of the automatic thoughts on a scale of 0 to 100. Cross out your original rating and put in your revised estimate. Then re-rate your negative feelings on a scale of 0 to 99 so you can evaluate how much you have improved.

Source: Figure 4 was adapted from David D. Burns, *Feeling Good: The New Mood Therapy* (New York: William Morrow, 1980). © 1980 by David D. Burns, M.D.

head, that the self-help exercises wouldn't do any good, and that she had "every right" to feel angry and upset with her friend. Once she saw her negative thoughts on paper it was easier for her to see how illogical they were.

The fourth automatic thought on Susan's Daily Mood Log indicates that anger was one cause of her resistance. Anger will frequently undermine a patient's motivation to do self-help assignments because of the natural tendency to feel helpless and victimized rather than to take steps to cope with an unpleasant situation more constructively. Susan's therapist agreed that she had every right to feel angry and to express these feelings during her session, and encouraged her to do a Cost-Benefit Analysis to see if her anger was healthy and productive for her. Once she examined the advantages and disadvantages of feeling resentful toward her friend, Susan concluded that her anger wasn't serving any useful purpose, since she'd already expressed her feelings in the two letters she'd written. Her friend hadn't responded after several months and Susan wasn't planning to take any further action. Therefore, her resentment was simply eating away at her and making her feel unhappy. She then felt motivated to write down the negative thoughts that were making her feel angry. After she identified the distortions in these thoughts and substituted rational responses for them, she was able to put the problem in a more objective perspective and she began to feel better about herself (see Figure 5).

Sometimes the patient's anger will be directed at the therapist, rather than at a family member or friend. It can be useful to ask every patient for specific negative and positive feedback at the beginning and end of each therapy session. A therapist can say, "I'd like to hear about any positive or negative reactions you may have had as we talked today. Let's start with the negatives first. Was there anything I might have said that seemed unrealistic or hurt your feelings or rubbed you the wrong way? Was there anything you were trying to say or wanted to work on that I might have ignored or misunderstood?" This gives the patient a change to express the negative feelings before the completion of the session. Once the air is cleared, the patient will be more likely to cooperate by doing the self-help assignment. When patients express negative feelings about the therapy, it is crucial for therapists to respond empathically rather than defensively so the patient will not feel judged or criticized. Although most therapists believe they are empathic listeners, it can be surprisingly difficult for novice and advanced practitioners to respond in a nondefensive way when confronted by a critical, hostile patient. Oppositional patients and those with a diagnosis of borderline personality disorder can readily arouse a therapist's insecurities. If the therapist becomes defensive, the patient may feel a lack of trust that can seriously undermine therapy. The unwillingness to complete self-help assignments is often just a symptom of this lack of trust.

Therapists can also elicit positive and negative feelings about the therapeutic process by asking patients to fill out the Patient's Therapy Session Report (Burns & Epstein, 1983) between sessions (see Figure 6). This form

FIGURE 5
The daily mood log

Upsetting Event. Briefly describe the upsetting situation: Sarah has broken off our friend-ship without an explanation. This came on around the time I broke up with a fellow she was very close to and she got a new boyfriend. I also had an abortion, and she told me she didn't like the way I was reacting to these various situations. In spite of writing to her and trying to contact her by phone, she has refused to answer my letters or communicate with me.

Feelings. Specify sad, anxious, guilty, etc. and rate each feeling on a scale from 1 (the least) to 99 (the worst): Sad–90̶ 50 percent; Disappointed–75̶ 50 percent; Frustrated–99̶ 50 percent; Angry 99̶ 50 percent

Automatic thoughts	Rational responses
Write down each negative thought and rate how much you believe it on a scale of 0 (the least) to 100 (the most).	Identify the distortion(s) in each automatic thought and substitute a more realistic and positive one. Rate how much you believe it between 0 (the least) and 100 (the most).
1. She owes me an explanation if she wants to end the relationship. 100̶ 60	1. Should statement: It would be desirable for her to explain her feelings to me, but she's not obligated to. She may be inas-sertive and afraid of conflicts. 75
2. This is going to bug me for a long time. 100̶ 50	2. Fortune-telling: It will only bug me if I insist on thinking about it. Why not just forget about it and make some new friends? 75
3. How can I explain this to people who ask me about her? 100̶ 50	3. Mind reading: I can tell people she hasn't been interested in pursuing our friend-ship and I don't really understand why. 100
4. People will think I've done something wrong if she's not talking to me. 100̶ 25	4. Mind reading: That seems unlikely. I'm probably a lot harder on myself than other people would be. 90
5. She's deserted me. 100̶ 50	5. Jumping to conclusions: If she has, it's more of a reflection on her than on me. It's unfortunate to lose a friend, but a friend who won't sit down and talk out a problem really isn't a very good friend in the long run. 100

OUTCOME: After reviewing your rational responses, rate how much you believe each of the automatic thoughts on a scale of 0 to 100. Cross out your original rating and put in your revised estimate. Then re-rate your negative feelings on a scale of 0 to 99 so you can evaluate how much you have improved.

Source: Figure 5 was adapted from David D. Burns, *Feeling Good: The New Mood Therapy* (New York: William Morrow, 1980). © 1980 by David D. Burns, M.D.

asks the patient for specific technical and interpersonal feedback about the most recent session. This form can be helpful to unassertive patients who have difficulties verbalizing their negative and positive feelings directly to the therapist.

The bottom part of the sheet asks patients how much warmth, empathy, trust, and understanding they experienced during the session. Any ratings other than 1s ("weak feeling") or 4s ("extremely strong feeling") usually indicate a less-than-optimal therapeutic relationship. These reactions need to

FIGURE 6

Patient's report of therapy session*

1. How much progress do you feel you made in this session in dealing with your problems? How do you feel about the session?

   EXCELLENT   VERY GOOD   GOOD   SATISFACTORY   BARELY ADEQUATE   POOR

2. How pleased are you with the progress you've made in therapy thus far?

   EXCELLENT   VERY GOOD   GOOD   SATISFACTORY   BARELY ADEQUATE   POOR

3. How well do you feel you are getting along, emotionally and psychologically, at this time?

   EXTREMELY WELL   QUITE WELL   SATISFACTORILY   NOT WELL AT ALL   VERY POORLY

Using the scale from 1 to 4 below, rate the AMOUNT OF SUCCESS YOU HAD IN THE PAST SESSION in meeting each of these goals.

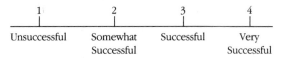

_____ 1. Better insight into and understanding of my problems.

_____ 2. Ideas for better ways of dealing with people and problems.

_____ 3. Help in being able to talk about what was troubling me.

_____ 4. Encouragement and confidence to try to do things differently.

_____ 5. Better control over my moods and/or actions.

_____ 6. Greater ability to respond rationally to my negative thoughts.

_____ 7. Greater ability to evaluate some basic values and assumptions about what is important to me.

_____ 8. Ways of scheduling my time better.

Using the scale from 1 to 4 below, rate the EXTENT TO WHICH YOU FEEL EACH OF THESE STATEMENTS IS TRUE TODAY.

_____ 1. The things my therapist says and does make me feel I can trust him or her.

_____ 2. My therapist often does not seem to be genuinely himself or herself.

_____ 3. My therapist pretends that s/he likes me or understands me more than s/he really does.

_____ 4. I feel that my therapist really thinks I'm worthwhile.

_____ 5. My therapist is friendly and warm toward me.

_____ 6. My therapist does not really care what happens to me.

_____ 7. My therapist usually understands what I say to him or her.

_____ 8. My therapist understands my words, but not the way I feel.

_____ 9. My therapist really sympathizes with my difficulties.

_____ 10. My therapist acts condescending and talks down to me.

* This form was adapted from one developed by Jeffrey H. Young.

be explored and resolved in order to develop a positive, collaborative therapeutic relationship. Recent studies by Persons and Burns (in press) have indicated that these ratings predict a significant proportion of the variance in emotional improvement patients experience during psychotherapy sessions. This suggests that the rate of improvement during sessions and the degree of collaboration with the therapist will be optimal when the patient perceives the therapist as empathic and caring.

Some patients with an Axis II diagnosis of borderline personality disorder will resist doing any self-help assignments because they feel sensitive to being controlled by others. They may resist any suggestions the therapist makes in order to maintain feelings of autonomy. This oppositional behavior can trigger feelings of frustration in therapists who may urge these patients to help themselves. The patient may then feel coerced and resist more intensely, and the therapist and patient may get locked into a struggle over power and control. If the patient feels pressured, he or she may threaten to terminate therapy, slash himself or herself, or make a suicide attempt.

It can be helpful to encourage oppositional patients to express their feelings of resentment and to focus on the fears and attitudes that make it difficult for them to experience the relationship in a collaborative manner. This can sometimes defuse the feelings of rebelliousness and encourage greater openness so the issue of self-help work can be negotiated more successfully. The therapist might encourage the oppositional patient to make a list of the advantages and disadvantages of doing self-help assignments between sessions using the Cost-Benefit Analysis described earlier. Therapists can also encourage oppositional patients to be more independent by choosing which problems they want to work on and by designing their own self-help assignments. Since these patients are usually quite dependent and have a great need for emotional support and ventilation, it can sometimes be helpful to propose that half of each therapeutic hour can be spent simply talking about feelings and problems, and the other half can be spent reviewing self-help assignments and working on solutions to problems.

In the event a patient still refuses to participate in the self-help aspect of treatment, therapists can emphasize their desire to continue with treatment and explain that self-help work is an inherent part of the therapy. The therapist can suggest that the patient try the techniques for one or two months to see if cognitive and behavioral methods are helpful and offer a referral to a therapist with a different therapeutic orientation if the patient is not satisfied. Most patients will not choose to terminate, but offering this option underscores the importance of the self-help work and emphasizes that the relationship must be negotiated in a way that is satisfactory to both the patient and therapist.

Hopelessness is one of the commonest reasons that patients don't complete their self-help assignments. Although feelings of hopelessness frequently result from the distorted belief that one's symptoms cannot change and that one's problems are insoluble (Burns & Persons, 1982), patients who feel this way are usually convinced that their feelings are entirely valid and that improvement is impossible. Therefore, they see no point in doing self-help assignments between sessions. This attitude tends to function as a self-fulfilling prophecy, since the lack of commitment to the treatment may cause the depression to intensify, and this reinforces the feelings of hopelessness.

When patients express feelings of hopelessness, therapists should explore whether any suicidal impulses are present because of the high correlation between hopelessness and suicide attempts (Beck, Kovacs, & Weissman,

1975; Wetzel, 1976; Wetzel, Margolies, & Davis, 1980). If the patient appears actively suicidal and no significant deterrent exists, hospitalization is indicated. One way to assess this is to ask the patient to list the advantages and disadvantages of living versus the advantages and disadvantages of dying. When the advantages of dying appear greater, the risk of a suicide attempt may be quite high.

When there are no significant suicidal urges, the therapist can help the patient work through these feelings of hopelessness and enlist his or her active collaboration in doing self-help assignments using the "experimental method." The therapist suggests the patient maintain his or her skepticism about the chances for improvement but test it objectively by doing the self-help assignments systematically for 30 minutes a day for an appropriate period of time (one or two months would be reasonable). The degree of improvement can be measured with a variety of parameters, such as a reduction in the patient's score on standardized depression or anxiety tests, an increase in daily activities, and improved social skills.

The advantage of the "experimental method" is that it allows patients to test their negative expectations in a collaborative way rather than getting into a nonproductive debate with the therapist about whether or not they really are hopeless. It is important that reasonable criteria for improvement be stipulated ahead of time so the patient's progress can be defined and measured objectively. For example, a 30 percent reduction in depression scores after doing several weeks of self-help assignments might indicate that improvement is occurring and could disconfirm the patient's belief that she or he is hopeless. However, if the criteria for improvement are not spelled out, patients may think about their symptoms in an all-or-nothing manner and conclude that anything short of total recovery proves they have not made any progress and really are hopeless.

It can be important to point out that if the patient does not experience the desired degree of improvement during the experimental period, the patient and therapist will evaluate why that happened and develop some new treatment strategies. This might involve a change in medication and/or the psychotherapeutic approach. This puts patients in a "can't lose" proposition—either they will improve, or they will learn that certain self-help techniques do not bear fruit and this information will be used to develop others that may be more beneficial.

One of the authors (Burns, in press) has recently developed an "Anti-Hopelessness Memo" which lists numerous interventions which can help patients overcome their feelings of hopelessness. After patients read about each intervention they rate how helpful it seems between 0 percent and 100 percent and record their comments. The patient and therapist can review the memo together to see which kinds of interventions are most likely to be helpful for that particular patient.

Many patients will experience a rapid improvement early in therapy. Usually they relapse within a few days or weeks of their first positive mood switch. During these relapses they nearly always feel disillusioned, frustrated, and hopeless and may refuse to continue doing self-help assignments.

These reactions can be minimized if therapists will prepare patients for relapses ahead of time. When patients begin to improve, the therapist can emphasize that it is probable that the patient will experience a setback before long. The therapist can explain that while this can be quite distressing, it is not unusual and can be turned into a productive growth experience if the patient will continue to apply the tools he or she has been learning about in therapy. Therapists can encourage patients to write down all the negative thoughts they're likely to have during these relapses. Typical thoughts might include, "This proves I really am hopeless," "My improvement was just a fluke," "The therapy didn't work because the effects didn't last," or "I really am worthless and inferior after all." Once the patient has listed these negative thoughts on a Daily Mood Log, she or he can identify the distortions in them and substitute more realistic thoughts.

Therapists can help patients learn to dispute these thoughts about relapses with a type of role-playing called the "externalization of voices" method developed by Burns (Moorey & Burns, 1983). After explaining the procedure to the patient, the therapist assumes the role of the patient's automatic thoughts and verbalizes the negative, self-critical cognitions that usually upset the patient. The patient assumes the role of the "rational responses" and attempts to talk back to these "automatic thoughts." It is important to keep in mind that this is not "assertiveness training" in which a patient learns to talk back to another person. In the "externalization of voices" method, both the therapist and patient are assuming the role of a part of the patient's mind. One voice represents the patient's negative, irrational thoughts, and the other voice represents a more realistic, compassionate way of thinking about problems. If the patient becomes upset and finds it difficult to talk back to the "automatic thoughts," the therapist and patient reverse their roles so the therapist can demonstrate ways of disputing them. Frequent role reversals may be necessary because depressed patients may find their negative thoughts quite convincing and flounder when they are in the "rational responses" role. A typical dialogue might evolve like this:

Therapist: [as "automatic thoughts"] Now I'm depressed again. This shows I'm hopeless.

Patient: [as "rational responses"] No, it just shows I'm feeling bad again. This will give me the opportunity to apply the same techniques that helped me the first time so I can master them.

Therapist: [as "automatic thoughts"] Ah, but that's just the point. The techniques didn't really help me before. I was just fooling myself into thinking I was a worthwhile person and that I could get better. But now I know the truth about myself—I'm really a loser after all.

Patient: [as "rational responses"] I'm not "a loser," I'm a human being who's suffering. I can find out what's bothering me and do something about it.

Therapist: [as "automatic thoughts"] That would be a waste of time because I *know* what's bothering me. I'm depressed because Linda rejected me. She rejected me because she found out what an inferior, second-rate person I really am. All my relationships will end up like this because I just don't have what it takes to form a good relationship with someone I care about.

Patient: [as "rational responses"] Wait a minute. Linda and I broke up because we found out we weren't suitable for each other on a long-term basis. Our relationship had a number of real strengths and weaknesses. I'm learning more and more about myself and others and I can look forward to better relationships in the future.

The "externalization of voices" method can be applied to any therapeutic problem once the patient has identified the upsetting automatic thoughts. The method allows the therapist to test the degree of conviction the patient has in the "rational responses" and to uncover areas of weakness that are in need of further therapy. During remissions, patients will usually be able to talk back to these "automatic thoughts" rather effectively. When patients are feeling depressed and overwhelmed, they may have great difficulties disputing them. Helping depressed individuals talk back to their negative thoughts requires considerable patience on the part of the therapist and frequent role reversals.

Some patients who clearly understand the rationale and purpose of self-help assignments may claim they "forget" to do them. These patients may be testing the therapist's conviction about the importance of this aspect of the treatment. Therapists can explain the logic and purpose of the self-help assignments and make a list of the specific assignments the patient agrees to complete prior to the next session. Therapists can ask the patient to call the office and leave a message when the next day's assignment has been completed. This usually leads to a significant increase in completed self-help assignments.

When efforts along these lines are not successful, a contingency contract can often be helpful. Contingency contracting is not needed for the great majority of patients and should only be done with a patient's consent. The therapist and patient first agree on a list of several simple assignments that are to be completed at home prior to the next session. The patient gets one point for each completed assignment. The list might include:

1. Locate my old resume so I can begin to revise it.
2–3. Write down my negative thoughts at least twice when I feel upset. (This would count as two assignments.)
4. Listen to the tape of the session.
5. Fill out the Beck Depression Test and bring it to the next therapy session.

The therapist asks if the patient would agree that the length of the next session will depend on the number of these assignments that have been completed. Patients who complete one of the five assignments would agree to pay for a full session but the length of the session would be 10 minutes instead of 50 minutes. Patients who complete two of the five assignments would receive a 20-minute session, and so on. The therapist should be extremely flexible and sensitive in the way this arrangement is "enforced." Patients will rarely lose any actual therapy time because they generally complete a reasonable amount of work once they have agreed to the contingency arrangement. If the patient does more than half the assignments, the therapist should reward the patient with a full session.

This technique should only be used when a therapist has good rapport with a patient and should never be used in a punitive manner as a way of subtly punishing an angry, uncooperative patient. Contingency contracting should probably never be used with severely depressed or suicidal patients and should only be used with the greatest caution with patients with a diagnosis of borderline personality disorder because they may see the arrangement as a rejection or a coercive maneuver and react by prematurely terminating treatment. It would not be wise to use the method for more than one or two weeks with any patient. The purpose of a contingency contract is to break a log jam so the therapy can get moving again. Using it on an ongoing basis would be likely to undermine trust and collaboration.

These are just a few examples of the types of interventions that can help motivate patients who resist self-help assignments. They are not to be applied in mechanical, cookbook fashion but in the context of a meaningful therapeutic relationship that takes into account the unique attitudes and feelings of each patient. A successful therapist will need to utilize numerous strategies and types of interventions for each of the 27 types of resistance listed in the "Concept of Self-Help" memo. This sometimes requires considerable therapeutic creativity and persistence. An approach which is extremely helpful for one patient is likely to be quite ineffective for the next. It is often necessary to try many approaches until a productive, collaborative relationship with the patient has been established.

Appendix

The Concept of Self-Help*

David D. Burns, M.D.

The purpose of treatment is to *feel* better, to *understand* why you got depressed or anxious and to learn to *master your moods* so your can cope with your problems more effectively in the future.

There are several reasons why you may feel better as a result of your therapy:

1. You may experience a mood lift because you learn something that helps you solve a personal problem.
2. You may appreciate the support of a therapist who understands you and approves of you.

---

* The appendix, "The Concept of Self-Help," was reprinted from David D. Burns, *The Feeling Good Workbook* (New York: New American Library, in press), with the permission of David D. Burns. © 1984, David D. Burns, M.D.

3. You may benefit from an antidepressant medication.

4. You may do things to help yourself between therapy sessions, such as scheduling more productive or pleasurable activities, becoming more assertive with people, writing down your negative thoughts and substituting more positive ones, and reading a self-help book.

Some of the newer forms of therapy are unique in emphasizing a structured self-help program to help you learn to feel better, become more productive, and improve your relationships with people. Research and clinical experience have confirmed that the speed of your improvement can depend on your willingness to do self-help assignments. Patients who are unwilling to help themselves are often very slow to improve. In contrast, patients who make an effort to participate in a systematic self-help program generally make the most rapid gains.

For this reason, it is crucial for you to decide whether you are willing to make an effort to help yourself as part of your treatment. Please answer the following questions and return this memo to your therapist so the two of your can review it together.

---

1. I understand that my therapist emphasizes a self-help program as a key to personal growth. ☐ Yes ☐ No ☐ Needs discussion

2. I am willing to do things to help myself between therapy sessions. ☐ Yes ☐ No ☐ Needs discussion.

3. The amount of time between sessions I agree to spend is _____ minutes/day (fill in).

4. I am willing to do this _____ days per week and to continue working in my own behalf for at least _____ weeks (fill in).

SELF-HELP FORMS AND METHODS

The following is a brief review of some of the types of self-help forms and methods that are commonly used by patients involved in therapy. It is not comprehensive but is just intended to give you an idea of what is available.

1. Activity Schedules.   A variety of forms are available to help your organize and utilize your time more productively.

2. Daily Mood Log.   This is a form for helping you learn to identify and change negative thoughts which lead to sadness, anxiety, anger, guilt, and frustration. You can freqently change the way you feel by changing the way you think about upsetting situation.

3. Checklist of Cognitive Distortions.   This is a list of the 10 types of twisted thinking that most frequently give rise to painful feelings. You can use it in conjunction with the "Daily Mood Log" to help you pinpoint the distortions in your negative thoughts.

4. The Pleasure Predicting Sheet.   This is a form for predicting and assessing the amount of satisfaction you get from various activities that have a potential for pleasure, achievement, learning, or personal growth. This form can help you test and modify certain self-defeating attitudes which can make you vulnerable to depression and anxiety, such as:

A. I cannot feel happy and fulfilled if I'm alone.

B. I cannot feel satisfied unless I do things perfectly.

C. I cannot be truly happy unless there's someone in my life who loves me.

5. *The Antiprocrastination Sheet.*   This form can help you overcome procrastination. You break a task down into its smallest component parts and predict how difficult and satisfying each part will be between 0 (the least difficult or satisfying) and 100 (the most). They you do each part and record how difficult and satisfying it actually turned out to be. Things you've been putting off frequently turn out to be considerably easier and more enjoyable than you predicted.

6. *Bibliotherapy.*   Many useful self-help books and pamphlets are available which can speed up your recovery. Some of these have to do with self-esteem, sex, assertiveness training, or other topics relevant to personal growth. Your therapist might be able to suggest some titles that would be especially valuable to you.

7. *The Beck Depression Inventory (BDI).*   This is a 21-question, multiple-choice inventory which acts as an "emotional thermometer" to measure the amount of depression you are experiencing. It can be filled out and scored in two or three minutes. You can take the BDI test once a week while your are in therapy for depression to monitor your progress. This can provide "quality control" to help you and your therapist determine whether or not you are feeling better as a result of therapy or taking an antidepressant medication.

8. *The Burns Anxiety Inventory (BAI).*   This is a 33 question, multiple-choice inventory which measures the symptoms of anxiety and panic. Like the depression inventory, it can be filled out and scored in several minutes. It can help you monitor your progress in therapy.

9. *Assertive Practice and Social Skills Training.*   Your therapist can teach you specific verbal skills during therapy sessions by role-playing difficult situations with you and demonstrating appropriate responses. You might want to learn how to communicate more effectively with family members, friends, strangers, or business associates. Common areas of difficulty include dealing with people who are excessively critical and angry as well as with complainers and people who make excessive demands on you. You might need to work on how to say no graciously, how to ask for a date, how to interview successfully, how to listen better, how to flirt, how to share angry feelings constructively, how to negotiate a business deal, how to deal with a rejection, how to communicate with people who refuse to talk to you, and so on. Once you have mastered a specific verbal skill in the office, your therapist can help you devise actual practice experiences outside of the office. You can report back on your degree of success or failure at the next session so you can improve your approach. Your therapist can also help you identify and modify self-defeating attitudes which may contribute to your difficulties in communicating openly and effectively.

10. *Decision-Making Form.*   This is a form which allows you to weigh the advantages and disadvantages of various options in a systematic manner when you are faced with a difficult decision.

11. *Patient's Report of Therapy Session.*   This form allows you to give your therapist positive and negative feedback about each therapy session. You can fill it out after the session and give it to your therapist at the beginning of the next session. This will help you bring any negative reactions to the attention of your therapist so they won't build up and undermine your treatment. Remember that your therapist is human and will make mistakes at times. He or she may say something that you disagree with or that rubs you the wrong way. Why not just acknowledge your feelings and develop a plan to deal with any problems frankly and openly? The resolution of these conflicts can improve your relationship with your therapist and give him or her valuable information about the best way to be helpful to you.

12. Taping of Sessions.   Many patients find it very beneficial to tape their sessions so they can listen to the tapes at home between sessions. During a productive session you may discover many exciting insights about yourself or learn to solve problems that have been troubling you. During the session these new ideas may all seem perfectly lucid and clear to you, but an hour or two later you may have trouble recalling just what it was that seemed so important and useful at the time. As you listen to the tape you will have the opportunity to review these ideas again. Many patients listen to the tapes of especially good sessions numerous times, and they report that the tapes can be more helpful than the actual sessions themselves.

When you listen to a tape you may also discover that you have a tendency to ignore or discount what the therapist says even though you felt convinced during the session that you were listening carefully. At times it can be uncomfortable to hear yourself because you will notice certain negative habits that you weren't aware of. Listening to yourself takes courage but it can be an important growth experience. You may also become aware of mistakes your therapist is making. Be sure to share this feedback at the next session.

REASONS FOR NOT DOING SELF-HELP

The following are some of the reasons why you may have difficulty doing self-help work between sessions. There is some overlap between a number of the categories and you will probably discover that several of them apply to you. These same attitudes may make you less productive and successful in other areas of your life. Once you pinpoint the problem that is holding you back, you can work with your therapist to develop a strategy for overcoming it. This is crucial because your willingness to work on your own between therapy sessions is an essential ingredient of your treatment. Resolving this problem might also make you more productive in other areas of your life.

After each of the following descriptions, put a check ($\checkmark$) in the box that indicates how accurately it describes the way you feel.

1. The Love Addiction.   You may feel convinced that love and closeness are the keys to happiness so you cannot conceive of finding satisfaction as a result of learning to cope with your problems on your own. Self-help techniques may seem cold and mechanical. You may resent having to help yourself because you feel convinced that the best way to overcome your depression involves sharing your feelings with a therapist or friend who cares about you and supports you.

This problem or attitude describes me:
☐ Not at all   ☐ Somewhat   ☐ Moderately   ☐ A lot

2. All-or-Nothing Thinking.   You may feel that if you do not do things perfectly there is no point in doing them at all. This distortion can defeat you in several ways. You may feel you have to do your self-help exercises so thoroughly and perfectly that you feel too overwhelmed to try. In fact, even 5 to 10 minutes a day of self-help work can contribute enormously to your improvement. You may be afraid that if you make a mistake or don't complete an exercise properly you will appear incompetent or stupid. In fact, you're permitted to make as many mistakes as you like because your therapist is teaching you something *new*. You can learn from your mistakes. You may also feel that a particular exercise must lead to a dramatic changes in the way you feel or else it wasn't successful. Actually, you can learn from self-help exercises that don't make you feel better if you will review your efforts with your therapist.

This problem or attitude describes me:

☐ Not at all   ☐ Somewhat   ☐ Moderately   ☐ A lot

3. *The Fear of Disapproval.* You may be afraid that your therapist will think less of you when s/he reviews your self-help efforts. You may think your negative thoughts and feelings are shameful or foolish. Paradoxically, this attitude may bring about the disapproval you're trying so hard to prevent. Since your therapist's primary job is to help you design and carry out a self-help program that will help you get in better control of your life, s/he might feel frustrated about your unwillingness to try to help yourself. This could make you feel disapproved of and then you will feel even less like trying to help yourself.

This problem or attitude describes me:

☐ Not at all   ☐ Somewhat   ☐ Moderately   ☐ A lot

4. *Putting the Cart before the Horse.* You may have the erroneous belief that motivation comes before effective action, so you wait around until you *feel* like doing something. Since the motivation doesn't come you end up doing nothing.

Actually, action must frequently precede motivation. Since depressed people often feel lethargic and unmotivated, you may have to make a decision to do something constructive *whether or not* you feel like it. Once you get started you will often feel more motivated. This, in turn, can make you feel like doing even more.

This problem or attitude describes me:

☐ Not at all   ☐ Somewhat   ☐ Moderately   ☐ A lot

5. *Unexpressed Anger.* You may resent something your therapist said or did or react negatively to his or her personality. Instead of expressing these feelings in a direct and open fashion, you may express them indirectly—by canceling sessions at the last minute, by being argumentative, or by not completing self-help assignments. This can make the feelings of tension worse and you may eventually drop out of treatment entirely.

This problem or attitude describes me:

☐ Not at all   ☐ Somewhat   ☐ Moderately   ☐ A lot

6. *Hopelessness.* One of the most painful aspects of depression and anxiety is the illogical sense of hopelessness that many patients experience. You may feel like your problems and suffering will go on forever no matter what. In spite of the fact that your therapist is convinced that your prognosis for recovery is excellent, you may feel hopeless and believe that all your efforts are pointless and doomed to failure. Then you give up and do nothing. Consequently, nothing changes. This reinforces the illusion that you're hopeless.

This problem or attitude describes me:

☐ Not at all   ☐ Somewhat   ☐ Moderately   ☐ A lot

7. Coercion Sensitivity.   You may at times feel like people are trying to *force* you to do various things. You may think your therapist or family members are being pushy or trying to control you. Consequently, you may dig in your heels and resist them because you don't want to give in. Then they get frustrated and put more pressure on you. You, in turn, feel stubborn and even more determined not to let them boss you around.

This problem or attitude describes me:
☐ Not at all   ☐ Somewhat   ☐ Moderately   ☐ At lot

8. Fatalism.   You may be convinced your moods are governed by forces that are beyond your control, such as hormones, drugs, biorhythms, fate, God, or the way other people treat you. Consequently there seems little point in trying to learn to master your moods. If you don't try, you may continue to feel bad. Then you'll conclude that you really can't control your feelings or solve your problems on your own.

This problem or attitude describes me:
☐ Not at all   ☐ Somewhat   ☐ Moderately   ☐ A lot

9. Fear of Blame.   Some people believe that if they accept the idea that they are responsible for their emotions, it follows that they will be *blamed* for them. Since they don't want to feel blamed they resist assuming any responsibility for their feelings and they refuse to do anything to help themselves. Paradoxically, others may get annoyed and blame them. Thus, the fear of being blamed often brings about the very blame they are trying to avoid.

This problem or attitude describes me:
☐ Not at all   ☐ Somewhat   ☐ Moderately   ☐ A lot

10. Internal versus External Expectations.   You may feel the need to meet the expectations of your parents, your spouse, your boss, and so on. You might base your self-esteem on the amount of praise or criticism you get. When you don't measure up to someone else's expectations, you might feel inadequate, resentful, or guilty. This can be so uncomfortable that it might seem preferable to adopt a low profile and do nothing at all. The less you do, the less you can be criticized for. You try to keep everybody's expectations low so no one will get their hopes up and be disappointed in you.

This problem or attitude describes me:
☐ Not at all   ☐ Somewhat   ☐ Moderately   ☐ A lot

11. Resistance to a Structured Fast-Acting Approach.   Some people feel that personal growth and insight must involve a long process of disclosing their feelings and childhood memories to a therapist over a period of years. The idea of trying to solve your problems in a short period of time using a structured training program may strike you as gimmicky and superficial. You may tend to write off therapies which focus on the here-and-now as "fads" or as psychological Band-Aids rather than as new developments which could speed up recovery just as penicillin improved the treatment of pneumonia.

This problem or attitude describes me:
☐ Not at all   ☐ Somewhat   ☐ Moderately   ☐ A lot

12. Self-Labeling.   Some people justify putting things off because they think of themselves as "lazy" or they call themselves "procrastinators." These labels set up the expectation that you must necessarily continue to be unproductive because of a deeply ingrained and irreversible aspect of your personality. You may even find that your family and friends buy into the ineffectual, helpless role you play. During a marital therapy session, a severely depressed woman announced: "I think I need a cigarette." Her obedient husband immediately picked up her pack of cigarettes from the table, took one of them out, placed it in her mouth, and lit it for her. His behavior rewarded her for acting like she couldn't do anything for herself and had to be waited on.

This problem or attitude describes me:
☐ Not at all   ☐ Somewhat   ☐ Moderately   ☐ A lot

13. *Different Priorities.* Some people are genuinely overcommitted and either forget to do their self-help assignments or they feel that they can't budget any time for them. They may feel overwhelmed and believe that the exercises the therapist suggests will only add to their burden instead of helping them solve their problems. You and your therapist may also have different ideas about what you should work on each session. If you don't set an agenda and tell the therapist the problems that are the most important to you, you may end up feeling controlled and taken advantage of. You may begin to feel like a "victim" and see your therapist as self-centered or insensitive to your needs.

This problem or attitude describes me:
☐ Not at all   ☐ Somewhat   ☐ Moderately   ☐ A lot

14. *Entitlement.* Some people feel they're entitled to happiness and fair treatment from others. They deeply resent the implication they are responsible for the way they feel and that they must put out energy and hard work to improve a difficult situation. They often have the attitude that they feel bad because other people don't treat them right. They resist personal change because it seems "unfair" that *they* should have to put out any effort to feel better. As one woman put it, "Why should *I* have to change? My husband is the one making me miserable!

This problem or attitude describes me:
☐ Not at all   ☐ Somewhat   ☐ Moderately   ☐ A lot

15. *Fear of Change.* Some people, in spite of their misery, fantasize that any change in the status quo might be even worse. The anxiety associated with change appears so great that the current painful state of affairs seems preferable. They may be afraid of rejection, failure, or success. They might feel that their personal identity depends on being depressed, angry or inadequate so they are reluctant to give up their symptoms for fear of being untrue to themselves.

This problem or attitude describes me:
☐ Not at all   ☐ Somewhat   ☐ Moderately   ☐ A lot

16. *Miscommunication.* Your therapist may not have explained the importance of self-help assignments or spelled out the rationale for the particular approach he or she is advocating. As a consumer, it is your right to request this information so you can make an enlightened decision about getting actively involved. If you are in the dark, ask your therapist to illuminate you!

This problem or attitude describes me:
☐ Not at all   ☐ Somewhat   ☐ Moderately   ☐ A lot

17. *Shame.* You may have a number of painful feelings and problems that you find it difficult to share with your therapist, such as alcoholism, a sexual indiscretion, or an angry reaction to something the therapist said. Since this may be what's bothering you the most, the self-help assignments the therapist suggests may not seem relevant to you.

This problem or attitude describes me:
☐ Not at all   ☐ Somewhat   ☐ Moderately   ☐ A lot

18. Emotional Reasoning.   This is one of the commonest distortions that can undermine your self-help efforts. You might reason: "I feel worse, therefore, I must not be getting anywhere in my therapy." You might also tell yourself, "I *feel* hopeless, therefore, I must *be* hopeless." The tendency to reason from the way you feel can be quite unrealistic and self-defeating because your emotions will often result from distorted thoughts that have no more validity than the grotesque images in the curved mirrors at an amusement park. Virtually all patients have setbacks and feel hopeless or unmotivated at times, but this doesn't mean they can't improve.

This problem or attitude describes me:
☐ Not at all   ☐ Somewhat   ☐ Moderately   ☐ A lot

19. Low Frustration Tolerance.   Many individuals find it difficult to stick with a task if they don't get immediate results, if they reach a plateau, or if they experience a setback. Since a number of ups and downs are an inevitable part of treatment or practically any activity, it would be to your advantage to learn to increase your frustration tolerance so that you can have the persistence required for optimal results.

This problem or attitude describes me:
☐ Not at all   ☐ Somewhat   ☐ Moderately   ☐ A lot

20. Superman/Superwoman.   You may feel the urge to do everything entirely on your own or else it means that you're "weak" or "inferior." If your therapist tries to help you, you may feel the urge to resist and come up with something entirely different that you alone thought of. This is just as illogical as going to a tennis coach and then refusing to follow through on his suggestions. If you insist on hitting the ball in your own way your style may be quite original, but you may not win as many matches!

This problem or attitude describes me:
☐ Not at all   ☐ Somewhat   ☐ Moderately   ☐ A lot

21. Rapid Improvement.   Feeling suddenly better is a common reason for avoiding self-help assignments and for terminating your treatment prematurely. When your depression lifts, the contrast with previous feelings of hopelessness and despair can be so profound that some clients conclude: "Hey, I'm okay now. I feel *great*! There's no need in going on with further therapy."

The problem is that there is a difference between *getting* better and *feeling* better. Even after you've experienced a dramatic improvement in the way you feel, you can still be vulnerable to bouts of depression or anxiety in the future. It can be helpful to work on these ahead of time instead of dropping out of therapy prematurely. It ordinarily requires *at least* 15 to 20 therapy sessions to learn to identify and restructure the attitudes and behavior patterns which lead to anxiety and depression. Unless this is accomplished, there is a significant chance your emotional difficulties will recur.

This problem or attitude describes me:
☐ Not at all   ☐ Somewhat   ☐ Moderately   ☐ A lot

22. Lack of Direction.   During periods of depression, some individuals experience slowed thinking and have difficulty concentrating. At these times you may have trouble defining your problems and find it difficult to identify your negative thoughts and feelings or to think of anything positive to do to help yourself.

This problem or attitude describes me:

☐ Not at all   ☐ Somewhat   ☐ Moderately   ☐ A lot

23. Conflict.   A good working relationship with your therapist is crucial to successful treatment. Sometimes a conflict will come up and you will begin to feel resentful, disappointed, guilty, or mistrustful. If these emotions are not adequately aired, they can undermine your therapy. In contrast, if you make a point of sharing them with your therapist, considerable benefit can result. It can be useful to take some time toward the beginning and end of each session to review and discuss anything your therapist did or said that might have rubbed your the wrong way. It's quite possible your therapist made a mistake or that you are misinterpreting something he or she said. Either way, there can be a benefit in airing these feelings so you can develop a good working relationship.

This problem or attitude describes me:

☐ Not at all   ☐ Somewhat   ☐ Moderately   ☐ A lot

24. The "Realism" of Depression.   Some people who are depressed are reluctant to work at getting better because they are convinced their problems are *real* and their misery is inevitable. They may feel there's no point in writing down their negative thoughts or trying to think more positively because this means ignoring reality or getting involved in the "Power of Positive Thinking."

This problem or attitude describes me:

☐ Not at all   ☐ Somewhat   ☐ Moderately   ☐ A lot

25. Reluctance to Give up Negative Feelings.   Some people are reluctant to give up feelings of anger, guilt, depression, or anxiety because they feel these emotions are healthy, appropriate, or beneficial to them. A psychologist who was petrified by the fear of failing her licensing examination didn't want to give up worrying because she was convinced it was helping her in some way, even though she was so nervous that she couldn't study. A woman who was considering separating from her husband didn't want to give up her anger, depression, and suicidal urges because she was afraid she'd get complacent and stuck in a bad marriage.

This problem or attitude describes me:

☐ Not at all   ☐ Somewhat   ☐ Moderately   ☐ A lot

26. The Medical Model.   If you go to a doctor because of a cough and a fever, you generally expect him to diagnose the cause and prescribe a treatment that will correct the problem. He may ask you to take an antibiotic and get plenty of bed rest, and the cure will usually take care of itself. When you have a personal problem such as depression or anxiety or a marital conflict, the expectation that your therapist will be responsible for solving the problem may actually make the situation worse. Your therapist can certainly help you pinpoint the causes of your problem and help you develop a step-by-step plan for solving it, but ultimately you will have to work actively between sessions to carry out that plan.

This problem or attitude describes me:

☐ Not at all   ☐ Somewhat   ☐ Moderately   ☐ A lot

27. Other.   Can you think of other specific attitudes or feelings you might have which might make you procrastinate or hold you back in your efforts to help yourself? If so, jot them down here so you can review them with your therapist: _____

_____

_____

References

Bandura, A. (1977). Self-efficacy: Toward a unifying theory of behavioral change. *Psychological Review, 84,* 191–215.

Beck, A. T. (1963). Thinking and depression. I. Idiosyncratic content and cognitive distortions. *Archives of General Psychiatry, 9,* 324–333.

Beck, A. T. (1964). Thinking and depression. II. Theory and Therapy. *Archives of General Psychiatry, 10,* 561–571.

Beck, A. T. (1967). *Depression: Clinical, experimental and theoretical aspects.* New York: Harper & Row.

Beck, A. T., Kovacs, M., & Weissman, A. (1975). Hopelessness and suicidal behavior: An overview. *Journal of the American Medical Association, 234,* 1146–1149.

Beck, A. T., Rush, A. J., Shaw, B. F., & Emery, G. (1979). *Cognitive therapy of depression.* New York: Guilford Press.

Blackburn, I. M., Bishop, S., Glen, A. I. M., Whalley, L. J., & Christie, J. E. (1981). The efficacy of cognitive therapy in depression: A treatment trial using cognitive therapy and pharmacotherapy, each alone and in combination. *British Journal of Psychiatry, 139,* 181–189.

Burns, D. D. (1980). *Feeling good: The new mood therapy.* New York: William Morrow (hardbound); New American Library (1981, paperback).

Burns, D. D. (1984). *Intimate connections.* New York: William Morrow.

Burns, D. D. (in press). *The feeling good workbook.* New York: New American Library.

Burns, D. D., & Epstein, N. (1983). Active and passive aggression: A cognitive approach. In R. D. Parsons & R. J. Wicks (Eds.), *Passive Aggressiveness: Research, theory and practice.* New York: Brunner/Mazel.

Burns, D. D., & Persons, J. (1982). Hope and hopelessness: A cognitive approach. In L. E. Abt & I. R. Stuart (Eds.), *The newer therapies: A sourcebook* (pp. 32–59). New York: Van Nostrand Reinhold.

Chesney, M., & Shelton, J. (1976). A comparison of muscle relaxation and electromyogram biofeedback treatments for muscle contraction headaches. *Behavior Therapy and Experimental Psychiatry, 7,* 221–226.

Dunlap, K. (1936). *Elements of psychology.* St. Louis, MO: C. V. Mosby.

Ellis, A. (1962). *Reason and emotion in psychotherapy.* Secaucus, NJ: Lyle Stuart.

Harmon, T. M., Nelson, R. O., & Hayes, S. C. (1980). Self-monitoring of mood versus activity by depressed clients. *Journal of Consulting and Clinical Psychology, 48,* 30–38.

Herzberg, A. (1941). Short treatment of neurosis by graduated tasks. *British Journal of Medical Psychology, 19,* 36–51.

Kanfer, F. H. (1970). Self-regulation: Research, issues, and speculations. In C.

Neuringer & J. L. Michael (Eds.), *Behavior modification in clinical psychology.* New York: Appleton Century-Crofts.

Kanfer, F., & Phillips, J. (1966). A survey of current behavior and a proposal for classification. *Archives of General Psychiatry, 15,* 114–128.

Karpman, B. (1949). Objective psychotherapy: Principles, methods, and results. *Journal of Clinical Psychology, 5,* 193–275.

Kazdin, A. E., & Mascitelli, S. (1982). Covert and overt rehearsal and homework practice in developing assertiveness. *Journal of Consulting and Clinical Psychology, 50,* 250–258.

Kelly, G. A. (1955). *The psychology of personal constructs.* New York: W. W. Norton.

Kopel, S., & Arkowitz, H. (1975). The role of attribution and self-perception in behavior change: Implications for behavior therapy. *Genetic Psychology Monographs, 92,* 175–212.

Kornblith, S. J., Rehm, L. P., O'Hara, M. W., & Lamparski, D. M. (in press). The contribution of self-reinforcement training and behavioral assignments to the efficacy of self-control therapy for depression. *Cognitive Therapy and Research.*

Kovacs, M. (1980). The efficacy of cognitive and behavior therapies for depression. *American Journal of Psychiatry, 137,* 1495–1501.

Lange, A., & Jakubowski, P. (1976). *Responsible assertive behavior: Cognitive-behavioral procedures for trainees.* Champaign, IL: Research Press.

Lewinsohn, P. M. (1974). Clinical and theoretical aspects of depression. In K. S. Calhoun, H. E. Adams, & K. M. Mitchell (Eds.), *Innovative treatment methods of psychopathology.* New York: John Wiley & Sons.

Masters, W., & Johnson, V. (1970). *Human sexual inadequacy.* Boston: Little, Brown.

Maultsby, M. C. (1971). Systematic written homework. *Psychotherapy: Theory, research, and practice, 8,* 195–198.

Moorey, S., & Burns, D. D. (1983). The apprenticeship model of cognitive therapy training. In A. Freeman (Ed.), *Cognitive therapy with couples and groups* (pp. 303–321). New York: Plenum Publishing.

Murphy, G. E., Simons, A. D., Wetzel, R. D., & Lustman, P. J. (1984). Cognitive and pharmacotherapy: Singly and together in the treatment of depression. *Archives of General Psychiatry, 41,* 33–41.

Persons, J., & Burns, D. (in press). Mechanisms of action of cognitive therapy: The relative contributions of technical and interpersonal interventions. *Cognitive Therapy and Research.*

Rehm, L. P. (1977). A self-control model of depression. *Behavior Therapy, 8,* 787–804.

Rush, A. J., Beck, A. T., Kovacs, M., & Hollon, S. (1977). Comparative efficacy of cognitive therapy and pharmacotherapy in the treatment of depressed outpatients. *Cognitive Therapy and Research, 1,* 17–37.

Salter, A. (1949). *Conditioned reflex therapy.* New York: Creative Age Press.

Shaw, B. (1977). Comparison of cognitive therapy and behavior therapy in the treatment of depression. *Journal of Consulting and Clinical Psychology, 45,* 543–551.

Shelton, J. (1975). The elimination of persistent stuttering by the use of home work assignments involving speech shadowing. *Behavior Therapy, 6,* 392–393.

Shelton, J., & Ackerman, J. M. (1974). *Homework in counseling and psychotherapy: Examples of systematic assignments for therapeutic use by mental health professionals.* Springfield, IL: Charles C. Thomas.

Shelton, J. L., & Levy, R. L. (1981). *Behavioral assignments and treatment compliance: A handbook of clinical strategies.* Champaign, IL: Research Press.

Teasdale, J. D., & Fogarty, S. J. (1979). Differential effects of induced mood on retrieval of pleasant and unpleasant events from episodic memory. *Journal of Abnormal Psychology, 88,* 248–257.

Wetzel, R. D. (1976). Hopelessness and suicidal intent. *Archives of General Psychiatry, 33,* 1069–1073.

Wetzel, R. D., Margolies, T. M., Davis, R., & Karm, E. (1980). Hopelessness, depression and suicidal intent. *Journal of Clinical Psychiatry, 41,* 159–160.

Zajonc, R. (1980). Feelings and thinking. *American Psychologist, 35,* 151–175.

Chapter 20

The Relationship of Depression to Other DSM-III *Axis I Disorders*

Laurent Lehmann

INTRODUCTION: THE NATURE OF DEPRESSION

The diagnostic and therapeutic implications of the coexistence of depression with other *DSM-III* Axis I disorders is the subject of this chapter. The occurrence of depression with other disorders should not be surprising given its ubiquitous presence in the normal.

In the 1980s, with the application of diagnosis-related group technology to the economic aspects of health care, the coexistence of disorders will acquire a new significance. Since such cases are more complicated, potentially generating higher costs and longer lengths of stay, it is likely that a new interest and study will arise in the area of "co-morbidity" in an effort to discover more efficient treatments.

Depression as an emotional state exists on a continuum from normal to pathological conditions. Its normative functions include serving as a form of nonverbal communication with others and, internally, acting as a stimulus to physiological arousal or withdrawal or for the initiation of psychological defenses (Klerman, 1980). As the depressive mood deepens, it becomes more pathological, yet in order to diagnose a depressive syndrome, additional features, a combination of psychological and somatic symptoms must be present. Pathological depression may exist as a symptom of another disorder or as a separate syndrome (Klerman, 1980).

The operational definition of depressive disorders has been established in the *DSM-III*, which provides two major innovations. First, *DSM-III* provides the definition of a mental disorder, identifying a pathological state as a syndrome associated with distress or disability due to behavioral, psychological, or biological dysfunction (American Psychiatric Association, 1980). Second, it helps, through specific diagnostic and exclusion criteria, to establish whether depression in a given case exists merely as a symptom or as a full syndrome, and if as a syndrome, then whether it is primary or secondary in relation to other disorders.

That issues of primary or secondary designation have not been fully resolved or may be subject to revision, rather than reflecting a defect in the current diagnostic system, suggests instead, a healthy capacity for growth and development (Spitzer & Williams, 1983).

The incidence of association between diagnosed depression and other disorders varies both with the disorders and the setting from which a sample is taken. A search of medical records of the Oklahoma City VA Medical Center for fiscal year 1982 revealed a total of 133 patients who had a depressive disorder as a primary, secondary, or tertiary diagnosis. Of these 23.3 percent (*n* = 31) had some other psychiatric diagnosis (exclusive of personality disorders). Of this group, 67.7 percent (21 of 31) had an alcohol-related diagnosis, most frequently alcohol dependence. This study reflects data recorded two years after *DSM-III* came into use in the VA system (G. Ward, personal communication, 1983).

DEPRESSION AND ANXIETY DISORDERS

Anxiety is a mood state which, like depression, is found in normal as well as pathological forms. While depressive disorders are often accompanied by anxiety, anxiety disorders are less commonly accompanied by depression (H. E. Lehmann, 1983). Leckman, Weissman, Merikangas, Pauls, & Prusoff (1983) reported a 58 percent incidence of anxiety symptoms meeting *DSM-III* criteria for agoraphobia, panic disorders, or generalized anxiety disorders in a group of depressed (by RDC criteria) probands. They suggested such patients had earlier onset of depression and a more severe degree of illness than depressed patients without associated anxiety symptoms.

In recent years, associations between anxiety disorders and depression have come under scrutiny because of success in treating previously refractory panic, phobic, and obsessional disorders with monoamine oxidase inhibitors (MAOI) and tricyclics which have been considered antidepressant medications. True depressive disorders do not respond to antianxiety treatments including anxiolytic medications and so it is important to correctly diagnose primary depressive disorders which may underlie symptoms of anxiety (H. E. Lehmann, 1983). Akiskal and Lemmi (1983) suggest that premorbid course holds the key to correct differential diagnosis. They note that anxiety states usually begin before age 40 and are characterized by a lifelong and continuous history of the tension-related complaints generally referred to as "neurotic." In contrast, depressive disorders tend to occur after age 40, and to be symptomatic episodically. Depressive disorders may also have the additional distinguishing features of positive family history of affective disease and abnormal responses on several biological tests for affective disease, such as shortened REM latency and nonsuppression of cortisol in the Dexamethasone Suppression Test (DST).

A significant incidence of depression in agoraphobics and in their first-degree relatives has been noted, suggesting a possible association between agoraphobia and depressive disorders (Munjack & Moss, 1981; Schapira, Kerr, & Roth, 1970). Other studies question this association, citing a low incidence of abnormal DST in patients with agoraphobia and panic disorder as well as response of panic and agoraphobic symptoms, but resistance of depressive features, to imipramine (Curtis, Cameron, & Nesse, 1982; Lieberman, Brenner, Lesser, Coccaro, Borenstein, & Kane, 1983; Nurnberg & Coccaro, 1982).

A close association has long been noted between depression and obsessions: compulsive and obsessional personality features were considered a characteristic of the prepsychotic personality of the involutional melancholic (Kolb, 1973). A study by Vaughn (1976) indicated that 31 percent of depressives with preexisting obsessional personalities manifested obsessions in a depressive episode while only 11 percent of depressives without obsessional personality developed obsessions when depressed. Gittleson (1966a, 1966b) in a series of studies, found that the presence of the phenomenon of obsessions during depressive episodes was related to an incidence of suicide attempts six and one half times less than that in depressed patients without obsessions. Gittleson did not speculate on why obsessions were "protective" except to note that this quality was related to the obsession remaining present throughout the course of the depressive episode and that it not develop into a delusion. The content of depressive obsessions had no effect on the suicide rate.

A broad range of antidepressant medications have recently been employed in an effort to control the symptoms of treatment-resistant obsessional disorders. Imipramine, MAOIs, and clomipramine have all been useful in relieving symptoms and improving patient functioning though not necessarily to the point of full recovery (Shader & Greenblatt, 1983; Thoren, Asberg, Cronholm, Jornestedt & Traskman, 1980). Once again, there is some question as to what this means about the pathophysiology of depressive and obsessional disorders. Thoren et al. (1980) showed a response to clomipramine whether patients had depressive features or not. Moreover, the DST is not particularly useful in predicting response of obsessional symptoms to clomipramine (Insel & Goodwin, 1983). At this time, it appears that antidepressant medications, though effective in controlling phobic, panic, and obsessional disorders, may do so by different mechanisms than those effective in depressive disorders.

Posttraumatic stress disorder (PTSD) includes features characteristic of depression among its diagnostic criteria: loss of interest, sleep disturbance, and survivor guilt (American Psychiatric Association, 1980). Walker (1982), reviewing the chemotherapy of Vietnam PTSD patients, states that "a high percentage" of patients who meet the criteria for PTSD also meet the criteria for major depression but he does not give any numbers. Friedman (1981), in a more general review of PTSD in Vietnam veterans, cites a higher incidence of depression in combat veterans. Helzer, Robins, & Davis (1976) reported that 18 percent of combat veterans had "probable depressive syndrome" (depressed mood and two associated symptoms) compared to only 5 percent of noncombat Vietnam veterans. That these symptoms can be chronic and derived from a variety of traumatic stressors is emphasized by Eaton and associates (Eaton, Sigal, & Weinfeld, 1982), who report a 48 percent incidence of depressive features in a sampling of Jewish Holocaust survivors some 30 years after the initial trauma.

Though depression is common to posttraumatic stress disorders, it is not considered to be a primary response to stress. Lesse (1982), in addressing this issue, notes anxiety as the initial response to stress in 80 percent of patients, with depression, which occurred in two thirds of patients, developing from a month to a year later. While his data is derived from psychotherapeutic investigations of an essentially nonmilitary population, the conclusions are consistent with the classification of PTSD with the anxiety disorders.

Antidepressant medications have been effective for PTSD patients, with tricyclics indicated particularly for those with typically endogenous depressive features, such as early morning awakening, anorexia, low energy, and decreased libido (Walker, 1982). MAOIs, especially phenelzine, have been helpful with some PTSD patients who show the more typical features of anxiety, panic attacks, nightmares, and violence. Hogben and Cornfeld (1981) detail a time course of several weeks for improvement with a characteristic pattern shown by all five patients in their series, of responses which include release of emotions in a manner beneficial to psychotherapeutic exploration. Unfortunately, the total number of patients reported in these studies is small and no information is given on any correlation of platelet MAO activity with clinical response.

Another topic for potential research in the area of PTSD is the correlation of clinical symptoms and response to medications with biological markers. There are discrepancies between the results of studies in REM latencies in U.S. and Israeli PTSD patients. Studies in the United States report shortened REM latencies, characteristic of depression, whereas the Israelis have found an increase in REM latency (Friedman, 1981).

DEPRESSION AND SCHIZOPHRENIA

One of the major results of the *DSM-III* diagnostic system has been the narrowing of the criteria for schizophrenia and the consequent broadening of the criteria for affective disorders. This change has been reinforced by the recent revision of the "decision tree" for psychotic diagnosis published in the third and subsequent printing of *DSM-III*, which requires a decision to be made about the presence or absence of affective disorder before a decision about relative prominence of psychotic (i.e., thought disorder) features. Only a decision ruling out organicity takes precedence (Spitzer, Williams, & Wynne, 1983a).

This major shift in diagnostic criteria moves the American diagnosis of schizophrenia away from the broader Bleulerian form, which might well include many affective features within diagnostic features of schizophrenia, toward the narrower Kraeplinian concept of schizophrenia preferred in Europe. The effects are reflected not only in the criteria for schizophrenia, but also in the criteria for affective disorders, in that *DSM-III* affective disorders may manifest formal thought disorder in terms of Schneiderian first-rank symptoms (Andreason & Akiskal, 1983; Stephens, 1978).

One must now be cautious in reading the pre-*DSM-III* literature on schizophrenia. For example, it is questionable how many of the "good prognosis" or "remitting" schizophrenics diagnosed prior to *DSM-III* in fact suffered from affective disorders (Fowler, 1978). A benefit of this shift in diagnosis is likely to be that formerly misdiagnosed affective disorder patients will now be successfully treated through antidepressants or lithium. Decreased neuroleptic usage and thus decreased overall risk of tardive dyskinesia should be another benefit associated with this change. One may also question, however, what percentage of "good prognosis schizophrenics" will become "poor prognosis affective disorders" because of the disabling affects of first-rank symptoms.

What can be said about the relationship of depression to schizophrenia in *DSM-III*? Some symptoms found in depressive disorders have been considered characteristic of schizophrenia as well. These negative symptoms of schizophrenia (flat affect, self-neglect, motor slowness), since they are used to diagnose schizophrenia, cannot be invoked to diagnose concurrent depression in the same patient. Excluding such negative symptoms, some studies, not all of them antedating *DSM-III*, suggest that depression can be found in schizophrenia. These reports by Knights and Hirsch (1981), Shanfield et al. (Shanfield, Tucker, Harrow, & Detre, 1970), and detailed studies by Planansky and Johnston (1971, 1973, 1978) suggest that certain depressive features may be an integral part of schizophrenia. Planansky and Johnston (1978) report depressive feelings of guilt and worthlessness in 57 percent of a group of 115 schizophrenics. They describe schizophrenic depression as phenomenologically and qualitatively different from affective depression, with schizophrenic depression characterized by global feelings of helplessness and impotence stemming from the psychotic disintegration of the personality.

It has been suggested that depression in schizophrenia may be secondary to treatment with neuroleptics. However, a specific test of this theory actually revealed an increase in depressive symptoms when neuroleptics are withdrawn (Wistedt & Palmstierna, 1983).

Another aspect of depression in schizophrenia is the phenomenon of postpsychotic depression "manifested by depressive affect . . . following remission of more florid psychotic symptoms" (McGlashan, 1976). McGlashan (1976) makes clear that postpsychotic depression is a complete depressive syndrome, including guilt feelings and vegetative signs. Incidence is variably reported in from 9–25 percent of patients. The patients' self-perceptions of being helpless, incompetent, and defective, are similar to Planansky and Johnston's descriptions cited above (Kendler & Hays, 1983; McGlashan, 1976). The etiology of postpsychotic depression has been considered by Planansky and Johnston (1978) as an extension of the depression of schizophrenia, and by Wildroe (1966) as a reaction to the patients' awareness of their degree of regression during psychosis, or as a consequence of having to cope with life after discharge from a hospital (Miller & Sonnenberg, 1973). Response to antidepressants is equivocal and the recommended treatment is a patient and persistent supportive psychotherapeutic approach helping the depressive to understand and accept the fact of his/her psychosis (McGlashan, 1976).

One of the clinically salient questions concerning depression in schizophrenia is its relation to suicide in schizophrenics. Data suggest that the majority of suicides among VA patients are schizophrenic (Veterans Administration, 1978). That suicidal behavior in schizophrenics may occur as their psychosis is resolving is consistent with the preoccupation with death and suicide reported in postpsychotic depression. Focusing on suicide in schizophrenics, Planansky and Johnston (1971, 1973) noted a 25 percent incidence of suicide attempts in a group of 205 hospitalized schizophrenics. Seventy-one percent of these patients gave no warning before their first suicide attempt but of the three who completed suicide, all had made prior attempts. The majority of suicide attempts were clustered in time, suggesting phases of suicidality which might last for months. Only 15.4 percent of the suicide attempters gave a depressive theme (feelings of guilt and worthlessness) as the reason for their suicidal behavior. Sixty percent of attempters related their suicidal behavior to an "alien" compulsion. It appears from this data that suicide could result from other aspects of schizophrenia than its depressive features, but this is clearly an area that requires further research.

In summary, despite the narrowing of the diagnosis of schizophrenia, depression is still a common coexistent symptom; one which is often resistant to antidepressant medications, though it may respond to neuroleptics and psychotherapy. The clinician must remain alert to the potential danger of suicide in the resolution, as well as in the acute phases, of a psychotic episode.

DEPRESSION AND SCHIZOAFFECTIVE DISORDER

The diagnosis of schizoaffective disorder is a diagnosis in transition, reflecting the above-noted changes in the overall concept of schizophrenia from a more global, to a more limited role in *DSM-III*. It is felt that many of the cases diagnosed before *DSM-III* as schizoaffective showed a greater affinity, by clinical signs, family history, and follow-up data, to the affective than to the schizophrenic disorders (Dunner & Rosenthal, 1979). Guze (1980) suggests that even *DSM-III* diagnosed schizoaffectives may, when followed over time, be found to represent atypical affective disorders. The frequency of change in diagnostic features manifested by patients over time is minimal, as reflected in a study by Tsuang et al. (Tsuang, Woolson, Winokur, & Crowe, 1981). They reported on 30- to 40-year follow-up of 525 patients and found only a 3.4 percent incidence of change in diagnosis from schizophrenia to affective disorder.

The possibility exists of a distinct entity of schizoaffective disorder which, in recurrent episodes, manifests similar and unique schizoaffective pathological signs. Spitzer and associates (Spitzer, Williams, & Wynne, 1983) have recently clarified the instances in which schizoaffective disorder should be diagnosed. These include: when psychotic symptoms persist after resolution of an affective syndrome; when it is unclear if affective symptoms appeared before psychotic symptoms; or when it is unclear whether affective symptoms were of brief duration compared to psychotic symptoms.

The treatment of schizoaffective disorder may be successful when neuroleptics are combined with antidepressants, or it may respond to the combination of neuroleptics and lithium. Electroconvulsive therapy (ECT) may be helpful in some cases (Guze, 1980).

In an effort to further define the entity of schizoaffective disorder, patients meeting these criteria can be followed longitudinally and monitored for changes in clinical presentation. Their family histories, particularly with regard to schizophrenic, affective or schizoaffective disorder can be elucidated to see if they will show the previously suggested link to affective disorder. Research involving schizoaffective patients and their relatives should also include examination for the presence of various biological markers of affective or schizophrenic disorder. Studies of platelet MAO levels suggest that schizoaffective patients may have higher platelet MAO level than either chronic schizophrenics, or bipolar or unipolar depressives (Schildkraut, Orsulak, Schatzberg, Cole, Gudeman, & Rohde, 1978). Newer research tools, such as nuclear magnetic resonance (NMR) and brain electrical activity mapping (BEAM), designed to identify physiological characteristics of psychiatric disorders will help to clarify the nature of schizoaffective disorder once groups of affective disordered and schizophrenic patients, large enough for statistical comparison have been studied (Brownell, Budinger, Lauterbur, & McGeer, 1982; Morihisa, Duffy, & Wyatt, 1983).

To summarize: we are not sure of the degree to which schizoaffective disorder is truly a separate entity. A research program such as outlined above should help resolve this uncertainty.

DEPRESSION AND PARANOID DISORDERS

It has long been clinically observed that paranoid features may be found in depression. Freedman and Schwab (1978) reported that 25 percent of patients on a psychiatric unit with paranoid ideation had affective disorders including manic-depression, involutional melancholia, and psychotic depression. Paranoid delusions can also be a major feature of depression in older age-groups (Post, 1980; Ward, Strauss & Ries, 1982). In the geriatric population, there is an increased incidence of false positive DSTs in nondepressed patients (H.E. Lehmann, 1982). It is recommended, when making the differential diagnosis between a paranoid and a depressive disorder in this age-group, to base the diagnosis of depression on the concurrence of multiple factors including prior history of depression, the presence of vegetative signs of depression and the agreement of several biological markers of depression such as DST, REM latency or TRH stimulation rather than relying on just one test (Ward et al., 1982). Another possible biological marker may be differences in EEG recording from right and left cerebral hemispheres. It has been reported that depressed patients show right hemisphere changes whereas cognitively disordered patients (paranoids, obsessive-compulsives) show predominant left hemisphere changes and that in each case the changes resolved with successful treatment. The results are not consistent, as shown by Rochford and associates (Rochford, Weinapple, & Goldstein, 1981) who found it easier to differentiate paranoids from normals than to differentiate paranoids from depressives based on hemispheric EEG recordings in adolescents.

Additional links between paranoid and affective disorders include the onset of both types of disorders in middle to late life and recent reports of responsiveness of paranoid disorders to antidepressants (Akiskal, Arana, Baldessarini, & Barreira, 1983; Kendler, 1982; Sheehy, 1983). These findings suggest a common underlying pathophysiology for at least some paranoid disorders and depression. Rudden et al. (Rudden, Sweeney, Francis, & Gilmore, 1983) note a significant incidence of depressive features in women suffering from erotomanic, heterosexual delusions, which Spitzer et al. (Spitzer, Williams, & Wynne, 1983) imply may be included as a variant of paranoid disorder in future revisions of *DSM-III*.

DEPRESSION AND SUBSTANCE USE DISORDERS

Depression is considered the most common condition found in association with alcoholism (Cadoret & Winokur, 1974). Reported rates of a depressive syndrome in alcoholism vary from 28 percent (G. Winokur, 1972) to 59 percent (Pottenger, McKernan, Patrie, Weissman, Ruben, & Newberry, 1978). The Oklahoma City VA Medical Center record review cited earlier found even higher rates of depressive symptoms (G. Ward, personal communication, 1983). Fifteen percent of female alcoholics and 5 percent of males can be diagnosed as having primary affective disorders: those in which the onset of depression antedates that of alcohol abuse and whose course and responses to treatment more closely approximate those of affective disorders than alcoholism (Schuckit, 1983b).

The increased incidence of depression in alcoholics over that in normals is explained differently by various authors. Schuckit (1983b) notes that incidence of depression that will meet *DSM-III* symptom criteria for affective disorder recorded in the first weeks of treatment by alcoholics may be as high as 98 percent, but that this reflects a response to the realistic stressors and losses that overwhelm the alcoholic and drive him/her to seek treatment. He suggests that, though this form of depression is serious and may include suicidal behaviors, it usually resolves with several days to two weeks of abstinence. The possibility of the physiological effects of alcohol causing alcoholic depression has been entertained, but most studies reject this theory for a variety of reasons including the multiplicity of depressive criteria met by these patients (Pottenger et al., 1978).

Winokur and associates (Winokur, Cadoret, Dorzab, & Baker, 1971) have proposed that there may be a genetic linkage between depression and alcoholism. They have proposed that "depressive-spectrum disorder" is characterized by chronic low-grade depression, and that it is less severe than "familial pure depression" in that there are fewer recurrences. Depressive-spectrum patients are said to have a high incidence of alcoholics among their first-degree relatives as opposed to the affective disorders found in relatives of familial pure depressives. In addition, depressive-spectrum patients tend not to show abnormal lack of suppression on the DST characteristic of familial pure depressives. Depressive-spectrum patients respond to ECT or to serotinergic antidepressants as opposed to noradrenergic ones (Van Valkenburg & Winokur, 1979). This group may correspond to Akiskal's (1983) "character-spectrum" dysthymic disorders who show high rates of alcohol and drug abuse in probands and family but lack biological markers or family history of depression and are generally poor responders to tricyclics or MAOIs.

The coexistence of depression in alcohol abusers is clearly a poor prognostic sign. There is a higher incidence of depression in alcohol abusers who have relapsed, though some component of this may be secondary to relapse rather than responsible for it (Hatsukami & Pickens, 1982). In addition, there is a greater frequency of suicide attempts as well as a higher rate of completed suicide in depressed, as opposed to nondepressed, alcoholics (Berensohn & Resnick, 1974; Cadoret & Winokur, 1974). The alcoholic may attempt suicide at the onset of a drinking bout, as the alcohol level rises rapidly to an intoxicating level, or, after a prolonged period of drinking when he/she is isolated and in despair. Alcohol can serve either to bolster the courage of the suicide to carry out the act, or as the means of suicide in overdoses. Indeed, alcoholism has been considered a form of chronic suicide (Menninger, 1938).

What are the treatment implications of the coexistence of depression and alcohol abuse? Hamm, Major, and Brown (1979), in a study of active duty military personnel referred for alcohol treatment, found a low incidence of both depression and anxiety in their subjects. This sample was unique in view of the tight screening and identification programs for alcohol and drug abuse in the military and they suggest that civilian alcoholics may be driven to treatment by their affective disorder, while those without affective disorder may not come to treatment.

The commonly accepted treatment of alcoholism involves a multidisciplinary approach focusing on group therapy and group support of the Alcoholics Anonymous type. The emphasis is on practical resolution of problems rather than on the development of insight (Fox, 1967). As noted above, depression may resolve in the first several weeks of treatment, but this is not always the case. Pottenger, et al. (1978) reported on a group of outpatients, 59 percent of whom appeared clinically depressed at the onset of alcohol treatment, and in whom virtually no change in the depressive symptoms were found at one-year follow-up, even if their alcohol abuse was improved. Only 10 percent of these patients received antidepressants, however, it is not clear whether they received an adequate trial. Pharmacotherapy with antidepressants and/or lithium is indicated and effective in alcoholics with significant depressive disorder features, particularly if they show evidence of primary affective disorder (Pottenger et al., 1978; Schuckit, 1983b). Such evidence should include: currently meeting criteria for depressive disorder, depression antedating alcoholism, positive family history of affective disorder, and positive biological tests for depressive disorder. The more depression-related factors are found, the greater the likelihood of good response to antidepressants.

This last point is of great significance when one notes the findings of REM latency, DST and TRH blunting studies in alcoholics. Abstinent alcoholics, challenged with ethanol and alcoholics in the first three weeks of abstinence show decreased REM latency which is considered a primary biological marker for depression (Mendelson, Gillin, & Wyatt, 1977; Williams & Rundell, 1981). DSTs during alcohol withdrawal may be falsely positive, but they normalize with three to four weeks of abstinence. The DST is a good test for depressive disorder in alcoholics since it has no false positive from alcoholism alone. Those alcoholics with abnormal DSTs when abstinent meet *DSM-III* criteria for major depression (Kahn, Ciraulo, Nelson, Becker, Nies, & Jaffe, 1984; Newsom & Murray, 1983). TRH blunting, however, appears to be strongly influenced by alcoholism alone. A study by Dackis et al. (Dackis, Bailey, Pottash, Stuckey, Extein, & Gold, 1984), using nondepressed alcoholics noted 53.3 percent of alcoholics in withdrawal to have TRH blunting, with 25 percent still showing TRH blunting after three weeks of sobriety. These findings are believed to reflect the effect of alcohol on the hypothalamic-pituitary-adrenal axis.

Unfortunately alcoholics tend to be medication noncompliant, and most antidepressants have significant potential lethality in overdoses. Additionally as Akiskal's and Winokur's previously cited work suggest, a cohort of these persistently depressed alcoholics may remain unresponsive to pharmacotherapeutic approaches (Akiskal, 1983; Van Valkenburg & Winokur, 1979). The dysthymic characteristics of these patients, and in particular their attitudinal components of pessimism and passivity, suggest that cognitive behavior therapy, which has shown significant results in the treatment of depression, might be indicated for these patients (Beck, 1976). This idea is reinforced by a study of the biological and adoptive parents of patients with affective disease or substance abuse. The study suggested that nongenetic factors such as cognitive styles of self-assessment (e.g., negative self-appraisal), acquired in childhood from the family environment, may influence the incidence of depression and substance abuse in patients (VonKnorring, Cloninger Bohman, & Sigvardsson, 1983). Reviewing the health records of 115 adoptees with affective disorder or substance abuse and comparing them with the records of their biological and adoptive parents, Von Knorring et al. (1983) found no significant concordance between specific diagnoses of biological parents and adopted away children. There was a fivefold excess of psychiatrically ill adoptive fathers, as compared with controls, found among psychiatrically ill adoptees. Most of the ill fathers had affective disorders. The children in these adoptive families were treated before the ill parents began treatment and father's diagnosis had no relation to the diagnosis of the child. This suggested to the authors a cultural inheritance of a parental attitudinal set which influenced vulnerability to illness or treatment seeking, rather than imitative illness behavior on the part of the impaired adoptees.

Depressed alcoholics have a greater tendency than nondepressed alcoholics to abuse other drugs in addition to alcohol (Schuckit, 1983a). Twenty-five to 33 percent of opiate addicts entering treatment are clinically depressed (Steer, Emery & Beck, 1980). The symptom pattern of these patients is similar to that of depressed alcoholics, with a chronic, low level of depressive symptoms punctuated by exacerbations when stressed. These exacerbations of depressive symptoms may lead to admission to treatment programs (Rounsaville, Weissman, Crits-Christoph, Wilber, & Kleber, 1982).

Again, as with alcoholics, depressed drug abusers often appear to be self-medicating to relieve dysphoric symptoms with their preferred drug of abuse (Fox, 1967; Steer et al., 1980). The catecholamine hypothesis of depression links low levels of catecholamines with depressed states. As it has been suggested that catecholamines may be decreased in opiate withdrawal, one can picture the opiate addict as trapped between the depression associated with sedative drug effects and that associated with the chronic withdrawal most of them suffer (Woody, O'Brien, & Rickels, 1975). Stafford (1977) citing the work of Salzman (1973) notes that obsessive-compulsive personality features are common in addicts. Their drug abuse habit wrests control of their lives from them, and in response to this loss, they experience depression (Stafford, 1977). Thus, a combination of psychodynamic, environmental, and physiological stressors combine to make the drug abuser particularly vulnerable to depression.

Another viewpoint on the association of substance abuse and depression comes from a study designed to identify "hidden" substance abuse in patients admitted to a psychiatry service with other diagnoses. Fifty percent of these patients had substance problems serious enough to meet diagnostic criteria for substance abuse. While it is not surprising that patients of a given diagnosis were consistent in their choice of preferred drug of abuse, it is interesting to note that patients with depressive disorders had a high incidence of sedative (barbiturates, alcohol, heroin) abuse and a low incidence of amphetamine-hallucinogen abuse (McLellan & Druley, 1977). The authors speculated that such a finding is consistent with a monoamine balance theory of mental disorder, in which barbiturates and sedatives, reducing the functional availability of central nervous system (CNS) catecholamines, should be associated with depression. Similarly they found an association of amphetamine and hallucinogen abuse which should result in the release of CNS monoamines at synapses, in paranoid schizophrenics. This would seem to suggest that the drug of abuse might have some etiologic role in the development of depression in these substance abusers; a finding exactly opposite to the conclusions of Pottenger et al. (1978) with alcoholics as cited above.

Methadone maintenance is a common pharmacological approach to opiate addiction. While methadone itself lacks antidepressant properties, studies have indicated a response of addiction-associated depression to traditional antidepressants prescribed in conjunction with methadone maintenance (Rounsaville, et al., 1982; Woody et al., 1975). Sedative-hypnotic, psychostimulant, and polydrug abusers, because of generally more diverse and regressive psychopathology and lack of a specific antagonist, such as methadone or disulfiram to help control drug-seeking behavior, present more difficulties in treatment than "pure" narcotic or alcohol abusers (Stafford, 1977).

DEPRESSION AND EATING DISORDERS

Depressive disorders have long been associated with problems in eating: loss of appetite and weight loss or overeating with weight gain are among the vegetative signs incorporated in *DSM-III* diagnostic criteria for depression (American Psychiatric Association, 1980). Anorexia nervosa and bulimia are two of the eating disorders described in the *DSM-III* section on the disorders of infancy, childhood, and adolescence. While this chapter primarily addresses adult Axis I disorders, anorexia nervosa and bulimia will be discussed here because of their significant association with depressive disorders and their continuation into adult life.

Anorexia nervosa is characterized by a phobic avoidance of food with weight loss and a refusal to maintain normal body weight. This is associated with the distorted perception of increased body size. Anorectics may display a preoccupation with food and no true loss of appetite, though they resist eating, while depressives experience loss of appetite. Anorectics frequently engage in ritualized exercise regimens which differ from the disorganized agitation of depressives (Bruch, 1977; Halmi, 1980).

Despite these differences, there is a significant incidence of depressive features in anorexia nervosa including depressed mood, crying spells, and suicidal behavior. These depressive symptoms are found in the 10–15 percent of anorectics who are males as well as the females who comprise the majority of these patients (Andersen & Mickalide, 1983). Depression may be found premorbidly, but in follow-up studies, depression is the most commonly identified psychiatric problem with up to 30 percent incidence noted (Cantwell, Sturzenberger, Burroughs, Salkin & Green, 1977; Hsu, 1980). A high incidence of affective disorders is found in the families of anorectics. Winokur, March, and Mendels (1980) report that 76 percent of families with an anorectic proband had primary affective disease compared with 48 percent of control families (lacking an anorectic proband). This incidence of primary affective disorder in relatives of anorectics approximates the findings in family studies of primary affective disease probands. Though biological markers for depression have also been reported in anorexia nervosa, some studies note that DST nonsuppression and low levels of urinary MHPG may be found in nondepressed anorectics. However, these phenomena may be a function of disordered norepinephrine metabolism in anorexia nervosa, not a sign of association of anorexia nervosa with affective disorder (Gerner & Gwirtsman, 1981).

Bulimia has only recently come to be diagnosed as a disorder separate from anorexia nervosa. Defined as binge eating of large amounts of food in a short time with awareness by the eater of the abnormality of such behavior, bulimia actually includes depressed mood among the criteria for its diagnosis (American Psychiatric Association, 1980). Bulimia, most often manifested as binging followed by vomiting or purging, is found in up to 47 percent of anorexia nervosa patients (Casper, Eckert, Halmi, Goldberg, & Davis, 1980). Alcohol abuse, suicidal behavior, and kleptomania are found more frequently in anorectics with bulimia than in anorectics without this symptom. Consequently, bulimic anorectics have a poorer prognosis than nonbulimic anorectics (Casper et al., 1980; Garfinkel, Moldofsky, & Garner, 1980). Attempts to control eating impulses with subsequent failure may cause guilt and depression. This is similar to a pattern of cognitive issues associated with addictions (Fremouw & Heyneman, 1983). Biological markers for depression are also found in bulimic patients: Gwirtsman, and associates (Gwirtsman, Roy-Byrne, Yager, & Gerner, 1983) reported not only a 67 percent rate of abnormal DST but also 80 percent incidence of abnormal TRH tests in bulimic patients.

A major impetus for studies on the association of depression with anorexia nervosa and bulimia comes from the hope for improved treatment methods given the 5–21.5 percent mortality rate of anorexia nervosa (Halmi, 1980). Current treatment paradigms for anorexia nervosa include behavioral therapy in which reinforcers, such as increased activity, are made contingent upon weight gain, and family therapy (Agras & Kraemer, 1983; Liebman, Minuchin, & Baker, 1974). A cognitive behavioral approach reported by Fairburn (1983) addresses the attitudinal set of bulimic patients concerning weight and shape, as well as improving self-control. The negative self-evaluations and irrational beliefs of bulimics are similar to the rigid and irrational attitudes of depressives, and similarly, they are challenged and altered through cognitive restructuring. Though reporting only preliminary results on a small number of patients (n = 11), 81.8 percent showed a marked improvement, reducing binging and vomiting to once a month from an average of three times a day. This level of improvement, accompanied by decreased depression, anxiety, and attitudinal abnormalities toward eating was maintained in 63.6 percent of the total for a mean of 9.6 months follow-up.

A variety of antidepressants have been used successfully in anorectic and bulimic patients. Pope, et al. (Pope, Hudson, Jonas, & Yurgelum-Todd, 1983), reported moderate to marked improvement of bulimia and depression in 90 percent of a group of 22 bulimics in an open trial of imipramine, though only 35 percent showed full remission of binging. Hudson et al. (1983) were successful in treating bulimics with imipramine achieving 70 percent reduction in binging and 50 percent decrease in depressive symptoms. Other antidepressants including amitriptyline, nortriptyline, desipramine, trazadone, phenelzine, and tranylcypromine have also been found effective for anorectic and bulimic symptoms (Hudson et al., 1983; Moore, 1977; Walsh, Stewart, Wright, Harrison, Roose, & Glassman, 1982). The dosages and time course for improvement are consistent with those for the treatment of depression. The dietary restrictions required of patients on MAO inhibitors appear not to present a major contraindication to the use of these drugs in bulimics as binging consists primarily of high carbohydrate, rather than tyramine rich, food (Walsh, et al., 1982).

While antidepressants appear to produce significant improvements in otherwise resistant aspects of anorexia and bulimia, treatment outcomes are in most cases not full remissions. The treatment of choice appears to be a combination of behavioral and family-oriented psychotherapies with antidepressant medications. Long-term follow-up studies using the consistent diagnostic criteria, standardized symptom-rating scales and neuroendocrine testing will resolve unanswered questions about this group of disorders.

DEPRESSION AND ORGANIC MENTAL DISORDERS

Since the issue of substance-induced depression has been touched on in the section on "Depression and Substance Use Disorders," it will not be commented on here except to note that sedatives and opioids can induce depressed mood. Rather, the current section of this chapter will discuss the association of depression with the dementia and organic brain syndrome.

Cognitive impairment is common to the dementias and depression so the differential diagnosis of true dementia from depressive pseudodementia is crucial, especially in the geriatric population. The quality of cognitive deficits is different in depressed and demented patients, as may be noted in open clinical interview or in a structured interview, such as the mini-mental status. Depressives will give more negativistic, "I don't know" responses, due to a lack of motivation and their memory and cognitive complaints tend to be more global and nonspecific than patients with an "organic" dementia (LaRue, 1982; McAllister, 1983). Patients with an organic dementia will show disorientation, impairment in recent (as opposed to remote) memory and deficits in new learning, as well as a tendency to affective lability, all of which help to differentiate them from depressives (Sloane, 1980). Differential diagnosis is based on the history of present illness (sudden onset of symptoms being more characteristic of depression); family history and past psychiatric history of the patient (both checked for prior affective disorders which, if found suggest a present recurrence); and current clinical presentation checked for vegetative signs of depression and the above-noted cognitive features (H. E. Lehmann, 1982). The efficacy of biological markers such as the DST in making a differential diagnosis is unclear at present. While in some reports abnormal DSTs have resulted in the correct identification of depressed patients with significant cognitive impairment (McAllister, 1983; McAllister, Ferrell, Price, & Neville, 1982), others cite high cortisol levels in the elderly and abnormal DST responses in demented, nondepressed geriatric patients (Lehmann, 1982; Spar & Gerner, 1982). In cases where a definitive diagnosis cannot be made, a trial with an antidepressant with low cardiotoxicity may be indicated given the presence of depressive features. (Lehmann, 1982). Reifler, Larson, and Hanley (1982) have raised the issue of the coexistence of depression and dementia. Using Research Diagnostic Criteria for depression and a rating scale for dementia, they determined that 15 percent of their depressed patients with cognitive impairment had depression only, while 85 percent had mixed depression and dementia (usually an early form of Alzheimer's disease). They suggest that antidepressants may be helpful for patients with mixed depression and dementia, though the cognitive impairment remains.

Depressive syndromes can occur in organic brain syndromes secondary to the physiological effects of Axis III physical disorders. Thus, depression can arise from hypoxia or cerebral metastases or primary tumors, such as those of the temporal lobe (Katz, 1982; Hall, 1980). Though depressive disorders are common in the medically ill, particularly in cancer patients, one study reported 26 percent of cancer patients referred to a consultation liaison service misdiagnosed as depressed when they were, in fact, suffering from organic brain syndrome (Levine, Silberfarb, & Kipowski, 1978).

DEPRESSION AND SOMATOFORM DISORDERS

The somatoform disorders are those in which physical symptoms are presented by the patient without any demonstrable organic or physiological basis and which presumably derive from psychological factors. The expression of emotional distress through somatic complaints is common. Katon, Kleinman, and Rosen (1982) suggest that 26 percent of patients presenting to physicians with "medical" complaints have an underlying depression which if not promptly recognized may well develop into one of these somatoform disorders. It has been suggested that non-Western cultures may have a higher incidence of somatization of emotional distress: it is stated, for example, that the Chinese language does not have a word to express depression (Escobar, Gomez, Tuason, 1983; Katon et al., 1982). Other writers indicate that patients in Western industrialized nations are similarily impaired in their ability to express feelings with words instead of physical symptoms (Cadoret & Wilson, 1983; Lesse, 1967).

Somatization disorder, previously known as Briquet's syndrome, usually has an onset before age 30 and is characterized by recurrent, multiple, and variable physical complaints, often associated with depression (American Psychiatric Association, 1980). If such a symptom complex were to commence after age 40, the most likely diagnosis would be an affective disorder. When patients with somatization disorder become depressed, their symptoms are similar to patients with primary depression but their perception of the experience is different. Patients with primary affective disorder perceive their depression as a marked change from their usual feeling state (hence an episodic phenomenon), while patients with somatization disorder report the onset of depression as a worsening of their usual state of suffering. Often, treating the depression with antidepressant medications will result in at least temporary relief of somatic complaints as well (Murphy, 1982).

In conversion disorder there is loss or alteration of physical function, usually motor or sensory in nature, as a result of unresolved psychological conflict. Thirty-three to 50 percent of conversion disorders may be associated with other psychopathology, such as depression, schizophrenia, or personality disorders (Lazare, 1981). A further identification of conversion disorder with depression is found in work with children, in whom resolution of the conversion symptom may reveal an underlying depressive disorder. A report cited by Weller and Weller (1983) noted 85 percent of a sample of children with conversion disorder had a clinically depressed parent. The implication of this report is that, in children, conversion disorder may be secondary to a depressive disorder.

Hypochondriasis, the unrealistic preoccupation with having serious illness, is construed dynamically as a defense against either unacceptable feelings of anger, feelings of depression, guilt, and low self-esteem (Barsky & Klerman, 1983; Brown & Vaillant, 1981). Depression is common among hypochondriacs and some authors have gone so far as to suggest that clear signs of depression are a good prognostic sign in a disorder which is otherwise difficult to treat (Brink & Yesavage, 1982). Lesse (1967) points out, however, that if the depression underlying hypochondriacal complaints is not identified early in the clinical course, more overt manifestations of depression may occur. He cites a 42 percent incidence of suicidal preoccupations in his study of patients with hypochondriasis and psychosomatic disorders.

While depression is commonly associated with the other somatoform disorders discussed above, it is most closely identified with psychogenic pain disorder. Blumer and Heilbronn (1982) have proposed that this be considered a variant of the affective disorders. The incidence of pain complaints in depressive disorders is cited as 60 percent to 100 percent while the incidence of definite and probable depression, by Research Diagnostic Criteria, in pain patients is given as 64 percent (Blumer & Heilbronn, 1982; Kramlinger, Swanson, & Maruta, 1983). Fifty percent of a cohort of psychogenic pain patients with insomnia had the depressive biological markers of shortened REM latency and nonsuppressive DSTs (Blumer, Zenick, Heilbronn, & Roth, 1982). Elevated cerebral spinal fluid (CSF) endorphins are found in depressed and psychogenic pain patients, whereas decreased endorphin levels would be expected in pain of organic etiology (Blumer & Heilbronn, 1982; Webb, 1983). A study of the families of chronic pain patients revealed 65 percent to have a positive family history of "depressive-spectrum disorder" including depression, alcoholism, or sociopathy, in at least one first-degree relative. Fifty-four percent of the total patient group studied were clinically depressed, and in this group the incidence of depression in first-degree relatives was 71 percent (Schaffer, Donlon & Bittle, 1980). The evidence accumulated to date is not convincing enough to shift psychogenic pain disorder into the diagnostic category of affective diseases but the close association to major depression may be acknowledged in future revisions of the *DSM-III* (Spitzer & Williams, 1982).

The treatment of psychogenic pain disorder and its associated depression are related to conceptions of the dynamics of the disorder. First, it must be noted that psychogenic pain disorder is a chronic disorder. Acute pain is a sensory phenomenon with anxiety being the primary associated affect. Chronic pain is construed as a motivational-affective phenomenon, with depression the commonly associated affect (Webb, 1983). Individuals prone to psychogenic pain disorder are described as industrious, physically active individuals, not given to verbalizing their emotions. Both dependency needs and aggression are denied and love is gained by work and effort. A significant loss, particularly if associated with some form of injury, can provoke the response of pain disorder and marked depression. It is here that the motivational aspect comes to prominence, as the patients often seem to lose all initiative and lapse into an "excused" gratification of previously denied dependency and escape from stressful demands to produce (Blumer & Heilbronn, 1982).

The treatment of psychogenic pain disorder may include antidepressants, with best results if the patients show positive signs or family history of depression (Blumer & Heilbronn, 1982). The psychotherapy of psychogenic pain disorder most frequently involves a multimodal behavioral approach involving operant conditioning methods. Treatment goals usually involve increased activity level, decreased use of analgesics and anxiolytics, and increased ability to cope with any residual pain using relaxation or hypnotic techniques (Fordyce, 1976). Results of such treatment programs vary in relation to the degree to which entrance requirements select for positive features, such as motivation for change, and away from negative features, such as drug addiction and long history of pain (Flinn & Yung, 1982). Kramlinger and associates (Kramlinger, Swanson, & Maruta, 1983) reported on a pain management program at the Mayo Clinic. While finding a high incidence of depression in their patients, they noted an improvement in depression as well as in pain in 90 percent of the depressed patients without need for antidepressants.

DEPRESSION AND DISSOCIATIVE DISORDERS

Dissociative disorders are those in which there is an impairment in the integrated functioning of consciousness, identity, or motor behavior. Psychogenic amnesia, the loss of memory for brief or extensive periods of one's past, occurs in response to some overwhelming stressor such as loss of, or abandonment by, a loved one. A severe depressive disorder, may also result in amnesia (American Psychiatric Association, 1980; Nemiah, 1980). The more extensive memory impairment of psychogenic fugue, characterized by inability to recall one's previous identity and traveling to a new locale, can also be associated with depression resulting from object loss. In the author's clinical experience, he has noted that a victim of fugue may develop a major depression upon the recollection of previous memories of loss. It is possible that the dissociation served a defensive function, to ward off grief, guilt feelings, and depression.

Depression may be found as a feature of one or more alternative personalities in multiple personality disorder. Greaves (1980) and Hall, et al. (Hall, LeCann, Schoolar, 1978), who comment on this phenomenon, also note changes in handedness and in lateralization of EEG findings with alternating personalities. As noted above (Rochford et al., 1981), depressive disorders have been associated with lateralization of EEG abnormalities to the right hemisphere, whereas cognitive disorders tend to show left hemisphere abnormalities. No reports to date have studied lateralization of EEG in multiple personality disorders where depression is a feature of one of the personalities. Such a study could note whether right hemisphere abnormalities are present in the depressive but then normalize as the patient shifts out of the depressive personality. There have been studies associating multiple personality as well as other dissociative phenomena with temporal lobe lesions which, in turn, have been associated with depression (Schenck & Bear, 1981). This suggests a common physiological basis for some dissociative and depressive phenomena.

Depersonalization disorder can also have depression as an associated finding, but it appears to be a secondary phenomenon, reactive to the sense of estrangement of the self, rather than an etiological feature (L. S. Lehmann, 1974; Nemiah, 1980). The use of antidepressants in depersonalization disorder appears to relieve associated depression but leave the depersonalization untouched. Liebowitz, McGrath and Bush (1980) report two cases of depersonalized patients becoming manic when treated with antidepressants suggesting an underlying genotype of bipolar disorder. Both patients were ultimately stabilized with lithium, which controlled both the affective symptoms and depersonalization.

DEPRESSION AND PSYCHOSEXUAL DISORDERS

Gender identity disorders frequently have associated depression, which may be attributed to the dissonance between the anatomically assigned and desired sexual roles. Pursuing this theory, Hunt, Carr, and Hampson (1981) suggest that a relevant study would evaluate transsexuals before and after surgical alteration of gender to determine if, and to what degree, the depression common to gender dysphoria is ameliorated by the sex change. Morgan (1978) has addressed the need for psychotherapeutic support for those individuals who are rejected as candidates for transsexual surgery. He notes their anger and despair, particularly in situations where prolonged periods on estrogens have resulted in irreversible anatomic and physiologic changes such as breast enlargement and testicular atrophy. Suicide or self-mutiliation may be associated with depression in transsexuals (American Psychiatric Association, 1980).

The paraphilias are those disorders in which unusual imagery or acts are required to achieve sexual excitement. These disorders were previously called sexual deviations or perversions and, particularly in the psychoanalytic literature, were related to impulse control disorders (Fenichel, 1945). While paraphiliacs experience pleasure in their symptomatic behavior, many suffer a secondary depression with shame and guilt over their indulgence in actions which are socially condemned but which they feel powerless to control.

Blair and Lanyon (1981) reviewing treatments for exhibitionism, noted that most controlled studies in this area were behavioral in orientation, often employing convert sensitization, a technique of associating aversive images with descriptions of exhibitionist behavior. While this should be and is an effective technique, considering the importance of fantasy in maintaining exhibitionism, the reports cited describe the effects on the target symptoms but tend not to comment on the presence or absence of other behavioral or psychological effects. Marks, Gelder, and Bancroft (1970) provide a description of a treatment program which used aversive stimuli (electric shocks) paired with paraphiliac behavior and fantasies and give a two-year follow-up. Results were generally positive with four out of five sadomasochists teminating their paraphiliac behavior as did one half of the combined group of nine transvestites and three fetishists. The six who continued to indulge in their paraphilia did so with less frequency and less enjoyment. Of greatest interest was the lack of symptom substitution noted in the group. While depression was noted briefly during treatment in 8 of the total 24 patients, it resolved before the course of treatment was ended. Six patients who reported episodic depression prior to the treatment program continued to report the same level of affective symptoms during the follow-up period. While depression was clearly present in many of these patients, it was not worsened by the loss of paraphiliac symptoms. The greatest need for these patients seems to be the inclusion in the treatment program of specific training to develop heterosexual skills, in addition to the elimination of paraphiliac behaviors. Thus, these studies would not suggest that paraphilias are a defense against depression, but rather that depression may be a result of loss of self-esteem secondary to paraphiliac behaviors.

Depression is frequently found in association with psychosexual dysfunctions: as an etiologic agent (the decreased libido of depression may lead to sexual dysfunction particularly male erectile dysfunction and male and female orgastic disturbance (Kaplan, 1974). Depression may also be reactive secondary to sexual dysfunction. Maurice and Guze (1970) in a review of the psychiatric profiles of a group of 20 marital couples in Master's and Johnson's clinic found a low incidence of psychiatric disorders. Depressive disorders, however, were the most frequently reported, with six individuals having had definite depressive episodes and two others probable episodes, though all prior to their sex therapy. Kaplan (1974) notes that mild depression, reactive to sexual dysfunction, may improve with successful treatment of dysfunction. She cautioned, though, against engaging in sexual therapy while one or the other partner is significantly depressed, both because the depressed partner may not be able to participate actively and enthusiastically in therapy and because improvements in one partner's sexual dysfunction might aggravate the other partner's depression. She recommends, instead, treatment of the depression first and working on any residual psychosexual dysfunction later.

The emotional distress that is a requirement for the diagnosis of ego dystonic homosexuality is often expressed as depression. This depression should be expected to resolve with the assumption of a heterosexual lifestyle, either through the application of psychoanalysis or behavior therapy techniques (aversion, desensitization, and heterosexual skill training). Green's (1980) review of homosexuality suggests that these approaches have at most a 33 percent success rate with regard to sustained heterosexual reorientation. Recently, gay counseling programs have begun to help homosexuals adjust to homosexual orientation but outcome studies for such programs have not been reported in detail (Green, 1980).

While ego-dystonic homosexuality may lead to depression, a nonclinical sample of single male homosexuals showed the same prevalence of psychiatric disorders as did a nonclinical sample of single male heterosexuals. Although the rate of depression in the homosexuals (29 percent) was only slightly higher than the heterosexuals (26 percent), the homosexual depressives had a more severe form of depression, manifesting more suicidal behavior, more alcohol abuse, and more overall disability. The depressed homosexuals sought out medical help for depression more than did the heterosexuals (Saghir, Robins, Walbran, & Gentry, 1970). One possible reason for the homosexuals' greater severity of depression may be found in Siegel and Hoefer's (1981) observation that a surviving homosexual may be denied the customary rituals of grieving by their deceased partner's family. At the same time they may experience isolation from homosexual support groups who may display the same discomfort as do heterosexuals coping with a new widow or widower. It must be remembered that homosexual individuals suffering from major depressive disorders who develop shame and guilt over their sexual orientation are not classified as having ego dystonic homosexuality. They may be expected to continue their homosexual lifestyle upon the successful treatment of the depression.

DEPRESSION AND IMPULSE CONTROL DISORDERS

The impulse control disorders were originally studied by psychoanalysts who considered them to be pathological ways of defending against intrapsychic dangers including depression (Fenichel, 1945). *DSM-III* represents the first attempt to incorporate these disorders into the official psychiatric nomenclature.

Pathological gambling, perceived as a gratification of pregenital, aggressive, and sexual urges, has been closely linked by dynamic theorists to guilt and depression (Greenson, 1948; Winer & Pollock, 1980). These dysphoric affects may derive either from indulgence in forbidden pleasures or from the realistic consequences of the gambler's financial losses and associated social ruin. Part of the gambler's pathology is theorized to be a drive to experience punishing losses (Bolen & Boyd, 1968; Greenson, 1948; Winer & Pollock, 1980). Alcoholism is common in first-degree relatives of gamblers (American Psychiatric Association, 1980). This suggests a connection with the depressive-spectrum disorders.

Gamblers generally come to treatment only when forced to, or as a consequence of depression and suicidal attempts subsequent to overwhelming stressors such as loss of job and family (Bolen & Boyd, 1968). Psychoanalysis has been a successful treatment in a few instances but suffers many dropouts. Reasons for this include limited motivation (beyond satisfying whoever forced the gambler to enter therapy) and/or a desire for only temporary symptomatic relief as opposed to fundamental change in personality. Behavior therapy, particularly aversive techniques, can effectively curtail gambling on a short-term basis but for longer term results, the patient must be taught alternative modes of gratification and may require periodic "booster" treatments (Lester, 1980). Gamblers Anonymous, an organization that operates in a way similar to Alcoholics Anonymous, seeks to provide social and psychological group support for the gambler and his family. In concluding his review of treatments for gambling, Lester (1980) indicates that the influence of the gambler's spouse is crucial in determining the outcome of therapy. Boyd and Bolen (1970), whom Lester cites, describe marital therapy for gamblers, noting how, as the gambler/husband improves, becoming more assertive, less depressed and gambling less, the wife becomes depressed as she recognizes the gambling as a symptom of marital discord and understands her role in supporting it. Moskowitz (1980) has reported on the use of lithium in two compulsive gamblers. Both patients had at least one depressed parent; one patient became depressed when he abstained from gambling and the other was described as "reckless" and "euphoric." In both cases the gambling ceased as the affective, "thrill" component was blunted by lithium and no symptom substitution was noted.

Kleptomaniacs may suffer depression over the possibility or actuality of being caught. In addition, these persons may perceive themselves as deprived, and their stealing may serve to ward off or relieve depression (Winer, & Pollock, 1980; Kenyon, 1976). One reason for the dearth of good studies of kleptomania is the fact that many shoplifters may go unidentified. Although changes in nomenclature make comparison difficult, a study by Arieff and Bowie (1947) suggests an incidence of depressive disorders in shoplifters that might be as high as 24 percent but is probably less than 14 percent. Features of low self-esteem over loss of control in kleptomaniacs are similar to findings in addictions and some eating disorders. The association of kleptomania and bulimia has been noted above (Casper et al., 1980).

Not much has been written that would suggest an association between pyromania and depression, though a review by Bradford (1982) of psychopathology in arsonists indicates a 17.6 percent incidence of "depressive neurosis," suggesting this may be significant in female arsonists. Alcohol abuse is also high in arsonists, raising speculation about an association of pyromania with depressive spectrum disorder.

The explosive disorders are by definition "intermittent," a characteristic found in affective disorders. Appropriate guilt feelings or depression are often noted after the symptomatic violent behavior (Winer & Pollock, 1980). The existence of affective distress is a positive prognostic sign in violence-prone patients. It has been used as a criterion for participation in at least one treatment program for violent behavior, which emphasized the development of appropriate social skills in coping with provocation to violence (Frederiksen & Rainwater, 1981). Antidepressants and lithium have been used with success in a number of individuals with explosive disorder, though some of these may have had undiagnosed affective disorders (Sheard, 1975; Winer & Pollock, 1980).

CONCLUSION

Several themes have emerged from this review of depression's coexistence with other psychiatric disorders. The first is that depression can be a common accompaniment to most of the other Axis I diagnostic groups. Usually its appearance suggests a worsening of the clinical situation; for example, it may increase the risk of suicide. But this is not always the case. The dysphoria of depression may benefically drive the drug addict or gambler into treatment. It may be seen as a potentially good prognostic sign, in schizophrenia or hypochrondriasis. One may wonder in some cases if its presence is not viewed positively by the therapist because it gives him/her something to treat that is more responsive in the original illness. Hard data on the prognostic significance of depression coexisting with other disorders is lacking, though there have been some efforts in this regard, including Vaillant's (1964) study which noted that 77 percent of schizophrenic patients with depression as an admitting symptom had full remission of schizophrenic symptoms in a long-term outcome study.

The second major theme revolves around the apparent breakthroughs in the treatment of previously resistant disorders with "antidepressant" medications and forms of cognitive behavioral therapy, which came into prominence in the treatment of depressive disorders. Does this mean that the various obsessive, phobic, bulimic, or pain disorders represent hidden affective disorders and should be reclassified? This is probably not the case, nor has it been the purpose of this chapter to re-label everything as a variant of affective disorder. Rather, depression appears to have a significant co-morbidity with these disorders, one whose proper identification may speed the treatment and promote the overall well-being of the patient.

It would seem that there are three logical possibilities that would explain the coexistence of depression as a syndrome associated with other Axis I disorders. First, depression could underlie another Axis I disorder, psychologically or biologically. The association of depression with conversion disorder, cited by Weller and Weller (1983) could represent either of these possibilities. The concept of depressive-spectrum disorder, suggesting genetic associations between depression, alcoholism, and impulse control disorders implies a biological depressive etiology for these disorders. The second logical possibility is that depression could be the result of another Axis I disorder, either psychologically or biologically, as suggested by the concept of depression in schizophrenia elaborated by Planansky and Johnston (1978). The final logical possibility is that depression and another Axis I disorder could arise from the same etiology. This could be on a psychological basis, as suggested by VonKnorring (VonKnorring et al., 1983) in postulating a common cognitive style as a basis for substance abuse and depression. It could be on a biological basis as suggested by depression and dissociative phenomena being linked to temporal lobe lesions (Schenck & Bear, 1981). It is unclear at this time how definitive the placement of a given disorder into any one of these categories is. For example, depressive-spectrum disorder might represent depression underlying other Axis I disorders or a common etiology for depression and the other disorders. Only future research on the psychology and biology of depressive disorders will resolve these questions.

References

Agras, W. S., & Kraemer, H. C. (1983). The treatment of anorexia nervosa: Do different treatments have different outcomes? *Psychiatric Annals, 13*, 928–935.

Akiskal, H. S. (1983). Dysthymic disorder: Psychopathology of proposed chronic depressive subtypes. *American Journal of Psychiatry, 140*, 11–20.

Akiskal, H. S., Arana, G. W., Baldessarini, R. J., & Barreira, P. J. (1983). A clinical report of thymoleptic-responsive atypical paranoid psychoses. *American Journal of Psychiatry, 140*, 1187–1190.

Akiskal, H. S., & Lemmi, H. (1983). Clinical, neuroendocrine, and sleep EEG diagnosis of "unusual" affective presentations: A practical review. *Psychiatric Clinics of North America, 6*, 69–83.

American Psychiatric Association (1980). *Diagnostic and statistical manual of mental disorders* (3rd ed.). Washington, DC: Author.

Andersen, A. E., & Mickalide, A. D. (1983). Anorexia nervosa in the male: An underdiagnosed disorder. *Psychosomatics, 24*, 1066–1075.

Andreasen, N. C., & Akiskal, H. S. (1983). The specificity of Bleulerian and Schneiderian symptoms: A critical reevaluation. *Psychiatric Clinics of North America, 6*, 41–54.

Arieff, A. J., & Bowie, C. G. (1947). Some psychiatric aspects of shoplifting. *Journal of Clinical Psychopathology, 8*, 565–576.

Barsky, A. J., & Klerman, G. L. (1983). Overview: Hypochondriasis, bodily complaints, and somatic styles. *American Journal of Psychiatry, 140*, 273–283.

Beck, A. T. (1976). *Cognitive therapy and the emotional disorders.* New York: International Universities Press.

Berensohn, H. S., & Resnik, H. L. P. (1974). A jigger of alcohol, a dash of depression and bitters: A suicidal mix. *Annals of the New York Academy of Sciences, 233,* 40–46.

Blair, C. D., & Lanyon, R. I. (1981). Exhibitionism: Etiology and treatment. *Psychological Bulletin, 89,* 439–463.

Blumer, D., & Heilbronn, M. (1982). Chronic pain as a variant of depressive disease. *Journal of Nervous and Mental Disease, 170,* 381–406.

Blumer, D., Zenick, F., Heilbronn, M., & Roth, T. (1982). Biological markers for depression in chronic pain. *Journal of Nervous and Mental Disease, 170,* 425–428.

Bolen, D. W., & Boyd, W. H. (1968). Gambling and the gambler. *Archives of General Psychiatry, 18,* 617–630.

Boyd, W., & Bolen, D. (1970). The compulsive gambler and spouse in group psychotherapy. *International Journal of Group Psychotherapy, 20,* 77–90.

Bradford, J. M. W. (1982). Arson: A clinical study. *Canadian Journal of Psychiatry, 27,* 188–193.

Brink, T. L., & Yesavage, J. A. (1982). Somatoform disorders. *Postgraduate Medicine, 72,* 189–198.

Brown, H. N., & Vaillant, G. E. (1981). Hypochondriasis, *Archives of Internal Medicine, 141,* 723–726.

Brownell, G. L., Budinger, T. F., Lauterbur, P. C. & McGeer, P. L. (1982). Positron tomography and nuclear magnetic resonance imaging. *Science, 215,* 619–626.

Bruch, H. (1977). Depressive factors in adolescent eating disorders. In W. E. Fann, I. Keracan, A. D. Pokorny, & R. L. Williams (Eds.), *Phenomenology and treatment of depression.* (pp. 143–152) New York: Spectrum Publication.

Cadoret, R. J., & Wilson, D. (1983). Somatization among depressed patients in industrialized nations (letter). *American Journal of Psychiatry, 140,* 1103–1104.

Cadoret, R. J., & Winokur, G. (1974). Depression in alcoholism. *Annals of the New York Academy of Sciences, 233,* 34–39.

Cantwell, D. P., Sturzenberger, S., Burroughs, J., Salkin, B., & Green, J. K. (1977). Anorexia nervosa, an affective disorder. *Archives of General Psychiatry, 34,* 1087–1093.

Casper, R. C., Eckert, E. D., Halmi, K. A., Goldberg, S. C., & Davis, J. M. (1980). Bulimia. *Archives of General Psychiatry, 37,* 1030–1035.

Curtis, G. C., Cameron, O. G., & Nesse, R. D. (1982). The dexamethasone suppression in panic disorder and agoraphobia. *American Journal of Psychiatry, 139,* 1043–1046.

Dackis, C. A., Bailey, J., Pottash, A. L., Stuckey, R. F., Extein, I. L., & Gold, M. S. (1984). Specificity of the DST and the TRH test for major depression in alcoholics. *American Journal of Psychiatry, 141,* 680–683.

Dunner, D. L., & Rosenthal, N. E. (1979). Schizoaffective states. *Psychiatric Clinics of North America, 2,* 441–448.

Eaton, W. W., Sigal, J. J., & Weinfeld, M. (1982). Impairment in holocaust survivors after 33 years: Data from an unbiased community sample. *American Journal of Psychiatry, 139,* 773–777.

Escobar, J. I., Gomez, I., & Tuason, V. B. (1983). Depressive phenomena in North and South American patients. *American Journal of Psychiatry, 140,* 47–51.

Fairburn, C. G. (1983). Bulimia: Its epidemiology and management. *Psychiatric Annals, 13,* 953–961.

Fenichel, O. (1945). *The psychoanalytic theory of neurosis.* New York: W. W. Norton.

Flinn, D., & Yung, C. (1982). Pain treatment: Recent approaches. *Psychosomatics, 23,* 33–40.

Fordyce, W. E. (1976). Behavioral concepts in chronic pain and illness. In P. O. Davidson (Ed.), *The behavioral management of anxiety, depression and pain* (pp. 147–188). New York: Brunner/Mazel.

Fowler, R. C. (1978). Remitting schizophrenia as a variant of affective disorder. *Schizophrenia Bulletin, 4,* 68–77.

Fox, R. (1967). Alcoholism and reliance on drugs as depressive equivalent. *American Journal of Psychotherapy, 21,* 585–595.

Frederiksen, L. W., & Rainwater, N. (1981). Explosive behavior: A skill development approach to treatment. In R. B. Stuart (Ed.), *Violent behavior: Social learning approaches to prediction, management and treatment* (pp. 265–288). New York: Brunner/Mazel.

Freedman, R., & Schwab, P. J. (1978). Paranoid symptoms in patients on a general hospital psychiatric unit. *Archives of General Psychiatry, 35,* 387–390.

Fremouw, W. J., & Heyneman, N. E. (1983). Cognitive styles and bulimia, *The Behavior Therapist, 6,* 143–144.

Friedman, M. J. (1981). Post-Vietnam syndrome: Recognition and management. *Psychosomatics, 22,* 931–943.

Garfinkel, R. E., Moldofsky, H., & Garner, D. M. (1980). The heterogeneity of anorexia nervosa. *Archives of General Psychiatry, 37,* 1036–1040.

Gerner, R., & Gwirtsman, H. E. (1981). Abnormalities of DST and urinary MHPG in anorexia nervosa. *American Journal of Psychiatry, 138,* 650–653.

Gittleson, N. L. (1966a). The effect of obsessions in depressive psychosis. *British Journal of Psychiatry, 112,* 253–259.

Gittleson, N. L. (1966b). The fate of obsessions in depressive psychosis. *British Journal of Psychiatry, 112,* 705–708.

Greaves, G. B. (1980). Multiple personality 165 years after Mary Reynolds. *Journal of Nervous and Mental Disease 168,* 577–596.

Green, R. (1980). Homosexuality. In H. I. Kaplan, A. M. Freedman, & B. J. Sadock (Eds.), *Comprehensive textbook of psychiatry* (3rd ed; Vol. 2; pp. 1762–1770). Baltimore: Williams & Wilkins.

Greenson, R. (1948). On gambling. *Yearbook of psychoanalysis, 4,* 110–123.

Guze, S. B. (1980). Schizoaffective disorders. In H. I. Kaplan, A. M. Freedman, & B. S. Sadock (Eds.), *Comprehensive textbook of psychiatry* (3rd ed; Vol. 2; pp. 1301–1304). Baltimore: Williams & Wilkins.

Gwirtsman, H. E., Roy-Byrne, P., Yager, J., & Gerner, R. H. (1983). Neuroendocrine abnormalities in bulimia. *American Journal of Psychiatry, 140,* 559–563.

Hall, R. C. W. (1980). Depression. In R. C. W. Hall (Ed), *Psychiatric presentations of medical illness: Somatopsychic disorders* (pp 37–63). New York: Spectrum Publications.

Hall, R. C. W., LeCann, A. F., & Schoolar, J. C. (1978). Amobarbital treatment of multiple personality. *Journal of Nervous and Mental Disease, 116,* 666–670.

Halmi K. A. (1980). Anorexia nervosa. In H. I. Kaplan, A. M. Freedman & B. J. Sadock (Eds.), *Comprehensive textbook of psychiatry* (3rd ed; Vol. 2, pp 1882–1890). Baltimore: Williams & Wilkins.

Hamm, J. E., Major, L. F., & Brown, G. L. (1979). The quantitative measurement of depression and anxiety in male alcoholics. *American Journal of Psychiatry 136*(4B), 580–582.

Hatsukami, D., & Pickens, R. W. (1982). Post-treatment depression in an alcohol and drug abuse population. *American Journal of Psychiatry, 139,* 1563–1566.

Helzer, J. E., Robins, L. N., & Davis, D. H. (1976). Depressive disorders in Vietnam returnees. *Journal of Nervous and Mental Disorders, 163,* 177–185.

Hogben, G. L., & Cornfeld, R. B. (1981). Treatment of traumatic war neurosis with phenelzine. *Archives of General Psychiatry, 38,* 440–445.

Hsu, L. K. G. (1980). Outcome of anorexia nervosa. *Archives of General Psychiatry, 37,* 1041–1046.

Hudson, J. I., Pope, H. G., Jr., & Jonas, J. M. (1983). Treatment of bulimia with antidepressants: Theoretical considerations and clinical findings. *Psychiatric Annals, 13,* 965–969.

Hunt, D. D., Carr, J. E., & Hampson, J. L. (1981). Cognitive correlates of biological sex and gender identity in transsexualism. *Archives of Sexual Behavior, 10,* 65–77.

Insel, T. R., & Goodwin, F. K. (1983). The dexamethasone suppression test: Promises and problems of diagnostic laboratory tests in psychiatry. *Hospital and Community Psychiatry, 34,* 1131–1138.

Kaplan, H. S. (1974). *The new sex therapy.* New York: Brunner/Mazel.

Katon, W., Kleinman, A., & Rosen, G. (1982). Depression and somatization: A review, part I. *American Journal of Medicine, 72,* 127–135.

Katz, I. R. (1982). Is there a hypoxic affective syndrome? *Psychosomatics, 23,* 846–853.

Kendler, K. S. (1982). Demography of paranoid psychosis (delusional disorder). *Archives of General Psychiatry, 39,* 890–902.

Kendler, K. S., & Hays, P. (1983). Schizophrenia subdivided by the family history of affective disorder. *Archives of General Psychiatry, 40,* 951–955.

Kenyon, J. M. (1976). A special type of theft. *Ohio State Medical Journal, 72,* 227–229.

Khan, A., Ciraulo, D. A., Nelson, W. H., Becker, J. T., Nies, A., & Jaffe, J. H. (1984). Dexamethasone suppression test in recently detoxified alcoholics: Clinical implications. *Journal of Clinical Psychopharmacology, 4,* 94–97.

Klerman, G. L. (1980). Overview of affective disorders. In H. I. Kaplan, A. M. Freedman, & B. J. Sadock (Eds.), *Comprehensive textbook of psychiatry* (3rd ed) (Vol. 2 pp. 1305–1319). Baltimore: Williams & Wilkins.

Knights, A., & Hirsch, S. R. (1981). "Revealed" depression and drug treatment for schizophrenia. *Archives of General Psychiatry, 38,* 806–811.

Kolb, L. C. (1973). *Modern clinical psychiatry* (8th ed). Philadelphia: W. B. Saunders.

Kramlinger, K. G., Swanson, D. W., & Maruta, T. (1983). Are patients with chronic pain depressed? *American Journal of Psychiatry, 140,* 747–749.

LaRue, A. (1982). Memory loss and aging: Distinguishing dementia from benign senescent forgetfulness and depressive pseudodementia. *Psychiatric Clinics of North America, 5,* 89–103.

Lazare, A. (1981). Conversion symptoms. *The New England Journal of Medicine, 305,* 745–748.

Leckman, J. F., Weissman, M. M., Merikangas, K. R., Pauls, D. L., & Prusoff, B. A. (1983). Paranoid disorders and major depression. *Archives of General Psychiatry, 40,* 1055–1060.

Lehmann, H. E. (1982). Affective disorders in the aged. *Psychiatric Clinics of North America, 5,* 27–44.

Lehmann, H. E. (1983). The clinician's view of anxiety and depression. *Journal of Clinical Psychiatry, 44,* 3–7.

Lehmann, L. S. (1974). Depersonalization. *American Journal of Psychiatry, 131,* 1221–1224.

Lesse, S. (1967). Hypochondriasis and psychosomatic disorders masking depression. *American Journal of Psychotherapy, 21,* 607–620.

Lesse, S. (1982). The relationship of anxiety to depression. *American Journal of Psychotherapy, 36,* 332–349.

Lester, D. (1980). The treatment of compulsive gambling. *International Journal of Addictions, 15,* 201–206.

Levine, P. M., Silberfarb, P. M., & Lipowski, Z. J. (1978). Mental disorders in cancer patients. *Cancer, 42,* 1385–1391.

Lieberman, J. A., Brenner, R., Lesser, M., Coccaro, E., Borenstein, M., & Kane, J. N. (1983). Dexamethasone suppression tests in patients with panic disorder. *American Journal of Psychiatry, 140,* 917–919.

Liebman, R., Minuchin, S., & Baker, L. (1974). An integrated treatment program for anorexia nervosa. *American Journal of Psychiatry, 131,* 432–436.

Liebowitz, M. R., McGrath, P. J., & Bush, S. C. (1980). Mania occurring during treatment for depersonalization: A report of two cases. *Journal of Clinical Psychiatry, 41,* 33–34.

Marks, I., Gelder, M., & Bancroft, J. (1970). Sexual deviants two years after electrical aversion. *British Journal of Psychiatry, 117,* 173–185.

Maurice, W. L., & Guze, S. B. (1970). Sexual dysfunction and associated psychiatric disorders. *Comprehensive Psychiatry, 11,* 539–543.

McAllister, T. W. (1983). Overview: Dementia. *American Journal of Psychiatry, 140,* 528–533.

McAllister, T. W., Ferrell, R. B., Price, T. R. P., & Neville, M. B. (1982). The dexamethasone suppression test in two patients with severe depressive pseudodementia. *American Journal of Psychiatry, 139,* 479–481.

McGlashan, T. H. (1976). Postpsychotic depression in schizophrenia. *Archives of General Psychiatry, 33,* 231–239.

McLellan, A. T., & Druley, K. A. (1977). Nonrandom relation between drugs of abuse and psychiatric diagnosis. *Journal of Psychiatric Research, 13,* 179–184.

Mendelson, W. B., Gillin, J. C., & Wyatt, R. J. (1977). *Human sleep and its disorders.* New York: Plenam.

Menninger, K. (1938). *Man against himself.* New York: Harcourt Brace & World.

Miller, J. B., & Sonnenberg, S. M. (1973). Depression following psychotic episodes: A response to the challenge of change? *Journal of the American Academy of Psychoanalysis, 1,* 253–270.

Moore, D. C. (1977). Amitriptyline therapy on anorexia nervosa. *American Journal of Psychiatry, 134,* 1303–1304.

Morgan, A. J. (1978). Psychotherapy for transsexual candidates screened out of surgery. *Archives of Sexual Behavior, 7,* 273–283.

Morihisa, J. M., Duffy, F. H., & Wyatt, R. J. (1983). Brain electrical activity mapping (BEAM) in schizophrenic patients. *Archives of General Psychiatry, 40,* 719–728.

Moskowitz, J. A. (1980). Lithium and lady luck: Use of lithium carbonate in compulsive gambling. *New York State Journal of Medicine, 80,* 785–788.

Munjack, D. J., & Moss, H. B. (1981). Affective disorder and alcoholism in families of agoraphobics. *Archives of General Psychiatry, 38,* 869–871.

Murphy, G. E. (1982). The clinical management of hysteria. *Journal of the American Medical Association, 247,* 2559–2564.

Nemiah, J. C. (1980). Dissociative disorders (hysterical neurosis, dissociative type). In H. I. Kaplan, A. N. Freedman, & B. J. Sadock (Eds.), *Comprehensive textbook of psychiatry* (3rd ed) (Vol 2, pp 1544–1561). Baltimore: Williams & Wilkins.

Newsom, G. & Murray, N. (1983). Reversal of dexamethasone suppression test nonsuppression in alcohol abusers. *American Journal of Psychiatry, 140,* 353–354.

Nurnberg, H. G., & Coccaro, E. F. (1982). Response of panic disorder and resistance of depression to imipramine. *American Journal of Psychiatry, 139,* 1060–1062.

Planansky, K., & Johnston, R. (1971). The occurrence and characteristics of suicidal preoccupation and acts in schizophrenia. *Acta Psychiatrica Scandinavica, 47,* 473–483.

Planansky, K., & Johnston, R. (1973). Clinical setting and motivation in suicidal attempts of schizophrenics. *Acta Psychiatrica Scandinavica, 49,* 680–690.

Planansky, K., & Johnston, R. (1978). Depressive syndrome in schizophrenia. *Acta Psychiatrica Scandinavica, 54,* 207–218.

Pope, H. G., Hudson, J. I., Jonas, J. M., & Yurgelun-Todd, D. (1983). Bulimia treated with imipramine: A placebo-controlled, double blind study. *American Journal of Psychiatry, 140,* 554–558.

Post, F. (1980). Paranoid, schizophrenia-like and schizophrenic states in the aged. In J. E. Birren & R. B. Sloane (Eds.), *Handbook of mental health and aging* (pp. 591–615). Englewood Cliffs, NJ: Prentice-Hall.

Pottenger, M., McKernan, J., Patrie, L. E., Weissman, M. M., Ruben, H. L., & Newberry, P. (1978). The frequency and persistence of depressive symptoms in the alcohol abuser. *Journal of Nervous and Mental Disease, 166,* 562–570.

Reifler, B. V., Larson, E., & Hanley, R. (1982). Coexistence of cognitive impairment and depression in geriatric outpatients. *American Journal of Psychiatry, 139,* 623–626.

Rochford, J. M., Weinapple, M., & Goldstein, L. (1981). The quantitative hemispheric EEG in adolescent psychiatric patients with depressive or paranoid symptoms. *Biological Psychiatry, 16,* 47–54.

Rounsaville, B. J., Weissman, M. M., Crits-Christoph, K., Wilber, C., & Kleber, H. (1982). Diagnosis and symptoms of depression in opiate addicts. *Archives of General Psychiatry, 39,* 151–156.

Rudden, M., Sweeney, J., Francis, A., & Gilmore, M. (1983). A comparison of delusional disorder in women and men. *American Journal of Psychiatry 140,* 1575–1578.

Saghir, M. T., Robins, E., Walbran, B., & Gentry, K. A. (1970). Homosexuality: III. Psychiatric disorder and disability in the male homosexual. *American Journal of Psychiatry, 126,* 1079–1086.

Salzman, L. (1973). *The obsessive personality.* New York: Jason Aronson.

Schaffer, C. B., Donlon, P. T., & Bittle, R. M. (1980). Chronic pain and depression: A clinical and family history survey. *American Journal of Psychiatry, 137,* 118–120.

Schapira, K., Kerr, T. A., & Roth, M. (1970). Phobias and affective illness. *British Journal of Psychiatry, 117,* 25–32.

Schenck, L., & Bear, D. (1981). Multiple personality and related dissociative phenomena in patients with temporal lobe epilepsy. *American Journal of Psychiatry, 138,* 1311–1316.

Schildkraut, J. J., Orsulak, P. J., Schatzberg, A. F., Cole, J. O., Gudeman, J. E., & Rohde, W. A. (1978). Elevated platelet MAO activity in schizophrenia-related depressive disorders. *American Journal of Psychiatry, 135,* 110–112.

Schuckit, M. A. (1983a). Alcoholic patients with secondary depression. *American Journal of Psychiatry, 140,* 711–714.

Schuckit, M. A. (1983b). Alcoholism and other psychiatric disorders. *Hospital and Community Psychiatry, 34,* 1022–1027.

Shader, R. I., & Greenblatt, D. J. (1983). Some current treatment options for the symptom of anxiety. *Journal of Clinical Psychiatry, 44,* 21–29.

Shanfield, S., Tucker, G. J., Harrow, M., & Detre, T. (1970). The schizophrenic patient and depressive symptomatology. *Journal of Nervous and Mental Disease, 151,* 203–210.

Sheard, M. H. (1975). Lithium in the treatment of aggression. *Journal of Nervous and Mental Disease, 160,* 108–118.

Sheehy, M. (1983). Successful treatment of paranoia with trazadone (letter). *American Journal of Psychiatry. 140,* 945.

Siegal, R. L., & Hoefer, D. D. (1981). Bereavement counseling for gay individuals. *American Journal of Psychotherapy, 35,* 517–525.

Siegal, R. B. (1980). Organic brain syndrome. In J. E. Birren & R. B. Sloane (Eds.), *Handbook of mental health and aging* (pp. 554–590). Englewood Cliffs, NJ: Prentice-Hall.

Spar, J. E., & Gerner, R. (1982). Does the dexamethasone suppression test distinguish dementia from depression? *American Journal of Psychiatry, 139,* 238–240.

Spitzer, R. L., & Williams, J. B. W. (1982). Idiopathic pain disorder: A critique of pain prone disorder, and a proposal for a revision of the *DSM-III* category of psychogenic pain disorder. *Journal of Nervous and Mental Disease, 170,* 415–419.

Spitzer, R. L., & Williams, J. B. W. (1983). The revision of *DSM-III. Psychiatric Annals, 13,* 808–811.

Spitzer, R. L., Williams, J. B. W., & Wynne, L. C. (1983). A revised decision tree for the *DSM-III* differential diagnosis of psychotic patients. *Hospital and Community Psychiatry, 34,* 631–633.

Stafford, J. R. (1977). The relationship and management of depressive and addictive syndromes. In W. E. Fann, I. Karacan, A. D. Pokorny, & R. L. Williams (Eds.), *Phenomenology and treatment of depression* (pp. 329–341). New York: Spectrum Publication.

Steer, R. A., Emery, G. D., & Beck, A. T. (1980). Correlates of self-reported and clinically assessed depression in male heroin addicts. *Journal of Clinical Psychology, 36,* 798–800.

Stephens, J. H. (1978). Long-term prognosis and follow-up in schizophrenia. *Schizophrenia Bulletin, 4,* 25–47.

Thoren, P., Asberg, M., Cronholm B., Jornestedt, L., & Traskman, L. (1980). Clomipramine treatment of obsessive compulsive disorder. *Archives of General Psychiatry, 37,* 1281–1285.

Tsuang, M. T., Woolson, R. F., Winokur, G., & Crowe, R. R. (1981). Stability of psychiatric diagnosis. *Archives of General Psychiatry, 38,* 535–539.

Vaillant, G. (1964). Prospective prediction of schizophrenic remission. *Archives of General Psychiatry. 11,* 509–518.

Van Valkenburg, G., & Winokur, G. (1979). Depression spectrum disease. *Psychiatric Clinics of North America, 2,* 469–482.

Vaughan, M. (1976). The relationships between obsessional personality, obsessions in depression and symptoms of depression. *British Journal of Psychiatry, 129,* 36–39.

Veterans Administration. (1978). *Management of the violent and suicidal patient.* Program Guide, Mental Health and Behavioral Sciences Services. Washington, DC: Author.

VonKnorring, A. L., Cloninger, R., Bohman, M., & Sigvardsson, S. (1983). An adoption study of depressive disorders and substance abuse. *Archives of General Psychiatry, 40,* 943–950.

Walker, J. I. (1982). Chemotherapy of traumatic war stress. *Military Medicine, 147,* 1029–1033.

Walsh, B. T., Stewart, J. W., Wright, L., Harrison, W., Roose, S. P., & Glassman, A. H. (1982). Treatment of bulimia with monoamine oxidose inhibitors. *American Journal of Psychiatry, 139,* 1629–1630.

Ward, G., (1983). Personal communication.

Ward, N. G., Strauss, M. M., & Ries, R. (1982). The DST as a diagnostic aid in late onset paranoia. *Journal of Nervous and Mental Disease, 170,* 248–250.

Webb, W. L., Jr. (1983). Chronic pain. *Psychosomatics, 24,* 1053–1063.

Weller, E. B., & Weller, R. A. (1983). Case report of conversion symptoms associated with major depressive disorder in a child. *American Journal of Psychiatry, 140,* 1079–1080.

Wildroe, H. J. (1966). Depression following acute schizophrenic psychosis. *Journal of Hillside Hospital, 15,* 114–122.

Williams, H. L. & Rundell, O. H., Jr. (1981). Altered sleep physiology in chronic alcoholics: Reversal with abstinence. *Alcoholism: Clinical and Experimental Research, 5,* 318–325.

Winer, J. A., & Pollock, G. H. (1980). Disorders of impulse control. In H. I. Kaplan, A. N. Freedman, & B. J. Sadock (Eds.), *Comprehensive textbook of psychiatry* (3rd ed) (Vol 2, pp 1817–1829). Baltimore: Williams & Wilkins.

Winokur, A., March, V., Mendels, J. (1980). Primary affective disorder in relatives of patients with anorexia nervosa. *American Journal of Psychiatry, 137,* 695–698.

Winokur, G. (1972). Family history studies. VIII. Secondary depression is alive and well, and . . . *Diseases of the Nervous System, 33,* 94–99.

Winokur, G., Cadoret, R., Dorzab, J., & Baker, M. (1971). Depressive disease a genetic study. *Archives of General Psychiatry, 24,* 135–144.

Wistedt, B., & Palmstierna, T. (1983). Depressive symptoms in chronic schizophrenic patients after withdrawal of long-acting neuroleptics. *Journal of Clinical Psychiatry, 44,* 369–371.

Woody, G. E., O'Brien, C. P., & Rickels, K. (1975). Depression and anxiety in heroin addicts: Placebo controlled study of doxepin in combination with methadone. *American Journal of Psychiatry, 132,* 447–450.

Chapter 21

The Relationship of Depression to Disorders of Personality

Theodore Millon
Doreen Kotik

A considerable amount of research and theory has been directed toward identifying individuals prone to develop clinical depressive illness. Examination of the relevant literature makes it clear that no consensus has been reached regarding the characteristics of the so-called depressive personality. Discrepant findings may, in large part, be attributed to the complexities and methodological difficulties in carrying out research of this sort (Chodoff, 1972). The accurate assessment and classification of both depression or personality are difficult enough themselves without having also to tease out the effects of depression on personality functions, or the impact of premorbid personality on the symptomatic expression of depression (Metcalf, 1968; Paykel & Weissman, 1973).

Of the numerous explanations offered to account for the relationship of depression and personality, the most widely held possibility is that personality is etiological; that is, that personality patterns precede the onset of depression and therefore, determine the vulnerability to symptom formation (Klerman, 1973). This viewpoint, most heavily supported by psychoanalytic theorists, emphasizes the developmental history and early family environment as factors that shape individuals and predispose them to the depressogenic feelings of helplessness, worthlessness, and dejection (McCranie, 1971). A related concept is that certain personalities may repeatedly elicit interpersonal conflict and create stressful life circumstances that favor the development of depressive episodes (Akiskal, Khani, & Scott-Strauss, 1979). Illustrative of this are borderline personalities with their erratic lifestyle and propensity toward tumultuous relationships and self-destructive behaviors. In a similar fashion, characterologic features may render an individual vulnerable to certain psychosocial stressors. The growing body of research on stress events and depression reflects the mounting interest in this theory. Studies have shown that depressions are frequently preceded by stressful events associated with separation or loss (Paykel, Myers & Dienelt, 1970). Since not all people who experience stress become depressed, it is felt that either a genetic predisposition and/or life history factors (e.g., personality style, effectiveness of coping mechanisms, or available suports) may predispose certain individuals toward a depressive response (Becker, 1977). The passive-dependent individual, for example, tends to be quite susceptible to feelings of depression under the conditions of interpersonal loss, abandonment, or rejection. An alternate viewpoint is that some "personality disorders" may actually represent subclinical or subaffective manifestations of major affective illness (Akiskal et al., 1979; Akiskal, Hirschfield, & Yerevanian, 1983). From this perspective, lifelong affective traits or "affective personalities" (e.g., the cyclothymic personality) may represent gradual stages of transition to full syndromic affective episodes (e.g., manic-depressive illness).

It might be argued further that rather than increasing vulnerability to depression, personality may exert a pathoplastic effect upon depression, in that it colors and molds the particular expression of the depressive symptoms (Paykel, Klerman, & Prusoff, 1976). Depending on the premorbid personality, depressive symptoms, such as hopelessness, helplessness, and self-deprecation, may serve a variety of goals. Among the secondary gains of depression are the eliciting of nurturance from others, an excuse for avoiding unwanted responsibilities, a rationalization for poor performance, or a method for safely (albeit indirectly) expressing anger toward others. Partly determined by the gains received, depressive symptoms may take the form of dramatic gestures, irritable negativism, passive loneliness, or philosophical intellectualizations. Finally, there is evidence to suggest that personality characteristics may influence a depressed individual's response both to psychopharmacological and psychotherapeutic treatment (Akiskal, Rosenthal, Haykal, Lemmi, Rosenthal, & Scott-Strauss, 1980; Charney, Nelson, & Quinlan, 1981).

Recently, several depressive subtypes (based upon symptomatic presentations) with corresponding typologies of depression-prone personalities have been proposed (Arieti & Bemporad, 1980; Beck, 1981; Blatt, 1974). While these theoretical endeavors represent an improvement over previous attempts to identify a single personality stereotype for depressive illness, they are still restrictive in that they deal with only a limited number of personality configurations.

It will be the task of this chapter to provide a more extensive review of the interaction between depression and personality characteristics drawing upon theoretical deduction, as well as the recent clinical and empirical literature. A "continuum" conception of depression will be employed in this evaluation rather than a clearly demarcated typology.

Depression will be viewed as a multifaceted syndrome that manifests affective, cognitive, and vegetative symptoms. The most prominent feature, of course, is a disturbance of mood, in which the individual feels sad, blue, apathetic, or hopeless. Expressions of discouragement, self-deprecation, and guilt frequently are present, along with somatic disturbances, such as loss of energy, social interest, and sexual desire, as well as disruptions in sleeping, eating, and ability to concentrate. In severe cases, preoccupation with suicidal ideation is often present.

Personality, like depression, may best be conceived as falling on a continuum of severity. The concept of personality refers to deeply etched characteristics which pervade all aspects of the individual's functioning. Derived from the complex and progressive interactions of constitutional and experiential factors, these patterns (including perceptions, attitudes, and behaviors) tend to persist with little change throughout the individual's lifetime, regardless of the adaptive level of the individual's functioning. Pathological personality patterns or personality disorders are distinguished from normal/healthy patterns by their adaptive inflexibility, their tendency to foster vicious circles of inefficient and self-defeating behaviors, and their tenuous stability under conditions of stress (Millon, 1969, 1981).

While the interpretations offered here may be extended to include the more adaptive and "healthy" personality traits and patterns, the focus of this chapter will be on the relationships between depression and the 11 disorders of personality depicted on Axis II of the *DSM-III* (American Psychiatric Association, 1980).

THE DEPENDENT PERSONALITY

Distinguished by their marked need for social approval and affection, and by their willingness to live in accord with the desires of others, dependent personalities are among the most likely individuals to become depressed. Characteristically, these individuals are docile, noncompetitive, and passive. Apart from requiring signs of belonging and acceptance, dependents make few demands on others. Their own needs are subordinated and their individuality denied, as these individuals assume a submissive, self-sacrificing, and placating role in relation to others. Social tension and interpersonal conflicts are carefully avoided, while troubling events are smoothed over or naively denied. Beneath their warm and affable presentation, however, may lie a plaintive and pessimistic quality. Dependents perceive themselves as weak, fragile, and ineffective. The recognition of their helplessness and utter reliance upon others may result in self-effacement and denigration. In addition, they may become excessively conciliatory in relationships to the point of submitting themselves to intimidation and abuse (Millon, 1981).

Given their pronounced susceptibility to separation anxiety, dependent personalities are quite likely to experience any number of affective disorders. Frequently, the underlying characterological pessimism of these individuals lends itself to a chronic, but mild depression or dysthmia. When faced with possible abandonment or the actual loss of a significant other, a major depression may ensue. Initially, these individuals may react with clinging helplessness and pleas for reassurance and support. Expressions of self-condemnation and guilt are also likely, as such verbalizations serve to deflect criticisms and evoke sympathetic reactions. Feelings of guilt can also act as a defensive maneuver to check outbursts of resentment or hostility. Fearful that their underlying feelings of anger might cause further alienation or retribution, dependents typically turn their aggressive impulses inward, discharging them through a despondency colored by self-derisive comments and contrition. On occasion, dependent personalities may make a desperate attempt to counter or deny emerging feelings of hopelessness and depression, through a temporary reversal of their typical passive, subdued style to that of hypomanic activity, excitement, and optimism. Such dramatic shifts in affective expression may resemble a bipolar disorder.

The dependent personality corresponds to the psychoanalytic "oral character" type, and more specifically, to what has been termed the *oral sucking* or *oral receptive* character. For both Abraham (1911/1968) and Freud (1917/1968), the orally fixated depressive or melancholic has great oral needs, manifested by sucking, eating, and insatiable demands for oral expressions of affection. Emphasis is also placed on affectional frustrations occurring during the pre-Oedipal period. In essence, the melancholic has experienced a pathological introjection, or identification with the ambivalently regarded love object through the process of oral incorporation. Thus, an interpersonal conflict is transformed to an intrapsychic conflict, with the angry desire to devour the frustrating love object being turned inward and experienced as depression.

As psychoanalytic theory developed, the concept of orality was extended to include the general feelings of warmth, nourishment, and security. The dependent personality's reliance on external approval and support for maintenance of self-esteem made it particularly vulnerable to depression resulting from the loss of a significant other. Rado (1968) described melancholia as a "despairing cry for love," while Fenichel (1968) describes the orally dependent depressive as a "love addict."

A theory of depressive subtypes, based on attained level of object representation has been developed by Blatt (1974). Of the two depressive subtypes offered, "anaclitic" and "introjective," the anaclitic depressive would correspond most closely to the dependent depressive. Individuals with this form of depression have histories of impaired object relations at the primitive, oral level of development. Anaclitic depression is associated with intense dependency on others for support and gratification, vulnerability to feelings of deprivation, and considerable difficulties in managing anger expression for fear of alienating the love object. Blatt, D'Afflitti and Quinlan (1976) provide empirical support for the division of depression into anaclitic and introjective subtypes. A Depressive Experiences Questionnaire was constructed to tap phenomenological experiences (rather than observed symptoms) of depression. Three stable factors emerging from this questionnaire included dependency, self-criticism, and efficacy. Corresponding with anaclitic depression is the dependency factor, which consists of items reflecting feelings of loneliness and helplessness, reliance on others, needs for closeness, fears of rejection and abandonment, and uneasiness about anger expression. Further empirical support was provided for Blatt's depressive subtypes in the study by Blatt, Quinlan, Chevron, McDonald and Zuroff (1982). Here clinical judges successfully predicted type of depression based on the case records of psychiatric patients. In the high-dependency patients, clinical records contained evidence of oral excesses (i.e., alcohol, food, and drug abuse), a history of early object loss or deprivation, and issues of abandonment and loneliness.

A depressive typology similar to that of Blatt (1974) is offered by Arieti and Bemporad (1980; see also Chapter 3). Depression is characterized as resulting from a "limitation of alternate ways of thinking and as self-inhibition from new experiences (p. 1360)." On the basis of clinical experience (i.e., long-term psychoanalytic therapy with 40 depressed patients), the three following premorbid types of depressive personality are proposed: (1) "dominant-other" type, (2) "dominant-goal" type, and (3) "chronic character structure," or personality disorder. Akin to the dependent or anaclitic depressive, the dominant-other depressive personality is characterized by "clingingness, passivity, manipulativeness, and avoidance of anger" (p. 1361). Depression in these individuals may be precipitated by the loss of an esteemed other.

While agreeing that depressives are typically orally dependent personality types, Bibring (1953) offers a slightly different emphasis from the traditional psychodynamic focus on orality in depression. He argues that depression is a basic ego state reflecting feelings of helplessness about fulfilling needs critical to the maintenance of self-esteem. According to Bibring, the infant's recurrent experiences of frustrated helplessness and ensuing depression result in the formation of a prototypical reaction pattern that is reactivated by similar events in the future. Thus, with the loss of a significant object, or the perceived inability to control an aversive event, a reactivation of the helpless ego state (rather than a regression due to oral fixation) results in passivity, inhibition, and the belief that striving is meaningless.

Bibring's emphasis on feelings of helplessness in depressives is quite similar to Seligman's (1974) behavioral theory of depression. Seligman hypothesizes that reactive depression is essentially a state of learned helplessness, characterized by the perception of noncontrol. A reformulation of Seligman's theory (Abramson, Seligman, & Teasdale, 1978) proposes that the severity and chronicity of depression is related to the attributions made to account for the perceived lack of control. If an individual assumes personal responsibility for his/her inability to control events, and further assumes that inner deficiencies are likely to continue to result in feelings of helplessness in future situations, then a rather chronic state of depression, associated with lowered self-esteem is likely to occur. An individual is then more likely to behave more helplessly, initiating fewer responses to control reinforcement, and having more difficulty in recognizing the successful responses that result in reinforcement. A related behavioral theory of depression is offered by Lewinsohn (1974) who proposes that a low rate of response-contingent positive reinforcement causes depression. Insufficient reinforcement can result from at least three causes: few events are reinforcing to the individual; few potentially reinforcing events are available in the environment, and/or the instrumental behaviors emitted by the individual infrequently elicit reinforcement (Blaney, 1977; Lewinsohn, 1974).

Both Seligman's (1974) and Lewinsohn's (1974) models of depression are relevant to the experience of depression in dependent personalities. Such individuals with their self-perceptions of inadequacy and ineffectiveness perpetuate behavioral helplessness by relying almost totally upon others for their support and reinforcement. By passively clinging to one or two individuals for nurturance, the dependents restrict their interpersonal and activity range, which in turn limits exposure to alternate sources of reinforcement and diminishes the probability of learning more appropriate coping skills. Lewinsohn's (1974) observation that "some depressed individuals are clearly overinvolved with one significant person to the exclusion of most other potential relationships" (p. 180), is reminiscent of Arieti and Bemporad's (1980) "dominant-other" depressive personality and their characterization of depressives as inhibiting themselves from new experiences and limiting alternate ways of thinking.

Critical in the dependent personalities propensity toward depression are their beliefs that they are ineffective, inferior, and unworthy of regard. This negative cognitive set of the depressive, that is, poor self-concept, disparaging view of the world, and the projection of continued hardships and frustrations in the future, is central to Beck's (1974) cognitive theory of depression. Recently (1981), Beck has extended his cognitive formulation to include other predisposing and precipitating factors, including personality attributes that may lead to depression. He proposes two basic personality modes, the "autonomous: and the "socially dependent," and describes the respective depressive symptom patterns of each. Individuals within the socially dependent cluster depend on others for safety, help, and gratification and are characterized by passive receiving. Such individuals require stability, predictability, and constant reassurance in relationships. As rejection is considered worse than aloneness to the socially dependent, no risks are taken that might lead to alienation from sources of nurturance (e.g., asserting oneself with others). Similarly, socially dependents avoid making changes and exposing themselves to novel situations, as they feel ill-equipped to cope with the unexpected. Depression in these individuals is usually precipitated by the experience of interpersonal rejection or loss, and is accompanied by a diminishment in confidence and self-esteem. The socially dependent depressive is more likely than the depressed autonomous personality to cry, complain of sadness and loneliness, and make demands for help. Such individuals evidence greater emotional lability and are more likely to experience an "anxious depression." They are also more optimistic about the benefits of help and respond better (at least temporarily) to support and reassurance.

Considerable overlap can be seen among the anaclitic depressive, the dominant-other depressive, and the socially dependent depressive. The emphasis on premorbid dependency in depressives is also apparent in the constructive-developmental model of depression, offered by Kegan, Rogers, and Quinlan (1981). Based on Kohlberg's (1976) sociomoral developmental stages, Kegan et al. (1981) have generated three subtypes of depression, relating to (1) egocentricity and control issues, (2) issues of interpersonal dependency, and (3) issues of self-definition and evaluation. Kegan's interpersonal dependency subtype correlates closely with depression in the dependent personality, in that feelings of dysphoria are directly related to the establishment and breaking of social bonds. Individuals with this form of depression often feel abandoned, unloved, betrayed, alienated, and unworthy of attention and regard. Again, problems with the expression of anger are common, as anger might threaten the stability of an established dependent relationship.

There also appears to be at least one dependent personality counterpart among the depressive typologies generated through factor analytic studies. In one of the earliest attempts to empirically classify subgroups of depression, Grinker and associates (Grinker, Miller, Sabshin, Nunn, & Nunnally, 1961) assessed feelings and concerns, as well as behavior of 96 depressed hospitalized patients and 10 nondepressed psychiatric controls. While many valid criticisms have been leveled at Grinker's study (Wittenborn, 1965), the five depressive patterns yielded by factor analysis in this landmark investigation still warrant consideration. "Factor Pattern B" seems particularly relevant to the current discussion on the dependent depressive. It depicts a depressed individual who is characterized by dismal, hopeless attitudes, low self-esteem, anxiety, and clinging demands for attention. It is speculated that some external event resulted in the release of repressed aggression in such an individual, which is, in turn, reacted to with guilt and self-punishment. Such patients are helped by support and kindness and typically do well in psychotherapy.

A number of correlational studies lend support to the role of dependency in depression. For example, Wittenborn and Maurer (1977) found that family informants, in describing the premorbid personalities of depressed patients, referred to low self-confidence, dependence on the opinions of others, and the tendency to deny anger and avoid confrontation. Paykel et al. (1976) found that depressives with a neurotic symptom pattern more frequently showed evidence of oral dependent personalities (according to both relatives' interviews and self-report personality inventories). Similarly, in a longitudinal, follow-up study of 40 depressed women, Paykel and Weissman (1973) found submissive dependency and family attachment to be closely related to symptomatology.

Altman and Wittenborn (1980) employing a self-descriptive inventory developed for their study, found that the following five factors discriminated formerly depressed women from a matched group of women with no psychiatric history: low self-esteem, unhappy outlook, narcissistic vulnerability, helplessness, and lack of self-confidence. In a follow-up and extension of Altman and Wittenborn's (1980) work, Cofer and Wittenborn again successfully discriminated depressed women in remission from a matched nonpsychiatric control group on the basis of a modified version of Altman and Wittenborn's (1980) self-descriptive inventory. Factor analysis identified three of the factors reported in the initial study (i.e., unhappy outlook, narcissistic vulnerability, and low self-esteem), as well as the additional factors of critical mother and dependency fostering father. The authors suggest that their findings lend corroboration to other studies and theories (e.g., Blatt et al., 1976;

Bibring, 1953; Seligman, 1974) that emphasize the role of low self-esteem and the perception of helplessness in the development of depression. More recently, Matussek and Feil (1983) found that on the basis of numerous self-report inventories, as well as psychiatric interviews, endogenous unipolar patients were characterized by a lack of autonomy and assertiveness, conformism, passive-submissiveness, dependency on others, and avoidance of responsibility.

THE HISTRIONIC PERSONALITY

Histrionic personalities, like dependent personalities, are characterized by intense needs for attention and affection. Unlike the passive receptive stance of the dependent, however, the histrionic actively solicits the interest of others through seductive, immaturely exhibitionistic, or self-dramatizing behaviors. Toward assuring a constant receipt of the admiration and esteem that they require, histrionics develop an exquisite sensitivity to the desires and moods of those they wish to please. While others may perceive them as being rather ingenuine or shallow, they are nonetheless typically viewed as gregarious, entertaining, and superficially charming. The histrionics extreme other-directedness and approval-seeking results in a capricious and fickle pattern of personal relationships. Unlike the dependent's blind loyalty and attachment to one significant other, the histrionic is lacking in fidelity and dissatisfied with single attachments. Their interpersonal relationships tend to be characterized by demandingness, manipulation, and at times, childish dependency and helplessness. These behaviors are particularly pronounced in heterosexual relationships where the histrionic demonstrates a marked appetite for fleeting romantic encounters (Millon, 1981).

Histrionics tend to be emotionally overreactive and labile. Frustration tolerance is quite low and there is a proneness toward immature stimulation seeking and impulsive responsiveness. Such individuals crave excitement, pleasure and change, and become easily bored with normal routines. A well-developed sense of inner identity is typically lacking in histrionics. Their perception of themselves is conceptualized in terms of their relationships and their effect upon others. In contrast to their hypersensitivity to the thoughts and moods of others, such individuals are lacking insight into their own feelings. Their orientation is toward external stimuli and only fleeting, impressionistic attention is paid to details. Their cognitive style is marked with difficulties in concentration and logical thinking. Experiences are poorly integrated and learned, and consequently, judgment is often lacking. In part, their cognitive flightiness results from their attempts to avoid potentially disrupting ideas and urges; for example, a recognition of their ravenous dependency needs and their resultant vulnerability to loss or rejection. Consequently, histrionic personalities will simply seal off, repress, or dissociate large segments of their memories and feelings.

The histrionics' virtually insatiable needs for attention and approval make them quite prone to feelings of dejection and anxiety, should they fail to evoke the recognition they desire. Signs of indifference or neutrality on the part of others are frequently interpreted as rejection and result in feelings of emptiness and unworthiness. Unlike the dependent's flat and somber symptom picture, dysthymic disorder in histrionic personalities is characteristically overplayed in dramatic and eye-catching gestures, characteristic of the histrionics exhibitionistic display of mood. Episodes of the milder forms of depression are usually prompted less by fear of abandonment than by a sense of emptiness and inactivity. Such dysphoria is likely to occur when histrionics find themselves stranded between one fleeting attachment and another, or between one transitory excitement and the next. At such times of noninvolvement, histrionics sense their lack of inner substance and direction, and begin to experience fears of an empty life and aloneness.

Depressive complaints in histrionic personalities tend to be expressed in current, fashionable, or intellectualized terms (e.g., *"existential anxiety"* or *"estrangement from the mass society"*). Expressing this distress through such popular jargon enables histrionics to rationalize their personal emptiness and confusion and, perhaps more importantly, provides them with a bridge to others, at a time when they feel most isolated from the social life they so desperately seek. Such pseudosophisticated expressions of disenchantment entertain and interest others and identifies the histrionic as being part of an "in" subgroup. Histrionics are also among the personality styles that may "mask" an underlying depression through psychosomatic disorders, hypochondriacal syndromes, or through acting-out behaviors, such as drug abuse, overeating, or sexual promiscuity (Akiskal, 1983; Lesse, 1974).

Major depressions in histrionics are primarily precipitated by anticipated losses in dependency security and are more likely to be evidenced in an agitated rather than a retarded form (Millon, 1981). In the hope of soliciting support and nurturance, histrionics may wail aloud and make well known their feelings of helplessness and abandonment. Suicidal threats or gestures are not uncommon at such times. Major depressions may also be colored with irritability and anger, although reproving reactions, especially from significant others, will cause histrionics to withdraw and substitute their anger with dramatic declarations of guilt and contrition.

Histrionic personalities may be particularly susceptible to bipolar and cyclothymic disorders, as these syndromes are consistent with their characteristic socially gregarious and exuberant style. Severe separation anxieties or the fear of losing social approval may intensify the histrionic's habitual behavior pattern until it reaches the forced and frantic congeniality of hypomania. To stave off the growing feeling of depressive hopelessness, tension may be released through hyperactivity and a frenetic search for attention.

Many of the psychoanalytic writings of the depressed oral dependent's pronounced affectional needs are equally applicable to depression in the histrionic personality. Freud (1932) wrote that a "dread of loss of love" governed the behavior of hysterics, while Rado (1951) referred to the predepressive's strong cravings for narcissistic gratification and low tolerance of affectional frustration. In addition, the active manipulative qualities of the histrionic are stressed. Bemporad (1971) describes a manipulative depressive who engages in "bargaining relationships" to ensure fulfillment of dependency needs and who decompensates if sufficient gratifications from others cannot be obtained. Chodoff (1972) describes the low frustration tolerance of the oral depression-prone individual and the various techniques, for example, "submissive, manipulative, coercive, piteous, demanding and placating" (p. 670) that are employed to satisfy their narcissistic needs. Finally, while Blatt (1974) characterizes anaclitic depressives as typically being more passive and helpless than oral dependents, case history studies of these patients also revealed evidence of histrionic features, such as impulsive behavior, suicidal gestures, and acting-out through oral excessives of drug and alcohol abuse (Blatt et al., 1982).

Considerable attention has been paid to the clinical presentation of depression in histrionic personalities. While it has been argued that the dramatic behavioral styles of histrionics may obscure a clear view of an underlying depression (Akiskal et al., 1983), others believe that the histrionic's "high" spirits and gregariousness protect against or mitigate the emergence of depressive feelings. Lazare and Klerman (1968) studied a small group of hospitalized depressed women who also carried the diagnosis of "hysterical personality." Assessment during the time of their illness revealed that hysterical patients, as compared to depressed patients without hysterical features, showed less intense feelings of depression, hopelessness and worthlessness, less retardation, fewer paranoid and obsessional symptoms, but more somatic complaints. Hysterical depressed patients also differed in their behavioral presentation while hospitalized, in that they were described as irritable, demanding, manipulative, and more hostile than patients without hysterical features. Follow-up studies (Paykel & Prusoff, 1973; Paykel et al., 1976) utilizing clinical interviews, self-report inventories, and ratings by relatives, supported the initial findings. Neurotic depressives showed more oral dependent traits, while depressed patients with hysterical personalities tended to be less severely ill, showing patterns of depression mixed with hostility and irritability, but little evidence of anxiety.

Such studies suggest that a key component in the histrionic personalities' apparent resistance to severe depression is their ability to express hostility. Classical psychodynamic formulations emphasize the depressive's turning of aggression against the self in punishment of the internalized, frustrating love object. Recent studies (Gershon, Cromer, & Klerman, 1968; Schless, Mendels, Kipperman, & Cochran, 1974) have challenged the universality of aggression turned inward as the depressive mechanism, arguing that depression is seen in those who overtly express hostility, as well as in individuals where hostility remains covert. There does appear to be at least some evidence, however, to suggest that hostility expressed outward may be associated with less severe depression, as well as hysterical features. In a rather extensive study of a very small group of hospitalized depressives, Gershon et al. (1968) found that while "hostility-in" was positively correlated with depressive symptoms, "hostility-out" appeared to be associated with depression only in the few subjects described as having hysterical personalities. For these patients, significantly fewer verbalizations of depression were noted, while the degree of hostility expressed appeared to be closely and positively related to the severity of depression.

Schless et al. (1974) found in their study group of 37 depressed patients, an approximately equal distribution of patients turning hostility inward and outward. Several indicators of outward hostility in this study were related to the presence of hysterical features and resentment. While the degree of turning hostility inward appeared to be related to the severity of depression, the most severely depressed patients had an increase in both inwardly and outwardly directed hostility. In addition, the more depressed patients felt their angry feelings to be relatively impotent, while anger in others was perceived as quite threatening. The authors proposed that depression, hostility, and anxiety are all signal emotions in reaction to certain stimuli. In their formulation, all of these "signals" have a parallel relationship and can occur together in different degrees and combinations. Hostility may thus serve as a secondary defense to depression. When this defense begins to fail in the highly depressed patients, they perceive their anger to be ineffective. The portrayal of hostility as a secondary defense in depression gains some support from Lazare and Klerman's (1968) study where hostility was quite pronounced in hysterical personalities during the time of their clinical depression, but diminished as the patients' depressive symptoms abated.

Consistent with the position that the histrionic personality structure confers protection against severe depression, is the association of histrionic features with neurotic rather than endogeneous depression (Charney et al., 1981; Paykel & Prusoff, 1973). A growing body of theory and research also suggests that the histrionic personality may be more prone toward chronic mild depression and characterological depressions (Akiskal et al., 1980).

Paykel (1971) conducted a cluster analysis on 35 rating variables derived from 165 depressed patients from varied treatment settings. Two major groups akin to the endogeneous and reactive dimensions were further divided into four depressive subtypes, two of which seem particularly relevant to depression in the histrionic. *Hostile depressives* were characterized by moderately young patients who evidenced moderately severe depression, flavored with hostility and self-pity. *Young depressives with personality disorders* were the youngest group (typically in their 20s) and evidenced relatively mild depression with situationally reactive mood fluctuations. Patients in this group (which overlaps somewhat with the hostile depressives) were high on neuroticism but also evidenced disturbed social relations suggestive of personality disorder. Support for the validity of Paykel's four depressive subtypes was derived from a second study (Paykel, 1972) where patient's self-reports and ratings by relatives revealed differences in symptomatology among the depressive subtypes. Hostile depressives and young depressives with personality disorders showed more evidence of hysterical personality features than the other two subgroups.

Grinker and associates' (1961) earlier factor analytic work also generated a depressive subtype with features that conform to the histrionic depressive. Patient's corresponding to "Factor Pattern C" evidenced less than average depressed affect, guilt, or anxiety. Their behavior is marked by agitated, demanding, hypochondriacal complaints, associated with psychosomatic symptoms. In contrast to the irrational, complaining attitudes noted in these patients is the very low loading on dismal and hopeless affect.

Charney et al. (1981) found histrionic, hostile, and borderline personality traits more frequently in the nonmelancholic forms of depression. Significantly more nonmelancholic as opposed to melancholic depressives also showed evidence of personality disorders. The subgroup of nonmelancholic depressives with personality disorder had an earlier onset of depressive illness and showed a poorer treatment response. Akiskal and colleagues (Akiskal, 1983; Akiskal et al., 1980) describe a similar type of depressive patient which they portray as predominantly neurotic, younger, mildly depressed, and possessing features consistent with personality disorder. Akiskal (1983) addresses the dysthymic disorder, and its associated conditions of chronic minor depression, characterologic depression, and hysteroid dysphoria. He divides chronic depressives into the following three groups: (1) primary depressives with residual chronicity, (2) chronic secondary dysphoria, and (3) characterologic depressions. The early onset, characterologic depressions are further divided into (*a*) character-spectrum disorders, and (*b*) subaffective dysthymic disorders. In discussing the poor response to treatment among characterologic depressives, Akiskal et al. (1980) refers to this subtype's "oral hysterical" features, but also emphasizes the antisocial, unstable, and even schizoid qualities that may be seen (e.g., immature and manipulative behaviors, impulsivity, interpersonal instability, and a high incidence of drug and alcohol abuse). Characterologic depressives typically have early histories of unstable object relations and evidence of a hypersensitivity to romantic disappointment, and other forms of separation events.

The characterologic depression described by the Akiskal group (Akiskal et al., 1980; Akiskal, 1983) shows considerable overlap with Liebowitz and Klein's (1981) "hysteroid dysphoria." Described as chronic, repetitive, nonpsychotic depressed moods, this disturbance is more frequent in women with pronounced needs for attention, approval, and praise, especially within a romantic relationship. Extreme intolerance of personal rejection is the hallmark of this disorder. Depression in these individuals is usually of short duration and manifested symptomatically in overeating or craving for sweets, oversleeping or extreme fatigue. Alcohol or drug abuse during episodes of depression may also be common. Described as "attention junkies" with "addictions" to approval, hysteroid dysphorics, on the surface, would seem to possess many of the features characteristic of the histrionic personality. As with Paykel's (1971) and Charney et al.'s (1981) young depressives, however, the hysteroid dysphorics also evidence considerably more "unstable" features (e.g., being prone toward angry outbursts, impulsive acting-out and physically self-damaging acts), which are suggestive of a more severe level of personality disorganization, such as the borderline personality.

THE SCHIZOID PERSONALITY

The essential features of the schizoid personality are a profound defect in the ability to form social relationships and an underresponsiveness to all forms of stimulation. Such individuals exhibit an intrinsic emotional blandness; an imperviousness to joy, anger, or sadness. Seemingly unmoved by emotional stimuli, the schizoid appears to possess a generalized inability to be aroused and activated; a lack of initiative and vitality. Their interpersonal passivity then, is not by intention or for self-protective reasons, but due to a fundamental imperceptiveness to the moods and needs of others (Millon, 1981).

Schizoid personalities typically prefer limited interpersonal contact and only a peripheral role in social and family relationships. They tend to choose interests and vocations that will allow them to maintain their social detachment. Colorless and lacking in spontaneity, they are usually perceived as unresponsive, boring, or dull in relationships. Their speech tends to be characterized by emotional flatness, vagueness, and obscurities, and there is a seeming inability to grasp the emotional components of human interactions and communications. They seem indifferent to both praise and criticism. Consistent with their interpersonal style, schizoids possess little awareness of themselves and employ only minimal introspection. Lacking in insight and relatively untroubled by intense emotions or interpersonal conflicts, the schizoid possesses limited and uncomplicated intrapsychic defenses.

Schizoid personalities' pervasive imperviousness to emotions puts them among the personality styles least susceptible to depression or other affective distress. Having failed to develop an "appetite" for social stimulation (including affection and attachment), these individuals are not vulnerable to dejection resulting from "object loss." In addition, since schizoids derive only limited pleasure from themselves, they are not particularly susceptible to loss of self-esteem or self-deprecation. Emotional distress may develop, however, when faced with unusual social demands or responsibilities, or when stimulation levels become either excessive or drastically curtailed. In addition, their inner barrenness and interpersonal isolation may occasionally throw them into a fear of nonbeing or petrification.

On rare occasions, schizoids may exhibit brief, frenzied episodes of maniclike excitement in an attempt to counter the anxieties of depersonalization. A fleeting and erratic course of frantic and rather bizarre conviviality may then temporarily replace the schizoid's characteristic impassive, unsociable pattern. More frequently, however, the schizoid reacts to disequilibrium with increased withdrawal and dissociation. Lacking an investment and interest in self, as well as external events, the schizoid fails to acquire a coherent and well-integrated inner identity. Disruptions to the consistency of the schizoid's lifestyle, as might result from unwanted social overstimulation or prolonged periods of social isolation, may consequently result in a kind of splitting or disintegration. During such periods of self-estrangement, schizoids may experience irrational thinking and compounding of their typical emotional poverty. Behaviorally, this might be manifested in profound lethargy, lifeless facial expressions, and inaudible speech, simulating but not reflecting a depressive mood.

Should depression be seen in the schizoid, certain aspects of behavioral theory may account for it. Lewinsohn's (1974) theory of depression stresses the role of low rates of response-contingent positive reinforcement. In the schizoid's case, few events (either within or without) are reinforcing. Schizoid personalities evidence a general state of unresponsiveness to innumerable sources of stimulus events, which for other individuals might cause pleasure, joy, or anger. In addition, few reinforcing events are available in the environment, because the schizoid lacks the perceptual capacities to perceive them, as well as the social skills to elicit them. Their infrequent social activities decrease opportunities for growth stimulation, and their insensitivity, impassivity, and disjointed thought and communicative skills make it unlikely that others will respond positively to them. Since this low rate of response-contingent positive reinforcement is characteristic or constant for the schizoid, it may not, by itself, explain the development of depression. However, should those few reinforcements suddenly drop, or a fear of nonbeing develop, the schizoid's inability to detect or elicit new reinforcement may contribute to depression.

While empirical data on affective disorders in schizoid personalities is lacking, at least two of the factor analysis generated subtypes would seem to fit the experience of depression in these individuals. "Factor Pattern A" generated in the 1961 study by Grinker et al. is described as a depressive who is not particularly anxious, clinging or attention-seeking, but rather isolated, withdrawn, and apathetic. A slowing in thought and speech, with some evidence of cognitive disturbance is also seen. The absence of large amounts of "gloomy affect," complaining, or attempts at restitution give this depressive subtype the appearance of an "empty person." While much of this description would fit the theoretical picture of depression in the schizoid, Grinker et al. (1961) give other features of this depressive factor pattern which might be more characteristic of a compulsive premorbid personality.

The "retarded depression" generated by Overall and Hollister (1980) might also be consistent with the symptomatic presentation of depression in the schizoid. Such depression is characterized by retardation in speech, gross motor behavior, and social interaction. A diminishment in affective responsiveness may frequently accompany the "generalized behavioral inhibition" (p. 376) that is present in this form of depression.

THE AVOIDANT PERSONALITY

While the schizoid and avoidant personalities may appear superficially rather similar, they differ in several important ways, including their susceptibility to depression. Both personalities may appear withdrawn, emotionally flat, and lacking in communicative and social skills. The affective flatness of the avoidant, however, is typically a defensive maneuver against underlying emotional tension and disharmony. Similarly, the apparent detachment and interpersonal withdrawal of avoidants develop in response to a fear of intimacy and a hypersensitivity to rejection and ridicule. Strong desires for affection and acceptance exist in these individuals, but are denied or restrained out of apprehension and fearful mistrust of others. Not infrequently, avoidants have had experiences of painful social derogation, which resulted in an acute sensitivity and alertness to signs of ridicule and humiliation. This hypersensitivity and vigilance often results in the misperceiving of innocuous social comments or events as critical rejection (Millon, 1981).

For the most part, avoidants engage in self-imposed isolation and social withdrawal. They will, however, enter into relationships with a limited number of people, if provided with strong guarantees of uncritical acceptance. Avoidants may become quite dependent on the one or two people they do allow into their lives. However, they are likely to remain rather cautious in relationships, engaging in frequent, subtle testing of their partner's sincerity.

While the avoidant may view people in general as critical, betraying and humiliating, they are usually very dissatisfied with the peripheral social role they feel forced to play and experience painful feelings of loneliness and alienation. Avoidants tend to be excessively self-critical, blaming themselves for their social undesirability. Consequently, they may become estranged from themselves as well as from others. They tend to resort to extreme defensive coping strategies to deal with the chronic feelings of interpersonal ambivalence and affective distress that they experience. In addition to active avoidance and withdrawal from threatening social situations, they may attempt to block and interfere with their own troubling cognitions, resulting in a fragmentation of their thoughts and disjointed verbal communications, as well as the appearance of being emotionally confused or socially irrelevant.

Avoidant types are among the most vulnerable of the personality patterns to psychiatric symptom disorders. Perhaps most frequently, the avoidant will suffer from feelings of anxiety and ruminative worry. Also, like the schizoid, prolonged estrangement from self and others can result in varied forms of dissociative disorders. Avoidants are also quite prone to feelings of deep sadness, emptiness, and loneliness. Frustrated yearnings for affection and approval, coupled with the self-deprecation they experience for their unlovability and ineffectuality may result in a chronic melancholic tone to these personalities. Depression may nonetheless be difficult to detect in the avoidant, given their characteristic affective flattening, and their typical presentation of slowness of speech and movement. Furthermore, avoidants will attempt to hide and contain their feelings of inner despair for fear that overt expressions of such weakness and suffering might render them even more vulnerable to social ridicule, humiliation, and rejection. While major depressive episodes in these individuals may be similar to the symptomatic presentation of depressed schizoids (i.e., psychomotor retardation, extreme social withdrawal, and apathy), avoidants may also experience anxiety or obsessive ruminations with their depression.

The avoidant's susceptibility to depression can be readily explained from a cognitive/behavioral framework. First is the avoidant's tendency to view things pessimistically; that is, contempt directed at the self, fear and suspicion of others, and a sense of future despair. Next is the limited possibility the avoidant has for experiencing reinforcing events. Characteristically, these individuals tend to be inflexible, confining themselves to a small range of potentially reinforcing experiences. Although possessing the innate capacity to experience pleasure, the interpersonal anxiety felt by avoidants may cause them to deny themselves the satisfaction they could derive from others, and to discount praise, compliments, and other social reinforcers. Similarly, the distorted view of self as ineffectual and unlovable, precludes the possibility of pleasure coming from within.

Although the avoidant personality is a relatively new concept to psychiatric nosology (Millon, 1969), the characteristics of this pattern have frequently been cited in the literature on depression. Arieti and Bemporad (1980), in their proposal of three premorbid types of depressive personality, describe a depressive personality structure that is characterized by constant feelings of depression lurking in the background, and an inhibition of nearly any form of gratification. Further, features of this form of chronic character structure are:

> A chronic, mild sense of futility and hopelessness which results from a lack of involvement in everyday activities . . . emptiness because they do not develop deep relationships for fear of being exploited or rejected . . . harsh, critical attitude towards themselves and others." (Arieti & Bemporad, 1980, p. 1362)

According to the authors, such depressive subtypes experience episodes of clinical depression when they are forced by some event to reevaluate their mode of existence, and confronted with the barrenness and meaninglessness of their lives.

Metcalfe (1968) described a group of recovered, depressed women as being characterized by ruminative worry, a denial of fantasy, and a rigid, limited, habit-bound lifestyle. He suggests that the depressive is not necessarily an individual who is prone to develop depression, but one who lacks the "resistance" necessary to recover from such illness. Hirschfeld and Klerman (1979) also described the depressed patients in their study to be more worrisome, insecure and sensitive, less socially adroit, and more likely to break down under stress. These individuals were further characterized as being more needy and obsessional than normal controls.

A similar personality subtype is proposed by Akiskal (1983; see also Chapter 17) in his discussion of the two characterologic depressive subtypes, the "character-spectrum disorders," and the "subaffective dysthymic disorders." In the latter subgroup, the depressive personality characteristics are considered as milder, but lifelong (subaffective) expressions of a primary depressive disorder. Individuals prone to subaffective dysthymic disorders exhibit anhedonic, "guilt-ridden," and retarded depressions. Akiskal views such patients as conforming to Schneider's (1958) depressive typology in that they are:

. . . (1) quiet, passive, and nonassertive, (2) gloomy, pessimistic and incapable of fun, (3) self-critical, self-reproaching, and self-derogatory, (4) skeptical, hyper-critical and complaining, (5) conscientious and self-disciplining, (6) brooding and given to worry, and (7) preoccupied with inadequacy failure and negative events to the point of a morbid enjoyment of one's failures." (Akiskal, 1983, p. 17)

The characteristics described thus far are obviously not exclusive to the avoidant personality. However, a great many of them are prominent features of the avoidant style. In a recent critical review of research on personality factors in affective disorders, Akiskal et al. (1983) suggest that introversion and low sociability have emerged as consistent and relatively robust premor-bid features of nonbipolar depressive disorders. Among the studies cited in their review was that of Hirschfeld, Klerman, Clayton, & Keller (1983) where personality data from recovered, depressed women was compared to similar data from formerly depressed female relatives as well as female relatives with no prior psychiatric history. The recovered depressives in this study were described as very introverted, "shy, withdrawn, reserved, restrained, serious, deliberate, and controlled" (p. 997). While these individuals showed an ex-treme dependence on one significant other, they tended not be very sociable or enjoying of company. The authors conclude social introversion to be "the most powerful personality characteristic associated with primary nonbipolar depression," while heightened interpersonal dependency is viewed as "mod-est second factor" (p. 997). Clearly the premorbid depressive features of introversion and low sociability have applicability to the avoidant personality.

THE SCHIZOTYPAL PERSONALITY

The hallmark of this disorder is a variety of peculiarities of behavior, speech, thought, and perception that are not severe enough to warrant the diagnosis of schizophrenia. There is considerable variability in the presentation of this syndrome (e.g., magical thinking, ideas of reference or suspiciousness, illu-sions, depersonalization, and hypersensitivity with undue social anxiety), and no single feature is invariably present. It is our contention that the schizotypal syndrome should be viewed as an advanced dysfunctional personality (akin in severity to the borderline or paranoid types), and that it is best understood as a more pathological version of the schizoid and avoidant patterns. Such a framework allows a greater appreciation of the schizotypal characteristics of social impoverishment, and the tendency toward distant rather than close interpersonal relationships. In fact, the observed oddities in behavior and thought, such as paranoid ideation, magical thinking, and circumstantial speech stem in part from the schizotypal's withdrawn and isolated existence. Without the stabilizing influences and repetitive corrective experiences that come with frequent human contact and social interactions, individuals may lose their sense of behavioral judgment and gradually begin the process of acting, thinking, and perceiving in peculiar and eccentric ways. In the ad-vanced stages of such a dysfunctional progression, schizotypals may merely drift aimlessly from one activity to another, leading meaningless and ineffectual existences, and remaining on the periphery of societal life.

Depending on which of the detached patterns (i.e., schizoid or avoidant) that schizotypals resemble, they may be emotionally flat, sluggish and apathetic, or hypersensitive, anxious and socially apprehensive. In a similar fashion, schizotypal personalities vulnerability to depression or other symptom disorders, is in part, dependent upon whether they have evolved from the sensitive and suffering avoidants or the innately bland, unfeeling schizoids. Empirical and theoretical literature on the relationship of affective disorder to the schizotypal personality is virtually nonexistent. To gain some appreciation of this phenomenon, the reader is referred to the preceding sections on the depressive experience in schizoid and avoidant personalities.

THE ANTISOCIAL PERSONALITY

The *DSM-III* provides a rather detailed listing of the delinquent, criminal, and socially undesirable behaviors that may be found among antisocial personalities, but fails, in our opinion, to deal with the personality characteristics from which such antisocial behaviors stem. In adopting a focus on the "criminal personality," insufficient attention is paid to individuals with similar propensities and basic traits who have managed to avoid criminal involvement (Millon, 1981). It is our contention that antisocial personalities are best characterized by: hostile affectivity, excessive self-reliance, interpersonal assertiveness, callousness, and a lack of humanistic concern or sentimentality. Such individuals exhibit rebelliousness and social "vindictiveness," with particular contempt being directed toward authority figures. Irascible and pugnacious, antisocials exhibit frequent, verbally abusive, and at times even physically cruel behaviors. Other notable features in the antisocial personality include a low tolerance for frustration, impulsivity, and an inability to delay gratification. Consistent with this is a tendency to become easily bored and restless with day-to-day responsibilities and social demands. Not only are such individuals seemingly undaunted by danger and punishment, they appear attracted to it, and may actually seek it out or provoke it. Our portrayal of the antisocial personality is more consistent with the concept of the sociopathic or psychopathic personalities as depicted in the incisive writings of Cleckley (1941). These individuals are most notable for their guiltlessness, incapacity for object love, impulsivity, emotional shallowness, superficial social charm, and an inability to profit from experience.

An argument may also be made for a "nonantisocial" variant of the sociopathic personality. Such individuals may view themselves as assertive, energetic, self-reliant, and hardboiled, but realistic, strong, and honest. In competitive society, these traits tend to be commended and reinforced. Consequently, such individuals may achieve positions of authority and power, which provide socially sanctioned avenues for expressing their underlying aggressiveness.

Antisocials tend to be finely attuned to the feelings, moods, and vulnerabilities of others, taking advantage of this sensitivity to manipulate and control. However, they typically evidence a marked deficit in self-insight and rarely exhibit foresight. While inner tensions, frustrations, and dysphoria may occur, such discomforts are not tolerated for very long, being discharged through acting-out, rather than intrapsychic mechanisms. Frequent references are made to the antisocials active avoidance of, and inability to tolerate awareness of depression (Reid, 1978). From this framework, conscious feelings of depression are viewed as a failure of the defensive mechanisms which permitted the previous involvement in antisocial behaviors (Cormier, 1966; Reid, 1978).

An appreciation of the antisocial's resistance to depression can be drawn from the psychoanalytic conceptualization of depression as a turning of hostility inward (Gershon, Cromer, & Klerman, 1968; Paykel & Prusoff, 1973; Schless et al., 1974), whereby the inherent hostile affectivity, resistance to social dependency, and interpersonal forcefulness of the antisocial all serve as safeguards against depression. This position is also consistent with cognitive-behavioral formulations.

Seligman (1974), for example, proposed that the individuals most resistant to depression (and helplessness) are those whose lives (especially childhood) have been filled with mastery and extensive experience controlling and manipulating sources of reinforcement, while Beck (1974) writes:

> The satisfactory expression of hostility seem to be a very powerful means of increasing a person's subjective feeling of effectiveness, thus increasing his self-esteem and combating the negative cognitions which I hold to be so important in the generation of depression." (1974, p. 21)

While the antisocial's active independence, internal locus of control, and appetite for stimulating change may militate against the impact of life stressors, these same characteristics can also make the antisocial vulnerable to occasional major depressive episodes. Precipitants for depression might include situations of forced interpersonal submissiveness or curtailed personal freedom (e.g., incarceration or required military service), as well as internal conditions (e.g., medical illness or age-related physical decline) that result in incapacitation, passivity, or immobility. It has also been suggested (Reid, 1978) that depression may ensue when antisocials are forced to confront their inner emptiness, emotional void, and tenuous object relations. Again, this forced recognition is most likely to occur when antisocials are made to feel inadequate or weakened in a way which strips from them their "resilient shell of narcissism" (Reid, 1978, p. 499).

Although rather meager in comparison to the attention paid to the dependent, introversive, and obsessive characteristics of depressives, a growing body of literature argues for a depressive subtype whose salient features are autonomy, self-control, and aggressiveness. In addition to his "socially dependent" mode of depression, Beck (1981) proposes an "autonomous mode" characterized by a great investment in "preserving and increasing his independence, mobility and personal rights" (p. 272). For such action-oriented individuals, their well-being is dependent on their ability to maintain their autonomy and direct their own activities without external constraint or interference. There is little sensitivity to the needs of others with a corresponding lack of responsiveness to external feedback and corrective influences. It should be noted that the autonomous individuals described by Beck are also characterized by excessively high-internalized standards and criteria for achievement, features which may be more indicative of the compulsive character structure, or the noncriminal variant of the antisocial personality. Such individuals tend to experience a hostile depression, characterized by social withdrawal, rejection of help, self-criticism, resistance to crying, and "active" violent forms of suicide attempts.

More recently, Matusek and Feil (1983) compared endogenous unipolar, endogenous bipolar, and nonendogeneous depressive patients with normal controls on numerous self-report personality inventories (completed during symptom-free periods), as well as on data derived from several hours of psychiatric interviewing. They reported nonendogenous depressives to have disproportionately high scores on measures of autonomy, describing them as "obstinate, nonadaptive, high-handed, independent and egocentric" (p. 788). These patients were further characterized as demonstrating aggressive self-assertiveness, with a dissatisfied, negative attitude toward life. Unlike the antisocial characterization, however, the nonendogeneous depressives also showed "autodestructive tendencies," including self-reproach, guilt, and fears of losing significant others.

Of particular relevance to the experience of depression in the antisocial personality is the "self-sacrificing depressive" included among the three subtypes in Kegan et al.'s (1981) sociomoral developmental formulation of depression. Characterized by egocentricity and control issues, these depressives experience dysphoria and discontent when unable to satisfy their desires due to external sources that constrain their freedoms or deprive them of the opportunity to act as they choose. To such individuals, issues of control, power, and influence are central. In a sense, a victim of their own impulses and desires, other people are viewed as either being instrumental, or as a source of opposition and threat toward achieving their needs.

> The fear is that to relinquish living in the flux of each moment and satisfying each want is to relinquish the self, to compromise away the core experiences of self. Where "guilt" is expressed or experienced, it is not a matter of self-punishment but of anxious anticipation that other parties will punish or curtail. (Kegan et al., 1981, p. 4)

When depression does occur in the antisocial personality, and if not "masked" through an exaggeration of acting-out behaviors, it is likely to be colored by bitterness, angry complaints, and accusations. Periods of self-loathing may occur at the perception of inner weakness and ineffectualness, and the sympathy of others would be actively shunned. Such features might be consistent with the "Factor Pattern D" depressive subtype described by

Grinker et al., (1961). Demonstrating the traits of gloom, hopelessness and anxiety with some guilt feelings, these patients do not cling or demand attention, nor do they evidence hypochondriacal symptoms. Described as the "angry depressives," these patients typically exhibit demanding, provocative behavior, and are most likely to have had narcissistic and overaggressive premorbid personalities. Having traditionally assumed the role of authority and power at home and in business, depression may be precipitated by frustration or the inability to continue this pattern due to external factors. Such patients are difficult to treat as they resist psychotherapy in their constant struggle to remain "on top," and may express their rage eruptions through serious suicide attempts. A similar, empirically derived, depressive subtype is offered by Overall and Hollister (1980). The hostile depressive is characterized by anxiety, irritable complaining, and anger with suspiciousness sometimes accompanying feelings of hostility.

THE NARCISSISTIC PERSONALITY

The essential feature of this personality style is an overvaluation of self-worth and a grandiose sense of self-importance and uniqueness. In seeming contradiction to the inflated self-concept is an inordinate need to be loved and admired by others. Unlike the ravenous affectional needs of histrionic and dependent personalities, however, narcissists believe that they are entitled to tribute and praise by virtue of their "specialness." These personalities also share the antisocial features of egocentricity, interpersonal exploitation, and exaggerated needs for power and success. Unlike the anger and vindictiveness of antisocials, however, narcissists are characterized by a benign arrogance and a sense that they are "above" the conventions and reciprocity of societal living. There is little real empathy for others but rather, a tendency to use people for self-enhancement and for indulging their desires. Those who satisfy their needs are idealized, while others who can serve no immediate purpose are devalued and even treated contemptuously. This shifting of overvaluation and denigration may occur frequently within the same relationship. There is an expectation of preferential treatment and special favors, without assuming reciprocal responsibilities.

Narcissistic personalities are cognitively expansive, enjoying fantasies of unrealistic goals, with a tendency to overestimate their abilities and achievements. However, these exaggerated feelings of personal importance can leave the narcissist quite vulnerable to injuries of self-esteem and pronounced feelings of unworthiness, should their grandiose self-expectations not be met. Although characteristically imperturbable and insouciant, repeated failure and social humiliations may result in uncertainty and a loss of self-confidence. Over time, with the growing recognition of inconsistencies between their self-perception and their actual performance, comes self-disillusionment, feelings of fraudulence, and in some cases, a chronic state of dysthymia. In other instances, a psychic blow generated from a single event (e.g., a humiliating defeat or a public criticism) may be precipitate a brief, but severe, major depressive episode. Such states rarely endure for extended periods, as depression is not experienced as consonant with the narcissist's self-image. The symptomatology of the narcissistic depression may be quite variable, shifting between dramatic expressions of worthlessness and self-deprecation to irritable demandingness and criticism of others. While feelings of helplessness may accompany their depression, such perceptions tend to be attributed to external, "universal" causes rather than to personal, inner inadequacies (Abramson et al., 1978). Consistent with this formulation, a narcissist may subtly accuse others of not supporting or caring for them enough. At other times, hostility may be directly expressed, as the narcissist becomes enraged at others being witness to his/her shame and humiliation.

Owing to the infrequency of enduring major depression in these individuals, little mention has been made of premorbid narcissistic characteristics in depressed patients. There appears to be some overlap, however, between the "oral" depressive's pronounced affectional needs, and the "narcissistic" depressive's craving for admiration. Rado (1928) characterized the depressive personality as having a low tolerance for narcissistic frustrations, with even trivial disappointments precipitating a marked loss of self-esteem. According to Rado, after actively courting and securing the affection and devotion of a love object, the predepressive may then proceed to treat this individual with a "sublime nonchalance" or tyrannical domination. Characteristically, unaware of this mistreatment of the love object, the predepressive may react with "embittered vehemence," should the love object withdraw or retaliate (1928, p. 422).

Klerman (1974) described depression as a response to fallen self-esteem, a signal of discrepancies within the self-system between "ideal expectations and practical reality" (p. 139). In a similar fashion, Salzman (1970, 1972) described the predepressive as an individual characterized by exceptionally high standards and an unwillingness to accept compromises. Depression in such individuals follows the inability to maintain the unreasonable expectations set for oneself and others. A premorbidly independent depressive is described by Salzman (1970) which shares features of Beck's (1981) "autonomous mode," depressive, Kegan and associates' (Kegan et al., 1981) "self-sacrificing" depressive, and the "angry depressive" reported by Grinker et al. (1961). The independent depressive's overvaluation of autonomy and personal abilities is also reminiscent of the depressive experience in narcissistic personalities.

> While he feels helpless and dependent, he is loath to accept any help, since his standards require total independence and omnipotence. He frequently rejects or distorts any sympathetic reassurance or aid, even while he needs and asks for it, insisting that it is insufficient or patronizing. (Salzman, 1970, p. 115)

It is Kernberg (1975) who provides perhaps the most relevant and eloquent description of the process of self-disillusionment and depression in the narcissistic.

> For them, to accept the breakdown of the illusion of grandiosity means to accept the dangerous, lingering awareness of the depreciated self—the hungry, empty, and lonely primitive self surrounded by a world of dangerous sadistically frustrating and revengeful objects. (1975, p. 311).

THE PARANOID PERSONALITY

The paranoid personality may be viewed as a more dysfunctional variant of the antisocial and narcissistic patterns, with each sharing an independent orientation, and preoccupation with matters of adequacy, power, and prestige. Among the more prominant features of paranoid personalities are a pervasive and unwarranted mistrust of others, hypersensitivity to signs of deception or malevolence, and restricted affectivity. These individuals are fearful of external sources of influence, and may be resistant to forming intimate relationships for fear of being stripped of their power of self-determination. In spite of their air of self-importance, invincibility and pride, paranoid personalities tend to experience extreme jealousy and envy at the "good fortune" of others. To justify these feelings of resentment, they constantly search for signs of deception and actively construct situations to "test" the sincerity of others. Inevitably, their provocative and abrasive behaviors elicit the very signs of malice that they project upon others. Even the slightest, most trivial cues are seized upon and magnified to justify their preconceptions. Data that contradicts their perceptions are ignored, with the paranoid accepting no responsibility or blame for his role. This distortion of events, while personally logical, is irrational, and at times verging on delusional.

In their attempts to remain constantly on guard and mobilized, the paranoid may exhibit an edgy tension, irritability, and rigid defensive posture. To protect themselves from the sadistic treatment and betrayal that they anticipate, these individuals maintain an interpersonal distance and attempt to desensitize themselves from tender and affectionate feelings toward others. They become hard and insensitive to the suffering of others, as well as alienated from their own emotions and inner conflicts.

Although dysfunctionally rigid this stance of social withdrawal, callousness, and projection of personal malevolence and shortcomings onto others provides the paranoid with a glorified self-image and relative freedom from intrapsychic distress. Under circumstances of real or imagined threats to their autonomy or challenges of their competency, however, the paranoid's tenuous sense of self-determination and superiority can be badly shaken. Initially, these individuals may construct new "proofs" to fortify their persecutory fantasies, while vigorously struggling to reestablish their former autonomy and esteem.

During the course of their self-assertion, considerable hostility may be unleashed upon others. In paranoids with prominent narcissistic features, threats to their illusion of omnipotence and superiority may elicit a self-exalted and pompous variant of manic disorder. With an exaggerated cheerfulness, excitement, and buoyancy, reminiscent of their former state of complacency, these individuals are frantically driven to recover their lost exalted status. In some instances, their previous sense of self-determination and confidence cannot be easily reconstructed. Time and again, the paranoid's competencies have been shown to be defective, and they have been made to look foolish. Defeated and humiliated, their past arrogance and self-assurance now submerged, a deep sense of helplessness and major depression may ensue. As with the other independently oriented personalities (i.e., the narcissist and antisocial), the weakness and dependency associated with depression is perceived as unacceptable and humiliating. Consequently, their depression may be colored with anger, agitation, and a suspicious mistrust, that precludes the acceptance of outside help. Many of these behavioral features would correspond to Grinker et al.'s (1961) Factor Pattern D, "angry depressive" pattern, as well as with Overall and Hollister's (1980) "hostile depression," which is described as:

> anxiety combined with depressive mood, but in this type irritable complaining, or angry feelings are also significantly present. Suspiciousness may accompany hostility in the hostile depression type which would suggest a mild paranoid-like syndrome (p. 376, 1980).

As the disorder is relatively infrequent in paranoid patterns, little has been written on the depressive experience in these personalities. Several components of the cognitive-behavioral models of depression, however, may be employed in understanding how and why depression may arise in such individuals. Beck's formulation (1974) for example, would emphasize the paranoid's proneness to distorted thought processes, such as arbitrary inference, selective abstraction, overgeneralization, personalization, and magnification. While paranoids do not characteristically hold negative self-perceptions, instead attributing any existing feelings of helplessness to external, unavoidable causes (Abramson et al., 1978), they do view others as malevolent and threatening. In Beck's (1974) terms, these individuals seem to possess a "template" or cognitive structure which predisposes them to distort perceptions and increase their sensitivity to certain events (e.g., social slights).

The Lewinsohnian model (Lewinsohn, 1974) which links low rates of reinforcement to depression, could also be applied to the paranoid. Sources of reinforcement from the environment are very limited for these individuals, due to their adaptive inflexibility, defensive rigidity, and the fears they harbor of interpersonal intimacy or unknown situations. As previously noted, once becoming depressed, these maladaptive characteristics make it very difficult for paranoids to seek or respond to potentially corrective experiences.

THE PASSIVE-AGGRESSIVE PERSONALITY

The *DSM-III* characterization and diagnostic criteria for the passive-aggressive syndrome is narrowly focused upon one essential trait: resistance to external demands. We propose a more comprehensive concept of a "negativistic personality" to reflect this general contrariness and disinclination to doing as others wish. Beyond the passive-resistance of these individuals is a capricious impulsiveness, an irritable moodiness, an unaccommondating, fault-finding pessimism that characterizes their behavior (Millon, 1981). The broader formulation of the passive-aggressive or negativistic personality taken here is consistent with the "oral sadistic melancholic" described in the writings of early psychoanalysts. Characterized by deep-seated and pervasive ambivalence, consequent to difficulties arising in the "oral biting" stage, these individuals have been described as spiteful, petulant, and overdemanding with a pessimistic mistrust of the world (Menninger, 1940). More recently, Small, Small, Alig & Moore (1970) in a study of 100 patients diagnosed as passive-aggressive personalities suggested that these individuals were characterized by:

> interpersonal strife, verbal (not physical) aggressiveness, emotional storms, impulsivity and manipulative behavior. Suicidal gestures and lack of attention to everyday responsibilities commonly accompanied this intensive style of relating. (p. 978)

Based on the characteristics most frequently reported in both the theoretical and research literature, we propose the following to be among the most essential features of the passive-aggressive or negativistic personality:

1. Irritable affectivity (e.g., quick-tempered and moody).
2. Behavioral contrariness (e.g., passive-aggressive, obstructive and sulking behaviors).
3. Discontented self-image (e.g., feels misunderstood, unappreciated, and disillusioned about life).
4. Deficient regulatory controls (e.g., capricious and poorly modulated emotional expression).
5. Interpersonal ambivalence (e.g., conflicts concerning dependency and self-assertion, unpredictable and exasperating social behaviors).

The characteristic vacillation, discontentment, and socially maladaptive behaviors of passive-aggressive personalities almost inevitably result in varying states of interpersonal conflict and frustration as well as emotional confusion and distress. Consequently, such individuals are highly susceptible to psychiatric symptomatology, including anxiety, somatoform disorders, and especially depression. While major depressive episodes are not uncommon, passive-aggressive personalities are probably most likely to experience chronic forms of dysthymic disorder. Typically, these individuals display an agitated form of dysphoria, shifting between states of anxious futility, self-deprecation and despair to demanding irritability and bitter discontent. They may struggle between their desire to act out defiantly and their social sense that they must curtail their resentments. Although passive-aggressive personalities are accustomed to directly venting their feelings, anger will be restrained and turned inward should they sense that such expression might result in rejection or humiliation. Their grumbling, moody complaints, and sour pessimism, however, serve as a vehicle of tension discharge, relieving them periodically of mounting inner and outer directed anger. A secondary, but important function of these behaviors is to intimidate others and induce guilt, which provides the passive-aggressive with some sense of retribution for the miseries others have caused them in the past. After a time, however, the sullen moodiness and complaining of the passive-aggressive may tend to annoy and alienate others. Although the piteous distress of these depressed individuals may inhibit others from directly expressing their frustration and annoyance, their exasperation is readily perceived by the hypersensitive passive-aggressive and taken as further evidence of the low esteem others hold for him/her.

The dynamics of the passive-aggressive's depressive cycle is well formulated in Salzman's (1972) interpersonal theory of depression, as well as Coyne's (1976) interactional description of depression. Both theorists describe a process of a downward depressive spiral which starts with the depressive's initial expression of helplessness and hopelessness successfully engaging others and eliciting support. Questioning the sincerity of the attention received or dissatisfied with the extent of it, the depressive may then proceed to test others or complain of their lack of caring. Although irritated, the increasingly guilt-ridden and inhibited members of the social environment may continue, initially, to provide gestures of reassurance and support. The continuing abnegating tendencies and bemoaning of the depressive may ultimately, however, cause others to replace their sympathy with annoyance and their compassion with contempt. As noted earlier, the downward depressive spiral is especially likely to occur in the negativisitic, passive-aggressive personality, who, in Lewinsohn's (1974) terms, lacks the social skills necessary to elicit and sustain consistent positive response from others.

Much of the theoretical and research literature on the young, hostile, unstable, and characterological depressives (Akiskal, 1983; Charney et al., 1981; Overall & Hollister, 1980; Paykel, 1972) is pertinent to the depressive experience in passive-aggressive personalities. In a study of characterological traits among a large group of depressed women, Wittenborn and Maurer (1977) noted the following features to persist before and after depressive episodes: a tendency to blame others; a demanding and complaining attitude, and low self-confidence. Two additional traits, obsessionalism and a tendency to dysphoria, manifested by worry and moodiness appeared as persisting traits among a subgroup of the depressed patients. In other patients, these latter traits, in addition to sulky-angry withdrawal, appeared in the prodromal phase of the depression. The authors speculate that the features appearing primarily at the onset of the depressive episode, might serve a defensive function against feelings of being overwhelmed and fears of losing control. An "atypical" or "hysteric" depressive subtype is described in the pharmacologic studies of British investigators, West and Dally (1959) and Sargant (1961). Patients within this category are described as being prone to both neurotic depression and anxiety hysteria. In contrast to the somatic symptoms of the endogenous depressives, atypical depressives manifested emotional overreactivity, anxiety, lethargy, irritability, and bitter complaining with a tendency to blame others. According to these investigators, such patients appear to have histories of good premorbid functioning, but were left depressed and feeling unable to cope by some precipitating stress event. Their emotional lability, hysterical exaggeration of their symptoms and fearfulness which appeared during their illness was not necessarily characteristic of their prior functioning.

In a factor analytic study of depressed woman, Rosenthal and Gudeman (1967) reported two clinically meaningful factors. The first formed an endogenous symptom pattern, while the second was associated with self-pity, hypochondriasis, complaining and demanding behavior, irritability, hostility, and anxiety. This second factor bears a resemblance to two of Paykel's (1972) depressive subtypes: the hostile depressives, characterized by verbal belligerance, and self-pity, and the young personality disordered depressives who evidenced negativism and persisting disturbances in social and interpersonal relationships. Two additional empirically derived depressive subtypes appear to be descriptive of the depressive experience in passive-aggressive personalities. The first is the "agitated depression," as reported by Overall and Hollister (1980). This profile is characterized as an anxious depression, accompanied by tension, excitement, and psychomotor agitation. The second subtype which shares some of the features of the passive-aggressive depressive is the "Factor Pattern C," generated by Grinker et al. (1961), which is characterized by agitation, demandingness, complaining, and hypochondriasis.

Finally, similarities can be drawn between characteristics of the passive-aggressive and the "autodestructive-neurotic" factor of depression recently reported by Matusek and Feil (1983). As described by the authors, this factor is associated with withdrawal tendencies and contact disturbances, but is characterized primarily by:

> mistrust (suspicion), dissatisfaction, a negative attitude toward life, anger, reproaches towards self and others, vulnerability and being easily hurt by petty matters. (p. 787)

It will be recalled that the authors of this study reported unipolar nonendogenous depressives to share many of the features previously reported to be associated with neurotic depressions, including chronic pessimism, loneliness, dissatisfaction, hostility, guilt feelings, and low-frustration tolerance.

THE BORDERLINE PERSONALITY

The term *borderline* rightfully has been criticized for its overinclusiveness and failure to convey a behavioral pattern with distinctive stylistic features (Akiskal, 1981; Millon, 1981; Perry & Klerman, 1978). Depending upon the theoretical orientation taken, the label has been used to connote:

1. A characterorganization existing at a level of personality cohesion midway between neurotic and psychotic (Kernberg, 1970; Knight, 1953).
2. An incipient precursor of schizophrenia.

3. A set of personality variants within the affective disorders spectrum (Akiskal, Khani, & Scott-Strauss, 1979; Stone, 1979).
4. A relatively stable and moderately severe level of functioning that encompasses a variety of different personality subtypes (Grinker, Werble, & Drye, 1968; Millon, 1969).

The borderline label is employed by the *DSM-III* to reflect a discrete syndromal entity. As described by Akiskal (1981), the borderline personality features an unstable sense of self, stemming from disturbances in the individuation-separation phase of development.

> the disorder is conceptualized in characterologic terms and defined by impulsivity, drug-seeking behavior, polymorphous sexuality, affective lability (i.e., display of unmodulated affects such as rage and panic), boredom, anhedonia, bizarre attempts at self-harm and "micropsychotic episodes." (Akiskal, 1981, p. 25)

From our perspective, the borderline concept is best used to represent a moderately severe level of functioning that may occur in virtually any of the personality disorders (perhaps with the exception of the schizoid and antisocial styles). Most frequently, however, the borderline personality appears as an advanced dysfunctional variant of the dependent, histrionic, compulsive, or most commonly, the passive-aggressive personality. Regardless of the background personality history, borderlines are characterized by intense, variable moods and irregular energy levels, both of which frequently appear to be unrelated to external events. The affective state characteristically may be either depressed or excited, or noted by recurring periods of dejection and apathy, interspersed with episodes of anger, anxiety, or euphoria. There is a notable fear of separation and loss with considerable dependency reassurance required to maintain psychic equilibrium. Dependence upon others is colored with strong ambivalent feelings, such as love, anger, and guilt. Chronic feelings of anxiety may be present as borderlines struggle between feelings of anger and shame at being so dependent, and fears that self-assertion will endanger the security and protection that they so desperately seek. In an attempt to secure their anger and constrain their resentment, borderlines often turn against themselves in self-critical, condemnatory manner, which at times may lead to self-mutilating and suicidal thoughts as well as self-damaging behaviors.

As a result of their instability of both affect and behavior, borderlines are prone to rather checkered histories in their personal relationships and in school and work performance. Most exhibit repeated setbacks, a lack of judgment and foresight, tendencies to digress from earlier aspirations and failures to utilize their natural aptitudes and talents. For the most part, despite their setbacks, borderlines manage to recoup and regain their equilibrium before slipping into a more pernicious and serious decompensation. At times, however, when overwhelmed with mounting internal pressures, the borderline's tenuous controls may break down, resulting in an eruption of bizarre behaviors, irrational impulses and delusional thoughts. These mini-psychotic episodes tend to be brief and reversible and seem to assist borderlines in regaining their psychic balance. Afterward such episodes are usually recognized by the individual as being peculiar or deviant.

As noted earlier, overt and direct expressions of hostility in borderlines tend to be exhibited only impulsively, for fear that such actions might result in abandonment or rejection. A characteristic form of anger control in these individuals is to turn feelings of resentment inward into hypochondriacal disorders and mild depressive episodes. Borderlines tend to overplay their helplessness and anguish, employing their depression as a means of avoiding responsibilities and placing added burdens upon others. Their exaggerated plight causes guilt and discomfort among family and friends, as they try to meet the borderline's "justified" need for attention and care. As with passive-aggressive personalities, the dour moods and excessive complaints of the borderline may evoke exasperation and rebuke from others. In this event, borderlines may turn their anger upon themselves even more intensely, voicing a flood of self-deprecatory comments about their worthlessness, evilness, and their inordinate demands upon others. This self-derision may be accompanied by thinly veiled suicidal threats, gambling, drug abuse, or other impulsively self-damaging acts that serve not only to discharge anger, but often succeed in eliciting forgiveness and reassurance, if not compassion from others.

As evident from the preceding, borderlines succumb frequently to major depressive episodes. While the symptomatic features of their affective disorder tend to be rather mixed or erratic, varying in quality and focus according to the individual's specific vulnerabilities, it is typically some composite of depression and hostility.

Agitated depressions are most common, with the borderline exhibiting an apprehensive and tense despondency, that is accompanied by a querulous irritability and hostile depressive complaints. Some borderlines may demonstrate a more intropunitive, self-deprecatory depression, manifest by expressions of self-doubt, feelings of unworthiness, delusions of shame and sin, and suicidal thoughts. In other borderlines, a retarded form of depression is expressed, where guilt and self-disparagement is accompanied by lethargy, feelings of emptiness, boredom, and "deadness."

Borderline personalities may also display periods of bipolar disorder, similar to schizoaffective states, displaying a scattering of ideas and emotions, and a jumble of disconnected thoughts and aimless behaviors. As the borderline's moods are quite changeable and inconsistent with their thoughts and actions, it is virtually impossible for others to comprehend or empathize with their experiences. In their more euphoric moments, the borderline's zestful energy and joviality may temporarily engage and entertain others. The irrational, self-expansive quality of the borderlines' forced sociability, along with their lapses into irritability, eventually exasperate and drain others, however, destroying any patience or goodwill that was previously evoked.

The literature on depression contains many references to atypical treatment-resistant variants of depressive illness (e.g., character-spectrum disorder, hysterical dysphoria) that appear to be strongly associated with unstable, hostile, and "borderline" personality features (Akiskal, 1981; Charney et al., 1981; Winokur, 1979). In Grinker et al.'s (1968) landmark study of the borderline syndrome, depression is mentioned in each of the four borderline subtypes: the Group I patients characterized by inappropriate and negative behaviors as well as hostile, angry depression; the Group II or "core" borderlines exhibiting a vacillating involvement with others and acting out of expressions of anger, alternating with a lonely, hopeless depression; the Group III patients, similar to *DSM-III*'s schizoid personality, with a withdrawn, affectless depression, and the Group IV borderlines characterized by gross defects in self-esteem and confidence and a depressive quality not associated with anger or guilt feelings.

More recently, a drift has occurred in theoretical and research literature toward conceptualizing the borderline syndrome as a personality variant that falls within the spectrum of affective disorders. On the basis of differential responsiveness to pharmacologic agents, Klein and colleagues (Klein, 1975; Liebowitz & Klein, 1981) have asserted that the borderline designation subsumes several heterogeneous subtypes that all share a vulnerability toward affective dysfunction. Of the three borderline personality subtypes that he proposes, the phobic-anxious, the emotionally unstable, and the hysterical dysphorics, it is the hysteroid dysphoric syndrome which has generated the most attention and controversy (Spitzer & Williams, 1982; Stone, 1979). It will be recalled that the disorder is defined as a chronic, nonpsychotic disturbance involving repeated episodes of abruptly depressed mood in response to feeling rejected. The predisposing characteristics of the disorder include an inordinate need for affection and approval with an extreme intolerance of personal (especially romantic) rejection. According to Liebowitz & Klein (1981):

> These vulnerabilities often give rise to a lifelong pattern of affective instability, difficulty being alone, and feelings of chronic emptiness, as well as to unstable or chaotic interpersonal and vocational functioning and a proneness toward angry outbursts, impulsive behavior, and physically selfdamaging acts. In essence, the vulnerabilities that we posit as the core of hysteroid dysphoria may be sufficient to produce many of the features of borderline personality disorder. (p. 73)

Stone (1979) concurs with the authors, reporting that in his own experience, hysteroid dysphorics almost invariably met the traditional borderline criteria, and in many cases, had at least one first-degree relative with a serious affective disorder.

Another group of contemporary biological researchers, led by Akiskal (Akiskal, 1983; Akiskal, 1981), has also argued strongly for the inclusion of the borderline syndrome within the subaffective spectrum. On the basis of affective family history, positive dexamethasone suppression test findings, major affective episodes, and high risk of suicide during prospective followup, Akiskal (1983) has suggested that approximately 50 percent of patients with severe characterologic disturbances, subsumed under the "borderline" rubric seem to suffer from lifelong affective disorders. He suggests that while about one fifth of borderline patients do suffer severe, primary characterological pathology in the form of somatization disorder and sociopathy, the largest group of borderlines exhibit "atypical, chronic and complicated forms of affective disorder with secondary personality dysfunction" (Akiskal, 1981, p. 31). Akiskal argues that while such patients may superficially present the picture of a personality disorder, an underlying biological affective illness may be "masked" by characterologic disturbances. He proposes a variety of subaffective disorders that may fall within the borderline realm. According to Akiskal, subaffective disorder, as opposed to major affective disorders, manifest only subsyndromal and intermittent (often lifelong) affective psychopathology, which only infrequently crystallizes into discrete syndromal episodes. The mood changes associated with such disorders may be quite subtle, with behavioral and interpersonal disturbances (in part having resulted from the affective instability) dominating the clinical picture.

Akiskal et al. (1979) have argued perhaps most strongly for the conceptualization of "cyclothymia" as a subclinical, borderline, affective disorder. They suggest that the bipolar spectrum may merge at one end with psychotic, schizoaffective states and overlap at the other extreme with certain characterological and temperamental disorders. The authors point out the difficulty in diagnostically differentiating the borderline personality disorder from the cyclothymic disorder, a position reflecting Millon's (1969) earlier formulation of the "borderline cycloid" personality. Akiskal notes that the two syndromes may share such features as irritable and angry outbursts, repeated conjugal or romantic failures, uneven work on academic records, geographic instability, and alcohol or drug abuse. A similar state of diagnostic confusion is suggested when the clinician is faced with differentiating the so-called bipolar II disorders from borderline characterologic psychopathology.

Both Akiskal and the authors of this chapter proposed that the unstable sense of self which is characteristic of the borderline may be less of an ego development problem and more a consequence of a constitutional affective disorder with associated unpredictable, uncontrollable mood swings. It is further suggested that the borderline's relatively poor response to psychotherapy may result in many cases, from a failure to provide pharmacologic treatment of the underlying, affective disorder. Stone (1979) also cites the similarities of the two disorders, observing that a large number of cyclothymic patients, in addition to having depressive and hypomanic bouts, favorably respond to lithium, and that relatives with bipolar or unipolar illness also exhibit characteristics that meet the criteria for borderline personality disorder.

The overlap between the borderline and dysthymic concepts has also been addressed (Akiskal, 1983; Snyder, Sajadi, Pitts, & Goodpaster, 1982). Similar to cyclothymia, dysthymic disorders are defined as chronic, intermittent, subaffective manifestations of unipolar depressive disorders. Akiskal offers a typology of chronic, low-grade dysphoric states, including "characterologic depression," which he considers to be closest to the *DSM-III* dysthymic syndrome. In this form of dysthymic disorder, onset typically occurs prior to adulthood and affective states are tightly interwoven with personality traits. On the basis of response to thymoleptic drugs, characterologic depressions are further divided into "subaffective dysthymic disorders," where personality features appear secondary to frequent low-grade endogenous depression, and "character-spectrum disorders," which are primarily characterologic pathology. This latter subtype reportedly occurs more frequently in female patients with "unstable" personality traits including substance abuse. Individuals falling within the character-spectrum group exhibit normal REM latency, typically poor response to somatic therapies, and an irritable dysphoria that is seldom complicated by discrete depressive episodes. Family history tends to be positive for alcoholism and sociopathy, but not for affective illness. Akiskal (1983) disagrees with Winokur's (1979) speculation that there is a genetic basis to this disorder. Instead, he emphasizes that the developmental histories of such individuals (e.g., parental loss and broken homes) lend themselves to characterologic disturbance and an exquisite sensitivity to separation, loss, or romantic disappointment during adult life. From this perspective, Akiskal (1981) argues that what Liebowitz & Klein (1981) have described as "hysteroid dysphoria," is best placed in the character-spectrum category, rather than with primary affective disorders.

Relevant to the issue of dysthymic disorder in borderline personalities is the work of Snyder et al. (1982). Using standardized observer- and subject-rated scales for depression, the authors compared patients satisfying the *DSM-III* criteria for both syndromes. While the scales as a whole failed to differentiate between the depressions of the borderline disorder and the dysthymic disorder, certain features, extracted from the rating scales (e.g., anger, affective instability, impulsiveness, and suspiciousness) were "strikingly" more common in the borderline patients.

THE COMPULSIVE PERSONALITY

The most prominent features of the compulsive personality include excessive emotional control and interpersonal reserve, preoccupation with matters of order, organization and efficiency, indecisiveness, and a tendency toward being overly conscientious, moralistic, and judgmental. It is our belief that much of the personality organization of the compulsive individual arises in reaction to marked underlying feelings of interpersonal ambivalence. Like passive-aggressive personalities, compulsive personalities are torn between their leanings toward submissive dependence on the one hand and defiant autonomy on the other (Millon, 1981). Unlike the overt emotional lability and chronic vacillation of passive-aggressives, however, compulsive personalities bind and submerge their rebellious and oppositional urges through a rigid stance of overcompliance, conformity, and propriety. By clinging grimly to rules of society and insisting upon regularity and uniformity in relationships and life events, these individuals help restrain and protect themselves against their own aggressive impulses and independent strivings. Although this behavioral and cognitive rigidity may effectively shield the individual from intra-psychic conflict as well as social criticism, it may also preclude growth and change, cause alienation from inner feelings and interfere with the formation of intimate and warm relationships.

To others, compulsives appear to be industrious and efficient, but lacking in flexibility, imagination, and spontaneity. They may also be viewed as stubborn or stingy and picayune, with a tendency to get lost in the minutiae, rather than appreciate the substance of everyday life. Compulsives are easily upset by the unfamiliar or by deviations from their accustomed routines. Their perfectionistic standards and need for certainty may result in a tendency toward indecisiveness and procrastination. While the social behavior of compulsives is typically polite and formal, there is a definite tendency to relate to others on the basis of their rank or status. Compulsives require considerable reassurance and approval from their superiors and consequently may relate to them in a deferential, ingratiating, and even obsequious manner. In contrast, compulsives may be quite autocratic and condemnatory with subordinates using their authority and the rules they represent to justify the venting of considerable hostility and criticalness.

Compulsives devalue self-exploration and exhibit little or no insight into their motives and feelings. Beset with deep ambivalence and contrary feelings, extensive defensive maneuvers must be employed to transmute or seal off frightening urges from conscious awareness. While rigid moralism and behavioral conformity bind much of their hidden feelings of defiance and anger, these individuals also find it necessary to compartmentalize or isolate their emotional responses to situations. They may particularly attempt to block or otherwise neutralize reactions to stressful events, for fear that signs of emotional weakness may become apparent and lead to embarassment or disapproval.

Despite their elaborate defensive strategies, compulsives tend to be among the personality styles that are most troubled by psychiatric symptoms. Their cognitive and behavioral organization make them particularly susceptible to affective disorders of virtually every type. Plagued by their own exacting standards, as well as the high expectations that they perceive others to hold for them, compulsives frequently feel as though they have fallen short of their criteria for acceptable performance. Although angry at themselves for being imperfect and resentful toward others for their unyielding demands, compulsives dare not expose either their own shortcomings or their hostility toward others. Rather than voicing their defiance or venting their resentment and thereby being subject to social rebuke, they turn their feelings inward, discharging their anger toward themselves. In this regard, the compulsives propensity toward experiencing guilt, expressing self-reproval, and acting contrite serves as a form of expiation for hidden, unacceptable feelings while preventing humiliation or condemnation from others. The anger-guilt, self-degradation sequence may occur quite frequently in compulsives, resulting in a chronic, mild depression, or dysthymic disorder. Major depressive states may be quite common among compulsives in later life, usually following a period of reflection and self-evaluation. At such times, compulsives are confronted with the realization that their lofty life goals and long-held standards of excellence have not been attained and further, that rigid conformity to external values has yielded a rather barren existence with the denial of a multitude of potentially satisfying experiences. Severe depression in compulsives tends to have an agitated and apprehensive quality, marked by feelings of guilt and a tendency to complain about personal sin and unworthiness. The tense and anxious coloring of their depression may be a reflection of their struggle to contain their hostility and resentments, as well as their fear that contrition and despondency will prompt derision and condemnation from others.

On occasion, in an exaggerated portrayal of their premorbid drive and achievement strivings, compulsives will attempt to counter a melancholic depression with brief periods of accelerated activity directed toward some unrealistic goal. Such maniclike episodes of grandiosity and self-assertion tend to be short lived, however, as they may generate considerable anxiety.

The compulsive personality (also known as the anankastic obsessive, or conforming personality) is undoubtedly the most frequently cited personality in depression literature. Its psychoanalytic counterpart, the anal character, has often been described in association with neurotic depression, manic-depression and involutional melancholia. Abraham (1924/1966), noting marked similarities between obsessive-compulsives and melancholics, suggested that both syndromes arose from fixations in the anal stage of psychosexual development, with obsessives emerging from the more advanced anal retentive phase and melancholics arising from complications in the more primitive anal-expulsive phase. Abraham cites a number of shared anal character traits between the obsessive-compulsive and the melancholic, including excessive punctuality, orderliness, obstinacy, parsimony, and marked feelings of ambivalence in interpersonal relationships.

A number of other theorists with analytic leanings have offered depressive subtypes akin to the anal-obsessive. A "subvalid" personality has been proposed by Swedish psychiatrist Sjöbring (1973) in his multidimensional theory of personality. The subvalid individual is described as cautious, reserved, precise, industrious, and scrupulous. Numerous researchers (Coppen, 1966; Nystrom & Lindegard, 1975; Perris, 1966) employing the Nyman-Marke Temperament Scale (NMTS), which objectifies Sjöbring's concepts, found depressed individuals (especially of the unipolar endogenous type) to exhibit a significant tendency toward subvalidity. As used on the NMTS, the subvalid concept has a somewhat broader meaning, referring to individuals who are bound to routine, easy to fatigue, cautious, tense, neurasthenic, and meticulous (Akiskal et al., 1983). Chodoff (1970) focused upon the interpersonal ambivalence and unexpressed hostility of premorbid depressives. He offered two behavioral paths that might be taken in response to such dependency conflicts: utilization of "extractive techniques" and the active manipulation of others, or the denial of such needs and the internalization of unrealistic self-standards. Chodoff (1970) suggested that the latter approach may lead to the development of a "perfectionistic, neurotically, prideful obsessive" (p. 58).

In Blatt's (1974) depressive typology, which is based on the level of object representation achieved, he describes a depression subtype associated with issues of "superego formation and the relatively advanced and complex phenomenon of guilt." The "introjective depression" is characterized by intense feelings of inferiority, guilt, and worthlessness. On the basis of a factor analytic study employing the Depressive Experiences Questionnaires, Blatt et al. (1976) identified a "self-criticism" factor that relates closely to the concept of introjective depression. According to the authors, the self-criticism factor in comparison with the other two factors identified, had the highest correlation with traditional psychometric measures of depression. This factor consisted of items relating to:

> concerns about feeling guilty, empty, hopeless, unsatisfied, and insecure, having failed to meet expectations and standards, and being unable to assume responsibility, threatened by change, feeling ambivalent about self and others, and tending to assume blame and feel critical toward self. (Blatt et al., 1976, p. 385)

A later study (Blatt et al., 1982) involving the identification of depressive subtypes on the basis of psychiatric case histories showed clinical records of the self-criticism group to be characterized by:

> social isolation, intense and self-critical involvement in work, professional and/or academic strivings, feelings of worthlessness and failure, a history of a very critical or idealized parent, obsessive and paranoid features, anxiety and agitation. (Blatt et al., 1982, p. 120)

In a similar fashion, Arieti and Bemporad (1980) propose a "dominant goal" predepressive among their three premorbid types of depressive personality. Described as "usually seclusive, arrogant, and often obsessive," this form of personality organization is reported to be more common in men. According to Arieti and Bemporad (1980) dominant-goal individuals have learned from their parents that achievement is rewarded with support and acceptance. Consequently, these individuals come to derive their sense of meaningfulness, satisfaction, and self-esteem from fantasies about obtaining some lofty objective. In pursuing their goals, other activities may be shunned as a diversion from their quest. For such individuals, the realization that a selected goal is unobtainable may threaten not only their sense of self-esteem, but the very structure upon which their life's meaning is based.

The two basic depressive personality modes of Beck (1981) have already been discussed. The "autonomous mode" shares several features of the compulsive including: internalized standards, goals, and criteria for achievement that tend to be higher than the conventionally accepted norms; an emphasis on independence, control and action, and a tendency to be direct, dogmatic, and authoritarian. Individuals operating within the autonomous mode are vulnerable to depression when they feel they have failed in their attempts to reach a crucial goal. Beck (1981) describes the "autonomous depression" as being permeated with the theme of defeat or failure, as the individual "blames himself continually for falling below his standard (self-attribution), and excoriates himself for his incompetence (self-punishment)" (Beck, 1981, p. 276). Beck also notes that such individuals experience a striking behavioral shift when depressed, from having been "self-sufficient, inner-directed, and active" to appearing "powerless, devoid of initiative and self-control" (Beck, 1981, p. 276).

From a slightly different theoretical perspective (i.e., sociomoral development), Kegan et al. (1981) proposed a "self-evaluative depression" in which "dysphoria and discontent are described in terms of the failure to live up to one's own hopes for oneself, falling short of one's standards" and "negative self-evaluation" (Kegan et al., 1981, p. 6). In this form of depression, there may also be a sense of not being whole, as "the price of self-determination and control has been the exclusion of important parts of oneself," and "self-imposed isolation, and the inability to experience true intimacy" (Kegan et al., 1981, p. 6–7).

As mentioned earlier, the compulsive personality has been frequently cited in association with involutional melancholia. While the syndrome of involutional depression has been the subject of considerable debate (Chodoff, 1972), the concept of an endogenous unipolar or psychotic depression, occurring for the first time in middle age, has received widespread clinical recognition. In association with this syndrome, a melancholic personality has been proposed that is characterized by some "oral," but predominantly "anankastic" features. Von Zerssen (1977) in his review of the international literature, found the clearest association between affective disorders and personality traits to be that between unipolar depressive psychosis (including involutional melancholia) and the melancholic personality. His description of the "melancholic type" includes the features of "orderliness, conscientiousness, meticulousness, high value achievement, conventional thinking and dependency on close personal relationships" (Von Zerssen, 1977, p. 97–98). The association of the late onset endogenous depression with anankastic, obsessional traits has been reported by a number of other researchers. Paykel et al. (1976) found older depressed patients in their study group to be significantly less neurotic, hysterical, and oral, but more obsessive. On symptomatic measures, these patients also evidenced a more severe endogenous pattern of depression, accompanied by a greater level of anxiety than seen in younger patients. Cadoret, Baker, Dorzab, and Winokur (1971), employing Cattell's personality inventory, found that scores on the factor denoting "superego strength" were highest in depressive patients having the onset of their illness after the age of 40. Scores on this factor were also higher in their healthy, first-degree relatives, as compared to early-onset depressive patients. On the basis of such studies, Yerevanian and Akiskal (1979) concluded that:

> there appears little reason to dispute the classic notion that portrays the late-onset (usually psychotic) depressive as a self-critical, conscientious, hard-work-

ing, and well-integrated (into the dominant culture) individual who has responded to losses and life reverses with self-punitive and self-denigrating cognitions. (p. 603)

In recognition of studies that have failed to confirm the age association between obsessionalism and unipolar depression (e.g., Snaith, McGuire & Fox, 1971; Kendell & Discipio, 1970), Chodoff (1972) drew a more conservative conclusion,

> among individuals suffering depressive breakdowns for the first time in middle life, there exists a certain well-defined subgroup, among men as well as women, who display premorbid obsessional personality characteristics. (1972, p. 667)

Interpretation of the apparent age effect upon personality and depressive features is not straightforward. As mentioned earlier, midlife reflection and self-evaluation may confront conforming, "obsessive" individuals with the realization that: (*a*) idealized internal standards have rarely been met; (*b*) productivity and the capacity to achieve are likely to decline sharply with advanced age, (*c*) the choice for an industrious, conforming lifestyle has been at the expense of interpersonal intimacy and emotional fulfillment. An alternate explanation for these age-associated features is that personality traits may actually be altered with age, leading to the development of "more obsessive, less hysterical, less dependent and less emotionally labile patterns" (Paykel et al., 1976, p. 332).

As with involutional melancholia, anankastic, compulsive personality traits have held a prominent place in the psychoanalytic literature on manic-depressive illness. Kolb, in his 1973 revision of Noye's original text, provides the following description of the premorbid personality of a depressed-type manic-depressive:

> Many have been scrupulous persons of rigid ethical and moral standards, meticulous, self-demanding, perfectionistic, self-depreciatory, prudish, given to self-reproach, and sensitive to criticism. Their obsessive-compulsive tendency have doubtless been defensive mechanisms for handling hostility, which characteristically they cannot express externally. (Kolb, 1973, p. 372–373)

A number of empirically based studies have suggested that bipolar disorders are not necessarily associated with cyclothymic, hyperthymic, or unstable characterologic features. Rather, there is evidence to suggest that the illness may occur most frequently among individuals who, except for "obsessive" features, are otherwise unremarkable (Donnelly, Murphy & Goodwin, 1976; Hirschfeld & Klerman, 1979; Perris, 1971). Consistent with this is the recent factor analytic study of Matussek and Feil (1983) which identified a "hypomanic success and achievement" factor that differentiated endogenous bipolar patients from "normals," as well as from other types of depressed patients. The authors report that this factor reflects a personality substructure that is characterized by:

hypomanic drive for success, high aspiration level, anankastic features, pedantry, subordinate to authority, perseverance in difficult tasks, and detachment for achievement. (Matussek & Feil, 1983, p. 787)

The authors note that the strong achievement orientation, exaggerated aspiration level, pronounced sense of duty, and scrupulousness of the endogenous bipolar patients all serve to make the individual exquisitely vulnerable to feelings of inadequacy and failure, while reaching a lofty goal may trigger a mania if it subjectively represents a great success after hard work.

Akiskal and his colleagues (Akiskal et al., 1983; Akiskal et al., 1979) have commented on the difficulty in differentiating the ambitious, driven, hyperthymic individual with an inordinate capacity for work, from the duty-bound and work-addicted compulsive individual. Similarities are also drawn between the premorbid adjustment of bipolar patients and the "Type A" coronary-prone behavior pattern, which is characterized by extremes of competitiveness, achievement striving, time urgency, and aggressiveness. It is suggested that future research might well be directed at detecting the incidence of frank manic-depressive illness in the families of people displaying the Type A pattern. Akiskal et al. (1979) also suggest similarities between compulsive personalities and manic-depressive patients in terms of pharmacological treatment response. They note the ample number of anecdotal reports which have suggested favorable and sometimes dramatic effects of lithium carbonate upon both the compulsive drivenness of manic-depressives during intermorbid periods, as well as the drivenness, indecisiveness, and anxious worry seen in several compulsive personality disorders.

Finally, this same group of researchers (Akiskal, 1983; Akiskal et al., 1983) have described a subaffective dysthmic disorder that is associated with: higher rates of familial bipolar illness, anhedonic, guilt-ridden, hypersomnic retarded depressions, occasional hypomanic responses to tricyclic antidepressant therapy, and favorable responses to lithium. Akiskal (1983) suggests that the depressive personality characteristics exhibited by such patients; that is, introversion with brief periods of hypomanic extraversion, are best considered lifelong, subaffective expressions of a primary depressive disorder. It will be recalled that this syndrome has been associated with numerous Schneiderian depressive features (e.g., nonassertiveness, pessimism, self-criticism, conscientiousness, and worried preoccupations about inadequacy and failure) that are also consistent with the compulsive personality organization.

At this point in the literature review, an important distinction must be made between compulsive personality traits and obsessive-compulsive symptoms as they occur in depression. While there is some evidence that obsessions, ruminative worry, and compulsive behaviors are more likely to occur in individuals with "obsessive" or compulsive premorbid personalities (Vaughan, 1976; Videbech, 1975), these same symptoms are frequent accompaniments of depressive episodes in a variety of other personality types. Studies that have attempted to carefully tease apart depressive symptomatology from enduring characterologic traits, however, have revealed considerable differences with respect to the intensity and duration of obsessive-compulsive symptoms in depression.

Wittenborn and Maurer's (1977) investigation of characterologic traits among depressives (reviewed earlier in this chapter) found two traits, worried moodiness and obsessionalism to be persistent features among only a subgroup of the depressed patients. In other patients, these features appeared as prodromal intensification of the episode, remitting with the development of the depression. Kendell and Discipio (1970) found that on measures of obsessionalism, recovered unipolar depressives had scores intermediate between those of obsessional neurotics and two "normal" groups. Comparisons between neurotic and psychotic depressives found neurotic depressives to be more obsessional premorbidly while psychotic depressives developed more new obsessional symptomatology during their depressive illness. Contrary to other reports (Gittleson, 1966; Videbech, 1975), obsessional traits did not appear to intensify during the depressive episode among premorbidly obsessional individuals. Vaughan (1976) found obsessive symptoms to occur more frequently in depression among a group of patients with obsessional personalities. He further reported that premorbidly obsessive patients evidenced less anxiety during their illness, while the presence of obsessive symptoms in other depressed patients tended to be associated with an agitated and anxious form of depression.

Of particular interest is the suggestion among some of these studies that obsessional symptoms and traits serve as a defense against depression. Wittenborn and Maurer (1977) hypothesize that intensification of obsessionalism and denial of anger at the onset of the depressive episode may serve a defensive function among individuals feeling overwhelmed by environmental stressors and sensing an impending loss of control. Kendell and Discipio (1970) suggested that marked premorbid obsessionalism seemed to offer protection against the development of manic episodes. Von Zerssen (1977), in his review of the literature, postulated that many of the traits of the "melancholic-type" resulted from the tendency to build defenses against the negative emotions involved in depression. He cites as an example, the melancholic's strivings toward self-confirmation in performance, as a strategy to avoid a lack of self-esteem. Consistent with this line of thought and in summary, Yerevanian and Akiskal (1979) have noted that:

> the psychoanalytical literature has suggested that the anankastic traits of orderliness, guilt and concern for others are a defense against the depressive's tendency for disorganization, hostility and self-preoccupation. (1979, p. 604)

CONCLUSIONS

A sizable body of literature has been reviewed in this chapter in an attempt to better elucidate the relationship between personality and depressive disorders. For the most part, our discussion has been restricted to the role that personality may play in the etiology and pathogenesis of affective disorders. While research in this area has been rather speculative, unsystematic, and for some personality disorders, quite sparse, it is our contention that a sufficient amount of both clinical and empirical evidence argues for the inclusion of a wide variety of characterologic features among the predisposing factors to depression. Furthermore once a depressive illness has emerged, it may be argued that disorders of personality, as well as specific personality traits may exert a pathoplastic effect, coloring the depressive symptom picture and influencing treatment compliance, responsivity and ultimately, outcome.

This chapter has paid only modest attention to the viewpoint that both personality and depressive disorders are expressions of shared genetic or constitutional endowments, whereby personality features may be conceptualized as a milder or alternative expression of affective illness. Similarly, we have not addressed the possibility that personality features may arise as complications or sequelae of affective illness. In this regard, Akiskal et al. (1983) have suggested the following possibilities as to how personality may be altered by affective illness: (1) personality presentation (i.e., behaviors, judgment, motivation, and emotional expression) may be changed during an affective episode, (2) interpersonal maladjustments and familial conflicts may immediately follow the resolution of a depressive or manic episode and (3) long-term alterations in personality organization as well as social deterioration may result from chronic affective illness or frequently recurring affective episodes.

To date, methodologic limitations have clouded our understanding of some of issues raised here. It remains the formidable task of future research to identify the range of genetic-constitutional, developmental, sociocultural, and experiential factors from which both personality and depression emerge. Only then can an appreciation of the complex interrelationship of the two be obtained.

References

Abraham, K. (1966). A short study of the development of the libido, viewed in the light of mental disorders. In B. D. Lewin (Ed.), *On character and development*. New York: W. W. Norton. (Original work published 1924).

Abraham, K. (1968). Notes on the psychoanalytical investigation and treatment of manic-deressive insanity and allied conditions. In W. Gaylin (Ed.), *The meaning of despair* (pp. 26–50). New York: Science House. (Original work published 1911)

Abramson, L. Y., Seligman M. E., & Teasdale J. (1978). Learned helplessness in humans: Critique and reformulation. *Journal of Abnormal Psychology, 87,* 49–74.

Akiskal, H. S. (1981). Subaffective disorders: Dysthymic, cyclothymic and bipolar II disorders in the "borderline" realm. *Psychiatric Clinics of North America, 4*(1), 25–46.

Akiskal, H. (1983). Dysthymymic disorder: Psychopathology of proposed chronic depressive subtypes. *American Journal of Psychiatry, 140*(1), 11–20.

Akiskal, H. S., Hirschfield, R., & Yerevanian, B. (1983). The relationship of personality to affective disorders. *Archives of General Psychiatry, 40,* 801–810.

Akiskal, H. S., Khani, M. K., & Scott-Strauss, A. (1979). Cyclothymic temperamental disorders. *Psychiatric Clinics of North America, 2*(3), 527–554.

Akiskal, H. S., Rosenthal, T. L., Haykal, R. F., Lemmi, H., Rosenthal, R. H., & Scott-Strauss, A. (1980). Characterological depressions: Clinical and sleep EEG findings separating "subaffective dysthymias" from "character-spectrum disorders." *Archives of General Psychiatry, 37,* 777–783.

Altman, J. H., & Wittenborn, J. R. (1980). Depression-prone personality in women. *Journal of Abnormal Psychology, 89,* 303–308.

American Psychiatric Association. (1980). *Diagnostic and Statistical Manual of mental disorders (DSM-III).* Washington DC: Author.

Arieti, S., & Bemporad, J. R. (1980). The psychological organization of depression. *American Journal of Psychiatry, 137,* 1360–1365.

Beck, A. T. (1974). The development of depression: A cognitive model. In R. J. Friedman, & M. M. Katz (Eds.), *The psychology of depression: Contemporary theory and research.* Washington: Winston, 3–19.

Beck, A. T. (1981). Cognitive therapy of depression: New perspectives. In P. Clayton & J. Barrett (Eds.), *Treatment of depression: Old controversies and new approaches.* New York: Raven Press.

Becker, J. (1977). *Affective disorders.* New York: General Learning Press.

Bemporad, J. (1971). New views on the psychodynamics of the depressive character. In S. Arieti (Ed.), *World biennial of psychiatry and psychotherapy* (Vol. 1; pp. 219–243). New York: Basic Books.

Bibring, E. (1953). The mechanism of depression. In P. Greenacre (Ed.), *Affective disorders,* New York: International Universities Press.

Blaney, P. H. (1977). Contemporary theories of depression: Critique and comparison. *Journal of Abnormal Psychology, 86,* 203–223.

Blatt, S. J. (1974). Levels of object representation in anaclinitic and introjective depression. *Psychoanalytic Study of the Child, 29,* 426–427.

Blatt, S. J., D'Afflitti, P., & Quinlan, D. M. (1976). Experiences of depression in normal young adults. *Journal of Abnormal Psychology, 85,* 383–389.

Blatt, S. J., Quinlan, D. M., Chevon, E. S., McDonald, C., & Zuroff, D. (1982). Dependency and self-criticism: Psychological dimensions of depression. *Journal of Consulting and Clinical Psychology, 50,* 113–124.

Cadoret, R., Baker, M., Dorzab, J., & Winokur, G. (1971). Depressive disease: Personality factors in patients and their relatives. *Biological Psychiatry, 3,* 85–93.

Charney, D. S., Nelson, J. C., & Quinlan, D. M. (1981). Personality traits and disorder in depression. *American Journal of Psychiatry, 138,* 1601–1604.

Chodoff, P. (1970). The core problem in depression: Interpersonal aspects. In J. Masserman (Ed.), *Depressions: Theories and therapies, science and psychoanalysis* (Vol. 17; pp. 56–65). New York: Grune & Stratton.

Chodoff, P. (1972). The depressive personality: A critical review. *Archives of General Psychiatry, 27,* 666–673.

Chodoff, P. (1973). The depressive personality. *International Journal of Psychiatry, 11*, 196–217.

Cleckley, H. (1941). *The mask of sanity.* St. Louis, MO: C. V. Mosby.

Cofer, D. H., & Wittenborn, J. R. (1980). Personality characteristics of formerly depressed women. *Journal of Abnormal Psychology, 89*, 309–314.

Coppen, A. (1966). The Marke-Nyman temperament scale: An English translation. *British Journal of Medical Psychology, 39*, 55–59.

Cormier, B. M. (1966). Depression and persistent criminality. *Canadian Psychiatric Association Journal, 11*, 208–220.

Coyne, J. C. (1976). Toward an interactional description of depression. *Psychiatry, 39*, 28–40.

Donnelly, E., Murphy, D., & Goodwin, F. (1976). Cross-sectional and longitudinal comparisons of bipolar and unipolar depressed groups on the MMPI. *Journal of Consulting and Clinical Psychology, 44*, 233–237.

Fenichel, O. (1968). Depression and mania. In W. Gaylin (Ed.), *The meaning of despair* (pp. 108–154). New York: Science House.

Freud, S. (1968) Mourning and melancholia. In W. Gaylin (Ed.), *The meaning of despair* (pp. 50–70). New York: Science House. (Original work published 1917)

Freud, S. (1932). Libidinal types. In *Collected Papers* (English translation, Vol. 5, 1950). London: Hogarth.

Gershon, E., Cromer, M., & Klerman, G. (1968). Hostility and depression. *Psychiatry, 31*, 224–235.

Gittelson, N. L. (1966). The effect of obsessions on depressive psychosis. *British Journal of Psychiatry, 112*, 253–259.

Grinker, R. R., Miller, J., Sabshin, M., Nunn, R., & Nunnally, J. (1961). *The phenomenon of depressions.* New York: Hoeber.

Grinker, R. R., Werble, B., & Drye, R. C. (1968). *Borderline Syndrome* New York: Basic Books.

Hirschfield, R., & Klerman, G. (1979). Personality attributes and affective disorders. *American Journal of Psychiatry, 136*, 67–70.

Hirschfield, R., Klerman, G., Clayton, P., & Keller, M. (1983). Personality and depression. *Archives of General Psychiatry, 40*, 993–998.

Kegan, R., Rogers, L., & Quinlan, D. (1981). *Constructive-developmental organizations of depression.* Invited paper presented to a symposium on New Approaches to Depression, American Psychological Association annual meeting, Los Angeles.

Kendell, R. E., & Discipio, W. J. (1970). Obsessional symptoms and obsessional personality traits in patients with depressive illness. *Psychological Medicine, 1*, 65–72.

Kernberg, O. F. (1970). A psychoanalytic classification of character pathology. *Journal of the American Psychoanalytic Association, 18*, 800–822.

Kernberg, O. F. (1975). *Borderline conditions and pathological narcissism.* New York: Jason Aronson.

Klein, D. F. (1975). Psychopharmacology and the borderline patient. In J. E. Mack (Ed.), *Borderline states in psychiatry.* New York: Grune & Stratton.

Klerman, G. L. (1973). The relationship between personality and clinical depressions: Overcoming the obstacles to verifying psychodynamic theories. *International Journal of Psychiatry, 11,* 227–233.

Klerman, G. L. (1974). Depression and adaptation. In R. J. Friedman, & M. M. Katz (Eds.), *The psychology of depression: Contemporary theory and research* (pp. 129–145). Washington, DC: V. H. Winston & Sons.

Knight, R. P. (1953). Borderline states. *Bulletin of the Menninger Clinic, 17,* 1–12.

Kohlberg, L. (1976). Moral stages and moralization: The cognitive developmental approach. In T. Lickona (Ed.), *Moral development and behavior.* New York: Holt, Rinehart & Winston.

Kolb, L. C. (1973). *Modern clinical psychiatry* (8th ed.). Philadelphia: W. B. Saunders.

Lazare, A., & Klerman, G. L. (1968). Hysteria and depression: The frequency and significance of hysterical personality features in hospitalized depressed women. *American Journal of Psychiatry, 11,* 48–58.

Lesse, S. (1974). Depression masked by acting-out behavior patterns. *American Journal of Psychotherapy, 28,* 352–361.

Lewinsohn, P. M. (1974). A behavioral approach to depression. In R. J. Friedman & M. M. Katz (Eds.). *The psychology of depression: Contemporary theory and research* (pp. 156–185). Washington, DC: V. H. Winston & Sons.

Lewinsohn, P. M., Zeiss, M. A., Zeiss, R. A., & Haller, R. (1977). Endogeneity and reactivity as orthogonal dimensions in depression. *The Journal of Nervous and Mental Disease, 164,* 327–332.

Liebowitz, M. R., & Klein, D. F. (1981). Interrelationship of hysteroid dysphoria and borderline personality disorder. *Psychiatric Clinics of North America, 4*(1), 67–87.

Lion, E. G. (1942). Anankastic depressions: Obsessive-compulsive symptoms occurring during depressions. *Journal of Nervous and Mental Disorders, 95,* 730–738.

Matussek, P., & Feil, W. (1983). Personality attributes of depressive patients. *Archives of General Psychiatry, 40,* 783–790.

McCranie, E. J. (1971). Depression, anxiety and hostility. *Psychiatric Quarterly, 45,* 117–133.

Mendelson, M. (1967). Neurotic depressive reactions. In A. M. Freedman & H. I. Kaplan (Eds.), *Comprehensive textbook of psychiatry.* Baltimore: Wilkins & Williams.

Mendelson, M. (1973). Some second thoughts on the depressive personality. *International Journal of Psychiatry, 11,* 222–226.

Menninger, K. (1940). Character disorders. In J. F. Brown (Ed.), *The psychodynamics of abnormal behavior.* New York: McGraw-Hill.

Metcalfe, M. (1968). The personality of depressive patients. In A. Coppen & A. Walk (Eds.), *Recent developments in affective disorders.* London: Royal Medico-Psychological Association.

Millon, T. (1969). *Modern psychopathology.* Philadelphia: W. B. Saunders.

Millon, T. (1981). *Disorders of personality: DSM-III: Axis II.* New York: John Wiley & Sons.

Nystrom, S., & Lindegard, B. (1975). Depression: Predisposing factors. *Acta Psychiatrica Scandinavica, 51,* 77–87.

Overall, J., & Hollister, L. (1980). Phenomenological classification of depressive disorders. *Journal of Clinical Psychology, 36*(2), 372–377.

Paykel, E. S. (1971). Classification of depressed patients: A cluster analysis derived grouping. *British Journal of Psychiatry, 118,* 275–288.

Paykel, E. S. (1972). Correlates of a depressive typology. *Archives of General Psychiatry, 27,* 203–210.

Paykel, E. S., Klerman, G. L., & Prusoff, B. A. (1976). Personality and symptom pattern in depression. *British Journal of Psychiatry, 129,* 327–334.

Paykel, E. S., Myers, J. K., & Dienelt, M. N. (1970). Life events and depression. *Archives of General Psychiatry, 21,* 753–760.

Paykel, E. S., & Prusoff, B. A. (1973). Relationships between personality dimensions: Neuroticism and extraversion against obsessive, hysterical and oral personality. *British Journal of Social and Clinical Psychology, 12,* 309–318.

Paykel, E. S., & Weissman, M. M. (1973). Social adjustment and depression. *Archives of General Psychiatry, 24,* 659–663.

Perris, C. (1966). A study of bipolar (manic-depressive) and unipolar recurrent depressive psychosis. *Acta Psychiatrica Scandinavica, 42* (Suppl.) 194.

Perris, C. (1971). Personality patterns in patients with affective disorders. *Acta Psychiatrica Scandinavica, 221* (Suppl.) 43.

Perry, J. C., & Klerman, G. L. (1978). The borderline patient. *Archives of General Psychiatry, 35,* 141–150.

Rado, S. (1928). The problem of melancholia. *International Journal of Psychoanalysis, 9,* 420–438.

Rado, S. (1951). Psychodynamics of depression from the etiologic point of view. *Psychosomatic Medicine, 13,* 51–55.

Rado, S. (1968). Psychodynamics of the depressive from the etiologic point of view. In W. Gaylin (Ed.), *The meaning of despair* (pp. 96–108). New York: Science House.

Reid, W. H. (1978). The sadness of the psychopath. *American Journal of Psychotherapy, 32,* 496–509.

Rosenthal, S., & Gudeman, J. (1967). The self-pitying constellation in depression. *British Journal of Psychiatry, 113,* 485–489.

Salzman, L. (1970). Depression: A clinical review. In J. Masserman (Ed.), *Depression: Theories and therapies Science and Psychoanalysis* (Vol. 17). New York: Grune & Stratton.

Salzman, L. (1972). Interpersonal factors in depression. In F. Flach & S. Draghi (Eds.), *The mature and treatment of depression.* New York: John Wiley & Sons.

Sargant, W. (1961). Drugs in the treatment of depression. *British Medical Journal, 1,* 225–227.

Schless, A., Mendels, J., Kipperman, A., & Cochrane, C. (1974). Depression and hostility. *The Journal of Nervous and Mental Disease, 159,* 91–100.

Schneider, K. (1958). *Psychopathic personalities.* trans. by M. W. Hamilton. London: Cassell.

Seligman, M. E. (1974). Depression and learned helplessness. In R. J. Friedman, & M. M. Katz (Eds.), *The Psychology of depression: Contemporary theory and research* (pp. 83–109). Washington: Winston.

Sjöbring, H. (1973). Personality structure and development: A model and its applications. *Acta Psychiatrica Scandinavica Supplement, 244,* 1.

Small, I., Small, J., Alig, V., & Moore, D. (1970). Passive-aggressive personality disorder: A search for a syndrome. *American Journal of Psychiatry, 126,* 973–983.

Snaith, R. P., McGuire, R. J., & Fox, K. (1971). Aspects of personality and depression. *Psychological Medicine, 1,* 239–246.

Snyder, S., Sajadi, C., Pitts, W. M., & Goodpaster, W. A. (1982). Identifying the depressive border of the borderline personality. *American Journal of Psychiatry, 139,* 814–817.

Spitzer, R. L., & Williams, J. B. W. (1982). Hysteroid dysphoria: An unsuccessful attempt to demonstrate its syndromal validity. *American Journal of Psychiatry, 139,* 1286–1291.

Stone, M. H. (1979). Contemporary shift of the borderline concept from a subschizophrenic disorder to a subaffective disorder. *Psychiatric Clinics of North American, 2*(3), 577–593.

Vaughn, M. (1976). The relationships between obsessional personality, obsessions in depression and symptoms of depression. *British Journal of Psychiatry, 129,* 36–39.

Videbech, T. (1975). A study of genetic factors, childhood bereavement, and premorbid personality traits in patients with anancastic endogenous depression. *Acta Psychiatrica Scandinavica, 52,* 178–222.

Von Zerssen, D. (1977). Premorbid personality and affective psychoses. In G. D. Burrows (Ed.), *Handbook of Studies on depression* (pp. 79–103). Amsterdam, The Netherlands: Excerpta Medica.

Von Zerssen, D. (1982). Personality and affective disorders. In E. S. Paykel (Ed.), *Handbook of affective disorders* (pp. 212–228). New York: Guilford Press,

Weissman, M. M., Prusoff, B. A., & Klerman, G. L. (1979). Personality and the prediction of long-term outcome of depression. *American Journal of Psychiatry, 136,* 555–558.

West, E. D., & Dally, P. J. (1959). Effects of iproniazid in depressive syndromes. *British Medical Journal, 1,* 1491–1494.

Winokur, G. (1979). Unipolar depression: Is it divisible into autonomous subtypes. *Archives of General Psychiatry, 36,* 47–52.

Wittenborn, R. R. (1965). Depression. In B. Wolman (Ed.), *Handbook of clinical psychology.* New York. McGraw-Hill.

Wittenborn, J. R., & Maurer, H. A. (1977). Persisting personalities among depressed women. *Archives of General Psychiatry, 34,* 968–971.

Yerevanian, B. I., & Akiskal, H. S. (1979). Neurotic, characterologic and dysthymic depressions. *Psychiatric Clinics of North America, 2,* 595–617.

Chapter 22

Depression Associated with Physical Disease

Roger G. Kathol

INTRODUCTION

Dysphoria is a prerequisite for the diagnosis of depression. Not all individuals with dysphoria, however, have the symptoms of a full depressive syndrome. It is rare in psychiatric textbooks to find mention that sadness or mild dysphoria (normal low mood) is an emotional state experienced by everyone. Sadness and dysphoria commonly occur in relation to daily events. It can also inherently change without reason from day to day (the "good" day and "bad" day phenomena) or persist for extended periods (the pessimist). Without some understanding of this normal experience of emotion there is a tendency among mental health professionals to consider that affective illness is present in any patient demonstrating dysphoria regardless of the number or degree of symptoms, until proven otherwise. Though sadness is similar to depression in that it is accompanied by the uncomfortable feelings of dejection and discouragement, it is distinctly different in its effect on an individual's ability to cope with routine life events. In this chapter "depression" or "depressive syndrome" will be used to connote dysphoria which is *continuous, pervasive,* and *severe* and which interferes with the performance of social, occupational, or personal activity.

In recent years, several classification systems—the St. Louis criteria (Feighner, Robins, Guze, Woodruff, Winokur, & Muñoz, 1972), the Research Diagnostic Criteria (Spitzer, Endicott, & Robins, 1978), and *DSM-III* (American Psychiatric Association, 1980)—have increased the clinician's ability to identify patients with a major depressive syndrome. Each requires a persistently low mood (one week to one month) associated with significant signs and symptoms (four to five) in the following areas: insomnia, appetite disturbance, fatigue, psychomotor disturbance, decreased interest, feelings of self-reproach or guilt, diminished ability to think or concentrate, and recurrent thoughts of death or suicide. Either incorporated into the definition or implied is some degree of social impairment resulting from the above symptomatology. Dysphoric individuals not meeting criteria for depression as defined above fall into the category of sadness. RDC and *DSM-III* criteria suggest that sadness may also occur in other disorders (Episodic Minor Depression, Chronic or Intermittent Minor Depressive Disorder—RDC; Dysthymic Disorder, Atypical Depression—*DSM-III*). The character of these disorders is still open to question since the information on these groups stems from poorly defined inclusion criteria and there is little knowledge about likely age of onset, course and duration, prognosis, or efficacy of treatment.

This chapter focuses on medically ill patients with symptoms of major depression, not simply sadness. While those with simple sadness may benefit from support, those with the depressive syndrome will require more specific assistance and will often evidence significant social, occupational, or interpersonal impairment as well as suicidal risk.

Recognition of the depressive syndrome is the most critical step in treating depression in medically ill patients. Mood disturbances may present in various circumstances; for example, with medical or preexisting psychiatric illness (Clayton & Lewis, 1980; Hall, 1980; Jefferson & Marshall, 1981; Koranyi, 1982; Weissman, Pottenger, Kleber, Rubin, Williams, & Thompson, 1977). These associated conditions often influence how patients are to be treated. For example, many patients with hypothyroidism and associated depression will respond completely to thyroid replacement (Asher, 1949; Tonks, 1964; Whybrow, Prange, & Treadway, 1969). Whether addition of antidepressant medication or electroconvulsive therapy (ECT) improves overall outcome with these cases is unknown. This example illustrates the need for a systematic approach to determine whether the affective symptoms are primary or secondary to the medical illness. Such a differential diagnosis is essential to appropriate treatment.

Major depression caused by known medical disorders is referred to as Organic Affective Syndrome in *DSM-III*. Organic affective syndrome requires more than the simple coexistence of depressive symptoms and a medical disorder. As shown in Table 1, a specific organic factor which is *etiologically* related to the mental disturbance is required. The mere temporal relationship of physical disease and depression does not imply a *causal* relationship. Different treatment approaches may be employed depending on this judgment.

Depressive symptoms and medical disorders may occur at the same time for various reasons:

1. The patient may have two unrelated conditions: primary affective syndrome and the medical disorder.
2. Depressive symptoms may be a reaction to the psychological and/or physical trauma associated with the medical disease.
3. Depressive symptoms may result from metabolic or structural central nervous system changes caused by the medical disorder.
4. The symptoms of the medical illness may be so similar to those of depression that they artifactually mimic the depressive syndrome.

TABLE 1

DSM-III *diagnostic criteria for organic affective syndrome*

A. The predominant disturbance is a disturbance in mood, with at least two of the associated symptoms listed in criterion B for manic or major depressive episode.

B. No clouding or consciousness, as in delirium; no significant loss of intellectual abilities, as in dementia; no predominant delusions or hallucinations, as in organic delusional syndrome or organic hallucinosis.

C. Evidence from the history, physical examinations, or laboratory tests, of a specific organic factor that is judged to be etiologically related to the disturbance.

In the first instance, one treats both the medical and psychiatric disorders independently. In the second, the primary focus is on helping the patient to cope with the difficulties associated with being in sick role. The third and fourth circumstances are best dealt with by effectively treating the underlying medical condition. In the third instance, other psychiatric interventions might also be needed if the medical illness is chronic or progressive.

Which medical illnesses cause depression? How is causality established? A wide variety of medical conditions are reportedly associated with depression. However, some of these associations are based on case reports, which in themselves are insufficient to establish causality. In other instances, symptoms of the physical condition itself may overlap with those of depression. Once association of a physical disease and depression is uncritically accepted, a causal relationship may be incorrectly inferred and the original evidence implying only association forgotten.

An etiologic relationship implies that structural, nutritional, or metabolic changes in the central nervous system caused by the medical disorder directly lead to the development of depressive symptoms (Organic Affective Syndrome). Such a causal relationship between depression and physical illness can be inferred in three ways: (1) the physical illness has been previously reported in the literature to manifest symptoms similar to those experienced by the patient; (2) the patient's psychiatric symptoms improved considerably or cleared completely with medical treatment; or (3) symptoms did not improve but physical examination and laboratory tests confirmed the presence of a medical illness known to produce psychiatric symptoms (Hall Gardner, Stickney, LeGann, & Popkin, 1980).

A close examination of Hall's criteria reveals a significant problem, however, because the previous association of a medical illness and depressive symptoms establishes only association, not causality. A critical appraisal of the nature of the reported evidence is needed. A more conservative set of guidelines is appropriate. At least one of the following is required for inferring causality: (1) depressive symptoms occur concurrently with the onset of the medical disorder and they resolve with treatment or spontaneous remission of the medical condition; (2) return of the medical symptoms is associated with the return of the depressive symptoms; or (3) direct pathologic central nervous system changes (metabolic or structural) could explain the depressive symptom picture; for example, depression in encephalitis or systemic lupus erythematosus.

Why is the issue of causality so important? If causality exists then treatment of the primary physical condition should improve or relieve depressive symptomatology without other psychiatric interventions. Hall et al. (Hall, Gardner, Popkin, LeCann, & Stickney, 1981) reported that over 60 percent of

TABLE 2
Medical conditions potentially causally linked to depression

Hormonal and Metabolic:

Hyperthyroidism	Postpartum
Hypothyroidism	Cushing's disease or syndrome
Hyperparathyroidism	Addison's disease
Hypoparathyroidism	Menopause

*Neoplastic:**
Carcinoid
Brain
Insulinoma
Carcinomatosis

Neurologic:
Stoke in the frontal or temporal lobes or in the limbic
    system
Multiple sclerosis
Huntington's chorea

Infectious:
Encephalitis

Nutritional:
Folate deficiency
Malnutrition

Drug-Induced:

Phenothiazines	Levodopa
Butyrophenones	Isoniazid
Reserpine	Cycloserine
Alpha-methyldopa	Ethambutol
Propranolol	Steroids
Birth control pills	Digitalis
Disulfiram	Barbiturates
Amphetamine withdrawal	Alcohol (and withdrawal)
Benzodiazepines	Narcotics

Other:
Lupus erythematosus
Arteritis
Uremia
Electrolyte disturbances

* Tumors which cause identifiable metabolic, hormonal, nutritional, or structural CNS changes linked to depression are not of themselves causes but the changes they produce are.

patients with depressive symptoms caused by a medical disorder (according to his criteria) were relieved of their psychiatric symptoms when the medical illness alone was treated. Clinicians, therefore, must search for medical conditions with physical examinations and laboratory studies (complete blood count, erythrocyte sedimentation rate, blood chemistry screen, electrolytes and creatinine, and thyroid function tests) in depressed patients. Otherwise, these patients might receive ineffective and inappropriate psychiatric treatment for otherwise remediable medical conditions (Kathol, 1984).

Table 2 lists those medical conditions for which a causal association with depression is reasonably well established. Other medical conditions, have been reported to be associated with depression, but the causal nature of this association is not well established.

Patients with depressive syndrome associated with, but not caused by, their medical conditions are diagnosed as having either Major Depression or Dysthymic Disorder using *DSM-III* criteria. The stress (acute or chronic, severe or benign) of having the medical condition may so emotionally burden the patient that a clinically significant depression ensues. For this reason, the psychological impact of the medical disorder must be evaluated, so that psychiatric treatment can be employed when relevant.

In this chapter, several aspects concerning the relationship of physical to psychiatric disease will be discussed. First, identifying depression in the medically ill presents special problems to the examiner. Some of the difficulties in this situation will be pointed out and suggestions made regarding patient evaluations. Second, the data showing the incidence of medical disease in depressed patients will be examined. Third, the studies which identify and discuss patients with depression secondary to medical illness will be reviewed. Fourth, psychological factors associated with having a physical disorder will be summarized. And fifth, the approach to treatment of these patients will be outlined.

DEFINING DEPRESSION IN THE MEDICALLY ILL

Common Symptoms

We have already discussed the general features which are required in making the diagnosis of depression. It is usually helpful to use one of the current classification systems such as that found in *DSM-III* (see book Appendix 1) to ensure that sufficient symptoms to diagnose a pathological mood disorder are present. A special problem, however, arises when evaluating patients with physical disease or suspected physical disorders because many of these conditions cause symptoms similar to those of depression (Table 3). If one examines the symptoms of an individual illness, such as hypothyroidism, the commonality of symptoms is quite evident (Table 4). Furthermore, severe medical illness leads to a greater frequency of these somatic complaints. Table 5 illustrates that physiological symptoms alone could account for or

TABLE 3
Comparison of physiological symptoms of depression in medical populations

	Medical Illness			
Symptom	Depressed (N = 31*)	Nondepressed (N = 122*)	Severe (N = 30†)	Nonsevere (N = 30†)
Decreased sleep	84	63	76	30
Decreased appetite	74	31	} 83	30
Decreased weight	48	28		
Fatigue	87	66	86	40
Retardation	100	76		
Somatic preoccupation	100	80		
Sexual indifference	32	18		
Indecisiveness	29	20		

*Schwab, Bialow, Brown, & Holzer, 1967.
†Stewart, Drake, & Winokur, 1965.

TABLE 4
Symptoms common to hypothyroidism and depression

Hypothyroidism (percent)	Depression
Loss of energy (25–98)	Loss of energy
Weakness (25–95)	Weakness
Poor concentration	Poor concentration
Memory loss (48–66)	Memory loss
Slowed actions (48–91)	Slowed actions
Decreased sex drive	Decreased sex drive
Constipation (38–61)	Constipation
Insomnia (25–98)	Insomnia
Nervousness (13–58)	Nervousness

TABLE 5
Physiologic questions used in screening for depression

	Number of items	Percentage of items with physiologic nature	Potential point score derived from physiologic questions alone
Zung*	20	35	35
Beck*	21	33	21
Hamilton*	24	42	27
Feighner†	8	63	5
RDC†	8	63	5
DSM-III†	8	63	5

*Zung items—4, 5, 7, 8, 9, 10, 13.
 Beck items—M, P, Q, R, S, T, U.
 Hamilton items—4, 5, 6, 8, 11, 12, 13, 14, 15, 16.
†Part B of criteria checklist

nearly account for a diagnosis of depression using several psychometric instruments (Beck, 1972a and b; Hamilton, 1960; Zung, 1965) or the commonly used symptom checklists for depression (American Psychiatric Association, 1980; Feighner, 1972; Spitzer et al., 1978) in the presence of medical illness. Schwab, Clemmons, Bialow, Duggan, and Davis (1965) concluded from a comparison of somatic symptoms in medical inpatients that 8 of 12 symptoms used in diagnosing depression were significantly more frequent in depressed patients. Unfortunately, their argument was circular; somatic symptoms contributed to the patients being placed in the depressive category which in turn led them to have more somatic symptoms. Inclusion of physiologic symptoms may account for part of the wide discrepancy in prevalence of depressive illness in the studies cited later in the chapter. An alternative list of criteria (Table 6) which places greater emphasis on the psychological symptoms of depression is required in this situation. These criteria include those symptoms which tended to discriminate depressed from nondepressed patients with hyperthyroidism (Kathol, Turner, & Delahunt, submitted for publication).

It could be objected that these new criteria will lead to missing the diagnosis of "masked" depression. This condition is presumably seen in patients who do not complain of feeling down or sad but have sufficient ancillary depressive symptoms (sleep disturbance, weakness, pain, appetite change, decreased interest, and the like) to suggest the presence of depression. Such an objection would fail to take into account that these ancillary symptoms can also be seen in a wide variety of nonpsychiatric diseases which do not manifest themselves on routine physical or laboratory examinations. It would be just as appropriate to say that these patients have "masked" cancer, "masked" hypothyroidism, or "masked" encephalitis since all of these can cause the symptoms described above in the absence of physical or basic laboratory abnormalities. Perhaps a better approach to patients presumed to have "masked" depression would be to leave them undiagnosed, treat them as is clinically indicated, and assure that they are followed lest an unrecognized organic condition be overlooked.

TABLE 6
Criteria for diagnosing depression in medically ill patients

1. Low mood which is a definite change from usual self and loss of interest persistently for three weeks or longer.
2. At least four of the following symptoms:
   a. Loss in interest in usual activities even if were well enough to do.
   b. Feelings of worthlessness/feelings of hopelessness.
   c. Difficulty doing anything because it's too much trouble and not because of physical incapacity.
   d. Crying a lot.
   e. Thinking of suicide/wanting to die/suicide attempt.
3. Social incapacity at school, home, work, and so on because of above symptoms.

The Question of Obscure Affective Illness

Psychiatrists and mental health professionals are often intimidated by physicians who refer patients in which they can find no evidence of organic disease. The assumption in these cases is that the symptoms *must* be occurring as a result of emotional distress. As a result psychiatrists have a tendency to overdiagnose or to presume that psychiatric illness (often depression) is present even when there are a paucity of emotional symptoms. Many of these patients have had inadequate medical examinations prior to referral. Even if an adequate examination was performed, many medical conditions do not manifest clinical or laboratory signs early in their course.

If a thorough psychiatric evaluation (Kathol, 1984) does not support the diagnosis of major affective disorder (or other psychiatric condition which could explain the symptoms), the psychiatrist should explain that the symptoms are unlikely to be the result of emotional problems and that the patient will need to be followed by the referring physician. This does not obviate instituting therapeutic measures (e.g., medical or psychiatric medications, physiotherapy, social support, reassurance) which may improve the symptoms giving discomfort.

Many patients do not fit conveniently into the categories defined by *DSM-III*. Rather than being a drawback, this helps to discriminate patients with significant psychiatric disease from those with less severe or less well-characterized emotional problems. For example, a 67-year-old patient was referred to us after a negative but thorough basic medical evaluation with a 12-month history of poor sleep, back pain, weakness, weight loss, and occasional crying spells (even during the interview). However, she had no prior psychiatric problems; was only intermittently sad because she couldn't get rid of her back pain; had a hopeful outlook toward the future; retained her sense of humor; had no suicidal thoughts; had no guilt feelings; and had good eye contact with a normal pattern of speech. Because she did not meet criteria of sustained dysphoria we recommended further evaluation to her referring physicians. Much to their surprise she was found to have a spinal cord tumor when a specialized back x ray was performed.

This is just one of many examples in which the diagnosis of "no psychiatric diagnosis" led to the identification of a condition which might otherwise have remained undiscovered.

MEDICAL ILLNESS IN DEPRESSED PATIENTS

Three studies (Davies, 1965; Hall, Popkin, Devaul, Faillace, & Stickney, 1978; Koranyi, 1972) have examined the frequency of medical illness in an outpatient psychiatric population. Only in Koranyi's paper (1972) is it possible to decide which patients had affective illness. Of the 10 patients so identified, 7 had some type of physical ailment. It is not clear whether the physical ailments were causative, aggravating, or coexisting. It should be pointed out, however, that depression was second only to organic mental disorders in the frequency of being associated with physical disease. Neither the study by Davies (1965) nor the one by Hall et al. (1978) reported data in such a way that the prevalence of medical illness in depressive outpatients can be determined. In both studies the commonest psychiatric disease thought to be associated with physical illness was depression. The total number of patients represented in these three studies is small ($N = 27$). It is, therefore, not possible to establish precisely which medical diseases are most commonly associated with depression.

There is more information regarding the association of dysphoria and physical disease in psychiatric inpatients (Hall et al., 1980; Herridge, 1960; Maguire & Granville-Grossman, 1968). A summary of the findings of Herridge (1960), Maguire and Granville-Grossman (1968), and Hall et al. (1980) may be found in Table 7. Maguire and Granville-Grossman (1968) retrospectively reviewed the occurrence of physical disease in psychiatric admissions and found that 95 of 200 (48 percent) admissions were for depression. Of these 95, 35 (37 percent) had physical disease. Sixty-seven of the 200 patients in this study were found to have physical disease. Fifty-two percent of those found to have physical disease had a concurrent diagnosis of depression. Maguire and Granville-Grossman (1968) made no attempt to establish a temporal or causal relationship between the physical disease and depression.

The first of two prospective studies of physical illness in psychiatric patients was performed by Herridge (1960). It is difficult in this paper to extract information about physical illness in the depressed subgroup. All that can be said is that 4 of 80 (5 percent) dysphoric patients had physical illness which was felt to cause the dysphoric symptoms. Depressive criteria are not defined, and the type of causality is not specified.

TABLE 7
Medical illness in depressive inpatients

	Depressed (N)	Criteria for inclusion	Prevalence
Herridge (1960)	80	None stated; prospective	4/80 (5 percent) of depressives have related physical disease
Maguire and Granville-Grossman (1968)	95	None stated; retrospective	34/95 (36 percent) of depressives have related or nonrelated physical disease
Hall et al. (1980)	29	Research Diagnostic Criteria prospective	12/29 (41 percent) of major and minor depressives have physical disease-causing symptoms

TABLE 8
Medical subspecialities likely to see serious depression

| | Maguire and Granville-Grossman (1968) | Hall et al. (1980) | |
	No causation established (N = 20)	No causation established (N = 18)	Causative (N = 18)
Endocrinology	3	6	6
Neurology	1	3	3
Cardiology	3	2	2
Gastroenterology	1	3	2
Rheumatology	5	2	0
Other	6	8	0

A second prospective study on psychiatric inpatients was reported by Hall et al. (1980). They screened 100 consecutive admissions to a psychiatric research ward with a thorough psychiatric and medical history, physical examination, sleep-derived electroencephalogram, electrocardiogram, psychological test battery, complete blood count, and extensive chemistry screen. Research Diagnostic Criteria (Spitzer et al., 1978) were used for the diagnosis of depression. When physical disease was identified an attempt was made to establish a causal relationship using the guidelines described in the introduction of this chapter. Hall et al. found that depression was the principal psychiatric diagnosis in 29 of their 100 patients. Of the total group of 29, 12 (41 percent) were found to have a medical disease either causing or exacerbating the depressive symptoms. As previously discussed, 63 percent of the questions in part B of the Research Diagnostic Criteria have a somatic orientation. Thus, the population of medically ill patients diagnosed as having depression might have been diagnosed inappropriately due to the inclusion criteria. A comparison of the medical diseases found in those patients with severe depression in Maguire and Granville-Grossman's study and major affective disorder in Hall's study may be found in Table 8. The organ systems Hall's group found most commonly to be associated with depression were the endocrine, central nervous, gastrointestinal, and cardiovascular systems, in decreasing order of frequency.

DEPRESSION IN THE MEDICALLY ILL

The point prevalence of major depression is 4.3 percent and for minor depression 2.5 percent in the general population, while the lifetime prevalence is estimated to be 20 percent for major depressive disorder and 9.2 percent for minor depression (Weissman & Meyers, 1978). Only six studies examine the prevalence of dysphoria in patients with medical illness (Frerichs, 1982; Glass, Allan, Uhlenhugh, Kimball, & Borinstein, 1978; Neilsen & Williams, 1980; Porter, 1970; Schwab et al., 1967; Stewart et al., 1965).

Porter (1970) concluded from the evaluation of 1,819 patients seen in a general medicine practice that 93 had dysphoria. In this study he did not describe what constituted depression and therefore the figure of 5 percent is highly suspect. His finding in this study that imipramine was ineffective in treating these patients cannot be relied upon.

Glass et al. (1978) used the St. Louis research criteria (Feighner et al., 1972) to evaluate 82 patients in general medicine clinics and found 26 (32 percent) had a depressive syndrome. Sixteen had primary depression and 20 secondary depression. This percentage is very high when compared to the 6.8 percent found by Weissman and Meyers (1978). This makes one suspicious of the validity of diagnoses dependent upon somatic criteria in medically ill populations.

Neilsen and Williams (1980) attempted to establish that the Beck Depression Inventory is a useful tool in screening a medical clinic population for depression. They found that 12 percent of patients had a total rating of greater than 13 on the Beck Depression Inventory, 3 percent had scores greater than 20, and 0.6 percent had scores greater than 30. These correspond to mildly, moderately, and severely dysphoric groups clinically (Beck, 1972b). When they, however, applied the Feighner criteria to a group of 41 patients with a Beck Depression Inventory greater than 10 (mean 13), they found that 58 percent had diagnosable depression.

Frerichs et al. (1982) examined 1,003 adults for depression in an ongoing community investigation using the Center for Epidemiological Studies—Depression Scale (CES-D). They found that 73 percent of persons with a score greater than 16 (a score suggesting significant depression) had some illness or injury whereas only 27 percent with a score greater than 16 were healthy at the time of interview. (It should be noted that the CES-D has 4 of 20 items which are somatic in nature. These four items can account for 12 of the 16 points needed for the diagnosis of depression using this scale. It is possible that these items contributed in a significant way to the total point score of the physically ill.) Frerichs et al. (1982) did not do a psychiatric assessment of the individuals interviewed using diagnostic criteria for depression. Therefore, it is difficult to tell how many had a clinically significant depression.

In the only published inpatient study, Schwab et al. (1967) judged 20 percent of all medical inpatients to be depressed. They used a complex mixture of depressive parameters called a rank sum to arrive at this conclusion. Their evaluation, however, did not include the results of a psychiatric interview assessment. In comparing patients included by each of the various individual parameters used (Beck Depression Inventory, Hamilton Depression Scale, provisional depressive diagnosis by the medical staff on admission and retrospective chart review) with the patients included by the rank sum, there was little correlation. Even if the estimate that 20 percent were depressed was an accurate guess (which remains to be proven), serious questions arise concerning the validity of diagnosis of the patients included in the depressive category. Due to this problem, conclusions about the patient's characteristics, frequency, and severity of medical illnesses, and symptom profiles arrived at in this paper, are not felt to warrant consideration.

The Beck Depression Inventory scores of the inpatients of Schwab et al. (1967) were generally higher than those of the outpatients of Neilsen and Williams (1980), suggesting that more severely ill medical inpatients are more dysphoric. Alternatively, this could merely reflect that inpatients were scoring higher on the Beck Depression Inventory because of greater somatic symptomatology.

Stewart et al. (1965) evaluated 30 patients judged to be terminally ill and 30 less severe medical controls. In assessing these patients for depression they exluded somatic symptoms yet included sufficient requirements for duration and symptoms so as to appropriately diagnose a depressive syndrome. He found the lifetime prevalence of depression in the severely ill versus the less severe medical controls to be 27 percent and 13 percent, respectively. The study of Stewart et al. (1965) is the only one of the six studies which correlates the onset of depression with the onset of medical disease. His findings reveal that 13 percent of the depressions in the severely ill population occurred at the onset or diagnosis of the disease and 3 percent occurred within six months of the diagnosis. This accounts for nearly two thirds of the depressions in the severely medically ill. There is no way to determine from the data presented whether the depression was a reaction to the trauma of finding out about the disease or whether it was a manifestation of the pathologic process.

PSYCHOLOGICAL REACTION TO PHYSICAL ILLNESS

A diagnosis of Organic Affective Syndrome implies a physiological causal relationship between central nervous system alteration and depression. A "causal" relationship can also exist if the physical illness is of sufficient magnitude to stress the individual's coping mechanisms beyond the point of adaptation. It is tempting in fact to assume that all depressions associated with physical illness, where an etiologically related organic factor is not present, are psychological reactions to the stress of the medical condition. On the other hand, it is known that affective disturbances can occur de novo in the absence of obvious psychological, social, or physical stressors. The question thus arises of how it can be established whether the depression in such circumstances is the result of an endogenous component.

Medical illness is an ideal stressor for the development of a depressive syndrome. It causes patients to lose control over their ability to associate with certain people, to do certain tasks, to go certain places, and the like. This loss of control leads to anger and frustration at the situation, the cause of the illness, the doctor, and the self. Because nothing can be done to alter this situation in the short term (and often for extended periods), the frustration is often expressed by demonstrating dysphoria.

Second, the patient must adjust to a new life situation, albeit sometimes temporarily, and accept a more limited lifestyle. This requires positive effort on the part of the patient. The adaptation techniques of the patient are maximally stressed.

And third, in addition to managing frustration and adapting one's lifestyle, the patient often has to adopt a new role in established relationships. This often involves increased dependency in relationships where they would otherwise maintain reasonable independence.

Despite impressive psychological reasons to develop depression, the human organism is amazingly resilient to these pressures and meets the challenge of change. The vast majority of individuals accept the occurrence of illness, an intrinsically unpleasant phenomena. They put up with frustration, alter their lifestyles, and accept new roles in their relationships. All this is done with the understanding that there is no choice. A feeling of sadness is a frequent and normal reaction. Nonetheless, the dysphoria is not typically pervasive, and patients typically do find a way to adapt.

Since a person's life might be viewed as a series of stressful events, of which the development of a physical illness is only one, an important question to ask to determine whether depressive symptoms are a psychological reaction to physical illness is whether the patient has undergone a similar stressor in the past without developing depression. If the patient has, then one must suspect that endogenous factors may be involved. For example, a diabetic who has had several episodes of ketoacidosis which required hospitalization in the past is found for the first time to be depressed during an episode of ketoacidosis. Though the depression could be a psychological reaction to the illness and hospitalization, it is more likely that the symptoms are related to some endogenous factor.

The following are suggested guidelines for determining whether an affective disorder is related to an external event by virtue of the psychological stress involved: (1) the depression began concurrently with the event (within three months after the event); (2) the depression disappeared when the stressor was terminated (in the absence of continuing consequences of the stressor); and (3) a prior similar stress was accompanied by a similar depressive picture. In the absence of similar prior stressors, it becomes difficult to establish the type of relationship between depression and stressor. As previously mentioned, a person's life is a series of stressful events, any one of which could be associated with depression.

DSM-III does not include a category for "reactive depression." Patients with sufficient symptoms would be diagnosed as having a major depressive disorder whether or not stressors are present. Persons experiencing dysphoria in relation to physical illness, which is not continuous and severe, or which does not have the required concommitant symptoms could be classified as having an adjustment disorder with depressed mood. Regardless of whether major or minor depressive symptoms are present in conjunction with the physical illness, common sense dictates that all measures possible be used to improve a condition, such as medical illness which is potentially related by virtue of the stress of the condition. Establishing whether a relationship exists helps the clinician to predict whether this manipulation alone will be effective or whether additional treatment for an endogenous component, such as pharmacotherapy or ECT will be necessary.

TREATMENT

As mentioned earlier, the identification of depression is only the first step in the care of patients presenting with emotional problems. Once the syndrome has been identified, it is of utmost importance to recognize any conditions which might be either physically or psychologically related to the development of symptoms. A thorough systematic approach for this is required.

The focus of treatment in most psychiatric treatment manuals is on psychological intervention or somatic therapies. The assumption seems to be that most depressions are primary in nature. Little attention is given to depression potentially related to physical illness. Yet the identification of a medical illness etiologically related to depression may lead to instituting forms of therapy which might not otherwise have been considered. Further, it might limit the use of other forms of therapy which are costly, time consuming, or potentially dangerous to the patient. For example, several patients with Cushing's syndrome have been described in which treatment of the hypercorticism led to complete cessation of symptoms of depression where prior psychiatric intervention had failed (Bochner, Burke, Lloyd, & Nurnberg, 1979; Pullan, Clement-Jones, Corder, Lowry, Rees, Rees, Besser, Macedo, & Galvao-Teles, 1980). The presumption in these cases is that the cortisol abnormalities in some way caused a metabolic encephalopathy leading to depressive symptoms.

It is not necessary that a medical illness be etiologically related to depression through physiology to be important in the treatment of patients with depression. As mentioned previously in the chapter, the stress of having a medical disease can be sufficient to aggravate the depressive symptoms thus making them clinically disruptive. In this situation, psychiatric intervention either in the form of supportive psychotherapy or somatic therapy can be greatly bolstered by effective treatment of the medical illness.

Some physical diseases associated with depressive symptoms are either untreatable or only partially treatable. Examples include brain tumors, central systemic lupus erythematosus, renal failure, and so on. In these instances the primary therapy, that is treatment of the medical illness, is ineffective because no adequate treatment is available. The use of other psychiatric interventions in these situations becomes more important. There is one controlled trial showing that the addition of antidepressant medication (nortriptyline) is efficacious in the care of poststroke depression (Lipsey, Robinson, Pearlson, Rao, & Price, 1984). Other conditions have not been studied. Nonetheless, antidepressant use should be attempted in the absence of contraindication, under close observation. If they prove unhelpful after a reasonable period of time or cause untoward side effects then they should be discontinued and support be given. As in any medical specialty, not all conditions have effective treatments. This is occasionally the case in patients with depression related to untreatable physical illness. Every effort should be made to assist these patients in the physical and emotional discomfort but not at the risk of adding to the cost and time requirements of the patient or to the symptoms in the form of side effects by instituting an ineffective treatment.

Regardless of how depressive symptoms are related to the associated physical disease, patients in this situation are adapting to a frustrating alteration in their life routine. Ventilation of feelings about this difficult position and discussion of coping options is often helpful. This function can frequently be performed by empathic concerned ward personnel; for example, nurses, social workers, and so on, or by relatives or friends. In fact, this is often preferable to enlisting the assistance of professional counselors because it does not carry with it the stigma of being "emotionally" unstable. Sometimes because of time constraints or other reasons, this approach is insufficient to meet the emotional needs of some patients. At this point, referral to mental health professionals, such as psychiatrists, psychiatric nurse clinicians, psychiatric social workers, or psychologists may be of benefit.

There is no data showing that any one type of intervention is more effective than another in helping patients with depression associated with medical disease. A time-limited cognitive approach would seem likely to improve such secondary depressions without leading to the development of a dependency relationship. Details concerning the use of this approach can be found in Chapter 1. This approach facilitates realistic appraisal of new lifestyle restrictions and allows patients to take an active part in adjusting to an otherwise undesirable circumstance. By encouraging the patients' participation, the therapist can show the patients that they can still exert control over their own existence; albeit, in a somewhat more limited fashion. This is a cardinal feature in treatment of patients who are otherwise relegated to a role which fosters dependency.

SUMMARY

Present studies suggest that depression is present in 5 to 30 percent of medically ill outpatients and 20 percent of medically ill inpatients. These figures may be artificially inflated since many of the symptoms of depression are common with symptoms seen in medical disease. Sustained dysphoric symptomatology with interferences in social and personal activities may be a better discriminator of depression in the medically ill than using multiple-somatic symptoms associated with dysphoria as is done in *DSM-III*.

A distinction is made between depression (continuous, pervasive, and severe dysphoria) and sadness (normal expression of dysphoric mood). This is important because the former implies the *need* for treatment because of interrupted activities and suicidal risk whereas the latter often requires no professional intervention though support or social manipulation may be helpful.

Depression which coexists with medical disease can be either causally or casually related. A causal relationship suggests that improvement of the causative disease will effect an improvement of the depressive symptomatology. Such a causal effect between medical disease and depression is most often found with diseases such as hypothyroidism, Cushing's disease, hyperthyroidism, among others. Medical disease may also be related to the development of depression by the real or perceived stress of having an illness. Treatment of the medical condition in these cases may shorten the course of depressive illness because it alleviates stress. Physical illness may also be a confounding variable in someone who has a propensity to develop depressive symptoms (primary affective disorder). The treatment for depression in these patients will primarily be psychiatric intervention.

References

American Psychiatric Association. (1980). *Diagnostic and statistical manual of mental disorders* (3rd ed.). Washington, DC: Author.

Asher, R. (1949). Myxoedematous madness. *British Medical Journal, 1,* 555–562.

Beck, A. T. (1972a). Measuring depression: The depressive inventory. In T. Williams, M. M. Kathy, & J. A. Shield (Ed.), *Recent advances in the psychobiology of the depressive illness.* Washington, DC: U.S. Government Printing Office.

Beck, A. T., (1972b). *Depression: Causes and treatment.* Philadelphia: University of Pennsylvania Press.

Bochner, F., Burke, C. J., Lloyd, H. M., & Nurnberg, B. I. (1979). Intermittent Cushing's disease. *The American Journal of Medicine, 67,* 507–510.

Burke, A. W. (1972). Physical illness in psychiatric hospital patients in Jamaica. *British Journal of Psychiatry, 121,* 321–322.

Clayton, P. M., & Lewis, C. E. (1980). The significance of Secondary Depression. *Journal of Affective Disorders, 3,* 25–35.

Davies, D. W. (1965). Physical illness in psychiatric outpatients. *British Journal of Psychiatry, 111,* 27–33.

Feighner, J. P., Robins, E., Guze, S. B., Woodruff, R. A., Winokur, G., & Muñoz, R. (1972). Diagnostic criteria for use in psychiatric research. *Archives of General Psychiatry, 26,* 57–63.

Frerichs, R. R., Aneshensel, C. S., Yokopenic, P. A., & Clark, V. A. (1982). Physical health and depression: An epidemiologic survey. *Preventive Medicine, 11,* 639–646.

Glass, R. M., Allan, A. T., Uhlenhugh, E. H., Kimball, C. P., & Borinstein, D. I. (1978). Psychiatric screening in a medical clinic: An evaluation of a self-report inventory. *Archives of General Psychiatry, 35,* 1189–1195.

Hall, R. C. W. (Ed.) (1980). *Psychiatric presentations of medical illness.* Jamaica, NY: SP Medical & Scientific Books.

Hall, R. C. W., Gardner, E. R., Popkin, M. K., LeCann, A. F., & Stickney, S. K. (1981). Unrecognized physical illness prompting psychiatric admission: A prospective study. *American Journal of Psychiatry, 138*(5), 629–634.

Hall, R. C. W., Popkin, M. K., Devaul, R. A., Faillace, L. A., & Stickney, S. K. (1978). Physical disease presenting as psychiatric disease. *Archives of General Psychiatry, 35,* 1315–1320.

Hall, R. C. W., Gardner, E. R., Stickney, S. K., LeCann, A. F., & Popkin, M. K. (1980). Physical illness manifesting as psychiatric disease. *Archives of General Psychiatry, 37,* 989–995.

Hamilton, M. (1960). A rating scale for depression. *Journal of Neurology, Neurosurgery and Psychiatry, 23,* 56–62.

Hedlund, J. L., & Vieweg, B. W. (1979). The Zung Self-Rating Depression Scale: A comprehensive review. *Journal of Operational Psychiatry, 10*(1), 51–64.

Herridge, C. F. (1960). Physical disorders in psychiatric illness: A study of 209 consecutive admissions. *Lancet, 2,* 949–951.

Hoffmann-LaRoche, Inc. (1975). *How to use the Beck Depression Inventory* ed. A. T. Beck (pp. 57–66). Nutley, NJ: Roche Laboratories.

Jefferson, J. W., & Marshall, J. R. (1981). *Neuropsychiatric features of medical disorders.* N.Y.: Plenum Medical Book Company.

Johnson, D. A. W. (1968). The evaluation of routine physical examination in psychiatric cases. *The Practitioner, 200,* 686–691.

Kathol, R. G. (1984). Patient evaluation. In R. A. Muñoz (Ed.), *Mood disorders clinics.* San Francisco: Jossey-Bass.

Kathol, R. G., Turner, R. D., & Delahunt, J. W. (submitted for publication). On diagnosing depression and anxiety in patients with hyperthyroidism.

Koranyi, E. K. (1972). Physical health and illness in a psychiatric outpatient department population. *Canadian Psychiatric Association Journal, 17,* 109–116.

Koranyi, E. K. (1982). *Physical illness in the psychiatric patient.* Springfield, IL: Charles C Thomas.

Lipsey, J. R., Robinson, R. G., Pearlson, G. D., Rao, K., & Price, T. R. (1984). Nortriptyline treatment of poststroke depression: A double-blind study. *The Lancet, 1,* 297–300.

Neilsen, A. C., & Williams, T. A. (1980). Depression in ambulatory medical patients: Prevalence by self-report questionnaire and recognition by nonpsychiatric physicians. *Archives of General Psychiatry, 37,* 999–1004.

New York State Psychiatric Institute, Biometrics Division. (1980). *Research diagnostic criteria* (3rd ed.): Author.

Maguire, G. P., & Granville-Grossman, K. L. (1968). Physical illness in psychiatric patients. *British Journal of Psychiatry, 115,* 1365–1369.

Porter, A. M. W. (1970). Depressive illness in a general practice: A demographic study and a controlled trial of imipramine. *British Medical Journal, 1,* 773–778.

Pullan, P. T., Clement-Jones, V., Corder, R., Lowry, P. J., Rees, G. M., Rees, L. H., Besser, G. M., Macedo, M. M., & Galvao-Teles, A. (1980). Ectopic production of methionine enkephalin and beta-endorphin. *British Medical Journal, 1,* 758–759.

Schwab, J. J., Bialow, M., Brown, J. M., & Holzer, C. E. (1967). Diagnosing depression in medical inpatients. *Annals of Internal Medicine, 67,* 695–707.

Schwab, J. J., Clemmons, R. S., Bialow, M., Duggan, V., & Davis, B. (1965). A study of the somatic symptomatology of depression in medical inpatients. *Psychosomatics, 17,* 273–277.

Spitzer, R. L., Endicott, J., & Robins, E. (1978). Research diagnostic criteria: Rationale and reliability. *Archives of General Psychiatry, 35,* 773–782.

Stewart, M. A., Drake, F., & Winokur, G. (1965). Depression among medically ill patients. *Diseases of the Nervous System, 26,* 479–485.

Tonks, C. M. (1964). Mental illnesses in hypothyroid patients. *British Journal of Psychiatry, 110,* 706–710.

Weissman, M. M., & Myers, J. K. (1978). Affective disorders in a U.S. urban community: The use of research diagnostic criteria in an epidemiological survey. *Archives of General Psychiatry, 35,* 1304–1311.

Whybrow, P. C., Prange, A. J., Jr., & Treadway, C. R. (1969). Mental changes accompanying thyroid gland dysfunction. A reappraisal using objective psychological measurement. *Archives of General Psychiatry, 20,* 48–63.

Zung, W. W. K. (1965). A self-rating scale. *Archives of General Psychiatry, 12,* 63–70.

Zung, W. W. K., Richards, C., & Short, M. J. (1965). Self-rating depression scale in an outpatient clinic. *Archives of General Psychiatry, 13,* 508–515.

PART 4

Basic Research

Chapter 23

Epidemiology of Depression

John K. Wing
Paul Bebbington
MRC Social Psychiatry Unit,
Institute of Psychiatry,
de Crespigny Park,
London, England

THE EPIDEMIOLOGICAL APPROACH

Epidemiology is the study of the distribution of disorders in populations, with the aim of discovering possible causes (as in the case of the association between cigarette smoking and cancer of the lung) or of throwing light on the way that public and private agencies serve to identify, prevent, or alleviate the disorders. When studying any particular disorder, therefore, the epidemiologist is faced with three major problems. The first is to enumerate the size and characteristics of the population under review, the second is to define the disorder sufficiently precisely to be able to count its frequency, and the third is to specify, on the basis of theory or at least of hypothesis, which subgroups of the population will be likely to yield disproportionate numbers of cases (MacMahon & Pugh, 1970).

The ratio of cases to unit population is known as a *rate*. When considering possible causal factors, the appropriate rate is the *incidence*—the number of new cases appearing in a defined population at risk during a given period of time, usually one year. The *relative risk* of new cases appearing in subgroups of the population characterized by the presence or absence of the supposedly causal factors, but otherwise thought to be comparable, can then be calculated.

Another useful rate, the *prevalence*, measures the number of cases in a defined population on a given day, or during a given period of time. The period prevalence includes cases that appeared for the first time during the period in question and those with an earlier onset that were still active at some time during the period. The point prevalance contains those cases that are active on a given day. The prevalence rate is more useful for studying the course of disorders and the extent of need, within the population, for various forms of treatment and service.

Specifying the two components of a rate—"cases" in the numerator and "population" in the denominator—and identifying factors on the basis of which to compare rates of disorder in subgroups of the population, comprise the *epidemiological method.* Its application to "depression" raises the same problems that arise in the study of any disorder where there is disagreement as to the criteria for definition and little possibility of appeal to an objective standard. The basic rule of interpretation in epidemiology—that any associations found can only provide clues or hypotheses as to the direction of cause and effect—applies *a fortiori* to the study of depression.

THE CONCEPT OF DISEASE

Mechanic (1970) pointed out that it is not uncommon for social scientists "to discover, on being introduced to the field of epidemiology, that this is what they have been doing all their professional lives." The same is true of many clinical psychologists. What distinguishes epidemiology from other applications of the survey method is the concept of *disease.* There have been many attempts to describe the essential elements involved in the concept and much disagreement between distinguished protagonists. (See, for example, the essays collected by Caplan, Engelhardt, & McCartney, 1981.)

Cohen (1961) suggested that two quite different concepts of disease can be distinguished from the earliest times. One of these, the *disease entity,* he regarded as no longer helpful because of its undue emphasis on classification and subclassification for its own sake; it could not be adapted to the increasingly rapid pace of the accumulation of knowledge. The second concept, which Cohen regarded with approval, is *deviation from the normal.* He was mainly concerned with "normal" anatomy and physiology, and the relationship between them. However, the concept of deviation from normal may be generalized to psychology and the social sciences and this approach may have a unifying influence.

Clinicians derive from their experience the notion that certain unusual experiences or behaviors cluster together as *syndromes.* As knowledge accumulates, it becomes clear that some of these syndromes are associated with deviations from normal that can be measured in completely different ways. Eventually, these deviations can be related to abnormality in the factors that keep the underlying functions within normal limits. In the case of diabetes mellitus this process is not yet complete, nearly 2,000 years after the physician Aretaeus first gave the name "diabetes" to a clinical syndrome. Nevertheless, the great advantage of the concept is that it is amenable to scientific method—theories regarding the pathology, causes, treatment, and likely outcome of *syndrome complexes* or *disorders,* can be tested and shown to be wrong if they are wrong (Wing, 1978).

CLINICAL SYNDROMES OF DEPRESSION

So far as the affective disorders are concerned (including manic and depressive disorders and states of anxiety under this broad heading) there has been relatively little consensus on classification and subclassification. The development of diagnostic concepts is traced in Chapter 11. In brief, Kraepelin (1913, 1921) simplified what had been a mass of conflicting ideas by postulating an inherited disease entity called *manic-depressive psychosis,* which could be distinguished from *dementia praecox* and other psychoses by reason of differences in course, outcome, and cause. Controversy continues, however, concerning the extent that the two types of psychoses can be differentiated. A high proportion of schizophrenics also manifest depression (Cooper, Kendell, Gurland, Sharpe, Copeland, & Simon, 1972; World Health Organization, 1973). Terms such as *schizoaffective psychosis, schizophreniform psychosis, cycloid psychosis, reactive psychosis,* and *bouffée délirante* have been coined to describe intermediate forms. In the third edition of the *Diagnostic and Statistical Manual of Mental Disorders* ([*DSM-III*]; American Psychiatric Association, 1980) no definition of schizoaffective disorder is offered at all.

There is more general agreement on a distinction between bipolar and unipolar affective disorders (Angst, 1966; Perris, 1966). The former, despite its name, depends on a history of mania, which is relatively easily recognized. Whether depression not associated with mania can be divided into two groups, psychotic and neurotic, is more problematic (Brockington, Altman, Hillier, Meltzer, & Nand, 1982; Katz, Robins, Croughan, Secunda, & Swann, 1982; Pfohl, Vasquez, & Nasrallah, 1982).

Another set of criteria for subclassification still used extensively is that between *endogenous* and *nonendogenous* depression. The former is said to be characterized by depressive delusions and hallucinations, psychomotor retardation, pathological guilt, and disorders of sleep, appetite, and other bodily functions. When severe, this is the classical *melancholia.* Charney and Nelson (1981), Glassman and Roose (1981), and Helms and Smith (1983) have provided recent evidence supporting the consistency of this traditional syndrome complex.

Concepts of bipolar, psychotic, or endogenous depression are largely derived from studies of patients referred to psychiatric specialists. Recent studies of samples of the general population have shown that depressed mood is common among people who have not been so referred, although endogenous symptoms are rare and there is often an admixture of anxiety (Wing, 1980). This has led to a ferment of new ideas about classification and subclassification and to speculation about the relationship between disorders identified in the two settings (Akiskal, Rosenthal, Haykal, Lemmi, Rosenthal, Scott-Strauss, 1980; Finlay-Jones, Brown, Duncan-Jones, Harris, Murphy & Prudo, 1980; Lewis, 1934; Rosenthal, Akiskal, Scott-Strauss, Rosenthal, & David, 1981; Winokur, 1973; Winokur, Behar, Van Valkenburg, & Lowery, 1978; Winokur, Clayton, & Reich, 1969). The range of subclassifications, together with others based on possible genetic and biochemical abnormalities (see Chapters 24 and 25) or on differential responses to various forms of medication, make it impossible for the epidemiologist to provide information about incidence that will be useful for all purposes. New subclassifications appear every year. It is not surprising, in the circumstances, that efforts have been made to provide standardized definitions that, at the very least, would allow comparison between studies carried out in different parts of the world, even though they could not subsume all the systems of diagnosis in clinical use.

Although little epidemiological information is available there is no doubt that physical factors can precipitate depressive disorders. The recovery period from viral infection is an example. Medication with reserpine is another. Puerperal depression is a third.

METHODS OF CASE FINDING IN EPIDEMIOLOGICAL SURVEYS

In the now classical Scandinavian and American surveys, experienced psychiatrists interviewed informants, using their clinical skills without much attempt at standardizing either the collection of relevant information (the *data base*) or the *rules,* approximately Kraepelinian, that were then applied in order to reach a diagnosis (e.g., Roth & Luton, 1942; Sjögren, 1948; Strömgren, 1938). The results of these surveys provided estimates of *expectancy* (lifetime incidence) that were remarkably similar for the major psychoses but much less satisfactory for the neuroses.

During the next phase of study, investigators used self-report schedules to introduce a degree of structure into data collection (Leighton, Harding, Macklin, MacMillan, & Leighton, 1963; Srole, Langner, Michael, Opler, & Rennie, 1962; Stouffer, Guttman, Suckman, Lazarfeld, Star & Clausen, 1950). The use of these techniques derived from a theory that the conditions under review were arranged continuously along a dimension stretching from health to abnormality, without any clear breaks that would allow classification. Lines could be drawn at various points but the resulting groupings were regarded as largely statistical. The self-report format allowed subjects to determine the meaning of each question for themselves with a consequent loss of comparability. Boyd and Weissman (1981) have pointed out that self-report scales dealing solely with depression (e.g., Beck, Ward, Mendelson, Mock, & Erbaugh, 1961; Radloff, 1977, Zung, 1965) have similar disadvantages, since there is little clinical agreement on the significance of disorders above the cutting points and no criteria are laid down for differential diagnosis.

More effective methods of providing reliability and comparability of measurement require more detailed specification of the data base and precise specification of the classifying rules. The methodological problems are formidable. The first element required is a glossary of differential definitions of items of subjectively described moods and experiences and of observed behaviors, that are regarded as abnormal, or for other reasons are deemed worthy of study. The definitions should not only cover the description of items in the glossary but how to differentiate each one from others with which it might be confused. The second element is a structured interview or other means of eliciting information about items that are present at a given time, and a standardized procedure for recording intensity and duration (clinical severity). The third element requires the addition of historical or observational data in order to delineate episodes and record relevant information concerning personality, cognitive development, putative causes, and so on. Fourth, algorithms have to be constructed to classify this material according to the diagnostic system(s) of particular interest to the investigator.

No system currently in use can be said to have overcome all the technical problems involved but progress has been made. Two systems of particular interest are the Diagnostic Interview Schedule (DIS) and the Present State Examination (PSE). The DIS (Robins, Helzer, Croughan & Ratliff, 1981) was developed to make "lifetime" diagnoses, using three sets of criteria: *DSM-III* (American Psychiatric Association, 1980), Feighner and colleagues (Feighner, Robins, Guze, Woodruff, Winokur, & Muñoz, 1972) and the Research Diagnostic Criteria (Spitzer, Endicott, & Robins, 1978). It was designed to be used by agency interviewers as well as psychiatrists and other professionals and, therefore, incorporates a highly questionnairelike structure, with little being left to the clinical judgment of the interviewer. There is no glossary of definitions of items. All historical information regarded as necessary is incorporated in the schedule and rated on the basis of the subject's answers. It is being used in an extensive program of research—the Epidemiological Catchment Area program (Eaton, Reiger, Locke, & Taube, 1981).

The Present State Examination (PSE), now in its 9th revision with a 10th under construction, is based on a glossary of definitions and a clinical-style interview that leaves the final choice of rating firmly in the hands of the interviewer. The PSE includes 140 items representing "functional" neurotic and psychotic symptoms likely to be present in the present "mental state." It was not originally constructed with diagnosis specifically in mind but to provide symptom and syndrome profiles and scores for use in comparative clinical research. It was found that standardizing the data base in itself helped to reduce the variability of the diagnoses based on it (Cooper et al., 1972; Wing, Birley, Cooper, Graham, & Issacs, 1967). An Index of Definition (ID) incorporates an algorithm designed to differentiate cases above defined threshold points—a case being a condition where sufficient symptoms are present to allow a classification to be made (Wing, Mann, Leff, & Nixon, 1978). A brief version of the PSE can be used by agency interviewers with fair reliability after special training, but there is a tendency to rate more abnormality than psychiatrists (Sturt, Bebbington, Hurry, & Tennant, 1981; Wing, Nixon, Mann, & Leff, 1977).

Separate instruments are used to cover previous episodes and any factors thought to be significant in causation. The CATEGO program operates on the combined data base to produce a variety of outputs, including a profile of eight categories each of which can be present at the same time, and a 50-part and 20-part classification which, within strictly limited specifications (Wing, 1983), can be regarded as equivalent to classes in the International Classification of Diseases (World Health Organization, 1978). The specifications are laid down in an instruction manual (Wing, Cooper & Sartorius, 1974). A comparison of results from surveys of a population sample, ambulatory clinics, and hospital admissions, suggests that the techniques have a degree of validity (Wing, Bebbington, Hurry, & Tennant, 1981).

The further development of such techniques promises well for the future, provided that instruments are not changed too rapidly to allow thorough testing and comparative study at each stage. Eventually, it should be possible to collect a data base comprehensive enough to allow the application of algorithms for several quite different types of classification, allowing a test of the advantages and disadvantages of each. Meanwhile, readers of this review will need to bear in mind the fact that most studies so far have used different case-finding techniques, many of which have been far from satisfactory.

THE FREQUENCY OF DEPRESSIVE DISORDERS

One method of establishing rates of depressive disorders is to use the data routinely collected about patients contacting psychiatric clinics in Western countries. Many such statistics relate to hospital admissions and are therefore subject to undefined and highly variable selection factors. Case registers are more satisfactory because contacts with day hospitals and nonhospital day centers, ambulatory clinics, and various forms of nonhospital residential units are recorded as well as admissions to hospital. Record linkage allows the computation of rates of "first-ever" contact with one of these services.

Table 1 presents the first-ever contact rates for Camberwell, an inner suburban area of London (Wing & Der, 1984). The mean annual rates for the period 1965–82 are shown, the population in 1973 being used in the denominator. Two categories of depressive disorders are used: "Severe affective disorder" includes all cases of mania or manic-depressive disorder, and depressions with delusions or hallucinations or severe "endogenous" features. Mania contributes to only a small fraction of this incidence. "Depression of moderate severity" includes all other disorders with a primary diagnosis of depression. The less severe variety of depression is nearly four times more common, overall, than the "psychotic" variety.

TABLE 1

First-ever contacts with psychiatric services, 1965–82 (overall and sex-specific rates per 100,000 Camberwell population in 1973)

Diagnostic group	Males	Females	Both sexes
Schizophrenias	14.6	13.9	14.2
Severe affective disorders	25.7	42.5	34.5
Other depressive disorders	85.6	156.2	122.5
Other neuroses	41.0	48.7	45.0
Dementias	12.6	33.1	23.3
Other disorders	129.9	103.8	116.2

It has been said that "melancholia" is particularly prevalent in spring. The results of studies of depression and mania provide no support for this hypothesis (Eastwood & Stiasny, 1978; Hare & Walter, 1978; Myers & Davies, 1978; Parker & Walter, 1982; Walter, 1977).

Figure 1 presents the age and sex-specific rates for the two kinds of depression. The rates for women are higher than those for men at virtually all ages. The pattern of distribution by age is quite different in the two groups (see also Comstock & Helsing, 1976).

Sturt, Kumakura, and Der (1984) have used Camberwell register data to calculate the lifetime risk for total depressive disorders. This comes to 11.9

FIGURE 1

Incidence of manic depressive disorders, Camberwell (1965–1982)
(Age and sex-specific rates per 100,000 population)

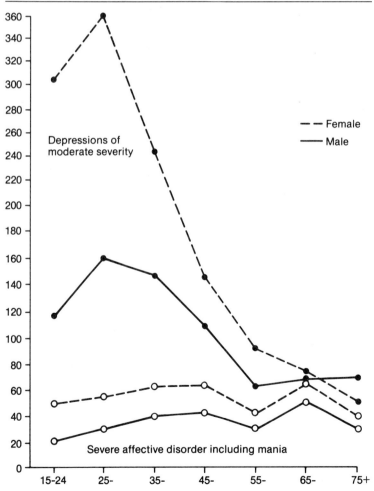

percent for men (s.e. 1.2 percent) and 20.2 percent for women (s.e. 1.5 percent), a highly significant difference. The result is closely similar to an earlier estimate for Bornholm, in Denmark (men 10.2 percent, women 22.4 percent), but lower than an estimate for Iceland (men 18.0 percent, women 24.6 percent). Both were based on the "birth cohort" method of study, using the excellent system of parish and clinic records available in the two countries (Fremming, 1951; Helgason, 1964).

When we come to consider American rates it is still more difficult to make comparisons because diagnostic rules and service provisions have probably differed systematically from those of Europe over much of the past 30 to 40 years. Kramer (1961) was the first to show that "the mental hospital first admission rate for England and Wales for manic-depressive psychosis in the age-group 55–64 was about 20 times the corresponding American rate" (Cooper et al., 1972). The U.S.-U.K. Diagnostic Project investigated the difference in great detail. Investigators using the Present State Examination (PSE) on the two sides of the Atlantic found a much higher rate of affective disorders diagnosed in New York than in London hospitals, but were unable to find any difference between their standardized diagnoses. They concluded that differences in diagnostic practice largely accounted for the differences in rates (Cooper et al., 1972).

Since that time, the introduction of new methods of treatment has given the differential diagnosis of manic and severe depression more importance and the introduction of *DSM-III* has sharpened the definitions of psychiatrists. The differences between America and Europe may now be much less prominent. Nevertheless, they give point to the necessity for adopting a degree of standardization and also for extending studies into the area of nontreated incidence and prevalence.

The methodological difficulties here are just as great but of a different kind. The most severe disorders are relatively rare and it is beyond the scope of most investigators to screen a large enough population to examine rates within all the subgroups that would be desirable. Compliance is much lower in population surveys—it is not uncommon for a quarter of the sample to be lost if there is a two-stage design (a first screen followed by a more intensive interview). Techniques of interview that are suitable for people referred to therapeutic agencies are not necessarily appropriate for a household survey and the threshold at which minimal "mental ill-health" becomes severe enough to be counted as a case is difficult to specify. Finally, the onset of a relatively mild disorder is usually determined retrospectively, since panel studies are expensive to mount, and is attended by a high likelihood of error (Duncan-Jones, 1981). Many population surveys are therefore restricted to measuring prevalence rather than incidence and inferences concerning causes must be appropriately cautious.

Table 2, adapted from a table presented by Bebbington, Hurry, Tennant, Sturt, and Wing (1981), lists prevalence estimates derived from recent sample population surveys in North America and Europe. Only studies that used a specified instrument to identify cases of depression are included. Both male

TABLE 2
Prevalence of depression in sample population surveys

Reference	N	Age range	Disorder	Prevalence (percent) M	Prevalence (percent) F	Instrument
Hare and Shaw (1965) Croydon, England	1,862	16+	Depression	4.0	11.8	Own scale
Warheit, Holzer, & Schwab (1973) Alachua Co, Fla.	2,333	16+	Depression inventory score	13.0	24.0	Beck, Zung, Leighton scales
Comstock and Helsing (1976) Kansas City, Mo. Washington Co, Md.	1,617 3,555	18+ 18+	Depression inventory score	15.7 11.9	22.4 20.7	CES/D CES/D
Weissman and Myers (1978) New Haven, Conn.	511	26+	Depression	5.5	7.9	SADS
Wing et al. (1978) Camberwell, London	237	18–64	ID 5+, Classes D, R, N	—	8.4	PSE-ID CATEGO
Henderson, Duncan-Jones, Byrne, Scott, & Adcock (1979) Canberra, Australia	157	18+	ID 5+, Classes D, R, N	2.6	6.7	CATEGO
Bebbington, Hurry, Tennant, Sturt, & Wing (1981) Camberwell, London	800	18–64	ID 5+ Classes D, R, N	4.5	9.0	CATEGO
Surtees, Dean, Ingham, Kreitman, Miller, & Sashidharan (1983) Edinburgh, Scotland	567 567	18–65 18–65	ID 5+, Classes D, R, N Depression	— —	5.9 8.7	CATEGO SADS

Source: Adapted from Bebbington, Hurry, Tennant, Sturt, and Wing (1981).

and female rates vary by a factor of three to four, with those that depend upon a cutoff score on a self-report inventory yielding the highest prevalence. If these are excluded, there is a fair degree of agreement: 2.6–4.5 percent in men and 5.9–9.0 percent in women.

All the rates so far reviewed have been concordant in one respect—women experience more depression than men, at all ages. Age differentiates "severe" (older) from "moderate" depressions in people contacting specialist services for the first time (Figure 1) but there seems to be little age-specificity in the general population prevalence rates (Bebbington, Hurry, Tennant, Sturt, & Wing, 1981). Contact with therapeutic agencies seems to suggest a more severe disorder (Wing et al., 1981).

None of the studies so far published provides data of sufficient accuracy and stability over a number of years to allow conclusions concerning the change in incidence or prevalence with time. Klerman (1978) and Schwab and colleagues (Schwab, Bell, Warheit, & Schwab, 1979) speculate that depression is becoming more common. Hagnell and colleagues (Hagnell,

Lanke, Rorsman, & Ojesjö, 1982), on the basis of much better data, collected in 1947, 1957, and 1972 in a Swedish rural community, suggest that the incidence of severe depression is decreasing, but that depression of mild to moderate severity is increasing, particularly in young adult males (who have a high rate of unemployment).

At this point, it becomes clear that the further analysis of rates of depression must be highly complex. Therefore, before considering the results of studies that deal with factors such as marital status, employment status, and the presence of young children at home, a word of warning may be in order. Most such studies are exploratory rather than hypothesis testing. It is particularly necessary to watch out for the "model builders" who do not provide critical tests for their theories but modify their models to take account of new results without regard to the foundations of the whole edifice. So far as depressive disorders are concerned, epidemiology is still in its infancy.

MACROSOCIAL FACTORS—SEX, MARITAL STATUS, FAMILY RESPONSIBILITY, EMPLOYMENT

The most robust finding in the field under review is that depressive disorders, however defined, whatever the sample, and irrespective of the instrument used for identification, are commoner in women than in men (Adelstein, Downham, Stein, & Susser, 1968). Weissman and Klerman (1977), in their comprehensive review of papers up to 1977, considered that the marital role involved more stress for women than for men. Many other studies have found that young married women looking after small children are particularly at risk (Baldwin, 1971; Bebbington, Hurry, Tennant, Sturt, & Wing, 1981; Brown & Harris, 1978; Grad de Alarcon, Sainsbury, & Costain, 1975; Moss & Plewis, 1977; Richman, 1974, 1977). Various endocrinologic theories have been put forward to explain the sex difference, mostly in terms of the hormone system in the female and there is also a theory of *depressive equivalents* in men; for example, alcohol misuse or psychopathy. The evidence, at best, is confusing.

Occupational class and employment status are also variables frequently claimed to be associated with rates of depression. Lower social class was found in the Midtown Manhattan survey (Srole et al., 1962) and in studies reviewed by Dohrenwend and Dohrenwend (1969) to be associated with higher rates of disorder. Brown and Harris (1978) found much higher rates in working-class than in middle-class women as did Surtees and colleagues (Surtees, Dean, Ingham, Kreitman, Miller, & Sashidharan, 1983) in Edinburgh. Although Bebbington and colleagues (Bebbington, Hurry, Tennant, Sturt, & Wing, 1981) were unable to show a relationship in either sex, or to find an association with either upward or downward mobility, the weight of the evidence is in favor of a social class effect.

Brenner (1973) suggested that higher rates of admission for mental illness were associated with periods of high unemployment though others have disputed the nature of the relationship (Gravelle, Hutchinson, & Stern, 1981). Banks and Jackson (1982) concluded from a longitudinal study of young people, that unemployment does have ill-effects on mental health and that, when work is obtained, the symptom level falls (Jackson, Stafford, Banks, & Warr, 1982). Fagin (1981) showed that the mental and physical health of families deteriorated when the chief wage earner became unemployed. Jenkins and colleagues (Jenkins, Hurst, & Rose, 1982) found similar effects when employees were threatened with redundancy; effects that were neutralized if the threat was removed.

Much depends on the meaning of "work" to the worker. The extent of any financial difficulty and of other commitments and burdens, and the availability of social support, are crucial. So is interest and involvement. Warr and Parry (1982) concluded that most evidence pointed to a protective effect of employment in the working-class but not in the middle-class women. Parry (in press) suggests that the important factor is whether work involves extra social support. If it does not, it may actually increase the burdens on women. Krause (1984) who conducted a telephone survey of married women living in Akron, Ohio, reported that work can reduce the effects of marital stress but does not provide relief from the stress of caring for children.

The relationships between the variables involved are extremely complex, as indicated in a recent survey in London. Table 3 shows the prevalence of "minor" psychiatric disorders (mostly depressions) in a sample community survey of Camberwell, an inner London suburb. The rates are given separately by sex, marital status, and whether one or other of two "risk" factors are present (unemployed, presence of young children at home). The differential association between marital status and disorder in the two sexes is clearly present even when the presence of one or both risk factors is controlled. In fact, the rate for men are very little increased, whereas they are doubled for married women and quadrupled for women who are not married.

TABLE 3

Prevalence of psychiatric disorder in sample of Camberwell population, ages 18–64 (by sex, marital status, and presence of risk factor)*

	Married (percent)	Single, widowed, divorced (percent)
Men:		
Neither risk factor	2.1	14.0
One or both	3.0	16.4
Total	2.6	13.8
Women:		
Neither risk factor	10.7	3.7
One or both	21.9	15.6
Total	18.4	9.5

* Risk factors: Unemployed; child aged <15 at home.

PRECIPITATION AND VULNERABILITY

The studies so far considered are unequivocally concordant in one respect—depressive disorders are more common in women than in men. There is also a majority view that the incidence and prevalence of depressive disorders in samples of the general population are associated with environmental stress factors, such as low occupational status, unemployment (particularly if it arrives suddenly in the form of redundancy), and the presence of a family burden (e.g., having to care for small children). It is generally agreed that depressive disorders referred for specialist advice and treatment tend to be more severe, and probably tend to have a different symptom pattern (e.g., more delusions and hallucinations, more guilt, more retardation, more vegetative disturbance and more likelihood of being associated with mania) than those found among nonreferred samples. Whether the more severe disorders are really clinically distinct from the less severe is still controversial. The question of whether they are also less likely to be precipitated by *environmental adversity* (i.e., are less *reactive*) deserves further examination.

The macrosocial "stress" factors already considered can be studied in more detail in terms of their components. Two major factors comprising current adversity are *life events* and *chronic problems*. Although they are not as independent as they might seem, since life events can occur repeatedly and also initiate chronic problems, and since chronic problems can have acute exacerbations, most studies have considered them separately. It is convenient to start in this way.

Some people are more likely to develop depressive disorders under stress than others. This *vulnerability* could be genetic, it could be due to the damaging effects of *earlier adversity,* and it could be due to an absence of the *social supports* that help most people to survive common misfortunes without too much damage. It could also be due to an interaction between these factors.

Underlying these issues is the further problem of how to define *normality*. In commonsense terms, a reaction of *distress* should be proportional to the severity of adversity. A young wife, whose newlywed husband is unexpectedly killed in a car accident, will not be considered abnormal if she is distracted with grief. On the other hand, she will not be expected to grieve "too long." To draw the line between normal grief and pathological reaction (i.e., to define deviance), is not at the moment possible using objective measures. The same is true the other way round, when someone appears to react to what most people regard as relatively minor stress with severe and disabling "symptoms."

Measurement of Life Events and Chronic Problems

The *inventory technique* is based upon a list of events thought to have potential for precipitating disorders (Dohrenwend, Krasnoff, Askenasy, & Dohrenwend, 1978; Holmes & Rahe, 1967; Paykel, Prusoff, & Uhlenhuth,

1971; Sarason, Johnson, & Siegel, 1978; Tennant & Andrews, 1976). The technique is economical when presented as a questionnaire for self-completion but it cannot cover all events, or provide adequate dating, or allow critical examination of what the event actually meant to the informant. Brown (1974), therefore, developed a standardized *interview technique,* providing for cross-examination about events, whether elicited or described spontaneously, and incorporating a technique for dating. Subsequently, he and other colleagues (Brown & Harris, 1978) devised a method of categorizing events as "logically independent," "possibly independent," and "dependent," the last category containing events that probably arose because a disorder was already present or developing.

Events are unlikely to be of equal importance and a need for quantifying their impact has always been recognized. The inventory technique for eliciting histories of events has been associated with the establishment of notional values for each event. These values are computed by averaging the ratings of a particular event made by members of a *rating sample* selected for the purpose. This provides a culturally relevant rating, at the cost of disregarding the variations in impact due to the specific circumstances of each event and of the characteristics of the individual experiencing the event.

This procedure is not available for events elicited by a semistructured interview of the Brown and Harris (1978) type, since they are not defined *a priori.* It is therefore necessary to rely on the rating of impact by a review panel able to take the social implications and context of the events into account. This also permits the raters to remain blind to the subject's own response to the event and psychiatric state. Some contamination is inevitable, because the individual who reports the event and its context also reports the symptoms. Nevertheless, two sources of bias are minimized and the commonsense meaning of each event is preserved.

Although these judgments are more meaningful and can be more reliable than is the case with the inventory technique (Mendels & Weinstein, 1972; Parry, Shapiro, & Davies, 1981; Tennant, Smith, Bebbington, & Hurry, 1979), they do not necessarily overcome the problem of contamination. The respondent provides information about the event, its severity and its date, and also about any disorder that might possibly be reactive, and *its* date. The problem is not overcome by having two interviews or two informants, and is only partially overcome by carrying out repeated interviews. The further problem of whether depressed people recall more events than others has not yet been resolved (Brown, Harris, & Peto, 1973; Bebbington, Tennant, & Hurry, 1981).

Another advantage of the interview over the inventory technique is that there is probably less decrement in memory over time and less need for another informant (Bebbington, Tennant, & Hurry, 1981; Brown et al., 1973; Brown & Harris, 1982; Jenkins et al., 1979; Schless & Mendels, 1978; Uhlenhuth, Balter, Lipman, & Haberman, 1977; Yager, Grant, Sweetwood, & Gerst, 1981). On the whole, therefore, in spite of some continuing disadvantages, it seems the better technique.

The measurement of "chronic problems" has received less attention. Some indexes, such as long-term physical illness or disability, or the presence of small children at home, are relatively easy to measure. Others, such as inadequate housing or behavior disturbance in children at school, or marital disharmony, present more difficult problems.

Does Adversity Precipitate Depression?

The epidemiological method is well suited to describing the patterns of association between variables such as those under consideration in this chapter. Most studies have been concentrated, however, either on series of people with relatively severe disorders who have been referred for specialist advice and treatment or on random samples of the general population. There have been few epidemiologically based investigations of all depressive disorders arising in a defined community over a defined period of time.

In general, studies of patients show that the absence or presence of precipitating factors is an important item in statistical functions that differentiate "endogenous" from "nonendogenous" or "reactive" disorders (Carney, Roth, & Garside, 1965; Feinberg & Carroll, 1982; Garside, Kay, Wilson, Deaton, & Roth, 1971; Kay, Garside, Beamish, & Roy, 1969; Kiloh & Garside, 1963; Mendels & Cochrane, 1968; Rosenthal & Gudeman, 1967; Rosenthal & Klerman, 1966). Copeland (1983), however, did not find this effect.

By contrast, studies in which indexes of adversity were tested for their ability to predict the presence or absence of endogenous symptoms provide little confirmation of the hypothesis (Benjaminsen, 1981; Brown, Ní Bhrolcháin, & Harris, 1979; Forrest, Fraser, & Priest, 1965; Hirschfeld, 1981; Katschnig, 1984, Katschnig, Brandl-Nebehay, Fuchs-Robetin, Sielig, Eichberger, Strobl, & Sint, 1981; Leff, Roatch, & Bunney, 1970; Thompson & Hendrie, 1972). Bebbington and colleagues (Bebbington, Tennant, & Hurry, 1981) did find that depressions characterized by retardation, agitation, and pathological guilt were less associated with adversity than other forms. Tennant and colleagues (Tennant, Smith, Bebbington, & Hurry, 1981), using follow-up data from the same sample population survey, found an association between life events that neutralize the effect of previous threatening events and improvement in depressive symptoms, but only in nonendogenous conditions.

A third method of analysis is to compare depressive disorders that seem to follow adversity with those that have no such relationship. Brown and colleagues (1979) found that some endogenous symptoms were less common following adversity but the effect was not substantial. Nelson and Charney (1980) found that 92 percent of an endogenous, compared with 45 percent of an nonendogenous group, had no apparent precipitating factors. The differentiating symptoms were psychomotor disorder, self-reproach, and difficulty in thinking—all characteristic of endogenous depression.

One possible explanation for conflicting results is variation in the age-composition of the groups included in published studies. The age of onset of endogenous depression is greater than that of other forms (Copeland, 1983;

Spicer, Hare, & Slater, 1973). Figure 1 provides some confirmation on the basis of a large series of referred patients. Increasing age is associated with decreasing adversity (Bebbington, Sturt, Tennant, & Hurry, 1984; Brown & Harris, 1978). Paykel (1974) showed that, if age was controlled, recent adversity lost its relationship to symptom picture. However, it seems most unlikely that age can account for all the discrepancies in results.

One further line of investigation has produced relevant data. Kendell and Di Scipio (1968) found that patients with endogenous depressions were less neurotic and less introverted following recovery than patients with neurotic depressions. Other workers reporting similar results are Benjaminsen (1981), Kerr and colleagues (Kerr, Shapira, Roth, & Garside, 1970), Paykel and colleagues (Paykel, Klerman, & Prusoff, 1976), and Perris (1971). Hirschfeld and Klerman (1979) did find that patients with unipolar depression were more introverted and neurotic than those with bipolar disorder, but the significance of this result for the discussion presented above is vitiated by the fact that their unipolar group contained a large proportion of endogenous cases. Recently, Charney and colleagues (Charney, Nelson, & Quinlan, 1981) reported that personality disorders were much less common in *melancholia* (severe endogenous depression) than in other depressive disorders. All these authors agree that nonendogenous depression is frequently precipitated by adverse environmental circumstances operating on someone whose personality is already somehow vulnerable.

Distress not amounting to a depressive disorder, the transient situational reaction of *DSM-III* (American Psychiatric Association, 1980), has been particularly thoroughly described by using follow-up interviews with people who have suffered bereavement or trauma. There is some disagreement as to the extent to which reactions can be called pathological (Clayton, 1975; Clayton, Halikas, & Maurice, 1972; Parkes, 1965, 1975) but, in general, they are not dissimilar to those of neurotic depression (Horowitz, Wilner, Kaltreider, & Alvarez, 1980).

Vulnerability to Stress

The concept of vulnerability involves an assumption that some prior condition or event has sensitized an individual to react adversely to a subsequent stressor. Genetic theories of vulnerability are considered in Chapter 24. Other theories suggest that early loss events, such as separation from or loss of one or both parents when a child, could have such an effect. Brown and Harris (1978) put forward the view that four factors, alone or in combination, predisposed those affected (their study involved only women age 18–65) to respond to severe adversity with a depressive reaction. The four factors were: (1) loss of mother before the age of 11; (2) absence of an intimate relationship (usually with husband or other partner); (3) not having a paid job; and (4) caring for three or more children under 14 years of age. Threatening life events or chronic personal problems would be less likely, by themselves, to precipitate a disorder.

There have been many further studies of the four factors, singly and in combination, and it is fair to conclude that the results are equivocal. For example, Tennant and colleagues (1981) were unable to demonstrate any effect of early loss on the prevalence of depression in a general population sample drawn from the same area as the series studied by Brown and Harris, thus reinforcing the negative conclusion of Granville-Grossman's review (1968). Costello (1982), in Calgary, found that lack of intimacy was sensitizing but that the other three factors were not. Solomon and Bromet (1982), who studied reactions to the Three Mile Island incident, came to a similar conclusion. Other workers have provided partial support for lack of "intimacy" as a vulnerability factor (Campbell, Cope, & Teasdale, 1983; Murphy, 1982; Paykel, Ems, Fletcher, & Ratsaby, 1980). Martin (1982), on the other hand, reported that lack of intimacy was related to disorder whether life events were present or not. Bebbington and colleagues (1984) found little evidence that the vulnerability model was useful in predicting disorder; an additive model, in which each potentially stressful factor, including life events, was accorded weight, seemed more satisfactory.

Psychosocial Support

Whether or not it is a vulnerability factor, psychosocial support emerges strongly as likely to be linked in some way with the onset of depressive disorders. So far, only the availability of an intimate or confiding relationship has been considered. This, however, is only part of the wider concept of *social network*. Certain groups of people are important to the individual in the sense that they confer value and provide a standard against which to measure attitudes and behavior—these are the primary groups of Cooley (1909) or the reference groups of Festinger (1957). The social network extends further than this, to include people who regularly interact with the individual or can, under certain circumstances, become important to him or her.

Parry and Shapiro (in press) provide evidence to suggest that of the two obvious functions of the social network—practical help and emotional support—the presence of the latter is more likely to be associated with a lower risk of developing minor affective disorder. They also point out that a lack of social support can result from depression. Henderson and colleagues (Henderson, Duncan-Jones, Byrne, & Scott, 1980) developed an Interview Schedule for Social Interaction (ISSI) to measure social support and found, both in ambulatory clinics and in population samples in Canberra, Australia, that affective disorders occurred in association with deficiencies in the social network (Henderson et al., 1979; Henderson, Byrne, Duncan-Jones, Scott & Adcock, 1980; Henderson, Duncan-Jones, McAuley, & Ritchie, 1978). Brugha and colleagues (Brugha, Conroy, Walsh, Delaney, O'Hanlon, Dondero, Daly, Hickey, & Bourke, 1982) came to a very similar conclusion after replicating the ambulatory clinic study in Dublin, Ireland.

As usual with epidemiological inquiries, and as was clear from the life event studies reviewed above, the direction of cause and effect cannot be determined from the associations alone. Henderson and colleagues (Henderson, Byrne, & Duncan-Jones, 1981), therefore, used a panel design with four waves of interviews in order to study factors associated with the onset of disorder. For example, people who were free of disorder in wave 1 could be divided into those who remained free in wave 2 or who had developed a disorder by then. The symptom measures used were the General Health Questionnaire ([GHQ]; Goldberg, 1972), the Zung Self-Rating Scale for Depression (Zung, 1965) and, in a subsample, the Present State Examination. All gave similar results. The Eysenck Personality Inventory (yielding estimates of *neuroticism* and *extraversion*) was used as a measure of personality and the ISSI was administered in each wave.

Several ISSI indexes were calculated, the most important distinction being between the *availability* of attachments or more diffuse relationships and the *adequacy,* from the respondent's point of view, of what was available. Those high in neuroticism tended to experience more adversity. Symptomatic measures were particularly associated with the adequacy indexes but this was mostly due to personality and background variables. Neuroticism explained 69 percent of the symptom variance and, when personality and background factors were controlled, the availability of social relationships made only a minor contribution to the onset of new symptoms.

The authors concluded that "the causes of neurosis lie much more within the person than within the social environment" (Henderson et al., 1981, p. 198). They point out that earlier studies had shown dissatisfaction with the environments to be highly characteristic of people with neurotic symptoms (Kay, Beamish, & Roth, 1964; Taylor & Chave, 1964). The design used by Henderson and colleagues is the most sophisticated so far reported and their results must be taken seriously so far as the minor depressive disorders are concerned.

A recent paper by Hirschfeld (1983) contains data on the personalities of 26 women who had recovered from unipolar depression, 134 first-degree female relatives who had similarly recovered, and 272 first-degree female relatives with no history of psychiatric disorder. "Social introversion" appeared to be the most powerful personality characteristic associated with primary nonbipolar depression.

CROSS-CULTURAL STUDIES

The wider problem of *social disorganization,* based on Durkheim's theory of *anomie* (1952), was studied in detail by Leighton and colleagues (1963) who thought it was highly associated with the prevalence of disorder. There is a substantial literature on the cross-cultural epidemiology of depression, but much of it is not based even on an approximate application of the epidemiological method. Moreover, the fundamental rule of translation from one language to another—translate concepts not words—often remains unheeded.

Orley records, on the basis of his studies in Uganda, the difficulties encountered when translating the Present State Examination into Luganda. Several terms could be used for depression, just as in English. *Munakuwavu* means sadness. *Obusongu* and *munyiivu* are terms for anger and irritability which can be associated with depression but must be distinguished from it. There is also a term for "crying in the heart without tears." The word *em-meme* (denoting the xiphisternum) is used in several ways to express emotion but, if it "falls," it means a loss of appetite and weight commonly associated with other disorders such as depression (Orley & Leff, 1972; Orley & Wing, 1979).

Clearly it is necessary to know the local language very well before attempting to match Western concepts. This does not mean that other, local, concepts may not turn out to have important implications. Investigating a defined and precisely measured factor carries no suggestion that other factors cannot be relevant.

In a large-scale collaborative study called the International Pilot Study of Schizophrenia (World Health Organization, 1973, 1979), over 1,200 patients in nine countries were assessed by standardized methods, including the Present State Examination, and followed up over five years. Among the non-schizophrenic groups included were 256 patients with depressive disorders. The participating psychiatrists had no difficulty in eliciting depressive symptoms in languages as structurally different from the Indo-European group (American, English, Czech, Danish, Hindi, Russian, Spanish) as Chinese and Yoruba. Depressive disorders were found in all nine centers.

A more recent international study (World Health Organization, 1983) used a specially constructed instrument to measure depressive symptomatology in hospital patients in Basel, Montreal, Nagasaki, Tehran, and Tokyo. Statistical analysis showed two main subgroups, interpreted as endogenous and psychogenic depression. The endogenous subgroup scored highly on a factor of anergia-retardation and the psychogenic subgroup on abnormal personality.

Perhaps the most famous subcultural study of depressive disorders was carried out by Eaton and Weil (1955) among an Anabaptist sect, the Hutterites, living in small closely knit farming communities along the U.S.-Canadian border. Their religious traditions dated from the 16th century and had been cemented by long periods of persecution and consequent migration. Property was owned in common, and everyday life was simple, austere, well regulated, and pious. Families were large, since there was no birth control. There was no poverty and practically no crime or violence (Hostetler & Huntington, 1967).

It was thought by many that such rural peace, community support, hard work, good order, and freedom from urban stresses would provide conditions in which mental disorders would be unlikely to develop. Eaton and Weil surveyed the colonies, some briefly, a few intensively, and concluded that about 6 per 1,000 of the total population of 8,500 had at some time suffered from a psychosis. This figure was mostly due to severe depressive disorders.

By contrast Böök (1953) carried out a survey in the extreme north of Sweden. The climate is severe, the summer short, and for six weeks in the winter the sun does not rise above the horizon. Many families lived under very primitive conditions and communications with neighbors, let alone with the rest of Sweden, were very poor. Using the extensive local parish and medical records, Böök calculated a rate of psychosis that was three times higher than that of the Hutterites and, moreover, in 85 percent of cases, was accounted for by schizophrenia, not depression. Manic-depressive disorder was almost nonexistent. Böök's explanation was in terms of genetics, a high rate of cousin marriages, and selective migration. He thought that a schizoid personality was an advantage for survival in those parts whereas people with more extravert personalities would escape toward the south. Such an explanation, reversed, would also be relevant to Eaton and Weil's results.

Further studies of the Amish communities in North America have more recently been carried out (Egeland & Hostetter, 1983). There was no sample survey of the population and little exploration of in- and out-migration. Much of the clinical information came from case records. Rather low-prevalence rates were found, particularly for schizophrenia but also for bipolar and unipolar depression. The minor depressive disorders and neuroses hardly appear in the figures at all.

Methods of case identification, population screening, and correction for population movement, have not yet developed far enough to allow firm estimates of prevalence, let alone incidence, in cultures without a well-developed system of services. The movement of individuals in and out of the Hutterite and Amish communities over a 20-year period is not known with any accuracy. However Murphy (1968) has "calculated the 1961 schizophrenia admission rate for the Mennonites and Hutterites combined, from Canada's Prairie Provinces, and that rate is not significantly below average." It seems probable that surveys so far have missed many cases of severe disorder.

Orley used the Ganda version of the PSE to interview all the 206 inhabitants of two small villages near Kampala (Orley & Wing, 1979). Twenty percent had disorders above threshold level and a further 5 percent had more severe disorders. The prevalence of depressive disorders among those age 65 or less was 14.3 percent in men and 22.6 percent in women, much higher than the rates found, using the same instruments, in southeast London (Bebbington, Hurry, Tennant, Sturt, & Wing, 1981). Four men over the age of 65 with depressive disorders were not counted in the overall Ugandan rate—if included, there is no difference between the rates for the two sexes. Pathological and somatic symptoms of depression were commoner than in the London sample. The result may partly be due to the fact that severe depressions are not treated in rural third-world communities, partly to a degree of debility due to parasitic infection and partly, perhaps, to environmental adversity, though this was not measured.

Symptom counts have also shown high prevalence in African populations compared with European or American. Leighton and colleagues (1963) found that depressive symptoms were four times more common in their Nigerian series than among the population of Stirling County, Canada, and that there were relatively small differences in this respect between Yoruba men and women. These authors found no difficulty in rating depression in the Nigerian population. They used complaints, such as sapped vitality, a sense of dwindling, continuous crying, loss of appetite, and loss of interest in life rather than subjective reporting of mood.

Carstairs and Kapur (1976) set out to design an instrument that would not be geared specifically to symptoms of disorders recognized in Western cultures and to apply this in a survey of an Indian village. Their results do not suggest that many new forms of psychopathology remain to be discovered. Local cultures add special color or flavor to well-known symptoms. The differences are in content rather than form. Worrying, for example, is much the same all over the world but the worry about loss of semen described by Carstairs (1959) in Indian men does not preoccupy men elsewhere to the same extent. They have their own local worries. Psychosomatic symptoms are also described in very different terms in different parts of the world, as are symptoms of hysteria.

SUMMARY AND CONCLUSIONS

The epidemiological method is useful for exploration, less good for firm conclusions. This is particularly true when the estimate of the numerator in prevalence rates is an approximate as it must be for depressive disorders. There is some evidence that subgroups of depressive disorders can be distinguished, in particular a relatively small group of severe disorders characterized by symptoms such as hallucinations, delusions, pathological guilt, retardation, and somatic dysfunctions, which tend to be called endogenous, and if associated with mania, bipolar. They occur at first contact with psychiatric services in London, at a rate estimated to be approximately 30–40 per 100,000 total population per year. A much larger subgroup of depressive disorders has fewer endogenous features and may have associated anxiety—the so-called neurotic or reactive depressions. They are much commoner (an incidence at first contact of about 120 per 100,000) and are markedly more frequent before the age of 45. The lifetime expectancy of the two groups together is 12 percent for men and 20 percent for women. Studies of general population samples produce high-point-prevalence rates—3–6 percent for men and 7–15 percent for women.

Frequency estimates of this kind have no absolute value. Depressive disorders used to be diagnosed in patients first admitted to U.S. mental hospitals at a far lower rate than in the United Kingdom but much of the difference was due to variation in the classificatory rules. The rates are useful only insofar as they can be compared with others made under approximately similar conditions; for example, within one large sample, or between samples if the methods of case identification are standardized. Equal thought needs also to be paid to the comparability of population structure.

The major macrosocial variables, apart from age and sex, that have been studied as possible causes, are marital status, the presence of small children at home, occupational classification, and unemployment. Marriage seems to be generally protective for men and stressful for women, if the associations are interpreted in causal terms. Marriage entails, for women, the likelihood of having to care for small children and of having to give up gainful employment—both factors that are associated with the presence of disorder. Lower occupational class is also generally associated with higher rates.

It has been suggested that certain factors are not so much precipitating in themselves as predisposing toward a liability to break down under the stress of adverse life events or long-term difficulties. Early loss of or separation from a parent, lack of a confiding relationship, unemployment, and caring for small children have been put forward as vulnerability factors. An alternative explanation is that such factors contribute, if at all, in additive fashion to the effect of adversity. On the whole, the evidence points to the latter conclusion. However, precipitating factors are less evidently involved in the onset of endogenous disorders.

Lack of psychosocial supports appears as a strong associate of depressive disorder, particularly of the nonendogenous kind. The best designed and most thorough study suggests that a personality factor (neuroticism) is so predominant that the availability of relationships adds little to prediction of breakdown. The adequacy of relationships (a measure of satisfaction) is highly related, both to neuroticism and to symptoms.

Subcultural and cross-cultural studies are less advanced in design and method and face the added difficulty of having to overcome translation problems. Results have received conflicting interpretations, with genetic and psychosocial theories competing.

Genetic factors have not been considered in this chapter, but it is a fair conclusion that they are likely to be of importance, in interaction with environmental factors, and that no satisfactory explanation for the depressive disorders will be developed unless the two approaches are combined. Together with more sophisticated designs and standardized measures, this is the direction in which future epidemiological research is likely to make most progress.

References

Adelstein, A. M., Downham, D. Y., Stein, Z., & Susser, M. W. (1968). The epidemiology of mental illness in an English city. *Social Psychiatry, 3,* 47–59.

Akiskal, H. S., Rosenthal, T. L., Haykal, R. F., Lemmi, H., Rosenthal, R. H., & Scott-Strauss, A. (1980). Characterological depression. Clinical and sleep EEG findings separating "sub-affective dysthymias" from "character spectrum disorders." *Archives of General Psychiatry, 37,* 777–783.

American Psychiatric Association. (1980). *Diagnostic and statistical manual of mental disorders (DSM-III)* (3rd ed.). Washington DC: Author.

Angst, J. (1966). Zur Ätiologie und Nosologie endogener depressiver Psychosen. *Monographien aus dem Gesamtgebrete der Neurologie und Psychiatrie* (No. 112 pp. 1–118). Berlin: Springer-Verlag.

Baldwin, J. A. (1971). *The mental hospital in the psychiatric service: A case-register study.* London: Oxford University Press.

Banks, M. H., & Jackson, P. R. (1982). Unemployment and risk of minor psychiatric disorders in young people: Cross-sectional and longitudinal evidence. *Psychological Medicine, 12,* 789–798.

Bebbington, P. E., Hurry, J., Tennant, C., Sturt, E., & Wing, J. K. (1981). The epidemiology of mental disorders in Camberwell. *Psychological Medicine, 11,* 561–580.

Bebbington, P. E., Sturt, E., Tennant, C., & Hurry, J. (1984). Misfortune and resilience: A community study of women. *Psychological Medicine, 14,* 347–363.

Bebbington, P. E., Tennant, C., & Hurry, J. (1981). Life events and the nature of psychiatric disorder in the community. *Journal of Affective Disorders, 3,* 345–366.

Beck, A. T., Ward, C. H., Mendelson, M., Mock, J., & Erbaugh, J. (1961). An inventory for measuring depression. *Archives of General Psychiatry, 4,* 561–571.

Benjaminsen, S. (1981). Primary non-endogenous depression and features attributed to reactive depression. *Journal of Affective Disorders, 3,* 245–259.

Böök, J. A. (1953). A genetic and neuropsychiatric investigation of a North-Swedish population. *Acta Genetica et Statistica Medica, 4,* 1–100.

Boyd, J. H., & Weissman, M. M. (1981). Epidemiology of affective disorders—A reexamination and future directions. *Archives of General Psychiatry, 38,* 1039–1046.

Brenner, M. H. (1973). *Mental illness and the economy.* Cambridge, MA: Harvard University Press.

Brockington, I. F., Altman, E., Hillier, V., Meltzer, H. V., & Nand, S. (1982). The clinical picture of bipolar affective disorder in its depressed phase: A report from London and Chicago. *British Journal of Psychiatry, 141,* 558–562.

Brown, G. W. (1974). Meaning, measurement and stress of life events. In B. S. Dohrenwend & B. P. Dohrenwend (Eds.), *Stressful life events: Their nature and effects* (pp. 217–243). New York: John Wiley & Sons.

Brown, G. W., & Harris, T. O. (1978). *Social origins of depression: A study of psychiatric disorder in women.* London: Tavistock.

Brown, G. W., & Harris, T. O. (1982). Fall-off in the reporting of life events. *Social Psychiatry, 17,* 23–28.

Brown, G. W., Harris, T. O., & Peto, J. (1973). Life events and psychiatric disorder. Part 2: Nature of causal link. *Psychological Medicine, 3,* 159–176.

Brown, G. W., Ní Bhrolcháin, M., & Harris, T. (1979). Psychotic and neurotic depression, Part 3. Aetiological and background factors. *Journal of Affective Disorders, 1,* 195–211.

Brugha, T., Conroy, R., Walsh, N., Delaney, W., O'Hanlon, J., Dondero, B., Daly, L., Hickey, N., & Bourke, G. (1982). Social networks, attachments and support in minor affective disorders: A replication. *British Journal of Psychiatry, 141,* 249–255.

Caplan, A. L., Engelhardt, H. T., & McCartney, J. K. (Eds.). (1981). *Concepts of health and disease.* Reading, MA: Addison-Wesley Publishing.

Carney, M. W. P., Roth, M., & Garside, R. F. (1965). The diagnosis of depressive syndromes and the prediction of ECT response. *British Journal of Psychiatry, 111,* 659–674.

Carstairs, G. M. (1959). *Mental illness. Medical surveys and clinical Trials.* New York: Oxford University Press.

Carstairs, G. M., & Kapur, R. L. (1976). *The great universe of Kota.* London: Hogarth Press.

Charney, D. S., & Nelson, J. C. (1981). Delusional and non-delusional unipolar depression: Further evidence for distinct sub-types. *American Journal of Psychiatry, 138,* 328–333.

Charney, D. S., Nelson, J. C., & Quinlan, D. M. (1981). Personality traits and disorder in depression. *American Journal of Psychiatry, 138,* 1601–1604.

Clayton, P. J. (1975). The effect of living alone on bereavement symptoms. *American Journal of Psychiatry, 132,* 133–137.

Clayton, P. J., Halikas, J. A., & Maurice, W. L. (1972). The depression of widowhood. *British Journal of Psychiatry, 120,* 71–78.

Cohen, H. (1961). The evolution of the concept of disease. In B. Lush (Ed.), *Concepts of medicine* (pp. 159–169). Elmsford, NY: Pergamon Press.

Comstock, G. W., & Helsing, K. J. (1976). Symptoms of depression in two communities. *Psychological Medicine, 6,* 551–563.

Cooley, C. H. (1909). *Social organization: A study of the larger mind.* New York: Charles Scribner's Sons.

Cooper, J. E., Kendell, R. R., Gurland, B. J., Sharpe, L., Copeland, J. R. M., & Simon, R. (1972). *Psychiatric diagnosis in New York and London.* (Maudsley Monograph No. 20). New York: Oxford University Press.

Copeland, J. R. M. (1983). Psychotic and neurotic depression: Discriminant function analysis and five-year outcome. *Psychological Medicine, 13,* 373–384.

Costello, C. G. (1982). Social factors associated with depression: A retrospective community study. *Psychological Medicine, 12,* 329–339.

Dohrenwend, B. S., Krasnoff, L., Askenasy, A. R., & Dohrenwend, B. P. (1978). Exemplification of a method for scaling life events: The PERI life events scale. *Journal of Health and Social Behaviour, 19,* 205–229.

Dohrenwend, B. P., & Dohrenwend, B. S. (1969). *Social status and psychological disorder. A causal inquiry.* New York: John Wiley & Sons.

Duncan-Jones, P. (1981). The natural history of neurosis. Probability models. In J. K. Wing, P. E. Bebbington, & L. N. Robins (Eds.). *What is a case? The problem of definition in psychiatric community surveys.* London: Grant McIntyre.

Durkheim, E. (1952). *Suicide: A study in sociology* (J. A. Spaulding & G. Simpson, Trans.). Boston: Routledge & Kegan Paul.

Eastwood, M. R., & Stiasny, S. (1978). Psychiatric disorder, hospital admission and season. *Archives of General Psychiatry, 35,* 769–771.

Eaton, J. W., & Weil, R. J. (1955). *Culture and mental disorders.* New York: Free Press.

Eaton, W. E., Regier, D. A., Locke, B. Z., & Taube, C. A. (1981). The NIMH epidemiological catchment area program. In J. K. Wing, P. Bebbington, & L. N. Robins (Eds.), *What is a case? The problem of definition in psychiatric community surveys.* London: Grant McIntyre.

Egeland, J. A., & Hostetter, A. M. (1983). Affective disorders among the Amish, 1976–1980. *American Journal of Psychiatry, 140,* 56–61.

Fagin, L. (1981). *Unemployment and health in families.* London: Department of Health and Social Security.

Feighner, J. P., Robins, E., Guze, S. B., Woodruff, R. A., Winokur, G., & Muñoz, R. (1972). Diagnostic criteria for use in psychiatric research. *Archives of General Psychiatry, 26,* 57–63.

Feinberg, M., & Carroll, B. J. (1982). Separation of sub-types of depression using discriminant analysis: I. Separation of unipolar endogenous depression from non-endogenous depression. *British Journal of Psychiatry, 140,* 384–391.

Festinger, L. (1957). *A theory of cognitive dissonance.* Evanston, IL: Row, Peterson.

Finlay-Jones, R., Brown, G. W., Duncan-Jones, P., Harris, T., Murphy, E., & Prudo, R. (1980). Depression and anxiety in the community: Replicating the diagnosis of a case. *Psychological Medicine, 10,* 445–454.

Forrest, A. D., Fraser, R. H., & Priest, R. G. (1965). Environmental factors in depressive illness. *British Journal of Psychiatry, 3,* 243–253.

Fremming, K. H. (1951). The expectation of mental infirmity in a sample of the Danish population. *Occasional Papers on Eugenics, No. 7* (p. 104). London: Eugenics Society.

Garside, R. F., Kay, D. W. K., Wilson, I. C., Deaton, I. D., & Roth, M. (1971). Depressive syndromes and the classification of patients. *Psychological Medicine, 1,* 333–338.

Glassman, A. H., & Roose, S. P. (1981). Delusional depression: A distinct clinical entity? *Archives of General Psychiatry, 38,* 424–427.

Goldberg, D. P. (1972). *The detection of psychiatric illness by questionnaire.* New York: Oxford University Press.

Grad de Alarcon, J., Sainsbury, P., & Costain, W. R. (1975). Incidence of referred mental illness in Chichester and Salisbury. *Psychological Medicine, 5,* 32–54.

Granville-Grossman, K. L. (1968). The early environment in affective disorder. In A. Coppen & A. Walk (Eds.), *Recent developments in affective disorders.* Ashford, Kent.: Headley Bros.

Gravelle, H. S. E., Hutchinson, G., & Stern, J. (1981). Morality and unemployment: A critique of Brenner's time series analysis. *Lancet, 2,* 675–679.

Hagnell, O., Lanke, J., Rorsman, B., & Ojesjö, L. (1982). Are we entering an age of melancholy? Depressive illness in a prospective epidemiological study over 25 years: The Lundby Study, Sweden. *Psychological Medicine, 12,* 279–289.

Hare, E. H., & Shaw, G. K. (1965). Mental health on a new housing estate: A comparative study of health in two districts in Croydon. Maudsley Monograph No. 12. London: Oxford University Press.

Hare, E. H., & Walter, S. D. (1978). Seasonal variation in admissions of psychiatric patients and its relation to seasonal variation in their birth. *Journal of Epidemiology and Community Health, 32,* 47–52.

Helgason, L. (1964). Epidemiology of mental disorders in Iceland. A psychiatric and demographic investigation of 5,395 Icelanders. *Acta Psychiatrica Scandinavica, 40,* 173.

Helms, P. M., & Smith, R. E. (1983). Recurrent psychotic depression: Evidence of diagnosis stability. *Journal of Affective Disorders, 5,* 51–54.

Henderson, A. S., Byrne, D. G., & Duncan-Jones, P. (1981). *Neurosis and the social environment.* Sydney, Australia: Academic Press.

Henderson, A. S., Byrne, D., Duncan-Jones, P., Scott, R., & Adcock, S. (1980). Social relationships, adversity and neuroses: A study of associations in a general population sample. *British Journal of Psychiatry, 136,* 574–583.

Henderson, A. S., Duncan-Jones, P., Byrne, D. G., & Scott, R. (1980). Measuring social relationships: The Interview Schedule for Social Interaction. *Psychological Medicine, 10,* 723–734.

Henderson, A. S., Duncan-Jones, P., Byrne, D. G., Scott, R., & Adcock, S. (1979). Psychiatric disorders in Canberra: A standardized study of prevalence. *Acta Psychiatrica Scandinavica, 60,* 355–374.

Henderson, A. S., Duncan-Jones, P., McAuley, H., & Ritchie, K. (1978). The patient's primary group. *British Journal of Psychiatry, 132,* 74–86.

Hirschfeld, R. M. A. (1981). Situational depression: Validity of the concept. *British Journal of Psychiatry, 139,* 297–305.

Hirschfeld, R. M. A. (1983). Personality and depression: Empirical findings. *Archives of General Psychiatry, 40,* 993–998.

Hirschfeld, R. M. A., & Klerman, G. L. (1979). Personality attributes and affective disorders. *American Journal of Psychiatry, 136,* 67–70.

Holmes, T. H., & Rahe, R. H. (1967). The Social Readjustment Rating Scale. *Journal of Psychomatic Research, 11,* 213–218.

Horowitz, M. J., Wilner, N., Kaltreider, N., & Alvarez, W. (1980). Signs and symptoms of post-traumatic stress disorder. *Archives of General Psychiatry, 37,* 85–92.

Hostetler, J. A., & Huntington, G. E. (1967). *The Hutterites in North America.* New York: Holt, Rinehart & Winston.

Jackson, P. R., Stafford, E. M., Banks, M. H., & Warr, P. B. (1982). Work involvement and employment status as influences on mental health: A test of an inter-actional model. *SAPU Memo 404.* University of Sheffield, England.

Jenkins, C. D., Hurst, M. W., & Rose, R. M. (1979). Life changes: Do people really remember? *Archives of General Psychiatry, 36,* 379–384.

Katschnig, H. (1984). Commentary to Paul Bebbington: Inferring causes—Some constraints in the social psychiatry of depressive disorders. *Integrative Psychiatry, 2,* 77–79.

Katschnig, H., Brandl-Nebehay, A., Fuchs-Robetin, G., Seelig, P., Eichberger, G., Strobl, R., & Sint, P. P. (1981). *Lebensverändernde Ereignisse, psychoziale Dispositionen und depressive Verstimmungzustände.* Wien. Abteilung für Sozialpsychiatrie und Dokumentation. Psychiatrische Universitätsklinik.

Katz, M. M., Robins, E., Croughan, J., Secunda, S., & Swann, S. (1982). Behavioural measurement and drug response characteristics of unipolar and bipolar depression. *Psychological Medicine, 12,* 25–36.

Kay, D. W. K., Beamish, P., & Roth, M. (1964). Old-age mental disorders in Newcastle-upon-Tyne. II. A study of possible social and medical causes. *British Journal of Psychiatry, 110,* 668–682.

Kay, D. W. K., Garside, R. F., Beamish, P., & Roy, J. R. (1969). Endogenous and neurotic syndromes of depression—A factor analytic study of 104 cases. Clinical features. *British Journal of Psychiatry, 115,* 377–388.

Kendell, R. E., & Di Scipio, W. J. (1968). Eysenck Personality Scores of patients with depressive illnesses. *British Journal of Psychiatry, 114,* 767–770.

Kerr, T. A., Shapira, K., Roth, M., & Garside, R. F. (1970). The relationship between the Maudsley Personality Inventory and the course of affective disorders. *British Journal of Psychiatry, 116,* 11–19.

Kiloh, L. G., & Garside, R. F. (1963). The independence of neurotic depression and endogenous depression. *British Journal of Psychiatry, 109,* 451–463.

Klerman, G. L. (1978). Affective disorders: In M. Armand & M. D. Nicholi (Eds.), *The Harvard guide to modern psychiatry.* Cambridge, MA: Harvard University Press.

Kraepelin, E. (1913). *Lectures on clinical psychiatry* (T. Johnstone, Ed., 8th ed. rev.). London: Bailliere, Tindall & Cox.

Kraepelin, E. (1921). *Manic-depressive insanity and paranoia* (R. M. Barclay, Trans.). *Psychiatrie* (8th ed.). Edinburgh: Livingstone.

Kramer, M. (1961). Some problems for international research suggested by observations on differences in first admission rates to mental hospital of England and Wales and of the United States. *Proceedings of the Third World Congress of Psychiatry* (Vol. 3). Montreal: McGill University Press.

Krause, N. (1984). Employment outside the home and women's psychological well-being. *Social Psychiatry, 19,* 41.

Leff, M. H., Roatch, J. F., & Bunney, W. E. (1970). Environmental factors preceding the onsets of severe depression. *Psychiatry, 33,* 293–311.

Leighton, A. H., Lambo, T. A., Hughes, C. C., Leighton, D. C., Murphy, J. M., & Macklin, D. B. (1963). *Psychiatric disorder among the Yoruba.* Ithaca, NY: Cornell University Press.

Leighton, D. C., Harding, J. S., Macklin, D. B., MacMillan, A. M., & Leighton, A. H. (1963). *The character of danger* (Stirling County Study, Vol. 3). New York: Basic Books.

Leonard, K. (1979). *The classification of endogenous psychoses* (R. Berman, Trans., 5th ed.). New York: Irvington Pubs.

Lewis, A. J. (1934). Melancholia—A historical review. *Journal of Men Science, 80,* 1–42.

MacMahon, B., & Pugh, T. F. (1970). *Epidemiology: Principles and methods.* Boston: Little, Brown.

Martin, C. (1982). *Psychosocial stress and puerperal psychiatric disorder.* Paper presented to the Marcé Society. Institute of Psychiatry, London, England.

Mechanic, D. (1970). Problems and prospects in psychiatric epidemiology. In E. H. Hare & J. K. Wing (Eds.), *Psychiatric epidemiology: An International Symposium.* New York: Oxford University Press.

Mendels, J., & Cochrane, C. (1968). The nosology of depression—The endogenous reactive concept. *American Journal of Psychiatry, 124*(Suppl.), 1–11.

Mendels, J., & Weinstein, N. (1972). The Schedule of Recent Experiences: A reliability study. *Psychosomatic Medicine, 34,* 527–531.

Moss, P., & Plewis, I. (1977). Mental distress in mothers of preschool children in inner London. *Psychological Medicine, 7,* 641–652.

Murphy, E. (1982). Social origins of depression in old age. *British Journal of Psychiatry, 141,* 135–142.

Murphy, H. B. M. (1968). Cultural factors in the genesis of schizophrenia. In D. Rosenthal, & S. Kety (Eds.), *The transmission of schizophrenia.* Elmsford, NY: Pergamon Press.

Myers, D. H., & Davies, P. (1978). The seasonal incidence of mania and its relationship to climatic variables. *Psychological Medicine, 8,* 433–440.

Nelson, C. J., & Charney, D. S. (1980). Primary affective disorder criteria and the endogenous-reactive distinction. *Archives of General Psychiatry, 37,* 787–793.

Orley, J. H., & Leff, J. (1972). The effect of psychiatric education on attitudes to illness among the Ganda. *British Journal of Psychiatry, 121,* 137–141.

Orley, J. H., & Wing, J. K. (1979). Psychiatric disorders in two African villages. *Archives of General Psychiatry, 36,* 513–520.

Parker, G., & Walter, S. D. (1982). Seasonal variation in depressive disorders and suicidal deaths in New South Wales. *The British Journal of Psychiatry, 140,* 626–632.

Parkes, C. M. (1965). Bereavement and mental illness. Part 1. A clinical study of the grief of bereaved psychiatric patients. *British Journal of Medical Psychology, 38,* 1–26.

Parkes, C. M. (1975). Determinants of outcome following bereavement. *Omega, 6,* 303–323.

Parry, G. M. (in press). The mental health of employed and unemployed mothers: Beyond the global comparison, *Journal of Health and Social Behaviour.*

Parry, G., & Shapiro, D. A. (in press). Social support and life events in working class women: Stress buffering or independent effects. *Archives of General Psychiatry.*

Parry, G., Shapiro, D. A., & Davies, L. (1981). Reliability of life-event ratings: An independent replication. *British Journal of Clinical Psychology, 20,* 133–134.

Paykel, E. S. (1974). Recent life events and clinical depression. In E. K. Gunderson & R. H. Rahe (Eds.), *Life stress and psychiatric illness.* Springfield, IL: Charles C Thomas.

Paykel, E. S., Ems, E. M., Fletcher, J., & Ratsaby, E. S. (1980). Life events and social support in puerperal depression. *British Journal of Psychiatry, 136,* 339–346.

Paykel, E. S., Klerman, G. L., & Prusoff, B. A. (1976). Personality and symptom pattern in depression. *British Journal of Psychiatry, 129,* 327–334.

Paykel, E. S., Prusoff, B. A., & Uhlenhuth, E. H. (1971). Scaling of life events. *Archives of General Psychiatry, 25,* 340–347.

Perris, C. (1966). A study of bipolar (manic-depressives) and unipolar recurrent affective psychoses. *Acta Psychiatrica Scandinavica, 42*(Suppl. 194).

Perris, C. (1971). Personality patterns in patients with affective disorders. *Acta Psychiatrica Scandinavica, 47*(Suppl. 221), 43–51.

Perris, C. (1974). A study of cycloid psychoses. *Acta Psychiatrica Scandinavica, 50*(Suppl. 253).

Pfohl, B., Vasquez, N., & Nasrallah, H. (1982). Unipolar versus bipolar mania: a review of 247 patients. *British Journal of Psychiatry, 141,* 453–458.

Radloff, L. S. (1977). The CES-D Scale: A self-report depression scale for research in the general population. *Applied Psychological Measurement, 1,* 385–401.

Richman, N. (1974). The effect of housing on pre-school children and their mothers. *Developmental Medicine and Child Neurology, 16,* 53–58.

Richman, N. (1977). Behaviour problems in pre-school children: Family and social factors. *British Journal of Psychiatry, 131,* 523–527.

Robins, L. N., Helzer, J. E., Croughan, J. L., & Ratcliff, K. (1981). The NIMH Diagnostic Interview Schedule: Its history, characteristics and validity. In J. K. Wing, P. Bebbington, & L. N. Robins (Eds.), *What is a case? The problem of definition in psychiatric community surveys.* London: Grant McIntyre.

Rosenthal, S. H., & Gudeman, J. E. (1967). The endogenous depressive pattern. *Archives of General Psychiatry, 16,* 241–249.

Rosenthal, S. H., & Klerman, G. L. (1966). Content and consistency in the endogenous depressive pattern. *British Journal of Psychiatry, 112,* 471–484.

Rosenthal, T. L., Akiskal, H. S., Scott-Strauss, A., Rosenthal, R. H., & David, M. (1981). Familial and developmental factors in characterological depressions. *Journal of Affective Disorders, 3,* 183–192.

Roth, W. F., & Luton, F. H. (1942). The mental health program in Tennessee. *American Journal of Psychiatry, 99,* 662–675.

Sarason, I. G., Johnson, J. H., & Siegel, J. M. (1978). Assessing the impact of life changes: Development of the Life Experiences Survey. *Journal of Consulting and Clinical Psychology, 46,* 932–946.

Schless, A. P., & Mendels, J. (1978). The value of interviewing family and friends in assessing life stressors. *Archives of General Psychiatry, 35,* 565–567.

Schwab, J. J., Bell, R. A., Warheit, G. J., & Schwab, R. B. (1979). *Social order and mental health: The Florida Health Study.* New York: Brunner/Mazel.

Sjögren, T. (1948). Genetic-statistical and psychiatric investigations of a west Swedish population. *Acta Psychiatrica et Neurologica Scandinavica, 23*(Suppl. 52).

Solomon, Z., & Bromet, E. (1982). The role of social factors in affective disorder: An assessment of the vulnerability model of Brown and his colleagues. *Psychological Medicine, 12,* 123–130.

Spicer, C. C., Hare, E. H., & Slater, E. (1973). Neurotic and psychotic forms of depressive illness: Evidence from age incidence in a national sample. *British Journal of Psychiatry, 123,* 535–541.

Spitzer, R. L., Endicott, J., & Robins, E. (1978). *Research Diagnostic Criteria (RDC) for a selected group of functional disorders* (3rd ed.). New York: New York State Psychiatric Institute.

Srole, L., Langner, T., Michael, S. T., Opler, M. K., & Rennie, T. A. C. (1962). *Mental health in the metropolis.* New York: McGraw-Hill.

Stouffer, S. A., Guttman, L., Suchman, E. A., Lazarsfeld, P. F., Star, S. A., & Clausen, J. A. (1950). Measurement and prediction. *In Studies in social psychology in World War II* (Vol. IV). Princeton, NJ: Princeton University Press.

Strömgren, E. (1938). *Beitrage zur psychiatrischen Erblehre,* Copenhagen, Denmark: Munksgaard.

Sturt, E., Bebbington, P., Hurry, J., & Tennant, C. (1981). The PSE used by interviewers from a survey agency. *Psychological Medicine, 11,* 185–192.

Sturt, E. S., Kumakura, N., & Der, G. (1984). How depressing live is: Lifelong risk of depression in the general population. *Journal of Affective Disorders, 7,* 109–22.

Surtees, P. G., Dean, C., Ingham, J. G., Kreitman, N. B., Miller, P. McC., & Sashidharan, S. P. (1983). Psychiatric disorder in women from an Edinburgh community: Associations with demographic factors. *British Journal of Psychiatry, 142,* 238–246.

Taylor, Lord, & Chave, S. (1964). *Mental health and environment.* London: Longman Green.

Tennant, C., & Andrews, G. (1976). A scale to measure the stress of life events. *Australian and New Zealand Journal of Psychiatry, 10,* 27–33.

Tennant, C., Bebbington, P., & Hurry, J. (1981). The short-term outcome of neurotic disorders in the community: The relation of remission to clinical factors and to "neutralizing" life events. *British Journal of Psychiatry, 139,* 213–220.

Tennant, C., Smith, A., Bebbington, P., & Hurry, J. (1979). The contextual threat of life events: The concept and its reliability. *Psychological Medicine, 9,* 525–528.

Tennant, C., Smith, A., Bebbington, P., & Hurry, J. (1981). Parental loss in childhood, adult psychiatric impairment and contact with psychiatric services. *Archives of General Psychiatry, 38,* 309–314.

Thompson, K. C., & Hendrie, H. C. (1972). Environmental stress in primary depressive illness. *Archives of General Psychiatry, 26,* 130–132.

Uhlenhuth, E., Balter, M. D., Lipman, R. S., & Haberman, S. J. (1977). Remembering life events. In J. S. Strauss, H. M. Babigian, & M. Roff (Eds.), *The origins and course of psychopathology* (pp. 117–132). New York: Plenum Publishing.

Walter, S. D. (1977). Seasonality of mania: A reappraisal. *British Journal of Psychiatry, 131,* 345–350.

Warheit, G. J., Holzer, C. E., & Schwab, J. J. (1973). An analysis of social class and racial differences in depressive symptomatology: A community study. *Journal of Health and Social Behaviour, 14,* 291–295.

Warr, P., & Parry, G. (1982). Paid employment and women's psychological well-being. *Psychological Bulletin, 91,* 498–516.

Weissman, M. M., & Klerman, G. L. (1977). Sex differences and the epidemiology of depression. *Archives of General Psychiatry, 34,* 98–112.

Weissman, M. M., & Myers, J. (1978). Rates and risk of depressive symptoms in a United States urban community. *Acta Psychiatrica Scandinavica, 57,* 219–231.

Wing, J. K. (1978). *Reasoning about madness.* New York: Oxford University Press.

Wing, J. K. (1980). The use of the PSE in general population surveys. In E. Strömgren, A. Dupont, & J. A. Nielsen (Eds.), *Epidemiological research as a basis for the organization of entramural psychiatry.* Acta Psychiatrica Scandinavica, 62(Suppl. 285), 230–240.

Wing, J. K. (1983). Use and misuse of the PSE. *British Journal of Psychiatry, 143,* 111–117.

Wing, J. K., Bebbington, P., Hurry, J., & Tennant, C. (1981). The prevalence in the general population of disorders familiar to psychiatrists in hospital practice. In J. K. Wing, P. Bebbington, & L. N. Robins (Eds.), *What is a case? The problem of definition in psychiatric community surveys.* London: Grant McIntyre.

Wing, J. K., Birley, J. L. T., Cooper, J. E., Graham, P., & Isaacs, A. (1967). Reliability of a procedure for measuring and classifying "present psychiatric state." *British Journal of Psychiatry, 113,* 499–515.

Wing, J. K., Cooper, J. E., & Sartorius, N. (1974). *Measurement and classification of psychiatric symptoms: An instruction manual for the PSE and CATEGO program.* Cambridge, MA: Harvard University Press.

Wing, J. K., & Der, G. (1984). *Report of the Camberwell Psychiatric Register 1964– 1983.* MRC Social Psychiatry Unit, London, SE5 8AF.

Wing, J. K., Mann, S. A., Leff, J. P., & Nixon, J. M. (1978). The concept of a "case" in psychiatric population surveys. *Psychological Medicine, 8,* 203–217.

Wing, J. K., Nixon, J. M., Mann, S. A., & Leff, J. P. (1977). Reliability of the *PSE* (9th ed.) used in a population survey. *Psychological Medicine, 7,* 505–516.

Winokur, G. (1973). The types of affective disorders. *Journal of Nervous and Mental Disease, 156,* 82–96.

Winokur, G., Behar, D., Van Valkenberg, C., & Lowry, M. (1978). Is a familial definition of depression both feasible and valid? *Journal of Nervous and Mental Disease, 166,* 764–768.

Winokur, G., Clayton, P. J., & Reich, T. (1969). *Manic-depressive illness.* St. Louis, MO: C.V. Mosby.

World Health Organization. (1973). *The International Pilot Study of Schizophrenia.* Geneva, Switz.: Author.

World Health Organization. (1978). *Mental disorders: Glossary and guide to their classification in accordance with the ninth revision of the International Classification of Diseases.* Geneva, Switz.: Author.

World Health Organization. (1979). *Schizophrenia: An international follow-up study.* Geneva, Switz.: Author.

World Health Organization. (1983). *Depressive disorders in different cultures.* Geneva, Switz.: Author.

Yager, J., Grant, I., Sweetwood, H. L., & Gerst, M. (1981). Life events reported by psychiatric patients, non-patients and their partners. *Archives of General Psychiatry, 38,* 343–347.

Zung, W. W. K. (1965). A self-rating depression scale. *Archives of General Psychiatry, 12,* 63–70.

Chapter 24

Genetic Research in Depressive Disorders

J. Mendlewicz
Professor and Head. Department of Psychiatry. University Clinics of
Brussels. Erasme Hospital, University of Brussels. Belgium.

DEPRESSIVE DISORDERS: EPIDEMIOLOGY AND HEREDITY

Prevalence

Leonhard (1959) and the Berlin School have proposed to discriminate between bipolar (manic-depressive) and unipolar (depressive) subtypes in depressive disorder research. Bipolar patients experience both mania and depression, whereas unipolar patients experience depression only. Most of the epidemiological studies on affective disorders have not made this distinction and various investigators have used different diagnostic criteria for classifying the affective psychoses. It is therefore difficult to assess reliably the prevalence of affective illness in the general population. Several investigators, however, have reported lifetime risks for bipolar (manic-depressive) illness in various geographical areas under specific conditions. The rates published vary from a low of 0.07 percent (Böök, 1953) to a high of 7.0 percent (Tomasson, 1938). The unusually low rate of 0.07 percent corresponds to only two cases of bipolar illness in a population of about 9,000 persons in a province of northern Sweden.

Zerbin-Rüdin (1967), who reviewed most population studies in manic-depressive illness, places the overall rate for this disease at around 1 percent. This rate is consistent with, although not identical to, the rates published by Slater (1953) for Great Britain (0.5–0.8 percent), Sjörgen (1948) for Sweden (0.6–0.8 percent), and Kallmann (1954) for New York state (0.4 percent). These differences in the prevalence of bipolar illness according to the country investigated could be partially explained by genetic factors: for example, breeding effects and higher consanguinity rates in isolates in Scandinavia, or differences in ethnic backgrounds. However, environmental factors may also lead to such differences.

Among these are sampling artifacts such as the different sizes of the samples studied, and the differences in the ethnic and socioeconomic composition of the populations investigated. Furthermore, some studies are based on admission to state hospitals and represent an incidence rate rather than a true prevalence; admissions to private and community facilities are rarely included in these surveys. This represents a serious bias since we know that population rates for a disease may fluctuate with time according to hospitalization policy or availability of beds. To illustrate this, the lifetime hospital admission risk for all affective disorders published by the Registrar General and the Ministry of Health (1969) in England in 1964 was 2.4 percent for males and 5.8 percent for females, a nearly 50 percent rise for both sexes when compared to 1954. These apparently high rates in certain areas may be true only under special demographic conditions. In addition to differences in sampling, investigators utilize different statistical procedures and, more important, various diagnostic criteria. American psychiatrists tend to diagnose schizophrenia more frequently and underdiagnose manic-depressive illness as compared to their British and Western European colleagues who are more prone to diagnose affective illness (Cooper, Kendall, Gurland, Sharp, Copeland, & Simon, 1972).

Nevertheless, one may conclude from the more reliable lifetime risk studies that 1 percent would be a conservative rate for the prevalence of bipolar manic-depressive illness in the general population (Ministry of Health, 1969). If one were to include milder forms of bipolar illness, where a considerable number of subjects are being treated as outpatients, the general prevalence may as well be as high as 10 percent.

Most studies have reported an appreciable difference between the sexes in the distribution of bipolar illness (Helgasson, 1964). The sex ratio generally accepted is two females to one male. The interpretation of this excess of females is still controversial. It is conceivable that for cultural reasons, women are more likely to be hospitalized for manic-depressive illness than men. If this were true, one would expect to find the same phenomenon for schizophrenia, something that remains to be proved. Another possible explanation is the fact that male suicides outnumber female suicides by a ratio of about 2 to 1 (Rüdin, 1923), leaving more females alive than males in the bipolar population. Finally, one could also invoke the hypothesis of sex-limited factors; for example, hormonal- (Zerbin-Rüden, 1967) or sex-linked genetic factors, increasing the expressivity of bipolar illness in females predisposed to this disorder.

Twin Studies

The twin method allows comparison of concordance rates for a trait between sets of monozygotic (MZ) and dizygotic (DZ) twins. Both types of twins share a similar environment, but they are genetically different. Monozygotic twins behave genetically as identical individuals, whereas DZ twins share only half of their genes and thus behave as sibs. Most twins studies show that the concordance rate for manic-depressive illness in MZ twins is significantly higher than the concordance rate for the disease in DZ Twins (Zerbin-Rüdin, 1969). This observation is taken as evidence in favor of a genetic factor in

TABLE 1
Concordance rates for manic-depressive
illness in twins

Study	Concordance rate (percent)	
	MZ	DZ
Rosanoff et al. (1934)	69.6	16.4
Kallmann (1954)	92.6	23.6
Da Fonseca (1959)	71.4	38.5
Harvald and Hauge (1965)	50.0	2.6
Kringlen (1967)	33.3	0.0

manic-depressive illness. Table 1 gives the concordance rate for affective disorder in MZ and DZ twins, according to various investigators who reported on 20 or more pairs (Da Fonseca, 1959; Harvald & Hauge, 1965; Kallmann, 1954; Kringlen, 1967; Rosanoff, Handy, & Rosanoff-Plesset, 1934). The concordance rates in MZ twins vary between 50 and 92.5 percent (mean 69.3 percent) as compared to 0–38.5 percent in DZ twins (mean 20 percent). These results strongly support the presence of a genetic factor in the etiology of manic-depressive illness.

Price (1968) reviewed the twin literature in order to locate pairs of identical twins who had been reared apart since early childhood and who were characterized by at least one of the twins being diagnosed as affectively ill. Price was able to find 12 such pairs of MZ twins. Among these pairs, eight were concordant for the disease, an observation suggesting that the predisposition to bipolar illness will usually express itself regardless of the early environment.

The complex interaction between hereditary and environmental factors underlying the etiology of bipolar illness cannot be elucidated by the twin method, or can it tell us the type of genetic mechanisms that may be involved in the transmission of manic-depressive illness.

Family Studies. Most of the early studies on manic-depressive illness have shown that this illness tends to be familial (Kallmann, 1954). The lifetime risk for the disease in relatives of bipolar probands is significantly higher than the risk in the general population. The risks published by Kallmann for parents of manic-depressive probands is 23.4 percent and for sibs 22.7 percent. With regard to morbidity risks in the more distant relatives (second-degree relatives), the rates usually range from 1 to 4 percent. It is thus clear that the risks for the illness are decreased as the degree of consanguinity is lowered, as expected, if there is a genetic component in the etiology of this disease. Most of the early family studies have been influenced by Kreapelin's classification as far as nosology is concerned. As a result of this, the aforementioned investigators have included among their probands patients suffering from mania and depression (bipolar) without distinguishing between these.

Thus, the samples investigated in the various studies are relatively heterogeneous. Leonhard (1959) in Berlin was one of the first investigators to make a clinical distinction between bipolar and unipolar forms of affective disorders on genetic grounds. The bipolar patients were shown to have a greater genetic loading for affective disorder than the unipolar patients. They also had more relatives with hypomanic temperaments as compared to the unipolar patients, whose relatives had depressive temperaments. It was concluded that bipolar and unipolar disorders may have different genetic etiologies. Two recent independent studies have investigated bipolar and unipolar probands separately (18–19). Both studies found that the morbidity risks for affective disorders were significantly higher in the relatives of bipolar as compared to unipolar patients. Bipolar and unipolar illnesses were present in the relatives of bipolar patients, whereas only unipolar illnesses were present in the relatives of unipolar patients. This genetic distinction between unipolar and bipolar illness has recently been confirmed by Winokur et al. (Winokur, Clayton, & Reich, 1969) in the United States. In this study, the lifetime risks for affective illness (i.e., bipolar and unipolar) in the first-degree relatives of bipolar patients were 34 percent for parents and 35 percent for sibs. These rates are similar to those we have found in studying the relatives of 134 bipolar probands in New York City (Mendlewicz & Rainer, 1974). Table 2 illustrates age-corrected risks found in various types of first-degree relatives of bipolar patients. This table indicates that the type of affective disorder found in the relatives of bipolar patients is not restricted to bipolar illness. The risk for unipolar illness is indeed quite significant in these relatives. The overall rates for affective illness are similar in sibs and parents; however, sibs are more likely to manifest bipolar illness than parents.

It can be seen that children of bipolar probands constitute a high-risk group. After reviewing all family studies, the risk for manic-depressive illness in the relatives of affected patients can be estimated at somewhere between 15 and 35 percent. There is, however, a large proportion of relatives of bipolar probands who exhibit unipolar illness only. When correction has been made for age, diagnoses, and statistical procedures, the morbidity risks for manic-depressive illness in different types of first-degree relatives (par-

TABLE 2
*Morbidity risks for affective illness in relatives of bipolar manic-depressive patients**

	All affective (percent)	Bipolar (percent)	Unipolar (percent)
Parents	33.7 ± 2.9	12.1 ± 2.0	22.0 ± 2.6
Sibs	39.2 ± 3.0	21.2 ± 2.5	18.6 ± 2.5
Children	59.9 ± 6.0	24.6 ± 5.0	41.3 ± 6.7

*N = 134.

Source: Adapted from J. Mendlewicz and J. D. Rainer, "Morbidity Risk and Genetic Transmission in Manic-Depressive Illness," *Nature* 268 (1977), pp. 327–329.

ents, sibs, children) are similar. This observation is consistent with a dominant mode of transmission in this disease.

Despite the high prevalence of unipolar depression in the general population, few genetic studies are available on subtypes of unipolar illness. We evaluated morbid risks for depression, alcoholism, and/or sociopathy in the relatives of early onset (before age 40) and late onset (after age 40) unipolar patients in a sample of 106 probands. Table 3 summarizes the results of this study (Mendlewicz & Baron, 1981).

Unipolar patients with an early onset disease had a greater familial morbidity for depression, alcoholism, and sociopathy than unipolar patients with a late onset disease. There was an excess of unipolar depression in female relatives of early onset unipolars when compared to late onset probands, regardless of the proband's sex (Table 3). Alcoholism and sociopathy were also more prevalent in the relatives of early onset unipolar versus late onset probands. Our morbidity risks show familial genetic differences between early and late onset forms of unipolar illness and partially confirm Winokur's concept of two subtypes of unipolar depression.

Linkage Studies

A number of studies have reported that the O blood group is most frequently found in manic-depressive patients (Barker, Theillie, & Spielberger, 1961;

TABLE 3

*Morbid risk for unipolar depression in parents and sibs of
unipolar probands, according to age of onset*

	Number ill	Number at risk	Morbid risk percent
Early Onset:			
Mothers	22	68	32.3 ± 5.6
Fathers	4	70	5.7 ± 1.8
Sisters	21	68	30.8 ± 6.1
Brothers	6	42	14.3 ± 5.5
Mothers and sisters	43	130	$33.0*\dagger \pm 5.2$
Fathers and brothers	10	112	8.9 ± 3.9
Late Onset:			
Mothers	10	60	16.6 ± 4.8
Fathers	4	59	6.7 ± 2.9
Sisters	10	40	25.0 ± 5.1
Brothers	8	63	12.7 ± 3.2
Mothers and sisters	20	106	18.8 ± 4.1
Fathers and brothers	12	122	9.8 ± 2.2

* $\chi^2 = 5.28$, $df = 1$, $P < 0.05$ versus morbid risk in mothers and sisters on late onset probands.

$\dagger \chi^2 = 22.5$, $df = 1$, $P < 0.001$ versus morbid risk in fathers and brothers of early onset probands.

Source: Adapted from J. Mendlewicz and M. Baron, "Morbidity Risks in Subtypes of Unipolar Depressive Illness: Differences between Early and Late Onset Forms," *British Journal of Psychiatry* 139 (1981), pp. 463–466.

Mendlewicz, Massart-Guiot, Wilmoth, & Fleiss, 1974). This potential association between a blood group factor and a major psychosis, although poorly understood, may indicate that the ABO genotype plays a role in the predisposition to manic-depressive illness. Association between traits is not to be confused with linkage; that is, the proximity of two traits on the same chromosome resulting in their dependent assortment during the process of meiosis. In this study, one tries to test a potential linkage relationship between a known genetic marker and a character known to be genetically determined, but which has not yet been mapped on the chromosomes. This method has been used successfully in the genetic study of several hereditary conditions, and has recently been used to test the hypothesis of genetic linkage in manic-depressive illness. Linkage to HLA combination has recently been suggested (Wirtkamp, Stancer, Persad, Flood, & Guttorsmen, 1981) for bipolar illness, but not confirmed in another study (Targum, Gershon, Van Eerdewegh, & Rogenline, 1979). Reich et al. (Reich, Clayton, & Winokur, 1969) studied two large families assorting for color blindness (an X-linked recessive marker) and bipolar illness. Mendlewicz, Fleiss, & Fieve (1972) reported on seven such families. In both studies the marker and the illness failed to show independent assortment. Winokur and Tanna (1969) described three more families assorting in a dependent fashion for manic-depressive illness and the Xg blood group (a dominant X-linked marker). We have confirmed these results in 11 other families assorting for the Xg blood group and the illness (Mendlewicz, Fleiss, & Fieve, 1975). In a more recent study, Mendlewicz and Fleiss (1974) were able to demonstrate close linkage between bipolar illness and both deutan and protan[1] color blindness in 17 informative pedigrees.

Linkage between bipolar illness and the Xg blood group, although measurable, was found to be less close in 23 informative families. Recent linkage data from our laboratory confirm a linkage relationship between color blindness and bipolar manic-depressive illness (Mendlewicz, Linkowski, Guroff, & Van Praag, 1979) and are at variance with the report of Gershon et al. (Gershon, Targum, Matthysse, & Bunney, 1979) who did not find such a linkage. A more comprehensive study undertaken as a project of the Biological Psychiatry Collaborative Program of the World Health Organization was conducted in four collaborative centers (Bethesda, Basel, Brussels, and Copenhagen) on 16 informative families, the overall results being consistent with the presence of linkage between bipolar illness and color blindness. Some families showed an X-linked pattern of inheritance while others did not, this last observation suggests the hypothesis of genetic heterogeneity in manic-depressive illness (Gershon, Mendlewicz, Gastpar, Bech, Goldin, Kielholz, Rafaelson, Vartanian, & Bunney, 1980). Figure 1 illustrates the distribution of deuteranopia and bipolar-unipolar disorders in successive generations of a family informative for the analysis of linkage between color blind-

---

[1] Deutan color blindness is a deficiency of green perception; protan is a deficiency of red perception. The chromosomal loci of these two conditions are closely linked but not identical.

FIGURE 1
*Pedigree informative for linkage analysis between
deuteranopia (D⁺) and affective illness*

CASE II

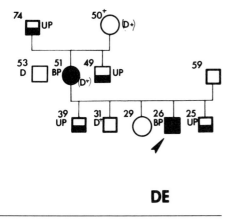

DE

ness and affective illness. The proband (age 26) has bipolar manic-depressive illness and normal color vision. His mother (age 51) carries the traits for bipolar manic-depressive illness and deuteranopia in repulsion (on separate X-chromosomes), according to the phenotypes of her brothers, who are either healthy and color blind (age 53 years) or have unipolar manic-depressive illness and are not color blind (49 years). The mother (51 years) could be homozygous for affective illness if she inherited a second allele for the illness from the grandmother (age 50 or more), as suggested by the phenotype of the uncle (age 49). This possibility however, is taken into acount in the LIPED program analysis, using likelihood estimates of the recombination fraction. The proband's older brother (aged 39 years) has unipolar manic-depressive illness and normal color vision. The next brother (age 31) is healthy and color blind, whereas the proband's younger brother (age 25) has unipolar manic-depressive illness and normal color vision. The traits being in repulsion, those subjects who have affective disorders have the allele for normal color vision, whereas unaffected male subjects have the allele for deuteranopia. This pedigree is thus compatible with X linkage because the presence of color blindness excludes the presence of affective illness. These linkage results, originating from different laboratories, suggest that an X-linked dominant factor is involved in the transmission of the manic-depressive phenotype in at least some families. The findings of close linkage between bipolar illness and the color vision loci, and of less close linkage between the illness and the Xg blood group have to be interpreted in the light of the fact that the loci for the Xg blood group and color blindness seem to be far apart. Thus, the locus for bipolar illness appears to be between the Xg locus and the color-blindness loci, probably closer to the latter. However, we were unable to measure linkage between unipolar depressive illness and either protanopia or the Xg blood group, in 14 *informative* families (Mendlewicz & Fleiss, 1974), an observation ruling out X-linked inheritance as the mode of transmission of unipolar illness. These negative results for unipolar illness are important in the light of the positive findings concerning X linkage in bipolar families, because all families studied by us were obtained from the same sample during the same period. The linkage studies conducted so far on manic-depressive illness are of great value since they are able to discriminate between sex-linked and sex-influenced types of inheritance and they do provide an estimate of the significance of the results. They all point to the presence of an X-linked dominant factor in the transmission of manic-depressive illness. This methodological approach is of great potential and should be extended to the study of other psychiatric conditions such as schizophrenia, using other genetic markers located on different chromosomes.

Adoption Studies

Few adoption studies are available for the affective disorders. In the study of Cadoret (1978), adopted away offspring of affectively ill biological parents presented significantly more depressive disorders (mainly unipolar illness) in adulthood as adoptees whose biological parents were well or had other psychiatric conditions. In our adoption study (Mendlewicz & Rainer, 1977) we investigated parents (biological and adoptive) of bipolar manic-depressive adoptees raised in adoptive families and parents of two control groups.

Comparison of adoptive parents of persons with a psychiatric disorder to the adoptees' biological parents provides a unique opportunity to separate the interacting etiological roles of heredity and environment.

The major finding of this investigation is that psychopathology in the biological parents is in excess of that found in the adoptive parents of the same manic-depressive offspring (Table 4). If we focus on disorders which we may call the *affective spectrum*, namely, bipolar affective disease (episodes of mania and depression), unipolar affective disease (psychotic depressions without mania), schizoaffective psychosis (schizophrenia and affective episodes), and cyclothymic personality), the difference is significant at the level of $P < 0.025$ ($\chi^2 = 5.10$). Previous genetic studies by us and others support the inclusion of unipolar and schizoaffective disorders as genetically related to bipolar illness when they are found in close relatives of bipolar patients (Mendlewicz & Rainer, 1974; Winokur et al., 1969). If we include other forms of psychopathology, the difference is highly significant ($\chi^2 = 7.29$, $P < 0.01$). The frequency of nonaffective psychopathology was no higher, in the biologi-

TABLE 4
Diagnosis of parents for bipolar adoptees and nonadoptees

| | Bipolar adoptees (N = 29) | | | | | | Bipolar nonadoptees (N = 31) | | |
| | Adoptive parents | | | Biological parents | | | Biological parents | | |
	Male	Female		Male	Female		Male	Female	
Bipolar	1	0	(1)*	3	1	(4)	2	0	(2)
Unipolar	3	3	(6)	1	11	(12)	3	8	(11)
Schizoaffective	0	0	(0)	0	2	(2)	1	0	(1)
Cyclothymic	0	0	(0)	0	0	(0)	1	1	(2)
Affective Spectrum:	4	3	(7)†	4	14	(18)†	7	9	(16)
Percentage	14	10	(12)	14	48	(31)	23	29	(26)
Schizophrenia	0	0	(0)	0	0	(0)	0	1	(1)
Alcoholism	2	0	(2)	2	1	(3)	1	1	(2)
Sociopathy	0	0	(0)	1	1	(2)	0	1	(1)
Other	0	0	(0)	0	0	(0)	0	0	(0)
All Psychopathology:	6	3	(9)‡	7	16	(23)‡	8	12	(20)
Percentage	21	10	(16)	24	55	(40)	26	39	(32)

* Figures in parentheses are totals.
† $\chi^2 = 5.10$, $P < 0.025$.
‡ $\chi^2 = 7.29$, $P < 0.01$.
Source: J. Mendlewicz and J. D. Rainer, "Adoption Study Supporting Genetic Transmission in Manic-Depressive Illness," *Nature* 268 (1977), pp. 327–329.

cal parents of bipolar adoptees (9 percent) (see Table 4) than in those of normal adoptees (16 percent) (see Table 5), indicating that it is by virtue of the affective disorders that the former differ from the latter (31 percent compared with 2 percent).

The degree of psychopathology in the biological parents of manic-depressive adoptees is similar to that of the parents of the nonadopted manic-depressives, and the rate of psychiatric disorder in the adoptive parents of the experimental group is similar to that of the adoptive parents of the normal offspring group. The degree of total psychopathology in the biological parents (of normal offspring) who gave their children for adoption is slightly greater than in adoptive parents who brought up those same individuals (Table 5). It is worth noting that this difference is due to an excess of alcoholism and sociopathy in the former group. Finally, the degree of psychopathology in the parents of polio patients is in the same range as in both groups of adoptive parents (Table 5). All these findings support our conclusion that our experimental sets of parents are truly representative of the degree of psychiatric disorder which is present respectively in those parents who bring up and those who contribute genetically to manic-depressive individuals.

In the follow-up process of this study, it was also possible to investigate a certain number of "biological" and "adoptive sibs" of the bipolar manic-depressive adoptees. Twelve "adoptive" sibs not biologically related to the

TABLE 5
Diagnosis of parents for normal adoptees and nonadoptees

| | Normal adoptees (N = 24) | | | | | | Poliomyelitis (N = 20) | | |
| | Adoptive parents | | | Biological parents | | | Biological parents | | |
	Male	Female		Male	Female		Male	Female	
Bipolar	0	0	(0)	0	0	(0)	0	0	(0)
Unipolar	1	2	(3)	1	0	(1)	3	1	(4)
Schizoaffective	0	0	(0)	0	0	(0)	0	0	(0)
Cyclothymic	1	0	(1)	0	0	(0)	0	0	(0)
Affective Spectrum:	2	2	(4)	1	0	(1)	3	1	(4)
Percentage	10	10	(10)	5	0	(2)	15	5	(10)
Schizophrenia	0	1	(1)	0	0	(0)	0	0	(0)
Alcoholism	0	0	(0)	1	2	(3)	1	0	(1)
Sociopathy	0	0	(0)	2	1	(3)	0	0	(0)
Other	0	0	(0)	0	1	(1)	0	0	(0)
All Psychopathology:	2	3	(5)	4	4	(8)	4	1	(5)
Percentage	9	14	(11)	18	18	(18)	20	5	(12)

Source: Adapted from J. Mendlewicz and J. D. Rainer, "Adoption Study Supporting Genetic Transmission in Manic-Depressive Illness," *Nature* 268 (1977), pp. 327–329.

adoptees (4 females, ages 28 to 34, and 8 males, ages 29 to 33) all biological children of the adoptive parents were compared to 9 biological sibs of the adoptees (4 females, ages 27 to 36, and 5 males, ages 31 to 37) all of them biological children of the biological parents of the bipolar adoptees. Out of these nine biological sibs, seven had not been separated from their biological family while two had been given away for adoption in other adoption families. The results of the psychopathological examination in sibs of bipolar adoptees are given in Table 6. There are three bipolar, two unipolar and one cyclothymic patients in the biological sibs as compared to no bipolar and one unipolar case in the "adoptive" sibs. The overall rate of psychopathology is 66

TABLE 6
Diagnosis in sibs of bipolar adoptees (N = 29)

| | Sibs | |
	Adoptive N = 12	Biological N = 9
Bipolar	0	3
Unipolar	1	2
Schizoaffective	0	0
Cyclothymic	0	1
Affective Spectrum	1 (8%)	6 (66%)
Schizophrenia	0	0
Alcoholism	0	0
Sociopathy	0	0
All psychopathology	1 (8%)	6 (66%)

percent in biological sibs for 8 percent in the adoptive sibs, the difference being exclusively made up by patients' belonging to the affective spectrum. These data in sibs also emphasize the importance of the genetic factor in the transmission of manic-depression.

Another finding of interest is that no father-to-son transmission of bipolar illness was seen in our entire sample. This is consistent with a sex-linked model of bipolar illness. Finally, bipolar illness, as would be expected, had an early onset in all parents in whom it was present; however, the onset of unipolar illness in the adopting parents occurred, in every case, after the onset of manic-depressive illness in their children, whereas in the biological parents, onset of unipolar disease occurred almost always previous to the onset in their children. This observation strengthens the genetic hypothesis by suggesting that the adoptive parents' unipolar illness might be more reactive and less severe than that of their biological counterparts; early onset is often considered to be an index of severity in psychiatric disorder.

Mode of Inheritance

There is no final consensus on the types of genetic mechanisms that operate in affective illness. Too little is known about the genetics of unipolar and schizoaffective illness to even propose specific genetic models for these syndromes in this chapter. It is even difficult, if not impossible, to draw definite conclusions on the mode of inheritance of bipolar manic-depressive illness. First, as we have said before, bias in selecting study populations must be carefully avoided, and second, clinical or genetic heterogeneity may foil the attempt to draw an unequivocal conclusion. There are, however, certain genetic models that can be ruled out from the genetic data published so far. Autosomal (nonsexual chromosome) recessive inheritance is one of these, since it cannot account for the appreciable number of families showing a two- and three-generation transmission of the illness. There is no increase in morbid risks in sibs and consanguinity, (i.e., unions between cousins), which would be expected under recessive inheritance. Sex-linked recessive inheritance is also very unlikely because there are no studies so far reporting an excess of affected males over affected females always present in sex-linked recessive transmission. In fact, the opposite has generally been observed.

There are some arguments in favor of a major dominant type of inheritance: (*a*) the illness has often been observed to be present in successive generations; (*b*) the morbidity risks in parents, sibs, and children are similar and some studies have shown the risks in sibs of probands with no affected parents to be equal to the risks in sibs with one affected parent (Mendlewicz & Fleiss, 1974; Winokur et al. 1969). and (*c*) when we tested our own data for consistency with a single-gene threshold model using a modification of a program developed by Kidd and Cavali-Sforza, the observed values for sibs and parents were compatible with various forms of single-gene inheritance, with dominant inheritance most likely (Mendlewicz & Rainer, 1974). Single-factor inheritance is consistent with these data. Some investigators have postulated a major autosomal dominant gene with reduced penetrance (expressivity) for bipolar disorder (Kallmann, 1954; Stenstedt, 1952; Strömgren, 1938). This autosomal hypothesis has the value of simplicity and fits most of the data except for the sex ratio differences found in patients and relatives; that is, a preponderance of affected females. Polygenic inheritance in bipolar manic-depressive illness has also been suggested by other investigators who used a computational model to test ancestral secondary cases for polygenic versus monogenic inheritance (Perris, 1972; Slater, Maxwell, & Price, 1972). However, another study using the same method has shown that one subgroup of the illness conformed to a monogenic model while a second subgroup behaved as a polygenic entity (Mendlewicz, Fieve, Rainer, & Fleiss, 1972). Finally, the linkage studies described in the preceding section contribute strong evidence which points to an X-linked dominant gene involved in the transmission of some manic-depressive illness. A more recent family study arrives at the same conclusion for early onset forms of bipolar illness (Taylor & Abrams, 1974). It is argued, however, that there are families where male-to-male transmission of the disease is apparent, an observation incompatible with X-linkage (Goetzl, Green, Whybrow, & Jackson, 1974; Perris, 1968). This is also the case in our own material (Mendlewicz & Rainer, 1974), where these families represent about 10 percent of our overall sample. Furthermore, the preponderance of affected females as compared to males in first-degree relatives (Angst, 1966; Mendlewicz & Rainer, 1974; Taylor & Abrams, 1974; Winokur et al., 1969) of bipolar patients is far from a universal finding (Brown, Elston, Pollitzer, Prange, & Wilson, 1973; Goetzl et al., 1974; Perris, 1968).

An interesting approach to the problem has recently been proposed by Crowe and Smouse (1974). These authors, working on Winokur's data, have derived an age-dependent penetrance function for manic-depressive illness. Their analysis revealed that a sex-linked dominant model was far more likely to explain the data than an autosomal dominant one. Although we are suggesting that the X-linked dominant model is the preponderant mode of transmission of manic-depressive illness, it seems quite clear that more than one genetic entity is involved in this disease.

Affective Disorders, Schizophrenia and Schizoaffective Illness: Genetic Considerations

There are few investigators who believe that schizophrenia and affective illness are genetically related. Most genetic studies have concluded that these two major psychoses are genetically different. The morbidity risks for schizophrenia in first-degree relatives (except for children) of manic-depressive probands are the same as in the general population (Angst, 1966; Perris, 1968; Winokur et al., 1969; Zerbin-Rüdin, 1967). There is, however, one exception to this rule: involutional melancholia. Kallman (1954) has reported the risks for schizophrenia to be three to four times higher in the relatives of involutional patients than in the general population. This finding is rather surprising since involutional disease is of late onset and schizophrenia usually starts early in life. He also reported the risk for schizophrenia in children of bipolar manic-depressive parents to be slightly elevated (~3 percent). On the other hand, the risk for manic-depressive illness in the relatives of schizophrenia probands has generally been reported to be low (Kallman, 1954). Another argument in favor of a genetic distinction between schizophrenia and affective illness is the absence of any reported instances of MZ twins where on twin is schizophrenic and the other affectively ill. In Slater's twin study (Slater, 1953), there is no single case of schizophrenia among the parents, sibs, or cotwins of DZ twins diagnosed as affective disorder. There seems to be little evidence, if any, favoring a genetic overlap between schizophrenia and affective illness. This does not mean that there is no overlap regarding the clinical manifestations of these illnesses. It is actually well documented that manic patients experience schizophrenialike symptoms (i.e., hallucinations, paranoid ideas, and so on) and other atypical symptoms. These patients are often misdiagnosed as schizophrenic, even although they present a recurrent type of disorder with full remissions between the episodes (Mendlewicz, Fieve, Rainer, & Fleiss, 1972; Weiner & Strömgren, 1958). We also know of schizophrenic patients suffering from a chronic condition who may experience mania or depression. At the present time, those disorders with mixed clinical symptomatology are often labeled "schizoaffective"; they seem to have a complex and unclear relationship to either schizophrenia or affective illness. Schizoaffective illness was previously classified according to the American Psychiatric Association nomenclature as a subgroup of schizophrenia, but we have to point out that so far there are no data to support this hypothesis. A natural inbreeding experiment can be found in the few studies describing matings between a schizophrenic and a manic-depressive parent (Elsasser, 1952; Schulz, 1940; Smith, 1925).

These studies have shown equal risks for schizophrenia and manic-depressive illness in the children. No children were diagnosed as schizoaffective, an observation indicating that the schizoaffective phenotype does not result from a combination of schizophrenic and manic genes. Some investigators have suggested that schizoaffective illness is genetically related to affective illness (Abrams, Taylor, & Gaztanaga, 1974; Clayton, Rodin, & Winokur, 1968; Weiner & Strömgren, 1958).

Clayton et al. conducted family studies on 39 schizoaffective patients (Clayton et al., 1968). They found a high prevalence of affective disorder in these families, while schizophrenia and schizoaffective psychosis was found to be rare in the relatives of their probands. On the basis of these results, they concluded that schizoaffective psychosis was just a variant of affective disorder. Asano in Japan, studying atypical cases of manic-depressive illness with schizophrenia-like symptoms, also found affective illness to be present in the relatives of the patients (Asano, 1967). The risks for affective illness in the relatives of atypical cases were, however, lower than in the relatives of typical manic-depressive patients.

In a large twin study on 15,909 twin pairs from VA hospitals, Cohen et al. (Cohen, Allen, Pollin, & Hrubec, 1972) reviewed the charts of 420 twin pairs where one or both twins had a psychotic diagnosis. The MZ pairwise concordance rate for schizoaffective illness was significantly higher than the one found for schizophrenia, and was much closer to the one found for manic-depressive illness. The similarity found in genotypic phenotypic variance between manic-depressive and schizoaffective twins led these authors to conclude that there exists common genetic determinants for these two illnesses. It is conceivable that the pathogenesis for schizoaffective psychosis may include some genetic factor similar to that of manic-depressive psychosis, but its full expression may require the presence of personality and environmental factors in the origin of schizophrenia. The possibility can also be considered that schizoaffective disorder represents an autonomous entity distinct from schizophrenia or affective illness or that a subject presenting schizoaffective symptoms has in fact two separate disorders. The latter hypothesis would explain why it is common to find in these families a mixed set of manic-depressive and schizophrenic relatives. We may admit the fact that being a schizophrenic does not necessarily confer immunity against becoming manic-depressive, although this "association" may be difficult to understand from a psychodynamic point of view. Furthermore even conservatively estimating the prevalence of schizophrenia and manic-depressive illness in the general population (~1 percent), the probability of one individual to carry both diseases would be about 1 out of 10,000, a rather rare event.

We have reasons to believe that schizophrenia and manic-depressive illness represent two distinct genetic illnesses. The syndrome defined as schizoaffective illness still remains a puzzling problem, with regard to both clinical and genetic aspects; it deserves further investigation of its long-term clinical course and heredity.

PRACTICAL APPLICATIONS OF GENETIC RESEARCH IN DEPRESSION

Genetic Criteria of Lithium Response

Progress in the knowledge of the basic mechanisms underlying lithium ion metabolism may provide some further clue to the understanding of the psychopathology and treatment of affective illnesses. Genetic factors determine transport of lithium into the erythrocyte, and the genetic approach is thus highly relevant in research studies attempting to investigate the mode of action of lithium salts in affective illness. Topics which need to be addressed by future long-term lithium studies include its efficacy for mood stabilization, depression, and mania prophylaxis. Several studies have proposed biological predictors of long-term lithium response. Bipolar patients with a positive family history of bipolar illness seem to have a better long-term lithium response than patients without such a family history (Mendlewicz, Fieve, & Stallone, 1973; Stallone, Shelley, & Mendlewicz, 1973). These results have now been confirmed by several groups (Ananth, Engelsmann, Kiriakos, & Kolivakis, 1979; Cazullo & Smeraldi, in press; Kupfer, Dickar, Himmelhoch, & Detre, 1975; Mendlewicz, Verbanck, Linkowski, & Wilmotte, 1978; Prien, Caffey, & Klett, 1974, Taylor & Abrams, 1975; Zvolsky, Vinarova, & Dostal, 1974). However, one study (Mistra & Berns, 1977) reported nonresponders to lithium prophylaxis to have more relatives with affective illness than lithium responders. This association was not observed, however, for the presence of unipolar illness in relatives of bipolar patients (Mendlewicz, Fieve, & Stallone, 1973; Stallone et al., 1973).

These results indicate that there may be several distinct genetic subgroups of bipolar illness showing different treatment responses to lithium. This genetic heterogeneity of long-term lithium response in bipolar illness is further evidenced by twin studies. A higher concordance rate for affective illness has been found in both monozygotic and dizygotic twin pairs when the proband had experienced good, long-term response to lithium (Mendlewicz, 1979; Perris, Strandman, & Wahlby, 1978). In those twin pairs where the proband was considered as a lithium nonresponder, the concordance rate for affective illness was much lower. These family and twin studies indicate that genetics factors are useful biological predictors of long-term lithium prophylaxis.

The histocompatibility antigen (HLA) system, a complex antigenic system used in immunogenetics (kidney transplants), has also been studied in an attempt to find immunogenetic markers of lithium prophylaxis (Mendels & Frazer, 1973). This is certainly an interesting observation relevant to the mempatients who were long-term lithium failures, while long-term lithium responders showed a reduction in the HLA-B18 antigen (Mendels & Frazer, 1973). This is certainly an interesting observation relevant to the membrane hypothesis of affective illness, since some of the antigens in the HLA system may be implicated in membrane transport mechanism. Nevertheless, this HLA study needs further replication. The membrane hypothesis of affective illness has recently stimulated considerable research into the physiological mechanism of lithium transport across the red blood cell (RBC). Claims were made that the lithium RBC/plasma ratio may serve as a pharmacokinetic indicator of short- and long-term lithium response in the affective illnesses (Frazer, Mendels, & Brunswick, 1978; Greil, Becker, & Duhm, 1979; Mendels, Frazer, & Baron, 1976). Although these claims have been disproved (Dorus, Pandey, Shaughnessy, Gaviria, Val, Ericksen, & Davis, 1979) and it is by now clear that the lithium RBC/plasma ratio is of little value in predicting lithium response in affectively ill patients, very important knowledge has been gained in the physiology of the transport of the lithium ion across the red blood cell membrane (Schless, Frazer, & Mendels, 1975). It is also clear now that genetic factors do play an important role in membrane lithium transport (Dorus et al., 1979; Dorus, Pandey, & Davis, 1975; Mendlewicz, 1979; Perris et al., 1978). The lithium RBC/plasma ratios have also been shown to have a heterogeneous distribution (two separate subgroups) in patients who are nonresponders to lithium prophylaxis. Patients responding well to lithium prophylaxis clearly showed a homogeneous pattern of lithium RBC/plasma ratio distribution (Mendlewicz, 1979; Perris et al., 1978). More recently, Dorus et al. have reported higher in vitro lithium RBC/plasma ratios in some relatives of bipolar patients, suggesting that higher lithium RBC/plasma ratios may be biological indicators of a membrane vulnerability to bipolar illness (Bert, Saier, Dufour, Scotto, Julien, & Sutter, 1977). Similar results have been found by us (higher lithium RBC/plasma ratios) in monozygotic and dizygotic twins concordant for affective illness when compared to discordant twins. We have compared lithium ratios between probands of concordant and discordant monozygotic twin pairs because concordant pairs are likely to be more genetically determined for manic-depressive illness than discordant pairs. Lithium rations were found to be significantly greater in concordant twins as compared to discordant twins. Our twin data confirmed Dorus et al.'s observation of hyper lithium accumulation in red blood cells of bipolar patients with a family history of affective illness. These results suggest the presence of a membrane anomaly in subjects with genetic vulnerability for affective illness. This observation may be of importance for genetic counseling in affective illness. Prospective studies will be needed for accurately predicting the risk of bipolar disorder in children of affectively ill patients.

Genetic Counseling

The genetic investigations reviewed above (family, twin, and adoption) can provide the research investigator with sophistication in diagnostic evaluation. This sophistication is essential for the clinician and indispensable for the genetic counselor. J. A. F. Roberts (1963) has stated his opinion that "genetic advice on mental disease must be left to psychiatrists. Some of those interviewed and the histories they give need psychiatric appraisal. What is even more important is the difficulty to anyone not a psychiatrist of interpreting and assessing psychiatric reports." Indeed, the psychiatrist does possess an advantage in interpreting genetic data to prospective parents. However, other mental health professionals when properly trained may also be able to perform the same task as well. A second contribution of psychiatry to genetic counseling concerns ways of presenting material and discussing it with persons who need help. Armed with clinical experience and the added knowledge derived from genetic studies of families, twins, adopted children, and high-risk children from early childhood on, the psychiatrist/counselor can provide responsible and sound advice to prospective parents regarding marriage choice, family planning, child rearing, adoption, and foster care. Empirically, risk for a major affective disorder runs from about 70 percent in the children of two bipolar parents down to about 15 percent in children of one bipolar parent. The theoretical risks of 25 percent for major affective illness for two affected parents under a recessive theory or 50 percent under a dominant gene theory have not been observed. Since most persons do not consider risks below 10 percent to be significant, the clearest indication for a warning of caution is in the case of dual mating. With one parent affected, the empirical risk for the offspring is low, but not negligible. It is necessary to help the family consider first, the effect of having a child on the course of illness in the disabled parent, and second, the effect of a possibly disrupted home on the development of the child regardless of genetic considerations.

References

Abrams, R., Taylor, M., & Gaztanaga, P. (1974). Manic-depressive illness and paranoid schizophrenia. A phenomenologic family history, and treatment response study. *Archives of General Psychiatry, 31,* 640–642.

Ananth, J., Engelsmann, F., Kiriakos, R., & Kolivakis, T. (1979). Prediction of lithium response. *Acta Psychiatrica Scandinavica, 60,* 279–286.

Angst, J. (1966). Zur Atiologie und Nosologie endogener depressiver Psychosen. *Monographien aus dem Gesamtgebrete der Neurologie und Psychiatrie.* Berlin: Springer-Verlag, No. 112.

Asano, N. (1967). Clinico-genetic study of manic-depressive psychoses. In. H. Mitsuda (Ed.), *Clinical genetics in psychiatry.* Kyoto, Japan: Bunko-Sha Co.

Barker, J. B., Theillie, A., & Spielberger, C. D. (1961). Frequency of blood types in an homogeneous group of manic-depressive patients. *Journal of Mental Science, 107,* 936–942.

Bert, J., Saier, J., Dufour, H., Scotto, J. C., Julien, R., & Sutter, J. M. (1977). Modification du sommeil provoqué par le lithium en administration aegüe et en administration chronique. *Electroencephalography and Clinical Neurophysiology, 43,* 745–748.

Böök, J. A. (1953). A genetic and neuropsychiatric investigation of a North-Swedish population. *Acta Geneticae Medicae et Genellologiae, 4,* 1–100.

Brown, R. J., Elston, R. C., Pollitzer, W. S., Prange, A., & Wilson, E. (1973). Sex ratio in relatives of patients with affective disorder. *Biological Psychiatry, 6,* 307–309.

Cadoret, R. J. (1978). Evidence for genetic inheritance of primary affective disorder in adoptees. *American Journal of Psychiatry, 134,* 463–466.

Carrol, B. J. (1979). Prediction of treatment outcome with lithium. *Archives of General Psychiatry, 10,* 133–146.

Cazullo, C. L., & Smeraldi, E. (in press). HLA system in psychiatry and psychopharmacology. *Progress in Neuropsychopharmacology.*

Clayton, P. J., Rodin, L., & Winokur, G. (1968). Family history studies. Schizoaffective disorder; Clinical and genetic factors, including a one- to two-year follow-up. *Comprehensive Psychiatry, 9,* 31–49.

Cohen, S. M., Allen, M. G., Pollin, W., & Hrubec, H. (1972). Relationship between schizoaffective psychosis to manic-depressive psychosis and schizophrenia. Findings in 15,909 veteran pairs. *Archives of General Psychiatry, 26,* 539–546.

Cooper, J. E., Kendall, R. E., Gurland, B. J., Sharp, L., Copeland, J. R. M., & Simon, R. (1972). *Psychiatric diagnosis in New York and London.* New York: Oxford University Press.

Crowe, R. R., & Smouse, P. E. (1974). Age-dependent penetrance in manic-depressive illness, and its implications for genetic analysis. Personal communication.

Da Fonseca, A. F. (1959). *Analise heredo-clinica das perturbacoes affectivas.* Dissertation, University of Porto, 1959.

Dorus, E., Pandey, G. N., & Davis, J. M. (1975). Genetic determinants of lithium ion distribution: An in-vitro and in-vivo monozygotic and dizygotic twin study. *Archives of General Psychiatry, 32,* 1097–1100.

Dorus, E., Pandey, G. N., Shaughnessy, R., Gaviria, M., Val, E., Ericksen, S., & Davis, J. M. (1979). Lithium transport across red cell membrane: A cell membrane abnormality in manic-depressive illness. *Science, 205,* 932–934.

Elsasser, G. (1952). Die Nachkommen geisteskranker Elternpaare. Stuttgart: Thieme.

Frazer, A., Mendels, J., & Brunswick, D. (1978). Erythrocyte concentrations of lithium ion: Clinical correlates and mechanisms of action. *American Journal of Psychiatry, 135,* 1005–1019.

Gershon, E. S., Mendlewicz, J., Gastpar, M., Bech, P., Goldin, L. R., Kielholz, P., Rafaelsen, O. J., Vartanian, F., & Bunney, W. E., Jr. (1980). A collaborative study of genetic linkage of bipolar manic-depressive illness and red/green color blindness. *Acta Psychiatrica Scandinavica, 61,* 319–338.

Gershon, E. S., Targum, S. D., Matthysse, S., & Bunney, W. E., Jr. (1979). Color blindness not closely linked to bipolar illness. *Archives of General Psychiatry, 36,* 1423–1431.

Goetzl, V., Green, R., Whybrow, P., & Jackson, R. (1974). X linkage revisited. A further family study of manic-depressive illness. *Archives of General Psychiatry, 31,* 665–672.

Greil, W., Becker, B. F., & Duhm, J. (1979). On the relevance of the red blood cell/plasma lithium ratio. In T. B. Cooper, S. Gershon, & S. Kline (Eds.), *Lithium controversies and unresolved issues.* Amsterdam, Netherlands: Excerpta Medica.

Harvald, B., & Hauge, M. (1965). Hereditary factors elucidated by twin studies. In J. V. Neel, M. W. Shaw, & W. J. Schull (Eds.), *Genetics and the epidemiology of chronic diseases.* Washington, DC: U.S. Department of Health, Education, and Welfare.

Helgasson, T. (1964). Epidemiology of mental disorders in Ireland. *Acta Psychiatrica Scandinavica, 173* (Suppl.) 1–258.

Kallmann, F. J. (1954). Genetic principles in manic-depressive psychoses. In P. Hoch and J. Zubin (Eds.), *Depression.* New York: Grune & Stratton.

Kringlen, E. (1967). Heredity and environment in the functional psychoses. An epidemiological-clinical twin study. Oslo, Norway: Universitstoforlaget.

Kupfer, D. J., Dickar, D., Himmelhoch, J. M., & Detre, T. P. (1975). Are there two types of unipolar depression? *Archives of General Psychiatry, 32,* 866–871.

Leonhard, K. (1959). Aufteilung der endogenen Psychosen. Berlin: Akademie-Verlag.

Mendels, J., & Frazer, A. (1973). Intracellular lithium concentration and clinical response: Towards a membrane theory of depression. *Journal of Psychiatric Research, 10,* 9–18

Mendels, J., Frazer, A., & Baron, J. (1976). Intra-erythrocyte lithium ion concentration and long-term maintenance treatment. *Lancet, 1,* 966.

Mendlewicz, J. (1979). Prediction of treatment outcome: Family and twin studies in lithium prophylaxis and the question of lithium red blood cell/plasma ratios. In T. B. Cooper, S. Gershon, & N. S. Kline (Eds.), *Lithium: Controversies and unresolved issues.* Amsterdam, Netherlands: Excerpta Medica.

Mendlewicz, J., & Baron, M. (1981). Morbidity risks in subtypes of unipolar depressive illness: Differences between early and late onset forms. *British Journal of Psychiatry, 139,* 463–466.

Mendlewicz, J., Fieve, R. R., Rainer, J. D., & Fleiss, J. L. (1972). Manic-depressive illness: A comparative study of patients with and without a family history. *British Journal of Psychiatry, 120,* 523–530.

Mendlewicz, J., Fieve, R. R., & Stallone, F. (1973). Relationship between the effectiveness of lithium therapy and family history. *American Journal of Psychiatry, 130,* 1011–1013.

Mendlewicz, J., & Fleiss, J. L. (1974). Linkage studies with X-chromosome markers in bipolar (manic-depressive) and unipolar (depressive) illnesses. *Biological Psychiatry, 9,* 261–294.

Mendlewicz, J., Fleiss, J. L., & Fieve, R. R. (1972). Evidence for X-linkage in the transmission of manic-depressive illness. *Journal of the American Medical Association, 222,* 1627.

Mendlewicz, J., Fleiss, J. L., & Fieve, R. R. (1975). Linkage studies in affective disorders: The Xg blood group in manic-depressive illness. In R. R. Fieve, D. Rosenthal, & H. Brill (Eds.), *Genetics and psychopathology.* Baltimore: Johns Hopkins Press.

Mendlewicz, J., Linkowski, P., Guroff, J. J., & Van Praag, H. M. (1979). Color blindness linkage to bipolar manic-depressive illness. New evidence. *Archives of General Psychiatry, 36,* 1442–1447.

Mendlewicz, J., Massart-Guiot, T., Wilmotte, J., & Fleiss, J. L. (1974). Blood groups in manic-depressive illness and schizophrenia. *Diseases of the Nervous System, 35,* 39–41.

Mendlewicz, J., & Rainer, J. D. (1974). Morbidity risk and genetic transmission in manic-depressive illness. *American Journal of Human Genetics, 26,* 692–701.

Mendlewicz, J., & Rainer, J. D. (1977). Adoption study supporting genetic transmission in manic-depressive illness. *Nature, 268,* 327–329.

Mendlewicz, J., Verbanck, P., Linkowski, P., & Wilmotte, J. (1978). Lithium accumulation in erythrocytes of manic-depressive patients: An in-vivo twin study. *British Journal of Psychiatry, 133,* 433–444.

Ministry of Health. (1969). Statistical report series, No. 4. *Psychiatric hospitals and units in England and Wales, in-patient statistics from the mental health enquiry for the years 1964, 1965, and 1966.* London: Her Majesty's Stationery Office, 1969.

Mistra, P. C., & Burns, B. H. (1977). Lithium nonresponders in a lithium clinic. *Acta Psychiatrica Scandinavica, 55,* 32–40.

Perris, C. (1968). Genetic transmission of depressive psychoses. *Acta Psychiatrica Scandinavica, 203* (Suppl.) 45–52.

Perris, C. (1972). Abnormality on paternal and maternal sides: Observations in bipolar manic-depressive and unipolar depressive psychosis. *British Journal of Psychiatry, 118,* 207–210.

Perris, C., Strandman, E., & Wahlby, L. (1978). (abstract) *HLA antigens and the response to prophylactic lithium.* 11th C.I.N.P. Congress, Vienna, 1978, *10,* 9–24.

Price, J. (1968). The genetics of depressive behavior. In A. Coppen & A. Walk (Eds.), *Recent developments in affective disorders. British Journal of Psychiatry,* Special Publication No. 2.

Prien, R. F., Caffey, E. H., & Klett, C. J. (1974). Factors associated with treatment success in lithium carbonate prophylaxis. *Archives of General Psychiatry, 31,* 189–192.

Reich, T., Clayton, P. J., & Winokur, G. (1969). Family history studies: V. The genetics of mania. *American Journal of Psychiatry, 125,* 1358–1359.

Roberts, J. A. F. (1963). *An introduction to medical genetics.* New York: Oxford University Press.

Rosanoff, A. J., Handy, L. M., & Rosanoff-Plesset, I. B. A. (1985). The etiology of manic-depressive syndromes with special reference to their occurrence in twins. *American Journal of Psychiatry, 91,* 725–762.

Rüdin, E. (1923). Ubert Vererbung geistiger Storungen. *Zeitschift für die Gesamte Neurologie und Psychiatrie, 81,* 459–496.

Schless A. P., Frazer, A., & Mendels J. (1975). Genetic determination of lithium ion metabolism: II. an in vivo study of lithium ion distribution across erythrocyte membranes. *Archives of General Psychiatry, 32,* 337–390.

Schulz, B. (1940). Kinder von Elternpaaren mit einem schizophrenen und einem affektpsychotischen Partner. *General Neurological Psychiatry, 170,* 441–514.

Sjörgen, T. (1948). Genetic, statistical and psychiatric investigations of a West Swedish population. *Acta Psychiatrica Scandinavica.* Suppl., *52.*

Slater, E. (1953). Psychotic and neurotic illness in twins. *Special Report. Series Medical Research Counsel 178.* London: Her Majesty's Stationery Office.

Slater, E., Maxwell, J., & Price, J. S. (1972). Distribution of ancestral secondary cases in bipolar affective disorders. *British Journal of Psychiatry, 118,* 215–218.

Smith, J. C. (1925). Atypical psychoses and heterologous hereditary taints. *Journal of Nervous Disease, 62,* 1–32.

Stallone, F., Shelley, E., & Mendlewicz, J. (1973). The use of lithium in affective disorders: III. A double-blind study of prophylaxis in bipolar illness. *American Journal of Psychiatry, 130,* 1006–1010.

Stenstedt, A. (1952). A study in manic-depressive psychoses. *Acta Psychiatrica et Neurologica Scandinavica* Suppl., 79.

Strömgren, E. (1938). Beitrage zür psychiatrischen Erblehere. Copenhagen, Denmark: Munksgaard.

Targum, S. D., Gershon, E. J., Van Eerdewegh, M., & Rogenline, N. (1979). Human leucocyte antigen (HLA) system not closely linked to or associated with bipolar manic-depressive illness. *Biological Psychiatry, 14,* 615–636.

Taylor, M., & Abrams, R. (1974). Manic states. A genetic study of early and late onset of affective disorders. *Archives of General Psychiatry, 28,* 656–672.

Taylor, M. A., & Abrams, R. (1975). Acute mania. *Archives of General Psychiatry, 32,* 863–865.

Tomasson, H. (1938). Further investigations on manic-depressive psychoses: (2) Investigations on heredity in Ireland. *Acta Psychiatrica et Neurologica Scandinavica, 13,* 517–526.

Weiner, J., & Strömgren, E. (1958). Clinical and genetic studies on benign schizophreniform psychoses based on a follow-up. *Acta Psychiatrica et Neurologica Scandinavica, 33,* 377–399.

Winokur, G., Clayton, P. J., & Reich, T. (1969). *Manic-depressive illness.* St. Louis, MO: C. V. Mosby.

Winokur, G., & Tanna, V. L. (1969). Possible role of X-linked dominant factor in manic-depressive diseases. *Diseases of the Nervous System, 30,* 89–94.

Wirtkamp, L. R., Stancer, H. C., Persad, E., Flood, C., & Guttorsmen, S. (1981). Depressive disorders and HLA. A gene on chromosome 6 that can affect behavior. *New England Journal of Medicine, 305,* 1301–1306.

Zerbin-Rüdin, E. (1967). Endogene Psychosen. In P. E. Becker (Ed.), *Human-Genetik: Ein kurzes Handbuch in funf Banden* (Vol. 2). Stuttgart, Germany: Thieme.

Zerbin-Rüdin, E. (1969). Zur Genetik der depressiven Erkrankungen. In H. Hippius and H. Selbach (Eds.), *Das Depressive Syndrom.* Munich: Urban and Schwarzenberg.

Zvolsky, P., Vinarova, E., & Dostal, T. (1974). Family history of manic-depressive and endogenous depressive patients and clinical effect of treatment with lithium. Abstracted, *Acta Nervosa Supplemental* (Praha), *16,* 194–195.

Chapter 25

Biological Processes in Major Depression

Michael E. Thase
Assistant Professor of Psychiatry

Ellen Frank
Associate Professor of Psychiatry and Psychology

David J. Kupfer
Professor and Chairman
Department of Psychiatry
University of Pittsburgh School of Medicine.
Western Psychiatric Institute and Clinic,
Pittsburgh, PA.

Depression is a complex phenomenon which may include disturbances in social and interpersonal spheres, changes in overt behavior and subjective experiences, and disruptions of basic functions such as sleep and appetite. As detailed in other chapters of this book, evidence has emerged to implicate the importance of recent and remote life events, social or interpersonal disturbances, and several intrapersonal factors (i.e., cognitive distortions or psychodynamic constructs) in the development and/or persistence of clinical depressions. In this chapter, research pertaining to biological aspects of depression will be reviewed. Considerable attention has been devoted to the investigation of this topic over the past two decades. While it is important to note from the beginning that the "biology" of major depression is not fully understood, a number of significant advances have been made. After a review of historical, conceptual, and methodological issues which can provide a basis for current psychobiological paradigms, we will review various hypotheses and empirical data regarding the role of altered neurotransmitter, neurophysiological, neuroendocrine, and circadian mechanisms in clinical depression. Evidence will be summarized which suggests that abnormalities in several biological systems discriminate depression from normal states or other psychopathological conditions. The heterogeneity within the broad category of major depressive disorder also will be emphasized. Finally, impli-

Acknowledgements: This work was supported in part by NIMH Grants MH24652, MH16804, and MH30915 as well as a grant from the John D. and Catherine T. MacArthur Research Network on the Psychobiology of Depression.

cations of current findings for treatment of depression and integration of research across disciplines will be considered.

HISTORICAL PERSPECTIVES

Interest in the possible role of biological factors in depression is not a recent development. For example, in the second century A.D. Galen proposed that an excess of black bile caused melancholia (Mora, 1980). Nevertheless, lack of knowledge about normal brain physiology and inability to study molecular or microelectrical processes kept notions about the biology of depression at the level of speculation until the late 1950s and early 1960s.

However, several lines of evidence began to emerge early in this century which indirectly pointed to the role of some form of biological abnormality in more severe depression (see Table 1). First, clinical studies of the phenomenology and longitudinal course of psychiatric patients, pioneered by Kraepelin (1921), were instrumental in separating affective psychoses (i.e., severe depressions and mania) from other types of disordered behavior. In particular, the natural history of depression was noted to be punctuated by an episodic course, with relatively clear periods of remission frequently alternating with episodes of depression and/or mania (Kraepelin, 1921; Lundquist, 1945; Poort, 1945; Rennie, 1942; Zis & Goodwin, 1979a).

Second, a relatively characteristic cluster of "somatic" symptoms also was noted in such patients, including disturbances in sleep, psychomotor behavior (agitation or retardation), appetite, libido, weight, and diurnal alterations in mood (Gillespie, 1929; Kraepelin, 1921). This constellation of symptoms subsequently formed the basis of what is now known as endogenomorphic (Klein, 1974), endogenous (Spitzer, Endicott, & Robins, 1978), or melancholic (American Psychiatric Association, 1980) depression. Moreover, increasing data on the neurophysiological correlates of normal behavior suggested that such "somatic" symptoms might reflect an underlying disturbance in the limbic system of the brain.

Third, early family history studies by Rosanoff and co-workers (Rosanoff, Handy, & Plesset, 1935), as well as investigations by Kallman, Luxemberger,

---

TABLE 1
Indirect evidence of the role of biological factors in depression

1. Longitudinal course marked by periods of recovery, alternating with episodes of recurrence and/or manic episodes, is suggestive of an episodic form of biological illness.

2. Constellation of symptoms suggestive of disruption of "vital" processes (i.e., sleep and appetite disturbances, reduced libido, diurnal mood variation, and psychomotor disturbances.)

3. Evidence of heritability.

4. Response to "somatic" treatment, particularly in patients with a constellation of vital disturbances, as well as occasional observations of drug-induced hypomania.

and Slater (see Nurnberger & Gershon, 1982) consistently documented higher concordance rates for affective psychoses in monozygotic (identical) twins when compared to fraternal (dizygotic) twins. Demonstration of an apparent genetic association pointed to some type of biological dysfunction underlying severe depression.

Finally, in the late 1940s and 1950s various "somatic" treatments were found to be effective for severe depressions which previously were refractory to psychosocial and milieu therapies. Treatments such as electroconvulsive therapy ([ECT]; Huston & Locher, 1948; Ulett, Smith, & Gleser, 1956), imipramine (Ball & Kiloh, 1959; Kuhn, 1958), and iproniazid (Loomer, Saunders, & Kline, 1958; West & Dally, 1959) were found to be relatively specific for depression. Antidepressant efficacy of these treatments also appeared most striking in patients with somatic or "endogenomorphic" symptoms of depression (e.g., Bielski & Friedel, 1976). The fact that such treatments occasionally appeared to induce manic or hypomanic episodes in vulnerable individuals further strengthened an association between affective disorders and biological dysfunction. Moreover, subsequent recognition of the in vitro effects of a variety of psychoactive substances stimulated interest in possible biological alterations in depression. For example, agents such as amphetamine, imipramine, and iproniazid were found to be amine-enhancing at the neuronal synapse. Conversely, reserpine, an antihypertensive agent with a pronounced tendency to cause depression, was found to be amine-depleting. In short, these observations set the stage for future investigations of possible neurotransmitter abnormalities in depression.

CONCEPTUAL ISSUES

Before turning attention to specific hypotheses and empirical findings, it is important to consider several conceptual issues related to the biology of major depression (see Table 2).

TABLE 2

Conceptual issues related to study of the biological aspects of major depression

1. Major depression is a syndromal diagnosis; several clinically distinct subtypes exist within this diagnostic grouping (i.e., bipolar, delusional, or melancholic forms of major depression).

2. It is conceivable that biological heterogeneity may exist even within a clinically distinct grouping.

3. The residual classification of nondelusional, nonbipolar, nonmelancholic major depression is a large and quite heterogeneous group; studies of biological disturbances often focus on more severely ill samples with endogenous or melancholic depressions.

4. Identification of a biological abnormality does not necessarily mean that the disturbance has etiopathogenetic significance.

5. A given disturbance may be present only during an episode (state marker) or may persist during recovery (trait marker).

First, it must be recognized that major depression is a syndromal classification and does not represent a specific disease entity. There is considerable clinical diversity within the major depression grouping. For example, while most depressives experience anxiety and/or agitation, some form of insomnia, and decreased appetite, a significant minority (about 20 percent) overeat, have little overt anxiety, and manifest hypersomnia. Other depressed patients experience delusions, while still others have a history of alternating episodes of depression and mania. Detailed reviews of clinical, genetic, and pharmacological studies indicate that such presentations represent distinct subtypes of depression (Coryell & Tsuang, 1982; Depue & Monroe, 1978; Glassman & Roose, 1981; Helms & Smith, 1983; Kupfer, Pickar, Himmelhoch, & Detre, 1975; Perris, 1982). It seems unlikely that a single biological disturbance will be found to underlie these diverse forms of major depression. Moreover, it is important to ascertain if clinical subtypes of depression (i.e., bipolar disorder or delusional depression) also represent distinct biological subgroupings (Kupfer & Thase, in press).

Second, it is conceivable that even within a relatively homogeneous grouping, such as bipolar disorder, several distinctly different biological types may exist (Kupfer & Thase, in press). Such a circumstance might easily be missed if investigators relied solely on grouped data (see Buchsbaum & Rieder, 1979). This would be particularly true if an abnormality was present in only a small number of cases.

Third, even after separately grouping bipolar and delusionally depressed patients, the residual category of nondelusional, nonbipolar major depression remains rather heterogeneous (Nelson & Charney, 1981). It is possible that a number of patients who meet criteria for major depression will have no evidence of biological disturbance (Kupfer & Thase, in press). At this time, biologically oriented investigators are focusing on patients with melancholia or endogenous subtype in order to maximize the probability of detecting pathophysiological abnormalities (Carroll, 1982; Kupfer & Thase, in press). However, conclusions drawn from studies of such severely depressed (and often hospitalized) patients may not be applicable to outpatients with milder, less pervasive nonbipolar depressive syndromes.

Fourth, demonstration of a replicable "biological" abnormality does not necessarily lead to the conclusion that a pathological alteration intimately related to the etiology of depression has been identified. The disturbance may simply reflect an objective amplification of a behavioral process or an epiphenomenon of some other disturbance (Kupfer & Thase, in press). An example of the former is use of muscle activity recording devices to objectify tension or agitation. Biological alterations which are the direct result of weight loss, decreased motoric activity, and/or insomnia would represent examples of epiphenomenal disturbances. While such parameters may be of some value in objectifying assessment of depression or even as diagnostic "markers," they do not provide useful information about the etiopathogenesis of depression. Other parameters, such as neuroendocrine measures, may provide useful indirect evidence of more fundamental disturbances by allowing inferences to be drawn about dysregulation of neurotransmitter or circadian mechanisms governing normal functioning. However, such conclusions can be reached only if the normal physiological regulatory mechanisms have been clearly elucidated. In most cases, regulation of neuroendocrine or sleep functions involve a number of complex interrelated processes and, therefore, exact conclusions cannot yet be reached (Kalin, Risch, Janowsky, & Murphy, 1981; Thase & Kupfer, in press-a).

Fifth, it should be determined if a proposed abnormality is state dependent or persists during periods of remission in a fashion analogous to a trait (Kupfer, 1982a). State-dependent "markers" of depression may be of use in elucidating pathophysiological mechanisms of the acute episode, as well as potentially providing important practical aids for diagnosis or treatment monitoring. However, such abnormalities also may be epiphenomena. Conversely, "trait" markers may prove particularly useful for genetic studies or as predictors of vulnerability in either recovered patients or their never-ill relatives. Unfortunately, one can never be certain if an apparent trait marker actually was present prior to development of the first episode of depression; that is, the abnormality may be a residual feature, or "scar," of the index episode of depression. Further, performing longitudinal biological and clinical studies of high-risk, but never-ill, relatives is an extremely expensive and time-consuming enterprise.

METHODOLOGIC ISSUES

Introduction of effective "somatic" treatments for depression led to renewed interest in classification of depression. Since not all depressed patients responded to such treatments, it seemed plausible that inconsistencies in diagnosis might account for a large portion of outcome variance. Indeed, psychiatric diagnoses as determined circa 1950–70 were consistently found to have poor or, at best, limited reliability (Matarazzo, 1983; Spitzer, Fleiss, & Endicott, 1978). Further, clinicians in the United States and Great Britain were found to differ in diagnosis of schizophrenia and affective disorder (Cooper, Kendell, Gurland, Sharpe, Copeland, & Simon, 1972).

With respect to diagnosis of depression, no single symptom or set of symptoms were found to be pathognomonic. Syndromal approaches had to suffice, yet initially there was little consensus as to what historical and symptomatic variables should be used to define the syndrome. In the United States, Kraepelin's concept of manic-depressive insanity had narrowed by relative exclusion of patients with delusions or hallucinations (Cooper et al., 1972), yet broadened to include patients with no history of mania.

Identification of the therapeutic effects of lithium (Baastrup & Schou, 1967; Carroll, 1979; Coppen, Peet, & Bailey, 1973; Goodwin, Murphy, & Bunney, 1969; Prien, 1979) resulted in renewed interest in differentiation between circular (bipolar) and recurrent unipolar forms of depression. Further, a diagnosis of manic-depression did not seem appropriate for many patients with milder, ambulatory depressions. Unfortunately, early alternative classifications for such patients were derived from unvalidated psychodynamic or social psychiatric formulations (i.e., anaclitic depression, depressive neurosis, or reactive depression; see Klerman & Barrett, 1973).

Limitations in reliability and validity of diagnoses posed similar problems for investigators seeking to study biological parameters in depression. The key factor seemed to be the lack of a widely accepted, standardized, and operationalized set of criteria for affective disorder diagnoses (Spitzer, Fleiss, & Endicott, 1978). Major progress was made through adoption of an atheoretical approach to classification based on symptomatic, syndromal criteria. Systems such as the St. Louis criteria (Feighner, Robins, Guze, Woodruff, Winokur, & Muñoz, 1972) and the expanded and slightly modified Research Diagnostic Criteria ([RDC]; Spitzer, Endicott, & Robins, 1978) achieved high levels of inter-rater agreement by explicitly defining the syndrome (primary or major depression) in terms of symptom cluster (depressed mood plus at least five common symptoms) and persistence (present nearly every day for at least two weeks). Such diagnostic systems reduced some variability within the depression grouping by separately classifying patients with affective syndromes developing historically secondary to other psychiatric disorders (i.e., schizophrenia, alcoholism, drug abuse, sociopathy, and so on) or severe, intercurrent medical illness (i.e., hypothyroidism, malignancies, Cushing's disease, and so on). Diagnostic variance was reduced further by use of semi-structured interviews, such as the Schedule for Affective Disorders and Schizophrenia ([SADS]; Endicott & Spitzer, 1978), to ensure uniform collection of data, and thorough collateral interviews with family members or significant others.

The St. Louis criteria and RDC gained wide acceptance and, for the first time, provided a common, reliable nomenclature for affective disorders researchers to define patient samples. Use of reliable rating scales of depressive severity, such as the Hamilton Rating Scale for Depression ([HRSD]; Hamilton, 1960), also facilitated comparisons and allowed investigators to set minimum thresholds of severity for inclusion in a study. While the rather arbitrary nature of exclusion and inclusion criteria for depression may at times detract from the external validity of research, this limitation appeared to be a small price to pay. Moreover, the success of such atheoretical, operationalized diagnostic systems led the American Psychiatric Association to adopt this format for the third edition of the *Diagnostic and Statistical Manual of Mental Disorders* (*DSM-III*), which was published in 1980 (see Spitzer Williams, & Skodol, 1980).

Aside from issues of diagnosis, several other methodological factors increasingly are recognized as potentially confounding variables. The effects of age, nutritional status, sex or menstrual phase may have manifold impact on multiple biological systems. Circadian variation in levels of a variety of hormones of interest to affective disorder researchers (e.g., cortisol, prolactin, and growth hormone) would indicate that even time of day is a critical experimental variable (G.M. Brown & J. Seggie, 1980; Wagner & Weitzman, 1980). Such variables necessitate careful selection and matching of normal control groups to ensure that an apparent biological abnormality is not due to artifact. Similarly, it also is important to use control groups of patients with clear-cut, nonaffective psychiatric disorders in order to rule out potentially confounding, nonspecific effects of stress, hospitalization, or patienthood. Further, potential effects of drugs (both prescribed and illicit) and alcohol on biological parameters must be recognized. It is entirely possible that an abnormal finding detected using a neurochemical or neurophysiological measure, which differentiates treated depressives from controls, actually might represent the effects of a particular form of treatment. More remote physiological effects of withdrawal from a given drug or illicit substance also must be taken into consideration. To control for such potential experimental hazards, study often is limited to patients who are medication free for a period of two weeks or longer (Kupfer & Thase, 1983).

Finally, a critical source of variance in studies employing biological parameters stems from the actual procedures and techniques employed in measurement of the variable(s) in question. With respect to neurochemical, receptor sensitivity, and certain neuroendocrine measurements, assays may involve levels in the microgram, nanogram, or even picogram range of sensitivity. Standardization and reliability of methods are as important here as they are with diagnosis. Determination of inter- and intra-assay coefficients of variation, comparisons across laboratories, and development of quality control standards are essential. Further, when several different assays are available for the same biological parameters, identification and acceptance of the most accurate technique is necessary.

Understanding of the importance of each of the methodological factors reviewed above has been an evolving process, taking place over the past several decades. Additional factors undoubtedly will be identified in the years to come. Nevertheless, adherence to the present "state of the art" can lessen the risk of false leads resulting from epiphenomena or experimental artifacts. Some suggested methodological guidelines for biological studies on depression recently have been published elsewhere (Kupfer & Rush, 1983). A summary of sources of methodological variance and suggested solutions is provided in Table 3.

With these conceptual and methodological issues in mind, we will briefly review key theories regarding possible neurochemical disturbances in depression. Next, empirical data pertaining to neurotransmitter, receptor, neurophysiological, neuroendocrine, and circadian abnormalities in depression will be considered. In each case, the theoretical rationale for studying a given parameter or system will be briefly reviewed, followed by an assessment of the replicability and specificity of the proposed abnormality in depression. The extent to which an abnormality may be due to experimental artifact or epiphenomenal factors will be discussed. When possible, incidence for various clinical subtypes of depression will be summarized.

TABLE 3
Sources of methodological variance in depression research

Problem	Suggested solution
1. Reliability of diagnosis.	Use of operationalized, descriptive diagnostic criteria. Use of standardized interviews and collateral sources of information.
2. Heterogeneity of diagnostic groupings.	Observe for biological subgroups. Separately study clinical subtypes of major depression.
3. Epiphenomenal effects (i.e., age, sex, weight loss, menstrual status or time of day).	Carefully match patient and control groups. Statistically control for relevant variables when matching is not possible.
4. Nonspecific effects of stress, patienthood, or hospitalization.	Use of matched control groups of patients with nonaffective disorders.
5. Direct biological effects of medication or withdrawal from drugs or alcohol.	Use of relatively long (i.e., greater than or equal to two weeks) medication-free washout prior to study.
6. Confounding effects of intercurrent medical illness.	Careful medical and neurological evaluation. Exclusion of subjects with potentially confounding conditions.
7. Accuracy and reliability of biological test parameters.	Determination of intra- and inter-assay reliability of measures. Development of norms for patient and control groups; Interlaboratory comparisons.

NEUROCHEMICAL ABNORMALITIES

Most biological theories of depression center around proposed disturbance of one or more neurochemical systems functioning within the brain. Particular attention has been given to the possible role of catecholamines, such as norepinephrine (NE) and dopamine (DA), as well as the indolamine serotonin (5-HT; see Figure 1). More recently, several groups of investigators have focused on possible abnormalities in the regulation of acetylcholine (ACH). Each of these substances are known to function as neurotransmitters within the central nervous system (CNS) and have been localized in high concentrations in several regions, nuclei, and tracts of the limbic system and brain stem; that is, areas involved with regulation of appetitive, sleep, and emotional processes (Cooper, Bloom, & Roth, 1978; Erickson, 1978; Kupfer & Edwards, 1978). A brief summary of the major precursors, metabolites, and enzymes involved in synthesis and degradation of these neurotransmitters is provided in Table 4.

FIGURE 1
Structural depictions of dopamine, norepinephrine, serotonin, and acetylcholine

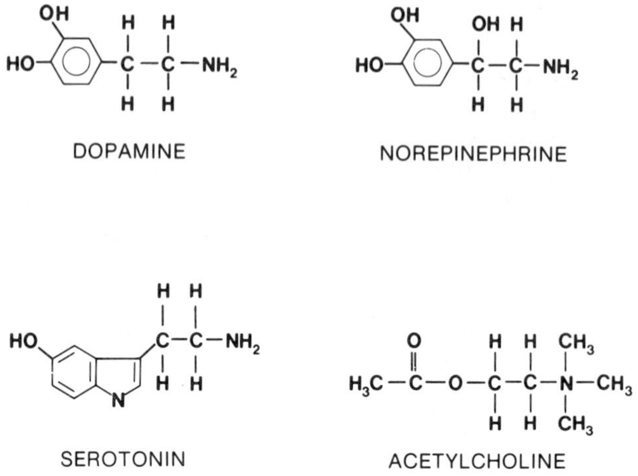

DOPAMINE

NOREPINEPHRINE

SEROTONIN

ACETYLCHOLINE

There also is increasing evidence that a variety of short-chain peptides function as neurotransmitters (Barchas, Akil, Elliott, Holman, & Watson, 1978; Cooper et al., 1978; Krieger & Liotta, 1979). However, while it is conceivable that these neuropeptides ultimately may prove to be of a great importance in depression, knowledge of their localization, regulation, and function as

TABLE 4
Summary of monoamine synthesis and metabolism

Neurotransmitter	Precursor(s)	Major metabolites	Enzymes	
			Synthetic	Degradative
1. Dopamine (DA)	Phenylalanine Tyrosine Dopa	Homavanillic acid (HVA) Norepinephrine	Tyrosine hydroxylase DOPA decarboxylase	Monoamine oxidase (MAO) Catechol-o-methyl transferase (COMT) Dopamine Beta Hydroxylase (DBH)
2. Norepinephrine (NE)	Phenylalanine Tyrosine Dopa Dopamine	Normetanephrine 3-methoxy-4-hydroxyphenyl-glycol (MHPG)	DBH	MAO COMT
3. Serotonin (5-HT)	Tryptophan 5-hydroxy-tryptophan	5-hydroxy-indol-acetic acid (5-HIAA)	Tryptophan hydroxylase	MAO
4. Acetylcholine (ACH)	Phosphatidyl-choline Choline	None	Choline acetyl-transferase	Cholinesterase

neurotransmitters is too incomplete at this time to permit inclusion in this review. In the next sections, we will review evidence pertaining to abnormalities of monoamines and acetylcholine in major depression.

Monoamines (MA)

Interest in the possible role in monoamines in depression intensified in the early 1960s, when it was discovered that antidepressant medications (i.e., imipramine and iproniazid) increased functional levels of NE and 5-HT within the synaptic cleft. All effective tricyclic antidepressants were subsequently shown to block neuronal reuptake of NE and/or 5-HT, and a heterogeneous group of antidepressants came to be known as monoamine oxidase inhibitors (MAOIs) by virtue of their common ability to inhibit this enzyme necessary for degradation of NE, DA, and 5-HT (Mindham, 1982; Nies & Robinson, 1982). Conversely, reserpine, an antihypertensive known to cause depression in vulnerable individuals, was found to deplete neuronal storage of both catecholamines and 5-HT. Several investigators drew upon these observations and advanced hypotheses of catecholamine (Bunney & Davis, 1965; Schildkraut, 1965) and indoleamine (Glassman, 1969) deficiencies in depression. When considered together, these formulations are referred to as the monoamine hypotheses of depression.

These early monoamine hypotheses were necessarily reductionistic and oversimplified (Bunney & Garland, 1982; Schildkraut, 1978). Nevertheless, it was anticipated that disturbances of NE or 5-HT might not account for all forms of depression (Glassman, 1969; Schildkraut 1965). Further, knowledge of neuronal functioning was sophisticated enough at that time to anticipate that a functional deficiency of neurotransmitter could arise through numerous mechanisms: decreased synthesis, increased degradation, impaired release or reuptake, or altered receptor function (Bunney & Davis, 1965; Schildkraut, 1965; see Figure 2). Thus, a functional deficiency of either monoamine might exist in certain conditions even if no deficit in actual amount of neurotransmitter was apparent.

Basic tenets of the monoamine hypotheses are summarized in Table 5. A substantial body of empirical data addressing these points has been collected over the past two decades, and a number of researchers have reviewed evidence for and against the monoamine hypotheses (e.g., Baldessarini, 1975; Kalin, Risch, & Murphy, 1981; Murphy, Campbell, & Costa, 1978; Schildkraut, 1978; van Praag, 1980a, 1980b; Zis & Goodwin, 1979b, 1982).

With respect to norepinephrine, extensive study of plasma, urine, and cerebrospinal fluid (CSF) samples collected from depressed individuals, as well as direct postmortem assays of brain tissue (usually obtained from suicide victims), has failed to reveal conclusive evidence of an NE deficiency state in major depression when compared to normals or nonaffective patient controls (Kupfer & Thase, in press; Zis & Goodwin, 1982).

Perhaps the best studied index of CNS noradrenergic function has involved determination of 3-methoxy-4-hydroxyphenylglycol (MHPG), a key

FIGURE 2
Schematic illustration of a monoamine synapse

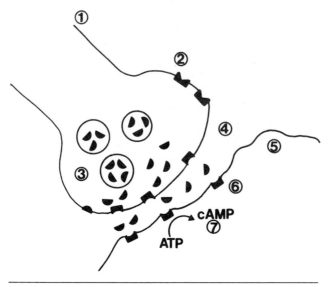

Key:
1. Representing the efferent terminal.
2. Presynaptic receptor sites.
3. Intracellular monoamine storage vesicles.
4. The synaptic cleft.
5. The afferent terminal.
6. Postsynaptic receptor sites.
7. Membrane-bound adenylate cyclase for conversion of the "second messenger" cAMP.

metabolite of brain norepinephrine (Maas, 1975; Schildkraut, 1982; van Praag, 1980b). A number of early studies indicated that at least a subgroup of major depressives had low 24-hour levels of excretion of urinary MHPG, which might suggest a deficiency of brain NE (see Goodwin & Post, 1975; Maas, 1975; Sacchetti, Allaria, Negri, Biondi, Smeraldi, & Cazzullo, 1979; Schildkraut, 1982). It also was proposed that major depression might consist

TABLE 5
Basic tenets of the monoamine (MA) hypothesis

1. Depressions are caused by decreased functional levels of catecholamines or indoleamines; mania is associated with increased levels of catecholamines.

2. Decreased functional levels of MA may be the result of impaired synthesis or storage, increased degradation, or altered receptor function.

3. Administration of MA precursors should produce an antidepressant effect; agents which deplete MA or impair synthesis should cause depression and/or treat mania.

4. Agents which result in persistent increases in synaptic MA should be effective antidepressants (tricyclic antidepressants, monoamine oxidase inhibitors and electroconvulsive treatment). Such agents also may produce hypomania in vulnerable individuals.

of two biochemically distinct subgroups: one with low levels of urinary MHPG ("noradrenergic" depression) and the other with normal or high levels (possibly "serotonergic" depression; see Maas, 1975; Schildkraut, 1978). Several studies documented significantly lower urinary MHPG levels in bipolar or schizoaffective depressions relative to patients with nonbipolar, nonendogenous syndromes (see DeLeon-Jones, Maas, Dekirmenjian, & Sanchez, 1975; Sacchetti et al., 1979; Schildkraut, 1982; Taube, Kirstein, Sweeney, Heninger, & Maas, 1978). Elevations in urinary MHPG levels also were reported in longitudinally studied bipolar patients following a shift into mania (Schildkraut, 1978). Similarly, high CSF levels of MHPG have been found in mania (Swann, Secunda, Davis, Robins, Hanin, Koslow, & Maas, 1983). Further, several investigators found that depressives with low urinary MHPG levels responded better to treatment with adrenergically active antidepressants, such as imipramine, desipramine, or maprotiline than to "serotonergic" agents like amitriptyline (Gaertner, Kreuter, Scharek, Wiatr, & Breyer-Pfaff, 1982; Kelwala, Jones, & Sitaram, 1983; Maas, 1975; Maas, Koslow, Katz, Gibbons, Bowden, Robins, & Davis, 1984; Schildkraut, 1978; 1982; Schatzberg, Orsulak, Rosenbaum, Maruta, Kruger, Cole, & Schildkraut, 1981).

However, continued study in this area has revealed a number of contradictory findings, which certainly limit inferences about the role of NE deficiency in the etiopathogensis of major depression. First, a number of groups have not been able to replicate the existence of a distinct, "low" MHPG subgroup of depressives (see Kelwala et al., 1983). Rather, division of samples into high and low groupings generally has remained an arbitrary and relative judgment, with only a modest number (approximately 25–40 percent) of nonbipolar major depressives having 24-hour urinary MHPG excretion values actually outside of the normal range (DeLisi, Karoum, Targum, Byrnes, & Wyatt, 1983; Kelwala et al., 1983). Second, studies employing plasma or cerebrospinal fluid determinations of MHPG (i.e., more direct and technically less difficult measurements than those based on collection of 24-hour urine specimens) have yielded conflicting results (see Kelwala et al., 1983; Koslow, Maas, Bowden, Davis, Hanin, & Javaid, 1983). Third, the proportion of urinary MHPG which is derived from brain NE may be lower than originally expected, with several investigators reporting that the CNS contribution is less than 50 percent of total urinary MHPG excretion (e.g., Hollister, 1981). Fourth, factors such as diet, psychomotor activity, psychotropic drug usage or withdrawal, and anxiety level all may impact on MHPG levels, and marked day-to-day variability in urinary MHPG excretion is noted in some patients (Muscettola, Potter, Gordon, & Goodwin, 1981; Sweeney, Maas, & Heninger, 1978; Tang, Stancer, Takahashi Shephard, & Warsh, 1981). Indeed, time of day appears to be more closely related to MHPG level than does a diagnosis of depression (Wehr, Muscettola, & Goodwin, 1980). Season of the year may even influence results (Wirz-Justice & Richter, 1979). Fifth, treatment with adrenergically active antidepressants does not consistently result in increases in urinary MHPG (Charney, Heninger, Sternberg, Redmond, Leckman, Maas, & Roth, 1981; Kelwala et al., 1983; Linnoila, Karoum, Calil, Kopin, & Potter, 1982).

Finally, implications of correlations between urinary MHPG levels and response to selected antidepressant agents are less straightforward than initially hoped for. For example, imipramine does not apparently only have effects on noradrenergic systems; it also has rather pronounced actions on serotonergic and antihistaminic systems (Richelson, 1983). Conversely, the "serotonergic" drug amitriptyline has metabolites which are quite adrenergic (Richelson, 1983). Thus, low urinary MHPG may have predictive value for antidepressant treatment in general. Furthermore, it is conceivable that urinary MHPG level is correlate of clinical features which predict tricyclic antidepressant response, such as psychomotor retardation or low anxiety levels, rather than an indicator of a biologically distinct subgroup of depressives (Thase & Kupfer, in press-a).

Investigations of other aspects of noradrenergic functioning, such as measurement of enzymes involved in synthesis or degradation, also have failed to demonstrate consistent evidence of a deficiency state. Levels of monoamine oxidase (MAO) in blood platelets, a physiological model of the neuron, have been variably reported to be decreased, unchanged, or even elevated in depression (Goodwin & Post 1975; Rotman, 1983; White, Macdonald, Razani, Shih, Boyd, Simpson, & Sloane, 1983). Such variability may be related, in part, to diagnostic subgroupings: low levels of MAO tend to be found in bipolar depressives while high platelet MAO values have been reported in nonbipolar patients with predominantly anxious, unstable, and "characterological" features (Davidson, McLeod, Turnbull, White, & Feuer, 1980; Gudeman, Schatzberg, Samson, Orsulak, Cole, & Schildkraut, 1982; Rotman, 1983; Schatzberg, Orsulak, Rothschild, Salomon, Lerbinger, Kizuka, Cole, & Schildkraut, 1983; White et al., 1983).

Attempts to treat depression with noradrenergic precursors, such as L-dopa or tyrosine, have not been particularly successful (van Praag, 1980; Zis & Goodwin, 1982). Conversely, there is little evidence that agents (other than reserpine) which specifically decrease the functional output of NE have pronounced depressogeneric effects in normals or remitted depressives (Zis & Goodwin, 1982).

There also is little evidence to implicate a deficiency of dopamine (DA), another catecholamine, in major depression (van Praag, 1980; Zis & Goodwin, 1982). Findings of one group of investigators indicate that decreased levels of the enzyme dopamine beta hydroxylase may be found in delusional depression (Meltzer, Cho, Carroll, & Russo, 1976). As this enzyme is responsible for conversion of dopamine to norepinephrine, a deficiency might result in increased levels of DA as well as decreased NE. This finding is of considerable interest since delusionally depressed patients generally do not respond to treatment with a tricyclic antidepressant unless combined with a dopamine-blocking antipsychotic (Avery & Lubrano, 1979; Glassman, Kantor, & Shostak, 1975; Thase & Kupfer, in press-a). Further, increased functional levels of dopamine frequently are implicated in a variety of psychotic states. However, a recent study by another research group failed to find decreased dopamine beta hydroxylase in psychotic depressives (Eisemann, Ericsson, von Knorring, Perris, & Ross, 1983).

Several groups have documented low post-probenecid levels of homovanillic acid, the principal CNS metabolite of DA, in the CSF of depressed patients (Banki, 1977; van Praag, 1980b; van Praag & Korf, 1971). However, such findings appear specifically related to degree of psychomotor retardation (Banki, 1977; van Praag, 1980b). As previously noted, administration of the DA precursor L-dopa does not reliably produce an antidepressant response, although a transient increase in motoric activity or even hypomania may be observed in some patients (van Praag, 1980b; Zis & Goodwin, 1982). Antidepressant treatment generally results in a lowering, rather than an increase, or peripheral excretion of both dopaminergic and noradrenergic metabolites (Linnoila, Karoum, Calil, Kopin, & Potter, 1982; Linnoila, Karoum, & Potter, 1982a; Linnoila, Karoum & Potter, 1983). Moreover, when elevations in excretion of dopamine and its metabolites are noted during antidepressant treatment, such changes usually are associated with development of agitation or hypomania (Linnoila, Karoum, & Potter, 1983).

More recently, investigators have studied the possibility of noradrenergic overactivity in depression. Results of a major collaborative study (Koslow et al., 1983), as well as findings from several other investigations (Esler, Turbott, Schwartz, Leonard, Bobik, Skews, & Jackman, 1982; Lake, Pickar, Ziegler, Lipper, Slater, & Murphy, 1982; Linnoila, Karoum, & Potter, 1982b) suggest that a significant minority of hospitalized depressives show evidence of elevated levels of catecholamines and their metabolites in CSF and peripheral specimens. These findings could relate to high levels of activity (agitation), panic or anxiety, and ruminative-obsessive thinking seen in some severely depressed, melancholic patients. One group of investigators developed a discriminant function based on urinary MHPG and peripheral metabolites of epinephrine and NE which reliably separated clinical samples of depressives into groups with either predominantly retarded, anergic bipolar depressions or anxious, agitated nonbipolar depressions (Schildkraut, 1982). Further, decreased platelet MAO activity was found in patients with low scores on this discriminate index (Schildkraut, 1978). Again, such findings might support an epiphenomenal relationship between biochemical correlates and clinical state, particularly with respect to psychomotor retardation and low anxiety levels.

Research examining the possible role of serotonergic deficiency in depression also has yielded mixed findings. Postmortem assays of serotonin (5-HT) and 5-hydroxy-indolacetic acid (5-HIAA) in the brains of suicide victims and nondepressed controls have yielded inconclusive results, which perhaps, at best, suggest slightly decreased levels in depression (see Murphy et al., 1978). Similarly, conflicting reports have been published with respect to the amount of serotonin precursors in plasma and CSF specimens of depressives relative to controls (Murphy et al., 1978).

A number of investigators have studied CSF levels of 5-HIAA as an index of brain serotonergic activity. Overall, most investigators have found decreased levels of 5-HIAA in depressives relative to controls, although frequently such differences are not statistically significant (Kalin, Risch, & Murphy, 1981; Murphy et al., 1978; van Praag, 1980a). Van Praag (1980a) reviewed ungrouped data and concluded that about 40 percent of endogenous depressives have 5-HIAA values which fall below the normal range; that is, that a distinct biochemical subtype exists within the major depression grouping which includes patients with a low-serotonin condition. This position is supported by observations of a bimodal distribution of 5-HIAA values (Asberg, Traskman, & Thoren, 1976), as well as the modest antidepressant effects of treatment with serotonin precursors, such as tryptophan and 5-hydroxy-tryptophan in depressed patients with low 5-HIAA (van Praag, 1980a).

Attempts to relate 5-HIAA levels to clinical subtypes suggest that reductions are most common in patients with severe melancholic or endogenous depressions (van Praag, 1980a). One group found that low levels of 5-HIAA characterized unipolar but not bipolar endogenous depressions. Similarly, Maas et al. (in press) found that low 5-HIAA levels were predictive of tricyclic response only in unipolar depressions. However, several other groups of investigators have not found such relationships (van Praag, 1980a). Other investigators have found low levels of 5-HIAA to predict risk or relapse (van Praag, 1980a) or violent suicidal behavior (Asberg & Traskman, 1981; G.L. Brown, Ebert, Goyer, Jimerson, Klein, Bunney, & Goodwin, 1982; Traskman, Asberg, Bertilsson, & Sjostrand, 1981). However, low CSF levels of 5-HIAA also have been associated with violent or suicidal behavior in individuals with diagnoses other than depression (Traskman et al., 1981). Thus, low 5-HIAA may occur in more nonspecific clinical states or actually be associated with a predisposition toward impulsive or violent acts rather than depression per se. However, Banki and Arato (1983a) were not able to find any relationship between low CSF 5-HIAA and personality indexes of impulsivity and instability.

Recently, several large well-controlled investigations have failed to confirm existence of a distinct subgroup of depressed patients with low 5-HIAA (Banki, Arato, & Papp, 1983; Koslow et al., 1983). Further, the influence of a number of methodological factors on CSF 5-HIAA levels, such as patient age, sex, diet, or use of probenecid prior to lumbar puncture, have not been fully controlled (Banki, Arato, Papp, & Kurcz, 1983; Cowdry, Ebert, Van Kammen, Post, & Goodwin, 1983; Kelwala et al., 1983; Koslow et al., 1983; Murphy et al., 1978).

Research on possible abnormalities of plasma levels of L-tryptophan, a major dietary precursor of serotonin, in depression has not yielded conclusive results (DeMyer, Shea, Hendrie, & Yoshimura, 1981; Menna-Perper, Swartzburg, Mueller, Rochford, & Manowitz, 1983; Moller, Honore, & Larsen, 1983). Further, attempts to treat depression with serotonergic dietary precursors have met with only limited success (Murphy et al., 1978; van Praag, 1980a). More recent research also indicates that clinical effects of 5-hydroxy-tryptophan, a serotonergic precursor, are most apparent when tyrosine (a NE and DA precursor) is concurrently administered (van Praag, 1983). Thus, it would be premature to conclude that a subgroup of depression with a serotonergic deficiency has been definitively identified.

More recent investigations have employed methods developed to measure the number of serotonin receptor sites in depressives relative to normal controls and individuals with nonaffective psychiatric disorders. Research in this area was facilitated by the discovery that the antidepressant imipramine attached to serotonin receptor sites in the brain and on blood platelets. Use of radioactively labeled ^{3}H-imipramine enabled investigators to measure the number of these high-affinity serotonin receptors. To date, a number of reports have documented decreased number of serotonin receptor sites in depressed individuals relative to normal controls or patients with other psychiatric conditions (Baron, Barkai, Gruen, Kowalik, & Quitkin, 1983; Briley, Langer, Raisman, Sechter, & Zarifan, 1980; Suranyi-Cadotte, Wood, Schwartz, & Nair, 1983). Further, Meltzer and associates (Meltzer, Arora, Tricou, & Fang, 1983) also found evidence of a decreased number of serotonin receptor sites in depression using a distinctly different technique involving measurement of radioactively labeled ^{14}C-serotonin. Clinical studies indicate that approximately 45 percent of major depressives have reductions in the number of serotonin receptors which fall outside the normal range (Meltzer et al., 1983). Such reductions are found across diagnostic subtypes; that is, unipolar and bipolar, delusional and nondelusional, or endogenous and nonendogenous subtypes (Paul, Rehavi, Skolnick, Ballenger, & Goodwin, 1981; Meltzer et al., 1983). Treatment with antidepressant pharmacotherapy appears to result in increased number of ^{3}H-imipramine sites (Suranyi-Cadotte et al., 1983). Of particular interest, Meltzer et al. (1983) recently found that reduced serotonin uptake measurements tend to aggregate in families. Thus decreased number of serotonin receptors in depression does not appear to be a secondary effect of antidepressant medication and may actually represent a traitlike phenomenon.

As previously noted, in vitro effects of tricyclic antidepressants and monoamine oxidase inhibitors have provided indirect support for a monoamine deficit hypothesis. However, agents such as amphetamine and cocaine are powerful potentiators of noradrenergic transmission at the synapse, yet are poor or ineffective antidepressants (Zis & Goodwin, 1982). Similarly, the amine enhancing effects of tricyclics at the synapse are apparent within hours or days after drug administration, yet clinical response does not occur until two to four weeks later (Mindham, 1982; Paul, Hauger, & Skolnick, 1983). Clinical efficacy of several novel antidepressant agents which do not enhance synaptic levels of NE or 5-HT, such as iprindole or mianserin, also weighs against more simplistic interpretations of the monoamine hypotheses (Zis & Goodwin, 1982). Nevertheless, all clinically effective antidepressants have manifold effects on a variety of presynaptic and postsynaptic neurotransmitter receptor mechanisms (Charney, Menkes, & Heninger, 1981; Paul et al., 1983). In particular, chronic antidepressant treatment with tricyclics, MAOIs, lithium, and novel heterocyclic antidepressant agents produce a down regulation or desensitization of both 5-HT receptors and certain types of noradrenergic receptors (Charney et al., 1981; Paul et al., 1983; Snyder & Peroutka, 1982). With respect to the several types of postsynaptic adrenergic receptors, chronic antidepressant treatment consistently down-regulates the affinity of the beta-type receptors; that is, sites which are linked to adenylate cyclase, the enzyme which triggers the so-called second messenger system of neural transmission (Paul et al., 1983).

Less consistent evidence is emerging regarding the activity of alpha-2 type of adrenergic receptors in depressed patients prior to and during antidepressant treatment (Charney, Heninger, Sternberg, Hafstad, Giddings, & Landis, 1982; Garcia-Sevilla, Zis, Hollingsworth, Greden, & Smith, 1981; Stahl, Lemoine, Ciaranello, & Berger, 1983). Alpha-2 adrenergic receptors are identified by their affinity for substances, such as the antihypertensive drug clonidine, and include a class of presynaptic receptors (known as autoreceptors) which inhibit release of neurotransmitter.

Receptor effects of various classes of antidepressant agents also may be synergistic: Lithium has been found to desensitize 5-HT receptors and may potentiate a partial response to tricyclic antidepressants (de Montigny, Cournoyer, Morisette, Langlois, & Caille, 1983; Heninger, Charney, & Sternberg, 1983). Thus, a variety of antidepressant agents appear to exert effects independent of possible increases in monoamine levels in the synaptic cleft.

Summary

Twenty years of research activity have failed to support the original monoamine hypotheses of depression. Some evidence indicates lower levels of CNS noradrenergic function (at least as reflected by 24-hour urinary MHPG levels) in a subset of patients, especially those with bipolar syndromes. Other depressives show evidence of overactivity of catecholaminergic function. Serotonergic deficits (as measured by CSF 5-HIAA levels) also may exist in some endogenously depressed patients. However, it is unclear if 5-HIAA level is inversely related to urinary MHPG. Such a finding would be necessary in order to conclude that distinct serotonergic and noradrenergic deficiency subgroups exist. Results from one recent study (Koslow et al., 1983) do not support an inverse relationship existing between noradrenergic and serotonergic metabolites. Moreover, when monoaminergic deficits are detected, it is difficult to ascertain if reduced metabolite levels have pathogenetic significance or, more simply, represent a secondary effect of psychomotor retarda-

TABLE 6
Summary of empirical studies of the monoamine hypotheses.

1. No evidence of abnormal synthesis or degradation of monoamines (MA); no consistently detected alterations in enzymatic processes.

2. Evidence of decreased MA limited to subgroups with low 24-hour urinary MHPG or low CSF 5-HIAA; some patients show increased levels of catecholamines.

3. Inconsistent evidence of antidepressant effects for MA precursors; reserpine (an amine-depleting agent) reliably induces depression in vulnerable individuals.

4. Anitidepressents rapidly increase MA in the synapse; clinical efficacy may be more closely related to slower developing receptor alterations.

tion or low-anxiety levels. Evidence of diminished number of platelet serotonin receptors in major depression may represent a possible exception, as reductions do not appear related to treatment, diagnostic subtype, or clincial state. Further research with this possible marker of major depression is needed. Finally, data from investigations studying the effects of antidepressant pharmacotherapy indicate that "somatic" treatments produce effects on receptor mechanisms which are independent of simple increases in synaptic monoamine levels. Results from investigations testing the monoamine hypotheses are summarized in Table 6.

Acetylcholine

Janowsky and associates (Janowsky, El-Yousef, Davis, & Sekerke, 1972; Janowsky, Risch, & Gillin, 1983) have expanded the original monoamine hypotheses to include consideration of the balancing neuroregulatory role of acetylcholine (ACH). This work is based upon growing knowledge of the interrelationship of ACH and the monoamines in the CNS, as well as observations of the effects of cholinergic agonists in normals and clinical samples. The chemical structure of ACH and a listing of its precursors and enzymes can be found in Figure 1 and Table 4.

In brief, increasing central cholinergic tone results in a relative (and perhaps transient) decrease in functional NE or 5-HT activity in several brain regions (Janowsky et al., 1983). Conversely, interventions which enhance monoaminergic activity affect a relative decrease in cholinergic tone. Administration of cholinergic agonists produces a state of lethargy, anergia, and low-grade dysphoria in normals, and may worsen or precipitate depression in patient samples (Janowsky et al., 1983). Further, administration of cholinergic agonists, such as physostigmine or phosphatidylcholine to acutely manic patients may have therapeutic effects (Janowsky et al., 1983).

Unfortunately, accurate noninvasive measurement of ACH and its metabolites in the CSF is not possible. Several recent reports have not established a clear-cut case for cholinergic hyperactivity using indirect neurochemical methods. No evidence of increased cholinergic receptor affinity was found in the brain tissue of suicide victims relative to tissues from controls (Stanley, 1983). Another group found no evidence of a deficiency of acetylcholinesterase (the enzyme responsible for metabolizing ACH) in depression (Deutsch, Mohs, Levy, Rothpearl, Stockton, Horvath, Coco, & Davis, 1983). Other investigations concerning a possible state of cholinergic hyperactivity have employed alternative indirect models, such as neuroendocrine or neurophysiological responses to pharmacological challenges. For example, administration of physostigmine, a cholinesterase inhibitor, to normals can induce changes in selected neuroendocrine parameters which mimic abnormalities seen in severely depressed patients (Carroll, Greden, Haskett, Feinberg, Albala, Martin, Rubin, Heath, Sharp, McLeod, & McLeod, 1980; Doerr & Berger, 1983). Similarly, pharmacological induction of a cholinergic receptor supersensitivity state via chronic pretreatment with scopolamine or acute administration of cholinergic agonists can reproduce alterations in sleep neurophysiology in normal individuals which are identical to those which characterize major depression (Berger, Lund, Bronisch, & von Zerssen, 1983; Gillin, Sitaram, & Duncan, 1979; Sitaram, Moore, & Gillin, 1979).

Application of such findings have led to use of the cholinergic agonist, arecholine, as a pharmacologic probe for vulnerability to depression. While intravenous administration of this agent reliably shortens the latency to onset of rapid eye movement (REM) sleep in normals, nearly all of the remitted, drug-free bipolar depressives studied by one group of investigators show a supersensitive REM response to arecholine (Sitaram, Nurnberger, & Gershon, 1980; Sitaram, Nurnberger, Gershon, & Gillin, 1982). Not only did altered REM response to arecholine clearly differentiate between controls and recovered bipolar patients, but several never-ill controls with a family history of depression also showed such increased sensitivity (Sitaram et al., 1982). However, Berger et al. (1983) were unable to replicate this finding in a more heterogeneous sample of patients with bipolar, unipolar endogenous, and nonendogenous depressive disorders. Several methodological differences between these investigations may account for discrepant findings, and the depressed patients studied by Berger et al. (1983) did show a hyperaroused EEG sleep response to cholinergic stimulation with physostigmine. Further research is needed to ascertain if this marker of cholinergic hypersensitivity also is present in recovered nonbipolar depressives. Results from a recent study by Kupfer, Targ, and Stack (1982) suggest that this may be the case, as the REM sleep response following administration of amitriptyline, an antidepressant with strong anticholinergic properties, discriminated nonbipolar depressives with a family history of depression from closely matched patients with no family history of affective disorder. Similarly, Nurnberger, Sitaram, Gershon, and Gillin (1983) found traitlike consistency in arecholine-REM response in identical twins.

With respect to drug treatment studies, there is essentially no evidence to support the antidepressant efficacy of agents with purely anticholinergic properties. While most tricyclic antidepressants have some anticholinergic effects, such properties are not correlated with clinical efficacy or potency (Klein, Gittleman, Quitkin, & Rifkin, 1980). Moreover, several of the MAOI antidepressants, such as phenelzine and tranylcypromine, have virtually no anticholinergic effects (Klein et al., 1980). Thus, anticholinergic properties do not appear to be a prerequisite for antidepressant efficacy. However, Dilsaver and associates (Dilsaver, Kronfol, Sackellares, & Greden, 1983) recently suggested that withdrawal symptoms following discontinuation of anticholinergic tricyclic antidepressant medication might provide indirect evidence of cholinergic overactivity in major depression.

Summary

There is some indirect evidence of cholinergic hyperactivity in major depression. However, what proportion of clinical samples may be characterized by these disturbances is unclear. Further, given the interrelationship of cholinergic and monoaminergic systems, it is conceivable that lowered functional activity of NE or 5-HT might induce an imbalance suggestive of increased cholinergic tone.

Other Neurochemical Studies

In addition to study of monoamines and acetylcholine, other investigations have dealt with possible abnormalities of trace biogenic amines, intracellular electrolyte and mineral regulation, membrane transport mechanisms, cyclic nucleotides and prostaglandins in depression. Although such studies have not yet yielded conclusive evidence of specific biological disturbances, we will briefly consider several promising areas of investigation.

Over a decade ago, Sabelli and Mosnaim (1974) reviewed evidence indicating the possible role of the trace amine 2-phenylethylamine (PEA) in depression. This substance has considerable structural similarity to amphetamine, and has an activating or stimulating effect when administered exogenously. Several preliminary studies, using relatively nonspecific assay procedures, suggested decreased levels of urinary PEA excretion in rather heterogeneous groups of depressed patients (see Sabelli & Mosnaim, 1974). Subsequently, low levels of phenylacetate, the oxidized metabolite of PEA, were found in more homogenous group of untreated major depressives (Sabelli, Gusovsky, Fawcett, Javaid, & Edwards, 1983).

As PEA is normally metabolized by the enzyme monoamine oxidase, it has been suggested that the energizing and mood-stabilizing effect of the MAOI antidepressants might be the direct effect of increased PEA levels (Sabelli & Mosnaim, 1974). Conversely, it should be recognized that low PEA levels could represent an epiphenomenon of other monoaminergic alterations which affect MAO activity. Further research in this area is needed, particularly with respect to study of patients with other psychiatric conditions and by simultaneous measurement of other neurochemical parameters. Nevertheless, it has been suggested that low PEA levels may prove related to the etiopathogenesis of a subgroup of depressives who manifest symptoms similar to amphetamine withdrawal (i.e., anergia, hypersomnia, and weight gain), crave chocolate (a foodstuff rich in PEA), and who show a preferential response to MAOI antidepressants (Liebowitz & Klein, 1979).

With respect to electrolyte and mineral regulation, a number of investigators have reported increased levels of intracellular sodium and/or calcium concentrations in depression, with such elevated values decreasing during periods of recovery (see Colt, Dunner, Wang, Ross, Pierson, & Fieve, 1982; Dubovsky & Franks, 1983). It is unclear if these findings reflect structural changes in membrane transport mechanisms or, more simply, are secondary effects of elevated corticosteroid levels on electrolyte balance in depression. Nevertheless, increasing attention is being given to possible alterations of the mechanism responsible for tranportation of sodium and lithium across the cellular membrane (Dorus, Cox, Gibbons, Shaughnessy, Pandey, &

Cloninger, 1983), as well as to membrane mechanisms involving the enzyme adenosine triphosphatase ([ATPase]; Belmaker, 1981; Dubovsky & Franks, 1983; Linnoila, MacDonald, Reinila, Leroy, Rubinow, & Goodwin, 1983). High levels of ATPase activity in depression are of conceptual interest because of their role in catalyzing formation of cyclic adenosine monophosphate (cAMP), the so-called second messenger of neuronal transmission (Dubovsky & Franks, 1983). Further, recent research indicates that treatment with lithium may alter or antagonize several of these membrane mechanisms (Belmaker, 1981; Dubovsky, & Franks, 1983). As recent evidence indicates that aspects of such membrane mechanisms involve traitlike heritability (Dorus et al., 1983), continued research in this area appears promising.

One group of investigators recently reported decreased levels of prostaglandins in the CSF of depressed patients when compared to patients with schizophrenia or normal controls (Linnoila, Whorton, Rubinow, Cowdry, Ninan, & Waters, 1983). Although this finding was relatively robust, it also was unexpected and, at this time, has not been convincingly linked to either other biological abnormalities or a theoretical model of the etiopathogenesis of depression.

NEUROPHYSIOLOGICAL ABNORMALITIES

Electroencephalographic Sleep Studies

Most depressed patients experience some form of difficulty sleeping. However, patient reports of sleep disturbance have not proven particularly useful as diagnostic criteria or as predictors of antidepressant treatment response (Nelson & Charney, 1981; Thase & Kupfer, in press-b). Further, self-ratings of sleep disturbances are not highly correlated with observer ratings or electroencephalographic measurements (Feinberg, Carroll, Greden, & Zis, 1982; Kupfer & Thase, 1983). Application of the electroencephalogram (EEG) for objective study of the neurophysiology of sleep has permitted more precise study of sleep disturbances in depression. Further, EEG sleep studies have enabled investigators to evaluate aspects of sleep architecture which are not observable or otherwise measurable.

Extensive study over the past 20 years has revealed four basic types of EEG sleep disturbance in major depression: (1) sleep continuity disturbances; (2) decreased slow-wave sleep (3) altered distribution of rapid eye movement (REM) sleep, and (4) shortened latency to the onset of the first REM period (i.e., REM latency; see Table 7).

Characteristic EEG sleep profiles for a normal individual and an age-matched depressed outpatient are provided in Figure 3.

Indexes of sleep continuity disturbance include the amount of difficulty falling asleep, the number of nocturnal awakenings, and the amount of early morning awakening. About 80 percent of major depressives experience such difficulties (Gillin, 1983a; Kupfer & Thase, 1983). Gillin and associates (Gillin, Duncan, Pettigrew, Frankel, & Snyder, 1979) were able to discriminate

TABLE 7
Summary of EEG sleep abnormalities in depression

1. Poor sleep efficiency (nonspecific)*
   a. Difficulty falling asleep.
   b. Frequent nocturnal awakenings.
   c. Early morning awakening.

2. Reduced slow-wave sleep (nonspecific).

3. Altered REM sleep (relatively specific)
   a. Increased REM activity.
   b. Shifted REM time and REM activity into first hours of sleep.

4. Shortened REM latency (relatively specific)
   a. 60–90 percent of major depressives have values less than 60 minutes.
   b. 20–30 percent have sleep onset REM (SOREM) periods (i.e., less than 20 minutes).

   * Specificity refers to presence in depression but not other psychopathological states.

FIGURE 3
EEG sleep graphs in a normal individual and a patient with characteristic sleep disturbances

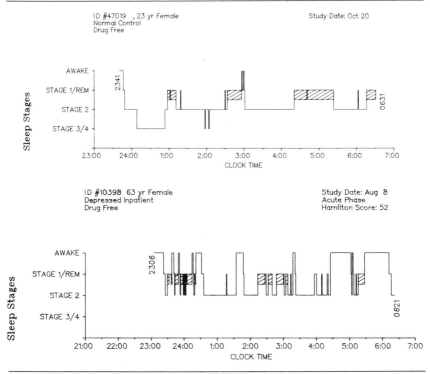

Source: Adapted from Kupfer and Thase, 1983.

reliably between a sample of hospitalized major depressives and normal controls using a multivariate function based on such EEG sleep measures. However, about 20 percent of major depressives do not experience significant sleep continuity disturbances (Kupfer & Thase, 1983). These patients often have bipolar disorder and exhibit either an absolute or a relative degree of hypersomnia (Kupfer, Foster, Detre, & Himmelhoch, 1975). When a discriminant function based on sleep continuity disturbance is applied to a bipolar sample, a number of patients may be misclassified as normal (Feinberg, Gillin, Carroll, Greden, & Zis, 1982). Further, sleep continuity disturbances are not specific to major depression: strong age-related effects are apparent and such changes are seen in a variety of psychopathological or medical-neurological conditions (Kupfer & Thase, 1983). Thus, while EEG measurement provides an objective assessment of sleep continuity disturbances, such data may not apply directly in understanding the pathophysiology of major depression. Further, improvements in sleep continuity noted during antidepressant treatment generally are not correlated highly with tricyclic drug blood levels (Thase & Kupfer, in press-b).

Similarly, decreased amount of slow-wave sleep (delta sleep; Stages 3 and 4) is a common, but relatively nonspecific phenomenon in major depression (Kupfer & Thase, 1983). Visually scorable delta sleep is often absent in depressives, which corresponds to patient reports of a light, restless sleep. Again aging and a variety of chronic nonaffective psychopathological and medical illnesses also are associated with decreased delta sleep (Kupfer & Thase, 1983). Nevertheless, the amount or percentage of delta sleep seen in depressives is substantially lower than observed in age-matched controls. This observation has led some investigators (Borbely & Wirz-Justice, 1982; Kupfer, Frank, Jarrett, Reynolds, & Thase, in press) to propose that a deficiency in a process related to generation of slow-wave sleep might underlie depression. Increases in delta sleep observed following sleep deprivation (a procedure with transient antidepressant effects; Gillin, 1983b) or during tricyclic antidepressant treatment support this hypothesis (Borbely & Wirz-Justice, 1982; Kupfer, Ulrich, Grochocinski, Doman, & Matthews, 1984). Further, the amount of slow-wave sleep increases in recovered depressives (Kupfer, 1981, 1982a). Additional research is needed to test the significance of deficits of slow-wave sleep in the etiopathogenesis of depression.

Unlike slow-wave sleep, REM sleep activity is frequently increased in major depression. While the actual percentage of REM sleep may not always be higher in depressed patients when compared to normals, the timing, distribution, and number of rapid eye movement sleep periods are characteristically altered. Normal individuals and most nonaffective patient populations experience the first REM period approximately 70–110 minutes after sleep onset, with successive REM periods of increasing length and intensity occurring at 90-minute intervals thereafter throughout the night (Williams, Karacan, & Hursch, 1974). In contrast, REM latency is substantially shortened in most major depressives (i.e., less than 60 minutes), with a corresponding shift of REM time and REM sleep activity into the first few hours of sleep

(Gillin, 1983a; Kupfer & Thase, 1983). Such REM disturbances are not solely the result of sleep continuity changes, as they also are observed in depressed patients with hypersomnia (Thase & Kupfer, in press-b).

Shortened REM latency in depression has now been replicated by at least 10 groups of independent investigators (see Kupfer & Thase, 1983; Thase, & Kupfer, in press-b). This degree of replicability is remarkable given the several alternative methods currently employed to measure REM latency (Reynolds, Taska, Jarrett, Coble, & Kupfer, 1983). Such findings cannot be attributed to effects of drug treatment, as most sleep researchers routinely employ a two-week, drug-free evaluation period prior to conducting all-night EEG studies (Kupfer & Thase, 1983). Shortened REM latency is found in outpatient as well as inpatient samples, and in unipolar, bipolar, and delusional forms of major depression (e.g., Duncan, Pettigrew, & Gillin, 1979; Feinberg et al., 1982; Kupfer & Thase, 1983). Overall, between 60–90 percent of a given clinical sample of depressed patients will evidence a shortened REM latency, compared to 5–30 percent of appropriately matched controls (see Kupfer & Thase, 1983; Thase & Kupfer, in press-b).

Several groups have described a bimodal distribution of REM latencies in samples of depressed patients, with one group showing modestly reduced values (i.e., 50–60 minutes) and another manifesting sleep onset REM periods (i.e., REM latency less than 20 minutes) (Coble, Kupfer, & Shaw, 1981; Schulz, Lund, Cording, & Dirlich, 1979). Review of REM latency data in a much larger sample of several hundred depressed patients studied in our sleep laboratory over the past 10 years does not reveal clear bimodality, and elsewhere we have suggested that this finding may be an artifact of sampling biases (Thase & Kupfer, in press-b). Extremely shortened REM latency values do, however, appear to be more common in older patients with severe agitated, melancholic, and/or delusional affective syndromes (Thase & Kupfer, in press-b). It is of interest that Schulz and Tetzlaff (1982) found that such patients also show extremely shortened latency to REM sleep following experimentally induced nocturnal awakenings. This suggests that while the normal 90-minute interval elapsing from onset of one REM period to onset of another REM period is not altered in depression, the mechanisms governing onset of the first REM period after sleep onset appear to be dysfunctional in more severely symptomatic patients.

Most investigators have found REM sleep disturbances to be more common in patients with more severe endogenous or melancholic depressions (Feinberg et al., 1982; Rush, Giles, Roffwarg, & Parker, 1982; Thase & Kupfer, in press-b). However, several groups report shortened REM latency in nonendogenous or atypical depressives as well (Berger, Doerr, Lund, Bronisch, & Von Zerssen, 1982; McNamara, Reynolds, Soloff, Mathias, Rossi, Spiker, Coble, & Kupfer, 1984; Quitkin, Schwartz, Liebowitz, Stewart, McGrath, Halpern, Puig-Antich, Tricamo, Sachar & Klein, 1982; Silberman & Post, 1982). Demonstration of shortened REM latency in patients with either agitated or anergic-retarded clinical presentations would indicate that this finding is not simply an epiphenomenon of level of motoric activity or anxiety. Indeed, EEG sleep of patients with depression can be readily distinguished from most individuals with insomnia (Gillin et al., 1979), generalized anxiety disorder (Reynolds, Shaw, Newton, Coble, & Kupfer, 1983), or panic disorder (Akiskal, 1983).

It is less certain that characteristic EEG sleep disturbances, such as REM latency, will be identified in children and adolescents with major depression (Lahmeyer, Poznanski, & Bellur, 1983; Puig-Antich, Goetz, Hanlon, Davies, Thompson, Chambers, Tabrizi, & Weitzman, 1982; Puig-Antich, Goetz, Hanlon, Tabrizi, Davies, & Weitzman, 1983; Thase & Kupfer, in press-b). Interestingly, Puig-Antich et al. (1982) found little evidence of specific EEG sleep abnormalities in acutely depressed children, yet shortened REM latency was seen in a follow-up study of the same sample of children after clinical recovery (Puig-Antich et al., 1983). Further work is needed in this area to clarify these discrepancies.

Cartwright (1983) recently extended the scope of EEG sleep research by demonstrating reduced REM latency in a number of women studied while in the process of divorce. Significant, albeit undiagnosed and untreated, depressive symptomatology was associated with REM sleep disturbances in this nonclinical sample (Cartwright, 1983). In contrast, more transient dysphoria in otherwise normal individuals is not associated with shortened REM latency (Cohen, 1979). Similarly, Zarcone and Benson (1983) found that most normal volunteers with modest elevations of self-reported depression scores do not have significantly shortened REM latency.

There is some question if shortened REM latency is specific to depression (Gillin, 1983a; Kupfer & Thase, 1983). For example, reduced REM latency is seen in a sizable proportion of patients with borderline personality disorder (Akiskal, 1981; Bell, Lycaki, Jones, Kelwala, & Sitaram, 1983; McNamara et al., 1984), obsessive-compulsive disorder (Insel, Gillin, Moore, Mendelson, Loewenstein, & Murphy, 1982; Rapoport, Elkins, Langer, Sceery, Buchsbaum, Gillin, Murphy, Zahn, Lake, Ludlow, & Mendelson, 1981), chronic pain syndromes (Blumer, Zorick, Heilbronn, & Roth, 1982), anorexia nervosa (Neil, Merikangas, Foster, Merikangas, Spiker, Neil, & Kupfer, 1980), and schizoaffective disorder (Kupfer, Broudy, Spiker, & Coble, 1979; Reich, Weiss, Coble, McPartland, & Kupfer, 1975). Although such findings might be considered to represent examples of "false positive" tests, considerable conceptual and clinical overlap exists between each of these conditions and the affective disorders.

Depressions developing in individuals with other, antecedent nonaffective psychopathological or medical conditions may also be associated with shortened REM latency. A recent study by our own group found that patients with depressions "secondary" to nonaffective psychiatric disorders had EEG sleep profiles which were indistinguishable from patients with uncomplicated major depression when samples were matched for age, severity, and endogeneity (Thase, Kupfer, & Spiker, 1984). However, many outpatients with "secondary" depressions have milder, nonendogenous syndromes, and EEG sleep studies in such patients frequently show REM latencies in the normal range (Akiskal, Lemmi, Yerevanian, King, & Belluomoni, 1982; Coble, Foster, & Kupfer, 1976).

REM latency generally becomes somewhat shorter with advancing age, such that many normal elderly individuals evidence REM latencies in the 40 to 60-minute range (Gillin, Duncan, Murphy, Post, Wehr, Goodwin, Wyatt, & Bunney, 1981; Reynolds, Spiker, Hanin, & Kupfer, 1983; Ulrich, Shaw, & Kupfer, 1980). Use of age-adjusted norms is needed to deal with this issue.

Some patients with narcolepsy also may evidence shortened REM latency (Kupfer & Thase, 1983). However Reynolds and his associates (Reynolds, Christiansen, Taska, Coble, & Kupfer, 1983) found that a number of sleep continuity and sleep architecture measures can be used to differentiate depression from narcolepsy.

Alcohol and drug-withdrawal states also may produce a transient shortening of REM latency (Kupfer & Thase, 1983). Since patients in such withdrawal states may present with either an agitated or anergic dysphoria, careful assessment and extended drug-free observation are needed to differentiate clinically significant secondary depressions from more transient syndromes. Postwithdrawal depressions which persist for several weeks after detoxification may have an EEG sleep profile which is virtually indistinguishable from "primary" major depression (Thase, Kupfer, & Spiker, 1984).

With respect to proposed biological mechanisms of depression, EEG sleep studies provide an indirect window to CNS neurophysiology. Investigations of sleep in normal individuals and animals suggest that serotonin and norepinephrine are reciprocally involved in induction and maintenance of non-REM sleep, with the timing and onset of REM sleep controlled by cholinergic processes (Gillin, Mendelson, Sitaram, & Wyatt, 1978; McCarley, 1982). Thus, alterations in any of these three neurotransmitter systems might underlie the sleep disturbances seen in depression (Thase & Kupfer, in press-b).

As we previously noted, some evidence does implicate the possibility of cholinergic receptor supersensitivity underlying the shortened REM latency and sleep efficiency disturbances seen in agitated unipolar depression (Gillin et al., 1979; Sitaram et al., 1979; Sitaram et al., 1982). In contrast, little evidence has emerged to support the role of purported monoaminergic disturbances in the sleep of depressed patients. Schildkraut et al. (Schildkraut, Keeler, Papouser, & Hartmann, 1973) reported an inverse relationship between urinary MHPG excretion and percentage of REM sleep time, although no such relationship was found in a larger, well-controlled study (Kupfer, Holzer, Edwards, Coble, Spiker, & Neil, 1980). Agren and Oreland (1982) found higher platelet MAO levels in unipolar patients who reported early morning awakening, although Kupfer and associates (Kupfer, Edwards, Spiker, Holzer, & Coble, 1979) did not find any relationship between MAO levels and EEG sleep indexes in unipolar depressives. Similarly Gaillard et al. (Gaillard, Iorio, Blois, & Tissot, 1981) found no association between alpha-adrenergic receptor sensitivity and EEG sleep. Finally Benson and associates (Benson, Zarcone, Faull, Barchas, & Berger, 1983) did find an inverse correlation between REM sleep density and CSF 5-HIAA levels in a heterogeneous group of psychiatric patients. However, this finding was most apparent in patients with schizophrenia. Thus, implications for the etiopathogenesis of depression seem questionable.

Results from studies of the effects of antidepressant treatments on the EEG sleep of depressed patients provide some additional information. At this time, it appears that most effective antidepressants produce a rapid and considerable suppression of REM sleep (Kupfer, 1981; Kupfer, 1982b; Thase & Kupfer, in press-b; Vogel, 1983). In particular, effective antidepressant treatment generally produces a > 50 percent decrease in the percentage of REM percent and a prolongation of REM latency to greater than 150 percent of the baseline time (Kupfer, 1981; Thase & Kupfer, in press-b). By contrast, improvements in sleep latency and sleep continuity disturbances appear to accompany clinical improvement in a more passive fashion (Thase & Kupfer, in press-b). Such REM-suppressing effects appear unrelated to the anticholinergic potency of the antidepressant agent, however, and it seems likely that multiple neurochemical mechanisms may affect REM suppression.

Vogel (1983) has suggested that REM suppression may be a common denominator of all effective antidepressant treatments. Indeed, the degree of REM rebound following either sleep deprivation (Duncan, Gillin, Post, Gerner, & Wehr, 1980; Gillin, 1983b; Vogel, 1983) or discontinuation of tricyclic antidepressants (Thase & Kupfer, in press-b) is correlated with antidepressant response. Conversely, patients who do not respond to pharmacotherapy generally do not evidence a significant sustained suppression of REM sleep or a pronounced REM rebound upon drug discontinuation (Kupfer, 1981; Thase & Kupfer, in press-b). However, the effects of ECT, perhaps the most efficacious treatment for severe depressive syndromes, on REM sleep are not clear cut, and even complete suppression of REM sleep with drug treatment does not invariably produce an antidepressant response (Thase & Kupfer, in press-b). Therefore, the possibility that a functional relationship exists between suppression of REM sleep and antidepressant response remains open to investigation. Further study is needed to elucidate the neurochemical mechanisms which underlie suppression of REM sleep.

Other Electroencephalographic Studies

There is no conclusive evidence to indicate that waking electroencephalographic rhythms of major depressives are abnormal in any consistent pattern (Kupfer & Reynolds, 1983). Of course, waking EEG studies may be of considerable use in differential diagnosis of atypical affective states, where unrecognized forms of epilepsy, particularly involving the temporal lobes, are sometimes detected (Himmelhoch, 1984).

More recent investigations have employed computers to provide quantitative and topographical measurements of waking EEG rhythms (see Kupfer & Reynolds, 1983). Unfortunately, research activity in this area generally has focused on patients with schizophrenia, with depressed patients often serving as control subjects (Kupfer & Reynolds, 1983). Further, many of the published studies employing these procedures suffer from a number of methodological problems, including imprecise sample definition, small sample sizes, and interlaboratory variability in experimental procedure.

Given these limitations, caution is needed in reviewing this literature. Several investigators have reported abnormal lateralization of waking EEG rhythms in major depression (d'Elia & Perris, 1973; Flor-Henry & Koles, 1980). The demonstration of either a relative increase in cerebral activity in the nondominant hemisphere or decreased function within the dominant hemisphere in clinically depressed patients is of some conceptual interest, since the nondominant cerebral hemisphere of the brain has been associated with the processing of negative affect and nonquantitative cognitive activity (Flor-Henry, 1979). However, other investigators have failed to find evidence of abnormal lateralization of EEG activity in depressives (see Kupfer & Reynolds, 1983; Lader, 1975). Further work in this area is needed to clarify these conflicting findings. It is relevant, however, that one group (Schaeffer, Davidson, & Saron, 1983) recently found hemispheric asymmetry of EEG rhythms in a very mildly depressed, nonpatient sample of student volunteers. Thus differences in hemispheric EEG activity may be more closely linked to a state of emotional arousal rather than to diagnostic groupings. If this is the case, then severely anergic, withdrawn depressed patients with marked psychomotor retardation might not be expected to manifest increased nondominant hemispheric activity.

Conflicting results also have been found using measurements of mean frequency and amplitude of EEG rhythms in depression (Kupfer & Reynolds, 1983). Research in this area is very complex, and many published studies suffer from the methodological limitations noted above. In particular, the effects of age, concurrent drug treatment, and recent withdrawal from either prescribed medications or alcohol and other nonprescription drugs on these EEG parameters must be controlled. Results from one relatively large and well-controlled investigation indicate that patients with major depression evidence a lower level of EEG activation than both age-matched normals and patients with schizophrenia or mania (Shagass, Roemer, & Straumanis, 1982). In particular, depressives had lower mean frequency and amplitude of EEG waves than controls, although few variables reliably discriminated between depressives and patients with personality disorders (Shagass et al., 1982). Indeed, across several studies the average EEG response amplitude in depressed patients is about 25 percent lower than seen in normals (Giedke, Bolz, & Heimann, 1980; Lader, 1975; Shagass, Roemer, Straumanis, & Amadeo, 1980; Shagass et al., 1982). Again, such a difference may be more closely related to clinical state rather than diagnosis, as manic and schizophrenic patients were found to have very similar quantitative EEG profiles (Shagass et al., 1982). Further, as 60 percent of Shagass et al.'s sample of depressives had bipolar disorder, it might be inferred that psychomotor retardation is linked to this pattern of low EEG activation (cf., Kupfer, Foster, Detre, & Himmelhoch, 1975). Nevertheless, the differences between diagnostic groups reported by Shagass et al. (1982) were not sufficiently specific to permit their application for differentiation of depression from normals or nonpsychotic patient groups (Kupfer & Thase, in press).

Buchsbaum and associates (Buchsbaum, 1975; Buchsbaum, Landau, Murphy, & Goodwin, 1973) have studied evoked EEG potentials in depressives, other patient groups, and normal controls. This sophisticated technique involves recording of specific EEG waves in response to an experimentally administered visual, auditory, or somatosensory stimulus. Briefly, several component wave alterations are noted to reliably occur in EEG leads following stimulation, and these wave forms are identified as P100, N120, and P200 on the basis of number of milliseconds elapsing following administration of the stimulus. P100 amplitude/intensity functions have been of particular interest, as patients with bipolar depression tend to augment P100 amplitude with increasing stimulus intensity, while nonbipolar depressives characteristically show a diminution of amplitude under such increasing stimulus intensity conditions. Validity of this "augmentor/reducer" dichotomy is indirectly supported by one pharmacological study, in which antidepressant response to lithium carbonate was predicted by an augmenting pattern on pretreatment evoked potential studies (Nurnberger, Gershon, Murphy, Buchsbaum, Goodwin, Post, Lake, Guroff, & McGinnis, 1979). Normal individuals generally show an intermediate type of response, although the pattern is perhaps closer to a "reducer" P100 response (Buchsbaum, 1975).

Several groups have studied the relationship between pain tolerance and evoked potential responses in patients with affective disorders (Buchsbaum, Davis, Goodwin, Murphy, & Post, 1980; von Knorring, Espvall, & Perris, 1974). Such studies are of interest because patients with nonbipolar forms of major depression frequently manifest a variety of pain-related complaints. However, neither an "augmenting" nor a "reducing" P100 evoked potential response has been consistently related to pain threshold, although a diminished N120 response is found in depressed patients with insensitivity to pain (Buchsbaum et al., 1980). As both the N120 and P200 evoked potential components appear more closely related to level of emotional arousal than to diagnostic subgroup (Buchsbaum, 1975), increased pain tolerance in depressed patients may, in part, be a function of attentional factors. This speculation is indirectly supported by the work of von Knorring et al. (1974), who found that increased pain tolerance characterized patients with more severe or psychotic forms of depression.

Results from a more recent investigation indicate that P100 evoked potential patterns normal volunteers tended to shift toward a "reducer" profile when subjects are stressed by 40 consecutive hours of sleep deprivation (Buchsbaum, Gerner, & Post, 1981). By contrast, a predominantly bipolar sample of depressed patients actually showed a modest improvement in mood following sleep deprivation, which was associated with increased visual evoked potential amplitude and augmenting response to stimulus intensity.

These findings illustrate that neurophysiological differences between clinically depressed patients and nondepressives may be qualitative as well as quantitative. Other work by Buchsbaum (1975) would suggest that the augmenting P100 response in bipolar depressives is not state dependent and, thus, may have traitlike properties. These findings require independent replication. Nevertheless, evoked potential differences between subgroups of depressives and normals are not striking enough to permit their use as a diagnostic aid. For example, Buchsbaum et al. (1981) found that pretreatment P100 evoked potential patterns did not discriminate either bipolar or unipolar depressives from normal controls in a study employing relatively small sample sizes. The value of evoked potential studies therefore may be limited to research examining the unipolar-bipolar diagnostic dichotomy or to investigations of the neurophysiological effects of various antidepressant therapies.

Abnormalities of Smooth Pursuit Eye Movements

Several groups have studied smooth pursuit eye movements in patients with affective disorders as compared to both normal controls and individuals with schizophrenia. Although abnormalities in smooth pursuit eye movements generally have been found to characterize schizophrenia (e.g., Lipton, Levy, Holzman, & Levin, 1983), a substantial minority (20–40 percent) of patients with bipolar or schizoaffective disorders show evidence of dysfunction (Holzman, Proctor, Yasillo, Meltzer, & Hurt, 1974; Iacono & Lykken, 1979; Klein, Salzman, Jones, & Ritzler, 1976; Lipton, Levin, & Holzman, 1980; Shagass, Amadeo, & Overton, 1974). However, it is conceivable that either effects of medication and/or diagnostic errors might account for such a high degree of overlap between patients' schizophrenia and affective disorders (Levy, Lipton, Yasillo, Peterson, Pandey, & Davis, in press; Spohn & Larson, 1983).

Results of two recent studies employing the RDC diagnostic system support this notion. First, Iacono and associates (Iacono, Peloquin, Lumry, Valentine, & Tuason, 1982) found that the proportion of patients with a diagnosis of unipolar or bipolar affective disorder who evidenced abnormal smooth pursuit eye movements was not significantly different from that of a sample of normal controls. Moreover, current treatment with lithium carbonate was found to be associated with an increased number of abnormal eye movements in the patients with affective disorders (Iacono et al., 1982). Second, in contrast to schizophrenia, first-degree, never-ill relatives of patients with affective disorder were no more likely than normal controls to have abnormal smooth pursuit patterns (Levy, Yasillo, Dorus, Shaughnessy, Gibbons, Peterson, Janicak, Gaviria, & Davis, 1983). Thus, it appears likely that once potential sources of error are controlled this neurophysiological abnormality may prove to be more specific to schizophrenic disorders than to the affective disorders.

Neuroradiological Abnormalities

Although early studies employing neuropathological methods, skull X rays, and pneumoencephalographic imaging of the cerebral cortex failed to identify any characteristic abnormalities in most depressed patients, use of more sophisticated neuroradiological techniques to study for possible structural and/or functional abnormalities in the brains of patients with the affective disorders is increasing.

Introduction of the computed axial tomograph (CAT) scan of the brain in the early 1970s has provided a much more detailed noninvasive method for visualizing brain structures than previously available. At the simplest level, this test is useful for identification of clinically silent tumors or mass lesions in patients with complex or atypical affective presentations. This particular use of the CAT scan appears justified in selected patients, although the low probability of finding such a lesion in an uncomplicated patient would not justify routine study of all depressed patients.

However, as was the case with quantitative EEG studies, there has been considerable interest in the CAT scans of schizophrenic patients. Again, both depressed and manic patients have been studied as nonschizophrenic controls. A number of investigators have documented that a substantial number of schizophrenic patients have atrophy of the cerebral cortex; that schizophrenic patients with cortical atrophy tend to respond poorly to neuroleptic medication; and that such patients have a more chronic (i.e., process) clinical course (Luchins, 1982; Nasrallah, Jacoby, McCalley-Whitters, & Kuperman, 1982; Tsai, Nasrallah, & Jacoby, 1983; Weinberger, DeLisi, Perman, Targum, & Wyatt, 1982). Several recent investigations have found a similar incidence of atrophy in patients with unipolar or bipolar affective syndromes (Kellner, Rubinow, Gold, & Post, 1983; Rieder, Mann, Weinberger, van Kammen & Post, 1983; Standish-Barry, Bouras, Bridges, & Bartlett, 1982). Jacoby and Levy (1980a) also found cortical atrophy in a subgroup of patients with late-onset affective disorders. Thus, the CAT scan may not be particularly useful for differentiating depression from senile dementia in elderly patients (Jacoby & Levy, 1980b, 1980c; Reynolds, Spiker, Hanin, & Kupfer, 1983).

There is no evidence that the cortical atrophy seen in patients with affective disorders is a toxic effect of previous treatment with either ECT or medication (Rieder et al., 1983; Standish-Barry et al., 1982). It remains to be seen whether a prior history of alcohol abuse is etiologically related to these changes, as a large percentage of patients with bipolar affective disorder have a concomitant or remote history of heavy drinking (Himmelhoch, Fuchs, May, Symons, & Neil, 1981). Kellner et al. (1983) found that bipolar patients with cortical atrophy also had elevated levels of excretion of urinary-free cortisol. Given an association between advancing age, clinical symptomatic profile (i.e., melancholic subtype of depression), and hypercortisolemia, it is conceivable that this finding is an artifact of sample characteristics (Kupfer & Thase, in press). Further work is needed to ascertain if depressed patients with cortical atrophy represent a subgroup who respond poorly to antidepressant therapies. This seems plausible since patients over age 60 are less likely to respond to tricyclic antidepressants than younger depressives (see Thase & Kupfer, in press-a). Moreover, Jacoby and Levy (1980a) found higher mortality in depressed patients with cortical atrophy during a longitudinal follow-up.

Recently, several groups have applied new methods for measurement of cerebral metabolism for study of affective disorders. Findings from these preliminary studies are pertinent to the question of abnormal hemispheric lateralization in depression, suggested earlier in this chapter. Among four investigations measuring cerebral blood flow in different brain regions as an index of cerebral metabolism, no significant differences were found between depressives and normals by two research groups (Gustafson, Johanson, Risberg, & Silfverskiold, 1981; Gustafson, Risberg, & Silfverskiold, 1981; Ingvar, unpublished paper, cited by Uytdenhoef, Portelange, Jacquy, Charles, Linkowski, & Mendlewicz, 1983), one group reported decreased cerebral blood flow in both hemispheres (Mathew, Meyer, Francis, Semchuk, Mortel, & Claghorn, 1980; Mathew, Meyer, Semchuk, Francis, Mortel, & Claghorn, 1980), and Uytdenhoef et al. (1983) found evidence of both left frontal hyper-vascularization and right posterior hypovascularization in major depression. Uytdenhoef et al. (1983) also found relatively normal regional cerebral blood flow in patients with subsyndromal, minor depressive conditions, as well as normal metabolic patterns in recovered bipolar depressives. Results of these four studies are difficult to reconcile, and it is conceivable that methodological differences may account for some degree of the variability. Nevertheless, the findings do not clearly support the hypothesis of increased nondominant lateralization in major depression at this time. As noted by Ingvar (1981), use of strategies to measure cerebral blood flow in psychopathological states is still in its infancy.

Positron emission tomography (PET) scanning recently has emerged as an alternative method for quantifying and visualizing disordered brain metabolism (Buchsbaum, Ingvar, Kessler, Waters, Cappelleti, van Kammen, King, Johnson, Manning, Flynn, Mann, Bunney, & Skoloff, 1982). This method employs intravenous administration of radioactively labeled 2-deoxyglucose, with use of a high-resolution tomographic scanner to visualize areas with low or high levels of cerebral metabolic activity. This sophisticated and extremely expensive procedure has been used in a small number of studies with psychiatric patients, and particular attention has been devoted to investigation of possible hypoactive cerebral metabolic activity in patients with schizophrenia (e.g., Buchsbaum et al., 1982). Preliminary evidence from one investigation studying a small number of depressed patients suggests relatively increased nondominant hemispheric cerebral glucose metabolism when compared to normals or patients with schizophrenia (Kling, Kuhl, Metter, Kurtz, Phelps, Riege, & Huellett, 1983). Treatment with antidepressants or ECT appeared to reverse this abnormality. Obviously, many more patients with affective disorders need to be studied with the PET scanner before firm conclusions can be reached. However, this method appears to have great promise with respect to resolving the question of abnormal hemispheric lateralization in major depression.

Measurement of Psychomotor Disturbances

Psychomotor disturbances are quite common in clinically depressed patients, with both retardation and agitation included as diagnostic criteria for major depression in the RDC and *DSM-III* systems. Development of relatively small and unobtrusive portable recording devices have enabled investigators to complement more traditional ratings of psychomotor behavior with more objective, around-the-clock measurements (Greden & Carroll, 1981). Not surprisingly, rather low correlations have been found between global clinical ratings and activity measurements, which suggests that the methods actually may tap into different dimensions of behavior (Kupfer & Reynolds, 1983). It remains to be seen whether activity measurements provide information which is clinically useful above and beyond that provided by traditional rating methods.

Studies of patients with bipolar affective disorder demonstrate rather striking changes in psychomotor activity level when patients shift from depression to hypomania or mania. Further, when compared to normals, manic patients demonstrate greater levels of activity during the evening and night (Kupfer, Foster, Detre, & Himmelhoch, 1975). Comparisons of bipolar and unipolar major depressives tend to support clinical observations of differences between these subtypes, with bipolar patients exhibiting lower activity levels while acutely depressed (Kupfer, Foster, Detre, & Himmelhoch, 1975). Such psychomotor activity differences also parallel characteristic EEG sleep findings, with low-activity levels correlated with the presence of hypersomnia, and high-activity levels associated with marked sleep continuity difficulties (Kupfer, Foster, Detre, & Himmelhoch, 1975). During treatment with tricyclic antidepressants, motor activity levels initially tend to decrease, reflecting a general sedating property of these medications (Kupfer et al., 1975b). Clinical recovery often is associated with normalization of activity patterns, although correlations between motor activity changes and degree of improvement are not striking (Kupfer & Reynolds, 1983).

Schwartz and associates (Schwartz, Fair, Salt, Mandel, & Klerman, 1976a, 1976b; 1979) have applied neuromuscular measurement techniques for study of more subtle disturbances of facial muscle expression in depression. Changes observed in depressed patients tend to mirror involuntary changes in facial muscle activity observed in normal subjects asked to visualize "sad" images. Further, asymmetry of facial muscle expression in depression indirectly supports the notion of increased nondominant cerebral hemispheric function in individuals with affective disorders (Schwartz et al., 1979). Greden and Carroll (1981) have suggested that this procedure might prove particularly useful in evaluating patients with "masked" depressive syndromes. At a broader level, video recording methods have been applied to analyze differences in posture and gait existing in normals and depressed patients. However, as was the case with other types of automated activity recording, it remains to be seen whether such measurements offer incremental validity over traditional observational methods.

Electrodermal Activity Recording

Given the dysphoria, agitation, and anxiety experienced by many clinically depressed patients, one might expect that major depression would be characterized by a state of autonomic overactivity. Indeed, tachycardia is frequently described in acutely depressed, unmedicated patients. However, a number of investigators have reported that major depression is often characterized by low tonic electrodermal activity when compared to normal values (Christie, Little, & Gordon, 1980; Giedke et al., 1980; Iacono, Lykken, Peloquin, Lumry, Valentine, & Tuason, 1983; LaPierre & Butter, 1980; Mirkin & Coopen, 1980; Ward, Doerr, & Storrie, 1983). In contrast, research with schizophrenic patients has yielded more variable results, with samples generally including distinct subgroups with either overactive or hypoactive electrodermal responses (Spohn & Patterson, 1979; Zahn, 1976).

Efforts to relate low electrodermal activity with clinical variables have produced some contradictory results. For example, low levels of electrodermal activity have generally been associated with psychomotor retardation and endogenous subtype of depression (see Christie et al., 1980), while normal or high levels have been reported in studies examining milder, reactive depressions or in patients with marked psychomotor agitation (Byrne, 1975; LaPierre & Butter, 1980; Lader & Wing, 1969; Mirkin & Coppen, 1980). However, several groups have failed to find such associations (Iacono et al., 1983; McCarron, 1973). Results of the Iacono et al. (1983) study are especially interesting, in that lowered electrodermal activity was found in both unipolar and bipolar patients. Further, a similar proportion of unipolar (58 percent and bipolar (54 percent) patients failed to emit an electrodermal response to a series of tones, compared to only 24 percent of age-matched normal controls ($p < .01$). Ward et al. (1983) found an even higher incidence of this abnormality in their sample of depressives, as well as fewer "false positive" test results in their control group.

Although not all studies in this area employed a drug-free, washout period prior to psychophysiological testing, data from several investigations do not indicate a pronounced effect for either antidepressant medications or lithium on electrodermal activity (Breyer-Pfaff, Gaertner, & Giedke, 1982; Iacono et al., 1983; Storrie, Doerr, & Johnson, 1981). Nevertheless, until an investigation is completed which employs both a sufficiently long drug-free, washout (i.e., greater than two weeks) and retesting of an untreated comparison group of depressed patients, the possibility of a drug-treatment artifact cannot be definitely ruled out.

The finding of lowered electrodermal activity is of some conceptual interest, given frequent reports of dry mouth and constipation in unmedicated depressed patients. These factors might point to a lowered peripheral cholinergic tone in some depressed patients (Christie et al., 1980). It is not clear how such observations relate to current theories of hyperactive cholinergic function in depressed patients (e.g., Janowsky et al., 1983). Relatively decreased peripheral cholinergic tone might be viewed as a compensatory consequence of elevated peripheral levels of catecholamines seen in some depressed patients. However, one would expect normalization of this transient phenomenon with clinical recovery. Several groups have studied electrodermal activity in depressed patients before and after somatic treatment. Generally, electrodermal activity remains low even following significant clinical improvement (Breyer-Pfaff et al., 1982; Stern, Sila, & Word, 1960; Storrie et al., 1981). Similarly, low electrodermal tone has been found in patients in a stable state of remission (Iacono et al., 1983). Long-term studies suggest that this measure is relatively stable, with a test-retest $r = 0.71$ ($p < .001$) reported over a one-year interval (Iacono et al., 1983). Thus, low electrodermal activity may prove useful as a vulnerability or trait marker for major depression, even though the etiopathogenetic meaning of this finding remains rather obscure.

Colonic Motility Studies

Lechin and associates (Lechin, Van der Dijs, Acosta, Gomez, Lechin, & Arocha, 1983; Lechin, Van der Dijs, Gomez, Arocha, Acosta, & Lechin, 1983) recently studied colonic motility patterns in depressed patients as an alternative index of autonomic nervous system function. Low levels of colonic neuromuscular tone were found to be associated with clinical ratings of anergia and psychomotor retardation, while patients with high levels were found to have agitated and anxious features (Lechin, Van der Dijs, Acosta, Gomez, Lechin & Arocha, 1983). Colonic motility ratings subsequently were found to predict differential treatment response to antidepressant pharmacotherapy, with patients having low motility scores showing marked intolerance to fenfluramine, a serotonergic agonist. These interesting findings warrant further study, particularly with respect to the apparent adverse interrelationship between psychomotor retardation, low levels of colonic motility, and poor response to treatments which do not directly affect adrenergic function.

Summary

Neurophysiological studies have detected a variety of abnormalities in depressed individuals. Unequivocal evidence documents several characteristic disturbances of EEG sleep rhythms in depression. Most notable is the presence of shortened REM sleep latency, an abnormality which may be linked to hyperactive cholinergic function. Study of waking EEG evoked potential responses in depression do not reveal major qualitative or quantitative differences from normal controls, although the pattern of response appears to reliably discriminate between bipolar and unipolar forms of affective disorder. By contrast, low electrodermal activity is relatively common in all clinical forms of severe depression. In both cases, however, the pathogenetic significance of the abnormalities is not yet known. Low levels of both psychomotor activity and colonic motility also are seen in a subgroup of depressives. Such findings have been linked closely to the clinical features of motor retardation and anergia, and therefore may represent either epiphenomena of the behavioral state or neurophysiological correlates of a core psychobiological distur-bance. Results from studies measuring facial muscle activity, cerebral blood flow, and spectral analysis of waking EEG rhythms suggest abnormal laterali-zation of brain activity in depression. This might take the form of either increased nondominant (i.e., right hemisphere) or decreased dominant cere-bral activity in depression. It should be recognized that these findings are consistent with results from analogous experiments of cerebral lateralization in normals during more transient period of unhappiness or dysphoria. Thus, abnormal lateralization in depression may reflect psychophysiological amplifi-cation of affective changes seen in depressed individuals. Such abnormal cerebral lateralization in depression is not associated with structural brain changes. However, diffuse cortical atrophy may be seen in a subset of individ-uals with severe or chronic affective syndromes. Research employing the recently introduced procedure known as positron emission tomography will help resolve many of these questions, since it provides direct, yet noninvasive visualization of cerebral metabolic activity. Finally, depressed patients do not appear to have a high rate of abnormality of smooth pursuit eye movements once effects of medication are controlled. This indicates that abnormal smooth pursuit eye movements are relatively specific for the diagnosis of schizophrenia.

NEUROENDOCRINE ABNORMALITIES

It has long been suspected that endocrinological changes might accompany the more severe depressive syndromes. For example, the now outdated con-cept of involutional melancholia was based on the premise that endocrino-logic changes of menopause led to an increased vulnerability for depression in women at midlife (see Weissman, 1979a). Moreover, it was clearly recog-nized that patients with a variety of diseases of the endocrine glands, includ-ing hypo- and hyperthyroidism, Cushing's disease, and hyperparathyroidism, occasionally presented with an endogenomorphic depressive syndrome. More detailed investigations of the interrelationship of depression and endo-crine dysfunction were made possible by numerous advances in the 1950s and 1960s, which ultimately led to the establishment of neuroendocrinology as a subspecialty area. Such advances, including development of sensitive assay procedures for measurement of small quantities of hormones and eluci-dation of the vascular channels connecting the hypothalamus and pituitary gland, have enabled sophisticated study of the regulation of endocrine func-tions (Bergland & Page, 1979; G. M. Brown & Seggie, 1980).

Identification of feedback regulation mechanisms by which the hypothal-amus and pituitary control hormonal secretion presented particularly inter-esting possibilities for affective disorders researchers (see G. M. Brown & Seggie, 1980). First, these areas are contiguous with brain centers involved in regulation of sleep, appetite, and sex drive; that is, behaviors which are frequently disturbed in severe depressions. Second, it subsequently was recognized that control of the hypothalamic releasing factors involved in neuro-endocrine regulation are mediated by the same neurotransmitters implicated in the various monoamine and cholinergic hypothesis of depression, (i.e., norepinephrine, serotonin, dopamine, and acetylcholine). Thus, not only did clinical data suggest a potential association between endocrinological dysfunction and depression, but a clear theoretical link also was apparent. Since the early 1970s, the neuroendocrinology of depression has been a topic of intense investigative efforts. In the next subsections, we will consider evidence pertaining to abnormalities of the hypothalamic-pituitary-adrenal cortex (HYPAC) systems, the hypothalamic-pituitary-thyroid axis, regulation of growth hormone, insulin and prolactin secretion, and endorphins. The possibility of neuroendocrine factors underlying observed sex differences in the incidence and prevalence of depression also will be briefly considered. We initially will focus on more basic abnormalities within each system, then subsequently address possible interrelationships between neuroendocrine parameters (when known) and associations between endocrine or neurochemical and EEG sleep disturbances.

HYPAC Axis Abnormalities

The relationship between stress and elevations of plasma cortisol with urinary 17-hydroxycorticosteroid levels has been known for some time, with hypercortisolemia viewed as part of a normal adaptational process to stress (Rose, 1980). Therefore, when a number of investigators reported elevated levels of cortisol in the plasma and urine of depressed patients, it seemed most parsimonious to conclude initially that such changes represented a nonspecific indicator of stress (Carroll, 1978; Sachar, Asnis, Halbreich, Nathan, & Halpern, 1980). However, even as early as 1966, Rubin and Mandell suggested that such elevations of cortical actually might be the result of an unidentified CNS dysfunction etiologically related to depression. Considerable efforts over nearly two decades have led to partial confirmation of this hypothesis (Carroll, 1982; Sachar, 1982).

Approximately one half to three quarters of most inpatient samples of depressed patients exhibit elevated secretion of cortisol (see Figure 4). Such elevations are detectable in the plasma and urine, as well as in the CSF of depressed patients (Gerner & Wilkins, 1983; Traskman, Tybring, Asberg, Bertilsson, Lanotto, & Schalling, 1980). In more severe cases, the degree of hypercortisolemia approaches the levels seen in Cushing's disease (Carroll, 1978). However, unlike patients with Cushing's disease, depressed patients generally do not show peripheral signs of hypercortisolemia, such as skin changes, truncal obesity, or development of a "buffalo hump" fat pad on the back. Increased levels of secretion of cortisol in depression also are generally higher than values seen in "stressed" normal individuals or in acutely distressed schizophrenic patients. Further, cortisol elevations may be seen in withdrawn, apathetic, or even catatonically immobile patients, which underscores the likelihood that the high levels of cortisol secretion in depression

FIGURE 4
24-hour plasma cortisol curves for normals and severely depressed
inpatients*

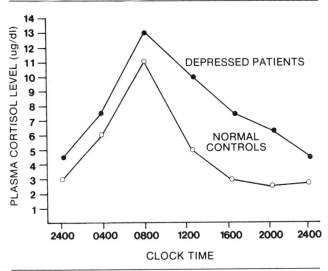

* Depressives show elevated mean cortisol values, elevations during the evening and night, and blunted diurnal cortisol rhythm.

Source: E. J. Sachar, G. Asnis, U. Halbreich, R. S. Nathan, and F. Halpern, "Recent Studies in the Neuroendocrinology of Major Depressive Disorders," *Psychiatric Clinics of North America,* 3 (1980), pp. 313–326.

are not secondary to increased activity level or overt distress (Carroll, 1982; Sachar, 1982).

In addition to hypersecretion of cortisol, many depressed patients show abnormalities of circadian regulation of the HYPAC. Unlike normals, who have peak cortisol levels in the morning (i.e., 6–10 A.M.) and low levels during the later afternoon and evening, severely depressed patients often show a blunted circadian cortisol rhythm, with relatively high values noted throughout the day (Carroll, 1982; Sachar, 1982). Particularly elevated cortisol levels are seen in depressed patients during the evening, with an early increase in cortisol secretory activity occurring after the onset of sleep (Carroll, 1978; Jarrett, Coble, & Kupfer, 1983; Sachar, 1982; Sachar, Asnis, Halbreich, Nathan, & Halpern, 1980; Sherman, Pfohl, & Winokur, 1984). Such abnormalities often are studied in inpatients because of the necessity for frequent collection of blood samples.

Secretion of cortisol normally is controlled by adrenocorticotropic hormone (ACTH), a long-chain neuropeptide. ACTH is secreted from the pituitary in short-lived bursts or "pulses" at times of stress or when plasma steroid levels are low. ACTH release, in turn, is triggered by a hypothalamic neuropeptide, corticotropin-releasing factor (CRF). The HYPAC system is regulated further by a negative feedback inhibition loop, in which high plasma levels of

FIGURE 5
Schematic illustration of the hypothalamic-pituitary-adrenal cortex
(HYPAC) axis.

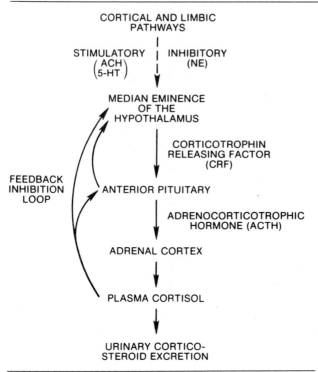

cortisol normally turn off release of both CRF and ACTH (see Figure 5). The system also may be "driven" by neural activity from pathways above the hypothalamus, including neural transmission from projections from the limbic system and the cerebral cortex.

Another index used in the study of hypersecretion of the HYPAC axis in depression involves administration of a potent, synthetic cortisol-like drug, dexamethasone, to try to suppress endogenous release of cortisol. This approach is referred to as the dexamethasone suppression test (DST). The DST has been widely used in clinical medicine since the mid-1960s as a rapid screening test for the diagnosis of Cushing's disease. In 90–95 percent of normal individuals, a test dose of one or two milligrams of dexamethasone provides sufficiently strong feedback inhibition to suppress adrenal secretion of plasma cortisol levels to less than 5 mcg/ml for 24 to 36 hours (Carroll, 1982; Sachar, Asnis, Halbreich, Nathan, & Halpern, 1980). In contrast, between 33 and 67 percent of hospitalized major depressives will show either a failure to suppress plasma cortisol levels following dexamethasone (i.e., elevated cortisol levels throughout the day) or early escape from suppression in the later afternoon or evening (Carroll, 1982; Kalin, Risch, Janowsky, & Murphy, 1981). The DST is now perhaps the most widely studied psychobiological parameter in patients with major depression (Kupfer & Thase, in press).

tions, type of cortisol assay, dosage and timing of dexamethasone administra-
The accuracy, reliability, and validity of the DST are dependent upon a number of methodological considerations. These factors include use of stringent medical exclusionary criteria, the number of plasma cortisol determinations, type of cortisol assay, dosage, and timing of dexamethasone administration, and length of drug-free interval (also see Hirschfeld, Koslow, & Kupfer, 1983). With proper standardization and rigorous control of such factors, it originally was felt that DST nonsuppression would prove to be highly specific for the more severely melancholic or endogenous forms of major depression (Carroll, 1982; Kalin, Risch, Janowsky, & Murphy, 1981). Indeed, studies employing milder samples of outpatient major depressives rather consistently have found relatively low rates of DST nonsuppression (i.e., 15–30 percent; see Amsterdam, Winokur, Caroff, & Conn, 1982; Coryell, Smith, Cook, Moucharafieh, Dunner, & House, 1983; Jaffe, Barnshaw, & Kennedy, 1983; Peselow, Goldring, Fieve, & Wright, 1983; Rabkin, Quitkin, Stewart, McGrath, & Puig-Antich, 1983; Rush, Schlesser, Roffwarg, Giles, Orsulak, & Fairchild, 1983). These observations are supported by several investigations studying symptomatic correlates of DST nonsuppression, which noted significant relationships between nonsuppression and various diagnostic criteria of endogenous depression, such as psychomotor disturbances, middle and early insomnia, weight loss, and so forth (Kasper & Beckmann, 1983; Nasr & Gibbons, 1983; Reus, 1982; Tosca, Fenoglio, Zerbi, Romani, Bezzi, Ferrari, & Canepari, 1982). Both hypercortisolemia and DST nonsuppression also have been linked to suicidal behavior (Banki & Arato, 1983b; Ostroff, Giller, Bonese, Ebersole, Harkness, & Mason, 1982; Targum, Rosen, & Capodanno, 1983). Investigation of HYPAC functioning in patients across recurrent episodes of depression suggests a rather high level of stability: approximately 70–80 percent of major depressives show identical DST test results in consecutive episodes (Brown & Qualls, 1982; Coryell & Schlesser, 1983; Grunhaus, Greden, Carroll, & Shein, 1983).

However, more recent studies have documented relatively high rates (i.e., 20–40 percent) of DST nonsuppression in some samples of patients with chronic schizophrenia (Carman, Wyatt, Crews, Hall, Scalise, Watts, & Hoppers, 1981; Dewan, Pandurangi, Boucher, Levy, & Major, 1982) or acute schizophreniform disorders (Targum, 1983c), senile dementia (Balldin, Gottfries, Karlsson, Lindstedt, Langstrom, & Walinder, 1983; Raskind, Peskind, Rivard, Veith, & Barnes, 1982; Spar & Gerner, 1982), obsessive-compulsive disorder (Insel, Kalin, Guttmacher, Cohen, & Murphy, 1982), borderline personality disorder (Carroll, Greden, Feinberg, Lohr, James, Steiner, Haskett, Albala, DeVigne, & Tarika, 1981), anorexia nervosa or bulimia (Gwirtsman, Roy-Byrne, Yager, & Gerner, 1983; Hudson, Laffer, & Pope, 1982), recently detoxified patients with a history of chronic alcoholism (Newsom & Murray, 1983; Swartz & Dunner, 1982; Targum, Wheadon, Chastek, McCabe, & Advani, 1982), and obese individuals who have recently lost 10 kg of body weight

(Edelstein, Roy-Byrne, Fawzy, & Dornfeld, 1983). High rates of DST nonsuppression also may be seen in mania or in patients with mixed affective states (Arana, Barreira, Cohen, Lipinski, & Fogelson, 1983; Evans, & Nemeroff, 1983; Graham, Booth, Boranga, Galhenage, Myers, Teoh, & Cox, 1982; Krishnan, Maltbie, & Davidson, 1983; Stokes, Stoll, Koslow, Maas, Daavis, Swann, & Robins, 1984). The relationships between HYPAC disturbances and mania is not yet clear, however, as other groups have found very low rates of DST nonsuppression in manic patients (Carroll, 1982; Schlesser, Winokur, & Sherman, 1979). Nevertheless, the specificity of this particular abnormality of the HYPAC system for endogenous depression appears lower than originally suspected.

Such diagnostic nonspecificity raises several interesting points. First, as both significant weight loss (i.e., >10 kg) and recent abuse of alcohol or sedative-hypnotic medications are known to affect the HYPAC system (see Kalin, Risch, Janowsky, & Murphy, 1981), high rates of DST abnormalities in nondepressed patients with either of these conditions illustrate the limits of application of the DST. Second, as typified by Blumer and associates' (1982) work with chronic pain patients, a number of patients with "false-positive" DST nonsuppression actually may have atypical or masked forms of depression. This explanation may be most relevant in understanding HYPAC disturbances in patients with personality disorders (Carroll et al., 1981), bulimia (Hudson et al., 1982), and obsessive-compulsive disorder (Insel, Kalin, Guttmacher, Cohen, & Murphy, 1982). As we noted earlier, clinical, natural history, and treatment response data suggest that such complicated conditions appear to share a common boundary with the affective disorders (Akiskal & Cassano, 1983; Kupfer & Thase, in press). Similarly, converging lines of research ultimately may support the validity of the diagnosis of major depression in children and adolescents, where preliminary evidence regarding high rates of DST nonsuppression is beginning to accumulate (Crumley, Clevenger, Steinfink, & Oldham, 1982; Extein, Rosenberg, Pottash, & Gold, 1982; Geller, Rogol, & Knitter, 1983; Poznanski, Carroll, Banegas, Cook, & Grossman, 1982; Robbins, Alessi, Yanchyshyn, & Colfer, 1982; Targum & Capodanno, 1983). Finally, in conditions such as senile dementia, where a large number of "false positive" test results have been noted, the DST may provide a useful experimental approach in order to improve understanding of the biochemical differences and similarities between conditions. In this regard, some evidence links advancing age with DST nonsuppression in both normals (Oxenkrug, Pomara, McIntyre, Branconnier, Stanley, & Gershon, 1983) and depressives (Berger et al., 1982; Spar & LaRue, 1983).

Within samples of major depressives, it has been rather consistently shown that the highest rates of DST nonsuppression are seen in patients with delusional syndromes (Caroff, Winokur, Rieger, Schweizer, & Amsterdam, 1983; Carroll, Greden, Feinberg, James, Haskett, Steiner, & Tarika, 1980; Mendlewicz, Charles, & Franckson, 1982; Rothschild, Schatzberg, Rosenbaum, Stahl, & Cole, 1982; Schatzberg, Rothschild, Stahl, Bond, Rosenbaum, Lofgren, MacLaughlin, Sullivan, & Cole, 1983). Patients with primary major depression are more likely to manifest DST nonsuppression than secondary depressives (see Carroll, 1982). However, it is possible that differences in age or severity between primary and secondary groupings might account for these findings (Thase, Kupfer, & Spiker, 1984). Overall, patients with endogenous (RDC) or melancholic *(DSM-III)* subtypes of major depression tend to have higher rates of DST nonsuppression, although several notable negative reports also have been published (Berger et al., 1982; Coryell, Gaffney, & Burkhardt, 1982a; Meltzer, Fang, Tricou, Robertson, & Piyaka, 1982; Stokes et al., 1984). Abnormal DSTs also may be found more often in patients with a family history of depression (Coryell, Gaffney, & Burkhardt, 1982b; Schlesser et al., 1979; Targum, Byrnes, & Sullivan, 1982a), although this difference appears to be diminished or absent in studies of patients with severe or psychotic depressive syndromes (Carroll, Greden, Feinberg, James, Haskett, Steiner, & Tarika, 1980; Mendlewicz et al., 1982; Rudorfer, Hwu, & Clayton, 1982). No consistent differences in DST nonsuppression rates have been found to discriminate between bipolar and unipolar depressions (Carroll, 1982).

Studies of hospitalized depressed patients receiving treatment usually reveals a normalization of the DSTs with clinical improvement (Carroll, 1982; Greden et al., 1980; Greden, Gardner, King, Grunhaus, Carroll, & Kronfol, 1983; Holsboer, Liebl, & Hofschuster, 1982). Conversely, preliminary data indicate that persistent nonsuppression during a course of treatment is associated with either nonresponse or a high risk of relapse (Greden et al., 1983; Holsboer, Liebl, & Hofschuster, 1982; Targum, 1983c; Yerevanian, Olafsdottir, Milanese, Russotto, Malon, Baciewicz, & Sagi, 1983). Curiously, the physiological effects of repeated seizures experienced during a course of ECT may induce a more transient normalization of the DST, which is not predictive of a subsequent positive outcome (Coryell & Zimmerman, 1983). Longitudinal study of a small number of remitted patients suggests that the DST may "revert" to nonsuppression prior to a clinical relapse (Carroll, 1982; Holsboer, Steiger, & Maier, 1983). Thus, it could be concluded that the DST has properties of a state marker for the more severe depressive syndromes.

If one speculates that this marker also has pathogenetic importance, then it might prove useful in selecting the proper biological treatment for depressed patients (Brown, Johnston, & Mayfield, 1979). To date, however, there is conflicting evidence as to whether DST results can be used to "tailor" an antidepressant treatment regimen (Brown et al., 1979; Coryell, 1982; Fraser, 1983; Greden et al., 1983; Greden, Kronfol, Gardner, Feinberg, Mukhopadhyay, Albala, & Carroll, 1981; Nelson, Orr, Stevenson, & Shane, 1982; Peselow, Fieve, Goldring, Wright, & Deutsch, 1983). In fact, several groups report relatively poorer response to pharmacotherapy in patients with DST nonsuppression (Amsterdam, Winokur, Bryant, Larin, & Rickels, 1983a; McLeod, 1972; Spar & LaRue, 1983). Such findings might have been anticipated, since an increased number of DST nonsuppressors are older patients with agitated or delusional melancholic depressive syndromes. Thus, a relatively high proportion of depressed patients with DST nonsuppression may require combination of a neuroleptic plus an antidepressant or ECT (Thase & Kupfer, in press-a). Very preliminary data (Rush, 1983; Thase & Kupfer, in press-a) indicate that DST nonsuppression may predict nonresponse to psychological treatments for depression. Similarly, Carroll (1982) has noted that hospitalized depressed patients who are DST nonsuppressors generally do not show a significant clinical response to milieu therapies during a drug-free observation period. Therefore, DST nonsuppression may represent a relative indication for the need for some form of somatic treatment rather than a psychosocial approach (Rush, 1983; Thase, 1983).

The relationship between DST nonsuppression and EEG sleep abnormalities has been studied by several groups (Asnis, Halbreich, Sachar, Nathan, Ostrow, Novacenko, Davis, Endicott, & Puig-Antich, 1983; Berger et al., 1982; Blumer et al., 1982; Feinberg, 1982; Rush, Giles, Roffwarg, & Parker, 1982; Rush, Schlesser, Roffwarg, Giles, Orsulak, & Fairchild, 1983). Results consistently indicate that nearly all depressed patients with DST nonsuppression also have shortened REM latency. Concordance of these measures is particularly striking when REM latency is very short (i.e., <40 minutes). This finding is especially interesting when one considers that REM latency is not closely associated with patterns of nocturnal cortisol secretion in normal individuals (Kupfer, Bulik, & Jarrett, 1983).

The close interrelationship between DST nonsuppression and short REM latency suggests a common neurobiological mechanism, as will be discussed below. Depressed patients who manifest both DST nonsuppression and shortened REM latency often show a cluster of clinical characteristics, including prominent endogenomorphic symptomatology, high global severity, presence of agitation and/or delusions, and relatively older age (i.e., >40 years old). When these tests have been concurrently obtained, approximately 20–40 percent of patients with normal DSTs (and an unequivocal clinical diagnosis of major depression) show shortened REM latency. A practical implication of this finding is recognition that shortened REM latency is a more sensitive biological indicator of endogenous depression than the DST (see Chapter 14 by Fawcett and Kravitz in this book). However, shortened REM latency also may prove to be a less specific marker of endogenous depression than the DST (Rush et al., 1982).

Haier (1983) studied the relationship between DST response and EEG evoked potentials. Contrary to the investigator's initial hypothesis, DST nonsuppression was closely linked to a stimulus-reducing evoked potential response, rather than a stimulus-augmenting pattern in this sample. Such a finding would suggest that DST nonsuppression is associated with a high level of neurophysiological arousal, a notion which also is supported by several studies employing neurochemical measures which are discussed below.

Efforts to identify the neurochemical disturbance(s) underlying HYPAC dysfunction have been only partially successful. Although multiple neurotransmitters impact on HYPAC axis regulation at various points, it can be concluded that hypercortisolemia and DST nonsuppression most likely reflects a disinhibition phenomenon mediated at the hypothalamic level by either excessive cholinergic activity and/or a norepinephrine deficiency state (see Carroll, Greden, Haskett, Feinberg, Albala, Martin, Rubin, Heath, Sharp, McLeod, & McLeod, 1980; Kalin, Risch, Janowsky, & Murphy, 1981). This hypothesis is supported by several reports documenting elevated ACTH levels in major depression, which indicates that an abnormality may exist above the pituitary (Demisch, Demisch, Bochnik, & Schulz, 1983; Kalin, Weiler, & Shelton, 1982; Nasr, Rodgers, Pandey, Altman, Gaviria, & Davis, 1983; Reus, Joseph, & Dallman, 1982; Yerevanian, Woolf, & Iker, 1983). However, it should be noted that one group failed to find high ACTH levels in depressives (Fang, Tricou, Robertson, & Meltzer, 1981).

Direct infusions of ACTH have yielded contradictory results in depressed patients, although one recent methodologically sound investigation found an exaggerated cortisol response to ACTH infusion (Amsterdam, Winokur, Abelman, Lucki, & Rickels, 1983). This might indicate hyperactivity of the adrenal cortex in depression, as well as a hypothalamic dysfunction (Amsterdam, Winokur, Abelman, Lucki, & Rickels, 1983). Other groups report that administration of dexamethasone is associated with blunted release of either aldosterone (Holsboer, Dorr, & Sippell, 1982) or prolactin (Meltzer et al., 1982) in depressed persons as compared to controls. Although the exact mechanisms of such effects are not known, it seems unlikely that a single hypothalamic dysfunction (i.e., disinhibited release of ACTH) accounts for these multiple neuroendocrine abnormalities (Meltzer et al., 1982).

Some evidence implicates a possible role for cholinergic overactivity in HYPAC axis abnormalities. Carroll et al. (Carroll, Greden, Haskett, Feinberg, Albala, Martin, Rubin, Heath, Sharp, McLeod, & McLeod, 1980) and Doerr and Berger (1983) found that administration of physostigmine, a cholinergic agonist, induces dexamethasone nonsupression in normal volunteers. These findings parallel the effects of cholinergic agonists on REM sleep reviewed earlier in this chapter. Of course, artificially reproducing a phenomenon does not necessarily ensure that the phenomenon is actually caused by in vivo disturbance of that neurotransmitter system in clinically depressed patients. For example, transiently perturbing the cholinergic-noradrenergic balance via administration of physostigmine might mimic an analogous, naturally occurring effect caused by a deficit of norepinephrine, or altered receptor mechanisms.

Several groups have studied the relationship between HYPAC function and catecholamines. Administration of a test dose of amphetamine or methamphetamine (i.e., drugs which are potent noradrenergic agonists) was found to paradoxically decrease plasma cortisol levels in depressed patients, while normal controls experienced a rise in plasma cortisol (Checkley, 1979; Sachar, Asnis, Nathan, Halbreich, Tabrizi, & Halpern, 1980; Sachar, Halbreich, Asnis, Nathan, Halpern, & Ostrow, 1981). Indeed, such paradoxical cortisol responses to amphetamine were found in about two thirds of a sample with endogenous major depression, and were most likely to occur in patients with baseline hypercortisolemia (Sachar et al., 1981). These findings suggest that administration of amphetaminelike drugs might transiently normalize a noradrenergic deficiency in the hypothalamus, which in turn leads to an increased inhibition of cortisol secretion. This hypothesis is supported by results from two investigations, in which depressed patients with DST nonsuppression were not found to exhibit an euphoric response following administration of the amphetaminelike stimulant methylphenidate (Brown & Brawley, 1983; Sternbach, Gwirtsman, & Gerner, 1981). However, it should be noted that the neurotransmitter mechanisms which mediate amphetamine's effects on the HYPAC are not yet fully understood (Sachar et al., 1981).

Siever and associates (Siever, Uhde, Jimerson, Post, Lake, & Murphy, 1984) recently tested the effects of clonidine, a drug with more specific effects on the noradrenergic system than amphetamine, on plasma cortisol in major depressives and matched controls. A test dose of clonidine was found to produce marked reduction in plasma cortisol levels in depressed patients when compared to either within-subjects changes observed during a placebo-administration period or the responses of normal controls following clonidine administration. Since clonidine preferentially stimulates presynaptic alpha-type adrenergic receptors, these findings would suggest hyporesponsivity of these sites in depression, rather than an actual norepinephrine deficiency. If such a hypothesis is correct, then both hypercortisolemia and diminished response to clonidine in depression should be associated with evidence of excessive peripheral adrenergic activity, which in turn is related to blunted presynaptic receptor function. Consistent with this, Siever et al. (1984) did report a significant inverse correlation ($r = -.54, p < .05$) between baseline cortisol levels and reductions in plasma MHPG concentrations following clonidine administration in their depressed patients. Thus, depressed patients with high cortisol levels fail to show a normal reduction in peripheral adrenergic activity in response to stimulation of inhibitory alpha-receptors by clonidine.

Several lines of evidence also support this hypothesis. Level of plasma unconjugated MHPG recently was found to be closely correlated with post-dexamethasone plasma cortisol level (Jimerson, Insel, Reus, & Kopin, 1983). Therefore, high levels of peripheral norepinephrine (at least as detected by plasma MHPG) are associated with DST nonsuppression and hypercortisolemia. Significant relationships also have been reported between urinary-free cortisol and both urinary MHPG excretion (Stokes, Fraser, & Casper, 1981; Rosenbaum, Maruta, Schatzberg, Orsulak, Jiang, Cole, & Schildkraut, 1983) and platelet MAO level (Schatzberg, Orsulak, Rothschild, Salomon, Lerbinger, Kizuka, Cole, & Schildkraut, 1983). Similarly, one group has reported elevations of plasma levels of norepinephrine and epinephrine in depressed patients who had high post-dexamethasone cortisol levels when compared to depressives with normal DSTs (Barnes, Veith, Borson, Verhey, Raskind, & Halter, 1983). Although results from one study are not in agreement (Davis, Hollister, Mathe, Davis, Rothpearl, Faul, Hsieh, Barchas, & Berger, 1981), overall, these findings would indicate a high level of peripheral adrenergic activation in depressions associated with HYPAC abnormalities. As previously noted, such a state would be compatible with a hypofunction of presynaptic noradrenergic receptor mechanisms in depression.

There is little direct evidence to suggest that serotonergic abnormalities are causally related to the HYPAC disturbances seen in depression (Banki & Arato, 1983a; Traskman et al., 1980; Westenberg, van Praag, de Jong, & Thijssen, 1982). Further, Meltzer et al. (1983) found that a diminished number of serotonin uptake sites in depressed patients was not related to DST nonsuppression. By contrast, experimentally induced elevations of corticosteroid levels actually may induce higher levels of both HVA and 5-HIAA in the CSF (Banki, Arato, Papp, & Kurcz, 1983; Rothschild, Schatzberg, Langlais, Cole, & Bird, 1983). Such an increase in HVA (i.e., the major metabolite of dopamine in the CSF), actually might be the cause of increased evening activity levels, agitation, and even delusions seen in severely depressed patients. Moreover, as such severely depressed patients often evidence DST nonsuppression and hypercortisolemia, this may provide a biochemical basis for the efficacy of adjunctive use of dopamine-blocking antipsychotic medications in agitated and/or psychotic depressives who have not responded to treatment with a tricyclic alone (Thase & Kupfer, in press-a). Further research is needed to establish the in vivo relationship between hypercortisolemia, CNS dopaminergic activity, clinical state, and treatment response.

Thyroid Axis Disturbances

Interest in the possible role of thyroid abnormalities in major depression also was prompted by clinical observations of affective changes in patients with thyroid disease. Hypothyroidism generally is characterized by fatigue, anergia, and weight gain, with a full depressive syndrome commonly seen in patients with myxedema (Gold & Pottash, 1983; Whybrow & Prange, 1981). Conversely, patients with hyperthyroidism often exhibit an anxious or agitated dysphoria, accompanied by weight loss and insomnia (Whybrow & Prange, 1981).

Surveys of thyroid hormone levels in large series of clinically depressed patients reveal chemical hypothyroidism in only a small number (e.g., 2–5 percent) of patients (Gold & Pottash, 1983; Whybrow & Prange, 1981). This percentage is somewhat higher in patient samples receiving lithium, as this agent is known to induce hypothyroidism (Jefferson & Greist, 1977; Vestergaard, Amidsen, & Schou, 1980). In addition to clinical hypothyroidism, high levels of a physiologically inactive thyroid hormone, reverse T3, have been found in a number of depressed and manic patients (Kirkegaard & Faber, 1981; Linnoila, Lamberg, Roseberg, Karonen, & Welin, 1979; Linnoila, Lamberg, Potter, Gold, & Goodwin, 1982). Such elevations appear to decrease with clinical recovery (Linnoila, Cowdry, Lamberg, Makinen, & Rubinow, 1983). The pathophysiological significance of high levels of reverse T_3 is not known, although reports of elevations in both mania and depression would indicate that such findings are probably not implicated in the anergia and psychomotor retardation seen in depression.

Curiously, a relatively high percentage of acutely depressed patients show mild elevations in levels of circulating thyroid hormone (Whybrow & Prange, 1981). Such transient increases in thyroxine levels are not attributable to thyroid disease per se: They normalize with clinical recovery and also are noted in acutely ill patients with other, nonaffective disorders (Whybrow & Prange, 1981). It has been suggested that increased levels of thyroxine might represent a compensation for low noradrenergic output (Whybrow & Prange, 1981).

More recently, development of accurate radioimmunoassay techniques for measurement of thyroid-stimulating hormone (TSH), as well as methods for synthesis of thyroid-releasing hormone (TRH), have enabled investigators to study the integrity of the hypothalamic-pituitary-thyroid axis in depression (see Figure 6).

Normal control of this axis is based on a feedback loop: low peripheral levels of circulating thyroid hormone trigger hypothalamic release of TRH, which in turn modulates increased pituitary secretion of TSH. In cases of thyroid failure, high levels of TSH are secreted in an attempt to increase production of thyroid hormone. In patients with milder, compensated forms of hypothyroidism (whether clinically depressed or not), an enlarged thyroid

FIGURE 6
Schematic illustration of the hypothalamic-pituitary-thyroid axis

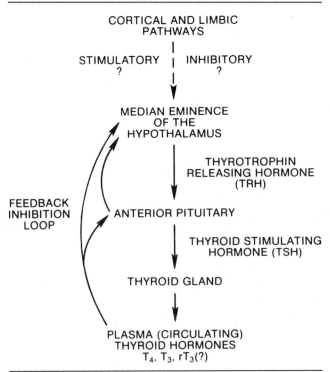

gland (i.e., goiter), high TSH levels, and, in certain cases, detectable levels of antithyroid autoantibodies are found. However, levels of circulating thyroid hormone may be maintained in the normal range. These patients also will show an exaggerated TSH response to intravenously administered thyroid-releasing hormone. Other individuals will have no evidence of a goiter and normal TSH levels, yet still show an *exaggerated* response to a test-dose of TRH. Longitudinal study of a number of depressed patients with exaggerated TSH responses indicates that this abnormality reflects an early (subclinical) form of slowly progressive thyroid disease (Gold & Pottash, 1983). Recent surveys of thyroid status employing both TSH levels and TRH-stimulation testing suggest that up to 8–15 percent of depressed patients will evidence milder or subclinical forms of hypothyroidism (Gold, Pottash, & Extein, 1981; Sternbach, Gold, Pottash, & Extein, 1983). Further, antidepressant medication often produces suboptimal results with these patients until the subtle thyroid deficiency is corrected by administration of supplemental thyroid hormone (Whybrow & Prange, 1981; Targum, 1983b).

Systematic application of the TRH stimulation test in large samples of major depressives rather consistently have found a blunted TSH response in 25–40 percent of patients (Kirkegaard, 1981; Loosen & Prange, 1982; Sternbach, Gerner, & Gwirtsman, 1982). This abnormality is not related to level of circulating thyroid hormone and is opposite of what is observed in hypothyroidism. Blunted response to a standardized test dose of TRH (i.e., <5 unit rise in TSH level over a 60-minute time period) is seen more often in depression than in normal controls or in patient groups with nonaffective psychiatric disorders (Kirkegaard, 1981; Loosen & Prange, 1982; Sternbach et al., 1982).

The TRH stimulation test is currently under investigation as a possible laboratory marker of major depression (see Chapter 14 in this volume for a more detailed discussion). However, several questions regarding the diagnostic specificity of the TRH test for depression remain to be answered (Kupfer & Thase, in press). As was the case with the DST, a number of medical illnesses and medications may affect TRH stimulation test results (see Kirkegaard, 1981; Loosen & Prange, 1982). In particular, high rates of blunted TSH responses are seen in alcoholics, and such "false-positive" test results may be observed in a high proportion of recovered, nondepressed alcoholics even after years of abstinence (Loosen, Wilson, Dew, & Tipermas, 1983). Blunted TSH response also occurs in a substantial minority of patients with mania (Extein, Pottash, Gold, Cadet, Sweeney, Davies, & Martin, 1980) or borderline personality disorder (Garbutt, Loosen, Tipermas, & Prange, 1983). Such findings have led to the suggestion that a blunted TSH response may be useful to rule out a diagnosis of schizophrenia (Extein, Pottash, Gold, & Martin, 1980). However Langer and associates (Langer, Aschauer, Koinig, Resch, & Schonbeck, 1983) found blunted responses to TRH in 4 of 11 patients with schizophrenia. While it is conceivable that these patients actually had an unrecognized form of bipolar affective disorder, this seems unlikely since schizophrenia was diagnosed according to the rather conservative RDC system. Further, even if TRH test differences between manic and schizophrenic patients are more extensively replicated, the possible confounding effects of alcohol abuse (TSH blunting) or neuroleptic treatment (increased TSH response) would limit clinical application.

Within the major depression diagnostic grouping, some evidence suggests higher rates of TSH blunting are observed in individuals with more severe, recurrent melancholic or endogenous depressions (Kirkegaard, 1981). Further, several groups have found a higher proportion of patients with blunted responses to TRH in unipolar samples relative to patients with bipolar depressions (Gold, Pottash, Ryan, Sweeney, Davis, & Martin, 1980; Gold, Goodwin, Wehr, & Rebar, 1977). However, these findings have not been widely replicated (Amsterdam, Winokur, Lucki, Caroff, Snyder, & Rickels, 1983; Davis, Hollister, Mathe, Davis, Rothpearl, Faul, Hsieh, Barchas, & Berger, 1981; Linkowski, Brauman, & Mendlewicz, 1981). Furthermore, a recent history of lithium treatment may alter TSH responses in some bipolar patients, leading to a higher proportion of patients with normal or even exaggerated responses. Unlike the DST, TSH blunting does not appear to be more common in depressed patients with a family history of affective disorder (Targum, Byrnes, & Sullivan, 1982b), although further study of this topic is needed.

Repeated study with TRH stimulation tests during the course of antidepressant treatment and longitudinal follow-up reveal that a majority of patients whose TSH responses are initially blunted experience a normalization of test results upon clinical recovery (Kirkegaard, 1981). Persistent TSH blunting generally has been found to be a correlate of either nonresponse to somatic treatment or a high risk of relapse (Kirkegaard, 1981; Targum, 1983a). Furthermore, persistent TSH blunting may have poor prognostic implications for patients with acute schizophreniform disorders (Langer et al., 1983; Targum, 1983c).

Results of TRH stimulation tests have been compared with other biological "markers" of major depression, including the DST and EEG sleep studies (Amsterdam, Winokur, Lucki, Caroff, Snyder, & Rickels, 1983; Berger et al., 1982; Gold, Pottash, Extein, & Sweeney, 1981; Kirkegaard & Carroll, 1980; Mendlewicz, Hoffman, Linkowski, Kerkhofs, Goldstein, van Haelst, L'Hermite, Robyn, van Cauter, Weinberg, & Weitzman, 1983; Rush et al., 1983; Targum, 1983a; Targum, Sullivan, & Byrnes, 1982; Winokur, Amsterdam, Caroff, Snyder, & Brunswick, 1982). Perhaps somewhat surprisingly, virtually no relationship has been found between TSH blunting and DST nonsuppression, with only a chance level of concordance (i.e., 10 percent) existing between these tests. This finding is of theoretical importance since it was originally suspected that the blunted TSH response was caused by hypercortisolemia (see Kirkegaard & Carroll, 1980). Further, the low concordance between TRH stimulation test and DST results would indicate that abnormalities of these two tests might be related to different pathophysiological disturbances.

As was the case with the DST, many patients with TSH blunting also have shortened REM latency (Berger et al., 1982; Rush et al., 1983). Again, shortened REM latency identifies about twice as many depressed cases as TRH test results. Combination of the TRH stimulation test and the DST achieve fairly high sensitivity for clinical diagnosis of endogenous major depression (e.g., 60–75 percent), a level approximating the prevalence of shortened REM latency in these patients (Berger et al., 1982; Mendlewicz et al., 1983; Rush et al., 1983). This might indicate that shortened REM latency is caused by several distinctly different neurochemical abnormalities.

Several investigators have attempted to relate TSH blunting to proposed neurochemical abnormalities in depression. Basic research on mechanisms controlling TRH release indicates that either a CNS norepinephrine deficiency or an excess of dopaminergic stimulation might account for TRH test blunting (Kirkegaard, 1981; Loosen & Prange, 1982). However, Davis et al. (1981) found that in patients with primary depression, urinary MHPG values were significantly higher in patients with blunted TRH tests. In contrast, Sternbach, Kirstein, Pottash, Gold, Extein, and Sweeney (1983) reported that low-urinary MHPG levels were associated with blunted TSH responses in men, but not women. Methodological differences between these investigations might account for such contradictory findings, and the limitations (reviewed earlier in this chapter) of urinary MHPG as an index of CNS noradrenergic function warrant caution in interpreting these results. Winokur and associates' (Winokur, Amsterdam, Oler, Mendels, Snyder, Caroff, & Brunswick, 1983) recent observation of a variety of abnormal pituitary hormone responses following TRH administration might indicate a heightened variability of neuroendocrinologic responsiveness to this neuropeptide, rather than a specific neurochemical deficit.

Insulin Tolerance Test Findings

Several investigators have described low utilization of glucose and relative insulin resistance in depressed patients (Heninger, Mueller, & Davis, 1975; Koslow, Stokes, Mendels, Ramsey, & Casper, 1982; Mueller, Heninger, & McDonald, 1969; Sachar, Finkelstein, & Hellman, 1971; Wright, Jacisin, Radin, & Bell, 1978). Insulin resistance refers to a blunted or diminished lowering of blood sugar following administration of an exogenous dose of the pancreatic hormone, insulin. Roughly 25–50 percent of endogenously depressed patients fail to show a normal hypoglycemic response to a test dose of insulin, and this abnormality usually reverses with clinical recovery (e.g., Sachar et al., 1971; Wright et al., 1978). Anecdotal reports also suggest improvements in glucose control in diabetic depressed patients following ECT. One group (Lewis, Kathol, Sherman, Winokur, & Schlesser, 1983) has reported persistent insulin resistance in about one half of recovered patients with bipolar depression, as well as a similar percentage of recovered unipolar patients with a family history of depression.

There is an obvious parallel in the data from these studies with the previously described work on HYPAC abnormalities in depression. In particular, it is known that high plasma cortisol levels diminish the sensitivity of cellular insulin receptors (Sachar, 1982). Further, significant correlations have been reported between afternoon and evening cortisol levels and degree of insulin resistance seen in depressed patients (Sachar, 1982). Results from the study by Lewis et al. (1983) indicate that persistent insulin resistance in recovered depressives may be related to persistent dexamethasone nonsuppression. Thus, it would appear that abnormal insulin resistance in depressed patients is secondary to HYPAC axis disturbance.

Growth Hormone Regulation

Unlike research on HYPAC and thyroid regulation, interest in growth hormone secretion in depression was not originally guided by a clinical correlation between a neuroendocrine illness and development of an affective syndrome. Rather, interest in growth hormone (GH) responses in depressed patients has been of a more theoretical nature, given the location of GH secreting cells in the anterior pituitary, the control of GH secretion by both a hypothalamic inhibiting factor (somatostatin) and/or excitatory noradrenergic and dopaminergic stimulation, and the predictable peak of secretion during slow-wave sleep (see Brown, Seggie, Chambers, & Ettigi, 1978). Thus, study of GH regulation in depression provides the opportunity to test the role of a variety of proposed neurochemical and neurophysiological disturbances in depressed patients.

Unfortunately, several aspects of GH regulation are not well suited for study in depressed patients. For example, secretion of GH generally occurs in several, short-lived bursts during the day, necessitating nearly constant measurement. Further, factors such as stress, physical activity, and food intake can provoke GH release, and level of circulating estrogen has a pronounced effect on GH regulation (Brown et al., 1978; Sachar, 1982).

Given so many variables potentially affecting secretion, it is not surprising that several promising leads involving GH abnormalities in depression have not been supported by subsequent investigations. In each case, negative results were obtained by investigators employing more rigorous control of potentially confounding variables. For example, Langer and associates (Langer, Heinze, Reim, & Matussek, 1976) reported that GH response to a test dose of amphetamine was markedly blunted in endogenously depressed patients when compared to normal controls or nonaffective psychiatric patients. Subsequently, Halbreich and associates (Halbreich, Sachar, Asnis, Quitkin, Nathan, Halpern, & Klein, 1982) found that such a diminished GH response was due to postmenopausal status, rather than depression per se. Similarly, apparent differences between GH response to L-dopa in bipolar and unipolar depressions (Gold, Goodwin, Wehr, Rebar, & Sack, 1976) also may be attributable to the estrogen status of the samples studied (Mendlewicz, Linkowski, & van Cauter, 1979).

More consistent evidence indicates that depressed patients are likely to evidence a diminished GH response to insulin (Gregoire, Brauman, de Buck, & Corvilain, 1977; Mueller et al., 1969; Sachar et al., 1971). In normal individuals, administration of a test dose of insulin results in a rise in plasma GH levels, mimicking the process which naturally follows eating a meal. With respect to abnormal GH responses in depression, two studies have controlled for the possible confounding effects of estrogen level: Gruen, Sachar, Altman, and Sassin (1975) found blunted GH response to insulin in postmenopausal female depressives when compared to carefully matched controls, and Puig-Antich and associates (Puig-Antich, Tabrizi, Davies, Goetz, Chambers, Halpern, & Sachar, 1981) reported similar findings in depressed prepubertal children.

The GH response to insulin is presumed to be mediated by a lowering of the blood sugar level (Brown et al., 1978) and, as previously noted, a substantial number of depressed patients fail to develop hypoglycemia following insulin administration. Therefore, it is possible that blunted GH response to insulin in depression simply reflects a failure to induce a physiologically significant degree of hypoglycemia (i.e., plasma glucose level of <50 mg percent). This position is supported by data from one recent study (Koslow et al., 1982), in which GH responses to insulin in both unipolar and bipolar depressives did not significantly differ from normals once analyses were limited only to those patients who experienced a sufficient degree of hypoglycemia.

In an earlier report, Garver, Pandey, Dekirmenjian, and DeLeon-Jones (1975) found a strong inverse correlation between urinary MHPG levels and growth hormone levels following insulin administration. However, as we have previously reviewed, a similar association also exists between high MHPG levels and hypercortisolemia (Jimerson et al., 1983; Rosenbaum et al., 1983; Stokes et al., 1981). Thus, Garver et al.'s (1975) finding may be secondary to a relationship between hypercortisolemia and high levels of urinary MHPG.

Other investigators have focused on GH responses to noradrenergic agonists, such as clonidine (Checkley, Slade, & Shur, 1981) and the tricyclic antidepressant desmethylimipramine (Laakmann, 1980). Using either of these adrenergically active medications, growth hormone responses were found to be deficient in depressives relative to closely matched controls. Such findings would again support theories of hyporesponsitivity of alpha-type noradrenergic receptors in depression. However, replication of these results by independent investigators is still needed, and the possible confounding effects of hypercortisolemia need to be controlled.

Results from several investigations indicate that levels of somatostatin may be decreased in the CSF of depressed individuals (Gerner & Yamada, 1982; Rubinow, Gold, Post, Ballenger, Cowdry, Bollinger, & Reichlin, 1983). While it is possible that such low levels of somatostatin are secondary to some other primary disturbance, increasing knowledge of the role of this neuropeptide as a CNS neurotransmitter also raises the possibility of a more causal association with development of depression (Rubinow et al., 1983). More detailed and comprehensive study of the neuroendocrine and neurochemical correlates of decreased somatostatin in depression clearly is needed. Preliminary data suggest that this abnormality is closely associated with low levels of 5-HIAA and high levels of NE in the CSF (Rubinow et al., 1983).

Surprisingly little research has dealt with secretion of growth hormone during sleep of depressed patients. As most depressed individuals show a virtual absence of visually scorable slow-wave sleep (Kupfer & Thase, 1983), some degree of disruption of the normal nocturnal pattern of GH secretion would be expected. However, the exact nature of this disturbance requires empirical identification. Of note, exogenous administration of somatostatin appears to result in reductions of the amounts of total sleep time, delta sleep and REM sleep (Rubinow, Gold, Post, Ballenger, & Cowdry, 1984a).

Prolactin Secretion

Regulation of prolactin in depression also is of interest because of its secretion by cells in the anterior pituitary. Several studies of basal prolactin secretion have shown significantly lower levels in acutely depressed patients when compared to either controls or retest values following clinical recovery (Asnis, Nathan, Halbreich, Halpern, & Sachar, 1980; Judd, Risch, Parker, Janowsky, Segal, & Huey, 1982; Linkowski, Brauman, & Mendlewicz, 1980). However, other groups have failed to find such relationships (Ehrensing, Kastin, Schalch, Friesen, Vargas, & Schally, 1974; Gregoire et al., 1977; Maeda, Kato, Ohgo, Chichara, Yoshimoto, Yamaguchi, Kuromaru, & Imura, 1975). Mendlewicz et al. (1983) found low basal prolactin to characterize bipolar, but not unipolar depressives. Abnormal circadian secretion of prolactin also has been reported in depression (Halbreich, Grunhaus, & Ben-David, 1979; Mendlewicz et al., 1983). Methodological differences, particularly with respect to diagnosis and medication status, probably account for such discrepancies. Further study is needed.

Diminished basal levels of prolactin in depression could suggest increased dopaminergically mediated inhibition, reduced serotonergic stimulation, or alterations in sleep-related prolactin secretion (Mendlewicz et al., 1983; Sachar, 1982). It is conceivable that elevations of cortisol in the CSF increases hypothalamic dopamine levels in some patients, which in turn results in lowered prolactin levels. This hypothesis is indirectly supported by the observation that the proportion of patients (i.e., 50 percent) who show reduced prolactin levels is similar to the prevalence of hypercortisolemia in depression (Judd et al., 1982). However, this possible relationship has not received direct empirical verification and available neurochemical data do not suggest increased CNS dopaminergic activity in most depressed patients.

A blunted prolactin response following administration of small doses of narcotic, such as methadone and morphine, also has been reported in patients with major depression (Extein, Pottash, Gold, Sweeney, Martin, & Goodwin, 1980; Judd et al., 1982). These findings support the possible role of abnormalities in regulation of central endogenous opiates in depression, as we will discuss in the next section.

Endorphins. Discovery of brain receptors for opiates, and subsequent identification of naturally occurring, endogenous opiatelike substances (endorphins) in the brain have raised several interesting questions with respect to the affective disorders. For example, since administration of morphine and other narcotics often induces a transient state of euphoria, one might speculate that depressions are associated with a deficiency of endorphins (e.g., Angst, Autenrieth, Brem, Koukkou, Meyer, Stassen, & Storck, 1979; Kline & Lehman, 1979). The agitated dysphoric syndrome experienced by individuals in opiate withdrawal would represent an indirect model of possible behavioral effects of endorphin deficiency (Gold & Rea, 1983). Conversely, increased pain tolerance observed in many depressives might reflect abnormally high levels of endorphins (Davis, 1983).

Attempts to test these competing assumptions by short-term administration of beta-endorphin to depressed patients have yielded inconclusive results: when improvements were noted, they were generally short lived (see Berger & Barchas, 1983). Treatment of depressed patients with narcotic antagonists also have not produced consistent clinical changes (Davis, Bunney, Buchsbaum, DeFraites, Duncan, Gillin, van Kammen, Kleinman, Murphy, Post, Reus, & Wyatt, 1979; Fink, Simeon, Itil, & Freedman, 1970; Terenius, Wahlstrom, & Agren, 1977). More recently, several groups have reported elevated levels of endorphin in either the plasma or CSF of depressed patients (Davis & Buchsbaum, 1981; Lindstrom, Widerlov, Gunne, Wahlstrom, & Terenius, 1978; Risch, 1982; Terenius, Wahlstrom, Lindstrom, & Winderlov, 1976). However, other investigators have failed to find differences in plasma or CSF endorphin levels between depressives and normal controls (Alexopoulos, Inturrisi, Lipman, Frances, Haycox, Dougherty, & Rossier, 1983; Naber, Pickar, Post, van Kammen, Waters, Ballenger, Goodwin, & Bunney, 1981). Unfortunately, the meaning of these contradictory results using plasma and CSF endorphin levels is not clear; several studies have failed to find significant correlations between such measurements (see Kalin & Loevinger, 1983).

A tentative association between depression and elevated CSF levels of beta-endorphin is of theoretical interest, as beta-endorphin and ACTH appear to be secreted simultaneously from the anterior pituitary (Risch, Janowsky, Judd, Gillin, & McClure, 1983). Furthermore, depressed patients may show evidence of an exaggerated beta-endorphin response following administration of physostigmine, a cholinergic agonist (Risch, 1982). It should be recalled that administration of physostigmine induces several other biological disturbances associated with depression (i.e., shortened REM latency and DST nonsuppression). Thus, Risch's report provides further evidence of cholinergic supersensitivity in depression. From this perspective, it might be concluded that elevated endorphin levels are part of a broader pattern of cholinergically mediated neuroendocrine abnormalities which are present in some forms of depression. Conversely, it is possible that high endorphin levels simply represent a secondary phenomenon: increased endorphin secretion occurs in a variety of stressful or noxious situations, and CSF endorphin levels correlate with both pain tolerance in depressed patients and depression scores in individuals with chronic pain (Almay, Johansson, von Knorring, Sedvall, & Terenius, 1980; Davis, 1983).

Sex Differences in Depression

It has long been an axiom of psychiatric epidemiology that women are at greater risk for depression. Indeed, most studies have placed the relative risk at greater than $2:1$ (e.g., Boyd & Weissman, 1981). The obvious hormonal differences which exist between men and women have been viewed for a similarly long time as possibly underlying the higher incidence and prevalence of depression in women (see Clayton, 1983).

Nevertheless, little firm evidence has emerged to directly link sex-related hormonal differences to the pathophysiological changes observed in major depression. Several groups have reported alterations in anterior pituitary secretion of luteinizing hormone and follicle stimulating hormone in depressed patients (see Amsterdam, Winokur, Lucki, Caroff, Snyder, & Rickels, 1983; Winokur et al., 1983). However, such changes are seen in both male and female patients and most likely reflect increased variability of anterior pituitary responsiveness in depression rather than a specific sex-related vulnerability. Similarly, abnormalities of HYPAC function and EEG sleep are not gender related once other clinically relevant factors, such as age and severity of depression, are accounted for (Carroll, 1982; Kupfer & Thase, 1983).

Several indirect factors affecting neuroendocrine function do appear to increase vulnerability to depression specifically in women. First, the incidence of hypothyroidism is higher in women, particularly when one focuses on the milder, subacute or "symptomless" forms of thyroid disease which are related to autoimmune disturbances and often present as a depressive syndrome (Gold & Pottash, 1983). Second, depression is a relatively common side effect of oral contraceptives, particularly those products containing high levels of progesterone (Parry & Rush, 1979). As these agents are almost exclusively used by women, this undoubtedly increases the rate of depression detected in community surveys of the female population between ages 15 and 50; that is, precisely the age-groups known to have increased affective vulnerability. However, it is unlikely that these sex-specific vulnerability factors, even when taken together, account for the large observed sex differences in rates of depression.

Other research on sex differences in depression has focused on high rates of postpartum depression and perimenstrual affective changes in women (e.g., Halbreich, Endicott, & Nee, 1983; Pitt, 1982). Of note, Pitt (1982) concluded that the risk of depression during pregnancy was similar to that noted during the postpartum period. Thus, dramatically different hormonal states seem to be associated with a similar vulnerability. Further, Pitt suggested that such states might be related to activated HYPAC axis function, in a fashion similar to that observed in postsurgical psychoses. With respect to perimenstrual affective changes, evidence indicates that a variety of clinical presentations exist, with prominent "atypical" features of depression (i.e., weight gain, hypersomnia, and irritability) seen in women with a history of both chronic depression and premenstrual mood changes (Halbreich et al., 1983).

Within the past few years, a number of reviewers have noted that sex-related differences in the incidence and prevalence of depression may to a large extent be the product of culturally sanctioned behaviors for expressing affective distress or seeking help (e.g., Boyd & Weissman, 1981; Clayton, 1983). In particular, it is assumed that the lower rate of depression in males results, in part, from expression of the depressive disorder in the form of alcoholism or antisocial behavior. Several recent studies support this hypothesis (see Clayton, 1983). Perhaps the most striking data come from an epidemiological survey of prevalence of affective disorders in the Amish; that is, a cultural group which strongly disapproves of alcohol abuse and antisocial behavior (Egeland & Hostetter, 1983; Egeland, Hostetter, & Eshleman, 1983). The ratio of Amish males and females diagnosed as having major affective disorder according to the SADS/RDC format was found to approach 1 : 1. Moreover, Kovacs and co-workers (Kovacs, Feinberg, Crouse-Novak, Paulauskas, & Finkelstein, 1984), studying a large sample of urban children, found increased incidence of depressive disorders in prepubertal girls, while boys of equivalent age showed higher rates of a variety of conduct-related problems. These findings would indicate that sex differences in symptomatic presentation are apparent even prior to the major hormonal changes of puberty. Thus, it seems likely that a major portion of the excess number of cases of depression in women should not be attributed to neuroendocrinological differences between the sexes.

Summary

Neuroendocrine parameters are studied with increasing frequency in depression research. Available data support the existence of multiple neuroendocrine abnormalities, an observation which illustrates the biological heterogeneity of depression. Aside from selected neuroendocrine diseases which may cause a depressive syndrome, it is now clear that over one half of severely depressed patients will show one or more neuroendocrine abnormalities. Further, in the case of hypercortisolemia, DST nonsuppression, and blunted response to TRH, such dysfunctions cannot be explained entirely as epiphenomena or nonspecific stress responses. By contrast, disturbances in certain aspects of growth hormone and insulin regulation may be secondary to hypercortisolemia. Neuroendocrine abnormalities occur most commonly in patients with severe, endogenomorphic depressions. Thus, there is a parallel with EEG sleep findings. Investigations of possible neurochemical correlates of endocrine changes point to alterations in cholinergic and presynaptic adrenergic mechanisms.

CHRONOBIOLOGY AND DEPRESSION

Increasing attention is being devoted to investigation of possible disturbances in a variety of biological rhythms in depression. Before reviewing this literature, it may be useful to provide a brief overview of some of the basics of chronobiology. Normal function of a number of neurophysiological, neuroendocrine, and thermoregulatory processes are characterized by a predictable periodicity within the 24-hour day; such patterns are referred to as circadian rhythms (Wehr & Goodwin, 1981). Examples of processes showing circadian rhythms in humans include cortisol secretion, the sleep-wake cycle, body temperature, and propensity to REM sleep (Wever, 1979). Other biological rhythms, such as the 90-minute REM sleep cycle, occur with a periodicity of less than 24 hours, and are referred to as ultradian rhythms. Finally, longer rhythms also are described in many lower mammals, including yearly (circannual) reproductive cycles. Circannual patterns recently have been noted in selected biochemical and neuroendocrine parameters in humans (Agren & Terenius, 1983; Wirz-Justice & Richter, 1979). There is now considerable evidence linking the length of the day with these circannual rhythms (Wehr & Goodwin, 1981).

Extensive basic research with both animals and humans has demonstrated that circadian biological rhythms apparently are driven by internal generators or biological "clocks" (Wehr & Goodwin, 1981). While these rhythms are influenced by external cues *(zeitgebers)*, they continue to function in settings in which all environmental stimuli are removed (Wever, 1979). Research with mammals indicates that the generator for the sleep-wake cycle is located in the suprachiasmatic nuclei (SCN) of the hypothalamus (Moore, 1978). Thus, there is an anatomical association between sleep-wake circadian rhythm generator and the area of the brain implicated in many of the biological disturbances of depression described in this chapter. Further, neural tracts have been identified which lead from the retina to the SCN, and from the SCN to the pineal gland (Wehr & Goodwin, 1981). These connections provide an anatomic pathway for transmission of visually processed environmental cues to brain areas which modulate the sleep-wake cycle.

The sleep-wake cycle is perhaps the most easily studied circadian rhythm. In normal situations, a variety of environmental cues serve to entrain this rhythm to the 24-hour clock. Examples of such cues in the natural environment include light-dark transitions, work schedules, and mealtimes. Generally, light-dark cycles are sufficient to control or entrain circadian rhythms. However, long-term isolation experiments conducted with hundreds of normal volunteers demonstrate that when environmental cues are carefully controlled, the average "free-running" sleep-wake cycle period increases to 25 hours (Wever, 1979). This means that normal individuals, in the absence of external cues, will go to bed and get up one hour later each day. Further, experimental manipulation of the light-dark cycle indicates that the range of entrainment is normally from 21- to 27-hour "days." Thus, humans can readily adapt to "days" shorter and longer than the conventional 24-hour clock.

During free-running isolation experiments, several circadian rhythms which normally are closely entrained become disassociated: the sleep-wake cycle begins to run independently from body temperature, REM propensity, and cortisol rhythms (Wever, 1979). In turn, these latter three circadian rhythms continue to oscillate together, suggesting existence of a second, albeit not yet localized, circadian generator in addition to the SCN (Wehr & Goodwin, 1981). Results from a number of investigations indicate that the sleep-wake rhythm is more readily influenced by environmental perturbations than the body temperature-REM propensity-cortisol secretion rhythm. Thus, relatively minor disruptions, such as the rapid time zone shift caused by transcontinental air travel, will affect changes in the sleep-wake cycle, yet not initially produce changes in other rhythms (Wehr & Goodwin, 1981). As those who have experienced "jet lag" will attest, transient dissociation of these two circadian rhythm systems frequently produces a subjective state of fatigue and a dulling of cognitive processes. Similar behavioral concomitants are observed during long-term isolation experiments at times in which the sleep-wake cycle and the body temperature rhythm are dissociated (Wever, 1979). In particular, dissociation of these circadian rhythm has been found to have an adverse effect on sleep: quality of sleep is poorer and duration of sleep is shorter when normal individuals retire during the rising phase of the diurnal temperature curve, rather than the descending body temperature phase which normally occurs at night (Czeisler, Weitzman, Moore-Ede, Zimmerman, & Kronauer, 1980).

Several clinical observations led to the suggestion that biological rhythm disturbances are present in depression: early morning awakening and diurnal variation in mood seen in many endogenously depressed patients might indicate a circadian disturbance, while predictable seasonal increases in the incidence of depression (highest in the fall and winter) and mania (highest in the spring) suggest annual cyclic abnormalities (Rosenthal, Sack, & Wehr, 1983; Wehr & Goodwin, 1981).

Theories of circadian rhythm disturbances in depression generally have focused on two possible types of abnormalities: 1) disorganization or blunting of daily rhythms, and 2) pathological desynchronization of circadian rhythms relative to each other (Wehr & Wirz-Justice, 1982). Particular attention has been given to the possibility of an abnormal phase-advance of the body temperature, REM propensity, and cortisol secretion circadian rhythms relative to the sleep-activity cycle (Wehr & Wirz-Justice, 1982). Such a dissociation could explain the phenomena of early morning awakening and diurnal mood variation noted earlier (Wehr & Wirz-Justice, 1982).

In addition, several of the biological abnormalities of endogenous depression reviewed earlier in this chapter might be viewed as consistent with the phase-advance hypothesis. First, shortened REM latency and increased length and density of the first REM period seen in endogenous depressions could be produced by a phase advance of four to six hours, since REM propensity normally reaches its maximum near dawn, rather than close to sleep onset (Wehr & Goodwin, 1981). Of note, experimentally induced delays in sleep onset generally result in some degree of shortening of REM latency in normal controls, although not all studies are in agreement (see Thase & Kupfer, in press-b). MacLean, Cairns, and Knowles (1983) applied a computer simulation to test the hypothesis that progressively longer phase delays of sleep onset in normals would begin to produce REM latency changes similar to those seen in depressed persons. Relatively long phase delays (i.e., greater than four hours) were found to produce reductions in REM latency which correspond to published values for severely depressed patients, thus supporting the phase-advancement hypothesis. However, a study of REM latency during daytime naps did not indicate phase advance: depressed patients continued to experience significantly shortened REM latency during daytime sleep, and these values were closely correlated with REM latency measurements from the previous night (Kupfer, Gillin, Coble, Spiker, Shaw, & Holzer, 1981). Results from another study of sleep during daytime naps in depression also failed to support the phase-advancement hypothesis (Pugnetti, Colombo, Cazzullo, Leccardi, Sicuro, & Scarone, 1982).

Second, high levels of psychomotor activity seen in some agitated depressed patients during the evening hours would go along with a similar degree of phase advancement. This is because the nocturnal activity recordings of persons with agitated depressions generally match or even surpass the levels seen in normal individuals during the peak activity periods of the daytime (Kupfer, Foster, Detre, & Himmelhoch, 1975). Such a pattern is reflected indirectly in studies or urinary and plasma levels of MHPG, which also demonstrate a phase advance of noradrenergic activity in depression (Halaris, DeMet, Gwirtsman, & Piletz, 1983; Wehr et al., 1980).

Third, nocturnal hypercortisolemia and early onset of cortisol secretion during the first few hours of sleep in some depressed patients (Jarrett et al., 1983) also might suggest a phase advance. It is of interest that an antidepressant response to sleep-deprivation procedures is seen most commonly in patients with hypercortisolemia or DST nonsuppression (Nasrallah & Coryell, 1982). It has been suggested that sleep deprivation may produce clinical improvement via a transient resetting of abnormally advanced circadian rhythms in depression (Wehr & Wirz-Justice, 1982). More specific alterations designed to produce phase advance of the sleep-wake cycle have induced striking clinical improvements, or even hypomania, in a small number of bipolar depressed patients (Wehr, Wirz-Justice, & Goodwin, 1979; Wehr & Wirz-Justice, 1982).

Additional evidence of an abnormal dissociation of circadian rhythms comes from several sources. Wehr and Goodwin (1981) reviewed and retrospectively analyzed published data for circadian rhythms of a number of biochemical and neurophysiological parameters in depressives and controls. Despite numerous methodological differences between these studies, a consistent pattern indicative of phase advance emerged in depressives relative to controls (Wehr & Goodwin, 1981).

One of the parameters covered in Wehr and Goodwin's (1981) review was body temperature. Abnormalities of body temperature in depressions are of interest, since this rhythm is linked to the same circadian oscillator as REM propensity and cortisol secretion. Thus, body temperature minimum should be closely related to several other biological disturbances noted in depression. Several recent preliminary reports, each based on small sample sizes, directly address this issue. Lee and Taylor (1983) found that a subset ($N = 2$) of their 10 patient sample had a phase advancement of the daytime temperature curve, and both of these depressed individuals had abnormal DSTs. Curiously, neither of these patients' depression ratings improved following a 36-hour sleep-deprivation procedure. In contrast, five patients had normal daytime temperature curves, yet also showed DST nonsuppression. Each of these patients responded to sleep deprivation. A third group ($N = 3$) evidenced a blunted temperature curve, showed no response to sleep deprivation, and had normal suppression of cortisol. Beersma, van den Hoofdakker, and van Berkestijn (1983) found no evidence of phase advance of temperature rhythm in a sample of 15 patients, despite documenting shortened REM latency in these endogenously depressed patients. However, similar to the findings of Lee and Taylor, a subgroup of this sample ($N = 7$) showed a blunted circadian temperature curve. Avery and associates (Avery, Wildschiodtz, & Rafaelson, 1982a) reported high nocturnal temperatures in their acutely depressed sample, (i.e., blunting of the normal nocturnal rhythm), but also found no evidence of phase advancement of the temperature curve. Such a blunting of nocturnal temperatures tended to normalize upon clinical recovery. In a related report, Avery, Wildschiodtz, and Rafaelson (1982b) did find a significant negative correlation between REM latency and temperature minimum in six depressed patients studied both before and after treatment. Similarly, Schulz and Lund (1983) found both shortened REM latency and elevated nocturnal temperature in endogenous depressives. In particular, patients with extremely shortened REM latency (i.e., less than 20 minutes) were found to have a blunted circadian temperature rhythm. Thus, the relationships between body temperature, REM latency, and cortisol secretion appear more complex than explained by the phase-advance hypothesis. Available data are more suggestive of blunted or disorganized circadian rhythms in depression. Definitive study in larger samples of depressed patients involving simultaneous measurement of all three parameters is needed to further explore these relationships.

In summary, evidence drawn from recent studies of EEG sleep, body temperature, and HYPAC axis function is not consistent with the existence of an advance of circadian rhythm phases in most depressed patients. Such studies do indicate, however, that circadian rhythms may be disorganized in a large number of severely depressed patients. Disorganization of circadian rhythms are clearly seen in patients with rapidly cycling bipolar affective disorder, where 48-hr, sleep-wake cycles commonly occur after a switch from depression into a manic clinical state (Wehr, Goodwin, Wirz-Justice, Breit-maier, & Craig, 1982).

A number of recent reports have addressed the neuropharmacology of circadian systems (see Wehr & Wirz-Justice, 1982; Wirz-Justice & Wehr, 1983). Briefly, circadian periodicity in the number or sensitivity of adrenergic, cho-linergic, dopaminergic, and opiate receptor sites in the brain has been dem-onstrated in animal experiments (Wirz-Justice & Wehr, 1983). Further, sev-eral hormones with clear behavioral effects (e.g., estrogen, testosterone, and thyroxine) have been found to influence the length or periodicity of sleep-wake circadian cycle (Wehr & Wirz-Justice, 1982). As might be predicted from the phase-advance hypothesis, many effective antidepressant agents, includ-ing lithium carbonate, clorgyline (an MAOI), and imipramine, produce lengthening or slowing of endogenous neurotransmitter receptor rhythms (Wirz-Justice & Wehr, 1983). By contrast, available data indicate that sleep deprivation procedures are not associated with demonstrable changes in receptor rhythms (Wehr & Wirz-Justice, 1982). This might explain why sleep deprivation usually only produces a transient response. Thus, although the phase-advance hypothesis of depression is not entirely supported by available studies employing neuroendocrine and neurophysiological methods, the ef-fects of antidepressants on various neurotransmitter receptors are consistent with this position.

If phase advancement of circadian rhythms does occur in major depres-sion, or even in a subgroup of patients with affective disorders, what etiologi-cal factors could conceivably produce such a shift? Several groups have sug-gested that depressed patients may have an abnormality of the SCN circadian pacemaker which results in an extremely short, intrinsic period for rhythms governed by this generator (Doerr, von Zerssen, Fischler, & Schulz, 1979; Wehr & Wirz-Justice, 1982). If this were the case, these rhythms would as-sume an earlier phase position relative to the light-dark and sleep-activity cycles under certain conditions of faulty entrainment. Unfortunately, determi-nation of the intrinsic period of these rhythms requires that depressed sub-jects be studied for extended periods in free-running isolation experiments to control for the masking effects of external time cues. There are virtually no data available to address this question, and it would be ethically questionable to subject clinically depressed patients to such a protocol. Further, it would be crucial to ascertain under what conditions faulty entrainment is provoked, or whether proposed abnormalities in the pacemaker are secondary to changes in either neurotransmitter or hormonal levels. Thus, phase advance could represent an epiphenomenon of more basic neurochemical processes.

Several recent studies suggest that seasonal changes in the amount of sunlight might produce faulty entrainment and, hence, phase advance. As previously noted, light-dark transitions are powerful *zeitgebers,* and fall and spring are the seasons in which dawn and dusk show the most critical changes. Higher prevalence of depression and mania during these periods provides some indirect support for the hypothesis of increased vulnerability to changes in sunlight. Further, Lewy and associates (1981) found that patients with bipolar affective disorder show an exaggerated melatonin response to bright light when compared to normal controls. As melatonin is secreted by the pineal gland, which in turn receives input from the retina via the SCN, a direct association between length of day and circadian disturbances appears possible. Moreover, attempts to treat patients whose depressions always occur in the fall or winter by extending the "day" with several additional hours of bright (1,000 lux) white light in the morning and/or evening have met with some success (Kripke, Risch, & Janowsky, 1983; Lewy, Kern, Rosenthal, & Wehr, 1982; Rosenthal, Sack, Gillin, Lewy, Goodwin, Davenport, Mueller, Newsome, & Wehr, 1984). Furthermore, such phototherapy does not seem to be an effective treatment for individuals with nonseasonal depressions.

Rosenthal et al. (1984) described a relatively large ($N = 29$) series of patients with recurrent fall or winter major depressions. Eighty-five percent of this sample reported that trips to sunny climates reliably improved their winter depressions and, as noted above, several extra hours of bright white light each morning (before dawn) and evening (after dusk) were found to produce statistically and clinically significant reductions in level of depression. Of note, 93 percent of this sample of community volunteers met diagnostic criteria for a bipolar affective disorder, and most patients presented with an atypical symptom profile: psychomotor retardation, irritability, increased appetite with weight gain and carbohydrate craving, and hypersomnia. A majority of these patients had previously received various somatic antidepressant therapies, although few patients (14 percent) had benefited enough to continue treatment with these agents.

Neuroendocrine data were not reported in this chapter, but EEG sleep studies were conducted during both summer and winter in nine patients. Results confirmed significant increases in sleep time and decreases in sleep latency, as well as diminution of delta sleep during winter depression. Although REM latency values were not reported, the authors noted that values did not significantly decrease during the winter depressions (Rosenthal et al., 1984).

Obviously, persons in this sample hardly seem representative of the broader grouping of patients with major depression seen in most hospital or clinic settings. Further, phenomenological and EEG sleep changes observed in these patients during periods of depression were not indicative of phase advancement: patients did not experience early morning awakening, difficulty falling asleep, evening agitation, or shortening of REM latency. While these are very interesting findings, they do not closely link changes in the light-dark cycle and seasonal depression with the circadian phase-advance hypothesis.

SUMMARY OF RESEARCH ON THE BIOLOGY OF MAJOR DEPRESSION

Review of research conducted over the past two decades leads to few firm conclusions regarding the role of biological factors in the etiopathogenesis of major depression. Investigation in this area is a dynamic and evolving process, however, and progress is being made. In particular, improvements in diagnosis and refinements in experimental methodology provide a necessary foundation for continued research efforts. Further, recognition of the effects of selected nondiagnostic variables, such as age, sex, menstrual status, and time of day, as well as appropriate control of these factors, improve replicability and increase confidence in the validity of research findings.

Available data do not fully support the classical monoamine hypotheses of depression. The complex regulatory and compensatory relationships of monoamines and acetylcholine undoubtedly mitigate against demonstration of specific, isolated deficits for a given neurotransmitter or enzyme. The apparent clinical heterogeneity of the major depressive syndrome also makes it quite unlikely that such a single specific deficit will be found in all depressed patients, even with development of the most precise and refined experimental methods. Recognition of biologically distinct subgroups within larger samples remains a useful strategy (e.g., Buchsbaum & Rieder, 1979). This is particularly true if clinical, family history, or treatment response data also support the independence of such a subgroup.

Nevertheless, consistent evidence of abnormalities in a number of neuroendocrine systems and, to a lesser extent, demonstration of reliable EEG sleep changes, provide compelling evidence of the existence of some underlying neurochemically mediated regulatory disturbance(s) involving the limbic system in many, if not most, severely depressed patients. At this time, it can be concluded that many of these findings are not attributable to methodological artifacts or nonspecific effects of stress (Kupfer & Thase, in press). Further study of presynaptic and postsynaptic receptor mechanisms should prove informative; such studies have already provided invaluable data on the multiple actions of antidepressant medications (e.g., Charney, Menkes, & Heninger, 1981). The strategy of simultaneous study of neurochemical, endocrine, and neurophysiological variables is increasingly employed in affective disorders research and represents a needed shift toward integration of multiple, diverse areas of potential biological dysfunction.

With respect to biological abnormalities in specific subtypes of major depression, we have summarized data reviewed in the previous sections in Table 8. On the whole, there is far greater evidence of biological disturbances in patients with the most pervasive and severe depressive syndromes. This is particularly true for the melancholic and delusional subtypes of major depression. Such patients often show multiple neuroendocrine and neurophysiological disturbances. The bipolar-unipolar dichotomy also receives some validation, although in many cases it is not possible to ascertain if biological differences are secondary to clinical differences in level of agitation or anxiety and amount of sleep or, conversely, if such symptomatic differences reflect a specific type of underlying biological dysfunction. On clinical grounds, division of the more severe depressive syndromes into either agitated-hyposomnic or retarded-hypersomnic subtypes (i.e., Kupfer, Foster, Detre, & Himmelhoch, 1975; Kupfer, Picker, Himmelhoch, & Detre, 1975) continues to show merit.

TABLE 8
Summary of biological abnormalities in clinical subtypes of major depression

Diagnostic subtype	Urinary MHPG	CSF 5-HIAA	Short REM latency	DST nonsuppression	Blunted TRH test
Melancholia (endogenous)	±	+	+ +	+	+
Bipolar (manic-depressive)	+ +	±	+ +	+	+
Delusional (psychotic)	±	±	+ +	+ +	+
Nonmelancholic, nonbipo-lar, nonpsychotic	—	—	+	±	±

+ + Present in a majority of patients.
+ Reliably detected in a smaller subgroup.
± Possibly detected in a subgroup.
— No clear relationship.

Patients with milder, nonbipolar-nondelusional-nonendogenous major depressions are the least likely to show evidence of biological dysfunction (Kupfer & Thase, in press). This observation has particularly important practical implications, since such individuals may constitute the majority of depressed patients seen in counseling centers and ambulatory clinic settings, as well as a high proportion of untreated depressives detected in community surveys. Preliminary evidence would indicate that shortened REM latency is found in some of the cases (Akiskal, 1981; Cartwright, 1983; Reynolds, Newton, Shaw, Coble, & Kupfer, 1982; Rush et al., 1982; Rush et al., 1983), while neuroendocrine tests results are frequently normal. It remains to be seen if other biological parameters which appear to "cut" across diagnostic subtypes, such as number of platelet serotonin receptors or electrodermal activity, also will characterize these patients.

Integration of biological and psychosocial research on depression is an especially promising and unfortunately neglected area. Far too much research pertaining to the psychosocial aspects of depression has been conducted with milder subclinical samples rather than actual patient populations (Doerfler, 1981; Rehm & Kornblith, 1979). Therefore, it is difficult, if not impossible, to generalize findings from such investigations to the samples of major depressives studied in biological research settings. Conversely, biologically oriented investigators need to give greater credence to the possible interrelationships of social, cognitive, and interpersonal variables with biological parameters. For example, although a vast literature has addressed the role of stressful life events in depression (see Paykel, 1982), it is unclear if individuals with underlying biological abnormalities are differentially sensitive to stress. Recognition of biological disturbances which persist in some recovered depressives, such as TRH blunting, supersensitivity to the REM-sleep inducing effects of arecholine, or low level of electrodermal activity, provides a basis for longitudinal study of stressful life events and vulnerability to relapse. Similarly, correlation of the impact of social and interpersonal disturbances on biological indexes is needed. This may be particularly important with respect to study of response and nonresponse to antidepressant treatments (Thase & Kupfer, in press-a).

One interesting area where integration has been attempted is study of the relationship between biological correlates and cognitive changes in depression. Limited evidence would suggest that EEG sleep abnormalities are not closely linked to decrements in cognitive performance (Shipley, Kupfer, Spiker, Shaw, Coble, Neil, & Cofsky, 1981). Conflicting data have recently been published with respect to the cognitive correlates of increased HYPAC axis activity (Caine, Yerevanian, & Bamford, 1984; Rubinow, Post, Savard, & Gold, 1984b). Results of the investigation by Rubinow et al. (1984) are of interest in that advancing age and depression appeared to interact on both HYPAC function and level of cognitive dysfunction, such that older depressed patients showed highest urinary cortisol levels and the greatest degree of neuropsychological impairment. Such findings are consistent with the phenomenological correlates of HYPAC axis hyperactivity reviewed earlier in this chapter.

With respect to the role of cognitive distortions in the etiopathogenesis of depression, available data from studies employing naturalistic follow-up designs (Hamilton & Abramson, 1983; Lewinsohn, Steinmetz, Larson, & Franklin, 1981; Silverman, Silverman, & Eardley, 1984) indicate that maladaptive cognitions are symptoms rather than a cause of depression. However, Giles and Rush (1982) did find that ratings of dysfunctional attitudes were significantly correlated with depressive severity in nonendogenous but not endogenous depressions. This might indicate that cognitive distortions are more intimately associated with the etiopathogenesis of milder depressions. Dexamethasone suppression test results did not appear to correlate with ratings of dysfunctional attitudes in this study (Giles & Rush, 1982).

By contrast, several groups are studying biological correlates of psychosocial models of depression in animals (e.g., Sherman, Sacquitne, & Petty, 1982; Suomi, Seaman, Lewis, DeLizio, & McKinney, 1978). For example, Sherman and Petty (1984) have reported the experimentally induced learned helplessness in rats is associated with a predictable decrease in the number of serotonin receptor sites, as measured using ^{3}H-imipramine. It should be recalled that this abnormality is observed in approximately 40 percent of clinically depressed persons. Moreover, chronic treatment with antidepressant drugs or ECT has been found to reverse animal models of depression (Sherman et al., 1982; Suami et al., 1978). We would suggest that experimental manipulations designed to produce cognitive and behavioral changes suggestive of depression in normal volunteers might be expected to be associated with some transient biological changes consistent with depressive states (i.e., increased nondominant cerebral activity or alterations in plasma MHPG levels), but that the effects of such manipulations are too short lived and not pervasive enough to cause the major psychobiological changes seen in severe endogenous depressions (cf., Cohen, 1979). Therefore, research employing experimentally induced dysphorias or decreased self-esteem in normals may not be a fruitful strategy with respect to the biology of the major depressive syndromes. However, the work of Cartwright (1983) clearly indicates the biological impact of severely stressful life events in a sample of community volunteers: over one half of a group of women going through divorce proceedings showed clinical evidence of depression and had shortened REM latency.

Another area of potential research integration of biological and psychosocial models would specifically address sex differences in the prevalence and incidence of depression. Although we have previously noted that higher rates of depression in women have not been conclusively linked to neuroendocrinological factors, longitudinal study of biological variables such as presence of premenstrual mood changes, or dysphoric response to contraceptives, concurrent with assessments of social support, use of coping strategies, and stressful life events may shed some light on the high rates of depression in women.

Perhaps the most interesting area of integration between psychosocial and biological approaches is study of the effectiveness of short-term psychotherapies for depression. Increasing evidence indicates that interpersonal, cognitive, and behavioral therapies may match or even exceed the effects of tricyclic antidepressants for outpatients with nonbipolar depression (see Rush, 1983; Steinbrueck, Maxwell, & Howard, 1983; Thase, 1983; Weissman, 1979b). While conventional clinical wisdom might indicate that such psychosocial treatments should be preferentially used for patients presenting with milder, nonendogenous depressions, preliminary evidence suggests that they might also be useful treatments for some outpatients with features of endogenomorphic depression (Blackburn, Bishop, Glen, Whalley, & Christie, 1981; Kovacs, Rush, Beck, & Hollon, 1981; Thase, Hersen, Bellack, Himmelhoch, Kornblith, & Greenwald, 1984). However, results from several investigations (Prusoff, Weissman, Klerman, & Rounsaville, 1980; Thase, Himmelhoch, Hersen, & Bellack, 1984) indicate that psychosocial treatments may be less useful than pharmacotherapy in a majority of patients with a full syndrome of melancholia or definite endogenous depression.

It has been proposed that the presence of selected biological disturbances in melancholic depressives, such as shortened REM latency or DST nonsuppression, will identify those nonbipolar outpatients who should receive pharmacotherapy in lieu of, or in combination with, a psychosocial treatment (Rush, 1983; Thase, 1983). Some preliminary evidence in this area does deserve further comment. Both Rush (1983) and our own group (see Thase & Kupfer, in press-a) have found that patients who have DST nonsuppression and/or shortened REM latency do not respond as well to cognitive therapy as those who do not show such biological changes. Similarly, Coble, Kupfer, Spiker, Neil, and McPartland (1979) found that inpatients with shortened REM latency did not improve markedly during a 28-day course of intensive psychosocial milieu therapy and placebo pharmacotherapy. While these findings support the hypothesis that patients with objective signs of biological dysfunction may require a "somatic" treatment, this important question merits considerable more empirical investigation. Of note, several controlled inpatient trials employing cognitive therapy are currently under way.

In summary, research on the biology of major depression has confirmed the existence of several distinct and relatively specific disturbances, as well as suggested the existence of numerous other abnormalities. The significance of these findings in etiology and pathogenesis of depression remains largely unproven, although the empirical and methodological foundations for continued investigation of this area are now quite firmly established. Research in the next decade needs to focus on the interrelationships of multiple purported biological disturbances, as well as integration of findings from such studies within the broader body of knowledge on the natural history and psychosocial aspects of depression.

References

Agren, H., & Oreland, L. (1982). Early morning awakening in unipolar depressives with higher levels of platelet MAO activity. *Psychiatry Research, 7,* 245–254.

Agren, H., & Terenius, L. (1983). Depression and CSF endorphin fraction I: Seasonal variation and higher levels in unipolar than bipolar patients. *Psychiatry Research, 10,* 303–311.

Akiskal, H. S. (1981). Subaffective disorders: Dysthymic, cyclothymic, and bipolar II disorders in the "borderline" realm. *Psychiatric Clinics of North America, 4,* 25–46.

Akiskal, H. S. (1983, December). *Interface of affective with character, anxiety and somatic disorders.* Paper presented at the annual meeting of the American College of Neuropsychopharmacology, San Juan, Puerto Rico.

Akiskal, H. S., & Cassano, G. B. (1983). The impact of therapeutic advances in widening the nosologic boundaries of affective disorders: Clinical and research implications. *Pharmacopsychiatry, 16,* 111–118.

Akiskal, H. S., Lemmi, H., Yerevanian, B., King, D., & Belluomoni, J. (1982). The utility of the REM latency test in psychiatric diagnosis: A study of 81 depressed outpatients. *Psychiatry Research, 7,* 101–110.

Alexopoulos, G. S., Inturrisi, C. E., Lipman, R., Frances, R., Haycox, J., Dougherty, J. H., & Rossier, J. (1983). Plasma immunoreactive β-endorphin levels of depression. *Archives of General Psychiatry, 40,* 181–183.

Almay, B. G. L., Johansson, F., von Knorring, L., Sedvall, G., & Terenius, L. (1980). Relationships between CSF levels of endorphins and monoamine metabolites in chronic pain patients. *Psychopharmacology, 67,* 139–142.

American Psychiatric Association (1980). *Diagnostic and statistical manual of mental disorders* (3rd ed.). Washington, DC: Author.

Amsterdam, J. D., Winokur, A., Abelman, E., Lucki, I., & Rickels, K. (1983). Cosyntropin (ACTH a1-24) stimulation test in depressed patients and healthy subjects. *American Journal of Psychiatry, 140,* 907–909.

Amsterdam, J. D., Winokur, A., Bryant, S., Larkin, J., & Rickels, K. (1983). The dexamethasone suppression test as a predictor of antidepressant response. *Psychopharmacology, 80,* 43–45.

Amsterdam, J. D., Winokur, A., Caroff, S. N., & Conn, J. (1982). The dexamethasone suppression test in outpatients with primary affective disorder and healthy control subjects. *American Journal of Psychiatry, 139,* 287–292.

Amsterdam, J. D., Winokur, A., Lucki, I., Caroff, J., Snyder, P., & Rickels, K. (1983). A neuroendocrine test battery in bipolar patients and healthy subjects. *Archives of General Psychiatry, 40,* 515–521.

Angst, J., Autenrieth, V., Brem, F., Koukkou, M., Meyer, H., Stassen, H. H., & Storck, U. (1979). Preliminary results of treatment with beta-endorphin in depression. In E. Usdin, W. E. Bunney, Jr., & N. S. Kline (Eds.), *Endorphins in mental health research* (pp. 518–528). New York: Macmillan.

Arana, G. W., Barreira, P. J., Cohen, B. M., Lipinski, J. F., & Fogelson, D. (1983). The dexamethasone suppression test in psychotic disorders. *American Journal of Psychiatry, 140,* 1521–1523.

Asberg, M., & Traskman, L. (1981). Studies of CSF 5-HIAA in depression and suicidal behavior. *Advances in Experimental Medicine and Biology, 133,* 739–752.

Asberg, M., Traskman, L., & Thoren, P. (1976). 5-HIAA in the cerebrospinal fluid. *Archives of General Psychiatry, 33,* 1193–1197.

Ashcroft, G. W., Blackburn, I. M., Eccleston, D., Glen, A. I. M., Hartley, W., Kinloch, N. E., Lonergan, M., Murray, L. G., & Pullar, I. A. (1973). Changes on recovery in the concentrations of tryptophan and biogenic amine metabolites in the cerebrospinal fluid of patients with affective illness. *Psychological Medicine, 3,* 319–325.

Asnis, G. M., Halbreich, U., Sachar, E. J., Nathan, R. S., Ostrow, L. C., Novacenko, H., Davis, M., Endicott, J., & Puig-Antich, J. (1983). Plasma cortisol secretion and REM period latency in adult endogenous depression. *American Journal of Psychiatry, 140,* 750–753.

Asnis, G. M., Nathan, R. S., Halbreich, U., Halpern, F. S., & Sachar, E. J. (1980). Prolactin changes in major depressive disorders. *American Journal of Psychiatry, 137,* 1117–1118.

Avery, D. H., & Lubrano, A. (1979). Depression treated with imipramine and ECT: The DeCarolis study reconsidered. *American Journal of Psychiatry, 136,* 559–562.

Avery, D. H., Wildschiodtz, G., & Rafaelson, O. (1982a). Nocturnal temperature in affective disorders. *Journal of Affective Disorders, 4,* 61–71.

Avery, D. H., Wildschiodtz, G., & Rafaelson, O. (1982b). REM latency and temperature in affective disorder before and after treatment. *Biological Psychiatry, 17,* 463–470.

Baastrup, P. C., & Schou, M. (1967). Lithium as a prophylactic agent. Its effect against recurrent depressions and manic-depressive psychosis. *Archives of General Psychiatry, 16,* 162–172.

Baldessarini, R. J. (1975). The basis of the amine hypothesis in affective disorders: A critical evaluation. *Archives of General Psychiatry, 32,* 1087–1093.

Ball, J. R. B., & Kiloh, L. G. (1959). A controlled trial of imipramine in treatment of depressive state. *British Medical Journal, 2,* 1052–1055.

Balldin, J., Gottfries, C. G., Karlsson, I., Lindstedt, G., Langstrom, G., & Walinder, J. (1983). Dexamethasone suppression test and serum prolactin in dementia disorders. *British Journal of Psychiatry, 143,* 277–281.

Banki, C. M. (1977). Correlation between cerebrospinal fluid amine metabolites and psychomotor activity in affective disorders. *Journal of Neurochemistry, 29,*255–257.

Banki, C. M., & Arato, M. (1983a). Amine metabolites, neuroendocrine findings, and personality dimensions as correlates of suicidal behavior. *Psychiatry Research, 10,* 253–261.

Banki, C. M., & Arato, M. (1983b). Amine metabolites and neuroendocrine responses related to depression and suicide. *Journal of Affective Disorders, 5,* 223–232.

Banki, C. M., Arato, M., & Papp, Z. (1983). Cerebrospinal fluid biochemical examinations: Do they reflect clinical or biological differences? *Biological Psychiatry, 18,* 1033–1044.

Banki, C. M., Arato, M., Papp, Z., & Kurcz, M. (1983). The effect of dexamethasone on cerebrospinal fluid monoamine metabolites and cortisol in psychiatric patients. *Pharmacopsychiatry, 16,* 77–81.

Barchas, J. D., Akil, H., Elliott, G. R., Holman, R. B., & Watson, S. J. (1978). Behavioral neurochemistry: Neuroregulators and behavioral states. *Science, 200,* 964–973.

Barnes, R. F., Veith, R. C., Borson, S., Verhey, J., Raskind, M. A., & Halter, J. B. (1983). High levels of plasma catecholamines in dexamethasone-resistant depressed patients. *American Journal of Psychiatry, 140,* 1623–1625.

Baron, M., Barkai, A., Gruen, R., Kowalik, S., & Quitkin, F. (1983). 3H-imipramine platelet binding sites in unipolar depression. *Biological Psychiatry, 18,* 1403–1409.

Beersma, D. G. M., van den Hoofdakker, R. H., & van Berkestijn, H. W. B. M. (1983). Circadian rhythms in affective disorders: Body temperature and sleep physiology in endogenous depressives. *Advances in Biological Psychiatry, 11,* 114–127.

Bell, J., Lycaki, H., Jones, D., Kelwala, S., & Sitaram, N. (1983). Effect of preexisting borderline personality disorder on clinical and EEG sleep correlates of depression. *Psychiatry Research, 9,* 115–123.

Belmaker, R. H. (1981). Receptors, adenylate cyclase, depression, and lithium. *Biological Psychiatry, 16,* 333–350.

Benson, K. L., Zarcone, V. P., Faull, K. F., Barchas, J. D., & Berger, P. A. (1983). REM sleep eye movement activity and CSF concentrations of 5-hydroxyindoleacetic acid in psychiatric patients. *Psychiatry Research, 8,* 73–78.

Berger, M., Doerr, P., Lund, R., Bronisch, T., & von Zerssen, D. (1982). Neuroendocrinological and neurophysiological studies in major depressive disorders: Are there biological markers for the endogenous subtype? *Biological Psychiatry, 17,* 1217–1242.

Berger, M., Lund, R., Bronisch, T., & von Zerssen, D. (1983). REM latency in neurotic and endogenous depression and the cholinergic REM induction test. *Psychiatry Research, 10,* 113–123.

Berger, P. A., & Barchas, J. D. (1983). Pharmacologic studies of beta-endorphin in psychopathology. *Psychiatric Clinics of North America, 6,* 377–391.

Bergland, R. M., & Page, R. B. (1979). Pituitary-brain vascular relations: A new paradigm. *Science, 204,* 18–24.

Bielski, R. J., & Friedel, R. O. (1976). Prediction of tricyclic antidepressant response. *Archives of General Psychiatry, 33,* 1479–1489.

Blackburn, I. M., Bishop, S., Glen, A. I. M., Whalley, L. J., & Christie, J. E. (1981). The efficacy of cognitive therapy in depression: A treatment trial using cognitive therapy and pharmacotherapy, each alone and in combination. *British Journal of Psychiatry, 139,* 181–189.

Blumer, D., Zorick, T., Heilbronn, M., & Roth, T. (1982). Biological markers for depression in chronic pain. *Journal of Nervous and Mental Disease, 170,* 425–428.

Borbely, A. A., & Wirz-Justice, A. (1982). Sleep, sleep deprivation, and depression. A hypothesis derived from a model of sleep regulation. *Human Neurobiology, 1,* 205–215.

Boyd, J. H., & Weissman, M. M. (1981). Epidemiology of affective disorders. A reexamination and future directions. *Archives of General Psychiatry, 38,* 1039–1046.

Breyer-Pfaff, U., Gaertner, H. J., & Giedke, H. (1982). Plasma levels, psychophysiological variables, and clinical response to amitriptyline. *Psychiatry Research, 6,* 223–234.

Briley, M. S., Langer, S. Z., Raisman, R., Sechter, D., & Zarifian, E. (1980). Tritiated imipramine binding sites are decreased in platelets of untreated depressed patients. *Science, 209,* 303–305.

Brown, G. L., Ebert, M. H., Goyer, P. F., Jimerson, D. C., Klein, W. J., Bunney, W. E., Jr., & Goodwin, F. K. (1982). Aggression, suicide, and serotonin: Relationship to CSF amine metabolites. *American Journal of Psychiatry, 139,* 741–746.

Brown, G. M., & Seggie, J. (1980). Neuroendocrine mechanisms and their implications for psychiatric research. *Psychiatric Clinics of North America, 3,* 205–221.

Brown, G. M., Seggie, J. A., Chambers, J. W., & Ettigi, P. G. (1978). Psychoendocrinology and growth hormone. A review. *Psychoneuroendocrinology, 3,* 131–153.

Brown, P., & Brawley, P. (1983). Dexamethasone suppression test and mood response to methylphenidate in primary depression. *American Journal of Psychiatry, 140,* 990–993.

Brown, W. A., Johnston, R., & Mayfield, D. (1979). The 24-hour dexamethasone suppression test in a clinical setting: Relationship to diagnosis, symptoms, and response to treatment. *American Journal of Psychiatry, 136,* 543–547.

Brown, W. A., & Qualls, C. B. (1982). Pituitary-adrenal regulation over multiple depressive episodes. *Psychiatry Research, 7,* 265–269.

Buchsbaum, M. S. (1975). Average evoked response augmenting/reducing in schizophrenia and affective disorders. In D. X. Freedman (Ed.), *The biology of major psychoses: A comparative analysis* (pp. 129–142). New York: Raven Press.

Buchsbaum, M. S., Davis, G. C., Goodwin, F. K., Murphy, D. L., & Post, R. M. (1980). Psychophysical pain judgments and somatosensory evoked potentials in patients with affective illness and in normal adults. *Advances in Biological Psychiatry, 4,* 63–72.

Buchsbaum, M. S., Gerner, R., & Post, R. M. (1981). The effects of sleep deprivation on average evoked responses in depressed patients and in normals. *Biological Psychiatry, 16,* 351–363.

Buchsbaum, M. S., Ingvar, D. H., Kessler, R., Waters, R. N., Cappelleti, J., Van Kammen, D. P., King, A. C., Johnson, J. L., Manning, R. G., Flynn, R. W., Mann, L. S., Bunney,

W. E., Jr., & Sokoloff, L. (1982). Cerebral glucography with positron tomography: Use in normal subjects and in patients with schizophrenia. *Archives of General Psychiatry, 39,* 251–259.

Buchsbaum, M. S., Landau, S., Murphy, D., & Goodwin, F. K. (1973). Average evoked response in bipolar and unipolar affective disorders: Relationship to sex, age of onset, and monoamine oxidase. *Biological Psychiatry, 7,* 199–212.

Buchsbaum, M. S., & Rieder, R. O. (1979). Biological heterogeneity and psychiatric research. *Archives of General Psychiatry, 36,* 1163–1169.

Bunney, W. E., Jr., & Davis, J. M. (1965). Norepinephrine in depressive reactions: A review. *Archives of General Psychiatry, 13,* 483–494.

Bunney, W. E., Jr., and Garland, B. L. (1982). A second generation catecholamine hypothesis. *Pharmacopsychiatry, 15,* 111–115.

Byrne, D. G. (1975). A psychophysiological distinction between types of depressive states. *Australian and New Zealand Journal of Psychiatry, 9,* 181–185.

Caine, E. D., Yerevanian, B. I., & Bamford, K. A. (1984). Cognitive function and the dexamethasone suppression test in depression. *American Journal of Psychiatry, 141,* 116–118.

Carman, J. S., Wyatt, E., Crews, E., Hall, K. R., Scalise, M., Watts, D., & Hoppers, L. (1981). Dexamethasone suppression test: Predictor of thymoleptic response in catatonic, paranoid, hebephrenic, and schizoaffective patients. In C. Perris, G. Strowe, & B. Jansson (Eds.), *Biological psychiatry 1981* (Vol. 5; p. 1189–1193). New York, Elsevier-North Holland Publishing.

Caroff, S., Winokur, A., Rieger, W., Schweizer, E., & Amsterdam, J. (1983). Response to dexamethasone in psychotic depression. *Psychiatry Research, 8,* 59–64.

Carroll, B. J. (1978). Neuroendocrine function in psychiatric disorders. In M. A. Lipton, A. DiMascio, & K. F. Killam (Eds.), *Psychopharmacology: A generation of progress* (pp. 487–497). New York: Raven Press.

Carroll, B. J. (1979). Prediction of treatment outcome with lithium. *Archives of General Psychiatry, 36,* 870–878.

Carroll, B. J. (1982). The dexamethasone suppression test for melancholia. *British Journal of Psychiatry, 140,* 292–304.

Carroll, B. J., Greden, J. F., Feinberg, M., James, N. M., Haskett, R. F., Steiner, M., & Tarika, J. (1980). Neuroendocrine dysfunction in genetic subtypes of primary unipolar depression. *Psychiatry Research, 2,* 251–258.

Carroll, B. J., Greden, J. F., Feinberg, M., Lohr, N., James, N. M., Steiner, M., Haskett, R. F., Albala, A. A., DeVigne, J. P., & Tarika, J. (1981). Neuroendocrine evaluation of depression in borderline patients. *Psychiatric Clinics of North America, 4,* 89–99.

Carroll, B. J., Greden, J. F., Haskett, R., Feinberg, M., Albala, A. A., Martin, F. I. R., Rubin, R. T., Heath, B., Sharp, P. T., McLeod, W. L., & McLeod, M. F. (1980). Neurotransmitter studies of neuroendocrine pathology in depression. *Acta Psychiatrica Scandinavica* (Suppl. 280), 183–200.

Cartwright, R. D. (1983). Rapid eye movement sleep characteristics during and after mood-disturbing events. *Archives of General Psychiatry, 40,* 197–201.

Charney, D. S., Heninger, G. R., Sternberg, D. E., Hafstad, K. M., Giddings, S., & Landis, D. H. (1982). Adrenergic receptor sensitivity in depression: Effects of clonidine in depressed patients and healthy subjects. *Archives of General Psychiatry, 30,* 290–294.

Charney, D. S., Heninger, G. R., Sternberg, D. E., Redmond, D. E., Leckman, J. F., Maas, J. W., & Roth, R. H. (1981). Presynaptic adrenergic receptor sensitivity in depression: The effect of long-term desipramine treatment. *Archives of General Psychiatry, 38,* 1334–1340.

Charney, D. S., Menkes, D. B., & Heninger, G. R. (1981). Receptor sensitivity and the mechanism of action of antidepressant treatment. *Archives of General Psychiatry, 38,* 1160–1180.

Checkley, S. A. (1979). Corticosteroid and growth hormone responses to methylamphetamine in depressive illness. *Psychological Medicine, 9,* 107–116.

Checkley, S. A., Slade, A. P., & Shur, E. (1981). Growth hormone and other responses to clonidine in patients with endogenous depression. *British Journal of Psychiatry, 138,* 51–55.

Christie, M. J., Little, B. C., & Gordon, A. M. (1980). Peripheral indices of depressive states. In H. M. Van Praag, M. H. Lader, O. J. Rafaelson, & E. J. Sachar (Eds.), *Handbook of biological psychiatry: Part II. Brain mechanisms and abnormal behavior-psychophysiology* (pp. 145–182). New York: Marcel Dekker.

Clayton, P. J. (1983). Gender and depression. In J. Angst (Ed.), *The origins of depression: Current concepts and approaches* (pp. 77–89). Berlin: Springer-Verlag.

Coble, P. A., Foster, F. G., & Kupfer, D. J. (1976). Electroencephalographic sleep diagnosis of primary depression. *Archives of General Psychiatry, 33,* 1124–1127.

Coble, P. A., Kupfer, D. J., & Shaw, D. H. (1981). Distribution of REM latency and depression. *Biological Psychiatry, 16,* 453–465.

Coble, P. A., Kupfer, D. J., Spiker, D. G., Neil, J. F., & McPartland, R. J. (1979). EEG sleep in primary depression: A longitudinal placebo study. *Journal of Affective Disorders, 1,* 131–138.

Cohen, D. B. (1979). Dysphoric affect and REM sleep. *Journal of Abnormal Psychology, 88,* 73–77.

Colt, E. W. D., Dunner, D. L., Wang, J., Ross, D. C., Pierson, R. N., & Fieve, R. R. (1982). Body composition in affective disorder before, during and after lithium carbonate. *Archives of General Psychiatry, 39,* 577–581.

Cooper, J. E., Kendell, R. E., Gurland, B. J., Sharpe, L., Copeland, J. R. M., & Simon, R. (1972). *Psychiatric diagnosis in New York and London: A comparative study of mental hospital admissions.* New York: Oxford University Press.

Cooper, J. R., Bloom, F. E., & Roth, R. H. (1978). *The biochemical basis of neuropharmacology* (3rd ed.). New York: Oxford University Press.

Coppen, A., Peet, M., & Bailey, J. (1973). Double-blind and open prospective studies of lithium prophylaxis in affective disorders. *Psychiatria, Neurologia, Neurochirurgia, 76,* 501–510.

Coryell, W. (1982). Hypothalamic-pituitary-adrenal axis abnormality and ECT response. *Psychiatry Research, 6,* 283–291.

Coryell, W., Gaffney, G., & Burkhardt, P. E., (1982a). *DSM-III* melancholia and the primary-secondary distinction: A comparison of concurrent validity by means of the dexamethasone suppression test. *American Journal of Psychiatry, 139,* 120–122.

Coryell, W., Gaffney, G., & Burkhardt, P. E. (1982b). The dexamethasone suppression test and familiar subtypes of depression: A naturalistic replication. *Biological Psychiatry, 17,* 33–40.

Coryell, W., & Schlesser, M. A. (1983). Dexamethasone suppression test response in major depression: Stability across hospitalizations. *Psychiatry Research, 8,* 179–189.

Coryell, W., Smith, R., Cook, B., Moucharafieh, S., Dunner, F., & House, D. (1983). Serial dexamethasone suppression test results during antidepressant therapy: Relationship to diagnosis and clinical change. *Psychiatry Research, 10,* 165–174.

Coryell, W., & Tsuang, M. T. (1982). Primary unipolar depression and the prognostic importance of delusions. *Archives of General Psychiatry, 39,* 1181–1184.

Coryell, W., & Zimmerman, M. (1983). The dexamethasone suppression test and ECT outcome: A six-month follow-up. *Biological Psychiatry, 18,* 21–27.

Cowdry, R. W., Ebert, M. H., van Kammen, D. P., Post, R. M., & Goodwin, F. K. (1983). Cerebrospinal fluid probenecid studies: A reinterpretation. *Biological Psychiatry, 18,* 1287–1299.

Cowdry, R. W., Wehr, T. A., Zis, A. P., & Goodwin, F. K. (1983). Thyroid abnormalities associated with rapid cycling bipolar illness. *Archives of General Psychiatry, 40,* 414–420.

Crumley, F. E., Clevenger, J., Steinfink, D., & Oldham, D. (1982). Preliminary report on the dexamethasone suppression test for psychiatrically disturbed adolescents. *American Journal of Psychiatry, 139,* 1062–1064.

Czeisler, C. A., Weitzman, E. D., Moore-Ede, M. C., Zimmerman, J. C., & Kronauer, R. S. (1980). Human sleep: Its duration and organization depends on its circadian phase. *Science, 210,* 1264–1267.

Davidson, J. R. T., McLeod, M. N., Turnbull, C. D., White, H. L., & Feuer, E. J. (1980). Platelet monoamine oxidase activity and the classification of depression. *Archives of General Psychiatry, 37,* 771–773.

Davis, G. C. (1983). Endorphins and pain. *Psychiatric Clinics of North America, 6,* 473–487.

Davis, G. C., & Buchsbaum, M. S. (1981). Pain sensitivity and endorphins in functional psychoses. *Modern Problems in Pharmacopsychiatry, 17,* 97–108.

Davis, G. C., Bunney, W. E., Jr., Buchsbaum, M. S., DeFraites, E. G., Duncan, W. J., Gillin, J. C., van Kammen, D. P., Kleinman, J., Murphy, D. L., Post, R. M., Reus, V., & Wyatt, R. J. (1979). The use of narcotic antagonists to study the role of endorphins in normal and psychiatric patients. In E. Usdin, W. E. Bunney, Jr., & N. S. Kline (Eds.), *Endorphins and mental health research* (pp. 393–406). New York: Macmillan.

Davis, K. L., Hollister, L. E., Mathe, A. A., Davis, B. M., Rothpearl, A. B., Faul, K. F., Hsieh, J. Y. K., Barchas, J. D., & Berger, P. A. (1981). Neuroendocrine and neurochemical measurements in depression. *American Journal of Psychiatry, 138,* 1555–1562.

DeLeon-Jones, F., Maas, J. W., Dekirmenjian, H., & Sanchez, J. (1975). Diagnostic subgroups of affective disorders and their urinary excretion of catecholamine metabolites. *American Journal of Psychiatry, 132,* 1141–1148.

d'Elia, G., & Perris, C. (1973). Cerebral functional dominance and depression. *Acta Psychiatrica Scandinavica, 49,* 191–197.

DeLisi, L. E., Karoum, F., Targum, S., Byrnes, S., & Wyatt, R. J. (1983). The determination of urinary 3-methoxy-4-hydroxy-phenylglycol excretion in acute schizophreniform and depressed patients. *Biological Psychiatry, 18,* 1189–1196.

Demisch, K., Demisch, L., Bochnik, H. J., & Schulz, F. (1983). Comparison of the ACTH suppression test and dexamethasone suppression test in depressed patients. *American Journal of Psychiatry, 140,* 1511–1512.

de Montigny, C., Cournoyer, G., Morissette, R., Langlois, R., & Caille, G. (1983). Lithium carbonate addition in tricyclic antidepressant-resistant unipolar depression. *Archives of General Psychiatry, 40,* 1327–1334.

DeMyer, M. K., Shea, P. A., Hendrie, H. C., & Yoshimura, N. N. (1981). Plasma tryptophan and five other amino acids in depressed and normal subjects. *Archives of General Psychiatry, 38,* 642–646.

Depue, R. A., & Monroe, S. M. (1978). The unipolar-bipolar distinction in the depressive disorders. *Psychological Bulletin, 85,* 1001–1029.

Deutsch, S. I., Mohs, R. C., Levy, M. I., Rothpearl, A. B., Stockton, D., Horvath, T., Coco, A., & Davis, K. L. (1983). Acetylcholinesterase activity in CSF in schizophrenia, depression, Alzheimer's disease, and normals. *Biological Psychiatry, 18,* 1363–1373.

Dewan, M. J., Pandurangi, A. K., Boucher, M. L., Levy, B. F., & Major, L. F. (1982). Abnormal dexamethasone suppression test results in chronic schizophrenic patients. *American Journal of Psychiatry, 139,* 1501–1503.

Dilsaver, S. C., Kronfol, Z., Sackellares, J. C., & Greden, J. F. (1983). Antidepressant withdrawal syndromes: Evidence supporting the cholinergic overdrive hypothesis. *Journal of Clinical Psychopharmacology, 3,* 157–164.

Doerfler, L. A. (1981). Psychological research on depression: A methodological review. *Clinical Psychology Review, 1,* 119–137.

Doerr, P., & Berger, M. (1983). Physostigmine-induced escape from dexamethasone suppression in normal adults. *Biological Psychiatry, 18,* 261–267.

Doerr, P., von Zerssen, D., Fischler, M., & Schulz, H. (1979). Relationship between mood changes and adrenal cortical activity in a patient with 48-hour unipolar-depressive cycles. *Journal of Affective Disorders, 1,* 93–104.

Dorus, E., Cox, N. J., Gibbons, R. D., Shaughnessy, R., Pandey, G. N., & Cloninger, C. R. (1983). Lithium ion transport and affective disorders within families of bipolar patients. *Archives of General Psychiatry, 40,* 545–552.

Dubovsky, S. L., & Franks, R. D. (1983). Intracellular calcium ions in affective disorders: A review and an hypothesis. *Biological Psychiatry, 18,* 781–797.

Duncan, W. C., Gillin, J. C., Post, R. M., Gerner, R. H., & Wehr, T. A. (1980). The relationship between EEG sleep patterns and clinical improvement in depressed patients treated with sleep deprivation. *Biological Psychiatry, 15,* 879–889.

Duncan, W. C., Pettigrew, K. D., & Gillin, J. C. (1979). REM architecture changes in bipolar and unipolar depression. *American Journal of Psychiatry, 136,* 1424–1427.

Edelstein, C. K., Roy-Byrne, P., Fawzy, F. I., & Dornfeld, L. (1983). Effects of weight loss on the dexamethasone suppression test. *American Journal of Psychiatry, 140,* 338–341.

Egeland, J. A., & Hostetter, A. M. (1983). Amish study: I. Affective disorders among the Amish. *American Journal of Psychiatry, 140,* 56–61.

Egeland, J. A., Hostetter, A. M., & Eshleman, S. K. (1983). Amish study III: The impact of cultural factors on bipolar diagnosis. *American Journal of Psychiatry, 140,* 67–71.

Ehrensing, R. H., Kastin, A. J., Schalch, D. S., Friesen, H. G., Vargas, J. R., & Schally, A. V. (1974). Affective states and thyrotropin and prolactin responses after repeated injections of thyrotropin-releasing hormone in depressed patients. *American Journal of Psychiatry, 131,* 714–718.

Eisemann, M., Ericsson, V., von Knorring, L., Perris, C., Perris, H., & Ross, S. (1983). Serum dopamine-beta-hydroxylase in diagnostic subgroups of depressed patients and in relation to their personality characteristics. *Neuropsychobiology, 9,* 193–196.

Endicott, J., & Spitzer, R. L. (1978). A diagnostic interview: The schedule for affective disorders and schizophrenia. *Archives of General Psychiatry, 35,* 837–848.

Erickson, C. K. (1978). Functional relationships among central neurotransmitters. In S. Ehrenpreis & I. Kopin (Eds.), *Reviews of Neuroscience* (Vol. 1, pp. 2–34). New York: Raven Press.

Esler, M., Turbott, J., Schwartz, R., Leonard, P., Bobik, A., Skews, H., & Jackman, G. (1982). The peripheral kinetics of norepinephrine in depressive illness. *Archives of General Psychiatry, 39,* 295–300.

Evans, D. L., & Nemeroff, C. B. (1983). The dexamethasone suppression test in mixed bipolar disorder. *American Journal of Psychiatry, 140,* 615–617.

Extein, I., Pottash, A. L. C., Gold, M. S., Cadet, J., Sweeney, D. R., Davies, R. K., & Martin, D. M. (1980). The thyroid-stimulating hormone response to thyrotropin-releasing hormone in mania and bipolar depression. *Psychiatry Research, 2,* 199–204.

Extein, I., Pottash, A. L. C., Gold, M. S., & Martin, D. M. (1980). Differentiating mania from schizophrenia by the TRH-test. *American Journal of Psychiatry, 137,* 981–982.

Extein, I., Pottash, A. L. C., Gold, M. S., Sweeney, D. R., Martin, D. M., & Goodwin, F. K. (1980). Deficient prolactin response to morphine in depressed patients. *American Journal of Psychiatry, 137,* 845–846.

Extein, I., Rosenberg, G., Pottash, A. L. C., & Gold, M. S. (1982). The dexamethasone suppression test in depressed adolescents. *American Journal of Psychiatry, 139,* 1617–1619.

Fang, V. S., Tricou, B. J., Robertson, A., & Meltzer, H. Y. (1981). Plasma ACTH and cortisol levels in depressed patients. *Life Sciences, 29,* 931–938.

Feighner, J. P., Robins, E., Guze, S. B., Woodruff, R. A., Winokur, G., & Muñoz, R. (1972). Diagnostic criteria for use in psychiatric research. *Archives of General Psychiatry, 26,* 57–63.

Feinberg, M. (1982). EEG studies of sleep and the dexamethasone suppression test in the diagnosis of depression. In I. Hanin & E. Usdin (Eds.), *Biological markers in psychiatry and neurology* (pp. 241–252). New York: Pergamon Press.

Feinberg, M., Carroll, B. J., Greden, J. F., & Zis, A. P. (1982). Sleep EEG, depressing rating scales, and diagnosis. *Biological Psychiatry, 17,* 1453–1458.

Feinberg, M., Gillin, J. C., Carroll, B. J., Greden, J. P., & Zis, A. P. (1982). EEG studies of sleep in the diagnosis of depression. *Biological Psychiatry, 17,* 305–316.

Fink, M., Simeon, J., Itil, T. M., & Freedman, A. M. (1970). Clinical antidepressant activity of cyclazocine-a narcotic antagonist. *Clinical Pharmacology and Therapeutics, 11,* 41–48.

Flor-Henry, P. (1979). On certain aspects of the localization of the cerebral systems regulating and determining emotion. *Biological Psychiatry, 14,* 677–698.

Flor-Henry, P., & Koles, Z. J. (1980). EEG studies in depression, mania and normals: Evidence for partial shifts of laterality in the affective psychoses. *Advances in Biological Psychiatry, 4,* 21–43.

Fraser, A. R. (1983). Choice of antidepressant based on the dexamethasone suppression test. *American Journal of Psychiatry, 140,* 786–787.

Gaertner, H. J., Kreuter, F., Scharek, G., Wiatr, G., & Breyer-Pfaff, U. (1982). Do urinary MHPG and plasma drug levels correlate with response to amitriptyline therapy? *Psychopharmacology, 76,* 236–239.

Gaillard, J. M., Iorio, G., Blois, R., & Tissot, R. (1981). Modifications of sleep in depressed patients: Possible physiological implications. *Advances in Biological Psychiatry, 6,* 81–86.

Garbutt, J. C., Loosen, P. T., Tipermas, A., & Prange, A. J. (1983). The TRH test in patients with borderline personality disorder. *Psychiatry Research, 9,* 107–113.

Garcia-Seville, J. A., Zis, A. P., Hollingsworth, P. J., Greden, J. F., & Smith, C. B. (1981). Platelet $\alpha2$-adrenergic receptors in major depressive disorder: Binding to tritiated clonidine before and after tricyclic antidepressant drug treatment. *Archives of General Psychiatry, 38,* 1327–1333.

Garver, D. L., Pandey, G. N., Dekirmenjian, H., & DeLeon-Jones, F. (1975). Growth hormone and catecholamines in affective disease. *American Journal of Psychiatry, 132,* 1149–1154.

Geller, B., Rogol, A. D., & Knitter, E. F. (1983). Preliminary data on the dexamethasone suppression test in children with major depressive disorder. *American Journal of Psychiatry, 5,* 620–622.

Gerner, R. H., & Wilkins, J. N. (1983). CSF cortisol in patients with depression, mania, or anorexia nervosa and in normal subjects. *American Journal of Psychiatry, 140,* 92–94.

Gerner, R. H., & Yamada, T. (1982). Altered neuropeptide concentrations in cerebrospinal fluid of psychiatric patients. *Brain Research, 238,* 298–302.

Giedke, H., Bolz, J., & Heimann, H. (1980). Evoked potentials, expectancy wave, and skin resistance in depressed patients and healthy controls. *Pharmakopsychiatry, 13,* 91–101.

Giles, D. E., & Rush, A. J. (1982). Relationship of dysfunctional attitudes and dexamethasone response in endogenous and nonendogenous depression. *Biological Psychiatry, 17,* 1303–1314.

Gillespie, R. D. (1929). The clinical differentiation of types of depression. *Guy's Hospital Reports, 79,* 306–344.

Gillin, J. C. (1983a). Sleep studies in affective illness: Diagnostic, therapeutic, and pathophysiological implications. *Psychiatric Annals, 13,* 367–384.

Gillin, J. C. (1983b). The sleep therapies of depression. *Progress in Neuro-Psychopharmacology and Biological Psychiatry, 7,* 351–364.

Gillin, J. C., Duncan, W. C., Murphy, D. L., Post, R. M., Wehr, T. A., Goodwin, F. K., Wyatt, R. J., & Bunney, W. E., Jr. (1981). Age-related changes in sleep in depressed and normal subjects. *Psychiatry Research, 4,* 73–78.

Gillin, J. C., Duncan, W., Pettigrew, K. D., Frankel, B. L., & Snyder, F. (1979). Successful separation of depressed, normal, and insomniac subjects by EEG sleep data. *Archives of General Psychiatry, 36,* 85–90.

Gillin, J. C., Mendelson, W. B., Sitaram, N., & Wyatt, R. J. (1978). The neuropharmacology of sleep and wakefulness. *Annual Review of Pharmacology and Toxicology, 18,* 563–579.

Gillin, J. C., Sitaram, N., & Duncan, W. C. (1979). Muscarinic supersensitivity: A possible model for the sleep disturbance of primary depression? *Psychiatry Research, 1,* 17–22.

Glassman, A. H. (1969). Indoleamines and affective disorders. *Psychomatic Medicine, 31,* 107–114.

Glassman, A. H., Kantor, S. J., & Shostak, M. (1975). Depression, delusions, and drug response. *American Journal of Psychiatry, 132,* 716–729.

Glassman, A. H., & Roose, S. P. (1981). Delusional depression. *Archives of General Psychiatry, 38,* 424–427.

Gold, M. S., & Pottash, A. L. C. (1983). Thyroid dysfunction or depression? In F. J. Ayd, I. J. Taylor, & B. T. Taylor (Eds.), *Affective disorders reassessed: 1983* (pp. 179–191). Baltimore: Ayd Medical Communications.

Gold, M. S., Pottash, A. L. C., & Extein, I. (1981). Hypothyroidism and depression: Evidence from complete thyroid function evaluation. *Journal of the American Medical Association, 245,* 1919–1922.

Gold, M. S., Pottash, A. L. C., Extein, I., & Sweeney, D. R. (1981). Diagnosis of depression in the 1980s. *Journal of the American Medical Association, 245,* 1562–1564.

Gold, M. S., Pottash, A. L. C., Ryan, N., Sweeney, D. R., Davis, R. K., & Martin, D. M. (1980). TRH-induced TSH response in unipolar, bipolar, and secondary depressions: Possible utility in clinical assessment and differential diagnosis. *Psychoneuroendocrinology, 5,* 147–155.

Gold, M. S., & Rea, W. S. (1983). The role of endorphins in opiate addiction, opiate withdrawal, and recovery. *Psychiatric Clinics of North America, 6,* 489–520.

Gold, P. W., Goodwin, F. K., Wehr, T., & Rebar, R. (1977). Pituitary thyrotropin response to thyrotropin-releasing hormone in affective illness: Relationship to spinal fluid amine metabolites. *American Journal of Psychiatry, 134,* 1028–1031.

Gold, P. W., Goodwin, F. K., Wehr, T., Rebar, R., & Sack, R. (1976). Growth-hormone and prolactin response to levodopa in affective illness (Letter to the Editor). *Lancet, 2,* 1308–1309.

Goodwin, F. K., Murphy, D. L., & Bunney, W. E., Jr. (1969). Lithium carbonate treatment in depression and mania: A longitudinal double-blind study. *Archives of General Psychiatry, 21,* 486–496.

Goodwin, F. K., & Post, R. M. (1975). Studies of amine metabolites in affective illness and in schizophrenia. In D. X. Freedman (Ed.), *Biology of the major psychoses* (pp. 299–332). New York: Raven Press.

Graham, P. M., Booth, J., Boranga, G., Galhenage, S., Myers, C. M., Teoh, C. L., & Cox, L. S. (1982). The dexamethasone suppression test in mania. *Journal of Affective Disorders, 4,* 201–211.

Greden, J. F., Albala, A. A., Haskett, R. F., James, N. M., Goodman, L., Steiner, M., & Carroll, B. J. (1980). Normalization of dexamethasone suppression test: A laboratory index of recovery from endogenous depression. *Biological Psychiatry, 15,* 449–458.

Greden, J. F., & Carroll, B. J. (1981). Psychomotor function in affective disorders: An overview of new monitoring techniques. *American Journal of Psychiatry, 11,* 1441–1448.

Greden, J. F., Gardner, R., King, D., Grunhaus, L., Carroll, B. J., & Kronfol, Z. (1983). Dexamethasone suppression test in antidepressant treatment of melancholia. *Archives of General Psychiatry, 40,* 493–500.

Greden, J. F., Kronfol, Z., Gardner, R., Feinberg, M., Mukhopadhyay, S., Albala, A. A., & Carroll, B. J. (1981). Dexamethasone suppression test and selection of antidepressant medications. *Journal of Affective Disorders, 3,* 389–396.

Gregoire, F., Brauman, H., de Buck, R., & Corvilain, J. (1977). Hormone release in depressed patients before and after recovery. *Psychoneuroendocrinology, 2,* 303–312.

Gruen, P. H., Sachar, E. J., Altman, N., & Sassin, J. (1975). Growth hormone responses to hypoglycemia in postmenopausal depressed women. *Archives of General Psychiatry, 32,* 31–33.

Grunhaus, L., Greden, J. F., Carroll, B. J., & Shein, H. (1983). The dexamethasone suppression test in repeated hospitalizations. *Biological Psychiatry, 18,* 1497–1502.

Gudeman, J. E., Schatzberg, A. F., Samson, J. A., Orsulak, P. J., Cole, J. O., & Schildkraut, J. J. (1982). Toward a biochemical classification of depressive disorders. VI: Platelet MAO activity and clinical symptoms in depressed patients. *American Journal of Psychiatry, 139,* 630–633.

Gustafson, L., Johanson, M., Risberg, J., & Silfverskiold, P. (1981). Regional cerebral blood flow in organic dementias, affective disorders and confusional states. In C. Perris, G. Struwe, & B. Jansson (Eds.), *Biological psychiatry* (pp. 276–279). New York: Elsevier-North Holland Publishing.

Gustafson, L., Risberg, J., & Silfverskiold, P. (1981). Cerebral blood flow in dementia and depression (Letter to the Editor). *Lancet, 1,* 275.

Gwirtsman, H. E., Roy-Byrne, P., Yager, J., & Gerner, R. H. (1983). Neuroendocrine abnormalities in bulimia. *American Journal of Psychiatry, 140,* 559–563.

Haier, R. J. (1983). Pain sensitivity, evoked potentials, and the dexamethasone suppression test in depressed patients. *Psychiatry Research, 10,* 201–206.

Halaris, A., DeMet, E., Gwirtsman, H., & Piletz, J. (1983, December). *Normal and abnormal circadian patterns of plasma 3-methoxy-4-hydroxyphenylglycol (MHPG).* Paper presented at the annual meeting of the American College of Neuropsychopharmacology, San Juan.

Halbreich, U., Endicott, J., & Nee, J. (1983). Premenstrual depressive changes. *Archives of General Psychiatry, 40,* 535–542.

Halbreich, U., Grunhaus, L., & Ben-David, M. (1979). Twenty-four-hour rhythm of prolactin in depressive patients. *Archives of General Psychiatry, 36,* 1183–1186.

Halbreich, U., Sachar, E. J., Asnis, G., Quitkin, F., Nathan, R. S., Halpern, F. S., & Klein, D. F. (1982). Growth hormone response to dextroamphetamine in depressed patients and normal subjects. *Archives of General Psychiatry, 39,* 189–192.

Hamilton, E. W., & Abramson, L. Y. (1983). Cognitive patterns and major depressive disorder: A longitudinal study in a hospital setting. *Journal of Abnormal Psychology, 92,* 173–184.

Hamilton, M. (1960). A rating scale for depression. *Journal of Neurology, Neurosurgery and Psychiatry, 23,* 56–62.

Helms, P. M., & Smith, R. E. (1983). Recurrent psychotic depression: Evidence of diagnostic stability. *Journal of Affective Disorders, 5,* 51–54.

Heninger, G. R., Charney, D. S., & Sternberg, D. E. (1983). Lithium carbonate augmentation of antidepressant treatment. *Archives of General Psychiatry, 40,* 1335–1342.

Heninger, G. R., Mueller, P. D., & Davis, L. S. (1975). Depressive symptoms in the glucose tolerance test and insulin tolerance test. *Journal of Nervous and Mental Disease, 151,* 421–431.

Himmelhoch, J. M. (1984). Major mood disorders related to epileptic changes. In D. Blumer (Ed.), *Psychiatric aspects of epilepsy* (pp. 271–294). Washington, DC: American Psychiatric Press.

Himmelhoch, J. M., Fuchs, C. Z., May, S. J., Symons, B. J., & Neil, J. F. (1981). When a schizoaffective diagnosis has meaning. *Journal of Nervous and Mental Disease, 169,* 277–282.

Hirschfeld, R. M. A., Koslow, S. H., & Kupfer, D. J. (1983). The clinical utility of the dexamethasone suppression test in psychiatry: Summary of a National Institute of Mental Health workshop. *Journal of the American Medical Association, 250,* 2172–2174.

Hollister, L. F. (1981). Excretion of 3-methoxy-4-hydroxyphenylglycol in depressed and geriatric patients and normal persons. *International Pharmacopsychiatry, 16,* 138–143.

Holsboer, F., Dorr, H. G., & Sippell, W. G. (1982). Blunted aldosterone response to dexamethasone in female patients with endogenous depression. *Psychoneuroendocrinology, 7,* 155–167.

Holsboer, F., Lieble, R., & Hofschuster, E. (1982). Repeated dexamethasone suppression test during depressive illness. *Journal of Affective Disorders, 4,* 93–101.

Holsboer, F., Steiger, A., & Maier, W. (1983). Four cases of reversion to abnormal dexamethasone suppression test response as indicator of clinical relapse: A preliminary report. *Biological Psychiatry, 18,* 911–916.

Holzman, P. S., Proctor, L. R., Yasillo, N. J., Meltzer, H. Y., & Hurt, S. W. (1974). Eye tracking dysfunctions in schizophrenic patients and their first-degree relatives. *Archives of General Psychiatry, 31,* 143–151.

Hudson, J. I., Laffer, P. S., & Pope, H. G. (1982). Bulimia related to affective disorder by family history and response to the dexamethasone suppression test. *American Journal of Psychiatry, 139,* 686–687.

Huston, P. E., & Locher, L. M. (1948). Manic-depressive psychosis: Course when treated and untreated with electric shock. *Archives of Neurology and Psychiatry, 50,* 37–48.

Iacono, W. G., & Lykken, D. T. (1979). Eye tracking and psychopathology. *Archives of General Psychiatry, 36,* 1361–1369.

Iacono, W. G., Lykken, D. T., Peloquin, L. J., Lumry, A. E., Valentine, R. H., & Tuason, V. B. (1983). Electrodermal activity in euthymic unipolar and bipolar affective disorders: A possible marker for depression. *Archives of General Psychiatry, 40,* 557–565.

Iacono, W. G., Peloquin, L. J., Lumry, A. E., Valentine, R. H., & Tuason, V. B. (1982). Eye tracking in patients with unipolar and bipolar affective disorders in remission. *Journal of Abnormal Psychology, 91,* 35–44.

Ingvar, D. H. (1981). Measurements of regional cerebral blood flow and metabolism in psychopathological states. *European Neurology, 20,* 294–296.

Insel, T. R., Gillin, J. C., Moore, A., Mendelson, W. B., Loewenstein, R. J., & Murphy, D. L. (1982). The sleep of patients with obsessive-compulsive disorder. *Archives of General Psychiatry, 39,* 1372–1377.

Insel, T. R., Kalin, N. H., Guttmacher, L. B., Cohen, R. M., & Murphy, D. L. (1982). The dexamethasone suppression test in patients with primary depressive-compulsive disorder. *Psychiatry Research, 6,* 153–160.

Jacoby, R. J., & Levy, R. (1980a). Computed tomography in the elderly. 3. Affective disorder. *British Journal of Psychiatry, 136,* 270–275.

Jacoby, R. J., & Levy, R. (1980b). Computed tomography in the elderly. 2. Senile dementia: Diagnosis and functional impairment. *British Journal of Psychiatry, 136,* 256–269.

Jacoby, R. J., & Levy, R. (1980c). CT scanning and the investigation of dementia. A review. *Journal of the Royal Society of Medicine, 73,* 366–369.

Jaffe, K., Barnshaw, H. D., & Kennedy, M. E. (1983). The dexamethasone suppression test in depressed outpatients with and without melancholia. *American Journal of Psychiatry, 140,* 492–493.

Janowsky, D. S., El-Yousef, M. K., Davis, J. M., & Sekerke, H. (1972). A cholinergic-adrenergic hypothesis of mania and depression. *Lancet, 2,* 632–635.

Janowsky, D. S., Risch, S. C., & Gillin, J. C. (1983). Adrenergic-cholinergic balance and the treatment of affective disorders. *Progress in Neuropsychopharmacology and Biological Psychiatry, 7,* 297–307.

Jarrett, D. B., Coble, P. A., & Kupfer, D. J. (1983). Reduced cortisol latency in depressive illness. *Archives of General Psychiatry, 40,* 506–511.

Jefferson, J. W., & Greist, J. H. (1977). *Primer of lithium therapy.* Baltimore: Williams & Wilkins.

Jimerson, D. C., Insel, T. R., Reus, V. I., & Kopin, I. (1983). Increased plasma MHPG in dexamethasone-resistant depressed patients. *Archives of General Psychiatry, 40,* 173–176.

Judd, L. L., Risch, S. C., Parker, D. C., Janowsky, D. S., Segal, D. S., & Huey, L. Y. (1982). Blunted prolactin response: A neuroendocrine abnormality manifested by depressed patients. *Archives of General Psychiatry, 39,* 1413–1416.

Kalin, N. H., & Loevinger, B. L. (1983). The central and peripheral opioid peptides: Their relationships and functions. *Psychiatric Clinics of North America, 6,* 415–428.

Kalin, N. H., Risch, S. C., Janowsky, D. S., & Murphy, D. L. (1981). Use of the dexamethasone suppression test in clinical psychiatry. *Journal of Clinical Psychopharmacology, 1,* 64–69.

Kalin, N. H., Risch, S. C., & Murphy, D. L. (1982). Involvement of the central serotonergic system in affective illness. *Journal of Clinical Psychopharmacology, 1,* 232–237.

Kalin, N. H., Weiler, S. J., & Shelton, S. E. (1982). Plasma ACTH and cortisol concentrations before and after dexamethasone. *Psychiatry Research, 7,* 87–92.

Kasper, S., & Beckmann, H. (1983). Dexamethasone suppression test in a pluri-diagnostic approach. Its relationship to psychopathological and clinical variables. *Acta Psychiatrica Scandinavica, 68,* 31–37.

Kellner, C. H., Rubinow, D. R., Gold, P. W., & Post, R. M. (1983). Relationship of cortisol hypersecretion to brain CT scan alterations in depressed patients. *Psychiatry Research, 8,* 191–197.

Kelwala, S., Jones, D., & Sitaram, N. (1983). Monoamine metabolites as predictors of antidepressant response: A critique. *Progress in Neuropsychopharmacology and Biological Psychiatry, 7,* 229–240.

Kirkegaard, C. (1981). The thyrotropin response to thyrotropin-releasing hormone in endogenous depression. *Psychoneuroendocrinology, 6,* 189–212.

Kirkegaard, C., & Carroll, B. J. (1980). Dissociation of TSH and adrenocortical disturbances in endogenous depression. *Psychiatry Research, 3,* 253–264.

Kirkegaard, C., & Faber, J. (1981). Altered serum levels of thyroxine, triiodothyronines and diiodo-thyronines in endogenous depression. *Acta Endocrinology, 96,* 199–207.

Klein, D. F. (1974). Endogenomorphic depression—A conceptual and terminological revision. *Archives of General Psychiatry, 31,* 447–454.

Klein, D. F., Gittleman, R., Quitkin, F., & Rifkin, A. (1980). *Diagnosis and drug treatment of psychiatric disorders: Adults and children* (2nd ed.). Baltimore: Williams & Wilkins.

Klein, R. H., Salzman, L. F., Jones, F., & Ritzler, B. (1976). Eye tracking in psychiatric patients and their offspring (Abstract). *Psychophysiology, 13,* 186.

Klerman, G. L., & Barrett, J. E. (1973). The affective disorders: Clinical and epidemiological aspects. In S. Gershon & B. Shopsin (Eds.), *Lithium: Its role in psychiatric research and treatment* (pp. 201–236). New York: Plenum Publishing.

Kline, N. S., & Lehman, H. E. (1979). Therapy with beta-endorphin in psychiatric patients. In E. Usdin, W. E. Bunney, Jr., & N. S. Kline (Eds.), *Endorphins in mental health research* (pp. 500–517). New York: Macmillan.

Kling, A. S., Kuhl, D. E., Metter, E. J., Kurtz, N., Phelps, M. E., Riege, W., & Huellett, J. (1983, May). *Positron computed tomography and CT scans in schizophrenia and depression.* Paper presented at the New Research section of the annual meeting of the American Psychiatric Association, New York.

Koslow, S. H., Maas, J. W., Bowden, C. L., Davis, J. M., Hanin, I., & Javaid, J. (1983). CSF and urinary biogenic amines and metabolites in depression and mania. *Archives of General Psychiatry, 40,* 999–1010.

Koslow, S. H., Stokes, P. E., Mendels, J., Ramsey, A., & Casper, R. (1982). Insulin tolerance test: Human growth hormone response and insulin resistance in primary unipolar depressed, bipolar depressed and control subjects. *Psychological Medicine, 12,* 45–55.

Kovacs, M., Feinberg, T. L., Crouse-Novak, M. A., Paulauskas, S. L., & Finkelstein, R. (1984). Depressive disorders in childhood. I. A longitudinal prospective study of characteristics and recovery. *Archives of General Psychiatry, 41,* 229–237.

Kovacs, M., Rush, A. J., Beck, A. T., & Hollon, S. D. (1981). Depressed outpatients treated with cognitive therapy or pharmacotherapy. *Archives of General Psychiatry, 38,* 33–39.

Kraepelin, E. (1921). *Manic depressive insanity and paranoia.* Edinburgh: Livingstone.

Krieger, D. T., & Liotta, A. S. (1979). Pituitary hormones in brain: Where, who and why? *Science, 205,* 366–372.

Kripke, D. F., Risch, S. C., & Janowsky, D. (1983). Bright white light alleviates depression. *Psychiatry Research, 10,* 105–112.

Krishnan, R. R., Maltbie, A. A., & Davidson, J. R. T. (1983). Abnormal cortisol suppression in bipolar patients with simultaneous manic and depressive symptoms. *American Journal of Psychiatry, 140,* 203–205.

Kuhn, R. (1958). The treatment of depressive states with G-22355 (imipramine hydrochloride). *American Journal of Psychiatry, 115,* 459–464.

Kupfer, D. J. (1981). EEG sleep and tricyclic antidepressants in affective disorders. In E. Usdin (Ed.), *Clinical pharmacology in psychiatry* (pp. 325–388). New York: Raven Press.

Kupfer, D. J. (1982a). EEG sleep as biological markers in depression. In I. Hanin & E. Usdin (Eds.), *Biological markers in psychiatry and neurology* (pp. 387–396). New York: Pergamon Press.

Kupfer, D. J. (1982b). Interaction of EEG sleep, antidepressants, and affective disease. *Journal of Clinical Psychiatry, 43*(Sec. 2), 30–35.

Kupfer, D. J., Broudy, D., Spiker, D. G., Neil, J. F., & Coble, P. A. (1979). EEG sleep and affective psychoses: I. Schizoaffective disorders. *Psychiatry Research, 1,* 172–178.

Kupfer, D. J., Bulik, C. M., & Jarrett, D. B. (1983). Nighttime plasma cortisol secretion and EEG sleep—Are they associated? *Psychiatry Research, 10,* 191–199.

Kupfer, D. J., & Edwards, D. J. (1978). Multi-transmitter mechanisms and treatment of affective disease. In P. Denber, C. Radouco-Thomas, & A. Villeneuve (Eds.), *Neuropsychopharmacology* (pp. 609–623). New York: Pergamon Press.

Kupfer, D. J., Edwards, D. J., Spiker, D. G., Holzer, B. C., & Coble, P. A. (1979). MAO Activity and EEG sleep in primary depression. *Psychiatry Research, 1,* 241–247.

Kupfer, D. J., Foster, F. G., Detre, T. P., & Himmelhoch, J. (1975). Sleep and motor activity as indicators in affective states. *Neuropsychobiology, 1,* 296–303.

Kupfer, D. J., Frank, E., Jarrett, D. B., Reynolds C. F. III, & Thase, M. E. (in press). The interrelationship of EEG sleep, chronobiology, and depression. In D. J. Kupfer, S. Matthysse, & J. D. Barchas (Eds.), *Biological clocks and the psychobiology of depression: Ultradian, circadian sleep mechanisms.* Chicago: University of Chicago Press.

Kupfer, D. J., Gillin, J. C., Coble, P. A., Spiker, D. G., Shaw, D., & Holzer, B. (1981). REM sleep, naps, and depression. *Psychiatry Research, 5,* 195–203.

Kupfer, D. J., Holzer, B. C., Edwards, D. J., Coble, P. A., Spiker, D. G., & Neil, J. F. (1980). MHPG excretion and EEG sleep in primary depression. *Psychiatry Research, 3,* 133–140.

Kupfer, D. J., Pickar, D., Himmelhoch, J. M., & Detre, T. P. (1975). Are there two types of unipolar depression? *Archives of General Psychiatry, 32,* 866–871.

Kupfer, D. J., & Reynolds, C. F. III (1983). Neurphysiologic studies of depression: State of the art. In J. Angst (Ed.), *The origins of depression: Current concepts and approaches* (pp. 235–252). New York: Springer-Verlag.

Kupfer, D. J., & Rush, A. J. (1983). Recommendations for depression publications (Letter to the Editor). *Archives of General Psychiatry, 40,* 1031.

Kupfer, D. J., Targ, E., & Stack, J. (1982). EEG sleep in unipolar depressive subtypes: Support for a biologic and familial classification. *Journal of Nervous and Mental Disease, 170,* 494–498.

Kupfer, D. J., & Thase, M. E. (1983). The use of the sleep laboratory in the diagnosis of affective disorders. *Psychiatric Clinics of North America, 5,* 3–25.

Kupfer, D. J., & Thase, M. E. (in press). Validity of major depression: A psychobiological perspective. In G. L. Tischler & M. M. Weissman (Eds.), *DSM:III: An interim appraisal.* Washington, DC: American Psychiatric Association.

Kupfer, D. J., Ulrich, R. F., Grochocinski, V., Doman, J., & Matthews, G. (1984). *Automated sleep analyses in depression and prediction of clinical response.* Manuscript submitted for publication.

Kupfer, D. J., Wyatt, R. J., & Snyder, F. (1970). Comparison between electroencephalographic and systematic nursing observations of sleep in psychiatric patients. *Journal of Nervous and Mental Disease, 151,* 361–368.

Laakmann, G. (1980). Neuroendocrinological findings in affective disorders after administration of antidepressants. *Advances in Biological Psychiatry, 5,* 67–84.

Lader, M. H. (1975). *The psychophysiology of mental illness.* Boston: Routledge, Kegan Paul.

Lader, M. H., & Wing, L. (1969). Physiological measures in agitated and retarded depressed patients. *Journal of Psychiatric Research, 7,* 89–100.

Lahmeyer, H. W., Poznanski, E. O., & Bellus, S. N. (1983). EEG sleep in depressed adolescents. *American Journal of Psychiatry, 140,* 1150–1153.

Lake, C. R., Pickar, D., Ziegler, M. G., Lipper, S., Slater, S., & Murphy, D. L. (1982). High plasma norepinephrine levels in patients with major affective disorders. *American Journal of Psychiatry, 139,* 1315–1318.

Langer, G., Aschauer, H., Koinig, G., Resch, F., & Schonbeck, G. (1983). The TSH response to TRH: A possible predictor of outcome to antidepressant and neuroleptic treatment. *Progress in Neuropsychopharmacology and Biological Psychiatry, 7,* 335–342.

Langer, G., Heinze, G., Reim, B., & Matussek, N. (1976). Reduction of growth hormone response in endogenous depressive patients. *Archives of General Psychiatry, 33,* 1471–1475.

Langer, S. Z., Zarafian, E., Briley, M., Raisman, R., & Sechter, D. (1981). High-affinity binding of 3H-imipramine in brain and platelets and its relevance to the biochemistry of affective disorders. *Life Sciences, 29,* 211–220.

LaPierre, Y. D., & Butter, H. G. (1980). Agitated and regarded depression: A clinical psychophysiological evaluation. *Neuropsychobiology, 6,* 217–223.

Lechin, F., Van der Dijs, B., Acosta, E., Gomez, F., Lechin, E., & Arocha, L. (1983). Distal colon motility and clinical parameters in depression. *Journal of Affective Disorders, 5,* 19–26.

Lechin, F., Van der Dijs, B., Gomez, F., Arocha, L., Acosta, E., & Lechin, E. (1983). Distal colon motility as a predictor of antidepressant response to fenfluramine, imipramine and clomipramine. *Journal of Affective Disorders, 5,* 27–35.

Lee, M. A., & Taylor, M. A. (1983). Cortisol suppression and circadian rhythm in endogenous depression: A preliminary report. *Biological Psychiatry, 18,* 1127–1132.

Lewinsohn, P. M., Steinmetz, J. L., Larson, D. W., & Franklin, J. (1981). Depression-related cognitions: Antecedent or consequence? *Journal of Abnormal Psychology, 90,* 213–219.

Levy, D. L., Lipton, R. B., Yasillo, N. J., Peterson, J., Pandey, G., & Davis, J. M. (in press). Psychotropic drug effects on smooth pursuit eye movements: A summary of recent findings. In A. G. Gale & F. Johnson (Eds.), *Theoretical and applied aspects of eye movement research.* New York: Elsevier-North Holland Publishing.

Levy, D. L., Yasillo, N. J., Dorus, E., Shaughnessy, R., Gibbons, R. D., Peterson, J., Janicak, P. G., Gaviria, M., & Davis, J. M. (1983). Relatives of unipolar and bipolar patients have normal pursuit. *Psychiatry Research, 10,* 285–293.

Lewis, D. A., Kathol, R. G., Sherman, B. M., Winokur, G., & Schlesser, M. A. (1983). Differentiation of depressive subtypes of insulin insensitivity in the recovered phase. *Archives of General Psychiatry, 40,* 167–170.

Lewy, A. J., Kern, H. A., Rosenthal, N. E., & Wehr, T. A. (1982). Bright artificial light treatment of a manic-depressive patient with a seasonal mood cycle. *American Journal of Psychiatry, 139,* 1496–1498.

Lewy, A. J., Wehr, T. A., Goodwin, F. K., Newsome, D. A., & Rosenthal, N. E. (1981). Manic-depressive patients may be supersensitive to light. *Lancet, 1,* 383–384.

Liebowitz, M. R., & Klein, D. F. (1979). Hysteroid dysphoria. *Psychiatric Clinics of North America, 2,* 555–575.

Lindstrom, L. H., Widerlov, E., Gunne, L. M., Wahlstrom, A., & Terenius, L. (1978). Endorphins in human cerebrospinal fluid: Clinical correlations to some psychotic states. *Acta Psychiatrica Scandinavica, 57,* 153–164.

Linkowski, P., Brauman, H., & Mendlewicz, J. (1980). Prolactin secretion in women with unipolar and bipolar depression. *Psychiatry Research, 3,* 265–271.

Linkowski, P., Brauman, H., & Mendlewicz, J. (1981). Thyrotropin response to thyrotropin-releasing hormone in unipolar and bipolar affective illness. *Journal of Affective Disorders, 3,* 9–6.

Linnoila, M., Cowdry, R., Lamberg, B. A., Makinen, T., & Rubinow, D. (1983). CSF triiodothyronine (rT_3) levels in patients with affective disorders. *Biological Psychiatry, 18,* 1489–1492.

Linnoila, M., Karoum, F., Calil, H. M., Kopin, I. J., & Potter, W. Z. (1982). Alteration of norepinephrine metabolism with desipramine and zimelidine in depressed patients. *Archives of General Psychiatry, 39,* 1025–1028.

Linnoila, M., Karoum, F., & Potter, W. Z. (1982a). Effect of low-dose clorgyline on 24-hour-urinary monoamine excretion in patients with rapidly cycling bipolar affective disorder. *Archives of General Psychiatry, 39,* 513–516.

Linnoila, M., Karoum, F., & Potter, W. Z. (1982b). High correlation of norepinephrine and its major metabolite excretion rates. *Archives of General Psychiatry, 39,* 521–523.

Linnoila, M., Karoum, F., & Potter, W. Z. (1983). Effects of antidepressant treatments on dopamine turnover in depressed patients. *Archives of General Psychiatry, 40,* 1015–1017.

Linnoila, M., Lamberg, B. A., Potter, W. Z., Gold, P. W., & Goodwin, F. K. (1982). High reverse T$_3$ levels in manic and unipolar depressed women. *Psychiatry Research, 6,* 271–276.

Linnoila, M., Lamberg, B. A., Roseberg, G., Karonen, S. L., & Welin, M. G. (1979). Thyroid hormones and TSH, prolactin and LH response to repeated TRH and LRH injections in depressed patients. *Acta Psychiatrica Scandinavica, 59,* 536–544.

Linnoila, M., MacDonald, E., Reinila, M., Leroy, A., Rubinow, D. R., & Goodwin, F. K. (1983). RBC membrane adenosine triphosphatase activities in patients with major affective disorders. *Archives of General Psychiatry, 40,* 1021–1026.

Linnoila, M., Whorton, A. R., Rubinow, D. R., Cowdry, R., Ninan, P. T., & Waters, R. N. (1983). CSF prostaglandin levels in depressed and schizophrenic patients. *Archives of General Psychiatry, 40,* 405–406.

Lipton, R. B., Levin, S., & Holzman, P. S. (1980). Horizontal and vertical pursuit eye movements, the oculocephalic reflex, and the functional psychoses. *Psychiatry Research, 3,* 193–203.

Lipton, R. B., Levy, D. L., Holzman, P. S., & Levin, S. (1983). Eye movement dysfunctions in psychiatric patients: A review. *Schizophrenia Bulletin, 9,* 13–32.

Loomer, H. P., Saunders, J. C., & Kline, N. S. (1958). A clinical and pharmacodynamic evaluation of iproniazid as a psychic energizer. *American Psychiatric Association Research Reports, 8,* 329.

Loosen, P. T., & Prange, A. J. (1982). The serum thyrotropin response to thyrotropin-releasing hormone in psychiatric patients: A review. *American Journal of Psychiatry, 139,* 405–416.

Loosen, P. T., Wilson, I. C., Dew, B., & Tipermas, A. (1983). Thyrotropin-releasing hormone (TRH) in abstinent alcoholic men. *American Journal of Psychiatry, 140,* 1145–1149.

Luchins, D. J. (1982). Computed tomography in schizophrenia. *Archives of General Psychiatry, 39,* 859–860.

Lundquist, G. (1945). Prognosis and course in manic-depressive psychoses. A follow-up study of 319 first admissions. *Acta Psychiatrica et Neurologica, 35*(Suppl. 1), 1–96.

Maas, J. W. (1975). Biogenic amines and depression: Biochemical and pharmacological separation on two types of depression. *Archives of General Psychiatry, 32,* 1357–1361.

Maas, J. W., Koslow, S. H., Katz, M. M., Gibbons, R. L., Bowden, C. L., Robins, E., & Davis, J. M. (1984). Pretreatment neurotransmitter metabolites and tricyclic antidepressant drug response. *American Journal of Psychiatry, 141,* 1159–1171.

MacLean, A. W., Cairns, J., & Kowles, J. B. (1983). REM latency and depression: Computer simulations based on the results of phase delay of sleep in normal subjects. *Psychiatry Research, 9,* 69–79.

Maeda, K., Kato, Y., Ohgo, S., Chihara, K., Yoshimoto, Y., Yamaguchi, N., Kuromaru, S., & Imura, H. (1975). Growth hormone and prolactin release after injection of thyrotropin-releasing hormone in patients with depression. *Journal of Clinical Endocrinology and Metabolism, 40,* 501–505.

Matarazzo, J. D. (1983). The reliability of psychiatric and psychological diagnosis. *Clinical Psychology Review, 3,* 103–145.

Mathew, R. J., Meyer, J. S., Francis, D. J., Semchuk, K. M., Mortel, K., & Claghorn, J. L. (1980). Cerebral blood flow in depression. *American Journal of Psychiatry, 137,* 1449–1450.

Mathew, R. J., Meyer, J. S., Semchuk, K. M., Francis, D. J., Mortel, K., & Claghorn, J. L. (1980). Regional cerebral blood flow in depression: A preliminary report. *Journal of Clinical Psychiatry, 41* (12, Sec. 2), 71–72.

McCarley, R. W. (1982). REM sleep and depression: Common neurobiological control mechanisms. *American Journal of Psychiatry, 139,* 565–570.

McCarron, L. (1973). Psychophysiological discriminants of reactive depression. *Psychophysiology, 10,* 223–230.

McLeod, W. R. (1972). Poor response to antidepressants and dexamethasone nonsuppression. In B. Davis, B. J. Carroll, & R. M. Mowbray (Eds.), *Depressive illness: Some research studies* (pp. 202–206). Springfield, IL: Charles C Thomas.

McNamara, E., Reynolds, C. F. III., Soloff, P. H., Mathias, R., Rossi, A., Spiker, D., Coble, P. A., & Kupfer, D. J. (1984). Electroencephalographic sleep evaluation of depression in borderline patients. *American Journal of Psychiatry, 141,* 182–186.

Meltzer, H. Y., Arora, R. C., Baber, R., & Tricou, B. J. (1981). Serotonin uptake in blood platelets of psychiatric patients. *Archives of General Psychiatry, 38,* 1322–1326.

Meltzer, H. Y., Arora, R. C., Tricou, B. J., & Fang, V. S. (1983). Serotonin uptake in blood platelets and the dexamethasone suppression test in depressed patients. *Psychiatry Research, 8,* 41–47.

Meltzer, H. Y., Cho, H. W., Carroll, B. J., & Russo, P. (1976). Serum dopamine-beta-hydroxylase activity in affective psychosis and schizophrenia. *Archives of General Psychiatry, 33,* 585–591.

Meltzer, H. Y., Fang, V. S., Tricou, B. J., Robertson, A., & Piyaka, S. K. (1982). Effect of dexamethasone on plasma prolactin and cortisol levels in psychiatric patients. *American Journal of Psychiatry, 139,* 763–768.

Mendlewicz, J., Charles, G., & Franckson, J. M. (1982). The dexamethasone suppression test in affective disorder: Relationship to clinical and genetic subgroups. *British Journal of Psychiatry, 141,* 464–470.

Mendlewicz, J., Hoffman, G., Linkowski, P., Kerkhofs, M., Goldstein, J., van Haelst, L., L'Hermite, M., Robyn, C., van Cauter, E., Weinberg, V., & Weitzman, E. D. (1983). Chronobiology and manic depression neuroendocrine and sleep EEG parameters. *Advances in Biological Psychiatry, 11,* 128–135.

Mendlewicz, J., Linkowski, P., & van Cauter, E. (1979). Some neuroendocrine parameters in bipolar and unipolar depression. *Journal of Affective Disorders, 1,* 25–32.

Menna-Perper, M., Swartzburg, M., Mueller, P. S., Rochford, J., & Manowitz, P. (1983). Free tryptophan response to intravenous insulin in depressed patients. *Biological Psychiatry, 18,* 771–780.

Mindham, R. H. S. (1982). Tricyclic antidepressants and amime precursors. in E. S. Paykel (Ed.), *Handbook of affective disorders* (pp. 231–245). New York: Guilford Press.

Mirkin, A. M., & Coppen, A. (1980). Electrodermal activity in depression: Clinical and biochemical correlates. *British Journal of Psychiatry, 137,* 93–97.

Moller, S. E., Honore, P., & Larsen, O. B. (1983). Tryptophan and tyrosine ratios to central amino acids in endogenous depression: Relation to antidepressant re-

sponse to amitriptyline and lithium + L-tryptophan. *Journal of Affective Disorders,*
5, 67–79.

Moore, R. Y. (1978). Central neural control of circadian rhythms. In W. F. Ganong, & L.
Martini (Eds.), *Frontiers in neuroendocrinology* (vol. 5, pp. 185–206). New York:
Raven Press.

Mora, G. (1980). Historical and theoretical trends in psychiatry. In H. I. Kaplan, A. M.
Freedman, & B. J. Sadock (Eds.), *Comprehensive textbook of psychiatry* (3rd ed.,
Vol. I, pp. 4–98). Baltimore: Williams & Wilkins.

Mueller, P. S., Heninger, G. R., & McDonald, R. K. (1969). Insulin tolerance test in
depression. *Archives of General Psychiatry, 21,* 587–594.

Murphy, D. L., Campbell, I., & Costa, J. L. (1978). Current status of the indoleamine
hypothesis of the affective disorders. In M. A. Lipton, A. DiMascio, & K. F. Killam
(Eds.), *Psychopharmacology: A generation of progress* (pp. 1235–1247). New York:
Raven Press.

Muscettola, G., Potter, W. Z., Gordon, E. K., & Goodwin, F. K. (1981). Methodological
issues in the measurement of urinary MHPG. *Psychiatry Research, 4,* 267–276.

Naber, D., Pickar, D., Post, R. M., Van Kammen, D. P., Waters, R. N., Ballenger, J. C.,
Goodwin, F. K., & Bunney, W. F. (1981). Endogenous opioid activity and β-en-
dorphin immunoreactivity in CSF of psychiatric patients and normal volunteers.
American Journal of Psychiatry, 138, 1457–1462.

Nasr, S. J., & Gibbons, R. D. (1983). Depressive symptoms associated with dexamethasone resistance. *Psychiatry Research, 10,* 183–189.

Nasr, S. J., Rodgers, C., Pandey, G., Altman, E. G., Gaviria, F. M., & Davis, J. M. (1983).
ACTH and the dexamethasone suppression test in depression. *Biological Psychiatry, 18,* 1069–1073.

Nasrallah, H. A., & Coryell, W. H. (1982). Dexamethasone nonsuppression predicts the
antidepressant effects of sleep deprivation. *Psychiatry Research, 6,* 61–64.

Nasrallah, H. A., Jacoby, C. G., McCalley-Whitters, M., & Kuperman, S. (1982). Cerebral
ventricular enlargement in subtypes of chronic schizophrenia. *Archives of General
Psychiatry, 39,* 774–777.

Neil, J. F., Merikangas, J. R., Foster, F. G., Merikangas, K. R., Spiker, D. G., & Kupfer, D. J.
(1980). Waking and all-night sleep EEGs in anorexia nervosa. *Clinical Electroencephalography, 11,* 9–15.

Nelson, J. C., & Charney, D. S. (1981). The symptoms of major depressive illness.
American Journal of Psychiatry, 138, 1–13.

Nelson, W. H., Orr, W. W., Stevenson, J. M., & Shane, S. R. (1982). Hypothalamic-
pituitary-adrenal axis activity and tricyclic response in major depression. *Archives
of General Psychiatry, 39,* 1033–1036.

Newsom, G., & Murray, N. (1983). Reversal of dexamethasone suppression test nonsuppression in alcohol abusers. *American Journal of Psychiatry, 140,* 353–354.

Nies, A., & Robinson, D. S. (1982). Monoamine oxidase inhibitors. In E. S. Paykel (Ed.),
Handbook of affective disorders (pp. 246–261). New York: Guilford Press.

Nurnberger, J. I., & Gershon, E. S. (1982). Genetics. In E. S. Paykel (Ed.), *Handbook of
affective disorders* (pp. 126–145). New York: Guilford Press.

Nurnberger, J. I., Gershon, E. S., Murphy, D. L., Buchsbaum, M. S., Goodwin, F. K., Post,

R. M., Lalio, C. R., Guroff, J. J., & McGinniss, M. H. (1979). Biological and clinical predictors of lithium response in depression. In T. B. Cooper, S, Gershon, N. S. Kline, & M. Schou (Eds.), *Lithium: Controversies and unresolved issues*. Amsterdam, The Netherlands: Excerpta Medica.

Nurnberger, J. I., Sitaram, N., Gershon, E. S., & Gillin, J. C. (1983). A twin study of cholinergic REM induction. *Biological Psychiatry, 18,* 1161–1165.

Ostroff, R., Giller, E., Bonese, K., Ebersole, E., Harkness, L., & Mason, J. (1982). Neuroendocrine risk factors of suicidal behavior. *American Journal of Psychiatry, 139,* 1323–1325.

Oxenkrug, G. F., Pomara, N., McIntyre, I. M., Branconnier, R. J., Stanley, M., & Gershon, S. (1983). Aging and cortisol resistance to suppression by dexamethasone: A positive correlation. *Psychiatry Research, 10,* 125–130.

Parry, B. L., & Rush, A. J. (1979). Oral contraceptives and depressive symptomatology: Biologic mechanisms. *Comprehensive Psychiatry, 20,* 347–358.

Paul, S. M., Hauger, R. L., & Skolnick, P. (1983). The effects of antidepressants on neurotransmitter receptors: Implications for their mechanism(s) of action. In F. J. Ayd, I. J. Taylor, & B. T. Taylor (Eds.), *Affective disorders reassessed: 1983* (pp. 244–250). Baltimore: Ayd Medical Communications.

Paul, S. M., Rehavi, M., Skolnick, P., Ballenger, J. C., & Goodwin, F. K. (1981). Depressed patients have decreased binding of tritiated imipramine to platelet serotonin "transporter." *Archives of General Psychiatry, 38,* 1315–1317.

Paul, S. M., Rehavi, M., Skolnick, P., & Goodwin, F. K. (1980). Demonstration of specific high-affinity binding sites for H3 imipramine on human platelets. *Life Sciences, 26,* 953–959.

Paykel, E. S. (1982). Life events and early environments. In E. S. Paykel (Ed.), *Handbook of affective disorders* (pp. 146–161). New York: Guilford Press.

Perris, C. (1982). The distinction between bipolar and unipolar affective disorders. In E. S. Paykel (Ed.), *Handbook of affective disorders* (pp. 45–58). New York: Guilford Press.

Peselow, E. D., Fieve, R. R., Goldring, N., Wright, R., & Deutsch, S. I. (1983). The DST and clinical symptoms in predicting response to tricyclic antidepressants. *Psychopharmacology Bulletin, 19,* 642–645.

Peselow, E. D., Goldring, N., Fieve, R. R., & Wright, R. (1983). The dexamethasone suppression test in depressed outpatients and normal control subjects. *American Journal of Psychiatry, 140,* 245–257.

Pitt, B. (1982). Depression in childbirth. In E. S. Paykel (Ed.), *Handbook of affective disorders* (pp. 361–378). New York: Guilford Press.

Poort, R. (1945). Catamnestic investigations on manic-depressive psychoses with special reference to the prognosis. *Acta Psychiatrica et Neurologica, 20,* 59–74.

Poznanski, E. O., Carroll, B. J., Banegas, M. C., Cook, S. C., & Grossman, J. A. (1982). The dexamethasone suppression test in prepubertal depressed children. *American Journal of Psychiatry, 139,* 321–324.

Prien, R. J. (1979). Lithium in the prophylactic treatment of affective disorders. *Archives of General Psychiatry, 36,* 847–848.

Prusoff, B. A., Weissman, M. M., Klerman, G. L., & Rounsaville, B. J. (1980). Research diagnostic criteria subtypes of depression: Their role as predictors of differential response to psychotherapy and drug treatment. *Archives of General Psychiatry, 37,* 796–801.

Pugnetti, L., Colombo, A., Cazzullo, C. L., Leccardi, G., Sicuro, F., & Scarone, S. (1982). Daytime sleep patterns of primary depressives: A morning nap study. *Psychiatry Research, 7,* 287–298.

Puig-Antich, J., Goetz, R., Hanlon, C., Davies, M., Thompson, J., Chambers, W. J., Tabrizi, M. A., & Weitzman, E. D. (1982). Sleep architecture and REM sleep measures in prepubertal children with major depression. *Archives of General Psychiatry, 39,* 932–939.

Puig-Antich, J., Goetz, R., Hanlon, C., Tabrizi, M. A., Davies, M. A., & Weitzman, E. D. (1983). Sleep architecture and REM sleep measures in prepubertal major depressives: Studies during recovery from the depressive episode in a drug-free state. *Archives of General Psychiatry, 40,* 187–192.

Puig-Antich, J., Tabrizi, M. A., Davies, M., Goetz, R., Chambers, W. J., Halpern, F., & Sachar, E. J. (1981). Prepubertal endogenous major depressives hyposecrete growth hormone in response to insulin-induced hypoglycemia. *Biological Psychiatry, 16,* 801–817.

Quitkin, F. M., Schwartz, D., Liebowitz, M. R., Stewart, J. R., McGrath, P. J., Halpern, F., Puig-Antich, J., Tricamo, E., Sachar, E. J., & Klein, D. F. (1982). Atypical depressives: A preliminary report of antidepressant response and sleep patterns. *Psychopharmacology Bulletin, 18,* 78–80.

Rabkin, J. G., Quitkin, F. M., Stewart, J. W., McGrath, P. J., & Puig-Antich, J. (1983). The dexamethasone suppression test with mildly and moderately depressed outpatients. *American Journal of Psychiatry, 140,* 926–927.

Rapoport, J., Elkins, R., Langer, D. H., Sceery, W., Buchsbaum, M. S., Gillin, J. C., Murphy, D. L., Zahn, T. P., Lake, R., Ludlow, C., & Mendelson, W. (1981). Childhood obsessive-compulsive disorder. *American Journal of Psychiatry, 138,* 1545–1554.

Raskind, M., Peskind, E., Rivard, M. F., Veith, R., & Barnes, R. (1982). Dexamethasone suppression test and cortisol circadian rhythm in primary degenerative dementia. *American Journal of Psychiatry, 139,* 1468–1471.

Rehm, L. P., & Kornblith, S. J. (1979). Behavior therapy for depression: A review of recent developments. *Progress in Behavior Modification, 7,* 277–318.

Reich, L., Weiss, B. L., Coble, P. A., McPartland, R. J., & Kupfer, D. J. (1975). Sleep disturbance in schizophrenia: A revisit. *Archives of General Psychiatry, 32,* 51–55.

Rennie, T. A. C. (1942). Prognosis in manic-depressive psychosis. *American Journal of Psychiatry, 98,* 801–814.

Reus, V. I. (1982). Pituitary-adrenal disinhibition as the independent variable in the assessment of behavioral symptoms. *Biological Psychiatry, 17,* 317–326.

Reus, V. I., Joseph, M. S., & Dallman, M. F. (1982). ACTH levels after the dexamethasone suppression test in depression. *New England Journal of Medicine, 306,* 238–239.

Reynolds, C. F. III, Christiansen, C. L., Taska, L. S., Coble, P. A., & Kupfer, D. J. (1983). Sleep in narcolepsy and depression. Does it all look alike? *Journal of Nervous and Mental Disease, 171,* 290–295.

Reynolds, C. F. III, Newton, T. F., Shaw, D. H., Coble, P. A., & Kupfer, D. J. (1982). Electroencephalographic sleep findings in depressed outpatients. *Psychiatry Research, 6,* 65–75.

Reynolds, C. F. III, Shaw, D. F., Newton, T. F., Coble, P. A., & Kupfer, D. J. (1983). EEG sleep in outpatients with generalized anxiety: A preliminary comparison with depressed outpatients. *Psychiatry Research, 8,* 81–89.

Reynolds, C. F. III, Spiker, D. G., Hanin, I., & Kupfer, D. J. (1983). Electroencephalographic sleep, aging, and psychopathology: New data and state of the art. *Biological Psychiatry, 18,* 139–155.

Reynolds, C. F. III, Taska, L. S., Jarrett, D. B., Coble, P. A., & Kupfer, D. J. (1983). REM latency in depression: Is there one best definition? *Biological Psychiatry, 18,* 849–863.

Richelson, E. (1983). Are receptor studies useful for clinical practice? *Journal of Clinical Psychiatry, 44* (*9, Sec. 2*), 4–9.

Rieder, R. O., Mann, L. S., Weinberger, D. R., van Kammen, D. P., & Post, R. M. (1983). Computed tomographic scans in patients with schizophrenia, schizoaffective, and bipolar affective disorder. *Archives of General Psychiatry, 40,* 735–739.

Risch, S. C. (1982). Beta-endorphin hypersecretion in depression: Possible cholinergic mechanisms. *Biological Psychiatry, 17,* 1071–1079.

Risch, S. C., Janowsky, D. S., Judd, L. L., Gillin, J. C., & McClure, S. F. (1983). The role of endogenous opioid systems in neuroendocrine regulation. *Psychiatric Clinics of North America, 6,* 429–441.

Robbins, D. R., Alessi, N. E., Yanchyshyn, G. W., & Colfer, M. V. (1982). Preliminary report on the dexamethasone suppression test in adolescents. *American Journal of Psychiatry, 139,* 942–943.

Rosanoff, A. J., Handy, L., & Plesset, I. R. (1935). The etiology of manic-depressive syndromes with special reference to their occurrence in twins. *American Journal of Psychiatry, 91,* 725–762.

Rose, R. M. (1980). Endocrine responses to stressful psychological events. *Psychiatric Clinics of North America, 3,* 251–276.

Rosenbaum, A. H., Maruta, T., Schatzberg, A. F., Orsulak, P. J., Jiang, N. S., Cole, J. O., & Schildkraut, J. J. (1983). Toward a biochemical classification of depressive disorders, VII: Urinary-free cortisol and urinary MHPG In depression. *American Journal of Psychiatry, 140,* 314–318.

Rosenthal, N. E., Sack, D. A., Gillin, J. C., Lewy, A. J., Goodwin, F. K., Davenport, Y., Mueller, P. S., Newsome, D. A., & Wehr, T. A. (1984). Seasonal affective disorder: A description of the syndrome and preliminary findings with light therapy. *Archives of General Psychiatry, 41,* 72–80.

Rosenthal, N. E., Sack, D. A., & Wehr, T. A. (1983). Seasonal variation in affective disorders. In T. A. Wehr & F. K. Goodwin (Eds.), *Circadian rhythms in psychiatry* (pp. 185–200). Pacific Grove, CA: Boxwood Press.

Rothschild, A. J., Schatzberg, A. F., Langlais, P. J., Cole, J. O., & Bird, E. D. (1983, December). *Dexamethasone elevates dopamine in human plasma and rat brain.* Paper presented at the annual meeting of the American College of Neuropsychopharmacology, San Juan.

Rothschild, A. J., Schatzberg, A. F., Rosenbaum, A. H., Stahl, J. B., & Cole, J. O. (1982). The dexamethasone suppression test as a discriminator among subtypes of psychotic patients. *British Journal of Psychiatry, 141,* 471–474.

Rotman, A. (1983). Blood platelets in psychopharmacological research. *Progress in Neuropsychopharmacology and Biological Psychiatry, 7,* 135–151.

Rubin, R. T., & Mandell, A. J. (1966). Adrenal cortical activity in pathological emotional states: A review. *American Journal of Psychiatry, 123,* 387–400.

Rubinow, D. R., Gold, P. W., Post, R. M., Ballenger, J. C., & Cowdry, R. W. (1984a). Somatostatin in patients with affective illness and in normal volunteers. In R. M. Post & J. C. Ballenger (Eds.), *Neurobiology of mood disorders* (pp. 369–387). Baltimore: Williams & Wilkins.

Rubinow, D. R., Gold, P. W., Post, R. M., Ballenger, J. C., Cowdry, R., Bollinger, J., & Reichlin, S. (1983). CSF somatostatin in affective illness. *Archives of General Psychiatry, 40,* 409–412.

Rubinow, D. R., Post, R. M., Savard, R., & Gold, P. W. (1984b). Cortisol hypersecretion and cognitive impairment in depression. *Archives of General Psychiatry, 41,* 279–283.

Rudorfer, M. V., Hwu, H. G., & Clayton, P. J. (1982). Dexamethasone suppression test in primary depression: Significance of family history and psychosis. *Biological Psychiatry, 17,* 41–48.

Rush, A. J. (1983). Cognitive therapy of depression: Rationale, techniques, and efficacy. *Psychiatric Clinics of North America, 6,* 105–127.

Rush, A. J., Giles, D. E., Roffwarg, H. P., & Parker, C. R. (1982). Sleep EEG and dexamethasone suppression test finding in outpatients with unipolar major depressive disorders. *Biological Psychiatry, 17,* 327–341.

Rush, A. J., Schlesser, M. A., Roffwarg, H. P., Giles, D. E., Orsulak, P. J., & Fairchild, C. (1983). Relationships among the TRH, REM latency, and dexamethasone suppression tests: Preliminary findings. *Journal of Clinical Psychiatry, 44* (8, Sec. 2), 23–29.

Sabelli, H. C., Gusovsky, F., Fawcett, J. A., Javaid, J. I., & Edwards, J. (1983, May). *Urinary phenylacetate in unipolar depression.* Paper presented at the annual meeting of the American Psychiatric Association, New York.

Sabelli, H. C., & Mosnaim, A. D. (1974). Phenylethylamine hypothesis of affective behavior. *American Journal of Psychiatry, 131,* 695–699.

Sacchetti, E., Allaria, E., Negri, F., Biondi, P. A., Smeraldi, E., & Cazzullo, C. L. (1979). 3-methoxy-4-hydroxyphenylglycol and primary depression: Clinical and pharmacological considerations. *Biological Psychiatry, 14,* 473–484.

Sachar, E. J. (1982). Endocrine abnormalities in depression. In E. S. Paykel (Ed.), *Handbook of affective disorders* (pp. 191–201). New York: Guilford Press.

Sachar, E. J., Asnis, G., Halbreich, U., Nathan, R. S., & Halpern, F. (1980). Recent studies in the neuroendocrinology of major depressive disorders. *Psychiatric Clinics of North America, 3,* 313–326.

Sachar, E. J., Asnis, G., Nathan, R. S., Halbreich, U., Tabrizi, M. A., & Halpern, F. S. (1980). Dextroamphetamine and cortisol in depression: Morning plasma cortisol levels suppressed. *Archives of General Psychiatry, 37,* 755–757.

Sachar, E. J., Finkelstein, J., & Hellman, L. (1971). Growth hormone responses in depressive illness. I. Response to insulin tolerance test. *Archives of General Psychiatry, 25,* 263–269.

Sachar, E. J., Halbreich, U., Asnis, G. M., Nathan, R. S., Halpern, F. S., & Ostrow, L. (1981). Paradoxical cortisol responses to dextroamphetamine in endogenous depression. *Archives of General Psychiatry, 38,* 1113–1117.

Schaeffer, C. E., Davidson, R. J., & Saron, C. (1983). Frontal and parietal electroencephalogram asymmetry in depressed and nondepressed subjects. *Biological Psychiatry, 18,* 753–762.

Schatzberg, A. F., Orsulak, P. J., Rosenbaum, A. H., Maruta, T., Kruger, E. R., Cole, J. O., & Schildkraut, J. J. (1981). Toward a biochemical classification of depressive disorders. III. Pretreatment urinary MHPG levels as predictors of response to treatment with maprotiline. *Psychopharmacology, 75,* 34–38.

Schatzberg, A. F., Orsulak, P. J., Rothschild, A. J., Salomon, M. S., Lerbinger, J., Kizuka, P. P., Cole, J. O., & Schildkraut, J. J. (1983). Platelet MAO activity and the dexamethasone suppression test in depressed patients. *American Journal of Psychiatry, 140,* 1231–1233.

Schatzberg, A. F., Rothschild, A. J., Stahl, J. B., Bond, T. C., Rosenbaum, A. H., Lofgren, S. B., MacLaughlin, R. A., Sullivan, M. A., & Cole, J. O. (1983). The dexamethasone suppression test: Identification of subtypes of depression. *American Journal of Psychiatry, 140,* 88–91.

Schildkraut, J. J. (1965). The catecholamine hypothesis of affective disorder: A review of supporting evidence. *American Journal of Psychiatry, 122,* 509–522.

Schildkraut, J. J. (1978). Current status of the catecholamine hypothesis of affective disorders. In M. A. Lipton, A. DiMascio, & K. F. Killam (Eds.), *Psychopharmacology: A generation of progress* (pp. 1223–1234). New York: Raven Press.

Schildkraut, J. J. (1982). The biochemical discrimination of subtypes of depressive disorders: An outline of our studies on norepinephrine metabolism and psychoactive drugs in the endogenous depressions since 1967. *Pharmakopsychiatry, 15* 121–127.

Schildkraut, J. J., Keeler, B. A., Papouser, M., & Hartmann, E. (1973). MHPG excretion in depressive disorders: Relation to clinical subtypes and desynchronized sleep. *Science, 181,* 762–764.

Schlesser, M. A., Winokur, G., & Sherman, B. M. (1979). Genetic subtypes of unipolar primary depressive illness distinguished by hypothalamic-pituitary-adrenal axis activity. *Lancet, 1,* 739–741.

Schulz, H., & Lund, R. (1983). Sleep onset REM episodes are associated with circadian parameters of body temperature. A study in depressed patients and normal controls. *Biological Psychiatry, 18,* 1441–1426.

Schulz, H., Lund, R., Cording, C., & Dirlich, G. (1979). Bimodal distribution of REM sleep latencies in depression. *Biological Psychiatry, 14,* 595–600.

Schulz, H., & Tetzlaff, W. (1982). Distribution of REM latencies after sleep interruption in depressive patients and control subjects. *Biological Psychiatry, 17,* 1367–1376.

Schwartz, G. E., Ahern, G. L., & Brown, S. L. (1979). Lateralized facial muscle response to positive and negative emotional stimuli. *Psychophysiology, 16,* 561–571.

Schwartz, G. E., Fair, P. L., Salt, P., Mandel, M. R., & Klerman, G. L. (1976a). Facial expression and imagery in depression: An electromyographic study. *Psychosomatic Medicine, 38,* 337–347.

Schwartz, G. E., Fair, P. L., Salt, P., Mandel, M. R., & Klerman, G. L. (1976b). Facial muscle patterning to affective imagery in depressed and nondepressed subjects. *Science, 192,* 489–491.

Shagass, C., Amadeo, M., & Overton, D. A. (1974). Eye tracking performance in psychiatric patients. *Biological Psychiatry, 9,* 245–260.

Shagass, C., Roemer, R. A., & Straumanis, J. J. (1982). Relationship between psychiatric diagnosis and some quantitative EEG variables. *Archives of General Psychiatry, 39,* 1423–1435.

Shagass, C., Roemer, R. A., Straumanis, J. J., & Amadeo, M. (1980). Topography of sensory evoked potentials in depressive disorders. *Biological Psychiatry, 15,* 183–207.

Sherman, A. D., & Petty, F. (1984). Learned helplessness decreases ^{3}H imipramine binding in rat cortex. *Journal of Affective Disorders, 6,* 25–32.

Sherman, A. D., Sacquitne, J. L., & Petty, F. (1982). Pharmacologic specificity of the learned helplessness model of depression. *Pharmacology, Biochemistry, and Behavior, 16,* 449–454.

Sherman, B., Pfohl, B., & Winokur, G. (1984). Circadian analysis of plasma cortisol levels before and after dexamethasone administration. *Archives of General Psychiatry, 41,* 271–275.

Shipley, J. E., Kupfer, D. J., Spiker, D. G., Shaw, D. H., Coble, P. A., Neil, J. F., & Cofsky, J. (1981). Neuropsychological assessment and EEG sleep in affective disorders. *Biological Psychiatry, 16,* 907–918.

Siever, L. J., Uhde, T. W., Jimerson, D. C., Post, R. M., Lake, C. R., & Murphy, D. L. (1984). Plasma cortisol responses to clonidine in depressed patients and controls: Evidence for a possible alteration in noradrenergic-neuroendocrine relationships. *Archives of General Psychiatry, 41,* 61–68.

Silberman, E. K., & Post, R. M. (1982). Atypically in primary depressive illness: A preliminary survey. *Biological Psychiatry, 17,* 285–304.

Silverman, J. S., Silverman, J. A., & Eardley, D. A. (1984). Do maladaptive attitudes cause depression? *Archives of General Psychiatry, 41,* 28–30.

Sitaram, N., Moore, A. M., & Gillin, J. C. (1979). Scopolamine-induced muscarinic supersensitivity in normal man: Changes in sleep. *Psychiatry Research, 1,* 9–16.

Sitaram, N., Nurnberger, J. I., & Gershon, E. S. (1980). Faster cholinergic REM sleep induction in euthymic patients with primary affective illness. *Science, 208,* 200–202.

Sitaram, N., Nurnberger, J. I., Gershon, E. S., & Gillin, J. C. (1982). Cholinergic regulation of mood and REM sleep: Potential model and marker of vulnerability to affective disorders. *American Journal of Psychiatry, 139,* 571–576.

Snyder, S. H., & Peroutka, S. J. (1982). A possible role of serotonin receptors in antidepressant drug action. *Pharmacopsychiatry, 15,* 131–134.

Spar, J. E., & Gerner, R. (1982). Does the dexamethasone suppression test distinguish dementia from depression? *American Journal of Psychiatry, 139,* 238–240.

Spar, J. E., & LaRue, A. (1983). Major depression in the elderly: *DSM-III* criteria and the dexamethasone suppression test as predictors of treatment response. *American Journal of Psychiatry, 140,* 844–847.

Spitzer, R. L., Endicott, J., & Robins, E. (1978). Research diagnostic criteria. *Archives of General Psychiatry, 34,* 773–782.

Spitzer, R. L., Fleiss, J. L., & Endicott, J. (1978). Problems of classification: Reliability and validity. In M. A. Lipton, A. DiMascio, & K. F. Killam (Eds.), *Psychopharmacology: A generation of progress* (pp. 857–869). New York: Raven Press.

Spitzer, R. L., Williams, J. B. W., & Skodol, A. E. (1980). *DSM-III:* The major achievements and an overview. *American Journal of Psychiatry, 137,* 151–164.

Spohn, H. E., & Larson, J. (1983). Is eye tracking dysfunction specific to schizophrenia? *Schizophrenia Bulletin, 9,* 50–55.

Spohn, H. E., & Patterson, T. P. (1979). Recent studies of psychophysiology in schizophrenia. *Schizophrenia Bulletin, 5,* 581–611.

Stahl, S. M., Lemoine, P. M., Ciaranello, R. D., & Berger, P. A. (1983). Platelet alpha2-adrenergic receptor sensitivity in major depression. *Psychiatry Research, 10,* 157–164.

Standish-Barry, H. M. A. S., Bouras, N., Bridges, P. K., & Bartlett, J. R. (1982). Pneumoencephalographic and computerized axial tomography scan changes in affective disorder. *British Journal of Psychiatry, 141,* 614–617.

Stanley, M. (1983, May). *Central nervous system cholinergic receptors are unchanged in suicide.* Paper presented at the New Research section of the annual meeting of the American Psychiatric Association, New York.

Steinbrueck, S. M., Maxwell, S. E., & Howard, G. S. (1983). A metaanalysis of psychotherapy and drug therapy in the treatment of unipolar depression with adults. *Journal of Consulting and Clinical Psychiatry, 51,* 856–863.

Stern, J. A., Sila, B., & Word, T. J. (1960). Observations on the effect of electroconvulsive therapy and pharmacotherapy on the psychogalvanic response. *Journal of Neuropsychiatry, 2,* 149–152.

Sternbach, H. A., Gerner, R. H., & Gwirtsman, H. E. (1982). The thyrotropin-releasing hormone stimulation test: A review. *Journal of Clinical Psychiatry, 43,* 4–6.

Sternbach, H. A., Gold, M. S., Pottash, A. C., & Extein, I. (1983). Thyroid failure and protirelin (thyrotropin-releasing-hormone) test abnormalities in depressed outpatients. *Journal of the American Medical Association, 249,* 1618–1620.

Sternbach, H. A., Gwirtsman, H., & Gerner, R. H. (1981). The dexamethasone suppression test and response to methylphenidate in depression. *American Journal of Psychiatry, 138,* 1629–1631.

Sternbach, H. A., Kirstein, L., Pottash, A. L. C., Gold, M. S., Extein, I., & Sweeney, D. R. (1983). The TRH and urinary MHPG in unipolar depression. *Journal of Affective Disorders, 5,* 233–237.

Stokes, P. E., Fraser, A., & Casper, R. (1981). Unexpected neuroendocrine relationships. *Psychopharmacology Bulletin, 17,* 72–75.

Stokes, P. E., Stoll, P. M., Koslow, S. H., Maas, J. W., Daavis, J. M., Swann, A. C., & Robins, E. (1984). Pretreatment DST and hypothalamic-pituitary-adrenocortical function in depressed patients and comparison groups. *Archives of General Psychiatry, 41,* 257–267.

Storrie, M. C., Doerr, H. O., & Johnson, M. H. (1981). Skin conductance characteristics of depressed subjects before and after therapeutic intervention. *Journal of Nervous and Mental Disease, 69,* 176–179.

Suomi, S. J., Seaman, S. F., Lewis, J. K., DeLizio, R. D., & McKinney, W. T. (1978). Effects of imipramine treatment of separation-induced social disorders in Rhesus monkeys. *Archives of General Psychiatry, 35,* 321–325.

Suranyi-Cadotte, B. E., Wood, P. L., Schwartz, G., & Nair, N. P. V. (1983). Altered platelet 3H-imipramine binding in schizoaffective and depressive disorders. *Biological Psychiatry, 18,* 923–927.

Swann, A. C., Secunda, S., Davis, J. M., Robins, E., Hanin, I., Koslow, S. H., & Maas, J. W. (1983). CSF monoamine metabolites in mania. *American Journal of Psychiatry, 140,* 396–400.

Swartz, C. M., & Dunner, F. J. (1982). Dexamethasone suppression testing of alcoholics. *Archives of General Psychiatry, 39,* 1309–1312.

Sweeney, D. R., Maas, J. W., & Heninger, G. R. (1978). State anxiety physical activity and urinary 3-methoxy-4-hydroxyphenylethylene glycol excretion. *Archives of General Psychiatry, 35,* 1418–1423.

Tang, S. W., Stancer, H. C., Takahashi, S., Shephard, R. J., & Warsh, J. J. (1981). Controlled exercise elevates plasma, but not urinary MHPG and VMA. *Psychiatry Research, 4,* 13–20.

Targum, S. D. (1983a). The application of serial neuroendocrine challenge studies in the management of depressive disorder. *Biological Psychiatry, 18,* 3–19.

Targum, S. D. (1983b). Neuroendocrinc challenge studies in clinical psychiatry. *Psychiatric Annals, 13,* 385–395.

Targum, S. D. (1983c). Neuroendocrine dysfunction in schizophreniform disorder: Correlation with six-month clinical outcome. *American Journal of Psychiatry, 140,* 309–313.

Targum, S. D., Byrnes, S. M., & Sullivan, A. C. (1982a). Subtypes of unipolar depression distinguished by the dexamethasone suppression test. *Journal of Affective Disorders, 4,* 21–27.

Targum, S. D., Byrnes, S. M., & Sullivan, A. C. (1982b). The TRH stimulation test in subtypes of unipolar depression. *Journal of Affective Disorders, 4,* 29–34.

Targum, S. D., & Capodanno, A. E. (1983). The dexamethasone suppression test in adolescent psychiatric inpatients. *American Journal of Psychiatry, 140,* 589–591.

Targum, S. D., Rosen, L., & Capodanno, A. E. (1983). The dexamethasone suppression test in suicidal patients with unipolar depression. *American Journal of Psychiatry, 140,* 877–879.

Targum, S. D., Sullivan, A. C., & Byrnes, S. M. (1982). Neuroendocrine interrelationships in major depressive disorder. *American Journal of Psychiatry, 139,* 282–286.

Targum, S. D., Wheadon, D. E., Chastek, C. T., McCabe, W. J., & Advani, M. T. (1982). Dysregulation of hypothalamic-pituitary-adrenal axis function in depressed alcoholic patients. *Journal of Affective Disorders, 4,* 347–353.

Taube, S. L., Kirstein, L. S., Sweeney, D. R., Heninger, G. R., & Maas, J. W. (1978). Urinary 3-methoxy-4-hydroxyphenylglycol and psychiatric diagnosis. *American Journal of Psychiatry, 135,* 78–82.

Terenius, L., Wahlstrom, A., & Agren, H. (1977). Naloxone (Narcan) treatment in depression: Clinical observations and effects on CSF endorphins and monoamine metabolites. *Psychopharmacology, 54,* 31–33.

Terenius, L., Wahlstrom, A., Lindstrom, L., & Widerlov, E. (1976). Increased CSF levels and endorphines in chronic psychosis. *Neuroscience Letters, 3,* 157–162.

Thase, M. E. (1983). Cognitive and behavioral treatments for depression: A review of recent developments. In F. J. Ayd, I. J. Taylor, & B. T. Taylor (Eds.), *Affective disorders reassessed: 1983* (pp. 234–243). Baltimore: Ayd Medical Communications.

Thase, M. E., Hersen, M., Bellack, A. S., Himmelhoch, J. M., Kornblith, S. J., & Greenwald, D. (1984). Social skills training and endogenous depression. *Journal of Behavior Therapy and Experimental Psychiatry, 15,* 101–108.

Thase, M. E., Himmelhoch, J. M., Hersen, M., & Bellack, A. S. (1984). *Poor response to psychosocial treatments in melancholia.* Paper presented at the annual meeting of the American Psychiatric Association, Los Angeles, May 1984.

Thase, M. E., & Kupfer, D. J. (in press-a). Characteristics of treatment resistant depression. In J. Zohar & R. H. Belmaker (Eds.), *Special treatments for resistant depression.* New York: Spectrum Publications.

Thase, M. E., & Kupfer, D. J. (in press-b). Current status of EEG sleep in the assessment and treatment of depression. In G. D. Burrows & J. S. Werry (Eds.), *Advances in human psychopharmacology* (Vol. 4). Greenwich CT: JAI Press.

Thase, M. E., Kupfer, D. J., & Spiker, D. G. (1984). EEG sleep secondary depression: A revisit. *Biological Psychiatry, 19,* 805–814.

Tosca, P., Fenoglio, L., Zerbi, F., Romani, A., Bezzi, G., Ferrari, E., & Canepari, C. (1982). Neuroendocrinological aspects of depression and symptomatological picture. *Psychiatria Clinica, 15,* 153–159.

Traskman, L., Asberg, M., Bertilsson, L., & Sjostrand, L. (1981). Monoamine metabolites in CSF and suicidal behavior. *Archives of General Psychiatry, 38,* 631–636.

Traskman, L., Tybring, G., Asberg, M., Bertilsson, L., Lanotto, O., & Schalling, D. (1980). Cortisol in the CSF of depressed and suicidal patients. *Archives of General Psychiatry, 37,* 761–767.

Tsai, L. Y., Nasrallah, H. A., & Jacoby, C. G. (1983). Hemispheric asymmetries on computed tomographic scans in schizophrenia and mania. *Archives of General Psychiatry, 40,* 1286–1289.

Ulett, G. A., Smith, K., & Gleser, G. C. (1956). Evaluation of convulsive and subconvulsive shock therapies utilizing a control group. *American Journal of Psychiatry, 112,* 795–802.

Ulrich, R. F., Shaw, D. H., & Kupfer, D. J. (1980). Effects of aging on EEG sleep in depression. *Sleep, 3,* 30–40.

Uytdenhoef, P., Portelange, P., Jacquy, J., Charles, G., Linkowski, P., & Mendlewicz, J. (1983). Regional cerebral blood flow and lateralized hemispheric dysfunction in depression. *British Journal of Psychiatry, 143,* 128–132.

van Praag, H. M. (1980a). Central monoamine metabolism in depressions. I. Serotonin and related compounds. *Comprehensive Psychiatry, 21,* 30–43.

van Praag, H. M. (1980b). Central monoamine metabolism in depressions. II. Catecholamines and related compounds. *Comprehensive Psychiatry, 21,* 44–54.

van Praag, H. M. (1983, December). *Psychological and biochemical effects of serotonin precursors in depression.* Paper presented at the annual meeting of the American College of Neuropsychopharmacology, San Juan, Puerto Rico.

van Praag, H. M., & Korf, J. (1971). Retarded depression and dopamine metabolism. *Psychopharmacologica, 29,* 199–203.

Vestergaard, P., Amidsen, A., & Schou, M. (1980). Clinically significant side effects of lithium treatment: A survey of 237 patients in long-term treatment. *Acta Psychiatrica Scandinavica, 62,* 193–200.

Vogel, G. W. (1983). Evidence for REM sleep deprivation as the mechanism of action of antidepressant drugs. *Progress in Neuro-Psychopharmacology and Biological Psychiatry, 7,* 343–349.

von Knorring, L., Espvall, M., & Perris, C. (1974). Averaged evoked responses, pain measures, and personality variables in patients with depressive disorders. *Acta Psychiatrica Scandinavica, 255,* 99–108.

Waegner, D. R., & Weitzman, E. D. (1980). Neuroendocrine secretion and biological rhythms in man. *Psychiatric Clinics of North America, 3,* 223–250.

Ward, N. G., Doerr, H. O., & Storrie, M. C. (1983). Skin conductance: A potentially sensitive test for depression. *Psychiatry Research, 10,* 295–302.

Wehr, T. A., & Goodwin, F. K. (1981). Biological rhythms and psychiatry. In S. Arieti & H. K. H. Brodie (Eds.), *American handbook of psychiatry* (Vol. 7, pp. 46–74). New York: Basic Books.

Wehr, T. A., Goodwin, F. K., Wirz-Justice, A., Breitmaier, J., & Craig, C. (1982). 48-hour sleep-wake cycles in manic-depressive illness. *Archives of General Psychiatry, 39,* 559–565.

Wehr, T. A., Muscettola, G., & Goodwin, F. K. (1980). Urinary 3-methoxy-4-hydroxy-phenylglycol circadian rhythm. Early timing (phase-advance) in manic-depressives compared with normal subjects. *Archives of General Psychiatry, 37,* 257–263.

Wehr, T. A., & Wirz-Justice, A. (1982). Circadian rhythm mechanisms in affective illness and in antidepressant drug action. *Pharmacopsychiatry, 15,* 31–39.

Wehr, T. A., Wirz-Justice, A., & Goodwin, F. K. (1979). Phase advance of the circadian sleep-wake cycle as an antidepressant. *Science, 206,* 710–713.

Weinberger, D. R., DeLisi, L. E., Perman, G. P., Targum, S., & Wyatt, R. J. (1982). Computed tomography in schizophreniform disorders and other acute psychiatric disorders. *Archives of General Psychiatry, 39,* 778–783.

Weissman, M. M. (1979a). The myth of involutional melancholia. *Journal of American Medical Association, 242,* 742–744.

Weissman, M. M. (1979b). The psychological treatment of depression. *Archives of General Psychiatry, 36,* 1261–1269.

Weissman, M. M., & Klerman, G. L. (1977). Sex differences and the epidemiology of depression. *Archives of General Psychiatry, 34,* 98–111.

West, E. D., & Dally, P. J. (1959). Effects of iproniazid in depressive syndromes. *British Medical Journal, i,* 1491–1494.

Westenberg, H. G. M., van Praag, H. M., de Jong, J. T. V. M., & Thijssen, J. H. H. (1982). Postsynaptic serotonergic activity in depressive patients: Evaluation of the neuroendocrine strategy. *Psychiatry Research, 7,* 361–371.

Wever, R. A. (1979). *The circadian system of man: Results of experiments under temporal isolation.* New York: Springer-Verlag.

White, K., Macdonald, N., Razani, J., Shih, J., Boyd, J., Simpson, G., & Sloane, R. B.

(1983). Platelet MAO activity in depression. *Comprehensive Psychiatry, 24,* 453–458.

Whybrow, P. C., & Prange, A. J. (1981). A hypothesis of thyroid catecholamine-receptor interaction. *Archives of General Psychiatry, 38,* 106–113.

Williams, R. L., Karacan, I., & Hursch, C. J. (1974). *Electroencephalography (EEG) of human sleep: Clinical applications.* New York: John Wiley & Sons.

Winokur, A., Amsterdam, J., Caroff, S., Snyder, P. J., & Brunswick, D. (1982). Variability of hormonal responses to a series of neuroendocrine challenges in depressed patients. *American Journal of Psychiatry, 139,* 39–44.

Winokur, A., Amsterdam, J. D., Oler, J., Mendels, J., Snyder, P. J., Caroff, S. N., & Brunswick, D. J. (1983). Multiple hormonal responses to protirelin (TRH) in depressed patients. *Archives of General Psychiatry, 40,* 525–531.

Wirz-Justice, A., & Richter, R. (1979). Seasonality in biochemical determinations: A source of variance and clue to the temporal incidence of affective illness. *Psychiatry Research, 1,* 53–60.

Wirz-Justice, A., & Wehr, T. A. (1983). Neuropsychopharmacology and biological rhythms. *Advances in Biological Psychiatry, 11,* 20–34.

Wright, J. H., Jacisin, J. J., Radin, N. S., & Bell, R. A. (1978). Glucose metabolism in unipolar depression. *British Journal of Psychiatry, 132,* 386–393.

Yerevanian, B. I., Olafsdottir, H., Milanese, E., Russotto, J., Mallon, P., Baciewicz, G., & Sagi, E. (1983). Normalization of the dexamethasone suppression test at discharge from hospital: Its prognostic value. *Journal of Affective Disorders, 5,* 191–197.

Yerevanian, B. I., Woolf, P. D., & Iker, H. P. (1983). Plasma ACTH levels in depression before and after recovery. Relationship to the dexamethasone suppression test. *Psychiatry Research, 10,* 175–181.

Zahn, T. P. (1976). On the bimodality of the distribution of electrodermal orienting response in schizophrenic patients. *Journal of Nervous and Mental Disease, 162,* 195–199.

Zarcone, V. P., & Benson, K. L. (1983). Increased REM eye movement density in self-rated depression. *Psychiatry Research, 8,* 65–71.

Zis, A. P., & Goodwin, F. K. (1979a). Major affective disorder as a recurrent illness. *Archives of General Psychiatry, 36,* 835–839.

Zis, A. P., & Goodwin, F. K. (1979b). Novel antidepressants and the biogenic amine hypothesis: The case for iprindole and mianserin. *Archives of General Psychiatry, 36,* 1097–1107.

Zis, A. P., & Goodwin, F. K. (1982). The amine hypothesis. In E. S. Paykel (Ed.), *Handbook of affective disorders* (pp. 175–190). New York: Guilford Press.

Chapter 26

The Learned Helplessness Model of Depression: Current Status of Theory and Research

Christopher Peterson
Associate Professor, Department of Psychology
Virginia Polytechnic Institute and State University

Martin E. P. Seligman
Professor, Department of Psychology
University of Pennsylvania

Our purpose in this chapter is to describe the learned helplessness model of depression in its original (Seligman, 1972, 1974, 1975) and reformulated (Abramson, Seligman, & Teasdale, 1978; Peterson & Seligman, 1984) versions. We evaluate helplessness theory and research and discuss directions for future investigation.

BASIC ISSUES AND QUESTIONS FOR A THEORY OF DEPRESSION

Any research-driven theory of the depressive disorders must grapple successfully with certain basic issues and questions. In the past, the helplessness model has been criticized for ignoring some of these matters (Depue & Monroe, 1978), so we wish to be explicit here about ground rules for judging any psychological theory of depression, including learned helplessness. Most basically, a good theory must be based on empirical research. Further, to be a good account of depression, it must be able to explain what is known about the symptoms, causes, consequences, and therapies of depression. It must take a clear stance with respect to controversial issues in the psychology of depression. Finally, a good explanation of depression must be useful in the

The research described in this chapter was supported by U.S. Public Health Service Grant MH-19604 to Martin E. P. Seligman.

future as the diagnosis, classification, treatment, and even prevention of the depressive disorders become more sophisticated.

These criteria elaborate Abramson and Seligman's (1977) earlier discussion of how to establish a laboratory phenomenon as a model for a psychopathology, by documenting parallels between the model and the psychopathology. Here are 13 current issues in depression which a good theory should illuminate:

1. Caseness: What Is Being Explained? *Depression* is a term with many meanings, ranging from a transient low mood to a chronic psychiatric disorder. It may refer to an aspect of everyday living or to a severe dysfunction. A theory of depression must be explicit about what type of depression it attempts to explain. If the theory purports to be general, accounting for many types of depression, it must explain when and how these types are similar as well as when and how they are different. If the theory is circumscribed, it must explain why the boundaries have been drawn tightly.

2. Continuity: Are Mild Depression and Severe Depression Different in Degree or in Kind? This issue is closely related to the question of what is being explained by a theory of depression. Of the numerous distinctions among types of depression, one of the most consistently made is between mild and severe depression (e.g., Arieti & Bemporad, 1978). Considerable debate has ensued regarding the relationship of mild and severe depression. A theory of depression must take a stance with respect to this debate, a debate with important implications for diagnosis, research, and treatment.

3. Symptoms: Why Do the Various Symptoms of Depression Co-occur? Depression is typically regarded as a disorder of mood, but it also involves characteristic physiological, appetitive, motivational, cognitive, behavioral, and interpersonal symptoms (Beck, 1967). A theory of depression must explain why the depressive syndrome coheres in the way it does. If one class of symptoms is held to be causal, then the theory should state how these primary symptoms give rise to the other symptoms.

4. Causes: What Are They and How Do They Work? Research has identified a number of causes of depression. To be a good explanation of depression, a theory must be consistent with what is known about risk factors. Further, the theory must specify the mechanism by which a given risk factor produces depression and not some other psychopathology.

5. Therapies: What Are They and How Do They Work? In recent years, several effective therapies for the depressive disorders have been described. A theory of depression must be able to explain why these various therapies are effective. A good theory of depression should also suggest ways in which depression can be prevented in the first place.

6. Spontaneous Recovery: Why Is Depression Usually Episodic? For most depressed individuals, an effective "therapy" for depression is simply waiting it out. Depression often goes away in three to six months. A theory of depression must be able to explain spontaneous recovery. For which depressives does it occur? For which depressives does it not?

7. Recurrence: Why Does Depression Sometimes Return? Some number of individuals experience recurring episodes of depression, while other individuals experience only a single episode. A good theory of depression must account for this aspect of the disorder, specifying who is at risk for recurrence and who is not.

8. Sex Differences: Why Do They Exist?   Among adults, women are much more likely to be depressed than men (Radloff, 1975). Some of our research suggests that this sex difference may be present as early as eight years of age (Seligman, Peterson, Kaslow, Tanenbaum, Alloy, & Abramson, 1984), but the difference seems to appear most clearly following puberty (Rutter, 1982). To date, a fully satisfactory explanation of this sex difference in depression has proved elusive (Amenson & Lewinsohn, 1981). A good theory of depression must attempt to explain why depression occurs more frequently among women than men. More generally, a theory should speak to epidemiological variation in depression, but the sex difference is better documented than other differences, such as SES.

9. Developmental Differences: Do They Exist and If so Why? Another controversial topic in the psychology of depression is its manifestation across the lifespan. It is now agreed that children can be depressed (e.g., Schulterbrandt & Raskin, 1977), but legitimate debate occurs regarding the continuity of childhood depression and adult depression. Are they fundamentally different or essentially the same? A theory of depression must be explicit about how it regards childhood depression. Similarly, a good theory must be clear about depression among the aged. Again, is it essentially the same disorder that appears among young and middle-aged adults, or is it a problem with unique causes and consequences, requiring different psychotherapies?

10. Suicide: Why Does It Accompany Depression?   The most frequent precursor of suicide in our society is depression, and conversely, depressed individuals are often considered at risk for suicide. A theory of depression must explain why individuals who are depressed attempt to take their lives.

11. Biochemistry: What Is Its Role in Depression?   Recent research has documented the involvement of several biochemical factors in depression, and perhaps points to a genetic predisposition. Antidepressant medication is often highly effective in the treatment of depression. Can a psychological theory account for the role of physiology in depression? Minimally, a psychological theory of depression must not be incompatible with what is known about the biochemistry of depression.

12. Adaptiveness: Is Depression ever Functional? Depression is usually regarded as a dysfunction. However, some writers have suggested that depression can sometimes be adaptive (Rippere, 1977), a signal that one's commerce with the world is disturbed and a means of ensuring withdrawal from a dead-end pursuit (Klinger, 1975). A theory of depression must take a stance with respect to the possible adaptiveness of depression, stating when the "disorder" is advantageous and when it is not. More generally, why do people have the capacity to become depressed?

13. Typology: What Are the Basic Forms of Depression? Current classification schemes like the *DSM-III* (American Psychiatric Association, 1980) are symptom based. As understanding of the depressive disorders increases, we expect that symptom-based classification will give way to etiology-based classification, as in other fields of medicine. When this occurs, a theory of depression must be useful in suggesting "basic categories" of diagnosis, presumably using the causes regarded as important by the theory. Will suggested diagnostic categories have different prognoses and treatments of choice?

In sum, these basic issues and questions represent topics of contemporary concern within the psychology of depression. While no single theory currently addresses each issue and each question, the success with which a theory does so is a measure of its adequacy. In the present chapter, we evaluate learned helplessness in this way, and we invite other theorists to examine their theories similarly.

THE ORIGINAL HELPLESSNESS MODEL

Learned helplessness was first described systematically by animal learning researchers at the University of Pennsylvania (Overmier & Seligman, 1967; Seligman & Maier, 1967). These researchers discovered that dogs given inescapable electric shock in a Pavlovian hammock showed several classes of deficits 24 hours later in a shuttlebox where the simple act of crossing a barrier would terminate shock. In contrast to dogs who had not previously experienced shock, these dogs showed: *(a)* motivational deficits, rarely initiating attempts to escape; *(b)* learning deficits, not following an occasionally successful escape response with another; and *(c)* emotional deficits, passively enduring the shock without overt signs of emotionality.

It was proposed that these deficits were the consequence of learning by the dogs in the Pavlovian hammock that responses and outcomes (i.e., shocks) were independent of each other, that nothing they did mattered. This learning was represented as an expectation of future uncontrollability (i.e., helplessness) which was generalized to the new situation where it produced the observed deficits. This expectation constituted the basic explanation of the phenomenon, and the explanation, along with the phenomenon, was dubbed "learned helplessness." Figure 1 depicts the process hypothesized by original helplessness theory.

A number of experiments strongly suggest that it is the uncontrollability of the aversive events and not their traumatizing properties per se which is responsible for the various helplessness deficits (see a review by Maier & Seligman, 1976). Central to these demonstrations is the triadic design. In a correctly done helplessness experiment, three groups are used. One (the escapable group) is exposed to controllable events, such as electric shock which may be terminated by some response. A second (the inescapable group) is yoked to the first group and subjected to the physically identical events. Crucially different, however, is that for subjects in this second group the termination of these events is independent of all responses. A third group (the no-pretreatment control) is exposed to no events, controllable or uncontrollable. All three groups are then tested on a task which involves learning some new response. Learned helplessness is present when the inescapable group has trouble relative to the other two groups.

The helplessness explanation of deficits in animals following uncontrollable events has been attacked by theorists inclined to explain them in peripheral or biochemical terms, and many of the studies conducted by learned helplessness proponents have been attempts to defend the cognitive account against these reinterpretations (see Maier & Jackson, 1979; Maier & Seligman, 1976; Seligman & Weiss, 1980). The success of helplessness theory in maintaining its cognitive emphasis while explaining animal behavior attracted the attention of psychologists interested in helplessness in people. Two lines of inquiry into human helplessness ensued.

In the first, researchers attempted simply to demonstrate learning impairment following uncontrollable events (see a review by Wortman & Brehm, 1975). Although some of these early studies were methodologically flawed, and others were unsuccessful in producing helplessness, a substantial number indeed showed helplessness deficits in people (e.g., Hiroto & Seligman, 1975). Most studies borrowed the triadic design from the animal paradigm. The controllable events were typically noises or shocks escapable by pushing a button or solvable concept identification problems. The uncontrollable events were inescapable noises or shocks or unsolvable problems.

In the second line of helplessness research with people, applied psychologists using the phenomenon and its cognitive explanation to model a variety of failures of human adaptation involving passivity. Thus, learned helplessness was proposed as analogous to failure in school (Dweck & Reppucci, 1973), the stagnation of the lower class (Bresnahan & Blum, 1971), sex differ-

---

FIGURE 1
The process of learned helplessness: Original theory

NONCONTINGENT ⟶ EXPECTATION OF ⟶ DEFICITS
EVENTS   UNCONTROLLABILITY

ences in achievement (Dweck & Bush, 1976), drug use (Berglas & Jones, 1978), responses to victimization (Peterson & Seligman, 1983), and so on. The best-known of these applications was Seligman's (1972, 1974, 1975) suggestion that learned helpless was a laboratory model of depression.

Many of the applications of learned helplessness to failures of human adaptation have been overly metaphorical, failing to show that the uncontrollability of bad events is critical in producing deficits (Peterson, 1982b). However, its application to depression has been the most attentive to the necessity for establishing parallels between the laboratory model and the out-of-the-laboratory dysfunction at a number of points: causes, symptoms, therapies, and preventions. In a series of studies, Seligman (1974) and his colleagues compared the responses of individuals made helpless in the experimental laboratory with those of individuals suffering from naturally occurring depression. Table 1 summarizes some of the parallels established in this research.

Original Helplessness Theory and the 13 Issues

We will consider each in turn. First, the original helplessness model attempts to explain many types of unipolar depression, from depression as a transient mood to depression as a psychiatric disorder. According to the model, at the core of many forms of depression is an expectation of response-outcome independence engendered by experience with uncontrollable events. However, the original helplessness model is unable to explain what is different about the various forms of depression ostensibly involving an expectation of helplessness. When do uncontrollable events result merely in a sad mood, and when do they result in a profound disorder? Common sense suggests that

TABLE 1
Parallels between laboratory helplessness and depression

Parallels between symptoms:
  1. Passivity.
  2. Retarded response-relief learning.
  3. Lowered aggression.
  4. Loss of appetite.
  5. Feelings of helplessness, hopelessness, and powerlessness.
  6. Negative expectations.
  7. Catecholamine and indoleamine depletion.

Parallels between causes:
  8. Uncontrollable bad events.

Parallels between therapies:
  9. Exposure to contingencies.
  10. Electroconvulsive shock.
  11. Antidepressant drugs.

Parallels between preventions:
  12. Early mastery training.

such factors as the amount of experience with uncontrollable events, the importance of the events, and so on may be invoked to distinguish among types of depression modeled by learned helplessness, but these factors are not explicitly incorporated within the original model.

Second, the original helplessness model regards mild and severe depression as continuous. Severe depression is a more intense version of mild depression; their difference is one of degree but not of kind. However, as already noted, the model does not address the difference in degree. Further, whether mild and severe unipolar depression are similar is an empirical question, at least with respect to specific causes and consequences. The early research applying learned helplessness to depression may be criticized for not frequently employing severely depressed research subjects (Depue & Monroe, 1978). Instead, mildly depressed college students were usually studied, and continuity was assumed rather than demonstrated.

Third, the original helplessness model does a good job of explaining why most of the symptoms of depression cohere as they do. Deficits induced by uncontrollability in the animal and human laboratory include physiological, appetitive, motivational, cognitive, behavioral, and interpersonal disturbances, just like depression (Seligman, 1974). According to helplessness theory, the core depressive symptom is cognitive: the expectation of response-outcome independence. This cognitive emphasis is consistent with some theories of depression, notably Beck's (1967) cognitive model. Depression researchers have not yet established the priority of any given symptom. This is not a fault of the helplessness model, although it points to the need for longitudinal investigations of the development of depressive symptoms.

One striking symptom of depression, however, is inconsistent with the original helplessness model. Most clinical descriptions of depression, from Freud's (1917/1957) to Beck's (1967), emphasize self-blame. Depressed individuals blame themselves for a variety of bad events in the world. As Abramson and Sackeim (1977) observed, self-blame by depressives is paradoxical if these individuals additionally perceive no control over events, as the helplessness model proposes. How can one blame oneself for events beyond control? Peterson (1979) demonstrated that this "paradox in depression" indeed exists, and the original learned helplessness model is unable to explain it.

Fourth, helplessness theory is consistent with the situational factors known to put individuals at risk for depression (Lloyd, 1980). In particular, research has shown that life events are most apt to precipitate depressive reactions when they involve losses or exits that are aversive and uncontrollable, as helplessness theory predicts (Paykel, 1974; Thoits, 1983). Helplessness theory does not easily explain genetic and biological risk factors for depression, nor personality predispositions. However, the helplessness model proposes sufficient but not necessary conditions for depression, so its silence on genetics and personality is not a major flaw. (It should be pointed out that biological theories of depression have the converse flaws. To expect any theory of depression—cognitive or biological—to account fully for both cognitive and physiological symptoms is to expect a solution to the mind-body problem.)

Fifth, a therapy technique for depression that involves forcible exposure to contingencies was suggested by the original helplessness model (Seligman, Maier, & Geer, 1968), and this procedure may alleviate some types of depression (Seligman, 1975). However, helplessness theory may be criticized for making the therapy of depression seem too simple, a matter merely of correcting erroneous beliefs about contingencies (Peterson, 1982a). In actuality, depressive beliefs show considerable inertia, and successful therapies probably involve much more than redressing beliefs about response-outcome contingencies (e.g., Beck, Rush, Shaw, & Emery, 1979).

Sixth, helplessness theory can explain spontaneous recovery. The expectation of helplessness is presumably a generalized and stable belief, one that resists change. However, it should be remembered that animal helplessness dissipates in time under some conditions (Maier & Seligman, 1976), and proactive interference of earlier experiences of control have been invoked to explain this.

Seventh, the original helplessness model is unable to explain in a simple way the recurrence of depression. Common sense suggests that some individuals are more apt than others to encounter repeatedly uncontrollable events and thus be put at risk for repeated episodes of helplessness-produced depression. But helplessness theory implies that repeated uncontrollability should result in chronic depression, not recurrent depression.

Eighth, sex differences in depression can be explained by the original helplessness model in three ways. One is that women experience more uncontrollable events than do men. Alternatively, as a result of early socialization that restricts their range of coping responses, women may be more likely than men to perceive bad events as uncontrollable. Finally, women may be taught giving up responses to uncontrollable events, while men may be taught to try repeatedly. Research is equivocal with respect to these possibilities, however, and there is no consistent evidence that women are more vulnerable than men to laboratory-produced helplessness. Thus, although the model's explanations of sex differences are reasonable, they have not been supported by research.

Ninth, helplessness theory takes a strong stance that depression exists across the life span in essentially the same form. Accounts of childhood depression that emphasize separation and loss are quite compatible with helplessness theory (e.g., Bowlby, 1969; Spitz, 1946), as are descriptions of depression among the aged that stress loss of family, friends, pursuits, and functions.

Tenth, the co-occurrence of suicide with depression is not explained by the original helplessness theory. If anything, the model predicts that depressed individuals would be less likely than the nondepressed to make the active responses involved in suicide.

Eleventh, helplessness research with animals has shown that uncontrollable aversive events result in catecholamine and indoleamine changes (Sherman, Sacquitine, & Petty, 1982), biological correlates of depression (Schildkraut, 1965). Similarly, antidepressant drugs and electroconvulsive shock may also break up learned helplessness in animals (e.g., Sherman et al., 1982; Weiss, Glazer, & Pohorecky, 1976). So, the learned helplessness phenomenon has an important biochemical parallel with depression. However, learned helplessness theory is not clear about how norepinephrine depletion is related to cognition. According to the theory, the primary cause of the helplessness phenomenon and of the depressions modeled by the phenomenon is the expectation of response-outcome independence. Thus, biochemical changes should follow the expectation, while the research suggests a bidirectional influence. This possibility is not incorporated within the helplessness model.

Twelfth, depression is regarded as dysfunctional by helplessness theory, in the sense that it precludes learning advantageous responses in situations where such learning is possible. That depression might be adaptive in some circumstances can be explained by reference to the special case in which real outcomes continue to be independent of responses. In such situations, there is probably some advantage to passivity. Helplessness theory does not conceive depression as centrally involving secondary gain. Indeed, recent research shows that depressed individuals are not rewarded by others for their symptoms (e.g., Coates & Wortman, 1980).

Thirteenth, the original learned helplessness model does not give rise to a classification scheme for the depressive disorders. As already noted, the model does not make distinctions among types of depressives, and this must be considered a shortcoming of the theory (cf., Depue & Monroe, 1978).

In sum, the original learned helplessness model has some success in addressing fundamental issues and questions about depression, but more often than not, it falls short. Depression is much more complex than the original helplessness model. Learned helplessness may model some of depression, but it is incomplete. In particular, the original learned helplessness model is inattentive to the boundary conditions of depression, and it fails to distinguish among types of depression.

THE ATTRIBUTIONAL REFORMULATION

At the same time that learned helplessness was being scrutinized as an account of depression, researchers were also evaluating the theory as an explanation of problem-solving deficits in people following uncontrollable events. A number of anomalies vis-à-vis the theory were documented, suggesting—as is the case for learned helplessness applied to depression—that laboratory-produced helplessness in people is more complicated than the theory implies (Peterson & Seligman, 1981). Among the puzzling laboratory findings were:

1. Some studies failed to produce helplessness, and a few even found that uncontrollability facilitated problem solving (the reactance effect; Wortman & Brehm, 1975).
2. Laboratory-produced helplessness sometimes generalized beyond the specific pretreatment, and sometimes not. For instance, changing the experimental room between the pretreatment and the test task precluded helplessness deficits for some subjects.
3. Information about how other people had performed and about the nature of the pretreatment and test tasks affected helplessness.
4. In some studies, helplessness followed uncontrollable events for subjects with certain personality characteristics but not for other subjects.

So, critics of both basic and applied learned helplessness research agreed that a more complex theory was needed. Most also agreed that such a theory should incorporate the individual's causal interpretation of the original uncontrollable events. In response, Abramson et al. (1978) reformulated helplessness theory along attributional lines (for similar revisions, see Miller & Norman, 1979; Roth, 1980).

According to the reformulation, when people face uncontrollable events, they ask why? Their answer affects how they will react to the events. Abramson et al. (1978) proposed that three explanatory dimensions are relevant. First, the cause may be something about the person (internal explanation), or it may be something about the situation or circumstances (external explanation). Second, the cause may be a factor that will persist across time (stable explanation), or it may be transient (unstable explanation). Third, the cause may affect a variety of outcomes (global explanation) or may be limited just to the event of concern (specific explanation). Table 2 gives examples of such explanations as they might be made about the bad event: "I failed my midterm examination."

TABLE 2
Causal explanations for the bad event: "I failed my midterm examination"

A. Internal explanation
   1. Stable explanation
     a. Global explanation: "I'm stupid."
     b. Specific explanation: "I'm stupid in this subject."
   2. Unstable explanation
     a. Global explanation: "I was feverish that day."
     b. Specific explanation: "I had trouble concentrating on that topic the other day."

B. External explanation
   1. Stable explanation
     a. Global explanation: "All evaluations are unfair."
     b. Specific explanation: "That teacher writes bad tests."
   2. Unstable explanation
     a. Global explanation: "It was Friday the 13th."
     b. Specific explanation: "My test booklet was missing a page."

The reformulation assigns particular roles to each of these three dimensions. Internality of causal beliefs affects self-esteem loss following bad events. If the person explains a bad event by an internal factor, then self-esteem loss is more likely to occur. If a person explains the event by an external factor, then self-esteem loss is less likely to occur. Stability of causal beliefs is thought to affect the chronicity of helplessness and depression following bad events. If a bad event is explained by a cause that persists, depressive reactions to that event will tend to persist. If the event is explained by a transient factor, then depressive reactions will tend to be short lived. Finally, globality of causal beliefs influences the pervasiveness of deficits following bad events. If one believes that a global factor has caused a bad event, then helplessness deficits will tend to occur in across a variety of different situations. If one believes that a more specific factor is the cause, the deficits will tend to be circumscribed.

The reformulation of helplessness theory further proposes that people show consistent explanatory styles. People offer the same sorts of causal explanations for different bad events. If a person habitually invokes internal, stable, and global causes, we call this a depressive explanatory style and expect the person to be particularly at risk for depression when bad events are encountered.

The attributional reformulation in part embodies the "man-as-scientist" metaphor popular in social-cognitive theorizing (e.g., Kelley, 1973; Kelly, 1955). It assumes that individuals' thoughts and beliefs are primary determinants of their actions and that actions are usually logically consistent with thoughts and beliefs. This metaphor contrasts with other points of view that regard drives and motives as primary determinants of actions (e.g., Freud, 1917/1957). However, the reformulation does not embrace the entire "man-as-scientist" metaphor. It does not assume that people necessarily arrive at their beliefs logically, or that they continually attempt to falsify them (cf., Nisbett & Ross, 1980). Beck (1967, 1976) has argued that depressives reason erroneously about themselves and the social world. In contrast, Alloy and Abramson (1979) have suggested that nondepressives, rather than depressives, evidence cognitive distortion. The helplessness reformulation does not take a position on depressive irrationality versus rationality.

We used qualified language above in stating the central predictions of the reformulation. An internal explanation for a bad event is said to make self-esteem loss "more likely," but not to cause self-esteem loss. It is important to realize that explanations and their precursor, explanatory style, are not sufficient to produce depressive deficits but rather are risk factors for such deficits.

The relationship among variables in the reformulated theory is diagrammed in Figure 2. It depicts the general process by which the symptoms of helplessness—passivity, cognitive deficits, emotional deficits (including sadness, anxiety, and hostility), a lowering of aggression, a lowering of appetitive drives, a set of neurochemical deficits, and an increase in susceptibility to disease—are produced. In addition, the symptom of self-esteem loss is sometimes one of the symptoms of helplessness and depression.

The process of learned helplessness: Reformulated theory

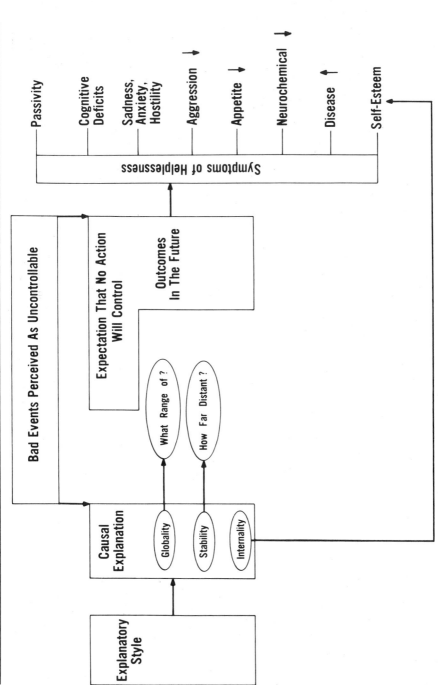

Source: Reproduced from C. Peterson & M. E. P. Seligman. Causal Explanations as a Risk Factor for Depression: Theory and Evidence, *Psychological Review,* 91 (1984), pp. 347–374. Copyright 1984 by the American Psychological Association. Reprinted by permission.

As in the original helplessness theory, the reformulation proposes that the expectation of future uncontrollability is a sufficient condition for the production of all of these symptoms of helplessness except self-esteem loss. This expectation is represented in the center of Figure 2. Whenever and wherever this expectation occurs, the symptoms will develop. The expectation is usually triggered when bad events are perceived as uncontrollable. The reality of the bad uncontrollable events influences the content of the expectation. For example, if the bad event is blindness, and one's job is proofreading, the range of outcomes to which the expectation applies will include work.

In addition to reality, there are two more variables shown in Figure 2 which influence the expectation that no action will control outcomes in the future: explanations and explanatory style. Explanatory style makes certain explanations more likely than others, and the stability and globality of the explanations modulate the range of situations to which the expectation will apply and how far into the future the expectation will be applicable. So, explanatory style and particular explanations are used to explain when the symptoms occur in many situations and when the symptoms are long lasting.

Explanations involving global causes tend to produce the expectation that action will not control many outcomes, which in turn produces deficits in exactly that large range of situations. In parallel, if the cause of a bad event is explained by stable factors, the expectation will tend to occur for a long time into the future, and therefore, the deficits will also be long lasting. If the explanation for a bad event is internal, then the symptom of lowered self-esteem will tend to be displayed.

The particular causal explanation an individual makes for the bad event influences the generality and time course of the symptoms of helplessness, as well as the loss of self-esteem. In the model, there are two influences on the particular explanation chosen. The first is the reality of the bad events themselves. If the bad event that sets off the expectation of helplessness is the death of one's spouse, this is a stable and global loss. The spouse will not return, and many of the activities in which one has customarily engaged will be undermined. The second influence on what particular explanation is made is explanatory style: the habitual tendency to choose certain kinds of explanations for bad versus good events. We have been able to identify individual patterns in the selection of causes over a variety of events. The particular style that most concerns us is the depressive style, in which one tends to give internal, stable, and global explanations for bad events (it's me; it's going to last forever; and it's going to affect everything I do).

It should now be apparent why a particular explanation or explanatory style is not sufficient for the symptoms of helplessness and depression to appear. These variables influence the expectation, but it is the expectation which is sufficient. Usually, causal explanations for an event and expectations about the consequences of an event are similar. But sometimes the properties of a cause and its consequences can be dissimilar. Knowing an individual's explanation and explanatory style will often predict helplessness deficits. But because of the dissimilarity, an individual's causal explanation and explanatory style do not actually bring about the deficits. We will speak of these variables as risk factors (just as smoking is a risk factor for lung cancer), rather than sufficient conditions for helplessness and depression. Our research has focused on measuring explanations and explanatory style, because a methodological framework already existed for doing so (e.g., Harvey, Ickes, & Kidd, 1976, 1978, 1981).

We have used a variety of research strategies: *(a)* cross-sectional correlational studies; *(b)* causal modeling with longitudinal data; *(c)* experiments of nature; *(d)* laboratory experiments; and *(e)* case studies. Each class of investigation addressed a more stringent prediction about the relationship of causal explanations to depression. The cross-sectional studies sought merely to correlate explanatory style and depressive symptoms. The longitudinal studies investigated whether a "depressive" style precedes depression, consistent with a predisposing role. The experiments of nature looked at how naturally occurring bad events and explanatory style interact to produce a subsequent depressive reaction. The laboratory experiments investigated whether experimentally manipulated bad events interact with explanatory style to result in laboratory helplessness, a depressive analogue. Finally, the case studies ascertained the applicability of the reformulation to real lives.

Taken together, these lines of research allow a multimethod test of the central prediction of the helplessness reformulation: that internal, stable, and global causal explanations for bad events are risk factors for depression (Peterson & Seligman, 1984). We consider each line of evidence in turn.

The cross-sectional studies we have conducted employed a variety of populations (e.g., college students, female welfare recipients, children, psychiatric patients), a variety of ways of assessing depression (e.g., self-report questionnaire, psychiatric diagnosis), and a variety of measures of explanatory style (e.g., self-report questionnaire, interview, content analysis). In most of our studies, internal, stable, and global explanations correlate with depressive symptoms (see Peterson & Seligman, 1984, for a complete review). Indeed, Peterson and Villanova (1984) recently summarized more than 60 different tests of the reformulation using a cross-sectional strategy. About 60 percent of these investigations supported the reformulation, and a number of studies which did not were flawed by inadequate sample size and/or unreliable measurement of style. Thus, cross-sectional tests of the reformulation have yielded quite strong support.

However, such tests do not answer a critical question: Does explanatory style put one at risk for later depression? Several other possibilities are compatible with the demonstrated correlation. First, there is the possibility of a tautological relationship of depressive explanatory style and depressive symptoms. For example, many answers that count toward the self-report of depression are phrased in terms of *internal, stable,* and *global* causes; for example, "I will always fail at whatever I do." Perhaps a bad explanatory style is just a special symptom of depression. Second, there is the possibility that depression causes the depressive style. On this view, when one becomes depressed, the style is activated as a result. Third, there is the possibility that some third variable, such as biochemical deficits or a preexisting tendency to turn anger inward, causes both depression and the depressive explanatory style. The remaining lines of research we conducted untangled these various possibilities from the causal process predicted by the reformulation.

Longitudinal investigations were used to test the next most stringent prediction of the reformulation: that depressive explanatory style precedes depression. In two studies with children, we showed that the depressive style predicted depressive symptoms six months later, even when initial level of depression was held constant (Seligman et al., 1984). Other researchers have conducted similar studies with adults, finding support that internal, stable, and global explanations for bad events precede the development of depressive symptoms (e.g., Cutrona, 1983; Golin, Sweeney, & Shaeffer, 1981; O'Hara, Rehm, & Campbell, 1982).

These longitudinal studies are consistent with the helplessness reformulation. Explanatory style thus precedes depression, allowing identification of individuals at risk by the way they explain bad events. The general flaw of longitudinal studies as tests of the reformulated model is that they do not manipulate or assess bad life events. According to Abramson et al. (1978), a depressive style per se is not sufficient for depression. It is only when bad events occur and are interpreted in terms of internal, stable, and global causes that depressive symptoms are more likely to ensue. Because these studies did not look at bad events, they did not test this prediction.

However, we have conducted several studies that investigated whether a preexisting depressive explanatory style followed by naturally occurring bad events makes depression more likely. In one study, the bad event we assessed was a poor grade on a college midterm. Depressive mood was measured before and after the midterm examination. A poor grade coupled with the depressive style increased depressed mood; neither a poor grade nor an explanatory style per se resulted in depression (Metalsky, Abramson, Seligman, Semmel, & Peterson, 1982). In a similar study, we showed that the depressive style predicted depression among men following imprisonment in federal penitentiaries (Peterson, Nutter, & Seligman, 1982). Other researchers have reported similar experiments of nature consistent with the helplessness reformulation (see Peterson & Seligman, 1984).

Each of these studies is open to the criticism that experimental control over the bad events was not possible, and so potential confounds might underlie the obtained correlations. For this reason, we also conducted several laboratory experiments in which bad events were presented to randomly chosen subjects. Does explanatory style affect such laboratory-induced helplessness in the same way that it affects naturally occurring depressive symptoms? Alloy, Peterson, Abramson, and Seligman (1984) found this to be the case for global versus specific style. In a standard helplessness experiment with college students, subjects who explained bad events with global causes showed general problem-solving deficits following uncontrollable events, while subjects who explained bad events with specific causes showed deficits only at a task similar to the pretreatment. As predicted by the helplessness reformulation, globality of causal explanations determines the pervasiveness of deficits following uncontrollability.

We have also obtained some evidence that stable versus unstable style affects the time course of laboratory helplessness (Peterson & Seligman, 1981). Other researchers have investigated the role of internal versus external explanations, and they have found that internal explanations affect self-esteem loss following uncontrollable events, just as the reformulation predicts (McFarland & Ross, 1982; Miller & Norman, 1981).

These laboratory data indicate that explanations and explanatory style, when accompanied by experimental control over bad events, support the helplessness reformulation. Revising the original model improves not only its applicability to depression but also its fit with the laboratory helplessness phenomenon.

Finally, we have conducted several case studies that show the reformulation to apply powerfully to the lives of depressed individuals. These studies overcome the obtrusive and reactive nature of the questionnaires we have usually employed to assess explanations by using content analysis. Causal explanations were extracted from written transcripts of psychotherapy sessions and rated for internality, stability, and globality (Peterson & Seligman, 1984). In one study with four depressed patients, we used this method to predict levels of depression across successful psychotherapy (Peterson & Seligman, 1981). In a second study, we were able to predict the mood swings of a patient in and out of depression by taking into account the internality, stability, and globality of his explanations for bad events prior to mood swings (Peterson, Luborsky, & Seligman, 1981).

Taken together, these five lines of research support the predictions of the attributional reformulation of the learned helplessness model of depression. Each type of research may be criticized, but the convergence of results across different strategies of investigation, different operationalizations, and different populations argues strongly for the validity of the reformulation (Campbell & Fiske, 1959).

The Reformulation and the 13 Issues

Has the reformulation improved the helplessness model as a theory of depression? We believe so. First, the helplessness reformulation allows the model to be applied to a number of different types of unipolar depression while at the same time explaining what is different about them: the nature of the expectation about future uncontrollability. Different expectations are under the sway of different causal explanations, and attention to various explanatory patterns among depressives is indicated. Chronic depression results from stable explanations, pervasive depression results from global explanations, and so on.

Second, the reformulation similarly explains that the distinction between mild and severe unipolar depression is one of degree, not quality. The intensity and variety of depressive symptoms following uncontrollable events are a function of the importance of these events and of the way that they are explained.

Third, the reformulated theory now accounts for the one depressive symptom that was unexplained by the original model: self-blame. There is no inconsistency in proposing that depressives believe events to be uncontrollable, and that the cause of these events is internal, say, a defect of character.

Fourth, the helplessness reformulation goes beyond the environmental risk factors for depression. Explanatory style is proposed as a dispositional risk factor for depression. Future research should investigate its relationship to the depression-prone personality (Carver & Ganellan, 1983). The reformulation remains silent with respect to the role of genetic risk factors, but perhaps explanatory style is partly heritable.

Fifth, behavioral and cognitive therapies for depression are interpretable within the framework of the helplessness reformulation, which makes clear predictions about what should be the active ingredients in their effective treatments (see Seligman, 1981). Future therapy outcome research is needed to evaluate these predictions.

Sixth, spontaneous recovery is thought to occur among individuals who interpret bad events in unstable terms. They may suffer depression in response to bad events, but these reactions are not long lasting. Eaves and Rush (1984) reported that the length of depressive episodes correlates with stability of causal explanations for bad events.

Seventh, the reformulation suggests that recurring depression is most likely to occur among individuals who explain bad events internally, unstably, and globally. It might be that these people frequently experience transient depression. Whether this is a reasonable explanation of recurring depression needs to be ascertained.

Eighth, according to the reformulated model, the sex difference in depression may involve different explanatory styles. Dweck and Licht (1980) argued that boys and girls may explain failure differently, with girls employing more internal, more stable, and more global explanations. This style may persist into adulthood, perhaps rendering women more vulnerable to depression when bad events occur.

Ninth, the helplessness reformulation suggests that the process of depression underlying depression is the same across the life span but that the specific manifestation of depression reflects developmental differences in the use of explanations (Seligman & Peterson, in press). So, differences between children and adults with respect to cognitive abilities may make children less likely to entertain stable and global explanations. Childhood depression may thus be briefer and more circumscribed than adult depression. As explained in the next paragraph, suicide may be less likely. And so on.

Tenth, the co-occurrence of suicide and depression is better explained by the revised model than by the original model. Hopelessness, a robust predictor of suicide, readily translates into stable and global explanations for bad events. The extrapolation of present helplessness into the future and across many situations transforms it into hopelessness. There is still an inconsistency between suicide conceived as an active response and depression conceived as passivity, but the helplessness reformulation no longer regards the depressive as completely passive. Domains of passivity are a function of causal explanations, and we predict that suicidal depressives are those who regard the solution of life's problems as under their control, even if causes are seen as uncontrollable. Again, research is needed to investigate this hypothesis.

Eleventh, the helplessness reformulation does not add to the original model's account of biochemistry in depression. Thus, it is compatible with the models implicating the role of biological amines, but it is silent about the mechanism linking cognitions and biochemistry.

Twelfth, depression is regarded as possibly adaptive by the reformulation not only in the special case of an unresponsive environment (where responses continue to be independent of responses) but additionally in situations where the causal texture of reality matches the "depressive" explanatory style. Theorists have proposed that causal explanations aid an individual in anticipating events in the world and coping with their consequences (Heider, 1958). To the degree that depressed individuals have more accurate causal beliefs than nondepressed individuals, depression is in some sense adaptive. Of course, severe depression carries with it a number of symptoms that are dysfunctional regardless of the context (e.g., susceptibility to illness), and the aspects of depression that may be adaptive will rarely compensate for these.

Thirteenth, one of the most promising uses to which the reformulation might be put is the generation of a typology of depressives in terms of explanatory styles (Seligman, 1978). Work in this direction has not yet begun, because helplessness researchers have mainly investigated whether depressive symptoms covary with internal, stable, and global explanations. This proposition has now been established for a number of depressives, and attention might now turn profitably to those depressives who do not make internal, stable, and global explanations for bad events. These individuals may show a different etiology of depression, and may need different forms of therapy.

For instance, one of us (CP) has done psychotherapy with Vietnam veterans suffering from posttraumatic stress syndrome. For some patients, this problem seems to involve a form of depression characterized by *external,* stable, and global explanations for bad events and a pattern of alcoholism, violence, and other antisocial behaviors. Therapy was directed at increasing internal explanations for bad events, not at decreasing them as we usually recommend (Seligman, 1981).

For another example, consider burnout, the emotional exhaustion sometimes occurring to individuals providing social services. Burnout is mostly indistinguishable from depression, except that it surrounds work. In many ways, burnout is a 40-hour-a-week depression. We would expect, therefore, that individuals suffering from burnout make internal, stable, and *specific* causal explanations for bad events. This would explain the pattern of work avoidance and withdrawal that sometimes accompanies burnout. Therapy might attempt to decrease internal and stable explanations for events that are already seen as circumscribed.

As a final example, a depressed individual who makes internal, *unstable,* and global explanations for bad events is a candidate for crisis intervention. The particular depressive episode should lift rather quickly with the passage of time, and the therapist's goal is to help the person make it through this period.

The typology of depression suggested by the helplessness reformulation has not yet been elaborated, and so any therapy implications are tentative at best. Although most depressives show the depressive explanatory style (internal, stable, and global explanations), there are some who do not. We believe that changes in explanatory style mediate effective cognitive therapy of depression, and a typology based on explanatory style would direct particular interventions (Seligman, 1981).

To conclude, when evaluated in terms of basic issues and questions about depression, the helplessness reformulation is a noticeable improvement over the original model. It promises to do as good a job explaining depression as any contemporary psychological theory.

FUTURE DIRECTIONS

The helplessness model of depression is not a finished product. As a research-based theory, it demands continued theoretical and empirical scrutiny. Toward this end, it particularly welcomes studies to disconfirm it. We now draw attention to several topics for future attention:

1. The Role in Depression of Causal Explanations for Good Events. The helplessness reformulation does not explicitly address such causal beliefs, but they seem to have at least a weak empirical relationship with depressive symptoms. We have assessed such beliefs, and generally found them to have effects on depression opposite to those of causal explanations about bad events, but at less robust levels (Peterson & Seligman, 1984). Internal, stable, and global explanations of good events correlate with the absence of depressive symptoms. However, some of our findings do not fit these generalizations. In our longitudinal investigations of children, explanatory style for bad events correlated with and predicted subsequent depression, while style for good events only correlated with depression. In our study of prisoners, the explanation of good events to internal, stable, and global causes was positively, not negatively, correlated with later depression. A sound theoretical treatment of these results is awaited.

We speculate that our pattern of findings with children may be related to the sorts of events that adults take for granted that children do not. When do we engage in explanatory analysis, and when do we forego it? C. S. Peirce (1955) suggested that the function of thought is to allay doubt (see also Wong

& Weiner, 1981). It seems likely that we ask "why?" more often when we are in doubt, when our path is suddenly obstructed, than when things are going smoothly. Indeed, consciousness itself may emerge only when our routine actions fail (cf., Langer, 1978). This implies that the explanatory analysis of failure among adults would be much more articulate than the analysis of success. Children, on the other hand, newer at the game, may analyze the causes of both failure and success closely, before they get older and come to relegate the analysis of success to routine causes. Such a developmental process would render children's explanatory style more useful than that of adults in predicting depression.

2. *The Relationship of Explanatory Style to Other Characteristics of Depressive Cognition.* The helplessness reformulation is only one of several contemporary cognitive theories of depression; it emphasizes explanations and explanatory style. Other theories emphasize the interplay between mood and memory (e.g., Bower, 1981), cognitive illusions (e.g., Alloy & Abramson, 1979), errors in information processing (e.g., Beck, 1976), characterological self-blame (e.g., Janoff-Bulman, 1979), beliefs about coping skills (e.g., Bandura, 1982), and so on. The helplessness reformulation does not necessarily "compete" with other cognitive accounts of depression, since it attempts to specify sufficient but not necessary conditions for depressive symptoms. Nevertheless, an integrated theory of the cognitive factors involved in depression would be valuable.

3. *Internality, Stability, and Globality as the "Basic" Dimensions of Causal Explanations.* The research we have conducted shows these to be important, but these dimensions are rarely orthogonal. In all of our samples with all of our assessment techniques, the three explanatory dimensions have been intercorrelated, within good events and within bad events. Stability and globality in particular co-occur. We believe that this is not a procedural artifact, and that it reflects the usual way people actually offer causal explanations. These dimensions could be teased apart by the laboratory studies, with the effect predicted by the helplessness reformulation (Peterson & Seligman, 1984). This does not imply, however, that in nature the dimensions are independent. The strong empirical correlation of stability and globality may reflect a more basic dimension of hopelessness versus hopefulness.

4. *The Origins of Explanatory Style.* The helplessness reformulation is silent about antecedents. We are turning our research attention to this issue, and it promises to be exciting. A preliminary finding is worth mentioning. In our study of explanatory style and depressive symptoms among children (Seligman et al., 1984), we obtained corresponding scores from the mothers and fathers of the children in our sample. Explanatory style for bad events and depressive symptoms were correlated for mothers and their children. Scores for fathers were unrelated to those of their children, and to those of their mates.

This finding does not point to the exact mechanisms by which causal explanations and levels of depressive symptomatology in mothers and their children converge. The likely direction seems from mother to child, but it is also likely that the effect is at least partly bidirectional. The intrapsychic vicious circle of the depressive (Beck, 1967) may be embedded in an interpersonal vicious circle. The depressive symptoms of mother and child may maintain each other because they both interpret the "bad" behavior of the other in internal, stable, and global terms.

5. Explanatory Style as a Trait.   We view explanatory style as a trait, analogous to liberalism in politics or vanity in interpersonal relations. We believe this for several reasons. We usually have measured explanatory style by assessing explanations across a variety of events (Peterson & Seligman, 1984). Explanatory style is derived from cross-situational consistency, and this is part of what is meant by "trait." Also, some people show more or less consistency across situations. When individuals who are inconsistent are discarded from our samples, correlations with depression and other outcomes go up. Finally, explanatory style shows fairly high stability across time.

However, we do not believe that explanatory style is invariant. Although we have argued that explanatory style affects depression, we also suspect that depression affects explanatory style. Hamilton and Abramson (1983), for instance, found that explanatory style changed for the better among patients as their depression lifted. Thus, therapy and other good or bad life events may change explanatory style (Seligman, 1981). We do after all acquire it at some time in our lives.

Future investigations should adopt a more sophisticated view of explanatory style. It should be treated as a dependent variable that can be modified by life events, as well as an independent variable that modifies future events. Also, the likelihood that there is a bidirectional influence between depression and explanatory style should be explored. And finally, the term *style* should be reserved for individuals whose causal explanations show low variability across time and situations.

To conclude, we have described the helplessness model of depression. The reformulation does a good job of addressing some of the basic questions and issues concerning depression. We also have briefly sketched some areas in need of further theoretical and empirical scrutiny. Explanations and explanatory style, in conjunction with actual bad events, often precede the development of depressive symptoms. Attention to them may be a practical means of predicting who is at risk for depression. Measuring them may help diagnose depression. And interventions directed at changing them may be an effective means of combating depression.

References

Abramson, L. Y., & Sackeim, H. A. (1977). A paradox in depression: Uncontrollability and self-blame. *Psychological Bulletin, 84,* 835–851.

Abramson, L. Y., & Seligman, M. E. P. (1977). Modeling psychopathology in the laboratory: History and rationale. In J. D. Maser & M. E. P. Seligman (Eds.), *Psychopathology: Experimental models* (pp. 1–26). San Francisco: Freeman.

Abramson, L. Y., Seligman, M. E. P., & Teasdale, J. D. (1978). Learned helplessness in humans: Critique and reformulation. *Journal of Abnormal Psychology, 87,* 49–74.

Alloy, L. B., & Abramson, L. Y. (1979). Judgment of contingency in depressed and nondepressed students: Sadder but wiser? *Journal of Experimental Psychology: General, 108,* 441–485.

Alloy, L. B., Peterson, C., Abramson, L. Y., & Seligman, M. E. P. (1984). Attributional style and the generality of learned helplessness. *Journal of Personality and Social Psychology, 46,* 681–687.

Amenson, C. S., & Lewinsohn, P. M. (1981). An investigation into the observed sex difference in prevalence of unipolar depression. *Journal of Abnormal Psychology, 90,* 1–13.

American Psychiatric Association (1980). *Diagnostic and statistical manual of mental disorders* (3rd ed.). Washington, DC: author.

Arieti, S., & Bemporad, S. (1978). *Severe and mild depression: The psychotherapeutic approach.* New York: Basic Books.

Bandura, A. (1982). Self-efficacy mechanisms in human agency. *American Psychologist, 37,* 122–147.

Beck, A. T. (1967). *Depression: Clinical, experimental, and theoretical aspects.* New York: Hoeber.

Beck, A. T. (1976). *Cognitive therapy and the emotional disorders.* New York: International Universities Press.

Beck, A. T., Rush, A. J., Shaw, B. F., & Emery, G. (1979). *Cognitive therapy of depression.* New York: Guilford.

Berglas, S., & Jones, E. E. (1978). Drug choice as a self-handicapping strategy in response to noncontingent reinforcement. *Journal of Personality, 36,* 405–417.

Bower, G. H. (1981). Mood and memory. *American Psychologist, 36,* 129–148.

Bowlby, J. (1969). *Attachment and loss, I: Attachment.* New York: Basic Books.

Bresnahan, J. L., & Blum, W. L. (1971). Chaotic reinforcement: A socioeconomic leveler. *Developmental Psychology, 4,* 89–92.

Campbell, D. T., & Fiske, D. W. (1959). Convergent and discriminant validation by the multitrait-multimethod matrix. *Psychological Bulletin, 56,* 81–105.

Carver, C. S., & Ganellan, R. J. (1983). Depression and components of self-punitiveness: High standards, self-criticism, and overgeneralization. *Journal of Abnormal Psychology, 92,* 330–337.

Coates, D., & Wortman, C. B. (1980). Depression maintenance and interpersonal control. In A. Baum & J. E. Singer (Eds.), *Advances in environmental psychology,* Vol. 2, *Applications of personal control* (pp. 149–182). Hillsdale, NJ: Erlbaum.

Cutrona, C. E. (1983). Causal attributions and perinatal depression. *Journal of Abnormal Psychology, 92,* 161–172.

Depue, R. A., & Monroe, S. M. (1978). Learned helplessness in the perspective of the depressive disorders: Conceptual and definitional issues. *Journal of Abnormal Psychology, 87,* 3–20.

Dweck, C. S., & Bush, E. S. (1976). Sex differences in learned helplessness: I. Differential debilitation with peer and adult evaluators. *Developmental Psychology, 12,* 147–156.

Dweck, C. S., & Licht, B. (1980). Learned helplessness and intellectual achievement. In J. Garber & M. E. P. Seligman (Eds.), *Human helplessness* (pp. 197–221). New York: Academic Press.

Dweck, C. S., & Reppucci, N. D. (1973). Learned helplessness and reinforcement responsibility in children. *Journal of Personality and Social Psychology, 25,* 109–116.

Eaves, G., & Rush, A. J. (1984). Cognitive patterns in symptomatic and remitted unipolar major depression. *Journal of Abnormal Psychology, 93,* 31–40.

Freud, S. (1957). Mourning and melancholia. In J. Strachey (Ed. and Trans.), *Standard edition of the complete psychological works of Sigmund Freud* (pp. 243–258). Vol. 14. London: Hogarth. (Originally published, 1917)

Golin, S., Sweeney, P. D., & Shaeffer, D. E. (1981). The causality of causal attributions in depression: A cross-lagged panel correlational analysis. *Journal of Abnormal Psychology, 90,* 14–22.

Hamilton, E. W., & Abramson, L. Y. (1983). Cognitive patterns and major depressive disorder: A longitudinal study in a hospital setting. *Journal of Abnormal Psychology, 92,* 173–184.

Harvey, J. H., Ickes, W. J., & Kidd, R. F. (1976). *New directions in attribution research.* Vol. 1. Hillsdale, NJ: Erlbaum.

Harvey, J. H., Ickes, W. J., & Kidd, R. F. (1978). *New directions in attribution research.* Vol. 2. Hillsdale, NJ: Erlbaum.

Harvey, J. H., Ickes, W. J., & Kidd, R. F. (1981). *New directions in attribution research.* Vol. 3. Hillsdale, NJ: Erlbaum.

Heider, F. (1958). *The psychology of interpersonal relations.* New York: John Wiley & Sons, 1958.

Hiroto, D. S., & Seligman, M. E. P. (1975). Generality of learned helplessness in man. *Journal of Personality and Social Psychology, 31,* 311–327.

Janoff-Bulman, R. (1979). Characterological versus behavioral self-blame: Inquiries into depression and rape. *Journal of Personality and Social Psychology, 37,* 1798–1809.

Kelley, H. H. (1973). The processes of causal attribution. *American Psychologist, 28,* 107–128.

Kelly, G. A. (1955). *The psychology of personal constructs.* New York: W. W. Norton.

Klinger, E. (1975). Consequences of commitment to and disengagement from incentives. *Psychological Review, 82,* 1–25.

Langer, E. J. (1978). Rethinking the role of thought in social interaction. In J. H. Harvey, W. J. Ickes, & R. F. Kidd (Eds.), *New directions in attribution research* (pp. 35–58). Vol. 2. Hillsdale, NJ: Erlbaum.

Lloyd, C. (1980). Life events and depressive disorder reviewed: I. Events as predisposing factors. II. Events as precipitating factors. *Archives of General Psychiatry, 37,* 529–548.

Maier, S. F., & Jackson, R. L. (1979). Learned helplessness: All of us were right (and wrong): Inescapable shock has multiple effects. In G. H. Bower (Ed.), *The psychology of learning and motivation* (pp. 155–218). Vol. 13. New York: Academic Press.

Maier, S. F., & Seligman, M. E. P. (1976). Learned helplessness: Theory and evidence. *Journal of Experimental Psychology: General, 105,* 3–46.

McFarland, C., & Ross, M. (1982). Impact of causal attributions on affective reactions to success and failure. *Journal of Personality and Social Psychology, 43,* 612–617.

Metalsky, G. I., Abramson, L. Y., Seligman, M. E. P., Semmel, A., & Peterson, C. (1982). Attributional styles and life events in the classroom: Vulnerability and invulnerability to depressive mood reactions. *Journal of Personality and Social Psychology, 43,* 612–617.

Miller, I. W., & Norman, W. H. (1979). Learned helplessness in humans: A review and attribution theory model. *Psychological Bulletin, 86,* 93–119.

Miller, I. W., & Norman, W. H. (1981). Effects of attributions for success on the alleviation of learned helplessness and depression. *Journal of Abnormal Psychology, 90,* 113–124.

Nisbett, R., & Ross, L. (1980). *Human inference: Strategies and shortcomings of social judgment.* Englewood Cliffs, NJ: Prentice–Hall.

O'Hara, M. W., Rehm, L. P., & Campbell, S. B. (1982). Predicting depressive symptomatology: Cognitive-behavioral models and postpartum depression. *Journal of Abnormal Psychology, 91,* 457–461.

Overmier, J. B., & Seligman, M. E. P. (1967). Effects of inescapable shock upon subsequent escape and avoidance learning. *Journal of Comparative and Physiological Psychology, 63,* 23–33.

Paykel, E. S. (1974). Life stress and psychiatric disorder: Applications of the clinical approach. In B. S. Dohrenwend & B. P. Dohrenwend (Eds.), *Stressful life events: Their nature and effects* (pp. 135–149). New York: John Wiley & Sons.

Peirce, C. S. (1955). *The philosophical writings of Peirce.* J. Buchler (Ed.). New York: Dover.

Peterson, C. (1979). Uncontrollability and self-blame in depression: Investigation of the paradox in a college population. *Journal of Abnormal Psychology, 88,* 620–624.

Peterson, C. (1982a). Learned helplessness and attributional interventions in depression. In C. Antaki & C. Brewin (Eds.), *Attributions and psychological change: A guide to the use of attribution theory in the clinic and classroom* (pp. 97–115). Academic Press, 1982.

Peterson, C. (1982b). Learned helplessness and health psychology. *Health Psychology, 1,* 153–168.

Peterson, C., Luborsky, L., & Seligman, M. E. P. (1983). Attributions and depressive mood shifts: A case study using the symptom-context method. *Journal of Abnormal Psychology, 92,* 96–103.

Peterson, C., Nutter, J., & Seligman, M. E. P. (1982). Unpublished data, Virginia Polytechnic Institute and State University.

Peterson, C., & Seligman, M. E. P. (1981). Helplessness and attributional style in depression. *Tiddsskrift for Norsk Psykologforening, 18,* 3–18; 53–59.

Peterson, C., & Seligman, M. E. P. (1983). Learned helplessness and victimization. *Journal of Social Issues, 39,* 103–116.

Peterson, C., & Seligman, M. E. P. (1984). Causal explanations as a risk factor for depression: Theory and evidence. *Psychological Review, 91,* 347–374.

Peterson, C., & Villanova, P. D. (1984). *Attributional style and depressive symptoms: A quantitative review.* Unpublished manuscript, Virginia Polytechnic Institute and State University.

Radloff, L. (1975). Sex differences in depression: The effects of occupational and marital status. *Sex Roles, 1,* 249–265.

Rippere, V. (1977). Comments on Seligman's theory of helplessness. *Behaviour Research and Therapy, 15,* 207–209.

Roth, S. (1980). A revised model of learned helplessness in humans. *Journal of Personality, 48,* 103–133.

Rutter, M. (1982). *The developmental psychopathology of depression: Issues and perspectives.* Paper delivered at Conference on Depression and Depressive Disorders: Developmental Perspectives, Temple University.

Schildkraut, J. J. (1965). The catecholamine hypothesis of affective disorders: A review of supporting evidence. *American Journal of Psychiatry, 112,* 509–522.

Schulterbrandt, J. G., & Raskin, A. (1977). *Depression in children: Diagnosis, treatment and conceptual models.* New York: Raven Press.

Seligman, M. E. P. (1972). Learned helplessness. *Annual Review of Medicine, 23,* 407–412.

Seligman, M. E. P. (1974). Depression and learned helplessness. In R. J. Friedman & M. M. Katz (Eds.), *The psychology of depression: Contemporary theory and research* (pp. 83–113). Washington, DC: Winston.

Seligman, M. E. P. (1975). *Helplessness: On depression, development, and death.* San Francisco: Freeman.

Seligman, M. E. P. (1978). Comment and integration. *Journal of Abnormal Psychology, 87,* 165–179.

Seligman, M. E. P. (1981). A learned helplessness point of view. In L. P. Rehm (Ed.), *Behavior therapy for depression: Present status and future directions* (pp. 123–141). New York: Academic Press.

Seligman, M. E. P., & Maier, S. F. (1967). Failure to escape traumatic shock. *Journal of Experimental Psychology, 74,* 1–9.

Seligman, M. E. P., Maier, S. F., & Geer, J. (1968). The alleviation of learned helplessness in the dog. *Journal of Abnormal Psychology, 73,* 256–262.

Seligman, M. E. P., & Peterson, C. (in press). A learned perspective on childhood depression: Theory and research. In M. Rutter, C. Izard, & P. Read (Eds.), *Depression in childhood: Developmental perspectives.* New York: Guilford.

Seligman, M. E. P., Peterson, C., Kaslow, N. J., Tanenbaum, R. L., Alloy, L. B., & Abramson, L. Y. (1984). Attributional style and depressive symptoms among children. *Journal of Abnormal Psychology, 93,* 235–238.

Seligman, M. E. P., & Weiss, J. M. (1980). Coping behavior: Learned helplessness, physiological activity, and learned inactivity. *Behaviour Research and Therapy, 18,* 459–512.

Sherman, A. D., Sacquitine, J. L., & Petty, F. (1982). Specificity of the learned helplessness model of depression. *Pharmacology, Biochemistry, and Behavior, 16,* 449–454.

Spitz, R. (1946). Anaclitic depression. *The Psychoanalytic Study of the Child, 2,* 313–342.

Thoits, P. A. (1983). Dimensions of life events that influence psychological distress: An evaluation and synthesis of the literature. In H. Kaplan (Ed.), *Psychosocial stress: Trends in theory and research* (pp. 33–103). New York: Academic Press.

Weiss, J. M., Glazer, H. I., & Pohorecky, L. A. (1976). Coping behavior and neurochemical changes: An alternative explanation for the original "learned helplessness" experiments. In G. Serban & A. Kling (Eds.), *Animal models of human psychobiology* (pp. 141–173). New York: Plenum.

Wong, P. T. P., & Weiner, B. (1981). When people ask "why" questions, and the heuristics of attribution search. *Journal of Personality and Social Psychology, 40,* 649–663.

Wortman, C. B., & Brehm, J. W. (1975). Response to uncontrollable outcomes: An integration of reactance theory and the learned helplessness model. In L. Berkowitz (Ed.), *Advances in experimental social psychology* (Vol. 8, pp. 277–336). New York: Academic Press.

Chapter 27

Psychosocial Stressors, Coping, and Depression

Andrew G. Billings

Research Psychologist
Social Ecology Laboratory
Department of Psychiatry and Behavioral Sciences
Stanford University School of Medicine
Palo Alto VA Medical Center

Rudolf H. Moos

Research Career Scientist and Professor
Veterans Administration and Stanford University Medical Centers
Palo Alto, CA

INTRODUCTION

Psychosocial stressors and stress-mediating factors such as coping resources are of major concern in current research on the onset and treatment of depression. We present a conceptual framework to summarize and integrate the rapidly expanding theoretical, empirical, and clinical literature in this area. The framework views depression as influenced by the interplay of several domains of variables, including personal and environmental resources, life stressors, and the individual's appraisal and coping responses to stressful events. We review research on each of these domains and their interplay with special emphasis on coping processes. We also consider the implications of the framework for developing and evaluating treatment and prevention programs.

Psychosocial factors in depression are receiving increased interest among researchers and clinicians. This focus on psychosocial factors has spawned a diversity of conceptual models and empirical methods to explore

Acknowledgements: We express our appreciation to Dani Lawler and Susan Spinrad for their assistance in manuscript preparation. This work was supported in part by NIAAA Grant AA02863 and Veterans Administration Medical and Health Services Research and Development Service research funds. This chapter is an expansion and adaptation of a previous article, A. Billings and R. Moos (1982), "Psychosocial theory and research on depression: An integrative review," *Clinical Psychology Review, 2,* pp. 213–217.

intrapsychic, cognitive-phenomenological, social, and behavioral aspects of depression. Much of the research in this area has considered the role of stressful life events in the onset and course of depression, but a number of important research and clinical issues remain unresolved. Why do stressful life circumstances lead to depression among some persons but not others? Can apparently different conceptual approaches to understanding depression be reconciled? How can one explain the finding that different psychosocial interventions appear to have similar effects on depression? Toward what areas should prevention efforts be targeted?

In this chapter, we will formulate a framework to organize these questions and to explore commonalities among diverse areas of research and treatment. The framework considers personal and environmental factors that influence the occurrence of stressful events and the likelihood that will lead to depression, as well as possible compensatory factors, such as coping resources. Thus, we will review and integrate research on the interplay of a set of conceptual domains, including environmental stressors, personal and environmental resources, and appraisal and coping responses. Given its pivotal role in our framework, we will emphasize new concepts and research on appraisal and coping responses. The framework will then be used to analyze the effectiveness of conceptually different treatment strategies, to explore the recovery process, to identify interventions that maximize the durability of treatment gains, and to develop implications for designing effective prevention programs.

AN INTEGRATIVE FRAMEWORK

The framework shown in Figure 1 hypothesizes that the depression-related outcomes of stressful life circumstances are influenced by individuals' personal and environmental resources as well as by their appraisal and coping responses. These resources can affect the occurrence of stressors, shape the nature of the coping responses selected to deal with them, and influence the adaptive outcome of the stressful episode. Thus, the link between *life stressors* and depression is seen as mediated by individuals' personal and environmental resources, their cognitive appraisal and coping responses, and the interrelationships among these domains. Stressful life circumstances develop from personal and environmental factors and include specific events (divorce, death of a spouse, job loss), chronic life strains associated with major social roles (a stressful job, marital discord), and medical conditions and illnesses (arthritis, cancer).

Personal resources include dispositional characteristics, such as self-concept, sense of environmental mastery and attributional styles, as well as social skills and problem-solving abilities. *Environmental resources* refer to the informational, material, and emotional support provided by intimates, other family members, and nonkin social network members. It is in the context of these environmental and personal resources that individuals use *coping re-*

FIGURE 1

An integrative framework for the analysis of adaptive processes and depression

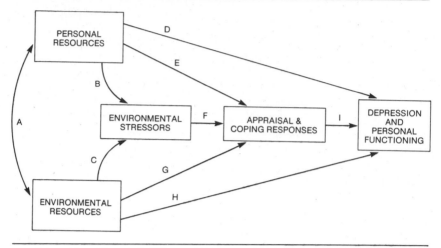

Source: Adapted from A. G. Billings and R. H. Moos, (1982), Psychosocial theory and research on depression: An integrative framework and review, *Clinical Psychology Review, 2* pp. 213–237. Reprinted with permission.

sponses that are intended to minimize the adverse effects of stress. We include *appraisals* of stressors; that is, perceptions and interpretations of specific events, as part of the coping process. The outcome of this process influences the individual's level of *functioning* and adaptation. From this perspective, functioning includes not only depressive symptoms but also cognitive and behavioral aspects of adjustment that may be disrupted in the depressive syndrome.

The model highlights the interplay among the domain affecting depression. For instance, the impact of life stressors on functioning is mediated by the other domains identified. A stressor elicits appraisal and coping responses (path F), whose nature and effectiveness determine whether the stressful event leads to depression and disruptions in functioning (path I). These processes are conditioned by personal and environmental resources. Personal resources such as high self-esteem may mitigate depressive outcomes by reducing the occurrence of stressors (path B), by facilitating stress-reducing coping (path E), or by fostering healthy functioning in the absence of stress (path D). Environmental resources can affect adaptation in similar ways. Moreover, personal resources can influence depression indirectly by promoting such environmental resources as supportive interpersonal ties (path A) that also affect functioning (path H). Finally, depressed mood and related aspects of functioning can affect each of the "preceding" sets of factors. We describe existing research in terms of these paths or processes and use the model to highlight relationships between sets of factors.

Framework Boundaries

Formulating such a framework involves certain simplifications. First, we recognize the presence of genetic and biologic "determinants" of depression (Akiskal & McKinney, 1975), as well as the role of developmental factors. For example, early parental loss or death may increase the chance of subsequent depression by curtailing important socialization experiences that bolster adult-coping resources (Crook & Eliot, 1980). Such macrosystem factors as aspects of the physical environment (crowding, urban traffic congestion, airport noise) and social conditions (economic factors, racial prejudice, sexism) also may be distal determinants of depression. An adequate treatment of these factors is beyond the scope of this chapter. However, we see all three of these sets of factors (biological, developmental, sociogeographic) as potentially affecting depression via their influence on the domains within the framework.

Second, the model highlights the unidirectional "causal" effects typically considered in the literature, even though the domains can have reciprocal effects on each other, such as when changes in coping and functioning affect personal and environmental resources. We refer to these reciprocal effects by adding a prime ($'$) to the letter of the relevant path. For example, depression may lead to the use of less effective coping strategies (path I$'$) and attributions of uncontrollability (path D$'$). Such strategies may alienate members of the individual's social network and thereby reduce future social support (path H$'$). We incorporate some findings on such effects in our review.

Lastly, considerable attention has been given to the diagnosis and description of depressive disorders (Endicott & Spitzer, 1978; Overall & Zisook, 1980), as well as to distinctions between depressive moods, symptoms, and syndromes. We hypothesize that the salient variables and processes that effect depressed moods and behaviors among "healthy" individuals are similar to those involved in the development of "diagnosable" depressions. We distinguish between clinical and nonclinical populations in reviewing the literature, but we believe that the basic nature of the framework is applicable to both groups. We also believe that the framework applies to different subtypes of depressive disorders, although the relative importance of the sets of factors may vary among subtypes (e.g., life stressors appear to be more relevant to acute rather than to chronic depressives; Billings & Moos, 1984a).

We turn now to a review of research on each of the domains in the framework. We indicate how variables in each domain may affect depression directly, as well as indirectly by preventing stress and by mediating the effects of stress and of the other domains on adaptation. We later consider how such demographic factors as socioeconomic status and gender relate to depression through their influence on the components of the framework. Finally, we consider how the framework can guide the formulation and evaluation of clinical interventions.

STRESSFUL LIFE CIRCUMSTANCES

Much of the literature on stress and depression is concerned with the effects of major life events, such as divorce, job loss, and death. Recent studies indicate the need to expand the concept of stress to include continuing life strains arising from major social roles, as well as more minor but frequent stresses encountered in daily living (Pearlin, 1982). We consider each of these factors in examining the role of stressful life circumstances in depression. Until quite recently, this research has focused primarily on the overall association between stressors and depression without considering the mediating factors noted in our framework.

Stressful Events

Life stressors are clearly implicated in the development and maintenance of depression (Paykel, 1979). The conceptual and methodological issues involved in this area are summarized elsewhere (Dohrenwend & Dohrenwend, 1974, 1981) and will not be reviewed here. In brief, this line of inquiry has identified depressogenic effects of undesirable (negative) life changes in the areas of health, finances, and interpersonal relationships, particularly those representing exits or losses in the social field (such as deaths and separations). These events, which apparently have cumulative effects that may manifest themselves over several months, are three to six times more common among depressed individuals as compared to demographically matched general population controls (Billings, Cronkite, & Moos, 1983; Brown & Harris, 1978; C. G. Costello, 1982).

Life Strains

Another significant source of stress stems from chronic strains associated with an individual's major social roles of spouse, parent, and provider. For example, Pearlin and Schooler (1978) found that such strains as frustration of marital role expectations, children's deviations from parental standards of behavior, and difficulty affording food and clothing were associated with more depressed moods among community residents. Physical and emotional dysfunction of one's spouse or children also creates strain and is linked to depression. Recent research has focused on the work setting as an important source of such stressors (for a review, see Holt, 1982). Work pressure, a lack of autonomy in decision making, and ambiguity about job roles and criteria of adequate performance have been associated with psychological distress and depression (Billings & Moos, 1982c). The comparability of findings on life strains (examined primarily among community samples) and stressful events (typically explored among clinical samples) suggests an underlying commonality in the role of environmental stressors in minor and major depressive outcomes (Mitchell, Cronkite, & Moos, 1983).

Microstressors

Lazarus and Cohen (1977) have noted the potential impact of daily "hassles," those comparatively minor but frequent irritants and frustrations associated with both the physical and social environment (such as noise, rush hour traffic, concerns about money, family arguments). In a short-term longitudinal study of a middle-aged community sample, indexes of daily hassles were better predictors of current and subsequent depression than were indexes of major life events (Kanner, Coyne, Schaefer, & Lazarus, 1981). Hassles may have "direct" effects on adaptation and may also be the functional subunits that comprise the stressful aspects of major life events.

Despite these conceptual and methodological advances, stressful life circumstances provide only a partial explanation for the development of serious depression or for the prevalence of depressive mood and reactions among essentially "normal" individuals. While up to three quarters of depressed patients may have experienced a provoking stressful event or strain recently, only one person in five in a nonpatient sample will become clinically depressed after facing a severe stressor (Brown & Harris, 1978). Among general community samples, typically less than 10 percent of the variance in depressive symptoms can be "accounted for" by life stressors (Billings & Moos, 1981; Warheit, 1979). Stressors may have "direct," that is, immediate effects, on functioning as well as effects on other domains, such as reducing social resources and leading to maladaptive appraisals and ineffective coping responses, all of which contribute to depression. We turn our attention now toward factors that may help to explain individual variability in response to stressful circumstances.

PERSONAL RESOURCES

Personal resources include relatively stable psychological characteristics and behavioral skills that affect functioning and provide a "psychological context" for coping. We focus here on several aspects of personal resources that are particularly relevant to depression: sense of environmental mastery, attributional styles relating to environmental stressors, and interpersonal orientation and skills. These resources tend to be more consistent across situations than event-specific appraisal and coping responses that vary according to the nature of the stressor. These stable personal resources accrue from the outcomes of previous coping episodes and may be shaped by demographic factors which we will consider later.

Personal resources can affect depression in several related ways. They may have "direct" effects on functioning (path D), as suggested, for instance, by the finding that individuals who enjoy high self-esteem are less likely to become depressed. In fact, there is some conceptual overlap in measures of personal resources and depression, since low self-esteem may be considered to be one aspect of a depressive syndrome. Personal resources may have indirect effects on depression by reducing stressors (path B) and by fostering social resources (path A) and coping responses (path E) that can attenuate the effects of stress.

Sense of Environmental Mastery

A lack of global personal resources, such as perceived competence and a sense of mastery, is present in many disorders, particularly depression (for reviews, see Becker, 1979; Sundberg, Snowden, & Reynolds, 1978). A focal construct in this area is an internal locus of control; that is, a generalized belief in one's ability to affect the environment so as to maximize rewards and minimize unpleasant outcomes (for reviews, see Lefcourt, 1981; Perlmuter & Monty, 1979). An external locus of control, a perceived inability to master one's environment either by controlling important events or by managing the consequences of uncontrollable events, has been directly associated with depression. For example, an external locus of control is related to serious depression as well as more frequent dysphoria among college students and community samples (Calhoun, Cheney, & Dawes, 1974; E. J. Costello, 1982; Warren & McEachren, 1983).

An internal control orientation may affect well-being directly as well as afford some resistance to the adverse effects of stress. For instance, Johnson and Sarason (1978) found that negative life events were less likely to be associated with depression among college students with an internal locus of control than among those with an external locus. Similarly, in comparsion to externally oriented corporation executives, internally oriented executives were more likely to remain healthy while under high stress (Kobasa, Maddi, & Kahn, 1982). A sense of environmental mastery, along with high self-esteem and freedom from self-denigration, has also been found to attenuate the depressive effects of life strains among members of a community group (Pearlin & Schooler, 1978).

The development and maintenance of a sense of mastery has been considered by several important theorists including Bandura, Beck, and Seligman. For example, Bandura's model of adaptational behavior (1977, 1980) suggests that an internal control orientation and feelings of self-efficacy are related to the generalized expectancy of being able to cope successfully with prospective stressors. Self-efficacious persons will typically persist in active efforts to reduce stress, while those who see themselves as less efficacious tend to lack persistence and to utilize avoidance responses (path E). Active coping responses should reduce exposure to stress (path F′) as well as moderate the effects of stress when it occurs (path I). Mastery of previous stressful circumstances can increase feelings of self-efficacy and reduce the use of defensive and avoidance-oriented coping styles. The effects of a sense of mastery may also extend to the development and use of social-environmental resources (path A) which themselves affect coping and depression (paths G and H).

Attributional Styles

Cognitive styles that are thought to be relatively stable and to affect perceptions of stressful circumstances have received considerable attention. Much of this work centers on the issue of perceived control and personal attribution of causality of the outcomes of stressful situations. The learned helplessness model hypothesizes that the lack of contingency between an individual's coping responses and environmental outcomes produces a generalized belief in the uncontrollability of the environment which relates to depression directly (path D) and indirectly by inhibiting active-coping responses (path E; Seligman, 1975). With its associated behavioral passivity (path E) and depressive affect (paths D and I), this belief insulates the individual from future counteractive experiences of environmental control.

Beck's cognitive theory holds that persons with a strong predisposition to assume personal responsibility for negative outcomes are prone to depression (Beck, 1967, 1974). Such individuals are filled with self-blame that may cause depression (path D) and their pessimistic view of their future effectiveness can adversely affect their coping responses (path E). Beck postulates that depressed persons' cognitive appraisals are characterized by several distortions: arbitrary inferences—conclusions unwarranted by the situation; selective abstractions—not considering all elements of a situation; magnification/minimization—distortions of the significance of an event; and overgeneralization—drawing inappropriate conclusions from minimal evidence. By promoting attributions of failure in mastery situations to personal rather than environmental factors, such appraisals reinforce depressive cognitive schemas (path E').

The learned helplessness and cognitive self-blame theories have been viewed as complementary (e.g., Akiskal & McKinney, 1975). However, Abramson and Sackeim (1977) point out that these two theories take conceptually contradictory positions on the role of perceived controllability of stressful events. Merging these models would create "the paradoxical situation of individuals blaming themselves for outcomes they believe they neither caused nor controlled" (p. 843). In exploring this paradox, Peterson (1979) found that depressed individuals do have a tendency toward contradictory attributions in that they see stressful events as externally controlled yet blame themselves for unsuccessful resolutions of such events. Additional theory development (Abramson, Seligman, & Teasdale, 1978; Garber & Hollon, 1980) has suggested that depressed persons view themselves as lacking the competence to handle stressful situations which they believe are handled adequately by other persons (i.e., those who are internally controlled).

While research has indicated an association between certain attributional patterns and depression, we know little of how such factors shape the appraisal of specific environmental stressors (path E). Thus, the degree of generality of these presumably "dispositional" cognitions over time and different stressful situations is unclear. In a controlled longitudinal study, Lewinsohn and his colleagues (Lewinsohn, Steinmetz, Larson, & Franklin, 1981) observed that such "depressive cognitions" were more common when persons were actually experiencing a depressive episode but not either before or after such an episode. We consider attributional responses that have been measured within the context of specific events later in discussing the appraisal and coping domain. We also explore the mechanisms whereby treatment procedures that focus on attributions may alleviate or prevent depression.

Interpersonal Skills and Orientation

Interpersonal skills and social competence are important components of personal resources (Tyler, 1978). Behavioral models tend to emphasize that deficits in social competence and an inability to serve as a source of positive social reinforcement to others are linked to depression (McLean, 1982). Depressed persons do seem to be characterized by inadequate social problem-solving skills (Dobson & Dobson, 1981; Fisher-Beckfield & McFall, 1982). Low social competence has also been reflected by social passivity, dysfunctional interpersonal cognitions, inadequate verbal and nonverbal communication skills, and difficulties in enacting family role skills (e.g., Hammen, Jacobs, Mayol, & Cochran, 1980; Paykel, Weissman, & Prusoff, 1978; Sanchez & Lewinsohn, 1980). Effective interpersonal skills may prevent depression by promoting social resources and coping responses (paths A and E) that can help to avoid stressors or to moderate the impact of stressors that do occur. Moreover, marital communication and conflict-resolution skills can preserve major sources of environmental support (path A) and reduce exposure to such stressors as marital separation and divorce (paths B and C). There is also evidence that improving social skills can enhance depressed persons' levels of social reinforcement and ease their discomfort in social situations and their stress levels (Youngren & Lewinsohn, 1980).

Certain individuals may not be oriented toward utilizing their interpersonal skills and social resources to deal with stressors. Although there is little research on this issue among depressed patients, Tolsdorf (1976) noted that psychiatric patients are not inclined to tap the resources of their social environments. In a community sample, B. B. Brown (1978) identified subsets of nonhelp seekers who were either unaware of existing sources of informal help or viewed them as ineffective. These groups displayed lower self-esteem and less effective coping responses than other help seekers or self-reliant nonhelp seekers. In probing an individual's orientation toward their social environments, psychiatric patients may be more sensitive to rejection and have weaker affiliative drives than controls (Henderson, Byrne, & Duncan-Jones, 1981). Such personality factors were inversely correlated with the extent and perceived adequacy of their social resources. A negative orientation toward use of social resources, combined with a lack of interpersonal skills, reduces the development of supportive social ties (path A). Subsequent experiences of stress and depression thus might confirm depressive persons' negative appraisals of their social environments (path G′) and thereby compound the adversity of their life circumstances.

Personal Resources: Directions for Research

A diverse set of personal factors has been linked to a susceptibility to depression. While we have sought to explicate some of the connections comprising the subdomains mentioned, additional integrative research is needed. For instance, what roles do self-concept factors such as self-esteem and sense of mastery play in developing and applying social skills? How can attributional styles or other resources compensate for deficits in certain personal resources? To move beyond an examination of isolated sets of person-centered variables, researchers need to consider coping and social resources as mediators through which personal factors can affect depression. For example, we have noted that persons with an internal locus of control are less likely to become depressed given the occurrence of stressful events. Such an effect may be mediated by the direct effects of this personal resource on functioning (path D) as well as its indirect effect via appraisal and coping (paths E and I). We also need to examine how depression can adversely affect future personal resources as well as how successful coping with potentially depressogenic stressors can promote the development and maintenance of such resources (paths D′ and E′).

ENVIRONMENTAL RESOURCES

An adequate model of depression must consider the type of social context in which depression is or is not likely to occur. We emphasize supportive interpersonal relationships as a major component of a person's social-environmental resources. Such social resources can provide companionship, emotional support, cognitive guidance and advice, and material aid and services. Social relationships also serve to affirm normative role expectations which provide an individual with behavioral guidelines to guide their adaptive efforts. Access to new sources of support may also be provided via the interpersonal relationships that characterize social networks. The development of these resources is influenced by a number of factors: an individual's personal resources (path A), the physical and architectural features of community settings, and the organizational and suprapersonal characteristics (that is, average characteristics of individuals inhabiting a setting) of these interpersonal contexts (Moos & Mitchell, 1982).

Social-environmental factors may have both positive and negative effects on personal functioning. Theorists have suggested that deficits in social resources may lead to depression (path H) due to either the unavailability or reduced effectiveness of social reinforcers, or both (C. G. Costello, 1972; Lewinsohn, 1974). A direct relationship between a lack of support and depression has been noted in surveys of community residents (for reviews, see C. G. Costello, 1982; Mitchell, Billings, & Moos, 1982). Social-environmental factors may also have indirect effects. For instance, impaired communication processes and friction in interpersonal relationships can indirectly promote depressive symptomatology (Bothwell & Weissman, 1977) by fostering stress or leading to ineffective coping responses (paths C and G).

Among positive effects, many investigators have hypothesized a stress-buffering value for social support (Mitchell et al., 1982). There is evidence that social support attenuates the relationship between depressed mood and stressful life events among community (e.g., Billings & Moos, 1981; Wilcox, 1981) and depressed patient respondents (e.g., G. W. Brown, 1979), as well as among individuals experiencing such stressors as pregnancy and child rearing (Wandersman, Wandersman, & Kahn, 1980), job strain and job loss (Gore, 1978; LaRocco, House, & French, 1980), and bereavement (Hirsch, 1980). Social support may positively influence stressor-related appraisals and provide the resources for effective coping that underlie the "buffering" effect (path G). Although relationships with friends and community organizations are important sources of support, we focus here on family and work settings as two primary sources of environmental resources.

Family Support

Depression is associated with marital dissatisfaction (Coleman & Miller, 1975) as well as with disruption of the marital relationship (Bloom, Asher, & White, 1978). Billings et al. (1983) contrasted patients with unipolar depression with sociodemographically matched nondepressed community controls. Relative to the controls, depressed patients had less supportive marital relationships and their family environments were characterized by less cohesion and interpersonal expressiveness and more conflict. Exposure to family conflict and a lack of family support may affect the course of depression. In a study of depressed patients, Vaughn and Leff (1976) found that the amount of criticism expressed toward the patient by family members at the time of hospitalization was a significant predictor of relapse during the posthosptialization period.

A similar pattern has been identified for depressed mood among nonpatient samples. In a community survey, Billings and Moos (1982b) noted that persons living in families that were less cohesive and expressive and had more interpersonal conflict reported more symptoms of depression than those living in more supportive families. In another community survey, Pearlin and Johnson (1977) found that married persons reported less depression than did the unmarried, even after controlling for such sociodemographic factors as gender, age, and ethnicity. In probing the determinants of this difference, persons who were married were shown to be less exposed to various life strains (path C) such as occupational stress and economic hardship. Married persons were still less depressed than the unmarried after equating for levels of strain, indicating that married persons are less vulnerable to the effects of such strains, possibly because they have more sources of available support.

Work Support

The work setting is a potential source of support and stress. Work support is highest for persons who are highly involved in their jobs, have cohesive relationships with co-workers, and have supportive supervisors who encourage job involvement through work innovation and participation in decision making (Cooper & Marshall, 1978). Depressed patients have been found to hold jobs that are less supportive on these dimensions (Billings et al., 1983). The relationship of these work factors to depression has been observed for community samples (Billings & Moos, 1981). These support factors also attenuated the depressive effects of work stress among men, but less so among women (Billings & Moos, 1982c; House, 1981). A supportive work setting may diversify one's social resources by serving as an alternate source of interpersonal support. Conversely, work stress can erode family support (path C'). For instance, Billings and Moos (1982c) noted that men whose wives were employed in stressful job settings tended to report less family support and more depression than men whose wives had nonstressful jobs.

Indirect and Reciprocal Effects

Environmental resources may prevent depression by facilitating effective coping with minor stressors, thereby circumventing the occurrence of major stressors (path G; see Mitchell et al., 1982). The availability of social relationships can also provide the necessary context for certain coping responses (such as help seeking and comparing one's situation to that of others) that may be particularly effective in preventing or alleviating stress (path C). In addition, the appraised severity of a stressor may be attenuated by the awareness that supportive resources are available to resolve a problematic situation (path G). For instance, Gore (1978) found that persons with high support perceived less financial stress due to a job loss than did those with less support, even though there were no differences between high- and low-support groups in their objective financial condition.

Conversely, established dysphoria may reduce future environmental resources by eroding social support (path H'). Depressed persons appear to elicit negative reactions from those in their social environments. Strack and Coyne (1983) found that strangers who had a brief conversation with a depressed person experienced negative feelings themselves and felt hostile and rejecting toward the depressed person. Thus, it is not surprising that depressed persons often elicit negative reactions from friends and family members (McLean, 1982; Weissman & Paykel, 1974). When friends and relatives are unsuccessful in controlling and reducing the individual's distress they may become hostile, withdraw their support, and eventually avoid interaction

(Coates & Wortman, 1980). Concurrent elevations in the depressive symptomatology of spouses and family members of depressed patients (Rubinstein & Timmins, 1978) may reflect a cyclic process that reduces family support and exacerbates stress for all members. Depression can also reduce future support by impairing the social initiative and skills needed to maintain social resources (via paths D' and A).

APPRAISAL AND COPING RESPONSES

Our framework indicates that cognitive appraisal and coping responses can help an individual avoid depression by moderating the potential effects that stressors have on functioning (paths F and I) as well as by avoiding future stressors (path F'). An appraisal involves the perception and interpretation of environmental stimuli. Appraisals are a continuing aspect of the coping process in which initial appraisals are followed by specific coping responses and then by reappraisal and possible modification of coping strategies (Lazarus, 1981). Our inclusion of appraisal and coping in a common domain reflects the closely interconnected nature of these processes. We use appraisal and coping to refer to cognitive and behavioral responses to specific events. Such responses are influenced by the dispositional attribution factors described earlier as personal resources and by the individual's environmental resources, which provide the context for coping. However, current research has not always observed this distinction between dispositional attribution patterns and stressor-specific appraisal and coping responses.

While several attempts have been made to formulate a classification system for categorizing appraisal and coping responses, no accepted method has yet emerged. We organize these dimensions into three subdomains: (1) appraisal-focused coping—efforts to define the personal meaning of a situation; (2) problem-focused coping—behavioral responses to modify or eliminate the source of stress or its consequences by dealing with the reality of the situation; and (3) emotion-focused coping—functions oriented toward managing stress-related emotions and maintaining affective equilibrium (Folkman & Lazarus, 1980; Moos & Billings, 1982).

Appraisal of Stressors

Much of the research on appraisal has evolved from the self-blame and learned helplessness theories of depression. For example, among college students and depressed patients, Krantz and Hammen (1979) found a consistent relationship between depressive symptoms and scores on the Cognitive Bias Questionnaire, a measure of the distortions outlined by Beck. Hollon and Kendall (1980) have also shown that depressed persons score higher on an inventory of stress-related cognitive distortions and negative self-statements. Although depression may exacerbate "depressive" appraisals (path I),

Golin, Sweeney, and Schaeffer (1981) found that such appraisals were more likely to precede than to follow an increase in depressive symptomatology (i.e., path I is stronger than path I').

The attribution of causality is an important aspect of the reformulated learned helplessness model. Abramson et al. (1978) hypothesize that individual attributions of the *causes* of a stressful event and perceived coping ability vary along three dimensions: (*a*) internal versus external to self, (*b*) stable versus unstable, and (*c*) global versus situation- or role-specific. For example, given the stressor of unemployment and an unsuccessful job search, attributions might be to either internal and personal causes, such as lack of employment-related skills, or to external causes such as job discrimination. Stable causal attributions imply that future job-seeking efforts are likely to result in a similar lack of success. Global causal attributions, such as a general lack of perceived self-efficacy, would involve role performances in addition to employment and a job search.

This model holds that persons are more likely to remain free of depression if they attribute causality of negative outcomes to characteristics of stressors that are external to the self, that vary across situations, and that relate to a restricted area of performance. Operationalizing these factors with their Scale of Attributional Style, Seligman and his colleagues (Seligman, Abramson, Semmel, & von Baeyer, 1979) found that the appraisal of depressed and nondepressed college students differed in the expected directions along these dimensions.

However, some studies have not found consistent relationships between these three attributional dimensions (internality, stability, and globality) and depression among college students (e.g., Golin et al., 1981; Hammen, Krantz, & Cochran, 1981; Harvey, 1981; Pasahow, 1980). Extending research on these attributional processes to patient populations, Gong-Guy and Hammen (1980) used an attribution questionnaire to assess respondents' appraisals of recent stressful events as internal, stable, global, expected, and intended. Depressed and nondepressed outpatients showed expected differences along these dimensions in the appraisal of their most upsetting event, but not in their appraisal of all recent stressors (see also Hammen & Cochran, 1981).

There has been relatively little longitudinal study of these attribution processes. Hamilton and Abramson (1983) found evidence of such negative appraisals among depressed persons as they entered the hospital, but noted substantial reductions at discharge when their depression was in remission. Peterson, Schwartz, and Seligman (1981) noted that self-blame occurred during depression among college students but did not precede it. Thus it is unclear whether such appraisals antedate depression or are concomitants or consequences of it. Lastly, the integration of this research is complicated by divergence in the content of current measures. For example, the Cognitive Bias Questionnaire and the Scale of Attributional Style are both correlated with depressive symptoms, even though they are only moderately related to each other (Blaney, Behar, & Head, 1980).

Stressor-Appraisal Specificity

Our framework indicates that the appraisal process is at least partially determined by the type of stressor (path F). In fact, studies employing heterogeneous samples of stressors (e.g., Dohrenwend & Martin, 1979; Fontana, Hughes, Marcus, & Dowds, 1979) have indicated that appraisals may be more closely related to event characteristics (path F) than personal characteristics (path E). For example, Hammen and Mayol (1982) found that different stressful life events elicited consistently different appraisal patterns. Divorce was consistently seen as more likely to be personally controllable and due to internal, stable, and global personal factors than, for instance, illness or death of a friend or family member. Most studies have focused on the appraisal and effect of success versus failure outcomes in experimental tasks such as solving anagram problems. There is much less information on the extent to which stable attributional styles are linked to specific appraisal responses to naturally occurring stressors (paths E and E').

While increasing attention has been directed toward conceptual and measurement issues, we know little of the actual appraisals seriously depressed persons make in their natural environment. Differences between depressed and nondepressed respondents in their appraisal of questionnaire-based scenarios of stressful events may not reflect their appraisal of actual personal stressors (Hammen & Cochran, 1981). Studies are needed to examine the extent to which the attributional styles of depressed individuals are related to their appraisal of real-life stressors. Current conceptualizations also should be reviewed and elaborated. For instance, depressed persons may be "accurate" in perceiving stressors as uncontrollable and their personal and environmental resources as being inadequate. In this regard, nondepressed individuals may have positively biased and self-serving attributions of causality (for a review, see Miller & Ross, 1975), while depressed persons may have "accurate" perceptions rather than negative biases. During recovery, depressed persons' perceptions of their competence and control may become somewhat less realistic by moving toward the self-enhancing bias of nondepressed persons (Lewinsohn, Mischel, Chaplin, & Barton, 1980).

Coping Responses

We now consider the problem-focused and emotion-focused cognitions and behaviors that occur in response to appraised stressors. While empirical studies are not numerous, some relevant work has examined the coping responses of depressed patients as well as the responses associated with depression among community groups. As with other domains, coping responses may directly affect functioning, attenuate the depressive effects of stress (paths F and I), or directly reduce or prevent the stressor (path F').[1]

---

[1] A number of conceptual and statistical questions have recently been raised about how to evaluate the modifier effects of social support and of coping. These issues are beyond our scope and the interested reader is referred to other sources (Cleary & Kessler, 1982; Finney, Mitchell, Cronkite, & Moos, 1984).

The interplay between appraisal and coping responses among a community group was explored by Coyne, Aldwin, and Lazarus (1981), who compared the coping responses of 15 persons falling within the depressed range of the Hopkins Symptom Checklist on two occasions with 72 persons who did not meet this criterion at either assessment. Although the depressed and nondepressed group did not differ in the type or perceived significance of stressful events encountered, there were differences in appraisal and coping responses. Depressed persons tended to appraise situations as requiring more information before they could act, and to view fewer events as necessitating acceptance and accommodation. They were also more likely to use such responses as seeking advice and emotional support and engaging in wishful thinking. However, there were no differences in the amount of problem-focused coping or use of self-blame, as might be predicted from the learned helplessness model. These findings are consistent with the idea that depressed persons find it difficult to make decisions and wish to be relatively certain prior to either taking action or electing to view the objective characteristics of the stressor as outside of their control (Beck, Rush, Shaw, & Emery, 1979).

Billings and Moos (1981) evaluated the efficacy of various classes of coping responses among a representative community sample. Coping responses to a recent stressful event were assessed according to their method (active-behavioral, active-cognitive, and avoidance) and focus (problem-focused, emotion-focused) of coping. The use of avoidance responses, which serve to avoid actively confronting a problem or to reduce emotional tension by such behavior as increased eating or smoking, was associated with more depressed mood. In contrast, the use of active-cognitive and active-behavioral coping attenuated the depressogenic effects of stressful life events.

Although coping holds a pivotal position in our model, very few studies have considered how clinically depressed persons cope with naturally occurring stressors. Using a sample of depressed patients, we developed a coping inventory in which respondents selected a recent stressful event and rated their frequency of use of 32 coping responses (Billings & Moos, 1984b). These responses were grouped into categories in three areas: (1) appraisal-focused coping (logical analysis), (2) problem-focused coping (seeking information, problem solving), and (3) emotion-focused coping (affective regulation, emotional discharge). We found that the coping responses of patients with unipolar depression differed from those of demographically matched, community controls (Billings et al., 1983). All types of coping were used to some extent by both patients and controls, though patients made more use of information seeking and less problem-solving responses. Depressed patients relied much more heavily on emotional discharge than did controls. These results are consistent with theoretical models suggesting that depressed persons find it hard to make decisions and take action. Their overreliance on emotional discharge coping, which was strongly related to depression severity and other indexes of dysfunction, indicates that the coping patterns of depressed persons may be characterized by the overuse of maladaptive strategies as much as by underuse of adaptive responses.

Parker and Brown (1982) also sought to identify coping patterns that mediated between life events and depressive disorders. In two preliminary studies, nondepressed respondents were asked to imagine a breakup of a close relationship or someone important becoming increasingly critical of them and to rate their anticipated use of 86 coping responses to reduce stress. Factor analyses reduced the item pool to 22 items and 6 coping dimensions: recklessness, socialization, distraction, problem solving, self-consolation, and passivity (e.g., read, ignore problem). As expected, persons reported that they would engage in behaviors rated as effective in preventing or reducing depression. In the second study, the coping responses of 20 depressed patients in psychotherapy were compared to those of matched nondepressed controls. At the beginning of therapy when seriously depressed, the patients were less likely than controls to socialize and to seek distraction and more likely to be passive. They also reported socialization, distraction, and problem solving to be less effective in reducing stress. Later in treatment when the patients were not seriously depressed, these patient-control differences were reduced substantially. This may indicate that the coping patterns of depressed persons are state dependent, as the authors suggest, though it is also possible that psychotherapy had positive effects on patients' coping repertoires.

Stone and Neale (1984) developed a coping inventory that differs in several respects from the measures described thus far. Rather than focusing on major life events, their inventory is concerned with coping with daily problems and is designed for daily administrations. Instead of a listing of individual coping items, their instrument provides global descriptions of eight coping categories (distraction, situation redefinition, direct action, catharsis, acceptance, seeking social support, relaxation, and religion). For each category, respondents check whether they used responses that served that function, and, if so, write a narrative description of these responses. Using a community sample, they found that the same coping response could serve multiple functions and were occasionally assigned to different categories at different times. However, there was fairly high agreement between the classifications subjects made of their narrative responses and those made by independent raters that were blind to the subjects' classifications. Coping responses were found to vary with the subject's problem appraisals which were measured separately. For instance, appraisals of low internal control over the problem were associated with greater use of catharsis and acceptance. Intercategory correlations showed that problem-solving categories such as direct action and seeking support were positively correlated but negatively correlated with emotion-focused categories such as distraction and acceptance. The association of these coping categories with depression and personal functioning was not reported.

Coping patterns may also be influenced by the fact that depression can develop into a syndrome that requires further coping efforts (path I'). Anticipation of problems in coping with the consequences of stressors, including depression, may distinguish the appraisal of depression-prone individuals. Moreover, dysphoria, insomnia, weight loss, and memory problems can influence current coping responses and may require additional coping efforts to alleviate the stress they themselves engender. Several investigators have examined how individuals cope with depression itself.

Funabiki and his colleagues (Funabiki, Bologna, Pepping, & Fitzgerald, 1980) developed a method of assessing the thoughts and behaviors college students use in coping with a depressive episode (see also Bloor, 1983; McLean, 1982; Rippere, 1976). Depressed students were more likely to be preoccupied with their stress-related emotions and to seek help from other depressed persons. However, these students also reported the use of efforts to counteract depression (tell myself things to cheer me up and try something new). Self-preoccupations may not be entirely maladaptive, as it may provide an opportunity to identify environmental and intrapsychic contingencies relevant to depression. In this regard, structured self-monitoring of mood and activity can be effective in treating depressed patients (Harmon, Nelson, & Hayes, 1980).

Doerfler and Richards (1981) also examined self-initiated attempts to cope with depression among adult women. In comparison to women who were unsuccessful in dealing with their depression, women who were successful in alleviating depression were more likely to believe the positive reappraisals made of themselves or their situations, to engage in problem-solving actions, and to attempt to increase their social support. However, such coping differences were not fully replicated in a study of college women (Doerfler & Richards, 1984). Using depressed patients, Beckham and Adams (1984) developed an inventory that included 133 coping responses to both depression and environmental stressors as well as depressive symptoms such as passivity that might serve a coping function. Ten coping categories were established: blame, emotional expression, emotional containment, social support, religious support, cognitive restructuring, general activity, avoidance-denial, problem solving, and passivity. Greater use of cognitive restructuring, religious support, and general activity were associated with less severe depressive symptomatology whereas blame, emotional expression, and passivity were more likely to occur in patients with high levels of depression. The correlational nature of their study leaves it unclear whether cognitive restructuring, religious support, and general activity are effective coping strategies that control depressive symptoms or whether they are simply more likely to be used when a patient is less depressed. Patients viewed the coping strategies of problem solving, obtaining religious support, and general activity as most helpful, and blame, passivity, and emotional containment as least helpful.

Help-Seeking

Given the importance of social resources in depression, help-seeking behaviors that tap or generate social resources are a key class of coping responses.

Indeed, over half the individuals who experience a troubling event will seek some help (Gourash, 1978). While preliminary, there is some evidence that the nature and success of help seeking may differentiate depressed and non-depressed groups. The nature of these differences is complex, as shown by the finding of Pearlin and Schooler (1978) that those who sought help in handling a stressful event actually reported more depression than those who relied on their own personal resources.

To understand the link between help-seeking responses and depression, we need to consider the impact that coping responses and depressive symptomatology may have on an individual's social resources (paths G' and H'). Help seeking, when combined with the expression of distress, may have mixed effects on these resources. Howes and Hokanson (1979) found that undergraduates expressed more overt reassurance and sympathetic support to a "depressive" than to a normal role confederate. However, Coyne (1976a) found that subjects conversing with a depressed patient were themselves more depressed and anxious, and tended to covertly reject the patient (see also Strack & Coyne, 1983). Hammen and Peters (1978) also report results indicating the rejection of depressed partners, although depressive behavior was more acceptable from women than from men partners. Thus, certain patterns of help seeking may be more intense than is appropriate for the strength, intimacy, and context of the relationship.

While help seeking in the context of depression may elicit superficial support in brief encounters with strangers, its longer term consequences on intimate relationships may be negative. Intimates may initially offer mollifying support to aid the depressed person and to control that person's aversive expression of dysphoria. Intimates may initially suppress the direct expression of their own negative reactions to the depressed person's behavior (Coyne, 1976b). However, such responses often fail to provide the validation that depressed individuals seek for the appropriateness of their stress reactions. Such ambiguity in the "supportive" communications of others would exacerbate stress (path C) and fail to provide corrective feedback on the depressed person's dysfunctional coping responses (path G).

Escalated help seeking and expression of depressive behaviors, so as to draw more convincing and effective support, may lead to an increase in intimates' efforts to control and minimize depressive symptomatology (Coates & Wortman, 1980). The failure of social network members to alleviate the expression of distress may produce frustration and even more negative attitudes toward the depressed person. It may be at this point that the negative and rejecting responses of intimates and family members (e.g., McLean, 1982; Salzman, 1975) are frankly expressed. Network members' expression of negative reactions and withdrawal from their relationship with the stressed individual would likely have adverse effects on that individual's coping and functioning (paths G and H) and heighten susceptibility to depression by decreasing the individual's self-esteem (path A).

The effects of help-seeking responses should be explored in the context of particular stressors. For instance, the chronicity of the stressor may be a particularly relevant dimension. In this regard, obtaining help from informal sources may be most advantageous in coping with discrete, time-limited stressors. When the stressor is of a more chronic nature (e.g., long-term unemployment or physical disability), individuals may "burn out" their social resources by overreliance on an informal social network. Professional or institutionalized sources of support may be especially important in handling chronic or major stressors that surpass the individual's social resources. Similarly, normative life stage stressors such as marriage and childbirth elicit culturally sanctioned support responses while there are no guidelines for seeking help with unexpected events such as divorce.

SOCIAL BACKGROUND FACTORS

Epidemiological research has shown that depression is related to such demographic factors as socioeconomic standing and gender (Radloff, 1977; Weissman & Klerman, 1977; Weissman & Myers, 1978). We view these factors as distal determinants of depression via their influence on the other domains in the framework.

Social Status

Individuals of lower social status (i.e., those with lower education, income, and occupational levels) are more likely to become depressed. As suggested by the "social causation" and "social selection" hypotheses, social status has links to each of the domains in our framework that may help to explain its association with depression (Liem & Liem, 1978). The social causation hypothesis holds that those of lower status experience more environmental stressors. For example, such persons are more exposed to unemployment, financial setbacks, poor health, and a variety of other stressors (Kessler, 1979).

The social selection hypothesis holds that persons of lower social status are more vulnerable to the effects of stress. Such vulnerability may be due to a lack of supportive social resources (Myers, Lindenthal, & Pepper, 1975), fewer personal resources, or less effective coping responses. In this regard, Pearlin and Schooler (1978) found that less efficacious coping responses were overrepresented among those of lower social standing. In comparison to upper class women, lower class women tend to use fewer active and preparatory coping responses and more avoidance and fatalistic responses in dealing with childbearing (Westbrook, 1979). These responses were associated with greater anxiety and sense of helplessness. Parker and Brown (1982) found that lower SES persons made less use of problem-solving coping. Our framework suggests that factors related to both social causation and social selection underlie the link between social status and depression.

Gender Differences

Depression is more common among women than among men, but the determinants of this gender difference remain controversial. While space does not permit a complete review of the extensive literature, we indicate how our framework can be used to explore this issue. In general, women are more exposed to environmental stressors (Dohrenwend, 1973). More specifically, variations in the types of events experienced may mediate differences in the amount of stress. For example, men report more work and economic stressors while women report more health and family-related events (Billings & Moos, 1981; Folkman & Lazarus, 1980).

Women may also be more vulnerable to the effects of stressors (Radloff & Rae, 1979). This vulnerability may derive from gender differences in personal and environmental resources. For instance, women are more likely to be pessimistic and lack self-esteem (Cofer & Wittenborn, 1980) and to favor a field-dependent cognitive style that may sensitize them to social and interpersonal stressors (see Witkin & Goodenough, 1977). Furthermore, marriage per se does not afford women the "protection" against depression that it does for men (Weissman & Klerman, 1977). However, women's vulnerability to depression can be reduced by the presence of an intimate and confiding relationship with a husband or male partner (Brown & Harris, 1978).

Gender differences in appraisal and coping are largely unexplored. There is some evidence that women use coping responses that are less effective in attenuating the depressive effects of stress. We found that women made more use of avoidance coping, which was itself associated with depression (Billings & Moos, 1981). This difference remained even after controlling for gender differences in the source and severity of stressors. This finding is consistent with analyses of other community samples, which have identified a tendency for women to use less effective coping methods (Folkman & Lazarus, 1980; Pearlin & Schooler, 1978). Funabiki et al. (1980) also noted several gender differences among a group of depressed students. Compared to depressed men, depressed women ate more, more frequently engaged in self-deprecation, and avoided large social gatherings but sought personal contact from meetings with friends. Last, differences between men and women in each of the domains may interact in a synergistic process which contributes to gender differences in the incidence, duration, and prevalence of depression.

CLINICAL AND RESEARCH APPLICATIONS

Having reviewed research on each of the domains in the framework, we now consider the clinical and research implications of our perspective. We first describe applications to assessment and treatment. Since treatment research on depression is mainly concerned with developing and comparing the outcomes of varied treatment regimens, we use our framework to interpret the results of such clinical trials. We then show how the domains we have identified provide a way of describing the recovery and relapse process and of evaluating the determinants of posttreatment functioning. Last, we consider the potential role of these domains in the design and effectiveness of prevention programs.

Assessment of the Domains in the Framework

We have suggested that specific personal, environmental, and coping factors are related to the onset and recovery from depression. Thus, treatment for depressed persons can be aimed at one or more of these domains. The assessment of each of the domains can be the basis for individualizing treatment procedures. Systematic assessment methods should provide treatment-relevant diagnostic information, require a minimum amount of time to administer and score, and preferably be amenable to feedback to patients and their family members. Such criteria are satisfied by only a few existing assessment procedures.

In the area of stressors and social resources, inventories of recent life events may help clinicians to identify general areas of stress that can affect the onset of a disorder or threaten recovery. Such measures have been developed for both adult (Dohrenwend, Krasnoff, Askenasy, & Dohrenwend, 1982) and adolescent groups (Sandler & Block, 1979). Family stressors can be assessed by McCubbin and Patterson's (1981) Family Stress Inventory that taps stressors impinging on any family member in such categories as marital strains, financial problems, losses. Some standardized measures of the resources in family and work settings are available. For example, the Family Environment Scale (FES) assesses support and stress in three general domains: interpersonal relationships, personal growth orientation, and family organization and control (Moos & Mitchell, 1982). The Work Environment Scale (WES) measures the interpersonal relationships, emphasis on goal orientation (such as task orientation and work pressure), and degree of structure and openness to change in the work setting (Billings & Moos, 1982c). Friends and social groups may be especially important among single and unemployed persons. Information can be obtained about network size (number of members) and density (number of members who also interact with each other), as well as the intensity, mutuality, and multidimensionality (number of different functions served) of each relationship. Interview and questionnaire protocols to assess these aspects of social networks have recently become available (for a review, see Moos & Mitchell, 1982). For example, Henderson and his colleagues (Henderson et al., 1981) have developed the Interview Schedule for Social Interaction (ISSI) that identifies the number and adequacy of relationships with intimates, friends, and acquaintances.

Basic research on coping responses, with its diverse conceptual approaches and methods, has led to an array of coping inventories that have only limited clinical applicability at present. There is a growing consensus that coping should be assessed relative to naturally occurring stressors in the individual's life rather than to standard or experimental stressors. Some self-report inventories tap appraisal processes; for example, the Cognitive Bias Questionnaire (Hammen et al., 1981); Scale of Attributional Style (Seligman et al., 1979); and the Dysfunctional Attitude Scale (Weissman & Beck, 1978). Several instruments allow individuals to describe how they handle specific stressful events (e.g., Billings & Moos, 1981; Folkman & Lazarus, 1980; Horowitz & Wilner, 1980; McCubbin & Patterson, 1981). Although no single classification scheme of the most relevant coping dimensions has yet emerged, such inventories can provide a clinician with useful information about a patient's preferred coping response.

The development of an integrated battery of measures of the type and amount of environmental stress, along with assessments of the individual's relevant social environments (e.g., work, family) and methods of coping, would be valuable in planning treatment and aftercare. Better understanding of these factors could increase patient compliance and reduce the number of early dropouts. It would be informative to study concurrent changes in stress levels and social resources that may reduce depression and lead to early termination of treatment. Assessment of such changes may clarify the differential role of formal and informal sources of assistance in recovering from depression.

Developing and Evaluating Psychosocial Treatments

The new treatment approaches that are being developed currently seem to be directed primarily at one or more of the domains in the framework. For example, some interventions are aimed primarily at personal resources by attempting to enhance self-concept and change maladaptive cognitive styles or to modify depressogenic attributional styles. Cognitive therapies also seek to change appraisal and coping responses by teaching the patient to identify distorted appraisals and to replace them with more realistic perceptions (Beck et al., 1979; Rush, Beck, Kovacs, & Hollon, 1977). Since depressed persons tend to exaggerate the negative aspects of their environment and behavior, such treatment often leads to a decrease in negative and self-derogatory thoughts and an increase in positive self-statements and cognitive self-reinforcement.

Other interventions aim to enhance environmental resources by improving the supportiveness of family and other interpersonal relationships and by modifying how patients cope with the social consequences of their disorder (e.g., McLean, 1982; Shaw, 1977; Weissman, 1979). A number of treatment approaches include coping skills training components. According to our framework, these interventions typically focus on personal resources such as problem solving and interpersonal skills. They also address immediate coping responses such as self-monitoring of positive and negative events (appraisal), solving current problems (problem-focused coping), and self-reward and relaxation (emotion-focused coping) strategies (e.g., Fleming & Thornton, 1980; Lewinsohn, Biglan, & Zeiss, 1976).

Controlled clinical trials have demonstrated that each of these interventions reduces depression for a significant number of patients (Hollon & Beck, 1978). While comparisons between psychosocial interventions sometimes show differential effectiveness, the most compelling conclusion is that all treatments are more effective in alleviating depression (alone and in combination with pharmacotherapy) than placebo or nonintervention control conditions (Kovacs, 1980; Weissman, 1979). For example, Zeiss, Lewinsohn, and Muñoz (1979) found that different treatment programs involving interpersonal skills training (a personal resource), cognitive modification (appraisal and coping), or pleasant events scheduling (environmental resources and coping) were equally effective in reducing depression (see also Fleming & Thornton, 1980). All three groups of treated patients increased their social skills and pleasant activities and decreased their dysfunctional cognitions. Differential improvement in the three areas was not specifically related to receiving the treatment that targeted one of these modalities.

Why are conceptually different interventions comparable in their effectiveness in alleviating depression? Zeiss and her colleagues view their results as reflecting nonspecific effects that combine to increase personal self-efficacy. Frank (1974) states that the central determinant of treatment effectiveness lies in the amelioration of clients' frustration with their unsuccessful problem-solving efforts and in the restoration of their morale. Alternatively, our framework suggests that multiple sources of treatment effectiveness can be identified in different treatment procedures.

Since there are complex linkages between the domains shown in the framework, changes in a domain targeted by a specific treatment procedure may affect, or be affected by, changes in other domains. This situation makes it hard to infer the reasons for changes "resulting from" an intervention intended to affect a cluster of variables within a single domain. For example, although cognitive treatment specifically seeks to modify maladaptive cognitive schemas, this intervention may also affect appraisal and preferred coping responses (path E), and the orientation toward social resources (path A), all of which may influence depression. Similarly, interventions designed to improve social skills and increase positive events may also reduce stress (path B), increase supportive social resources (path A), and provide new coping alternatives (path E), all of which may affect depression. Different treatment procedures may thus obtain similar effects because of the links among the sets of factors involved in depression.

These considerations indicate that treatment effectiveness might be maximized by targeting multiple domains within a broad-spectrum program. For example, recent efforts have combined cognitive and behavioral techniques with social resource interventions by including the functioning and attitudes of the depressed person's spouse and family members within the scope of treatment (McLean & Hakistan, 1979; Rush, Shaw, & Khatami, 1980). Programs of training in the development of more effective coping responses to ongoing or expected stressors can decrease the risk of stress-related relapse. Such programs may achieve their effectiveness by increasing the supportiveness of important relationships, reducing the negative attitudes that social network members have developed toward the depressed patient, and facilitating the generalization of treatment gains to a range of natural settings.

Exploring the Determinants of Posttreatment Functioning

Treatment increases the probability of recovery and even untreated depression usually shows remission. However, the longer term outcomes of clinical depression are less positive. More than 50 percent of depressed patients seem to relapse within one year regardless of whether they have received either psychosocial therapy or pharmacotherapy, or a combination of the two (Keller & Shapiro, 1981; Kovacs, Rush, Beck, & Hollon, 1981; Weissman, 1979). What factors determine whether individuals will relapse or maintain recovery? While socioeconomic status, pretreatment functioning, and treatment experiences are related to outcome, these factors typically account for less than 25 percent of the variance in posttreatment functioning, depending on the outcome criterion involved.

Given that the domains identified in our framework contribute to the onset of depression, they also warrant consideration as determinants of posttreatment functioning. For example, patients who experience stressful life events are more likely to relapse. However, those with adequate personal and environmental resources and effective coping responses may be most able to "resist" relapse-inducing influences that occur subsequent to the termination of treatment. In assessing these domains as determinants of the posttreatment functioning of alcoholic patients, Cronkite and Moos (1980) found that stressors, coping, and family resources have a strong impact on outcome. The long-term effects of pretreatment and treatment-related variables (e.g., amount and type of treatment) may be mediated by these posttreatment factors. Cross, Sheehan, and Kahn (1980) noted that treated patients subsequently made more use of informal social resources for guidance and problem solving than did untreated controls. Two treatment approaches which varied in their overall effectiveness were also associated with differential increases in patients' use of these social resources. Thus, persons who are initially more severely depressed are likely to experience more extratreatment stressors, to use less effective coping resources, and to show poorer posttreatment functioning.

Developing Prevention Programs

The effectiveness of prevention programs is often viewed as stemming from one of two sources: a reduction in exposure to stressors or an increase in individuals' resistance to such stressors (Kessler & Albee, 1977; Mitchell et al., 1982). Given the interconnectedness of the domains included in our framework, preventive interventions may simultaneously focus on both these sources. Prevention programs may, of course, seek to reduce the incidence of depression among adults. Programs might also be directed at preventing the negative effects that an individual's depression may have on other persons in their social network. For instance, children and spouses of depressed adults have been found to have increased risks of psychological, social, and physical impairments (Billings & Moos, 1983; Mitchell, Cronkite, & Moos, 1983).

Preventive interventions aimed at bolstering personal and social resources may decrease stressors as well as increase resistance. For example, community interventions such as block clubs and neighborhood social organizations (Wandersman & Giamartino, 1980) promote neighborhood improvements in housing and safety and thereby enhance members' physical and social-environmental resources. These interventions may simultaneously reduce such stressors as the amount of actual and feared crime. Changes in work settings such as reorganizing assembly-line workers into work groups responsible for a more substantial proportion of the final product may promote cooperation and social support from co-workers and reduce such work stressors as boredom, lack of involvement in decision making, and uncontrolled work pressure.

Community groups and agents such as neighborhood and parent groups, lawyers, youth recreation leaders, hairdressers, and bartenders may provide important sources of informal social support (Gottlieb, 1981). Programs designed to foster the support-giving skills of such individuals may increase the social and coping resources in depressed persons' extended social networks and thereby serve to enhance their adaptation. Similarly, preventive interventions may be aimed at smaller social units such as families and at particular stressors such as bereavement and divorce that are especially likely to elicit depressive outcomes. A self-help program for widows might have multiple intervention foci, providing increased social support, cognitive guidance and modeling of effective coping responses to grief, and assistance in resolving economic, social, and personal stressors that can accompany the death of a spouse (Rogers, Vachon, Lyall, Sheldon, & Frieman, 1980). The framework presented here can be a guide for planning prevention programs and program evaluations which yield information on the process as well as the outcome of interventions.

SUMMARY

We have presented an integrative conceptual framework that considers stressful life circumstances and personal and social resources that foster well-being and protect against depressive outcomes. This framework suggests that there are multiple pathways to depression. A lack of personal and environmental resources may be "sufficient" to lead to depression. While stressful circumstances may predispose to depression, the presence of supportive resources and appraisal and coping responses may moderate the adverse effects of stress and thus prevent a serious depressive outcome. Future research and clinical interventions should benefit from considering a broad spectrum of factors and utilizing the interconnectedness of the domains we have identified. Since personal and environmental factors are often slow to change, and since the elimination of stress is neither feasible nor desirable, appraisal and coping is a pivotal factor to be addressed by treatment and prevention programs. Most importantly, a conceptual framework such as the one we have presented here can help clinicians and researchers to organize the rapidly expanding information on the development and treatment of depression and to formulate more integrated plans for future research and intervention.

References

Abramson, L. Y., & Sackeim, H. (1977). A paradox in depression: Uncontrollability and self-blame. *Psychological Bulletin, 84,* 838–851.

Abramson, L. Y., Seligman, M. E. P., & Teasdale, J. D. (1978). Learned helplessness in humans: Critique and reformulation. *Journal of Abnormal Psychology, 87,* 49–74.

Akiskal, H. S., & McKinney, W. T. (1975). Overview of recent research in depression. *Archives of General Psychiatry, 32,* 285–305.

Andrews, G., Tennant, C., Hewson, D., & Vaillant, G. (1978). Life event stress, social support, coping style, and risk of psychological impairment. *Journal of Nervous and Mental Disease, 166,* 307–316.

Bandura, A. (1977). Self-efficacy: Toward a unifying theory of behavioral change. *Psychological Review, 84,* 191–215.

Bandura, A. (1980). Self-referent thought: The development of self-efficacy. In J. H. Flavell & L. D. Ross (Eds.), *Cognitive social development: Frontiers and possible futures* (pp. 200–239). New York: Cambridge University Press.

Beck, A. T. (1967). *Depression: Clinical, experimental and theoretical aspects.* New York: Harper & Row.

Beck, A. T. (1974). The development of depression: A cognitive model. In R. Friedman & M. Katz (Eds.), *The psychology of depression: Contemporary theory and research* (pp. 3–27). Washington, DC: V. H. Winston & Sons.

Beck, A. T., Rush, A. J., Shaw, B. F., & Emery, G. (1979). *Cognitive therapy of depression.* New York: Guilford Press.

Becker, J. (1979). Vulnerable self-esteem as a predisposing factor in depressive disorders. In R. A. Depue (Ed.), *The psychobiology of the depressive disorders: Implications for the effects of stress* (pp. 317–334). New York: Academic Press.

Beckham, E. E., & Adams, R. L. (1984). Coping behavior in depression: Report on a new scale. *Behavior Research and Therapy, 22,* 71–75.

Billings, A. G., Cronkite, R. C., & Moos, R. H. (1983). Social-environmental factors in unipolar depression: Comparisons of depressed patients and nondepressed controls. *Journal of Abnormal Psychology, 92,* 119–133.

Billings, A. G., & Moos, R. H. (1981). The role of coping responses and social resources in attenuating the impact of stressful life events. *Journal of Behavioral Medicine, 4,* 139–157.

Billings, A. G., & Moos, R. H. (1982a). Psychosocial theory and research on depression: An integrative framework and review. *Clinical Psychology Review, 2,* 213–237.

Billings, A. G., & Moos, R. H. (1982b). Social support and functioning among community and clinical groups: A panel model. *Journal of Behavioral Medicine, 5,* 295–311.

Billings, A. G., & Moos, R. H. (1982c). Work stress and the stress-buffering roles of work and family resources. *Journal of Occupational Behavior, 3,* 215–232.

Billings, A. G., & Moos, R. H. (1983). Comparisons of children of depressed and nondepressed parents: A social environmental perspective. *Journal of Abnormal Child Psychology, 11,* 463–485.

Billings, A. G., & Moos, R. H. (1984a). Chronic and nonchronic unipolar depression: The differential role of environmental stressors and resources. *Journal of Nervous and Mental Disease, 172,* 1–11.

Billings, A. G., & Moos, R. H. (1984b). Coping, stress, and social resources among adults with unipolar depression. *Journal of Personality and Social Psychology, 46,* 877–891.

Blaney, P. H., Behar, V., & Head, R. (1980). Two measures of depressive cognitions: Their association with depression and with each other. *Journal of Abnormal Psychology, 89,* 678–682.

Bloom, B., Asher, S. J., & White, S. W. (1978). Marital disruption as a stressor: A review and analysis. *Psychological Bulletin, 85,* 867–894.

Bloor, R. (1983). "What do you mean by depression"—A study of the relationship between antidepression activity and personal concepts of depression. *Behavior Research and Therapy, 21,* 43–50.

Bothwell, S., & Weissman, M. M. (1977). Social impairments four years after an acute depressive episode. *American Journal of Orthopsychiatry, 47,* 231–237.

Brown, B. B. (1978). Social and psychological correlates of help-seeking behavior among urban adults. *American Journal of Community Psychology, 6,* 425–439.

Brown, G. W. (1979). The social etiology of depression. In R. A. Depue (Ed.), *The psychobiology of the depressive disorders: Implications for the effects of stress* (pp. 263–290). New York: Academic Press.

Brown, G. W., & Harris, T. O. (1978). *Social origins of depression: A study of psychiatric disorder in women.* New York: Free Press.

Calhoun, L. G., Cheney, T., & Dawes, A. S. (1974). Locus of control, self-reported depression, and perceived causes of depression. *Journal of Consulting and Clinical Psychology, 42,* 736.

Cleary, P. D., & Kessler, R. C. (1982). The estimation and interpretation of modifier effects. *Journal of Health and Social Behavior, 23,* 159–168.

Coates, D., & Wortman, C. B. (1980). Depression maintenance and interpersonal control. In A. Baum & J. E. Singer (Eds.), *Advances in environmental psychology* (Vol. 2, pp. 149–182). Hillsdale, NJ: Lawrence Erlbaum.

Cofer, D. H., & Wittenborn, J. R. (1980). Personality characteristics of formerly depressed women. *Journal of Abnormal Psychology, 89,* 309–314.

Coleman, R. E., & Miller, A. G. (1975). The relationship between depression and marital maladjustment in a clinic population: A multitrait-multimethod study. *Journal of Consulting and Clinical Psychology, 43,* 647–651.

Cooper, G. L., & Marshall, J. (1978). Sources of managerial and white-collar stress. In C. L. Cooper & R. Payne (Eds.), *Stress at work* (pp. 81–106). New York: John Wiley & Sons.

Costello, C. G. (1972). Depression: Loss of reinforcers or loss of reinforcer effectiveness? *Behavior Therapy, 3,* 240–247.

Costello, C. G. (1982). Social factors associated with depression: A retrospective community study. *Psychological Medicine, 12,* 329–339.

Costello, E. J. (1982). Locus of control and depression in students and psychiatric outpatients. *Journal of Clinical Psychology, 38,* 340–343.

Coyne, J. C. (1976a). Depression and the response of others. *Journal of Abnormal Psychology, 85,* 186–193.

Coyne, J. C. (1976b). Toward an interactional description of depression. *Psychiatry, 39,* 28–40.

Coyne, J. C., Aldwin, C., & Lazarus, R. S. (1981). Depression and coping in stressful episodes. *Journal of Abnormal Psychology, 90,* 439–447.

Cronkite, R. C., & Moos, R. H. (1980). The determinants of posttreatment functioning of alcoholic patients: A conceptual framework. *Journal of Consulting and Clinical Psychology, 48,* 305–316.

Crook, T., & Eliot, J. (1980). Parental death during childhood and adult depression: A critical review of the literature. *Psychological Bulletin, 87,* 252–259.

Cross, D. G., Sheehan, P. W., & Kahn, J. A. (1980). Alternative advice and counsel in psychotherapy. *Journal of Consulting and Clinical Psychology, 48,* 615–625.

Dobson, D. J. G., & Dobson, K. S. (1981). Problem-solving strategies in depressed and nondepressed college students. *Cognitive Therapy and Research, 5,* 237–249.

Doerfler, L. A., & Richards, C. S. (1981). Self-initiated attempts to cope with depression. *Cognitive Therapy and Research, 5,* 367–371.

Doerfler, L. A., & Richards, C. S. (1984). College women coping with depression. *Behaviour Research and Therapy, 21*(3), 221–224.

Dohrenwend, B. S. (1973). Social status and stressful life events. *Journal of Personality and Social Psychology, 28,* 225–235.

Dohrenwend, B. S., & Dohrenwend, B. P. (Eds.). (1974). *Stressful life events: Their nature and effects.* New York: John Wiley & Sons.

Dohrenwend, B. S., & Dohrenwend, B. P. (1981). *Stressful life events and their contexts.* New York: Neale Watson.

Dohrenwend, B. S., Krasnoff, L., Askenasy, A. R., & Dohrenwend, B. P. (1982). The psychiatric epidemiology research interview life events scale. In L. Goldberger & S. Breznitz (Eds.), *Handbook of stress: Theoretical and clinical aspects* (pp. 332–363). New York: Free Press.

Dohrenwend, B. S., & Martin, J. L. (1979). Personal versus situational determination of anticipation and control of the occurrence of stressful life events. *American Journal of Community Psychology, 7,* 453–468.

Endicott, J., & Spitzer, R. L. (1978). A diagnostic interview: The schedule for affective disorders and schizophrenia. *Archives of General Psychiatry, 35,* 837–844.

Finney, J. W., Mitchell, R. E., Cronkite, R. C., & Moos, R. H. (1984). Methodological issues in estimating main and interactive effects: Examples from the coping, social support, and stress field. *Journal of Health and Social Behavior, 25,* 85–98.

Fisher-Beckfield, D., & McFall, R. M. (1982). Development of a competence inventory for college men and evaluation of relationships between competence and depression. *Journal of Consulting and Clinical Psychology, 50,* 697–705.

Fleming, B. M., & Thornton, D. W. (1980). Coping skills training as a component in the short-term treatment of depression. *Journal of Consulting and Clinical Psychology, 48,* 652–654.

Folkman, S., & Lazarus, R. S. (1980). An analysis of coping in a middle-aged community sample. *Journal of Health and Social Behavior, 21,* 219–239.

Fontana, A. F., Hughes, L. A., Marcus, J. L., & Dowds, B. N. (1979). Subjective evaluation of life events. *Journal of Consulting and Clinical Psychology, 47,* 906–911.

Frank, J. D. (1974). Psychotherapy: The restoration of morale. *American Journal of Psychiatry, 131,* 271–274.

Funabiki, D., Bologna, N. C., Pepping, M., & Fitzgerald, K. C. (1980). Revisiting sex differences in the expression of depression. *Journal of Abnormal Psychology, 89,* 194–202.

Garber, J., & Hollon, S. D. (1980). Universal versus personal helplessness in depression: Belief in uncontrollability or incompetence? *Journal of Abnormal Behavior, 89,* 56–66.

Golin, S., Sweeney, P. D., & Schaeffer, D. E. (1981). The causality of causal attributions in depression: A cross-lagged panel correlational analysis. *Journal of Abnormal Psychology, 90,* 14–22.

Gong-Guy, E., & Hammen, C. L. (1980). Causal perceptions of stressful events in depressed and nondepressed outpatients. *Journal of Abnormal Psychology, 89,* 662–669.

Gottlieb, B. H. (Ed.) (1981). *Social networks and social support.* Beverly Hills, CA: Sage Publications.

Gore, S. (1978). The effect of social support in moderating the health consequences of unemployment. *Journal of Health and Social Behavior, 19,* 157–165.

Gourash, N. (1978). Help seeking: A review of the literature. *American Journal of Community Psychology, 6,* 413–423.

Hamilton, E. W., & Abramson, L. Y. (1983). Cognitive patterns and major depressive disorder: A longitudinal study in a hospital setting. *Journal of Abnormal Psychology, 92,* 173–184.

Hammen, C. L., & Cochran, S. D. (1981). Cognitive correlates of life stress and depression in college students. *Journal of Abnormal Psychology, 90,* 23–27.

Hammen, C. L., Jacobs, M., Mayol, A., & Cochran, S. D. (1980). Dysfunctional cognitions and the effectiveness of skills and cognitive-behavioral training. *Journal of Consulting and Clinical Psychology, 48,* 685–695.

Hammen, C., Krantz, S. E., & Cochran, S. D. (1981). Relationships between depression and causal attributions about stressful life events. *Cognitive Therapy and Research, 5,* 351–358.

Hammen, C., & Mayol, A. (1982). Depression and cognitive characteristics of stressful life-event types. *Journal of Abnormal Psychology, 91,* 165–174.

Hammen, C. L., & Peters, S. D. (1978). Interpersonal consequences of depression: Responses to men and women enacting a depressed role. *Journal of Abnormal Psychology, 87,* 322–332.

Harmon, T. M., Nelson, R. O., & Hayes, S. C. (1980). Self-monitoring of mood versus activity by depressed clients. *Journal of Consulting and Clinical Psychology, 48,* 30–38.

Harvey, D. M. (1981). Depression and attributional style: Interpretations of important personal events. *Journal of Abnormal Psychology, 90,* 134–142.

Henderson, S., Byrne, D. G., & Duncan-Jones, P. (1981). *Neurosis and the social environment.* New York: Academic Press.

Hirsch, B. (1980). Natural support systems and coping with major life changes. *American Journal of Community Psychology, 8,* 159–172.

Hollon, S. D., & Beck, A. T. (1978). Psychotherapy and drug therapy: Comparison and combinations. In S. L. Garfield & A. E. Bergin (Eds.), *Handbook of psychotherapy and behavior change: An empirical analysis* (2nd ed., pp. 437–490). New York: John Wiley & Sons.

Hollon, S. D., & Kendall, P. C. (1980). Cognitive self-statements in depression: Development of an automatic thoughts questionnaire. *Cognitive Therapy and Research, 4,* 383–395.

Holt, R. R. (1982). Occupational stress. In L. Goldberger & S. Breznitz (Eds.), *Handbook of stress: Theoretical and clinical aspects* (pp. 419–444). New York: Free Press.

Horowitz, M., & Wilner, N. (1980). Life events, stress, and coping. In L. W. Poon (Ed.), *Aging in the 1980s.* Washington, DC: American Psychological Association.

House, J. S. (1981). *Work stress and social support.* Reading, MA: Addison-Wesley Publishing.

Howes, M. J., & Hokanson, J. E. (1979). Conversational and social responses to depressive interpersonal behavior. *Journal of Abnormal Psychology, 88,* 625–634.

Johnson, J. H., & Sarason, I. G. (1978). Life stress, depression and anxiety: Internal-external control as a moderator variable. *Journal of Psychosomatic Research, 22,* 205–208.

Kanner, A. D., Coyne, J. C., Schaefer, C., & Lazarus, R. S. (1981). Comparison of two modes of stress measurement: Daily hassles and uplifts versus major life events. *Journal of Behavioral Medicine, 4,* 1–39.

Keller, M. B., & Shapiro, R. W. (1981). Major depressive disorder: Initial results from a one-year prospective naturalistic follow-up study. *Journal of Nervous and Mental Disorders, 169,* 761–768.

Kessler, R. (1979). A strategy for studying differential vulnerability to the psychological consequences of stress. *Journal of Health and Social Behavior, 20,* 100–108.

Kessler, M., & Albee, G. W. (1977). An overview of the literature of primary prevention. In G. W. Albee & J. M. Joffe (Eds.), *Primary prevention of psychopathology: The issues* (Vol. 1, pp. 351–399). Hanover, NH: University Press of New England.

Kobasa, S. C., Maddi, S. R., & Kahn, S. (1982). Hardiness and health: A prospective study. *Journal of Personality and Social Psychology, 42,* 168–177.

Kovacs, M. (1980). The efficacy of cognitive and behavior therapies for depression. *The American Journal of Psychiatry, 137,* 1495–1501.

Kovacs, M., Rush, A. J., Beck, A. T., & Hollon, S. D. (1981). Depressed outpatients treated with cognitive therapy or pharmacotherapy. *Archives of General Psychiatry, 38,* 33–39.

Krantz, S., & Hammen, C. L. (1979). Assessment of cognitive bias in depression. *Journal of Abnormal Psychology, 88,* 611–619.

LaRocco, J. M., House, J. S., & French, J. R. P. (1980). Social support, occupational stress, and health. *Journal of Health and Social Behavior, 21,* 202–218.

Lazarus, R. S. (1981). The stress and coping paradigm. In C. Eisdorfer, D. Cohen, A. Kleinman, & P. Maxim (Eds.), *Models for clinical psychopathology* (pp. 177–214). New York: Spectrum Publications.

Lazarus, R. S., & Cohen, J. B. (1977). Environmental stress. In I. Altman & J. F. Wohlwill (Eds.), *Human behavior and the environment: Current theory and research* (Vol. 2, pp. 89–127). New York: Plenum Publishing.

Lefcourt, H. M. (Ed.) (1981). *Research with the locus of control construct.* New York: Academic Press.

Lewinsohn, P. M. (1974). A behavioral approach to depression. In R. Friedman & M. Katz (Eds.), *The psychology of depression: Contemporary theory and research* (pp. 157–178). New York: John Wiley & Sons.

Lewinsohn, P. M., Biglan, T., & Zeiss, A. (1976). Behavioral treatment of depression. In P. O. Davidson (Ed.), *Behavioral management of anxiety, pain, and depression* (pp. 91–146). New York: Brunner/Mazel.

Lewinsohn, P. M., Mischel, W., Chaplin, W., & Barton, R. (1980). Social competence and depression. The role of illusory self-perceptions. *Journal of Abnormal Psychology, 89,* 203–212.

Lewinsohn, P. M., Steinmetz, J. L., Larson, D., & Franklin, F. (1981). Depression related cognitions: Antecedent or consequence? *Journal of Abnormal Psychology, 90,* 213–219.

Liem, R., & Leim, J. (1978). Social class and mental illness reconsidered: The role of economic stress and social support. *Journal of Health and Social Behavior, 19,* 139–156.

McCubbin, H. I., & Patterson, J. M. (1981). Systematic assessment of family stress, resources and coping: Tools for research, education, and clinical intervention. St. Paul, MN: Family Stress Project.

McLean, P. D. (1982). Behavioral therapy: Theory and research. In A. J. Rush (Ed.), *Short-term therapies for depression* (pp. 19–49). New York: Guilford Press.

McLean, P. D., & Hakistan, A. R. (1979). Clinical depression: Comparative efficacy of outpatient treatments. *Journal of Consulting and Clinical Psychology, 47,* 818–836.

Miller, D. T., & Ross, M. (1975). Self-serving biases in the attribution of causality: Fact or fiction? *Psychological Bulletin, 82,* 213–225.

Mitchell, R. E., Billings, A. G., & Moos, R. H. (1982). Social support and well-being: Implications for prevention programs. *Journal of Primary Prevention, 3,* 77–98.

Mitchell, R. E., Cronkite, R. C., & Moos, R. H. (1983). Stress, coping and depression among married couples. *Journal of Abnormal Psychology, 92,* 443–448.

Moos, R. H., & Billings, A. G. (1982). Conceptualizing and measuring coping resources and processes. In L. Goldberger & S. Breznitz (Eds.), *Handbook of stress: Theoretical and clinical aspects* (pp. 212–230). New York: Macmillan.

Moos, R. H., & Mitchell, R. E. (1982). Conceptualizing and measuring social network resources. In T. A. Wills (Ed.), *Basic processes in helping relationships* (pp. 213–232). New York: Academic Press.

Myers, J. K., Lindenthal, J. J., & Pepper, M. P. (1975). Life events, social integration and psychiatric symptomatology. *Journal of Health and Social Behavior, 16,* 421–427.

Overall, J. E., & Zisook, S. (1980). Diagnosis and the phenomenology of depressive disorders. *Journal of Consulting and Clinical Psychology, 48,* 626–634.

Parker, G. B., & Brown, L. B. (1982). Coping behaviors that mediate between life events and depression. *Archives of General Psychiatry, 39,* 1386–1391.

Pasahow, R. J. (1980). The relation between an attributional dimension and learned helplessness. *Journal of Abnormal Psychology, 89,* 358–367.

Paykel, E. S. (1979). Recent life events in the development of the depressive disorders. In R. A. Depue (Ed.), *The psychobiology of the depressive disorders: Implications for the effects of stress* (pp. 245–262). New York: Academic Press.

Paykel, E. S., Weissman, M. M., & Prusoff, B. A. (1978). Social maladjustment and severity of depression. *Comprehensive Psychiatry, 19,* 121–128.

Pearlin, L. I. (1982). The social contexts of stress. In L. Goldberger & S. Breznitz (Eds.), *Handbook of stress: Theoretical and clinical aspects* (pp. 367–379). New York: Free Press.

Pearlin, L. I., & Johnson, J. (1977). Marital status, life strains, and depression. *American Sociological Review, 42,* 704–715.

Pearlin, L. I., & Schooler, C. (1978). The structure of coping. *Journal of Health and Social Behavior, 19,* 2–21.

Perlmuter, L. C., & Monty, R. A. (1979). *Choice and perceived control.* Hillsdale, NJ: Lawrence Erlbaum.

Peterson, C. (1979). Uncontrollability and self-blame in depression: Investigation of the paradox in a college population. *Journal of Abnormal Psychology, 88,* 620–624.

Peterson, C., Schwartz, S. M., & Seligman, M. E. P. (1981). Self-blame and depressive symptoms. *Journal of Personality and Social Psychology, 41,* 253–259.

Radloff, L. S. (1977). The CES-D Scale: A self-report depression scale for research in the general population. *Applied Psychological Measurement, 1,* 385–410.

Radloff, L. S., & Rae, D. S. (1979). Susceptibility and precipitating factors in depression: Sex differences and similarities. *Journal of Abnormal Psychology, 88,* 174–181.

Rippere, V. (1976). Antidepressive behaviour: A preliminary report. *Behaviour Research and Therapy, 14,* 289–299.

Rogers, J., Vachon, M. L., Lyall, W. A., Sheldon, A., & Freeman, S. J. (1980). A self-help program for widows as an independent community service. *Hospital and Community Psychiatry, 31,* 844–847.

Rubinstein, D., & Timmins, J. F. (1978). Depressive dyadic and triadic relationships. *Journal of Marriage and Family Counseling, 4,* 13–23.

Rush, A. J., Beck, A. T., Kovacs, M., & Hollon, S. D. (1977). Comparative efficacy of cognitive therapy and pharmacotherapy in the treatment of depressed outpatients. *Cognitive Therapy and Research, 1,* 17–36.

Rush, A. J., Shaw, B. F., & Khatami, M. (1980). Cognitive therapy of depression: Utilizing the couples system. *Cognitive Therapy and Research, 4,* 103–113.

Salzman, L. (1975). Interpersonal factors in depression. In F. F. Flach & S. C. Draghi (Eds.), *The nature and treatment of depression* (pp. 43–56). New York: John Wiley & Sons.

Sanchez, V., & Lewinsohn, P. M. (1980). Assertive behavior and depression. *Journal of Consulting and Clinical Psychology, 48,* 119–120.

Sandler, I. N., & Block, M. (1979). Life stress and maladaptation of children. *American Journal of Community Psychology, 7,* 425–440.

Seligman, M. E. P. (Ed.) (1975). *Helplessness: On depression, development, and death.* San Francisco: W. H. Freeman.

Seligman, M. E. P., Abramson, L. Y., Semmel, A., & von Baeyer, C. (1979). Depressive attributional style. *Journal of Abnormal Psychology, 88,* 242–247.

Shaw, B. (1977). Comparison of cognitive therapy and behavior therapy in the treatment of depression. *Journal of Consulting and Clinical Psychology, 45,* 543–551.

Stone, A. A., & Neale, J. M. (1984). A new measure of daily coping: Development and preliminary results. *Journal of Personality and Social Psychology, 46,* 892–906.

Strack, S., & Coyne, J. C. (1983). Social confirmation of dysphoria: Shared and private reactions to depression. *Journal of Personality and Social Psychology, 44,* 798–806.

Sundberg, N. D., Snowden, L. R., & Reynolds, W. M. (1978). Toward assessment of personal competence and incompetence in life situations. *Annual Review of Psychology, 29,* 179–221.

Tolsdorf, C. C. (1976). Social networks, support, and coping: An exploratory study. *Family Process, 15,* 407–417.

Tyler, F. B. (1978). Individual psychological competence: A personality configuration. *Educational and Psychological Measurement, 38,* 309–323.

Vaughn, C. E., & Leff, J. P. (1976). The influence of family and social factors on the course of psychiatric illness: A comparison of schizophrenic and depressed neurotic patients. *British Journal of Psychiatry, 129,* 125–137.

Wandersman, A., & Giamartino, G. A. (1980). Community and individual difference characteristics as influences on initial participation. *American Journal of Community Psychology, 8,* 217–228.

Wandersman, L., Wandersman, A., & Kahn, S. (1980). Social support in the transition to parenthood. *Journal of Community Psychology, 8,* 332–342.

Warheit, G. J. (1979). Life events, coping, stress, and depressive symptomatology. *American Journal of Psychiatry, 136,* 502–507.

Warren, L. W., & McEachren, L. (1983). Psychosocial correlates of depressive symptomatology in adult women. *Journal of Abnormal Psychology, 92,* 151–160.

Weissman, A. N., & Beck, A. T. (1978). *Development and validation of the Dysfunctional Attitude Scale.* Paper presented at the 12th annual meeting of the Association for the Advancement of Behavior Therapy, Chicago.

Weissman, M. M. (1979). The psychological treatment of depression: Evidence for the efficacy of psychotherapy alone, in comparison with, and in combination with pharmacotherapy. *Archives of General Psychiatry, 36,* 1261–1269.

Weissman, M. M., & Klerman, G. L. (1977). Sex differences and the epidemiology of depression. *Archives of General Psychiatry, 34,* 98–111.

Weissman, M. M., & Myers, J. (1978). Affective disorders in a U.S. urban community: The use of Research Diagnostic Criteria in an epidemiological survey. *Archives of General Psychiatry, 35,* 1304–1311.

Weissman, M. M., & Paykel, E. S. (1974). *The depressed woman: A study of social relationships.* Chicago: University of Chicago Press.

Westbrook, M. T. (1979). Socioeconomic differences in coping with childbearing. *American Journal of Community Psychology, 7,* 397–412.

Wilcox, B. L. (1981). Social support, life stress, and psychological adjustment: A test of the buffering hypothesis. *American Journal of Community Psychology, 9,* 371–386.

Witkin, H. A., & Goodenough, D. R. (1977). Field dependence and interpersonal behavior. *Psychological Bulletin, 84,* 661–689.

Youngren, M. A., & Lewinsohn, P. M. (1980). The functional relationship between depression and problematic interpersonal behavior. *Journal of Abnormal Psychology, 89,* 333–341.

Zeiss, A. M., Lewinsohn, P. M., & Muñoz, R. F. (1979). Nonspecific improvement effects in depression using interpersonal skills training, pleasant activity schedules, or cognitive training. *Journal of Consulting and Clinical Psychology, 47,* 427–439.

PART 5

Appendixes

DSM-III *Criteria for Major Depressive Episode and Dysthymic Disorder**

Diagnostic Criteria for Major Depressive Episode

A. Dysphoric mood or loss of interest or pleasure in all or almost all usual activities and pastimes. The dysphoric mood is characterized by symptoms such as the following: depressed, sad, blue, hopeless, low, down in the dumps, irritable. The mood disturbance must be prominent and relatively persistent, but not necessarily the most dominant symptom, and does not include momentary shifts from one dysphoric mood to another dysphoric mood; e.g., anxiety to depression to anger, such as are seen in states of acute psychotic turmoil. (For children under six, dysphoric mood may have to be inferred from a persistently sad facial expression.)

B. At least four of the following symptoms have each been present nearly every day for a period of at least two weeks (in children under six, at least three of the first four).

   1. Poor appetite or significant weight loss (when not dieting) or increased appetite or significant weight gain (in children under six, consider failure to make expected weight gains).
   2. Insomnia or hypersomnia.
   3. Psychomotor agitation or retardation (but not merely subjective feelings of restlessness or being slowed down) (in children under six, hypoactivity).
   4. Loss of interest or pleasure in usual activities, or decrease in sexual drive not limited to a period when delusional or hallucinating (in children under six, signs of apathy).
   5. Loss of energy; fatigue.
   6. Feelings of worthlessness, self-reproach, or excessive or inappropriate guilt (either may be delusional).

---

* American Psychiatric Association, *Diagnostic and Statistical Manual of Mental Disorders,* Third Edition. Washington, DC, APA, 1980. Used with Permission.

7. Complaints or evidence of diminished ability to think or concentrate, such as slowed thinking, or indecisiveness not associated with marked loosening of associations or incoherence.
8. Recurrent thoughts of death, suicidal ideation, wishes to be dead, or suicide attempt.

C. Neither of the following dominate the clinical picture when an affective syndrome (i.e., criteria A and B above) is not present, that is, before it developed or after it has remitted:

  1. Preoccupation with a mood-incongruent delusion or hallucination (see definition below).
  2. Bizarre behavior.

D. Not superimposed on either schizophrenia, schizophreniform disorder, or a paranoid disorder.

E. Not due to any organic mental disorder or uncomplicated bereavement.

Fifth-digit code numbers and criteria for subclassification of major depressive episode

(When psychotic features and melancholia are present the coding system requires that the clinician record the single most clinically significant characteristic.)

6— *In Remission*
This fifth-digit category should be used when in the past the individual met the full criteria for a major depressive episode but now is essentially free of depressive symptoms or has some signs of the disorder but does not meet the full criteria.

4— *With Psychotic Features*
This fifth-digit category should be used when there apparently is gross impairment in reality testing, as when there are delusions or hallucinations, or depressive stupor (the individual is mute and unresponsive). When possible, specify whether the psychotic features are mood-congruent or mood-incongruent. (The non-ICD-9-CM fifth-digit 7 may be used instead to indicate that the psychotic features are mood-incongruent; otherwise, mood-congruence may be assumed.)

  Mood-Congruent Psychotic Features. Delusions or hallucinations whose content is entirely consistent with the themes of either personal inadequacy, guilt, disease, death, nihilism, or deserved punishment; depressive stupor (the individual is mute and unresponsive).

  Mood-Incongruent Psychotic Features. Delusions or hallucinations whose content does not involve themes of either personal inadequacy, guilt, disease, death, nihilism, or deserved punishment. Included here are such symptoms as persecutory delusions, thought insertion, thought broadcasting, and delusions of control, whose content has no apparent relationship to any of the themes noted above.

3— *With Melancholia*
Loss of pleasure in all or almost all activities, lack of reactivity to usually pleasurable stimuli (doesn't feel much better, even temporarily, when something good happens), and at least three of the following:

a. Distinct quality of depressed mood; that is, the depressed mood is perceived as distinctly different from the kind of feeling experienced following the death of a loved one
b. The depression is regularly worse in the morning.
c. Early morning awakening (at least two hours before usual time of awakening).
d. Marked psychomotor retardation or agitation.
e. Significant anorexia or weight loss.
f. Excessive or inappropriate guilt.

2– ***Without Melancholia***

0– ***Unspecified***

Diagnostic Criteria for Dysthymic Disorder

A. During the past two years (or one year for children and adolescents) the individual has been bothered most or all of the time by symptoms characteristic of the depressive syndrome but that are not of sufficient severity and duration to meet the criteria for a major depressive episode.
B. The manifestations of the depressive syndrome may be relatively persistent or separated by periods of normal mood lasting a few days to a few weeks, but no more than a few months at a time.
C. During the depressive periods there is either prominent depressed mood (e.g., sad, blue, down in the dumps, low) or marked loss of interest or pleasure in all, or almost all, usual activities and pastimes.
D. During the depressive periods at least three of the following symptoms are present:

1. Insomnia or hypersomnia.
2. Low-energy level or chronic tiredness.
3. Feelings of inadequacy, loss of self-esteem, or self-deprecation.
4. Decreased effectiveness or productivity at school, work, or home.
5. Decreased attention, concentration, or ability to think clearly.
6. Social withdrawal.
7. Loss of interest in or enjoyment of pleasurable activities.
8. Irritability or excessive anger (in children, expressed toward parents or caretakers).
9. Inability to respond with apparent pleasure to praise or rewards.
10. Less active or talkative than usual, or feels slowed down or restless.
11. Pessimistic attitude toward the future, brooding about past events, or feeling sorry for self.
12. Tearfulness or crying.
13. Recurrent thoughts of death or suicide.

E. Absence of psychotic features, such as delusions, hallucinations, or incoherence, or loosening of associations.
F. If the disturbance is superimposed on a preexisting mental disorder, such as obsessive compulsive disorder or alcohol dependence, the depressed mood, by virtue of its intensity or effect on functioning, can be clearly distinguished from the individual's usual mood.

Interview Questions for Symptoms of Major Depression and Endogenous Subtype from the Schedule for Affective Disorders and Schizophrenia.*

Depressive Mood

Subjective feelings of depression based on verbal complaints of feeling depressed, sad, blue, gloomy, down in the dumps, empty, "don't care." Do not include such ideational aspects as discouragement, pessimism, or worthlessness; suicide attempts, or depressed appearance (all of which are rated separately).

How have you been feeling? Describe your mood.
Have you felt depressed (sad, blue, moody, down, empty, as if you didn't care)? (Have you cried or been tearful?) (How often? Does it come and go?) (How long does it last?) (How bad is the feeling? Can you stand it?)

Guilt

Feelings of self-reproach or excessive or inappropriate guilt for things done or not done, including delusions of guilt (not simply a negative evaluation of self).

Do you blame yourself for anything you have done or not done?
What about feeling guilty?
Do you feel you have done anything wrong? (Do you deserve punishment?)
Do you feel you have brought this on yourself?

Feelings of Worthlessness

Negative evaluation of himself, including feelings of inadequacy, failure, or worthlessness.

How do you feel about yourself?
Are you down on yourself? (What is your opinion of yourself compared to other people?) (Worthless? A failure?) (How often do you feel this way about yourself?)

---

* Developed by Robert L. Spitzer and Jean Endicott; quoted with permission.

Suicidal Tendencies

Includes preoccupation with thoughts of death or suicide. (Do not include mere fears of dying.)

> When a person gets upset, depressed, or feels hopeless, he may think about dying or even killing himself. Have you? (Have you thought how you would do it?) (Have you told anybody [about suicidal thoughts]?) (Have you actually done anything?)

Insomnia

Sleep disturbance, including initial, middle, and terminal difficulty in getting to sleep or staying asleep. Do not rate if person feels no need for sleep. Take into account the estimated number of hours slept and subjective sense of lost sleep. If subject is using medications, ask what he or she thinks it would be like without medication.

> Have you had trouble sleeping? (What about falling asleep?) (. . . or waking up in the middle of the night?) (. . . or early in the morning before you want to get up?) (How bad does it get?)

Sleeps more than usual.

> Are you sleeping longer or more than usual? (Do you go back to sleep or reset the alarm?) (How much more?) (How often?) (What about taking long naps during the day?)

Fatigue

Subjective feeling of lack of energy or fatigue. (Do not confuse with lack of interest). Rate as present even if clearly due to medication.

> Have you had less energy than usual to do things—or have you been getting tired more easily? (I am not talking about *interest* in things, but your physical *energy* to do things.)

Loss of Appetite Compared to Usual

> What about your appetite for food compared to the way it usually is? (Do you have to force yourself to eat?) (Are you eating less than usual?) (How much?)

Weight Loss

Total weight loss from usual weight during present episode (or maximum of one year) without dieting (even if later regained weight).

> Have you lost any weight since. . ?

Increase in Appetite

> Have you had an increase in appetite? (How much have you been eating?)

Weight Gain

Total weight gain from usual weight during present episode (or maximum of one year) not including gaining back weight previously lost.

> Have you gained any weight since. . . ?

Diminished Concentration

Complaints or evidence of diminished ability to think or concentrate including slowed thinking (Do not include if apparently due to obvious formal thought disorder).

Have you had trouble concentrating?
Is your thinking slowed down? (When do you have trouble?) (What difficulties does it cause?) (Does it affect your work?) (Is that because you can't concentrate or just that you're not interested?)

Difficulty Making Everyday Decisions

Have you had any difficulty making everyday decisions?
Has it taken longer to make decisions than when you were feeling good, like what to wear, what to cook, where to go, what to buy? (Are there things that you don't get done because you can't decide what to do?)

Loss of Interest

Pervasiveness of loss of interest or pleasure in work, family, friends, sex, hobbies, and other leisure-time activities. Severity is determined by the number of important activities in which the subject has less interest or pleasure compared to usual level.

Do you find that you have lost interest in or get less pleasure from things that you used to enjoy—like your job, friends, your family, sex, hobbies, watching TV, eating?
Which things have you lost interest in?
Which things do you still enjoy?
Are there things that you still enjoy as much as usual?

Agitation

Agitation lasting at least a few days (not associated with manic syndrome). Includes inability to sit still, pacing, fidgeting, movements of lips or fingers, wringing hands, pulling at clothes, not limited to isolated periods when discussing something upsetting. Do not include mere subjective feeling of tension or restlessness, which is often incorrectly called agitation.

Were there times that you were unable to sit still or did you always have to be moving or pacing up and down? (Did you wring your hands?) (Did you pull or rub on your clothing, hair, skin, or other things?) (Were there times when you shouted or complained loudly to the people around you?)

Retardation

Psychomotor retardation *lasting at least* a week; that is, visible generalized slowing down of physical reactions, movement, and speech, including latency in speech. Make certain that the slowing down actually occurred and is not merely a subjective feeling. Does not include discrete periods of catatonic-like rigidity.

When you did things, were you slowed down because you couldn't move as quickly as usual?

Was your speech slowed down? (Did you find it hard to start talking?) (Did you talk a lot less than usual?) (Did you feel like you were moving in slow motion?) (How long did that last?)

Additional Items Used for Research Diagnostic Criteria Diagnosis of Endogenous Depression. (These questions can be used to probe for the symptoms of DSM-III Major Depression with Melancholia).

Distinct Quality of Mood

Extent to which the depressed feelings are felt by the subject to be qualitatively different from the kind of feeling he would have or has had following the death of a loved one (not just more severe, or mixed with other symptoms, such as loss of interest).

Is this feeling of (use patient's terms) different from the usual feelings that you would get, or have had after someone close died? (Or from a sad movie or story?) (How is the feeling different?)

Reactivity

Extent to which temporary improvement in mood or ideation or loss of interest or pleasure was associated with positive environmental events during the week when he was most upset.

During the week when you were feeling the worst, did that feeling ever go away when you got your mind on other things or when something pleasant happened—like talking to a friend, or hearing good news, or did you feel bad no matter what was happening? (If someone tried to cheer you up, could they?)

Diurnal Mood Variation

Extent to which, for at least one week, there is a constant fluctuation of depressed mood and other symptomatology coinciding with the first or second half of day. Generally, if the mood is worse in one part of the day it will be better in the other. However, for occasional subjects who are better in the afternoon and worse both in the morning and evening, both may be present, or for other subjects there may have been a period when it was clearly worse in the morning and another period when it was worse in the evening. Both items should be rated independently. Rate regardless of regular environmental changes such as feeling better while at work.

Was there any part of the day in which you usually felt better or worse, or didn't it make any difference?

(Researchers interested in obtaining copies of the SADS may write to Dr. Endicott at the Research Assessment and Training Unit, New York State Psychiatric Institute, 722 West 168th Street, New York, New York, 10032.)

Beck Depression Inventory*

On this questionnaire are groups of statements. Please read each group of statements carefully. Then pick out the one statement in each group which best describes the way you have been feeling the *PAST WEEK, INCLUDING TODAY!* Circle the number beside the statement you picked. If several statements in the group seem to apply equally well, circle each one. *Be sure to read all the statements in each group before making your choice.*

1. 0 I do not feel sad.
1 I feel sad.
2 I am sad all the time and I can't snap out of it.
3 I am so sad or unhappy that I can't stand it.

2. 0 I am not particularly discouraged about the future.
1 I feel discouraged about the future.
2 I feel I have nothing to look forward to.
3 I feel that the future is hopeless and that things cannot improve.

3. 0 I do not feel like a failure.
1 I feel I have failed more than the average person.
2 As I look back on my life, all I can see is a lot of failures.
3 I feel I am a complete failure as a person.

4. 0 I get as much satisfaction out of things as I used to.
1 I don't enjoy things the way I used to.
2 I don't get real satisfaction out of anything anymore.
3 I am dissatisfied or bored with everything.

---

5. 0 I don't feel particularly guilty.
   1 I feel guilty a good part of the time.
   2 I feel quite guilty most of the time.
   3 I feel guilty all of the time.

6. 0 I don't feel I am being punished.
   1 I feel I may be punished.
   2 I expect to be punished.
   3 I feel I am being punished.

7. 0 I don't feel disappointed in myself.
   1 I am disappointed in myself.
   2 I am disgusted with myself.
   3 I hate myself.

8. 0 I don't feel I am any worse than anybody else.
   1 I am critical of myself for my weaknesses or mistakes.
   2 I blame myself all the time for my faults.
   3 I blame myself for everything bad that happens.

9. 0 I don't have any thoughts of killing myself.
   1 I have thoughts of killing myself, but I would not carry them out.
   2 I would like to kill myself.
   3 I would kill myself if I had the chance.

10. 0 I don't cry any more than usual.
   1 I cry more now than I used to.
   2 I cry all the time now.
   3 I used to be able to cry, but now I can't cry even thought I want to.

11. 0 I am no more irritated by things than I ever am.
   1 I am slightly more irritated now than usual.
   2 I am quite annoyed or irritated a good deal of the time.
   3 I feel irritated all the time now.

12. 0 I have not lost interest in other people.
   1 I am less interested in other people than I used to be.
   2 I have lost most of my interest in other people.
   3 I have lost all of my interest in other people.

13. 0 I make decisions about as well as I ever could.
   1 I put off making decisions more than I used to.
   2 I have greater difficulty in making decisions than before.
   3 I can't make decisions at all anymore.

14. 0 I don't feel that I look any worse than I used to.
   1 I am worried that I am looking old or unattractive.
   2 I feel that there are permanent changes in my appearance that make me look unattractive.
   3 I believe that I look ugly.

15. 0 I can work about as well as before.
    1 It takes an extra effort to get started at doing something.
    2 I have to push myself very hard to do anything.
    3 I can't do any work at all.

16. 0 I can sleep as well as usual.
    1 I don't sleep as well as I used to.
    2 I wake up one–two hours earlier than usual and find it hard to get back to sleep.
    3 I wake up several hours earlier than I used to and cannot get back to sleep.

17. 0 I don't get more tired than usual.
    1 I get tired more easily than I used to.
    2 I get tired from doing almost anything.
    3 I am too tired to do anything.

18. 0 My appetite is no worse than usual.
    1 My appetite is not as good as it used to be.
    2 My appetite is much worse now.
    3 I have no appetite at all anymore.

19. 0 I haven't lost much weight, if any, lately.
    1 I have lost more than five pounds.
    2 I have lost more than 10 pounds.
    3 I have lost more than 15 pounds.

    I am purposely trying to lose weight by eating less.
    Yes _____ No _____

20. 0 I am no more worried about my health than usual.
    1 I am worried about physical problems such as aches and pains, or upset stomach, or constipation.
    2 I am very worried about physical problems and it's hard to think of much else.
    3 I am so worried about my physical problems that I cannot think about anything else.

21. 0 I have not noticed any recent change in my interest in sex.
    1 I am less interested in sex than I used to be.
    2 I am much less interested in sex now.
    3 I have lost interest in sex completely.

Official scoring criteria have not been published. However, clinical experience suggests that persons scoring 11–16 have mild depression, persons with scores from 17–26 have moderate levels of depression, and persons with scores above 26 have severe depression. (E.E.B. & W.R.L)

Hamilton Rating Scale for Depression

The Hamilton Rating Scale for Depression has been published in several forms. The first form printed in this appendix is the 1967 version published by Dr. Max Hamilton. It is reprinted here with the permission of Dr. Hamilton, the British Psychological Society, and the British Medical Association. Following that version is another developed in the NIMH Early Clinical Drug Evaluation Program (ECDEU version) with anchor points for different rating levels on each item. These anchor points have been widely used in American research. The ECDEU version was modified for use in the NIMH Treatment of Depression Collaborative Research Program to include items on hypersomnia, increased appetite, and weight gain. That is the ECDEU version printed here. Dr. Hamilton does not feel that the ECDEU anchors in and of themselves constitute an adequate version of his scale. We agree. The ECDEU version is included here because it has become widely used in American research and is a useful adjunct to the original scale.

The Hamilton Rating Scale for Depression has been used in research in both the 17-item version (Dr. Hamilton's original 17 items which do not include hypersomnia, increased appetite, and weight gain) and as a 20-item scale including items on depersonalization, paranoia, and obsessional symptoms. Research with the scale should specify which version is used.

There are no universally accepted questions to probe for information for Hamilton items. Suggested probes have been printed by G. L. Klerman et al. in *Interpersonal Psychotherapy of Depression* (New York: Basic Books, 1984) and by J. Mark G. Williams in *The Psychological Treatment of Depression* (New York: Free Press, 1984).

Below is the version published by Dr. Hamilton in 1967 in the *British Journal of Social and Clinical Psychology*.

References
Hamilton, M. (1960). A rating scale for depression. *Journal of Neurology, Neurosurgery and Psychiatry, 12,* 56–62.

Hamilton, M. (1967). Development of a rating scale for primary depressive illness. *British Journal of Social and Clinical Psychology, 6,* 278–296.

The Rating of Male Patients

1. Depression (0–4)

Depressed mood is not easy to assess. One looks for a gloomy attitude, pessimism about the future, feelings of hopelessness and a tendency to weep. As a guide, occasional weeping could count as 2, frequent weeping as 3, and severe symptoms allotted 4 points. When patients are severely depressed they may "go beyond weeping." It is important to remember that patients interpret the word "depression" in all sorts of strange ways. A useful common phrase is "lowering of spirits."

2. Guilt (0–4)

This is fairly easy to assess but judgement is needed, for the rating is concerned with pathological guilt. From the patient's point of view, some action of his which precipitated a crisis may appear as a "rational" basis for self-blame, which persists even after recovery from his illness. For example, he may have accepted a promotion, but the increased responsibility precipitated his breakdown. When he "blames" himself for this, he is ascribing a cause and not necessarily expressing pathological guilt. As a guide to rating, feelings of self-reproach count 1, ideas of guilt 2, belief that the illness might be a punishment 3, and delusions of guilt, with or without hallucinations, 4 points.

3. Suicide (0–4)

The scoring ranges from feeling that life is not worth living 1, wishing he were dead 2, suicidal ideas and half-hearted attempts 3, serious attempts 4. Judgement must be used when the patient is considered to be concealing this symptom, or conversely, when he is using suicidal threats as a weapon, to intimidate others, obtain help and so on.

4., 5., 6. Insomnia (Initial, Middle and Delayed) (0–2)

Mild, trivial, and infrequent symptoms are given 1 point, obvious and severe symptoms are rated 2 points; both severity and frequency should be taken into account. Middle insomnia (disturbed sleep during the night) is the most difficult to assess, possibly because it is an artifact of the system of rating. When insomnia is severe, it generally affects all phases. Delayed insomnia (early morning wakening) tends not to be relieved by hypnotic drugs and is not often present without other forms of insomnia.

7. Work and Interests (0–4)

It could be argued that the patient's loss of interest in his work and activities should be rated separately from his decreased performance, but it has been found too difficult to do so in practice. Care should be taken not to include fatiguability and lack of energy here; the rating is concerned with loss of efficiency and the extra effort required to do anything. When the patient has to be admitted to hospital because his symptoms render him unable to carry on, this should be rated 4 points, but not if he has been admitted for investigation or observation. When the patient improves he will eventually return to work, but when he does so may depend on the nature of his work; judgement must be used here.

8. Retardation (0–4)

Severe forms of this symptom are rare, and the mild forms are difficult to perceive. A slight flattening of affect and fixity of expression rate as 1, a monotonous voice, a delay in answering questions, a tendency to sit motionless count as 2. When retardation makes the interview extremely prolonged and almost impossible, it is rated 3, and 4 is given when an interview is impossible (and symptoms cannot be rated). Although some patients may say that their thinking is slowed or their emotional responsiveness has been diminished, questions about these manifestations usually produce misleading answers.

9. Agitation (0–4)

Severe agitation is extremely rare. Fidgetiness at interview rates as 1, obvious restlessness with picking at hands and clothes should count as 2. If the patient has to get up during the interview he is given 3, and 4 points are given when the interview has to be conducted "on the run," with the patient pacing up and down, picking at his face and hair and tearing at his clothes. Although agitation and retardation may appear to be opposed forms of behaviour, in mild form they can co-exist.

10. Anxiety (Psychic Symptoms) (0–4)

Many symptoms are included here, such as tension and difficulty in relaxing, irritability, worrying over trivial matters, apprehension and feelings of panic, fears, difficulty in concentration and forgetfulness, "feeling jumpy." The rating should be based on pathological changes that have occurred during the illness and an effort should be made to discount the features of a previous anxious disposition.

11. Anxiety (Somatic Symptoms) (0–4)

These consist of the well-recognized effects of autonomic overactivity in the respiratory, cardiovascular, gastrointestinal and urinary systems. Patients may also complain of attacks of giddiness, blurring of vision and tinnitus.

12. Gastrointestinal Symptoms (0–2)

The characteristic symptom in depression is loss of appetite and this occurs very frequently. Constipation also occurs but is relatively uncommon. On rare occasions patients will complain of "heavy feelings" in the abdomen. Symptoms of indigestion, wind and pain, etc. are rated under Anxiety.

13. General Somatic Symptoms (0–2)

These fall into two groups: the first is fatiguability, which may reach the point where the patients feel tired all the time. In addition, patients complain of "loss of energy" which appears to be related to difficulty in starting up an activity. The other type of symptom consists of diffuse muscular achings, ill-defined and often difficult to locate, but frequently in the back and sometimes in the limbs; these may also feel "heavy."

14. Loss of Libido (0–2)

This is a common and characteristic symptom of depression, but it is difficult to assess in older men and especially those; e.g., unmarried, whose sexual activity is usually at a low level. The assessment is based on a pathological change, i.e., a deterioration obviously related to the patient's illness. Inadequate or no information should be rated as zero.

15. Hypochondriasis (0–4)

The severe states of this symptom, concerning delusions and hallucinations of rotting and blockages, etc., which are extremely uncommon in men, are rated as 4. Strong convictions of the presence of some organic disease which accounts for the patient's condition are rated 3. Much preoccupation with physical symptoms and with thoughts of organic disease are rated 2. Excessive preoccupation with bodily functions is the essence of a hypochondriacal attitude and trivial or doubtful symptoms count as 1 point.

16. Loss of Insight (0–2)

This is not necessarily present when the patient denies that he is suffering from mental disorder. It may be that he is denying that he is insane and may willingly recognize that he has a "nervous" illness. In case of doubt, enquiries should be directed to the patient's attitude to his symptoms of guilt and hypochondriasis.

17. Loss of Weight (0–2)

The simplest way to rate this would be to record the amount of loss, but many patients do not know their normal weight. For this reason, an obvious or severe loss is rated as 2 and a slight or doubtful loss as 1 point.

18. Diurnal Variation (0–2)

This symptom has been excluded from the rating scale as it indicates the type of illness, rather than presenting an addition to the patient's disabilities. The commonest form consists of an increase of symptoms in the morning, but this is only slightly greater than worsening in the evening. A small number of patients insist that they feel worse in the afternoon. The clear presence of diurnal variation is rated as 2 and the doubtful presence is 1 point.

The following three symptoms were excluded from the rating of symptoms because they occur with insufficient frequency, but they are of interest in research.

19. Derealization and Depersonalization (0–4)

The patient who has this symptom quickly recognizes the questions asked of him; when he has difficulty in understanding the questions it usually signifies that the symptom is absent. When the patient asserts that he has this symptom it is necessary to question him closely; feelings of "distance" usually mean nothing more than that the patient lacks concentration or interest in his surroundings. It would appear that the severe forms of this symptom are extremely rare in patients diagnosed as depressive.

20. Paranoid Symptoms (0–4)

These are uncommon, and affirmative answers should always be checked carefully. It is of no significance if the patient says that others talk about him, since this is usually true. What is important in the mild symptom is the patient's attitude of suspicion, and the malevolence imputed to others. Doubtful or trivial suspicion rates as 1, thoughts that others wish him harm rates as 2, delusions that others wish him harm or are trying to do so rates as 3, and hallucinations are given 4 points. Care should be taken not to confuse this symptom with that of guilt, "people are saying that I am wicked."

21. Obsessional Symptoms (0–2)

These should be differentiated from preoccupations with depressive thoughts, ideas of guilt, hypochondriacal preoccupations and paranoid thinking. Patients usually have to be encouraged to admit to these symptoms, but their statements should be checked carefully. True obsessional thoughts are recognized by the patient as coming from his own mind, as being alien to his normal outlook and feelings, and as causing great anxiety; he always struggles against them.

The Rating of Female Patients

The same general principles apply to the rating of women as of men, but there are special problems which need to be considered in detail.

1. Depression (0–4)

It is generally believed that women weep more readily than men, but there is little evidence that this is true in the case of depressive illness. There is no reason to believe, at the moment, that an assessment of the frequency of weeping could be misleading when rating the intensity of depression in women.

* * * * *

7. Work and interests (0–4)

Most women are housewives and therefore their work can be varied, both in quantity and intensity, to suit themselves. Women do not often complain of work being an effort, but they say they have to take things easily, or neglect some of their work. Other members of the family may have to increase the help they give. It is rare for a housewife to stop looking after her home completely. If she has an additional job outside the home she may have to change it to part-time, or reduce her hours of work or even give it up completely. Women engage in hobbies less frequently than men. Loss of interest, therefore, may not be as obvious. Patients may complain of inability to feel affection for their families. This could be rated here, but it could be rated under other symptoms, depending upon its meaning and setting. Care should be taken not to rate it in two places. It is a very valuable and important symptom if the patient mentions it spontaneously but could be very misleading as a reply to a question.

* * * * *

11. Anxiety (Somatic) (0–4)

These last three symptoms appear to be more common in women than in men.

* * * * *

13. Somatic Symptoms (General) (0–2)

It is not uncommon for women to complain of backache and to ascribe it to a pelvic disorder. This symptom requires careful questioning.

14. Loss of Libido (0–2)

In women whose sexual experience is satisfactory, this symptom will appear as increasing frigidity, progressing to active dislike of sexual intercourse. Women who are partially or completely frigid find that their customary toleration of sex also changes to active dislike. It is difficult to rate this symptom in women who have had no sexual experience or, indeed, in widows since loss of libido in women tends to appear not so much as a loss of drive but as a loss of responsiveness. In the absence of adequate information of a pathological change a zero rating should be given.

Disturbed menstruation and amenorrhoea have been described in women suffering from severe depression, but they are very rare. Despite the difficulties in rating, it has been found that the mean score for women is negligibly less than men.

ECDEU Version Used in the Treatment of Depression Collaborative Research Program

Instructions.   Using the key beneath each symptom, please fill in the blank to the far right with the number that best describes that symptom's severity.

1. Depressed Mood (sadness, hopeless, helpless, worthless)   _____
  - 0 = Absent.
  - 1 = These feeling states indicated only on questioning.
  - 2 = These feeling states spontaneously reported verbally.
  - 3 = Communicates feeling states nonverbally—that is, through facial expression, posture, voice, and tendency to weep.
  - 4 = Patient reports VIRTUALLY ONLY these feeling states in his spontaneous verbal and nonverbal communications.

2. Feeling of Guilt   _____
  - 0 = Absent.
  - 1 = Self-reproach, feels he has let people down.
  - 2 = Ideas of guilt or rumination over past errors or sinful deeds.
  - 3 = Present illness is a punishment. Delusions of guilt.
  - 4 = Hears accusatory or denunciatory voices and/or experiences threatening visual hallucinations.

3. Suicide   _____
  - 0 = Absent.
  - 1 = Feels life is not worth living.
  - 2 = Wishes he were dead or any thoughts of possible death to self.
  - 3 = Suicide ideas or gesture.
  - 4 = Attempts at suicide (any serious attempt rates 4).

4. Insomnia Early   _____
  - 0 = No difficulty falling asleep.
  - 1 = Complains of occasional difficulty falling asleep—that is, more than a half hour.
  - 2 = Complains of nightly difficulty falling asleep.

5. Insomnia Middle   _____
  - 0 = No difficulty.
  - 1 = Patient complains of being restless and disturbed during the night.
  - 2 = Waking during the night—any getting out of bed rates 2 (except for purposes of voiding).

6. Insomnia Late   _____
  - 0 = No difficulty.
  - 1 = Waking in early hours of the morning but goes back to sleep.
  - 2 = Unable to fall asleep again if he gets out of bed.

7. Hypersomnia   _____
  - 0 = No difficulty.
  - 1 = Frequently sleeps at least one hour or more (or spends one hour or more in bed) than when not depressed.
  - 2 = Frequently sleeps two or more hours (or spends two or more hours in bed) than when not depressed.

8. Work and activities _____
  0 = No difficulty.
  1 = Thoughts and feelings of incapacity, fatigue, or weakness related to activities: work or hobbies.
  2 = Loss of interest in activity: hobbies or work—either directly reported by patient, or indirect in listlessness, indecision and vacillation (feels he/she has to push self to work or activities).
  3 = Decrease in actual time spent in activities or decrease in productivity.
  4 = Stopped working because of present illness.
9. Retardation (slowness of thought and speech; impaired ability _____
  to concentrate; decreased motor activity)
  0 = Normal speech and thought.
  1 = Slight retardation at interview.
  2 = Obvious retardation at interview.
  3 = Interview difficult.
  4 = Complete stupor.
10. Agitation _____
  0 = None.
  1 = Fidgetiness.
  2 = Playing with hands, hair, etc.
  3 = Moving about, can't sit still.
  4 = Handwringing, nail-biting, hair-pulling, biting of lips.
11. Anxiety Psychic _____
  0 = No difficulty.
  1 = Subjective tension and irritability.
  2 = Worrying about minor matters.
  3 = Apprehensive attitude apparent in face or speech.
  4 = Fears expressed without questioning.
12. Anxiety Somatic (physiological concomitants of anxiety such as: _____
  Gastrointestinal—dry mouth, wind, indigestion, diarrhea, cramps, belching Cardiovascular—palpitations, headaches Respiratory—hyperventilation, sighing; Urinary frequency; Sweating)
  0 = Absent.
  1 = Mild.
  2 = Moderate.
  3 = Severe.
  4 = Incapacitating.
13. Somatic Symptoms Gastrointestinal _____
  0 = None.
  1 = Loss of appetite but eating without encouragement. Heavy feeling in abdomen.
  2 = Difficulty eating without urging. Requests or requires laxatives or medication for bowels or medication for G.I. symptoms.
14. Increased Appetite _____
  0 = Not present.
  1 = Mild to moderate increase in hunger, increased eating.
  2 = Hungry all the time, uncontrolled eating.

15. Somatic Symptoms General   _____
    0 = None.
    1 = Heaviness in limbs, back, or head. Backaches, headaches, muscle aches. Loss of energy and fatigability.
    2 = Any clear-cut symptom rates 2.

16. Genital Symptoms (symptoms such as: loss of libido, menstrual   _____
disturbances)
    0 = Absent.
    1 = Mild.
    2 = Severe.

17. Hypochondriasis   _____
    0 = Not present.
    1 = Self-absorption (bodily).
    2 = Preoccupation with health.
    3 = Frequent complaints, requests for help, etc.
    4 = Hypochondriacal delusions.

18. Loss of Weight   _____
    0 = No weight loss.
    1 = Probable weight loss associated with present illness.
    2 = Definite (according to patient) weight loss.

19. Weight Gain   _____
    0 = No weight gain.
    1 = Probable weight gain associated with present illness.
    2 = Definite (according to patient) weight gain.

20. Insight   _____
    0 = Acknowledges being depressed and ill (or no longer depressed).
    1 = Acknowledges illness but attributes cause to bad food, climate, overwork, virus, need for rest, etc.
    2 = Denies being ill at all

21. Diurnal Variation
    A. Note whether symptoms are worse in morning or evening. If NO diurnal variation, record "0"   _____
        0 = No variation.
        1 = Worse in A.M.
        2 = Worse in P.M.
    B. When present, mark the severity of the variation. Record "0" if NO variation   _____
        0 = None.
        1 = Mild.
        2 = Severe.

22. Depersonalization and Derealization (such as feelings of unreality, nihilistic ideas)   _____
    0 = Absent.
    1 = Mild.
    2 = Moderate.
    3 = Severe.
    4 = Incapacitating.

23. Paranoid Symptoms _____

   0 = None.

   1 = Suspicious.

   2 = Ideas of reference.

   3 = Delusions of reference and persecution.

24. Obsessional and Compulsive Symptoms _____

   0 = Absent.

   1 = Mild.

   2 = Severe.

25. Helplessness _____

   0 = Not present.

   1 = Subjective feelings which are elicited only by inquiry.

   2 = Patient volunteers his helpless feelings.

   3 = Requires urging, guidance, and reassurance to accomplish work, household, and other chores.

   4 = Despite urging, does not perform necessary chores because of feelings of helplessness.

26. Hopelessness _____

   0 = Not present.

   1 = Intermittently doubts that "things will improve," but can be reassured.

   2 = Consistently feels "hopeless" but accepts reassurance.

   3 = Expresses feelings of discouragement, despair, pessimism regarding the future which cannot be dispelled.

   4 = Spontaneously and inappropriately perseverates, "I'll never get well" or equivalent.

27. Worthlessness—Ranges from mild loss of esteem, feelings of inferiority, self-depreciation to feelings of total worthlessness _____

   0 = Not present.

   1 = Indicates feelings of worthlessness (loss of self-esteem) only on questioning.

   2 = Spontaneously indicates feelings of worthlessness (loss of self-esteem).

   3 = Different from "2" by degree: patient volunteers that he/she is "no good," "inferior," etc.

   4 = Expresses feelings of total worthlessness—e.g., "I'm a heap of garbage" or its equivalent.

The ECDEU version of the scale printed here includes anchor points developed in the NIMH Early Clinical Drug Evaluation Program and items on hypersomnia, increased appetite, and weight gain added from the NIMH Treatment of Depression Collaborative Research Program. The ECDEU scale has most often been scored in either the seventeen item version (# 1–20, excluding hypersomnia, increased appetite, and weight gain) or as a 20-item scale (the 17-item version plus items 22 through 24 as printed here). Research with the scale should specify which version was used.

Carroll Rating Scale for Depression

Complete *all* the following statements by *circling yes* or *no,* based on how you have felt during the *past few days.*

1.	I feel just as energetic as always.*	Yes	No
2.	I am losing weight.	Yes	No
3.	I have dropped many of my interests and activities.	Yes	No
4.	Since my illness I have completely lost interest in sex.	Yes	No
5.	I am especially concerned about how my body is functioning.	Yes	No
6.	It must be obvious that I am disturbed and agitated.	Yes	No
7.	I am still able to carry on doing the work I am supposed to do.*	Yes	No
8.	I can concentrate easily when reading the papers.*	Yes	No
9.	Getting to sleep takes me more than half an hour.	Yes	No
10.	I am restless and fidgety.	Yes	No
11.	I wake up much earlier than I need to in the morning.	Yes	No
12.	Dying is the best solution for me.	Yes	No
13.	I have a lot of trouble with dizziness and faint feelings.	Yes	No
14.	I am being punished for something bad in my past.	Yes	No
15.	My sexual interest is the same as before I got sick.*	Yes	No
16.	I am miserable and often feel like crying.	Yes	No
17.	I often wish I were dead.	Yes	No
18.	I am having trouble with indigestion.	Yes	No
19.	I wake up often in the middle of the night.	Yes	No
20.	I feel worthless and ashamed about myself.	Yes	No
21.	I am so slowed down that I need help with bathing and dressing.	Yes	No
22.	I take longer than usual to fall asleep at night.	Yes	No
23.	Much of the time I am very afraid but don't know the reason.	Yes	No
24.	Things which I regret about my life are bothering me.	Yes	No
25.	I get pleasure and satisfaction from what I do.*	Yes	No
26.	All I need is a good rest to be perfectly well again.	Yes	No

Reprinted by permission of Bernard J. Carroll and the *British Journal of Psychiatry.*

27.	My sleep is restless and disturbed.	Yes	No
28.	My mind is as fast and alert as always.*	Yes	No
29.	I feel that life is still worth living.*	Yes	No
30.	My voice is dull and lifeless.	Yes	No
31.	I feel irritable or jittery.	Yes	No
32.	I feel in good spirits.*	Yes	No
33.	My heart sometimes beats faster than usual.	Yes	No
34.	I think my case is hopeless.	Yes	No
35.	I wake up before my usual time in the morning.	Yes	No
36.	I still enjoy my meals as much as usual.*	Yes	No
37.	I have to keep pacing around most of the time.	Yes	No
38.	I am terrified and near panic.	Yes	No
39.	My body is bad and rotten inside.	Yes	No
40.	I got sick because of the bad weather we have been having.	Yes	No
41.	My hands shake so much that people can easily notice.	Yes	No
42.	I still like to go out and meet people.*	Yes	No
43.	I think I appear calm on the outside.*	Yes	No
44.	I think I am as good a person as anybody else.*	Yes	No
45.	My trouble is the result of some serious internal disease.	Yes	No
46.	I have been thinking about trying to kill myself.	Yes	No
47.	I get hardly anything done lately.	Yes	No
48.	There is only misery in the future for me.	Yes	No
49.	I worry a lot about my bodily symptoms.	Yes	No
50.	I have to force myself to eat even a little.	Yes	No
51.	I am exhausted much of the time.	Yes	No
52.	I can tell that I have lost a lot of weight.	Yes	No

---

* Reverse items.

Rosenbaum Self-Control Schedule

Directions

Indicate how characteristic or descriptive each of the following statements is of you by using the code given below.

> +3 = Very characteristic of me, extremely descriptive.
> +2 = Rather characteristic of me, quite descriptive.
> +1 = Somewhat characteristic of me, slightly descriptive.
> −1 = Somewhat uncharacteristic of me, slightly undescriptive.
> −2 = Rather uncharacteristic of me, quite undescriptive.
> −3 = Very uncharacteristic of me, extremely nondescriptive.

1. When I do a boring job, I think about the less boring parts of the job and the reward that I will receive once I am finished.
2. When I have to do something that is anxiety arousing for me, I try to visualize how I will overcome my anxieties while doing it.
3. Often by changing my way of thinking, I am able to change my feelings about almost everything.
4. I often find it difficult to overcome my feelings of nervousness and tension without any outside help.*
5. When I am feeling depressed I try to think about pleasant events.
6. I cannot avoid thinking about mistakes I have made in the past.*
7. When I am faced with a difficult problem, I try to approach its solution in a systematic way.
8. I usually do my duties quicker when somebody is pressuring me.*
9. When I am faced with a difficult decision, I prefer to postpone making a decision even if all the facts are at my disposal.*
10. When I find that I have difficulties in concentrating on my reading, I look for ways to increase my concentration.
11. When I plan to work, I remove all the things that are not relevant to my work.
12. When I try to get rid of a bad habit, I first try to find out all the factors that maintain this habit.

Used with permission of Michael Rosenbaum.

13. When an unpleasant thought is bothering me, I try to think about something pleasant.
14. If I would smoke two packages of cigarettes a day, I probably would need outside help to stop smoking.*
15. When I am in a low mood, I try to act cheerful so my mood will change.
16. If I had the pills with me, I would take a tranquilizer whenever I felt tense and nervous.*
17. When I am depressed, I try to keep myself busy with things that I like.
18. I tend to postpone unpleasant duties even if I could perform them immediately.*
19. I need outside help to get rid of some of my bad habits.*
20. When I find it difficult to settle down and do a certain job, I look for ways to help me settle down.
21. Although it makes me feel bad, I cannot avoid thinking about all kinds of possible catastrophies in the future.*
22. First of all, I prefer to finish a job that I have to do and then start doing things I really like.
23. When I feel pain in a certain part of my body, I try not to think about it.
24. My self-esteem increases once I am able to overcome a bad habit.
25. In order to overcome bad feelings that accompany failure, I often tell myself that it is not so catastrophic and that I can do something about it.
26. When I feel that I am too impulsive, I tell myself "stop and think before you do anything."
27. Even when I am terribly angry at somebody, I consider my actions very carefully.
28. Facing the need to make a decision, I usually find out all the possible alternatives instead of deciding quickly and spontaneously.
29. Usually I do first the things that I really like to do even if there are more urgent things to do.*
30. When I realize that I cannot help but be late for an important meeting, I tell myself to keep calm.
31. When I feel pain in my body, I try to divert my thoughts from it.
32. I usually plan my work when faced with a number of things to do.
33. When I am short of money, I decide to record all my expenses in order to plan more carefully for the future.
34. If I find it difficult to concentrate on a certain job, I divide the job into smaller segments.
35. Quite often I cannot overcome unpleasant thoughts that bother me.*
36. Once I am hungry and unable to eat, I try to divert my thoughts away from my stomach or try to imagine that I am satisfied.

---

* Reverse items.

Dysfunctional Attitude Scale (Form A)

This Inventory lists different attitudes or beliefs which people sometimes hold. Read *each* statement carefully and decide how much you agree or disagree with the statement.

For each of the attitudes, show your answer by placing a check mark ($\sqrt{}$) under the column that *best describes how you think*. Be sure to choose only one answer for each attitude. Because people are different, there is no right or wrong answer to these statements.

To decide whether a given attitude is typical of your way of looking at things, simply keep in mind what you are like *most of the time*.

EXAMPLE

Attitudes	Totally Agree	Agree very much	Agree slightly	Neutral	Disagree slightly	Disagree very much	Totally disagree
1. Most people are OK once you get to know them.			$\sqrt{}$				

Look at the example above. To show how much a sentence describes your attitude, you can check any point from totally agree to totally disagree. In the above example, the check mark at "agree slightly" indicates that this statement is somewhat typical of the attitudes held by the person completing the inventory.

Remember that your answer should describe the way you think *most of the time*.

NOW TURN THE PAGE AND BEGIN

DAS

Attitudes	Totally agree	Agree very much	Agree slightly	Neutral	Disagree slightly	Disagree very much	Totally disagree
REMEMBER, ANSWER EACH STATEMENT ACCORDING TO THE WAY YOU THINK *MOST OF THE TIME.*							
1. It is difficult to be happy unless one is good looking, intelligent, rich, and creative.							
2. Happiness is more a matter of my attitude toward myself than the way other people feel about me.							
3. People will probably think less of me if I make a mistake.							
4. If I do not do well all the time, people will not respect me.							
5. Taking even a small risk is foolish because the loss is likely to be a disaster.							
6. It is possible to gain another person's respect without being especially talented at anything.							
7. I cannot be happy unless most people I know admire me.							
8. If a person asks for help, it is a sign of weakness.							
9. If I do not do as well as other people, it means I am an inferior human being.							
10. If I fail at my work, then I am a failure as a person.							
11. If you cannot do something well, there is little point in doing it at all.							
12. Making mistakes is fine because I can learn from them.							
13. If someone disagrees with me, it probably indicates he does not like me.							
14. If I fail partly, it is as bad as being a complete failure.							
15. If other people know what you are really like, they will think less of you.							
16. I am nothing if a person I love doesn't love me.							
17. One can get pleasure from an activity regardless of the end result.							

DAS (continued)

Attitudes	Totally Agree	Agree very much	Agree slightly	Neutral	Disagree slightly	Disagree very much	Totally disagree
18. People should have a reasonable likelihood of success before undertaking anything.							
19. My value as a person depends greatly on what others think of me.							
20. If I don't set the highest standards for myself, I am likely to end up a second-rate person.							
21. If I am to be a worthwhile person, I must be truly outstanding in at least one major respect.							
22. People who have good ideas are more worthy than those who do not.							
23. I should be upset if I make a mistake.							
24. My own opinions of myself are more important than other's opinions of me.							
25. To be a good, moral, worthwhile person, I must help everyone who needs it.							
26. If I ask a question, it makes me look inferior.							
27. It is awful to be disapproved of by people important to you.							
28. If you don't have other people to lean on, you are bound to be sad.							
29. I can reach important goals without slave driving myself.							
30. It is possible for a person to be scolded and not get upset.							
31. I cannot trust other people because they might be cruel to me.							
32. If others dislike you, you cannot be happy.							
33. It is best to give up your own interests in order to please other people.							
34. My happiness depends more on other people than it does on me.							

DAS (*continued*)

Attitudes	Totally Agree	Agree very much	Agree slightly	Neutral	Disagree slightly	Disagree very much	Totally disagree
35. I do not need the approval of other people in order to be happy.							
36. If a person avoids problems, the problems tend to go away.							
37. I can be happy even if I miss out on many of the good things in life.							
38. What other people think about me is very important.							
39. Being isolated from others is bound to lead to unhappiness.							
40. I can find happiness without being loved by another person.							

DAS Scoring

1. Every item on the DAS (Form A or Form B) is scored from one to seven. Depending on the content, either totally agree or totally disagree will be the anchor point of one and each category from that point will be one more; that is, if totally agree = +1 then the next category, agree very much, will be = +2, and so on to totally disagree which will be = +7.

2. The following items are scored in the adaptive way if a "totally agree response" is given:

Form A (No.)		Form B (No.)	
2	29	1	20
6	30	5	26
12	35	12	30
17	37	14	33
24	40	19	36

That is, totally agree = +1; agree very much = +2; agree slightly = +3; neutral = +4; disagree slightly = +5; disagree very much = +6; totally disagree = +7.

3. All the other items on Form A and Form B of the DAS are scored in the reverse direction of what was stated in number 2 above; that is, totally disagree = +1; . . . totally agree = +7.

4. The total score on DAS-A or DAS-B is obtained by summing the item scores for each individual.

5. Omits have been coded as zero (missing data). However, if by some chance, the individual omits a large proportion of the items, the test should be ignored.

The alternate form of the DAS, Form B, may be obtained from Dr. Arlene Weissman, at Towers, Perrin, Forster, & Crosby, 1500 Market Street, Philadelphia, PA 19102-2183.

Pleasant Events Schedule Form III-S

This schedule is designed to find out about the things you have enjoyed during the past month. The schedule contains a list of events or activities which people sometimes enjoy. You will be asked to go over the list twice, the first time rating each event on how many times it has happened in the past month and the second time rating each event on how pleasant it has been for you. There are no right or wrong answers.

Please rate every event. Work quickly; there are many items and you will not be asked to make fine distinctions on your ratings. The schedule should take about an hour to complete. Please make your ratings on the answer sheets provided. You should find two of them. Use the answer sheet labeled A to answer Question A; use the sheet labeled B to answer Question B. When you mark the answer sheet, be very careful to completely fill the little box corresponding to your rating. Use only a soft pencil, and erase completely any answers you have changed.

Directions—Question A

On the following pages you will find a list of activities, events, and experiences. *How often have these events happened in your life in the past month?* Please answer this question by rating each item on the following scale:

0 = This has *not* happened in the past 30 days.
1 = This has happened *a few times* (1 to 6) in the past 30 days.
2 = This has happened *often* (7 or more) in the past 30 days.

Place your rating for each item on the answer sheet labeled A.
Here is an example:

Item 1 is "Being in the country." Suppose that you have been in the country three times during the past 30 days. Then you would mark a 1 on the answer sheet in the row of boxes for item number 1. On answer sheet A your mark would look like this:

1.   0   1   2
    ☐   ■   ☐

Important

Some items will list *more than one event*; for these items, mark how often you have done *any* of the listed events. For example, item 12 is "Doing art work (painting, sculpture, drawing, movie-making, etc.)". You should rate item 12 on how often you have done *any* form of artwork in the past month.

Since this list contains events that might happen to a wide variety of people, you may find many of the events have not happened to you in the past 30 days. It is not expected that anyone will have done all of these things in one month.

Now begin.

1. Being in the country.
2. Wearing expensive or formal clothes.
3. Making contributions to religious, charitable, or other groups.
4. Talking about sports.
5. Meeting someone new of the same sex.
6. Taking tests when well prepared.
7. Going to a rock concert.
8. Playing baseball or softball.
9. Planning trips or vacations.
10. Buying things for myself.
11. Being at the beach.
12. Doing artwork (painting, sculpture, drawing, movie-making, etc.)
13. Rock climbing or mountaineering.
14. Reading the Scriptures or other sacred works.
15. Playing golf.
16. Taking part in military activities.
17. Rearranging or redecorating my room or house.
18. Going naked.
19. Going to a sports event.
20. Reading a "How to Do It" book or article.
21. Going to the races (horse, car, boat, etc.)
22. Reading stories, novels, poems, or plays.
23. Going to a bar, tavern, club, etc.
24. Going to lectures or hearing speakers.
25. Driving skillfully.
26. Breathing clean air.
27. Thinking up or arranging songs or music.
28. Getting drunk.
29. Saying something clearly.
30. Boating (canoeing, kyaking, motorboating, sailing, etc.).
31. Pleasing my parents.
32. Restoring antiques, refinishing furniture, etc.
33. Watching TV.
34. Talking to myself.
35. Camping.
36. Working in politics.
37. Working on machines, (cars, bikes, motorcycles, tractors, etc.).
38. Thinking about something good in the future.
39. Playing cards.
40. Completing a difficult task.
41. Laughing.
42. Solving a problem, puzzle, crossword, etc.
43. Being at weddings, baptisms, confirmations, etc.
44. Criticizing someone.
45. Shaving.
46. Having lunch with friends or associates.
47. Taking powerful drugs.
48. Playing tennis.
49. Taking a shower.
50. Driving long distances.
51. Woodworking, carpentry.
52. Writing stories, novels, plays, or poetry.
53. Being with animals.
54. Riding in an airplane.

55. Exploring (hiking away from known routes, spelunking, etc.).
56. Having a frank and open conversation.
57. Singing in a group.
58. Thinking about myself or my problems.
59. Working on my job.
60. Going to a party.
61. Going to church functions (socials, classes, bazaars, etc.).
62. Speaking a foreign language.
63. Going to service, civic, or social club meetings.
64. Going to a business meeting or convention.
65. Being in a sporty or expensive car.
66. Playing a musical instrument.
67. Making snacks.
68. Snow skiing.
69. Being helped.
70. Wearing informal clothes.
71. Combing or brushing my hair.
72. Acting.
73. Taking a nap.
74. Being with friends.
75. Canning, freezing, making preserves, etc.
76. Driving fast.
77. Solving a personal problem.
78. Being in a city.
79. Taking a bath.
80. Singing to myself.
81. Making food or crafts to sell or give away.
82. Playing pool or billiards.
83. Being with my grandchildren.
84. Playing chess or checkers.
85. Doing craft work (pottery, jewelry, leather, beads, weaving, etc.).
86. Weighing myself.
87. Scratching myself.
88. Putting on makeup, fixing my hair, etc.
89. Designing or drafting.
90. Visiting people who are sick, shut in, or in trouble.

91. Cheering, rooting.
92. Bowling.
93. Being popular at a gathering.
94. Watching wild animals.
95. Having an original idea.
96. Gardening, landscaping, or doing yard work.
97. Shoplifting.
98. Reading essays or technical, academic, or professional literature.
99. Wearing new clothes.
100. Dancing.
101. Sitting in the sun.
102. Riding a motorcycle.
103. Just sitting and thinking.
104. Social drinking.
105. Seeing good things happen to my family or friends.
106. Going to a fair, carnival, circus, zoo, or amusement park.
107. Talking about philosophy, or religion.
108. Gambling.
109. Planning or organizing something.
110. Smoking marijuana.
111. Having a drink by myself.
112. Listening to the sounds of nature.
113. Dating, courting, etc.
114. Having a lively talk.
115. Racing in a car, motorcycle, boat, etc.
116. Listening to the radio.
117. Having friends come to visit.
118. Playing in a sporting competition.
119. Introducing people who I think would like each other.
120. Giving gifts.
121. Going to school or government meetings, court sessions, etc.
122. Getting massages or back rubs.
123. Getting letters, cards, or notes.
124. Watching the sky, clouds, or a storm.
125. Going on outings (to the park, a picnic, or a barbecue, etc.).
126. Playing basketball.

127. Buying something for my family.
128. Photography.
129. Giving a speech or lecture.
130. Reading maps.
131. Gathering natural objects (wild foods or fruit, rocks, driftwood, etc.).
132. Working on my finances.
133. Wearing clean clothes.
134. Making a major purchase or investment (car, appliance, house, stocks, etc.).
135. Helping someone.
136. Being in the mountains.
137. Getting a job advancement (being promoted, given a raise, or offered a better job, accepted into a better school, etc.).
138. Hearing jokes.
139. Winning a bet.
140. Talking about my children or grandchildren.
141. Meeting someone new of the opposite sex.
142. Going to a revival or crusade.
143. Talking about my health.
144. Seeing beautiful scenery.
145. Eating good meals.
146. Improving my health (having my teeth fixed, getting new glasses, changing my diet, etc.).
147. Being downtown.
148. Wrestling or boxing.
149. Hunting or shooting.
150. Playing in a musical group.
151. Hiking.
152. Going to a museum or exhibit.
153. Writing papers, essays, articles, reports, memos, etc.
154. Doing a job well.
155. Having spare time.
156. Fishing.
157. Loaning something.
158. Being noticed as sexually attractive.
159. Pleasing employers, teachers, etc.
160. Counseling someone.
161. Going to a health club, sauna bath, etc.
162. Having someone criticize me.
163. Learning to do something new.
164. Going to a "Drive-in" (Dairy Queen, MacDonald's, etc.).
165. Complimenting or praising someone.
166. Thinking about people I like.
167. Being at a fraternity or sorority.
168. Taking revenge on someone.
169. Being with my parents.
170. Horseback riding.
171. Protesting social, political, or environmental conditions.
172. Talking on the telephone.
173. Having daydreams.
174. Kicking leaves, sand, pebbles, etc.
175. Playing lawn sports (badminton, croquet, shuffleboard, horseshoes, etc.).
176. Going to school reunions, alumni meetings, etc.
177. Seeing famous people.
178. Going to the movies.
179. Kissing.
180. Being alone.
181. Budgeting my time.
182. Cooking meals.
183. Being praised by people I admire.
184. Outwitting a "superior."
185. Feeling the presence of the Lord in my life.
186. Doing a project in my own way.
187. Doing "odd jobs" around the house.
188. Crying.
189. Being told I am needed.
190. Being at a family reunion or get-together.
191. Giving a party or get-together.
192. Washing my hair.
193. Coaching someone.
194. Going to a restaurant.
195. Seeing or smelling a flower or plant.
196. Being invited out.

197. Receiving honors (civic, military, etc.).
198. Using cologne, perfume, or after-shave.
199. Having someone agree with me.
200. Reminiscing, talking about old times.
201. Getting up early in the morning.
202. Having peace and quiet.
203. Doing experiments or other scientific work.
204. Visiting friends.
205. Writing in a diary.
206. Playing football.
207. Being counseled.
208. Saying prayers.
209. Giving massages or back rubs.
210. Hitchhiking.
211. Meditating or doing yoga.
212. Seeing a fight.
213. Doing favors for people.
214. Talking with people on the job or in class.
215. Being relaxed.
216. Being asked for my help or advice.
217. Thinking about other people's problems.
218. Playing board games (Monopoly, Scrabble, etc.).
219. Sleeping soundly at night.
220. Doing heavy outdoor work (cutting or chopping wood, clearing land, farm work, etc.).
221. Reading the newspaper.
222. Shocking people, swearing, making obscene gestures, etc.
223. Snowmobiling or dune-buggy riding.
224. Being in a body-awareness, sensitivity, encounter, therapy, or "rap" group.
225. Dreaming at night.
226. Playing Ping-Pong.
227. Brushing my teeth.
228. Swimming.
229. Being in a fight.
230. Running, jogging, or doing gymnastic, fitness, or field exercises.
231. Walking barefoot.
232. Playing frisbee or catch.
233. Doing housework or laundry; cleaning things.
234. Being with my roommate.
235. Listening to music.
236. Arguing.
237. Knitting, crocheting, embroidery, or fancy needlework.
238. Petting, necking.
239. Amusing people.
240. Talking about sex.
241. Going to a barber or beautician.
242. Having house guests.
243. Being with someone I love.
244. Reading magazines.
245. Sleeping late.
246. Starting a new project.
247. Being stubborn.
248. Having sexual relations with a partner of the opposite sex.
249. Having other sexual satisfactions.
250. Going to the library.
251. Playing soccer, rugby, hockey, lacrosse, etc.
252. Preparing a new or special food.
253. Bird-watching.
254. Shopping.
255. Watching people.
256. Building or watching a fire.
257. Winning an argument.
258. Selling or trading something.
259. Finishing a project or task.
260. Confessing or apologizing.
261. Repairing things.
262. Working with others as a team.
263. Bicycling.
264. Telling people what to do.
265. Being with happy people.
266. Playing party games.
267. Writing letters, cards, or notes.
268. Talking about politics or public affairs.
269. Asking for help or advice.

270. Going to banquets, luncheons, potlucks, etc.
271. Talking about my hobby or special interest.
272. Watching attractive women or men.
273. Smiling at people.
274. Playing in sand, a stream, the grass, etc.
275. Talking about other people.
276. Being with my husband or wife.
277. Having people show interest in what I have said.
278. Going on field trips, nature walks, etc.
279. Expressing my love to someone.
280. Smoking tobacco.
281. Caring for houseplants.
282. Having coffee, tea, a coke, etc., with friends.
283. Taking a walk.
284. Collecting things.
285. Playing handball, paddleball, squash, etc.
286. Sewing.
287. Suffering for a good cause.
288. Remembering a departed friend or loved one, visiting the cemetery.
289. Doing things with children.
290. Beach-combing.
291. Being complimented or told I have done well.
292. Being told I am loved.
293. Eating snacks.
294. Staying up late.

295. Having family members or friends do something that makes me proud of them.
296. Being with my children.
297. Going to auctions, garage sales, etc.
298. Thinking about an interesting question.
ing on community service projects.
300. Water skiing, surfing, scuba diving.
301. Receiving money.
302. Defending or protecting someone; stopping fraud or abuse.
303. Hearing a good sermon.
304. Picking up a hitchhiker.
305. Winning a competition.
306. Making a new friend.
307. Talking about my job or school.
308. Reading cartoons, comic strips, or comic books.
309. Borrowing something.
310. Traveling with a group.
311. Seeing old friends.
312. Teaching someone.
313. Using my strength.
314. Traveling.
315. Going to office parties or departmental get-togethers.
316. Attending a concert, opera, or ballet.
317. Playing with pets.
318. Going to a play.
319. Looking at the stars or moon.
320. Being coached.

STOP

If you have just gone through the list for the first time, follow the directions for Question B.

If you have just finished answering Question B you have completed the test.

Directions—Question B

Now please go over the list once again. This time the question is: *How pleasant, enjoyable, or rewarding was each event during the past month?* Please answer this question by rating each event on the following scale:

0 = This was *not* pleasant. (Use this rating for events which were either neutral or unpleasant.)

1 = This was *somewhat* pleasant. (Use this rating for events which were mildly or moderately pleasant.)

2 = This was *very* pleasant. (Use this rating for events which were strongly or extremely pleasant.)

Important

If an event has happened to you *more than once* in the past month, try to rate roughly how pleasant it was *on the average.*

If an event has not happened to you during the past month, then rate it according to how much fun you think it would have been.

When an item lists *more than one event,* rate it on the events *you have actually done.* (If you haven't done any of the events in such an item, give it the average rating of the events in that item which you would like to have done.)

Place your rating for each event on the answer sheet labeled B. Here is an example:

Event number 1 is "Being in the country." Suppose that each time you were in the country in the past 30 days you enjoyed it a great deal. Then you would rate this event "2", since it was "very pleasant." On answer sheet B your mark would look like this:

1.   0   1   2
     ☐   ☐   ■

The list of items may have some events which you would not enjoy. The list was made for a wide variety of people, and it is not expected that one person would enjoy all of them.

Now go back to the list of events, start with item 1, and go through the entire list rating each event on *roughly how pleasant it was (or would have been) during the past 30 days.* Please be sure that you rate each item and that your marks completely fill the boxes on the answer sheet.

A Selected Listing
of Other Depression Inventories
and Depression-Related Instruments
for Adults

Attributional Style Questionnaire (ASQ)

The ASQ is designed to assess habitual ways that individuals construe causality. It is divided into six good and six bad scenes for which subjects provide a cause if this event were to happen to them. The cause is then rated along the dimensions of internality, stability, and globality.

Address Where It May Be Obtained
Martin E. P. Seligman, Ph.D., Department of Psychology, University of Pennsylvania, 3813 Walnut Street, Philadelphia, Pennsylvania 19104.

Restrictions on Availability
The scale is available for use by qualified investigators.

Reference
Peterson, C., Semmel, A., von Baeyer, C., Abramson, L. Y., Metalsky, G. I., & Seligman, M. E. P. (1982). The Attributional Style Questionnaire. *Cognitive Therapy and Research, 6,* 287–300.

Automatic Thoughts Questionnaire (ATQ)

The ATQ is a 30-item instrument developed by having unselected college students report their ruminations the last time they were "depressed." Reported ruminations were then cross-validated in a psychometrically identified sample of depressed college students. Each cognition is rated for frequency of occurrence on a 1 to 5 scale, with total scores generated by summing over the 30 items. The measure provides an index of frequency of depressotypic ruminations. The scale is printed in:
Hollon, S. D., & Kendall, P. C. (1980). Cognitive self-statements in depression: Development of an Automatic Thoughts Questionnaire. *Cognitive Therapy and Research, 4,* 383–396.

Center for Epidemiological Studies Depression Scale (CES-D)

This is a 20-item self-report scale of symptoms of depression, scaled by frequency of occurrence during the "past week." It is suitable for use in general populations and can be self-administered or scored by an interviewer.

Address Where It May Be Obtained
Lenore Radloff or Anita Green, National Institute of Mental Health, 5600 Fishers Lane, Room 18-105, Rockville, Md. 20857.

Cost
None.

Restrictions on availability
None.

References
Radloff, L. S. (1977). The CES-D Scale: A self-report depression scale for research in the general population. *Applied Psychological Measurement, 1,* 385–401.

Radloff, L. S., & Locke, B. Z. (in press). The Community Mental Health Assessment Survey and the CES-D Scale. In M. Weissman, J. Myers, & C. Ross (Eds.), *Community surveys.* New Brunswick: Rutgers University.

Cognitive Bias Questionnaire (CBQ)

This instrument is designed to test Beck's hypotheses regarding negativistic cognitive bias in interpreting information about the self, the world, and the future. Six vignettes are presented with questions about interpretation, and each gives response options representing depressed or nondepressed and biased or nonbiased cognitions. Research has supported its use in discriminating between depressed and nondepressed samples.

Address Where It May Be Obtained
Dr. Constance Hammen, Department of Psychology, University of California, Los Angeles, California 90024.

Cost
Free.

Restrictions on Availability
None.

References
Krantz, S., & Hammen, C. (1979). The assessment of cognitive bias in depression. *Journal of Abnormal Psychology, 88,* 611–619.

Blaney, P., Behar, V., & Head, R. (1980). Two measures of depressive cognitions: Their association with depression and with each other. *Journal of Abnormal Psychology, 89,* 678–682.

Cognitive Response Test (CRT)

The CRT was developed to assess clients' immediate thoughts that occur in conjunction with potentially depressogenic situations. The person responds to 36 open-ended vignettes by writing his/her first thought. The test discriminates depressed subjects who have high and low levels of irrational-depressed cognitions.

Address Where It May Be Obtained
John T. Watkins, Ph.D., Department of Psychiatry and Behavioral Sciences, University of Oklahoma Health Sciences Center, P.O. Box 26901, 5SP 464, Oklahoma City, Oklahoma 73190.

Cost
$4.00.

Restrictions on Availability
None.

References
Watkins, J. T., & Rush, A. J. (1983). Cognitive Response Test. *Cognitive Therapy and Research, 7,* 425–436.

Coping Strategies Scales (COSTS)

The Coping Strategies Scales consist of 10 subscales and 142 items designed to measure ways in which people respond to their depression. Scales include blame, emotional expression, emotional containment, social support seeking, religious coping, philosophical/cognitive restructuring, general activity, avoidance/denial, problem solving, and passivity.

Address Where It May Be Obtained
E. E. Beckham, Ph.D., Department of Psychiatry and Behavioral Sciences, University of Oklahoma Health Sciences Center, P.O. Box 26901, Oklahoma City, Oklahoma 73190.

Cost
Free.

Restrictions on Availability
None.

References
Beckham, E. E., & Adams, R. L. (1984). Coping behavior in depression: Report on a new scale. *Behaviour Research and Therapy, 22,* 71–75.

Depression Adjective Checklists (DACL)

The DACL are self-report objective measures of depressive mood, or affect. There are state ("today") and trait ("in general") versions. There is one set of four equivalent forms (32 adjectives each) and another set of three equivalent forms (34 adjectives each).

Address Where It May Be Obtained
EdITS, P.O. Box 7234, San Diego, California 92107.

Cost
Check with EdITS for cost and user qualifications.

References
Lubin, B. (1965). Adjective checklists for the measurement of depression. *Archives of General Psychiatry, 12,* 57–62.

Lubin, B. (1981). *Depression Adjective Checklists: Manual* (2nd ed.). San Diego: Educational and Industrial Testing Service.

Geriatric Depression Scale (GDS)

The GDS was specifically created for aged subjects. It was designed to be simple to administer, reliable, and valid with an elderly population. The test consists of 30 yes/no items which may be administered orally or in writing.

Address Where It May Be Obtained
T. L. Brink, 1044 Sylvan, San Carlos, California 94070.

Cost
Free.

Restrictions on Availability
None.

References
Brink, T. L., Yesavage, J. A., Lum, O., Heersema, P., Adey, M., & Rose, T. L. (1982). Screening tests for geriatric depression. *Clinical Gerontologist, 1,* 37–43.

Yesavage, J. A., Brink, T. L., Rose, T. L., Lum, O., Huang, V., Adey, M., & Leirer, V. O. (1983). Development and validation of a geriatric depression screening scale. *Journal of Psychiatric Research, 17,* 37–49.

Hopelessness Scale (HS)

The Hopelessness Scale consists of 20 items about one's personal future which subjects answer as true or false. The scale is often used as a measure of pessimism and hopefulness, especially in suicide research.

Address Where It May Be Obtained
Center for Cognitive Therapy, 133 South 36th Street, Philadelphia, Pennsylvania 19104.

Cost
Check with the Center for Cognitive Therapy for cost and user qualifications.

References
Beck, A. T., Weissman, A., Lester, D., & Trexler, L. (1974). The measurement of pessimism: The Hopelessness Scale. *Journal of Consulting and Clinical Psychology, 42,* 861–865.

Irrational Beliefs Test (IBT)

The Irrational Beliefs Test consists of 100 statements which subjects register degree of agreement or disagreement with on a seven-point Likert scale. There are 10 different scales developed through factor analysis which are aimed at representing Albert Ellis's concepts of "irrational ideas."

Address Where It May Be Obtained
Test Systems International, Ltd., P.O. Box 18347, Wichita, Kansas 67218.

Cost
Specimen set $25. Instruments alone, $75 per hundred.

Restrictions on Availability
The publisher considers this to be a classified instrument according to American Psychological Association standards and requires at least Ph.D. supervision for purchasers.

References
Jones, R. G. (1969). A factored measure of Ellis' irrational belief system, with personality and maladjustment correlates. *Dissertation Abstracts International, 29,* 11–13.

Nelson, R. E. (1977). Irrational beliefs and depression. *Journal of Consulting and Clinical Psychology, 45,* 1190–1191.

Montgomery-Åsberg Depression Rating Scale

This is a clinician-rated instrument covering 10 of the most common symptoms of depression. Items were chosen which were likely to show the greatest change during treatment. All items are rated from 0–6. The scale is published in Montgomery and Åsberg (1979).

Reference
Montgomery, S. A., & Åsberg, M. C. (1979). A new depression scale designed to be sensitive to change. *British Journal of Psychiatry, 134,* 382–389.

Raskin Three-Area Scale

This scale is a clinician-rated instrument measuring depressive symptomatology in the three areas of "verbal report," "behavior," and "secondary symptoms of depression." Each is rated on a five-point scale from 1 = "not at all" to 5 = "very much." The three area scores are summed, producing total scores from 3–15.

Address Where It May Be Obtained
Allen Raskin, Ph.D., Chief of Anxiety Disorders Section, Pharmacologic and Somatic Treatments Research Branch, National Institute of Mental Health, Room 10C06, 5600 Fishers Lane, Rockville, Maryland 20857.

Cost
None.

Restrictions on Availability
None.

References
Raskin, A., Schulterbrandt, J. G., Reatig, N., Crook, T. H., & Odle, D. (1974). Depression subtypes and response to phenelzine, diazepam, and a placebo: Results of a nine-hospital collaborative study. *Archives of General Psychiatry, 30,* 66–75.

Raskin, A., Schulterbrandt, J., Reatig, N., & Rice, C. E. (1967). Factors of psychopathology in interview, ward behavior, and self-report ratings of hospitalized depressives. *Journal of Consulting Psychology, 31,* 270–278.

Symptom Checklist 90-R Depression Scale (SCL-90-R)

The SCL-90-R is composed of nine primary symptom scales, one of which measures depression and is composed of 13 items. Subjects rate each item on a five-point scale for how well the statement describes the patient. Norms are provided in a manual.

Address Where It May Be Obtained

Clinical Psychometric Research, P.O. Box 425, Riderwood, Maryland 21139.

Cost

Tests are $28 per 100. The manual is $15.

Restrictions on Availability

Restricted to qualified professionals in accord with American Psychological Association standards.

References

Derogatis, L. R., & Cleary, P. A. (1977). Confirmation of the dimension structure of the SCL-90: A study in construct validation. *Journal of Clinical Psychology, 33,* 981–989.

Derogatis, L. R., Rickels, K., & Rock, A. F. (1976). The SCL-90 and the MMPI: A step in the validation of a new self-report scale. *British Journal of Psychiatry, 128,* 280–289.

Visual Analog Scale (VAS)

The VAS consists of a 100 mm horizontal line marked at one end "normal mood" and at the other end "extreme depression." Subjects place an X on the line to indicate their level of depression. The scale is scored by measuring the distance from the end marked "normal mood" to the X.

References

Aitken, R. C. B. (1969). Measures of feeling using analogue scales. *Proceedings of the Royal Society of Medicine, 62,* 989–993.

Zealley, A. K., & Aitken, R. C. B. (1969). Measurement of mood. *Proceedings of the Royal Society of Medicine, 62,* 993–997.

Zung Self-Rating Depression Scale (SDS)

The SDS includes 20 items intended to measure various aspects of the depressive syndrome. Each item is rated on a four-point scale. Items are balanced between being stated positively and negatively. The instrument is reproduced in Zung (1965).

References

Zung, W. W. K. (1965). A self-rating depression scale. *Archives of General Psychiatry, 12,* 63–70.

Zung, W. W. K., Richards, C. B., & Short, M. J. (1965). Self-rating depression scale in an outpatient clinic. *Archives of General Psychiatry, 13,* 508–515.

For more information on depression scales, the reader is referred to Chapters 12 and 13 in this volume and to Moran and Lambert (1983) and Levitt and Lubin (1975).

Moran, P. W., & Lambert, M. J. (1983). A review of current assessment tools for monitoring changes in depression. In M. J. Lambert, E. R. Christensen, & S. S. DeJulio (Eds.), *The assessment of psychotherapy outcome.* New York: John Wiley & Sons.

Levitt, E. E., & Lubin, B. (1975). *Depression: Concepts, controversies, and some new facts.* New York: Springer.

A Selected Listing
of Measures of Depression
for Children

Compiled by **Eldon Marshall, Ph.D.**
Department of Psychiatry and Behavioral Sciences
University of Oklahoma Health Sciences Center

Bellevue Index of Depression (BID)

The Bellevue Index of Depression is a structured interview and clinician rating form applicable with children, parents, or significant others. It consists of 29 items that inquire into the severity and duration of depressive symptomatology. Clinicians rate symptom severity on a five-point scale ("no problem" to "very much of a problem") and duration on a three-point scale ("recent or new," "long time," and "always")

Ages for Whom Suitable
Six to 12 years.

Address Where It May Be Obtained
Theodore A. Petti, M.D., Western Psychiatric Institute and Clinic, University of Pittsburgh School of Medicine, Webster Hall-O.E.R.P., 4415 5th Avenue, Pittsburgh, Pennsylvania 15213.

Cost
None

Restrictions on Availability
None

References
Petti, T. A. (1978). Depression in hospitalized child psychiatry patients. *Journal of the American Academy of Child Psychiatry, 17,* 49–50.

Child Assessment Schedule (CAS)

The Child Assessment Schedule is a semi-structured interview for the clinical assessment of children. It employs a format of standardized questions and response items. Part I contains approximately 75 items and records the child's verbal responses to clinical inquiries about school, friends, activities and hobbies, family, fears and anxieties, worries, self-image, mood, somatic concerns, expression of anger and thought disorder symptomatology. Part II records the examiner observations and consists of approximately 53 items that probe insight, grooming, motor coordination, activity level, other physical movement and behavior, cognitive abilities, quality of verbalization, quality of emotional expression and quality of interpersonal interaction. For each response item, the child's responses are coded as either "yes" (presence of symptoms), "no" (absence of symptoms), "ambiguous," "no response," or "not applicable." Part III obtains information about the onset and duration of symptoms. A form for parents is available.

Ages for Whom Suitable
6 to 18 years. (The CAS can be used with adolescents with some modifications.)

Address Where It Can Be Obtained
Administrative Assistant, Department of Psychiatry, University of Missouri, Rm. 107 MMMHC, 3 Hospital Drive, Columbia, Missouri 65201.

Cost
$3.00

Restrictions on Availability
None.

References
Hodges, K., McKnew, D., Burbach, D., & Roebuck, L. (1984). *Diagnostic concordance between two structured interviews for children: The Child Assessment Schedule and Kiddie-SADS.* Paper presented at the annual meeting of the American Psychological Association, Toronto, Canada.

Hodges, K., McKnew, D., Cytryn, L., Stern, L., & Kline, J. (1982). The Child Assessment Schedule (CAS) diagnostic interview: A report on reliability and validity. *Journal of the American Academy of Child Psychiatry, 21*(15), 468–473.

Child Behavior Checklist (CBCL)

The Child Behavior Checklist contains items relevant to childhood depression. On a three-point rating scale, parents indicate the extent to which each of 113 items describes their child's behavior. The checklist yields a profile of special competence and problem behavior along the dimensions of schizoid, depressed, uncommunicative, obsessive-compulsive, somatic complaints, social withdrawal, hyperactive, aggressive, delinquent, internalizing and externalizing. A Teacher Report Form (113 items), Youth Self-Report Form (112 items), and Direct Observation Report Form (97 items) are also available.

Ages for Whom Suitable
4–16 years.

Address Where It May Be Obtained
Thomas Achenbach, Ph.D., University Associates in Psychiatry, 1 South Prospect St., Burlington, Vermont 05401.

Cost
The Child Behavior Checklist is $25 for 100 forms or 25 cents per form. Cost of the manual is $18.

Restrictions on Availability
None.

References

Achenbach, T. M., & Edelbrock, C. S. (1979). The child behavior profile II: Boys aged 12–16 and girls aged 6–11 and 12–16. *Journal of Consulting and Clinical Psychology, 47*, 223–233.

Achenbach, T. M. & Edelbrock, C. S. (1983). *Manual for the Child Behavior Checklist and Revised Child Behavior Profile.* Burlington, Vermont: Department of Psychiatry, University of Vermont.

Children's Depression Adjective Checklist (C-DACL)

The Children's Depression Adjective Checklist assesses dysphoric mood in present state. Forms H and I each contain 34 items that include 22 depression-connoting adjectives and 12 nondepression-connoting adjectives, respectively. (The Depression Adjective Checklist referenced in Appendix 9 contains forms appropriate for adolescents.)

Ages for Whom Suitable
8–12 years.

Address Where It May Be Obtained
Bernard Lubin, Ph.D., Department of Psychology, University of Missouri, 5100 Rockhill Road, Kansas City, Missouri 64110.

Cost
None.

Restrictions on Availability
Available for research purposes.

References

Sokoloff, R. M. & Lubin, B. (1983). Depressive mood in adolescent, emotionally disturbed females: Reliability and validity of an adjective checklist (C-DACL). *Journal of Abnormal Child Psychology, 11*, 531–536.

Children's Depression Inventory (CDI)

The Children's Depression Inventory is a 27-item self-rated symptom-oriented scale on which the child chooses the one alternative out of three presented that best describes his/her own feelings/ideas for the past two weeks. Alternatives reflect the nature and frequency of symptoms characteristic of childhood depression ranging from sadness, anhedonia, suicidal ideations to sleep and appetite disturbances. Based on a modification of the Beck Depression Inventory, items on the CDI have been selected to cover affective, cognitive, psychomotor, and vegetative aspects of depression.

Ages for Whom Suitable
8–13 years.

Address Where It May Be Obtained
Maria Kovacs, Ph.D., Western Psychiatric Institute and Clinic, University of Pittsburgh School of Medicine, 3811 O'Hara Street, Pittsburgh, Pennsylvania 15213.

Cost
None.

Restrictions on Availability
None.

References
Kovacs, M. (1983). *The Children's Depression Inventory: A self-rated depression scale for school-age youngsters.* Unpublished manuscript, University of Pittsburgh, Pittsburgh, Pennsylvania.

Children's Depression Rating Scale (CDRS)—Revised

The Children's Depression Rating Scale—Revised is a clinician-rated scale for measuring the severity of depression. Following a structured interview clinicians use a seven-point scale to rate the degree of symptomatology in the areas of school work, anhedonia, social withdrawal, sleep, appetite, excessive fatigue, physical complaints, irritability, guilt, self-esteem, depressed feelings, morbid ideation, suicide/ideation, weeping, depressed affect, tempo of speech, hypoactivity, and lability of mood.

Ages for Whom Suitable
6–12 years.

Address Where It May Be Obtained
Department of Psychiatry, Rush-Presbyterian Hospital, 1720 West Polk Street, Chicago, Illinois 60612.

Cost
$5.

Restrictions on Availability
None.

References
Poznanski, E. O., Cook, S. C., & Carroll, B. J. (1979). A depression rating scale for children. *Pediatrics, 6*(4), 442–450.

Poznanski, E. D., Grossman, J. A., Buchsbaum, Y., Baneges, M., Freeman, L., & Gibbons, R. (1984). Preliminary studies of the reliability and validity of the Children's Depression Rating Scale. *Journal of the American Academy of Child Psychiatry 23*(2), 191–197.

Children's Depression Scale (CDS)

The Children's Depression Scale is a self-rated scale consisting of 66 items (48 depressive and 18 positive). Six aspects of childhood depression are measured including affective responses, social problems, self-esteem, preoccupation with own sickness and death, guilt and pleasure. Items are presented on cards which the child sorts into boxes labeled "very wrong," "wrong," "don't know," "not sure," "right," and "very right." The CDS-Adult Form consists of a separate set of cards reworded for use with parents, siblings, teachers, and relatives.

Cost
$100 for kit including manual and forms.

Ages for Whom Suitable
9–16 years.

Address Where It May Be Obtained
Consulting Psychologist Press, P.O. Box 60070, Palo Alto, California 94306

Restrictions on Availability
None

References
Lang, M., & Tisher, M. (1983). *Children's Depression Scale (Revised)*. Melbourne, Australia: Australian Council for Educational Research.

Tisher, M., & Lang, M. (1983). The Children's Depression Scale: Review and further developments. In D. P. Cantwell & G. A. Carlson (Eds.), *Affective disorders in childhood and adolescence: An update* (pp. 181–203). New York: Spectrum Publications.

Diagnostic Interview Schedule for Children and Adolescents (DICA)

The Diagnostic Interview for Children and Adolescents and the companion interview schedule for parents, DICA-P, are semistructured interviews yielding information on the onset, duration, and severity of symptoms including those related to depression. Both are keyed to the *DSM-III* and assess a broad range of psychopathology.

Ages for Whom Suitable
6–17 years.

Address Where It May be Obtained
Zila Welner, M.D., Department of Psychiatry, Washington University School of Medicine, 4940 Audubon Avenue, St. Louis, Missouri 63110.

Cost
$15

Restrictions on Availability
None

References
Herjanic, B., & Campbell, W. (1977). Differentiating psychiatrically disturbed children on the basis of a structured interview. *Journal of the Association of Child Psychology, 5,* 127–134.

Reich, W., Herjanic, B., Welner, Z., & Gandhy, P. R. (1982). Development of a structured psychiatric interview for children: Agreement on diagnosis comparing child and parent interviews. *Journal of Abnormal Child Psychology, 10,* 325–336.

Interview Schedule for Children (ISC)

The Interview Schedule for Children is a semistructured, symptom-oriented psychiatric interview covering the major symptoms of depression and a broad range of psychopathology. Clinicians rate symptoms on degree of severity. Two parallel forms are available.

Ages for Whom Suitable
8–13 years.

Address Where It May Be Obtained
Maria Kovacs, Ph.D., Western Psychiatric Institute and Clinic, University of Pittsburgh School of Medicine, 3811 O'Hara Street, Pittsburgh, Pennsylvania 15213.

Cost
None.

Restrictions on Availability
None.

References
Feinberg, T. L. (1983). *The formalization of clinical decision making.* Unpublished manuscript, University of Pittsburgh School of Medicine, Pittsburgh, Pennsylvania.

Kovacs, M. (1983). *The Interview Schedule for Children.* Unpublished manuscript, University of Pittsburgh School of Medicine, Pittsburgh, Pennsylvania.

Kiddie Schedule for Affective Disorders and Schizophrenia (K-SADS)

The K-SADS is a comprehensive-structured psychiatric interview for use with parents and children to assess major symptomatology. It records symptoms relevant to *DSM-III* criteria for the following diagnostic categories: major/minor depression, mania, hypomania, schizophrenia, schizoaffective disorder, autism, eating disorders, attention deficit disorder, conduct disorders, anxiety disorders, alcohol and substance abuse, and suicidal behavior. Form E assesses whether a past symptom or behavior ever occurred and whether the problem is current. Form P focuses on present episode and symptom severity.

Ages for Whom suitable
6–16 years.

Address Where It May Be Obtained
Joaquim Puig-Antich, M.D., Western Psychiatric Institute and Clinic, University of Pittsburgh School of Medicine, 3811 O'Hara Street, Pittsburgh, Pennsylvania 15213.

Cost
$10

Restrictions on Availability
None.

References
Chambers, W., Puig-Antich, J., Hirsch, M., Paez, P., Ambrosini, P., Tabrizi, M., & Davis, M. (in press). The assessment of affective disorders in children and adolescents by a semi-structured interview: Test-retest reliability of the K-SADS-P. *Archives of General Psychiatry.*

Orvaschel, H., Puig-Antich, J., Chambers, W., Tabrizi, M. A., & Johnson, R. (1982). Retrospective assessment of prepubertal major depression with the Kiddie-SADS-E. *Journal of the American Academy of Child Psychiatry, 21*(4), 392–397.

Peer Nomination Inventory of Depression (PNID)

The Peer Nomination Inventory of Depression is based on the assumption that symptoms of depression in children can be easily detected by peers. It consists of 20 items that ask children in a given group to nominate their peers on such questions as "Who often seems alone?" or "Who often looks sad?" Subscales include depression, happiness, and popularity.

Ages for Whom Suitable
7–13 years.

Address Where It May Be Obtained
Monroe M. Lefkowitz, Ph.D., Department of Psychology, Long Island University, Brooklyn Center, University Plaza, Brooklyn, New York 11201-9926.

Cost
None.

Restrictions on Availability
None.

References

Tesiny, E. P., & Lefkowitz, M. M. (1983, August). *The Peer Nomination Inventory of Depression: 1975–Present.* Paper presented at the annual meeting of the American Psychological Association, Anaheim, California.

Lefkowitz, M. M., & Tesiny, E. P. (1982, August). *Depressive symptoms in children: Prevalence and correlates.* Paper presented at the annual meeting of the American Psychological Association, Washington, DC.

Personality Inventory for Children (PIC)

The Personality Inventory for Children is a standardized instrument for the assessment of children's personality. It is completed by parents, consists of 600 true-false items, and yields 12 clinical scales including achievement, intellectual screening, development, somatic concerns, depression, family relations, delinquency, withdrawal, anxiety, psychosis, hyperactivity and social skills.

Ages for Whom Suitable
3–16 years.

Address Where It May Be Obtained
Western Psychological Services, 1231 Wilshire Blvd., Los Angeles, California 90025.

Cost
A kit containing all materials pertinent to the inventory costs over $100, but portions of the kit can be purchased separately at lower cost.

Restrictions on Availability
Professional use only.

References

Wirt, R. D., Lacher, D., Klinedinst, J. K., & Seat, P. D. (1984). *Multidimensional description of child personality: A manual for the personality inventory for children* (rev. ed). Los Angeles: Western Psychological Services.

Froman, P. K. (1971). *The development of a depression scale for the personality inventory for children (PIC).* Unpublished manuscript, University of Minnesota, Minneapolis.

Self-Rating Scale (SRS)

The Self-Rating Scale consists of 18 items found to discriminate depressed from nondepressed children. Children are presented 18 statements like "I feel very bored," or "I feel very lonely" and asked to check whether each applied "most times," "sometimes," or "never" over the past weeks.

Ages for Whom Suitable
7–17 years.

Address Where It May Be Obtained
Peter Birleson, M.D., Royal Edinburgh Hospital, The Young Peoples Unit, Tipperlin House, Tipperlin Road, Edinborough, EH. 105 HF. United Kingdom.

Cost
None.

Restrictions on Availability
None.

References
Birleson, P. (1981). The validity of depressive disorder in childhood and the development of a self-rating scale: A research report. *Journal of Child Psychology and Psychiatry. 22,* 73–88.

Name Index

A

Aarons, S., 254
Abelson, R. P., 45
Abernethy, D. R., 248
Abood, L. G., 238
Abou-Saleh, M. T., 269
Abraham, K., 82, 83, 84, 703, 733
Abrami, D. L., 22
Abramowitz, S. I., 226
Abrams, A., 263
Abrams, R., 228, 257, 274, 275, 277, 354, 806, 807, 809
Abramson, L. Y., 15, 21, 23, 46, 153, 208, 413, 414, 415, 416, 417, 418, 432, 435, 436, 528, 537, 538, 704, 721, 723, 880, 914, 915, 916, 920, 923, 924, 928, 933, 934, 947, 953, 1012
Absenour, P., 270
Achenbach, T. M., 524, 527, 535, 1019, 1020
Ackenheil, M., 468
Ackerman, J. M., 634
Acosta, E., 850
Adam, K. S., 608, 609
Adams, H. E., 23
Adams, M., 257
Adams, Russell L., 331, 429, 634, 957, 1014
Adcock, S., 773, 780
Adelstein, A. M., 774
Aden, G. C., 247, 575
Adey, M., 1015
Adland, M., 353
Adragna, N., 476
Advani, M. T., 855
Aghajanian, G. K., 237, 238
Agis, Y., 270
Agnoli, A., 269
Agras, W., 376, 681
Agren, H., 449, 614, 841, 869, 872
Aitken, R. C. B., 392, 1017
Akil, H., 824
Akins, W. T., 73
Akiskal, Hagop S., 151, 156, 157, 204, 205,
352, 354, 350, 375, 396, 478, 479, 481, 587, 588–96, 598, 599–601, 670, 673, 676, 678, 700, 701, 708–11, 715, 716, 725, 726, 727, 729, 730, 733, 735, 737, 738, 767, 840, 841, 856, 879, 943, 947
Alarcon, R. D., 317
Albala, A. A., 455, 460, 462, 474, 832, 855, 857, 859
Albee, G. W., 964
Albert, N., 526
Alberti, R. E., 58
Alden, L. E., 22
Aldridge, D. M., 596
Aldwin, C., 428, 955
Alessi, N. E., 856
Alexopoulos, G. S., 279, 869
Alig, V., 724
Allan, A. T., 754
Allari, E., 454, 826
Allen, M. G., 808
Allen, R., 234
Allen, W., 458
Allman, E. G., 238
Alloy, L. B., 23, 46, 432, 435, 538, 916, 924, 933
Alltop, L. B., 451, 454, 463, 465
Almay, B. G. L., 870
Almeida, M., 234
Alper, T., 42, 153
Alterman, I. S., 228, 254
Altesman, R. J., 269
Altman, E., 767, 859
Altman, J. H., 19, 706
Altman, N., 467, 468, 867
Alton, H., 450
Altschule, M. D., 220
Alvarez, W., 779
Amadeo, M., 843, 845
Aman, M. G., 228
Ambrosini, P., 1023
Amidisen, A., 259, 260, 261, 262, 861
Amenson, C. S., 44, 423, 916

American Psychiatric Association, 343, 520, 566, 587, 609, 671, 680, 681, 683, 685, 689, 745, 751, 769, 817
Amies, P. L., 29, 320
Amin, M., 281
Aminoff, A. K., 463
Amsterdam, J. D., 462, 470, 559, 855, 857, 864, 865, 870
Ananth, J., 228, 232, 266, 269, 597, 809
Anastopoulos, Arthur D., 634
Anderson, A. E., 680
Anderson, C. M., 167, 354, 479
Anderson, E., 425
Anderson, G., 271
Anderson, J. C., 540
Anderson, J. L., 117
Anderson, K., 246
Anderson, M., 616
Anderson, M. S., 264, 465
Anderson, P. J., 450
Anderson, T., 449
Andrasik, F., 228
Andreason, N. C., 349, 351, 355, 673
Andreoli, V., 269
Andrews, G., 220
Andrulonis, P. A., 596
Anggaard, E., 449
Angle, C. R., 543, 621
Angrist, B., 472
Angst, J., 270, 353, 767, 806, 869
Anisman, H., 221
Annable, L., 268
Antelman, S. M., 279
Anthony, E. J., 174, 517, 526, 527
Anthony, J. C., 557
Anton, R. F., 246
Antonuccio, D. O., 61, 62, 73
Aperia, B., 280, 463
Applebaum, S. A., 107
Apter, A., 454, 524
Arana, G. W., 676, 856
Arato, M., 280, 830, 855, 861
Arieff, A. J., 689
Arieti, S., 87, 88, 91, 98, 701, 705, 715, 734, 915
Arkowitz, H., 637
Arocha, L., 850
Aronoff, M. S., 454
Arora, R. C., 468, 831
Artiss, K. L., 458
Asano, N., 807
Asarch, K. B., 237
Asberg, M., 228, 234, 451, 454, 463, 614, 671, 830, 852, 1016
Aschauer, H., 863
Aserinsky, E., 477
Asher, R., 746
Asher, S. J., 950
Ashford, J. W., 575
Askenasy, A. R., 776, 961

Asnis, G. M., 467, 474, 482, 852, 853, 854, 858, 859, 866, 868
Asnis, L., 157
Astor-Dubin, L., 429
Astrom, G., 463
Atkins, R. N., 262
Atsman, A., 454
Atwood, G., 42
Autenrieth, V., 869
Autry, A. H., 125, 326, 379
Avery, D., 240, 480, 576, 828, 875
Axelrod, J., 235, 249, 269, 448, 453
Ayd, F. J., Jr., 247, 560, 592, 597
Ayuso Gutierrez, J. L., 268
Azrin, N. H., 68, 69

B

Baarfusser, B., 469
Baastrup, P. C., 262, 820
Baber, R., 468
Baciewicz, G., 857
Badawy, A. A. C., 268
Bader, T. F., 241
Baer, L., 261, 454
Bagley, C. R., 615
Bagri, S., 455, 471, 472, 473
Bailey, J., 262, 269, 678, 820
Baker, L., 681
Baker, M., 268, 354, 677, 735
Balbi, A., 269
Baldessarini, R. J., 249, 448, 454, 455, 461, 465, 676, 825
Baldwin, J., 155, 774
Balka, E. B., 228
Ball, J. R. B., 818
Balldin, J., 855
Ballenger, J., 227, 266, 449, 468, 831, 867, 868, 869
Balter, M. D., 777
Bamford, K. A., 880
Ban, T. A., 264, 331
Bancroft, J., 22, 24, 687
Bandura, A., 43, 637, 933, 946
Banegas, M., 532, 856, 1021
Banki, C. M., 829, 830, 855, 861
Banks, M., H., 775
Barbaccia, M. L., 256
Barber, J. G., 19
Barbero, G. J., 525
Barchas, J. D., 450, 455, 824, 841, 860, 864, 869
Barkai, A., 831
Barker, J. B., 799
Barker, K., 482
Barlow, D., 376
Barnes, G., 191
Barnes, R., 569, 855
Barnes, R. F., 573, 860
Barnes, R. H., 562
Barnshaw, H. D., 855

Baron, M., 157, 257, 353, 799, 809
Barraclough, B., 538, 615
Barranco, S. F., 230
Barreira, P. J., 676, 856
Barrera, M., 62
Barrett, J. E., 821
Barsky, J., 223, 252, 684
Bartels, P. H., 484
Bartko, J., 524
Bartlett, D., 252, 558
Bartlett, J., 598, 846
Bartolini, A., 471
Barton, R., 46, 426, 432, 954
Barwick, C., 607
Bassett, D. L., 226
Bateson, G., 152
Bauer, G. P., 101
Baumann, A., 455
Baumoff, M., 386
Beamesderfer, A., 384, 385, 781
Beamish, P., 778
Bear, D., 686, 691
Beardslee, W. R., 174
Beauchemin, J. A., 258
Beavin, J., 152
Bebbington, Paul, 765, 769, 772, 773, 774,
    777–80, 783
Bech, P., 235, 380, 800
Beck, A., 376, 396, 397
Beck, Aaron T., 3–8, 15–21, 23, 24, 25, 27,
    28, 30, 39, 47, 125, 153, 164, 205, 208,
    213, 216, 230, 239, 319, 320, 328, 333,
    373, 374, 375, 383, 384, 385, 397, 409,
    412, 413, 421, 424, 433, 435, 436, 526,
    528, 530, 578, 610, 612, 613, 617, 618,
    634, 635, 637, 638, 642, 645, 653, 678,
    679, 701, 705, 718, 721, 723, 734, 735,
    750, 751, 768, 881, 915, 920, 921, 924,
    934, 946, 947, 952, 955, 962, 963, 964,
    1015
Beck, R. W., 384, 385
Beck-Friis, J., 280, 463
Becker, B. F., 809
Becker, Ernest, 90
Becker, J., 23, 39, 127, 946
Becker, J. T., 678, 701
Becker, Robert, 213, 324
Beckham, Ernest Edward, 30, 316, 331, 343,
    373, 411, 429, 434, 957, 1014
Beckman, H., 232, 450, 454, 855
Bedford, P., 247
Bedrosian, R. C., 6, 28, 320
Beersma, D. G. M., 875
Behar, V., 21, 410, 767, 953, 1013
Beigel, A., 257, 354, 399, 400
Beiman, I., 23
Beitman, B. D., 598
Belensky, G. L., 279
Bell, J., 840
Bell, R., 164, 773, 865

Bellack, Alan S., 39, 66, 67, 73, 118, 204, 205,
    209, 210, 211, 216, 228, 323, 324, 325,
    327, 328, 332, 378, 881
Bellack, L., 616
Bellodi, L., 454
Belluomini, J., 478, 479, 600, 841
Bellus, S. N., 840
Belmaker, R. H., 262, 836
Belyea, M., 349
Bemis, K., 207, 399, 424, 432, 433
Bemporad, Jules R., 82, 87, 174, 526, 527,
    545, 701, 704, 705, 709, 715, 734, 915
Ben-David, M., 868
Bendz, H., 260
Benjaminsen, S., 350, 778
Benson, H., 57
Benson, K. L., 840, 841
Berblinger, K. W., 589
Berensohn, H. S., 677
Berger, M., 833, 834, 839, 856, 857, 858, 859,
    864
Berger, P. A., 238, 450, 454, 455, 465, 832,
    841, 860, 864, 865, 869
Bergey, B., 264
Bergland, R. M., 851
Berglas, S., 919
Bergner, P. E. E., 260
Berman, A. L., 542
Berne, Eric, 184, 186–89, 192
Berniker, K., 260
Berns, B. H., 809
Bernstein, N. R., 166
Bert, J., 810
Bertani, L. M., 448
Bertelsen, A., 353
Bertilsson, L., 228, 451, 454, 852
Bertolino, A., 269
Besalel, V. A., 68, 69
Besser, G. M., 459, 758
Beutler, Larry, 322
Bezzi, G., 855
Bhat, A. V., 251
Bhrolchain, M., 155
Bialow, M., 380, 751
Bianchi, E. C., 524
Bibring, E., 86, 562, 704, 707
Biel, J. H., 238
Bielman, P., 269
Bielski, R., 66, 230, 231, 232, 325, 454, 818
Bigelow, A., 264
Bigger, J. T., Jr., 240, 513
Biggs, J. T., 234, 381, 386, 389
Biglan, T., 44, 51, 72, 125, 962
Billings, Andrew G., 334, 350, 428, 429, 940,
    942, 943, 944, 945, 950, 951, 952, 955,
    960, 961, 963, 965
Binder, J., 101–4, 108, 116
Biondi, P. A., 454, 826
Birchler, G. R., 154
Bird, E. D., 861

Bird, J., 613
Birleson, P., 530, 1025
Birley, J. L. T., 156, 374, 769
Birmacher, B., 227
Birtchnell, J., 155
Bischofs, W., 280, 281
Bishop, F. M., 454
Bishop, M. E., 262
Bishop, S., 28, 320, 397, 642, 881
Bitar, A. H., 156, 587, 588
Bittle, R. M., 685
Bivens, C. H., 469
Bjorum, N., 258, 464
Blackburn, I. M., 28, 30, 31, 320, 327, 328,
    397, 642, 645, 881
Blackhard, W. G., 467
Blair, C. D., 687
Blaney, P. H., 21, 25 n, 39, 45, 410, 411, 417,
    704, 953, 1013
Blaser, R., 384
Blashfield, R. K., 346, 360, 361, 373
Blashki, T. G., 389
Blaszkiewicz, F., 280, 281
Blatt, S. J., 20, 279, 701, 706, 709, 734
Blau, S., 546, 701
Blazer, Dan G., 556, 557, 562, 579
Bleuler, E., 224
Bloch, R. G., 223
Block, B., 261
Block, M., 961
Blois, R., 841
Blombery, P. A., 449
Bloom, B., 950
Bloom, F. E., 823
Bloom, P. M., 384
Bloom, V. L., 226, 234, 454, 592
Bloor, R., 957
Blum, I., 454
Blum, M. R., 253
Blum, W. L., 918
Blumberg, S., 5, 425
Blumer, D. P., 242, 600, 684, 685, 840, 856,
    858
Boag, L., 480, 518
Bobik, A., 829
Bochner, F., 758
Bochnik, H. J., 859
Bohman, M., 678
Bolander, F. D., 525
Bolen, D. W., 689
Bollinger, J., 867
Bologna, N. C., 957
Bolwig, T., 380
Bolz, J., 843
Bond, M., 61
Bond, T. C., 460, 856
Bonese, K., 614, 855
Bonge, D., 414
Bonner, K. M., 277
Bonnet, A. M., 270
Boodoosingh, L. A., 611

Book, J. A., 783, 795
Booth, J., 856
Boranga, G., 856
Borbely, A. A., 838
Borengasser, M. A., 524
Borenstein, M., 671
Borinstein, D. I., 671
Borison, R. L., 447, 452, 453, 471, 473
Borland, B. L., 264
Bornstein, M., 545
Borson, S., 860
Bos, E. R. H., 265
Boswell, J. W., 613
Botez, M. I., 269
Botez, T., 269
Bothwell, S., 164, 950
Bottiglieri, T., 269
Boucher, M. L., 855
Bouckous, A., 608
Boulton, A. A., 452, 453
Bouras, N., 846
Bourke, G., 780
Bourne, H. R., 558
Boverman, H., 545
Bowden, C. L., 234, 449, 827
Bowen, M., 152
Bower, G. H., 21, 424, 433, 933
Bowers, M. B. J., 234, 348, 450, 454
Bowie, C. J., 689
Bowlby, J., 128, 921
Bowman, R. E., 558
Boyar, R., 467
Boyd, J. H., 346, 390, 391, 557, 768, 828, 870,
    871
Boyd, M., 481
Boyd, W. H., 689
Boyer, Jenny L., 376, 606
Bracha, H., 262
Bradford, J. M. W., 690
Bradley, C. F., 417
Brady, J. P., 384
Branchey, L., 280
Branchey, M., 280
Branconnier, R. J., 856
Brandl-Nebehay, A., 778
Brandsma, J. M., 22
Braucht, G., 610
Brauman, H., 468, 864, 866, 868
Brawley, P., 473, 474, 860
Breese, G. R., 448, 451, 454, 463, 465
Brehm, J. W., 918, 923
Breiter, H. J., 21, 412
Breitman, J., 281, 876
Brem, F., 869
Bremer, W., 280, 281
Bremkamp, H., 261
Brenner, M. H., 774
Brenner, R., 259, 671
Bresnahan, J. L., 918
Brewer, D., 530, 531
Breyer-Pfaff, U., 454, 827, 849, 850

Bridges, C. I., 228
Bridges, P., 598, 846
Bridges, P. K., 280
Bridges, T. P., 615
Briley, M. S., 237, 831
Brill, H., 346
Brink, T. L., 684, 1015
Briscoe, C. W., 128, 151
Broadhurst, A. D., 268
Brockington, I. F., 767
Brodie, H. K. H., 450
Brogan, D., 389
Bromet, E. J., 157, 780
Bronisch, T., 834
Brooksbank, B. W. L., 449
Brotman, A. W., 228
Broudy, D., 478, 840
Brown, B. B., 948
Brown, C., 155
Brown, F., 534
Brown, G. L., 389, 614, 677, 830
Brown, G. M., 464, 467, 470, 822, 851, 866, 867
Brown, G. W., 128, 151, 155, 156, 158, 160, 169, 204, 215, 216, 350, 386, 767, 774, 777, 778, 779, 780, 944, 945, 950, 960
Brown, H. H., 684
Brown, J. R., 241
Brown, J. T., 564, 571
Brown, L. B., 430, 435, 956, 959
Brown, P., 473, 474, 860
Brown, R., 61, 62, 63, 72, 254
Brown, R. J., 806
Brown, T. R., 612
Brown, W. A., 462, 467, 468, 474, 855, 857
Brownell, G. L., 485, 675
Bruch, H., 680
Brugha, T., 780
Brumback, R. A., 518, 524, 525, 536
Bruno, R. L., 573
Brunswick, D., 467, 470, 559, 809, 864, 865
Bryant, S., 462, 857
Buchanan, D., 260
Buchberg, A. S., 223
Buchbinder, R., 255
Buchsbaum, M., 257, 281, 484, 840, 844, 845, 847, 869, 878
Buchsbaum, Y., 432, 819, 1021
Buchwald, A., 424
Buck, P., 429
Budinger, T. F., 485, 675
Budman, S., 107
Bueno, J. R., 450
Bulik, C. M., 850
Bullock, R. C., 156
Bumberry, W., 384
Bunch, J., 538
Bunney, W. E., Jr., 89, 224, 231, 236, 254, 263, 266, 268, 399, 447, 448, 449, 456, 458, 475, 479, 521, 558, 610, 614, 778, 800, 820, 825, 830, 841, 847, 869

Burbach, D. J., 535, 1019
Burchfiel, J., 484
Burckhardt, D., 573
Burgess, E., 42
Burke, C. J., 758
Burke, J. D., Jr., 557
Burkhardt, P. E., 857
Burkhart, B. R., 384, 387
Burns, David D., 17, 634, 642–51, 653, 654–57
Burroughs, J., 680
Burrows, G., 392, 573
Burton, N., 517, 518
Bush, E. S., 919
Bush, S. C., 686
Buss, D. M., 45
Busse, E. W., 562, 564, 577
Bussod, N., 211
Butcher, J. N., 117
Butler, P. W. P., 459
Butler, R. N., 563, 577
Butter, H. G., 849
Byck, R., 263, 354, 479
Byck, T. C., 597
Byrne, D. G., 156, 773, 780, 781, 849, 948
Byrnes, S. M., 466, 827, 857, 864

C

Cade, J. F. J., 222, 256, 258, 259, 261
Cadet, J., 465, 863
Cadoret, R. J., 225, 354, 355, 676, 677, 683, 735, 802
Cadotte, M., 269
Caffey, E. H., 809
Cagnasso, P., 454
Caille, G., 832
Caine, E. D., 880
Cairns, J., 479, 482, 874
Caldwell, A. B., 226
Caldwell, H. C., 260
Caldwell, J. H., 573
Calhoun, L. G., 946
Calil, H. M., 273, 454, 827
Cameron, O. G., 671
Cammer, L., 156
Campbell, D. R., 258
Campbell, D. T., 929
Campbell, I. C., 254, 255, 451, 825
Campbell, S. B., 21, 413, 928
Campbell, W., 534, 1022
Candy, J., 227
Canepari, C., 855
Canessa, M., 476
Cannon, D. S., 73
Cantwell, D. P., 517, 520, 521, 523, 524, 525, 541, 542, 544, 545, 546, 621, 680, 1022
Caplan, A. L., 766
Caplan, G., 175
Capodanno, A. E., 855, 856
Capparell, H. V., 228
Cappelleti, J., 847

Carlson, G., 384, 517, 521, 523, 524, 525, 526, 531, 539, 540, 541–54, 546, 621, 1022
Carlsson, A., 268
Carlsson, G. A., 353
Carman, J. S., 258, 855
Carney, M. W. P., 269, 778
Caroff, S., 470, 559, 855, 856, 864, 865, 870
Carr, J. E., 686
Carroll, B. J., 349, 387, 388, 389, 396, 451, 455, 456, 459, 460, 461, 462, 467, 468, 474, 479, 525, 559, 598, 778, 819, 820, 828, 833, 836, 838, 848, 852, 853–59, 864, 870, 996, 1021
Carskadon, M. A., 559
Carson, T. P., 23
Carstairs, G. M., 784
Carter, A. L., 613
Cartwright, R. D., 480, 481, 840, 879, 881
Carver, C. S., 19, 44, 45, 47, 930
Casacchia, M., 269
Case, W. G., 239
Casey, J. F., 264
Casper, R., 225, 234, 467, 468, 681, 689, 860, 865
Cassano, G. B., 156, 856
Cath, S., 562
Cattell, W. R., 262
Caveny, E. L., 346
Cazzullo, C. L., 874
Cazzulo, C. O., 454, 809, 826
Cerbo, R., 269
Cerleth, Ugo, 221, 271
Chace, P. M., 276
Chadwick, O., 529
Chambers, C., 257
Chambers, J. W., 467, 866
Chambers, W. J., 480, 532, 533, 546, 840, 867, 1023
Chanarin, I., 269
Chandra, O., 469
Chang, S., 225, 234, 261, 273
Chaplin, W., 46, 426, 432, 954
Charbonneau-Powis, M., 26, 29
Charles, G., 462, 847, 856
Charney, D. S., 349, 352, 447, 449, 455, 701, 710, 711, 725, 729, 767, 778, 779, 819, 827, 831, 832, 836, 878
Chastek, C. P., 855
Chatham, T., 73
Chatterji, D. C., 266
Chave, S., 781
Checkley, S., 249, 456, 468, 470, 472, 717, 859, 867
Cheney, T., 946
Chernick, D. A., 263, 480
Chesney, M., 634, 639
Chevron, Eve S., 20, 124, 125, 161, 168, 318, 360, 703
Chiappa, K. H., 484
Chihara, K., 868
Childers, P., 543

Chiles, J., 376, 531, 606, 607, 613
Chioda, L. A., 279
Cho, D. W., 609, 828
Chodoff, P., 127, 273, 700, 709, 733, 735, 736
Chouinard, G., 268
Christenfeld, R., 392
Christensen, E. R., 1017
Christensen, P. G., 481
Christiansen, C. J., 841
Christiansen, J., 235
Christie, J. E., 28, 320, 397, 642, 881
Christie, M. J., 849
Christodoulou, G. N., 262
Chung, H. R., 239
Ciaranello, R. D., 832
Claeys, M. M., 234
Claghorn, J. L., 847
Clark, D. M., 436
Clarke, G., 73
Clarkin, John F., 151, 160, 161, 164, 166, 167
Clarkson, S. E., 540
Clausen, J. A., 768
Clayton, P., 353, 716
Clayton, P. J., 358, 360, 593, 716, 767, 769, 798, 800, 807, 857, 870
Clayton, P. M., 746
Cleary, P. A., 1017
Cleary, P. D., 954 n
Clement-Jones, V., 758
Clemmons, R. S., 951
Clevenger, J., 856
Cloninger, C. R., 476, 836
Cloninger, R., 258, 676
Clovet, D., 265
Clum, G. A., 610
Clyde, D., 392
Co, B. T., 234
Coates, D., 922, 952, 958
Cobbin, D. M., 232, 454
Coble, P., 226, 233, 280, 477, 478, 481, 482, 546, 559, 839, 840, 841, 853, 874, 879, 880, 881
Coccaro, E. F., 227, 671
Cocco, A., 833
Cocheme, M., 268
Cochran, S., 24, 436, 948, 954
Cochran, S. D., 953
Cochrane, C., 349, 709, 778
Cofer, D. H., 19, 706, 960
Cofsky, J., 478, 880
Cohen, B. M., 246, 269, 856
Cohen, D., 238, 479
Cohen, D. B., 840, 880
Cohen, H., 766
Cohen, H. W., 388
Cohen, J., 380
Cohen, L. M., 271
Cohen, M. R., 455, 468
Cohen, N. H., 259
Cohen, R. M., 236, 237, 250, 254, 255, 455, 468, 855, 856

Cohen, S. M., 808
Cohen, W. J., 259
Cohen-Sandler, R., 542, 543
Cohler, B. J., 174
Cohn, D., 464
Colburn, R. W., 558
Cole, J. O., 232, 242, 246, 448, 449, 454, 460, 675, 827, 828, 856, 860, 861
Coleman, J. H., 241
Coleman, R. E., 23, 151, 950
Colfer, M. V., 856
Colgin, R., 386
Collins, G. L., 613
Colombo, A., 874
Colonna, L., 270
Colpaert, F. C., 239
Colt, E. W. D., 835
Comrey, A., 386
Comstock, G. M., 771, 773
Conn, J., 855
Conners, C. K., 546
Connolly, T. M., 476
Connor, S. M., 260
Connors, C. K., 545
Conroy, R., 780
Conwell, G., 59
Cook, B., 855
Cook, S. C., 525, 856, 1021
Cooley, C. H., 780
Coopen, A. J., 558
Cooper, D. S., 246
Cooper, G. L., 951
Cooper, J., 374, 383
Cooper, J. E., 767, 769, 772, 796, 820
Cooper, J. R., 823, 824
Cooper, R., 475, 476
Cooper, T., 265
Cooper, T. B., 235, 238, 259, 260, 560, 598
Conte, H. R., 540
Copas, J. B., 609, 610
Copeland, J. R., 128, 151, 767, 778, 796, 820
Coppen, A., 236, 262, 263, 269, 354, 449, 450, 451, 452, 454, 820, 849
Corbett, J. A., 269
Corder, B. F., 544
Corder, R. F., 544, 758
Cording, C., 478, 839
Corfman, E., 179
Cormier, S., 429, 718
Cormier, W., 429
Cornelison, S. F., 152
Corner, T., 454
Cornfield, R. B., 228, 672
Corriveau, D. P., 467
Corvilain, J., 468, 866
Coryell, W., 232, 274, 348, 355, 482, 819, 855, 857, 874
Costa, E., 236, 256
Costa, J. L., 451, 825
Costain, W. R., 774
Costall, B., 471

Costello, C. G., 42, 350, 780, 944, 949, 950
Costello, E. J., 946
Coulam, C. M., 485
Cournoyer, G., 832
Covi, L., 317, 325, 327, 378
Cowdry, R. W., 239, 265, 454, 830, 836, 861, 867, 868
Cowitz, B., 388
Cox, G. B., 531
Cox, L. S., 856
Cox, M., 174
Cox, N. J., 258, 476, 835
Cox, R., 174
Cox, W. H., Jr., 228
Coyne, J. C., 5, 128, 152, 153, 154, 329, 413, 425, 426, 428, 429, 432, 725, 945, 951, 955, 958
Craig, C., 281, 876
Craig, K. A., 73
Craig, T., 390
Craighead, W. E., 8, 20, 22, 23, 39
Crammer, J., 258, 468
Crandell, C. J., 21, 415, 436
Crane, G. E., 223
Creasey, D. E., 243
Crews, E., 855
Crews, F. T., 236
Cristol, A. H., 216
Crits-Christoph, K., 679
Cromer, M., 709, 718
Cronholm, B., 228, 234, 451, 454, 671
Cronkite, R. C., 350, 428, 944, 954 n, 964, 965
Crook, T. H., 331, 943, 1016
Cropley, A. J., 385
Cross, A. J., 279
Cross, D. G., 964
Croughan, J., 254, 278, 767, 769
Crouse-Novak, M. A., 524, 871
Crovitz, H. F., 277, 278
Crow, J. F., 157
Crowe, R. R., 674, 806
Crowne, D., 385
Crumley, F. E., 621, 856
Csanalosi, I., 233, 239
Culbreth, D. M. R., 258
Curtis, G. C., 460, 671
Curtius, H. Ch., 270
Cutrona, C. E., 24, 417, 928
Cutter, N. R., 230, 239
Cytryn, L., 518, 521, 524, 526, 528, 529, 534, 540, 1019
Czeisler, C. A., 873

D

Dackis, C. A., 678
D'Afflitti, P., 703
DaFonseca, A. F., 797
Dahlstrom, W., 386
Dalby, M. A., 266
Dale, H. H., 447
Dallman, M. F., 859

Dallob, A., 239
Dally, P. J., 597, 725, 818
Daly, L., 780
Damiel, W. F., 277, 278
Damlouji, N. F., 247
Danker-Brown, Pamela, 343, 373
Dashwood, M. J., 279
Davanloo, H., 100, 102, 106, 108, 109, 110, 111, 119, 130
Davenport, Y. B., 162, 282, 353, 877
David, M., 590, 767
Davidson, J., 252, 253, 273, 349
Davidson, J. R. T., 593, 594, 828, 856
Davidson, N. E., 255
Davidson, P. O., 417
Davidson, R. J., 843
Davidson, S., 454
Davies, B., 251, 392, 459
Davies, D. W., 752, 753
Davies, L., 777
Davies, M., 480, 533, 840, 867
Davies, P., 771
Davies, R. K., 465, 863
Davis, B., 751, 860
Davis, B. M., 864
Davis, D. H., 671
Davis, G. C., 869, 870
Davis, H., 19, 434
Davis, John M., 220, 226, 232, 236, 237, 238, 243, 245, 247, 258, 273, 356, 447, 448, 449, 452, 453, 467, 468, 472, 475, 476, 558, 681, 809, 825, 827, 833, 845, 856,
Davis, J. N., 558
Davis, K. L., 238, 448, 449, 450, 454, 455, 465, 833, 860, 864, 865
Davis, L. S., 865
Davis, M., 482, 858, 1023
Davis, R., 654
Davis, R. K., 864
Davison, G. C., 422
Davison, K., 253
Dawes, A. S., 946
Dawling, S., 468
Dawson, S., 482
Deakin, J. F. W., 279
De Alarcon, R., 564
Dean, C., 773, 774
Deaton, I. D., 778
de Buck, R., 468, 866
Dedauw, G., 200
Deffenu, G., 471
Defraites, E., 238
de Jong, J. T. V. M., 861
Dekirmenjian, H., 448, 449, 454, 467, 468, 469, 827, 867
Delahunt, J. W., 751
Delamater, A., 545
Delaney, W., 780
De la Vergne, P. M., 242
Delay, J., 384
DeLeon-Jones, Frank, 220, 449, 450, 451, 469, 827, 867

Delgado, I., 249
d'Elia, G., 278, 843
DeJulio, S. S., 1017
Delini-Stula, A., 251, 454
DeLisi, L. E., 827, 846
DeLizio, R. D., 880
Delva, N., 480
DeMane, N., 161, 167
DeMartini, W. J., 452
DeMayo, R., 19
Demel, I., 270
Dement, W., 477, 559
DeMet, E. M., 449, 874
Demisch, K., 859
Demisch, L., 859
DeMonbreun, B. G., 20
de Montigny, C., 237–38, 832, 597
Dempsey, P., 386, 387
DeMyer, M. K., 830
Dencker, S. J., 235
DePue, R. A., 204, 353, 373, 608, 819, 914, 920
Der, G., 770, 771
Derogatis, L. E., 317, 378, 382, 1017
Derry, P. A., 19
DeRubeis, R. J., 39, 207, 214, 321, 327, 328, 329
Deschenes, J. P., 597
Detre, T., 354, 479, 597, 673, 809, 819, 838, 843, 848, 874, 878
Deutsch, S. I., 234, 833, 857
Devaul, R. A., 752
deVigne, J. P., 460, 474
Dew, B., 863
Dewan, M. J., 855
DeWitt, K., 118, 120
Diamond, B. I., 473
Diamond, E., 228
Diamond, J. M., 475, 476
Diaz-Guerrero, R., 477
Dibble, E. D., 162
Dick, P., 257
Dickar, D., 809
Dickson, H., 593
Dienelt, M. N., 151, 700
Diener, U., 260
Dietz, S. J., 522
Dietz-Schmidt, S. G., 518, 524
Dillon, D., 227
Dilsaver, S. C., 243, 834
DiMascio, A., 124, 125, 146, 147, 151, 157, 206, 216, 241, 317, 318
Dingell, J. V., 471
Dirlich, G., 478, 839
Discipio, W. J., 736, 738, 779
Divoli, M., 248
Dixon, H., 520
Dobson, D. J. G., 948
Dobson. K. S., 20, 21, 412, 948
Docherty, J. P., 225, 335
Doerfler, L. A., 879, 957
Doerr, P., 833, 839, 849, 859, 876

Dohn, H. H., 613
Dohrenwend, B. P., 774, 776, 944, 961
Dohrenwend, B. S., 774, 776, 944, 954, 960, 961
Doller, J. C., 246
Dominian, J., 264
Donaldson, D., 269
Dondero, B., 780
Donlon, P. T., 685
Donnelly, E. F., 258, 736
Dooneief, A. S., 223
Doorenbos, H., 265
Dopat, T. L., 613
Doren, R., 116, 153
Dornbush, R. L., 277
Dornfeld, L., 856
Dorr, H. G., 859
Dorus, E., 258, 476, 809, 835, 845
Dorzab, B., 354, 677, 735
Dostal, T., 809
Dougherty, J. H., 279, 869
Dow, M. G., 51, 72
Dowds, B. N., 954
Dowdy, S. B., 266
Dowie, C., 227
Downham, D. Y., 774
Dragstedt, C. A., 252
Draguns, J. G., 346, 360, 361
Dranon, M., 352
Draper, R., 606, 614, 615
Draskoczy, P. R., 448, 471
Dreyfus, Jack, 266
Druley, K. A., 679
Drummer, E. J., 598
Dubovsky, S. L., 835, 836
Duffy, F. H., 484, 675
Dufour, H., 810
Duggan, V., 751
Duhm, J., 809
Duncan, W., 226, 478, 479, 482, 834, 836, 839, 841, 842, 869
Duncan-Jones, P., 156, 767, 772, 773, 780, 781, 948
Dunlap, K., 635
Dunn, V., 5
Dunner, D. L., 254, 258, 263, 268, 450, 598, 674, 835, 855
Durden, D. A., 452, 453
Durell, J., 448, 454
Durkheim, E., 781
Duval, S., 44, 45
Dweck, C. S., 918, 919, 930
Dyck, D., 436, 453
Dysken, M. W., 232
Dyson, W. L., 257, 258
D'Zuriela, T., 430

E

Eardley, D. A., 880
Eastwood, M. R., 771
Eaton, J. W., 782

Eaton, W. E., 769
Eaton, W. W., 671, 672
Eaves, G., 5, 412, 413, 417, 418, 435
Ebersole, E., 614, 855
Ebert, M. H., 228, 448, 449, 467, 830
Ebstein, R., 262
Eccleston, E., 450
Eckert, E., 270, 681
Eckman, E., 606, 615
Edelbrock, C., 524, 535, 1020
Edelstein, P., 225, 856
Edwards, A. L., 612
Edwards, D., 232, 454
Edwards, D. J., 823, 841
Edwards, J., 452, 453, 835
Edwards, P., 266
Egeland, J. A., 783, 871
Eggers, J., 22
Ehrensing, R. H., 264, 265, 465, 868
Ehrlich, B. E., 475, 476
Eichberger, G., 778
Eichman, W. G., 386
Eisdorfer, C., 560
Eisemann M., 828
Ekman, P., 376
el-Guebaly, N., 232
Eliot, J., 943
Elithorn, A., 280
Elizur, A., 454
Elliott, G. R., 824
Ellis, A., 59, 153, 415, 635
Elkin, I. E., 125, 148, 378
Elkins, R., 546, 840
Elsasser, G., 807
Elsinga, S., 281
Elston, R. C., 806
Elsworth, J. D., 254
El-Yousef, M. K., 238, 453, 454, 472, 832
Emery, G., 3, 125, 153, 333, 397, 421, 578, 579, 618, 634, 679, 821, 955
Emmons, M. L., 58
Emrich, H. M., 270
Ems, E. M., 780
Endicott, J., 47, 124, 131, 146, 226, 345, 348, 363, 373, 374, 378, 380, 382, 386, 482, 533, 588, 745, 769, 817, 820, 821, 858, 870, 943
Endo, J., 468
Endo, M., 468, 469
Eneroth, P., 463
Engel, G. L., 445
Engelhardt, H. T., 625, 766
Engelman, K., 450, 451
Engelsmann, F., 228, 269, 809
Enna, S. J., 236, 238
Epstein, D., 73, 580
Epstein, M., 436, 650
Epstein, P., 471, 473
Epstein, S., 380
Erbaugh, J., 47, 164, 383, 768
Ereshefsky, L., 246
Erickson, C. K., 823

Erickson, J. J., 485
Erickson, S., 258, 273, 476, 809
Ericsson, V., 828
Erman, M. K., 278
Erskine, R. G., 200
Escobar, J. I., 683
Eshleman, S. K., 871
Esler, M., 829
Espvall, M., 844
Esveldt-Dawson, K., 9, 542
Ettigi, P. G., 467, 470, 474, 866
Evans, D., 374
Evans, D. L., 242, 462, 856
Evans, J. R., 167
Evans, M., 268
Evans, M. D., 207
Evans, W. E., 241
Evenson, R. C., 609
Everett, G. M., 447
Extein, I., 237, 259, 264, 273, 454, 465, 466,
    470, 598, 600, 678, 856, 863, 865, 868
Eysenck, H. J., 41

F

Faber, J., 265, 464–65, 861
Fabre, L. F., 247, 575
Faden, V. B., 228
Fagin, L., 775
Faillace, L. A., 752
Fair, P. L., 848
Fairchild, C., 855, 858
Faithorn, P., 416
Falk, J. R., 270
Fang, V. S., 461, 559, 831, 859
Fankhauser, M. P., 235
Fann, W. E., 248
Faragella, F. F., 258
Faravelli, C., 351
Farberow, N. L., 612, 614
Farkas, T., 268
Faschingbauer, T. R., 386
Faull, K. F., 450, 455, 841, 860
Fava, G. A., 261
Fawcett, Jan, 232, 333, 445, 448, 449, 452,
    453–56, 458, 471–74, 608, 610, 835, 858
Fawcett, R., 473
Fawzy, F. I., 856
Fazio, C., 269
Feather, N. T., 19
Feiger, A., 232, 681
Feighner, J. P., 226, 247, 248, 351, 356, 357,
    361, 363, 522, 575, 745, 750, 751, 755,
    769
Feil, W. B., 158, 707, 719, 726, 736, 737
Feinberg, I., 559
Feinberg, M., 260, 349, 387, 388, 396, 451,
    460, 461, 462, 474, 479, 778, 833, 836,
    838, 839, 857, 858, 859
Feinberg, T. C., 424
Feinberg, T. L., 871, 1023
Feldman, J. M., 469

Feldman, L. B., 152
Feldstein, S., 277
Felner, A. E., 255
Fenichel, O., 80, 687, 688, 703
Fennell, M. J. V., 24, 29, 320, 334
Fenoglio, L., 855
Ferguson, J. M., 247
Ferrari, E., 855
Ferrell, R. B., 683
Ferris, C., 45
Ferris, R., 471
Ferster, C. B., 41
Feschbach, S., 542
Festinger, L., 780
Fetsch, R. J., 200
Feuer, E. J., 828
Fialkov, M. J., 545
Fibel, B., 20
Fielding, J. M., 389
Fieve, R. R., 157, 234, 254, 258, 261, 263, 268,
    270, 462, 800, 806, 807, 808, 809, 835,
    855, 857
Filippo, J. R., 153
Finch, C. E., 557
Fine, E. W., 398
Fink, Max, 221, 274, 275, 277, 278, 279, 479,
    869
Finkelstein, J., 468, 865
Finkelstein, R., 524, 871
Finlay-Jones, R., 767
Finley, P. R., 235
Finney, J. W., 954 n
Fisch, J., 376
Fisch, R., 152
Fischer, E., 452, 473
Fischer, J. R., 351
Fischer, P., 538, 539
Fischler, M., 876
Fischman, M. W., 334
Fisher, P., 543
Fisher-Beckfield, D., 425, 427, 430, 433, 948
Fiske, D. W., 929
Fitzgerald, K. C., 957
Fitzgerald, R. G., 157
Fitzpatrick, J., 520
Flach, F. F., 258
Fleischhacker, W. W., 270
Fleiss, J. L., 231, 232, 380, 800, 802, 806, 807,
    820, 821
Fleming, B. M., 415, 962
Fletcher, J., 780
Flinn, D., 685
Flood, C., 800
Flor-Henry, P., 843
Flynn, R. W., 847
Fog, R., 450
Fogarty, S. J., 23, 424
Fogelson, D., 856
Folkman, S., 428, 952, 960, 962
Folks, D. G., 266
Follette, W. C., 154

Folstein, M. F., 392
Fontana, A. F., 954
Ford, C. V., 575
Fordyce, W. E., 685
Forrest, A. D., 778
Forrest, T., 97
Foster, F. G., 232, 477, 478, 479, 838, 840, 843, 848, 874, 878
Foster, G., 226
Fouts, J. R., 223
Fowler, R. C., 225, 673
Fowles, D. C., 396
Fox, K., 736
Fox, R., 677, 679
Fram, D. H., 255, 264, 481
Frame, C., 545
Frances, A., 254, 279
Frances, R., 869
Francis, A., 676
Franckson, J. M., 462, 856
Frank, Ellen, 816, 838
Frank, J., 127, 963
Frankel, B. L., 226, 478, 836
Frankenburg, F., 269
Franklin, F., 947
Franklin, J., 208, 421, 880
Franks, R. D., 835, 836
Frantz, A. G., 467, 468
Fras, I., 600
Fraser, A., 462, 860
Fraser, A. R., 857
Fraser, R. H., 778
Frazer, A., 234, 237, 257, 258, 447, 454, 467, 475, 476, 809
Frederick, C. J., 616, 617
Frederickson, L. W., 690
Fredman, D. J., 245
Freedman, A. M., 869
Freedman, R., 675
Freeman, F. R., 480
Freeman, L., 532, 1021
Freeman, S. J., 965
Fremming, K. H., 772
Fremouw, W. J., 681
Fremoux, W., 429
French, A. P., 545
French, J. R. P., 950
French, N. H., 19, 542
Frerichs, R. R., 754, 755
Freud, Sigmund, 82, 84, 85, 477, 561, 703, 708, 920, 924
Frey, J., 230
Frey, S., 376
Friedel, R. O., 226, 230, 231, 232, 234, 235, 455, 592, 818
Friedman, A. S., 160, 327, 328, 388
Friedman, E., 238, 256, 317
Friedman, M. J., 235, 238, 560, 671, 672
Friedman, R., 384, 537
Friesen, D., 239
Friesen, H. G., 868

Friesen, W., 376
Frith, C. D., 227
Froese, A., 542
Frohman, L. A., 456
Frolich, J. C., 260
Froman, P. K., 1024
Fromm-Auch, D., 278
Frommer, E. A., 546
Fromuth, M. E., 384, 387
Frost, L. L., 562
Frost, R. O., 23, 410, 411, 437
Fuchs, C. Z., 25, 62, 65, 66, 209, 423, 846
Fuchs-Robetin, G., 778
Fuentes, J. A., 250
Fuhr, R., 164
Fukushima, D. K., 458
Funabiki, D., 957, 960
Fuxe, K., 452
Fyer, A., 227, 230

G

Gaensbauer, T. J., 529
Gaertner, J. H., 454, 827, 849
Gaffney, F., 857
Gaillard, J. M., 841
Galhenage, S., 856
Gallagher, D., 72, 73, 384, 580
Gallagher, D. E., 26, 28, 322
Gallagher, P., 273
Gallagher, T. F., 458
Gallaper, D., 263, 475
Galvao-Teles, A., 758
Galzenati, M., 269
Gambrill, E., 60
Gammon, G. D., 246
Gampel, D., 480
Gandhy, P. R., 1022
Gandolfi, O., 256
Ganellen, R. J., 19, 930
Garber, J., 537, 947
Garbutt, J. C., 863
Garcia-Sevilla, J. A., 236, 832
Gardner, E., 390
Gardner, E. R., 747, 748
Gardner, M., 253
Gardner, R. W., 462, 857
Garfield, S. L., 208, 321
Garfinkel, B. D., 542
Garfinkel, R., 174, 681
Garland, B. L., 263, 825
Garmezy, N., 174
Garner, D., 399, 448, 467, 681
Garrick, N. A., 254
Garside, R. F., 227, 397, 778, 779
Garver, D. L., 225, 468, 469, 867
Gaspar, M., 587
Gasperini, M., 157
Gastpar, M., 800
Gaultieri, C. T., 228
Gaviria, M., 258, 476, 809, 845, 859
Gawin, F. H., 243

Gaztanaga, P., 811
Geagea, K. C., 266
Geer, J., 921
Gelder, M., 687
Gelenberg, A. J., 246
Geller, B., 856
Gentry, K. A., 688
George, L., 235
Gerber, C. J., 560
Gerlach, J., 450
Gerner, R., 28, 322, 461, 462, 473, 569, 597,
     681, 683, 842, 852, 855, 860, 863, 867
Gersh, F., 396
Gershon, E. J., 800
Gershon, E. S., 162, 238, 257, 353, 482, 524,
     709, 718, 818, 834, 844
Gershon, S., 234, 237, 244, 256, 262, 279,
     448, 449, 454, 459, 472, 856
Gerst, M., 777
Geschwind, J., 571
Ghadirian, A. M., 262, 269
Ghrist, S. L., 385
Giamartino, G. A., 965
Giardina, W. J., 447
Giardini, E. V., 573
Gibbons, J. S., 615
Gibbons, R., 532, 1021
Gibbons, R. D., 258, 273, 476, 481, 835, 845,
     855
Gibbons, R. L., 827
Giddings, S., 832
Giedke, H., 843, 849
Giles, D. E., 479, 843, 855, 858, 880
Gillam, J., 227
Giller, E., 614, 855
Gillespie, R. D., 349, 817
Gilliland, A. R., 386
Gillin, J. C., 226, 228, 238, 282, 453, 469, 478,
     479, 480–83, 678, 832, 834, 836, 838–42,
     869, 874, 877
Gilmore, M., 676
Gilpin, D. C., 545
Girlin, M. J., 598
Gitlow, S. E., 448
Gittelman-Klein, R., 227, 518
Gittleman, R., 834
Gittleson, N. L., 671, 738
Givirtsman, H. E., 598
Glaser, H. I., 822
Glaser, K., 518, 543, 545
Glass, D. R., 60, 379, 380, 381, 382, 410, 424
Glass, G. V., 117, 200
Glass, R. M., 227, 334, 754, 755
Glasser, William, 198, 199
Glassman, A. H., 228, 232, 234, 240, 348, 467,
     573, 682, 767, 819, 825, 828
Glaubman, H., 542, 543
Glazer, W., 125, 164
Glen, A., 397
Glen, A. I. M., 28, 320, 642, 881
Gleser, G. C., 818

Glick, Ira D., 151, 160, 161, 166, 167
Gliklich, J., 227
Gloger, S., 227
Glover, V., 254
Glowinski, J., 235
Glueck, B. C., 596
Goetz, R., 480, 533, 840, 867
Goetzl, V., 806
Goklaney, M., 124, 206, 216, 318
Gold, A., 227
Gold, M. S., 465, 466, 599, 678, 856, 861, 863,
     864, 865, 869, 870
Gold, P., 454
Gold, P. W., 465, 467, 846, 861, 864, 866, 867,
     868, 880
Goldberg, D., 320
Goldberg, D. P., 781
Goldberg, H. L., 241
Goldberg, I. J. L., 454
Goldberg, I. K., 462
Goldberg, S., 474
Goldberg, S. C., 228, 681
Golden, R. N., 242
Goldfried, M., 430
Goldin, J. C., 26, 29
Goldin, L. R., 800
Goldman, E., 384
Goldman, R., 101, 103, 112
Goldney, R. D., 609, 610
Goldring, N., 85, 857
Goldstein, J., 864
Goldstein, L., 676
Goldstein, M. J., 167
Golin, S., 21, 24, 417, 928, 953
Golub, S., 200
Gomez, F., 850
Gomez, I., 683
Gong-Guy, E., 953
Gonzales, L., 73
Goodall, McC., 448, 450
Goodell, H., 128
Good-Ellis, M., 161
Goodenough, D. R., 960
Goodman, P., 195
Goodnick, P. J., 258
Goodpaster, W. A., 730
Goodstein, J. L., 606, 607, 613
Goodwin, A. M., 411
Goodwin, B. L., 452, 454
Goodwin, D. W., 346
Goodwin, F. K., 233, 234, 235, 237, 239, 254,
     258, 262, 264, 265, 273, 279, 280, 282,
     447, 449, 450, 451, 454, 465, 467, 468,
     479, 482, 484, 614, 671, 736, 817, 820,
     825–31, 836, 841, 844, 861, 864, 866,
     868, 869, 872–77
Gordon, A. M., 849
Gordon, E. K., 448, 449, 450, 454, 827
Gordon, F. G., 477
Gordon, J., 234
Gordon, N. H., 535, 536

Gore, S., 950, 951
Gorham, D. R., 397
Gorman, J. M., 227
Gotlib, I. H., 20, 413, 432, 435, 437
Gottfries, C. G., 855
Gottlieb, B. H., 965
Gottlieb, J. S., 477
Gould, J. W., 384, 385
Goulding, M. M., 186, 187, 193
Goulding, R. L., 186, 187, 193
Gourash, N., 958
Goyer, P. F., 830
Grab, E. L., 232, 448, 449, 454
Grad, B., 558
Grad de Alarcon, J., 774
Graf, M., 60, 423
Graff, M., 23
Graham, J. R., 386, 393
Graham, P., 374, 529, 769
Graham, P. M., 856
Gram, L. F., 235
Granick, S., 388
Grant, I., 777
Granville-Grossman, K. L., 753, 780
Grau, T. G., 481
Grauer, L., 64, 160
Gravelle, H. S. E., 774
Graves, D. J., 20
Greaves, G. B., 686
Greden, J. F., 236, 243, 389, 396, 451, 455,
   456, 460, 461, 474, 479, 832, 833, 834,
   836, 838, 848, 855, 857, 859
Green, A., 1013
Green, J., 384, 531
Green, J. K., 680
Green, J. P., 238
Green, R., 235, 448, 688, 806
Greenberg, D. A., 232
Greenberg, M. S., 571
Greenberg, R., 480
Greenberg, R. D., 264
Greenberg, R. L., 8
Greenblatt, D. J., 240, 248, 671
Greene, B. L., 157
Greene, N. M., 448
Greene, R. F., 266
Greengard, P., 238
Greengrass, P. M., 454, 455
Greenhill, L. L., 546
Greenson, R., 689
Greenspan, K., 454
Greenwald, D. P., 216
Greenwood, F. C., 467
Greer, S., 615, 616
Gregoire, F., 468, 469, 866, 868
Greil, W., 809
Greist, J. H., 72, 262, 861
Gresock, C., 386
Griesemer, E. C., 252
Griffin, H., 524
Griffin, N. J., 537, 538

Griffing, G., 271
Grimson, R. C., 524
Gringras, M., 454
Grinker, R. R., 388, 706, 711, 713, 720, 721,
   723, 726, 727, 729
Grobecker, H., 452
Grof, P., 258, 260, 384
Groom, G., 263
Gross, H. A., 228
Gross, M. D., 247
Gross, V., 542
Grosscup, S. J., 43, 44, 50, 205, 423, 424
Grossman, J. A., 532, 856, 1021
Grove, W. M., 349
Groves, J. E., 248
Gruen, P. H., 467, 468, 867
Gruen, R., 157, 831
Gruenau, C., 228
Grunberg, F., 597
Grunberger, J., 269
Grundy, G., 450
Grunebaum, H., 174
Grunhaus, L., 462, 855, 857, 868
Gudeman, J. E., 448, 675, 726, 778, 828
Guerriero, L. A., 200
Gulomb, M., 454
Gumbrecht, G., 573
Gunn, R. B., 476, 869
Gur, R. C., 571
Gurland, B. J., 767, 796, 820
Gurman, A., 107, 154, 160, 164
Guroff, J. J., 800, 844
Gurtman, M. B., 20
Gusovsky, F., 452, 453, 471, 835
Gustafson, J. P., 102, 106
Gustafson, L., 847
Guthrie, Leslie, 376, 606
Guttmacher, L. B., 855, 856
Guttman, L., 768
Guttorsmen, S., 800
Guze, S. B., 522, 591, 674, 675, 687, 745, 769,
   821
Gwirtsman, H., 461, 473, 681, 855, 863, 874

H

Haas, Gretchen L., 151, 161, 167
Haas, J., 476
Haas, M., 475
Haberman, S. J., 777
Hackett, E., 230
Hadley, S. W., 125, 326, 379
Hafstad, K. M., 832
Hagnell, O., 773
Haier, R. J., 462, 858
Hajioft, J., 227
Hakami, N., 525
Hakstian, A. R., 64, 71, 117, 209, 323, 325,
   327, 963
Halaris, A. E., 449, 874
Halbreich, U., 467, 474, 482, 852, 853, 854,
   858, 859, 866, 868, 870, 871

Hale, W. D., 20
Haley, J., 152
Halikas, J. A., 358, 779
Hall, K. R., 855
Hall, R. C. W., 248, 683, 686, 746, 747, 752, 753, 754
Haller, R., 349
Hallstrom, C., 598
Halmi, K. A., 270, 680, 681
Halpern, F. S., 458, 467, 468, 474, 481, 533, 839, 852, 853, 854, 859, 866, 867, 868
Halter, J. B., 860
Hamer, R. M., 474
Hamilton, E. W., 21, 208, 413, 418, 435, 436, 880, 934, 953
Hamilton, M., 131, 147, 164, 274, 350, 374, 379, 380, 381, 396, 750, 751, 821, 987
Hamlet, G., 454
Hamm, J. E., 677
Hammen, Constance, 19, 21, 24, 60, 408–11, 421, 424, 425, 426, 429, 436, 437, 948, 952, 953, 954, 958, 962, 1013
Hamovit, J., 524
Hampson, J. L., 686
Hanaoka, M., 266
Handy, L. M., 797, 817
Hanin, I., 232, 233, 449, 454, 479, 481, 827, 841, 846
Hankoff, L. D., 609, 610, 611, 616
Hanley, R., 683
Hanlon, C., 480, 533, 840
Hanlon, T. E., 384
Hannum, T. E., 385
Hansen, C., 246
Hansen, H. E., 262
Hanson, B., 124, 318
Hanson, L. C. F., 471
Hardiker, T. M., 232
Harding, J. S., 768
Hare, E. H., 264, 771, 773
Harkness, L., 614, 855
Harmon, R. J., 529
Harmon, R. L., 264
Harmon, T. M., 60, 638, 639, 957
Harper, D., 608
Harper, R. A., 59, 153
Harrell, T. H ., 412
Harrington, J. B., 390
Harris, E., 161
Harris, I. S., 558
Harris, P., 269
Harris, P. Q., 246
Harris, T., 128, 151, 156, 158, 160, 169, 185, 187, 767
Harris, T. O., 350, 774, 777, 778, 779, 780, 944, 945, 960
Harris, W. G., 72
Harris, W. H., 258
Harrison, R., 436
Harrison, W., 228, 230, 251, 252, 254, 255, 593, 682
Hartel, F. W., 334

Hartford, J. M., 558
Hartman, B., 239
Hartmann, E., 448, 471, 841
Hartney, L. M., 20
Harvald, B., 353, 797
Harvey, D. M., 953
Harvey, J. H., 927
Haskett, R. F., 396, 455, 456, 461, 462, 474, 857, 859
Hathaway, S. R., 385, 399
Hatotani, N., 468
Hatsukami, D., 677
Hattox, S. E., 448
Hauge, M., 353, 797
Hauger, R., 254, 831
Hauri, P., 3, 21, 480
Havdala, H. S., 473
Hawkins, D., 479, 480
Hawkins, J. W., 543
Hawthorne, B. C., 613
Hawton, K., 615
Haycox, J., 27, 869
Hayes, P. E., 474
Hayes, S. C., 60, 72, 638, 957
Haykal, R. F., 355, 396, 478, 589, 701, 767
Hays, P., 673
Head, R., 21, 410, 953, 1013
Healey, S., 226
Hearn, M., 374
Heath, B., 455, 832, 859
Heckman, H. H., 264
Hedley, L. R., 238
Hedlund, B., 73
Hedlund, J., 380, 381
Heersema, P., 1015
Hefferling, R. F., 195
Heider, F., 931
Heidingsfelder, S. A., 467
Heilbronn, M., 684, 685, 840
Heimann, H., 843
Heimberg, Richard, 213, 324
Heinze, G., 467, 866
Heiser, J. F., 230, 239
Helgason, L., 772
Helgasson, T., 796
Heller, B., 452
Heller, N., 559
Hellman, L., 458, 468, 865
Hellon, C. P., 607
Helms, P. M., 767, 819
Helsing, K. J., 771
Helzer, J. E., 360, 378, 671, 769
Hemmingsen, R., 242
Henderson, A. S., 773, 780, 781
Henderson, S., 128, 156, 948, 961
Hendin, A., 620
Hendrie, H. C., 778, 830
Heninger, G. R., 447, 449, 450, 454, 455, 468, 827, 831, 832, 865, 878
Herceg-Baron, R., 138, 151, 318
Herjanic, M., 351, 534, 1022
Herman, I., 612

Herridge, C. F., 753
Herrman, R. S., 346
Hersen, M., 39, 66, 67, 73, 118, 204, 205, 209, 210, 211, 214, 216, 228, 323, 324, 378, 386, 881
Hertting, G., 249
Herz, A., 270
Herzog, C., 247
Herzog, D. B., 228
Heseltine, G. F. D., 227
Hestbech, J., 262
Hetherington, E. M., 174
Heyes, J., 454
Heyneman, N. E., 681
Hibbert, G. A., 29
Hickey, N., 780
Hill, M. A., 580
Hillier, V., 767
Himmelhoch, J. M., 66, 67, 73, 118, 204–5, 209, 210, 216, 323, 324, 354, 479, 597, 809, 819, 838, 842, 843, 846, 848, 874, 878
Himwich, H. E., 450
Hinchcliffe, M., 159, 425
Hinson, J., 6126
Hippins, H., 468
Hirata, F., 269
Hiroto, D. S., 918
Hirsbrunner, H., 376
Hirsch, B., 950
Hirsch, M., 533, 1023
Hirsch, S. R., 606, 609, 614, 615, 673
Hirschfeld, M. A., 151
Hirschfeld, R. M. A., 348, 588, 596, 701, 715, 716, 736, 778, 779, 781, 855
Hirschowitz, J., 225
Hitzemann, R., 279
Ho, B., 453
Hoberman, Harry, M., 39, 44, 53, 62, 63, 154, 213, 528
Hodges, Kay Kline, 517, 518, 524, 534, 535, 573, 1019
Hodgson, J. W., 26, 28
Hoefer, D. D., 688
Hoeper, E. W., 528
Hoffman, G., 864
Hoffman, L., 152
Hofschuster, E., 462, 857
Hogan, B. K., 152
Hogan, P., 152
Hogarty, G. E., 167
Hogben, G. L., 228, 672
Hokanson, J. E., 5, 19, 376, 425, 426, 968
Hokfelt, T., 447
Holaday, J. W., 279
Hole, G., 232
Holinger, P. E., 539, 544
Hollingsworth, P. J., 236, 832
Hollister, L. E., 233, 238, 264, 449, 454, 455, 465, 713, 720, 723, 725, 726, 827, 860, 864

Hollon, S. D., 3, 4, 8, 21, 23, 25 n, 26, 27, 28, 30, 31, 39, 207, 214, 319, 320, 321, 332, 333, 409, 412, 413, 424, 432, 433, 436, 645, 881, 947, 952, 962, 963, 964, 1012
Holman, R. B., 824
Holmes, T. H., 63, 128, 776
Holsboer, F., 462, 857, 859
Holt, R. R., 944
Holzer, B., 479, 841, 874
Holzer, C., 380, 557, 773
Holzman, P. S., 845
Honore, P., 830
Hood, J., 542
Hooper, D., 159
Hoppers, L., 855
Hops, H., 154
Hornblow, A. R., 608, 609
Hornstra, R. K., 392
Hornum, I., 258
Horowitz, H. M., 153
Horowitz, L. M., 116
Horowitz, M., 101, 102, 105, 108, 112, 113, 114, 118, 119, 120, 962
Horowitz, M. J., 137, 779
Horvath, T., 833
Hostetler, J. A., 782
Hostetter, A. M., 783, 871
House, D., 855
House, J. S., 950
Howard, E., 465
Howard, G. S., 70, 205, 325, 881
Howard, K. I., 116
Howes, M., 376, 426, 958
Hoya, W. K., 238
Hoyt, M. F., 112
Hrubec, H., 811
Hsieh, J. Y. K., 455, 860, 864
Hsu, L. K. G., 680
Hu, R., 240
Huang, H., 559, 1015
Hudson, J. I., 228, 681, 682, 855, 856
Huellett, J., 847
Huey, L. Y., 868
Hugdens, R. W., 542
Huggins, P., 227
Hughes, L. A., 954
Hughes, M. D., 390
Hungerbuhler, J. P., 57
Hunt, D. D., 686
Hunt, H. F., 164
Hunt, W. A., 346
Huntington, G. E., 782
Hurry, J., 769, 770, 772, 773, 774, 777, 778, 779, 783
Hursch, C. J., 838
Hurst, M. W., 775
Hurt, S. W., 475, 845
Hurvish, M. S., 21
Husain, A., 518, 524–25, 528, 545
Husaine, B. A., 390
Huston, P. E., 818
Hutchinson, G., 774

Hutchinson, J. C., 239
Hwu, H. G., 857

I

Iacono, W. G., 845, 849, 850
Ibsen, L., 235
Ickes, J., 45
Ickes, W. J., 927
Iker, H. P., 859
Ilfeld, F. N., 128, 155
Imhof, P., 573
Imura, H., 868
Inamdar, S. C., 524, 526, 621
Inanga, K., 266
Ingham, J. C., 773, 774
Ingvar, D. H., 847
Innes, I. R., 471
Insel, T. R., 228, 473, 480, 671, 840, 855, 856, 860
Inturrisi, C. E., 279, 869
Inwang, E. E., 452, 473
Iorio, G., 841
Irwin, G. H., 239
Isaacs, A., 374, 769
Isberg, R. S., 228
Isherwood, J., 608, 609
Ishino, H., 257
Ithenhuth, E. H., 334
Itil, T. M., 264, 869
Ives, J. O., 235, 252, 560
Ivey, A., 374

J

Jacisin, J. J., 865
Jack, R. A., 266
Jackel, 454
Jackman, G., 829
Jackoway, M. K., 525
Jackson, D. D., 152
Jackson, P. R., 775
Jackson, R., 806
Jackson, R. L., 918
Jacobs, D., 610, 611, 616
Jacobs, J., 542, 543
Jacobs, L. S., 469
Jacobs, M., 436, 948
Jacobsen, G., 227
Jacobsen, O., 235
Jacobson, A., 167
Jacobson, E., 57, 87 n, 91, 98, 562
Jacobson, M., 425
Jacobson, N. S., 154, 211
Jacoby, C. J., 846
Jacquy, J., 847
Jaffe, K., 855
Jaffee, J. H., 678
Jakubowski, P., 635
James, A. E., 485
James, M., 184
James, N., 396
James, N. McI., 460, 461, 462, 474, 855, 857

Jamison, K. R., 270
Janicak, P. G., 273, 845
Janowsky, D. S., 238, 243, 263, 282, 453, 454, 461, 472, 483, 820, 833, 849, 854, 859, 868, 869, 877
Jarrett, D. B., 482, 838, 839, 853, 858, 874
Jarrett, R. B., 72
Jarvik, L. F., 322, 325, 327, 380
Jatlow, P., 234
Javaid, J., 449, 452, 453, 455, 471, 472, 473, 827, 835
Jeanneret, O., 544
Jefferson, J. W., 262, 746, 861
Jeffriess, H., 452, 453, 471
Jeger, A. M., 616, 619
Jenike, M. A., 228, 558
Jenkins, C. D., 775, 777
Jenner, F. A., 262
Jennings, C., 615
Jerkovich, G., 239
Jerrett, I., 540
Jiang, N. S., 860
Jimerson, D., 254, 449, 450, 830, 860, 867
Jobson, K., 227, 228
Joffee, W. G., 87
Johanson, M., 847
Johansson, F., 870
Johansson, O., 447
Johnson, G., 262
Johnson, J., 950
Johnson, J. E., 20
Johnson, J. H., 72, 777
Johnson, J. J., 22
Johnson, J. L., 847
Johnson, K., 422
Johnston, R., 462, 673, 674, 857, 1023
Johnstone, E. C., 227, 253
Jonas, J. M., 228, 681
Jonas, W. Z., 257
Jones, B., 269
Jones, D., 827, 840
Jones, E. E., 919
Jones, F., 448, 845
Jones, M., 66, 325
Jones, R. G., 409, 414, 415, 420, 1016
Jones, S. L., 73
Jongeward, D., 184
Jonsson, J., 452
Jope, R. S., 263
Jornestedt, L., 228, 671
Jortner, S., 386
Joseph, M. S., 859
Jouvent, R., 270
Judd, L. L., 263, 868, 869
Juel-Neilson, N., 222
Juergens, S., 247
Julien, R., 810
Junge, C., 261
Jurjevich, R. M., 386

K

Kafka, M. S., 236, 263
Kagedol, B., 465
Kahn, A., 678
Kahn, J. A., 964
Kahn, S., 946, 950
Kakimoto, Y., 452
Kales, A., 226
Kales, J. D., 226
Kalin, N. H., 453, 461, 473, 820, 825, 829, 854, 856, 859, 869
Kalinowski, L., 222
Kallman, F. J., 795, 797, 806, 807, 817
Kaltreider, N., 101, 120, 779
Kane, J., 546, 671
Kanfer, R., 19, 418, 635
Kanner, A. D., 425, 945
Kanof, P. D., 238
Kanter, D. R., 225
Kantor, S. J., 232, 240, 573
Kantrowich, J., 448, 449
Kaplan, B. H., 524
Kaplan, H. S., 687, 688
Kaplan, R. D., 254
Kapur, R. L., 784
Karacan, I., 480, 838
Karasu, T. B., 116
Karlberg, B. E., 465
Karlsson, I., 855
Karoly, P., 19, 20
Karones, S. L., 861
Karoum, F., 254, 453, 827, 829
Karpman, B., 635
Karst, T. O., 414
Kashani, J. H., 518, 524, 525, 528, 540, 545
Kaslow, N. J., 70, 419, 421, 526, 537, 538, 545, 916
Kasper, S., 855
Kassir, S., 261
Kastin, A. J., 264, 265, 465, 868
Kathol, Roger G., 397, 745, 751, 752, 865
Kato, Y., 868
Katon, W., 375, 683
Katschnig, H., 778
Katz, G., 264
Katz, I. R., 683
Katz, M. M., 354, 378, 767, 827
Kauffman, C., 174
Kay, D. W. K., 778, 781
Kaye, I. S., 558
Kaye, W., 228
Kazdin, A. E., 19, 20, 41, 58, 209, 393, 530, 542, 545, 639
Keeler, B. A., 448, 449, 841
Kegan, R., 705, 719, 721, 735
Keisling, R., 267
Keller, K. E., 414
Keller, M., 716
Keller, M. B., 174, 589, 964
Kelley, H. H., 924

Kellner, C. H., 846
Kelly, D., 598
Kelly, G. A., 635, 924
Kelly, J., 227
Kelwala, S., 244, 249, 827, 830, 840
Kendall, D. A., 236, 238
Kendall, P. E., 21, 409, 412, 413, 433, 436, 537, 952, 1012
Kendall, R. E., 796
Kendell, R. E., 348, 593, 736, 738, 779, 820
Kendell, R. R., 767
Kendler, K. S., 673, 676
Kennard, J., 155
Kennedy, M. E., 855
Kennedy, P., 615
Kenyon, J. M., 689
Kerkofs, M., 864
Kern, H. A., 877
Kernberg, O., 105, 721
Kerr, T. A., 670, 779
Kessler, K., 239, 264
Kessler, M., 964
Kessler, R., 847, 954 n, 959
Kety, S. S., 268, 454
Khani, M. K., 700, 727
Khatami, M., 6, 963
Kidd, K. K., 174
Kidd, R. F., 927
Kielholz, P., 587, 591, 598, 800
Kiev, A., 617, 619
Kikowski, J., 450
Kilmann, P. R., 272, 273
Kiloh, L. G., 220, 397, 569, 778, 818
Kim, W. Y., 247
Kimball, C. P., 754
Kimball, R. R., 258
Kinard, K., 261
Kincel, R. L., 611
King, A. C., 847
King, D., 227, 353, 462, 478, 479, 589, 600, 841, 857
King, L. D., 266
King, R. A., 542
Kipperman, A., 709
Kirchheimer, W. F., 223
Kiriakos, R., 809
Kirk, L., 262
Kirkegaard, C., 265, 464, 466, 861, 863
Kirsten, L. S., 827, 864
Kissling, W., 270
Kizuka, P. P., 828, 860
Kjellberg, O., 450
Kjellman, B., 463, 465
Kleber, H. D., 125, 351, 679, 746
Klee, S. H., 21, 410, 417
Klein, D., 156
Klein, D. F., 227, 228, 230, 232, 252, 345, 356, 396, 397, 481, 593, 594, 596, 711, 729, 731, 834, 839, 866
Klein, M. H., 72
Klein, R. H., 845

Klein, W. J., 830
Kleinman, A., 683
Kleinman, J., 869
Kleitman, N., 477
Klerman, Gerald L., 115, 124, 125, 132, 145, 151, 155, 157, 161, 168, 174, 204, 205, 206, 216, 248, 317, 318, 319, 327, 333, 335, 348, 350, 353, 360, 526, 588, 589, 591, 609, 684, 700, 701, 709, 715, 716, 718, 721, 726, 736, 773, 774, 778, 779, 821, 848, 881, 959, 960
Klett, C. J., 809
Kline, J., 534, 1019
Kline, N. S., 223, 265, 598, 818, 869
Klinedinst, J. K., 535, 1024
Kling, A. S., 847
Klinger, E., 917
Klotz, J., 353
Knapp, S., 263
Knight, R. G., 389
Knight, R. P., 726
Knights, A., 673
Kniskern, D. P., 154, 160, 164
Knitter, E. F., 856
Knoll, J., 254, 256
Knott, J. R., 477
Knowles, J. B., 479, 480, 482, 874
Knox, A., 264, 454
Kobasa, S. C., 946
Kobos, J. C., 101
Kocsis, J., 234, 254, 449
Koe, B. K., 471
Kohlberg, L., 705
Koinig, G., 863
Kolb, L. C., 93, 671, 736
Koles, K. Z., 843
Kolivakis, T., 809
Kolmer, H. S., 458
Kondo, H., 469
Koomen, J. C., 266
Kopel, S., 637
Kopin, I. J., 235, 448, 827, 829, 860
Koranyi, E. K., 746, 752
Koresko, R., 559
Korf, J., 450, 829
Kornblith, S. J., 39, 65, 66, 209, 216, 419, 423, 638, 639, 879
Kosky, R., 542, 543
Koslow, S. H., 449, 455, 468, 827, 829, 830, 832, 855, 856, 865, 867
Koss, M. P., 117
Kotik, Doreen, 700
Kotin, J., 268, 353
Koukkou, M., 869
Kovacs, M., 3, 16, 20, 27, 30, 205, 216, 319, 376, 524, 528, 529, 530, 533, 610, 612, 645, 653, 871, 881, 962, 964, 1020, 1021, 1023
Kowalik, S., 831
Kraemer, H., 450, 681
Kraepelin, E., 127, 347, 361, 797, 817, 820

Kraft, T. B., 247
Kraft, W., 374
Kral, V. A., 558
Kramer, M., 557, 772
Kramlinger, K. G., 226, 684
Kramp, P., 380
Krane, R. V., 23
Krantz, Susan E., 21, 24, 408, 409, 410, 411, 416, 421, 436, 437, 952, 953, 1013
Kranzler, G., 59
Krasner, L., 345
Krasnoff, L., 776, 961
Krause, N., 775
Krautwald, O., 235
Kravitz, Howard M., 445, 858
Kreitman, N., 152, 613, 773, 774
Kreuter, F., 827
Krieger, D. T., 458, 468, 824
Krieger, H. P., 458
Krieger, J. N., 247
Kringlen, E., 797
Kripke, D. F., 282, 451, 897
Krishnan, R. R., 856
Kronauer, R. S., 873
Kronfol, Z., 243, 460, 462, 474, 834, 857
Krueger, A., 238
Krueter, J., 454
Kruger, E. R., 449, 454, 827
Krupnick, J., 101
Kufferle, B., 269
Kuhl, D. E., 847
Kuhn, R., 223, 447, 546, 818
Kuhn, V., 546
Kuiper, N. A., 19
Kulcsar, A., 237
Kulik, F. A., 247
Kumakura, N., 771
Kumar, P., 254
Kumbaraci, T., 263
Kuperman, S., 482, 846
Kupfer, David J., 226, 232, 233, 280, 332, 354, 375, 454, 477, 478, 479, 480, 481, 482, 546, 559, 569, 597, 598, 809, 816, 819, 820, 822, 823, 825, 828, 834, 836–44, 846, 848, 853, 855–58, 861, 863, 868, 870, 874, 878–81
Kupietz, S. S., 228
Kurcz, M., 830, 861
Kurelek, William, 271
Kurland, A. A., 384
Kuromaru, S., 868
Kurtz, N., 847

L

Laakman, G., 468, 867
LaBrie, R. A., 448
Lache, D., 535, 1024
Ladame, F., 544
Lader, M., 252, 843, 849
Laffaw, J. A., 608

Laffer, P. S., 855
Lahmeyer, H. W., 840
Lajtha, A., 265
Lake, C. R., 236, 449, 829, 840, 844, 860
Lakein, A., 59
Lamberg, B. A., 265, 861
Lambert, M. J., 1017
Lambourne, J., 253
Lamela, M., 621
Lamour, M., 529
Lamparski, D. M., 71, 419, 638
Lancashire, M., 425
Lancee, W., 607
Landau, S., 484, 844
Landis, D. H., 448, 832
Landon, J., 467
Landrum, G. C., 425
Landsdrum, G., 5–6
Landsman, S. G., 200
Lang, M., 530, 531, 1022
Lange, A., 635
Langer, D. H., 840
Langer, E., 45
Langer, E. J., 933
Langer, G., 467, 863, 866
Langer, S. Z., 237, 831
Langevin, R., 385
Langley, G. E., 564
Langlois, P. J., 861
Langlois, R., 832
Langner, T., 768
Langstrom, G., 855
Lanke, J., 774
Lankford, A., 23
Lantta, O., 451, 852
Lanyon, R. I., 687
Lapierre, Y. D., 246, 849
Lapin, I. P., 236, 268
Lapointe, K. A., 21, 23, 27, 415, 436
Lara, P. P., 463, 465
Larkin, J., 462, 857
LaRocco, J. M., 950
Larsen, J. K., 280
Larsen, O. B., 830
Larson, D. W., 19, 208, 421, 880, 947
Larson, E., 683
Larson, J., 845
LaRue, A., 558, 682, 856, 857
Laski, E., 265
Laughton, E. M., 559
Launier, R., 430
Lauridsen, U. B., 465
Lauterbur, P. C., 485, 675
Law-Vone, B., 273
Layne, C., 20
Lazare, A., 684, 709
Lazarsfeld, P. F., 768
Lazarus, A. A., 42
Lazarus, R., 425, 428, 430, 945, 952, 955, 960, 962
Leaf, P. J., 557

Leber, William, 30, 316, 343, 373, 411, 434
Lebovitz, H. E., 469
LeCann, A. F., 686, 747, 748
Leccardi, G., 874
Lechin, F., 850
Leckman, J. F., 353, 449, 450, 670, 827
Lecrubier, Y., 270
Ledwidge, B., 227
Lee, J. S., 261
Lee, M. A., 875
Lee, R. R., 157
Leeavathi, D. E., 234, 240
Lees, A. J., 254
Lefcourt, H. M., 946
Lefebvre, M. F., 21, 421
Leff, J. P., 156, 169, 769, 782, 950
Leff, M. H., 778
Leff, M. J., 231
Leff, M. L., 89, 174, 610
Lefkowitz, M. M., 517, 518, 524, 525, 535, 537, 1024
Lefton, W., 20
Leftwich, R., 260
Lehman, H. E., 262, 265, 266, 670, 675, 682, 683, 686, 869
Lehman, Laurent, 669
Leibl, R. D., 200
Leighton, A. H., 768, 781, 783
Leighton, D. C., 768
Leirer, V. O., 1015
Leiser, L. A., 238
Leitch, L., 227
Lemmi, H., 355, 396, 478, 479, 589, 593, 598, 600, 670, 701, 767, 841
Lemoine, M., 832
Lemperiere, T., 384
Leon, G. R., 537
Leonard, D. P., 232
Leonard, P., 829
Leonhard, K., 352, 795, 798
Lepine, J. P., 270
Lerbinger, J., 828, 860
Lerer, B., 279
Leroy, A., 836
Lesar, T., 247
Lesko, L. M., 255
Lesse, S., 226, 672, 683, 684, 708
Lesser, I., 246
Lesser, M., 671
Lester, D., 20, 385, 612, 689, 1015
Lester, Gregory W., 184
Letmendia, F. J., 480
Letofsky, K., 607
Lettieri, D. J., 613
Leveille, J., 269
Leventhal, B., 235
Leventhal, J., 565
Levin, S., 845
Levine, J. L., 321, 322
Levine, P. M., 683
Levine, R. A., 270

Levine, S., 91
Levitt, E. E., 1017
Levitt, M., 227
Levy, B. F., 833, 855
Levy, D. L., 845
Levy, R. L., 634, 636, 640
Lewi, P. J., 239
Lewinsohn, Peter M., 5, 19, 20, 21, 25, 39,
    42–46, 48–50, 53, 56, 60–63, 66, 72, 73,
    125, 153, 154, 164, 205, 208, 213, 324,
    349, 376, 391, 421, 423–27, 432, 435,
    528, 580, 639, 704, 705, 713, 723, 725,
    880, 916, 947, 948, 954, 962, 963, 1005
Lewis, A., 161
Lewis, A. J., 767
Lewis, C. E., 593, 746
Lewis, D. A., 865, 866
Lewis, D. O., 621
Lewis, J. K., 880
Lewis, N. D. C., 221
Lewy, A., 236, 282, 876, 877
L'Hermite, M., 470, 864
Lhermitte, F., 270
Li, C. H., 265
Liberman, H., 558
Liberman, P. R., 606, 615
Libet, J., 153, 423
Licht, B., 930
Liddle, G., 458
Lidz, T. A. R., 152
Lieberman, J. A., 39, 128, 155, 168, 259, 671
Liebl, R., 462, 857
Liebman, R., 681
Liebowitz, M., 230, 252, 254, 329, 481, 593,
    594, 596, 686, 711, 729, 731, 839
Liem, J., 959
Liem, R., 959
Lijerly, S. B., 378
Lindberg, M. L., 280
Lindegard, B., 733
Lindemann, E., 136
Linden, R. D., 245
Lindenthal, J. J., 151, 959
Lindsay, R., 537
Lindstedt, G., 855
Lindstrom, L., 869
Linehan, M., 375, 376, 606, 607, 608, 612, 613
Ling, W., 522, 532
Linkowski, P., 280, 470, 800, 809, 847, 864,
    866, 868
Linnoila, M., 227, 228, 235, 252, 254, 265,
    273, 827, 829, 836, 861
Liotta, A. S., 824
Lipinsky, J. F., 267, 269, 856
Lipman, R., 279, 317, 378, 777, 869
Lipowski, Z. J., 683
Lipper, S., 254, 255, 829
Lippman, L., 240
Lippmann, S., 247
Lipsedge, M. S., 227

Lipsey, J. R., 758
Lipton, M. A., 264, 454
Lipton, R. B., 844
Lishman, W. A., 20, 424
Littin, E. M., 600
Little, B. C., 849
Litvack, S. B., 22
Liu, K., 475
Ljingdahl, A., 447
Ljunggren, J. G., 463
Lloyd, C., 920
Lloyd, G. G., 20, 424
Lloyd, H. M., 758
Lobban, M. C., 280
Lobitz, C., 20
Locher, L. M., 818
Locke, B. Z., 769, 1013
Loevinger, B. L., 869
Loewenstein, R. J., 480, 840
Lofgren, S. B., 460, 856
Lohr, J. M., 414
Lohr, N., 460, 474, 855
Lohrenz, J. C., 608
Lombroso, C. T., 484
Loomer, H. P., 223, 818
Loomis, M. E., 200
Loosen, P. T., 264, 265, 463, 464, 465, 466,
    598, 863, 865
Lopez-Ibor Alino, J. J., 268
Lourie, R. S., 540, 544
Lovallo, W., 385
Love, A., 392
Lovelace, R., 255
Lovenberg, W., 270, 450
Low, D., 384
Lowery, M., 355, 767
Lowry, F., 115
Lowry, P. J., 758
Lubin, B., 50, 391, 392, 530, 531, 1014, 1015,
    1017, 1020
Luborsky, L., 23, 117, 215, 329, 330, 929
Lubrano, A., 576, 828
Luchins, D., 597, 846
Lucki, I., 470, 859, 864, 870
Ludlow, C., 840
Ludmer, L. I., 473
Lum, O., 1015
Lumry, A. E., 845, 849
Lund, R., 478, 834, 839, 875
Lundberg, J. M., 447
Lundquist, G., 817
Lupatkin, W., 533
Luria, R. E., 392
Lustig, N., 157
Lustman, P. J., 29, 208, 320, 645
Luton, F. H., 768
Lyall, W. A., 965
Lycaki, H., 840
Lykken, D. T., 845, 849
Lynn, C. W., 451

M

Maany, I., 228, 467
Maas, J. W., 448, 449, 450, 454, 455, 471, 472, 473, 474, 826, 827, 830, 856
Maayani, S., 238
MacDonald, E., 836
Macdonald, N., 828
Macedo, M. M., 758
Macklin, D. B., 768
MacLean, A. W., 479, 480, 482, 874
MacMahon, B., 765
MacMillan, A. M., 768
MacPhillamy, D. J ., 44, 48, 56, 60, 164, 422, 423, 424, 1005
MacSweeney, D. A., 268, 449
Maddi, S. R., 946
Maeda, K., 868
Maggini, C., 156
Maguire, G. P., 753
Mahoney, M. J., 59
Mahura, C. C., 613
Maier, S. F., 917, 918, 921
Maier, W., 857
Maiorano, M., 473
Maitre, L., 251, 255, 454, 455
Major, L. K., 855
Makinen, T., 265, 861
Malan, D., 100, 102–5, 108, 109, 112, 118, 130
Malleson, A., 450
Mallinger, A. G., 260
Mallinger, J., 260
Mallon, P., 857
Malloy, F. W., 277
Malmquist, C. P., 524
Maloof, F., 246
Maltbie, A. A., 856
Mamidanna, S. R., 613
Mandel, M. R., 278, 848
Mandell, A. J., 263, 456, 458, 852
Manly, P. C., 417
Mann, E., 240
Mann, J., 100, 102, 103, 108, 112, 118
Mann, J. D., 448
Mann, J. J., 237, 254
Mann, L. S., 484, 846, 847
Mann, S. A., 769
Manning, R. G., 847
Manowitz, P., 830
Manshadi, M., 247
Marangos, P. J., 263
March, V., 680
Marchenko, L., 611
Marcus, J. L., 954
Marder, S. R., 225
Mardh, G., 449
Margolies, T. M., 654
Marini, J. L., 228
Markey, S. P., 234, 449
Markianos, E., 450

Markoff, R. A., 243
Markowitz, J. S., 252, 593
Marks, I., 687
Marks, T., 426
Marlowe, D., 385
Marmar, C., 101, 118
Marmor, J., 101, 118, 323
Marone, J., 392
Marsh, W., 253
Marshall, Eldon, 1018
Marshall, J., 950
Marshall, J. R., 746
Marshall, W. L., 26, 27
Martensson, B., 463
Martin, B. R., 454
Martin, C., 780
Martin, D. J., 417
Martin, D. M., 465, 863, 864, 868
Martin, F. I. R., 455, 459, 832, 859
Martin, J. B., 464, 467
Martin, J. L., 954
Martin, R., 269
Maruta, T., 226, 232, 449, 454, 684, 685, 827, 860
Marx, N., 546
Mascitelli, S., 639
Mason, J., 614
Mason, J. W., 458, 855
Massart-Guiot, T., 800
Master, R. S., 220
Matarazzo, J. D., 820
Mathe, A. A., 455, 860, 864
Mather, S., 247
Mathia, G., 459
Mathias, R., 839
Matson, J. L., 329, 545
Matthew, R. J., 847
Matthews, D. M., 269
Matthews, J., 459
Matthysse, S., 800
Mattison, R., 520
Mattson, A., 254, 543
Matussek, N., 467, 468, 469
Matussek, P., 158, 349, 707, 719, 726, 736, 737, 866
Matuzas, W., 227, 232, 334
Maultsby, M. C., 639
Maurer, H. A., 706, 725, 738
Maurice, W. L., 358, 687, 779
Mavissakalian, M., 227, 228
Maxwell, J., 806
Maxwell, R., 471
Maxwell, S. E., 70, 205, 325, 880
May, A. E., 385
May, J. R., 22
May, P. R. A., 167
May, S. J., 846
Mayer, A., 597
Mayeux, R., 565
Mayfield, D., 462, 857

Mayo, J. A., 157, 166
Mayol, A., 436, 948, 954
McAbee, R. S., 477, 482
McAllister, T. W., 569, 682, 683
McAuley, H., 780
McBride, P. A., 237
McBride, W. G., 241
McCabe, M. S., 225
McCabe, Scott B., 372
McCabe, W. J., 855
McCall, R. B., 237
McCalley-Whitters, M., 846
McCarley, R. W., 580, 841
McCarron, L., 849
McCartney, J. K., 766
McClane, T. K., 264, 454
McClure, D. J., 227
McClure, J. N., 384
McClure, S. F., 869
McConville, B. J., 480, 518, 526, 527
McCranie, E. J., 700
McCubbin, H. I., 961, 962
McCunney, S., 263
McDonald, C., 703
McDonald, D. W., 154
McDonald, R. K., 468, 865
McEachren, L., 19, 946
McFall, R. M., 425, 427, 430, 432, 948
McFarland, C., 929
McGee, R. O., 540
McGeer, P. L., 675
McGinniss, M. M., 903
McGlashen, T. H., 673, 674
McGrath, P., 230, 251, 252, 254, 481, 593, 686, 839, 855
McGreer, P. L., 485
McGuire, R. J., 736
McHugh, P. R., 484
McInnis, D. J., 410, 411, 437
McIntire, M. S., 543, 621
McIntyre, I. M., 856
McKay, G., 61
McKenry, P. C., 542
McKeon, J., 390
McKernan, J., 676
McKinley, J. C., 385, 399
McKinney, W. T., 167, 587, 880, 943, 947
McKnew, D. H., 518, 521, 524, 526, 528, 529, 534, 535, 540, 1019
McKnight, D. L., 72
McLaughlin, R. A., 460, 856
McLean, P., 49, 51, 54, 55, 63, 64, 71, 72, 117, 160, 209, 323, 325, 327, 948, 951, 957, 958, 962, 963
McLellan, A. T., 679
McLeod, M. F., 455, 833, 859
McLeod, M. N., 252, 253, 273, 828
McLeod, W. L., 455, 833, 859
McLeod, W. R., 857
McMahon, R. J., 417
McNamara, E., 839, 840

McPartland, R. J., 477, 478, 479, 481, 840, 881
McPherson, I. C., 227
Mednick, S. A., 174
Meduna, Laszlo, 221
Meichenbaum, D., 58
Meites, J., 559
Meites, K., 385
Melby, J., 271
Melica, A. M., 157
Mellerup, E. T., 258
Mellstrom, B., 228, 454
Meltzer, H. L., 258
Meltzer, H. V., 767
Meltzer, H. Y., 238, 461, 468, 559, 828, 831, 845, 859, 861
Mendels, J., 252, 257, 258, 263, 349, 447, 454, 460, 467, 468, 475, 476, 479, 480, 559, 597, 598, 680, 709, 777, 778, 809, 865
Mendelsohn, M., 164
Mendelson, M., 47, 114, 383, 612, 768, 840, 841
Mendelson, W., 228, 282, 469, 480, 678
Mendlewicz, J., 157, 249, 256, 280, 353, 462, 795, 798, 799, 800, 802–10, 847, 856, 857, 864, 865, 866, 868
Mendlowitz, M., 448
Menkes, D. B., 237, 447, 455, 831, 878
Menna-Perper, M., 830
Menninger, K., 677, 724
Merbaum, M., 71
Merikangas, K. R., 157, 158, 670, 840
Merry, J., 20
Metalsky, G. I., 415, 415, 928, 1012
Metcalfe, M., 354, 384, 700, 715
Methven, R. J., 520
Metter, E. J., 847
Meyer, Adolph, 127
Meyer, D., 381
Meyer, H., 869
Meyer, J. S., 847
Miccoli, L., 269
Michael, S. T., 768
Michelson, L., 227, 228
Mickalide, A. D., 680
Mielke, D. H., 241, 242
Mikhalenko, I. N., 280
Mikkelson, E. J., 228
Miklowitz, D., 436
Milana, S. A., 5
Milanese, E., 857
Miller, A. G., 151, 950
Miller, Alice, 90
Miller, D. T., 954
Miller, I. W., 21, 23, 410, 417, 418, 923
Miller, J., 388, 706
Miller, J. B., 674
Miller, M. J., 277
Miller, M. L., 531
Miller, P., 454
Miller, P. McC., 773, 774
Miller, R. D., 593

Miller, T. I., 117
Miller, W. R., 72
Millon, Theodore, 700, 702, 707, 712, 714, 715, 717, 724, 726, 730, 731
Mills, M. J., 272
Milner, G., 269
Milstein, V., 277
Milstoc, M., 263
Mindham, R. H. S., 825, 831
Mintz, J., 322, 580
Minuchin, S., 152, 681
Mirin, S. M., 243
Mirkin, A. M., 849
Miro, A. V., 452
Mirouze, R., 384
Mischel, W., 46, 426, 432, 434, 954
Misra, C. H., 234
Missel, T., 19
Mistra, P. C., 809
Mitchell, R. E., 944, 949, 950, 951, 954 n, 964, 965
Mizruchi, M. S., 541, 542, 621
Mock, J., 47, 164, 383, 768
Modai, I., 454
Mohs, R. C., 833
Molander, L., 450
Moldofsky, H., 681
Moller, S. E., 830
Molnar, G., 261
Monagan, B., 73
Monroe, S. M., 73, 204, 353, 373, 819, 914, 920
Montejo Iglesias, M. L., 268
Montgomery, D., 609, 615
Montgomery, S. A., 609, 615, 1016
Monty, R. A., 946
Moody, J. P., 257
Moore, A., 480, 840
Moore, A. J., 238
Moore, A. M., 483, 834
Moore, D., 154, 724
Moore, D. C., 228, 682
Moore, K. E., 471
Moore, R. Y., 872
Moore-Ede, M. C., 873
Moorey, S., 655
Moos, B. S., 164
Moos, Rudolph H., 164, 334, 350, 428, 940, 942, 943, 944, 945, 949, 950, 951, 952, 954 n, 955, 960, 961, 962, 964, 965
Mora, G., 817
Moran, P. W., 1017
Morgan, R. A., 20
Morgan, D. E., 274
Morihisa, J. M., 675
Morissette, R., 832
Morland, J., 253
Morris, J. B., 230, 239
Morris, L. A., 30
Morris, N. E., 26, 27
Morrison, J. R., 610

Mortel, K., 847
Moschitto, L. J., 248
Moskop, J., 625
Moskowitz, J. A., 689
Mosnain, A. D., 447, 451, 452, 453, 471, 473, 835
Moss, H. B., 670
Moss, P., 774
Motoike, P., 580
Motto, J. A., 609
Moucharafieh, S., 855
Mountjoy, C. Q., 227
Moyal, B. R., 537
Mueller, E. A., 465, 600
Mueller, P. D., 865
Mueller, P. S., 242, 281, 282, 468, 830, 865, 866, 877
Muir, W., 385
Mukherji, B. R., 417
Mukhopadhyay, S., 462, 857
Muller, F., 468
Müller, V., 573
Mullins, L., 524, 537
Munjack, D. J., 670
Munmkvad, I., 450
Muñoz, R. F., 19, 25, 44, 61, 226, 351, 421, 522, 745, 769, 821, 963
Munro, J. J., 231
Murphy, D. L., 228, 232, 236, 237, 250, 254, 255, 257, 258, 264, 268, 323, 327, 328, 334, 354, 399, 400, 451, 454, 461, 473, 479, 480, 484, 736, 820, 825, 829, 830, 840, 841, 844, 853, 854, 856, 859, 860, 869
Murphy, E., 767, 780
Murphy, G. E., 29, 31, 208, 321, 351, 607, 608, 645, 686
Murphy, H. B. M., 783
Murray, N., 678, 855
Musa, M. N., 234
Muscetola, G., 234, 264, 269, 454, 482, 827
Mushrush, J., 467
Myers, C. M., 856
Myers, D. H., 771
Myers, E. D., 609
Myers, J. K., 151, 390, 391, 557, 700, 754, 755, 773, 959, 1013

N

Naber, D., 263, 455, 468, 869
Nagel, D., 349
Nagy, A., 235, 268
Nair, N. P. V., 237, 831
Nakajima, T., 452, 453
Nammalvar, N., 720
Nand, S., 767
Napier, L., 227
Narasimhachari, N., 454, 473, 474
Narrol, H., 537
Narsapur, S. L., 269
Nasr, S. J., 232, 238, 262, 855, 859

Nasrallah, H. A., 482, 767, 846, 874
Natale, M., 22, 23
Nathan, P. E., 345
Nathan, R. S., 468, 474, 482, 852, 853, 954,
    858, 859, 866, 868
Naylor, G. J., 257, 269
Naylor, R. J., 471
Neale, J. M., 956
Neckers, L. M., 454
Nee, J., 870
Nee, L. E., 228, 380
Needleman, H. L., 228
Neff, J. A., 390
Neff, N. H., 250
Negri, F., 157, 454, 826
Neil, J. F., 232, 233, 280, 454, 478, 480, 481,
    559, 840, 846, 880, 881
Neilson, A. C., 754, 755, 756
Neilson, M., 220
Nelson, C. J., 778
Nelson, H. B., 266
Nelson, J. C., 234, 348, 349, 352, 597, 701,
    767, 779, 819, 836
Nelson, R. E., 20, 21, 415, 1016
Nelson, R. O., 60, 72, 638, 957
Nelson, W. H., 232, 462, 678, 857
Nemeroff, C. B., 462, 856
Nemiah, J. C., 685, 686
Nerup, J., 465
Nesse, R. D., 671
Neu, C., 124, 157, 206, 216, 318
Neubauer, H., 573
Neuringer, C., 613
Nevid, J. S., 612
Neville, M. B., 683
Newberry, P. B., 391, 676
Newman, J., 161, 167
Newman, K., 241
Newmark, C. S., 386
Newsom, G., 678, 855
Newsome, D. A., 282, 877
Newton, T. F., 478, 479, 840, 879
Ní Bhrolcháin, M., 778
Niederweiser, A., 270
Nielson, A., 384
Nielson, S. L., 606, 612, 613
Nies, A., 235, 252, 558, 560, 678, 825
Nies, G., 73, 384, 580
Ninan, R. T., 836
Nisbett, R. E., 431
Nishikubo, M., 468
Nissenbaum, H., 269
Nixon, J. M., 769
Nixon, R. A., 271
Noguera, R., 449, 451
Nolen, W. A., 267
Noll, Katherine M., 220, 226
Norman, W. H., 21, 23, 410, 417, 923
Norris, E., 230
Norvich, M. R., 471
Novacenko, H., 482, 858

Novaco, R. W., 58
Nuhfer, P. A., 238
Nuller, J. L., 462
Nunally, J. C., 388, 706
Nunn, R., 388, 706
Nunn, W. D., 459
Nurnberg, B. I., 758
Nurnberg, H. G., 227, 671
Nurnberger, J. I., Jr., 238, 483, 818, 834, 844
Nussbaum, K., 384, 386
Nuttall, E. A., 609
Nutter, J., 928
Nystrom, S., 733

O

Oates, J. A., 260
Obayuwana, A. D., 613
O'Brien, C. P., 679
O'Brien, J. C., 609
Ochi, Y., 469
O'Conner, J., 386
Odle, D., 1016
O'Donohue, T. L., 263
Offer, D., 539, 544
Oftedal, G., 522
Ogston, K., 64, 160
O'Hanlon, J., 780
O'Hara, M., 381, 413, 414, 419
O'Hara, M. W., 21, 24, 71, 417, 638, 928
Ohgo, S., 868
Ojesjo, L., 774
O'Keefe, R., 449
Okonek, A., 476
Okuma, T., 266, 597
Olafsdotter, H., 857
Oldham, D., 856
Oler, J., 559, 865
Oliver, J. M., 384
Olsen, H., 253
Olsen, S., 262
Olson, D. H., 164
O'Malley, S. S., 117
Opler, M. K., 768
Orbach, I., 540, 542, 543
Ordy, J. M., 557
Oreland, L., 841
Orley, J. H., 782, 783
Orlinsky, D. E., 116
Ornstein, G. C., 223
Orr, W. W., 232, 462, 857
Orsulak, P. J., 232, 246, 448, 449, 454, 675,
    827, 828, 855, 858, 860
Ortman, J., 235
Orton, I. K., 23
Orvaschel, H., 174, 557, 1023
Osborne, G., 66, 325
Osborne, M., 524
Osswald, M., 469
Ostroff, R., 614, 855
Ostroumova, M. N., 462
Ostrow, D., 475, 476, 477, 482

Otsuki, S., 257, 266
Ottosson, J. O., 278
Overall, J., 204, 264, 397, 449, 713, 720, 723, 725, 726, 943
Overmier, J. B., 917
Overton, D. A., 845
Owen, F., 279
Owens, D. G. C., 227
Owens, M. L., 471
Oxenkrug, G. F., 236, 268, 280, 856

P

Padesky, C., 429
Padfield, M., 329
Padian, N., 115, 216, 319
Paez, P., 533, 1023
Page, R. B., 851
Palmstierna, T., 673
Pambakian, R., 360
Pandey, G. N., 237, 238, 258, 261, 467, 468, 469, 475, 809, 835, 845, 859, 867
Pandurangi, A. K., 855
Paporisek, M., 448, 449
Papouser, M., 841
Papp, Z., 830, 861
Pare, C. M. B., 252, 450, 597, 598
Parker, C. R., 479, 839, 858
Parker, D. C., 868
Parker, G., 771
Parker, G. B., 430, 435, 956, 959
Parker, R. R., 251, 253
Parker, W., 66, 325
Parkes, C. M., 779
Parloff, M. B., 116, 117, 125, 326, 379
Parrack, S., 454
Parry, B. L., 282, 870
Parry, G., 775, 777, 780
Parsons, Talcott, 133
Partain, C. L., 485
Pasahow, R. J., 953
Patrie, L. E., 676
Patterson, C. D., 264
Patterson, G. A., 613
Patterson, G. R., 154
Patterson, J. M., 961, 962
Patterson, T. P., 849
Patterson, W. M., 613
Pattison, J. H., 317
Patton, J. A., 485
Paul, S. M., 237, 273, 468, 831, 832
Paulauskas, S. L., 524, 871
Pauls, D. L., 670
Paykel, E. S., 5, 124, 128, 145, 151, 155, 156, 157, 159, 169, 174, 206, 242, 251, 252, 253, 317, 318, 350, 397, 425, 593, 608, 700, 701, 706, 709, 710, 711, 718, 725, 726, 735, 736, 776, 779, 780, 879, 920, 944, 948, 951
Pearce, J., 525, 527

Pearlin, L. I., 128, 350, 944, 946, 950, 958, 959, 960
Pearlman, C. A., 480
Pearlson, G. A., 484
Pearlson, G. D., 758
Pearsall, D. T., 272
Pearson, J. S., 600
Pechnick, R., 263
Pecknold, J. C., 228
Pecknold, L. C., 264
Pedemonte, W. A., 447
Peet, M., 257, 820
Peirce, C. S., 932
Peloquin, L. J., 845, 849
Penick, E. C., 522
Pepeu, G., 471
Pepper, M. P., 151, 959
Pepping, M., 957
Pereira-Ogan, J., 233
Perel, J. M., 227, 232, 240, 533, 573
Perini, G. I., 261
Perlmuter, L. C., 946
Perlow, M., 467
Perls, Frederick, S., 194–97
Perman, G. P., 846
Peroutka, S. J., 237, 831
Perrier, D., 235
Perris, C., 353, 354, 733, 736, 767, 779, 806, 809, 810, 819, 828, 843, 844
Perris, H., 828
Perry, J. C., 726
Perry, P. J., 274
Persad, E., 265, 800
Persons, J., 653
Pert, A., 263, 475
Pert, C. B., 263, 475
Peselow, E. D., 234, 254, 462, 855, 857
Peskind, E. R., 560, 569, 855
Peters, S. D., 425, 426, 958
Peterson, Christopher, 19, 21, 23, 416, 417, 537, 914, 916, 919, 920, 922, 925, 927–30, 932–34, 947, 953, 1012
Peterson, G. O., 235
Peterson, J., 246, 845
Petit, M., 270
Peto, J., 777
Petrie, W. M., 266, 269
Petterson, U., 280, 463
Petti, T. A., 228, 523, 525, 530, 545, 546, 1018
Pettigrew, K. D., 226, 478, 836, 839
Pettinati, H. M., 277
Petty, F., 880, 920
Petzel, T. P., 20
Pfeffer, C. R., 540, 541, 542, 543, 577, 621
Pflug, B., 280
Pfohl, B., 767, 853
Phelps, M. E., 847
Philips, I., 174, 175, 526, 527
Phillips, J., 635
Phillips, L., 346, 360
Phupradit, P., 254

Pi, E. H., 235, 254
Pick, G. R., 459
Pickar, D., 236, 254, 255, 454, 455, 468, 819, 829, 869, 878
Pickens, R. W., 677
Picot, P., 384
Pierce, J., 227
Pierce, W. E., 528
Pierson, R. N., 835
Pike, D. J., 227
Piletz, J., 874
Pilowsky, I., 226
Pinder, R. M., 249
Pinsker, E. J., 200
Pinzello, A., 269
Piotrowski, Z. A., 221
Piper, W. E., 119
Pishkin, V., 385
Pitt, B., 870
Pitts, W. M., 248, 730
Planansky, K., 673, 674
Plenge, P. K., 258
Plesset, I. R., 817
Plewis, I., 774
Plutchik, R., 540, 541, 542, 621
Pohl, R., 255
Pohorecky, L. A., 922
Pokorny, A. D., 264, 451, 809, 611
Poli, E., 351
Polinsky, R. J., 450
Pollin, W., 808
Pollitzer, W. S., 806
Pollock, G. H., 689
Polvan, N., 264
Pomara, N., 856
Poort, R., 817
Pope, H. G., Jr., 228, 267, 681, 855
Popkin, M. K., 747, 748, 752
Porro, V., 269
Portelange, P., 847
Porter, A. M. W., 754, 755
Portner, J., 164
Post, D., 20
Post, F., 569, 675
Post, R. M., 258, 264, 266, 267, 281, 449, 450, 451, 454, 479, 484, 826, 828, 830, 839, 841, 844, 846, 860, 867, 869, 880
Potkin, S. G., 453
Pottash, A., 465, 466, 600, 678, 856, 861, 863, 864, 865, 868, 870
Pottenger, M., 351, 676, 678, 680, 746
Potter, W. Z., 234, 235, 254, 273, 449, 454, 827, 829, 861
Poust, R. J., 260
Poynton, C., 392
Poznanski, E., 522, 525, 532, 840, 856, 1021
Prabhu, V., 232
Prakash, R., 269
Prakhje, I., 280
Prange, A. J., Jr., 264, 265, 448, 451, 454, 463–66, 598, 746, 806, 861, 862, 863, 865

Pratt, R. T. C., 253
Preece, J. M., 269
Preskorn, S. H., 239
Preston, T. A., 226
Price, J., 797, 806
Price, J. S., 588, 598
Price, L. H., 597
Price, R. G., 262
Price, R. R., 485
Price, T. R. P., 683, 758
Price Evans, D. A., 253
Prien, R. F., 809, 820
Priest, R. G., 778
Prinz, P. N., 560, 570
Privatera, M. R., 462
Proctor, L. R., 845
Prudo, R., 767
Prusoff, B. A., 115, 124, 132, 138, 151, 157, 161, 206, 216, 317, 318, 319, 350, 391, 589, 670, 701, 709, 710, 718, 776, 779, 800, 881, 948
Pry, G., 20
Puech, A., 270
Pugh, T. F., 765
Pugnetti, L., 874
Puhringer, W., 232
Puig-Antich, J., 480, 481, 482, 521, 532, 533, 534, 546, 596, 839, 840, 855, 858, 867, 1023
Puite, J., 450
Pullan, P. T., 758
Purohit, A. P., 518
Putnam, P. L., 262
Puzantian, V. R., 156, 352, 587, 588

Q

Qualls, C. B., 462, 855
Quinlan, D. M., 20, 234, 701, 703, 705, 779
Quinton, D., 155
Quitkin, F., 230, 232, 251, 252, 254, 255, 468, 481, 593, 831, 834, 839, 855, 866

R

Rabin, A. S., 70, 419, 421
Rabkin, J., 252, 254, 593, 855
Rabon, A. M., 264
Racy, J., 242
Radin, N. S., 865
Radke-Yarrow, M., 529
Radloff, L. S., 48, 390, 391, 768, 912, 959, 961, 1013
Rado, Sandor, 85, 703, 708, 721
Radwan, M., 454
Rae, D. S., 960
Raeder, E., 573
Rafaelson, O. J., 242, 258, 380, 480, 800, 875
Raft, D., 227, 309
Ragheb, M., 260
Rahe, R. H., 63, 776
Rainer, J., 353, 798, 802, 804, 805, 806, 807
Rainwater, N., 690

Raisman, R., 237, 831
Rama Rao, V. A., 454
Ramirez, A. L., 247
Ramsey, A., 257, 468, 865
Ramsey, T. A., 258
Randrup, A., 450
Rao, B., 268
Rao, K., 758
Rapoport, J. L., 228
Rapp, S., 429
Raps, C. S., 21, 23, 417
Raskin, A., 145, 331, 390, 517, 917, 1016
Raskind, M., 558, 560, 569, 573, 575, 855, 860
Ratcliff, K. S., 378, 767
Ratsaby, E. S., 780
Ravaris, C. L., 235, 252, 254, 560
Rawson, S. G., 387, 388
Rayner, J., 225
Razani, J., 254, 828
Rea, W. S., 869
Reatig, N., 145, 390, 1016
Rebar, T., 465, 467, 864, 866
Redmond, D. E., 449, 450, 827
Reed, K., 240
Rees, G. M., 758
Rees, L., 251, 597
Reese, L. H., 758
Regier, D. A., 769
Rehavi, M., 237, 468, 831
Rehm, L., 20, 21, 25, 39, 60, 62, 65, 66, 70, 71,
    153, 209, 210, 214, 325, 381, 413, 418,
    419, 421, 423, 425, 526, 528, 538, 545,
    635, 638, 879, 928
Reich, J., 226
Reich, L., 226, 232, 481, 840
Reich, T., 353, 360, 767, 798, 800
Reich, W., 534, 1022
Reichlin, S., 464, 467, 867
Reid, J. B., 154
Reid, W. H., 718
Reifler, B. V., 683
Reigle, G. D., 559
Reim, B., 467, 866
Reiman, M., 260
Reimann, I. W., 260
Reinhard, K. E., 21, 23, 417
Reinila, M., 836
Reisberg, B., 262
Reisdy, N., 235
Reiss, D. J., 167
Rencker, S. J., 235
Rennie, T. A. C., 768, 817
Reppucci, N. D., 918
Requin-Blow, B., 232, 454
Resch, F., 863
Resnik, H. L. P., 613, 677
Reus, V. I., 855, 859, 860, 869
Reveley, A. M., 351
Reveley, M. A., 351, 360
Reynolds, C. F., 478, 479, 480, 838–43, 846,
    848, 879

Reynolds, E. H., 269
Reynolds, G. P., 254
Reynolds, W. H., 384, 385, 946
Rezin, V., 18
Reznikoff, M., 542, 544
Rholes, W. S., 22, 411
Rice, C. E., 1016
Rich, C. L., 272, 276
Rich, M., 227
Richards, C. B., 386, 1017
Richards, C. S., 957
Richelson, E., 574, 828
Richey, C. A., 60
Richman, N., 774
Richter, R., 827, 872
Rickels, K., 233, 239, 462, 470, 575, 679, 857,
    859, 864, 870, 1017
Ridges, P. P., 454, 455
Rie, H. E., 517, 527
Rieder, R. O., 484, 819, 846, 878
Riege, W., 847
Rieger, W., 856
Ries, R., 675
Rifkin, A., 227, 230, 232, 259, 834
Rihmer, Z., 280
Riley, G., 227
Rimm, D. C., 22
Rimon, R., 384
Ringberger, V. A., 451, 454
Rinne, J., 239
Rippere, V., 429, 917, 957
Risberg, J., 847
Risch, S. C., 282, 453, 461, 473, 820, 825, 829,
    832, 854, 859, 868, 869, 877
Riskind, J. H., 22, 23, 396, 411, 413, 414, 436,
    437
Ritchie, J. C., 462, 573
Ritchie, K., 780
Ritzler, B., 845
Rivard, D., 558, 569, 855
Rizzo, F., 458
Roatch, J. F., 89, 231, 778
Robbins, D. R., 856
Roberts, F. J., 159, 425
Robertson, A., 859
Robertson, M. M., 270
Robin, A., 609, 610
Robins, A. J., 540
Robins, C., 422
Robins, E., 47, 124, 146, 226, 348, 351, 354,
    373, 449, 522, 588, 591, 688, 745, 767,
    817, 821, 827, 856
Robins, L. N., 174, 360, 378, 671, 769
Robinson, D. S., 235, 252, 253, 558, 560, 589,
    825
Robinson, J. C., 42
Robinson, R. G., 758
Robitzek, E. H., 223
Robyn, C., 470, 864
Rochford, J. M., 676, 686, 830
Rock, A. F., 1017

Rodgers, C., 859
Rodin, L., 807
Rodnick, E. H., 167
Rodnight, R., 450
Roebuck, L., 535, 1019
Roemer, R. A., 484, 843
Roffwarg, H., 458, 479, 839, 855, 858
Rogenline, N., 800
Rogers. H. G., 277
Rogers, J., 607, 965
Rogers, L., 705
Rogers, T., 8, 22
Rogol, A. D., 856
Rohde, W. A., 448, 449, 454, 675
Rollo, F. D., 485
Rolsten, C., 557
Romani, A., 855
Romano, J. M., 66, 71, 209, 419, 423
Roos, B. E., 268
Roose, S. P., 228, 348, 573, 682, 767, 819
Ropper, A. H., 484
Rorsman, B., 774
Rosanoff, A. J., 797, 817
Rosanoff-Plesset, I. B. A., 797
Rose, J. T., 350
Rose, R. M., 775, 852
Roseberg, G., 861
Rosen, G., 683
Rosen, G. M., 57
Rosen, J., 565
Rosen, L., 448, 855
Rosen, R., 581
Rosen, S., 381
Rosenbaum, A. H., 232, 449, 454, 460, 827, 856, 860
Rosenbaum, J. F., 248
Rosenbaum, M., 70–71, 331, 419, 420, 998
Rosenbaum, R., 118
Rosenberg, G. N., 558
Rosenberg, Saul E., 100
Rosenblatt, J., 263, 475
Rosenthal, N. E., 281, 282, 674, 873, 877
Rosenthal, R. H., 355, 396, 478, 590, 701, 767
Rosenthal, S., 726, 778
Rosenthal, T. L., 156, 352, 355, 396, 478, 587, 588, 589, 590, 593, 595, 701, 767
Rosnick, L., 230
Ross, C., 1013
Ross, D. C., 835
Ross, D. R., 246
Ross, E. D., 570
Ross, M., 929, 954
Ross, R. J., 254
Ross, S., 828
Rossi, A., 481, 839
Rossier, J., 279, 869
Roth, D., 20, 209, 325, 328, 423
Roth, D. M., 66
Roth, M., 227, 670, 778, 779, 781
Roth, R. H ., 449, 823, 827
Roth, T., 684, 840

Roth, W. F., 768
Rothpearl, A. B., 455, 833, 860, 864
Rothschild, A. J., 460, 828, 856, 860, 861
Rotman, A., 828
Rotrosen, J., 472
Rotter, J. B., 43
Roubicek, J., 277
Rounsaville, Bruce J., 124, 125, 132, 138, 147, 151, 161, 168, 213, 318, 335, 336, 350, 360, 589, 679, 680, 881
Rowan, P. R., 251, 253
Roy, A., 608, 609, 610
Roy, B. F., 236, 250, 450, 451
Roy, J. R., 778
Roy-Byrne, P., 681, 855, 856
Rozensky, R. H., 20
Ruben, H. L., 351, 676
Rubenstein, D., 152
Rubin, R. T., 455, 456, 458, 746, 832, 852, 859
Rubinow, D., 265, 836, 846, 861, 867, 868, 880
Rubinstein, D., 952
Rudden, M., 676
Rude, S. S., 416, 419, 420, 421
Rudolf, von G. A. E., 280, 281
Rudorfer, M. V., 857
Rudy, V., 257
Ruehlman, L., 19, 20
Rundell, O. H., Jr., 678
Rush, A. J., 3, 5, 6, 18, 26, 27, 30, 31, 39, 125, 153, 205, 208, 216, 319, 321, 327, 332, 333, 359, 375, 397, 412, 413, 417, 418, 421, 422, 435, 479, 578, 592, 617, 634, 645, 822, 839, 855, 858, 864, 865, 870, 879, 880, 881, 921, 955, 962, 963, 964, 1014
Ruskin, R., 597
Russell, A., 153
Russell, A. T., 520
Russell, H. L., 200
Russell, L., 153
Russell, P. L., 22
Russell, R. W., 263
Russo, P., 828
Russotto, J., 857
Ruther, E., 469
Ruthven, C. R. J., 452, 454
Rutman, J., 522
Rutter, M., 155, 174, 518, 525, 526, 528, 529, 539, 540, 916
Ryan, N., 465, 864
Ryon, N. B., 412

S

Saavedra, J. M., 453
Sabelli, H. C., 447, 451, 452, 453, 455, 471, 472, 473, 835
Sabshin, M., 388, 706
Sacchetti, E., 454, 826, 827
Sacco, William P., 3, 5, 17, 19, 20, 425

Sachar, E. J., 458, 467, 468, 474, 481, 482,
    533, 839, 852, 853, 854, 858, 859, 865–68
Sack, D. A., 282, 873
Sack, R., 450, 467, 866, 877
Sackellares, J. C., 243, 834
Sackheim, H. A., 571, 920, 947
Sacquitne, J. L., 880, 922
Saenz, M., 62, 63
Sager, C. J., 154
Saghir, M. T., 688
Sagi, E., 857
Saier, J., 810
Sainsbury, M. J., 597
Sainsbury, P., 538, 774
St. Laurent, J., 454
Sajadi, C., 248, 730
Sakel, M., 221
Salkin, B., 680
Salkind, M. R., 384
Salomon, M. S., 828, 860
Salter, A., 635
Salzman, C., 272, 560
Salzman, L., 679, 721, 725, 845, 958
Samorajski, T., 557, 558
Sampson, H., 114, 115
Samson, J. A., 828
Sanchez, J., 827, 948
Sandele, J. A., 117
Sandler, I. N., 961
Sandler, J., 87
Sandler, M., 254, 450, 452, 454
Sano, I., 452
Sara, V., 463
Sarantakos, S., 380
Sarason, I. G., 777
Sargant, W., 725
Sarkadi, B., 476
Saron, C., 843
Sartorias, N., 383, 769
Sashidharan, S. P., 773, 774
Sassin, J., 467, 468, 867
Sathananthan, G. L., 234, 448
Satin, M., 392
Satir, V., 154
Saunders, J. C., 223, 818
Savage, I., 252
Savard, R., 880
Scalise, M., 855
Scarone, S., 874
Sceery, W., 840
Schact, T., 345
Schaefer, C., 425, 428, 945
Schaffer, C. B., 685, 843
Schaffer, J. D., 331
Schaffer, N., 116
Schalch, D. S., 264, 465, 868
Schalling, D., 451, 852
Schally, A. V., 868
Schanberg, S. M., 448
Schank, R., 45
Schapira, K., 670

Scharek, G., 454, 827
Schatzberg, A. F., 232, 242, 243, 449, 454,
    460, 625, 827, 828, 856, 860, 861
Schaublin, A., 384
Schaultz, N. L., 228
Scheel-Kruger, J., 450
Scheiber, S. C., 235
Scheier, M. F., 44, 45, 46
Scheinin, M., 254
Schenck, L., 686, 691
Scher, M., 247
Schict, M. L., 62
Schiff, J. L., 192, 193
Schildkraut, J. J., 232, 236, 268, 448, 449, 454,
    471, 675, 825, 826, 827, 828, 829, 841,
    860, 922
Schilgen, von, B., 281
Schilkrut, R., 469
Schless, A., 709, 710, 718, 777, 809
Schlesser, M. A., 355, 462, 855, 858, 865
Schmidt, M., 72
Schneider, K., 595, 715
Schoenbach, V. J., 524
Schonbeck, G., 863
Schoolar, J., 234, 240, 686
Schooler, C., 350, 944, 946, 958, 959, 960
Schooler, J., 475
Schotte, D. E., 610
Schou, M., 222, 256, 257, 261, 262, 560, 820,
    861
Schroder, H. Th., 468
Schroeder, K. G., 22
Schubert, H., 270
Schuckit, M. A., 676, 678, 679
Schuele, J. G., 22
Schulsinger, R., 174
Schulterbrandt, J. G., 145, 390, 517, 916, 1016
Schultz, J. R., 225
Schultzberg, M., 447
Schulz, B., 807
Schulz, F., 859
Schulz, H., 480, 839, 875, 876
Schuyler, D., 612
Schwab, J., 380, 384
Schwab, J. J., 751, 754, 755, 756, 773
Schwab, P. J., 675
Schwab, R. B., 773
Schwarcz, G., 247
Schwartz, D., 481, 839
Schwartz, G., 237, 831, 848
Schwartz, L., 247
Schwartz, M., 537
Schwartz, R., 829
Schwartz, S. M., 953
Schweizer, E., 856
Scott, N. A., 385
Scott, R., 773, 780, 781
Scott-Strauss, A., 396, 478, 589, 590, 700, 701,
    727, 767
Scotto, J. C., 810
Scovern, A. W., 272, 273

Seaman, S. F., 880
Seat, P. D., 535, 1024
Sechrest, L., 25
Sechter, D., 237, 831
Secord, G. J., 474
Secunda, S. K., 257, 354, 384, 767, 827
Sedlucek, S., 454
Sedvall, G., 870
Seese, L. R., 543
Segal, D. S., 868
Segal, R. M., 153, 421
Seggie, J., 467, 822, 851, 866
Seifert, R., 261
Seitz, F. C., 42
Sekerke, H. J., 453, 454, 472, 832
Seligman, Martin E. P., 15, 21, 23, 153, 154,
    169, 415, 416, 417, 418, 435, 528, 537,
    538, 562, 704, 707, 718, 914–22, 925,
    927, 928–34, 946, 947, 953, 962, 1012
Selikoff, T. J., 223
Selmi, P. M., 72
Seltzer, R. L., 254
Selye, H., 456
Semchuk, K. M., 847
Semmel, A., 415, 416, 928, 953, 1012
Sendbuehler, J. M., 611
Senogles, S., 263
Settle, E. C., Jr., 247
Sexauer, J. D., 246
Shader, R. I., 240, 248, 671
Shaeffer, D. E., 21, 417, 928, 953
Shaffer, D., 538, 539, 540, 543, 621
Shaffer, M., 49, 153
Shaffner, I., 559
Shagass, C., 484, 843, 845
Shane, S. E., 232, 462, 857
Shanfield, S., 673
Shanok, S. S., 621
Shapira, K., 779
Shapiro, A. K., 30
Shapiro, A. L., 596
Shapiro, D. A., 777, 780
Shapiro, R. W., 589
Sharp, L., 796
Sharp, P. T., 455, 832, 859
Sharpe, L., 264, 767, 820
Shaughnessy, R., 258, 476, 809, 835, 845
Shaw, Brian F., 3, 6, 20, 26, 27, 125, 153, 208,
    209, 210, 216, 333, 372, 397, 421,
    478–81, 558, 578, 617, 634, 645, 921,
    955, 962, 963
Shaw, D., 874
Shaw, D. A., 42
Shaw, D. F., 840
Shaw, D. H ., 280, 559, 839, 841, 879, 880
Shaw, D. M., 449, 450, 597
Shaw, F. H., 454
Shaw, K. M., 254
Shea, C., 534
Shea, P. A., 830
Sheard, M. H., 228, 690

Sheehan, D., 227
Sheehan, P. P., 232
Sheehan, P. W., 964
Sheehy, M., 676
Sheffield, B., 269
Shein, H., 855
Shekim, W. O., 518
Shelat, H., 234
Sheldon, A., 607, 965
Shelley, E., 808
Shelton, J., 634, 636, 639, 640
Shelton, S. E., 859
Shephard, R. J., 827
Sheran, T. J., 612
Sherick, R. B., 19, 542
Sherman, A., 237
Sherman, A. D., 880, 921–22
Sherman, B. M., 355, 462, 853, 856, 865
Sherwood, G. G., 22, 23
Shih, J. C., 237, 828
Shipley, J. E., 880
Shneidman, E. S., 610, 611, 619
Sholomskas, D., 115, 132, 216, 242, 319, 589
Shopsin, B., 244, 247, 249, 256, 262, 268, 448,
    449, 454, 459
Shorr, W., 544
Short, M. J., 386
Shostak, M., 232
Shulz, H., 478
Shur, E., 249, 468, 867
Shure, M., 437
Shy, G. M., 562
Sicuro, F., 874
Siegel, J. M., 777
Siegel, L. J., 517, 524, 537, 538
Siegel, R., 156, 688
Sielig, P., 778
Siever, Lawrence J., 236, 237, 250, 473, 860
Sifneos, P., 100, 102, 106, 108, 113, 118, 119,
    130
Sigal, J. J., 672
Siggins, L., 136
Sigvardsson, S., 678
Sila, B., 850
Silberfarb, P. M., 683
Silberman, E. K., 839
Silfverskiold, P., 847
Silva, P. A., 540
Silva, W. J., 479
Silverman, A. J., 562
Silverman, J. A., 880
Silverman, J. S., 880
Simeon, J., 869
Simmons, Rebecca C., 375, 587
Simon, P., 270
Simon, R., 767, 796, 820
Simonds, J. F., 525
Simons, A. D., 29, 208, 321, 322, 331, 645
Simpson, D., 228
Simpson, G. M., 235, 254, 260, 828
Simpson, S., 239

Singer, B., 117, 215, 329
Sint, P. P., 778
Siogvist, F., 228
Siomopoulos, V., 232, 471, 473, 474, 524, 526, 527, 621
Sippell, W. G., 859
Siris, S. G., 259, 573
Sitarem, N., 238, 453, 482, 827, 834, 840
Siwers, B., 454
Sjöbring, H., 733
Sjögren, T., 768
Sjohn, A., 463
Sjoquist, B., 448, 451, 454
Sjörgen, T., 795
Sjostrand, L., 451, 830
Sjostrom, R., 450
Skerke, H. J., 238
Skews, H., 829
Skinner, B. F., 40, 41
Skinner, H., 373
Skinner, T., 228
Skodol, A. E., 116, 821
Skolnick, P., 237, 468, 831
Skott, A., 268
Skovgaard, B., 280
Skuja, A., 102
Slade, A. P., 468, 867
Slater, E., 779, 795, 806, 807
Slater, J., 608
Slater, P. C., 277
Slater, S., 829
Sleeman, M., 454
Sloan, K., 481
Sloane, R., 216, 254, 682, 828
Sloman, G., 573
Small, I., 277, 724
Small, J., 724
Smeraldi, E., 157, 454, 809, 826
Smith, A., 357, 777
Smith, B., 374
Smith, C. B., 236, 832
Smith, C. C., 237
Smith, J. B., 128, 151
Smith, J. C., 807
Smith, J. E., 317
Smith, K., 818
Smith, M. L., 117, 200
Smith, R., 855
Smith, R. B., 248
Smith, R. C., 234, 240
Smith, R. E., 274, 767, 819
Smith, V. K., 317
Smith, W. T., 575
Smouse, P. E., 387, 388, 806
Smucker, M. R., 413
Snaith, R. P., 736
Snowden, L. R., 946
Snyder, D. K., 165
Snyder, F., 226, 255, 478, 481, 836
Snyder, P., 470, 864, 870
Snyder, P. J., 559, 864

Snyder, S., 248, 730, 731
Snyder, S. H., 232, 237, 240, 831
Sokoloff, L., 847
Sokoloff, R. M., 531, 1020
Söldner, M., 349
Solerian, A. J., 264
Soloff, P. H., 839
Solomon, G., 541
Solomon, H. S., 476
Solomon, M. I., 607
Solomon, Z., 780
Solyom, C., 227
Solyom, L., 227
Sommer, D., 19
Sondergard, I., 238
Sonis, W. A., 545
Sorisio, D., 481
Sotsky, S., 379, 380, 381, 382
Sourkes, T. L., 268, 558
Spanier, G. B., 164, 165
Spar, J. E., 462, 558, 569, 683, 855, 856, 857
Sparks, S., 475
Spatz, H., 473
Spatz, N., 473
Spears, G. F., 389
Spector, N., 234
Spector, S., 234, 558
Spellman, S., 223
Spencer, J. H., 161, 167
Spencer, R. F., 389
Spicer, C. C., 779
Spiegel, R., 91
Spielberger, C. D., 799
Spiker, D. G., 157, 232, 233, 280, 454, 478, 479, 480, 481, 559, 839, 840, 846, 857, 874, 880, 881
Spitzer, R. L., 47, 124, 131, 146, 226, 348, 356, 357, 360, 363, 373, 374, 378, 397, 519, 520, 533, 588, 670, 672, 675, 676, 729, 745, 751, 754, 769, 817, 820, 821, 943, 980
Spivack, G., 437
Spohn, H. E., 845, 849
Sprinkle, R. L., 200
Squillace, K. M., 266–67
Squire, L. R., 276, 277
Srole, L., 768, 774
Stachura, M. E., 456
Stack, J., 480, 834
Stafford, E. M., 775
Stafford, J. P., 679, 680
Stahl, J. B., 460, 856
Stahl, S. M., 246, 832
Stallone, F., 808, 809
Stamler, J., 475
Stamp, T. C. B., 467
Stancer, H. I., 265, 385, 800, 827
Standish-Barry, H. M. A. S., 846
Stanley, M., 237, 244, 279, 832, 856
Staples, F. R., 216
Star, S. A., 768

Stassen, S. H., 869
Staye, J., 228
Steer, R. A., 397, 679
Stefic, E., 386
Steiger, A., 857
Stein, M. K., 233
Stein, Z., 774
Steinberg, D., 227
Steinberg, G., 227
Steinberg, M. R., 167
Steinbrueck, S. M., 70, 205, 325, 327, 881
Steiner, C. M., 188, 193
Steiner, M., 396, 454, 460, 461, 462, 474, 855, 857
Steinfeld, B., 429
Steinfink, D., 856
Steinmetz, J. L., 61, 62, 72, 73, 208, 215, 421, 880
Stenbeck, A., 384
Stengel, E., 344, 346
Stenstedt, A., 806
Stephens, J. H., 673
Stern, G. M., 254
Stern, J., 774
Stern, J. A., 850
Stern, L., 534, 1019
Stern, S. L., 252, 597, 598
Stern, Y., 564
Sternbach, H., 461, 473, 859, 865
Sternberg, D. E., 449, 827, 831
Steuer, J., 322, 580
Stevenson, J. M., 232, 462, 857
Stewart, M. A., 754, 756
Stewart, J. R., 839
Stewart, J. W., 228, 230, 251, 252, 255, 593, 682, 855
Stiasny, S., 771
Stickney, S. K., 747, 748, 752
Stikeleather, R. A., 451
Stiller, R. L., 534
Stockton, D., 833
Stokes, P. E., 459, 468, 456, 460, 465, 867
Stoll, P., 234, 459, 856
Stoltzman, R., 557
Stone, A. A., 956
Stone, M. H., 727, 729, 730
Stone, R. H., 390
Storck, U., 869
Storrie, M. C., 849, 850
Stoudemire, Alan, 556, 564, 571, 572
Stouffer, S. A., 768
Stout, J. R., 277
Strack, S., 426, 951, 958
Stramentinoli, G., 269
Strandman, E., 809
Straumanis, J. J., 484, 843
Strauss, M. M., 675
Streiner, D., 608
Strickland, R., 349
Strober, M., 384, 518, 526, 530, 531, 532
Stroble, R., 778

Stroebel, C. F., 59
Strömgren, E., 222, 768, 806, 807
Stromgren, L. S., 278
Struempler, L. J., 543
Strupp, H. H., 101, 102, 103, 104, 106, 108, 116, 117
Stuart, R. B., 154
Stuckey, R. F., 678
Stulemeijer, S. M., 249
Stuntz, E. C., 189
Sturt, E. S., 769, 771, 772, 773, 774, 779, 783
Sturzenberger, S., 680
Subrahmanyan, S., 449
Suchman, E. A., 768
Sudershan, P., 238
Sugerman, J. A., 452
Suhl, M., 449
Sullivan, A. C., 466, 857, 864
Sullivan, Harry Stack, 127
Sullivan, J., 252
Sullivan, J. L., 227, 593
Sullivan, J. M., 50
Sullivan, L., 522
Sullivan, M. A., 460, 856
Sulser, F., 237, 471
Sun, M., 266
Sundberg, N. D., 946
Sunderland, T., 246
Suomi, S. J., 880
Suranyi-Cadotte, B., 237, 831
Surtees, P. J., 773, 774
Susman, P., 609, 610
Susser, M. W., 774
Sutter, J. M., 810
Svendsen, K., 481
Svensson, T. H., 236, 237
Swade, C., 263
Swaminathan, S., 247
Swann, A., 354, 827, 856
Swann, S., 767
Swanson, D. W., 226, 684, 685
Swartz, C. M., 855
Swartzburg, M., 353, 479, 597, 830
Sweeney, D. R., 450, 465, 827, 863, 864, 865, 868
Sweeney, J., 676
Sweeney, P. D., 21, 417, 454, 928, 953
Sweetwood, H. L., 777
Swenson, B. R., 266
Swilling, M., 157
Symons, B. J., 846
Szasz, T. S., 344, 345, 625

T

Tabrizi, M. A., 474, 480, 533, 534, 840, 859, 867, 1023
Taibleson, M., 360
Takahashi, S., 469, 827
Takezabi, H ., 266
Talkington, J., 44, 422, 424
Tallman, J., 237, 453

Tamura, K., 480
Tanenbaum, R. C., 537, 538
Tanenbaum, R. L., 916
Tang, F., 471, 827
Tanna, V. L., 800
Tarau, J., 385
Targ, E., 480
Targum, S. D., 162, 236, 264, 265, 465, 466, 470, 800, 827, 846, 855, 856, 857, 864
Tarika, J., 396, 460, 461, 462, 474, 855, 857
Tashjian, R., 593
Taska, L. S., 839, 841
Taube, C. A., 769
Taube, S. L., 827
Taylor, F. G., 26, 27
Taylor, Lord, 781
Taylor, M., 806, 807, 809
Taylor, M. A., 228, 257, 277, 354, 875
Teasdale, J. D., 15, 18, 21, 22, 23, 24, 29, 31, 154, 320, 328, 334, 415, 424, 433, 436, 528, 704, 914, 947
Teicher, J. D., 542, 543
Tenen, S. S., 471
Tennant, C., 709, 770, 772, 773, 774, 777, 778, 779, 780, 783
Teoh, C. L., 856
Teplitz, T. A., 258
Terenius, L., 869, 870, 872
Teri, L., 44, 61, 62, 63, 72, 391, 528
Termansen, P., 609
Terry, D., 152
Terzani, S., 587
Tesiny, E. P., 524, 525, 535, 536, 537, 1024
Tetzlaff, W., 839
Thaler, M., 562
Thase, Michael E., 210, 324, 328, 336, 478, 479, 598, 816, 819, 820, 822, 825, 828, 836–39, 840, 842, 844, 855–58, 861, 863, 868, 870, 874, 878–81
Theillie, A., 799
Thijssen, J. H. H., 861
Thompson, J., 480, 840
Thompson, K. C., 778
Thompson, K. S., 232, 481
Thompson, L. W., 26, 28, 72, 73, 322, 384, 580
Thompson, T. L., 572
Thompson, W. D., 351, 390
Thoren, P., 228, 451, 454, 463, 614, 671, 830
Thoresen, C. E., 59
Thorley, G., 264
Thorndike, E. L., 40
Thornton, D. W., 415, 962, 963
Thornton, J. E., 246
Thrash, M. L., 230
Thurmond, A. J., 477, 481, 482
Timmins, J. F., 952
Tipermas, A., 863
Tilson, M., 62
Timmens, J. F., 152
Tisher, M., 530, 531, 1022

Tishler, C. L., 542, 447
Tissot, R., 841
Tizard, J., 174, 525
Tohen, M., 269
Tolle, R., 280, 281
Tollefson, G., 247, 263
Tolsdorf, C. C., 948
Toman, J. E. P., 447
Tomasson, H., 795
Tomba, P., 463
Tonks, C. M., 746
Toolan, J. M., 543, 621
Toomey, T., 389
Toone, B. K., 269
Topol, P., 542, 544
Tortella, F. C., 279
Tosca, P., 855
Tosteson, D. C., 258, 475, 476
Tourigny-Rivard, M. F., 558
Trachtenberg, J., 558
Traskman, L., 228, 451, 454, 614, 671, 830, 852, 861
Traskman-Bendz, L., 463
Treadway, C. R., 746
Tredre, R. E., 280
Trevisan, M., 475, 476
Trexler, L., 20, 385, 414, 612, 1015
Tricamo, E., 252, 481, 593, 839
Tricou, B. J., 468, 831, 859
Trimble, M. R., 269, 270
Trojan, B., 480
Troudart, T., 227
Trzebialowski-Trzeciak, O., 353
Tsai, L. Y., 846
Tsuang, M. T., 232, 274, 348, 674, 819
Tuason, V. B., 683, 845, 849
Tuck, D., 234, 451, 454
Tucker, G. J., 673
Tuckman, I., 613
Tuomisto, J., 237
Tupin, J., 226
Turbott, J., 829
Turk, D., 58
Turnbull, C. D., 227, 252, 349, 593, 828
Turner, D. J., 72
Turner, R. D., 751˙
Turner, R. W., 72, 73
Turner, S. M., 288
Turunen, M., 384
Tybring, G., 451, 454, 852
Tyler, F. B., 948
Tyrer, P., 227, 252, 253, 593

U

Uhde, T., 266, 473, 860
Uhlemann, M., 374
Uhlenhugh, E. H., 754, 776
Ulenhuth, E. M., 776, 777
Ulett, G. A., 818
Ullman, L. P., 345
Ulrich, R., 280, 478, 479, 480, 481, 559, 841

Unden, F., 463
Unis, A. S., 19, 228, 542
U'Prichard, D. C., 232, 236
Unruh, W. R., 19, 434
Urquart, A., 385
Usdin, T., 236
Utiger, R. D., 559
Uytdenhoef, P., 847

V

Vachon, M. L., 965
Vaillant, G. E., 684
Val, E., 476, 809
Valentine, R. H., 845, 849
Vallis, T. Michael, 372
Van Bemmel, A. L., 281
van Berkestiju, H. W. B. M., 875
Van Cauter, E., 470, 864, 866
van den Burg, W., 264
Van den Hoofdakker, R. H., 281, 875
Van den Steen, N., 228
Van der Dijs, B., 850
Van der Kolk, B. A., 240
Van der Vis-Melsen, M. J. E., 264
Van Eerdewegh, M., 800
van Hallst, L., 864
Van Kammen, D. P., 225, 232, 236, 264, 484,
    830, 846, 847, 869
VanNatta, P., 39
Van Orden, L. S., 223
Van Orth, R., 249
Van Praag, H. M., 265, 268, 450, 454, 614,
    800, 825, 826, 828, 829, 830, 861
Van Valkenburg, C., 355, 593, 677, 678, 767
van Zanton, A. K., 265
Vareltzides, A. G., 262
Vargas, J. R., 868
Varpila-Hannson, R., 463
Vartanian, F., 800
Vasquez, A. J., 447
Vasquez, N., 767
Vaughan, P. W., 159
Vaughn, C. E., 156, 169, 174, 950
Vaughn, M., 671, 737
Veith, R. C., 454, 455, 569, 573, 855, 860
Velten, E., 22, 23
Venkoba, Rao, A., 220
Verbanck, P., 809
Vereby, K., 265
Verghese, A., 459
Verhey, J., 860
Veroff, A. E., 484
Vestergaard, P., 261, 262, 861
Videbech, T., 737, 738
Vieweg, B., 380, 381
Vijayalakshmy, P., 254
Villanova, P. D., 927
Vinar, O., 384
Vinarova, E., 809
Vitaliano, P. O., 560
Vogel, C., 247

Vogel, F., 477
Vogel, G. W., 477, 481, 482
Vogel, N. G., 596
Vogt, P., 270
Vohra, J., 573
Vojtechovsky, M., 281
Volavka, J., 265, 277
Volby, H., 222
Volkin, J. I., 419
Von Baeyer, C., 415, 416, 953, 1021
Von Knorring, A. L., 678, 691, 828, 844, 870
Von Zerssen, D., 735, 738, 834, 839, 878

W

Waal-Manning, H. G., 389
Wadeson, H. S., 157
Waegner, D. R., 822
Wagner, E., 228
Wagner, E. H., 524
Wahlby, L., 809
Wahlstrom, A., 869
Walbran, B., 688
Waldman, I. N., 258
Waldmeier, P. C., 251, 255, 454, 455
Waldron, J., 480
Walinder, J., 268, 855
Walker, J. I., 246, 671, 672
Walker, M., 481
Walker, P., 352
Walker, P. W., 156, 587, 588
Wallach, M. B., 238
Wallerstein, R., 101, 108
Walsh, B. T., 228, 573, 682
Walsh, C., 606, 612, 613
Walsh, N., 780
Walter, S. D., 771
Walters, D., 20
Walton, L. A., 540
Wanderer, Z. W., 42
Wandersman, A. G., 950, 965
Wandersman, L., 950
Wang, J., 835
Ward, C. H., 3, 21, 164, 383, 612, 768
Ward, G., 670
Ward, G. H., 47
Ward, J., 230
Ward, M. F., 72
Ward, N. G., 226, 234, 562, 675, 676, 849
Ward-Racy, E. A., 242
Warheit, G. J., 350, 773, 945
Waring, E. M., 153
Warr, P. B., 775
Warren, L. W., 19, 946
Warsh, J. J., 827
Wasilewski, B., 468
Waskow, I., 116, 326
Watanabee, S., 257
Waternaux, C., 269
Waters, B. G. H., 611
Waters, R. N., 836, 847, 869
Watherhouse, G. J., 117

Watkins, J. T., 26, 208, 216, 322, 422, 618, 1014
Watson, R., 448, 471
Watson, S. J., 824
Watts, D., 855
Watzlawick, P., 152
Waxer, P., 376, 425
Weakland, J., 152
Weaver, L., 275
Webb, L., 154
Webb, W. L., Jr., 684, 685
Weber, D., 228
Webster, M. H., 239, 454
Weckler, D. A., 116, 153
Weckowicz, T. E., 385
Wehl, C. W., 73
Wehr, T. A., 254, 263, 265, 280, 281, 282, 454, 465, 467, 479, 482, 841, 842, 864, 866, 872–77
Weil, B. J., 782
Weiler, S. J., 859
Weiman, A. L., 571
Wein, S. J., 20
Weinapple, M., 676
Weinberg, U., 280, 864
Weinberg, W. A., 518, 522, 523, 524, 525, 532
Weinberger, D. R., 240, 484, 846
Weiner, A., 541
Weiner, B., 933
Weiner, J., 807
Weiner, R., 576
Weiner, R. D., 277
Weinfeld, M., 672
Weinstein, M., 42, 153
Weinstein, N., 777
Weinstock, M., 238
Weintraub, M., 153, 421
Weise, C. C., 233, 239
Weiss, B., 233, 479, 481, 840
Weiss, D., 118, 120
Weiss, J., 114, 115, 193, 252, 918, 922
Weiss, L., 193
Weiss, R. L., 154, 211
Weissenberger, J., 319
Weissman, A., 17, 20, 21, 385, 409, 414, 436, 437, 470, 653, 1000, 1015
Weissman, Myrna M., 115, 124, 125, 128, 132, 138, 145, 146, 151, 155, 156, 157, 159, 161, 164, 168, 169, 174, 346, 350, 351, 353, 360, 390, 391, 412, 413, 425, 557, 589, 591, 609, 610, 670, 676, 679, 700, 706, 746, 754, 755, 768, 773, 774, 851, 870, 871, 881, 948, 950, 951, 959, 960, 962, 963, 964, 1013
Weissman, M. W., 216
Weitzman, E. D., 280, 467, 480, 533, 822, 840, 864, 873
Welch, C. A., 278
Welin, M. G., 861
Weller, E. B., 684, 691
Weller, R. A., 684, 691

Wells, C. E., 569
Wells, J. A., 252
Wells, K. C., 67
Werry, J. S., 228, 518, 520, 530, 532, 546
West, E. D., 725, 818
West, E. M., 597
West, P. S., 253
Westbrook, M. T., 959
Westenberg, H. G. M., 861
Westlake, W. J., 260
Wetterberg, L., 280, 463
Wetzel, C. D., 277
Wetzel, R. D., 29, 208, 321, 607, 608, 645, 654
Wever, R. A., 872, 873
Whalley, L. J., 28, 320, 397, 642, 881
Wharton, A. R., 836
Wheadon, D. E., 855
Wheatt, T., 534
Whipple, K., 216
Whitby, L. G., 249
White, H. L., 252, 828
White, J., 350, 374
White, J. H., 228
White, K., 235, 254, 828
White, R. H., 271
White, S. W., 950
Whitford, M., 253
Whitmore, K., 174, 525
Whybrow, P. C., 451, 464, 466, 587, 746, 806, 861, 862, 863
Wiatr, G., 454, 827
Wicklund, R., 44, 45
Widerlov, E., 869
Widlocher, D., 270
Wieder, G. B., 211
Wiener, J. D., 264
Wiesenfeld, A. R., 22
Wijsenbeck, H., 454
Wikoff, R. L., 621
Wilber, C. H., 125, 679
Wilbur, R., 247
Wilcox, B. L., 950
Wildroe, H. J., 673
Wildshiodtz, G., 480, 875
Wilk, E. K., 448
Wilk, S., 448, 449
Wilkins, J. N., 852
Will, L., 520
Willard, R., 70, 419, 421
Williams, B. W., 467
Williams, C. D., 557
Williams, D., 351
Williams, H. L., 678
Williams, J., 376, 378, 384, 397
Williams, J. B., 345, 346, 356, 360, 670, 672, 675, 676, 729, 821
Williams, J. M. G., 411
Williams, L. R., 232, 454
Williams, R. L., 480, 838
Williams, R. W., 275
Williams, S., 540

Williams, T., 384, 754, 755, 756
Williams, W. O., 232, 454
Wilmotte, J., 800, 809
Wills, T. A., 154
Wilner, N., 101, 779, 962
Wilson, A. R., 23
Wilson, D., 683
Wilson, E., 806
Wilson, I. C., 264, 451, 454, 463, 465, 466, 778, 863
Wilson, P. H., 26, 29, 324, 325, 327, 328
Wilson, P. T., 345
Wilson, S. B., 613
Wilson, T. D., 431
Wilson, W., 478, 600
Wimmer, M., 543
Windle, C., 386
Winer, J. A., 689
Winfield, D. C., 386
Wing, John K., 156, 374, 383, 765, 766, 767, 769, 770, 772, 773, 774, 782, 783, 849
Winokur, G., 204, 225, 226, 240, 274, 351, 353, 354, 355, 462, 470, 480, 522, 559, 569, 674, 676, 677, 678, 680, 729, 731, 735, 745, 767, 769, 798, 800, 806, 807, 821, 853, 855, 856, 857, 859, 864, 865, 870
Winston, F., 597
Wirt, R. D., 535, 1024
Wirtkamp, L. R., 800
Wirz-Justice, A., 233, 263, 280, 281, 282, 450, 482, 827, 838, 872, 873, 874, 876
Wish, E. D., 360
Wistedt, B., 673
Witkin, H. A., 960
Wittenborn, J. R., 19, 706, 725, 738, 960
Wittig, B. A., 384
Wittson, L. L., 346
Woerner, M. G., 227
Woggon, B., 270
Wolberg, L. R., 117, 323
Wolf, R. C., 558
Wolfe, B. E., 116
Wolpe, J., 42
Wong, P. T. P., 932
Wonnacott, T. H., 389
Wood, C. A., 241
Wood, J. B., 609
Wood, K., 263, 354
Wood, P. L., 237, 831
Woodruff, R. A., 226, 351, 360, 522, 745, 769, 821
Woods, S. W., 228, 248
Woody, G. E., 679, 680
Woolf, P. D., 859
Woolf, S., 128
Woolson, R. F., 674
Worall, E. P., 257
Word, T. J., 850
Wortman, C. B., 918, 922, 923, 952, 958
Wright, J. H., 865

Wright, L., 228, 682
Wright, L. B., 573
Wright, R., 855, 857
Wyatt, E., 855
Wyatt, R. J., 255, 453, 469, 479, 480, 481, 482, 675, 678, 827, 841, 846, 869
Wylie, L. T., 386
Wynn, V., 467
Wynne, L., 152, 672, 675, 676

Y

Yager, J., 681, 777, 855
Yalom, I. D., 62
Yamada, T., 867
Yamaguchi, M., 868
Yamaguchi, T., 468
Yamamura, H. J., 240
Yanchyshyn, G. W., 856
Yasillo, N. J., 845
Yeaton, W. H ., 25
Yerevanian, B. I., 151, 204, 478, 479, 593, 596, 600, 701, 735, 738, 841, 857, 859, 880
Yesavage, J. A., 272, 684, 1015
Yorkston, N. J., 216
Yoshimoto, Y., 868
Yoshimura, M., 469, 830
Youdin, M. B. H., 256
Young, E., 460, 474
Young, J. E., 320
Young, Jeffrey, H., 652
Young, S. N., 268
Young, W., 480
Youngman, W. F., 613
Youngren, M. A., 43, 61, 153, 205, 423, 425, 426, 427, 948
Yule, W., 529
Yung, C., 685
Yurgelan-Todd, D., 228, 681

Z

Zacharko, R. M., 221
Zahn, T. P., 840, 849
Zahn-Waxler, C., 524, 528, 529
Zajonc, R., 645
Zarcone, V. P., 450, 840, 841
Zarifan, E., 237, 831
Zavadil, A., 228, 235
Zealley, A. K., 1017
Zeigler, B., 73
Zeigler, M. G., 829
Zeigler, V. E., 234, 381, 386
Zeiss, A. M., 19, 25, 44, 61, 70, 71, 73, 125, 349
Zeiss, M. A., 349, 962, 963
Zeller, E. A., 223, 252
Zemcuznikov, N., 560
Zenick, F., 684
Zerbi, F., 855
Zerbin-Rudin, E., 353, 795, 796, 806
Zetzel, E., 561
Zigler, E., 346, 360

Zimznova, J., 281
Zimmerman, J. C., 873
Zimmerman, M., 274, 857
Zis, A. P., 236, 265, 279, 450, 451, 454, 479,
    817, 825, 828, 829, 831, 832, 836, 838
Zisook, S., 204, 248, 397, 943
Zitrin, C. M., 227
Zorick, T., 840
Zrull, J. P., 522, 525
Zsilla, G., 256

Zubenko, G. S., 271
Zubin, J., 345
Zuckerman, D. M., 319
Zuliani, R., 157
Zung, W. W. K., 47, 220, 245, 384, 386, 388,
    389, 390, 750, 751, 768, 1017
Zuroff, D., 703
Zvolsky, P., 809
Zwelling, M., 318
Zwilling, M., 124

Subject Index

A

Acetylcholine (ACH), 557, 823–24, 833–35
Acetylcholine neurotransmission, 238, 823
Acetylcholinesterase, 833
ACTH (Adreno-corticotropic hormone), 458, 558, 853
Adapin, 230, 233
Addison's disease, 461
Adenosine triphosphatase (ATPase), 836
Adenylate cyclase, 832
Adjustment disorder, 212, 343, 353, 358, 366, 568, 757
Adolescent depression, 517, 525–26; see also Childhood depression
  suicidal behavior, 538–44
Adoption studies, 802
Adreno-corticotropic hormone (ACTH), 458, 558, 853
Adult ego state, 90–91
Affective disorders; see Depression
Affective expression, 42–43
Ageism, 563, 579
Aggressive behavior
  children, 518
  convicts, 228
Agitated delusional depression, 349
Agitation; see Psychomotor agitation
Agoraphobia, 227, 670–71
Akiskal classification of dysthymia, 355–56
Alcoholics Anonymous, 677
Alcoholism, 101, 367, 461
  depression, 676–79
  genetic component, 799
  suicide, 610
All-or-none thinking, 5
Allopurinol, 268
Alpha-receptors, 236, 832
Alpha-2 adrenergic receptors, 832
Alprazolam, 244–48
Alzheimer's disease, 683

American Psychiatric Association, 343, 769, 821
  classification of depression, 356–59
  Task Force on Nomenclature and Statistics, 345, 519
American Veterans Administration, 264
Amish community study, 783
Amitriptyline, 31, 67, 145–46, 160, 227, 229–33, 235, 239–40, 242, 317, 324, 560
Amnesia, 685–86
Amoxapine, 244–46
Amphetamines, 263–64, 472, 474
Anaclitic depression, 703–5
Anafranil, 230
Anal-obsessive personality, 733
Analytic treatment of depression, 82–97
  depressive personality, 88–90
  effectiveness, 97
  historical review, 82–88
  medication, 97
  outcome studies, 97–98
  psychotherapy, 90–97
Anankastic obsessive personality, 733
Anectine, 275
Anergia, 166, 600
Anger, 84, 661, 721
Anhedonia, 166
Animal models of depression, 557
Anomie, 781
Anorexia nervosa, 228, 242, 398, 461, 680–81
Anorgasmia, 255
Antecedents, 45–46
Anterograde amnesia, 276
Anticholinergic effects of antidepressant drugs, 238, 240–41, 243, 246, 256
Anticonvulsants, 266
Antidepressant medication, 115, 470–75
  anticholinergic effects, 238, 240–41, 243, 246, 256
  anticonvulsants, 266

Antidepressant medication—*Cont.*
  chemical structure, 230, 244, 250
  eating disorders, 681–82
  elderly, 573
  hormones and neuropeptides, 265–66
  methylation, 268–69
  obsessional disorders, 671
  posttraumatic stress disorder, 672
  second generation, 243–49
  stimulants, 263–64
  transmitter precursors, 267–68
  trycyclic, 229–43
Antidepressive Behavior Measure, 430
Antihistamic effects of antidepressant drugs,
    238
Anti-Hopelessness Memo, 654
Antihypertensive medication, 239–40
Antipsychotic drugs, 270, 574–75
Antipsychotic neuroleptics, 601
Antisocial personality, 717–20
Anxiety, 87, 227, 385
  beta-receptors, 237
  depression, 247–48, 396, 593, 670–72, 704
  Hamilton Rating Scale, 989
  MAOI responders, 252
Anxiolytic medication, 670
Anxious depression, 704
Appetite disorders, 680–82, 981
Aprosodias, 570–71
Arbitrary inference, 4
Arecholine, 834
Articulated Thoughts during Simulated
    Situations (ATSS), 422, 433
Asendin, 244–45
Assertiveness training, 42, 58, 66–67, 209
Assessment of depression, 47
Attributional model of depression, 415–18
  learned helplessness, 922–32
Attributional style, 538, 947–48
Attributional Style Questionnaire (ATQ),
    416–18, 435, 1012
Atypical depression, 366, 594
Automatic thoughts, 8–16, 58
  Dysfunctional Thoughts Record, 9–11, 15
  negative, 12–14
Automatic Thoughts Questionnaire, 321,
    412–13, 1012
Autonomous depression, 221, 349
Autonomous personality mode, 705
Aventyl, 230, 233
Avoidant personality, 713–16

B

Beck Depression Inventory (BDI), 7, 47, 54,
    62–63, 72, 164, 214, 319, 322, 325, 333,
    383–85, 395, 410, 412, 530–31, 612, 659,
    755–56, 984–86
Beck Hopelessness Scale, 612
Beck's Center for Cognitive Therapy, 208
Behavior therapy, 17–18, 39–73, 208–10
  compared to pharmacotherapy, 323–25

Behavior therapy—*Cont.*
  conceptual foundations, 40–41
  evaluation, 54
  history, 41–43
  operant reinforcement, 68–70
  outcome studies, 54, 71–75
  patient compliance, 55
  self-control therapy, 65–66
  social interaction therapy, 63–64
  social skills training, 66–68
  specific skills training, 53–54
  strategies for treating
    assessment, 47–49
    conceptualization of problem, 49–51
    contracting and self-reinforcement,
      52–53
    goal attainment, 51–52
    tactics, 55–63
  theories of depression, 43–46
  time limits, 54, 59
Behavioral approaches to depression, 422–31
  causality/vulnerability issues in
    measurement, 435–36
  coping, 427–31
  outcome studies, 54, 71–75
  Pleasant Events Schedule, 422–24
  reinforcement, 422–25
  social skill assessment, 425–27
  specificity issues in measurement, 436–37
  Unpleasant Events Schedule, 424–25
Bellah v. *Greenson,* 625
Bellevue, Index of Depression (BID), 532,
    1018
Beta-adrenergic receptors, 237
Billings and Moos Coping Responses, 428–29
Biochemical basis of depression, 49, 220–21,
    227, 235–36, 267, 271
Biogenic amine hypothesis, 446–56
  catecholamine measures, 448–50
  central cholinergic factors, 453
  indoleamine measure, 450–51
  monoamine hypotheses, 446–48
  PEA measures, 451–53
Biogenic causes of unipolar depression, 49
Biological axis of depression assessment, 163
Biological clock, 872
Biological markers of depression, 232
Biological processes in major depression,
    163, 816–82
  chronobiology, 872–77
  conceptual issues
    classification, 819–20
    symptoms, 819
  historical perspective, 817–18
  methodological issues, 820–23
  neurochemical abnormalities, 823–36
  neurophysical abnormalities, 836–51
  summary of research, 877–82
Biological psychiatry, 445
Biological Psychiatry Collaborative Program
    of the World Health Organization, 800

Biological rhythms of depressed patients, 280
Biopsychosocial model, 445
Bipolar depression, 156, 167, 347, 352–54, 373
  anticonvulsants, 266–67
  antipsychotic drugs, 270
  compared to unipolar, 767
  course of illness, 353
  demographic and social characteristics, 353
  elderly, 564
  genetic transmission, 352–53
  lithium, 257
  schizophrenia compared, 224–25
  stimulants, 263
Bipolar II-type disorder, 282
Block Design, Coding and Digit Span subtests, 537
Borderline personality, 726–31
  cyclothymic disorder, 730
Bouffée délirante, 767
Boyce v. *California*, 623
Brain electrical activity mapping (BEAM), 484, 675
Brain imaging, 484–85
Brief dynamic psychotherapy, 100
  compared to medication, 325
  focal themes, 103–6
  outcome studies, 117–20
  principles, 107–15
  research, 115
Brief Psychiatric Rating Scale, 397
Briquet's syndrome, 228, 683
British General Practitioner's Research Group, 264
Bromocriptine, 270
Bulimia, 228, 680, 681
Buprenorphine, 270
Bupropion, 244, 245–46, 249
Burnout, 931
Burns Anxiety Inventory, 659

C

Camberwell, England, epidemiological survey, 770, 775
Captopril, 270
Carbamazepine, 266–67
Cardiovascular effects of antidepressant drugs, 239–40
Carroll Rating Scale for Depression (CRS), 387–88, 395, 996–97
Causality/vulnerability issue in depression, 435
CAT (computed axial tomography) scan, 846
Cataplexy, 228
Catatonia, 228
Catecholamine (CA), 447, 448–50, 823
Catecholamine Hypothesis of depression, 236, 267, 679
Catecholamine neurotransmitters, 254
Catecholamine receptor, 236

Catech-o-methyltransferase (COMT), 558
CATEGO program, 769
Center for Cognitive Therapy, 7
Center for Epidemiologic Studies-Depression Scale (CES-D), 47–48, 390–91, 395, 755, 1013
Central cholinergic factors, 453–54
Central nervous system (CNS), 446–48, 823, 825
  dysfunction related to depression, 852
Cerebral angiography, 484
Cerebral metabolism, measurement of, 847
Cerebrospinal fluid (CSF), 448–51, 614, 825
  suicide, 451
CES-D; *see* Center for Epidemiologic Studies-Depression Scale
Character-spectrum disorder, 396, 595, 677, 715, 731
Characterological depression, 156–58, 212, 223, 251, 282, 347, 355–56, 568, 589, 593–96
  case history, 172–74
"Cheese effect", 251, 254
Child Assessment Schedule (CAS), 534, 1018–19
Child Behavior Checklist, 524, 1019–20
Child ego-state, 186–87
Childhood depression, 83–84, 517–46
  assessment, 529–36
    clinician-rated scales, 532
    diagnostic interviews, 532–35
    future research needs, 536
    parent scales, 535
    self-rating scales, 530–32
  cognitive features, 537–38
    attributional styles, 538
    locus of control, 537–38
    problem-solving skills, 537
  diagnosis/classification, 519–24
  prevalence and epidemiology, 524–26
  selective listing of depression measures, 1018–25
  suicidal behavior, 538–44
  symptoms, 518–19, 522
  treatment and outcome studies, 544–46
Childhood enuresis, 228, 518
Children's Depression Adjective Checklist (C-DACL), 530–31, 1020
Children's Depression Inventory, 530, 537, 541, 621, 1020–21
Children's Depression Rating Scale (CDRS), 532, 1021
Children's Depression Scale, 530, 1021–22
Chlorpromazine, 222–23, 227, 229, 238
Cholinergic hypothesis of depression, 852
Cholinergic overdrive hypothesis, 243
Cholinergic supersensitivity, 256, 833–34
Chronic and refractory depressions, 102, 587–601
  classification, 589–91
  intractable depression, 596–601

Chronic and refractory depressions—*Cont.*
   treatment
      chronic residual phase of unipolar
         depression, 591–92
      chronic secondary dysphoria, 593
Chronic secondary dysphoria, 593
Chronobiology, 872–77
Cingulotomy, 598
Circadian rhythm, 279–80, 282, 477, 480, 482,
   872–77
Classification of depression
   Akiskal classification of dysthymia, 355–56
   biological, 359
   criteria for evaluating classification
      systems, 360–62
   diagnoses, 224, 344
   DSM III, 356–59, 977–79
   endogenomorphic depression, 356
   hysteroid dysphoria, 356
   neurotic-psychotic distinction, 347–48
   primary-secondary distinction, 351–52
   psychosocial processes, 359–60
   reactive-endogenous distinction, 348–51
   Research Diagnostic Criteria, 356–57
   subclassifications, 767–68
   unipolar-bipolar distinction, 352–54
   Winokur-Iowa classification, 354–55
Clinical Checklist of Suicidality, 625–27
Clomipramine, 31, 230, 245–46, 671
Clonidine, 468
Clorgyline, 253, 255
Clyde Mood Scale, 392
CNS noradrenergic function, 825
Cocaine, 263
Cognition, 6
   assessments of, 431–34
      measurement, 431–32
      methodological concerns, 432–34
      situational stability, 434
      definition, 431
Cognitive approaches to depression, 408–22;
   see also Cognitive theory of depression
   and Cognitive therapy of depression
   attributional model, 415–18
      Attributional Style Questionnaire,
         416–18
   cognitive distortion model, 408–15
      Automatic Thoughts Questionnaire, 321,
         412–13
      Cognitive Bias Questionnaire, 409–12
      Dysfunctional Attitude Scale, 321,
         413–14
      Irrational Beliefs Test, 414–15
   issues in assessment, 431
   self-control model, 418–21
      Self-Control Questionnaire, 419–20
      Self-Control Schedule, 420–21
Cognitive-behavioral therapy (CBT), 25–31,
   320
Cognitive bias, 432, 435
Cognitive Bias Questionnaire, 409–12, 1013

Cognitive distortions, 20–21
Cognitive Error Questionnaire, 421–22
Cognitive Events Schedule, 421
Cognitive features of childhood depression,
   536–38
Cognitive Response Test, 321, 422, 1013–14
Cognitive schemas, 4–5
Cognitive state, measure of, 164
Cognitive theory of depression, 3–6, 153–55
   research on validity of, 18–24
      causal evidence, 21–24
      correlational studies, 19–21
Cognitive therapy of depression, 3, 6, 153,
   207–8
   behavioral techniques, 17–18, 25–31,
      58–59, 70
   compared to pharmacotherapy, 319–23
   efficacy, 24–32
   elderly, 578–79
   group therapy, 322
   negative triad, 578
   outcome studies, 25–31
Collaborative empiricism, 8–9
Colonic motility studies, 850
Color blindness, 800–801
Communication analysis, 144
Communication patterns of depressed
   patients, 158–60
Compulsive personality, 731–38
Computed axial tomography (CAT) scan, 484,
   846
Concentration deficits, 982
Concept of Self-Help, 657–66
Conduct disorders, 596
Confluence, 196
Conforming personality, 733
Contracting, 52–53
   contingency, 656–57
Control
   impulse, 618–19, 687–90
   lack of, 704
   locus of, 537
   self-, 25, 65–66, 321, 331, 418–21
Control Your Depression, 61
Conversion disorder, 684
Convulsive therapy; *see* Electroconvulsive
   therapy
Coping
   Billings and Moos coping responses,
      428–29
   Coping Strategies Scale, 429–30
   definition, 427
   depression, 427–28
   environmental resources, 941–42, 952–59
   marital/family therapy, 169
   personal resources, 941, 945
   Problem Inventory for College Students,
      430–31
"Coping With Depression," 8
Coping with Depression (CWD) course,
   61–63, 72–73

Coping Strategies Scale, 429–30, 1014
Correlational research, 19–21
Corticotropin releasing factor (CRF), 458, 853
Cortisol, 456, 558, 614, 670, 852–53
Covert sensitization, 687
Cross-cultural epidemiological studies, 781–84
Crying, 979, 991
CSF; *see* Cerebrospinal fluid
Cushing's syndrome, 458, 460–61, 851–52, 854
Cycloid psychoses, 767
Cyclothymic disorder, 366, 732
Cyproheptadine, 270

D

Daily Mood Log, 645
Daily Record of Dysfunctional Thoughts, 9–11
Defense and resistance, 109–11
Delta sleep, 838, 877
Delusional depressions, 232, 348, 564
Dementia, 568, 682
Dementia praecox, 767
Demoralization, 564
Denervation supersensitivity, 237
Dependent personality, 702–7
    chronic character structure, 704
    dominant-goal type, 704
    dominant-other type, 704–05
Depersonalization disorder, 686, 990
Deprenyl, 253, 256
Depression
    assessment of outcome, 214–17
    biological processes in major depression;
        see Biological processes in major depression
    clinical syndromes of, 766–68
    cognitive theories; *see* Cognitive theories of depression
    definition, 126, 226, 396, 669
    diagnosis; *see* Diagnosis of depression
    epidemiology; *see* Epidemiology, frequency of depressive disorders
    interpersonal elements, 152–55
    medical model concept, 126–27
    medication; *see* Medication in treatment of depression
    physical disease, 745–59
    psychological assessment, 373–400
    psychosocial context, 152
    psychotherapy research, 204–17
    subtypes; *see* Subtypes of depression
    symptoms; *see* Symptoms of depression
    theoretical issues, 914–17
Depression in Late Life, 562
Depressive Adjective Checklist (DACL), 50, 164, 391–92, 396, 1014–15
Depressive bias, 432
Depressive equivalents, 226, 397, 518, 774

Depressive Experiences Questionnaire, 703, 734
Depressive mood, 980
Depressive personality, 88–90
    characteristics, 700
Depressive Spectrum Disease, 274
Depressogenic behavior, 437
Depressogenic cognitive schemas, 4–6
    errors in logic, 4–5
Depressogenic processes, measures of, 435–36
    causality/vulnerability issue, 435–36
    specificity issue, 436–37
Derealization, 990
Desipramine, 229–31, 233–35, 239, 241, 600
Desyrel, 244–45
Deuteranopia, 801
Dexamethasone suppression test (DST), 232, 327, 458–63, 478, 593, 599, 670, 854–55, 858
    elderly, 558, 569
    standardization of, 460–63
Dextroamphetamine (D-AMPH), 471–72
Diabetes insipidus, 261
Diagnosis of depression, 47–49, 211–15, 224–28, 820
    classification of depression and other disorders; *see* Classification of depression
    criteria for depression, 343–66
    DSM III, 366, 977–79
    interviewing, 362–65
    medical diagnostic procedures, 445
    medical model, 345
    psychological assessment techniques, 373
    purpose of, 346–47
Diagnostic Interview for Children and Adolescents (DICA), 534–35, 1022
Diagnostic Interview Schedule (DIS), 378, 769
Diagnostic and Statistical Manual of Mental Disorders; *see* DSM III
Diathesis-stress model of depressive disorder, 156
Dilantin, 266
Diphenylhidantoin, 266
Disease, concept of, 766
Disease entity, 766
Dissociative disorders, 685–86
Diurnal mood variation, 983
Divorce, 141–42
    case history, 171–72
Dominant goal type of depression, 88–89
Dominant other, 88, 92
Dopamine, 250–51, 270, 557, 823–24
Double delta value for predicting outcome, 466
Double depression, 589
Down regulation, 237
Doxepin, 230, 233, 239
Dreams, 477

Dreyfus Fund, 266
Drug abuse, 101
Drug-free baseline, 599
Drug refractory depression, 73
Drugs; *see also* Medication in treatment of
    depression *and* Pharmacological therapy
    depression, 676–80
    elderly, 560
    suicide, 610
DSM-II
DSM-III, 115–17, 124, 126, 205, 212, 226, 251,
    343, 350, 356–57, 373, 377–79, 396,
    587–90, 745, 747, 749, 767
    Axis I disorders related to depression,
        669–89
    Axis II disorders, 702
    childhood depression, 519–20, 522–23,
        535
    Criteria for Major Depressive Episode and
        Dysthymic Disorder, 977–79
    current issues, 358–59
    evaluation, 360–62
    major depressive disorder, 566, 821
Dyadic Adjustment Scale, 165
Dynamic psychotherapy; *see* Brief dynamic
    psychotherapy
Dysfunctional Attitude Scale, 321, 413–14,
    435, 1000–1004
Dysfunctional automatic thoughts, 8–16
Dysfunctional Thoughts Record, 9–11, 15
Dysphasia, 242
Dysphoria, 42–43, 45–47, 49, 58, 166, 356,
    745
    childhood depression, 519
    versus depression, 87
    search for causes, 92–93
Dysthymic disorder, 212, 348, 366, 396, 587,
    588
    childhood depression, 520
    diagnostic criteria, 979
    DSM criteria, 115, 568, 749, 977

E

Early Clinical Drug Evaluation Program
    (ECDEU), 987, 992–95
Eating disorders and depression, 680–82,
    981
Edwards Social Desirability Scale, 612
EEG sleep studies, 569–79, 599–600, 836–42,
    877
Effect, law of, 40
Ego disintegration, 458
Ego dystonic homosexuality, 688
Elavil, 230–31, 233
Elderly
    biological aspects of aging, 557–61
    biopsychosocial model of illness, 556
    diagnosis of depression, 563–66, 566–71
    effects of antidepressant drugs, 240–41
    endocrine changes, 558–59
    epidemiology of depression, 557

Elderly—*Cont.*
    grief, 571–72
    lithium, 560–61, 575–76
    metabolic disturbances, 560
    pseudodementia, 462
    psychological aspects of aging, 556, 561
    sleep patterns, 559–60
    sociological aspects of aging, 563
    treatment of depression, 572–77
        electroconvulsive therapy, 576–77
        psychopharmacological, 572–76
        psychotherapy, 577–81
Electroconvulsive therapy (ECT), 165,
    222–23, 271–79
    effectiveness, 272
    elderly, 570, 576–77
    major depression, 818
    memory impairment, 76–78
    mode of use, 274–76
    proposed mechanisms of action, 278–79
    treatment machines, 275
    unilateral versus bilateral, 277–78
Electrodermal activity recording, 849
Electroencephalographic data, 484
    sleep, 836–42
    waking rhythms of major depression,
        642–45
Electrophysiological studies, 484–85
Enalapril, 271
Endep, 230, 233
Endocrine abnormalities; *see*
    Neuroendocrine abnormalities
Endocrine treatment, 244–46
Endogenomorphic depression, 356, 359,
    817–18
Endogenous depression, 155–58, 162–63,
    167, 212–13, 318, 348–49, 361, 396–97,
    767
Endogenous/psychotic depression, 348
Endorphins, 265, 869
Environmental adversity, 776
    chronic problems, 776–78
    life events, 776–78
Environmental mastery, 946
Environmental resources, 941, 949–52
    family support, 950–51
    work support, 951
Epidemiological Catchment Area program,
    769
Epidemiological method, 766
Epidemiology
    case finding methods in surveys, 768–70
    clinical syndrome depression, 766–68
    concept of disease, 766
    cross-cultural studies, 781–84
    definition, 765
    environmental adversity, 776–78
    frequency of depressive disorders, 470–74
    incidence rate, 765, 796
    macrosocial factors, 774–75
    precipitation and vulnerability, 776–81

Epidemiology—*Cont.*
  prevalence, 765 66, 795
  relative risk rate, 765, 796
Epilepsy, 266
Esalen Institute, 194
Eskalith, 259
Etiological model of depression, 44–46
Eutonyl, 250–51
Exogenous depression, 158
Explosive disorders, 690
Extinction, 41
Externalization of voices method, 655–56
Eysenck Personality Inventory, 781

F

Familial Pure Depressive Disease, 274
Family Environment Scale, 961
Family Stress Inventory, 961
Family support, 950–51
Family therapy; *see* Marital and family
  therapy
Fatigue, 977, 980
Feeling Good: The New Mood Therapy, 643
Feighner criteria for depression, 357, 361
5-hydroxy-indoleacetic acid, 613, 829–30
5-hydroxytryptophan, 268
Funkenstein test, 274

G

Gambling, 689
Gender differences in depression, 870–71,
  960, 991
Gender identity disorders, 686–87
General Health Questionnaire, 781
Genetic counseling, 810–11
Genetic polymorphism, 476
Genetic research, 795
  adoption studies, 802–5
  counseling, 810–11
  family studies, 797–99
  linkage studies, 799–802
  lithium response, 808–10
  mode of inheritance, 805–6
  schizophrenia, 806–8
  twin studies, 796–802
Genetic transmission of bipolar depression,
  352–53
Geriatric Depression Scale (GDS), 1015
Gestalt therapy, 194–98, 200–202
  depression treatment, 197
  need cycle, 194–95
Glaucoma, 240
Gonadotropine, 470
Grief, 112–13, 135–38
  normal and abnormal, 358, 564, 571–72
Group treatment therapy, 25, 42, 62, 209
  suicide, 620
Growth hormone (GH), 466–69
  regulation, 866–68
Guilt, 114–15, 365, 980, 988

H

Hallucinations, 242, 347–48, 566, 978
Halsted Reitan Battery, 537
Hamilton Rating Scale for Depression
  (HRSD), 131, 147, 164, 320, 325, 332–33,
  350–51, 364, 379–82, 389, 396, 532, 581,
  755, 821, 987–95
Helplessness, 413–14, 704
  learned, 15, 153–54, 415
Heredity, 795; *see also* Genetic research
Heterocyclic antidepressants, 597
Hirsch v. *State of New York,* 623
Histocompatibility antigen (HLA), 809
Histrionic personality, 709–12
Homework, 67; *see also* Self-help
  assignments
Homosexuality, 688
Hope Index Scale, 613
Hopelessness, 378, 388, 542, 653, 661
  suicide, 612, 653
Hopelessness Scale, 385, 612, 1015
Hopkins Symptom Checklist, 428, 955
Hormones, 264–66
Hostile depressive patient, 710
*How to Get Control of Your Time and Your
  Life,* 59
Hutterite community study, 782
HYPAC; *see* Hypothalamic-pituitary-adrenal
  cortex
Hyperactivity and attention deficit disorder,
  228
Hypercortisolemia, 858–59
Hypersomnia, 364, 479
Hypersomnolence, 480
Hyperthyroidism, 851
Hypochondriasis, 568, 589, 684, 989–90
Hypomanic symptomatology, 399
Hypothalamic-pituitary-adrenal (HPA) axis,
  456
Hypothalamic-pituitary-adrenal cortex
  (HYPAC), 852, 865–66
  abnormalities, 852–61
Hypothalamic-pituitary-growth hormone
  (GH) system, 466–69
Hypothalamic-pituitary-thyroid (HPT) axis,
  463–64
Hypothalamus, 466
Hypothyroidism, 560–61, 851
  symptoms, 750
Hysteroid dysphoria, 252, 594, 711, 729

I

ICD-9, 348
Idomethacin, 566
Imipramine, 27, 223, 227, 229–31, 233–35,
  237, 239, 241, 247, 256, 319, 560, 671,
  825
Impulse control, 618–19
Impulse control disorders, 687, 688–90
  explosive disorders, 690

Impulse control disorders—*Cont.*
  gambling, 689
  kleptomania, 689
  pyromania, 690
Inderal, 237, 262
Index of Definition (ID), 769
Indoleamine (IA), 447, 450–51
Indoleamine deficiencies in depression, 825
Indoleamine hypothesis of depression, 236
Inpatient family intervention (IFI), 167
Insomnia, 226, 232, 364, 981, 988
Insulin tolerance test findings, 865–66
Intermittent depression disorder, 573, 983
International Classification of Diseases, 769
International Pilot Study of Schizophrenia, 782
Interpersonal deficits, 143–44
Interpersonal element in depression, 152
Interpersonal Events Schedule, 427
Interpersonal psychiatry (IPT), 124, 206–7, 318–19
  efficiency data, 145–48
    acute treatment, 146–47
    maintenance treatment, 145–46
    methadone maintained opiate addicts, 147–48
  goals, 130
  need for short-term treatment, 128
  practitioner training, 130
  strategies, 130–44
  theoretical framework, 27
Interpersonal role disputes, 135, 138–40
Interpersonal skills, 948–49
Interpersonal style, 426
Interview Schedule for Children, 533, 1022–33
Interview Schedule for Social Interaction, (ISSI), 780, 961
Interviewing depressed patient, 104–6, 374–83, 772, 777
  children, 532–35
  compared to self-support method, 393–95
  diagnostic, 362–65
  Hamilton Rating Scale for Depression, 379–82
  Present State Examination, 383
  Schedule for Affective Disorders and Schizophrenia, 377–79
Intractable depressive
  recommendations for treatment, 597–98
  terminologic aspects, 596–97
Intrapsychic axis of depression assessment, 163
Introjections, 195
Inventory technique, 777
Involutional depression, 735
Iprindole, 249
Iproniazid, 223, 235, 249, 252, 254, 818, 825
Irrational Beliefs Test, 414–15, 1015–16
Isocarboxazid, 250–53

J–K

Janimine, 230, 233
Katz Adjustment Scale, 378
Kiddie Schedule for Affective Disorders and Schizophrenia, 532, 1023
Kleptomania, 689
Kynurenine pathway, 268

L

L-dopa, 267, 467
L-thyroxine, 265
L-triiodothyronine, 598
L-tryptophan, 598, 830
Learned helplessness, 15, 153–54, 562, 704, 914–34
  attributional reformulation, 922–32, 947–48
  causal explanation for bad events, 923, 953
  future directions of research, 932–34
  original model, 917–22
Libido loss, 989, 991
Librium, 247
Life events, 776
Life History Questionnaire, 375
Life script, 191
Life strains, 528
Light therapy, 281–82
Limbic system-hypothalamic pituitary function, 463–70
  growth hormone, 466–69
  thyroid-releasing hormone stimulation test, 463–66
Lithium, 204, 224–25, 254, 256–63
  dosage and kinetics, 258–60
  effectiveness, 256–58
  elderly, 560, 575–76
  genetic criteria, 808–10
  major depression, 820
  proposed mechanism of action, 262–63
  toxicity and side effects, 261
  transport, 475–77
Lithobid, 259
Locke-Wallace Marital Adjustment Test, 165
Locus of control, 537
Long-term analytic treatment of depression; *see* Analytic treatment of depression
Ludiomil, 244–45, 247

M

Macrosocial factors of depression, 774–75
  employment status, 774–75
  marital status, 775
  occupational class, 774–75
  sex, 776
Magnification, 5
Major depressive disorders (MDD), 372–73, 396, 591
  biological processes; *see* Biological processes in major depression

Major depressive disorders (MDD)—*Cont.*
  children, 519–20, 530
  diagnosis, 746, 749
  DSM criteria, 977–79
  elderly, 566
  histrionic personality, 708
  symptoms, 566–67
Mania, 767, 817
  measures of, 399–400
Manic-depressive psychoses, 767
Manic-State Rating Scale, 399–400
MAOIs; *see* Monoamine oxidase inhibitors
Maprotilene, 244–46, 247
Marital and family therapy, 151, 210–11,
    317
  assessment strategies, 162–65
  case histories, 170–73
  cognitive-behavioral models of depression,
    355
  interpersonal therapies, 152–55
  outcome studies, 160–61
  preventive intervention, 174–75
  psychosocial dysfunction, 155–60
  specific models of treatment, 167
  stress, 156
  theoretical and practical considerations,
    160–61
  therapist's role, 169
  treatment goals and strategies, 165–68
  typical issues in treatment, 167–70
Marital Satisfaction Inventory, 165
Marlowe-Crowne Social Desirability Scale,
    385, 392
Marplan, 250–51
Masked depression, 226, 397, 518, 521, 564,
    751
Matching Familiar Figures Test, 537
Materia Medica and Pharmacology, 258
Maudsley Personality Inventory, 415
Medical conditions underlying depression;
    see Physical disease and depression
Medical diagnostic procedures, 445–85
  biogenic amines, 446–56
  brain imaging, 484–85
  lithium transport, 474–77
  neurophysiological studies, 477–83
  psychoneuroendocrine studies, 456–70
  stimulant challenge, 470–75
Medical Journal of Australia, 222
Medication in treatment of depression,
    26–31, 115, 125, 220–83; *see also*
    Pharmacological therapy
  analytic therapy, 91
  anticonvulsants, 266–67
  antidepressant; *see* Antidepressant
    medication
  behavioral therapy, 67, 70
  cause of depression symptoms, 566
  differential diagnosis, 224–28
  elderly, 560
  endocrine treatments, 264–66

Medication in treatment of
    depression—*Cont.*
  history, 221–23
  interpersonal psychotherapy, 132, 145–46
  lithium, 256–63
  marital/family treatment, 110, 162, 166–68
  methylation, 268–70
  monoamine oxidase inhibitors, 249–56
  nondepressive illness, 227–28
  second-generation antidepressants, 229,
    243–47
  stimulants, 263–64
  transmitter precursors, 267–68
  trycyclic antidepressants, 229–43
Melancholia, 83–84, 86, 126, 251–52, 257,
    272, 463, 767, 978–79
  distinguished from mourning, 561
Mellaril, 270
Menninger Psychotherapy Research Project,
    108
Mental disorder, definition, 344–45
Methadone maintenance, 680
Methylation, 268–69
Methyldopa, 560
Methylene blue, 269
Methylphenidate, 264, 472–73, 598
Metrazol, 221
MHPG; *see* 3-methoxy-4-hydroxyphenylglycol
Mianserin, 244–46, 249
Microstressors, 945
Midtown Manhattan survey, 774
Minimization, 5
Minnesota Multiphasic Personality Inventory
    (MMPI), 73, 258, 274, 385–87, 395
  mania scale, 399
Minor depression, 347, 393, 757, 775
Mixed anxiety depression, 593
MMPI; *see* Minnesota Multiphasic Personality
    Inventory
Monoamine hypothesis of depression,
    825–32, 852
  basic tenets, 826
  empirical studies, 832
Monoamine oxidase, 240, 250, 558
Monoamine oxidase inhibitors (MAOIs),
    249–56, 825, 831
  anxiety disorders, 593, 670–72
  chemical structure, 250–51
  dosage, 251–52
  effectiveness, 249–51
  elderly, 575
  hysteroid disphoria, 356
  kinetics and degree of inhibition, 252–53
  MAO-A versus MAO-B inhibitors, 250,
    252–54
  mechanisms of action, 255–56
  side effects, 254–55
Monoamine neurotransmitters, 255–56, 456,
    613
Montgomery-Asberg Depression Rating Scale,
    1016

Mood, 50–51, 60, 126, 164, 447
  defining symptom of depression, 226, 373
  diurnal variation, 983
  Profile Mood States, 411
  thyroid gland, 463
Motivation, 52, 119
Mourning, 136–38
  distinguished from melancholia, 561
Multiple Adjective Affect Checklist, 411
Multiple personality disorder, 686

N

Narcissistic personality, 720–22
Narcolepsy, 841
Nardil, 250
National Institute of Mental Health (NIMH),
  125, 254
  Collaborative Program on the
    Psychobiology of Depression, 449
  diagnosis of childhood depression, 520
  Early Clinical Drug Evaluation Program,
    995 n
  Treatment of Depression Collaborative
    Research Program, 206–7, 326, 355,
    379–80, 995 n
Navane, 270
Negative assertion, 67
Negative cognitive triad, 4, 20, 578
Neuroamine transmission, 447
Neurochemical abnormalities, 823–36
  acethylcholine, 833–35
  monoamines, 825–33
Neuroendocrine abnormalities, 558, 851–71;
  see also Psychoneuroendocrine studies
  of depressive disorders
  HYPAC axis abnormalities, 852–61
  insulin tolerance test finding, 865–66
  prolactin secretion, 868–70
  sex differences, 870–71
  thyroid axis abnormalities, 861–65
Neuroleptics, 348, 574, 601, 615
Neuropeptides, 265
Neurophysiological abnormalities, 836–51
  colonic motility studies, 850
  electrodermal activity recording, 849–50
  electroencephalographic sleep studies,
    836–45
  neuroradiological, 845–47
  psychomotor disturbances, 848
  smooth pursuit eye movement, 845
Neurophysiological studies, 477–83
  brain imaging, 484–85
  sleep markers in depression, 477–83
Neuroradiological abnormalities, 845–47
Neuroradiological studies, 484–85
Neurotic depression, 155, 347–48, 396, 588
Neurotic illness, 227
Neurotransmitters, 235–36, 447, 823–24
  second messenger system, 832
New Haven-Boston Collaborative Depression
  Project, 145

New Haven Methadone Clinic, 147
Niacinamide, 268
NIMH; *see* National Institute for Mental
  Health
Nomifensine, 244–46
Nonautonomous depression, 349
Nonendogenous depression, 156, 162–63,
  168, 212–13, 318, 347, 396–97, 767
Nonpsychotic depression, 100–101, 212–13
Noradrenergic depression, 827
Norepinephrine, 235–37, 447, 557–58,
  823–25
Normality
  defined, 779
  deviation from, 766
Norpramin, 230–31, 233, 250
Nortriptylene, 31, 213, 229–31, 233–35, 239,
  324, 560
Nyman-Marke Temperament Scale, 733

O

Obsessive-compulsive personality, 731
Obsessive disorders, 227–28, 670–71, 990
Oedipal themes in depression, 113–14
Oklahoma City VA Medical Center, 670, 676
Operant reinforcement, 68–70
Opiates, 265
Oral sucking (receptive) character, 705
Organic Affective Disorder, 343, 746–47, 756
Organic mental disorders, 682–83
Orthostatic hypotension, 254–55, 573
Outcome studies; *see* Treatment outcome
  studies
Overgeneralization, 4

P

Pamelor, 230–31, 233
Panic attacks, 227, 670
Paranoid disorders, 675–76, 990
Paranoid personality, 722–23
Paraphilias, 687
Parasuicides, 613, 615
Parathesias, 255
Parent ego-state, 185–86
Pargyline, 250–51, 256
Parkinson's disease, 565
Parnate, 250–51
Passive-aggressive personality, 723–26
Pathological depression, 88
Pathological grief, 571–72
Patterns of Individual Change Scores, 119–20
Pavlovian hammock, 917
PEA; *see* Phenylethylamine
Peer inventories, 535
Peer Nomination Inventory of Depression
  (PNID), 535, 1023–24
Pentylenetrozol, 221–22
Periactin, 270
Peripheral neuropathy, 255
Permissive hypothesis, 454
Personal Beliefs Inventory, 421

Personal resources, 941, 945–49
Personality, concept of, 701–2
Personality disorders, 610, 700–39
  depressive subtypes; *see* Subtypes of
    depression
  relation to depression, 700–2
Personality Inventory for Children, 535, 1024
Personalization, 5
Pertofrane, 230, 233
PETT scan (positron emission [transaxial]
    tomography), 485, 847
Pharmacological therapy, 26–31, 91, 132,
    145–46, 151, 160, 162, 204–5
  alcoholism, 678
  compared to psychotherapy, 316–35
    behavior therapy, 323–25
    clinical implications, 335
    cognitive therapy, 319–23
    limitations on generalizability of
      research, 329
    meta-analysis of comparative efficiency,
      325–26
    NIMH research program, 326–27
    research issues, 329–34
    short-term analytic therapy, 325
  elderly, 572–77
    unipolar depression, 592
Phenelzine, 250–51, 253, 255, 600
Phenylethylamine (PEA), 249, 447, 451–53,
    835
Phobias and depression, 670–71
Physical disease and depression; *see also*
    Medical diagnostic procedures
  common symptoms, 749–51
  depression in the mentally ill, 749–52,
    754–56
  medical conditions potentially causally
    linked to depression, 565, 748
  medical illness in depressed patients,
    752–54
  obscure affective illness, 752
  psychological reaction to physical illness,
    756–58
  treatment, 758–59
Physostigmine, 225
Piagetian stages, 527
Pituitary gland, 466
Pleasant Events Schedule (PES), 48, 50–51,
    54, 56, 59–60, 164, 324, 422–24,
    1005–11
Pleasure predicting experiments, 17
Pleasure Predicting Sheet, 643–45
Positive assertion, 66–67
Positron emission (transaxial) tomography
    (PETT scan), 485, 847
Postpsychotic depression, 673
Postsynaptic receptors, 237, 831–32
Posttraumatic disorder (PTSD), 671–72, 931
Precursor load strategy, 267
Pregnancy, effects of antidepressant drugs,
    241

Present State Examination (PSE), 383, 396,
    769, 772, 781–82
Presynaptic autoreceptors, 237
Priapism, 247
Primal parathymia, 83
Primary depression, 156, 684
  distinguished from secondary, 351–52
Problem Inventory for College Students
    (PICS), 430–31
Problem-solving skills, 537
Profile of Mood States, 411, 413
Projection, 195–96
Prolactin, 470
Propranolol (Inderal), 237, 262
Protirelin test measures, 599
Protriptylene, 230–31, 233, 239
Pseudodementia, 462, 565, 569, 682
Psychoanalysis; *see* Analytic treatment of
    depression
Psychobiology, 446
Psychodynamic evaluation, 358–59
Psychodynamic therapy; *see* Brief dynamic
    therapy
Psychogenic amnesia, 685
Psychogenic fugue, 686
Psychogenic pain disorder, 684–85
Psychological games, 188–89
Psychological theories of depression
  behavioral theories, 422–31, 436–37
  cognitive distortion model, 408–22,
    433–37
Psychomotor agitation, 349, 365, 388, 848,
    874, 977, 983
Psychomotor retardation, 376, 388, 977, 982
Psychoneuroendocrine studies of depressive
    disorders, 456–70
  cortisol, 456
  Dexamethasone Suppression Test, 456–63
  gonadotropins, 470
  growth hormones, 466–69
  prolactin, 470
  thyroid-releasing hormone stimulation test,
    463–66
Psychopharmacotherapy, 165–66; *see also*
    Pharmacological therapy
Psychosexual disorders, 686
  gender identity, 686
  homosexuality, 688
  paraphilias, 687
Psychosocial axis in depression assessment,
    163
Psychosocial dysfunction, 155
Psychosocial stressors; *see* Stressors
Psychostimulants, 575
Psychotherapy
  analytic; *see* Analytic treatment of
    depression
  behavioral; *see* Behavioral therapy
  cognitive; *see* Cognitive therapy of
    depression
  elderly, 577–81

Psychotherapy—*Cont.*
interpersonal; *see* Interpersonal
psychotherapy
research, 204–17
Psychotic depression, 347, 348
Psychotrophic drugs, 560
Pure depressive disease, 354–55, 359
Pyridoxine, 268
Pyromania, 690

R

Racket feelings, 189–91
Radioisotope brain scans, 484
Rapid eye movement (REM) sleep; *see* REM
sleep
reciprocal inhibition model, 483
Raskin Depression Scale, 145–46, 320, 1016
Ratio of depression cases to unit population,
765
RDC; *see* Research Diagnostic Criteria
Reactive depression, 347, 348–50, 757, 767,
983
Reality therapy, 198–202
treatment of depression, 199–200
Reasons for Living Inventory (RFL), 613–14
Reason for Living Questionnaire, 376
Receptors, 236, 248
alpha-adrenergic, 236
beta-adrenergic, 237
catecholamine, 236
postsynaptic, 237
presynaptic autoreceptors, 237
serotonin, 237–38
Redecision therapy, 193
Reinforcement, 42–44, 52–53, 68–70, 153,
422–23
Rejection sensitivity, 252
Relaxation training, 42, 57–58
REM sleep, 559, 569, 600, 838–42, 873, 875,
877
reciprocal inhibition model, 483
Reparenting, 192–93
Research Diagnostic Criteria (RDC), 47, 124,
146, 226, 318, 348, 364, 373, 377, 577,
683, 745, 769, 821
Reserpine, 825
Retardation, 982–83, 988–89
Retarded anhedonic depression, 349
Retroflection, 196
Retrograde amnesia, 276
Reuptake blockade, 236–37, 249
Role-playing, 144
Role transitions, 140–43
Rorschach scales, 274
Rosenbaum Self-Control Schedule, 321,
998–99

S

S-adenosylmethione (SAMe), 269
SAD PERSONS Scale, 613

Sadness, 745
St. Louis criteria, 745, 821
Salbutamol, 270
SAMe (S-adenosylmethone), 269
Scale of Attributional Style, 953
Scale for Suicidal Ideation, 612
Schedule for Affective Disorders and
Schizophrenia (SADS), 47, 131, 147, 358,
363–64, 377–79, 821, 980–83
interview questions, 980–83
Schedule for Affective Disorders and
Schizophrenia for School Age Children
(K-SADS), 533–34
Schemas, 4–5
Schizoaffective disorders, 674–75, 767
genetic considerations, 806–8
Schizoid personality, 712–13
Schizophrenia, 221, 224–26
depression, 610
distinguished from manic depression,
224–25
electroconvulsive therapy, 272
genetic considerations, 806–8
suicide, 610
transmethylation hypothesis, 269
Schizphreniform psychosis, 767
Schizotypal personality, 716–17
School phobia, 227, 518
Science and Human Behavior, 41
Scripted behavior patterns, 45
Second generation antidepressants, 243–49
chemical structure, 244
dosage, 245
effectiveness, 245
proposed mechanism of action, 248–49
side effects and adverse effects, 245–48
Secondary depression, 56, 593
distinguished from primary, 351–52
Selective abstraction, 4
Selective attention, 107
Self-awareness, 45–46
Self-control model of depression, 418–21
Self-Control Questionnaire (SCQ), 419–20
Self-Control Schedule (SCS), 321, 331,
420–21
Self-control therapy, 25, 65–66
Self-esteem, 19, 169, 537, 562
Self-help assignments
Concept of Self-Help, 657–66
cost-benefit analysis, 646–48
Daily Mood Log, 645–47, 649–50
empirical support, 638–40
historical review, 635
methods, 642–48
motivating resistant patients, 649–57
patient introduction to, 640–42
Pleasure Predicting Sheet, 643–45
prevalence, 635–36
rationale, 636–37
resistance, 648–49
Self-Rating Scale (SRS), 531, 1025

Self-rating scales, 530–32
Self-reinforcement, 52–53, 65
Self-report methods of assessment, 383–95
  Beck Depression Inventory, 383–85
  Carroll Rating Scale for Depression, 387–88
  Center for Epidemiologic Studies Depression Scale, 390–91
  Depression Attitude Checklist, 391–92
  interview method compared, 393–95
  Minnesota Multiphasic Personality Interview, 385–87
  Visual Analogue Scale, 388, 392–93
  Zung Self-Rating Depression Scale, 388–90
Self-sacrificing depressive, 719, 721
Serotonergic depression, 827
Serotonin, 250–51, 256, 268, 824
Serotonin receptor, 237–38
Sex differences in depression, 870–71, 960, 991
Sexual deviations, 687
Shagass test, 274
Short-term psychodynamic therapy; *see* Brief dynamic therapy
Sick role, 133, 166
Silent assumptions, 16–17, 21
Sinequan, 230, 233
Situational depression, 319, 350, 779
Sleep
  circadian rhythm, 279–80, 282, 477–78, 480, 482
  deprivation treatments, 280–81
  disorders, 226, 232, 349, 355
  EEG procedures, 599–600, 836–42
  elderly, 560, 564
  marker in depression, 280, 477–83, 559
  REM, 477–83
  ultradian rhythm, 279
Sleep apnea, 48
Sleep-wake cycle, 872–73
Slow wave sleep, 559, 838
SK-amitriptylene, 230, 233
Smooth pursuit eye movement, 845
Social Adjustment Scale, 145
  self-report, 164
Social background factors of depression, 959–60
  gender differences, 960
Social competence, 427
Social desirability, 385, 612
Social interaction therapy, 63–64
Social introversion, 781
Social learning theory, 43
Social Means-Ends Problem Solving Procedures, 537
Social network, 780
Social Skill subscale, 426
Social skills assessment, 425–27
Social skills training, 66–68, 154, 209–10, 213, 323, 328
Social support, 941–42, 949–50

Socially dependent personality mode, 705
Somatic therapies, 165–67, 220–83, 271–79, 817–18
Somatoform disorders, 683–85
Speech disorders as depression symptom, 376
Spiroperidol, 237
Sporadic Depressive Disease, 274
State-dependent markers of depression, 820
Stimulant, 263–64, 470–75
Stimulant Challenge Test, 473–74
Stress, 940–54
  appraisal, 952–54
  chronic problems, 776
  clinical and research applications, 960–65
  coping responses, 941–42, 952–59
  environmental resources, 941, 949–52
  life events, 776
  marital/family, 156–58, 162
  medical illness leading to depression, 756–57
  personal resources, 941, 945–49
  relation to depression, 156–58
  vulnerability to, 779–80
Stress management, 58
Stressful events, 350, 944
Stressful life circumstances, 944–45
Stressors, 5, 45, 156, 162, 756–57, 940–41
  appraisal of, 952–54
Stroking, 188–89, 193
Structural Clinical Interview for Diagnosis (SCID), 378
Subaffective disorder, 396
Subaffective dysthymia, 255, 359, 595–96, 715, 731
Subjective Probability Questionnaire, 421
Substance abuse
  depression, 676–80
  suicide, 610
Subtypes of depression
  anaclitic, 703–4
  antisocial personality, 717–20
  avoidant personality, 713–16
  borderline personality, 726–31
  compulsive personality, 731–38
  dependent personality, 702–7
  factor analytic studies, 706, 711, 713, 719–20, 723, 726, 729
  histrionic personality, 709–12
  introjective, 703
  narcissistic personality, 720–22
  paranoid personality, 722–23
  passive-aggressive personality, 723–26
  schizoid personality, 712–13
  schizotypal personality, 716–17
Subvalid personality, 733
Succinylcholine, 275
Suicidal ideation, 6–7, 365, 375–76, 540–44, 981
Suicide, 6–7, 606–27
  alcoholism, 538, 544

Suicide—*Cont.*
  antidepressant drugs, 241, 254
  assessment of risk, 606–11
  biochemical assessment, 613
  case history, 170
  children and adolescents, 538–44, 620
  Clinical Checklist of Suicidality, 625–27
  CSF tests, 451
  depression, 606, 609, 930–31
  dexamethasone test, 463
  diagnosis, 609–10
  drug abuse, 610
  dynamic therapy, 101
  environmental stressors, 608
  ethics, 625
  Hamilton Rating Scale, 988
  ideation, 365
  intent, 611
  legal issues, 621–25
    confidentiality, 624–25
    involuntary commitment, 621–22
    malpractice, 622–24
  lethality, 611
  mood change preceding, 373
  outcome studies, 614–15
  parasuicide, 613, 615
  personality factors, 610–11
  predictor of
    Hopelessness Scale, 612
    Reasons for Living Inventory, 613
    SAD PERSONS Scale, 613
    Scale for Suicidal Ideation, 612
    Suicidal Intent Scale, 612
  psychological assessment instruments,
      612–13
  risk factors, 607–8
  treatment, 614–30
    control strategies, 618–20
    support strategies, 616–18
Suicide Ideation Scale, 375, 612
Suicide Interest Scale (SIS), 612
Surmontil, 230–31, 233, 245
Symptom Checklist 90 (SCL 90-R), 118, 378,
    1016–17
Symptoms of depression, 126, 131, 134,
    362–65
  appetite disturbances, 680–82, 981
  assessment of severity and patterns,
      372–400
  concentration deficits, 982
  fatigue, 977, 980
  guilt, 114–15, 365, 980, 988
Syndrome
  compared to symptoms, 373
  definition, 363, 766

T

Tachycardia, 849
Tarasoff v. *The Regents of the University of
    California,* 622, 624
Tardive dyskinesia, 262

Taylor Manifest Anxiety Inventory, 385
TCA; *see* Tricyclic antidepressants
Tegretol, 266
Tennessee Mood Clinic, 597
Termination of therapy, 111–12
Tetrahydrobiopterin, 270
Therapeutic window phenomenon, 234, 276
Thioridazine, 270
Thioxanthine, 270
Thought counting, 9
3-methoxy-4 hydroxphenylglycol (MHPG),
    447–50, 825, 829
Thyroid axis abnormalities, 861–65
Thyroid Challenge Test, 327
Thyroid function tests, 599
Thyroid gland, 265, 463, 862–63
Thyroid hormone, 264–65
Thyroid-releasing hormone (TRH), 862–65
Thyroid-Releasing Hormone (TRH)
    Stimulation Test, 463–66
Thyroid stimulating hormone (TSH), 463–66,
    559, 598–99, 862
Thyrotropin-releasing hormone (TRH), 559,
    598–99
Thyrotropin test measures, 599
Time management, 54, 59
  setting limits of therapy, 107
Time projection, 42
Tofranil, 230–31, 233
Trail Making Test, 537
Training Manual for Inpatient Family
    Intervention, 167
Trait, 355, 934
Trait markers for depression, 820
Transactional analysis, 185–93, 200–2
  child ego state, 186–87
  life positions, 187–88
  life scripts, 191
  parent ego state and depression, 185–86
  personality theory, 185
  psychological games, 188–89
  racket feeling, 189–90
  stroking, 188, 193
  treatment of depression, 191
Transexuals, 687
Transference, 109
Transmethylation hypothesis of
    schizophrenia, 269
Transmitter precursors, 267–68
Tranylcypromine, 250–51, 256
Traumatic war neurosis, 228
Trazodone, 244–47
Treatment of Depression Collaborative
    Research Program, 206–7
Treatment outcome studies
  analytic therapy, 97–98
  assessment of, 214–17
  behavioral treatment, 54, 71–73
  biology of major depression, 877–82
  brief dynamic therapy, 117–20
  childhood depression, 544–45

Treatment outcome studies—*Cont.*
  chronic and refractory depressions,
    597–601
  cognitive therapy of depression, 25–31
  coping responses, 954–57
  cross-cultural studies, 781–84
  elderly, 680–81
  interpersonal psychotherapy, 145–48
  medication compared to psychotherapy,
    317–28
  self-help, 638–40
  suicide, 614–15
Treatment as usual (TAU), 320–21
TRH stimulation test, 569, 572
Trial therapy, 105–6
Tricyclic antidepressant (TCA), 125, 132, 145,
    204, 229–43, 447
  chemical structure, 230
  dosage, 233
  effectiveness, 229–33
  elderly, 561, 572–74
  kinetics and plasma concentration, 233–35
  proposed mechanism of action, 235–39
  side effects and adverse effects, 239–43
Trimipramine, 230–31, 233, 245–46
Tryptamine, 447
Tryptophan, 268
Twin studies, 796–802, 818
Type A coronary-prone behavior pattern, 737
Tyramine, 249
Tyrosine, 830

U

Ultradian rhythm, 279
Uncomplicated bereavement, 358
Uncontrollable events, 922
Unipolar depression, 39–40, 44, 156–57, 167,
    352–54
  biogenic cause, 49
  chronic residual phase, 591–92

Unipolar depression—*Cont.*
  compared to bipolar, 767
  episodic, 592
  short-term dynamic therapy, 100
University of Tennessee Mood Clinic,
    597–601
Unpleasant Events Schedule (UES), 48,
    50–51, 54, 56, 60, 424–25
U.S.-U.K. Diagnostic Project, 772

V

Valium, 247
Velton-Mood Induction Procedure (VMIP),
    22–23
Viloxazine, 245
Visual Analogue Scale (VAS), 388, 392–93,
    396, 1017
Vivactil, 230–31, 233
Vulnerability factors in depression, 435–36,
    799–80

W

Ward Behavior Check, 376
Ways of Coping Checklist, 428
Weeping, 979, 991
Weight loss or gain, 981, 990
Wellbutrin, 244
Wilk's lambda test, 361
Winokur-Iowa classification, 354–55
Work Environment Scale (WES), 961
Work support, 951
World Health Organization, 767, 769, 782
  Biological Psychiatry Collaboration
    Program, 800

X–Z

Xanax, 244–45, 247
Your Perfect Right, 58
Zimelidine, 244, 246
Zung Self-Rating Depression Scale (SDS), 47,
    351, 388–90, 392, 395

*This book has been set Linotron 202, in 10 and 9 point
ITC Garamond Light, leaded 2 points. Part and chapter
numbers are 18 point ITC Garamond Light; part titles are
36 point and chapter titles are 18 point Garamond Book
italic. The size of the type page is 27 by 47½ picas.*